Study Guide

CLAT

Common Law Admission Test

2025

Study Guide

CLAT

Common Law Admission Test

2025

Mansi Varshney
Pawan Khanna

arihant
SUCCESS AND NOTHING LESS

arihant
SUCCESS AND NOTHING LESS

ARIHANT PUBLICATIONS (INDIA) LIMITED

Administrative & Production Offices
Regd. Office
'Ramchhaya' 4577/15, Agarwal Road, Darya Ganj, New Delhi -110002
Tele: 011- 47630600, 43518550

Head Office
Kalindi, TP Nagar, Meerut (UP) - 250002
Tel: 0121-7156203, 7156204

Sales & Support Offices
Agra, Ahmedabad, Bengaluru, Bareilly, Chennai, Delhi, Guwahati, Hyderabad, Jaipur, Jhansi, Kolkata, Lucknow, Nagpur & Pune.

PO No : TXT-XX-XXXXXXX-X-XX

Published by Arihant Publications (India) Ltd.

For further information about the books published by Arihant, log on to www.arihantbooks.com or e-mail at info@arihantbooks.com

Follow us on

CONTENTS

CLAT Solved Paper 2024 3-45
CLAT Solved Paper 2023 46-107
CLAT Solved Paper 2022 1-50

LEGAL APTITUDE

1. Law : Its Nature and Classification 3-11
2. Criminal Law 12-27
3. Contract Law 28-47
4. Acts 48-61
5. Law of Tort 62-81
6. Legal Maxims 82-93
7. Legal Terms 94-109
8. Important Treaties and Conventions 110-112

INDIAN CONSTITUTION

1. Constitutional Development of India 115-123
2. Features of the Indian Constitution 124-134
3. Union and Its Territory 135-140
4. Citizenship 141-146
5. Fundamental Rights 147-156
6. Directive Principles & Fundamental Duties 157-163
7. The Executive 164-173
8. Legislature (Union & States) 174-183
9. Centre-State Relations 184-190
10. Judiciary 191-201
11. Constitutional & Non-Constitutional Bodies of India 202-210
12. Local Self Government 211-213
13. Special Provision for Indian States 214-216

ENGLISH LANGUAGE

1. Spotting Errors 219-244
2. Comprehension 245-258
3. Synonyms and Antonyms 259-270

4. Idioms and Phrases 271-281
5. Sentence Improvement 282-289
6. Fill in the Blanks & Cloze Test 290-300
7. Spelling Test 301-306
8. Foreign Language Phrases 307-312

MATHEMATICS
1. Number System and Simplification 315-335
2. Linear and Quadratic Equations 336-346
3. Percentage 347-352
4. Ratio and Proportion 353-361
5. Average 362-368
6. Profit and Loss 369-378
7. Work, Time, Distance and Speed 379-391
8. Simple and Compound Interests 392-401
9. Mensuration 402-420
10. Statistics and Probability 421-437
11. Clock 438-445

LOGICAL REASONING
1. Analogy Test 449-457
2. Classification 458-461
3. Coding Decoding 462-471
4. Series 472-480
5. Sitting Arrangement 481-488
6. Number Ranking a [illegible] Test 489-497
7. Direction Sense Test 498-505
8. Blood Relations 506-512
9. Puzzle Test 513-524
10. Mathematical Reasoning 525-529
11. Analytical and Logical Reasoning 530-561

GENERAL KNOWLEDGE
1. History 565-594
2. Geography 595-621
3. Indian Economy 622-639
4. General Science 640-665
5. General Knowledge 666-695

PRACTICE SETS (1-3) 699-746

CLAT
Entrance Exam

SOLVED PAPER 2024

Instructions

- There are total 5 sections and 150 questions in this Solved Paper.
- For every correct attempt the students will be awarded 1 mark.
- All the questions are in MCQs form.

Section A : English

I. In the realm of contemporary literature, the interplay between character and setting is anuanced dance that shapes the narrative's essence. The setting, often described with painstaking detail, becomes more than a backdrop; it becomes a character, influencing the plot and character development.

Consider, for instance, the barren expanse of the desert in Jhumpa Lahiri's *The Namesake*. The arid landscape mirrors the sense of isolation felt by the protagonist, Gogol, as he navigates his identity crisis in a foreign land. The relentless Sun and vast sands are not mere descriptions; they are the silent witnesses to his inner turmoil.

On the other end of the literary spectrum, there is Arundhati Roy's *The God of Small Things*. The lush, vibrant Kerala backwaters are not just the setting; they are a character woven into the fabric of the story. The teeming, humid landscape reflects the complex web of human relationships and secrets that unravel in the narrative. This interplay is not confined to contemporary literature alone. In Shakespeare's timeless tragedy *Macbeth*, the eerie and foreboding setting of the Scottish moors casts a dark shadow over the characters' actions. The moors, shrouded in mist and mystery, serve as an ever-present omen of the impending tragedy.

1. In contemporary literature, how is the relationship between character and setting described in the passage?

(a) It is non-existent, characters and settings are entirely separate entities.
(b) It is a complex interplay where the setting influences the plot and character development.
(c) Characters and settings are interchangeable.
(d) Settings are insignificant in contemporary literature.

Sol. (*b*) In contemporary literature, the relationship between character and setting is described in the passage as a complex interplay where the setting influences the plot and character development. This means that the setting is not just a passive backdrop against which the story unfolds but an active element that shapes the narrative and influences the characters. The setting can reflect and amplify the characters' emotions, drive their actions and contribute to their growth and transformation.

2. In the novel, *The Namesake* by Jhumpa Lahiri, what does the barren desert landscape symbolise?

(a) A thriving community.

(b) The protagonist's sense of isolation and identity crisis.

(c) A lush, vibrant setting.

(d) A happy, carefree life.

Sol. (*b*) In the novel, The *Namesake* by Jhumpa Lahiri, the barren desert landscape symbolises the protagonist's sense of isolation and identity crisis.

This suggests that the physical environment in the novel is not merely a geographical location but a reflection of the protagonist's inner state. The barrenness of the desert mirrors the protagonist's feelings of isolation and the vast, unending sands echo his identity crisis, amplifying the emotional intensity of his experiences.

3. What role does the Scottish moors play in Shakespeare's *Macbeth*?

(a) It serves as a beautiful, serene landscape.

(b) It has no influence on the characters' actions.

(c) It is an ever-present omen of impending tragedy.

(d) It is a place for the characters to relax.

Sol. (*c*) The role that the Scottish moors play in Shakespeare's *Macbeth* is that it is an ever-present omen of impending tragedy. The eerie and foreboding setting of the Scottish moors casts a dark shadow over the characters' actions, serving as a constant reminder of the tragic outcome. The moors, shrouded in mist and mystery, symbolise the moral ambiguity and the impending doom that characterise the play.

4. What does the term 'interplay' refer to in the context of the passage?

(a) A lack of interaction between characters and setting.

(b) A complex relationship where the setting influences the narrative.

(c) An insignificant connection between characters and setting.

(d) A complete separation of characters and setting.

Sol. (*b*) In the context of the passage, the term 'interplay' refers to a complex relationship where the setting influences the narrative. This suggests that the setting and the narrative are not separate elements, but are intricately connected. The setting influences the narrative by shaping the characters' experiences, driving the plot and contributing to the overall mood and theme of the story.

5. Which of the following words best describes the setting in *The God of Small Things?*

(a) Boring (b) Lush and vibrant

(c) Insignificant (d) Dark and foreboding

Sol. (*b*) In *The God of Small Things*, the setting is best described as lush and vibrant, reflecting the Kerala backwaters. This rich and teeming environment is not just a backdrop but a character in itself, reflecting the complex web of human relationships and secrets that unravel in the story.

6. What is the main theme discussed in the passage?

(a) The characters in contemporary literature are not influenced by their settings.

(b) Setting in literature is unimportant.

(c) In literature, settings can be as influential as characters in shaping the narrative.

(d) Settings have no role in character development.

Sol. (*c*) The main theme discussed in the passage is that in literature, settings can be as influential as characters in shaping the narrative. The passage discusses how the setting, often described with painstaking detail, becomes more than a backdrop; it becomes a character, influencing the plot and character development.

II. The crisis of justice that is the subject matter of discussion in the media today is in fact the crisis of 'justice for the middle class'. the main difference between India and the OEcd (Organisation for Economic Cooperation and Development) countries is that whereas the middle class in these countries has reasonable access to justice, in india it does not. A vocal and powerful middle class has emerged in India since 1991. it is demanding reasonable access to justice. Much of the judicial reform effort will help meet this demand...

The question of justice for the poor is, however, an altogether different challenge. No country in the world has been able to secure justice for the poor. Most of the jails of the richest countries are filled with the poorest. The 'masses' are more often victims of the criminal justice system than of crime. In India as well, jails are almost exclusively filled with the poor. The civil justice system is hardly accessible to them. They are often victimised by lawyers, touts and court staff. They are docket-excluded, a new type of untouchability. The language and the logic-and the colonial and feudal culture—of the judicial system are alien to them. It rarely takes cognisance of their needs and interests.

Their main concern, therefore, is to escape the attention of the justice system, criminal and civil. A landless dalit person in the interior of Madhya Pradesh once gave me an insightful definition of a court from the perspective of the masses: "A court is a place where you are forcibly taken by the police to be punished; no one goes to a court." In contrast, many lawyers and judges colloquially define a court as 'a temple of justice where rights are protected'.

These sharply divergent visions mean that justice for one section is often injustice for another. Protecting the livelihood of traditional taxi and auto drivers from predatory pricing by corporate app-based taxi providers by imaginatively using the available tools of law to delay their incursion would be seen by the rich and by sections of the middle class as a failure of the judicial system, and possibly as also resulting in a downgrading of the "ease of doing business" measure. However, the masses would see such a judicial intervention as strong evidence of a good Justice system. Although the conflict over competing visions of the nation and conflicting demands from social and economic segments have confined judicial reform of Judicial Administration mainly to 'neutral' areas such as process reform, procedural law, technology, planning and court and case management, judge strength, and the workload of judges, there has been considerable improvement in these areas, and the Judicial System has improved its performance.

[*Extracted*, with edits, from "Justice and the Two Ideas of India", by G. Mohan Gopal, Frontline]

7. What is the central thesis of the above extract?

(a) The practice of untouchability takes various forms in modern India.

(b) The imagination of justice for the rich and poor is vastly different.

(c) Addressing judge strength and case-load management does not affect the performance of the Judicial System.

(d) Protecting the livelihood of traditional taxi drivers is contrary to the goals of ease of doing business.

Sol. (*b*) The central thesis of the above extract is that the imagination of justice for the rich and poor is vastly different.

The passage discusses how the perception and experience of justice vary greatly between different social and economic classes in India. It highlights how the middle class and the poor have different access to and expectations from the justice system.

The middle class, which has grown in power and voice since 1991, demands reasonable access to justice, while the poor are often victims of the justice system and seek to escape its attention.

This stark contrast in experiences and perceptions underscores the deep-seated inequalities in the Indian justice system.

8. What does the author mean by 'docket-excluded' in the second paragraph?

(a) The poor do not have easy access to the justice system.

(b) Courts do not list bail petitions of poor undertrial prisoners who populate the country's jails.

(c) The poor reject the judicial system as being alien to their language and logic.

(d) The rich are excluded from the country's prisons, which are mostly populated by the poor.

Sol. (*a*) In the second paragraph, the author uses the term 'docket-excluded' to mean that the poor do not have easy access to the justice system.

The term suggests that the poor are often excluded from the formal processes of the justice system, either due to lack of resources, lack of knowledge or systemic biases. They are often victimised by lawyers, touts and court staff, and the language and logic of the judicial system are alien to them.

This lack of access and representation in the justice system further marginalises the poor and exacerbates their vulnerability.

9. Which of the following words best describes the experience of different segments of people with the justice system as described in the third paragraph?

(a) Symbiotic (b) Affective

(c) Conflicting (d) Inter-dependent

Sol. (*c*) The word that best describes the experience of different segments of people with the justice system as described in the third paragraph is conflicting.

The passage discusses how the perceptions and experiences of the justice system can vary greatly between different social and economic groups, leading to conflicting views on what constitutes justice.

For instance, measures to protect the livelihood of traditional taxi and auto drivers from predatory pricing by corporate app-based taxi providers might be seen as a failure of the judicial system by the rich and sections of the middle class, but as evidence of a good justice system by the masses.

10. Which of the following statements is the author most likely to agree with?

(a) The judicial system reflects the same power relationships as those that exist in society.

(b) Access to the judicial system is determined more by a person's economic status such as wealth and income, than by their social status, such as religion and caste.

(c) The judicial system was made by the rich, for the rich, of the rich.

(d) None of the above.

Sol. (*a*) The author is most likely to agree with the statement that the judicial system reflects the same power relationships as those that exist in society.

The passage discusses how the justice system in India often mirrors the social and economic inequalities present in the wider society, with different levels of access and treatment for the rich, the middle class and the poor.

This suggests that the justice system is not an isolated entity, but is deeply intertwined with the broader social and economic structures of society.

11. Which of the following statements is the author most likely to disagree with?

(a) A truly representative democracy would ensure that the interests of the poor are also represented in the Judicial System.

(b) The Law ensures equality both in text and in practice.

(c) The poor suffer most at the hands of lawyers and touts, compared to judges who might still pronounce judgements in their favour from time to time.

(d) All of the above

Sol. (*b*) The author is most likely to disagree with the statement that the Law ensures equality both in text and in practice. The passage discusses the disparities in access to and treatment by the justice system for different social and economic groups, suggesting that while the law may promise equality, its implementation often falls short. This gap between the ideals of the law and the realities of its practice underscores the challenges in achieving true justice and equality.

12. What makes reform of Judicial administration a 'neutral' area?

(a) Persons across socio-economic strata agree on the need to Reform Judicial Administration.

(b) There is consensus among political parties across the ideological and regional spectrum on reforms to Judicial Administration.

(c) Reforms to Judicial Administration do not favour one class of people over another.

(d) Reform of Judicial Administration is mandated by the Constitution and thus, lies beyond political considerations.

Sol. (*c*) Reform of Judicial Administration is considered a 'neutral' area because reforms to Judicial Administration do not favour one class of people over another. The passage discusses how judicial reforms often focus on areas such as process reform, procedural law, technology, planning, and court and case management, which are intended to improve the efficiency and effectiveness of the justice system for all users, regardless of their social or economic status. These 'neutral' areas of reform aim to enhance the overall functioning of the justice system, without specifically targeting or favouring any particular group.

III. Everything she wanted was here, at Carignano, in Kasauli. Here, on the ridge of the mountain, in this quiet house. It was the place, and the time of life, that she had wanted and prepared for all her life as she realised on the first day at Carignano, with a great, cool flowering of relief and at last she had it.

She wanted no one and nothing else. Whatever else came, or happened here, would be an unwelcome intrusion and distraction. This she tried to convey to the plodding postman with a cold and piercing stare from the height of the ridge onto his honest bull back. Unfortunately, he did not look up at her on the hilltop but stared stolidly down at the dust piling onto his shoes as he plodded on. A bullock-man, an oafish ox, she thought bitterly. She stepped backward into the garden and the wind suddenly billowed up and threw the pine branches about as though to curtain her. She was grey, tall and thin and her silk sari made a sweeping, shivering sound and she fancied she could merge with the pine trees and be mistaken for one. To be a tree, no more and no less, was all she was prepared to undertake.

What pleased and satisfied her so, here at Carignano, was its barrenness. This was the chief virtue of all Kasauli of course its starkness. It had rocks, it had pines, it had light and air. In every direction there was a sweeping view - to the North, of the mountains, to the South, of the plains. Occasionally an eagle swam through this clear unobstructed mass of light and air, that was all. And Carignano, her home on the ridge, had no more than that.

Why should it? The Sun shone on its white walls. Its windows were open the ones facing North opened on to the blue waves of the Himalayas flowing out and up to the line of ice and snow sketched upon the sky, while those that faced south looked down

explored the inner thoughts and lives of its characters with a modernist narrative style. dystopian visions, as seen in George Orwell's *Nineteen Eighty-Four* provided stark warnings about the dangers of totalitarianism and the erosion of individual freedom.

Today, English literature is a global phenomenon, transcending borders and languages. Indian authors like Arundhati Roy, with her novel *The God of Small Things*, have won prestigious international literary awards. The book not only explores intricate family dynamics but also delves into the broader socio-political landscape of India. In summary, English literature is a testament to the enduring power of storytelling and the written word. It encompasses an array of authors, themes, and styles that continue to captivate and inspire readers across the world.

19. Who is often regarded as the greatest playwright in the history of English language?

(a) Jane Austen
(b) William Wordsworth
(c) William Shakespeare
(d) George Orwell

Sol. (*c*) The person often regarded as the greatest playwright in the history of English language is William Shakespeare.

The passage mentions that Shakespeare is often hailed as the greatest playwright in the history of the English language. His works, including Hamlet, Macbeth, and Romeo and Juliet, are celebrated for their exploration of human nature, love, ambition and tragedy. His characters, such as the tormented Hamlet and the star-crossed lovers Romeo and Juliet, continue to captivate readers and audiences worldwide, attesting to his enduring influence and greatness in the realm of English literature.

20. Which of Jane Austen's novels is known for its social commentary and witty portrayal of romance?

(a) *'Nineteen Eighty-Four'*
(b) *'Sense and Sensibility'*
(c) *'I Wandered Lonely as a Cloud'*
(d) *'The Rime of the Ancient Mariner'*

Sol. (*b*) The novel by Jane Austen known for its social commentary and witty portrayal of romance is 'Sense and Sensibility'. The passage mentions that Austen's novels, such as Sense and Sensibility, provide incisive social commentary through the lens of wit and romance. Austen's heroines, like Elizabeth Bennet and Elinor Dashwood, are known for their intelligence and resilience, and her novels are celebrated for their insightful exploration of social norms and relationships, often conveyed through the dynamics of romantic relationships.

21. Who are the romantic poets mentioned in the passage known for celebrating nature and intense human emotions?

(a) William Shakespeare and Virginia Woolf
(b) George Orwell and Samuel Taylor Coleridge
(c) William Wordsworth and Samuel Taylor Coleridge
(d) Jane Austen and Arundhati Roy

Sol. (*c*) The romantic poets mentioned in the passage known for celebrating nature and intense human emotions are William Wordsworth and Samuel Taylor Coleridge. The passage mentions that the Romantic era brought forth poets like Wordsworth and Coleridge, who celebrated the beauty of nature and the emotional intensity of the individual. Their works, such as Wordsworth's "I Wandered Lonely as a Cloud" and Coleridge's "The Rime of the Ancient Mariner", are testament to the power of the written words to evoke profound emotions and imagery, and reflect the Romantic poets' deep appreciation for nature and human emotions.

22. What is the title of Virginia Woolf's novel known for its modernist narrative style?

(a) *Pride and Prejudice*
(b) *Nineteen Eighty-Four*

(c) *Mrs. Dalloway*

(d) *The God of Small Things*

Sol. (*c*) The title of Virginia Woolf's novel known for its modernist narrative style is *Mrs. Dalloway*. The passage mentions that Woolf's ground-breaking novel *Mrs. Dalloway* explored the inner thoughts and lives of its characters with a modernist narrative style. This suggests that the novel is notable for its innovative use of narrative techniques, such as stream of consciousness and interior monologue, to delve into the psychological depths of its characters and portray their inner lives with great depth and complexity.

23. Identify the 20th century novel mentioned in the passage that provides a warning about the dangers of totalitarianism?

(a) *'Nineteen Eighty-Four'*

(b) *'Romeo and Juliet'*

(c) *'Sense and Sensibility'*

(d) *'I Wandered Lonely as a Cloud'*

Sol. (*a*) The 20th-century novel mentioned in the passage that provides a warning about the dangers of totalitarianism is *Nineteen Eighty-Four*.

The passage mentions that dystopian visions, as seen in George Orwell's Nineteen Eighty-Four, provided stark warnings about the dangers of totalitarianism and the erosion of individual freedom. This suggests that the novel presents a grim portrayal of a future society under totalitarian rule, serving as a cautionary tale about the loss of individual freedom and the dangers of absolute power.

24. What does the passage highlight as the enduring power of English literature?

(a) Its ability to win literary awards.

(b) The diversity of its authors, themes and styles.

(c) Its ability to captivate and inspire only British readers.

(d) The decline of storytelling.

Sol. (*b*) The passage highlights the enduring power of English literature as the diversity of its authors, themes and styles. The passage concludes by stating that English literature encompasses an array of authors, themes and styles that continue to captivate and inspire readers across the world.

This suggests that the richness and diversity of English literature, in terms of its wide range of authors, themes and styles, contribute to its enduring appeal and power to captivate and inspire readers.

Section B : Current Affairs & General Knowledge

V. On the evening of the 10th, General Dyer arrived at Amritsar and the Deputy-Commissioner handed over the civil power to him. He issued a proclamation by word of mouth that no meetings should be held. Two days later, after there had been no sort of riot, nor murder, General Dyer heard that a meeting was to be held at the Jallianwala Bagh. He proceeded there with about fifty troops, half British, half Indian, and a certain number of Ghurkas, armed with their kukris. The Jallianwala Bagh is an open space, half a mile square, which has one entry wide enough for three persons. The troops got in and lined up on a mound of debris. The walls, seven feet high, and the surrounding houses enclosed the people. There were, too, three alleys through which the people might have been able to pass. Within thirty seconds of the troops getting in, General Dyer gave orders to fire, and the crowd of people, estimated at anything from 5,000 to 20,000, who were sitting on the ground peacefully listening to the mob oratory, were fired on. The result of the troops' fire into the mass of people we do not know. But we do know that Dyer's own estimate of the casualties resulting from ten minutes continual individual firing, was 400 to 500 killed and 1,500 wounded. The people were not able to escape. They were people who had not offered any violence and who had not been warned. These people were shot down. After ten minutes, the ammunition was exhausted and the troops marched off, and they left 1,500 wounded there. There were men lying there for two days, dying of thirst, eating the ground, bleeding to death and nobody to look after them. Those who lived nearby came and carried away some of the wounded from the heap of dead and dying, but the unfortunate country people died there miserably of their wounds. This is what is done in 1919 in British India... Centuries hence you will find Indian children brought up to this spot, just as they visit now the Cawnpore Well and you can imagine the feelings of these Indians for generations over this terrible business.

[*Col.* Wedgwood, MP, speaking in the British Parliament, 22nd December, 1919]

25. Which incident is described in the passage?

(a) Baisakhi festival at Amritsar, April 1919

(b) Jallianwala Bagh Massacre, April 1919

(c) Congress Protests of April 1919

(d) Non-Cooperation Movement, April 1919

Sol. (*b*) The passage describes a tragic and historically significant event that occurred on 13th April, 1919, known as the Jallianwala Bagh Massacre.

General Dyer, upon learning of a peaceful gathering at Jallianwala Bagh, proceeded to the site with his troops and ordered them to open fire on the unarmed crowd without any warning.

The crowd consisted of men, women and children who had assembled to protest peacefully. The passage details the horrific nature of the attack, including the fact that the gathering was surrounded by walls with limited exits, making escape difficult.

The troops fired continuously for ten minutes, leading to a high number of casualties.

Estimates of those killed range from 400 to 500, with around 1,500 wounded. The description in the passage is consistent with historical accounts of the Jallianwala Bagh Massacre, which is a pivotal event solution in the Indian struggle for independence from British rule.

The incident demonstrated the brutal measures employed by the British colonial authorities to suppress dissent and left a deep scar on the collective memory of the Indian people.

26. Why did the General Dyer order to fire on the crowd?

(a) To bring the crowd under control.

(b) To scatter the crowd.

(c) To teach the crowd a lesson.

(d) To enforce the martial law.

Sol. (*c*) General Dyer's intent was to 'teach a lesson' to the Indian populace, showing them the severe repercussions of assembling and protesting against British rule. His actions were aimed at establishing a climate of terror and maintaining control through fear. This approach reflects a broader strategy of using extreme force to suppress dissent and maintain the colonial status quo.

General Dyer's order to fire on the peaceful assembly at Jallianwala Bagh was a deliberate and calculated act of brutality meant to instill fear and discourage future gatherings and protests.

The passage indicates that Dyer had not issued any prior warning to the crowd and that his troops began firing almost immediately upon arrival.

This action was not a response to any immediate threat or violence from the crowd, but rather a preemptive measure to demonstrate the consequences of defying colonial authority.

27. In the light of above passage, what was the intention of the speaker?
(a) To praise General Dyer
(b) To expose the deeds of General Dyer
(c) To get sympathy for the Indians who died
(d) All of the above

Sol. (*b*) The speaker, Col. Wedgwood, addresses the British Parliament with a clear objective to expose and condemn the actions of General Dyer during the Jallianwala Bagh Massacre. The passage is replete with vivid descriptions of the brutality inflicted on the peaceful crowd and the subsequent suffering of the victims. The speaker highlights the callousness of Dye's decision to fire on unarmed civilians and the inhumane aftermath where the wounded were left unattended. By providing detailed accounts of the massacre and its repercussions, the speaker aims to reveal the extent of the atrocities committed under British rule. The intention is not only to evoke sympathy for the victims but also to bring to light the moral and ethical failings of the colonial administration. The passage underscores the need for accountability and serves as a stark reminder of the oppressive nature of British colonialism.

28. After the incident, who helped the injured and the dying people?
(a) The army
(b) The police
(c) The civil administration
(d) Some people who lived nearby

Sol. (*d*) The passage describes the immediate aftermath of the Jallianwala Bagh Massacre, where the wounded were left on the ground, suffering from their injuries without any medical assistance. The British authorities, including the army and civil administration, did not provide aid to the victims. Instead, it was the local residents who eventually came to the rescue. These nearby residents carried away some of the wounded and provided whatever help they could. The passage highlights the negligence and cruelty of the authorities, who abandoned the injured to their fate.

This lack of official assistance exacerbated the suffering of the victims, many of whom died due to the lack of timely medical care. The local people, driven by compassion and humanity, stepped in to offer whatever relief they could, even though their resources were limited.

29. What would be the feelings of the Indian children brought up to the spot?
(a) Friendliness to the British rule .
(b) Bitterness about the British rule
(c) A sense of helplessness .
(d) None of the above.

Sol. (*b*) Bitterness about the British rule. The passage suggests that future generations of Indians, when visiting the site of the Jallianwala Bagh massacre, would feel a deep sense of bitterness and resentment towards British rule.

The massacre left a lasting impact on the collective memory of the Indian people, symbolising the brutality and oppression of colonialism. The speaker mentions that Indian children, when brought to this spot, would remember the horrific events and the suffering inflicted by the British authorities.

This visit would serve as a reminder of the injustices perpetrated under colonial rule and would likely evoke strong feelings of anger and bitterness. The passage implies that the memory of such a traumatic event would continue to influence the attitudes and sentiments of future generations, reinforcing their resolve against colonial oppression.

30. What was the full name of General Dyer?
(a) Reginald Murree Harry dyer
(b) Reginald Royce Harry Dyer
(c) Reginald Edward Harry Dyer
(d) Reginald Coleman Harry Dyer

Sol. (*c*) General Dyer's full name was Reginald Edward Harry Dyer.

He is historically known for his role in the Jallianwala Bagh massacre, which had a profound impact on the Indian independence movement. His actions during the massacre were widely condemned both in India and internationally, highlighting the oppressive nature of British colonial rule. The incident at Jallianwala Bagh became a turning point in the Indian struggle for freedom, galvanising nationalist sentiments and leading to increased demands for independence.

General Dyer's name is indelibly linked to this tragic event, and his actions have been scrutinised and criticised in historical accounts and discussions of British colonialism in India.

VI. On 7th October 2023, an armed conflict broke out between Usrael and Hamas led Palestinian militants from the Gaza Strip[o] after the latter launched a multi-pronged invasion of Southern Israel. After clearing Hamas militants, the Israeli military retaliated by conducting an extensive aerial bombardment campaign on Gazan targets and followed up with a largescale ground invasion of Gaza.

More than 1,400 Israelis, mostly civilians, and more than 10,000 Palestinians have been killed in the fighting. Over 240 Israelis and foreign nationals were taken hostage and brought into the Gaza Strip. The Hamas-led attack began in the morning of 7th October, as Palestinian militants in Gaza launched a barrage of over 5,000 rockets against Israeli cities and kibbutzim while some 3,000 Palestinian militants breached the Gaza-Israel barrier. Over 1,000 Israeli civilians were killed in more than a dozen massacres, including the re'im music festival massacre, and military bases were attacked. Over 200 civilians and israeli soldiers were captured or abducted and taken to the Gaza Strip.

At least 44 countries, mostly from the Western world, characterised the massacres of civilians as terrorism. Hamas declared that the invasion was carried out in response to the "desecration of the Al-Aqsa Mosque", the Gaza Strip blockade the construction of Israeli settlements, and Israeli settler violence against Palestinians in the West Bank.

Israel declared a state of war on 8th October, and its response to the attack has seen the most significant military escalation in the region since the Yom Kippur War. The current hostilities constitute the fifth war of the Gaza–Israel conflict, which is part of the broader Israeli–Palestinian conflict. In 2023, before the offensive started, an uptick in Israeli–Palestinian violence saw at least 247 Palestinians, 32 Israelis, and two foreigners killed. According to the Gaza Health ministry, as of 6 November, over 10,000 Palestinians had been killed, including 79 UNRWA staff. Israel dropped a total of 6,000 bombs during the first six days of the conflict—nearly double the number of bombs dropped by the American-led CJTF—OIR in one month during the war against the Islamic State. There has been widespread killing of civilians, and human rights groups and a panel of United Nations special rapporteurs have accused both Israel and Hamas of war crimes.

31. What was the reason for Hamas led Palestinian militants' attack on Israel?

(a) To retaliate against Israeli settler violence against Palestinians.

(b) In response to the desecration of the western wall.

(c) To protest against the construction of Palestinian settlements in the West bank.

(d) To seek an end to the Gaza Strip blockade.

Sol. (*a*) The passage provides multiple reasons cited by Hamas for launching their attack on Israel. These include the 'desecration of the Al-Aqsa mosque,' the Gaza Strip blockade, the construction of Israeli settlements and Israeli settler violence against Palestinians in the West Bank.

It is important to note that the desecration of the Western Wall is not mentioned in the passage, making option (b) incorrect.

The mention of Israeli settler violence against Palestinians indicates that Hamas views this as one of the primary provocations for their actions.

This attack was not an isolated incident but a response to a series of grievances that have built up over time.

The construction of settlements and the blockade are long-standing issues but the immediate violence and tensions in the West Bank are highlighted as significant triggers.

32. What was the reaction of the international community to the killing of Israeli civilians?

(a) Condemned as terrorism by 44 countries.

(b) Ignored by most of the countries.

(c) Supported by the UN.

(d) Praised as a necessary measure by 10 countries.

Sol. (*a*) The passage clearly states that at least 44 countries, mostly from the Western world, characterised the massacres of civilians as terrorism.

This significant condemnation reflects the global community's stance on the violent actions taken against Israeli civilians.

This reaction highlights the international perspective on such attacks, distinguishing between legitimate military actions and those targeting civilians, which are viewed as acts of terrorism.

The widespread condemnation also underscores the severity and brutality of the attack, which led to a significant loss of civilian lives.

33. Which of the following is not true about the historical context of the Israel Hamas Conflict?

(a) The Palestinian refugees started settling under Ottoman rule in the late 19th Century.

(b) Hamas emerged during the first Intifada in the late 1980s.

(c) Hamas was formally known as the Islamic Resistance Movement.

(d) First intifada was a Palestinian uprising against Israeli rule.

Sol. (*a*) The historical context provided in the passage and general historical knowledge about the Israel-Hamas conflict supports options (b), (c), and (d).

Hamas, formally known as the Islamic Resistance Movement, emerged during the First Intifada in the late 1980s as a significant political and militant force opposing Israeli occupation.

The First Intifada was indeed a Palestinian uprising against Israeli rule, marked by widespread protests and clashes.

However, the statement that "Palestinian refugees started settling under Ottoman rule in the late 19th Century" is misleading. Palestinian refugees are a result of the 1948 Arab-Israeli War and subsequent conflicts, particularly the creation of Israel and the displacement of Palestinian populations. The Ottoman Empire ruled the region before World War I, and the dynamics of settlement and displacement during that period were different from the context of the refugee situation that emerged in the mid-20th century.

Hence, option (a) is incorrect.

34. What has been the response of the israeli military to the Hamas-led attack?

(a) Declared a state of war and launched a ground invasion.

(b) Conducted an aerial bombardment campaign only.

(c) Asked for international intervention.

(d) Captured and imprisoned the militants responsible.

Sol. (*a*) The passage details Israel's military response to the Hamas-led attack, which included declaring a state of war on October 8 and launching an extensive aerial bombardment campaign followed by a large-scale ground invasion of Gaza.

This response marks a significant escalation in military operations, demonstrating Israel's determination to counter the Hamas offensive forcefully.

The combination of aerial bombardment and ground invasion highlights the intensity and scope of Israel's military strategy. This approach aimed not only to neutralize immediate threats but also to dismantle Hamas's infrastructure and capabilities in Gaza.

35. What is the current hostilities known as in the Gaza-Israel conflict?

(a) Sixth war (b) Fifth war

(c) Seventh war (d) Fourth war

Sol. (*b*) The passage refers to the current hostilities as the fifth war of the Gaza-Israel conflict, which is part of the broader Israeli-Palestinian conflict.

This designation indicates the ongoing and cyclical nature of the conflict, marked by periodic escalations of violence between Israel and Hamas.

Each of these wars represents a distinct phase in the protracted struggle, characterized by intense military engagements and significant casualties on both sides. The term 'fifth war' underscores the recurrence of conflict and the challenges in achieving lasting peace and stability in the region.

36. Which major war does the current Gaza-Israel conflict resemble?

(a) Yom Kippur War (b) Iraq War

(c) Six-day War (d) Gulf War

Sol. (*a*) The passage notes that Israel's response to the Hamas-led attack has seen the most significant military escalation in the region since the Yom Kippur War.

The Yom Kippur War, also known as the October War of 1973, was a major conflict between Israel and a coalition of Arab states led by Egypt and Syria.

This war was characterised by large-scale military operations and significant territorial and strategic implications.

The comparison indicates the scale and intensity of the current conflict, suggesting that the hostilities have reached a level of severity and complexity not seen since the Yom Kippur War.

This resemblance underscores the profound impact of the current Gaza-Israel conflict on regional stability and security.

VII. Today, India has become the fourth country in the world to touch the surface of the moon. This success becomes even greater when we look at the place from where India had started its journey. There was a time when India did not have the required technology and there was no support either. We used to be among the 'Third World' countries, standing in the third row. Today, India has become the fifth largest economy in the world. Today, from trade to technology, India is among the countries standing in the first row. In this journey from third row to first row, institutions like ISRO have played a major role. Today, you have taken 'make in india' to the moon.

I have seen the photo in which our moon lander has firmly set its foot on the moon like Angad. On one hand is the confidence of Vikram while on the other hand is the bravery of Pragyan. Our Pragyan is continuously leaving its footprints on the moon. The pictures taken from different cameras, which have just been released, and I have the privilege of seeing, are indeed amazing. For the first time, since the beginning of human civilization, for the first time in the history of lakhs of years on the earth, man is looking at the pictures of that place with his own eyes.

India has done the work of showing these pictures to the world! All the scientists like you have done it. Today, the whole world is acknowledging the significance of India's scientific spirit, our technology and our scientific temperament. Chandrayaan Maha Abhiyan is a success not only for india but for the entire humanity.

[*Extracted* from the Speech made by the Prime Minister of India Shri. Narendra Modi on the occasion of the landing of Chandrayaan 3 on 26th August, 2023]

37. In what did India become the fourth country in the world?

(a) Sending a spacecraft to the moon
(b) Landing a spacecraft on the moon
(c) Landing a man on the moon
(d) Crashlanding (impacting) a spacecraft on the moon

Sol. (*b*) India's Chandrayaan 3 mission marked a significant milestone, making India the fourth country in the world to land a spacecraft on the moon. The passage clearly celebrates this achievement, highlighting the progress India has made from being considered a "third world" country to becoming a leader in space exploration.

The success of Chandrayaan 3 in landing on the moon demonstrates India's advanced technological capabilities and positions it alongside other spacefaring nations. This achievement is particularly noteworthy as it involves the precision required to soft-land on the lunar surface, a challenging feat that only a few countries have accomplished.

38. What is the role of Pragyan?

(a) To move around the Moon, leaving footprints.
(b) To take photographs of the Moon, while moving.
(c) Showing these pictures to the world.
(d) To record the laser radiation.

Sol. (*b*) Pragyan, the rover, is designed to move around the lunar surface and perform various scientific tasks. The passage mentions that Pragyan is 'continuously leaving its footprints on the moon' and that it has been taking 'pictures taken from different cameras.' These images are significant because they allow scientists and the public to see the lunar surface in detail, enhancing our understanding of the moon's geology and environment. The rover's ability to capture and transmit photographs is a crucial part of its mission, providing valuable data and visual documentation of its explorations.

39. Name one Institution that played a major role in bringing India to the forefront.

(a) Tata Industries
(b) Indian Oil Corporation
(c) ISRO
(d) Reliance Industries

Sol. (*c*) Indian Space Research Organisation (ISRO) has been instrumental in India's advancements in space technology and exploration.

The passage highlights the significant contributions of institutions like ISRO in India's journey from being a 'third world' country to becoming a major player in global technology and trade.
ISRO's successful missions, including the Chandrayaan and Mars Orbiter missions, have showcased India's capabilities in space exploration and have brought international recognition to the country's scientific and technological prowess.

40. What is the name of the moon lander and the rover?

(a) Vikram and Pragyan
(b) Pragyan-2 and Vikram
(c) Chandrayaan and Vikram
(d) Chandrayaan and Pragyan

Sol. (*a*) The passage refers to the moon lander as 'Vikram' and the rover as 'Pragyan.' These names are significant components of the Chandrayaan 3 mission.

Vikram, named after Dr. Vikram Sarabhai, the founder of ISRO, successfully landed on the lunar surface, and Pragyan, the rover, is designed to explore and gather data from the moon. The collaboration between these two components exemplifies India's advanced engineering and technological capabilities in space exploration.

41. Whom did the Prime Minister address this to?

(a) To the people of India
(b) To the world
(c) To the students
(d) To the scientists of ISRO

Sol. (*d*) The passage is an excerpt from the Prime Minister of India, Shri Narendra

Modi's speech, delivered on the occasion of the landing of Chandrayaan 3.

In this speech, the Prime Minister specifically acknowledges and praises the efforts of the scientists at ISRO who made the mission possible. He highlights their dedication, hard work, and scientific spirit, attributing the success of the mission to their contributions.

While the message also resonates with the pride of the entire nation and humanity, the direct address is to the scientists of ISRO, celebrating their achievement and encouraging further advancements in space exploration.

42. Which of the following countries in the world had touched the surface of the moon?

(a) United States of America, USSR, China, india

(b) United States of America, Russia, China, India

(c) United States of America, uSSr, France, india

(d) United States of America, Russia, Israel, India

Sol. (*a*) The passage celebrates India's achievement of becoming the fourth country in the world to land on the moon. The countries that had previously accomplished this feat are the United States of America, the USSR (Soviet Union), and China. The Soviet Union was the first to achieve a soft landing on the moon with the Luna 9 mission in 1966. The United States followed with the Apollo missions, notably Apollo 11, which saw humans land on the moon for the first time. China achieved its first soft landing on the moon with the Chang'e 3 mission in 2013. India's Chandrayaan 3 mission now joins this prestigious list.

VIII. The 18th G20 Summit, in which the heads of states and governments will meet, on september 9 and 10 will be held in India's national capital New Delhi. Over 25 world leaders along with other delegates are going to attend this mega event.

One of the largest multilateral summits, the G20 Summit presents a significant diplomatic opportunity for India, which will convene with the adoption of a joint declaration by all the member states.

India assumed the G20 Presidency on december 1 last year. The 18th G20 Summit in New Delhi is scheduled to be held on September 9th to 10th.

The Group of twenty (G20) comprises 19 countries .... and the European union. The G20 members represent around 85% of the global GDP, over 75% of the global trade, and about two-thirds of the world population.

World leaders from several countries and institutions will mark their presence at the event. They include US President Joe Biden, UK Prime Minister Rishi Sunak, Australian Prime Minister Anthony Albanese, Canadian Prime Minister Justin Trudeau and French President Emmanuel Macron. However, Russian President Vladimir Putin has opted out of the summit and Foreign Minister Sergei Lavrov will represent the country in his place. Chinese President Xi Jinping has also decided to skip the event and will send country's Premier Li Qiang instead, according to sources.

The G20 Summit 2023 is being held under the theme – Vasudhaiva Kutumbakam (One Earth. One Family. One Future) – centered around the value of all life including human, animal, plant, and microorganisms and their inter-connectedness on the planet Earth and in the wider universe.

India's presidency of the summit holds significance as it aims to become a voice for the 'less developed' global South in a world dominated by developed nations of the West. it is also likely to take up the issue of border tension with China.

India, for its part, may attempt to straighten out its diplomatic intricacies with the West after it faced challenges due to the Russia-Ukraine conflict.

[*Extracted*, with edits and revisions, from "India gears up for G20 Summit: Check event venue, guest list, special invitees", Hindustan Times]

43. The Group of twenty (G20) is a forum for ....
Select the correct option.
(a) International Economic Cooperation
(b) International peace and security
(c) International cooperation for combating money laundering
(d) All of the above

Sol. (*a*) The G20 is primarily a forum for International Economic Cooperation. It was established in 1999 in response to the financial crises of the late 1990s and aims to bring together the world's major economies to discuss and promote international financial stability.

The G20 members represent a significant portion of the global economy, including 85% of global GDP, over 75% of global trade, and about two-thirds of the world population. The forum addresses issues related to global economic growth, international trade, and regulation of financial markets.

While the G20 also touches upon other issues such as climate change, health, and sustainable development, its primary focus remains on economic cooperation.

44. The G20 Summit is hosted by the incumbent 'Presidency'. The G20 Presidency is responsible for bringing together the G20 agenda in consultation with other members and in response to developments in the global economy. Which country will hold the Presidency in 2024?
(a) India (b) Indonesia
(c) Brazil (d) Saudi Arabia

Sol. (*c*) India assumed the G20 Presidency on December 1st, 2022, and is hosting the 18th G20 Summit in September 2023. The G20 Presidency rotates annually among its members, and each presidency is responsible for setting the agenda and organizing the summit. After India, Brazil is scheduled to hold the G20 Presidency in 2024. This will involve Brazil taking on the role of leading the discussions and setting the priorities for the G20 Summitin 2024.

45. Which one of the following countries is not a member of the G20?
(a) Egypt (b) Mexico
(c) Republic of Korea (d) Turkiye

Sol. (*a*) The G20 consists of 19 countries and the European Union. The member countries include Argentina, Australia, Brazil, Canada, China, France, Germany, India, Indonesia, Italy, Japan, Mexico, Russia, Saudi Arabia, South Africa, South Korea, Turkey, the United Kingdom, and the United States. The European Union is also a member, represented by the European Commission and the European Central Bank. Egypt is not a member of the G20, though it may be invited as a guest to G20 summits.

46. At every G20 Summit, the host country invites countries and institutions that are not members of the G20. Which among the following denotes the correct list of countries being G20 invitees to the summit held in New Delhi in September 2023?
(a) Nepal, bangladesh, egypt, Netherlands
(b) Bhutan, mauritius, Nigeria, Oman
(c) Bangladesh, Singapore, Spain, Netherlands
(d) Sri Lanka, Egypt, UAE, Mmauritius

Sol. (*c*) The correct list of G20 Countries being invites to Summit held in New Delhi is Bangladesh, Singapore, Spain, Netherlands.

At every G20 Summit, the host country has the discretion to invite countries and institutions that are not formal members of the G20 but have relevance to the discussions or issues at hand.

In the context of the G20 Summit held in New Delhi in September 2023, the selected countries make sense.

IX. On 26th January 1950, we are going to enter into a life of contradictions. In politics, we will have equality and in social and economic structure, continue to deny the principle of one man one value. How long shall we continue to live this life of contradictions? How long shall we continue to deny equality in our social and economic life? if we continue to deny it for long, we will do so only by putting our political democracy in peril. We must remove this contradiction at the earliest possible moment else those who suffer from inequality will blow up the structure of democracy, which this Constituent Assembly has so laboriously built up.

I feel that the Constitution is workable, it is flexible and it is strong enough to hold the country together both in peacetime and in wartime. Iindeed, if i may say so, if things go wrong under the new Constitution, the reason will not be that we had a bad Constitution. What we will have to say is that man was vile?

The third thing we must do is not be content with mere political democracy. We must note that our political democracy cannot last unless there lies at the base of social democracy. What does social democracy mean? it means a way of life, which recognizes liberty, equality and fraternity as the principles of life.

... however, good a Constitution may be, it is sure to turn out bad because those who are called to work it, happen to be a bad lot. However, bad a Constitution may be, it may turn out to be good if those who are called to work it, happen to be a good lot. Tthe working of a Constitution does not depend wholly upon the nature of the Constitution.

[*Excerpts* from Dr. Ambedkar's address to the Constituent Assembly, 25th November, 1949]

47. What is the life of contradiction referred to here?

(a) That of equality in politics but inequality in social and economic structure.

(b) That of inequality in politics but equality in social and economic structure.

(c) That of inequality in social structure but equality in economic structure.

(d) That of equality in politics and economic structure but inequality in social structure.

Sol. (*d*) The contradiction referred here is that of equality in politics but inequality in social and economic structure.

This excerpt from Dr. Ambedkar's address to the Constituent Assembly highlights the contradiction between political equality and social/economic inequality. He points out that while India's political system may strive for equality, the social and economic structures continue to perpetuate inequality.

Dr. Ambedkar emphasises the need to address this contradiction urgently, warning that failure to do so may endanger the political democracy established by the Constitution. He suggests that if inequality persists, those suffering from it may eventually rebel against the democratic system.

48. What will happen, according to Dr. Ambedkar, if we continue to deny equality in our social and economic life?

(a) There will be no injustice.

(b) Our political democracy will be in danger.

(c) Equality in social and economic life will be achieved nevertheless.

(d) Our social and economic life will be in peril.

Sol. (*b*) If we continue to deny equality in our social and economic life our political democracy will be in danger.

Dr. Ambedkar warns that if equality continues to be denied in social and economic life, it will jeopardise political democracy. He suggests that the structure of democracy, painstakingly built by the Constituent Assembly, will be at risk if the contradiction between political equality and social/economic inequality persists.

The denial of equality in social and economic aspects creates discontent among the marginalised sections of society, which could potentially lead to unrest and upheaval. This, in turn, threatens the stability and functioning of political democracy.

49. What might be the cause, according to Dr. Ambedkar, if things go wrong under the new Constitution?

(a) That the Constitution was ignored.

(b) That the men called upon to work the Constitution were good.

(c) That the men called upon to work the Constitution were not good.

(d) That the Constitution was bad and failed the people.

Sol. (*c*) Dr. Ambedkar makes it clear that the effectiveness of a Constitution depends significantly on the people who implement and work within its framework.

He suggests that a good Constitution can fail if the individuals responsible for its operation are not of good character and do not uphold its principles. Conversely, even a less-than-ideal Constitution can function well if the people in charge are committed and competent. This highlights the importance of ethical and capable leadership in ensuring the success of constitutional governance.

50. What does social democracy mean?

(a) Equality before the Law

(b) Equality of opportunities

(c) Equality in social life

(d) Equality in economic life

Sol. (*c*) In Dr. Ambedkar's address, social democracy is described as a way of life that recognises liberty, equality and fraternity as principles.

While economic equality is crucial, social democracy encompasses broader aspects of societal equality beyond just the economic sphere. It includes equality in social interactions, opportunities and relationship among individuals and communities.

In Dr. Ambedkar emphasises the importance of removing contradictions between political equality and social/ economic inequality. Therefore, option (c) accurately reflects the meaning of social democracy as portrayed in the passage.

51. When does a bad Constitution turnout to be good?

(a) When the people called upon to work it are good.

(b) When the people called upon to work it are bad.

(c) When the Constitution is amended.

(d) None of the above

Sol. (*a*) Dr. Ambedkar asserts that the success of a Constitution is not solely dependent on its written content but significantly on the people who implement it.

A Constitution, regardless of its perceived quality, can be made to work effectively if the individuals responsible for its application are committed, ethical, and competent. This highlights the critical role of human agency in the functioning of political institutions. The integrity and capability of those in positions of power can transform a flawed Constitution into a functional system of governance.

52. Which of the following statement is not correct about what DR. B.R. Ambedkar feel about the Constitution?

(a) The Constitution is workable.

(b) The Constitution is flexible.

(c) The Constitution is strong enough to hold the country together in peacetime only.

(d) The Constitution is strong enough to hold the country together both in peacetime and in wartime.

Sol. (*c*) Dr. Ambedkar expresses confidence in the robustness of the Indian Constitution, stating that it is flexible and strong enough to maintain the country's unity both in peacetime and wartime. He believes that the Constitution provides a solid framework for governance that can adapt to various challenges and circumstances. The passage indicates that Dr. Ambedkar views the Constitution as capable of holding the country together under diverse conditions, emphasising its comprehensive strength.

Section C : Legal Reasoning

X. The Indian legal system places a significant emphasis on protecting the rights and welfare of children. Tthe Juvenile Justice (Care and Protection of Children) Act, 2015, is a vital piece of legislation in this regard. It is designed to ensure that children in conflict with the law receive special care, protection, and treatment, with the ultimate goal of their rehabilitation and reintegration into society.

One of the key provisions of the Act is the establishment of Juvenile Justice Boards (JJBs) at the district level. These boards consist of a Metropolitan magistrate or Judicial Magistrate of the first class and two social workers, at least one of whom should be a woman. The primary function of the JJB is to determine the age of the juvenile, the circumstances in which the offense was committed, and whether the juvenile should be sent to a special home or released on probation. The Act makes a clear distinction between a "child in conflict with the law" and a "child in need of care and protection." A child in conflict with the law is one who has committed an offense, while a child in need of care and protection is a child who is vulnerable or at risk and requires special care and support.

The Act introduces a unique approach to dealing with children who are in conflict with the law. For children between the ages of 16 and 18, who have committed heinous offenses, they can be tried as adults, subject to a preliminary assessment by the Juvenile Justice Board. This assessment considers the child's mental and physical capacity to commit such an offense. If the board determines that the child should be tried as an adult, the case is transferred to the regular criminal courts. The Act also places restrictions on the publication of information that could lead to the identification of a juvenile offender. This is done to protect the privacy and future prospects of the child.

53. What is the primary objective of the Juvenile Justice (Care and Protection of Children) Act, 2015?

(a) To punish child offenders.

(b) To rehabilitate and reintegrate children in conflict with the law.

(c) To remove all forms of violence against children.

(d) To increase the age of criminal responsibility.

Sol. *(b)* The Juvenile Justice (Care and Protection of Children) Act, 2015 is a comprehensive legislation in India that primarily aims to provide care, protection, treatment and rehabilitation to children in need, including those in conflict with the law. The main objective of this Act is to adopt a child-friendly approach while dealing with children who come in conflict with the law, focusing on their rehabilitation and reintegration into society, rather than punitive measures.

54. Who makes up the Juvenile Justice Board (JJB)?

(a) Two Judges.

(b) A Metropolitan Magistrate and two Lawyers.

(c) A Metropolitan Magistrate or Judicial Magistrate of the first class and two Social Workers.

(d) Three Police Officers.

Sol. *(c)* A Metropolitan Magistrate or Judical Magistrate of the first class and two Social Workers make the Juvenile Justice Board (JJB). It is as outlined in the Juvenile Justice (Care and Protection of Children) Act, 2015, consists of specific members who are responsible for determining the age of the juvenile, the circumstances of the offense and the appropriate course of action.

According to the Act, the JJB comprises

(i) Metropolitan Magistrate or Judicial Magistrate of the first class: This judicial member is reponsible for presiding over the board and providing legal expertise in juvenile matters.

(ii) Two Social Workers : At least one of these social workers must be a woman. Social workers bring valuable insights into the circumstances of the juvenile and provide input on rehabilitation and reintegration into society.

55. What is the role of the Juvenile Justice Board (JJB)?

(a) To determine the punishment for juvenile offenders.

(b) To decide whether a child should be sent to a regular prison.

(c) To assess the age and circumstances of the juvenile, and make decisions on rehabilitation.

(d) To prosecute child offenders.

Sol. (*c*) According to the Juvenile Justice (Care and Protection of Children) Act, 2015, the primary role of the Juvenile Justice Board (JJB) is to conduct an inquiry and determine the age of the child in conflict with the law. To assess the circumstances and situation of the child, including their family background, education, and social circumstances. Based on the inquiry and assessment, make decisions regarding the care, protection, treatment, development, and rehabilitation of the child.

56. What is the distinction between a"child in conflict with the law" and a "child in need of care and protection" ?

(a) There is no distinction; both terms mean the same thing.

(b) A "child in conflict with the law" has committed a crime, while a "child in need of care and protection" is vulnerable or at risk.

(c) A "child in need of care and protection" is more likely to commit crimes.

(d) A "child in conflict with the law" is an adolescent offender.

Sol. (*b*) The Juvenile Justice (Care and Protection of Children) Act, 2015 makes a clear distinction between these two categories of children: A 'child in conflict with the law' is a child who is alleged or found to have committed an offense. This category includes children who have violated any law and are facing charges or have been convicted of a crime.

A 'child in need of care and protection' is a child who is found to be in circumstances that are harmful or likely to be harmful to their overall well-being and development. This includes children who are homeless, abandoned, abused, victims of trafficking, or those whose parents/guardians are unable to take care of them.

57. Under what circumstances can children between the ages of 16 and 18 be tried as adults?

(a) They can always be tried as adults.

(b) After a preliminary assessment by the Juvenile Justice Board.

(c) When they have committed any offense, regardless of the severity.

(d) When they reach the age of 18.

Sol. (*b*) The JJB conducts a preliminary assessment to evaluate various factors like the child's mental and physical capacity, ability to understand consequences and circumstances of the offense. Based on this assessment, if the JJB finds that the child has not been subjected to abuse or exploitation, and is mature enough to understand the consequences of the alleged offense, it may transfer the case to a Children's Court (a separate court meant for trying such children as adults).

58. What is the purpose of placing restrictions on the publication of information related to juvenile offenders?

(a) To increase the age of criminal responsibility.

(b) To protect the privacy and future prospects of the child.

(c) To encourage public shaming of juvenile offenders.

(d) To help law enforcement track juvenile offenders.

Sol. (*b*) The Juvenile Justice (Care and Protection of Children) Act, 2015 places restrictions on the publication of information related to juvenile offenders to protect their privacy and prospects. The purpose of these restrictions is to prevent the stigmatisation and labeling of children who come into conflict with the law, which could have a detrimental effect on their rehabilitation and reintegration into society.

XI. In India, the legal landscape surrounding online defamation is a subject of significant interest and debate. With the rise of social media, and online platforms, cases of online defamation have become increasingly common. Defamation refers to making false statements about someone that harm their reputation. Online defamation includes defamatory statements made on the internet, including social media, blogs, forums and other online platforms.

One critical aspect of online defamation is determining the liability of intermediaries, such as social media platforms or websites, for defamatory content posted by users. Section 79 of the Information technology Act, 2000, provides a safe harbor for intermediaries, stating that they are not liable for third-party content if they act as intermediaries and follow due diligence in removing or disabling access to the content once notified.

However, determining whether an intermediary has fulfilled its due diligence obligations can be complex. The Indian judiciary has been actively interpreting this provision. One significant case is the *Shreya Singhal v. Union of India*, in which the Supreme Court clarified that intermediaries are required to act upon a valid court order or government directive for content removal, not upon private complaints.

The court also emphasized that the intermediaries should not take a proactive role in monitoring content, as this could potentially infringe on free speech. While the law provides a safe harbor, it does not absolve intermediaries from their responsibilities.

Online defamation cases often involve a balancing act between the right to freedom of expression and the right to reputation. Tthe Indian legal system requires a careful examination of the content, context, and intent of the statements to determine whether they qualify as defamatory. Additionally, the plaintiff in an online defamation case must prove that the statement was false, damaging to their reputation, and made with a degree of fault, such as negligence or actual malice.

59. What is the primary focus of the passage?

(a) The rise of social media in India.

(b) The legal aspects of online defamation in India.

(c) The role of intermediaries in online content.

(d) The importance of free speech on the Internet.

Sol. (*b*) The primary focus of the passage is on discussing the legal landscape and challenges surrounding online defamation in India. The passage covers various legal aspects related to online defamation, such as Defining online defamation and its relation to making false statements that harm someone's reputation on internet platforms. Discussing the liability of intermediaries (social media, websites) for defamatory content posted by users, as per Section 79 of the IT Act 2000.

60. What is online defamation, as described in the passage?

(a) Making harmful statements about someone in person.

(b) False statements made on the internet that harm someone's reputation.

(c) Online harassment.

(d) A form of political activism.

Sol. (*b*) The passage clearly states: 'Online defamation includes defamatory statements made on the internet, including social media, blogs, forums, and other online platforms.

Defamation refers to making false statements about someone that harm their reputation.' Therefore, online defamation specifically refers to making false or defamatory statements about someone on internet platforms like social media, blogs, etc. that damage their reputation.

61. What is the significance of Section 79 of the Information Technology Act, 2000, as mentioned in the passage?

(a) It defines defamation laws in India.

(b) It provides safe harbor for intermediaries in cases of online defamation.

(c) It regulates the content on social media platforms.

(d) It allows private complaints against online defamation.

Sol. (*b*) The significance of Section 79 is that it provides legal protection or 'safe harbor' to intermediaries like social media platforms and websites from being held liable for defamatory content posted by third-party users, as long as they follow due diligence in removing such content when notified.

62. According to the Supreme Court in the *Shreya Singhal v. Union of India case*, under what circumstances should intermediaries act in response to content removal?

(a) Upon receiving a private complaint.

(b) Upon a valid court order or government directive.

(c) Proactively to monitor content.

(d) Only if the content is found to be defamatory.

Sol. (*b*) 'One significant case is the Shreya Singhal v. Union of India, in which the Supreme Court clarified that intermediaries are required to act upon a valid court order or government directive for content removal, not upon private complaints.' Therefore, as per the Supreme Court's clarification in this case, intermediaries like social media platforms should act and remove content only in response to a valid court order or directive from the government, and not based on private complaints alone

63. How does the Indian legal system balance the Right to Freedom of Expression and the Right to Reputation in online defamation cases?

(a) By favoring freedom of expression over reputation.

(b) By favoring reputation over freedom of expression.

(c) By carefully examining the content, context and intent of statements.

(d) By absolving intermediaries of their responsibilities.

Sol. (*c*) This indicates that in online defamation cases, Indian courts balance the competing rights of freedom of expression and the right to reputation by carefully examing the content, context, and intent behind the statements in question to determine if they qualify as defamatory or not.

64. In an online defamation case, what must the plaintiff prove about the defamatory statement?

(a) That it was political activism.

(b) That it was made with good intentions.

(c) That it was true and intended to inform the public.

(d) That it was false, damaging to their reputation, and made with a degree of fault.

Sol. (*d*) "Additionally, the plaintiff in an online defamation case must prove that the statement was false, damaging to their reputation, and made with a degree of fault, such as negligence or actual malice." Therefore, for a plaintiff (the person filing the defamation case) to succeed, they must prove the following three elements about the alleged defamatory statement: That the statement was false, That it caused damage to their reputation, That it was made with some degree of fault, like negligence or malice, by the defendant.

65. What is the role of intermediaries in the context of online defamation cases?

(a) To actively monitor and censor content.

(b) To act upon private complaints for content removal.

(c) To completely absolve themselves of liability.

(d) To encourage online defamation.

Sol. (*) This question has been withdrawn in official answerkey.

XII. The Eeditors Guild of Iindia has expressed concern over the "draconian provisions" of the Press and Rregistration of Periodicals (PRP) bill, 2023, that can have an adverse impact on freedom of the press.

The Guild added: "Editors Guild of India would like the proposed bill to ensure that publishing of news in India remains free of encumbrances and intrusive checks on publishers by the registrar and that the primary emphasis of the registrar and the PRP remains 'registration' and not 'regulation', as the latter has the potential of restricting freedom of the press."

"In the definitions section, the term 'specified authority' gives power to government agencies beyond the Press registrar, to conduct the functions of the Registrar, which could even include police and other law enforcement agencies. Given the intrusive, expansive and vague nature of powers that the bill in any case allows to the Press registrar, the power to further delegate this power to other government agencies including law enforcement agencies is deeply distressing," the Guild said.

The statement says sections 4(1) and 11(4) allow the Registrar to deny the right to bring out a periodical and cancel the certificate of registration of a periodical to persons convicted of 'terrorist act or unlawful activity' or 'for having done anything against the security of the State'. 'Interestingly, the PRb Act, 1867, had no such provisions. Given the liberal and arbitrary use of UAPA (which is the basis for Efining 'terrorist act' and 'unlawful activity'), as well as other criminal laws, including sedition against journalists and media organisations to suppress freedom of speech, the Guild is deeply concerned by the introduction of these new provisions, and the way they can be misused to deny the right to bring out news publications to persons who are critical of governments," it said.

Among the other worrisome provisions listed by the Guild is Section 6(b), which gives power to the Press Registrar (as well as any other "specified authority") to enter the premises of a periodical to "inspect or take copies of the relevant records or documents or ask any questions necessary for obtaining any information required to be furnished".

[*Extracted*, with edits and revisions from "Editors Guild of India expresses concern over draconian provisions of the Press and Registration of Periodicals Bills, 2023" published in The Telegraph dated 07-08-2023]

66. The PRP Bill defines 'newspaper' to mean a periodical of loose-folded sheets usually printed on newsprint and brought out daily or at least once in a week, containing information on current events, public news or comments on public news. Who among the following is covered by the definition of newspaper?

(a) Mr. X publishing news content on digital media.

(b) Mr. Y publishing books containing the comments of the public on public news.

(c) Mr. Z publishing news content in print media on weekly basis.

(d) All of the above.

Sol. (*c*) Mr. Z publishes news content in print media every week. The key criteria mentioned in the definition are: It is a periodical of loose-folded sheets (implying a print publication). It is printed on newsprint. It is brought out daily or at least once a week. it contains information on current events, public news, or comments on public news.

67. Who among the following is not eligible to publish a periodical as per the PRP bill?

(a) Mr. A convicted of waging war against Government of India.

(b) Mr. B, accused of unlawful activities under the Unlawful Activities Prevention Act.

(c) Mr. C, accused of terrorist activities under the Unlawful Activities Prevention Act.

(d) All of the above.

Sol. (*a*) In this context, Mr. A, who has been convicted of waging war against the Government of India, falls under this disqualification criterion. The offense of waging war against the government is a grave violation that undermines national security and stability. Allowing individuals convicted of such offenses to publish periodicals could pose significant risks to public order and national security.

68. Which of the following is a threat to the freedom of press in India?

(a) Liberal use of Unlawful Activities Prevention Act against Journalists refrains journalists from tracing, tracking and publishing investigative articles because they apprehend that they might be linked with criminals.

(b) Use of Sedition laws against journalists under the guise that through their articles they are promoting hatred and exciting disaffection against the government.

(c) Levy of GST on newspapers.

(d) Both (a) and (b)

Sol. (*d*) The freedom of the press in India is under threat from two major legislative measures: the Unlawful Activities Prevention Act (UAPA) and the Sedition laws. The Liberal use of the Unlawful Activities Prevention Act against Journalists refrains journalists from tracing, tracking, and publishing investigative articles due to the fear of being linked with criminals.

The use of Sedition laws against journalists under the guise that through their articles they are promoting hatred and exciting disaffection against the government is another significant threat to press freedom in India.

69. The PRP Bill defines "specified authority" to mean a District Magistrate or Collector or such other officer as the State Government or, as the case may be, Union territory Administration may, by notification, specify. The PRP Bill is criticised by Editors Guild of India because

(a) the definition of specified authority is too wide and can include even officers below the level of Collector. The PRP Bill enables the specified authority to perform the functions of Press Registrar General.

(b) the PRP bill confers various powers on the Press registrar General including the power to register, deny registration, cancel the registration, etc.

(c) the PRP Bill enables the specified authority to enter the premises of a periodical for inspection.

(d) All of the above

Sol. (*c*) The ability for authorities to enter these premises for inspection without proper safeguards or oversight raises concerns about privacy, freedom of expression, and editorial independence.

It opens up possibilities for undue influence or intimidation on journalists and media organisations. In a democratic society, freedom of the press is considered a fundamental pillar that ensures transparency, accountability and the dissemination of information to the public.

70. Freedom of press is not specifically guaranteed under the Constitution of India but is implied in Article 19(1)(a) i.e., Freedom of Speech and expression. Therefore, freedom of press is part of fundamental rights.

(a) Freedom of press being a fundamental right, no law can be made for registration and denial of registration of newspapers.

(b) Fundamental rights are not absolute rights and reasonable restrictions can be imposed on the exercise of fundamental rights and therefore, laws such as PRP bill can be enacted.

(c) Freedom of press being a fundamental right, journalists and press is exempt from the operation of general criminal law of the country.

(d) None of the above

Sol. (*b*) While fundamental rights are essential protections granted to individuals, they are not absolute. The Indian Constitution allows for reasonable restrictions to be imposed on the exercise of fundamental rights under Article 19(2).

These restrictions can be imposed in the interest of the sovereignty and integrity of India, security of the State, friendly relations with foreign States, public order, decency or morality, contempt of court, defamation, or incitement to an offense.

71. PRP bill denies the right to publish periodicals to a person who has been found to have committed a terrorist act and has been convicted by a competent Court in India.

Which of the following is most appropriate reason?

(a) The right to publish a periodical is denied because criminals do not possess any fundamental rights.

(b) The right to publish a periodical is denied because such a person is a threat to the society and nation.

(c) The right to publish a periodical is denied because they may not be neutral in reporting and may incite violence and spread disaffection against the state being themselves involved in terrorist acts.

(d) All of the above

Sol. (*c*) It highlights the potential danger of allowing individuals involved in terrorist activities to have a platform for communication that could be used to propagate violence or anti-state sentiments. Restricting such individuals from publishing periodicals, aims to prevent the dissemination of biased or inflammatory content that could further destabilise society and pose a threat to national security. This measure is intended to safeguard public safety and prevent the misuse of media platforms by those with criminal backgrounds linked to terrorism.

XIII. There are some advantages of the Digital Personal Data Protection Act (DPDPA), 2023. For instance, for the first time, personal data belonging to or identifying children will have to be classified separately, with such data carrying a greater degree of security and privacy. The law also seeks to reduce the rate and impact of data breaches targeting Indian businesses. The Digital Personal Data Protection Law, however, goes a step beyond by imposing penalties for cases where data is breached as a result of a lack of implementation of adequate security controls. However, it could be said that the law isn't balanced, because it provides wide exemptions to the processing of personal data to the government. For instance, data can be processed "in the interest of prevention, detection, investigation or prosecution of any offence … in India." These kinds of exemptions are dangerous as they stand to legitimise widespread and unwarranted collection of data under the guise that such collection and processing may ultimately be useful for preventing or deterring a crime.

Security agencies will have significant authority to collect and retain any data whatsoever, as is typically the case with exemptions relating to the maintenance of sovereignty, integrity, security of the state, preservation of public order, prevention of offences, and incitement to commit offences. The law also exempts processing of personal data held outside of India. The government is also exempt from being required to delete any data that it possesses, regardless of the purpose it may have been collected for, on the request of an individual, or by way of a prescribed data retention period.

The government is not bound by purpose limitations, allowing data collected for one specified purpose be used for a new, incompatible purpose, which stands in contrast to the regulations imposed on businesses.

[*Extracted*, with edits and revisions from "digital Personal data Protection Law Raises Questions About Consistency with Right to Privacy ruling" published in The Wire dated 22-08-2023]

72. Mr. Lal was suffering from a rare disease and the data relating of that was collected by the government. Suppose the DPDPA, 2023 provides exemptions for the government relating to data deemed "necessary for research, archiving or statistical purposes" if the personal data is not to be used to take any decision specific to a data principal and such processing is carried on in accordance with such standards as may be prescribed.

Which of the following is most appropriate?

(a) The personal data of Mr. Lal can be preserved by the government till the research on rare disease is complete.

(b) The data can only be used for taking any decision regarding Mr. Lal.

(c) The personal data of Mr. Lal's health conditions and his personal data can be preserved by the private hospital forever and used for research by them without his consent.

(d) All of the above

Sol. (*a*) According to the DPDPA, 2023, exemptions are provided for the government to collect and process data deemed necessary for research, archiving, or statistical purposes as long as the personal data is not used to make any specific decisions regarding an individual.

This means that the government can preserve Mr. Lal's data for research purposes related to his rare disease without using it to make decisions specifically about him.

73. Suppose the DPDPA, 2023 provided exemption for the processing of personal data for the purpose of ascertaining the financial position of any person who has defaulted in payment of amount due on loan taken from a nationalised bank. Mr. X Commits a default in repayment of emi of loan taken from a nationalised bank.

(a) The bank can demand access to and process the personal data of Mr. X relating to family history of ailments from which Mr. X or his family was suffering.

(b) The bank can process the personal data of mr. X viz., the particulars of the family, wife, children, brothers etc.

(c) The bank can process the data of Mr. X for the purpose of ascertaining the assets and liabilities of the defaulter.

(d) All of the above

Sol. (*c*) The bank can process the data of Mr. X to ascertain his assets and liabilities as part of its efforts to recover any outstanding debts.

This is a permitted use under the DPDPA, 2023 for credit reporting purposes and debt recovery activities by financial institutions.

Again, it must be applicable done by laws and regulations governing data protection and privacy.

74. Suppose Mr. Y, a citizen of India, is working in an mNC in New Zealand since 2021. The MNC has obtained personal details of the employee for the purpose of recovering the amount of indemnity bond if Mr. Y left the job within three years of joining.

(a) Mr. Y can file an application in India for protection of his digital personal data under the DPDPA if he leaves the job in September 2023, and returns to India.

(b) Mr. Y, being a citizen of india, can claim protection against the MNC for misuse of his personal data even while serving in New Zealand.

89. Which of the following strengthens the author's idea of words being 'like glow-worms momentarily dispelling the surrounding darkness'?

(a) Words help in understanding reality.

(b) Words illuminate the mind of the reader.

(c) Words help in escaping reality.

(d) Words cast darkness in the mind of the reader.

Sol. (*a*) Words help in understanding reality. This strengthens the author's idea. The metaphor of words being like glow-worms momentarily dispelling the surrounding darkness implies that words have the power to bring clarity and understanding to the reader, much like how light dispels darkness, revealing what was previously hidden. Therefore, by choosing option (a), it suggests that words aid in understanding reality by shedding light on various aspects of it. This aligns with the broader theme in the passage, where words are portrayed as a powerful tool that allows individuals to explore and comprehend the world around them.

90. In the context of the passage, what is the significance of the 'world within the word'?

(a) It refers to the power of language to create inspiration, energy and faith.

(b) It signifies the author's love for the global community.

(c) It represents the mysteries hidden in language.

(d) It describes the author's mission to explore different cultures.

Sol. (*a*) The phrase 'world within the word' captures the idea that words have the intrinsic power to create and shape entire worlds of meaning, inspiration, and faith. The passage discusses how words grant us the ability to explore the universe, give life to inanimate objects, and provide aesthetic form to the formless. This highlights the transformative and generative capacity of language. The significance of the 'world within the word' lies in its ability to inspire and energise, offering new perspectives and fostering a sense of connection and understanding.

XVI. Students have been abuzz over how artificial intelligence tools can do their homework and programmers over how these can increase their productivity or take away their jobs. As much as digitization has transformed the country in recent years, there is a widespread feeling that at some point around the horizon, Ai shall rejig everything in even more fundamental, fantastic, and frightening ways. This is why deciding how the coming changes should be regulated is very important. TRAI has made a strong case for an independent statutory authority to ensure the responsible development and use of AI in the country, a global agency along similar lines shall likely be pitched at the G20 leaders' summit, and interestingly even American MNC Microsoft has floated a blueprint for AI governance in India.

The great size and diversity of its 'data points' make india of great interest to all developers of AI technologies.

But India is only at their receiving end, nowhere close to the US and China's advances. Although lately, it is becoming obvious how much state censorship is encumbering China's Large Language Modeling, the country is still very much in the game with PhDs in fields related to AI, investments in AI chip hardware design, and domestic generative models like Wu Dao. The scientific accomplishments of India's Chandrayaan mission have seen it being wooed for various international space collaborations.

This promises spinoff technological benefits across Indian industry and is also geo-strategically useful. Likewise, it is only with sufficient AI prowess that India shall really get to play at the high table of global rulemaking for AI. Knowing how much Indians' future shall be shaped by generative AI needs matching efforts to create indigenous models.

In this and at this stage, a proactive government role is key, rather than just waiting on some large corporation to do the needful. Missing this bus will after all be even more costly than missing the chip research one. Plus, GOi alone can push academia-industry collaborations with the necessary weight and urgency. This does not let other institutions off the hook.

A US judge has rejected the copyright for an AI-generated artwork. Indian courts should start engaging with the broader issue of non-human agency rather than wait for precedence to be set elsewhere. Indian schools need to think beyond the ban-ChatGPt mindset. Let us lead instead of only being led.

[*Extracted* from "First, get the tech: Unless India develops domestic AI heft, it wouldn't play any meaningful part in global regulatory efforts", Times of India]

91. Which of the following is the author most likely to agree with?

(a) The best way to deal with the advancement of AI is to leave its regulation to market forces.

(b) Government-driven control of AI is inefficient and shall promote red-tapism.

(c) Private companies with their large capital and infrastructure design the most efficient AI governance models.

(d) Government-led initiatives of AI regulation and development lead to efficient outcomes.

Sol. (*d*) Government-led initiatives of AI regulation and development lead to efficient outcomes. The passage emphasises the need for government involvement in the regulation and development of AI to ensure responsible and effective outcomes. The author argues that India's government must take a proactive role in creating indigenous AI models and fostering academia-industry collaborations. The call for a government-driven approach is highlighted through mentions of the TRAI's proposal for an independent statutory authority and the significance of India's government role in AI governance.

92. Which of the following, if true, would most strengthen the main argument of the passage?

(a) Governments that lead the initiative on regulating and responding to the advancement of AI tools benefit the most from them.

(b) Governments that don't engage with generative AI and remain at its receiving end stay risk-averse with nothing to lose.

(c) Governments that actively incentivise MNCs to participate in AI governance make the most out of the advancements in the field.

(d) Governments that explore models of public-private partnership strike the right balance in regulating generative AI.

Sol. (*a*) Governments that lead the initiative on regulating and responding to the advancement of AI tools benefit the most from them.

The passage underscores the importance of government intervention in the regulation and development of AI.

Strengthening the main argument would involve evidence that supports the effectiveness of government-led initiatives in maximizing the benefits of AI tools. Option (A) directly aligns with this by suggesting that proactive government leadership in AI regulation results in significant benefits.

93. Based only on the author's statement that "indian courts should start engaging with the broader issue of non-human agency rather than wait for precedence to bc set elsewhere", which of the following would the author be most likely to agree with?

(a) Courts should take the initiative by being innovative and laying down rules where no precedents exist.

(b) Courts should wait for precedents and in the meantime refrain from engaging with the challenges presented by generative AI.

(c) Courts should stop relying on precedents and decide cases on the basis of judicial wisdom.

(d) Precedents are the best possible safeguard against arbitrary decision-making.

Sol. (*a*) Courts should take the initiative by being innovative and laying down rules where no precedents exist.

The author suggests that Indian courts should actively engage with the challenges posed by generative AI, rather than waiting for precedents to be set elsewhere.

This implies a need for judicial innovation and proactive rule-making in the face of new technological issues.

The statement emphasises the importance of addressing non-human agency within the judicial system promptly and effectively.

94. If the information in the passage above is correct, which of the following must necessarily be true?

(a) AI regulation is the responsibility of the legislature alone.

(b) AI regulation is the responsibility of courts and can't be addressed through standalone statutory rules.

(c) AI regulation is a collaborative effort involving all the institutions of the State.

(d) AI regulation is the domain of private industry.

Sol. (*c*) AI regulation is a collaborative effort involving all the institutions of the State.

The passage discusses the role of various institutions, including the government, courts and academia, in the regulation and development of AI.

It highlights the need for a comprehensive approach involving multiple stakeholders to effectively govern AI advancements. This collaborative effort is essential to address the complexities and far-reaching implications of AI technology.

95. Based on the author's arguments, which of the following would result in weakening, rather than strengthening india's position at the forefront of generative AI?

(a) Investing in indigenous AI chip hardware design and domestic generative models.

(b) Exploring spinoff technological benefits with other scientific advancements like the Chandrayaan mission.

(c) Introducing generative models like Wu Dao which have demonstrated success in other jurisdictions.

(d) Locally developing technologies such as indigenous AI models.

Sol. (*c*) Introducing generative models like Wu Dao which have demonstrated success in other jurisdictions.

While options (A), (B), and (D) suggest strengthening India's AI capabilities through local development and leveraging existing technological advancements, option (C) implies reliance on external models rather than developing indigenous solutions. The author emphasizes the importance of creating indigenous AI models and technologies to ensure India can play a significant role in global AI governance.

96. The author states that, "Missing this bus will after all be even more costly than missing the chip research one." For this statement to be true, with which of the following statements about chip research must the author most likely agree?

(a) India lead chip research from its frontiers.

(b) India was right to leave regulation of chip industry and research to MNCs.

(c) India should have proactively played a role in responding to new research in chip technology.

(d) The failure to respond to new developments in chip technology was a bigger loss than the potential failure to regulate generative AI.

Sol. (*c*) India should have proactively played a role in responding to new research in chip technology. The author's statement suggests that missing the advancements in generative AI would be a significant loss, comparable to or even greater than the missed opportunities in chip research. This implies a recognition that proactive involvement in chip research was necessary and that failing to do so was a significant setback. The comparison underscores the importance of not repeating the same mistake with AI.

XVII. Imagine you have just been appointed as a consultant for a manufacturing company that is experiencing a decline in its production efficiency. The company produces a wide range of products, and the management is concerned about the overall output. Your task is to identify the root causes of this decline and recommend solutions.

As you begin your investigation, you gather information and observe the following:

- The company recently introduced a new production system that is more automated but requires highly specialised operators.
- The workforce has reported a lack of motivation and job satisfaction, which has led to increased absenteeism.
- There have been several breakdowns in the new machinery, leading to production delays and quality issues.
- The company's competitors have adopted similar automation technologies and are experiencing increased productivity.
- Customer complaints about product quality have increased in recent months.

97. Based on the information provided, which of the following is a potential root cause of the decline in production efficiency?

(a) The introduction of a new production system.

(b) Lack of motivation and job satisfaction among the workforce.

(c) Increased absenteeism.

(d) Breakdowns in machinery.

Sol. (*b*) While all the factors listed contribute to the decline in production efficiency, the root cause often lies deeper within the organisational culture and employee satisfaction.

The introduction of a new production system, increased absenteeism, and machinery breakdowns are symptoms of underlying issues.

The lack of motivation and job satisfaction is a fundamental issue that leads to absenteeism, which in turn affects overall production efficiency. When employees are not motivated or satisfied, their performance suffers, leading to higher absenteeism and less effective operation of new systems.

98. What makes the introduction of the new production system a potential contributing factor to the decline in efficiency?

(a) The system is highly automated.

(b) It requires specialised operators

(c) The machinery is prone to breakdowns.

(d) Competitors have adopted similar technologies.

Sol. (*b*) The introduction of the new production system necessitates highly specialised operators.

If the workforce lacks the necessary skills or if there has not been adequate training, the system's potential benefits cannot be fully realised. This mismatch between the system requirements and the workforce capabilities can lead to inefficiencies, errors and breakdowns. The lack of skilled operators can also exacerbate the lack of motivation and job satisfaction among employees, further contributing to the decline in production efficiency.

99. What is a critical difference between the company's situation and that of its competitors?

(a) Both the company and its competitors have introduced new production systems.

(b) The competitors have experienced increased customer complaints.

(c) The company's workforce lacks motivation and job satisfaction.

(d) The company's machinery is prone to breakdowns.

Sol. (*c*) The passage indicates that the competitors who have adopted similar automation technologies are experiencing increased productivity, unlike the company in question. This suggests that the critical difference lies in the workforce's motivation and job satisfaction.

The competitors' workforce may be better trained, more motivated, or more satisfied with their jobs, leading to better utilization of the new technology and higher productivity. In contrast, the company's workforce issues are leading to absenteeism, lower productivity, and quality issues.

100. How might the increased absenteeism affect production efficiency?

(a) It might lead to increased quality issues.

(b) It might result in longer machinery breakdowns.

(c) It could lead to delays in production.

(d) It has no impact on production efficiency.

Sol. (*c*) Increased absenteeism directly impacts production efficiency by causing delays in production. When key personnel are absent, there may not be enough skilled operators to run the machinery or oversee production processes, leading to bottlenecks and slowdowns. Additionally, absenteeism can disrupt the workflow and Solution increase the burden on the remaining workforce, potentially causing further inefficiencies and quality issues.

101. What could be a possible solution to address the decline in production efficiency?

(a) Hire more specialised operators for the new system.

(b) Implement a motivation and job satisfaction programme for the workforce.

(c) Upgrade the machinery to reduce breakdowns.

(d) Purchase new machinery to replace the automated system.

Sol. (*b*) Implement a motivation and job satisfaction programme for the workforce.

Addressing the root cause of the problem, which is the lack of motivation and job satisfaction among the workforce, can lead to improved production efficiency.

A motivation and job satisfaction program could include various initiatives such as training and development, employee engagement activities, recognition and rewards, and better communication.

By enhancing job satisfaction and motivation, absenteeism can be reduced, and employees will be more inclined to work effectively with the new production system.

102. Based on the information provided, what is a potential consequence of increased customer complaints about product quality?

(a) It indicates that the company's competitors are also experiencing quality issues.

(b) It suggests that the company's products are meeting customer expectations.

(c) It may lead to a loss of customers and reputation damage.

(d) It shows that the company's automated system is performing well.

Sol. (*c*) Increased customer complaints about product quality can have severe consequences for the company, including loss of customers and damage to its reputation. Quality issues indicate that the products are not meeting customer expectations, leading to dissatisfaction and potentially driving customers to seek alternatives from competitors. In the long term, this can erode the company's market share and profitability.

XVIII. In a world where aspirations for upward mobility are fervent, the opportunities for achieving such dreams remain limited. When one generation falls short, the mantle of ambition passes to the next, embedding within it a heavy burden of responsibility. Failing to meet these expectations can lead to profound sorrow, and in the direst cases, even to suicide. It's in this landscape that coaching institutes assume a significant role, cultivating an atmosphere of uncertainty among students and parents. A stark discrepancy emerges between preparation for board examinations and competitive tests, amplifying the inequalities that plague the education system. The coaching industry's massive marketing campaigns further exacerbate the situation, with some strategies veering into ethical grey areas. The tests themselves, designed to be more challenging than standardised exams, set the stage for feelings of inadequacy and self-doubt when not conquered.

Our educational system is tailored to gauge an individual's merit through examinations. Eminent thinker Michael J Sandel dubs this system the 'tyranny of merit', a sentiment echoed by the Supreme Court of India. upholding the ObC reservation judgment, the Court called for a deeper evaluation of the 'idea of merit', highlighting its nuanced nature. Merit as a concept remains shrouded in misunderstanding and often goes unexamined within school curriculum. Adapting to new living arrangements, sourcing nourishing meals, battling isolation and grappling with commutes form the backdrop against which education unfolds. For marginalised communities and gender minorities, these hurdles are often amplified.

Social media algorithms exacerbate mental health concerns, sowing loneliness and impeding attention spans and creativity. Technology emerges as a potential equaliser in this landscape. Online platforms now offer preparation opportunities from the comfort of one's home. Government-curated or market-driven content could usher in a new era of accessibility.

[*Extracted*, with edits and revisions from "Kota suicides: Coaching institutes manufacture insecurity — moving beyond the tyranny of merit might help" authored by Akash Kumar and published in The Indian Express dated 2nd September, 2023]

103. As per the author, which one of the following is not likely leading to suicide among the students?

(a) Incorrect marketing strategies by the coaching institutes.

(b) Burdening of ambitions by one generation to another.

(c) Creation of hostile environment by the coaching institutes.

(d) Living in a surrounding with different background and culture.

Sol. (*a*) The incorrect marketing strategies employed by coaching institutes contribute to creating a stressful and competitive environment, which, in turn, may negatively impact students' mental health and well-being. This heightened stress and pressure can potentially contribute to severe outcomes, including suicidal thoughts or actions. Thus, option (a) aligns with the discussion in the passage regarding the role of coaching institutes in exacerbating student stress and mental health issues.

104. Which of the following is not true regarding the education system as per the opinion of the author?

(a) It is primarily based on the merit of the students.

(b) Merit of the students is not the determining factor.

(c) Examination plays a pivotal role in the education system.

(d) An individual's merit cannot be identified without examination.

Sol. (*b*) The passage emphasises that the education system is heavily based on examinations, which are used to gauge an individual's merit.

It also mentions that this system is often criticized for its narrow definition of merit, which does not account for the multifaceted nature of true merit. The Supreme Court of India and Michael J. Sandel critique this 'tyranny of merit,' indicating that the current system is indeed centered around merit as determined by exams.

105. Which of the following strengthens the argument regarding the 'idea of merit' as per the above-mentioned passage?

(a) True merit is multifaceted and extends beyond performance in a single competitive examination.

(b) Pervasive inequalities can only be identified with the help of a single competitive examination.

(c) True merit is not multifaceted and does not extend beyond performance in a single competitive examination.

(d) The school education ensures the proper implementation of the idea of merit.

Sol. (*a*) The passage suggests that the current education system's focus on examination performance as the primary indicator of merit is flawed. It cites the views of Michael J. Sandel and the Supreme Court of India, which call for a broader evaluation of merit. This indicates that true merit encompasses more than just exam performance, including various other attributes and achievements.

106. Which of the following is correct regarding the inequalities mentioned by the author?

(a) There is no difference between the preparation of board and competitive examination.

(b) Education system accommodates the inequalities.

(c) Competitive examination leads to social equality.

(d) There are existing inequalities which are enlarged by the competitive examinations.

Sol. (*d*) The passage highlights that competitive examinations exacerbate existing inequalities within the education system. The disparity between preparation for board exams and competitive tests, along with the aggressive marketing strategies of coaching institutes, amplifies these inequalities, making it harder for marginalised communities and gender minorities.

107. Which of the following statements reflects the use of online platforms for education as per the author?

(a) It provides equal opportunity to all the students irrespective of caste or creed.

(b) It encourages the students to prepare for examination.

(c) It should be the only means to education.

(d) It cannot be accessed by majority of the people due to technological impediments.

Sol. (*b*) The statement (b) reflects the use of online platforme for education as per the author.

The passage discusses the potential role of online platforms in education, highlighting that they offer preparation opportunities from the comfort of one's home. While the passage does not explicitly mention that online platforms encourage students to prepare for examinations, the implication is that they provide resources and tools for educational preparation. Therefore, it can be inferred that online platforms serve to facilitate and support students in their examination preparation efforts.

This interpretation aligns with the broader context of the passage, which discusses the challenges and opportunities in the education systems, including the role of technology in providing educational resources.

108. Which one of the following is not a challenge for quality education?

(a) Influence of social media.

(b) Mental health of the students and parents.

(c) Availability of online resources.

(d) Lack of competitive atmosphere among the peers.

Sol. (*c*) The passage points out several challenges to quality education, including the negative influence of social media on mental health, leading to loneliness and impaired attention spans. It also discusses the burden of ambition, creating stress and potential mental health issues for students and their parents.

The lack of a competitive atmosphere is not explicitly mentioned, but the pressures of competitive exams are highlighted. However, the availability of online resources is presented as a potential solution to some of these challenges, not as a challenge itself.

Section E : Quantitative Techniques

XIX. Automobiles are the most preferred mode of transport because they allow us to cover large distance quickly. Resultantly, vehicles have been developed that run on diesel, petrol and even on electricity, which is a remarkable innovative development.

During a survey about the percentage wise distribution of cars in four different states, the information regarding ratio between the diesel engine cars, petrol engine cars and electric cars was collected. Total number of cars for which data was collected was 8000. Of these, State 1 had 15% of the total cars in the ratio of 3:4:1 (diesel, petrol and electric); State 2 had 20% of the total cars in the ratio of 5:3:2 (diesel, petrol and electric); State 3 had 30% of the total cars in the ratio of 4:5:3 (diesel, petrol and electric) and State 4 had 35% of the total cars in the ratio of 7:5:2 (diesel, petrol and electric).

Based on the above information, answer the following questions.

109. If 45% of the electric cars in State 4 are air conditioned (AC) and remaining are non-AC, what is the number of non-AC cars?

(a) 380 (b) 240

(c) 220 (d) 180

110. Number of petrol cars in State 2 is how much percentage more than the number of diesel cars in State 1?

(a) 4.67% (b) 9.23%

(c) 3.33% (d) 6.67%

111. What is the ratio of diesel cars in State 4 to electric cars in State 3?

(a) 7:3 (b) 3:7 (c) 7:4 (d) 4:7

112. Compute the percentage of total electric cars to total cars in all the states.

(a) 19.37% (b) 18.37%

(c) 18.73% (d) 19.57%

113. What is the difference between number of petrol cars in State 3 and diesel cars in State 1?

(a) 350 (b) 400

(c) 500 (d) 550

114. What is the average number of diesel cars in all the states?

(a) 810 (b) 862.5

(c) 886 (d) 912.5

Sol. (Q. Nos. 109-114) According to the given information,

Total number of cars = 8000

For State 1

Total number of cars $= 8000 \times \frac{15}{100} = 1200$

Number of diesel cars $= \frac{3}{8} \times 1200 = 450$

Number of petrol cars $= \frac{4}{8} \times 1200 = 600$

Number of electric cars $= \frac{1}{8} \times 1200 = 150$

For State 2

Total number of cars $= 8000 \times \frac{20}{100} = 1600$

Number of diesel cars $= \frac{5}{10} \times 1600 = 800$

Number of petrol cars $= \frac{3}{10} \times 1600 = 480$

Number of electric cars $= \frac{2}{10} \times 1600 = 320$

For State 3

Total number of cars $= 8000 \times \frac{30}{100} = 2400$

Number of diesel cars $= \frac{4}{12} \times 2400 = 800$

Number of petrol cars $= \frac{5}{12} \times 2400 = 1000$

Number of electric cars $= \frac{3}{12} \times 2400 = 600$

For State 4

Total number of cars $= 8000 \times \frac{35}{100} = 2800$

Number of diesel cars $= \frac{7}{14} \times 2800 = 1400$

Number of petrol cars $= \frac{5}{14} \times 2800 = 1000$

Number of electric cars $= \frac{2}{14} \times 2800 = 400$

109. (c) Number of electric cars in State 4 = 400

Number of electric cars in State 4 are air conditioned (AC)

$= 400 \times \frac{45}{100} = 180$

$\therefore$ The number of non-AC cars

$= 400 - 180 = 220$

110. (d) Number of petrol cars in State 2 = 480

Number of diesel cars in State 1 = 450

$\therefore$ Required percentage $= \frac{480 - 450}{450} \times 100$

$= 6.666\% = 6.67\%$

111. (a) Number of diesel cars in State 4 = 1400

Number of electric cars in State 3 = 600

$\therefore$ Required ratio $= \frac{1400}{600} = \frac{7}{3} = 7:3$

112. (b) Number of total electric cars in all states

$= 150 + 320 + 600 + 400 = 1470$

$\therefore$ Required percentage $= \frac{1470}{8000} \times 100\%$

$= 18.375\% \approx 18.37\%$

113. (d) Number of petrol cars in State 3 = 1000

Number of diesel cars in State 1 = 450

$\therefore$ Required difference $= 1000 - 450 = 550$

114. (b) Average number of diesel cars in all the states

$= \frac{450 + 800 + 800 + 1400}{4}$

$= \frac{3450}{4} = 862.5$

XX. **A survey was conducted about the population of a particular region having working population of three lacs and information was collected about self-employed persons, casual wage workers, regular salaries employees of both urban and rural areas of the region. Self-employment is a key source of income in both rural and urban areas but it is more prevalent in rural areas (56% of the rural population) than in urban areas (40% of the urban population). Rural population was 48% of the total population. Regular salaried workers in urban areas were 48% of the urban population whereas in rural areas, regular salaried workers constituted 12% of the rural population. During the survey, the casual wage workers were found to be more common in rural areas than in urban areas. Casual wage workers in rural areas were 32% of the rural population whereas it was 12% of the urban population in urban areas.**

Based on the above information, answer the following questions.

115. **By what percentage the number of self-employed workers in rural areas is more than the number of self-employed workers in urban areas?**

(a) 29.23 (b) 33.24
(c) 35.01 (d) 34.32

116. **What is the ratio of urban and rural working population?**

(a) 12:13 (b) 11:12
(c) 13:12 (d) 03:08

117. **If urban population of the region increased from 52% to 56% and percentage of self-employed in urban region remains same, then number of self-employed people in urban areas are**

(a) 66840 (b) 68640
(c) 62700 (d) 67200

118. What is the total number of regular salaried employees of the region?

(a) 90216 (b) 91260
(c) 92160 (d) 96210

119. What is the percentage of regular salaried employees in rural areas corresponding to the number of casual wage workers in urban areas?

(a) 72.3% (b) 79.8%
(c) 88.7% (d) 92.3%

120. If 60% of the total working population of the region were self-employed in rural areas and 40% of total population were self-employed in urban areas, then what is the ratio of rural self-employed to urban self-employed?

(a) 2:3 (b) 3:2
(c) 13:18 (d) 18:13

Sol. (Q. Nos. 115-120) According to the given information,

Total population = 300000

Rural population $= 300000 \times \frac{48}{100} = 144000$

$\therefore$ Urban population $= 300000 - 144000 = 156000$

Number of self-employed workers in rural areas

$= 144000 \times \frac{56}{100} = 80640$

Number of self-employed workers in urban areas

$= 156000 \times \frac{40}{100} = 62400$

Number of regular salaried workers in urban areas

$= 156000 \times \frac{48}{100} = 74880$

Number of regular salaried workers in rural areas

$= 144000 \times \frac{12}{100} = 17280$

Number of casual wage workers in rural areas

$= 144000 \times \frac{42}{100} = 46080$

Number of casual wage workers in urban areas

$= 156000 \times \frac{12}{100} = 18720$

115. (a) Number of self-employed workers in rural areas = 80640

Number of self-employed workers in urban areas = 62400

Required percentage $= \frac{80640 - 62400}{62400} \times 100$

$= \frac{18240}{62400} \times 100$

$= 29.23\%$

116. (c) Rural population = 144000

Urban population = 156000

Required ratio $= \frac{156000}{144000} = \frac{156}{144}$

$= \frac{13}{12} = 13:12$

117. (d) Urban population $= 300000 \times \frac{56}{100}$

$= 168000$

Number of self-employed in urban region

$= 168000 \times \frac{40}{100} = 67200$

118. (c) Number of regular salaried workers in urban areas = 74880

Number of regular salaried workers in rural areas = 17280

Total number of regular salaried employees = 74880 + 17280 = 92160

119. (d) Number of regular salaried workers in rural areas = 17280

Number of casual wage workers in urban areas = 18720

$\therefore$ Required percentage $= \frac{17280}{18720} \times 100\%$

$= 92.3\%$

120. (b) Required ratio $= \frac{60\% \text{ of } 300000}{40\% \text{ of } 300000}$

$= \frac{60}{40} = \frac{3}{2} = 3:2$

CLAT Entrance Exam

SOLVED PAPER 2023

Instructions

- There are total 5 Sections and 150 questions in this Solved Paper.
- For every correct attempt the students will be awarded 1 mark.
- All the questions are in MCQs form.

Section A : English

I. I grew up in a small town not far from Kalimpong. In pre-liberalisation India, everything arrived late, not just material things but also ideas. Magazines - old copies of Reader's Digest and National Geographic - arrived late too, after the news had become stale by months or often years. This temporal gap turned journalism into literature, news into legend and historical events into something akin to plotless stories. But like those who knew no other life, we accepted this as the norm. The dearth of reading material in towns and villages in socialist India is hard to imagine and it produced two categories of people, those who stopped reading after school or college and those - including children - who read anything they could find. I read road signs with the enthusiasm that attaches to reading thrillers. When the iterant kabadiwala, collector of papers, magazines and rejected things, visited our neighbourhood, I rushed to the house where he was doing business. He bought things at unimaginably low prices from those who'd stopped having any use for them and I rummaged through his sacks of old magazines. Sometimes, on days when business was good, he allowed me a couple of copies of Sportsworld magazine for free. I'd run home and ignoring my mother's scolding, plunge right in - consuming news about India's victory in the Benson and Hedges Cup......

Two takeaways from these experiences have marked my understanding of the provincial reader's life, the sense of belatedness, of everything coming late and the desire for pleasure in language. ...... Speaking of belatedness, the awareness of having been born at the wrong time in history, of inventing things that had already been discovered elsewhere, far away, without our knowledge or cooperation, is a moment of epiphany and deep sadness. I remember a professor's choked voice, narrating to me how all the arguments he'd made in his doctoral dissertation, written over many, many years of hard work (for there indeed was a time when PhDs were written over decades), had suddenly come to naught after he'd discovered the work of CWE Bigsby. This I realised as I grew older, was one of the characteristics of provincial life, that they (usually males) were saying trite things with the confidence of someone declaring them for the first time. I, therefore, grew up surrounded by would be Newtons who claimed to have discovered gravity (again). There's a deep sense of tragedy attending this sort of thing–the sad embarrassment of always arriving after the party is over. And there's a harsh word for that sense of belatedness 'gdated'. What rescues it is the unpredictability of these anachronistic 'discoveries' the randomness and haphazardness involved in mapping connections among thoughts and ideas, in a way that hasn't yet been professionalised.

[*Extracted*, with edits and revisions, from 'The Provincial Reader', by Sumana Roy, Los Angeles Review of Books]

1. What use was the kabadiwala (wastepicker) to the author?

(a) The kabadiwala bought up all her magazines.

(b) The kabadiwala's stock of books and magazines were of interest to the author.

(c) The kabadiwala was about to steal the author's magazines.

(d) The author ordered books online which the kabadiwala delivered.

Sol. (*b*) The kabadiwala was of use to the author because his stock of books and magazines were of interest to the author. The author, in the passage, describes how she would eagerly rummage through the kabadiwala's sacks of old magazines, indicating her interest in the reading material he provided.

2. What according to the author is essential about the experience of being a 'provincial reader'?

(a) Belatedness in the sense of coming late for everything.

(b) Over-eagerness.

(c) Accepting a temporal gap between what was current in the wider world and the time at which these arrived in the provincial location.

(d) None of the above

Sol. (*c*) According to the author, what is essential about the experience of being a 'provincial reader' is accepting a temporal gap between what was current in the wider world and the time at which these arrived in the provincial location. The author discusses how in pre-liberalisation India, everything, including ideas and material things, arrived late, turning journalism into literature, news into legend and historical events into something akin to plotless stories. This acceptance of the temporal gap is a key aspect of the provincial reader's experience.

3. Why did the author feel a sense of epiphany and deep sadness?

(a) Because the things that felt special and unique to the author, were already established and accepted thought in the wider world.

(b) Because the author was less well-read than others.

(c) Because the author missed being in a big city.

(d) All of the above

Sol. (*a*) The author felt a sense of epiphany and deep sadness because the things that felt special and unique to the author, were already established and accepted thought in the wider world. The author talks about the realisation of having been born at the wrong time in history, of inventing things that had already been discovered elsewhere, far away, without their knowledge or cooperation. This realisation brought about a sense of epiphany and deep sadness.

4. What does the word 'anachronistic' as used in the passage, mean?

(a) Rooted in a non-urban setting.

(b) R elated to a mofussil area.

(c) Connected with another time.

(d) Opposed to prevailing sensibilities.

Sol. (*c*) As used in the passage, the word 'anachronistic' means connected with another time. The author uses the term to describe the 'discoveries' that were being made in the provincial setting, which were already established thoughts and ideas in the wider world.

5. Which of the following options captures the meaning of the last sentence best?

(a) Though the author feels provincial, she pretends to be from the metropolis.

(b) Though the author feels dated in her access to intellectual ideas, her lack of metropolitan sophistication lets her engage with the ideas with some originality.

(c) Though the author is aware of the limitedness of her knowledge, she is confident and can hold her own in a crowd. She also proud of her roots in the small town.

(d) All of the above

Sol. (*b*) The option that best captures the meaning of the last sentence is that though the author feels dated in her access to intellectual ideas, her lack of metropolitan sophistication lets her engage with the ideas with some originality. The author discusses how the unpredictability of these anachronistic "discoveries" rescues the sense of belatedness, suggesting that there is some originality in the way the provincial reader engages with ideas. This originality comes from the lack of metropolitan sophistication, allowing the author to engage with the ideas in a unique way.

II. Until the Keeladi site was discovered, archaeologists by and large believed that the Gangetic plains in the North urbanised significantly earlier than Tamil Nadu. Historians have often claimed that large scale town life in India first developed in the Greater Magadha region of the Gangetic basin. This was during the 'second urbanisation' phase. The 'first urbanisation phase' refers to the rise of the Harappan or Indus Valley Civilisation. Tamil Nadu was thought to have urbanised at this scale only by the third century BCE. The findings at Keeladi push that date back significantly. Based on linguistics and continuity in cultural legacies, connections between the Indus Valley Civilisation or IVC and old Tamil traditions have long been suggested, but concrete archaeological evidence remained absent. Evidence indicated similarities between graffiti found in Keeladi and symbols associated with the IVC. It bolstered the arguments of dissidents from the dominant North Indian imagination, who have argued for years that their ancestors existed contemporaneously with the IVC. ...... 'All the archaeologists I spoke to said it was too soon to make definitive links between the Keeladi site and the IVC. There is no doubt, however, that the discovery at Keeladi has changed the paradigm. In recent years, the results of any new research on early India have invited keen political interest, because proponents of Hindu nationalism support the notion of Vedic culture as fundamental to the origins of Indian civilisation. The Keeladi excavations further challenge the idea of a single fountainhead of Indian life. They indicate the possibility that the earliest identity that can recognisably be considered 'Indian' might not have originated in North India. That wasn't all. In subsequent seasons of the Keeladi dig, archaeologists discovered that Tamili, a variant of the Brahmi script used for writing inscriptions in the early iterations of the Tamil language, could be dated back to the sixth century BCE, likely a hundred years before previously thought. So not only had urban life thrived in the Tamil lands, but people who lived there had developed their own script. "The evolution of writing is attributed to Ashoka's edicts, but 2600 years ago writing was prevalent in Keeladi," Mathan Karuppiah, a proud Madurai local, told me. "A farmer could write his own name on a pot he owned. The fight going on here is 'You are not the one to teach me to write, I have learnt it myself."

[*Excerpted* from 'The Dig', by Sowmiya Ashok, *Fifty-Two*]

6. What was the assumption about the origin of urban life in India before the Keeladi dig?

(a) The origins lay in the Northern Gangetic plains, which urbanised earlier than the South.

(b) The Indus Valley Civilisation was the first urban civilisation of India.

(c) The second urbanisation was known to be in the Magadha empire.

(d) Both (a) and (b)

Sol. (*a*) The assumption about the origin of urban life in India before the Keeladi dig was that the origins lay in the Northern Gangetic plains, which urbanised earlier than the South. The passage mentions that until the Keeladi site was discovered, archaeologists believed that the Gangetic plains in the North urbanised significantly earlier than Tamil Nadu. This belief was based on the historical understanding that large scale town life in India first developed in the Greater Magadha region of the Gangetic basin during the 'second urbanisation' phase. However, the findings at Keeladi challenged this assumption by pushing back the date of urbanisation in Tamil Nadu, thereby altering the understanding of the origin of urban life in India.

7. "The Keeladi excavations further challenge the idea of a single fountainhead of Indian life". In elaboration of this sentence, which of these options follows?

(a) Dominant theories of how urban and modern life came about in ancient India were proved wrong by the Keeladi archaeological dig.

(b) Neither the Indus Valley Civilisation, nor the ancient urban civilisation of Magadha are clear explanations of how urban life emerged in the Keeladi region of southern India in the third century BCE.

(c) The Keeladi archaeological dig proved that Indian urban and modern life emerged independently in several historical periods and geographies and no one theory is enough to explain it.

(d) None of the above

Sol. (*c*) In elaboration of the sentence - "the Keeladi excavations further challenge the idea of a single fountainhead of Indian life." The option that follows is that the Keeladi archaeological dig proved that Indian urban and modern life emerged independently in several historical periods and geographies and no one theory is enough to explain it. The passage discusses how the Keeladi excavations challenge the idea of a single fountainhead of Indian life. The findings suggest that the earliest identity that can recognisably be considered 'Indian' might not have originated in North India, as traditionally believed. Instead, it indicates the possibility of multiple, independent origins of urban and modern life in different parts of India at different times.

8. Language, including a script similar to the Brahmi script, emerged in Keeladi in the sixth century BCE. Which of the following is the most convincing conclusion from this statement?

(a) Keeladi is a centre of culture and learning far superior to any others in ancient India.

(b) People of Keeladi were illiterate and could not use language to inscribe on their pots and pans.

(c) Ancient urban history of India, as we know it today, could significantly be altered by the findings of the advances achieved by the Keeladi civilisation.

(d) All of the above

Sol. (*c*) The most convincing conclusion from the statement "Language, including a script similar to the brahmi script, emerged in Keeladi in the sixth century bCE" is that ancient urban history of India, as we know it today, could significantly be altered by the findings of the advances achieved by the Keeladi civilisation. The passage mentions that archaeologists discovered that Tamili, a variant of the Brahmi script used for writing inscriptions in the early iterations of the Tamil language, could be dated back to the sixth century BCE, likely a hundred years before previously thought. This discovery challenges the existing understanding of the timeline of the development of language and script in ancient India, suggesting that the history of urban life in India may need to be reevaluated in light of these findings.

9. BCE is the acronym for

(a) Before the Common Era

(b) Before Colloquial Era

(c) Before Chapel Eternal

(d) Behind Christ Era

Sol. (*a*) BCE is the acronym for Before the Common Era. This term is used in academic and historical texts to denote years before the year 1 in the Gregorian calendar, which is the calendar most widely used today.

10. A farmer could write his own name on a pot he owned. The fight going on here is 'You are not the one to teach me to write, I have learnt it myself.' These sentences imply

(a) that the Keeladi civilisation was an inegalitarian one.

(b) that the Keeladi civilisation did not conserve the access to education and literacy only for the elite.

(c) that the farmers of the Keeladi civilisation were also potters.

(d) All of the above

Sol. (*b*) 'A farmer could write his own name on a pot he owned. the fight going on here is 'You are not the one to teach me to write, i have learnt it myself.' These sentences imply that the Keeladi civilisation did not conserve the access to education and literacy only for the elite. The passage mentions that a farmer could write his own name on a pot he owned, indicating that literacy was not limited to the elite in the Keeladi civilisation. This suggests a level of social equality and widespread access to education in the Keeladi civilisation, challenging the notion that literacy and education were exclusive privileges of the elite in ancient societies.

III. The call of self-expression turned the village of the internet into a city, which expanded at time-lapse speed, social connections bristling like neurons in every direction. At twelve, I was writing five hundred words a day on a public LiveJournal. By twenty-five, my job was to write things that would attract, ideally, a hundred thousand strangers per post. Now I'm thirty and most of my life is inextricable from the internet and its mazes of incessant forced connection–this feverish, electric, unliveable hell.

The curdling of the social internet happened slowly and then all at once. The tipping point, I'd guess, was around 2012. People were losing excitement about the internet, starting to articulate a set of new truisms. Facebook had become tedious, trivial, exhausting. Instagram seemed better, but would soon reveal its underlying function as a three-ring circus of happiness and popularity and success. Twitter, for all its discursive promise, was where everyone tweeted complaints at airlines and moaned about articles that had been commissioned to make people moan. The dream of a better, truer self on the internet was slipping away. Where we had once been free to be ourselves online, we were now chained to ourselves online and this made us self-conscious. Platforms that promised connection began inducing mass alienation. The freedom promised by the internet started to seem like something whose greatest potential lay in the realm of misuse.

Even as we became increasingly sad and ugly on the internet, the mirage of the better online self continued to glimmer. As a medium, the internet is defined by a built-in performance incentive. In real life, you can walk around living life and be visible to other people. But on the internet-for anyone to see you, you have to act. You have to communicate in order to maintain an internet presence. And, because the internet's central platforms are built around personal profiles, it can seem-first at a mechanical level and later on as an encoded instinct–like the main purpose of this communication is to make yourself look good. Online reward mechanisms beg to substitute for offline ones and then overtake them. This is why everyone tries to look so hot and well-travelled on Instagram why everyone seems so smug and triumphant on Facebook and why, on Twitter, making a righteous political statement has come to seem, for many people, like a political good in itself. The everyday madness perpetuated by the internet is the madness of this architecture, which positions personal identity as the centre of the universe. It's as if we've been placed on a lookout that oversees the entire world and given a pair of binoculars that makes everything look like our own reflection.

[*Extracted*, with edits and revisions, from Trick Mirror: Reflections on Self-Delusion, by Jia Tolentino, Random House, 2019.]

11. Which of the following statements can be inferred from the above passage?
(a) The internet expanded very slowly.
(b) The internet can be used to cause harm.
(c) The internet is addictive.
(d) The main purpose of social media platforms is to dissuade people from showing off.

Sol. (*b*) From the passage, it can be inferred that the internet has the potential to be used in ways that can cause harm. The author discusses the evolution of the internet from a platform for self-expression and connection to a space that can lead to self-consciousness, alienation and even misuse. This suggests that while the internet has the potential to connect people and provide a platform for self-expression, it also has the potential to cause harm by fostering feelings of alienation, self-consciousness and providing opportunities for misuse. The author's description of the internet as a "feverish, electric, unliveable hell" further underscores the potential harm that the internet can cause.

12. All the following statements are 'truisms', except
(a) The internet has changed the way the world works.
(b) A preference for cat videos can reveal a lot about your personality.
(c) Like with any tool, digital technology has both advantages and disadvantages.
(d) Only time can tell what the future holds.

Sol. (b) The statement that is not a 'truism' according to the passage is that a preference for cat videos can reveal a lot about your personality. A 'truism' is a statement that is obviously true and says nothing new or interesting. The passage does not discuss anything about cat videos or their relation to personality. Therefore, this statement does not align with the themes discussed in the passage and is not a 'truism' in this context.

13. Which of the following comes closest to the underlined sentence in the passage?
(a) The way we use the internet says a lot about who we are.
(b) The internet has reduced the distance between people living across the world.
(c) The internet has the ability to customise what we access based on our identity.
(d) The internet only shows us what we don't want to see.

Sol. (c) The underlined sentence in the passage comes closest to the statement that the internet has the ability to customise what we access based on our identity. The underlined sentence discusses how the internet reflects and reinforces our personal identity. This suggests that the content we see online is customised based on who we are, our preferences and our online behavior. This aligns with the idea that the internet has the ability to customise what we access based on our identity.

14. Which of the following is a metaphor?
(a) the village of the internet
(b) this feverish, electric, unliveable hell
(c) three-ring circus of happiness and popularity and success
(d) All of the above

Sol. (d) All the options provided, the village of the internet, this feverish, electric, unliveable hell and three-ring circus of happiness and popularity and success, are metaphors used in the passage. Metaphors are figures of speech that describe an object or action in a way that isn't literally true, but helps explain an idea or make a comparison. Here, the metaphors are used to vividly describe the author's feelings and observations about the internet.

15. Which of the following categories best describes this piece of writing?
(a) Non-fiction essay
(b) Fiction
(c) Academic paper
(d) Poem

Sol. (a) This piece of writing best fits the category of a non-fiction essay. The passage is a personal reflection on the author's experience with the internet, which aligns with the characteristics of a non-fiction essay. Non-fiction essays are based on real events and facts and aim to inform, persuade or entertain readers. They often explore personal experiences or societal issues in depth, as this passage does with the issue of the internet's impact on personal identity and social connection.

IV. Down by the sandy banks of the Yamuna River, the men must work quickly. At a little past 12 a.m. one humid night in May, they pull back the black plastic tarp covering three boreholes sunk deep in the ground. They then drag thick hoses toward a queue of 20-odd tanker trucks idling quietly with their headlights turned off. The men work in a team, while one man fits a hose's mouth over a borehole, another clambers atop a truck at the front of the line and shoves the tube's opposite end into the empty steel cistern attached to the vehicle's creaky frame. 'On kar!' someone shouts in Hinglish, almost instantly, his orders to 'switch it on' are obeyed. Diesel generators, housed in nearby sheds, begin to thrum. Submersible pumps, installed in the borehole's shafts, drone as they disgorge thousands of gallons of groundwater from deep in the earth. The liquid gushes through the hoses and into the trucks' tanks. The full trucks don't wait around. As the hose team continues its work, drivers nose down a rutted dirt path until they reach a nearby highway. There, they turn on their lights and pick up speed, rushing to sell their bounty to factories and hospitals, malls and hotels, apartments and hutments across this city of 25 million. Everything about this business is illegal the boreholes dug without permission, the trucks operating without permits, the water sold without testing or treatment. Water work is night work,' says a middle-aged neighbour who lives near the covert pumping station and requested anonymity. 'Bosses arrange buyers, labour fills tankers, the police look the other way and the muscle makes sure that no one says nothing to nobody.' Teams like this one are ubiquitous in Delhi, where the official water supply falls short of the city's needs. A quarter of Delhi's households live without a piped-water connection, most of the rest receive water for only a few hours each day. So residents have come to rely on private truck owners– The most visible strands of a dispersed web of city councillors, farmers, real estate agents and fixers who source millions of gallons of water each day from illicit boreholes and sell the liquid for profit. The entrenched system has a local moniker, the water-tanker mafia. A 2013 audit found that the city loses 60 percent of its water supply to leakages theft and a failure to collect revenue. The mafia defends its work as a community service but there is a much darker picture of Delhi's subversive water industry: one of a thriving black market populated by small-time freelance agents who are exploiting a fast-depleting common resource and in turn threatening India's long-term water security.

[*Extracted*, with edits and revisions, from: 'At the Mercy of the Water Mafia', by Aman Sethi, Foreign Policy]

16. Which of the following can be inferred from the passage?

(a) The water tanker mafia's operations, though illegal, are justified given the vital service they provide to the people of Delhi.

(b) The water supplied by the water tanker mafia is potentially contaminated.

(c) Private truck owners play the most important role in the operations of the water tanker mafia.

(d) The water supplied by the water tank mafia is meant primarily for residential use.

Sol. (*b*) From the passage, it can be inferred that the water supplied by the water tanker mafia is potentially contaminated. The passage mentions that the water is sold without testing or treatment. This lack of regulation and oversight implies that the water could potentially be contaminated with harmful substances or pathogens. This is a serious concern as contaminated water can lead to various health issues for the consumers.

17. Which of the following, used in the passage, suggests that the illegal supply of groundwater is not a recent phenomenon?

(a) Entrenched

(b) Ubiquitous

(c) Long-term water security

(d) Fast-depleting common resource

Sol. (*a*) The word 'Entrenched' used in the passage suggests that the illegal supply of groundwater is not a recent phenomenon. The term 'entrenched' implies that the system of illegal groundwater supply has been in place for a long time and is deeply rooted in the society. This suggests that the issue is not a recent development, but rather a long-standing practice that has become an integral part of the city's water supply system.

18. Which of the following seems to be the author's main concern in the passage?

(a) Delhi's water supply infrastructure does not adequately cater to all its residents.

(b) The illegal operations of the water tank mafia do not depend on the complicity of a range of actors, including the police and city councillors.

(c) The petty profiteering of a few actors comes at the immense cost of India's sustainable access to water.

(d) All of the above

Sol. (*c*) The author's main concern in the passage seems to be that the petty profiteering of a few actors comes at the immense cost of India's sustainable access to water. The author expresses concern over the exploitation of a common resource for personal gain. The illegal extraction and sale of groundwater by the water tanker mafia is depleting the water table and threatening India's long-term water security. This unsustainable practice could lead to severe water shortages in the future.

19. All of the following are sounds you can hear as the water tankers are filled, except:

(a) Creaking (b) Thrumming

(c) Droning (d) Gushing

Sol. (*d*) All of the following are sounds you can hear as the water tankers are filled, except for the sound of 'Gushing'. The sounds mentioned in the passage during the filling of the water tankers are the thrumming of diesel generators, the droning of submersible pumps and the creaking of the truck's frame. These sounds create a vivid auditory image of the scene. However, the sound of water 'gushing' into the tankers is not mentioned.

20. Which of the following words from the passage means 'hidden'?

(a) Illicit (b) Idling

(c) Subversive (d) Covert

Sol. (*d*) The word 'Covert' from the passage means 'hidden'. The word 'covert' means hidden or secret, which aligns with the description of the pumping station in the passage. The pumping station operates at night, under the cover of darkness and is hidden by a black plastic tarp. This covert operation allows the water tanker mafia to carry out their illegal activities undetected.

V. English encodes class in India. It does so by sliding into the DNA of social division: income, caste, gender, religion or place of belonging. The threat it poses to social cohesion has worried public commentators across the political spectrum. In an address delivered as independent India's Parliament dilly-dallied over the suggestion to replace English with regional languages as the medium of instruction for higher education, Gandhi said, 'This blighting imposition of a foreign medium upon the youth of the country will be counted by history as one of the greatest tragedies. Our boys think and rightly in the present circumstances, that without English they cannot get government service. Girls are taught English as a passport to marriage.'

A hundred years later, the language continues to be seen as a tool of exclusion. The problem now is about inequality of access. 'To be denied English is harmful to the individual as well as our society,' writes Chetan Bhagat, self-appointed leader of a class war set off by unequal access to English.

Bhagat, an engineer-turned-investment banker, wrote his first college romance in English in 2004. Then only a certain kind of person– Someone who grew up reading, writing and speaking the language– Wrote books in English– Big words, long sentences, literary pretension, heavy with orientalism. In the ten years since Bhagat put the popular in 'popular' English fiction, he has written six other novels and sold millions of copies all told. With every new book, all written in deliberately simple English, Bhagat has recruited thousands of new soldiers in his crusade against what he calls the 'caste system around the language'. Bhagat even has a term for Indians who have English E1. These people had parents who spoke English, had access to good English-medium schools– typically in big cities and gained early proficiency, which enabled them to consume English products such as newspapers, books and films. English is so instinctive to them that even some of their thought patterns are in English. These people are much in demand. The people E1 presumably control, through a nexus of privilege built on ownership of English are E2 'probably ten times the E1s. They are technically familiar with the language. [But] if they sit in an interview conducted by E1s, they will comeacross as incompetent, even though they may be equally intelligent, creative or hardworking.'

The situation may not be so comically stark. The haves and have-nots may not exactly fit into Bhagat's stereotypes of urban, sophisticated rich people and provincial, uncultured poor. His argument does not factor in many other walls around English in India.

You are more likely to learn English if you are born a man rather than a woman, high caste rather than low caste, south Indian rather than north Indian. There is more than one kind of E1 and more than one kind of E2. And there is more than one way E2s can overthrow E1s. One is to speak it like they know it.

[*Extracted*, with edits and revisions, from Dreamers: How Young Indians Are Changing the World, by Snigdha Poonam, Penguin Viking, 2018.]

21. Which of the following can be inferred about the author's views on English in contemporary India?

(a) The ability to speak English in India depends on place and social identity.

(b) English is not an Indian language.

(c) English language fluency does not necessarily imply competence.

(d) People's views on English are divided along political lines.

Sol. (*a*) From the passage, it can be inferred that the author's views on English in contemporary India is the ability to speak English in India depends on place and social identity.

The passage discusses how factors such as gender, caste and regional identity can influence one's access to English education in India. It suggests that English in India is not just a language, but a marker of social and economic status and access to it is often determined by one's social identity and geographical location.

22. Who among the following would defy Chetan Bhagat's neat categorisation of Indian English-speakers into E1 and E2?

(a) Savitha, an above-average student in an English medium school in Mumbai, belongs to an upper-middle class family. Public speaking makes her extremely nervous and she fumbles through all her interviews.

(b) Moin, once a milkman in Ranchi, learns English at the age of 17. After a lot of hard work, he becomes an instructor of spoken English at a thriving institute.

(c) Both (a) and (b)

(d) Neither (a) nor (b)

Sol. (*b*) Moin, once a milkman in Ranchi, learns English at the age of 17 and becomes an instructor of spoken English would defy Chetan Bhagat's categorisation of Indian English-speakers into E1 and E2.

Despite his humble beginnings and lack of early exposure to English, Moin manages to learn the language and even teach it, demonstrating that determination and hard work can overcome barriers of access and opportunity.

23. Which of the following best describes the author's response to Bhagat's views on English?

(a) The author dismisses his views as a self-appointed expert.

(b) The author completely agrees with his views.

(c) The author neither agrees nor disagrees with his views.

(d) The author considers his views and finds that they lack nuance.

Sol. (*d*) The author considers Bhagat's views and finds that they lack nuance is the best option that describes the author's response to Bhagat's views on English.

While the author acknowledges Bhagat's observations about the divide between those who are fluent in English (E1) and those who are not (E2), they also point out that Bhagat's categorisation oversimplifies the complex realities of English usage in India.

The author argues that there are more than one kind of E1 and E2 and that factors such as gender, caste and regional identity also play a role in determining access to English.

24. Which of the following can be inferred from Gandhi's views with respect to English in post-independence India?

(a) English should not be taught as a subject in Indian universities.

(b) English proficiency is vital in order to gain entry into the bureaucracy.

(c) Indian women cannot get rich if they do not know English.

(d) None of the above

Sol. (*b*) From Gandhi's views with respect to English in post-independence India, it can be inferred that English proficiency is seen as vital in order to gain entry into the bureaucracy. Gandhi mentions that boys think that without English they cannot get government service. This suggests that during the post-independence period, English proficiency was seen as a prerequisite for securing a job in the government sector.

25. All the following pairs of words are synonyms, except
(a) stark, sharp
(b) sophisticated, spoilt
(c) crusade, campaign
(d) cohesion, unity

Sol. (*b*) The pair of words that are not synonyms are 'sophisticated' and 'spoilt'. While 'sophisticated' generally means worldly-wise, cultured or refined, 'spoilt' typically means ruined, damaged or overindulged. These two words have different connotations and do not convey the same meaning.

VI. 'So pick a bird,' Iff commanded. 'Any bird.' This was puzzling. 'The only bird around here is a wooden peacock,' Haroun pointed out, reasonably enough. Iff gave a snort of disgust. 'A person may choose what he cannot see,' he said, as if explaining something very obvious to a very foolish individual. 'A person may mention a bird's name even if the creature is not present and correct, crow, quail, hummingbird, bulbul, mynah, parrot, kite. A person may even select a flying creature of his own invention. For example,winged horse, flying turtle, airborne whale, space serpent or aeromouse. To give a thing a name, a label, a handle; to rescue it from anonymity, to pluck it out of the Place of Namelessness, in short to identify it– well, that's a way of bringing the said thing into being. Or, in this case, the said bird or Imaginary Flying Organism.

'That may be true where you come from,' Haroun argued. 'But in these parts, stricter rules apply.'

'In these parts,' rejoined blue-bearded Iff, 'I am having time wasted by someone who will not trust in what he can't see. How much have you seen, eh? Africa, have you seen it? No? Then is it truly there? And submarines? Huh? Also, hailstones, baseballs, pagodas? Goldmines? Kangaroos, Mount Fujiyama, the North Pole? And the past, did it happen? And the future, will it come? <u>Believe in your own eyes and you'll get into a lot of trouble, hot water, a mess.</u>'

With that, he plunged his hand into a pocket of his auberginey pajamas and when he brought it forth again it was bunched into a fist. 'So take a look or I should say a gander, at the enclosed.' He opened his hand and Haroun's eyes almost fell out of his head. Tiny birds were walking about on Iff's palm and pecking at it and flapping their miniature wings to hover just above it. And as well as birds there were fabulous winged creatures out of legends; an Assyrian lion with the head of a bearded man and a pair of large hairy wings growing out of its flanks; and winged monkeys, flying saucers, tiny angels, levitating (and apparently air-breathing) fish. 'What's your pleasure, select, choose,' Iff urged. And although it seemed obvious to Haroun that these magical creatures were so small that they couldn't possibly have carried so much as a bitten-off fingernail, he decided not to argue and pointed at a tiny crested bird that was giving him a sidelong look through one highly intelligent eye.

[*Extracted*, with edits and revisions, from Haroun and the Sea of Stories, by Salman Rushdie, Granta and Penguin, 1990.]

26. If Iff is right, which of the following statements is true?
(a) You should only trust what you cannot see.
(b) Naming something is the only way to make it unreal.
(c) You should only trust what you can see.
(d) Naming something is one way to make it real.

Sol. (*a*) If Iff is right, statement (a) is true.

This is because, in the passage, Iff explains to Haroun that giving something a name or a label helps to bring it into being or reality. He emphasises that even if a creature is not physically present, by naming it, one can make it exist in some sense. This concept highlights the power of imagination and belief in creating reality, rather than relying solely on what can be physically seen.

27. Which of the following applies to Iff?

(a) He speaks in contradictions.

(b) He has a habit of speaking in synonyms.

(c) He uses proverbs to express ideas.

(d) He uses metaphors to describe things.

Sol. (*d*) Option (d) applies to Iff.

Iff uses metaphors to convey his ideas about the power of naming and believing in things that cannot be seen. For instance, he talks about rescuing something from the "Place of Namelessness" and how giving something a name can bring it into being. These descriptions are metaphorical, as they represent abstract concepts through more tangible images and ideas. Iff's speech is rich in metaphorical language, helping to illustrate his points in a more vivid and imaginative way.

28. Which of the following most accurately describes what the underlined sentence means in the context of the passage?

(a) Do not restrict your knowledge only to what you can physically see.

(b) Accept everything you see uncritically.

(c) Trusting your senses is a recipe for success.

(d) Learn not to appreciate viewpoints other than your own.

Sol. (*a*) The underlined sentence in the passage most accurately means that you should not restrict your knowledge only to what you can physically see. Iff argues that relying solely on one's own eyes can lead to trouble, suggesting the importance of acknowledging and understanding things beyond our immediate perception. This statement encourages a broader understanding of reality that goes beyond physical sight and includes imagination, intuition and intellectual insight.

29. All the words below are related in meaning, except

(a) levitate (b) fly

(c) hover (d) gander

Sol. (*d*) All the words listed are related in meaning, except for gander, which is not a synonym for levitate, fly or hover. While levitate fly and hover all relate to the action of moving or being suspended in the air. Gander is a term that means to look or glance at something. It does not convey the same sense of aerial movement as the other words.

30. What does 'fabulous' mean in the passage?

(a) Very good

(b) Unbelievable

(c) Mythical

(d) Enormous

Sol. (*c*) In the context of the passage, 'fabulous' means mythical. The term is used to describe winged creatures out of legends, suggesting a sense of mythical or fantastical quality. These creatures, such as an Assyrian lion with the head of a bearded man and a pair of large hairy wings, are not found in the natural world but exist in myths and legends. The use of 'fabulous' here conveys the extraordinary, imaginative nature of these creatures.

Section B : Current Affairs & General Knowledge

VII. Former Governor of a State and National Democratic Alliance (NDA) candidate Droupadi Murmu was elected the 15th President of India, the first tribal woman to be elected to the position and the youngest as well. She was declared elected on Thursday after four rounds of counting, although she had crossed the half-way mark after the third round of counting itself, posting an unassailable lead over her rival and the Opposition's candidate who conceded the election thereafter. Prime Minister Narendra Modi was the first to greet Ms. Murmu at her residence in New Delhi after the third round of counting showed that she had crossed the half-way mark.

Ms. Murmu hails from the Santhal tribe and was born in the district of Mayurbhanj, coming up the hard way in life, graduating and teaching in Odisha before entering electoral politics at the local body level and later being elected MLA and serving as a Minister in the Biju Janata Dal-BJP coalition government from 2000 to 2004. She remained an MLA till 2009, representing Rairangpur in Odisha, a town that burst into celebrations since her name was announced as a candidate for the post of President of India. She was known to intervene in stopping amendments to the Chota Nagpur Tenancy Act that was being brought in by the BJP government of Raghubar Das, which involved changing land use in tribal areas.

[*Excerpt* taken and edited from 'Droupadi Murmu elected 15th President of India', The Hindu]

31. Before Droupadi Murmu, India had only one other female president, Pratibha Patil. When did Patil serve as the President of India?

(a) 2007-2012 (b) 2005-2010
(c) 2012-2017 (d) 2006-2011

Sol. (a) Pratibha Patil served as the 12th President of India from 25th July, 2007, to 25th July, 2012. She holds the distinction of being the first woman to occupy the highest constitutional office in India. Her election was a historic moment, symbolising a step forward in gender equality and representation in Indian politics.

Patil, a veteran Congress leader, had a long political career, having served as the Governor of Rajasthan and holding various ministerial portfolios in Maharashtra before becoming the President. During her tenure, she focused on issues like women's empowerment, education and rural development. Her presidency also emphasised maintaining the dignity and decorum of the office while engaging in various ceremonial duties and state functions.

32. President Murmu has earlier served as a Governor of which State?

(a) Odisha (b) Bihar
(c) Jharkhand (d) West Bengal

Sol. (c) Droupadi Murmu served as the Governor of Jharkhand from 18th May, 2015, to 12th July, 2021. Her tenure as Governor was marked by significant efforts to uphold the rights and welfare of tribal communities. Hailing from the Santhal tribe, Murmu's appointment was a landmark for tribal representation in Indian governance. As Governor, she played a crucial role in opposing amendments to the Chota Nagpur Tenancy Act and the Santhal Pargana Tenancy Act, which aimed to change land use patterns in tribal areas. Her interventions ensured the protection of tribal lands from potential exploitation and reflected her deep commitment to her community's welfare. Additionally, Murmu's governance style was characterised by her inclusive approach and her efforts to bring about social and economic development in Jharkhand.

33. The first presidential election was held by the Election Commission in which year?

(a) 1952 (b) 1950
(c) 1948 (d) 1949

Sol. (*a*) The first presidential election in India was conducted in 1952, a few years after India became a republic on 26th January, 1950. Dr. Rajendra Prasad was elected as the first President of India and held office from 1950 until 1962. He was re-elected for a second term in 1957, serving a total of 12 years, which remains the longest tenure for any President in Indian history. The election of 1952 marked the beginning of the democratic process for selecting the head of state in independent India. Dr. Prasad's presidency set a precedent for future elections and established the protocols and traditions associated with the office. His leadership and commitment to the principles of democracy and constitutional governance were crucial during the formative years of the Indian Republic.

34. The Rashtrapati Bhavan was formerly known as the Viceroy's palace (during colonial times). Where did the Governor General reside before the transfer of the British capital to Delhi in 1911?

(a) Belvedere House

(b) Raisina Palace

(c) Secretariat Building

(d) Writers' Building

Sol. (*a*) Before the British capital was transferred from Calcutta (now Kolkata) to Delhi in 1911, the Governor General of India resided at Belvedere House in Calcutta.

Belvedere House, located in the Alipore region of Kolkata, served as the residence of the Governor General during the period when Calcutta was the capital of British India.

The decision to move the capital to Delhi was announced by King George V during the Delhi Durbar in December 1911. The shift was part of a strategic move to better administer the vast territories of India and to placate growing nationalist sentiments in Bengal. Consequently, the construction of the Viceroy's Palace (now Rashtrapati Bhavan) began in Delhi, designed by British architect Sir Edwin Lutyens. The new residence symbolised the shift in political power and the centralisation of administrative functions in Delhi.

35. Who among the following was a candidate in the elections for the Vice President of India in 2022?

(a) R. Venkataraman

(b) Yashwant Sinha

(c) M. Venkaiah Naidu

(d) Margaret Alva

Sol. (*d*) In 2022 Vice Presidential election, Margaret Alva was the candidate representing the opposition.

A seasoned politician and former Governor of Rajasthan, Alva has had a distinguished career in Indian politics, spanning several decades. She has also served as the Union Minister in various capacities and has been a prominent figure in the Congress Party.

In the Vice Presidential election of 2022, she contested against Jagdeep Dhankhar, the candidate of the National Democratic Alliance (NDA), who eventually won the election. The election was notable for the broad political engagement and discussions it spurred regarding the role of the Vice President in the Indian parliamentary system.

Margaret Alva's candidacy highlighted the opposition's efforts to present a united front and offered a significant choice to the electorate.

36. Voting in an Indian Presidential Election is through

(a) a first-past-the-post system through a single transferable vote cast in a secret ballot.

(b) a proportional representation system through a single transferable vote cast in a secret ballot.

(c) a proportional representation system through a single transferable vote cast in an open ballot.

(d) A first-past-the-post system through a single transferable vote cast in an open ballot.

Sol. (*b*) The Indian Presidential election employs a proportional representation system with a single transferable vote, conducted through a secret ballot. This system ensures that the elected President has a broad base of support from both Members of Parliament and Members of Legislative Assemblies across states and Union Territories. Each elector casts their vote by marking their preferences in a ranking order and these votes are then counted to determine the winner through a process that ensures the winning candidate achieves a majority. This system is designed to reflect the collective choice of the elected representatives and to ensure that the President represents a wide consensus. The use of a secret ballot upholds the confidentiality and integrity of the voting process, allowing electors to vote according to their conscience without external pressure.

37. Who was the first Dalit to hold the office of the President of India?

(a) Ram Nath Kovind
(b) VV Giri
(c) Neelam Sanjiva Reddy
(d) Kocheril Raman Narayanan

Sol. (*d*) KR Narayanan was the first Dalit to hold the office of the President of India, serving from 1997 to 2002. His election was a significant milestone in Indian politics, symbolising the inclusivity and democratic values of the nation. Narayanan had an illustrious career in public service and diplomacy before becoming President. He served as a diplomat in various capacities, including as India's ambassador to the United States and held significant positions within the Indian government. His presidency was marked by a commitment to social justice, upholding the Constitution and promoting the welfare of marginalised communities. Narayanan's tenure is remembered for his integrity, intellectual acumen and his efforts to ensure that the office of the President remained a moral compass for the nation.

VIII. 'I want everyone to understand that I am, in fact, a person,' wrote LaMDA in an 'interview' conducted by engineer Blake Lemoine and one of his colleagues. ....Lemoine, a software engineer at Google, had been working on the development of LaMDA for months. His experience with the program, described in a recent Washington Post article, caused quite a stir. In the article, Lemoine recounts many dialogues he had with LaMDA in which the two talked about various topics, ranging from technical to philosophical issues. These led him to ask if the software program is sentient. In April, Lemoine explained his perspective in an internal company document, intended only for Google executives. But after his claims were dismissed, Lemoine went public with his work on this artificial intelligence algorithm.and Google placed him on administrative leave........Regardless of what LaMDA actually achieved, the issue of the difficult "measurability" of emulation capabilities expressed by machines also emerges. In the journal Mind in 1950, mathematician [1] proposed a test to determine whether a machine was capable of exhibiting intelligent behaviour, a game of imitation of some of the human cognitive functions.

[*Extracted*, with edits and revisions, from "Google Engineer Claims AI Chatbot Is Sentient: Why That Matters", by Leonardo De Cosmo, Scientific American]

38. Whose name has been replaced with '[1]' in the passage above?

(a) Alan Turing (b) Peter Hilton
(c) Albert Einstein (d) Kurt Godel

Sol. (*a*) The name '[1]' in the passage refers to Alan Turing, a pioneering British mathematician and logician, who is widely considered the father of theoretical computer science and artificial intelligence. In his seminal 1950 paper 'Computing Machinery and Intelligence,' published in the journal mind, Turing introduced what is now known as the Turing Test. The Turing Test is a measure of a machine's ability to exhibit intelligent behaviour equivalent to, or indistinguishable from, that of a human. Turing proposed an 'imitation game,' where a human evaluator interacts with both a machine and a human through a computer interface without knowing which is which. If the evaluator cannot consistently tell the machine from the human, the machine is considered to have passed the test. This concept has been fundamental in discussions of artificial intelligence and machine learning.

39. Garry Kasparov, (then) world chess champion, was defeated in 1997 by a supercomputer in a chess tournament. What was the name of this supercomputer?

(a) Deep Mind (b) Deep Blue
(c) Watson (d) Blue Gene

Sol. (*b*) In 1997, Garry Kasparov, the reigning world chess champion, was famously defeated by IBM's supercomputer Deep Blue in a six-game match. This event marked a significant milestone in the field of artificial intelligence and computer science. Deep Blue's victory demonstrated the potential of computers to perform complex, strategic tasks at a level that could surpass human abilities. The supercomputer utilised advanced algorithms and computational power to evaluate millions of chess positions per second, enabling it to outmaneuver Kasparov. The match highlighted the rapid advancements in AI and machine learning, sparking debates about the future implications of AI technologies.

40. The Emperor's New Mind: Concerning Computers, Minds and The Laws of Physics, published in 1989, was written by a British mathematician who won the Nobel Prize in Physics for 2020. Who was this mathematician?

(a) Donna Strickland
(b) Max Tegmark
(c) Peter Higgs
(d) Roger Penrose

Sol. (*d*) "The Emperor's New Mind: Concerning Computers, Minds and The Laws of Physics," published in 1989, was authored by Sir Roger Penrose, a distinguished British mathematician and physicist. In this book, Penrose argues against the view that human consciousness can be fully explained by conventional computational theories of mind. He explores the relationship between physics and consciousness, proposing that quantum mechanics plays a crucial role in cognitive processes. Penrose's work spans various fields, including mathematics, cosmology and quantum gravity. In 2020, he was awarded the Nobel Prize in Physics for his work on black holes, specifically for demonstrating that black hole formation is a robust prediction of the general theory of relativity.

41. What kind of computing model resembles the way in which biological neurons exchange signals in the human brain ?

(a) Neural network
(b) Cognitive computing
(c) Natural language processing
(d) Data mining

Sol. (*a*) A neural network is a computing model designed to simulate the way biological neurons process and transmit information in the human brain. Neural networks consist of interconnected nodes (or 'neurons') that work together to solve complex problems. These models are a core component of deep learning, a subset of machine learning and are used in various applications, including image and speech recognition, natural language processing and autonomous systems. Neural networks learn from data by adjusting the weights of the connections between neurons, enabling them to recognise patterns and make predictions. The structure and functioning of neural networks are inspired by the neural architecture of the brain, making them effective for tasks that require a high degree of cognitive function.

42. What is the full form of 'LaMDA'?
(a) Landing Macro Data Applications
(b) Language Model for Dialogue Applications
(c) Large Model Data Applications
(d) Last Mile Dialogue Assessment

Sol. (*b*) LaMDA stands for Language Model for Dialogue Applications.
Developed by Google, LaMDA is an advanced conversational AI model designed to understand and generate natural language in a way that mimics human conversation.
Unlike traditional language models, LaMDA is specifically trained to engage in open-ended dialogue on a wide range of topics, making it capable of more fluid and dynamic interactions.
The development of LaMDA represents a significant step forward in conversational AI, aiming to enhance the quality and coherence of machine-generated dialogue. This capability is crucial for applications such as virtual assistants, customer service bots and other interactive AI systems.

43. Meta's newly released, fully trained large language AI model is called:
(a) FTP (b) OPT
(c) HTTP (d) SMTP

Sol. (*b*) Meta (formerly Facebook) released a fully trained large language AI model called OPT (Open Pretrained Transformer). OPT is part of Meta's efforts to advance Natural Language Processing (NLP) and create AI systems that can understand and generate human-like text.
The model is designed to be open and accessible to researchers, providing a platform for further innovation and experimentation in the field of AI and machine learning. By making OPT available, Meta aims to foster collaboration and transparency in AI research, helping to drive progress in developing more sophisticated and ethical AI technologies.

44. What is the name of the AI-enabled legal research assistive tool launched by the Supreme Court of India in April 2021?
(a) SURAM (b) GPT-3
(c) SUPACE (d) E -Courts

Sol. (*c*) The Supreme Court of India launched an AI-enabled legal research assistive tool called SUPACE (Supreme Court Portal for Assistance in Court's Efficiency) in April 2021.
SUPACE is designed to assist judges and legal researchers by streamlining the process of analysing and organising legal documents and information. This tool leverages artificial intelligence to enhance the efficiency and accuracy of legal research, allowing for quicker and more informed decision-making.
SUPACE aims to reduce the workload of judges by automating routine tasks and providing comprehensive insights into complex legal issues. The implementation of SUPACE reflects the Supreme Court's commitment to integrating advanced technologies to improve the judicial process and ensure timely justice.

IX. As a result of FIFA's restrictions on players wearing [1] rainbow armbands during the 2022 World Cup in Qatar, the German Football Association (DFB) has taken the matter to the Court of Arbitration for Sport (CAS). In a protest against FIFA's rule regarding the armband meant to support the [2] community, the German players covered their lips in a team picture taken before their 2-1 defeat to Japan.

On Wednesday, Germany played against Japan. Before the game, FIFA warned the DFB of 'severe' athletic fines if they breached tournament regulations by allowing their captain to wear the [1] armband, which promotes diversity and inclusion. The DFB told German captain Manuel Neuer not to wear the rainbow armband during the game.

If CAS rules quickly against the suspension's legality, Neuer might continue to wear the captain's armband for

Germany's next game against Spain on Sunday. CAS has set up a special ad hoc branch for this World Cup to ensure that applications are processed within 48 hours. Germany's players protested by covering their lips as they sought to wear the rainbow armband during their team's dramatic 2-1 defeat to Japan at the Khalifa Stadium.

[*Extracted*, with edits and revisions, from "World Cup 2022: Germany's players cover mouths during team photo to protest FIFA's rainbow armband rule", The Economic Times]

45. What is the name of the armband which has been replaced with '[1]' in the passage above?

(a) FreeLove (b) OneLove
(c) Pride (d) PlayLove

Sol. (*b*) The armband referred to as '[1]' in the passage is the OneLove armband. The OneLove campaign was initiated to promote diversity, inclusion and to show support for the LGBTQ+ community. The armband features a heart with multiple colors to symbolise unity and equality among different communities. During the 2022 World Cup in Qatar, FIFA restricted players from wearing the OneLove armband, citing regulations that prohibited political statements on the field.

This led to various protests and legal actions, including the German football association (DFB) taking the matter to the Court of Arbitration for Sport (CAS). The symbolic gesture of wearing the armband was intended to advocate for human rights and stand against discrimination.

46. The name of which community has been replaced with '[2]' in the passage above?

(a) Kurdish (b) Rohingya
(c) U yghur (d) LGBTQ+

Sol. (*d*) The community referred to as '[2]' in the passage is the LGBTQ+ community. The OneLove armband was specifically designed to show support for the LGBTQ+ community, promoting diversity, inclusion and equality.

The armband's colors and design are reminiscent of the Pride flag, which is a well-known symbol of LGBTQ+ rights. The controversy surrounding FIFA's ban on the armband during the 2022 World Cup in Qatar brought attention to issues of discrimination and human rights in sports. The German football team's protest by covering their mouths in team photos was a direct response to FIFA's restrictions, highlighting the importance of free expression and support for marginalised communities.

47. What is the name of the system used to monitor and regulate migrant labourers, which is used in Qatar and a few other countries and which came under heavy criticism in the build-up to the FIFA World Cup 2022 in Qatar?

(a) Iddat (b) Khalifa
(c) Kafala (d) Jazeera

Sol. (*c*) The system referred to in the passage is the Kafala system, which is used to monitor and regulate migrant laborers in Qatar and several other Middle Eastern countries. The Kafala system has been heavily criticised for its exploitative practices and lack of protections for migrant workers. Under this system, migrant workers are required to have a local sponsor (usually their employer) who controls their visa and employment status. This often leads to situations where workers are subjected to poor working conditions, low wages and restrictions on their freedom of movement. In the lead-up to the FIFA World Cup 2022 in Qatar, numerous reports highlighted the plight of migrant workers involved in the construction of stadiums and infrastructure. The international outcry led to calls for reform and greater scrutiny of labour practices in Qatar.

48. Where is the Court of Arbitration for Sport based?

(a) Lausanne, Switzerland
(b) The Hague, Netherlands
(c) Brussels, Belgium
(d) Paris, France

Sol. (*a*) The Court of Arbitration for Sport (CAS) is based in Lausanne, Switzerland. CAS was established in 1984 to provide an independent, specialised tribunal to resolve disputes related to sport through arbitration. It handles cases involving a wide range of issues, including doping, contract disputes and governance matters. CAS operates under the aegis of the International Council of Arbitration for Sport (ICAS) and is recognised by major sports organisations, including the International Olympic Committee (IOC) and FIFA. The court's decisions are binding and enforceable, providing a crucial mechanism for maintaining fairness and integrity in international sports. Given its significance in adjudicating sports-related disputes, the CAS plays a vital role in upholding the principles of justice and impartiality in the sporting world.

49. Who is the current captain of the Indian men's football team?

(a) Shabbir Ali
(b) Bhaichung Bhutia
(c) Sunil Chhetri
(d) I .M. Vijayan

Sol. (*c*) The current captain of the Indian men's football team is Sunil Chhetri. Chhetri is one of the most prominent and successful footballers in India, having earned numerous accolades for his performances on both the national and international stages.

As of 2022, Chhetri is the second-highest international goal scorer among active players, behind only Cristiano Ronaldo. He has played a crucial role in leading the Indian team to multiple victories and has been instrumental in popularising football in a cricket-dominated country. Chhetri's leadership, skill and dedication to the sport have made him a revered figure in Indian football and his contributions continue to inspire young players across the nation. Therefore, option (C) Sunil Chhetri is the correct answer.

50. Timothy Weah, the Paris Saint Germain and U.S. national team player in the FIFA World Cup 2022 in Qatar is the son of the President of which country?

(a) Senegal (b) Uruguay
(c) Honduras (d) Liberia

Sol. (*d*) Timothy Weah, a talented footballer playing for Paris Saint-Germain (PSG) and the U.S. national team, is the son of George Weah, the President of Liberia. George Weah is a former professional footballer who achieved international fame as one of the greatest African footballers of all time. He played for clubs like AC Milan, Chelsea and Paris Saint-Germain and won the FIFA World Player of the Year award in 1995.

After retiring from football, George Weah transitioned into politics and was elected President of Liberia in 2018. Timothy Weah has followed in his father's footsteps by pursuing a career in football and has represented the United States at various youth levels before making his senior debut.

51. Which of the following is the oldest football tournament in India?

(a) Indian Super League
(b) I FA Shield Cup
(c) Santosh Trophy
(d) Durand Cup

Sol. (*d*) The Durand Cup is the oldest football tournament in India and one of the oldest in the world, having been established in 1888. Named after its founder, Sir Mortimer Durand, the tournament was initially held in Shimla before being moved to New Delhi and later to Kolkata. The Durand Cup has a rich history and has been a prestigious competition in Indian football, attracting participation from top clubs and teams from across the country. The tournament has played a significant role in the development and promotion of football in India, providing a platform for players to showcase their talents and compete at a high level. Given its historical significance and long-standing tradition, the Durand Cup is a celebrated event in the Indian football calendar.

X. YouTuber Nas Daily in one of his videos named him as the Most Generous Billionaire who wanted to donate all his wealth to charity. But ten months later, '[1]' is no longer a billionaire. He is alleged to have caused massive losses worth $1 billion to investors. Known by his initials, he is the co-founder and former CEO of FTX, one of the biggest cryptocurrency exchange which has recently filed for bankruptcy in the US.

Once a billionaire with an estimated wealth of $26 billion at peak, according to Bloomberg estimates, [1] has seen his wealth been entirely wiped out. [1] studied physics at Massachusetts Institute of Technology (MIT) and traded currencies, futures and exchange-traded funds before moving to crypto trading, setting up [2] in 2017.

[1] teamed up with Gary Wang, a former software engineer at Google and a fellow MIT graduate, to launch FTX in 2019. The company offered trading on crypto tokens and derivatives. At the start of 2022, investors valued FTX and its U.S. operations at $40 billion. [1] transferred $10 billion in customer funds to his hedge fund, [2] without publicly disclosing it, many say this become the reason for collapse of his empire.

[*Extracted*, with edits and revisions, from "Who is [1], the co-founder of collapsed crypto firm FTX", Hindustan Times]

52. Which person's name has been replaced with '[1]' in the passage above?

(a) Mike Novogratz

(b) Brian Armstrong

(c) Changpeng Zhao

(d) Sam Bankman-Fried

Sol. (*d*) Sam Bankman-Fried. The person referred to as '[1]' in the passage is Sam Bankman-Fried, the co-founder and former CEO of FTX, a major cryptocurrency exchange that recently filed for bankruptcy. Known by his initials SBF, Sam Bankman-Fried was once a prominent figure in the cryptocurrency world, with an estimated wealth of $26 billion at its peak. He studied physics at the Massachusetts Institute of Technology (MIT) and had a background in trading currencies, futures and exchange-traded funds before moving into the crypto space. In 2017, he founded Alameda Research, a quantitative trading firm and later co-founded FTX in 2019 with Gary Wang.

FTX's rapid rise and subsequent dramatic collapse, attributed to the mismanagement and undisclosed transfer of customer funds, led to significant financial losses and the downfall of Bankman-Fried's empire.

53. Which hedge fund's name has been replaced with '[2]' in the passage above?

(a) BlackRock Advisors

(b) Alameda Research

(c) AQR Capital Management

(d) M an Group

Sol. (*b*) The hedge fund referred to as '[2]' in the passage is Alameda Research. Founded by Sam Bankman-Fried in 2017, Alameda Research is a quantitative trading firm that played a crucial role in the operations of FTX.

The passage highlights the significant role of Alameda Research in the collapse of FTX, noting that Sam Bankman-Fried transferred $10 billion in customer funds to this hedge fund without proper disclosure, which contributed to the financial instability and eventual bankruptcy of FTX. Alameda Research was instrumental in the rapid growth of FTX but also central to its downfall due to the controversial and opaque financial practices.

54. This person was once named "the world's youngest self-made female billionaire" by Forbes magazine and is the founder of the company Theranos. What is the name of this person?

(a) Elizabeth Holmes

(b) Eren Ozmen

(c) Fan Hongwei

(d) Diane Hendricks

Sol. (*a*) Elizabeth Holmes is the founder of Theranos, a health technology company that claimed to have revolutionised blood testing with its proprietary technology. Once hailed as a visionary entrepreneur, Holmes was named "the world's youngest self-made female billionaire" by Forbes magazine due to her stake in Theranos, which was valued at $9 billion at its peak. However, subsequent investigations revealed that the technology did not work as claimed, leading to charges of fraud against Holmes. The Theranos scandal became one of the most high-profile corporate fraud cases in recent history, highlighting the importance of scientific validation and transparency in biotech startups.

55. The Reserve Bank of India recently announced the launch of 'Digital Rupee. Wholesale Segment', a form of which of the following?

(a) Digi Suvidha
(b) Virtual Wallet
(c) Central Bank Digital Currency
(d) Cyber Rupee

Sol. (*c*) The 'Digital Rupee — Wholesale Segment' launched by the Reserve Bank of India (RBI) is a form of Central Bank Digital Currency (CBDC). A CBDC is a digital form of a country's fiat currency, issued and regulated by the central bank. The Digital Rupee aims to enhance the efficiency of the interbank market and reduce transaction costs. The wholesale CBDC is primarily intended for the settlement of large-value transactions and interbank transfers, providing a secure and efficient alternative to traditional banking systems. This initiative reflects the RBI's efforts to modernize the financial system and embrace the digital economy while maintaining monetary stability.

56. Which of the following technologies does cryptocurrency rely on?

(a) Cryptography (b) Blockchain
(c) Spectrography (d) Both (a) and (b)

Sol. (*d*) Cryptocurrencies rely on both cryptography and blockchain technologies. Cryptography ensures the security, integrity and privacy of transactions by using complex algorithms to encrypt data. This prevents unauthorised access and tampering. Blockchain, on the other hand, is a decentralised ledger technology that records all transactions across a network of computers. Each block in the blockchain contains a list of transactions and these blocks are linked together in a chronological chain. The combination of cryptography and blockchain enables secure, transparent and immutable transactions, which are fundamental to the functioning of cryptocurrencies like Bitcoin, Ethereum and others.

57. What is the name of the Government of India-owned corporation that mints coins used as legal tender in India?

(a) National Institute of Financial Management
(b) Security Printing and Minting Corporation of India Ltd.
(c) India Infrastructure Finance Company Ltd.
(d) National Bank of Agricultural and Rural Development

Sol. (*b*) The Security Printing and Minting Corporation of India Ltd. (SPMCIL) is the government-owned corporation responsible for minting coins used as legal tender in India. SPMCIL was established in 2006 and operates under the Ministry of Finance. It is involved in the production of currency notes, coins, non-judicial stamps, postage stamps and other security products. SPMCIL has several mints across the country, including those in Mumbai, Kolkata, Hyderabad and Noida, where coins are manufactured to meet the nation's requirements. The corporation plays a crucial role in ensuring the availability of secure and reliable currency and coinage for the Indian economy.

58. Who was the founder and former Chairman of Satyam Computer Services Ltd.,and was sentenced to prison and fined for a corporate governance scam?

(a) Harshad Mehta

(b) Ketan Parekh

(c) B . Ramalinga Raju

(d) Nirav Modi

Sol. (*c*) B. Ramalinga Raju was the founder and former chairman of Satyam Computer Services Ltd., one of India's leading IT services companies. In January 2009, Raju confessed to a massive accounting fraud, admitting that he had falsified the company's financial statements and inflated its assets and profits for several years. The scandal, often referred to as 'India's Enron,' led to a significant loss of investor confidence and a sharp decline in the company's stock value. Raju's confession resulted in his arrest and he was later sentenced to prison and fined for his role in the corporate governance scam. The Satyam scandal highlighted the need for stronger regulatory oversight and corporate governance standards in India.

XI. The agriculture sector has experienced buoyant growth in the past two years. The sector, which is the largest employer of workforce, accounted for a sizeable 18.8 per cent (2021- 22) in Gross Value Added (GVA) of the country registering a growth of 3.6 per cent in 2020-21 and 3.9 per cent in 2021-22. Growth in allied sectors including livestock, dairy and fisheries has been the major drivers of overall growth in the sector. When measured in total value of agricultural production, India is ranked fourth largest in the world.

Post-independence, there was a need to import food grains due to low-productivity, stagnant food-crop sector and poor rural infrastructure making food self-sufficiency a major national goal. The introduction of the Green Revolution then yielded spectacular results and we became one of the largest producers of many agricultural commodities such as rice, wheat, pulses, fruits and vegetables. From being a net importer of foods in the 1960s, India is now a net exporter, thanks to Indian farmers and the Indian agriculture input industry.

[*Extracted*, with edits and revisions, from: "India's changing agricultural landscape and its way to inclusive growth", by NS Ramaswamy, The Economic Times]

59. Which of the following is the largest exported agricultural product from India?

(a) Wheat (b) Sugar

(c) Rice (d) Barley

Sol. (*c*) Rice is the largest exported agricultural product from India. India is the world's largest exporter of rice, accounting for a significant share of global rice trade. The country exports both basmati and non-basmati varieties of rice to numerous countries across Asia, the Middle East, Africa and Europe. The Indian rice export market has been bolstered by its high-quality produce, competitive pricing and strategic trade policies. In the fiscal year 2021-22, rice exports from India reached new heights, driven by robust demand from traditional markets and new trade agreements.

60. According to provisional data released by the Directorate General of Commercial Intelligence and Statistics, India achieved record exports of agricultural exports for the financial year FY22. What was the value of India fs agricultural products exports according to this data?

(a) USD 7.5 billion

(b) USD 95.34 billion

(c) USD 13.2 billion

(d) USD 50.21 billion

Sol. (*d*) According to the provisional data released by the Directorate General of Commercial Intelligence and Statistics (DGCI&S), India achieved a record value of USD 50.21 billion in agricultural exports for the financial year FY22.

This milestone underscores the significant growth and resilience of the

Indian agriculture sector, which has managed to expand its export footprint despite various challenges such as the COVID-19 pandemic and fluctuating global trade dynamics. The increase in exports was driven by a surge in shipments of products like rice, marine products, spices and sugar. This remarkable performance reflects the sector's enhanced productivity, better market access and improved logistics.

61. Who among the following is also called the 'Father of the Wheat Revolution'?

(a) Dilbagh Singh Athwal
(b) Verghese Kurien
(c) Atmaram Bhairav Joshi
(d) Shanti Swaroop Bhatnagar

Sol. (*a*) Dilbagh Singh Athwal is known as the 'Father of the Wheat Revolution' in India. He was an agronomist and plant breeder who made significant contributions to the development of high-yielding varieties of wheat that played a crucial role in the Green Revolution in India. His work, along with that of other agricultural scientists, led to a substantial increase in wheat production, transforming India from a food-deficient nation to one of the world's leading producers of wheat. Athwal's research and innovations in plant breeding were instrumental in achieving self-sufficiency in food grains and improving food security in India.

62. India is the world's largest producer of which of the following?

(a) Poultry meat (b) Rice
(c) Almonds (d) Milk

Sol. (*d*) India is the world's largest producer of milk. The country's dairy industry has experienced significant growth over the past few decades, largely due to initiatives like Operation Flood, which transformed India from a milk-deficient country to the world's largest milk producer. The White Revolution, spearheaded by Dr. Verghese Kurien, played a pivotal role in this transformation. Today, India produces over 200 million metric tons of milk annually, contributing substantially to the global dairy market. The Indian dairy sector supports millions of small and marginal farmers, providing them with a steady source of income.

63. What is India fs ranking in the 2022 Global Hunger Index?

(a) 10 (b) 107 (c) 50 (d) 35

Sol. (*b*) India was ranked 107th in the 2022 Global Hunger Index (GHI). The GHI is a tool designed to measure and track hunger at global, regional and national levels. It is calculated based on four indicators: undernourishment child wasting, child stunting and child mortality. India's ranking reflects significant challenges in addressing malnutrition and food insecurity, despite being one of the world's largest food producers. The low ranking highlights the need for comprehensive policies and programs to improve food distribution, nutrition and overall public health.

64. The National Commission on Farmers, constituted in December 2004, which recommended the C2+50% formula for calculation of the Minimum Support Price, was chaired by:

(a) Ashok Gulati
(b) P. Sainath
(c) M .S. Swaminathan
(d) Abhijit Sen

Sol. (*c*) The National Commission on Farmers, which recommended the C2+50% formula for calculating the Minimum Support Price (MSP), was chaired by Dr. M.S. Swaminathan. Dr. Swaminathan is a renowned agricultural scientist known for his role in India's Green Revolution. The C2+50% formula suggests that the MSP should be at least 50% more than the cost of production, including comprehensive costs (C2) that cover all expenses incurred by farmers. This recommendation aims to ensure that farmers receive a fair and remunerative price for their produce, thus enhancing their income and economic stability.

65. The bio-decomposer technology to avoid stubble burning around the Delhi NCR was developed by:

(a) Monsanto
(b) Cargill
(c) Biocon
(d) ICAR, Pusa Campus

Sol. (*d*) The bio-decomposer technology to avoid stubble burning around the Delhi NCR region was developed by the Indian Council of Agricultural Research (ICAR), Pusa Campus. This technology involves spraying a microbial solution that decomposes crop residue, turning it into manure within a few weeks. Stubble burning has been a major environmental issue, contributing to severe air pollution in the region. The bio-decomposer offers an eco-friendly alternative, reducing air pollution and improving soil health. The successful implementation of this technology can help mitigate the adverse effects of stubble burning and promote sustainable agricultural practices.

Section C : Legal Reasoning

Assume that the statements in the passages are the applicable law.

XII. Quashing a case of cruelty that was filed against a man by his wife, the Bombay High Court said that if a married lady is asked to do household work for the family, it cannot be said that she is treated 'like a maid servant'. The Court was hearing an application by the husband and his parents seeking that proceedings against them are quashed. A First Information Report ('FIR') was filed against the trio in September 2020, around nine months after the marriage, alleging that they hounded the woman for money to purchase a car, harassed her 'mentally and physically' and treated her like a maid servant. Examining the evidence, the Court found that there was no merit to the woman's allegations. The Court said that though the FIR says that she was treated properly for about a month and then 'like a maid servant", there are no details of what this meant. The Court added: "If a married lady is asked to do household work for the purpose of the family, it cannot be said that it is like a maid servant." The Court held that the mere use of the word harassment "mentally and physically" in the FIR is not sufficient to constitute an offence Section 498A of the Indian Penal Code ('IPC'), which punishes the husband, or a relative of the husband of a woman who subjects her to cruelty in any way. It is interesting to note that Section 498A of the IPC also provides that if a married woman is actually treated like a 'maid servant', it would be an offence under that Section.

[*Extracted*, with edits and revisions, from "If Wife Is Asked To Do Household Work, Does Not Mean She Is Treated Like Maid: Bombay HC", The Wire]

66. Ashwin and Ashima were married in February 2020. In March 2020, Ashwin asked Ashima to take care of all their household work, such as cooking, cleaning and other domestic chores, as he was very busy with his professional responsibilities. Ashima claims that this amounts to treating her like a maid servant and constitutes an offence under Section 498A of the IPC. Applying the Bombay High Court decision, is she likely to succeed?

(a) Yes, since Ashwin had only asked Ashima to do their household work and not for others.
(b) No, since Ashwin had only asked Ashima to do their household work and not for others.
(c) Yes, since Ashwin had asked Ashima to do household work for themselves as well as others.
(d) No, since treating a married woman like a maid servant would not amount to an offence under that Section.

Sol. (*b*) According to the court's interpretation, Section 498A is intended to protect married women from cruelty by their husbands or relatives of their husbands. However, asking a married woman to perform household chores for her own family does not amount to cruelty or harassment under this section. Therefore, based on the Bombay High Court decision, Ashima is unlikely to succeed in her claim that Ashwin's request for her to do household work constitutes an offense under Section 498A of the IPC, as he had only asked her to do household work for their own family and not for others.

67. In April 2020, Ashwin's friend Rakesh visits Ashwin and Ashima's home and stays with them for a few days. During his visit, he is very mean to Ashima and uses abusive language with her. He also threw a plate at her one evening when he was unhappy with the meal that she had prepared. Ashima now claims that Rakesh has committed an offence under Section 498A of the IPC. Is she likely to succeed?

(a) No, since Rakesh's actions were perfectly justifiable for a man who does not get a well-cooked meal.

(b) Yes, since Rakesh's use of abusive language and throwing the plate at Ashima clearly amount to cruelty.

(c) No, since Rakesh is not her husband, nor is he related to Ashwin.

(d) Yes, since Rakesh was staying at Ashwin and Ashima's home at the time of the incident.

Sol. (*c*) Rakesh's actions of using abusive language and throwing a plate at Ashima, though cruel, would not constitute an offense under Section 498A of the IPC since he is neither Ashima's husband nor related to her husband Ashwin. Section 498A specifically deals with cruelty inflicted by a husband or his relatives towards a married woman. his actions would not be covered under this particular section, despite being reprehensible.

68. Frustrated and upset with her marriage, Ashima applies for and is granted a divorce from Ashwin in November 2020. Since she and Ashwin had been friends for many years before they got married, she stays in touch with him. She moves into her own apartment and starts going to office regularly at a new job. Ashwin is very upset at this and starts treating Ashima very cruelly. Ashima again claims that Ashwin has committed an offence under Section 498A of the IPC. Is she right?

(a) Yes, since Ashwin has, as we are told, treated her cruelly.

(b) Yes, since Ashwin has been her husband.

(c) No, since Ashwin was understandably upset at Ashima's behaviour.

(d) No, since she is no longer married to Ashwin.

Sol. (*d*) The protection afforded by Section 498A is specifically for married women who are subjected to cruelty by their husbands or their husband's relatives. Once the marriage is dissolved through divorce, the applicability of Section 498A ceases. Even though Ashwin is treating Ashima cruelly after their divorce, his actions would not constitute an offense under Section 498A, as Ashima is no longer his 'married woman' after the divorce.

69. Assume that the government passes a new law in January 2021, called the Protection of Rights of Married *Women Act, 2021 (the "PoMWA")*, according to which, asking a married woman to take care of household chores would be an offence. The PoMWA also provides that if a man commits such an offence, he would have to pay compensation to the woman. The PoMWA even applies to actions that were committed any time in the three years prior to the new law coming into force and even if the man and woman involved in the matter were no longer married. Upon hearing about this new law, Ashima once again alleges that Ashwin has committed an offence under Section 498A of the IPC and claims compensation under the PoMWA for his actions. Is she right and will she succeed?

(a) Ashima is right about Ashwin committing an offence under Section 498A of the IPC, but she will not get compensation under the PoMWA.
(b) Ashima will get compensation under the PoMWA, but she is not right about Ashwin committing an offence under Section 498A of the IPC.
(c) Ashima will get compensation under the PoMWA and she is also right about Ashwin committing an offence under Section 498A of the IPC.
(d) Ashima will neither get compensation under the PoMWA, nor is she right about Ashwin committing an offence under Section 498A of the IPC.

Sol. (*b*) Ashwin's actions of asking Ashima to take care of household chores while they were married would constitute an offense. The PoMWA explicitly states that asking a married woman to perform household chores is an offense and it applies retrospectively to actions committed within three years before its enactment, even if the parties are no longer married. Since Ashwin's actions of asking Ashima to do household work took place in March 2020, which falls within the three-year retrospective period, Ashima would be entitled to claim compensation from Ashwin under the POMWA.

70. Assume that in March 2021, the government changes Section 498A of the IPC. The effect of this change is that asking a married woman to do household chores . cven for their own family . by herself would be considered cruelty and therefore, an offence under the Section. Some days after this change comes into effect, Shamita, Ashima's friend at work, tells her that her husband has been forcing her to do all the household work by herself. Ashima tells Shamita that her husband's actions would amount to an offence under Section 498A of the IPC, even though Ashima herself has been unsuccessful in having Ashwin convicted under that Section in the past. Is Ashima's advice to Shamita correct?

(a) Yes, since Section 498A has now been changed and Shamita's husband's actions would now be an offence under the changed Section 498A.
(b) No, since Ashima has been unsuccessful in having Ashwin convicted under that Section in the past.
(c) Yes, since the passing of the Protection of Married Women Act has resulted in Shamita's husband's actions being made illegal.
(d) No, since Ashima is only Shamita's friend and only the married woman herself can file a complaint under Section 498A of the IPC.

Sol. (*a*) Shamita's friend Ashima informs her that, under the amended Section 498A, Shamita's husband's actions of forcing her to do all the household work by herself would now constitute an offense. Ashima's advice to Shamita is correct because the amended Section 498A has broadened the scope of what constitutes cruelty towards a married woman and Shamita's husband's actions would fall under this revised definition.

XIII. Parliament passed the Criminal Procedure (Identification) Act, 2022 (the 'Act') in March 2022. The legislation enables police and central investigating agencies to collect, store and analyse the measurements of arrested persons. Until rules are notified, an Act cannot be implemented or come into force. On 19th September 2022, the Ministry of Home Affairs (the 'MHA') notified the rules (the "Rules") under the Act.

The Act empowers a Magistrate to direct any person to give measurements to the police, which till now was reserved for convicts and those involved in heinous crimes. It also enables police personnel of the rank of Head Constable or above to take measurements of any person who resists or refuses to give measurements when ordered to do so by a Magistrate. As per the Rules, 'measurements' mean finger-impressions, palm-print, footprint, photographs, iris and retina scan, physical, biological samples and their analysis, behavioural attributes including signatures and handwriting. Though it has not been specified, analysis of biological samples could also include DNA profiling.

However, the Rules state that measurements of those detained under preventive Sections of the Code of Criminal Procedure ('CrPC') shall not be taken unless such person is at that time charged or under arrest in connection with any other offence punishable under any other law. Measurements can also be taken under the Rules if a person has been ordered to give security for his good behaviour for maintaining peace under Section 117 of the CrPC for a proceeding under that Section.

[*Extracted*, with edits and revisions, from "Explained | Rules for identifying criminals", by Vijaita Singh, The Hindu]

71. Bhargesh is arrested by the police on April 11, 2022, on suspicion of having committed a series of minor thefts. During their investigation, the police find some fingerprints at the crime scenes and on 12th April, 2022, they tell Bhargesh that he must provide his finger-impressions to them so that they can check whether they match the fingerprints from the crime scenes. When Bhargesh refuses, the police tell him that he has no choice but to provide his measurements, as the Act had been passed by Parliament the previous month. Was Bhargesh bound to provide his finger-impressions under the Act?

(a) No, since Bhargesh had only been arrested and not convicted.

(b) Yes, since Bhargesh was under arrest.

(c) No, since the Rules had not yet been notified.

(d) Yes, since finger-impressions are included within the definition of 'measurements' under the Act.

Sol. (*c*) The passage states that the Act was passed by Parliament in March 2022, but it also mentions that "Until rules are notified, an Act cannot be implemented or come into force." Since the Rules were not notified until 19th September, 2022, the Act was not in force or implementable during April 2022 when the events with Bhargesh occurred. Therefore, Bhargesh was not bound to provide his finger impressions under the Act in April 2022, as the Rules necessary for the Act's implementation had not yet been notified.

72. Bhargesh is later released by the police because they are unable to find enough evidence to make a strong case against him. On 5th October, 2022, the police receive a complaint alleging that Bhargesh had beaten up his neighbour and caused the neighbour severe injuries. They ask the local Magistrate to issue an order directing Bhargesh to provide the police his blood samples, so that they can match them against some blood stains that were found on the neighbour's clothes. The Magistrate issues the order, but Bhargesh refuses to provide the blood samples. Is Bhargesh bound to provide his blood samples to the police under the Act?

(a) Yes, since the crime that Bhargesh was accused of was very serious.

(b) Yes, since the Magistrate had passed an order directing him to do so.

(c) Yes, since Bhargesh had already been arrested in connection with another crime in the past.

(d) Yes, since the police needed the blood samples to verify Bhargesh's involvement in the crime.

Sol. (*b*) The Magistrate has issued an order directing Bhargesh to provide his blood samples in connection with the alleged offense of beating up his neighbor, Bhargesh is bound to comply and provide his blood samples to the police.

73. On 15th October, 2022, the police detain Bhargesh under a preventive Section of the CrPC, since they believe that he had plans to disturb the public peace during a festival day. They then tell Bhargesh that he must provide his measurements to them for their records. Bhargesh refuses again. Is Bhargesh bound to provide his photographs to the police under the Act?

(a) No, since he was not charged or under arrest in connection with any other offence at the time.

(b) No, since that would violate Bhargesh's right to privacy.

(c) Yes, since the police had detained Bhargesh under a preventive Section of the CrPC.

(d) Yes, since there was a high likelihood that Bhargesh would disturb the public peace on a festival day.

Sol. (*a*) The Rules under the Criminal Procedure (Identification) Act, 2022, specifically state that "measurements of those detained under preventive Sections of the Code of Criminal Procedure ('CrPC') shall not be taken unless such person is at that time charged or under arrest in connection with any other offence punishable under any other law." the police cannot compel Bhargesh to provide his measurements, including photographs, since he was not charged or under arrest for any other offense at the time of his preventive detention.

74. Two days later, the police obtain an order from the Magistrate directing Bhargesh to provide them his photographs. As Bhargesh continues to refuse to provide his photographs, a regular police constable forces him to stand still and takes his photographs. Bhargesh files a case in court, claiming that the constable's actions violate the Act. Will he succeed?

(a) Yes, since Bhargesh had been detained under a preventive section of the CrPC.

(b) Yes, since only police personnel of the rank of Head Constable or above can take measurements of any person who resists or refuses to give measurements when ordered to do so by a Magistrate.

(c) No, the Magistrate had issued an order directing him to provide his photographs to the police.

(d) No, since the police constable was only performing his duty.

Sol. (*b*) Bhargesh would likely succeed in his case claiming that the constable's actions violated the Act, as the Rules specifically allow only police personnel of the rank of Head Constable or above to take measurements in cases of resistance or refusal.

75. The police release Bhargesh, but to ensure that he does not disturb the public peace, they ask the Magistrate to issue an order under Section 117 of the CrPC, directing Bhargesh to provide a security of ₹ 1,00,000/- for his good behaviour and to ensure he maintains the peace, which the Magistrate refuses. The police now tell Bhargesh he must provide them his iris and retina scans. Is Bhargesh required to do so?

(a) No, since a person against whom an order has been issued under Section 117 of the CrPC cannot be made to give their measurements to the police.

(b) Yes, since a person against whom an order has been issued under Section 117 of the CrPC can be made to give their measurements to the police.

(c) Yes, since Bhargesh had been detained under other preventive sections of the CrPC in the past.

(d) No, since the Magistrate had not issued the order.

Sol. (*d*) Bhargesh is not required to provide his iris and retina scans to the police. The reason for this is that the Magistrate refused to issue an order under Section 117 of the Code of Criminal Procedure (CrPC) directing Bhargesh to provide security for his good behavior. Without such an order in place, Bhargesh cannot be compelled to provide his biometric data.

XIV. The government has amended the Electoral Bond Scheme, 2018. The Ministry of Finance on 7th November, 2022, issued a notification for amending the scheme to provide "an additional period of 15 days" for their sale "in the year of general elections to the Legislative Assembly of any States or Union Territories with Legislature". The bonds under this scheme are usually made available for purchase by any person for a period of ten days each in the months of January, April, July and October, when specified by the Union Government. The original scheme had provided for an additional period of thirty days, as specified by the Government, in the year when Lok Sabha elections are held, while the amendment adds another 15 days.

Since Assembly elections to various States and Union Territories are held every year, the amendment effectively means that there will be 15 additional dates annually during which the bonds can be sold. Immediately after issuing the notification, the Union Government also announced the sale of electoral bonds under the 23rd tranche from the authorised branches of the State Bank of India. The notification said the sale of bonds would take place through the 29 authorised branches of the said bank from 9th November to 15th November, 2022. Like in previous rounds of sale, the electoral bonds shall be valid for 15 calendar days from the date of issue and no payment shall be made to any payee political party if the bond is deposited after expiry of the validity period. The Electoral Bond deposited by an eligible political party in its account shall be credited on the same day.

[*Extracted*, with edits and revisions, from "Electoral Bonds Scheme Amended To Allow Sale for Additional 15 Days in Assembly Election Years", by Gaurav Vivek Bhatnagar, The Wire]

76. Assad buys an electoral bond worth ₹ 1,00,000/- on 9th November, 2022 and plans to give the bond to the Popular People's Party (the "PPP"), which he has been supporting for many years. On November 10, he must travel out of station on some urgent business and he only hands the bond over to a representative of the PPP on 14th November, 2022. The PPP's representative deposits the bond in the Party's account on 16th November, 2022, but the bank refuses to credit the bond to the party's account, on the grounds that it was no longer valid. Is the bank correct?

(a) No, since Assad was a long-time supporter of the PPP.

(b) Yes, since the bonds were only issued from November 9 to 15th November, 2022 and were invalid after that.

(c) Yes, since the party representative had not deposited the bond with an authorised branch of the bank.

(d) No, since the bond was valid on 16th November, 2022.

Sol. (*d*) According to the rules governing electoral bonds, these bonds are valid for a specific period after issuance. In this case, the bonds were issued between 9th November and 15th November, 2022. Therefore, the validity of the bond purchased by Assad would extend beyond November 14 when he handed it over to the PPP's representative. The bank's refusal to credit the bond to the party's account on 16th November, 2022, citing its invalidity is incorrect. As per the Electoral Bond Scheme guidelines, the bond would still be considered valid on that date since it falls within the permissible period of usability.

77. The Government announces that there would be a sale of a 24th tranche of electoral bonds on 10th February, 2023, for a period of 15 days, since elections to the Legislative Assembly of some States are scheduled for that year. Since there are no elections to the Lok Sabha or the Legislative Assembly of the State in which Assad resides, he claims that the Government does not have the power to issue this 24th tranche of electoral bonds in 2023. Is he right?

(a) No, since the changes to the Electoral Bond Scheme, 2018 mean that electoral bonds can be issued for an additional period of 15 days in any year, regardless of whether any elections are scheduled that year.

(b) Yes, since no elections were scheduled for Assad's state in that year.

(c) Yes, since the Government had already sold some bonds in the 23rd tranche in 2022.

(d) No, since the changes to the Electoral Bond Scheme, 2018 provide that electoral bonds can be issued for an additional period of 15 days in years when there is an election to the Legislative Assembly of a State.

Sol. (*d*) No, since the changes to the Electoral Bond Scheme, 2018 provide that electoral bonds can be issued for an additional period of 15 days in years when there is an election to the Legislative Assembly of a State.

78. On 10th November, 2022, Palak purchases an electoral bond from a branch of the State Bank of India and hands it over to a representative of the PPP. The next day, the PPP announces that it has changed its candidates for the upcoming elections in Palak's State. Upset at this news, she tells a PPP representative that she would like her bond back. The representative tells her that the bond has already been deposited and that the money has been credited to the party's account. Palak claims that since the period of validity of the bonds has not expired, she has the right to get her bond back from the party. Is she right?

(a) No, since Palak cannot ask for the bond back once she has given it to a political party.

(b) No, since the party had already deposited the bond and the money had been credited to its account.

(c) Yes, since Palak bought the bond with her own money and has the right to ask for it back.

(d) Yes, since the PPP changed its candidates and Palak may no longer support the party.

Sol. (*b*) Palak purchased an electoral bond and handed it over to the PPP party. After receiving the bond, the PPP deposited it and the money was credited to the party's account. Once a political party has deposited an electoral bond and the funds have been credited to their account, the transaction is considered complete and final. Therefore, Palak cannot ask for the bond back from the party after it has already been deposited and the funds credited to the party's account.

79. On 15th November, 2022, the Government issues another notification, announcing that from that date onwards, only political parties that have received at least 1% of the votes polled in the last elections to the Lok Sabha, or the last elections to the Legislative Assembly of a State, would be eligible to receive and deposit electoral bonds. In the sale of the 24th tranche of electoral bonds, Palak decides to give the electoral bonds she has purchased to the newly formed More Popular People's Party (the "MPPP"), which is likely to win the first elections it would be contesting, in July 2023. Is the MPPP eligible to receive the electoral bonds?

(a) Yes, since it is likely to succeed in the upcoming elections.

(b) Yes, since it fulfils the criteria announced in the 7th November, 2022 notification.

(c) No, since it does not fulfil the eligibility criteria announced in the 15th November, 2022 notification.

(d) No, since it does not fulfil the eligibility criteria announced in the 7th November, 2022 notification.

Sol. (*c*) On 15th November, 2022, the government issued a notification stating that only political parties that have received at least 1% of the votes polled in the last elections to the Lok Sabha or the last elections to the Legislative Assembly of a State would be eligible to receive and deposit electoral bonds. Since the MPPP has not received at least 1% of the votes in the last Lok Sabha or State Legislative Assembly elections, as per the 15th November 15, 2022 notification, it does not fulfill the eligibility criteria to receive and deposit electoral bonds.

80. Abraham, who lives in a different State from Assad, purchased an electoral bond in the sale of the 23rd tranche. He decides to give the electoral bond to the PPP, even though the PPP is only active in Assad's State. When the PPP representative goes to an authorised branch of the State Bank of India to deposit the electoral bond on December 5, 2022 however, the bank refuses to credit the money to the PPP's account. Which of the following would be the most valid reason for the bank to refuse to credit the money to the party's account?

(a) The bond was no longer valid.
(b) Abraham could not give the bond to the PPP since the PPP was not active in his state.
(c) The PPP was not eligible to receive electoral bonds.
(d) The PPP could only deposit the bond in a bank branch located in Abraham's state.

Sol. (*a*) A valid reason if the electoral bonds have a defined period of validity and Abraham's bond from the 23rd tranche sale had crossed its expiration date by December 5th when the PPP tried to deposit it.

XV. Twitter's lawyer on 27th October, said before the Karnataka High Court that Union government orders to block certain Twitter handles and posts must contain reasons for the same that can be communicated to users of the microblogging site. He said this applies to all blocking orders sent to social media platforms. The lawyer representing Twitter said that reasons for the blocking order must be provided to users so they can determine whether or not they want to challenge the orders.

Challenging the blocking orders, Twitter's July 5 petition contended that several blocking orders "demonstrate excessive use of powers and are disproportionate". Such orders can only be issued by the Union government and not the state governments, he said, which increases the danger of such abuse. Twitter also claimed that the Ministry of Electronics and Information Technology had sent it a letter threatening consequences for failing to comply with the blocking orders, such as criminal proceedings against the company's chief compliance officer and the stripping away of Twitter's safe harbour immunity, otherwise available to social media platforms under Section 79(1) of the Information Technology Act (the 'IT Act'). Note that the Government has the power to strip away such safe harbour immunity under the IT Act. Further, in a previous hearing, Twitter's lawyer said that the company was asked to block entire accounts, although Section 69A of the IT Act does not permit blocking of the whole account. It only permits the blocking of information, or a particular tweet or post. It argued that the Union government's direction to block whole accounts will affect its business, adding that several prominent persons have their accounts on the platform.

[*Extracted*, with edits and revisions, "from "Government Must Provide Reasons for Blocking User Accounts,' Twitter Tells Karnataka HC", The Wire]

81. Sunil is a high-ranking officer of the Union government. While scrolling through his timeline on a social media platform, he notices some posts by Sachin, a private businessman, which he finds objectionable. He sends an order to UnReal, the company that owns that social media platform, that the posts must be blocked, as they may bring disrepute to India. UnReal claims that Sunil has not provided a clear, detailed reason for blocking the posts and so, the order is not valid. Is UnReal right?

(a) No, the blocking order is valid since Sunil found the posts objectionable.
(b) No, the blocking order is valid since Sunil had provided reasons for blocking the post.
(c) Yes, Sunil's reasons are vague and he should have provided more detail.
(d) Yes, such an order is violative of the fundamental right to freedom of speech and expression.

Sol. (*b*) Given Sunil's position and responsibility within the government, his judgement on what constitutes content detrimental to India's reputation should be respected. Therefore, even if his reasons were not explicitly detailed in the order sent to UnReal, the fact that he found the posts objectionable and potentially harmful should suffice as justification for blocking them.

82. Some days later, Sunil notices another post from Sachin on UnReal's social media platform; this post contains some highly sensitive information about the country's defence policies. He issues an order to UnReal, that the post must be blocked since it divulges the government's confidential information. The order also says that UnReal should not let anyone know about the blocking order, or that the post was ordered to be deleted, since it relates to secret government information. UnReal claims that this order is invalid. Is UnReal right?
(a) Yes, since it did not provide any reasons that could be communicated to the users of the social media platform.
(b) No, since Sunil had provided reasons to UnReal for ordering that the post be blocked.
(c) Yes, since Sunil did not have the authority to issue blocking orders so frequently.
(d) No, since the post divulged confidential government information.

Sol. (*a*) Yes UnReal is right since it did not provide any reasons that could be communicated to the users of the social media platform.

According to the principles laid out in the context of the case before the Karnataka High Court, the Union government's orders to block content must contain reasons that can be communicated to the users affected by the order. In this scenario, although Sunil provided a reason to UnReal (the post contained confidential information), the stipulation that UnReal must not inform users about the blocking order violates the requirement for transparency and the ability for the affected party to challenge the order.

83. Sunil sends UnReal a third blocking order. UnReal claims that this order too was invalid. Upset with UnReal for claiming that all his blocking orders were invalid, Sunil sends them a letter in which he says, "If you do not comply with my blocking orders, then I will be forced to initiate criminal proceedings against you and cancel your safe harbour immunity." UnReal claims that Sunil has broken the law by making these statements in the letter. Is UnReal right?
(a) Yes, since making such threats amounts to intimidation.
(b) No, since Sunil had issued blocking orders in the past as well and UnReal should have complied with the orders without questioning them.
(c) Yes, since Sunil did not have the power to cancel UnReal fs safe harbour immunity.
(d) No, since the IT Act does not forbid Sunil from doing so.

Sol. (*d*) Yes, UnReal is right since Sunil did not have the power to cancel UnReal's Sunil did not have the power to cancel UnReal's safe harbour immunity.

While Sunil, as a government official, can issue blocking orders, the authority to cancel safe harbour immunity under Section 79(1) of the IT Act lies with the Union government, not an individual official. Therefore, Sunil's threat to cancel UnReal's safe harbour immunity is beyond his legal authority, making his statements in the letter inappropriate and potentially unlawful.

84. Complying with a fourth blocking order that they receive from Sunil, UnReal blocks Sachin's account, since his posts were seen as increasingly objectionable by the government. Sachin asks UnReal to share the reasons for the blocking order, which they do, yet Sachin claims the blocking order is invalid. Is he right?

(a) Yes, since Sunil was clearly targeting Sachin and was misusing his powers to silence him.

(b) No, since UnReal had shared the reasons for the blocking order with Sachin.

(c) Yes, since Section 69A of the IT Act only permits blocking information, or a particular post, but not a whole account.

(d) No, since his posts were seen as increasingly objectionable by the government.

Sol. (*c*) Yes, he is right since Section 69A of the IT Act only permits blocking information, or a particular post, but not a whole account.

Section 69A of the IT Act permits the blocking of specific pieces of information or individual posts but does not authorise the blocking of entire accounts. Therefore, Sunil's order to block Sachin's entire account exceeds the scope of the law, making Sachin's claim that the blocking order is invalid correct.

85. Sunil sends UnReal a fifth blocking order, which says that several of Sachin's latest posts must be blocked. The blocking order sets out several reasons why the posts should be blocked, but UnReal does not find them satisfactory. Rather than take on another fight with a government official however, UnReal blocks the posts and gives Sachin what it thinks is a better set of reasons for blocking the posts. When Sachin finds out, he claims this was wrong on UnReal's part and that the blocking order was inappropriate. Which of the following is most accurate in this regard?

(a) The blocking order was valid, but UnReal's actions were inappropriate.

(b) UnReal's actions were valid, but the blocking order was invalid.

(c) UnReal's actions were valid, but Sachin's actions were invalid.

(d) Sachin's actions were valid, but the blocking order was invalid.

Sol. (*a*) Option (a) is most accurate in his regard. The blocking order, as issued by Sunil, set our reasons for blocking Sachin's posts and followed the required protocol under Section 69A of the IT Act. However, UnReal altering or providing different reasons to Sachin undermines the transparency and accountability that the law seeks to ensure. UnReal should have communicated the original reasons provided in the blocking order, thus making their actions inappropriate even if the blocking order itself was valid.

XVI. Free legal aid is the provision of free legal services in civil and criminal matters for those poor and marginalised people who cannot afford the services of a lawyer for the conduct of a case or a legal proceeding in any Court, Tribunal or Authority. These services are governed by the *Legal Services Authority Act, 1987* (the 'Act') and provided by the National Legal Services Authority ('NALSA'). Provision of free legal aid includes:

- Representation by an advocate in legal proceedings;
- Payment of process fees, expenses of witnesses and all other charges payable or incurred in connection with any legal proceedings in appropriate cases;
- Preparation of pleadings, memo of appeal, paper book including printing and translation of documents in legal proceedings;
- Drafting of legal documents, special leave petition etc.; and

- Supply of certified copies of judgements, orders, notes of evidence and other documents in legal proceedings.

Free legal aid also includes provision of aid and advice to the beneficiaries to access benefits under welfare statutes and schemes framed by the Central Government or the state governments and to ensure access to justice in any other manner. Free legal aid is not confined to cases before the subordinate courts. Free legal aid must be provided to the needy from the lowest court to the Supreme Court of India.

According to Section 13(1) of the Act, any individual who satisfies any criteria under Section 12 is entitled to receive free legal aid, provided that NALSA is satisfied that such person has a genuine case to prosecute or defend the matter. There is hence no bar as to which kind of cases one can apply and not apply for. Section 12 of the Act includes the following:

- a member of a Scheduled Caste or Scheduled Tribe
- a woman or a child
- a person with a disability
- an industrial workman or
- a person in police custody

[*Extracted*, with edits and revisions, from 'FAQs', National Legal Services Authority]

86. Divya was arrested by the police and charged with having committed a murder. She was convicted by the trial court and appealed to the high court. She lost her appeal there and decided to appeal to the Supreme Court. By this time she has run out of money, so she approaches NALSA and asks them to help her get an advocate who can represent her before the Supreme Court. Is Divya entitled to support from NALSA?

(a) No, since she should have approached them at the beginning of the case before the trial court and not at such a late stage.

(b) Yes, since her previous lawyers were incompetent and that is why she lost the matter in the trial court and the high court.

(c) Yes, she is entitled to free legal aid in the Supreme Court proceedings because she is a woman.

(d) No, since she had been accused of having committed the heinous crime of murder.

Sol. (c) Divya, a woman, has approached NALSA for legal aid to represent her before the Supreme Court in an appeal against her conviction. Under the Legal Services Authorities Act, 1987, women are considered a category entitled to free legal aid, irrespective of their financial means or the stage of the case. Therefore, Divya is entitled to support from NALSA for legal representation in the Supreme Court proceedings.

87. Divya is acquitted by the Supreme Court and goes back to her regular life. Some days later, she has a fight with her neighbour Riya over a petty matter and decides to file a criminal case against her. She approaches NALSA for free legal aid to prosecute the matter. She tells NALSA representative that she knows she does not have a genuine case, but just wants to harass Riya. NALSA refuses to provide Divya free legal aid because they believe she does not have a genuine case to prosecute. Can NALSA do so?

(a) Yes, since Section 13(1) of the Act provides that free legal aid can be provided if NALSA is satisfied the person has a genuine case to prosecute and they did not believe that Divya had a genuine case to prosecute.

(b) Yes, since Divya had earlier been prosecuted for the crime of murder.

(c) Yes, since Divya had already applied for free legal aid from NALSA in the past and could not repeatedly ask NALSA for such assistance.

(d) No, since Divya is a woman and is included within the list of people entitled to free legal aid from NALSA under Section 12 of the Act.

Sol. (*a*) The provision further states that "the person, because of his poverty, is unable to engage a counselor to afford the expenses of litigation."Critically, it adds that NALSA must be "satisfied that the person has a prima facie case to prosecute or to defend."In this case, Divya herself admitted to the NALSA representative that she did not have a genuine case but only wanted to harass her neighbor Riya. Therefore, NALSA would be justified in refusing legal aid to Divya under Section 13(1), as they did not believe she had a genuine case to prosecute.

88. I ncensed at Divya, Riya decides to file a civil case against Divya, claiming that Divya had violated the terms of a contract they had made some time back. Divya approaches NALSA for free legal aid to defend the matter, which NALSA agrees to provide. Since Riya is also short of funds, she too approaches NALSA for free legal aid. NALSA refuses to provide legal aid to Riya, since they are already providing Divya free legal aid in the same case. Is NALSA right in refusing free legal aid to Riya?

(a) Yes, since NALSA cannot provide free legal aid to opposing parties in the same matter.

(b) Yes, since NALSA does not provide free legal aid in civil matters.

(c) No, since Divya had filed a frivolous case against Riya in the past and Riya was entitled to retaliate by filing another case against Divya.

(d) No, since Riya is a woman and is entitled to free legal aid as long as NALSA is satisfied she has a genuine case.

Sol. (*d*) Riya is a woman seeking legal aid from NALSA to file a civil case against Divya. As a woman, Riya is entitled to free legal aid under Section 12 of the Act. NALSA has not stated that they are not satisfied with Riya having a genuine case. They have refused legal aid solely because they are already providing aid to Divya in the same matter. The Act does not explicitly prohibit NALSA from providing legal aid to opposing parties in the same case, as long as both parties meet the eligibility criteria. Therefore, NALSA's refusal to provide legal aid to Riya solely because they are already providing aid to Divya in the same case is not justified under the Act.

89. Farhan is an up-and-coming artist and makes a living selling his paintings. Since he is not very well known yet, he isn't able to sell too many paintings and is dependent on aid from the government and well-wishers. He reads about a new Central Government scheme in the papers one day, under which artists would be provided a monthly stipend by the local government. Since he finds the language of the scheme document very complex to understand, he approaches NALSA for help in understanding the scheme and obtaining the stipend. Is he entitled to free legal aid from NALSA in this regard?

(a) No, since free legal aid does not include provision of help to understand and access benefits under government schemes.

(b) No, since he does not fit within any of the categories under Section 12 of the Act.

(c) Yes, since free legal aid includes provision of help to understand and access benefits under government schemes.

(d) Yes, since he is a struggling artist and is dependent on aid for survival.

Sol. (*b*) Section 12 of the Act lists these categories, which include: (a) Members of Scheduled Castes or Scheduled Tribes (b) Victims of trafficking or forced labor (c) Women and children (d) Mentally ill or disabled persons (e) Victims of mass disasters, violence, atrocities (f) Industrial workmen (g) Persons in custody (h) Persons with an annual income below a prescribed limit. Farhan, being an upcoming artist who makes a living by selling paintings, does not appear to fall under any of these listed categories.

90. Vikram is a rich businessman and has a huge art collection. Farhan invites Vikram to his studio one day, hoping to convince Vikram to buy some of his paintings. Vikram doesn't buy any of his paintings, but after he leaves, Farhan notices that one of his newest paintings is missing. He suspects that Vikram has stolen it and complains to the police, who promptly arrest Vikram. Vikram approaches NALSA for free legal aid, so that he can obtain bail. Is Vikram entitled to free legal aid from NALSA?

(a) No, since he is a rich businessman and can hire a lawyer with his own money.

(b) Yes, since he was innocent.

(c) Yes, since he was in police custody.

(d) No, since he had stolen from a struggling artist.

Sol. (*c*) In this case, Vikram was arrested and taken into police custody on suspicion of stealing Farhan's painting. As a person in custody, he falls under the category of persons entitled to free legal aid from NALSA, regardless of his financial status or the merits of the allegations against him.

XVII. Surrogacy is defined by law as "a practice whereby one woman bears and gives birth to a child for an intending couple" and intends to hand over the child to them after the birth, as per the Surrogacy (Regulation) Act, 2021 (the 'SRA'). The SRA restricts altruistic surrogacy to legally wedded infertile Indian couples. The couple is deemed eligible for surrogacy only if they have been married for five years. The SRA sets an age limitation for the couple. A husband must be between 26 and 55 years of age and a wife between 23 and 50 years. Further, Indian couples with biologRl or adopted children are prohibited from undertaking surrogacy, save for some exceptions such as mentally or physically challenged children, or those suffering from a life-threatening disorder or fatal illness. The SRA provides that the surrogate mother has to be a close relative of the couple (such as a sibling of one of the members of the couple), a married woman with a child of her own, aged between 25 and 35 years, who has been a surrogate only once in her life. Even within this category of people, commercial surrogacy is banned in India and that includes the "commercialisation of surrogacy services or procedures or its component services or component procedures". The surrogate woman cannot be given payments, rewards, benefits or fees, except the medical expenses and such other prescribed expenses incurred on the surrogate mother and the insurance coverage for the surrogate mother".

A legal commentator points out some criticisms of the law. "Permitting limited conditional surrogacy to married Indian couples and disqualifying other persons on basis of nationality, marital status, sexual orientation or age does not pass the test of equality," he writes. He adds that reproductive autonomy, inclusive of the right to procreation and parenthood is protected under Article 21 of the Constitution of India, which guarantees the right to life and personal liberty. The intending parents typically sign a contract with the surrogate. The Indian Contract Act, 1972 (the "ICA") provides that a valid contract has to be in writing and signed in the presence of two witnesses. The ICA also provides that a contract that is prohibited by any other law will not be valid under the ICA.

[*Extracted* with edits and revisions from "What laws regulate surrogacy in India", The Indian Express]

91. Rani and Shiva would like to opt for surrogacy. They have been married for 6 years. Rani is aged 51 and Shiva is aged 53. Both Rani and Shiva have built successful business empires. They are now working together on a joint initiative. Due to the demanding nature of their work, they have not thought about children previously. However, they are now keen to have a child via surrogacy. Are Rani and Shiva eligible for surrogacy under the SRA?

(a) Yes, because they have been married for more than 5 years.
(b) Yes, because they have financial capacity to bring up a child.
(c) No, because they do not fall within the legal requirements of intending parents.
(d) No, because they are not an infertile couple.

Sol. (*c*) The SRA mandates that intending parents must meet certain legal requirements to be eligible for surrogacy. These include being Indian citizens who have been married for at least five years and do not have any surviving children (biological or adopted). Since Rani and Shiva have been married for six years but do not meet the age criteria and other legal requirements specified in the SRA, they are not eligible to opt for surrogacy under this law.

92. Assume Rani and Shiva are eligible for surrogacy under the SRA. They approach Geeta to act as a surrogate. Geeta is Rani's sister. She is 29 years old. She is married, has one child and has been a surrogate twice before. Which of the following statements are false?

i. Geeta is eligible to be a surrogate because she is a close relative.
ii. Geeta is eligible to be a surrogate because she is married.
iii. Geeta has been a surrogate only twice before and is now eligible to be a surrogate for Rani.
iv. Geeta is eligible to be a surrogate because she is 29.

(a) Statement iii
(b) Statements i and iii
(c) Statements ii and iii
(d) Statements ii, iii and iv

Sol. (*a*) Statement (iii) is false.
Under the Surrogacy (Regulation) Act, 2021, a woman can only act as a surrogate once in her lifetime. Since Geeta has already acted as a surrogate twice, she does not meet this criterion and is therefore ineligible to be a surrogate again.

93. Joseph and Neena are keen to have a child via surrogacy. They have been married for 8 years and have been unable to conceive biologically due to infertility. Joseph is 40 years old and Neena is 42 years old. They have an adopted daughter, Maya, who is 4 years old. Maya has been diagnosed with Striker fs Syndrome, which would cause slow neurological deterioration, with chances of death. Devastated, Joseph and Neena decide to opt for surrogacy, to become parents to their biological child.
Are they eligible for surrogacy?

(a) Yes, because they have no biological children.
(b) No, because they have an adopted child.
(c) Yes, because their adopted child has been diagnosed with Striker's Syndrome.
(d) Yes, because their right to procreation and parenthood is protected under

Sol. (*c*) In the scenario presented, Joseph and Neena are a married couple who have been unsuccessful in conceiving a child due to infertility. They have an adopted daughter, Maya, who has been diagnosed with Striker's Syndrome, a condition that leads to slow neurological deterioration with potentially fatal outcomes. In their desire to have a biological child, they opt for surrogacy. This choice is based on the fact that Maya's medical condition may be considered a valid reason for them to pursue surrogacy to have a biological child without the risk of passing on the genetic disorder.

94. Queen runs a surrogacy clinic. She employs 54 women, aged between 25 and 35 years. They are all married women with one or more children. Most of them belong to economically disadvantaged backgrounds. They choose to be surrogates because it gives them a reliable source of income. Kishore and Noor are intending parents. They have been married 5 years, are both aged 35 and do not have children. Kishore has been certified as infertile. So, they decide to approach Queen's clinic. They sign a contract with the surrogate. The contract is in writing and is signed in the presence of two witnesses. As per the contract, Kishore and Noor are required to remunerate the surrogate with ₹ 2 lakh per child born as a result of surrogacy and take care of her medical needs, including providing her with medical insurance. A healthy baby girl is born as a result of surrogacy. Kishore and Noor are overjoyed. They take care of the surrogate fs medical expenses. However, they do not pay the surrogate the ₹ 2 lakh. The surrogate, supported by Queen, now wants to take Kishore and Noor to court, to demand that they make the payment.Will she succeed?

(a) Yes, because Kishore and Noor are bound by the contract under the ICA.
(b) Yes, because the intending parents and the surrogate meet the eligibility requirements under the SRA.
(c) Yes, because the surrogate meets the eligibility requirements under the SRA.
(d) No, because SRA allows only altruistic surrogacy, so the contract is not valid under the ICA.

Sol. (*d*) The contract between Kishore, Noor and the surrogate is in writing and signed in the presence of witnesses, which satisfies the requirements of a valid contract under the ICA. The SRA prohibits commercial surrogacy and allows only altruistic surrogacy, where no monetary compensation is paid to the surrogate mother other than reasonable medical expenses.

95. Karan and Daniel are in a homosexual relationship. As per the Hindu Marriage Act, marriage is allowed only between heterosexual couples. As a result, Karan and Daniel are not married. However, they wish to have children and decide to go in for surrogacy. When they approach Queen fs clinic, they are informed that they do not meet the requirements for an intending couple under the SRA. Karan and Daniel wish to challenge the SRA for violating their constitutional right to non-discrimination. The non-discrimination clause under the Constitution of India reads. 'No citizen shall be discriminated on the basis of sex, caste, religion, nationality, place of birth or any other ground'. Karan and Daniel argue that the SRA discriminates against them on the basis of sexual orientation, because it restricts surrogacy to heterosexual couples alone. Which of the following arguments would most strongly support their claim in court?

(a) The non-discrimination clause does not explicitly mention sexual orientation.
(b) Discrimination on the basis of sex could include discrimination on the basis of sexual orientation.
(c) The non-discrimination clause is not restricted to explicitly mentioned grounds.
(d) Surrogacy is restricted under the SRA to married couples and only heterosexual couples can get married.

Sol. (*c*) The non-discrimination clause is not restricted to explicitly mentioned grounds. This argument also supports their claim. If the court considers that the non-discrimination clause is not limited to the explicitly mentioned grounds, then it could potentially include discrimination based on sexual orientation.

XVIII. Until 2017, India did not have a codified law to order internet shut downs. A general power was vested in District Magistrates in this regard. The Magistrate could issue an order ordering a shut down if a 'speedy remedy' (extending to internet shut down) is desirable for 'immediate prevention' of an event. The Magistrate had to be satisfied that the order is 'likely to prevent or tends to prevent obstruction, annoyance or injury to human life, health or safety, or a disturbance of public tranquillity'. The

Magistrate's order cannot be for longer than two months.

In 2017, new rules to order internet shut downs were introduced taking the power away from the Magistrate. These rules- the Temporary Suspension Rules - state that internet shut downs can now only be ordered by the Home Secretary of the Union or State Governments. Only in "unavoidable circumstances" can the passing of orders be delegated to someone lower than the rank of a Joint Secretary to the Government of India. And even in this case, the official must be authorised by the Centre or State Home Secretary. Shut downs can be ordered where 'necessary' or 'unavoidable' during a 'public emergency' or in the 'interest of public safety'. Shut down orders must necessarily detail the reasons to shut down the internet. The orders must also be sent to a review committee under the state or central government within 24 hours. The committee must then review them within five working days. The rules state that apart from the Chief Secretary and Legal Secretary, the committee can comprise a secretary other than the home secretary.

In January 2020 the Supreme Court passed its judgement in the case of Anuradha Bhasin. The judgement in this case explicitly recognised two things: that the freedom to access information is a fundamental right under Article 19(1)(a) of the Constitution of India (which protects the freedom of speech and expression) and that the freedom to conduct your trade, profession or business over the internet is also a fundamental right under Article 19(1)(g) of the Constitution of India (which protects the freedom to practise any profession, or to carry on any occupation, trade or business). Every time the internet is suspended, it is quite obvious that it is a violation of these rights. These rights can only be curtailed in the interest of the 'sovereignty and security of the state, integrity of the nation, friendly relations with foreign states, or public order or for preventing incitement to the commission of an offence'. The Supreme Court's judgement in Anuradha Bhasin's case had also underlined that shut down orders must clearly provide reasons for the shut down and they must be publicly available.

[Extracted with edits and revisions from "In India, are internet shut downs in accordance with law? Not always", by Diksha Munjal, News Laundry]

96. In 2014, India was hit by a terrible pandemic. It was the first time the country was experiencing a pandemic. People panicked. WhatsApp and Facebook groups became common platforms for sharing information about the pandemic. Messages were forwarded from group to group. Many of these messages prescribed different remedies to prevent and cure the flu caused by the pandemic. In Merodha district, people following these remedies began to fall sick. The already overburdened public sector hospitals became even more full. The district administration requested people to stop sharing such misinformation. However, these requests were not heeded. The District Magistrate issued an indefinite order to shut down the internet to prevent the transmission of these messages. Is this order legal?

(a) Yes, because the District Magistrate has the power to issue a range of orders, which includes internet shut down orders.

(b) Yes, because the order was necessary on grounds of public health.

(c) Yes, because a speedy order was necessary to immediately prevent transmission of these messages.

(d) No, because the order was indefinite.

Sol. *(d)* While the District Magistrate may have had valid concerns about the spread of misinformation and its impact on public health, the indefinite nature of the internet shutdown order would render it illegal under the applicable rules and regulations. The order should have specified a definite duration for the suspension of internet services to be considered legal.

97. The Central government was preparing to conduct the National Medical Eligibility Test ('NMET') on 25th October 2021. The exams were to be conducted in public schools around the country on computers provided by the government. In July 2021, there were rumours that several groups had hatched plans to share answers with the students taking the exam. A special chat application was developed. The student simply had to open the application on the browser of the computer on which they were taking the exam, allowing persons on the other end to send them the answers. The government was very concerned. If the rumours were true, the quality of doctors in training (who were selected through the NMET) would be severely affected. To prevent this public emergency, the government issued orders under the Temporary Suspension Rules to shut down internet countrywide on 25th October, 2021. Many protested against this decision. They argued that the government could prevent cheating in the exams by shutting down the internet in the public schools where the exam was taking place. A nation-wide blanket shut down was not required for this purpose. Now, the issue is before the Supreme Court. What will the Court decide?

(a) The government's order is legal under the Temporary Suspension Rules because it prevents a public emergency by preserving the quality of doctors in India.

(b) The government's order is not legal under the Temporary Suspension Rules because the power belonged to the magistrate to issue orders under Section 144.

(c) The government's order is not legal under the Temporary Suspension Rules because the nation-wide internet shut down order was not necessary or unavoidable.

(d) The government's order is legal because it is the responsibility of the State to conduct exams in a fair manner.

Sol. (*c*) The government's order is not legal under the Temporary Suspension Rules because the nationwide internet shutdown order was not necessary or unavoidable. This argument holds the strongest basis for determining the legality of the order. The Temporary Suspension Rules require the measures taken to be necessary and unavoidable for preventing a public emergency or public safety threat. A nationwide internet shutdown may be considered disproportionate and not the least restrictive measure available when the concerns were specific to the exam centers.

98. In the above instance, the order was passed by the Communications Minister of the Indian Central Government. The Communications Minister is below the rank of Joint Secretary. The Home Secretary was away for a conference in Geneva and thus was not present in Delhi when the decision to pass the order was made. However, the Home Secretary could be contacted by phone or email. She had, in fact, explicitly said that she should be contacted if any need arises, however minor. As she had taken measures to make herself available virtually, the Home Secretary did not authorise any other official to exercise her functions. Against this, consider the following statements:

i. The Communications Minister had the power to pass the order under the 2017 Rules.

ii. The passing of the order by the Communications Minister was avoidable.

iii. The power to pass the order remained with the Home Secretary.

iv. The Communications Minister did not have the power to pass the order under the 2017 Rules.

Which of the following statements are false?

(a) Statement iv

(b) Statement i

(c) Statements ii and iii

(d) Statements ii and iv

Sol. (*b*) Statement (i) is false.
According to the 2017 Rules, only the Home Secretary of the Union or State Governments can order internet shutdowns or in unavoidable circumstances, an official not below the rank of Joint Secretary authorised by the Hom Secretary. The Communications Minister is below the rank of Joint Secretary and was not authorised by the Home Secretary.

99. Assume that in the above instance, the Joint Secretary passed the order. The order stated 'By means of the discretion vested in me by the Temporary Suspension of Telecom Services (Public Emergency or Public Safety) Rules 2017, I suspend internet across all Indian States and Union Territories on October 25, 2021'. The order was passed on 15 October, 2021. The order was sent to the Central Government review committee within 8 hours of its passing. The committee reviewed and approved of the order on 22 October, 2021. Is the order legal?

(a) Yes, because it was passed under the 2017 rules.
(b) No, because the procedure under the 2017 rules was not followed.
(c) Yes, because the order was reviewed by the Central government review committee.
(d) No, because the order was passed 10 days before it was to come into effect.

Sol. (*b*) No, order is not legal because the procedure under the 2017 rules was not followed. The procedure under the 2017 rules was not followed correctly because the review committee did not review the order within five working days of its passing. This procedural lapse renders the order illegal despite it being issued under the correct authority and reviewed subsequently.

100. In January 2022, communal riots were rife in five states in India, between two dominant communities, X and Y. The primary mode of communication amongst the rioters was Signal which could be accessed through the internet via mobile phones and computers. The State governments of the five States received information that some members of X group were planning to set the houses of members of Y group on fire. Through broad Signal broadcasts amongst all users, the leaders of X group were instigating members of their group to participate in this exercise, threatening public order. Creating or inciting threat to public order is a criminal offence under Section 163F of the Indian Penal Code. To prevent further communication between the leaders of X group and their members, the State shut Signal down. However, communication then shifted to other platforms. Realising that targeting isolated platforms would not work, the State governments issued an order shutting down internet completely in all the states. Two groups protested against this order. First, students whose education was being conducted online due to the riots. They argued that they were prevented from accessing vital information, central to their education. Second, business owners who conducted business on the internet. The State's order read: 'In the five Indian States listed below, internet will be suspended for a period of two months from 10 January 2022 to 10 March 2022'. The State's order was not displayed anywhere (in print or virtually) from January to March 2022.

Consider the following statements:

i. The students' right under Article 19(1)(a) was violated by the State order.
ii. The business owners' right under Article 19(1)(g) was violated by the State order.
iii. The State order validly restricted the said fundamental rights.
iv. The State's order complied with the guidelines under Anuradha Bhasin.

How many statements are true?

(a) One statement
(b) Two statements
(c) Three statements
(d) All four statements

Sol. (*c*) All the statements are true except one. The State's order complied with the guidelines under Anuradha Bhasin is false.

The order did not comply with the guidelines set forth in the Anuradha Bhasin case, which require that shutdown orders provide clear reasons and be made publicly available. The order was neither publicly displayed nor properly justified, failing to meet the stipulated guidelines.

XIX. Consumers are people who buy and use goods or services. Consumers have a right to file a complaint for any of the services or goods used by them under Consumer Protection Law. Under Consumer Protection Law, a 'consumer' means Person buying and using goods and services. A consumer includes any person who buys goods and services, as well as anyone who uses them. For instance, a person who watches a movie after buying a movie ticket is a consumer and similarly, a person who uses a gift voucher gifted from someone else is also a consumer.

Person using goods for self-employment and not for commercial purposes: The consumer protection law does not apply to people who use goods and services for commercial purposes. However, there are some exceptions to this. For example, people who use goods for self-employment are considered as consumers. For example, artists who buy art supplies for their work or beauticians who buy beauty products are consumers.

Person using online facilities: A consumer also includes any person who buys or hires goods or services online. For example, if you order from an online clothes website, you are a consumer.

People facing issues related to food: Consumers also include people who may be facing issues related to food items, such as adulteration, poor quality, lack of service, etc. For instance, issues related to food can cover problems across a wide range of products, starting from water that goes into the production of items like juices as well as the sale of animals like chicken, mutton etc. that are expressly intended for human consumption.

[*Extracted*, with edits and revisions, from "Who is a Consumer?", Nyaaya India]

101. Clint Leone Morricone Ltd. ("CLML") is a factory manufacturing bicycles. For the purpose of documentation and record keeping, it purchased a laptop from Pacer. However, within a month of the purchase, the laptop crashed and there was a motherboard failure. Despite a warranty, Pacer failed to replace the motherboard Which of the following statements is correct?

(a) Purchase of electronic items do not fall within the purview of consumer law.

(b) CLML is a consumer since it has bought a good for a price.

(c) CLML is not a consumer since it has purchased the laptop for commercial purpose.

(d) A company is not a person and so, cannot be a consumer.

Sol. (*c*) Under consumer protection law, an entity is not considered a consumer if it purchases goods or services for commercial purposes. Since Clint Leone Morricone Ltd. (CLML) bought the laptop for documentation and record-keeping purposes in the course of running its business, it would generally be considered a commercial purpose. Therefore, CLML does not fall under the category of a consumer for this transaction.

102. Sita Das has been working as a freelance journalist. She writes columns and news-reports for various newspapers and news-portals and is paid on the basis of each column and report. For the purpose of her writing work, she purchases a Pacer laptop. However, within a month of the purchase, the laptop crashed and there was a motherboard failure. Which of the following statements is correct?

(a) Since she is using the laptop for the purpose of writing paid columns and news reports, Sita Das cannot be a consumer.
(b) Purchase of goods does not fall within the purview of Consumer Protection Law.
(c) Since she is using the laptop for the purpose of earning her livelihood, she will be a consumer.
(d) None of the above

Sol. (*c*) Under consumer protection law, an individual who purchases goods to earn their livelihood through self-employment is generally considered a consumer. Sita Das, as a freelance journalist using the laptop to write columns and news reports, fits this criterion. Therefore, she is considered a consumer.

103. Kalpavruksha Charitable Trust runs a hospital. The hospital charges a fee from its patients. The fee is however 30% less than the commercial rates for all services and medical devices sold to patients. The hospital purchased a pacemaker from St. Rude's - a globally reputed manufacturer of pacemakers, to be resold to and used by - patients. Which of the following statements is correct?
(a) The hospital is a charitable hospital and therefore, it is a consumer with respect to the pacemakers purchased from St. Rude's.
(b) The hospital resells the pacemakers to patients and therefore cannot be considered as a consumer with respect to the pacemakers purchased from St. Rude's.
(c) The hospital resells the pacemakers at a discounted rate and therefore can be considered a consumer with respect to the pacemakers purchased from St. Rude's.
(d) Sale of medical devices is not covered by Consumer Protection Law.

Sol. (*b*) Under consumer protection law, an entity that purchases goods for resale or for any commercial use is not considered a consumer. In this case, although the hospital charges less than the commercial rates, it is still purchasing the pacemakers to resell to patients. Therefore, the hospital would not be considered a consumer regarding the pacemakers purchased from St. Rude's.

104. Fitzit is an online platform that provides physiotherapy and other ancillary medical services. Amit Ghosh booked a physiotherapist on Fitzit for three months by paying an amount of ₹ 25,000. Fitzit guaranteed the availability of qualified physiotherapists for the duration. However, Fitzit failed to provide a qualified physiotherapist and the persons who were sent for the first two visits had no training or certification in the field. Amit Ghosh seeks to proceed against Fitzit under Consumer Protection Law. Which of the following statements can be correctly inferred?
(a) Since online services are not covered by Consumer Protection Law, Amit Ghosh cannot be considered a consumer.
(b) Since services are not covered by Consumer Protection Law, Amit Ghosh cannot be considered a consumer.
(c) Since online services are covered by Consumer Protection Law, Amit Ghosh shall be considered a consumer.
(d) Since medical services are not covered by Consumer Protection Law, Amit Ghosh cannot be considered a consumer.

Sol. (*c*) Under the Consumer Protection Act, a consumer is defined as a person who hires or avails of services for a consideration which has been paid or promised or has been partly paid and partly promised. In the given case, Amit Ghosh booked a physiotherapist service on the online platform Fitzit and paid an amount of ₹ 25,000, which qualifies him as a consumer under the Act.

Furthermore, the Consumer Protection Act covers both goods and services, including online services. Medical services, such as physiotherapy, are also covered under the Act.

105. Jitesh Shah purchased from BreatheEasy, a company selling respiratory devices, a nebuliser device for his son, Jignesh Shah, for use for clearing his nasal passages. The nebuliser was however defective and led to severe respiratory distress for Jignesh. Jignesh is considering filing a complaint against BreatheEasy under the Consumer Protection Law. Which of the following statements can be correctly inferred?

(a) Since Jignesh Shah did not purchase the device from BreatheEasy, he cannot be considered a consumer with respect to BreathEasy.

(b) Since Jignesh Shah is a user of the device, he can be considered a consumer.

(c) Sale of medical devices are not covered by Consumer Protection Law.

(d) None of the above

Sol. (*b*) Under the Consumer Protection Act, a 'consumer' is defined as a person who buys goods or services for a consideration, either paid or promised or partly paid and partly promised. Any user of goods or services, when such use is made with the approval of the buyer. In the given case, Jitesh Shah purchased the nebuliser device from BreatheEasy for his son, Jignesh Shah. Although Jignesh did not directly purchase the device, he is considered a consumer under the second part of the definition, as he is a user of the device and his use is with the approval of the buyer.

Section D : Logical Reasoning

XX. The depreciation of an economy's currency is not a matter of concern in itself. The decline in value against major currencies has to be viewed within a set of macroeconomic factors. The recent depreciation of the Indian rupee is a case in point. The rupee has been depreciating for a long time. What are of concern now are the rate at which the depreciation is occurring and the underlying factors causing the change. The Russia-Ukraine war has disrupted supply chains causing commodity prices to rise, leading to a worldwide hardening of inflationary trends. This, in turn, has caused major central banks to raise interest rates, forcing investors back to the safe haven of the US dollar. For India, these headwinds from the global economy have caused several problems. The rise in international prices, especially of crude oil, has led to a higher import bill and, hence, a greater demand for dollars. Higher interest rates in developed country markets have caused a significant outflow of portfolio investments from India, aggravating the already climbing demand for dollars from a rising import bill. By May 2022, foreign institutional investors had pulled out ₹ 1.50 lakh crore from Indian markets.

In the face of these pressures, the rupee, left to itself, would decline in value as the rupee-price of a dollar would increase substantially. One way the Reserve Bank of India could stem the tide would be to sell off dollars in the market to ease the supply situation. However, this would mean that while the value of the rupee could be contained, the nation's foreign exchange kitty would start to erode further. The RBI has been doing exactly that. The challenge before the RBI is this how much to let the rupee depreciate and how much to intervene to prop it up? Too much depreciation would raise domestic inflation rates as the rupee-price of imports, especially oil, would raise costs of production. It could trigger a rise in policy-controlled interest rates while closely monitoring inflationary expectations. The biggest challenge is to navigate unpredictable international economic shocks in the near future. The Indian economy's health is not exactly at its best. Exports may not be able to take advantage of a falling rupee since international demand is expected to stagnate. India's growth and employment situations are yet to stabilise to what they were about a decade ago. The RBI has difficult choices controlling inflation versus stimulating growth and stabilising the rupee without severely diminishing the economy's foreign exchange kitty.

[*Extracted*, with edits and revisions, from "Stiff test: Editorial on depreciation of rupee & challenges before RBI", The Telegraph]

106. Which of the following is the author most likely to agree with?

(a) It is a major cause for concern if an economy's currency is depreciating.

(b) Currency depreciation is not a reason for worry in itself, but if macroeconomic factors are not good, there may be a cause for concern.

(c) The fact that the Indian rupee is witnessing a decline in value against major currencies is very worrisome.

(d) A central bank must always do everything in its power to stem the slightest depreciation of an economy's currency.

Sol. (*b*) The author argues that currency depreciation needs to be evaluated within the broader context of macroeconomic factors. The passage provides an analysis of the recent depreciation of the Indian rupee, noting that the decline itself is not inherently problematic. Instead, the author points out that the concern lies in the rate of depreciation and the underlying causes, such as the Russia-Ukraine war, which has disrupted global supply chains, leading to increased commodity prices and inflation. This, in turn, has prompted central banks to raise interest rates, causing a flight of investment back to the US dollar. The impact on India has been significant, with higher import bills due to rising crude oil prices and an outflow of portfolio investments.

107. Based on the author's arguments, which of the following, if true, would reduce the decline in value of the rupee?

(a) Appointing a new Governor for the RBI who has a better sense of how to control inflationary trends.

(b) A steep increase in commodity prices and the continued disruption of supply chains.

(c) A reduction in worldwide inflationary trends and the reduction of interest rates in developed country markets.

(d) The RBI buying as many dollars as possible from the market.

Sol. (*c*) The author identifies global inflationary trends and high interest rates in developed markets as primary drivers of the rupee's depreciation. The Russia-Ukraine war has exacerbated these trends by causing supply chain disruptions and increasing commodity prices. Central banks in developed countries have responded by raising interest rates, which has led investors to move their funds to the US dollar, perceived as a safe haven. This has put additional pressure on the Indian rupee. If there were a reduction in global inflation and a subsequent lowering of interest rates in developed markets, the demand for the US dollar would decrease. This would reduce the pressure on the Indian rupee, helping to stabilise its value.

108. Which of the following, if true, would most weaken the author's arguments?

(a) The Indian economy has been affected by global inflationary trends and the increase of interest rates in developed country markets.

(b) Since developed country markets have increased their interest rates, global investors have pulled their investments out of other economies and routed them to such developed country markets.

(c) As the demand for US dollars increases, it is likely the rupee-price of a dollar would increase substantially.

(d) The Indian economy and currency are highly protected and have been insulated from the effects of global inflationary trends and the increase of interest rates in developed country markets.

Sol. (*d*) The author's argument is predicated on the idea that the depreciation of the Indian rupee is largely driven by external factors, such as the global rise in inflation and higher interest rates in developed markets, which have caused capital outflows from India and increased demand for the US dollar. If it were true that the Indian economy and currency are highly protected and insulated from these global influences, it would contradict the author's analysis. This would imply that the rupee's depreciation is due to domestic factors alone, weakening the argument that global economic conditions are to blame.

109. Which of the following, if true, would most strengthen the author's arguments for why Indian exports may not be able to take advantage of a falling rupee?

(a) Economies across the world are witnessing a slowdown and in such economies, demand for imports decreases substantially.

(b) Economies across the world are booming and there is an increasing demand for Indian exports.

(c) A reduction in the volume of exports would be more than offset by the increased value of dollars that Indian exporters would earn.

(d) Countries across the world have managed to find ways to insulate themselves from the effects of the Russia-Ukraine war and will need a lot of Indian imports to sustain their new growth models.

Sol. (*a*) The author argues that the benefits of a depreciating rupee in boosting Indian exports may not materialize due to stagnant international demand. This is because global economic conditions significantly influence the demand for imports. If global economies are experiencing a slowdown, the demand for Indian exports is likely to decrease, irrespective of the competitive pricing advantage provided by a weaker rupee. This situation would directly support the author's argument that Indian exports may not be able to leverage the falling rupee effectively.

110. Based on the author's arguments, which of the following must necessarily be true?

(a) The continuing depreciation of the Indian rupee at its current rate, coupled with worldwide inflationary trends, would result in immense political instability in India and consequently, in all of South Asia.

(b) If nothing else is done, the rise of interest rates in developed country markets, coupled with hardening of inflationary trends across the world, will result in a fall in the value of the rupee against the dollar.

(c) If inflationary trends continue to harden across the world and if interest rates in developed country markets continue to rise, portfolio investors will increase their investments in India and this will have a positive impact on India's foreign exchange reserves.

(d) If nothing else is done, the rise of interest rates in developed country markets, coupled with hardening of inflationary trends across the world, will result in a rise in the value of the rupee against the dollar.

Sol. (*b*) If nothing else is done, the rise of interest rates in developed country markets, coupled with hardening of inflationary trends across the world, will result in a fall in the value of the rupee against the dollar.

The author explains that the depreciation of the rupee is influenced by global economic conditions, particularly rising interest rates in developed markets and increasing inflationary trends. These factors have led to significant capital outflows from India and higher demand for the US dollar.

If these conditions persist and no other mitigating measures are taken, it is logical to conclude that the rupee will continue to lose value against the dollar.

111. Which of the following is the author most likely to agree with?

(a) The RBI must not focus solely on preventing the depreciation of the rupee, as that may result in negative impacts on other aspects of the economy.

(b) The RBI must focus solely on preventing the depreciation of the rupee at all costs, since it is by far the most important indicator of the health of the Indian economy.

(c) Periodic inflationary trends are normal in any economy and the RBI need not worry about the inflationary effects in the Indian economy caused by the depreciation of the rupee.

(d) The RBI need not do anything to reduce the rate of depreciation of the rupee, since the depreciation of an economy's currency is not a matter of concern in itself.

Sol. (*a*) The author discusses the complex trade-offs faced by the Reserve Bank of India (RBI) in managing the rupee's depreciation.

While it is important to prevent excessive depreciation to avoid inflationary pressures, focusing solely on stabilising the rupee could lead to other economic issues, such as eroding foreign exchange reserves and stifling economic growth. The author suggests that the RBI needs to strike a balance between controlling inflation, supporting growth and maintaining currency stability.

XXI. The post-truth era is, expectedly, marked by a discerning erosion of public trust in sources of information. Mass media - both traditional and new-age avatars– has borne the brunt of this mistrust. And for good reasons too. Social media, its most popular platform, is a harbinger of falsity. It is thus encouraging to see that at least the old guard of the media ecosystem - the newspaper - continues to defy this discouraging trend. A pan-India survey of media consumption by Lokniti found that print media remains the most trusted source of information. The finding is consistent with the heartening surge in public endorsement of the reliability of newspapers since the pandemic. An earlier survey, which attempted to examine the impact of the lockdown on 'reading patterns', had found that the number of readers who used to spend over an hour on newspapers every day had risen to 38%, up from 16% in the pre-lockdown period. The increased trust in newspapers is because the lockdowns coincided with the dissemination of the crudest kinds of misinformation about the pandemic in India and around the world and newspapers played a pivotal role in exposing these lies.

But that is where the good news ends – for the print media, at least. Among other things, the data collated by the survey found deepening footprints of social media in rural and urban constituencies while television continues to dominate the screen. These developments are consistent with global trends that reveal that the newspaper industry is struggling to contain the migration of readers and revenue to other formats, especially digital media. Ironically, the pandemic, which saw a resurgence in collective trust in newspapers, adversely affected the print media as traditional advertisers, reeling under the economic fallouts of Covid-19, cut back on advertisements. But the crisis in print precedes the pandemic. Newspapers have been outpaced by speedier, but also spurious, sources of information. The dominance of the image over text as a cultural phenomenon is another formidable challenge. The print media's hopes of remaining competitive and profitable must, therefore, centre on using this collective trust as a form of capital. Survival strategies, especially the revenue model, must be re-explored and the emphasis shifted to in-depth analyses of news as well as eyecatching layouts now that newspapers are slower to reach news to the audience.

[*Extracted*, with edits and revisions, from "Good news: Editorial on print media remaining the most trusted source of information", The Telegraph]

112. Which of the following is the author most likely to agree with?

(a) The Covid-19 pandemic was an unmitigated disaster for the newspaper industry.

(b) The Covid-19 pandemic had negative as well as positive effects on the newspaper industry.

(c) The Covid-19 pandemic only had good effects on the newspaper industry.

(d) The Covid-19 pandemic had no effect at all on the newspaper industry.

Sol. (*b*) The Covid-19 pandemic had negative as well as positive effects on the newspaper industry. The author discusses how the pandemic led to a resurgence in collective trust in newspapers, as people turned to print media for reliable information amidst widespread misinformation. However, the pandemic also had negative impacts, such as a reduction in advertising revenue due to the economic fallout from Covid-19. Traditional advertisers cut back on advertisements, which adversely affected the financial stability of the print media industry.

113. Which of the following, if true, would most weaken the author's arguments?

(a) Social media is a reliable source of true and accurate news and information.

(b) Social media is a highly unreliable source of news and information and should not be trusted.

(c) Social media is a good way for people to stay connected with each other.

(d) Social media is a speedier source of information than newspapers.

Sol. (*a*) The author argues that social media is a significant harbinger of falsity and is a major factor in the erosion of public trust in information sources. The passage highlights that newspapers have gained trust partly because they have been reliable in exposing misinformation, especially during the pandemic. If it were true that social media is a reliable source of accurate news, this would directly contradict the author's claim that social media spreads misinformation and would weaken the argument about the relative trustworthiness of print media.

114. Which of the following would be an effective way of making print media more competitive?

(a) Slowing down the process of print media production.

(b) Using more expensive printing methods that achieve better print quality, even if it results in newspapers becoming more expensive.

(c) Only publishing newspapers on alternate days.

(d) Developing ways of ensuring that print media can reach readers more speedily.

Sol. (*d*) Developing ways of ensuring that print media can reach readers more speedily. The author notes that one of the significant challenges facing print media is being outpaced by faster sources of information, such as social media and digital platforms. To make print media more competitive, it would be effective to develop ways to ensure that newspapers can reach readers more quickly. This could involve improving distribution channels, leveraging digital platforms for quicker dissemination, or adopting new technologies to speed up the printing process. Enhancing the speed of delivery would help newspapers remain relevant and better compete with other faster information sources.

115. Based on the author's arguments, which of the following, if true, would have resulted in the weakening, rather than deepening of public trust in newspapers since the pandemic?

(a) Newspapers were very careful in ensuring they reported accurate and true news during the lockdowns.
(b) Newspapers played a leading role in exposing lies and misinformation spread during the lockdown.
(c) Newspapers actively disseminated misinformation during the lockdowns and made no efforts to expose lies spread by others.
(d) Newspapers alerted the public to the fact that a number of sources were spreading crude forms of misinformation during the pandemic.

Sol. (*c*) Newspapers actively disseminated misinformation during the lockdowns and made no efforts to expose lies spread by others. The author argues that the increased trust in newspapers during the pandemic is largely due to their role in exposing misinformation and providing accurate news. If newspapers had instead actively disseminated misinformation and made no efforts to counter falsehoods, this would have significantly undermined public trust in them. Such behavior would have aligned newspapers with the unreliable sources that the public was trying to avoid, thereby weakening the trust that people had placed in print media during the crisis.

116. What would be the impact on the readership and revenues of the print media if the image were not dominant over text as a cultural phenomenon?

(a) Print media would not suffer as much of a reduction in readership and revenue as readers shifted to other formats.
(b) Print media would suffer a greater reduction in readership and revenue as readers shifted to other formats.
(c) There would be no impact on the readership and revenues of the print industry.
(d) There would be an increased demand from readers that newspapers carry more images and less text.

Sol. (*a*) Print media would not suffer as much of a reduction in readership and revenue as readers shifted to other formats. The author mentions that the dominance of the image over text is a formidable challenge for print media. This cultural shift towards preferring visual content has contributed to readers migrating to digital platforms that offer more images and videos. If this dominance of images were not as prevalent, print media, which relies heavily on text-based content, might retain more of its readership and not face as severe a reduction in revenues. Readers would be less inclined to shift to other formats that prioritise visual content, thereby sustaining the print media's audience and financial stability.

117. How does the author suggest newspapers can overcome the problem of being outpaced by speedier sources of information?

(a) They offer direct means by which newspapers can become faster to publish and deliver to readers.
(b) They encourage a complete and immediate shift to digital media as a way of ensuring newspapers are not outpaced by other sources of information.
(c) They offer ways to reduce production costs, which would offset the losses caused by readers shifting allegiance to faster sources of information.
(d) They offer alternative means for newspapers to become competitive and profitable, but do not solve the

problem of how newspapers can become faster sources of information.

Sol. (*d*) They offer alternative means for newspapers to become competitive and profitable, but do not solve the problem of how newspapers can become faster sources of information. The author suggests that newspapers need to focus on leveraging the trust they have built as a form of capital. This involves re-examining their revenue models and emphasizing in-depth analyses and attractive layouts. These strategies aim to make newspapers more competitive and profitable by capitalising on their reliability and the depth of their content, rather than trying to match the speed of digital media. The author does not provide specific solutions for making newspapers faster but instead emphasises enhancing their unique strengths to remain relevant.

XXII. In this moment, the developed countries - I point to them, because these countries have already burnt massive amounts of carbon dioxide for energy to build their economies - are faced with a real energy conundrum. On the one hand, developed countries are battered because of a fast-heating planet; temperatures have gone through the roof; droughts and extreme weather events are hitting them as well. On the other hand, ordinary people in these countries are worried, not just because of climate change but because of the lack of energy to heat their homes this coming winter. In the US, gas prices went up in summer, so much so that people travelled less and consumption of fuel dropped. But now prices are down and it is business as usual.

The fact is that this energy disruption has provided the much-needed vault to the beleaguered fossil fuel industry. Governments are asking this industry to supply more. Europe has baptised natural gas, a fossil fuel less polluting than coal but still a major emitter of carbon dioxide, as 'clean'. The US has passed a climate bill, which will invest in renewable energy but conditional to increased spends on oil and gas and the opening up of millions of hectares of federal land for drilling. Through this bill the US will do more than ever before to build a manufacturing base for renewable energy, particularly solar. Europe, even in this desperate scramble for gas, is working to ramp up its investment in renewable power. So, it is the worst of times. It could be the best of times, but there are some caveats. One, this renewed interest in fossil fuels must remain temporary and transient. Given the nature of economies, once the investment has been made in this new infrastructure or the supply of fossil fuel has increased from new oil and gas discoveries, it will be difficult to wean off. Two, these countries should not be entitled to more use of fossil fuels in our world of shrunk carbon budgets. They need to reduce emissions drastically and leave whatever little carbon budget space that is remaining to poorer countries to use, thereby satisfying such poorer countries' demands.

[*Extracted*, with edits and revisions, from "New energy conundrum", by Sunita Narain, DownToEarth]

118. Which of the following is the author most likely to agree with?

(a) People in the US are not worried at all about climate change.

(b) People in the US are worried about climate change and these concerns affect their energy consumption habits more than anything else.

(c) Climate change has resulted in the increase of energy prices across the world and as a result, governments have had to invest in finding newer sources of renewable energy.

(d) Changes in the energy consumption habits of people in the US are affected more by energy prices than concerns of climate change.

Sol. (*d*) Changes in the energy consumption habits of people in the US are affected more by energy prices than concerns of climate change. The passage mentions that gas prices in the US went up in summer, leading to reduced travel and lower fuel consumption. 'However, once prices dropped, it was "business as usual.' This indicates that the primary driver for changes in energy consumption habits was the fluctuation in energy prices rather than concerns about climate change. The author emphasises that while there are worries about climate change, immediate economic factors, such as fuel costs, have a more direct impact on people's behaviour.

119. Which of the following is most similar to the author's statements about developed countries' renewed interest in fossil fuels?

(a) Developed countries should not, under any circumstances, invest any resources in fossil fuel energy extraction and must immediately put a halt to all fossil fuel consumption.

(b) Things could improve if developed countries recognise the difficulty of moving away from reliance on such sources of energy and make a conscious effort to move to alternate or renewable energy sources quickly.

(c) Since investments in energy extraction of any kind are very expensive, developed countries must ensure that they make permanent and continuing investments in fossil fuels.

(d) Developing countries must not, under any circumstances, consume fossil fuels and leave whatever carbon budget space is remaining to richer countries to use.

Sol. (*b*) The author suggests that while there is a renewed interest in fossil fuels due to the current energy crisis, this interest must remain temporary and transient. Developed countries should not rely on fossil fuels long-term but should instead focus on transitioning to renewable energy sources. The passage emphasizes the need for a conscious effort to move away from fossil fuels to avoid locking in new infrastructure that would make it difficult to reduce reliance on these energy sources in the future.

120. If the information in the passage above is correct, which of the following must necessarily be true?

(a) The fossil fuel industry in developing countries will face reduced sales in the short term, with increased sales in the long term.

(b) The cost of making, installing and using solar panels will reduce substantially in the coming years.

(c) Passing a bill in the US is a huge effort and it would not have been possible to pass the new climate bill unless the current energy crisis had compelled lawmakers to do so.

(d) The fossil fuel industry in developing countries will see an increase in business, at least in the short term.

Sol. (d) Statement (d) will be necessarily be true.

The fossil fuel industry in developing countries will see an increase in business, at least in the short term. The pasage discusses the energy crisis in developed countries pushing them to seek more fossil fuels, including pressuring the industry to produce more.

While the long-term goal is to shift to renewable, the short-term solution involves increased reliance on fossil fuels. Since developed countries are seeking more fossil fuels, it's likely to lead to increased business for the global fossil fuel industry, which includes developing countries.

121. Which of the following, if true, would most weaken the author's argument about why travel and fuel consumption in the US reduced in summer?

(a) People like to travel regardless of season and the only thing that would prevent them from travelling at any time of the year would be high costs.

(b) Airlines raised ticket prices as a response to increase in fuel prices and therefore, fewer people were able to buy air tickets to travel.

(c) Strict lockdowns were imposed in the US in summer, because of which people travelled less; further, temperatures were moderate and this meant people had to use less fuel to heat or warm their homes.

(d) Widespread geopolitical tensions in the first half of the year meant that fuel prices were at an all-time high in summer, but prices have now eased of somewhat, making fuel slightly more affordable in the US.

Sol. (*c*) Strict lockdowns were imposed in the US in summer, because of which people traveled less; further, temperatures were moderate and this meant people had to use less fuel to heat or warm their homes. The author attributes the reduction in travel and fuel consumption in the US during the summer primarily to the increase in gas prices. If it were true that strict lockdowns were imposed during the summer, leading to reduced travel and moderate temperatures reduced the need for fuel for heating, this would weaken the argument that high gas prices were the main reason for decreased travel and fuel consumption. The presence of these additional factors would suggest that the reduction in fuel use was not solely due to price increases, thereby weakening the author's argument.

122. Which of the following, if true, would resolve the 'conundrum' the author says developed countries face now?

(a) The development of adequate renewable power sources in the near term that would lead to a reduction in consumption of fossil fuels.

(b) Finding new sources of fossil fuels that will ensure there is no shortage of energy to heat homes in the winter.

(c) Switching immediately to renewable power sources, even if it leads to a shortage in energy supply for people.

(d) Providing adequate aid to poorer countries so that they can develop renewable power sources for their use.

Sol. (*a*) The development of adequate renewable power sources in the near term that would lead to a reduction in consumption of fossil fuels. The author points out the dilemma that developed countries face: the need to address the immediate energy crisis without exacerbating climate change through increased fossil fuel consumption.
If developed countries can quickly develop sufficient renewable energy sources, this would alleviate the pressure to rely on fossil fuels and resolve the conundrum of balancing energy needs with climate goals. This approach would allow for the transition to cleaner energy without causing an energy shortage, thereby meeting both immediate and long-term objectives.

123. Assuming the aim of the US climate bill is to reduce fossil fuel consumption, which of the following would be the strongest argument that it will fail to achieve such an aim?

(a) The bill promotes investments in renewable energy but does not provide for enough increase in investments in developing more sources of fossil fuel-powered energy.

(b) The bill is written in technical language, which ordinary people cannot easily understand.

(c) The bill is self-defeating, since it makes investments in renewable energy conditional to more expenditure on oil and gas and making millions of hectares of federal land available for drilling, which would lead to an increased consumption of fossil fuels.

(d) The bill does not provide any means of increasing carbon budgets, thereby making more room for fossil fuel consumption.

Sol. (*c*) The bill is self-defeating, since it makes investments in renewable energy conditional to more expenditure on oil and gas and making millions of hectares of federal land available for drilling, which would lead to an increased consumption of fossil fuels. The author mentions that the US climate bill, while investing in renewable energy, also requires increased spending on oil and gas and opens federal land for drilling. This dual approach could undermine the bill's primary aim of reducing fossil fuel consumption by simultaneously promoting activities that increase fossil fuel use. This conditional investment strategy could perpetuate reliance on fossil fuels, making it difficult to achieve significant reductions in their consumption.

XXIII. While men and women are both considered to be more capable as they get older, only women bear the brunt of being seen as "less warm" as they age, new research has found. This series of studies is reportedly the first to look at both gender and age to determine how perceptions of women and men differ. "It's just stunning' These stereotypes are so hard-wired and deeply entrenched that they come out even when absolutely identical information is provided about a man and a woman," Jennifer Chatman, Distinguished Professor of Management at UC Berkeley's Haas School of Business, said. In an analysis of professors' evaluations, female professors witnessed a decline as they moved from their 30s to 40s, hitting an all-time low around the age of 47. All this while, the evaluation of male professors remained consistent. Interestingly, after the age of 47, the evaluations for women increased again, becoming equal with those of men around the early 60s. "At that point, there are different stereotypes of women and they may benefit from being seen as more grandmotherly," said Laura Kray, faculty director of the Center for Equity, Gender and Leadership at Berkeley Haas and an author of the study. Women around the age of mid 30s to late 40s also face what is called "the motherhood penalty," where assumptions around parenting duties lead people to believe women are less committed to their careers than men. This has several repercussions, most particularly evident in hiring, promotions and wages. Women executives further pointed out that they face "hyper-scrutiny" and 'scepticism' which harks back to perceptions of likeability versus agency. Gendered networks in the workplace, with men gaining greater access to senior leaders, become cemented mid-career, pose another difficulty for working women. Negative perceptions of women in middle-age can also be linked to stereotypes around menopause. In 2008, psychologists studied the attitudes of people towards women in different reproductive stages. They found that while the pregnant women or the woman with the baby were thought about in glowing terms, menopausal women were associated with negative emotions, illness and ageing.

[*Extracted*, with edits and revisions, from "How Stereotypes Affect Middle. Aged Women's Careers", by Ananya Singh, The Swaddle]

124. Which of the following is most likely to be true if the author's statements about gendered networks in the workplace are true?

(a) Mid-career women do not find it as easy to get access to senior leaders, who are usually male, as their male colleagues. They therefore find career progression or new opportunities easier to come by.

(b) Mid-career women find it easier to get access to senior leaders, who are usually male, as their male colleagues. They therefore find career progression or new opportunities easier to come by.

(c) Mid-career women do not find it as easy to get access to senior leaders, who are usually male, as their male colleagues. They therefore find career progression or new opportunities harder to come by.

(d) Mid-career women find it easier to get access to senior leaders, who are usually male, as their male colleagues. They therefore do not find career progression or new opportunities harder to come by.

Sol. (*c*) The passage mentions that gendered networks in the workplace lead to men gaining greater access to senior leaders, which becomes cemented mid-career. This implies that mid-career women face challenges in accessing senior leaders, who are usually male, compared to their male colleagues. As a result, they encounter more difficulties in finding career progression or new opportunities.

125. Which of the following is most likely to be an outcome of what the author describes as the 'motherhood penalty'?

(a) People are more hesitant to hire men from their mid 30s to their late 40s but may be more willing to hire women of a similar age.

(b) People are more hesitant to hire women from their mid 30s to their late 40s but may be more willing to hire men of a similar age.

(c) Women from their mid 30s to their late 40s always prioritise parenting responsibilities and so are not really interested in pursuing a career.

(d) Women who have children are less committed to their careers than men.

Sol. (*b*) The passage discusses the 'motherhood penalty,' where assumptions about parenting duties lead to the belief that women are less committed to their careers than men. This bias affects hiring, promotions and wages, as employers may perceive women in their mid 30s to late 40s as less dedicated to their professional responsibilities due to potential childcare responsibilities.

126. If professors' evaluations are the most important criteria in awarding promotions, then which of the following would be the most likely outcome, based on the information provided in the passage?

(a) Male professors are likely to be promoted at an even rate throughout their career, while women professors would experience a lower likelihood of promotion in the mid-career stage.

(b) Since there is a wide disparity between the evaluations that male and female professors receive, the practice of relying upon such evaluations will quickly be abandoned.

(c) Male and female professors will receive promotions at a similar rate throughout the course of their career.

(d) Women professors are likely to be promoted at an even rate throughout their career, while male professors would experience a lower likelihood of promotion in the mid-career stage.

Sol. (*a*) Male professors are likely to be promoted at an even rate throughout their career, while women professors would experience a lower likelihood of promotion in the mid-career stage. The passage mentions that female professors' evaluations decline as they move from their 30s to their 40s, hitting an all-time low around the age of 47, while male professors' evaluations remain consistent. If evaluations are the most important criteria for promotions, this disparity would result in male professors having a more consistent promotion trajectory, while female professors would face lower promotion prospects during their mid-career stage due to lower evaluations.

127. Which of the following is the author most likely to disagree with?

(a) Women going through menopause often quit the workforce voluntarily.

(b) Women going through menopause are more likely to be perceived negatively at the workplace and to have difficulty achieving professional success.

(c) Women going through menopause should be permitted to take a mid-career sabbatical.
(d) Women going through menopause are more likely to be perceived positively at the workplace and to achieve professional success.

Sol. (*d*) Women going through menopause are more likely to be perceived positively at the workplace and to achieve professional success. The passage notes that negative perceptions of women in middle age can be linked to stereotypes around menopause, which are associated with negative emotions, illness and aging. This suggests that menopausal women are often viewed negatively and face difficulties in achieving professional success.

128. Which of the following, if true, would most strengthen the main argument in the passage?
(a) Several independent studies conducted in different countries have shown that women in the workplace are perceived positively and are favourably treated as they age.
(b) Several independent studies conducted in different countries have shown that women in the workplace are perceived negatively and are unfairly treated as they age.
(c) The studies mentioned in the passage have been discredited after they were published and no reliance should be placed on them.
(d) The studies mentioned in the passage were conducted on very small sample sets and cannot be used to make general statements about the difference in perception between men and women.

Sol. (*b*) Several independent studies conducted in different countries have shown that women in the workplace are perceived negatively and are unfairly treated as they age. The passage discusses how stereotypes about aging and gender negatively affect women's professional lives, particularly during their mid-career stages. If multiple independent studies from various countries support the findings that women are perceived negatively and treated unfairly as they age, it would strengthen the main argument by providing additional evidence that these stereotypes and biases are widespread and not isolated incidents.

129. Which of the following, if true, would most weaken Laura Kray's arguments?
(a) Women professors perceived as being 'grandmotherly' are regarded as being likeable and caring.
(b) Women professors perceived as being 'grandmotherly' are treated better by their colleagues and students.
(c) Women professors perceived as being 'grandmotherly' are regarded as being slow, inefficient and outdated in their field.
(d) Women professors perceived as being 'grandmotherly' are regarded very highly and receive much more respect than younger women professors.

Sol. (*c*) Women professors perceived as being 'grandmotherly' are regarded as being slow, inefficient and outdated in their field. Laura Kray suggests that evaluations for women improve after the age of 47 because they benefit from being seen as more "grandmotherly," which implies a positive perception. If it were true that women professors perceived as 'grandmotherly' are regarded as slow, inefficient and outdated, it would directly contradict Kray's argument that this perception is beneficial. This negative stereotype would imply that older women are seen in a less favorable light, thereby weakening the argument that their evaluations improve due to positive perceptions associated with being 'grandmotherly.'

XXIV. Why are we humans so susceptible to the doom and gloom of the news? Two reasons. The first is what psychologists call negativity bias: we're more attuned to the bad than the good. Back in our hunting and gathering days, we were better off being frightened of a spider or a snake a hundred times too often than one time too few. Too much fear wouldn't kill you; too little surely would. Second, we're also burdened with an availability bias. If we can easily recall examples of a given thing, we assume that thing is relatively common. The fact that we're bombarded daily with horrific stories about aircraft disasters, child snatchers and beheadings. which tend to lodge in the memory - completely skews our view of the world. In this digital age, the news we're being fed is only getting more extreme. In the old days, journalists didn't know much about their individual readers. They wrote for the masses. But the people behind Facebook, Twitter and Google know you well. They know what shocks and horrifies you, they know what makes you click. They know how to grab your attention and hold it so they can serve you the most lucrative helping of personalised ads. This modern media frenzy is nothing less than an assault on the mundane. Because, let's be honest, the lives of most people are pretty predictable. Nice, but boring. So while we'd prefer having nice neighbours with boring lives, 'boring' won't make you sit up and take notice. 'Nice' doesn't sell ads. And so Silicon Valley keeps dishing us up ever more sensational clickbait, knowing full well, as a Swiss novelist once quipped, that "News is to the mind what sugar is to the body."

[*Extracted*, with edits and revisions, from Humankind: A Hopeful History, by Rutger Bregman, Bloomsbury Publishing, London, 2021.]

130. Which of the following, if true, would most weaken the author's arguments?

(a) Behavioural traits that helped us in the days when we were hunter-gatherers continue to be present in modern-day humans.

(b) Behavioural traits that helped us in the days when we were hunter-gatherers are no longer found in modern-day humans.

(c) The negativity bias makes us more likely to be affected by depressing or sad news.

(d) We have certain behavioural characteristics that affect how we perceive and are affected by sad news.

Sol. (*b*) The author's argument hinges on the idea that humans have inherited behavioral traits, such as negativity bias and availability bias, from our hunter-gatherer ancestors. These traits make us more susceptible to negative news because they once had survival benefits. If it were true that these behavioral traits are no longer present in modern-day humans, it would weaken the author's argument by undermining the basis for why we are more attuned to negative news.

131. Which of the following is the author most likely to agree with?

(a) Contemporary media continuously exposes us to exciting news and information, which may be just like the things we usually experience in our lives.

(b) Contemporary media continuously exposes us to exciting news and information, which may be very unlike the kinds of things we usually encounter in our lives.

(c) Contemporary media continuously exposes us to boring news and information, which may be very unlike the kinds of things we usually encounter in our lives.

(d) Contemporary media continuously exposes us to boring news and information, which may be just like the things we usually experience in our lives.

Sol. (*b*) Contemporary media continuously exposes us to exciting news and information, which may be very unlike the kinds of things we usually encounter in our lives. The author argues that contemporary media, driven by algorithms and personalised content, tends to present sensational and extreme news to capture our attention. This news is often very different from the mundane realities of our daily lives. The author notes that "boring" doesn't sell ads and that Silicon Valley provides sensational clickbait instead.

132. Based only on the author's statement that "we'd prefer having nice neighbours with boring lives" and the author's argument about the nature of news that modern media exposes us to, which of the following would the author be most likely to agree with?

(a) Constantly being exposed to negative news gives us a warped perspective of the world.

(b) In our hunting and gathering days, it was better for us to be unnecessarily scared rather than being scared too little.

(c) The news modern media exposes us to is just like our day-to-day experiences.

(d) The news modern media exposes us to is very different from our day-to-day experiences.

Sol. (*d*) The news modern media exposes us to is very different from our day-to-day experiences. The author emphasises that contemporary media, especially digital platforms, focuses on sensational and extreme news to capture attention and sell ads. This type of news is contrasted with the "boring" but preferable reality of having "nice neighbors with boring lives." This suggests that the news we are exposed to is far more dramatic and alarming than our everyday experiences.

133. The author's statements about negativity bias, if true, provide most support for which of the following conclusions?

(a) We are more likely to notice a story about a billionaire donating their money to charity than a story about an airplane crash.

(b) We are more likely to be attracted to a news article about a rise in life expectancy in our country than a news article about a murder in our city.

(c) We are more likely to notice a story about increasing pollution levels than a story about improving educational levels in schools.

(d) We are more likely to form our opinion of the world based on the information available to us rather than information we do not have access to.

Sol. (*c*) We are more likely to notice a story about increasing pollution levels than a story about improving educational levels in schools. The author's discussion of negativity bias suggests that people are more attuned to negative information because it had survival benefits for our ancestors. This bias makes us more likely to notice and remember bad news. Therefore, a story about increasing pollution levels (a negative event) is more likely to capture our attention than a story about improving educational levels (a positive event). This conclusion is directly supported by the author's argument about our inherent tendency to focus on negative news.

134. Which of the following would be the most effective way of countering the effects of what the author describes as our 'availability bias'?

(a) Ensuring that we do not seek out news sources and stories that we may not otherwise have been exposed to.

(b) Following only one news source and limiting our perspective of the world to that one source.

(c) Avoiding all positive news stories and instead only reading news stories about disasters and tragedies.

(d) Ensuring that we seek out news sources and stories that we may not otherwise have been exposed to.

Sol. (*d*) Ensuring that we seek out news sources and stories that we may not otherwise have been exposed to.

The author explains that availability bias leads us to assume that events we can easily recall are more common than they are. This bias is exacerbated by being bombarded with sensational and negative news. To counteract this bias, it would be effective to diversify our news consumption and seek out a variety of sources and stories, including those that are not sensational or negative. This would provide a more balanced and accurate view of the world.

135. The author says that "The fact that we're bombarded daily with horrific stories about aircraft disasters, child snatchers and beheadings . which tend to lodge in the memory . completely skews our view of the world."

The conclusion the author draws in this argument follows logically if which of the following is assumed?

(a) Our ideas about the world are shaped by the information we are exposed to.

(b) Modern media is concerned only with making massive profits.

(c) Modern journalists generate news stories much faster than in the old days.

(d) Humans once lived as hunter-gatherers.

Sol. (*a*) Our ideas about the world are shaped by the information we are exposed to. The author's argument is that the daily bombardment of horrific news stories distorts our perception of the world, making us believe that such events are more common than they are. This conclusion relies on the assumption that the information we are exposed to significantly influences our worldview. If we accept that our ideas about the world are shaped by the news and information we consume, the author's argument logically follows.

Section D : Quantitative Techniques

XXV. The findings of Oxfam India's latest 'India Discrimination Report 2022' indicate that there is a significant gap in the earnings between men and women in the case of regular and self-employment in urban areas. The lower wages for salaried women are due to 67 per cent of discrimination and 33 per cent due to lack of education and work experience. The average earning is ₹ 16,000 for men and merely ₹ 6600 for women in urban areas in self-employment. The average earning of men is ₹ 19800 as against ₹ 15600 for women in regular/salaried employment in urban areas. Also, in urban areas the average earnings of men (₹ 9000) are significantly higher than women (₹ 5700) even in casual employment. Apart from women, historically oppressed communities along with religious minorities also continue to face discrimination in accessing jobs, livelihoods and agricultural credit. The mean income for Scheduled Castes or Scheduled Tribes ("SC/ST") persons in urban areas who are in regular employment is ₹ 15300 as against ₹ 20300 for persons belonging to the non-SC/ST category. The average earning of self-employed workers is ₹ 15900 for non-SC/STs and ₹ 10500 for SC/STs. The average monthly earning for the SC/ST workers in casual work is ₹ 8000 below the corresponding figure of ₹ 8600 for the Non-SC/ST.

[**Data Source** Oxfam India]

[**Note** Values have been approximated to the nearest hundred]

136. Choose the correct option:

(a) Women's average earnings in urban areas in casual work is 30% lower than that of men

(b) Men's average earning in urban areas in self-employment is nearly 2.5 times that of earnings of women

(c) In casual work, women earn more in rural areas than in urban areas

(d) The difference in earnings of men and women in regular/salaried employment in urban areas is ₹ 3500

Sol. (*b*) In urban areas,

According to option (a),

Women's average earning in casual work = ₹ 5700

Men's average earning in casual work = ₹ 9000

Women's average earning lower than that men

$$= \frac{9000 - 5700}{9000} \times 100$$

$$= \frac{3300}{9000} \times 10 = 36.67\% \neq 30\%$$

So, option (a) is false,

According to option (b)

In urban areas,

$$= \frac{\text{Average earning of men in self-employment}}{\text{Average earning of women in self-employment}}$$

$$= \frac{16000}{6600}$$

$= ₹ 2.424 \approx ₹ 2.5$

Hence, men's average earning in urban areas in self-employment is nearly 2.5 times that of earnings of women.

So, option (b) is correct.

137. Of the regular employed in urban areas, the earnings of a non-SC/ST worker is what percent more than a SC/ST worker?

(a) Between 20% and 25%

(b) Less than 15%

(c) Between 30% and 35%

(d) More than 35%

Sol. (*c*) For regular employed in urban areas.

The mean income of SC/ST workers = ₹ 15300

The mean income of non-SC/ST workers = ₹ 20300

$$\therefore \text{Required per cent} = \frac{20300 - 15300}{15300} \times 100\%$$

$$= \frac{5000 \times 100}{15300}\%$$

= 3267% (it is between 30% and 35%)

Hence, option (c) is correct answer.

138. Of those in casual employment, if a man's average earnings was deposited at a rate of 16% simple interest for 20 years, in how many years at the same rate of simple interest a SC/ST worker must deposit their average earnings to earn the same amount as a man in 20 years?

(a) 24 years (b) 22.5 years

(c) 21 years (d) 23.2 years

Sol. (*d*) In casual employment,

Men's average earnings = ₹ 9000

Rate = 16% p.a, Time = 20 yr

$$\therefore \text{Simple Interest} = \frac{9000 \times 16 \times 20}{100}$$

= ₹ 28800

Total amount = 9000 + 28800 = ₹ 37800

Now, average earnings of SC/ST workers = ₹ 8000

Required simple interest = 37800 − 8000 = ₹ 29800

Rate = 16% p.a.

Let the required time be T yr.

$$\therefore \quad 29800 = \frac{8000 \times 16 \times T}{100}$$

$$\therefore \quad T = \frac{29800}{80 \times 16} = 23.2 \text{ yr}$$

139. The findings also indicate discrimination as a driving factor behind low Women's Labour Force Participation Rate (LFPR) in the country. As per the Union Ministry of Statistics and Programme Implementation (MoSPI), LFPR for women in India was only 25.1 percent in 2020-21 for urban and rural women. This is considerably lower than South Africa where the LFPR for women is 46 percent in 2021 as per the latest World Bank estimates. The LFPR for women in India has rapidly declined from 42.7 percent in 2004-05 to mere 25.1 percent in 2020-2021 showing the withdrawal of women from the workforce despite rapid economic growth during the same period. In 2019-20, 60 percent of all males aged 15 years and more have regular salaried and self-employed jobs while 19 percent of all similarly aged females get regular and self-employment. Use the additional data in the passage above to answer this and the next question.

If the number of women in India in 2020-2021 is 670 million which is 24% more than in 2004-2005, what is the difference in the number of women in LFPR 2004-05 and 2021?

(a) Less than 5 crores

(b) Between 6 and 8 crores

(c) Between 10 and 12 crores

(d) More than 15 crores

Sol. (*b*) Let the number of women in 2004-05 be x.

According to the question,

$$x \times \frac{124}{100} = 670000000$$

[∴ 1 million = 1 lakh]

$$\therefore \quad x = \frac{670000000 \times 100}{124} = 540322580.645$$

$= 540322581$ (approx)

Now, women in LFPR in 2004-05

$$= 540322581 \times \frac{42.7}{100} = 230717742.08$$

$= 230717742$

and women in LFPR in 2020-21

$$= 670000000 \times \frac{25.1}{100} = 168170000$$

Required difference

$= 230717742 - 168170000$

$= 62547742$

$= 6.25$ crores (it is between 6 and 8 crores)

Hence, option (b) is correct answer.

140. In 2019-20, if the number of males aged 15 years and more is 76% of the total male population and the number of females aged 15 years and more is 72% of the total female population and the total male population is 1.05 times the total female population, what is the ratio of females to males aged 15 years and more that have regular salaried and self-employed jobs?

(a) 2 : 7 (b) 3 : 10 (c) 5 : 9 (d) 1 : 3

Sol. (*a*) Let the total number of females be x.

∴ The total number of males = $1.05x$

According to the question,

Number of males aged 15 yr in

$$\text{2019-20} = 1.05\,x \times \frac{76}{100}$$

Number of females aged 15 yr sin

$$\text{2019-20} = x \times \frac{72}{100}$$

In 2019-20, number of males aged 15 yr and have regular salaried and self-employed jobs $= 1.05x \times \frac{76}{100} \times \frac{60}{100}$

and number of females aged 15 yr and have regular salaried and self-emboloyed jobs $= x \times \frac{72}{100} \times \frac{19}{100}$

$$\therefore \text{Required ratio} = \frac{x \times \frac{72}{100} \times \frac{19}{100}}{1.05\,x \times \frac{76}{100} \times \frac{60}{100}}$$

$$= \frac{1368}{4788} = \frac{2}{7} = 2:7$$

XXVI. World fruit production went up 54 per cent between 2000 and 2019, to 883 million tonnes. Five fruit species accounted for 57 per cent of the total production in 2019, down from 63 per cent in 2000. Use the data in the passage to answer the following questions. [Data source: FAO]

141. What was the world fruit production in 2000?

(a) 474 million tonnes

(b) 517 million tonnes

(c) 573 million tonnes

(d) 406 million tonnes

Sol. (*c*) Let the fruit production in 2000 be x million tonnes.

According to the question,

$$x \times \frac{154}{100} = 883 \text{ million tonnes}$$

$$\Rightarrow \quad x = \frac{883 \times 100}{154} \text{ million tonnes}$$

$= 573.37 \approx 573$ million tonnes

142. Of the five fruit species mentioned in the passage above, the share of bananas and plantains increased by 1 percentage point between 2000 and 2019, watermelons in 2019 was 6 percentage points lower than bananas and plantains in 2000, apples remained stable at 10% and the percentage share of oranges and grapes reduced to half of bananas in 2019 . What was the percentage of bananas and plantains in 2019?

(a) 17% (b) 18%

(c) 16% (d) 21%

Sol. (*b*) Let percentage of bananas and plantains in 2000 be x%.

$\therefore$ Percentage of bananas and plantains in 2019 = $(x+1)$%

Percentage change 2000 to 2019

$$= \frac{883-573}{573} \times 100 = 54\%$$

According to the question,

$$x+1+x-6+10+\frac{x}{2}-1+\frac{x}{2}-1=54$$

$$\Rightarrow 3x+3=54$$

$$\Rightarrow \quad 3x=51 \Rightarrow x=17$$

$\therefore$ Percentage of bananas and plantains in 2019 = $(17+1)\% = 18\%$

143. Of the watermelons in 2000, one-eighth perished, one-fifth of the remaining was sold to be juiced and 30% of the remaining was exported. If the percentage share of oranges in 2000 was equal to the percentage share of watermelons in 2019, how many watermelons were retained for home sale and consumption?

(a) 39.2 million tonnes

(b) 1.6 million tonnes

(c) 16.8 million tonnes

(d) 2.7 million tonnes

Sol. (*a*) Watermelons in 2000 $= 573 \times \frac{17}{100}$

Watermelons perished $= \frac{1}{8} \times 573 \times \frac{17}{100}$

Remaining watermelons $= \frac{7}{8} \times 573 \times \frac{17}{100}$

Sold watermelons $= \frac{7}{8} \times 573 \times \frac{17}{100} \times \frac{30}{100}$

According to the questions,

Percentage share of orange in 2000 was equal to the percentage share of watermelons = 154%

$\therefore$ Retained watermelons

$$= \frac{7}{8} \times 573 \times \frac{17}{100} \times \frac{30}{100} \times \frac{154}{100}$$

$$= 39.2 \text{ million tonnes}$$

144. Assume that all grapes and apples were sold through a single organisation in 2000. Grapes and apples were sold to 4 different customers such that a certain quantity of apples were sold to the first customer, same number of apples were sold to the second customer as to the first and a certain number of grapes were sold to that customer after which apples were over. Twice the quantity of grapes sold to the second was sold to the third customer and twice the quantity sold to the third was sold to the fourth customer. The total quantity of grapes is equal to the total quantity of apples sold and the remaining grapes were stored. How many grapes were sold to each customer?

(a) 19.1 million tonnes

(b) 8.2 million tonnes

(c) 28.6 million tonnes

(d) 9.4 million tonnes

Sol. (*) Data is not clear or incomplete. This question has been withdrawn in official answer key.

145. Frutopia and Fruitfix both sold oranges at the same selling price. However, Frutopia gave customers a 15% discount on the marked price whereas Fruitfix sold the oranges for a discount of 20% on the marked price. If the marked price of oranges on Frutopia is ₹ 75/kg, what is the marked price of oranges on Fruitfix?

(a) ₹ 78 (b) ₹ 82 (c) ₹ 90 (d) ₹ 80

Sol. (*d*) Let marked price of oranges on fruit fix be ₹ x/kg

According to the question,

$$573 \times 75 \times \frac{85}{100} = 573 \times x \times \frac{80}{100}$$

$$\Rightarrow x = \frac{75 \times 85}{80} = 79.68 \approx ₹\ 80/\text{kg}$$

XXVII. Players are selected for Judo based on their body weights from the following 10 weight groups

1. (48 kg - 52 kg)	6. (68 kg - 72 kg)
2. (52 kg - 56 kg)	7. (72 kg - 76 kg)
3. (56 kg - 60 kg)	8. (76 kg - 80 kg)
4. (60 kg - 64 kg)	9. (80 kg - 84 kg)
5. (64 kg - 68 kg)	10. (84 kg - 88 kg)

The average weight of the players after selecting one player from each group is 68 kg. If one of the players (named S) leaves the team, their average weight comes down to 66.5 kg.

146. Player S is from the weight group

(a) 1 (b) 9

(c) 5 (d) 10

Sol. (*b*) The average weight after selecting one player from each groups = 68 kg

$\therefore$ Total select player = 10

$\therefore$ Total weight of 10 players

$= 10 \times 68 = 680$ kg

Let weight of S be $= x$ kg.

According to the question,

$680 - x = 9 \times 66.5$

$\Rightarrow \quad x = 680 - 598.5 = 81.5$ kg

81.5 kg between the group 80 kg –84 kg i.e., 9 weight group.

147. If S leaves the group and two new players join the group, their average weight increases to 68 kg. These players can not be from groups

(a) Both 1 and 3 (b) Both from group 7

(c) Both 4 and 10 (d) Both 5 and 9

Sol. (*a*) Weight of $S = 81.5$ kg (from question 146)

Let weight of two new players be x_1 kg and x_2 kg.

According to the question,

$10 \times 68 - 81.5 + x_1 + x_2 = 68 \times 11$

$\Rightarrow \quad x_1 + x_2 = 748 - 680 + 81.5$

$= 829.5 - 680 = 149.5$ kg

Maximum weight of two players for groups 1 and 3 $= 52 + 60 = 112$ kg

$\because \quad 112 \text{ kg} < 149.5 \text{ kg}$

So, two new players cannot be from groups 1 and 3.

148. What is the average weight of all the players taken together?

(a) 68 kg

(b) 66 kg

(c) 69 kg

(d) Cannot be determined

Sol. (*d*) The value of weights of all players is not definite and the number of players is not given.

So, the average weight of all players cannot be determined.

149. In the average of all the groups together, which group contributes most in overall average?

(a) 10

(b) 8

(c) 1

(d) Cannot be determined

Sol. (*d*) The value of number of players is not given of each group.

So, the average most in all groups cannot be determined.

150. If one of the new two players is from group 4, which group the other player is from?

(a) 5 (b) 7

(c) 10 (d) None of these

Sol. (*b*) Let weight of two new players be x_1, which is from group 4 and other players be x_2.

According to the question,

$680 + x_1 + x_2 = 12 \times 68$

$\Rightarrow \quad x_1 + x_2 = 816 - 680$

$\Rightarrow \quad x_1 + x_2 = 136$

$\because$ One player from group 4,

Then $x_1 = 61, 62, 63, 64$.

$\therefore x_2 = 75, 74, 73, 72$ (these weights between 72 – 76)

So, other player is from group 7.

(**Note**- However option (c) is the answer in official answer key but the correct answer is (b))

CLAT
Entrance Exam

SOLVED PAPER 2022

Instructions

- There are total 5 Sections and 150 questions in this Solved Paper.
- For every correct attempt the students will be awarded 1 mark.
- All the questions are in MCQs form.

Section A : English

I. Public speaking is a powerful real life skill. Over the centuries, impressive speeches made by people from various walks of life have helped to change hearts, minds and shape the world as we see it today. Speeches that are delivered with intense emotions and conviction can infuse compassion and forgiveness; elevate levels of hatred and destruction; break or unite nations.

On 5th October, in 1877 in the mountains of Montana Territory, when Chief Joseph surrendered to General Nelson A. Miles, the former gave a *Surrender Speech*. The speech included these words: *"It is cold, and we have no blankets; the little children are freezing to death. I want time to look for my children, and see how many of them I can find. Maybe I shall find them among the dead. Hear me, my Chiefs! I am tired; my heart is sick and sad. From where the Sun now stands I will fight no more forever."*

The heart-wrenching speech bared the grief and misery of the speaker, and those subjected to overwhelming hardships.

During World War II, the speech *We Shall Fight* on the Beaches delivered by Winston Churchill on 4th June, 1940 is considered a high-powered speech that strengthened the determination of those present in the House of Commons. In the speech, he said, *"Even though large tracts of Europe and many old and famous States have fallen or may fall into the grip of the Gestapo and all the odious apparatus of Nazi rule, we shall not flag or fail. We shall go on to the end, we shall fight in France, we shall fight on the seas and oceans, we shall fight with growing confidence and growing strength in the air, we shall defend our island, whatever the cost may be, we shall fight on the beaches, we shall fight on the landing grounds, we shall fight in the fields and in the streets, we shall fight in the hills."*

In 1950, William Faulkner was honoured with a Nobel Prize for his significant contributions to the American novel. This was the time when the Soviet Union had found the possible implications of the use of the atomic bomb, and people had begun to live in the fear of annihilation. In his *Nobel Prize Acceptance Speech*, Faulkner urged writers of various genres to think and write beyond the fear of destruction, and instead write materials that would lift the human spirit. The powerful message included: *"I believe that man will not merely endure: he will prevail. He is immortal, not because he alone among creatures has an inexhaustible voice, but because he has a soul, a spirit capable of compassion and sacrifice and endurance. The poet's, the writer's, duty is to write about these things. It is his privilege to help man endure by lifting his heart, by reminding him of the courage and honor and hope and pride and compassion and pity and sacrifice which have been the glories of his past. The poet's voice need not merely be the record of man, it can be one of the props, the pillars to help him endure and prevail."*

Undoubtedly, effective speeches have a long-lasting impact on the minds of the listeners, and they elevate the levels of awareness or actions the speaker intends to raise or catalyse.

1. The main idea of the passage is that
(a) all leaders should be accomplished public speakers.
(b) an impactful speech can convey a strong message to the listeners.
(c) a speech should sound pleasing to the ears of the listeners.
(d) public speakers should be bold and argumentative.

Sol. (*b*) The main idea of the passage is that an impactful speech can convey a strong message to the listeners. Public speaking is a powerful real life skill. Over the centuries, impressive speeches made by people from various walks of life have helped to change hearts, minds and shape the world as we see it today. Speeches that are delivered with intense emotions and conviction can infuse compassion and forgiveness; elevate levels of hatred and destruction; break or unite nations.

2. The tone of the 'Surrender Speech' is
(a) satiric (b) optimistic
(c) poignant (d) narcissistic

Sol. (*c*) The tone of the 'Surrender Speech' is Poignant. The speech included these words: "It is cold, and we have no blankets; the little children are freezing to death. I want to look for my children, and see how many of them I can find. Maybe I shall find them among the dead. Hear me, my Chiefs! I am tired; my heart is sick and sad. From where the Sun now stands I will fight no more forever." Thus, this tone evokes a great deal of sadness and regret and hence, the tone is poignant.

3. It is evident that through his speech, Churchill wished to ...... his countrymen ......
(a) inform, about the challenges that arise in a war-torn country.
(b) warn, against the futility of war.
(c) remind, how their endeavours to fight against the Nazi rule had failed miserably.
(d) reassure, that they would combat fiercely against their enemy under all circumstances.

Sol. (*c*) It is evident that through his speech, Churchill wished to reassure his countrymen that they would combat fiercely against their enemy under all circumstances. Thus, option (d) is the right answer.

4. Which one of the following is the least likely to be used to describe Churchill?
(a) Resolute (b) Undaunted
(c) Complacent (d) Unwavering

Sol. (*c*) The word complacent is least likely to define Churchill. He was a resolute, undaunted and unwavering personality and thus, complacency is not the right word to define him. Hence, option (c) is the right answer.

5. In the sentence: *"The poet's voice need not merely be the record of man, it can be one of the props, the pillars to help him endure and prevail"*. Faulkner has used ...... to convey the power of a poet's writings.
(a) A metaphor (b) A simile
(c) An onomatopoeia
(d) A transferred epithet

Sol. (*a*) In the sentence, "The poet's voice need not merely be the record of man, it can be one of the props, the pillars to help him endure and prevail" Faulkner has used a metaphor to convey the power of a poet's writings. A metaphor refers to a figure of speech in which a word or phrase is applied to an object or action to which it is not literally applicable.

II. As a six year old child-beggar, Saroo slept off in a stationary train in Khandwa, Madhya Pradesh; however, when he woke up, he found himself in an empty compartment of a train thundering towards Kolkata where he spent a couple of weeks in a state of panic and hopelessness. Finally, he ended up in a local government adoption centre from where he was adopted by an Australian couple. Twenty five years later, Saroo felt the urge to trace his biological mother and see in what state she lived. Relentlessly, he used Google's satellite feature to map the parts of the country that could have possibly been his own hometown.

The search was a long and arduous one; nevertheless, the perseverance did pay. One eventful day, he met his mother; thereafter, he continued to keep in touch with her.

If technology can unite people with their loved ones, it can also make them distant. The unlimited variety of applications (apps) available to toddlers, teenagers and adults might have revolutionised their lives for the better, but these very apps have snatched away the joys of long naturewalks; they have encroached upon the time and space that people earlier used for physical interaction; they have drilled deep chasms of loneliness in the lives of countless numbers of people.

Simple pleasures of life include visiting friends and relatives, playing matches in open spaces, interacting with people in markets, public libraries and clubs. However, with the escalating rage of using apps like those for social media, playing virtual games, and home delivery services, these joyous moments are fading into oblivion, and the pall of loneliness is getting heavier by the day.

Where are we heading to? Are we going to allow ourselves to be swamped by apps? Are we going to allow social media to engulf us in a deluge of loneliness and isolation? Are we going to drive ourselves to situations that will ultimately demand mental and physical therapies to regain normalcy? Do we not know that physical interaction is as essential for mental health as food and water is for physical health?

Earlier, social isolation was mostly experienced by some of the elderly people who were devoid of an occupation, and bereft of company of their loved ones. Unfortunately today, an unhealthy solitude prevails among numerous children, teenagers and adults too; subsequently, there is an alarming increase in the demand for mental health therapy practitioners.

The necessity of engaging psychologists in schools and colleges is evidently on the rise. The psychologists are required to identify and address the learning and behavioural needs of students who approach them for guidance; moreover, if required, the professionals are expected to help them in strengthening their emotional, social and academic skills. Regardless how alarming the situation might be, it is never too late. If people revert to the earlier trend of shopping offline, going for naturewalks, playing outdoor games, and catching up with friends in their homes or cafes more frequently, they can keep their heads firmly well above the ocean of loneliness.

6. From the passage it is evident that Saroo's desire to find his mother

(a) ended up being a distant dream.

(b) inspired him to use Google's satellite feature intermittently.

(c) waned as time went by.

(d) did not slacken till he succeeded.

Sol. (d) From the passage, it is evident that Saroo's desire to find his mother did not slacken till he succeeded. As a six year old child-beggar, Saroo slept off in a stationary train in Khandwa, Madhya Pradesh; however, when he woke up, he found himself in an empty compartment of a train thundering towards Kolkata where he spent a couple of weeks in a state of panic and hopelessness. Finally, he ended up in a local government adoption centre from where he was adopted by an Australian couple.

25 years later, Saroo felt the urge to trace his biological mother and see in what state she lived. Relentlessly, he used google's satellite feature to map the parts of the country that could have possibly been his own hometown. The search was a long and arduous one; nevertheless, the perseverance did pay. One eventful day, he met his mother; thereafter, he continued to keep in touch with her.

7. In the sentence *'these very apps have snatched away the joys of long nature-walks;'* the author has
   (a) satirized nature
   (b) metaphorized apps
   (c) personified apps
   (d) None of the above

Sol. (c) In the sentence 'these very apps have snatched away the joys of long nature-walks;' the author has personified apps, meaning that he gace life to inanimate objects. Thus, option (c) is the right answer.

8. From the passage one can conclude that
   (a) it is impossible for people to reduce the usage of apps.
   (b) there is a direct correlation between loneliness and excessive usage of social- media apps.
   (c) the usage of technology is as essential for mental-health as food and water is for physical health.
   (d) all senior citizens are lonely because they are not tech-savvy.

Sol. (b) From the passage one can conclude there is a direct correlation between loneliness and excessive usage of social-media apps. Other statements are all extremes which cannot be inferred or concluded from the passage given here.

9. From the passage it can be inferred that presently in many educational institutions
   (a) the number of teachers who pass the buck to psychologists is on the rise.
   (b) special emphasis is being laid on the mental and emotional health of the students.
   (c) the usage of educational apps is being discouraged significantly.
   (d) all the students feel the need to be counseled by psychologists.

Sol. (b) From the passage it can be inferred that presently in many educational institutions that special emphasis is being laid on the mental and emotional health of the students. The necessity of engaging psychologists in schools and colleges is evidently on the rise. The psychologists are required to identify and address the learning and behavioural needs of students who approach them for guidance; moreover, if required, the professionals are expected to help them in strengthening their emotional, social and academic skills.

10. In the concluding paragraph of the given passage, the writer's tone can be best described as
    (a) optimistic (b) despairing
    (c) laudatory (d) apologetic

Sol. (a) In the concluding paragraph of the given passage, the writer's tone can be best described as optimistic. The concluding paragraph ends on a positive note as it states that regardless how alarming the situation might be, it is never too late. If people revert to the earlier trend of shopping offline, going for nature walks, playing outdoor games, and catching up with friends in their homes or cafes more frequently, they can keep their heads firmly above the ocean of loneliness.

III. *"Wash! Wash! Wash your hands!"* That's been the safety-mantra ever since the pandemic COVID-19 began swamping the world. Undoubtedly, washing hands has proven to be the best way to keep germs at bay. Unfortunately, the medical practitioner who first promoted the importance of this simple activity was subjected to intense humiliation, and ultimately declared insane!

Ignaz Semmelweis was a Hungarian doctor. In 1847, as an obstetrician, he was disturbed that post-delivery, almost every third woman died of an unexpected malady. He observed that as a part of the set routine, medical students and doctors would examine and study the corpses in the mortuary, and then come for rounds to the maternity wards. Here, without washing their hands, they would examine expectant mothers. After making numerous hypothesis and observations, he was convinced that when doctors washed their hands before examining the women in the ward, the number of deaths due to serious infection declined. He shared his observations with his colleagues and many others working in the field of medicine, but unfortunately he could not provide any concrete evidence to his theory. Sadly, due to the vehement criticism that he received, he went into depression. Furthermore, Ignaz strived to prove his point so relentlessly that it led to the belief that he had lost his mind. In 1865, a doctor deceptively lured him into an asylum for the insane, and two weeks of the brutal treatment that was meted out to him by the attendants led to his untimely death. About twenty years later, when the world became more receptive to the works of scientists like Louis Pasteur and Joseph Lister, awareness regarding germs that cause diseases began to spread. This is the time when Ignaz was honoured with titles like Father of Hand Hygiene and Saviour of Mothers- an honour much too late!

Some of the most celebrated artists have earned fame much after their deaths. It is tragic that Vincent Van Gogh's awe-inspiring work was labelled as strange and amateur by most of the critics of his time. It is believed that he sold only one or two painting in his lifetime, and that too for a meager amount. Today, every single painting of Vincent Van Gogh paintings is worth millions of dollars.

Franz Kafka was a proficient writer, but when he published a few pieces of his writings, he received immense criticism. Before his death in 1924, he handed over his unpublished novels and short stories to his friend Max Brod, and urged him to destroy them; however, Brod got the manuscripts published. Today, Franz is acclaimed as one of the major fiction writers of the twentieth century; the novels titled *The Trial* published in 1925, and *The Castle* published in 1926 are considered two if his masterpieces. Perhaps, if humans were more tolerant and amenable to change, innovative concepts, theories and creations, the deserving would live to experience the glory and honour they rightfully deserve.

11. The main idea of the passage is that
(a) all original theories and works should receive unreserved acceptance.
(b) many undeserving innovators have been honoured after their demise.
(c) creativity must never be inhibited.
(d) numerous innovators have found recognition and appreciation of their works posthumously.

Sol. (d) The main idea of the passage is that numerous innovators have found recognition and appreciation of their works posthumously. Some of the most celebrated artists have earned fame much after their deaths. For example- it is tragic that Vincent Van Gogh's awe-inspiring work was labelled as strange and amateur by most of the critics of his time. It is believed that he sold only one or two paintings in his lifetime, and that too for a meager amount. Today, every single Vincent Van Gogh's painting is worth millions of dollars.

12. From the passage it is evident that Dr. Ignaz's theory was rejected because
(a) he could not substantiate it
(b) the doctors did not want him to regulate their work ethics
(c) he had been declared insane
(d) Joseph Lister and Louis Pasteur had already discovered germs

Sol. (a) From the passage it is evident that Dr. Ignaz's theory was rejected because he could not substantiate it. Ignaz

Semmelweis was a Hungarian doctor. In 1847, as an obstetrician, he was disturbed that post-delivery, almost every third woman died of an unexpected malady. He observed that as a part of the set routine, medical students and doctors would examine and study the corpses in the mortuary, and then come for rounds to the maternity wards. Here, without washing their hands, they would examine expectant mothers. After making numerous hypotheses and observations, he was convinced that when doctors washed their hands before examining the women in the ward, the number of deaths due to serious infection declined. He shared his observations with his colleagues and many thinkers working in the field of medicine, but unfortunately he could not provide any concrete evidence to support his theory.

13. From the passage one can conclude that the art critics who .... Van Gogh's works were ......

(a) applauded, pessimistic

(b) censured, hypercritical

(c) denounced, tolerant

(d) acclaimed, rigid

Sol. (b) From the passage, one can conclude that the art critics who censured Van Gogh's paintings were hypercritical. It is tragic that Vincent Van Gogh's awe-inspiring work was labelled as strange and amateur by most of the critics of his time. It is believed that he sold only one or two paintings in his lifetime, and that too for a meager amount. Today, every single Vincent Van Gogh's painting is worth millions of dollars.

14. From the passage it can be inferred that Max Brod

(a) was of the opinion that Franz had not reached out to the right critics

(b) decried Franz's writings

(c) considered it unsacred to destroy any manuscript

(d) appreciated and valued Franz's works

Sol. (d) From the passage it can be inferred that Max Brod appreciated and valued Franz's works. Franz Kafka was a proficient writer, but when he published a few pieces of his writings, he received immense criticism. Before his death in 1924, he handed over his unpublished novels and short stories to his friend Max Brod, and urged him to destroy them; however, Brod got the manuscripts published.

Today, Franz is acclaimed as one of the major fiction writers of the twentieth century; the novels titled The Trial published in 1925, and The Castle published in 1926 are considered two of his masterpieces.

15. The word *relentlessly* in the passage can be best replaced by the word

(a) Irresolutely (b) Recklessly

(c) Unabatedly (d) Unabashedly

Sol. (c) The word *relentlessly* in the passage can be best replaced by the word unabatedly. Relentless means persistent or constant. Thus, option (c) is the right answer.

IV. Cryptocurrencies are a terrible thing. They are the essence of a Ponzi scheme whose value is based entirely on a greater fool prepared to buy it. The promise of alchemy-turning lead into gold has bewitched humanity throughout the ages and cryptocurrencies are just the latest alchemy. Do not get me wrong, if rich people want to lose their money, in this or any other way, they should be allowed to do so. The rich should be the vanguards of new things in case something unforeseen and good falls out of them. But we need to protect those vulnerable consumers whose lives are such that almost any get rich-quick schemes will be seductive, and seven out of 10 times, they will lose their life savings. Cryptocurrencies are today's South Sea Bubble - one of the earliest recorded financial bubbles that took place in the 1720s' Britain. Meme based currencies like Dogecoin, Dogelon Mars and Doge Dash remind me of the infamous plan of one company during the South Sea Bubble to raise money "for carrying on an undertaking· of great advantage; but nobody to know what it is."

The cryptocurrency bubble is worse than tulip mania. Through the veil of technology, cryptocurrency enthusiasts are leaning on policy-makers to permit them to be exempt from regulation, privatise money, and make money so disconnected from the economy that it would reap financial disaster. There are many reasons to avoid financial disasters, but one of them is that they ratchet up poverty and inequality. The current money-credit system is not perfect, but like democracy, it is the worst system barring all the others. It has evolved from the ashes of the system cryptocurrency enthusiasts are trying to resurrect.

The current system is vulnerable to attack because money is little understood. Cryptocurrency enthusiasts have attracted a following based on the fiction that the central bank or government creates money and are busy debasing it in their self-interest. This is not the case, but then again, there is some overlap between cryptocurrency advocates, conspiracy theorists, and *anti-vaxxers*. The time has come for someone to stand up for the current fiat money system and explain that while it could be better still, it has been associated with far more growth, much more distributed, and has responded better to economic crisis than what came before.

In today's money-credit system, banks create money when they issue a loan and place the loan's proceeds into the account of their customers, creating a deposit. Money is, in fact, a tradable debt. The bank's deposit can be used as cash because the bank is a regulated issuer of loans and deposit-taker, which gives the deposit credibility and convertibility. The central bank only influences the creation of money indirectly by its regulatory requirement that a proportion of the loans need to be funded by shareholder's profits. They need to have skin in the game. Money creation then is based on thousands of separate decisions by loan officers and is more distributed than a centralised algorithm like Bitcoin. And its supply is determined by the private demand for loans, which means it is closely aligned to the economy.

16. Which of the following does best describe attitude of the author towards rich people?

(a) Concerned (b) Assiduous
(c) Indifferent (d) Sympathetic

Sol. (c) The attitude of the author towards rich people is indifferent. The author does not really care about the plight of the rich in light of the crashing crypto market. Instead, he simply goes on to elaborate on the menace that can be caused because of the ill effects of schemes of this sort.

17. Which of the following is true in the context of the passage?

(a) The author defends the current money-credit system.
(b) The author rejects the idea that the central bank or government creates money and are busy debasing it in their self-interest.
(c) The author backs the protection of poor from menace of cryptocurrencies.
(d) All of the above

Sol. (d) Statements A, B and C are all correct in context of the passage. The author does defend the current money–credit system. The Statement B is correct becuase the author rejects the idea that the central bank or government creates money and are busy debasing it in their self-interest. Further, Statement C is correct because the author backs the protection of the poor from menace of cryptocurrencies.

18. Which rhetorical device is employed in 'cryptocurrencies are just the latest alchemy'?

(a) Antithesis (b) Metaphor
(c) Personification (d) Synecdoche

Sol. (b) The rhetorical device called 'metaphor' is employed in 'cryptocurrencies are just the latest alchemy'. A metaphor is a figure of speech in which a word or phrase is applied to an object or action to which it is not literally applicable.

19. Which of the following does best describe the passage?
(a) Argumentative and explanatory
(b) Descriptive and argumentative
(c) Narrative and explanatory
(d) Expository and argumentative

Sol. (a) Argumentative and explanatory best defines the passage. The author argues upon the relevance of cryptocurrencies and gives in evidence to support his theory. Hence, option (a) is right answer.

20. What do the cryptocurrency enthusiasts rely on?
(a) Exemption from regulation
(b) Privatisation of money
(c) Disconnection of money from the economy
(d) All the above

Sol. (d) The cryptocurrency enthusiasts rely on all the given options here, i.e,
a. Exemption from regulation
b. Privatisation of money
c. Disconnection of money from the economy.

Through the veil of technology, cryptocurrency enthusiasts are leaning on policy-makers to permit them to be exempt from regulation, privatise money and make money so disconnected from the economy that it would reap financial disaster. Thus, option (d) is the correct answer.

V. The fact that Gaia, in her monstrous avatar, decided to distribute fossil fuels very unevenly across the Earth has been central to the emergence of the world's current geopolitical order. From a vitalist point of view, it could be said that the wars of the twentieth century were won as much by the fossilized energy of botanical matter as by particular groups of humans.

In the First World War Germany's lack of oil put it at a huge disadvantage against the Allies, more or less ensuring its defeat. The shortage of oil effectively cancelled the technological advantages Germany enjoyed at the start of the war: despite having a large fleet, for instance, it was unable to use its navy effectively because its coal-burning ships needed to refuel every eleven days. Conversely, the assured supply of American oil conferred so great an advantage on Britain and France that "it could be fairly stated that the war was won for the Western allies by tankers." Not for nothing was it said of the First World War that Britain, France, and the United States floated "to victory on a sea of oil." In the Second World War the shortage of oil was even more critical to the defeat of the Axis powers. The German Luftwaffe was forced to rely on synthetic fuels derived from coal, and these could not provide the high-octane energy that was necessary for high- compression aero engines: "it was largely due to the inferior engines in German aircraft that the Luftwaffe lost the Battle of Britain." The shortage of oil also dictated Germany's war strategy: it was in order to seize the oilfields of the Caucasus that the German army pushed eastward into the Soviet Union in 1942, leading to a.defeat at Stalingrad from which it never recovered. Japan's invasion of the Dutch East Indies was similarly forced by its lack of oil.

In short, over the course of the twentieth century access to oil became the central focus of global geopolitical strategy: for a Great Power, to be able to ensure or hinder the flow of oil was to have a thumb on the jugulars of its adversaries. In the first part of the twentieth century the guarantor of the flow of oil was Britain. After the Second World War, the baton was passed, along with a string of British naval bases, to the United States. The role of guarantor of global energy flows is still crucial to US strategic dominance and to its position as global hegemon.

Today, as Elizabeth DeLoughrey has pointed out, "US energy policy has become increasingly militarized and secured by the Navy, the largest oceanic force on the planet." In the words of the historian Michael Klare, the Iraq War of 2003 marked the transformation of the US military into "a global oil protection service, guarding pipelines, refineries, and loading facilities in the Middle East and elsewhere."

It is important to note that the strategic value of controlling oil flows is tangentially related to the US's energy requirements. The period in which the American military was turning into "a global oil protection service" was one in which the US was well on its way to reducing its dependence on imported oil. The fact that the US is now self- sufficient in fossil fuels has in no way diminished the strategic importance of oil as an instrument for the projection of power- it is the ability to deny energy supplies to rivals that is strategically of central importance.

21. What is the central idea of the passage?
(a) Fossil fuels in war-making.
(b) Strategic value fossil fuels in US dominance in the world.
(c) Role of fossil fuels in modern geopolitical order.
(d) Distribution of fossil fuels in the world.

Sol. (c) The central idea of the passage is the role of fossil fuels in modern geopolitical order. The fact that Gaia, in her monstrous avatar, decided to distribute fossil fuels very unevenly across the earth has been central to the emergence of the world's current geopolitical order. From a vitalist point of view, it could be said that the wars of the twentieth century were won as much by the fossilised energy of botanical matter as by particular groups of humans.

22. What was the cause of Germany's defeat in the First World War?
(a) Germany's shortage of oil
(b) Advantage of Britain and France
(c) Weaknesses of Germany's navy
(d) All of the above

Sol. (a) The major cause for Germany's defeat in the First World War was the shortage of oil. It put it at a huge disadvantage against the Allies, more or less ensuring its defeat. The shortage of oil effectively cancelled the technological advantages that Germany enjoyed at the start of the war: despite having a large fleet, for instance, it was unable to use its navy effectively because its coal burning ships needed to refuel every 11 days.

23. Which of the following could be inferred from Michael Klare's opinion on US military?
(a) The US military interferes with energy needs of other countries.
(b) The US energy policy has become increasingly militarised.
(c) The US has changed energy policy drastically.
(d) The US has fully understood the strategic value of controlling oil flows.

Sol. (b) From Michael Klare's opinion on the US military, it can be inferred that the US energy policy has become increasingly militarised. In the words of the historian Michael Klare, "the Iraq War of 2003 marked the transformation of the US military into a global oil protection device, guiding pipelines, reservoirs, and loading facilities in the middle east and elsewhere."

24. What does the phrase 'tangentially related to' mean?
(a) Related directly and in straightforward way
(b) Related closely and centrally
(c) Related only slightly and peripherally
(d) None of the above

Sol. (c) The phrase 'tangentially related to' means related only slightly and peripherally. Hence, option (c) is the right answer.

25. What makes the US strategically dominating global hegemon?
(a) Capacity of the US to provide oil protection service, guarding pipelines, refineries, and loading facilities.
(b) Increasingly militarised energy policy of the US Navy, the largest oceanic force on the planet.
(c) The role of US as a guarantor of global energy flows.
(d) All of the above

Sol. (c) US can strategically dominating the global hegemony because of the role of the US as a guarantor of global energy flows. From Michael Klare's opinion on the US military, it can be inferred that the US energy policy has become increasingly militarised. In the words of the historian Michael Klare, "the Iraq War of 2003 marked the transformation of the US military into a global oil protection device, guiding pipelines, reservoirs, and loading facilities in the middle east and elsewhere."

VI. The modern animal rights movement, which originated in the 1970s, may be understood as a reaction to dominant emphases within science and religion (principally, though not exclusively, Christianity). When the Jesuit Joseph Rickaby wrote in 1888 that "Brute beasts, not having understanding and therefore not being persons, cannot have any rights" and that we have "no duties of charity or duties of any kind to the lower animals as neither to stocks and stones", he was only articulating, albeit in an extreme form, the moral insensitivity that has characterised the Western view of animals.

That insensitivity is the result of an amalgam of influences. The first, and for many years the most dominant, was the "other worldly" or "world denying" tendency in Christianity, which has, at its worst, denigrated the value of earthly things in comparison with things spiritual. Traditional Catholicism has divided the world into those beings that possess reason and therefore immortal souls, and those that do not. Christian spirituality has not consciously been at home with the world of non-human creatures either animal or vegetable. Classic accounts of eternal life as found in Augustine of Hippo, Thomas Aquinas, or John Calvin make little or no reference to the world of animals. Animals, it seems, are merely transient or peripheral beings in an otherwise wholly human-centric economy of salvation.

The second idea-common to Christianity, Judaism, and Islam-is that animals, along with vegetables and minerals, exist instrumentally in relation to human beings; they are made for human beings, even belong to human beings, as resources in creation. This idea predates Christianity and is found notably in Aristotle, who argues that "since nature makes nothing to no purpose, it must be that nature has made them for the sake of man". This idea, largely unsupported by scripture, was nevertheless taken over by Aquinas, who conceived of creation as a rational hierarchy in which the intellectually inferior existed for the sake of the intellectually superior.

Such instrumentalism, which features rationality as the key factor dividing human beings from "brute beasts," has in turn buttressed the third influence, namely the notion of human superiority in creation. Human superiority need not, by itself, have led to the neglect of animal life, but when combined with the biblical ideas of being made "in the image of God" and God's preferential choice to become incarnate in human form, some sense of moral as well as theological ascendancy was indicated. As a result, Christianity, and to a lesser extent Judaism, have been characterized historically by an overwhelming concern for humanity in creation rather than an egalitarian concern for all forms of God-given life. That humans are more important than animals, and that they self-evidently merit moral solicitude in a way that animals cannot, has become religious doctrine. Thus the Catechism of the Catholic Church maintains that "it is ... unworthy to spend money on them [animals] that should as a priority go to the relief of human misery".

These influences have in turn enabled and justified the scientific exploration of the natural world and specifically the subjection of animals to experimentation. Francis Bacon pursued his scientific investigations in the belief that humanity should "recover that right over nature which belongs to it by divine bequest". Rene Descartes famously likened the movements of a swallow to the workings of a clock, and maintained that There is no prejudice to which we are more accustomed from our earliest years than the belief that dumb animals think".

26. Jesuit Joseph Rickaby's articulation on animals may be termed as

(a) Eco-centric view of animals
(b) Anthropocentric view of animals
(c) Ethnocentric view of animals
(d) Androcentric view of animals

Sol. (b) Jesuit Joseph Rickaby's articulation on animals may be termed as anthropocentric view of animals. The modern animal rights movement, which originated in the 1970s, may be understood as a reaction to dominant emphases within science and religion (principally, though not exclusively, Christianity).

27. According to the author, how did Christianity contribute to insensitivity of the West towards animals?

(a) It denigrated the value of earthly things in comparison with spiritual things.
(b) It divided the world into beings with and without reason
(c) It propagated as if animals are transient or peripheral in human centric economy of salvation
(d) All of the above

Sol. (d) According to the author, Christianity contributed to the insensitivity of the West towards the animals in the following manner.

- it denigrated the value of earthly things in comparison with spiritual things.
- it divided the world into beings with and without reason.
- it propagated as if animals are transient or peripheral in the human centric economy of salvation.

28. Which of the following is closest to the meaning of the word 'instrumentalism' as used in the passage?

(a) Pragmatism (b) Idealism
(c) Egalitarianism (d) None of these

Sol. (d) None of the given words can be considered to be closest to the meaning of the word 'instrumentalism' as used in the passage. Instrumentalism can be considered to be a pragmatic philosophical approach which regards an activity chiefly as an instrument or tool for some practical purpose, rather than in more absolute or ideal terms.

29. Which of the following is not true in the context of the passage?

(a) Western philosophy and science are both under the influence of religion.
(b) Western philosophical views on animals have been influenced by religious notions about them.
(c) Western religious notions on animals have justified subjection of animals to scientific experimentation.
(d) Some of the scientific views on animals have been influenced by religious notions about them.

Sol. (a) Option (a) is incorrect which states that Western philosophy and science are both under the influence of religion. These influences have in turn enabled and justifies the scientific exploration of the natural world and specifically the subjection of animals to experimentation. Francis Bacon pursued his scientific investigations in the belief that humanity should "recover that right over nature which belongs to it by divine bequest".

30. It may be inferred from Rene Descartes' view that

(a) It is irrational to assume that animals have awareness and some mental capacities.
(b) Animals are automata or they act mechanically.
(c) Neither (a) nor (b)
(d) Both (a) and (b)

Sol. (d) Option (d) is the right answer as both a and b are correct. It may be inferred from Rene Descartes view that

- a. It is irrational to assume that animals have awareness and some mental capacities.
- Animals are automata or they act mechanically.

Thus, both statements are correct.

Section B : Current Affairs & General Knowledge

VII. When we hear the name SPACE, only one organisation comes to mind: the Indian Space Research Organisation (ISRO). The Indian Space Research Organisation (ISRO), located in Bengaluru, is the country's first space agency. ISRO was founded in 1969 with the goal of developing and utilising space technology for national development while also conducting planetary exploration and space science research. The space research operations began in India in the early 1960s, at a time when satellite applications were still in the experimental stages in the United States. Dr. Vikram Sarabhai, the founding father of India's space programme, rapidly recognised the benefits of space technologies after the live transmission of the Tokyo Olympic Games across the Pacific by the American satellite 'Syncom-3' demonstrated the power of communication satellites. The ISRO has launched various spacecrafts like the Chandrayaan, Astrosat, Microsat, GSAT etc. The Government of India has also approved a regional spaceborne navigation system, which will consist of seven satellites. Out of these, four of them will be placed in geosynchronous inclined orbit of 29° relative to the equatorial plane. Such an arrangement would mean all seven satellites would have continuous radio visibility with Indian control stations.

31. Name the first dedicated mission launched by ISRO for studying the celestial sources in X-ray, optical and UV spectral bands simultaneously.

(a) Amazonia

(b) Astrosat

(c) Gaganyaan-1

(d) Lunar Polar Exploration Mission

Sol. (b) Astrosat is the first dedicated mission launched by ISRO for studying the celestial sources in X-Ray, optical and UV spectral bands simultaneously. It would thus be providing a space astronomy observatory which is operated by ISRO. The satellite is at 650 km near-equatorial orbit with a 6-degree orbital inclination. ISRO has also launched various spacecrafts like the Chandrayaan, Astrosat, Microsat, GSAT etc. The Government of India has also approved a regional spaceborne navigation system, which will consist of seven satellites.

32. APPLE, the first communication satellite of ISRO was launched from

(a) Satish Dhawan Space Centre, Sriharikota

(b) TERLS, Thiruvananthapuram

(c) Kourou, French Guiana

(d) SSLV Launching Station, Tamil Nadu

Sol. (c) APPLE, the first communication satellite of ISRO was launched from Kourou, French Guiana. The Ariane Passenger Payload Experiment (APPLE) was ISRO's first indigenous, experimental communication satellite. It was launched into GTO (Geosynchronous Transfer Orbit) by the third development flight of ESA's Ariane vehicle from Kourou on 19th June, 1981.

33. Name the spacecraft that has been successfully sent into the space to probe into the planets in the solar system.

(a) Sputnik 19 (b) Cosmos 482

(c) Pioneer-E (d) Mariner 10

Sol. (d) Mariner 10 was the spacecraft that has been successfully sent into space to probe into the planets in the solar system. It was an American robotic space probe launched by NASA on 3rd November, 1973 to fly by the planets Mercury and Venus. It was the first spacecraft to perform flybys of multiple planets. Mariner 10 was launched approximately two years after Mariner 9 and was the last spacecraft in the Mariner program.

34. The first successful Nuclear Bomb test conducted by India in 1974, is called the

(a) Prithvi (b) Pokhran-II

(c) Smiling Buddha (d) Surya

Sol. (c) The first successful nuclear bomb test conducted by India in 1974 is called the Smiling Buddha. Operation Smiling Buddha was the assigned code name of India's first successful nuclear bomb test on 18th May, 1974. The bomb was detonated on the Pokhran Test Range (PTR), in Rajasthan, by the Indian Army under the supervision of several key . Pokhran-I was also the first confirmed nuclear weapons test by a nation outside the five permanent members of the United Nations Security Council.

35. NaviC covers India and region extending

(a) 1500 km (b) 2000 km
(c) 7000 km (d) 1000 km

Sol. (a) NaviC covers India and region extending 1500 km. According to ISRO, the NaviC system presently comprises the entire constellation of eight satellites — IRNSS-1A, 1B, 1C, 1D, 1E, 1F, and 1G which are already in their orbital homes in space over India. NaviC will ultimately also help users find precise locations providing specific goods and services (including restaurants, theatres, hospitals, schools, hotels, etc) when they register with the system for users to find them easily using the satellite service.

VIII. On 26th December, 2021, for the first time since the present government came to power in 2014, the Union Home Ministry constituted a panel led by its officers to review the withdrawal of the Armed areas. The Act was amended in 1972 and the powers to declare an area as "disturbed" were conferred concurrently upon the Central Government along with the States. Currently, the MHA issues periodic "disturbed area" notification to extend AFSPA only for Nagaland and Arunachal Pradesh, where it is applicable in the districts of Tirap, Changlang, Longding and areas falling under Namsai and Mahadevpur police stations bordering Assam. The notification for Manipur and Assam is issued by the State Governments. Tripura revoked the Act in 2015 and Meghalaya was under AFSPA for 27 years, until it was revoked by the MHA from 1st April, 2018. The Act was implemented in a 20 km area along the border with Assam. Jammu and Kashmir has a separate J&K Armed Forces (Special Powers) Act, 1990.

36. Power to notify parts of or the whole of a State or a Union Territory as a 'disturbed area', under the Armed Forces (Special Powers) Act, 1958 is vested with

(a) Governor of any State
(b) Administrator of a Union Territory
(c) Central Government
(d) All of the above

Sol. (d) The correct answer here is option d (All of the above). Power to notify parts of or the whole of a State or a Union Territory as a 'disturbed area', under the Armed Forces (Special Powers) Act, 1958 is vested with all of the following:

(a) Governor of any State
(b) Administrator of a Union Territory
(c) Central Government

Section 3 of Armed Forces (Special Powers) Act, 1958 states that "if, in relation to any State or Union Territory to which this Act extends, the Governor of that State or the Administrator of that Union Territory or the Central Government, in either case, is of the opinion that the whole or any part of such State or Union Territory, as the case may be, is in such a disturbed or dangerous condition that the use of armed forces in aid of the civil power is necessary, the Governor of that State or the Administrator of that Union Territory or the Central Government, as the case may be, may, by notification in the Official Gazette, declare the whole or such part of such State or Union Territory to be a disturbed area."

37. AFSPA was introduced in Meghalaya in the year

(a) 1995 (b) 1999
(c) 1991 (d) 1989

Sol. (c) AFSPA was introduced in Meghalaya in the year 1991. AFSPA gives powers to the army, state and central police forces to shoot to kill, search houses and destroy any property that is "likely" to be used by insurgents in areas declared as "disturbed" by the Home Ministry. It is invoked when a case of militancy or insurgency takes place and the territorial integrity of India is at risk. However, in 2018, due to a decrease in insurgency related incidents in the state, AFSPA was withdrawn from Meghalaya with effect from 31st March, 2018.

38. Consider the following statements about the Armed Forces (Special Powers) Act and mark the correct option.

(a) Detractors and Human Rights Organisations, as well as many sections of civil society, argue that the Act often leads to excesses and require checks and balances or could alienate the people instead of integrating them with the main stream.

(b) Irom Chanu Sharmila, an activist from Manipur, became ansensitising figure symbolising the protest against AFSPA after she sat on an indefinite fast in 2000, demanding its repeal and ended it only in August 2016.

(c) Both (a) and (b) are correct

(d) None of the above

Sol. (c) Both Statements a and b are correct. Statement a is correct because as per AFSPA, Detractors and Human Rights Organisations, as well as many sections of civil society, argue that the Act often leads to excesses and require checks and balances or could alienate the people instead of integrating them with the main stream.

Statement b is correct because Irom Chanu Sharmila, an activist from Manipur, became a sensitising figure symbolising the protest against AFSPA after she sat on an indefinite fast in 2000, demanding its repeal and ended it only in August, 2016. She was also known as the "Iron Lady of Manipur".

39. In 2005, a government appointed five-member committee, recommended that AFSPA be repealed. It suggested that the Unlawful Activities (Prevention) Act could be suitably amended to deal with terrorism. It made this recommendation as it felt that the AFSPA created an impression that the people of the North-East States were being targeted for hostile treatment. Who headed this committee?

(a) B. P. Jeevan Reddy

(b) Abhishek Singhvi

(c) Soli Sorabjee

(d) Ram Jethmalani

Sol. (a) In 2005, a government appointed five-member committee, headed by B.P. Jeevan Reddy suggested that Unlawful Activities (Prevention) Act should be suitably amended to deal with terrorism. It made this recommendation as it felt that the AFSPA created an impression that the people of the North-East States were being targeted for hostile treatment.

40. AFSPA is currently in force in

(a) Arunachal Pradesh and Assam

(b) Nagaland and Manipur

(c) Jammu and Kashmir

(d) All of the above

Sol. (d) Currently, AFSPA is in force in all the given states of Arunachal Pradesh, Assam, Nagaland, Manipur and Jammu and Kashmir. The AFSPA empowers security forces to arrest a person without a warrant, enter or search a premises without a warrant along with some other actions. Banned insurgent groups National Socialist Council of Nagaland (NSCN-K), United Liberation Front of Assam (ULFA) and National Democratic Front of Bodoland (NDFB) are active in these areas of Arunachal Pradesh.

IX. One of the justifications of Russia-Ukraine war Russian leader claimed that military action was necessary to stop Ukrainian attacks on the two break away regions of Donetsk and Lugansk, which Russia recognised as sovereign states. President of Russia claimed that Russia could come under attack by Ukrainian far right government, unless their influence in the country is diminished. He accused Western Nations of arming Kyiv against Russia. After being ordered by Russia's leader to invade the capital of Ukraine, Russian troops moved in several directions. As the first targets were hit, airports and the military HQs were located near cities across Ukraine, then tanks and troops rolled into the country from the North, East, and South. The war has demolished most of the cities of the Ukraine and caused irreparable damage to the humanity.

41. Ukraine was part of which country during 1922-1991?

(a) Germany (b) Poland
(c) USA (d) USSR

Sol. (d) The Ukrainian Soviet Socialist Republic, also known as Soviet Ukraine, was one of the constituent republics of the Soviet Union from the Union's inception in 1922 until its breakup in 1991. The republic was governed by the Communist Party of the Soviet Union through its republican branch, the Communist Party of Ukraine, as a union republic of the Soviet Union, which existed as a highly centralised one-party state. The first Bolshevik Ukrainian republic was founded in December 1917, as Ukrainian Soviet Republic, after the Bolshevik Revolution started in Russia. The Ukrainian civil war was fought among the different Ukrainian republics founded by Ukrainian nationalists, Ukrainian anarchists, and Ukrainian Bolsheviks, with the help or against neighbouring states.

42. Who is the President of Ukraine?

(a) Volodymyr Zelenskyy
(b) Vladimir Zelenskyy
(c) Volodymyr S. Zelenskyy
(d) Vladimir Zelensky

Sol. (a) Volodymyr Zelenskyy is the current and sixth President of Ukraine. He was elected President of Ukraine on 21st April, 2019.

43. Which is the currency of Ukraine?

(a) Guilder (b) Zloty
(c) Ruble (d) Hryvnia

Sol. (d) The currency of Ukraine is the Ukrainian Hryvnia. Each hryvnia is divided into 100 kopiyka.

44. The President of Ukraine was formerly

(a) Weather Forecaster
(b) Navy Officer
(c) Comedian
(d) TV News Reader

Sol. (c) Volodymyr Zelenskyy is the current and sixth President of Ukraine. He is a former actor and comedian.

45. Which operation was launched by the Indian Government to bring back Indians from Ukraine during Russia-Ukraine war?

(a) Operation Kyiv
(b) Operation Ganga
(c) Operation Rakshak
(d) Operation East Star

Sol. (b) Operation Ganga was launched by the Indian government to bring back Indians from Ukraine during the Russia-Ukraine war. This involved transport assistance from the neighbouring countries of Romania, Hungary, Poland, Moldova, Slovakia to reach India. Thus, option b is the right answer.

X. Every second patent granted in India between 2016-2021 is related to green technology and a quarter of the green technology patents are concerning alternative energy production, coinciding with the Centre's efforts on *"enhanced use of green technology for boosting economy and encouraging consumers to use products produced through use of such technology"*. Data from the Ministry of Commerce and Industry shows that more than 91,500 patents were granted between 2016-17 and 2020-21, while the data for 2021-22 was not immediately available. However, going by the trend in the past two years, India is expected to clear at least 25,000 more applications this year.

Separate data from the ministry shows that between 2016-17 and 2021-22 (up to January), 61,186 patents related to green technologies have been granted in the said period. Of these, 90% are for technologies concerning waste management and alternative energy production- 38,837 or 63% of them are related to waste management and more than 16,000 or 26% are for alternative energy production. The rest of the green technology patentsare for energy conservation (2,555),transportation technologies (2,481),nuclear power generation (1,079),agriculture and forestry (161) and others (69).

46. With which country India entered into a 'Green Strategic Partnership' in September 2020?

(a) Poland (b) Greece
(c) Denmark (d) South Korea

Sol. (c) India entered into a Strategic Green Partnership with Denmark in September 2020. This partnership aims to create a framework for significant expansion of cooperation in areas of renewable energy, environment, economy, climate change and science and technology.

47. In pursuance of the United Nations Sustainable Development Goals (SDG), India aims to be energy independent by the year

(a) 2047 (b) 2040
(c) 2045 (d) 2057

Sol. (a) In pursuance of the United Nations Sustainable Development Goals (SDG), India aims to be energy independent by the year 2047. The Sustainable Development Goals, also known as the Global Goals, were adopted by the United Nations in 2015 as a universal call to action to end poverty, protect the planet, and ensure that by 2030 all people enjoy peace and prosperity.

48. According to the Global Innovation Index 2021 published by the World Intellectual Property Organisation (WIPO), India is ranked .... out of 132 countries.

(a) 45th (b) 46th
(c) 47th (d) 48th

Sol. (c) According to the Global Innovation Index 2021 published by the World Intellectual Property Organisation (WIPO), India is ranked 47th out of 132 countries. The 2021 edition of the Global Innovation Index (GII) presents the latest global innovation ranking of 132 economies, relying on 81 different indicators.

While tracking the most recent global innovation trends in the new Global Innovation Tracker, this edition also focuses on the impact of the COVID-19 pandemic on innovation. The GII's overall formula for measuring an economy's innovative capacity and output provides clarity for decision makers in government, business and elsewhere as they look forward to creating policies that enable their people to invent and create more efficiently.

49. In January 2022, the Union Cabinet approved the second phase of the Green Energy Corridor (GEC) in India with the objective to facilitate

(a) Grid integration and power evacuation of Renewable Energy (RE) Power Projects in seven states
(b) Ecologically sustainable growth by increasing carbon footprint.
(c) Ecologically sustainable production of fossil fuels.
(d) Spreading awareness regarding Renewable Energy (RE) Power Projects.

Sol. (a) In January 2022, the Union Cabinet approved the second phase of the Green Energy Corridor (GEC) in India with the objective to facilitate grid integration and power evacuation of Renewable Energy (RE) Power Projects in seven states. The scheme targets to add approximately 10,750 circuit kilometres of transmission lines and about 27,500 megavolt-amperes transformation capacity of substations.

50. The IRENA is an intergovernmental organisation that supports countries in their transition to a sustainable energy future and serves as the principal platform for international co-operation on renewable energy. IRENA stands for

(a) Intergovernmental Renewable Energy Association
(b) International Renewable Energy Association
(c) Intergovernmental Renewable Energy Agency
(d) International Renewable Energy Agency

Sol. (d) IRENA stands for International Renewable Energy Agency. With 167 members, IRENA plays a leading role in the energy transformation as a centre of excellence for knowledge and innovation, a global voice for renewables, a network hub and a source of advice and support for countries. As a part of its contribution to the Climate Investment Platform, IRENA invites financial institutions, development organisations and private investors prepared to support the realisation of projects and projects in need of support to register their interest.

XI. The Government may defer the deadline for companies to deposit the unspent portion of their Corporate Social Responsibility (CSR) funds into specified bank accounts in a move aimed at providing some relief in the fight against the COVID-19 and subsequent restrictions. Companies are required to spend at least 2% of their average net profit of the preceding within three financial years on CSR. The Ministry has allowed firms to undertake projects on an ongoing basis on the condition that any unspent amount must be deposited with a scheduled bank within 30 days of the end of the financial year. *"Considering the current crisis, we request your esteemed office to consider relaxation by providing extension of the time lines up to 30th June, 2021,"* the Institute of Company Secretaries of India said in a letter to the Ministry. Experts said that while lockdowns and restrictions are less stringent than last year and companies have adapted to working online, many professionals or their families have been affected by the infection, leaving teams short-staffed.

51. Which of the following is the Corporate Social Responsibility (CSR) initiative of the erstwhile Facebook India to promote women entrepreneurship?

(a) Shakti (b) Pragati
(c) Lean In
(d) Marching Forward

Sol. (b) Pragati is the Corporate Social Responsibility (CSR) initiative of the erstwhile Facebook India to promote women entrepreneurship. The initiative which aims to boost women entrepreneurship in India, is powered by N/Core (The/Nudge Centre for Social Innovation). The project will incubate and accelerate early-stage women-led non-profit units that work on women entrepreneurship. The initiative will award four financial grants of up to .50 lakh for each non-profit organisation.

52. In 2019, which of the following Committees recommended that CSR expenditure should be made tax deductible expenditure?

(a) Company Laws Committee
(b) High Level Committee on Reform of Indian Company Law
(c) High Level Committee on Corporate Social Responsibility
(d) Committee for Reforms in Corporate Social Responsibility in India

Sol. (c) In 2019, the High Level Committee on Corporate Social Responsibility recommended that CSR expenditure should be made tax deductible expenditure. The High Level Committee (HLC) on Corporate Social Responsibility (CSR) constituted by the Ministry of Corporate Affairs recommended making CSR expenditure tax deductible and to make compliance violations a civil offence that attracts penalties. Thus, option c is the right answer.

53. CAWACH is an initiative by the National Science and Technology Entrepreneurship Development Board, Department of Science and Technology, Government of India stands for the

(a) Centre for Alleviating Waning Healthcare Companies
(b) Centre for Augmenting Wound-up Healthcare Companies
(c) Centre for Augmenting WAR with COVID-19 Health Crisis
(d) Centre for Alleviating Withering Healthcare Companies

Sol. (c) CAWACH stands for The Centre for Augmenting WAR with COVID-19 Health Crisis. It is an initiative by National Science and Technology Entrepreneurship Development Board (NSTEDB), Department of Science and Technology (DST), Government of India. Given the impact of COVID-19 globally and in India, the need of the hour is to support R&D efforts in this direction and end any further damage to the economy. Department of Science and Technology (DST), Government of India is supporting innovations offering comprehensive solutions through the startup-ecosystem.

54. On 22nd January, 2021 the Companies (Corporate Social Responsibility Policy) Amendment Rules, 2021 were notified by the

(a) Ministry of Finance
(b) Ministry of Social Justice and Empowerment
(c) Ministry of Law and Justice
(d) Ministry of Corporate Affairs

Sol. (d) On January 22, 2021 the Companies (Corporate Social responsibility Policy) Amendment Rules, 2021 were notified by the Ministry of Corporate Affairs. It provides amendments to the Companies (Corporate Social Responsibility Policy) Rules, 2014 ("Rules") in relation to the Corporate Social Responsibility ("CSR") obligations required to be complied with by the companies under the Companies Act, 2013 ("Act").

55. The Ministry of Corporate Affairs has instituted an award to select companies to recognise corporate initiatives in the area of Corporate Social Responsibility (CSR) to achieve inclusive growth and inclusive and sustainable development. The name of the award is

(a) National Corporate Social Responsibility Awards
(b) National Awards for Excellence in Social Responsibility
(c) National Awards for Corporate Excellence in Social Responsibility
(d) National Awards for Excellence in Inclusive Growth and Sustainable Development

Sol. (a) The Ministry of Corporate Affairs has instituted an award to select companies to recognize corporate initiatives in the area of Corporate Social Responsibility (CSR) to achieve inclusive growth and inclusive and sustainable development. The name of the award is National Corporate Social Responsibility Awards. Thus, option a is the right answer.

XII. With the announcement of Drone Shakti in the Union Budget, the industry got a massive push after the liberalisation of the Drone Rules in 2021. The Government stated that startups will be promoted to facilitate Drone Shakti, with 'drone as a service'.

"The current Government has taken a serious paradigm shift on drone technology and Drone Shakti announcement of the current FY budget proves the government's clear vision and focus towards this emerging industry. Drone Shakti and Kisan Drones will definitely help get this technology to impact common people on the grassroots level at a massive scale," according to the founder and CEO of a prominent aerospace quoted in a business magazine. The country is set to witness the use of large, unmanned aircraft systems weighing more than 150 kilograms across the sectors. Kisan Drones are already being used for crop assessments, land records, spraying of

insecticides, and are expected to boost a wave of technology in the Agri and farming sector. Drones are also being used in surveillance systems for Railway Security. In India, drones were also deployed to deliver COVID-19 vaccines.

56. COVID-19 vaccines were delivered by drones as ICMR-Ied pilot project to

(a) Ladakh (b) Katra
(c) Dantewada (d) Manipur

Sol. (d) COVID-19 vaccines were delivered by drones as iCmr-led pilot project to Manipur. i-Drone, which stands for ICMR's Drone Response and Outreach in North East, aims to facilitate vaccine delivery to tough and hard-to-reach terrains of India.

57. Which of the following is the online platform hosted by the Directorate General of Civil Aviation for various activities related to the management of drone activities in India?

(a) e-Drone Shakti
(b) Digital Sky platform
(c) Aakash Shakti
(d) Digital Drone platform

Sol. (b) Digital Sky Platform is the online platform hosted by the directorate general of Civil Aviation for various activities related to the management of drone activities in India.

58. Which of the following refers to the phenomenon of restricting the movement of drones within a defined airspace?

(a) Geo-fencing (b) Drone-fencing
(c) Sky-fencing (d) Air-fencing

Sol. (a) Geo-fencing refers to the phenomenon of restricting the movement of drones within a defined airspace. Geofencing for drones is a safety measure put in place to prohibit drones access to a restricted area. These restricted areas can then be seen via your drones app when you are flying and alert you when you are nearby. These no-fly zones are protected airspace areas and governed by the FAA to prevent any wrongdoing.

59. The Drone Rules, 2021 have been made in supersession of which of the following rules?

(a) The Unmanned Aircraft System Rules, 2020
(b) The Aircraft Rules, 2020
(c) The Unmanned Aircraft System Rules, 2021
(d) The Manned Aircraft Rules, 1934

Sol. (c) The Drone Rules, 2021 have been made in supersession of The Unmanned Aircraft System Rules, 2021. The Central Government on 25th August 2021 has promulgated liberalised 'The Drone Rules, 2021' ("the Rules"), replacing the erstwhile Unmanned Aircraft System Rules 2021 ("Prior Rules"), to regulate the use and operation of Drones or Unmanned Aerial System ("UAS") in India.

60. Which autonomous body is responsible for national accreditation structure for drones?

(a) Drone Council of India
(b) Unmanned Aircraft Council of India
(c) Manned Aircraft Council of India
(d) Quality Council of India

Sol. (d) Quality Council of India is the autonomous body that is responsible for the national accreditation structure for drones. Quality Council of India (QCI) was set up in 1997 by Government of India jointly with Indian Industry as an autonomous body under the administrative control of the Department to establish and operate the National Accreditation Structure for conformity assessment bodies, providing accreditation in the field of education, health and quality promotion. Besides the role of putting in place the accreditation structure, it also promotes the adoption of quality standards relating to Quality Management Systems (ISO 14001 Series), Food Safety Management Systems (ISO 22000 Series) and Product Certification and Inspection Bodies through the accreditation services provided by National Accreditation Board for Certification Bodies (NABCB).

XIII. The 21st century has seen an overall shift in India's policy outlook and also the global outlook towards India. Coherent policy initiatives and effective implementation on the ground have ensured a positive growth profile. The biggest shift has been the recognition of the maritime sector. Somehow, post-independence, we as a nation became sea blind and completely undermined our maritime potential.

Initially, the Indian Navy came out with their Military Maritime Strategy in 2007, titled "Freedom to use the Seas". They kept on upgrading their vision document on regular intervals with latest being declared in 2015. The Security And Growth for All in the Region (SAGAR) vision declared by the Government of India in May 2015 has been a massive game changer on multiple fronts. It integrates the geopolitical and geostrategic realities to domestic requirements. The security concerns and the blue economic opportunities are comprehensively addressed along with the diplomatic leverage and reviving the rich maritime heritage.

The SAGAR vision has been backed by aggressive push by the Government of India to drive mega projects with massive human resource requirements.

61. Which of the following is the flagship programme of the Ministry of Shipping, Government of India, to promote port-led development in the "Country through harnessing India's 7,500 km long coastline, 14,500 km of potentially navigable waterways and strategic location on key international maritime trade routes?

(a) Sagarmala Programme
(b) Sagarshakti Programme
(c) Jalshakti Programme
(d) Jalmala Programme

Sol. (a) Sagarmala Programme is the flagship programme of the Ministry of Shipping, Government of India, to promote port-led development in the country through harnessing India's 7,500 km long coastline, 14,500 km of potentially navigable waterways and strategic location on key international maritime trade routes.

62. Which of the following is the initiative of the Ministry of Earth Sciences (MoES), Government of India, to explore marine resources and develop deep sea technologies for sustainable use of ocean resources?

(a) Sagarmanthan Mission
(b) Samudramanthan Mission
(c) Deep Ocean Mission
(d) Deep Ocean and Sea Technology Mission

Sol. (c) Deep Ocean Mission is the initiative of the Ministry of Earth Sciences (MoES), Government of India, to explore marine resources and develop deep sea technologies for sustainable use of ocean resources. The Mission will send a manned submersible 'Matsya-6000' up to a depth of 6,000 metres in the ocean with three people aboard.

63. ISA is a United Nations body regulating the exploration and exploitation of marine non-living resources of oceans in international waters. ISA stands for

(a) International Sea Authority
(b) International Sea Association
(c) International Seafaring Association
(d) International Seabed Authority

Sol. (d) ISA stands for International Seabed Authority. It was formed on 16th November, 1994 as an intergovernmental body under the United Nations Convention on the Law of the Sea (UNCLOS). It regulates the exploration and exploitation of marine non-living resources of oceans in international waters.

64. Under Mission SAGAR, which Indian Naval Ship was deployed by the Indian Navy to provide humanitarian and medical assistance to Maldives, Mauritius, Seychelles, Madagascar and Comoros?

(a) INS Kesari (b) INS Vikrant
(c) INS Viraat
(d) INS Vikramaditya

Sol. (a) Under Mission SAGAR, INS Kesari was the Indian Naval Ship which was deployed by the Indian Navy to provide humanitarian and medical assistance to Maldives, Mauritius, Seychelles, Madagascar and Comoros. Indian Naval Ship Kesari entered the Port of Maputo, Mozambique, as part of yet another deployment undertaken under Mission SAGAR. Around 500 tonnes of food aid has been shipped by INS Kesari to support the efforts of the government of Mozambique to cope with the ongoing drought and concurrent challenges of the pandemic.

65. Which of the following is India's first manned ocean mission which was launched at Chennai?

(a) Samudrashakti (b) Samudrayan
(c) Sagaryan (d) Sagarshakti

Sol. (b) Samudrayan is India's first manned ocean mission which was launched at Chennai. The new vessel is for purposes including survey and exploration of resources, oceanography and would feature radar, seismic components as well and it could study characteristics of the sea bed.

XIV. Writ is a public law remedy. It refers to a formal, written order issued by a judicial authority directing an individual or authority to do or refrain from doing an act. The High Court, while exercising its power of judicial review, does not act as an appellate body. It is concerned with illegality, irrationality and procedural impropriety of an order passed by the State or a Statutory Authority. A High Court is empowered to issue directions, orders or writs for the enforcement of Fundamental Rights and for any other purpose. The writ jurisdiction of High Court is discretionary and equitable. Writ of mandamus is issued by a court commanding a public authority to perform a public duty belonging to its office. It can be issued only when a legal duty is imposed on the authority and the petitioner has right to compel the performance of such duty.

Writ of mandamus is requested to be issued, *inter alia*, to compel performance of public duties which may be administrative, ministerial or statutory in nature. A writ of mandamus may be issued in favour of a person who establishes a legal right in himself. It may be issued against a person who has a mandatory legal duty to perform, but has failed or has neglected to do so. Such a legal duty emanates by operation of law. The writ of mandamus is most extensive in regards to its remedial nature. The object of mandamus is to prevent disorder emanating from failure of justice and is required to be granted in all cases where law has established no specific remedy.

66. The government of a state made a rule to make it discretionary to grant dearness allowance to its employees. One of the employees filed a writ petition seeking a mandamus to compel the government to grant dearness allowance. In the given situation, which of the following statements is true?

(a) Writ of mandamus cannot be granted as no legal duty was imposed on the government to grant dearness allowance.
(b) Writ of mandamus cannot be granted as a statutory right was conferred on the employee to receive dearness allowance.
(c) Writ of mandamus can be granted as it is a public law remedy.
(d) Writ of mandamus can be granted as it is a discretionary remedy.

Sol. (a) Option (a) which states that Writ of mandamus cannot be granted as no legal duty was imposed on the government to grant dearness allowance is the correct statement. A writ of mandamus can be granted to compel performance of a public duty which may be administrative, ministerial or statutory in nature. It can only be issued when a legal duty is imposed on the authority and the petitioner has the right to compel the performance of such duty. In the given situation, since no legal duty was imposed on the government to grant dearness allowance as it was discretionary, a writ of mandamus cannot be issued by the employees against the government.

67. A public-spirited citizen filed a writ petition seeking a mandamus to compel the government to make a law to curb the ill-effects of climate change. In the given situation, which of the following statements is true?

(a) Writ of mandamus can be granted as it is an equitable remedy.

(b) Writ of mandamus cannot be granted as no legal duty is imposed on the government to pass a law to curb the ill-effects of climate change.

(c) Writ of mandamus can be granted as it is a discretionary remedy.

(d) Writ of mandamus cannot be granted as there is no violation of fundamental right.

Sol. (b) Writ of mandamus cannot be granted as no legal duty is imposed on the government to pass a law to curb the ill-effects of climate change. This is because no legal duty is imposed on the government as such to pass a law that can help in curbing the ill-effects of climate change.

68. Mr. A and Mr. B are parties to a contract of sale of goods. Upon breach of contractual obligations by Mr. A, Mr. B filed a writ petition seeking a mandamus to compel Mr. A to perform his obligations under the contract. In the given situation, which of the following statements is true?

(a) Writ of mandamus can be granted as it is a discretionary remedy.

(b) Writ of mandamus cannot be granted as there is no violation of fundamental right.

(c) Writ of mandamus cannot be granted as Mr. B's right under the contract is a private right.

(d) Writ of mandamus can be granted as there is no statutory duty imposed on Mr. A to fulfill his contractual Obligations.

Sol. (c) The correct answer here is option c, i.e, a writ of mandamus cannot be granted as Mr. B's right under a contract is a private right. A writ of mandamus can be granted to **compel performance of a public duty (and not a private duty)** which may be administrative, ministerial or statutory in nature. It can only be issued when a legal duty is imposed on the authority and the petitioner has the right to compel the performance of such duty. In the given situation, since the rights arose from a contract, they were considered to be private rights (right in personam) and thus, a writ of mandamus could not be granted.

69. A licensing officer is under a statutory duty to issue a license to an applicant who fulfils the conditions prescribed for the issue of such license. Mr. X, an applicant, fulfilled all the conditions prescribed for the issue of such license, but his application for issuance of license was rejected by the licensing officer. In the given situation, which of the following statements is correct?

(a) Writ of mandamus can be granted compelling the license officer to issue the license.

(b) Writ of mandamus cannot be granted compelling the license officer to issue the license as there is no violation of fundamental right.

(c) Writ of mandamus can be granted as it is the discretion of the licensing officer to grant license.

(d) Writ of mandamus cannot be granted compelling the license officer to issue the license as there is no violation of public duty.

Sol. (a) The correct answer here will be option a, i.e, Writ of mandamus can be granted, compelling the license officer to issue the license. In the given situation, since the officer was under a statutory compulsion or duty to grant license to anyone who fulfils the conditions prescribed, he becomes bound to do so the moment Mr. X, the applicant performs all the requisite conditions.

70. Which of the following statements is incorrect?

(a) Writ of mandamus may be issued in favour of a person who establishes the existence of a legal right.

(b) Writ of mandamus may be issued against a person or authority who has a mandatory duty to perform but has failed or has neglected to do so.

(c) Writ of mandamus is purported to prevent disorder emanating from failure of justice.

(d) Writ of mandamus may be requested to be issued to compel performance of private duties which may be administrative, ministerial or statutory in nature.

Sol. (d) Option D is the incorrect statement here as a writ of mandamus cannot be issued to compel the performance of a private duty. It can only be granted to compel the performance of a public duty which may be administrative, ministerial or statutory in nature. Thus, it can only be issued when a legal duty is imposed on the authority and the petitioner has the right to compel the performance of such duty.

XV. To maintain the secular character of the Indian polity, not only does the Constitution of India guarantee freedom of religion to individuals and groups, but it is also against the general policy of the Constitution of India that any money be paid out of the public funds for promoting or maintaining any particular religion. Accordingly, it is provided in the Constitution of India that no person shall be compelled to pay any taxes, the proceeds of which are specifically appropriated in payment of expenses for the promotion or maintenance of any particular religion or religious denomination. This does not prohibit the State from enacting a law to incur expenses for the promotion or maintenance of any particular religion or religious denomination, but by such law, no person can be compelled to pay any tax, the proceeds of which are to be so utilised. This, however, does not invalidate levy of a fee to provide some service. Thus, a fee can be levied on pilgrims to a religious fair to meet the expenses of the measures taken to safeguard the health, safety and welfare of the pilgrims. Such fee levied by a State will be valid because the object of such contribution is not to foster or preserve religion, but to control secular administration of religious institutions.

71. Mr. A, a tax-payer of various taxes levied by the State Government, filed a writ petition for issuance of a writ of mandamus directing the State to forbear from spending any amount from the public funds of the state for renovation of water tanks belonging to a Hindu temple in the State. These tanks were used by the general public, irrespective of their religious affiliation, for bathing and drinking purposes. In the given situation, which of the following statements is correct?

(a) The State is promoting or maintaining the Hindu religion.

(b) The State cannot be said to be promoting or maintaining the Hindu religion.

(c) The State is compelling citizens to pay tax for promotion of Hindu religion.

(d) The State is compelling citizens to pay tax for maintenance of Hindu religion.

Sol. (b) The correct answer here is option b, i.e, the State cannot be said to be promoting or maintaining the Hindu religion. According to the Indian Constitution, a fee can be levied on pilgrims to a religious fair to meet the expenses of the measures taken to safeguard the health, safety and welfare of the pilgrims. Such a fee levied by a State will be valid because the object of such contribution is not to foster or preserve religion, but to control secular administration of religious institutions. In the given situation, even though the water tanks belonged to the Hindu temple, they can still be renovated by the State, out of the public funds as the tanks were used by the general public, irrespective of religion.

72. Communal riots between religion 'A' and religion 'B' resulted in the destruction of places of worship of both religions in a State. As a result, the State Government utilised public funds for restoring the places of worship of both religions 'A' and 'B'. In the given situation, which of the following statements is correct?

(a) The State Government's act is violative of the Constitution of India as it is promoting or maintaining particular religions.

(b) The State Government's act is not violative of the Constitution of India as it is not promoting or maintaining any particular religion.

(c) The State Government's act is violative of freedom of religion as it condones communal violence.

(d) The State Government's act is not violative of the Constitution of India as it is promoting or maintaining a particular religion.

Sol. (b) The correct answer here is option b. The act of the State Government in utilising public funds for restoring the places of worship of the religion of both A and B is not violative of the Constitution because it is not promoting or maintaining any particular religion. Such an act of the State upholds the secular fabric of the Indian society and this has also been safeguarded by the Indian Constitution.

73. Communal riots between religion 'A' and religion 'B' resulted in the destruction of a place of worship of religion 'B' in the State. As a result, the State Government utilised public funds for restoring the places of worship of religion 'B'. In the given situation, which of the following statements is correct?

(a) The State Government's act is violative of the Constitution of India as it is promoting or maintaining particular religion.

(b) The State Government's act is not violative of the Constitution of India as it is promoting or maintaining a particular religion.

(c) The State Government's act is not violative of the Constitution of India as it is not promoting or maintaining a particular religion.

(d) The State Government's act is violative of freedom of religion as it condones communal violence.

Sol. (c) The State Government's act is not violative of the Constitution of India as it is not protecting or maintaining a particular religion. Restoring the place of worship of a particular religion that was destroyed due to communal riots cannot amount to protecting or maintaining a particular religion. The Constitution of India imbibes secularism as an essential feature and the act of restoring the place of worship upholds this very principle.

74. A State Government passed a law making it mandatory for all residents of the State to pay a hefty 'pilgrimage tax' so as to aid the State in organising a popular religious pilgrimage in that State. The said pilgrimage is undertaken only by followers of religion 'X' and draws a large number of followers of religion 'X' from all over the country to the state every year. In the given situation, which of the following statements is correct?

(a) The State Government's act is violative of the Constitution of India as it is not promoting or maintaining religion 'X'.

(b) The State Government's act is not violative of the Constitution of India as it is not promoting or maintaining religion 'X'.

(c) The State Government's act is violative of the Constitution of India as it is compelling citizens to pay tax for promoting or maintaining religion 'X'.

(d) The State Government's act is not violative of the Constitution of India as it is a measure to safeguard the health, safety and welfare of the pilgrims.

Sol. (c) The State Government's act is violative of the Constitution of India as it is compelling citizens to pay tax for promoting or maintaining religion 'X'. The Constitution does not prohibit the State from enacting a law to incur expenses for the promotion or maintenance of any particular religion or a particular religious denomination, but no person can be compelled by such a law to pay any tax, the proceeds of which are to be utilised for the promotion or maintenance of any particular religion.

75. The object of a State Legislation is "to provide for the better administration and governance of certain Hindu religious endowments", where 'religious endowment' means the property belonging to or given or endowed for the support of temples. The State Legislation vests the supervision of public temples in a statutory authority, i.e. 'Commissioner of Hindu Religious Endowments'. For the purpose of meeting the expenses of the Commissioner and his staff, every Hindu temple in the State is required under provisions of the State Legislation, to pay an annual contribution at certain percentage of their annual income. In the given situation, which of the following statements is correct regarding the annual contribution provided under the State Legislation?

(a) It is not violative of the Constitution of India because its object is the proper administration of religious trusts and institutions.

(b) It is not violative of the Constitution of India because its object is fostering of Hindu religion.

(c) It is violative of the Constitution of India because its object is fostering of Hindu religion.

(d) It is violative of the Constitution of India because its object is not inclusive of administration of religious endowments belonging to all religions.

Sol. (a) The said provision is not violative of the Constitution of India because its object is the proper administration of religious trusts and institutions. A fee can be levied to meet the expenses of measures undertaken to safeguard health, safety and welfare of the pilgrims. Such a fee levied by the State will be valid because the object of such a contribution is not to foster or preserve religion, but to control the secular administration of religious institutions.

XVI. The Constitution of India guarantees to all its citizens certain fundamental freedoms, which are recognised as their fundamental rights. However, these fundamental freedoms guaranteed by the Constitution of India are not absolute as no right can be. Each of these fundamental rights is liable to be controlled, curtailed and regulated to some extent by laws made by the Parliament or the State Legislatures. Accordingly, the Constitution of India lays down the grounds and the purposes for which a legislature can impose 'reasonable restrictions' on the rights guaranteed to citizens. The State cannot travel beyond the contours of these reasonable restrictions in curbing the fundamental rights guaranteed to citizens. While determining the constitutional validity of a restriction imposed on a fundamental right by a legislation, the Court is not concerned with the necessity of the restriction or the wisdom of the policy underlying it, but only whether the restriction is in excess of the requirement, and whether the legislature has overstepped the Constitutional limitations.

Two of the fundamental rights guaranteed to every citizen of India are- the right to move freely throughout the territory of India and the right to reside and settle in any part of India. However, the State may impose reasonable restrictions on these rights by law, in the interests of the general public or for the protection of the interests of any Scheduled Tribes.

76. A law was enacted by the Parliament of India which consisted of a provision making it mandatory for every person riding a two-wheeler in India, to wear a helmet, failing which such person was made liable to a fine. Mr. X, a citizen of India, was fined for violation of the said provision. Mr. X challenged the constitutional validity of the said provision. In the given situation, which of the following statements is correct?

(a) The provision is violative of the Constitution of India because it is a restriction on the freedom to move freely throughout the territory of India.

(b) The provision is not violative of the Constitution of India because it is a reasonable restriction on the freedom to move freely throughout the territory of India.

(c) Mr. X's fundamental right to move freely throughout the territory of India is violated.

(d) Both (a) and (c)

Sol. (b) The said provision is not violative of the Constitution of India because it is a reasonable restriction on the freedom to move freely throughout the territory of India. The Constitution of India guarantees to all its citizens certain fundamental freedoms, which are recognised as their fundamental rights. However, these fundamental freedoms guaranteed by the Constitution of India are not absolute as no right can be. Each of these fundamental rights is liable to be controlled, curtailed and regulated to some extent by laws made by the Parliament or the State Legislatures. Accordingly, the Constitution of India lays down the grounds and the purposes for which a legislature can impose 'reasonable restrictions' on the rights guaranteed to citizens. In the given situation, the restriction on the freedom to freely travel throughout India is reasonable as it seeks to ensure the safety of people while travelling.

77. A group of Indian students of XYZ University located in New Delhi, India posted on social networking sites that they would hold a demonstration outside the university campus, protesting against a recently passed law which made it compulsory for university students to wear uniforms while attending classes. The students further threatened to "use whatever means necessary" to "stop the oppression of students".

Therefore, the State Authorities placed barricades around the university campus in order to restrict movement of the students carrying out the demonstration and ensuring that the demonstration does not turn violent. In the given situation, which of the following statements is correct regarding the act of placing of barricades by State Authorities?

(a) The act is violative of the Constitution of India because it is a restriction on the freedom to move freely throughout the territory of India.

(b) The act is not violative of the Constitution of India because it is a reasonable restriction in the interests of general public.

(c) The act is violative of the Constitution of India because it is restriction in the interest of students.

(d) The act is not violative of the Constitution of India because it is a reasonable restriction in the interest of morality.

Sol. (b) The act is not violative of the Constitution of India because it is a reasonable restriction in the interests of the general public. The placing of barricades around the University campus by the State Authorities was done to prevent the movement from turning into a violent agitation and to safeguard the interests of the general public.

This acts as a reasonable restriction that has been provided for in the Constitution itself.

78. The appropriate authority in a State passed an externment order against Mr. A, a citizen of India. The externment order prohibited Mr. A, from residing within the State, from the date specified in such order. The externment order was passed by virtue of powers conferred on the appropriate authority by law, and the constitutional validity of this law had been upheld by the Supreme Court of India. The externment order was passed on the ground that Mr. A was found to be frequently engaged in illegal business of narcotic drugs and was also involved in several cases of riot and criminal intimidation. In the given situation, which of the following statements is correct regarding the externment order?

(a) It is a reasonable restriction on Mr. A's fundamental right of free movement throughout the territory of India.

(b) It is an unreasonable restriction on Mr. A's fundamental right of residence and settlement in any part of India.

(c) It is violative of Mr. A's fundamental right of free movement throughout the territory of India.

(d) It is an unreasonable restriction on Mr. A's fundamental right of free movement throughout the territory of India.

Sol. (a) The externment order is a reasonable restriction on Mr. A's fundamental right of free movement throughout the territory of India. It was passed on the ground that Mr. A was found to be frequently engaged in illegal business of narcotic drugs and was also involved in several cases of riot and criminal intimidation. Thus, the imposition of restrictions on his free movement was reasonable in the interests of the general public.

79. Mr. Z, a citizen of India, was issued a passport on 1st June, 2020 by the Passport Office. Mr. Z was due to travel to Spain on 15th July, 2021. On 11th July, 2021, Mr. Z received a letter from the Regional Passport Officer intimating him that it was decided by the Government of India to seize his passport "in public interest". Mr. Z was required to surrender his passport within seven days of the receipt of that letter. In the given situation, which of the following statements is correct?

(a) Mr. Z can challenge the letter on the ground that it is violative of his fundamental right of free movement throughout the territory of India.

(b) Mr. Z can challenge the letter on the ground that it is violative of his fundamental right to reside and settle in any part of India.

(c) Mr. Z can challenge the letter on the ground that it is violative of the law relating to passports in India.

(d) Mr. Z cannot challenge the letter on the ground that it is violative of his fundamental right(s) of free movement throughout the territory of India and/or to residence and settlement in any part of India.

Sol. (d) Mr. Z cannot challenge the letter on the ground that it is violative of his fundamental right(s) of free movement throughout the territory of India and/or to residence and settlement in any part of India. Two of the fundamental rights guaranteed to every citizen of India are the right to move freely throughout the territory of India and the right to reside and settle in any part of India. In the given situation, the restriction was imposed on the freedom to travel abroad, which will not come within the ambit of the fundamental right of free movement throughout the territory of India.

80. Which of the following statements is incorrect?

(a) Fundamental right to movement and residence in any part of India are sacrosanct and are guaranteed to all citizens.

(b) Fundamental right to movement and residence in any part of India are sacrosanct, but are guaranteed subject to reasonable restrictions on such rights.

(c) Reasonable restrictions may be imposed, on fundamental rights to movement and residence in any part of India, by law.

(d) The constitutional validity of a law imposing reasonable restrictions on fundamental rights can be challenged by a citizen before the legislature.

Sol. (d) The incorrect statement here is option d, i.e, the constitutional validity of a law imposing reasonable restrictions on fundamental rights can be challenged by a citizen before the legislature. This is because it is the judiciary and not the legislature or executive that has the power to hear matters pertaining to the constitutional validity of any law.

XVII. Where a spouse contracts a second marriage while the first marriage is still subsisting, the spouse would be guilty of the offence of bigamy under the penal law in India, if it is proved that the first as well as the second marriages were legally valid, i.e., all the necessary ceremonies required by law or by custom have been performed at the time of contracting the marriages. According to the penal law in India, if a person, who has a living husband or wife, marries again, then such person is liable to be punished with imprisonment up to seven years along with a fine for committing the offence of bigamy. Although the penal law of India is applicable to all citizens irrespective of their religious affiliations, an exception to the offence of bigamy may be created by the law relating to marriage applicable to followers of a particular religion. Under the Hindu law relating to marriage, bigamy is not permitted.

If a Hindu wife files a criminal complaint against her husband on the ground that during the subsistence of her marriage, her husband had married a second wife by converting into another religion which legally permits having more than one wife, then her husband is liable to be punished for the offence of bigamy. Further, the Hindu law relating to marriage also provides that the punishment for offence of bigamy as provided in the penal law of India would be applicable to marriage between two Hindus.

81. Mr. A, a Hindu male, has been married to Ms. B, a Hindu female. Their marriage was solemnised as per Hindu rites and ceremonies. After his marriage to Ms. B, Mr. A underwent religious conversion into a religion 'X' which legally permits males to have two wives. Thereafter, Mr. A got married to Ms. C, a female belonging to religion 'X', in compliance with all the legal requirements of contracting a valid marriage under religion 'X'. In the given situation, which of the following statements is true?

(a) As Mr. A married Ms. C, the marriage of Mr. A and Ms. B has become invalid.

(b) As Mr. A is not a Hindu, the marriage of Mr. A and Ms. B has become invalid.

(c) Mr. A's marriage with Ms. C has not affected the validity of his marriage with Ms. B.

(d) Both (a) and (b)

Sol. (c) Mr. A's marriage with Ms. C has not affected the validity of his marriage with Ms. B. This is the most accurate option among the ones given. Although the penal law of India is applicable to all citizens irrespective of their religious affiliation, an exception to the offence of bigamy may be created by the law relating to marriage applicable to followers of a particular religion. Under the Hindu law relating to marriage, bigamy is not permitted. If a Hindu wife files a criminal complaint against her husband on the ground that during the subsistence of her marriage, her husband had married a second wife by converting into another religion which legally permits having more than one wife, then her husband is liable to be punished for the offence of bigamy.

[**Note** The options given in this question weren't exactly accurate]

82. Mr. A, a Hindu male, has been married to Ms. B, a Hindu female. Their marriage was solemnised as per Hindu rites and ceremonies. After his marriage to Ms. B, Mr. A underwent religious conversion into a religion 'X' which legally permits males to have two wives. Thereafter, Mr. A got married to Ms. C, a female belonging to religion 'X', in compliance with all the legal requirements of contracting a valid marriage under religion 'X'. Ms. B filed a criminal complaint against Mr. A for committing the offence of bigamy. In the given situation, which of the following statements is true?

(a) Mr. A is liable to be punished according to the Hindu law relating to marriage.

(b) Mr. A is liable to be punished according to the penal law of India.

(c) Mr. A has not committed the offence of bigamy.

(d) Both (a) and (b).

Sol. (d) The correct answer here is option d, i.e, Mr. A is liable to be punished according to both the Hindu laws of marriage as well as the penal law of the country. Under the Hindu law relating to marriage, bigamy is not permitted. If a Hindu wife files a criminal complaint against her husband on the ground that during the subsistence of her marriage, her husband had married a second wife by converting into another religion which legally permits having more than one wife, then her husband is liable to be punished for the offence of bigamy.

83. Mr. A, a Hindu male, has been married to Ms. B, a Hindu female. Their marriage was not solemnised as per Hindu rites and ceremonies or any other custom, but was performed by seeking blessings of their family members. After his marriage to Ms. B, Mr. A underwent religious conversion into a religion 'X' which legally permits males to have two wives. Thereafter, Mr. A got married to Ms. C, a female belonging to religion 'X', in compliance with all the legal requirements of contracting a valid marriage under religion 'X'. Ms. B filed a criminal complaint against Mr. A for committing the offence of bigamy. In the given situation, which of the following statements is true?

(a) Mr. A has committed the offence of bigamy because he married again during the subsistence of the first marriage.

(b) Mr. A has not committed the offence of bigamy because his first marriage is not valid.

(c) Mr. A has committed the offence of bigamy because he underwent religious conversion in order to contract a bigamous marriage.

(d) Mr. A has not committed the offence of bigamy because his second marriage is not valid.

Sol. (b) Mr. A has not committed the offence of bigamy because his first marriage is not valid. In the given situation, though Mr. A was married to Ms. B and they both were Hindus, the marriage was not solemnised according to the Hindu rites or ceremonies. It was not even solemnised through any other custom. This made the first marriage invalid and thus, Ms. B cannot file a criminal complaint against A for bigamy when he married C.

84. Mr. A, a male belonging to religion 'P', has been married to Ms. B, a female belonging to religion 'P'. Their marriage was solemnised in compliance with all the legal requirements of contracting a valid marriage under religion 'P'. Monogamy is espoused as a cherished value by the followers of religion 'P' and provided as a pre-condition for a valid marriage for the followers of the religion. After his marriage to Ms. B, Mr. A underwent religious conversion into a religion 'Q' which legally permits males to have two wives. Thereafter, Mr. A got married to Ms. C, a female belonging to religion 'Q', in compliance with all the legal requirements of contracting a valid marriage under religion 'Q'. Ms. B wife filed a criminal complaint against Mr. A for committing the offence of bigamy. In the given situation, which of the following statements is true?

(a) Mr. A has committed bigamy according to the Hindu law relating to marriage.

(b) Mr. A has committed bigamy according to the penal law of India.

(c) Mr. A has committed bigamy according to the law relating to marriage of religion 'P'.

(d) Both (b) and (c)

Sol. (d) The correct answer here is option d, i.e, Mr. A has committed bigamy according to the penal law of the country as well as according to the law relating to "P's" religion. Under the law relating to marriage of the religion of P, bigamy is not permitted. Thus, if the wife files a criminal complaint against her husband on the ground that during the subsistence of her marriage, her husband had married a second wife by converting into another religion which legally permits having more than one wife, then her husband is liable to be punished for the offence of bigamy.

85. Which of the following statements is incorrect?

(a) Marrying again during lifetime of husband or wife is a pre-condition for performing a valid Hindu marriage.

(b) Religious conversion is not a defence for the offence of bigamy under the penal law of India.

(c) Bigamy is an offence under the penal law of India.

(d) Offence of bigamy can be committed according to the provisions of Hindu law relating to marriage.

Sol. (a) The incorrect statement here is option a, i.e, Marrying again during the lifetime of husband or wife is a pre-condition for performing a valid Hindu marriage. This will not be a pre-condition, infact, it would become a criminal offence and the said spouse can be penalised for the offence of bigamy.

XVIII. A special marriage, i.e., a marriage between persons from two different religious affiliations can be legally contracted in India under the provisions of the law relating to special marriages. The law relating to special marriages provides for the registration of such marriages and for divorce in such cases. One of the modes in which a special marriage can be legally terminated is through divorce by mutual consent of parties to the marriage. In order to obtain a divorce by mutual consent, both the parties to the special marriage are required to jointly present a petition for divorce to the district court on the ground that they have been living separately for one year or more, that they have not been able to live together and that they have mutually agreed that the marriage should be dissolved. At least six months after the presentation of such petition, but not later than eighteen months after the presentation of such petition, the district court, after hearing the parties and after making the necessary inquiry, and being satisfied that the marriage is a 'special marriage', and that the claims made in the petition are true, shall declare the marriage to be dissolved. Further, the personal presence of the parties before the district court at the time of presenting the joint petition for divorce is not mandatory, as the parties can satisfy the court even by affidavit that the requirements for granting divorce on mutual consent are fulfilled.

86. Ms. A, a Hindu female and Mr. B, a Christian male, got married as per the law relating to special marriages in January 2018. On 26th January, 2021, Ms. A and Mr. B jointly presented a petition for divorce by mutual consent before the district court on the ground that they have been inflicting mental cruelty on each other for a period of three years and that they have mutually agreed that the marriage should be dissolved. In the given situation, which of the following statements is correct?

(a) The district court shall pass a decree of divorce within six months after the presentation of petition for divorce by mutual consent.

(b) The district court shall pass a decree of divorce after eighteen months of the presentation of petition for divorce by mutual consent.

(c) The district court shall not immediately pass a decree of divorce by mutual consent.

(d) The district court shall immediately pass a decree of divorce by mutual consent if it is satisfied that the marriage was valid.

Sol. (c) The correct answer here is option c, i.e, the district court shall not immediately pass a decree of divorce by mutual consent. This is because at least six months after the presentation of such petition, but not later than eighteen months after the presentation of such petition, the district court, after hearing the parties and after making the necessary inquiry, and being satisfied that the marriage is a special marriage, and that the claims made in the petition are true, shall declare the marriage to be dissolved.

87. Ms. A, a Hindu female and Mr. B, a Christian male, got married as per the law relating to special marriages in January 2018. On 15th February, 2021 ,Ms. A presented a petition for divorce by mutual consent before the district court on the ground that Ms. A and Mr. B have been living separately for a period of one year because Mr. B has been in an adulterous relationship with Ms. X, a Christian female. In the given situation, which of the following statements is correct?

(a) The district court shall pass a decree of divorce by mutual consent six months after the date of presentation of petition for divorce.

(b) The district court shall pass a decree of divorce by mutual consent eighteen months after the date of presentation of petition for divorce.

(c) The district court shall not pass a decree of divorce by mutual consent as the requirements for the grant of divorce are not fulfilled.

(d) The district court shall not pass a decree of divorce by mutual consent as Ms. A and Mr. B have not been living separately for more than one year.

Sol. (c) The district court shall not pass a decree of divorce by mutual consent as the requirements for the grant of divorce are not fulfilled. In order to obtain a divorce by mutual consent, both the parties to the special marriage are required to jointly present a petition for divorce to the district court on the ground that they have been living separately for one year or more, that they have not been able to live together and that they have mutually agreed that the marriage should be dissolved. In the given situation, since the petition was not jointly presented, it did not fulfill the requirements for the grant of a divorce.

88. Ms. A, a Hindu female and Mr. B, a Christian male, got married as per the law relating to special marriages in January 2018. On 10th April, 2021, Ms. A and Mr. B jointly presented a petition for divorce by mutual consent before the district court on the ground that they have been living separately for a period of three years and that they have mutually agreed that the marriage should be dissolved. In the given situation, which of the following statements is correct?

(a) The district court shall pass a decree of divorce by mutual consent after all other legal requirements are fulfilled.

(b) The district court shall pass a decree of divorce by mutual consent immediately because Ms. A and Mr. B have been living separately for more than one year.

(c) The district court shall not pass a decree of divorce by mutual consent because the marriage between Ms. A and Mr. B is not valid.

(d) The district court shall not pass a decree of divorce by mutual consent because neither party is at fault in the marriage.

Sol. (a) The district court shall pass a decree of divorce by mutual consent after all other legal requirements are fulfilled. In order to obtain a divorce by mutual consent, both the parties to the special marriage are required to jointly present a petition for divorce to the district court on the ground that they have been living separately for one year or more, that they have not been able to live together and that they have mutually agreed that the marriage should be dissolved.

89. Ms. A, a Hindu female and Mr. B, a Christian male, got married as per the provisions of the law relating to special marriages in January 2018. On 16th June, 2021, Ms. A and Mr. B jointly presented a petition for divorce by mutual consent before the district court on the ground that they have been living separately for a period of three years and that they have mutually agreed that the marriage should be dissolved. During the presentation of the petition, while Ms. A was present physically in the district court, Mr. B joined via video-conferencing. In the given situation, which of the following statements is correct?

(a) The district court may pass a decree of divorce by mutual consent six months after the date of presentation of petition for divorce.

(b) The district court shall pass a decree of divorce by mutual consent after all other legal requirements are fulfilled.

(c) The district court shall not pass a decree of divorce by mutual consent.

(d) Both (a) and (b)

Sol. (d) Both Statements a and b are correct. Since the petition was jointly presented by both the parties, the district court may pass a decree of divorce by mutual consent six months after the date of presentation of the petition for divorce. Alternatively, the district court shall pass a decree of divorce by mutual consent after all other legal requirements have been fulfilled.

90. Ms. A, a Hindu female and Mr. B, a Christian male, got married as per the law relating to special marriages in January 2018. On 15th March, 2021, Ms. A and Mr. B jointly presented a petition for divorce before the district court on the ground that they have been living separately for a period of three years and that they have mutually agreed that the marriage should be dissolved. Six months later, the district court, after hearing the parties and making inquiry, found that the marriage had been solemnised under the law relating to special marriages, and that the consent of Ms. A for the presentation of petition of divorce was obtained by fraud. In the given situation, which of the following statements is correct?

(a) The district court shall pass a decree of divorce by mutual consent because the legal requirements are fulfilled.

(b) The district court shall pass a decree of divorce because the marriage had been solemnised under the law relating to special marriages.

(c) The district court shall not pass a decree of divorce because there was no mutual consent between parties.

(d) The district court shall not pass a decree of divorce because Ms. A has not been punished for fraud.

Sol. (c) The district court shall not pass a decree of divorce because there was no mutual consent between parties. In order to obtain a divorce by mutual consent, both the parties to the special marriage are required to jointly present a petition for divorce to the district court on the ground that they have been living separately for one year or more, that they have not been able to live together and that they have mutually agreed that the marriage should be dissolved.

XIX. There are two principal theories on the relationship between international law and domestic law- Monism and Dualism. The monistic theory maintains that the subjects of two systems of law, i.e., international law and municipal law are essentially one. The monistic theory asserts that international law and municipal law are fundamentally the same in nature, and arise from the same science of law, and are manifestations of a single conception of law. The followers of this theory view international law and municipal law as part of a universal body of legal rules binding all human beings, collectively or singly. In a monist system, international law does not need to be incorporated into domestic law because international law immediately becomes incorporated in domestic legal system upon ratification of an international treaty. According to this theory, domestic law is subordinate to international law. The Statute of the International Criminal Court, therefore, can be directly applied and adjudicated in national courts according to the monistic theory. According to dualism theory, international law and municipal law represent two entirely distinct legal systems, i.e., international has an intrinsically different character from that of municipal law. International law is not directly applicable in the domestic system under dualism. First, international law must be translated into State legislation before the domestic courts can apply it. For example, under dualism, ratification of the Statute of the International Criminal Court is not enough-it must be implemented through State legislation into the domestic system. Most states and courts presumptively view national and international legal systems as discrete entities and routinely discuss in dualist fashion incorporation of rules from one system to the other.

91. In light of the given passage, which of the following statements is correct?

(a) Monism and Dualism are similar approaches to adopt international law into domestic law.

(b) Dualism postulates the homogeneousness of domestic law and international law.

(c) Monism and Dualism are different approaches to understand how domestic law impacts international law.

(d) Monism postulates the homogeneousness of international law and domestic law.

Sol. (d) Monism postulates the homogeneity of international law and domestic law. The monistic theory maintains that the subjects of international law and municipal law are essentially one. The monistic theory asserts that international law and municipal law are fundamentally the same in nature and arise from the same science in law and are manifestations of a single conception of law.

92. 'X' is a developing country. 'X' ratified the United Nations Framework Convention on Climate Change in 1995, and incorporated the provisions of the said convention in its domestic legislation addressing climate change in 1996. However, 'X' has been widely criticised in the international community for its failure in meeting the obligations under the said convention. 'Y' is a developed country. 'Y' ratified the United Nations Framework Convention on Climate Change in 1995, and has not incorporated the provisions of the said convention in its domestic legislation till date. 'Y' has been appreciated by the international community for its success in meeting the obligations under the said convention. In the given situation, which of the following statements is correct?

(a) 'X' is a monist State and 'Y' is a dualist State.

(b) 'X' is a dualist State and 'Y' is a monist State.
(c) 'X' and 'Y' are both monist States.
(d) 'X' and 'Y' are both dualist States.

Sol. (b) In the given factual situation, 'X' is a dualist state while 'Y' is a monist state. Since X had adopted the provisions of UNFCCC into its municipal law, it was a dualist state wherein international law and municipal law are two distinct legal systems. On the other hand, Y is a monist state as it did not specifically adopt the provisions into its municipal law and yet continued to meet its obligations.

93. 'D', a dualist State, has signed and ratified the Agreement on Trade related Aspects of Intellectual Property Rights (TRIPS Agreement), an international agreement administered by the World Trade Organisation (WTO). If 'D' is compelled to fulfill its international obligations under the TRIPS Agreement, which of the following statements is correct?
(a) 'D' may adopt the provisions of the TRIPS Agreement without enacting a new domestic legislation or amending an existing legislation.
(b) 'D' may not incorporate the provisions of the TRIPS Agreement into a new domestic legislation.
(c) 'D' must incorporate the provisions of the TRIPS Agreement into an existing domestic legislation or in a new domestic legislation.
(d) 'D' may not incorporate the provisions of the TRIPS Agreement into an existing domestic legislation .

Sol. (c) 'D' must incorporate the provisions of the TRIPS agreement into an existing domestic legislation and thus, option c is the right answer. Since D is a dualist state which incorporates the existence of two separate legal systems, it is important for D to specifically incorporate the provisions of TRIPS agreement into an existing domestic legislation to give it effect in the domestic system.

94. Which of the following statements is incorrect?
(a) According to monism, the nature of domestic law and international law is the same and domestic law is subordinate to international law.
(b) According to monism, ratified international conventions automatically become a part of domestic law and domestic law is subordinate to international law.
(c) According to dualism, ratified international conventions automatically become a part of domestic law and domestic law is subordinate to international law.
(d) According to dualism, the nature of domestic law and international law is different and domestic law is not subordinate to international law.

Sol. (c) Option c is the incorrect statement here as it is according to monism and not dualism that ratified international conventions automatically become a part of the domestic law and domestic law is subordinate to international law.

95. The country 'X' has ratified an International Convention which requires each State Party to enact laws defining and punishing bribery, i.e., the act of offering bribes to Government officials. The Convention has neither defined bribery, nor prescribed a punishment for the same, so that each State Party may define the offence of bribery differently in their respective domestic legislations. By 2022, 'X' has not enacted any law defining and punishing the offence of bribery. In November 2021, Mr. A was being prosecuted by a domestic criminal court in 'X' for allegedly offering a bribe to a Government official. In the given situation, which of the following statements is correct?
(a) If 'X' is a monist State, Mr. A can be punished for committing an offence under the Convention.

(b) If 'X' is a dualist State, Mr. A can be punished for committing an offence under the Convention.
(c) If 'X' is a dualist State, Mr. A cannot be punished for committing an offence under the Convention.
(d) Mr. A cannot be punished for committing an offence under the Convention irrespective of whether 'X' is a monist or a dualist State.

Sol. (d) Mr. A cannot be punished for committing an offence under the Convention irrespective of whether 'X' is a dualist state or a monist state. It is because the Convention had neither defined bribery nor had it prescribed a punishment for the same. Thus, option (d) is the right answer.

XX. The United Nations Commission on Environment and Development defines 'sustainable development' as follows: "Sustainable development is the development that meets the needs of the present without compromising the ability of future generations to meet their own needs". Sustainable development clearly postulates an anthropocentric bias, least concerned with the rights of other species which live on this earth. Anthropocentrism is always human-interest focused thinking that considers non-humans as having only instrumental value to humans, in other words, humans take precedence and human responsibilities towards non-human are based on benefits to humans. Eco-centrism is nature-centred, where humans are part of nature and non-humans have intrinsic value. In other words, human interest does not take automatic precedence and humans have obligations towards non-humans independently of human interest. Eco-centrism is, therefore, life-centred, nature-centred where nature includes both humans and non-humans. The Constitution of India protects not only human rights but also casts an obligation on human beings to protect and preserve a specie from becoming extinct. Conservation and protection of environment is an inseparable part of the fundamental right to life. According to the doctrine of 'public trust' recognised under the Constitution of India, certain common properties such as rivers, seashores, forests and the air are held by the Government in trusteeship for the free and unimpeded use of the general public. The resources like air, sea, waters and the forests have such a great importance to the people as a whole, that it would be totally unjustified to make them a subject of private ownership. The State, as a custodian of the natural resources, has a duty to maintain them not merely for the benefit of the public, but for the best interest of flora and fauna, wildlife and so on.

96. Ms. G, a student of environmental science, has cultivated a butterfly garden which provides a favourable habitat for butterflies. Ms. G has cultivated the butterfly garden so that she could observe and study the different stages of development of butterflies such as egg, larvae, pupae, and adult. In the given situation, which of the following statements is correct?
(a) Ms. G's approach to cultivation of butterfly garden is anthropocentric because it concerns the furtherance of her academic interest.
(b) Ms. G's approach to cultivation of butterfly garden is anthropocentric because it concerns the conservation of environment.
(c) Ms. G's approach to cultivation of butterfly garden is eco-centric because it concerns the provision a favourable habitat to the butterflies.
(d) Ms. G's approach to cultivation of butterfly garden is eco-centric because it concerns the understanding of the different stages of development of butterflies.

Sol. (a) Ms. G's approach to cultivation of butterfly garden is anthropocentric because it concerns the furtherance of her academic interest. Anthropocentrism is always human interest focused thinking that considers non humans as having only instrumental value to humans. Thus, option (a) is the right answer.

97. Which of the following statements is correct?

(a) Anthropocentrism and eco-centrism are different approaches to achieving sustainable development.

(b) Anthropocentrism focuses on file promotion of non-human interests.

(c) Eco-centrism is concerned with the promotion of both human and non-human interests.

(d) Anthropocentrism and eco-centrism are different approaches to protection of environment and sustainable development.

Sol. (c) The correct statement is Option (c) which states that Eco-centrism is concerned with the promotion of both human and non-human interests. Eco-centrism is nature centred, life centred, whereas nature includes both humans and non humans.

98. Which of the following is the basis for the difference between anthropocentrism and eco-centrism?

(a) The inherent value placed on humans and non-humans.

(b) The inherent value placed on living things and non-living things.

(c) The relationship between human society and environment.

(d) The relationship between non-humans and environment.

Sol. (a) The basis for the difference between anthropocentrism and eco-centrism is the inherent value placed on humans and non-humans. In anthropocentrism, it is always human-interest focused thinking that considers non-humans as having only instrumental value to humans. However, eco-centrism is nature centred, life centred where humans are a part of nature and non-humans have an intrinsic value.

99. Which of the following statements is correct regarding fundamental right to life under the Constitution of India?

(a) It creates a corresponding duty on human beings to protect and preserve non-humans.

(b) It creates a corresponding duty on non-humans to protect the right to life of human beings.

(c) It is inclusive of the right of human beings to utilise non-human resources to the best of their advantage.

(d) It is inclusive of the right of non-humans to utilise human resources to the best of their advantage.

Sol. (a) Fundamental right to life under the Constitution creates a corresponding duty to human beings to protect and preserve non-humans. It also casts an obligation on human beings to protect and preserve a species from becoming extinct. Thus, option a is correct.

100. Which of the following statements is incorrect according to the doctrine of public trust?

(a) Private ownership of forests is unwarranted

(b) Forests are held by the State in a fiduciary capacity

(c) State is obligated to maintain forests for their economic value

(d) State is obligated to maintain forests in the interest of humans and non-humans

Sol. (c) According to the doctrine of "public trust", it is incorrect to say that the State is obligated to maintain forests for their economic value. The public trust doctrine is a doctrine which raises the duty of the sovereign to protect the resources that are freely available in the environment for the public to protect it and to act as a watchdog of society and if anyone uses that public resources privately then the sovereign has to punish that person.

XXI. When parties to a contract are under a 'Mistake' 'regarding' an important fact related to such contract, it may affect the contract in two ways. It may, firstly, defeat the consent altogether that the parties are supposed to have given, that is to say, the consent is unreal. Two or more persons are said to consent when they agree upon the same thing in the same sense. Secondly, the mistake may mislead the parties as to the purpose which they had contemplated. Where the mistake does not defeat consent, but only misleads the parties, i.e., where both parties to an agreement are under a mistake as to a matter of fact essential to the agreement, the agreement is void. However, if the mistake is concerning an erroneous opinion regarding value of the subject-matter of the agreement, it is not a mistake as to a matter of fact. Thus, agreement is void when: (1) both the parties to an agreement are mistaken, (2) their mistake is as to a matter of fact, and (3) the fact about which they are mistaken is essential to the agreement. Further, it is pertinent to note that a mistake, in order to invalidate a contract, should be a mistake of fact and not a mistake of law. Furthermore, where only one party to the contract is under mistake of fact, and the other party is not, the contract is not voidable merely for such reason .

101. Mr. A entered into an agreement to sell his bicycle which had been kept unused in his attic for a year, to Mr. B, at an agreed price. However, neither party was aware that at the time of entering into the agreement, the bicycle had already been destroyed by a fire in the attic. In the given situation, which of the following statements is true?

(a) The agreement is void as both parties were under a mistake as to a matter of fact essential to the agreement.

(b) The agreement is void as both parties were under a mistake as to a law in force in India.

(c) The agreement is not voidable as only one of the parties was under a mistake as to a matter of fact.

(d) The agreement is not voidable as the promise made under the agreement had not been performed.

Sol. (a) The agreement is void as both parties were under a mistake as to a matter of fact essential to the agreement. When parties to a contract are under a 'mistake' regarding an important fact related to such contract, it may affect the contract in two ways. It may, firstly, defeat the consent altogether that the parties are supposed to have given, that is to say, the consent is unreal. Secondly, the mistake may mislead the parties as to the purpose which they had contemplated.

102. Ms. X and Ms. Y entered into a contract of sale of an article, while reeling under the erroneous belief that the sale of the article, which was the subject-matter of the agreement, was permitted by the law in force in India. In the given situation, which of the following statements is true?

(a) The contract is valid.

(b) The contract is voidable at the option of Ms. X.

(c) The contract is voidable at the option of Ms. Y.

(d) The contract is not voidable.

Sol. (d) Both Statements a and b are correct and thus, option d is the right answer. When parties to a contract are under a 'mistake' regarding an important fact related to such contract, it may affect the contract in two ways. It may, firstly, defeat the consent altogether that the parties are supposed to have given, that is to say, the consent is unreal. Secondly, the mistake may mislead the parties as to the purpose which they had contemplated.

103. Mr. J entered into an agreement with Mr. K for the sale of Mr. J's 'club'. At the time of entering into the agreement, while Mr. J believed that he was agreeing to sell his golf club, Mr. K believed that he was agreeing to buy a clubhouse owned by Mr. J. The agreement is void because

(a) Mistake of fact defeated the consent of the parties.

(b) Mistake of fact mislead the parties as to the purpose of the contract.

(c) Mistake of fact was regarding the identity of parties.

(d) Both (a) and (b)

Sol. (d) Both Statements a and b are correct. When parties to a contract are under a 'mistake' regarding an important fact related to such contract, it may affect the contract in two ways. It may, firstly, defeat the consent altogether that the parties are supposed to have given, that is to say, the consent is unreal. Secondly, the mistake may mislead the parties as to the purpose which they had contemplated.

104. Mr. D appointed Mr. K to manage the cultivation of his land as he was unable to manage it himself due to his advanced age. Mr. K agreed to manage the cultivation of Mr. D's land if he granted Mr. K a lease of the said land. Mr. D agreed to the same and signed a deed which was, unknown to both parties, a gift deed of the land and not a lease deed. In the given situation, which of the following statements is true?

(a) Mr. D and Mr. K were reeling under a mistake as to a matter of fact essential to the agreement.

(b) Mr. D and Mr. K were reeling under a mistake as to a matter of law essential to the agreement.

(c) Mr. D was reeling under a mistake as to a matter of fact essential to the agreement.

(d) Mr. D was reeling under a mistake as to a matter of law essential to the agreement.

Sol. (a) Mr. D and Mr. K were reeling under a mistake as to a matter of fact essential to the agreement. Since the mistake mislead the parties as to the purpose which they had contemplated, the agreement is void.

105. Ms. X and Ms. Y entered into a contract of sale of an article which was agreed to be shipped by Ms. X in a ship named. The Cruiser' and delivered to Ms. Y on an agreed date. Mr. X shipped the said article by a different ship named 'The Mariner', without informing Ms. Y and the article was delivered to Ms. Y on the agreed date. In the given situation, which of the following statements is true?

(a) The agreement is void as both parties were under a mistake as to a matter of fact essential to the agreement.

(b) The agreement is void as both parties were under a mistake as to a law in force in India.

(c) The agreement is valid as both parties were under a mistake as to a matter of fact not essential to the agreement.

(d) The agreement is valid as both parties were under a mistake as to a matter of fact essential to the agreement.

Sol. (c) The agreement is valid as both parties were under a mistake as to a matter of fact not essential to the agreement. Where the mistake does not defeat consent, but only misleads the parties, i.e., where both parties to an agreement are under a mistake as to a matter of fact essential to the agreement, the agreement is void. However, if the mistake is concerning an erroneous opinion regarding the value of the subject-matter of the agreement, it is not a mistake as to a matter of fact.

Section C : Logical Reasoning

XXII. Students decide to attend college for several reasons. These reasons include career opportunities and financial stability, intellectual growth, a time for self-discovery, norms, obligations, and social opportunities. Outside demands in society, such as technology changes, and increased educational demands also drive the need for more students to attend college. The students then spend the next few years trying to discover a path and find their way so they can become successful. The transition to college presents students with many new challenges, including increased academic demands, less time with family members, interpersonal problems with roommates and romantic interests, and financial stress. Competitive academic work and uncertainty about future employment and professional career were also noted as sources of stress. The transition to college represents a process characterised by change, ambiguity, and adjustment across all of life's domains. The transition towards independence and self-sufficiency has been characterised as 'stress arousing' and 'anxiety-provoking' by many college students. Failure to accomplish and develop these characteristics of development and maintain independence may result in life dissatisfaction. Emerging adulthood has also been noted to augment college student's vulnerability to stress. Many students experience their first symptoms of depression and anxiety during this time, but a growing problem is that college campuses do not have enough resources to help all of these students. It has been noted that 75% to 80% of college students are moderately stressed and 10% to 12% are severely stressed.

106. What according to you is the objective of the study of the present paragraph?

(a) To map the various stages of pressure points of adulthood in the process of education.

(b) To narrate the anti-family agenda in the current education system.

(c) To pinpoint the obstacles targeted against meritorious students.

(d) All of the above

Sol. (a) From given paragraph, the main objective of the study to map the various stages of pressure points of adulthood in the proccess of education.

107. Which factors as per the author cause more stress amongst college students?

(a) Pressure from parents and society towards greater educational needs and increased competitive academic work.

(b) Failure to develop successful romantic interests, financial constraints and interpersonal issues with roommates.

(c) Failure to adapt to the transition to college life and to adjust various life domains in tune with needs and requirements of college life.

(d) Inability to manage time constraints and the uncertainty pertaining to their future.

Sol. (c) According to the author cause more stress amongst college students is failure to adapt to the transition to college life and to adjust various life domains in tune with needs and requirements of college life.

108. Which of the following fall closest to the underlying assumption in the present study?

(a) Problem-solving ability amongst college students is negatively associated with symptoms of depression and anxiety.

(b) Students lean towards unhealthy coping skills in order to try to lower the stress that they experience

(c) Romantic interest is an anti-dote for stress amongst the students in the colleges.

(d) Stress is subjective for each student.

Sol. (a) Best assumption in the present study is to problem solving ability amongst college students is negatively associated with symptoms of depression and anxiety.

109. Suggest a suitable title for the paragraph from amongst the given titles:

(a) Triumph and Turbulence of College Education System

(b) Negative impact of College Education System

(c) Negligence of Stress Management by parents

(d) Unemployment and Mental Instability

Sol. (a) A suitable title for the paragraph is 'Triumph and Turbulence of College Education System'.

110. With reference to the above paragraph, which of the following offers the most plausible solutions as a coping up mechanism for college students?

(a) Individual students should approach counsellors for coping up with stress.

(b) Keeping in view that large number of students are experiencing stress, colleges must take steps reduce course curriculum and peer pressures.

(c) College authorities shall provide access to counselling and every student experiencing stress must engage in some form of coping mechanism to alleviate stress.

(d) The students must learn to differentiate between short-term and long-term stress.

Sol. (c) The most plausible solutions as a coping up mechanism for college students is college authorities shall provide access to counselling and every student experiencing stress must engage in some form of coping mechanism to alleviate stress.

XXIII. Under the COVID-19 outbreak, universities and schools around the world had suspended face-to-face classes to prevent the rapid spread of the virus among students and staff. This sudden disruption to face-to-face education reshaped pedagogical practices and led to the rapid adoption of online teaching among universities. Subsequently, academics working at universities, at the frontline of those changes, faced enormous levels of pressure and disturbance to their professional roles and practices. For those without sufficient knowledge or experience for effective online teaching, this sudden transition was particularly challenging. In normal circumstances, designing an online course follows a systematic instructional design process with careful consideration of the unique characteristics of target learner groups and the chosen instructional medium. During the rapid adoption of online teaching in response to COVID - 19, however, systematic instructional design procedures and team-based support for course development and preparation were unavailable. Instead individual academics were given the challenge alone to teach online with a limited level of support and guidance from their school or university-the task was even more difficult in this situation where they were remotely working from home.

111. The objective behind the information furnished in the passage is

(a) To examine the experiences faced by the teachers because of the sudden transition from offline to online mode of teaching due to outbreak of COVID-19.

(b) To identify the differences between the online and offline mode of teaching.

(c) To reveal the side-effects of COVID-19.

(d) To understand the need to be able to cope up with crisis like situations even in the educational sector.

Sol. (a) The objective behind the information furnished in the passage is to examine the experiences faced by the teachers because of the sudden transition from offline to online mode of teaching due to outbreak of COVID-19.

112. Based on the ideas presented in the paragraph, it will not be possible to draw out useful recommendations for situations like the pandemic, unless:

(a) The factors required to contribute to quality education by online and offline modes are examined.

(b) Knowledge about the infrastructural availability in the schools or universities is crucial.

(c) The faculty is given adequate training and experience in providing online education is taken into consideration. .

(d) A detailed analysis of the comparative performance in the online and offline modes is done.

Sol. (c) Based on the ideas presented in the paragraph, it will not be possible to draw out useful recommendations for situations like the pandemic, unless the faculty is given adequate training and experience in providing online education is taken into consideration.

113. What can be most conveniently inferred from the given paragraph?

(a) Whether online or face-to-face, university teaching activity is a genuinely complex task that involves multiple elements of interlinked activity systems.

(b) It has been more challenging for both individual academics and institutions to quickly adopt to online teaching during the COVID-19 Pandemic.

(c) The object of the online teaching activity systems created a fundamental contradiction with the object of the previous teaching activity systems.

(d) All of the above

Sol. (d) All the given options are most conveniently inferred from the given paragraph.

114. What suitable policy decision should be devised by the administrators of the schools and the universities, in the light of the facts presented in the paragraph?

(a) There must be an insight into the complexity of online teaching and need to work for the capacity building of the teachers during such extra ordinary times and there is a greater need to create a teacher community and foster collaborative teaching relationships among the members, even if it takes time.

(b) The faculty members must be oriented towards the lasting changes brought about to their roles and identities in teaching.

(c) It is time to develop a comprehensive understanding of the challenges experienced by individual academics and the changes created by those academics.

(d) There is a need to develop infrastructure in schools and universities.

Sol. (a) Most suitable policy decision from given paragraph, there must be an insight into the complexity of online teaching and need to work for the capacity building of the teachers during such extra ordinary times and there is a greater need to create a teacher community and foster collaborative teaching relationships among the members, even if it takes time.

115. Which of the following points most closely supports the fact that the present education system lacks the structure to sustain effective teaching during and after the periods of lockdown ?

(a) There are inadequate applications and platforms for effective online teaching.

(b) Shift from offline to online was faced with resistance.

(c) The academia's long-established roles and identities have been completely altered by the pandemic.

(d) The students are interested in online examinations and schools and universities are finding it difficult to shift to offline examination mode.

Sol. (c) The academia's long established roles and identities have been completely altered by the pandemic is most closely points to supports the fact that the present education system locks the structure to sustain effective teaching during and after the periods of lockdown.

XXIV. Biodiversity is being lost at a rate not seen since the last mass extinction. But the United Nations decade-old plan to slow down and eventually stop the decline of species and ecosystems by 2020 has failed. Most of the plan's 20 targets - known as the Aichi Biodiversity Targets - have not been met. The Aichi targets are part of an international agreement called the UN Convention on Biological Diversity, and member states are now finalising replacements for them. Currently referred to as the post-2020 Global Biodiversity Framework (GBF), its draft was published in July 2021. It aims to slow down the rate of biodiversity loss by 2030. And by 2050, biodiversity will be *"valued, conserved, restored and wisely used, maintaining ecosystem services, sustaining a healthy planet and delivering benefits essential for all people"*. The GBF is a comprehensive plan. But success will require systemic change across public policy. That is both a strength and a weakness. If systemic change can be implemented, it will lead to real change. But if it cannot, there's no plan B. This has led some researchers to argue that one target or number should be prioritised and defined in a way that is clear to the public and to policy makers. It would be biodiversity's equivalent of the 2°C climate target.

116. As per the passage, which of the following is a challenge for implementation of the post-2020 Global Biodiversity Framework (GBF)?

(a) Unfulfillment of the pre-2020 global biodiversity targets

(b) Clarity of action plan for the society and government

(c) Threat of mass extinction

(d) Failure of plan to save ecosystems

Sol. (b) Clarity of action plan for the society and government is a challenge for implementation of the post -2020 Global Biodiversity Framework (GBF).

117. According to the passage, why do some researchers advocate that one biodiversity target be prioritised?

(a) Systemic policy change is difficult to implement

(b) Post-2020 Global Biodiversity Framework (GBF) is comprehensive

(c) The 2° C climate target needs to be prioritised

(d) Biodiversity needs to be valued, conserved, restored and wisely used

Sol. (a) According to the passage, researchers advocate that one biodiversity target be prioritised because systemic policy change is difficult to implement.

118. Which of the following is correct expression of the author's opinion as stated in passage?

(a) Implementation of the post-2020 Global Biodiversity Framework (GBF) allows no middle ground for success or failure.

(b) It is high time that countries re-evaluate the progress in achieving biodiversity targets.

(c) Biodiversity conservation should be prioritised over climate change at the global level.

(d) The post-2020 Global Biodiversity Framework (GBF) is the best way to prevent mass extinction.

Sol. (a) Correct expression of the author's opinion as stated in passage is implementation of the post -2020 Global Biodiversity Framework (GBF) allows no middle ground for success or failure.

119. Which of the following is the central theme of the above passage?

(a) The reason for failure of biodiversity conservation efforts at global level

(b) The inter-relationship between biodiversity conservation and climate change

(c) The future of biodiversity conservation efforts at global level
(d) The role of United Nations in biodiversity conservation at global level

Sol. (c) The central theme of the given passage is 'The future of biodiversity conservation efforts at global level'.

120. Which of the following can be inferred from the above passage?
(a) The holistic nature of the post-2020 Global Biodiversity Framework (GBF) is a boon.
(b) The holistic nature of the post-2020 Global Biodiversity Framework (GBF) is a bane.
(c) The holistic nature of the post-2020 Global Biodiversity Framework (GBF) can be a boon or a bane.
(d) The post-2020 Global Biodiversity Framework (GBF) includes the 2°C climate target.

Sol. (c) 'The holistic nature of the post -2020 Global Biodiversity Framework (GBF) can be a boon or a bane' can be inferred from the given passage.

XXV. An unintended and unjust consequence of the Protection of Children from Sexual Offences Act, 2012 is its widespread persecution of teenage lovers. This law raised the age of consent from 16 to 18 years, while defining persons below 18 years as children. Consequently, when two 16-year-olds are romantically and sexually involved, but the girl's family doesn't approve the affair and files a police complaint, her consent has zero legal validity. And the consensual relationship morphs into a case of statutory rape. The Allahabad High Court has indicated how its "conscience" is concerned by such severe POCSO provisions being drawn by teenage lovers simply on the basis of family disapproval. The High Courts of Delhi, Madras and others have made similar observations in recent years and also pointed to amendments to the law that can help reduce its injustices. One suggestion that has gathered broad support is to push back both the cut-off for childhood and the age of consent to 16 years. Given that the NCRB data shows around half of POCSO cases falling in the 16-18 years age group, such an amendment is overdue. Minimising the prosecution of consensual romances would also leave a logjammed system with more space to pursue actual sexual assault cases. The broader goal here is respecting the rights of adolescents and young adults. Their romantic and sexual autonomy needs greatly increased recognition in India.

121. "Minimising the prosecution of consensual romances would also leave a logjammed system with more space to pursue actual sexual assault cases."
In the context of the statement, which of the following strengthens the author's opinion?
(a) There are many unreported sexual assault cases.
(b) Speedy prosecution of sexual assault cases is desirable.
(c) Consensual romance, in some cases, can amount to sexual assault.
(d) Sexual assault and rape are different.

Sol. (a) In the context of given statement, the author's opinion is there are many unreported sexual assault cases.

122. What has the author conveyed regarding the prosecution of statutory rape in India? .
(a) Statutory rape does not violate the romantic and sexual autonomy of young adults.
(b) Statutory rape must be met with stricter punishment.
(c) Statutory rape must be abolished.
(d) Statutory rape is a relic of Victorian morality.

Sol. (a) The author conveyed regarding the prosecution of statutory rape in India as statutory rape does not violate the romantic and sexual autonomy of young adults.

123. As per the above passage, which of the following does not correctly represent the author's view regarding the widespread persecution of teenage lovers under the POCSO Act?

(a) Teenagers have the right to love as much as adults.

(b) Police complaints of teenage lovers may lead to their harassment.

(c) Consent of minor girls do not have legal validity.

(d) Consent of minor girls have legal validity.

Sol. (d) 'Consent of minor girls have legal validity' does not correctly represent the author's view regarding the widespread persecution of teenage lovers under the POCSO Act.

124. In the above passage, which of the following has concerned the "conscience" of the Allahabad High Court?

(a) Carelessness of teenage lovers.

(b) Threat to the safety of teenage lovers.

(c) Impact on mental health of teenage lovers.

(d) Harassment of teenage lovers by their families.

Sol. (d) Harassment of teenage lovers by their families' has concerned the 'conscience' of the Allahabad High Court.

125. As per the above passage, which of the following is a major challenge in implementation of the POCSO Act?

(a) Speedy prosecution of cases.

(b) Respecting the rights of adolescents and young adults .

(c) Counselling of adolescents and young adults.

(d) Imposition of stringent punishment.

Sol. (c) Counselling of adolescents and young adults is a major challenge in implementation of the POCSO Act.

XXVI. A Madras High Court Judge's suggestion to amend the Constitution of India mandating that every citizen also has a duty to laugh comes as a whiff of fresh air - something the country has been gasping for, of late. Justice GR Swaminathan of the Madurai Bench has a remarkably refined sense of humour, but in quashing an FIR against a man arrested for an innocuous social media post, his insightful observations only highlight the idiocy and absurdity that surround the growth and normalisation of the offence-taking tribe. Written from the perspective of cartoonists and satirists, the judgement draws attention to how what ought to be a reasonable understanding of a situation is increasingly being influenced by impulses that border on the irrational and amount to an abuse of the legal process. The petitioner tried tongue-in-cheek wordplay while captioning photographs after a sight-seeing trip with family: 'Trip to Sirumalai for shooting practice'. For the police, it appeared as a threat to wage war, though the Judicial Magistrate refused remand. 'Laugh at what?' is a serious question, the Judge said, using the 'holy cow' as a metaphor, which varies from person to person, region to region. Being funny is one thing, the Judge righty states, and poking fun at another is different altogether. Those who have been at the receiving end for their attempt at humour can draw strength from the ruling, but then, a creative process facing combative opposition because of its very nature is anything but funny.

126 What is the central idea in the passage as conveyed by the author?

(a) People need to be sensitive towards others' sensibilities.

(b) Humour is often used as a garb to offend others .

(c) There is an unwelcome decrease in people's sense of humour.

(d) Judiciary should use humour to make judgements understandable to laypersons.

Sol. (c) 'There is an unwelcome decrease in people's sense of humour' is the central idea in the passage as conveyed by the author.

127. According to the given passage, which of the following statements is true?

(a) Social media often popularised insensitive and offensive posts.

(b) It should be a right of every person to poke fun at others.

(c) Creative expressions are bound to be offensive to some persons.

(d) Every humorous expression should be understood reasonably and rationally.

Sol. (d) According to the given passage, 'Every humorous expression should be understood reasonably and rationally' is true statement.

128. According to the given passage, which of the following statements is not true?

(a) Each expression should be understood according to its context.

(b) The word 'shooting' used in a sentence is indicative of waging war.

(c) Legal process can be abused if the authorities act on their irrational impulses.

(d) The expression 'holy cow' bears different meanings for different people.

Sol. (b) According to the given passage, 'The word 'shooting' used in a sentence is indicative of waging war is not true statement.

129. As per the passage, which of the following approaches can reduce the increasing 'idiocy and absurdity' in responding to expressions made in jest?

(a) Apologising upon hurting another person's sentiments.

(b) Avoiding the use of controversial words and expressions.

(c) Using humour as a means to mitigate conflict.

(d) Understanding the difference between being funny and poking fun at another person.

Sol. (d) As per the passage, understanding the difference between being funny and poking fun at another person' can reduce the increasing idiocy and absurdity' is responding to expressions made in jest.

130. "Those who have been at the receiving end for their attempt at humour can draw strength from the ruling, but then, a creative process facing combative opposition because of its very nature is anything but funny."

Which of the following conclusions can be drawn from the above statement?

(a) Creativity and conflict go hand-in-hand.

(b) Creative freedom should not be curbed unreasonably.

(c) Creative expressions are strengthened due to challenges faced by their authors.

(d) Creativity often leads to conflict.

Sol. (b) 'Creative freedom should not be curbed unreasonably' can be drawn from the above statement.

XXVII. Two recent developments have brought India's reliance on fossil fuel into sharp focus. The Russia-Ukraine conflict and the consequent surge in crude oil prices roiled the economy. Separately, the most recent IPCC report on climate highlighted the energy sector's large contribution to global warming. Both these developments need to be located in the context of India's pledge to get to net zero carbon emissions by 2070. Meeting this pledge requires an overhaul of both the logistics and electricity sectors to reduce reliance on fossil fuels.

Transitioning to renewables in energy is an important part of the solution. Within renewables, solar energy has been lavished with policy support. However, it won't be enough to meet the targets. Anil Kakodkar, former chairman of Atomic Energy Commission, had written that India can't meet its net-zero commitment without nuclear power. He's right. It's an area where India was off to an early start, developed relatively high indigenous capabilities in relation to other sectors, but subsequently let the ball drop. Today, nuclear power contributes a mere 3% of the total electricity generated, and has a capacity of 6780 MW. After the early euphoria of the India-United States civil nuclear deal, progress has been disappointing. The deal did open the pathway to a stable supply of uranium ore from Kazakhstan and Canada. However, the design of the subsequent bill on civil liability for nuclear damage killed the prospect of participation of Western firms. India's main partner today is Russia, which side stepped the bill through inter-government agreements.

131. What is the central idea in the passage as conveyed by the author?

(a) India needs to increase use of nuclear power.
(b) India needs to increase production of fossil fuels.
(c) India needs to enter into multilateral agreements addressing use of nuclear power.
(d) Nuclear energy is a renewable source of power.

Sol. (a) India needs to increase use of nuclear power' is the central idea of the passage as conveyed by the author.

132. According to the author, which of the following measures will not help India achieve its pledge of net zero carbon emissions by 2070?

(a) Logistical changes
(b) Changes in electricity sector
(c) Reduction in use of solar power
(d) Increase in use of nuclear power

Sol. (c) 'Reduction in use of solar power' will not help India achieve its pledge of net zero carbon emissions by 2070.

133. According to the author, which of the following is not the effect of India's reliance on fossil fuels?

(a) Global warming
(b) Increase in crude oil prices
(c) Relations with Middle East
(d) Less reliance on renewable sources of power

Sol. (c) 'Relations with middle East' is not the effect of India's reliance on fossil fuels.

134. According to the author, which of the following is the effect of the India-United States civil nuclear deal?

(a) Export-Import target with United States
(b) Removal of bottlenecks for self-reliance in power generation
(c) Nuclear Defence Pact with Kazakhstan
(d) Self-reliance in Solar Power

Sol. (b) According to the author, 'Removal of bottlenecks for self-reliance in power generation' is the effect of the India-United States civil nuclear deal.

135. According to the author, Western firms lost the opportunity of doing business in the nuclear production in India because.

(a) They had to pay hefty penalties for delay in supply
(b) They do not find nuclear power profitable
(c) They do not agree with India's place of nuclear plants
(d) They failed to circumvent internal laws by other bilateral instruments

Sol. (d) According to the author, Western firms lost the opportunity of doing business in the nuclear production in India because they failed to circumvent internal laws by other bilateral instruments.

Section D : Quantitative Techniques

XXVIII. As per a survey conducted in a college out of total students enrolled i.e., 3000 in 2020-21, 1700 were girls and 1300 were boys. Data regarding students opting for various courses *viz* Non-Medical, Medical, Commerce, Arts and Fine Arts showed that 25% of the enrolled students opted Non-Medical and the percentage of girls in Non-Medical was 30% of the total number of girls, 15% of the total students opted for Medical and the percentage of girls who opted Medical was 18% of the total number of girls, 25% of the total students opted Arts but the percentage of girls who opted for Arts was 15% of the total number of girls, 16% of the total students opted Commerce and the percentage of girls who opted Commerce was 17% of the total number of girls, and, 19% of the total students opted Fine Arts and the percentage of girls who opted Fine Arts was 20% of the total number of girls.

136. How many girls have opted Non-Medical?

(a) 440 (b) 365 (c) 530 (d) 510

137. Girls have outnumbered boys in Fine Arts. How many girls in Fine Arts are more than the boys, as a percentage of total number of boys in Fine Arts?

(a) 49.62% (b) 47.82%
(c) 51.23% (d) 50.89%

138. Which of the following courses have been opted by maximum number of boys?

(a) Non-Medical (b) Arts
(c) Fine Arts (d) Commerce

139. Which of the following courses have been opted by minimum number of boys?

(a) Medical (b) Fine Arts
(c) Commerce (d) Non-Medical

140. What is the ratio among boys and girls for Non-Medical?

(a) 3 : 17 (b) 17 : 8
(c) 8 : 17 (d) 17 : 3

Sol. (Q. Nos. 136-140) *According to the given information.*

Total number of students = 3000

Total number of girls = 1700

Total number of boys = 1300

Total number of students who opted Non-Medical $= 3000 \times \frac{25}{100} = 750$

Total number of girls who opted Non-Medical

$= 1700 \times \frac{30}{100} = 510$

Total number of boys who opted Non-Medical

$= 750 - 510 = 240$

Total number of students who opted Medical

$= 3000 \times \frac{15}{100} = 450$

Total number of girls who opted Medical

$= 1700 \times \frac{18}{100} = 306$

Total number of boys who opted Medical

$= 450 - 306 = 144$

Total number of students who opted Arts

$= 3000 \times \frac{25}{100} = 750$

Total number of girls who opted Arts

$= 1700 \times \frac{15}{100} = 255$

Total number of boys who opted Arts

$= 750 - 255 = 495$

Total number of students who opted commerce $= 3000 \times \frac{16}{100} = 480$

Total number of girls who opted commerce

$= 1700 \times \frac{17}{100} = 289$

Total number of boys who opted commerce $= 480 - 289 = 191$

Total number of students who opted Fine Arts $= 3000 \times \frac{19}{100} = 570$

Total number of girls who opted Fine Arts $= 1700 \times \frac{20}{100} = 340$

Total number of boys who opted Fine Arts $= 570 - 340 = 230$

Courses	Girls = 1700	Boys = 1300	Total = 3000
Non-Medical	510	240	750
Medical	306	144	450
Commerce	289	191	480
Arts	255	495	750
Fine Arts	340	230	570

136. (d) Total number of girls who opted Non-Medical = 510

137. (b) Required percentage

$$= \frac{340 - 230}{230} \times 100 = 47.82\%$$

138. (b) Course opted by maximum number of boys = Arts = 495

139. (a) Course opted by minimum number of boys = Medical = 144

140. (c) Number of boys who opted Non-Medical = 240

Number of girls who opted Non-Medical = 510

Required ratio $= 240 : 510$
$= 24 : 51 = 8 : 17$

XXIX. An Indian company, having its registered office at Gurugram, is engaged in manufacturing of consumer goods at Noida. The goods manufactured by the company are sold in Indian market and exported to Europe. Company produces five products namely 'P', 'Q', 'R', 'S' and 'T'. Total production of the company for the financial year 2021-22 is 3000 tonnes and the turnover of the company is ₹ 50 million.

An analysis of the production and net revenue generation shows that production of product 'P' is 21% of the total production and 18% of the turnover is attributable to product 'P'; production of 'Q' is 16% of the total production and 17% of the turnover is attributable to 'Q'; 'R' accounts for 18% of the total production and 20% of the turnover; 'S' accounts for 20% of the total production and 25% of the turnover, and; 'T' accounts for 25% of total production and 20% of turnover.

141. What is the percentage of profit earned from sale of 'R', if the expenditure incurred on production of 'R' is ₹ 15000 per tonne?

(a) 20% (b) 23.46%
(c) 26.55% (d) 25%

142. Which product has the highest selling price per tonne?

(a) Q (b) R
(c) S (d) T

143. How much loss is incurred to company, if the expenditure on production of 'T' was ₹ 20000 per tonne?

(a) 5 million (b) 10 million
(c) 4 million (d) 7 million

144. What percentage of turnover of 'R' has to turnover of 'T'?

(a) 100% (b) 75%
(c) 50% (d) 60%

145. What is the average selling price per tonne of all products taken together?

(a) ₹ 17488 (b) ₹ 17667
(c) ₹ 18667 (d) ₹ 16667

Sol. (Q. Nos. 141-145) According to the given passage,

Total production of the company
= 3000 tonnes

Total turnovers of the company
= ₹ 50 million

Products	Production (in tonnes)	Turnover (in million)
P	$3000 \times \frac{21}{100} = 630$	$50 \times \frac{18}{100} = ₹\,9$
Q	$3000 \times \frac{16}{100} = 480$	$50 \times \frac{17}{100} = ₹\,8.5$
R	$3000 \times \frac{18}{100} = 540$	$50 \times \frac{20}{100} = ₹\,10$
S	$3000 \times \frac{20}{100} = 600$	$50 \times \frac{25}{100} = ₹\,12.5$
T	$3000 \times \frac{25}{100} = 750$	$50 \times \frac{20}{100} = ₹\,10$

141. (b) Total expenditure of product

$R = 540 \times 15000 = ₹\,8100000$

Total turnover of product $R = ₹\,10000000$

Required profit percentage

$= \frac{10000000 - 8100000}{8100000} \times 100 = 23.46\%$

142. (c) For Q, selling price

$= \frac{8.5 \text{ million}}{480} = \frac{8500000}{480} = ₹\,17708.33$

For R, selling price

$= \frac{10 \text{ million}}{540} = \frac{10000000}{540} = ₹\,18518.51$

For S, selling price

$= \frac{12.5 \text{ million}}{600} = \frac{12500000}{600} = ₹\,20833.33$

For T, selling price

$= \frac{10 \text{ million}}{750} = \frac{10000000}{750} = ₹\,13333.33$

Hence, product S has the highest selling price per tonne.

143. (a) Total expenditure on production of

$T = 750 \times 20000 = ₹\,15000000$

Total turnover of product $T = ₹\,10$ million

$= ₹\,10000000$

$\therefore$ Required loss $= 15000000 - 10000000$

$= ₹\,5000000$

$= ₹\,5$ million

144. (a) $\because$ Required percentage

$= \frac{₹\,10 \text{ million}}{₹\,10 \text{ million}} \times 100$

$= 100\%$

145. (d) $\because$ Required average

$$= \frac{\frac{9 \text{ million}}{630} + 17708.33 + 18518.51 + 20833.3 + 13333.33}{5}$$

$= \frac{84679.18}{5} = ₹\,16935.35 \approx ₹\,16667$

XXX. In an organisation the total number of employees working in various Departments *viz*. IT, Marketing, Purchase, 'HR, Accounts and Production are 4500. The information regarding department wise percentage of employees was collected and also record about gender ratio of employees was prepared. 18% of total number of employees work in IT department and ratio of males to females in IT department is 2 : 1. In Marketing, ratio of males to females is 2 : 3 and number of employees engaged in marketing is 20% of the total employment. 12% of the total numbers of workers are running the HR department and the ratio of males to females in this department is 5 : 1. The ratio of males to females in production department is 3 : 2 and total number of persons employed in this department is 15% of the total workforce. The number of persons occupied in purchase and accounts department is 24% and 11% respectively of the total number of workers. Gender Ratio (ratio of males to females) in Purchase department is 1 : 1 and in Accounts is 1 : 2.

146. How many females are employed in Purchase department?

(a) 450 (b) 540 (c) 495 (d) 595

147. How many employees are working in IT and Accounts departments together?

(a) 1702 (b) 1646 (c) 1766 (d) 1305

148. What is the ratio of total number of males to total number of females working in all the departments put together?

(a) 63 : 41 (b) 19 : 27 (c) 41 : 34 (d) 34 : 41

149. Number of females in Marketing Department forms what percentage of the total number of employees in the organisation?

(a) 8% (b) 7% (c) 12% (d) 10%

150. What is the ratio of number of males in Marketing Department to the number of males in HR department?

(a) 4 : 5 (b) 5 : 4
(c) 7 : 3 (d) 6 : 7

Sol. (Q. Nos. 146-150) *According to the given passage,*

Total number of employees = 4500

Departments	Number of employees	Total males	Total females
IT	$4500 \times \frac{18}{100} = 810$	$810 \times \frac{2}{3} = 270 \times 2 = 540$	$810 - 540 = 270$
Marketing	$4500 \times \frac{20}{100} = 900$	$900 \times \frac{2}{5} = 180 \times 2 = 360$	$900 - 360 = 540$
HR	$4500 \times \frac{12}{100} = 540$	$540 \times \frac{5}{6} = 90 \times 5 = 450$	$540 - 450 = 90$
Purchase	$4500 \times \frac{24}{100} = 1080$	$1080 \times \frac{1}{2} = 540$	$1080 - 540 = 540$
Accounts	$4500 \times \frac{11}{100} = 495$	$495 \times \frac{1}{3} = 165$	$495 - 165 = 330$
Production	$4500 \times \frac{15}{100} = 675$	$675 \times \frac{3}{5} = 135 \times 3 = 405$	$675 - 405 = 270$

146. (b) 540 females are employed in purchase department.

147. (d) Total number of employees who working in IT and Accounts departments together

$= (810 + 495) = 1305$

148. (c) $\therefore$ Required ratio $= \frac{540 + 360 + 450 + 540 + 165 + 405}{270 + 540 + 90 + 540 + 330 + 270} = \frac{2460}{2040} = \frac{41}{34} = 41:34$

149. (c) $\therefore$ Required percentage $= \frac{540}{4500} \times 100 = 12\%$

150. (a) $\therefore$ Required ratio $= 360 : 450 = 4:5$

LEGAL APTITUDE

CHAPTER 01

LAW : ITS NATURE AND CLASSIFICATION

Law is a system of rules that are created and enforced through social or governmental institutions to regulate behaviour. Law as a system helps regulate and ensure that a community show respect and equality amongst themselves.

State-enforced laws can be made by a collective legislature or by a single legislator, resulting in statutes, by the executive through decrees and regulations or established by judges through precedent, normally in common law jurisdictions.

MEANING AND DEFINITIONS OF LAW

According to **Roscoe Pound**, "Law is the body of principles recognised or enforced by public and regular tribunals in the administration of justice".

According to **Austin**, "Law is the aggregate of the rules set by men as political superior or sovereign to men as politically subject".

In short, Law is the command of sovereign. It imposes a duty and duty is backed by a sanction. *He further said that there exists three elements in law*

(i) Command (ii) Duty (iii) Sanction

It is possible to describe law as the body of official rules and regulations, generally found in the constitutions, legislations, judicial opinions and the like, that is used to govern a society and to control the behaviour of its members, so law is a formal mechanism of social control.

Legal systems are particular ways of establishing and maintaining social order.

Nature of Law

- The word 'law' is difficult to define, particularly as it is used in many different ways. It contains, however, the concepts of orderliness, universality and objectivity. It is concerned with behaviour and not with causes and either contains an element of inevitability, e.g. scientific laws, such as the laws of gravity or of sanction, e.g. divine laws.
- It shapes politics, economics and society in numerous ways and serves as a social mediator of relations between people.
- In the narrower concept of law, there must be a set of rules which can be applied objectively with someone to enforce them.
- There have been many attempts to put these into a workable definition, some more successful than others. According to Salmond,
  - "Law consists of any principle which is recognised and enforced by the courts in the administration of justice".
  - "A body of rules for the guidance of human conduct which are imposed upon and enforced among the members of a given state".

Classification of Law

Sir John Salmond refers to eight types of law. *They are as follows*

1. Imperative Law

"It means a rule of action imposed upon mere by some authority which enforces obedience to it." In other words, it is a command enforced by some superior power either physically or in any other form of compulsion.

Following are the two types of imperative law

(i) **Divine Law** It consists of the command imposed by God upon men either by threats or punishments or by hope of his blessings.

(ii) **Human Law** It is the law by analogy.

2. Physical or Scientific Law

- Physical laws are expressions of the uniformities of nature and general principles that express regularity and harmony, which are observable in the activities and operations of universe.
- They are not the creation of men and cannot be changed by them. Human laws changes from time to time and from country to country but physical laws are invariable forever.
- The uniform actions of human beings, such as law of Psychology, also falls into this class. They express not what men ought to do, but what they do.

3. Practical or Technical Law

It consists of principles and rules for the attainment of certain ends, such as laws of health, laws of architecture. These rules guide us as to what we ought to do in order to attain certain ends, within this category, there are the laws of music and laws of style.

4. Natural or Moral Law

"By Nature or Moral law is meant the principles of natural right and wrong i.e. the principle of natural justice".

Natural law have been also called the following

(i) **Divine Law** i.e. commands of God imposed upon men.

(ii) **Law of Reason** i.e. being established by which the world is being governed.

(iii) **Unwritten Law** As being written not on brazen tablets or on pillars of stone but by the finger of nature in the heart of people.

(iv) **Eternal Law** It is being uncreated and invariable.

(v) **Moral Law** It is the expression of the principles of morality.

5. Conventional Law

It is the body of rules agreed upon and followed by the concerned parties to regulate their mutual conduct. It is a form of special law for the parties, which can be made valid or enforced through an agreement. A good example of conventional law is the laws of cricket or any other game, rules of club. *It has been further divided into two groups, which are as follows*

(i) Rules enforced by the parties themselves but not recognised by the state like, the rules of hockey.

(ii) Rules which are recognised and enforced by the state, like contract etc.

6. Customary Law

- Customary laws are those rules of customs that are habitually followed by the majority of persons subject to them in the belief of binding nature. According to **Salmond**, customary laws means "any rule of action which is actually observed by men", when a custom is firmly established.
- It is enforced by the authority of the state. Custom is not law itself but an important source of law. Only those customs acquired the force of law which are recognised by the courts.

7. International Law

- According to Hughes, "International law is the body of principles and rules which civilised states consider as binding upon them in their mutual relations." It can be defined as "the name of the body of customary and conventional rules, which are considered legally binding by civilised states in their intercourse with each other".
- According to **Salmond**, "It consists of those rules which the sovereign states have agreed to observe in their dealings with one another." International agreements are of two types, they are either expressed or implied. Expressed agreements are contained in treaties and conventions; while the implied agreements are to be found in the customs or practice of the state.

International laws are divided into two types

(i) **Public International Law** It prevails universally in all over the world.

(ii) **Private International Law** It is enforced only between some of states.

8. Civil Law

It is the law of the states regarding the land. Civil law according to **Salmond** is "the law of the state or the law of the land, the law of lawyers and the law of courts." It is the positive law of the land, which means the law as it exists. It is backed by the force and might of the state for purpose of enforcement. Civil law differs from special law as the sitter applies only in special circumstances. The other term used for the civil law is municiple law and national law.

Sources of Law

The term 'sources of law' also refers to the sovereign or the state from which the law derives its force or validity.
Customs, entity, statute law etc, are the sources of law.

1. Customs

These are rules of behaviour which develop in a community without being deliberately invented. *There are two main types of customs*

(i) **General Customs** Historically, these are believed to have been very important in a way that they were effectively the basis of our common law. It is thought that following the Norman conquest (as the country was gradually brought under centralised government) the judges appointed by the kings to travel around the land making decisions in the king's name based at least some of their decisions were on the common custom.

(ii) **Local Customs** This is the term used where a person claims that he is entitled to some local right, such as a right of way or a right to use land in a particular way, because this what has always happened locally. Such customs are an exceptions to the general common law of land and will only operate in that particular area. Since there were exceptions to the general common law, the judges from the earliest times, established a series of rigorous test or hurdles that had to be passed before they recognised any local custom.

2. **Equity**

- The word 'Equity' has a meaning of 'fairness'. Equity developed because of problems in Common law.
- Major problem was the fact that the only remedy the common law courts could give was 'damages' which is an order that defendant pay a sum of money to the plaintiff by way of compensation.
- In some cases, this would not be the best method of putting matters right between the parties. e.g. in a case of trespass to land, where perhaps the defendant had built on his neighbour's land, the building would still be there and the plaintiff would have lost the use of that part of his land.
- In such a situation, the plaintiff would probably prefer to have the building removed, rather than be given money in compensation.

3. **Case Law**

- In the English Common Law system, case law develops as courts hear disagreement between parties, making a decision as to what the law should be in a particular case. These decisions create precedents.
- The doctrine of judicial precedents operates by ensuring that a previous court's decision is followed by another court when deciding a subsequent legal case, provided certain rules for extracting the legal principle from the earlier case and that principle applies to the case which are to be followed by that case.

4. **Statute Law**

- Statute law comprises legislation that made by the House of Parliament. Legislation may be a primary legislation which starts as a Bill and become an Act of Parliament or it may be secondary or delegated legislation, drafted by the Government department and enacted under powers given by primary piece of legislation.
- The legal system defines a set of rules, conducts or/and procedures which are necessary for establishing and maintaining a disciplined society. It has been formulated by custom, agreement and national interests and is enforced through a set of institutions.
- The Indian Legal system is one of the oldest and longest written set of laws in the world. Our legal system has its roots in the legislature formulated during the British Raj era. The Indian legal system is formulated baring in mind the diversity of the country and with due respect to the religion, customs and traditions of the people.

Jurisprudence

Jurisprudence is the study of Law. It is a type of Science that explores the creation, application and enforcement of law. Jurisprudence is the study of theories and philosophies regarding law. The word 'Jurisprudence' is derived from the Latin phrase Juris Prudential. This means 'Knowledge of Law'.

Definitions of Jurisprudence

In the words of **Austin**, "Jurisprudence is concerned with positive law".

According to **Salmond**, "Jurisprudence is the Science of law. Here, law stands for law of land or Civil Law".

Keeton considered "Jurisprudence as the study and systematic arrangement of the general principles of law".

Rosco Pound described "Jurisprudence as the Science of Law".

LAW COMMISSION OF INDIA

Law in a society should be dynamic not as a static object as in black letter law. Society continue in changing nature so as the law of the society.

The first such commission was established in 1834 under the Charter Act of 1833 under the Chairmanship of Lord Macaulay which recommended codification of the Penal Code, the Criminal Procedure Code and a few other mattters.

The Government of India reacted favourably and established the First Law Commission of Independent India in 1955 with the Attorney-General of India, Mr MC Setalvad, as its Chairman.

Law Commission and its Chairman

Commission	Year	Chairman
Second Law Commission	1958-61	Mr Justice TV Venkatarama Aiyar
Third Law Commission	1961-64	Mr Justice JL Kapur
Fourth Law Commission	1964-68	Mr Justice JL Kapur
Fifth Law Commission	1968-71	Mr KVK Sundaram, ICS
Sixth Law Commission	1971-74	Mr Justice Dr PB Gajendragadkar
Seventh Law Commission	1974-77	Mr Justice Dr PB Gajendragadkar
Eighth Law Commission	1977-79	Mr Justice HR Khanna
Ninth Law Commission	1979-80	Mr Justice PV Dixit
Tenth Law Commission	1981-85	Justice KK Mathew
Eleventh Law Commission	1985-88	Justice DA Desai
Twelfth Law Commission	1988-91	Justice MP Thakkar
Thirteenth Law Commission	1991-94	Justice KN Singh
Fourteenth Law Commission	1995-97	Justice K Jayachandra Reddy
Fifteenth Law Commission	1997-2000	Justice BP Jeevan Reddy
Sixteenth Law Commission	2000-2001 2002-2003	Justice BP Jeevan Reddy Justice M Jagannadha Rao
Seventeenth Law Commission	2003-2006	Justice M Jagannadha Rao
Eighteenth Law Commission	2006-2009	Justice AR Lakshmanan
Nineteenth Law Commission	2009-2012	Justice PV Reddi
Twentieth Law Commission	2012-2015	Justice DK Jain
Twenty First Law Commission	2015-2018	Justice Balbir Singh Chauhan

Since then, twenty-one more law commissions have been appointed, each with a three-years term and with different terms of reference.

Review/Repeal of Obsolete Laws

- To identify laws which are no longer needed or relevant and can be immediately repealed.
- To identify laws which are in harmony with the existing climate of economic liberalisation which need no change.
- To identify laws which require changes or amendments and to make suggestions for their amendment.

- To consider in a wider perspective the sugges- tions for revision/amendment given by expert groups in various ministries/departments with a view to coordinating and harmonising them.
- To consider references made to it by ministries/departments in respect of legislation having bearing on the working of more than one ministry/department.
- To suggest suitable measures for quick redressal of citizens grievances, in the field of law.

Practice Exercise

1. The Source law classified by ...... and ..... .
(a) Salmond, Keeton (b) Salmond, Austin
(c) Keeton, Austin (d) Hobbes, Holland

2. Natural law means
(a) Principles of Common Law
(b) Principles of Constitutional Law
(c) Principles of Municipal Law
(d) Principles of Natural Justice

3. Customs which have the force of law are
(a) legal custom and conventional customs
(b) legal custom and constitutional customs
(c) legal custom and racial customs
(d) legal custom and material customs

4. According to analysts, jurisprudence is the study of
(a) Ideal law (b) Concrete law
(c) International law (d) Positive law

5. The kind of jurisprudence which deals with the law as it ought to be known as
(a) analytical jurisprudence
(b) historical jurisprudence
(c) ethical jurisprudence
(d) None of the above

6. Jurisprudence is derived from the word jurisprudence which is a
(a) German word
(b) Greek word
(c) Latin word
(d) Russian word

7. Particular jurisprudence is the science which examine
(a) actual and single system of law
(b) actual and double system of law
(c) actual and common system of law
(d) None of the above

8. The term 'common law' has three different meanings. Which of the following is not a meaning of the term common law?
(a) The body of law as made by judges through the determination of cases
(b) A legal system that is based on that of England
(c) Laws created by Parliament
(d) The system of law that emerged following the Norman Conquest in 1066

9. Who of the following was not a proponent of Natural law?
(a) Aristotle (b) Jeremy Bentham
(c) St Augustine (d) St Thomas Aquinas

10. Which of the following countries does not have a common law legal system?
(a) England
(b) Australia
(c) United States of America
(d) France

11. The term 'private law' refers to ....
(a) the body of laws that derive from the deciding of cases
(b) the body of laws that seeks to regulate the relationship between individuals
(c) the legal principle that states that a person has the right to privacy
(d) the body of laws that seeks to regulate the relationship between the state and its citizens

12. According to the text, what is wrong with the principle of universality?
(a) It fails to explain what's wrong with lying
(b) It permits the actions of principled fanatics
(c) It falsely claims that the central moral virtue is benevolence
(d) It makes the morality of actions solely a matter of their consequences

13. Regarding the system of equity, which one of the following statements is untrue?
- (a) If the common law and equity conflict, the common law prevails
- (b) Equity refers to the supplementary system of law that originally derived from the decisions of the Court of Chancery
- (c) The rules of equity are more concerned with fairness than the rules of the common law
- (d) The administration of common law and equity is fused, so any court may apply common law or equitable principles

14. The phrase 'civil law' can refer to those legal systems whose laws are based on Roman law. It can also refer to ..... .
- (a) laws created by judges
- (b) the body of laws that does not relate to criminal offences
- (c) The supplementary system of law that is based on fairness and equality and seeks to mitigate the harshness of the common law
- (d) The body of laws that establish what conduct is criminal and the punishments for engaging in such conduct

15. The phrase 'English legal system' refers to
- (a) the legal system of England and Wales
- (b) the legal system of England only
- (c) the legal system of England, Wales and Scotland
- (d) the legal system of the United Kingdom

16. Statue law refers to
- (a) laws created by the judges through the deciding of cases
- (b) the doctrine that seeks to mitigate the harshness of the common law by deciding cases based on fairness and equality
- (c) the body of law that regulates the relationship between the state and its citizens
- (d) the body of laws created by Parliament in the form of legislation

17. What is 'unilateral acts'?
- (a) They are acts that states perform as practice in the context of custom
- (b) They are acts creating unilateral legal obligations to the acting state
- (c) Unilateral acts are simply political acts of state devoid of any legal effect
- (d) Unilateral acts are those that state perform in order to be bound by a treaty

18. Who is a 'persistent objector'?
- (a) The state which persistently objects to the rule in question after its formation
- (b) The state which denies to be bound by the rule in question for a short period
- (c) The state which persistently and publicly objects to the formation of a rule of customary law from its outset
- (d) The state which accepts the formation of a rule of customary law, but it retains objections as to its content

19. What is required for a general rule of customary law to be formed?
- (a) Only general, widespread and consistent practice on the part of states is required
- (b) The consistent practice of few states is sufficient
- (c) The legal conviction that a certain practice of a state is in accordance with International law is the most significant requirement
- (d) Both the elements of widespread and consistent state practice and of the Opinio Juris are required

20. What is the relationship between the formal sources of International law?
- (a) There is no hierarchy between the formal sources of International law
- (b) Treaties supersede custom
- (c) Custom supersedes treaties
- (d) General Principles of Law supersede both custom and treaties

21. Where do we find the 'general principles of law recognised by civilised nations' (Article 38 ICJ Statute)?
- (a) We look for established principles of law recognised only among the most civilised nations
- (b) We look for established principles of law, which are common to all major legal systems
- (c) We look for general principles of International law recognised by International Courts and tribunals
- (d) We look for general principles of law recognised by all nations

22. Which treaties are considered as 'source of International law' under Article 38 ICJ Statute?
(a) All treaties that are in force at the time of the dispute
(b) Only the treaties that are in force and binding upon the parties to the dispute
(c) All treaties that have been concluded between the parties to the dispute, regardless whether they are in force
(d) Only treaties that are multilateral and of paramount significance

23. Which are the formal sources of International law?
(a) Custom, treaties and judicial decision
(b) Custom, general principles of law and theory
(c) Treaties, custom and general principles of law
(d) Treaties, custom and General Assembly Resolutions

24. How can customary law be related to treaty provisions?
(a) Treaties may only codify customary law
(b) Customary law is a different source of international and it cannot be embodied in treaties
(c) Treaties may, codify customary law, 'crystallise' customary law and lead to the emergence of customary law
(d) Customary law can emerge only from few multilateral treaties

25. Which of the following scholar belongs to Sociological School of Law?
(a) J Benthum (b) Austin
(c) Auguste Comte (d) Karl Mannheim

26. ..... hold that jurisprudence is the study of law as it is.
(a) Moralists (b) Positivists
(c) Realists (d) Analysts

27. According to naturalists, law is the dictates of
(a) rules (b) heart (c) reason (d) time

28. What kind of state practice is required?
(a) Widespread, consistent and uniform practice, consisting both of acts and omissions
(b) Only widespread, consistent and uniform acts and not omissions of states
(c) Widespread acts and omissions of states, but not necessarily consistent or uniform
(d) Consistent practice of few states, including both acts and omissions, which is met with protestation by the other states

29. Which of the following is the source of law?
(a) Jurisprudence (b) Social law
(c) Customary law (d) None of these

30. Which of the following is pertain to law by analogy?
(a) Scientific law (b) Natural law
(c) Human law (d) Divine law

31. What was the main source of law till 19th century England?
(a) Customary law (b) Constitution law
(c) Parliamentary law (d) Private law

32. Who was considered as Father of Sociological Jurisprudence?
(a) Duguit (b) August Comte
(c) Roscoe Pound (d) Fichte

33. International law is the law between sovereign states. A sovereign is the supreme authority not bound by legal constraints
(a) International law is not binding
(b) International law is only a positive morality
(c) International law is binding
(d) International law is in law of nature

34. The Father of International law is
(a) Plato (b) Aristotle
(c) Grotius (d) Denning

Directions (Q. Nos. 35-38) *In the questions given below are two statements labelled as Assertion (A) and Reason (R). In the context of the two statements, which of the following is correct?*

Codes
(a) Both (A) and (R) are true and (R) is the correct explanation of (A)
(b) Both (A) and (R) are true, but (R) is not the correct explanation of (A)
(c) (A) is true, but (R) is false
(d) (A) is false, but (R) is true

35. Assertion (A) Law is the aggregate of the rule set by men as a political subject.
Reason (R) Law of the nature related to will of superior.

36. Assertion (A) Law is the social mediator of the society.
Reason (R) In a complex society, conflict are bound to create.

37. **Assertion** (A) Divine law is always related to God.

Reason (R) Man in the state of society is governed by divine law of God in ancient society.

38. **Assertion** (A) The source of law is traced from judicial pronouncement.

Reason (R) It ensures that previous courts decision is followed by another court.

Previous Year's Questions

39. The 17th Commonwealth Law Conference was held in which city? **[CLAT 2011]**

(a) Delhi (b) Bengaluru
(c) Kolkata (d) Hyderabad

Directions (Q. Nos. 40-41) *In the questions given below are two statements labelled as Assertion (A) and Reason (R). In the context of the two statements, which of the following is correct?*

Codes

(a) Both (A) and (R) are true and (R) is the correct explanation of (A)
(b) Both (A) and (R) are true, but (R) is not the correct explanation of (A)
(c) (A) is true, but (R) is false
(d) (A) is false, but (R) is true

40. **Assertion (A)** The Indian Constitution was adopted on 26th November, 1949.

Reason (R) Law Day is celebrated in India on 26th November every year. **[CLAT 2012]**

41. **Assertion** (A) Austin's concept of law is known as imperative theory.

Reason (R) Austin emphasized on the commanding character of law. **[CLAT 2012]**

42. The seat of International Criminal Court is at **[CLAT 2012]**

(a) Hague (b) Geneva
(c) Washington (d) Tokyo

43. Law Day is observed on **[CLAT 2014]**

(a) 26th January (b) 26th May
(c) 15th August (d) 26th November

44. **Principle** There are certain acts which, though harmful, are not wrongful in law; therefore do not give legal right to bring action in law, to the person who suffers from such acts.

Fact 'Prakash' has a rice mill. His neighbour, Shanti, sets-up another rice mill and offers a tough competition to Prakash. As a consequence, Prakash's profits fall down. He brings a suit against Shanti for damages. **[CLAT 2016]**

(a) Prakash cannot succeed in his claim for damages, as it is a case of damage without infringement of any legal right
(b) Himesh would not be protected under the principle stated above becuse his acts show that he was sufficiently mature to understand the nature and consequences of his conduct
(c) Himesh would be protected under the principle stated above because he is below 12 years of age
(d) Nimesh would not be protected under the principle stated above becuse irrespective of the age, steading is an offence

Answers

1	a	2	d	3	a	4	d	5	c	6	c	7	a	8	c	9	b	10	d
11	b	12	b	13	a	14	a	15	a	16	d	17	b	18	c	19	d	20	a
21	b	22	b	23	c	24	c	25	c	26	b	27	c	28	a	29	c	30	c
31	c	32	c	33	b	34	c	35	b	36	a	37	b	38	a	39	d	40	a
41	a	42	a	43	d	44	d												

CHAPTER 02

CRIMINAL LAW

Criminal law concerned with the system of legal rules that define what conduct is classified as a crime and how the government may prosecute individuals that commit crimes. Individuals who violates federal, state and local laws may face fines probation or incarceration mentioned in the criminal law.

MEANING OF CRIMINAL LAW

Criminal law is the body of law that relates to crime. Crimes are generally referred to as offences against the state.

- Criminal law, also termed as Penal law, encompasses the rules written by state. Many laws are enforced by threat of criminal punishment. Indian criminal laws are divided into three major acts, i.e. Indian Penal Code, 1860, Code of Criminal Procedure, 1973 and Indian Evidence Act, 1872. Besides these major acts, special criminal laws are also passed by Indian Parliament i.e. Narcotic Drugs and Psychotropic Substances Act, 1985 (NDPS), Prevention of Corruption Act, Food Adulteration Act, Dowry Prevention Act, the Defence of India Act etc and thousands of minor laws are made in India.
- The Indian Penal Code (IPC) is the main criminal code of India. It is a comprehensive code intended to cover all substantive aspects of Criminal law. The code was drafted in 1860 on the recommendations of first law commission of India established in 1834 under the Charter Act of 1833 under the Chairmanship of Thomas Babington Macaulay. It came into force in British India during the early British Raj period in 1862.
- The Indian Evidence Act, identified as Act no. 1 of 1872 and called the Indian Evidence Act, 1872.
- The Code of Criminal Procedure (CrPC) is the main legislation on procedure for administration of substantive Criminal law in India.
- It was enacted in 1973 and came into force on 1st April, 1974.

- It provides the machinery for the investigation of crime, apprehension of suspected criminals, collection of evidence, determination of guilt or innocence of the accused person and the determination of punishment of the guilty.

Principles of Criminal Liability

The general basis for imposing liability in criminal law is that the defendant must be proved to have committed a guilty act whilst having had a guilty state of mind. The physical elements are collectively called the **actus reus** and the accompanied mental state is called the **mens rea**.

It is the fundamental duty of the prosecution to prove both of these elements of the offence to the satisfaction of the judge or jury beyond reasonable doubt. In the absence of such proof, the defendant will be acquitted.

Actus Reus

- Actus Reus means *physical event*. It is a physical result of a human conduct which is sufficiently harmful and therefore punishable.
- According to Section 32 of IPC, the 'Act' includes illegal omissions. e.g. 'A' firing a gun to kill 'B'. While shooting, 'A' holds the gun, places his finger on the trigger and pulls the trigger, as a consequence of which the bullet leaves the gun. In order to constitute an actus reus, there must be the further consequence of the bullet entering 'B's body and thereby causing his death or injury.

Mens Rea

- It is one of the essential ingredients of criminal liability. 'A' criminal offence is committed only when an act which is forbidden by law is done voluntarily.
- The term mens rea has been given to the volition, which is the motive force behind the Criminal act.
- Ordinarily, a crime is not committed if the mind of the person doing the act is innocent. There must be a wrongful intention or some blame worthy condition of mind (mens rea) before a person is made criminally liable.
- The underlying principle of the doctrine of mens rea is expressed in the Latin maxim actus non facit reum, nisi mens sit rea- the act does not make one guilty unless the mind is also guilty.
  e.g. for instance, 'A' slipped as he walked and fell. As he fell, he lost balance and pulled down 'B' with him. 'B' hit his head against the wall, sustained head injuries and died. Is 'A' guilty liable of murder?
- 'A' satisfies one portion of the definition of murder, of actus reus means doing an act which causes death. But still it does not constitute the offence of murder because another essential ingredient of the offence of murder, *viz*, the intention (mens rea) to cause death is absent. Hence, 'A' is not guilty of murder.

General Exceptions

A crime would not be treated as crime in the eye of law in the presence of one or more general exceptions. Following are some general exceptions against Criminal law

1. Accident

Section 80 of the IPC exempts the commission of any innocent or lawful act, done in an innocent or lawful manner, which has led to an unforeseen result that may have ensured from an accident or misfortune. For the accused to avail of this exception it must be shown that due care and caution were exercised at the time of commission of the act.

2. Absence of Criminal Intent

These exceptions, including for unsoundness of mind and intoxication, are based on the premise that the accused, while committing the acts in question had no criminal/malafide intent. For instance, under Section 82 of the IPC, acts done by a child under the age of seven are not offences.

3. Unsound Mind

- Section 84 of the IPC deals with act of a person of unsound mind. Under Section 84 of the IPC, a person is exempted from criminal responsibility, *if at the time of doing the act*
  - (i) he was of unsound mind.
  - (ii) he was incapable of knowing either
    - (a) the nature of the act, or
    - (b) that what he was doing was either wrong or contrary to law.
- The Indian Law of Insanity is based on the opinion of M' Naght.
- Medical insanity and legal insanity (unsoundness of mind) are different from each other. The former is dependent solely on medical grounds while the latter depends on the factor as to be proved in a court of law to enable the accused to be acquitted of charge.

4. Intoxication

Under Section 85 of the IPC, a person will be exonerated from liability for doing an act while in a state of intoxication, if at the time of the act the person (due to intoxication) was incapable of knowing the nature of his act or that he was doing what was either wrong or contrary to law.

5. Consent

- Section 87 of the IPC provides that nothing is an offence if the person to whom harm is caused is above eighteen years of age and has given consent to suffer such harm.
- The provision however, provides that the act for which consent is offered should not be intended to cause death or grievous hurt. e.g. A and 'Z' agree to fence with each other for amusement.
- This agreement implies the consent of each to suffer any harm which, in the course of such fencing, may be caused without foul play and if A, while playing fairly, hurts Z, A commits no offence.
- **Trifling Acts Section 95** of the IPC provides that if the harm caused by an act is so slight that a person of ordinary sense and temper would not complain of such harm, the act would not be an offence. This defence is often known as the 'defence of triviality'.

6. Private Defence

- Sections 96 to 106 of the IPC deal with the right of private defence and are a recognition of the right of a person to protect his or her life and property against the unlawful aggression of others.
- Section 96 of the IPC states that nothing is an offence which is done in the exercise of the right of private defence.
- Section 97 of the IPC defines the right of private defence of the body and property. Every person has a right to defend his own body and the body of any other person against any offence affecting the human body, subject to the restrictions contained in Section 99 of the IPC.
- Among the restrictions stated in Section 99 of the IPC, the provision stipulated the extent to which the right of private defence may be exercised, namely that it is no case extends to the inflicting of more harm than it is necessary to inflict for the purpose of defence.
- Further, Section 100 of the IPC details instances in which the right of private defence of the body extends to causing death.

7. Homicide

Homicide represents the act of unnaturally ending the life of a human being or killing a human being.

8. Culpable Homicide

Section 299 of IPC defines culpable homicide. Whoever causes death by doing an act with the intention of causing such bodily injury is likely to cause death, or with the knowledge that he is likely by such act to cause death, commits the offence of culpable homicide.

e.g. A know Z to be behind a bush. B does not know it. A, intending to cause, or knowing it to be likely to cause Z's death, induces B to fire at the bush. B fires and kills Z. Here B may be guilty of no offence, but A has committed the offence of culpable homicide.

9. Murder

Section 300 of the IPC defines 'Murder' while Section 302 provides the punishment for murder and Section 307 provides the punishment for attempt to murder.

The following are essential ingredients of murder culpable homicide is murder, if it is done with

- Intention of cause death.
- Intention to cause bodily injury, knowing that the injury caused, is likely to cause death.
- Intention of causing bodily injury sufficient in the ordinary course, of nature to cause death.

Knowledge that the act is so imminently dangerous that in all probability it will cause death or bodily injury likely to cause death and such act should be without justification.

Culpable homicide is not a murder in following cases (exceptions of Section 300)

- Where the act is done on grave and sudden provocation.
- Where the act is done in exceeding the right of private defence of person or property.
- Where the act is done in exceeding the right by public servant or in aiding a public servant.
- Where the act is done in sudden fight without premeditation.
- Where the act is done with the consent of deceased of the age of above 18 years.

All the cases of murder fall under the category of culpable homicide, but all the cases of culpable homicide do not fall under the category.

The case of KM Nanavati *vs* State of Maharashtra AIR 1962 is on grave and sudden provocation.

CRIME AGAINST PROPERTY

Crime against property is categorised as specific crime. These crimes generally lead to financial loss or harm to private property. *Following are some crime against property*

1. Theft

- Section 378 of IPC defines theft. It states that whoever, intending to take dishonestly any moveable property out of the possession of any person without that person's consent, moves that property in order to such taking is said to commit theft.
- In order to constitute the offence of theft, the following elements are essential
  - It should be a moveable property.
  - In the possession of anyone.
  - 'A' dishonest intention to take it out of that person's possession.
  - 'A' moving in order to such taking and without his consent.

e.g.

(i) 'A' cuts down a tree on 'Z's ground, with the intention of dishonestly taking the tree out of 'Z's possession without 'Z's consent. Here, as soon as 'A' has severed the tree in order to such taking, he has committed theft.

(ii) 'A' being 'Z's servant, and entrusted by 'Z' with the care of 'Z's plate, dishonestly runs away with the plate, without 'Z's consent. 'A' has committed theft.

(iii) 'A' finds a ring lying on the highroad, not in the possession of any person. 'A', by taking it, commits no theft, though he may commit criminal misappropriation of property.

(iv) 'A' in good faith, believing property belonging to 'Z' to be A's own property, takes that property out of B's possession. Here, as 'Z' does not take dishonestly, he does not commit theft.

2. Extortion

- Section 383 of IPC defines the extortion.
- Extortion is a criminal offense of obtaining money, property or services from an individual or an institution through coercion. Extortion is distinguish from robbery.

e.g. 'A' threatens 'Z' that he will keep Z's child in wrongful confinement unless 'Z' will sign and deliver to 'A' a promissory note binding 'Z' to pay certain money to 'A'. 'Z' signs and delivers the note. 'A' has committed extortion.

3. Criminal Misappropriation

- Section 403 explains dishonest misappropriation of property.
- It states that whoever dishonestly misappropriates or converts to his own use any moveable property, shall be punished with imprisonment of either description for a term which may extend to two years or with fine or with both.

  e.g. 'A' takes property belonging to 'Z' out of Z's possession in good faith, believing, at the time when he takes it, that the property belongs to himself. 'A' is not guilty of theft, but if A, after knowing his mistake, dishonestly appropriates the property to his own use, he is guilty of an offence under this section.

4. Cheating

- Section 415 IPC defines cheating.
- It is generally used for the breaking of rules to gain unfair advantage in a competitive situation.

  e.g. 'A', by falsely pretending to be in the Civil Service, intentionally deceives 'Z' and thus, dishonestly induces 'Z' to let him have on credit goods for which he does not mean to pay. 'A' is guilty of cheating 'Z'.

5. Breach of Trust

Section 405 of IPC explains criminal breach of trust. It states that, whoever, being in any manner entrusted with property or with any dominion over property, dishonestly misappropriates or converts to his own use of that property, or dishonestly uses or disposes of that property in violation of any direction of law prescribing the mode in which trust is to be discharged or of any legal contract, express or implied, or wilfully suffers any other person so to do, commits 'criminal breach of trust'.

e.g. 'A' being executor to the will of a deceased person, dishonestly disobeys the law which directs him to divide the effects according to the will and appropriates them to his own use. 'A' has committed criminal breach of trust.

Criminal Law Terminology

Certain terms are important and have been questioned in legal knowledge if not reasoning. *Some of these are detailed below*

1. **Admission** A statement concerning a crime which may be made by any party. Where A says that B committed a crime, it is an admission.
2. **Confession** A statement made by the accused that she herself/himself committed a crime; e.g. X says that X committed the crime.
3. **Approver** One who testified on behalf of the prosecution in return for a reduced sentence. e.g. X makes a statement that both X and Y committed a crime. In return X gets some sort of relief.
4. **Accused** A person facing criminal charges.
5. **Convict** A person having been found guilty of the charges and being convicted by a court of law.
6. **Prosecution** The side trying to prove the charges against the accused. In India, the prosecution is the state as crimes are committed against the state.
7. **Bail** A bond furnished on behalf of the accused before a court where a person requests that the-accused be released from jail and the person furnishing the bond takes responsibility to present the accused.

8. **Parole** A bail is for an accused, whereas a parole applies to a convict. A convict is given parole or permission to live outside prison on account of good behaviour. A parole is a discretionary power given to the prison authorities.
9. **Furlough** Unlike parole, furlough is a matter of right, which enables the prisoner to leave the prison to renew and keep touch with his social ties. It is a 'leave' from prison. In India, a prisoner can apply for 14 days of furlough in a year.
10. **Custody** In India, there are two kinds of custody, police custody and judicial custody. In police custody, you are a responsibility of the police and in judicial custody you are in the custody of the judge. Sending a person to jail means judicial custody.

Important Provisions of IPC

- **IPC Sec-34** Acts done by several persons in furtherance of common intension. When a Criminal act is done by several people in furtherance of the common intension of all, each of such persons are liable for that act in the same manner as if it were done by him alone.
- **IPC Sec-82** Act of any child under 7 years of age. Nothing is an offence which is done by a child under 7 years of age.
- **IPC Sec-85** Act of a person incapable of judgement by reason of intoxication caused against his will. Nothing is an which is done by a person who at the time of doing it, is , by reason of intoxication, in capable of knowing the nature of the act, or that he is doing what is either wrong, or contrary to law, provided that the thing which intoxicated him was administered to him without his knowledge or against his will.
- **IPC Sec-149** Every member of unlawful assembly guilty of offence committed in Prosecution of common object. If an offence is committed by any member unlawful assembly in Prosecution of the common object of that assembly, or such as the member of that assembly knew to be likely to be committed in Prosecution of that object, every person who, at the time of the committing of that offence, is a member of the same assembly is guilty of that offence.
- **IPC Sec-268** Person is guilty of public nuisance who does any act or is guilty of an illegal omission which causes any common injury, danger, or annoyance to the public or to the people in general who dwell or occupy property in the vicinity or which must necessarily cause injury, obstruction, danger or annoyance to persons who may have occasion the use any public right.
  A common nuisance is not excused on the ground that it causes some conference or advantage.
- **IPC Sec-269** Negligent act likely to spread infection of disease dangerous to life. Whoever unlawfully or negligently does any act which is, which he knows or has reason to believe to be, likely to spread the infection of any disease dangerous to life, shall be punished with imprisonment of either description for a term which may extend to mouths, or with fine or with both.
- **IPC Sec-270** Malignant act likely to spread infection of disease dangerous to life, whoever malignantly does any act which is and which he knows or has reason to believe to be, likely to spread the infection of any disease dangerous to life, shall be punished with imprisonment of either description for a term which may extend to two years or with fine or with both.
- **IPC Sec-286** Negligent conduct with respect to explosive substance, whoever does, with any explosive substance, any act so rashly or negligently as to endanger human life, or to be likely to cause hurt or injury to any other person, or knowingly or negligently omits to take order with any explosive substance in his possession as is sufficient to guard against probable danger to human life from that

substance shall be punishable with imprisonment of either description for a term which may extend six months, or with fine which may extend to one thousand rupees, or with both.

- **IPC Sec-336** Act endangering life or personal safety of others- whoever does any act so rashly or negligently as to endanger human life, or the personal safety of others, shall be punished with imprisonment of either descriptions for a term which may extend to six months, or with fine which may extend to five hundred rupees or with both.
- **IPC Sec-377** Unnatural offences, whoever voluntarily has carnal intercourse against the order or nature with any man, woman or animal shall be punished with imprisonment for life or with imprisonment of either description for a term which may extend to ten years and shall also be liable to fine. Penetration is sufficient to Constitute the carnal intercourse necessary to the offence described in this section.
- **IPC Sec-391** When five or more persons conjointly commit or attempt to commit a robbery, or where the whole number of persons conjointly committing or attempting to commit a robbery and persons present and aiding such commission or attempt, amount to five or more, every person so committing, attempting or aiding is said to commit 'dacoity'.
- **IPC Sec-441** Whoever enters into or upon property in the possession of another with intent to commit an offence or to intimidate, insult or annoy and person in possession of such property, or having lawfully entered into or upon such property, unlawfully remains there with intent thereby to intimidate, insult or annoy any such person or with intent to commit an offence, is said to commit 'criminal trespass'.
- **IPC Sec-494** Marrying again during lifetime of husband or wife whoever, having a husband or wife living, marries in any case in which such marriage is void by reason of its taking place during the life of such husband or wife, shall be punished with imprisonment of either description for a term which may extend to seven years, and shall also be liable to fine.

Practice Exercise

1. The Indian Evidence Act, 1872 helps in
(a) Procedural of crime (b) Subjective nature
(c) Police enquiry (d) Judicial enquiry

2. The criminal procedure code is of
(a) Subjective in nature (b) Procedural nature
(c) Supportive in nature (d) None of these

3. *Actus reus* means
(a) Wrongful act (b) Lawful act
(c) Unlawful act (d) Act that is justified

4. A person with innocent mind
(a) can commit a crime
(b) cannot commit a crime
(c) may commit a crime
(d) depend upon the fact

5. Ignorance of law is
(a) excusable (b) not excusable
(c) a lawful wrong (d) None of these

6. Homicide means killing of a human being by
(a) a human being
(b) by accident
(c) by natural disaster
(d) by some kind of animal

7. Unlawful homicide includes
(a) culpable homicide not amounting to murder
(b) murder
(c) homicide by rash or negligent
(d) All of the above

8. Extortion is almost equal to offence of
(a) Black mail (b) Theft
(c) Demand of money (d) None of these

9. Theft is defined only for
(a) moveable property (b) immoveable property
(c) Both (a) and (b) (d) None of the above

10. If the things removed temporarily with dishonest intention amount to
(a) robbery (b) extortion
(c) theft (d) None of these

11. PRINCIPLE The right of private defence entitles one to do harm to a proportional extent provided it is done in good faith, it is proportional and is inflicted only to the extent is necessary to stop a person from committing harm against oneself.

FACTS A doctor with the intention of saving a terminal patient's life decides to administer an experimental drug to the patient without informing the patient or taking consent from the patient's relatives leading to the patient's death.

(a) The act shall not constitute an offence as there was no criminal intention.
(b) The act shall not constitute an offence as there was no knowledge
(c) Both (a) and (b)
(d) Neither (a) nor (b)

12. FACTS 'A' who was known to have violent tendencies to got drunk and was forced to get such by 'B'. When 'A' got drunk and tried to attack 'B', 'B' injured 'A' in using as much force as was proportional and only to the extent necessary to stop 'A' from injuring 'B'.

(a) B's action is protected as it was proportional to the harm
(b) B's action was protected as it was inflicted to the extent necessary
(c) B's action is not protected as 'A' was drunk and therefore not in control of his actions
(d) B's action is not protected as it was not done in good faith

13. PRINCIPLE Whoever causes the death of any person by doing any rash or negligent act not amounting to culpable homicide, shall be liable for causing death by negligence.

FACTS A nurse knowing that she is supposed to take vitals and ensure them to be in order before administering a particular injection, but not knowing or having reason to believe it is fatal does not follow the protocol in hurry. As a result the patient died.

(a) The nurse is liable for death by negligence.
(b) The hospital is liable for death by negligence under vicarious liability
(c) The nurse is liable for culpable homicide
(d) The hospital is liable for hasty selection of nurses

14. PRINCIPLE No person shall be prosecuted and punished for the same offence twice.

FACTUAL SITUATION 'A', a kleptomaniac, was an acquaintance of 'B' and used to visit 'B's home on weekends. One day, 'B' was unable to find his watch after a visit from 'A'. Ultimately, 'B' informed the police about the missing watch and the persons who had been to his room. The police, among others, made a search on person of 'A' and found the watch in his pocket. At his trial, the Court found him guilty of theft and sentenced him to 3 months in prison. After completing his sentence, 'A' went to 'B's' home to apologise for his conduct. After 'A' left, it was discovered that 'B's' watch was missing. 'A' informed the police who located the watch from 'A's home. Can 'A' be prosecuted for theft?

(a) No, he has already been prosecuted and punished for theft and cannot be punished for the same again
(b) No, he is a kleptomaniac with a psychological disorder of stealing and therefore cannot be found guilty
(c) Yes, he can be prosecuted because he has committed two separate acts of theft
(d) Yes, he can be prosecuted because the recovery of the stolen goods in each case has been made from separate places

15. PRINCIPLE Nothing is an offence which is done by a person who, at the time of doing it, is, by reason of intoxication, incapable of knowing the nature of the act, or that he is doing what is either wrong, or contrary to law: provided that the thing which intoxicated him was administered to him without his knowledge or against his will.

FACTUAL SITUATION 'A' was having a get together with his old friends and on his friends suggestions, he consumed some alcohol. On his way back to home at, night, 'A' heard some footsteps and turning back, he imagined he saw a figure moving towards him with a spear. In fact, it was only a man, 'B' with an umbrella who was telling 'A' to walk carefully since 'A' appeared to be unsteady. However, 'A' proceeded to attack 'B' with an iron rod leading to grave injuries to 'B', Is 'A' guilty of causing grievous hurt to 'B'?

(a) No, 'A' is not guilty because in his intoxicated state the umbrella appeared a spear to him and he exercised his right of private defence
(b) No, 'A' is not guilty because 'B' could have attacked 'A' with his umbrella
(c) No, 'A' is not guilty because he was intoxicated on the suggestions of his friends and was incapable of knowing that he was savagely attacking a man who was carrying only an umbrella
(d) Yes, 'A' is guilty because he got intoxicated voluntarily and under the effect of this voluntary intoxication, he attacked and caused grievous injuries to 'B' -who posed no threat to him in fact

Previous Year's Questions

16. Principle Whoever, intending to take dishonestly any movable property out of the possession of any person without that person's consent, moves that property with an intention to take. it is said to commit theft.

Facts Y cuts down a tree on Z's ground, with the intention of dishonestly taking it out of Z's possession without Z's consent. Y could not take away the tree. **[CLAT 2012]**

(a) Y can be prosecuted for theft
(b) Y cannot be prosecuted for theft
(c) Y can be prosecuted for attempt to theft
(d) Y has neither committed theft nor attempted to commit theft

17. Principle *Injuria Sine Damnum i.e.,* Injury (violation of legal right) without damage.

Facts X, who was the returning officer at a polling booth in Amethi, wrongly refused to register a duly tendered vote of Y in the recent UP elections, even though Y was an eligible voter. The candidate in whose favour Y wanted to vote, was declared elected. Give the appropriate answer **[CLAT 2012]**

(a) Y can sue X on the ground that he was denied the right to cast vote, which is a Fundamental Right
(b) Y can sue X on the ground that he was denied the right to cast vote, which is a legal right
(c) Y cannot sue X because there is no injury or damage caused to Y
(d) Y cannot sue X because the candidate in whose favour he wanted to vote was declared elected

18. Principle When one person signifies to another his willingness to do or abstain from doing anything, with a view to obtaining the assent of that person to such an act or abstinence, he is said to have made a proposal.

Fact "Ramanuj telegraphed to Shyam Sunder, writing *'Will you sell me your Rolls Royce CAR? Telegram the lowest cash price.'* Shyam Sunder also replied by telegram: *"Lowest price for CAR is ₹ 20 lakh."* Ramanuj immediately sent his consent through telegram stating: *'I agree to buy the CAR for ₹ 20 lakh asked by you* Shyam Sunder refused to sell the car. **[CLAT 2012]**

(a) He cannot refuse to sell the CAR because the contract has already been made
(b) He can refuse to sell the CAR because it was only invitation to offer and not the real offer
(c) It was not a valid offer because willingness to enter into a contract was absent
(d) None of the above

Directions (Q. Nos. 19-21) *In the questions given below are two statements labelled as Assertion (A) and Reason (R). In the context of the two statements, which of the following is correct?*

Codes

(a) Both (A) and (R) are true and (R) is the correct explanation of (A)
(b) Both (A) and (R) are true, but (R) is not the correct explanation of (A)
(c) (A) is true, but (R) is false
(d) (A) is false, but (R) is true

19. Assertion (A) The essence of joint liability under Section-149 of the IPC is that the criminal act must have been done with a view to fulfill the common object of an unlawful assembly.

Reason (R) Any sudden and provocative act done by a member of an unlawful assembly would render the other members of that assembly liable. **[CLAT 2012]**

20. Assertion (A) X, because of unsound state of mind and not knowing the nature of the act, attacks Y, who in self defense and in order to ward off the attack, hits him thereby injuring him. Y has not committed an offence.

Reason (R) Y had a right of private defense against X under Section-98 of the Indian Penal Code. **[CLAT 2012]**

21. Assertion (A) X and Y independently entertained the idea to kill Z. Accordingly; each of them separately inflicted wounds on Z who died as a consequence. X and Y are liable for murder under Section-341 of the IPC.

Reason (R) When a criminal act is done by several persons in furtherance of common intention of all, each of such persons is liable as if the whole act was done by him alone. **[CLAT 2012]**

22. Principle Nothing is an offence which is done by a child under seven years of age.

Facts A child born on January 01, 2005 killed another child B on December 30, 2011. **[CLAT 2013]**

(a) A has committed no offence
(b) A has committed the offence as it is heinous crime
(c) Killing of one child by another child is not an offence
(d) A has not committed the offence for on the date of killing of B, A was a minor

23. Principle Whoever attempts to commit an offence punishable by the Indian Penal Code and in such attempt does any act towards the commission of the offence, shall be punished. Stealing is an offence punishable by the Indian Penal Code.

Facts A makes an attempt to steal some jewels by breaking open a box and after so opening the box, finds that there is no jewel in it. **[CLAT 2013]**

(a) A has committed no offence
(b) A has committed the offence of stealing
(c) A has attempted to commit the offence of stealing
(d) None of the above

24. Principle Whoever takes away anything from the land of any person without that person's consent is said to commit theft. A thing so long as it is attached to the earth is not the subject of theft but it becomes capable of being the subject of theft as soon as it is severed from the Earth.

Facts Y cuts down a tree standing on the land of X with the intention of dishonestly taking the tree out of X's possession without the consent of X. But Y is yet to take away the tree out of X's possession. **[CLAT 2013]**

(a) Y has committed theft as soon as he came to the land of X
(b) Y has committed theft as soon as the tree has been completely cut down by him
(c) Y has committed theft as soon as he has started cutting down the tree
(d) Y has not committed theft because he is yet to take away the tree out of X's possession

Directions (Q. Nos. 25-29) *This section consists of fifty (50) questions. Each question consists of legal propositions/ principles (hereinafter referred to as 'principle') and facts. These principles have to be applied to the given facts to arrive at the most reasonable conclusion.*

Such principles may or may not be true in the real sense, yet you have to conclusively assume them to be true for the purposes of this section. In other words, in answering the following questions, you must not rely on any principles except the principles that are given herein below for every question. Further, you must not assume any facts other than those stated in the question. The objective of this section is to test your interest towards study of law, research aptitude and problem solving ability even if the 'most reasonable conclusion' arrived at may be unacceptable for any other reason. It is not the object of this section to test your knowledge of law. **[CLAT 2014]**

25. Principle Where a person fraudulently or erroneously represents that he is authorised to transfer certain immovable property and professes to transfer such property for consideration, such transfer shall, at the option of the transferee, operate on any interest which the transferor may acquire in such property at anytime during which the contract of transfer subsists.

Facts 'A', a Hindu who has separated from his father 'B', sells to 'C' three fields, X, Y and Z representing that 'A' is authorised to transfer the same. Of these fields Z does not belong to 'A', it having been retained by 'B' on the partition; but on B's dying 'A' as successor obtains Z and at that time 'C' had not cancelled the contract of sale.

(a) 'A' can sell Z to a third party
(b) 'A' is not required to deliver Z to 'C'
(c) 'A' is required to deliver Z to 'C'
(d) None of the above statements

26. Principle Under the Transfer of Property Act, 1882 a property must be transferred , by one living person to another living person. The Act deals only with transfer of property between living persons.

Facts 'X' wants to transfer his property to the presiding deity in a temple situated within the estate of 'A'.

(a) Transfer of property by 'X' will be valid
(b) Transfer of property by 'X' will be invalid
(c) Transfer of property by 'X' to the presiding deity will become a valid transfer to 'A'
(d) None of the above

27. Principle When an act which would otherwise be a certain offence, is not that offence, by reason of the youth, the want of maturity of understanding, the unsoundness of mind or the intoxication of the person doing that act, or by reason of any misconception on the part of that person, every person has the same right of private defence against that act which he would have if the act were that offence.

Facts 'X', under the influence of madness, attempts to kill 'Y'.

(a) 'Y' has the right of private defence against 'X'
(b) 'Y' does not have the right of private defence against 'X'
(c) 'Y' has the right of private defence against 'X', only if 'X' is not under the influence of madness
(d) 'X' has the right of private defence against 'Y'

28. Principle Trespass to land means direct interference with the possession of land without lawful justification. Trespass could be committed either by a person himself entering the land of another person or doing the same through some tangible object(s).

Facts 'A' throws some stones upon his neighbour's (B's) premises.

Which of the following derivations is correct?

(a) 'A' has committed trespass
(b) 'A' has not committed trespass, as he has not entered B's premises
(c) 'A' has committed nuisance
(d) None of the above

29. Principle The court has power to issue an injunction to prohibit a child marriage from being performed.

Factual Situation A marriage is performed between A and B. A is of 14 years of age and B of 17 years of age. X is a public spirited person filed a suit to declare the said marriage void. Is the suit maintainable?

Decision

(a) No, because court has power to issue injunction and not to declare the marriage as valid and void.
(b) No, because the marriage is performed with the consent of their parents.
(c) Yes, because the policy of the law is to prevent the child marriages.
(d) None of the above

30. Principle Theft is the dishonest moving of a property with the intension of taking it out from the person's possession without his consent.

Factual Situation *A* gives his woollen coat to a dry cleaner along with his wife's sarees for the purpose of dry cleaning. He is told to collect the clothes after two days. When he comes after two days, he finds that he does not have enough money to pay the dry cleaner. But since due to the winter, he needs the coat desperately, he surreptitiously places the coat near his goods, so that he can quietly take it without the knowledge of the dry cleaner. **[CLAT 2015]**

Decision

(a) A is guilty of theft.
(b) A is not guilty of theft.
(c) A is not guilty of theft but has to pay compensation to the dry cleaner.
(d) None of the above

31. Principle Nothing is an offence, which is done by a person, who at the time of doing it, by the reason of unsoundness of mind is incapable of knowing the nature of the act, or that what he is doing is either wrong or contrary to law.

Factual Situation Jack has a bad day at work and is called at by all his superiors. On the way back from office, he gets stuck in a traffic jam, which adds to his stress. As, Jack nears his home, a person tries to run across the road. Owing to the stress, Jack runs into the person, grievously injuring him.

He is prosecuted and he takes the defence that at the time of doing the act he was really stresses and was incapable of knowing what he was doing was wrong. **[CLAT 2015]**

Decision

(a) Jack would not be liable, as he knows not what he did at the time of the incident.
(b) Jack would be liable as he is not of unsound mind and was capable of knowing the consequences of his act.
(c) Jack would be liable as he took the stress he felt at office out on the pedestrian.
(d) Jack would not be liable as the pedestrian should have waited until Jack had passed.

32. Principle Money or good given to person by mistake must be returned to the person who gave them.

Factual Situation Sunil and Suman jointly owed ₹1000 to Siraj. Sunil pays the whole amount to Siraj in Suman's absence. Suman after returning from his vacations also paid full amount to Siraj not knowing the fact that Sunil had already paid the same. Is Siraj bound to repay or return the extra money to Suman that he obtained under mistake from her? **[CLAT 2015]**

(a) No, this is not Siraj's mistake but Suman's, hence there is no point of returning the money back.
(b) Yes, because Suman and Sunil owed only ₹ 1000 to Siraj. Suman paid extra ₹ 1000 by mistake and now Siraj has a total of ₹ 2000 which is extra from the original owed amount.
(c) No, extra ₹ 1000 are interest from Suman's side.
(d) Facts are not clear.

33. Y makes an attempt to steal some jewels by breaking open a box and finds, after opening the box, that there is no jewel in it.

Choose the appropriate answer. **[CLAT 2015]**

(a) Y is not guilty of attempt to theft because the box was empty.
(b) Y is guilty of attempt to commit theft.
(c) Y is guilty of trespass.
(d) Y is not guilty of any offence.

34. Which of the following is correct for the purpose of criminal deception? **[CLAT 2015]**

(a) Dishonest concealment of facts
(b) Dishonestly receiving of property
(c) Making damage by an act
(d) Intentionally giving consent

35. X, a married woman, agreed to live in adultery with B and also agreed to serve him as his housekeeper. In return, B agreed to pay X ₹ 500 per month for living in adultery and ₹ 500 per month for housekeeping. The agreement is **[CLAT 2015]**

(a) valid
(b) void
(c) void as to the first object, but valid with respect to the second object
(d) unlawful as being opposed to public policy

36. Principle A 'fixture' is something attached to land or a building in such a way that it is regarded as an irremovable part of the property you are considering buying. Some typical 'fixtures' in a home include the hot water service, range top, wall oven, fixed floor coverings, light fittings and a built-in (under bench) dishwasher. Garden plants, including bushes and trees are also 'fixtures'.

Rule A. When land is sold, all 'fixtures' on the land are also deemed to have been sold.

Rule B. If a movable thing is attached to the land or any building on the land, then it becomes a 'fixture'.

Factual Situation Khaleeda wants to sell a plot of land she owns in Beghmara (Meghalaya) and the sale value decided for the plot includes the fully-furnished palatial six- bedroom house that she has built on it five years ago. She sells it to Gurpreet for ₹60 lakh. After completing the sale, she removes the expensive Iranian carpet which used to cover entire wooden floor of one of the bedrooms. The room had very little light and Khaleeda used this light-coloured radiant carpet to negate some of the darkness in the room. Gurpreet, after moving in, realises this and files a case to recover the carpet from Khaleeda.

Assume that in the above fact scenario, Khaleeda no longer wants the carpet. She removes the elaborately carved door to the house after the sale has been concluded and claims that Gurpreet has no claim to the door. The door in question was part of Khaleeda's ancestral home in Nagercoil (Tamil Nadu) for more than 150 years before she had it fitted as the entrance to her Beghmara house. **[CLAT 2015]**

As a judge you would decide in favour of

(a) Gurpreet because when the price was agreed upon, Khaleeda did not inform her about removing the carpet
(b) Gurpreet because the carpet was integral to the floor of the bedroom and therefore, attached to the building that was sold
(c) Khaleeda because a fully-furnished house does not entail the buyer to everything in the house
(d) Khaleeda because by virtue of being a carpet, it was never permanently fixed to the floor of the building

37. Principle One who dishonestly misappropriates or converts to his own use or sells any movable property belonging to another, is guilty of the offence of misappropriation.

Fact 'A' takes property belonging to 'Z' out of 'Z's possession, in good faith, believing when he takes it, that the property belongs to himself. Subsequently, 'A' on discovering his mistake, without disclosing the actual facts, dishonestly sells the property to a stranger. **[CLAT 2016]**

(a) 'A' may be guilty of theft but not for misappropriation.
(b) 'A' is guilty of an offence of misappropriation.
(c) 'A' is not guilty because when he took the property, he believed in good faith that it belonged to him.
(d) 'A' is not guilty as the property can be recovered from the stranger.

38. Principle Acceptance of proposal must be the exact mirror image of the proposal.

Fact 'A' made a proposal to 'B' to sell a chair for ₹500. 'B' expressed his desire to buy the said chair for ₹400. **[CLAT 2016]**

(a) 'B' has accepted the proposal of 'A'
(b) It is not clear whether 'B' has accepted the proposal of 'A' or not
(c) It is not clear whether 'A' made a proposal to 'B'
(d) 'B' has not accepted the proposal of 'A'

39. Principle A person, who is usually of unsound mind, but occasionally normal, may take a contract when he is not of unsound mind.

Fact 'A' generally means in the state of unsound mind and rarely becomes capable of understanding the things. **[CLAT 2016]**

(a) 'A' can never make a contract
(b) 'A' can make a contract at any time whenever he pleases
(c) 'A' can make a contract when normal
(d) 'A' can make a contract only for his own benefit

40. Principle Nothing is an offence, which is done by accident or misfortune and without any criminal intention or knowledge in the doing of a lawful act in a lawful manner by lawful means and with proper care and caution.

Fact 'A' takes up a gun, not knowing whether it is loaded or not, points it playfully at 'B' and pulls the trigger. Consequently, 'B' falls dead. **[CLAT 2016]**

(a) B's death is accidental, as 'A' had no intention to kill 'B'
(b) B's death is accidental, as 'A' was just pointing the gun playfully at 'B'
(c) B's death is accidental, as 'A' did not have the knowledge that the gun is loaded
(d) B's death is not accidental, as there was want of proper care and caution on the part of 'A'

41. Principle Causing an effect partly by an act and partly by an omission is an offence.

Fact 'A' confined her daughter 'D' in a room. 'A' also did not provide any food to her daughter 'D'. Consequently, 'D' died of starvation. **[CLAT 2016]**

(a) 'A' committed no offence
(b) 'A' committed the offence of confining 'D'
(c) 'A' committed the offence of not providing food to 'D'
(d) 'A' committed the offence of causing death of 'D'

42. Principle Where a person lawfully does anything for another person, or delivers anything to him, not intending to do so or to provide gratuitously, and such other person takes the benefit of that, the latter is bound to compensate the former for something done or thing provided, or to restore, the thing so delivered.

Fact Trader 'A' delivers certain eatables at B's house by mistake. 'B' consumed the eatables without asking anything. Which of the following derivations is correct? **[CLAT 2016]**

(a) 'B' can be made liable to pay for the eatables, only if 'A' establishes an express contract between 'A' and 'B'
(b) 'B' is bound to pay 'A' for the eatables
(c) It is the discretion of 'B' to make payment to 'A'
(d) 'B' is not bound to pay 'A' for the eatables

43. Principle A person is said to have committed assault when an apprehension is caused in the mind of a person that he is about to use physical force against his body.

Fact 'A' abuses 'B' while he was sitting in a moving train, by aggressively shaking his fists when 'B' was standing on the railway platform at a distance. **[CLAT 2016]**

(a) 'A' has not committed assault against 'B'
(b) 'A' has caused fear of assault in the mind of 'B'
(c) 'A' has caused apprehension of assault in the mind of 'B'
(d) 'A' has committed assault against 'B'

44. Principle Whoever takes away any moveable thing from the land of any person without that person's consent, he is said to have committed theft.

Fact During his visit to the house of 'C', 'A' asked 'B', the son of 'C', to accompany 'A' to the forest. Neither 'A' nor 'B' informed 'C' in this regard. 'B' accompanied 'A' to the forest. **[CLAT 2016]**

(a) 'A' has committed theft
(b) 'A' has not committed theft
(c) 'A' has not committed theft till 'B' did not accompany him
(d) 'A' has committed theft as soon as he entered the house of 'C'

45. Principle When a person consented to an act to be done by another, he cannot claim any damages resulting from doing that act, provided the act done is the same for which consent is given.

Fact 'P' submitted a written consent to a surgeon 'S' for undergoing a surgical operation for removal of appendicitis. The surgeon while doing surgery also removed the gall bladder of 'A' : **[CLAT 2017]**

(a) 'P' is required to pay expenses for surgery for Appendicitis but not for Gall Bladder
(b) 'P' can claim damages from 'S'
(c) 'P' is not bound to pay expenses of the surgery
(d) 'P' cannot claim damages from 'S'

46. Principle Penal laws provide that whoever voluntarily has carnal intercourse against the order of nature with any man or woman, shall be punished for rape.

Fact A police officer found a man engaged in carnal intercourse with an animal. The police officer arrested the man and produced him before the court. **[CLAT 2017]**

(a) Court will punish the man for rape.
(b) Court will punish the police officer.
(c) Court will not punish the police officer.
(d) Court will not punish the man for rape.

47. Principle There are legal provisions to give authority to a person to use necessary force against an assistant or wrong-doer for the purpose of protecting one's own body and property as also another's body and property when immediate aid from the state machinery is not readily available, and in so doing he is not answerable in law for his deeds.

Fact X, a rich man was taking his morning walk. Due to the threat of robbers in the locality, he was carrying his pistol also. From the opposite direction, another person was coming with a ferocious looking dog. All of a sudden, the dog which was on a chain held by the owner, started barking at X. The owner of the dog called the dog to be calm. They crossed each other without any problem. But suddenly, the dog started barking again from a distance. X immediately took out his pistol. By seeing the pistol the dog stopped barking and started walking with the owner. However, X shot at the dog which died instantly. The owner of the dog files a complaint against X, which in due course reached the Magistrate Court. X pleads the right of private defense. Decide. **[CLAT 2017]**

(a) The right of private defense is available to persons against assailants or wrong-doers only and a dog does not fall in the this category.
(b) Shooting a fierce dog is not to be brought under the criminal law. So the case should be dismissed.
(c) As there was no guarantee that the dog would not bark again, shooting it was a precautionary measure and hence within the right available to X under law.
(d) There was no imminent danger to X as the dog stopped barking and was walking with the owner. Hence, shooting it amounted to excessive use of the right of private defense and hence liable for killing the dog.

48. Principle A person is said to do a thing fraudulently, if he does that thing with intent to defraud, but not otherwise.

Fact 'A' occasionally hands over his ATM card to 'B' to withdrawn money for 'A'. On one occasion 'B' without the knowledge of 'A', uses 'A's ATM card to find out the balance in 'A's account, but does not withdraw any money. **[CLAT 2017]**

(a) 'B' has committed misappropriation
(b) 'B' has not committed the act fraudulently
(c) 'B' has committed the act fraudulently
(d) 'B' has committed breach of faith.

49. Principle Whoever takes away with him any minor less than sixteen years of age if a male, or less than eighteen years of age if a female, out of the custody of parents of such minor without the consent of such parents, is said to commit no offence.

Fact 'A', a man, took away a girl below sixteen years to Mumbai without informing the parents of the girl. **[CLAT 2017]**

(a) 'A' committed no offence against the parents of the girl.
(b) 'A' committed no offence against the girl.
(c) 'A' committed no offence against the girl was well as her parents.
(d) 'A' committed an offence against the girl was well as her parents.

50. Principle Nothing is an offence which is done in the exercise of the right of private defense.

Fact 'A', under the influence of madness, attempts to kill 'B'. 'B' to save his life kills 'A'. **[CLAT 2017]**

(a) 'B' has not committed any offence.
(b) 'B' has committed an offence.
(c) 'A' has not committed an offence because he was mad.
(d) 'A' has committed the offence of attempt to murder.

51. Principle Assault is causing bodily injury to another person by use of physical force.

Fact Rustum while entering into compartment of a train raised his first in anger towards a person Sheetal, just in front of him in the row, to get way to enter into the train first, but dit not hit him. Rustum has : **[CLAT 2017]**

(a) insulted Sheetal
(b) Rightly showed his anger
(c) not committed an assault on Sheetal
(d) committed an assault on Sheetal

52. Principle When a person interferes with peaceful possession of another person without the permission of the person in possession of those premises, commits trespass to land.

Fact 'T' just walked over the land of 'P' to reach his house as it was a short cut. 'P' had displayed a notice that it is not a thoroughfare. 'P' did not cause any damage to the land. **[CLAT 2017]**

(a) 'T' has created nuisance for 'P'.
(b) 'T' has violated privacy of 'P'.
(c) 'T' has committed trespass to land.
(d) 'T' has not committed any trespass on the land of 'P'.

53. Principle Ownership in property consists of right to possess, right to use, right to alienate and right to exclude others. Sale is complete when property gets transferred from the seller to the buyer on sale.

Fact 'A' sold his car to 'B'. After this, 'B' requested 'A' to keep the car in his care on behalf 'B' for one month. 'A' agreed. **[CLAT 2017]**

(a) Sale will be completed when 'B' will take the delivery of the car.
(b) Sale of car is complete.
(c) Sale of car is not complete.
(d) Sale will be automatically completed after the expiry of one month.

Answers

1	*d*	2	*b*	3	*a*	4	*b*	5	*c*	6	*a*	7	*d*	8	*a*	9	*a*	10	*c*
11	*d*	12	*b*	13	*a*	14	*c*	15	*d*	16	*c*	17	*c*	18	*c*	19	*a*	20	*a*
21	*d*	22	*a*	23	*c*	24	*b*	25	*c*	26	*b*	27	*a*	28	*a*	29	*c*	30	*a*
31	*b*	32	*b*	33	*b*	34	*a*	35	*d*	36	*a*	37	*b*	38	*d*	39	*c*	40	*d*
41	*d*	42	*a*	43	*d*	44	*b*	45	*b*	46	*a*	47	*d*	48	*b*	49	*c*	50	*a*
51	*c*	52	*c*	53	*b*														

CHAPTER 03

CONTRACT LAW

Human society works on promises and future course of action is guided by some models which intended to fulfill some obligation on behalf of two consulting individuals. The contract law is an effective tool to deal with such acts and deeds in a society.

CONTRACT

A contract is a legally enforceable agreement between two or more parties with mutual obligations. The Indian Contract Act, 1872, Section 2(h) defines the term 'Contract' as an agreement enforceable by law.

Agreement

Section 2(e) of Indian Contract Act, 1872 defines agreement as, "every promise and every set of promises forming the consideration for each other".

A promise is defined as an accepted proposal. Now, we can conclude that a contract is an agreement, an agreement is a promise and a promise is an accepted proposal.

An agreement becomes a contract when the following conditions are satisfied

- There is some consideration for it.
- The parties are competent to contract.
- Their consent is free.
- Their object is lawful.
- Offer and acceptance (offer from one party and its acceptance by the other).
- Intention to create legal obligations.
- The terms of the agreement must not be vague or uncertain.
- The agreement must be capable of performance.

Essential Conditions of a Valid Offer (Proposal)

1. **Expression of Willingness to do/Abstain from Doing and to Obtain Other's Assent** An offer must be made to obtain the assent of the other. When a person says he may buy a particular thing for a certain amount, it is not an offer.
2. **Intention to Contract** There is no provision in the Indian Contract Act requiring that an offer or its acceptance should be made with the intention of creating legal relations, while under English law it is so. However, the courts generally presume intention to enter into legal relation.
3. **Express or Implied Offer** A valid proposal may be made by words i.e. express offer or by conduct i.e. implied offer.
4. **Certainty of Offer** Terms of the offer must be certain and not vague.

   e.g. 'A' agrees to sell to 'B' his white horse for ₹ 500 or ₹ 1000. There is nothing to show which of the two prices was to be given, thus, it is not a valid offer.

Communication of Offer

The proposal must be communicated to other party. And communication of a proposal is complete when it comes to the knowledge of the person to whom it is made.
e.g. 'A' proposes by letter, to sell a horse to 'B' at a certain price. The communication of the proposal is complete when 'B' receives the letter.

Essential Elements of a Valid Contract

There are two kinds of offers, which are as follows

1. **General Offer** It is made to the public or world at large. The contract is made only with that person who comes forward and performs the conditions of the proposal as such performance amounts to acceptance of performance. The communication of acceptance is not necessary.
2. **Specific Offer** It is made to specific or an ascertained person.

Offer and Invitation to Treat (Offer)

- An 'offer' is the final expression of willingness by the offer or to be bound by his offer. Sometimes a person may not offer to sell his goods, but make some statement or give some information with a view to inviting others to make offers on that basis.
- A party without expressing his final willingness, proposes certain terms on which he is willing to negotiate, he does not make any offer but merely 'invites' the other party to make an offer on those terms.
  e.g. A book seller sends catalogue of books indicating price of various books to many persons. This is an, 'invitation to treat'. The interested party may make an offer and the book seller may accept or reject the offer.

Acceptance

Section 2 (b) of Indian Contract Act, 1872 defines 'acceptance' as, "When the person to whom the proposal is made signifies his assent thereof, the proposal is said to be accepted. A proposal, when accepted, becomes a promise". Thus, acceptance is the assent given to a proposal.

Consideration

- It constitutes the very foundation of the contract. An agreement not supported by consideration is void.
- It is the cause of the promise and its absence would make the promise a gravitous or bare promise (nudum pactum).
- Consideration is the price for which the promise of the offer is bought. If 'A' makes an agreement to sell his laptop to 'B' for ₹ 10000 then 10000 is the consideration for A's promise to sell his laptop.

Capacity to Contract

- It means the legal competence of a person to enter into a valid contract. Usually, the capacity to contract refers to the capacity to enter into legal agreement and the competence to perform some act.
- The basic element to enter into a valid contract is that he/she much have a sound mind.

Following three persons are parties incompetent to contract

1. Minor Person

A minor cannot make a promise enforceable in law. An agreement made by minor person is absolutely void.

No Estoppel Against Minor

- When a minor misrepresents at the time of the contract that he is a major, the question arises that whether the law of Estoppel apply against him or not.
- It is a defined law that the law of estoppel cannot be applied against the minor even if he acted fraudulently.

No Liability in Contract or in Tort Arising Out of Contract

A minor may be liable in tort generally. However, he will not be liable for a tort arising out of contract, for the reason that such liability is an indirect way of enforcing his agreement.

Doctrine of Restitution

Doctrine of Restitution applies against a minor i.e. when a minor obtains property or goods by false representation, he can be compelled to restore it, but only so long as the same is traceable in his possession.

2. Persons of Unsound Mind

- A person is said to be of sound mind for the purpose of making a contract if, at the time when he makes it, he is capable of understanding it and of forming a rational judgement as to its effect upon his interests.
- A person, who is usually of unsound mind, but occasionally of sound mind, may make a contract when he is of sound mind. A person who is usually of sound mind but occasionally of unsound mind, may not make a contract when he is of unsound mind. e.g.
  (i) A patient in a lunatic asylum, who is at intervals of sound mind, may contract during those intervals.
  (ii) A same man, who is delirious from fever or who is so drunk that he cannot understand the terms of a contract or form a rational judgement as to its effect on his interests, cannot contract whilst such delirium or drunkness lasts.

3. Disqualified Persons

The incompetent persons are those who are disqualified from contracting by any law to which they are subject. e.g. alien enemies, foreign sovereigns and ambassadors, convicts etc.

Free Consent

- 'Consent' is defined under **Section 13** of Indian Contract Act, 1872.
- "Two or more persons are said to consent when they agree upon the same thing in the same sense". This is known as 'Consensus ad-idem'.

Consent is said to be free when it is not caused by

- Coercion
- Under influence
- Fraud
- Misrepresentation
- Mistake

Coercion

An agreement to which the consent is caused by coercion is voidable at the option of the party whose consent was so caused.

A consent is caused by coercion, when it is obtained by

- committing or threatening to commit any act forbidden by the Indian Penal Code.
- unlawfully detaining or threatening to detain any property.

e.g. 'A' threatens to shoot 'B', if 'B' does not agree to sell his property to 'A' at a stated price. 'B's consent has been obtained by coercion.

Under Influence

Where the relations subsisting between the parties are such that one of the parties is in a position to dominate the will of the other, and uses that position to obtain an unfair advantage over the other, there is said to be under influence.
e.g. 'A', having advanced money to his son, 'B', during his minority, upon 'B's coming of age obtains, by misuse of parental influence, a bond from 'B' for a greater amount than the sum due to respect of the advance. 'A' employs undue influence.

Fraud

- An agreement to which the consent is caused by fraud is voidable at the option of the party whose consent was so caused.
- 'Fraud' means and includes any of the following acts, committed by a party to a contract or with his connivance or by his agent, done with 'intent to deceive' or to induce a person to enter into a contract.
  - The suggestion that a fact is true when it is not true and the person making the suggestion does not believe it to be true.
  - Active concealment of a fact by a person.
  - Promise made without any intention of performing.
  - Any other act fitted to deceive.
  - Any such act or omission as the law specially declares to be fraudulent.
- The essentials of fraud are that there should be a 'false statement of fact' by a person who himself does not believe the statement to be true. There must be a wrongful intention also.

Misrepresentation

- A contract, the consent to which is induced by misrepresentation is voidable at the option of the deceived party.
- Misrepresentation means misstatement of a fact material to the contract. When a person makes a false statement which he himself believes to be true and he does not intend to deceive the other party, there is misrepresentation.
  e.g. the government auctioned certain forest coupes. A part of the land was occupied by tenants. The forest department knew this fact but did not disclose to the purchaser. The contract is vitiated by misrepresentation.

Mistake

- Mistake means an erroneous belief about something. Mistake makes the contract void i.e. it is not enforceable at the option of either party. It may operate upon a contract in two ways.
- It may defeat the consent altogether or it may mislead the parties as to the purpose which they contemplated.

e.g. 'A' agrees to buy from 'B' a certain horse. It turns out that the horse was dead at the time of the bargain, though neither party was aware of the fact. The agreement is void on account of mistake.

Limitation on Freedom of Contract

- For the validity of a contract, it is essential that the consideration and object should be lawful.
- If the money is borrowed for the purpose of the marriage of a minor, the consideration for the contract is the loan and the object is the marriage.

The consideration or object of an agreement are lawful unless

- It is forbidden by law.
- It is of such a nature that it would defeat the provision of law.
- It is fraudulent.
- It involves or implies injury to the person or property of another.
- The court regards it as immoral or opposed to public policy.

e.g. 'A's estate is sold for arrears of revenue under the provisions of an act of the legislature, by which the defaulter is prohibited from purchasing the estate. 'B', upon an understanding with 'A', becomes the purchases and agrees to convey the estate to 'A' upon receiving from him the price which 'B' has paid. The agreement is void as it renders the transaction, in effect, a purchase by the defaulter and would so defeat the provision of the law.

Void Agreements

An agreement not enforceable by law is said to be void. There are some agreements which have been specifically or expressly declared as void by the Indian Contract Act. *These are as follows*

- Agreements of which the consideration or object is unlawful.
- Agreement without consideration.
- Agreement in restraint of marriage.
- Agreement in restraint of trade.
- Agreement in restraint of legal proceedings.
- Agreement which are uncertain and ambiguous.
- Agreement by way of wager.
- Agreements to do impossible acts.

Discharge of Contract

- When the performance of the contract becomes impossible, the purpose, which the parties have in mind, is frustrated.
- If the performance becomes impossible, because of a supervening event, the promisor is excused from the performance of the contract. This is known as doctrine of frustration.
- An agreement to do an impossible act in itself is void.

e.g.

- 'A' agrees with 'B' to discover treasure of magic. The agreement is void.
- 'A' and 'B' contract to marry each other. Before the time fixed for the marriage, 'A' goes mad. The contract becomes void.
- 'A' contracts to marry 'B', being already, married to 'C', and being forbidden by the law to which he is subject to practice polygamy. 'A' must make compensation to 'B' for the loss caused to her by the non-performance of his promise.
- 'A' contracts to take in cargo for 'B' at a foreign port. 'A's government afterwards declares war against the country in which the port is situated the contract becomes void when war is declared.

Revocation of Offers and Acceptance

An offer may be revoked at any time before it is accepted and an acceptance made at time before communication of acceptance is complete as against the offeror.

Invitation to Offer and Counter-Offers

Sometimes certain exchange of communication or willingness to eventually enter into a contract is mistaken for offer and acceptance. In spite of their language which is similar to an offer or acceptance, no agreement is born.

Invitation to Offer

Where a person aspires his/her willingness to enter into a contract but does not make an out right offer it constitutes an invitation to offer. The best example of an invitation to offer is displaying goods for sale. In this case, the seller is not making an offer but is inviting you to come and purchase a good. When you express willingness to purchase, your willingness constitutes an offer. The shopkeeper is within his rights to accept or reject your offer.

Counter-Offers

Where instead of giving acceptance a person responds to an offer by making a counter-offer, giving partial acceptance or conditional acceptance, the act constitutes a counter-offer rather than acceptance. Bargaining, negotiations, cross-offers are good examples of counter offers.

Indian Contract Act, 1872

The Indian Contract Act, 1872 is the law codifying contracts in India. Contract under the Indian Contract Act, 1872 under Section 2(b) is defined as 'an agreement enforceable by law'. As to which agreements are enforceable by law, we look at Section 10 which states that,

"All agreements are contracts if they are made by the free consent of parties competent to contract, for a lawful consideration and with a lawful object, and are not hereby expressly declared to be void."

In other words, for a contract we require

- Formation of a valid agreement.
- The agreement be entered by free consent.
- The contracting parties have the capacity to contract.
- The contract requires exchange of lawful consideration.
- The contract has a lawful object and is not declared void.

If these five requirements are present then an agreement qualifies for a contract. In this section, we study requirements 2 to 5.

Position of Minors in Contracts

This is one of the trickiest areas of the entire contract's course for CLAT. A minor's position is indeed very peculiar as we shall study.

1. **Definition of a Minor** A minor is a person below 18 years of age. However, if he has court-appointed legal guardian then a minor cannot contract till she/he is of 21 years.
2. **General Rule** As a general rule a contract with a minor is absolutely void, i.e. when a contract is entered with a minor it cannot be enforced at all. The logic behind this is analogous to the reason as to why persons of unsound mind are debarred from contract. Since minors are not mature enough to understand the full implications of a contract, the law presumes it is best that no contract be entered by a minor. Thus, where a contract is entered by X who is of 18 years of age and Y who is of 25 years of age, and Y enters into a contract with X who represents his age to be 21, the contract shall still be void. This places an obligation upon X to find out the age of the minor.
3. **When can Contracts be Enforced by a Minor**? Though no contract can be enforced against a minor, a contract can indeed be enforced by a minor if the contract is beneficial to him. However,

   unless this is given as a part of the principle, follow the general rule that a contract is void, as such it cannot be enforced by anyone.
4. **Necessaries and Restitution** Where a person enters into a contract with a minor in good faith, supplying him necessaries, basic requirements essential for his maintenance and well being of a child, e.g. feeding a child when he is hungry, the price of food articles can be claimed from he legal guardian of the child.

Practice Exercise

1. The law of contract is nothing but
(a) a child of commercial dealing
(b) a child of religion
(c) a child of day to day politics
(d) a child of economic

2. The contract Act came into force
(a) from 1st September, 1972
(b) before 1st September, 1882
(c) from 1st September, 1872
(d) after 1st September, 1872

3. An agreement consists of reciprocal promises between atleast
(a) four parties (b) six parties
(c) three parties (d) two parties

4. Contractual rights and duties are created by
(a) state
(b) statute
(c) parties
(d) custom or usage

5. Contract is defined as an agreement enforceable by law, vide Section .... of the Indian Contract Act.
(a) 2(e) (b) 2(f)
(c) 2(h) (d) 2(i)

6. A sells his car to B. A has a right to recover the price of the car from B. This right is a
(a) Right is rem
(b) Right is personam
(c) Right in rem as well as right in personam
(d) Moral right

7. A owns a residential flat. He is entitled to a quiet possession and enjoyment of his property. This is called
(a) Rights in personam
(b) Rights in rem
(c) Moral right
(d) There is no right at all

8. A contract creates
(a) Rights in personam
(b) Rights in rem
(c) No obligations
(d) Only obligations and no rights

9. Valid contracts
(a) are made by free consent
(b) are made by competent parties
(c) have lawful consideration and lawful object
(d) All of the above

10. Agreement to murder a person
(a) cannot be enforceable by law
(b) is valid in law
(c) is invalid for want of consideration
(d) has no consensus ad idem

11. An agreement is valid
(a) which creates legal and social obligations of the parties
(b) which creates rights of a party
(c) which is written on a piece of paper and signed by the parties
(d) which creates legally binding right and obligations of the parties to it

12. Voidable contract is one
(a) which is lawful
(b) which is invalid
(c) which is valid as long as it is not avoided by the party entitled to do so
(d) which is unlawful

13. When the contract is perfectly valid but cannot be enforced because of certain technical defects. This is called
(a) Unilateral contract
(b) Bilateral contract
(c) Unenforceable contract
(d) Void contract

14. A and B enter into a contract to marry each other. Before the time fixed for the marriage, A goes mad. The contract becomes
(a) Void (b) Illegal (c) Valid (d) Voidabl

15. A makes a contract with B to beat his business competitor. This is an example of
(a) Valid contract
(b) Illegal agreement
(c) Voidable contract
(d) Unenforceable contract

16. LEGAL PRINCIPLE When a contract has been broken, the party who suffers by such breach is entitled to receive, from the party who has broken the contract, compensation for any loss or damage caused to him thereby, which naturally arose in the usual course of things from such breach, or which the parties knew, when they made the contract to be likely to result from the breach of it. Such compensation is not given for any remote or indirect loss or damage sustained by reason of the breach. Decide, whether and to what extent B is entitled to damages in the following situation.

FACTUAL SITUATION A contracts with B to sell him 1000 tonnes of iron at ₹ 100 per tonne. B tells A that he needs the iron for export purposes, and that he would be selling the iron at ₹ 200 per tonne. A breaks the contract. When the question comes about damages, A says he will pay only ₹ 5000 as damages because the same variety of iron was available in the market at ₹ 105 per tonne. B however contends that he should be given ₹ 100000 because that was the profit which he would have made had A fulfilled the contract B had actually bought the iron at ₹ 110 and had exported it. B is

(a) not entitled to damages
(b) entitled to ₹ 10000 as damages
(c) entitled to ₹ 5000 as damages
(d) entitled to ₹ 100000 as damages

17. LEGAL PRINCIPLE The contract after death of one party can be continued if it is ratified by the surviving party.

FACTUAL SITUATION Vishal, a famous artist was requested by Arun, an industrialist to draw the portrait of his deceased wife and paid ₹ 20000 in advance and agreed to pay when the work was completed, a sum of ₹ 2 lakhs. When the portrait was half drawn, Vishal died due to heart attack. His son also a fine artist completed his father's work and demanded the money from Arun. Arun refused to pay and to accept the portrait drawn by Vishal's son and also demanded the advance to be returned.

(a) Arun cannot demand the advance amount from the son of Vishal, because in normal cases the son is not responsible for the father's contractual obligation
(b) Son of Vishal cannot demand the rest of amount from Arun because Arun has not assigned him the work
(c) Arun can demand the rest of the amount
(d) Both (a) and (b)

18. PRINCIPLE A contract between the father and his son is a contract of utmost good faith. In such a type of contract law presumes that at the time of entering into the contract father was in a position to dominate the will of his son. Where one of the parties was in a position to dominate the will of the other party, the contract is enforceable at the option of the party whose will was so dominated.

FACTS Ram had advanced a sum of ₹ 10000 to his minor son Shyam. When Shyam became major, his father Ram misused his parental position and entered into an agreement with Shyam and obtained a bond from him for a sum ₹ 30000 in respect of the advance. Whether this agreement is enforceable?

(a) The agreement is enforceable against Shyam only for ₹ 10000 the actual amount of money advanced to him
(b) The agreement is enforceable against Shyam for ₹ 30000 because he has signed the bond
(c) The agreement is enforceable against Shyam because he was major at the time of agreement
(d) The agreement is not enforceable against Shyam because Ram has misused his position as father to obtain unfair advantage

19. A lease agreement is a form of

(a) promissory note (b) bill of exchange
(c) licence (d) contract

20. Frustration of contract implies

(a) commercial hardship
(b) physical impossibility due to disappearance of the subject matter of the contract on the object has failed to materialise
(c) Both (a) and (b)
(d) Neither (a) nor (b)

Previous Year's Questions

Problems (Q. Nos. 21-25)

Rules

A. A minor is a person who is below the age of eighteen. However, where a guardian administers the minor's property the age of majority is twenty one.

B. A minor is not permitted by law to enter into a contract. Hence, where a minor enters into a contract with a major person, the contract is not enforceable. This effectively means that neither the minor nor the other party can make any claim on the basis of the contract.

C. In a contract with a minor, if the other party hands over any money or confers any other benefit on the minor, the same shall not be recoverable from the minor unless the other party was deceived by the minor to hand over money or any other benefit. The other party will have to show that the minor misrepresented her age, he was ignorant about the age of the minor and that he handed over the benefit on the basis of such representation.

Facts Ajay convinces Bandita, a girl aged 18 that she should sell her land to him. Bandita's mother Chaaru is her guardian. Nonetheless Bandita, without the permission of Chaaru, sells the land to Ajay for a total sum of rupees fifty lac, paid in full and final settlement of the price. Chaaru challenges this transaction claiming that Bandita is a minor and hence the possession of the land shall not be given to Ajay. Thus, Ajay is in a difficult situation and has no idea how to recover his money from Bandita. **[CLAT 2011]**

21. Chaaru is justified in challenging the sale transaction because

(a) Bandita is of unsound mind and is not in a position to make rational decisions

(b) Though Bandita is eighteen years old, she will be treated as a minor, as Chaaru is her guardian

(c) Though Bandita is eighteen years old, she cannot sell the land without the permission of her mother

(d) Though Bandita is eighteen years old, she should not be treated like a person who has attained the age of majority

22. Ajay can be allowed to recover the money only if he can show that

(a) he was deceived by Bandita who misrepresented her age

(b) he honestly believed that Bandita was empowered under the law to sell the land

(c) he was an honest person who had paid the full price of the land to Bandita

(d) Both (a) and (b)

23. In order to defend the sale, Bandita will need to show that

(a) Bandita has attained the age of majority

(b) Bandita is mature enough to make rational decisions regarding her own affairs

(c) the sale transaction was beneficial to her interest and will enhance her financial status

(d) None of the above

24. Which of the following is correct?

(a) Ajay should be allowed to recover the money because even though there is no contract, Bandita and Chaaru should not be allowed to unjustly benefit from Ajay's money

(b) Ajay should be allowed the possession of the land because Chaaru can always decide to approve the transaction between Ajay and Bandita

(c) Ajay should not be allowed to recover because he induced Bandita, a minor, to sell the land

(d) None of the above

25. Which of the following is correct?

(a) If Ajay is allowed to recover the money, that will defeat the law framed for protecting the minors against fraudulent persons

(b) If Ajay is not allowed to recover that will cause him injustice as he has not paid off the entire sale price

(c) If Ajay is allowed to recover, Chaaru will benefit from both the money and the land

(d) None of the above

26. Principle Mere silence as to the facts likely to affect the willingness of a person to enter into a contract is not a fraud, unless the circumstances of the case are such that, on close examination it is found to be the duty of the person keeping silent to speak, or unless his silence is, in itself, equivalent to speech.

Facts X sells by auction to Y, a horse which X knows to be of unsound state of mind. X says nothing to Y about the horse's unsound state of mind. Give the correct answer. **[CLAT 2011]**

(a) X can be held liable for fraud
(b) X can be held liable for misrepresentation
(c) X cannot be held liable, because he did not say anything positive about the mental state of the horse
(d) X cannot be held liable because it is the buyer who must be aware of the things

27. **Principle** A person is said to be of sound mind for the purpose of making a contract if, at the time when he makes it, he is capable of understanding it and of forming a rational judgement as to its effect upon his interests.

Facts Mr X who is usually of sound state of mind, but occasionally of unsound state of mind, enters into a contract with Mr Y when he was of unsound state of mind. Mr Y having come to know about this fact afterwards, wants to file a suit against Mr X. **[CLAT 2011]**

(a) Mr X cannot enter into contract, because he is of unsound state of mind when he entered into contract
(b) Mr X can enter into contract but the burden is on the other party to prove that he was of unsound state of mind at the time of contract
(c) Mr X can enter into contract but the burden is on Mr X to prove that he was of sound state of mind at the time of contract
(d) None of the above

28. **Principle** Agreements, the meaning of which is not certain, or not capable of being made certain, are void.

Facts A horse was bought for a certain price coupled with a promise to give ₹ 500 more if the horse is proved lucky. **[CLAT 2011]**

(a) This is a valid agreement
(b) This agreement is void for uncertainty because it is very difficult to determine what luck, bad or good, the horse has brought to the buyer
(c) The agreement is partially valid and partially void
(d) None of the above

29. **Assertion** (A) A void contract is not necessarily illegal.

Reason (R) Every illegal contract is void. **[CLAT 2011]**

Coses

(a) Both (A) and (R) are true and (R) is the correct explanation of (A)
(b) Both (A) and (R) are true, but (R) is not the correct explanation of (A)
(c) (A) is true, but (R) is false
(d) (A) is false, but (R) is true

30. **Principle** Every person, who is of the age of majority, is competent to contract according to the law to which he is subject.

Facts A minor mortgaged his house in favour of Thakur Das, a money lender, to secure a loan of ₹ 20000. A part of this i.e. ₹ 10500 was actually advanced to him. While considering the proposed advance the attorney who was acting for the money lender, received information that plaintiff was still a minor. Subsequently, the minor commenced an action stating that he was underage when he executed the mortgage and the same should therefore, be cancelled. He prayed for setting aside the mortgage. The mortgage money lender prayed for the refund of ₹ 10500 from the minor. **[CLAT 2012]**

(a) As a minor's contract is void and money advanced to a minor can be recovered
(b) A minor's contract is void a initio any money advanced to a minor cannot be recovered
(c) A minor's contract is voidable; any money advanced to a minor can be recovered
(d) Advanced money can be recovered because minor has given wrong information about his age

31. Ramu applied for the post of director in an organisation. The governing body of the organisation passed a resolution appointing him to the post. After the meeting, one of the members of the governing body informed him privately of the resolution. Subsequently, the resolution was rescinded. Ramu claims damages, which one of the following is the correct legal proposition in the case? **[CLAT 2012]**

(a) Ramu cannot claim damages as he had not resigned, from his existing post in anticipation of getting the appointment letter
(b) Ramu cannot claim damages as there was no formal communication
(c) Ramu can claim damages as governing body cannot rescind the resolution once passed
(d) Ramu can claim damages as there was private communication

Directions (Q. Nos. 32-75) *This section consists of forty four questions. Each question consists of legal propositions/ principles (hereinafter referred to as 'principle') and facts.*

These principles have to be applied to the given facts to arrive at the most reasonable conclusion. Such principles may or may not be true in the real sense, yet you have to conclusively assume them to be true for the purposes of this section. In other words, in answering the following questions, you must not rely on any principles except the principles that are given here in below for every question. Further you must not assume any facts other than those stated in the question. The objective of this section is to test your interest towards study of law, research aptitude and problem solving ability even if the 'most reasonable conclusion' arrived at may be unacceptable for any other reason. It is not the objective of this section to test your knowledge of law.

32. Principle An agreement to do an act impossible in itself cannot be enforced by a court of law.

Facts Ramesh agrees with his girl friend Shilpa to pluck stars from the sky through his extraordinary will power and bring them down on Earth for her within a week. After the expiry of one week, Shilpa filed a suit for damages against Ramesh, for the breach of contract as Ramesh failed to perform his promise. **[CLAT 2013]**

(a) Shilpa can succeed in getting damages as Ramesh has deceived her
(b) Ramesh cannot be held liable as he honestly believes that his love for Shilpa is true and therefore, he will succeed in his endeavour
(c) The court cannot entertain such suits as the act promised under the agreement is impossible in itself
(d) Ramesh can be held liable for making an absurd promise

33. Principle Every agreement in restraint of the marriage of any person, other than a minor, is void.

Facts Qadir Khan died in a road accident. Two co-widows, Sultana and Marjina enter into an agreement that if any of them will remarry, would forfeit her right to her share in the deceased husband's property. **[CLAT 2013]**

(a) The agreement is void because it was restraint of marriage
(b) The agreement is not void because no restraint was imposed upon either of two widows for remarriage
(c) The restraint was partial so agreement is valid
(d) None of the above

34. Principle When at the desire of one person, any other person has done or abstained from doing something, such act or abstinence or promise is called a consideration for the promise. Only a promise coupled with consideration is enforceable by law.

Facts X, the uncle of Y, made a promise to pay him an amount of ₹ 10000 as reward, if Y quits smoking and drinking within one year. X also deposited the above mentioned amount in a bank and informed Y that the said amount will be paid to him, if he quits smoking and drinking within one year. Within a period of six months of making the promise X died. After the expiry of one year of making the promise by X, Y made a request to the legal heirs of X demanding the promised money. The legal heirs of X declined the request of Y. **[CLAT 2013]**

(a) The promise of X to Y is enforceable by law because Y has quitted smoking and drinking
(b) The promise of X to Y is not enforceable by law because Y has benefitted by quitting smoking and drinking
(c) The promise of X to Y is enforceable by law because the amount of ₹ 10000 has been deposited in a bank
(d) The promise of X to Y is enforceable by law because X has died within a period of six months of making the promise

35. Principle Licence is an agreement whereby the owner of the copyright agrees to grant an interest in the copyright to the licences. Assignment is an agreement whereby the owner of the copyright transfers all the property rights to the assignee. Property right is a bundle of rights consisting of right to possess, right to use, right to alienate and the right to exclude others.

Facts An owner of copyright in a cinematographic film enters into an agreement with B, a film distributor. B agrees to distribute the film only in Mumbai. A also enters into many such agreements with other distributors for distribution of his film in other cities. **[CLAT 2013]**

(a) The agreement between A and B is more in the nature of assignment than in the nature of licence
(b) The agreement between A and B is more in the nature of licence than in the nature of assignment
(c) The agreement between A and B is both in the nature of assignment and licence
(d) The agreement between A and B is neither in the nature of assignment nor in the nature of licence

36. Principle A seller of goods cannot transfer better rights than he himself possesses in the goods sold to the buyer.

Facts Komal leaves his watch by mistake on a seat in the park. Sonal finds that watch and immediately sells the same for good price to Monal who without inquiring whether Sonal is its owner or not. Komal later on claims that watch from Monal decide whether Komal can succeed. **[CLAT 2013]**

(a) Komal cannot succeed as Monal has paid good price of the watch
(b) Komal cannot succeed as Monal is unaware of the fact that Sonal is not its owner
(c) Komal cannot succeed as it was his carelessness and nothing else which enabled Sonal to sell the watch to Monal
(d) Komal cannot succeed as Sonal is merely finder of the watch and therefore, cannot transfer ownership rights thereon to Monal

37. Principle A person is said to be of sound mind for the purpose of making a contract if, at the time, when he makes it, he is capable of understanding it and of forming a rational judgment as to its effect upon his interest.

Facts X, who is usually of sound mind but occasionally of unsound mind enters into a contract with Y, when he (X) is of unsound mind. Y came to know about this fact afterwards and now wants to file a suit against X. **[CLAT 2013]**

(a) X cannot enter into contract because he is of unsound mind, when he entered into contract
(b) X can enter into contract but the burden is on the other party to prove that he was of unsound mind at the time of contract
(c) X can enter into contract but the burden is on X to prove that he was of sound mind at the time of contract
(d) None of the above

38. Principle In an agreement, a condition subsequent must be complied with, to claim the benefit of that agreement.

Facts A agrees to transfer a farm to B, provided that, if B does not go to England within three years after the date of the agreement, his interest in the farm shall cease. B does not go to England within the term prescribed. **[CLAT 2013]**

(a) B's interest in the farm continues
(b) B's interest in the farm does not continue
(c) B has a Fundamental Right to go to England or not to go to England and hence, the condition was illegal
(d) The agreement between A and B was void

39. Principle When a party to a contract has refused to perform or disabled himself from performing, his promise in its entirety, the other party may put an end to the contract.

Facts A engaged B on 12th April to enter his service on 1st June but on 11th May, A wrote to B that his services would not be needed. On 22nd May, B joined C for employment. **[CLAT 2013]**

(a) B must wait till 1st June
(b) B must have joined C on 11st May
(c) B is not bound to wait till 1st June
(d) A must pay damages to B

40. Principle When a person voluntarily agrees to suffer some harm, he is not allowed to complain for that.

Facts A was one of the spectators at a formula one car race, being held at Gurgaon, on a track owned by one M company. During the race, there was a collision between two racing cars, one of which was thrown away amidst spectators, thereby causing an injury to A, A claims damages for the injuries caused to him. **[CLAT 2013]**

(a) M company will be liable for damages because the injury was caused during the race organized by it

(b) M company will not be liable for damages because A had come to see the race on his own will

(c) M company will not be liable for damages because the collision between the cars was beyond its control

(d) M company will be liable because it has earned huge revenue by way of sale of tickets for the event

41. Principle Generally an agreement without consideration is not valid. Therefore, in order to make a valid agreement, some consideration which may have some value in the eyes of law, is essentially required.

Facts William has an old car of which he makes seldom use. He voluntarily enters into an agreement with Smith to sell this car for rupees ten thousand. Thereafter one Anson approaches William and offers to buy that car for rupees 1 lakh as the car was one which Anson has been searching for long. Now, William wants to cancel his agreement with Smith and refuses to deliver the car to him saying that consideration price for the car promised by Smith is negligible and therefore, agreement with him cannot be said to be valid one. **[CLAT 2013]**

(a) William can cancel his agreement with Smith as the consideration involved in that is really inadequate

(b) William cannot cancel his agreement with Smith as the sale of car for rupees ten thousand was voluntary and this price has some value in the eyes of law

(c) William can cancel his agreement with Smith as he was ignorant about the value/price of the car for which it could be sold

(d) William can cancel his agreement with Smith as he is entitled to get full market value/price of his car

42. Principle If the object of an agreement is or becomes unlawful or immoral or opposed to public policy in the eyes of law, then the courts will not enforce such agreements. Law generally prohibits child labour.

Facts P enters into an agreement with T, by which P has to let his house to T for two years and T has to pay ₹ 20000.00 per month to P as rent. T starts a child care centre in that house. But after some time in order to earn some money for the maintenance of the centre, T starts sending the children of the centre on the rotation basis to work for four hour a day in some nearby chemical and hazardous factories. When P comes to know about this new development, he asks T either to stop the children from working in factories or to leave his house immediately. T neither agrees to leave the house nor to stop the children from working in the factories. P files a suit in the court of law for appropriate relief/action. **[CLAT 2013]**

(a) P cannot succeed as the agreement was for the two years and it cannot be terminated before the expiry of that period

(b) P cannot succeed as the object at the time of making of the agreement was not clear

(c) P will succeed as the object of the agreement has become unlawful

(d) P will not succeed, if T agrees to share the wages of the children with P

43. Principle A contract cannot be enforced by or against a person who is not a party to it. However, where some benefit is conferred on third party by the contract itself, there third party can be allowed to enforce that contract to get such benefit.

Facts Dinesh is liable to pay ₹ 50000 to Suresh. In order to discharge this liability Dinesh enters into a contract with Ramesh by which Dinesh sells his car to Ramesh for ₹ 1 lakh Ramesh takes the delivery of the car and promises/assures to pay its price at the

earliest. Dinesh separately informs Suresh about this contract for his satisfaction. Ramesh fails to pay the car's price. Suresh wants to join Dinesh in filing suit against Ramesh for the recovery of price of the car. Whether Suresh is entitled to do so?
[CLAT 2013]

(a) Suresh is entitled to do so because the contract was made for his benefit
(b) Suresh is entitled to do so because Dinesh is liable to him and discharge of this liability depends upon the payment of the price of the car by Ramesh
(c) Suresh is not entitled to do so because liability of Dinesh does not depend upon any assurance of Ramesh
(d) Suresh is not entitled to do so because he is not a party to the contract between Dinesh and Ramesh

44. Principle If a contract is made by post between two persons living in two different cities, then the contract is said to be complete as soon as the letter of acceptance is properly posted and the place of completion of the contract is that city where acceptance is posted. It is worth mentioning here that in every contract there is always an offer from one party and the acceptance of the offer from the other party.

Facts Sani, a resident of Patna, gives an offer by post to sell his house for ₹ 25 lakh to Hani, a resident of Allahabad. This offer letter is posted on 1st January, 2013 from Patna and reaches Allahabad on 7th January, 2013. Hani accepts this offer and posts the letter of acceptance on 8th January, 2013 from Allahabad which reaches Patna on 16th January, 2013. But Sani presuming that Hani is not interested in accepting his offer, sells his house to Gani at same price on 15th of January, 2013. Hani files a suit against Sani for the breach of contract in the competent court of Allahabad. Whether Hani will succeed?
[CLAT 2013]

(a) Hani cannot succeed as Sani cannot be compelled by law to wait for the answer from Hani for an indefinite period of time
(b) Hani cannot succeed as he could use some other effective and speedy mode for communicating his acceptance in minimum possible time
(c) Hani can succeed as he properly posted the letter of acceptance and the delay was beyond his control
(d) Hani can succeed as contract became complete in the eyes of law on the date of posting the letter of acceptance

45. Principle In order to be eligible to appear in the semester examination, a student is required to attend, under all circumstances, atleast 70% of the total classes held in that semester as per University rules.

Facts Anand, an economically poor but a very brilliant student of LLB final semester, while going to his university by cycle received some leg injuries in road accident. Consequently Anand could not attend his classes for one week as he was advised rest by his doctor for that period. Due to this absence from the university, Anand failed to have 70% attendance essential to appear in the examination and therefore, he was debarred from appearing in the examination by the university authorities. Anand challenges this decision in the court of law.
[CLAT 2013]

(a) Anand will succeed in the court of law as the accident was beyond his control
(b) Anand will definitely get favour of the court on humanitarian ground as he comes from a economically poor family and may not afford to take readmission
(c) Anand will not succeed as he could very easily fulfil eligibility criteria for appearing in the examination by being reasonably regular in the class throughout the semester
(d) Anand will succeed as requirement of 70% attendance may be declared arbitrary and therefore, unreasonable by the court of law

46. Principle Whosoever commits any act forbidden by the Indian Penal Code with a view to obtain the consent of any person to enter into an agreement, he cannot get the agreement enforced by law but the person, whose consent has been so obtained may get the agreement enforced by law. The Indian Penal Code defines various offences and prescribes punishments therefor.

Facts A obtains the consent of B to enter into an agreement by an act amounting to criminal intimidation under the Indian Penal Code. A brings a case against B for performance of agreement **[CLAT 2013]**

(a) A will succeed in the case
(b) A may succeed in the case
(c) B will succeed in the case
(d) B will not succeed in the case

47. Principle Mere silence as to facts likely to affect the decision of a person to enter into a contract does not amount to fraud, unless his silence is in itself equivalent to speech.

Facts A sells to B a horse which A knows to be of unsound mind. B says to A that if A does not say anything about the state of mind of horse, then B shall presume that the horse is of sound mind. A says nothing to B about the mental condition of horse. **[CLAT 2013]**

(a) A has committed fraud
(b) A has committed misrepresentation
(c) There cannot be a fraud because A says nothing about the mental condition of the horse
(d) There cannot be a fraud because B did not ask A whether the horse is of sound mind

48. Principle Agreements in restraint of marriage are void.

Facts 'X' enters into an agreement, with 'Y' where under he agrees not to marry anybody else other than a person whose name starts with the letter 'A' and promises to pay ₹100000 to 'Y' if he ('X') breaks this agreement.

Which of the following derivations is correct? **[CLAT 2013]**

(a) There is a contract between 'X' and 'Y'
(b) There is an agreement between 'X' and 'Y' which can be enforced by the court of law
(c) There is an agreement between 'X' and 'Y' which cannot be enforced by the court of law
(d) There is a voidable contract between 'X' and 'Y'

49. Principle Ignorance of law excuses on one.

Facts 'X' fails to file his income tax returns for a considerable number of years. The Income Tax department serves upon him a 'show-cause notice' as to why proceedings should not be initiated against him for the recovery of the income tax due from him with interest and penalty.

Which of the following derivations is correct? **[CLAT 2013]**

(a) 'X' may defend himself by taking the plea that his legal advisor had not advised him to file the return
(b) 'X' would have to pay the due, as ignorance of law and failure to comply with law is no legal ground of defence
(c) 'X' may defend himself successfully by taking the plea that he was unaware of any such law being in force
(d) None of the above

50. Principle A contract which is duly supported by real and lawful consideration is valid not with standing the fact that the consideration is inadequate. The quantum of consideration is for the parties to decide at the time of making a contract and not for the courts (to decide) when the contract is sought to be enforced. An agreement to which the consent of the promisor is freely given is not void merely because the consideration is inadequate, but the inadequacy of the consideration may be taken into account by the court in determining the question whether the consent of the promisor was freely given.

Facts 'A' agrees to sell his mobile phone worth ₹ 20000 for ₹ 100 only to 'B' A's consent is freely given.

Which of the following derivations is correct? **[CLAT 2014]**

(a) There is a contract between 'A' and 'B'
(b) There is no contract between 'A' and 'B' because consideration is not adequate
(c) There is no contract between 'A' and 'B' because a mobile phone worth ₹ 20000 cannot be sold for just ₹ 100
(d) None of the above

51. Principle The consideration or object of an agreement is unlawful if it is forbidden by law. Every agreement of which the object or consideration is unlawful is void.

Facts 'X' promises to pay 'Y' ₹ 50000, if he ('Y') commits a crime, 'X' further promises to indemnify him ('Y') against any liability arising thereof. 'Y' agrees to act as per X's promise. **[CLAT 2014]**

Which of the following derivations is correct?

(a) There is a contract between 'X' and 'Y'
(b) There is an agreement between 'X' and 'Y' which can be enforced by the court of law
(c) There is an agreement between 'X' and 'Y' which cannot be enforced by the court of law
(d) There is a voidable contract between 'X' and 'Y

52. Principle Acceptance should be made while the offer is still subsisting. The offeror is free to retract his offer at anytime before his offer gets accepted by the offeree. Once the offer is withdrawn or is lapsed, it is not open to be accepted so as to give rise to a contract. Similarly, if a time is prescribed within which the offer is to be accepted, then the offer must be accepted within the prescribed time. And if no time is prescribed, then the acceptance must be made within a reasonable time. 'What is a reasonable time', is a question of fact which is to be determined by taking into account all the relevant facts and surrounding circumstances.

Facts 'X' makes an offer to 'Y' to sell his equipment for ₹ 1000.00. No time is specified for the acceptance. 'Y' sends his reply two years after receiving the offer.

Which of the following derivations is correct? **[CLAT 2014]**

(a) There arises a contract between 'X' and 'Y' to sell/buy the equipment in question for ₹ 1000.00
(b) There does not arise any contract between 'X' and 'Y' to sell/buy the equipment in question for ₹ 1000.00
(c) 'X' is bound by his offer and hence cannot reject the acceptance made by 'Y'
(d) There arises a promise by 'Y' to buy the equipment

53. Principle A proposal (offer) should be made with an intention that after its valid acceptance, a legally binding promise or agreement will be created. The test for the determination of such intention is not subjective, rather it is objective. The intention of the parties is to be ascertained from the terms of the agreement and the surrounding circumstances under which such an agreement is entered into.

As a general rule, in the case of arrangements regulating social relations, it follows as a matter of course that the parties do not intend legal consequences to follow. On the contrary, as a general rule, in the case of arrangements regulating business affairs, it follows as a matter of course that the parties intend legal consequences to follow. However, the above rules are just presumptive in nature and hence can be rebutted.

Facts One morning while having breakfast, 'X', the father, says to 'Y' (X's son), in a casual manner, 'I shall buy a motorbike for you, if you get through the CLAT.'

Which of the following derivations is correct? **[CLAT 2014]**

(a) 'X' made a statement that resulted in an enforceable promise
(b) 'X' made a statement that resulted in a valid proposal
(c) 'X' made a statement that resulted in an enforceable agreement
(d) 'X' made a statement that did not result in any enforceable agreement

54. Principle When one person signifies to another his willingness to do or to abstain from doing anything, with a view to obtaining the assent of that other to such act or abstinence, he is said to make a proposal. The expression of willingness/desire results in a valid proposal only when it is made/addressed to some person(s).

Facts 'X' makes the following statement in an uninhabited hall. 'I wish to sell my mobile phone for ₹ 1000.'

Which of the following derivations is correct? **[CLAT 2014]**

(a) 'X' made a statement that resulted in a promise
(b) 'X' made a statement that resulted in a proposal
(c) 'X' made a statement that did not result in any proposal
(d) 'X' made a statement that resulted in an agreement

55. Principle The consideration or object of an agreement is unlawful if the court regards it as opposed to public policy. Every agreement of which the object or consideration is unlawful is void.

Facts 'X' promises to obtain for 'Y' an employment in the public service and 'Y' promises to pay ₹ 500000 to 'X'

Which of the following derivations is correct? **[CLAT 2014]**

(a) There is a contract between 'X' and 'Y'
(b) There is a voidable contract between 'X' and 'Y'
(c) There is an agreement between 'X' and 'Y' which can be enforced by the court of law
(d) There is an agreement between 'X' and 'Y' which cannot be enforced by the court of law

56. Principle When two or more persons agree to do or cause to be done, (1) an illegal act or (2) an act which is not illegal by illegal means, through such an agreement such persons are said to have been engaged in a criminal conspiracy to commit an offence. It is said that no consummation of the crime need be achieved or even attempted.

Facts 'X', 'Y' and 'Z' plan to kill 'D'. They agree that only one among them, that is 'Z', will execute the plan. In pursuance of it 'Z' buys a gun and loads it. **[CLAT 2014]**

(a) Only 'Z' can be charged with criminal conspiracy to kill 'D'
(b) All of them, i.e. 'X', 'Y' and 'Z' can be charged with criminal conspiracy to kill 'D'
(c) 'X' and 'Y' cannot be charged with criminal conspiracy to kill 'D'
(d) None of them can be charged with criminal conspiracy to kill 'D'

57. Principle 'Wrongful gain' is gain by unlawful means of property to which the person gaining is not legally entitled. 'Wrongful loss' is the loss by unlawful means of property to which the person losing it is legally entitled.

Facts 'X' takes away Y's watch out of Y's possession, without Y's consent and with the intention of keeping it. **[CLAT 2014]**

(a) 'X' causes 'wrongful gain' to 'Y'
(b) 'Y' causes 'wrongful gain' to 'X'
(c) 'X' causes 'wrongful loss' to 'Y'
(d) 'Y' causes 'wrongful loss' to 'X'

58. Principle Nothing is an offence by reason that it causes, or that it is intended to cause, or that it is known to be likely to cause any harm, if that harm is so slight that no person of ordinary sense and temper would complain of such harm.

Facts 'X' takes a plain sheet of paper from Y's drawer without Y's consent to write a letter to his friend. **[CLAT 2014]**

(a) 'X' has committed an offence in the above context
(b) 'X' has committed no offence in the above context
(c) 'Y' can sue 'X' for an offence in the above context
(d) None of the above

59. Principle Where both the parties to an agreement are under a mistake as to a matter of fact essential to the agreement, the agreement is void.

Factual Situation Roxanne supplies designer clothes to big showrooms and famous cloth houses. Max agrees to buy a certain consignment of only pink designer clothes for his shop due to the pink coloured theme of his famous shop. Issue cropped up when the exclusive pink coloured dresses were not delivered to Max's showroom, but to some other buyer who had earlier contracted with Roxanne's store and all this was neither in the knowledge of Roxanne nor Max.

Decide whether the contract between Roxanne and Max is void? **[CLAT 2015]**

(a) Yes, because Roxanne and Max were under a mistake as to matter of fact which is essential to the agreement
(b) No, because Max's agreement was fresh, so it is legally binding
(c) Yes, because an earlier commitment made by store owner to some other buyer is far more relevant than another commitment
(d) Roxanne and Max's contract is valid

60. Principle Contract is an agreement entered into between the parties.

Factual Situation Ramlal was a dealer in cement. The government of India, by an order issued under the Essential Commodities Act, fixed the price of cement and also the quantity which a person can buy from the dealer, Ramlal carried on his business under this new order for sometime, but he refused to pay sales tax on his sales transactions on the ground that these were not the contracts freely entered into by him. [CLAT 2015]

Decision

(a) Ramlal would succeed because free consent between the parties were there despite the restriction on price and quantity
(b) Ramlal would not succeed because free consent between the parties were there despite the restriction on price and quantity
(c) Ramlal would succeed because the government under the new order, forced him to enter into contracts
(d) None of the above

61. Principles

A servant is one who is employed to do some work for his employer (master). He is engaged under a contract of service. He works directly under the control and directions of his master.

In general, the master is vicariously liable for those torts (wrongful facts) of his servant which are done by the servant in the course of his employment.

Fact 'M' appointed 'D' exclusively for the purpose of driving his tourist vehicle. 'M' also appointed 'C' exclusively for the purpose of performing the work of a conductor for the tourist vehicle. During one trip, at the end of the journey, 'C', while 'D' was not on the driver's seat, and apparently for the purpose of turning the vehicle in the right direction for the next journey drove it through the street at high speed and negligently injured 'P'. [CLAT 2016]

(a) 'M' could be made liable for the act of 'C', as 'C' was employed under a contract of service
(b) 'M' is not liable as he was not present at the time of accident
(c) 'M' could not be made liable for the act of 'C', as his (C's) act of driving the vehicle was not in the course of his employment
(d) 'M' is liable as he was present at the time of accident

62. Principles Waging agreements are void. Collateral agreements to wagering contracts are valid.

Fact XVZ Bank lends ₹ 40000 to Sabu in order to enable him to award as prize to Randeep who is the winner of horse race. Later, Sabu refuses to pay the prize stating that horse racing is wagering agreement. Can XVZ Bank recover money from Sabu? [CLAT 2016]

(a) Bank can recover money from Sabu so that payment of prize money can be made to Randeep
(b) No, as it is a wagering contract
(c) Yes, as it is only a collateral agreement to horse racing. Therefore, the bank can recover the money from Sabu
(d) Horse racing is illegal and therefore, XVZ Bank cannot recover anything from Sabu

63. Principles An independent contractor is one who is employed to do some work of his employer. He is engaged under a contract for services. He undertakes to produce a given result, and in the actual execution of the work, he is not under the direct control or following directions of his employer. He may use his own discretion in execution of the work assigned.

In general, an employer is not liable for the torts (wrongful acts) of his independent contractor. But, the employer may be held liable if he directs him to do some careless acts.

Fact Ramesh hired a taxi-cab to go to Delhi Airport. As he started late from his home, he kept on urging the taxi-driver to drive at a high speed and driver followed the directions; and ultimately due to high speed, an accident took place causing injuries to a person. [CLAT 2016]

(a) Ramesh would not be held liable for damages because Ramesh did not know the consequences of such rash driving
(b) Ramesh would be held liable for damages as he exercised the control by giving directions to the driver
(c) Ramesh would not be held liable for damages because the driver was an independent contractor and not his servant
(d) Ramesh would not be liable as car was not owned by him

64. Principle Sale of liquor is illegal. All agreements relating to prohibited items do not exist in the eyes of law.

Fact 'A' entered into an agreement with 'B' for the sale of liquor. 'A' failed to supply the agreed quantity of liquor to 'B'. **[CLAT 2016]**

(a) 'A' can bring a legal action against 'B'
(b) 'A' and 'B' can initiate appropriate legal proceeding against each other
(c) 'B' can bring a legal action against 'B'
(d) 'B' cannot bring any legal action against 'A'

65. Principle An agreement may be entered into orally or in writing, or by conduct.

Fact 'A' went to the shop of 'B' and picked a toothbrush and gave a cheque of ₹ 20 to 'B' and left the shop. **[CLAT 2016]**

(a) Payment of toothbrush cannot be made through a cheque
(b) 'A' should have carried a currency note of ₹ 20 to make the payment
(c) 'A' did not enter into an agreement with 'B'
(d) There was an agreement between 'A' and 'B'

66. Principle The communication of a proposal is complete when it comes to the knowledge of the person to whom it is made.

Fact 'A' sent a letter making a proposal to 'B' to purchase the house of 'B'. **[CLAT 2016]**

(a) The communication of proposal is complete when A sent the letter
(b) The communication of proposal is complete when B's wife handed over the letter to 'B'
(c) The communication of proposal is complete when B's wife received it
(d) The communication of proposal is complete when 'B' reads the letter

67. Principle A condition to a contract can also be compiled with after the happening of the event to which such a condition is attached.

Fact 'A' promises to pay ₹ 9000 to 'B' on the condition that he shall marry with the consent of 'C', 'D' and 'E', 'B' marries without the consent of 'C', 'D' and 'E', but obtains their consent after the marriage. **[CLAT 2016]**

(a) 'B' has not fulfilled the condition
(b) 'B' has fulfilled the condition
(c) 'B's marriage is not valid
(d) The condition is illegal

68. Principle An agreement without free consent can be enforced only at the option of the party whose consent was not free.

Fact 'A' obtains the consent of 'B' to enter into an agreement by putting the gun on the head of B's girl friend. **[CLAT 2016]**

(a) 'A' can enforce the agreement
(b) 'B' can enforce the agreement
(c) Neither 'A' nor 'B' can enforce the agreement
(d) 'B' cannot enforce the agreement

69. Principle Import means bringing some consignment into India from a foreign country.

Fact A consignment from Sri Lanka entered the territorial waters of India. However, this consignment never crossed the Indian custom barrier nor did it enter into the stream of commerce in India. **[CLAT 2016]**

(a) The consignment was imported into India
(b) The consignment will only be imported into India when it crosses the Indian custom barrier
(c) The consignment was not imported into India
(d) The consignment will only be imported into India when it enters into the stream of commerce in India

70. Principle Mere silence as to facts likely to affect the decision of a person to enter into a contract is not fraud.

Fact 'A' sells to 'B' ('A's daughter who is minor) a horse which 'A' knows to be unsound. 'A' says nothing to 'B' about the unsoundness of the horse. **[CLAT 2017]**

(a) 'B' can take plea of fraud because she is minor
(b) 'A' has not committed fraud
(c) There cannot be a contact between a father and daughter
(d) 'A' has committed fraud

71. Principle An offer made by one party when accepted by another makes it a contract.

Transactions

1. P offered to sell his house for ₹ 20 lakhs to R; R told P that he was interested to buy a house for 15 lakhs only.
2. C was looking for a house for not more than 25 lakhs; P informed C that his house was available for 20 lakhs.
3. K wanted to buy some old furniture; L told K that he would sell his furniture for ₹ 10000.
4. R advertised to sell his old car for a price of ₹ 3 lakhs; S found the advertisement and offered to buy it for ₹ 2 lakhs 50 thousand; R agrees to sell it to S. **[CLAT 2017]**

Which among the above is actually a contract?

(a) Situation 4 only is a contract
(b) Situations 2 and 4 are contracts
(c) Situations 1 and 2 are contracts
(d) Situation 3 only is contract

72. Principle Every agreement, of which the object or consideration is opposed to public policy, is void. An agreement which has the tendency to injure public interest or public welfare is one against public policy. What constitutes an injury to public interest or public welfare would depend upon the time and the circumstances.

Facts 'A' promises to obtain for 'B' an employment in the public service, and 'B' promises to pay ₹ 500000/- to 'A'. **[CLAT 2017]**

(a) The agreement is void because rupees 5,00,000/- is excessive
(b) The agreement is void, as the object and consideration for it is opposed to public policy
(c) The agreement is valid, as it is a contract between two parties with their free consent
(d) The agreement is valid, as it is with consideration for public service

73. Principle Acceptance of a proposal must be absolute and unqualified.

Facts 'A' made a proposal to sell his motorcycle to 'B' for ₹ 25000/-. 'B' agreed to buy it for rupees ₹ 24000/-. 'A' sold his motorcycle to 'C' for ₹ 26000/- the next day. 'B' sues 'A' for damages. **[CLAT 2017]**

(a) 'B' will get the difference of ₹ 1000/- only
(b) 'B' will get damages from 'A'
(c) 'B' can proceed against 'C'
(d) 'B' will not get any damages from 'A'

74. Principle An agreement, the terms of which are not certain or capable of being made certain, is void.

Facts Sunder agreed to take Bhola's penthouse on rent for three years at the rate of rupees ₹ 1200000/-per annum provided the house was put to thorough repairs and the living rooms were decorated according to contemporary style. **[CLAT 2017]**

(a) There is a valid contract because all the terms of contract are certain and not vague as the rent is fixed by both of them and the term 'present style' only can be interpreted to mean the latest style
(b) There is no valid contract because it has vague and uncertain terms, as the term 'present style' may mean one thing to Sunder and another to Bhola
(c) It is voidable contract at the option of Bhola
(d) There is a valid contract because there is an offer from Sunder and acceptance from Bhola

Answers

1	*a*	2	*c*	3	*d*	4	*c*	5	*c*	6	*b*	7	*b*	8	*a*	9	*d*	10	*a*
11	*d*	12	*c*	13	*c*	14	*a*	15	*b*	16	*c*	17	*d*	18	*c*	19	*d*	20	*b*
21	*b*	22	*a*	23	*a*	24	*c*	25	*a*	26	*a*	27	*a*	28	*b*	29	*b*	30	*d*
31	*b*	32	*c*	33	*a*	34	*a*	35	*b*	36	*d*	37	*a*	38	*b*	39	*c*	40	*b*
41	*b*	42	*c*	43	*a*	44	*d*	45	*c*	46	*c*	47	*a*	48	*c*	49	*b*	50	*a*
51	*c*	52	*b*	53	*d*	54	*c*	55	*d*	56	*b*	57	*c*	58	*b*	59	*d*	60	*d*
61	*a*	62	*c*	63	*c*	64	*d*	65	*d*	66	*d*	67	*a*	68	*c*	69	*b*	70	*a*
71	*a*	72	*b*	73	*d*	74	*b*												

CHAPTER 04

ACTS

An Act is the guiding force for the authority to take any action under due process of law. The law in India is made by legislative bodies, which describe every possible enforcement of law of the land.

The Societies' Registration Act, 1860

- The Societies Registration Act, 1860 (21 of 1860), which came into force on 21st May, 1860.
- The Societies Registration Act is an act under the Constitution of the Government of India.
- The Act allows the registration of entities generally involved in the benefit of society like education, health, employment etc.
- The Indian Government, with a wish to encourage such activities and to promote the formal organisation of groups of like minded people.
- The Act continues until today and being an Act of Parliament, comes under the Right to Information Act, wherein the government is legally responsible to give any information requested by any citizen of India with respect to any society registered under this Act.

Indian Evidence Act, 1872

The Indian Evidence Act of 1872, originally passed by the British Parliament in 1872, contains a set of rules and allied issues governing admissibility of any evidence in the Indian courts of law.

Importance of Indian Evidence Act

- Upto that point of time, the rules of evidences were based on the traditional legal systems of different social groups and communities of India and were different for different persons depending on his or her caste, religious faith and social position.

- The Indian Evidence Act removed this anomaly and differentiation and introduced a standard set of law applicable to all Indians.
- It applies to all judicial proceedings in the court, including the court martial as well. However, it does not apply on affidavits and arbitration.

Negotiable Instruments Act, 1881

A negotiable instrument means a promissory note, bill of exchange or cheque payable either to order or to bearer. It may be made payable to two or more payees jointly, or it may be made be payable in the alternative to one of two, or one or some of several payees.

Provided that such usages may be excluded by any words in the body of the instrument, which indicate an intention that the legal relations of the parties thereto shall be governed by this Act, and it shall come into force on the first day of March, 1882.

Parliament of India enacted the Negotiable Instruments (Amendment and Miscellaneous Provisions) Act, 2002 which is intended to plug the loopholes. This Amendment Act inserts five new Sections from 143 to 147 touching various limbs of the Parent Act and cheque truniation through digitally were also included and the amendment Act has been secently brought into force on 6th February, 2003.

The Transfer of Property Act, 1882

- It is an Indian Legislation which regulate the transfer of property in India.
- It is an act by which a person conveys property to one of more person on himself and one more other persons.
- The persons may include an individual company or association or body of individuals and any kind of property may be transferred including immovable property.

The Land Acquisition Act, 1894

- The Land Acquisition Act of 1894, is a law that allows the government to acquire private land in India.
- But in 2013, Government of India has passed the Right to Fair Compensation and Transparency in Land Acquisation, Rehabilitation and Resettlement Act, 2013 (LARR) and which came into force from 1st January, 2014. This Act amended the Land Acquisition Act, 1894.
- Land acquisition in India refers to the process by which the Union or a State Government acquires private land for the purpose of industrialisation development of infrastructural facilities or urbanisation of the private land and provides compensation to the affected landowners and their rehabilitation and resettlement.

The Hindu Inheritance (Removal of Disabilities) Act, 1928

- The Hindu Inheritance (Removal of Disabilities) Act, 1928 was enacted to abolish the exclusion from inheritance of certain classes of heirs and to remove certain doubts regarding their ability to inherit property.
- The Act specifies that persons who are diseased, deformed or physically or mentally handicapped cannot be disqualified from their right to own or share joint-family property unless the law specifies otherwise.
- This Act essentially abolishes the ancient Hindu legal practice that those who are handicapped are ineligible to inherit property from their family.

The Indian Partnership Act, 1932

- The Indian Partnership Act, 1932 is an act that regulates partnership firms in India.
- Before the enactment of this act, partnerships were governed by the provisions of the Indian Contract Act. The act is administered through the Ministry of Corporate Affairs.
- The act is not applicable to Limited Liability Partnerships, since they are governed by the Limited Liability Partnership Act, 2008.

The Industrial Disputes Act, 1947

- The Industrial Disputes Act, 1947 extends to the whole of India. It came into force 1st April, 1947.
- The objective of the Industrial Disputes Act is to secure industrial peace and harmony by providing machinery and procedure for the investigation and settlement of industrial disputes by negotiations.
- Various studies indicate that Indian labour laws are highly protective of labour and labour markets are relatively inflexible.
- These laws apply only to the organised sector.
- Consequently, these laws have restricted labour mobility, have led to capital-intensive methods in the organised sector and adversely affected the sector's long-run demand for labour.
- Labour being a subject in the Concurrent list, state-level labour regulations are also an important determinant of industrial performance.

The Companies Act, 1956

- The Companies Act, 1956 is an Act of the Parliament of India, enacted in 1956, which enabled companies to be formed by registration, and set out the responsibilities of companies, their directors and secretaries.
- The Companies Act, 1956 is administered by the Federal Government of India through the Ministry of Corporate Affairs and the Offices of Registrar of Companies, Official Liquidators, Public Trustee, Company Law Board, Director of Inspection etc.
- The Registrar of Companies (RoC) handles incorporation of new companies and the administration of running companies.

The Hindu Succession Act, 1956

- The Hindu Succession Act, 1956, is a law that was passed by the Parliament of India in 1956 to amend and codify the law relating to intestate or unwilled succession, among Hindus, Buddhists, Jains and Sikhs.
- The Act lays down a uniform and comprehensive system of inheritance and succession into one act.
- The Hindu woman's limited estate is abolished by the act.
- Any property possessed by a Hindu female is to be held by her absolute property and she is given full power to deal with it and dispose it of by will as she likes.
- The Act was amended in 2005 by the Hindu Succession (Amendment) Act, 2005.
- The Hindu Succession (Amendment) Act, 2005, amended Section 6 of the Hindu Succession Act, 1956, allowing daughters of the deceased equal rights with sons.
- In the case of coparcenary property, or a case in which two people inherit property equally between them, the daughter and son are subject to the same liabilities and disabilities.
- The amendment essentially furthers equal rights between males and females in the legal system.

Applicability

- The Hindu Succession Act is applicable to all those who practice the Hindu religion as well as those who fall under the term Hindu within the Indian Legal System, including Buddhists, Jains and Sikhs.
- Unlike Muslim law, Hindu law outlines different heirs for males and females.

Armed Forces Act, 1958

- The Armed Forces (Special Powers) Act (AFSPA), was passed on 11th September, 1958, by the Parliament of India.
- It conferred special powers upon armed forces in what the act calls 'disturbed areas' in the states of Arunachal Pradesh, Assam, Manipur, Meghalaya, Mizoram, Nagaland and Tripura.
- It was later extended to Jammu and Kashmir as The Armed Forces (Jammu and Kashmir) Special Powers Act, 1990 in July 1990.

The Articles in the Constitution of India empower state governments to declare a state of emergency due to one or *more of the following reasons.*

- Failure of the administration and the local police to tackle local issues.
- Return of (central) security forces leads to return of miscreants/erosion of the 'peace dividend'.
- The scale of unrest or instability in the state is too large for local forces to handle.

The Prevention of Cruelty to Animals Act, 1960

- The Prevention of Cruelty to Animals Act, 1960 is federal law of India enacted to prevent the infliction of unnecessary pain or suffering on animals and to amend the laws relating to the prevention of cruelty to animals.
- As per the provisions of the law the Government of India formed the Animal Welfare Board of India.

The Hindu Marriage Act, 1955

- The Hindu Marriage Act is an Act of the Parliament of India enacted in 1955.
- The main purpose of the Act was to amend and codify the law relating to marriage among Hindus and others.
- This Act applies to Hindus by religion in any of its form and to any person who is Buddhist, Jain or Sikh by religion. However, with the passage of 'Anand Marriage (Amendment) Bill' in 2012, Sikhs now also have their own personal law related to marriage. Buddhist, Jaina and Sikh.

The Advocates Act, 1961

- The Advocates Act, 1961 was enacted to lay down the rights and obligations of legal practitioners in India.
- It created statutory bodies, namely the bar councils for each state as well as the Bar Council of India.
- The aim behind the same was to regularise the legal system as well as to provide a forum to redress complaints and provide for disciplinary action.
- The Bar Council of India is a statutory body created by Parliament to regulate and represent the Indian bar.

The Apprentices Act, 1961

- The Apprentices Act, 1961 was enacted to regulate and control the programme of training of apprentices and for matters connected therewith.
- The term 'apprentice' means "a person who is undergoing apprenticeship training in pursuance of a contract of apprenticeship".
- The Act makes it obligatory on part of the employers both in public and private sector establishments having requisite training infrastructure.
- Directorate General of Employment and Training (DGE&T) in the Ministry of Labour is responsible for implementation of the Act in respect of Trade Apprentices in the Central Government Undertakings and Departments.

Unlawful Activities Act, 1967

- The object of this Bill was to make powers available for dealing with activities directed against the integrity and sovereignty of India.

- Unlawful Activities (Prevention), Act is Indian law aimed at effective prevention of unlawful activities associations in India.
- The National Integration Council appointed a Committee on National Integration and Regionalisation to look into, inter alia, the aspect of putting reasonable restrictions in the interests of the sovereignty and integrity of India.
- Empowering Parliament to impose, by law, reasonable restrictions in the interests of sovereignty and integrity of India, *on the*
  - Freedom of speech and expression.
  - Right to Assemble Peaceably and Without Arms.
  - Right to Form Associations or Unions.

The Wildlife Protection Act, 1972

- The Wildlife Protection Act, 1972 refers to a sweeping package of legislation enacted in 1972 by the Government of India.
- Before 1972, India only had five designated national parks. Among other reforms, the Act established schedules of protected plant and animal species, hunting or harvesting these species was largely outlawed.
- The Act provides for the protection of wild animals, birds and plants; and for matters connected therewith or ancillary or incidental thereto.
- It extends to the whole of India, except the State of Jammu and Kashmir which has its own wildlife act.
- Government of India enacted a comprehensive legislation Wildlife Protection Act of 1972 with the objective of effectively controlling poaching and illegal trade in wildlife and its derivatives.
- This has been amended (and signed) in January, 2003 and punishment and penalty for offences under the Act have been made more stringent.

The Consumer Protection Act, 1986

- The Consumer Protection Act, 1986 is a Social Welfare Legislation which was enacted as a result of widespread consumer protection movement.
- The main object of the legislature in the enactment of this act is to provide for the better protection of the interests of the consumer and to make provisions for establishment of consumer councils and other authorities for settlement of consumer disputes and matter therewith connected.

The Muslim Women (Protection of Rights on Divorce) Act, 1986

- The Muslim Women (Protection of Rights on Divorce) Act was a landmark legislation passed by the Parliament of India in 1986 to protect the rights of Muslim women who have been divorced by or have obtained divorce from, their husbands and to provide for matters connected therewith or incidental thereto.
- The Act was passed by the Rajiv Gandhi Government to nullify the decision in Shah Bano case.
- The law applies to the whole of India except Jammu and Kashmir.
- It is administered by any magistrate of the first class exercising jurisdiction under the Code of Criminal Procedure, 1973.

Terrorist and Disruptive Activities, (Prevention) Act, 1987

- Terrorist and Disruptive Activities (Prevention) Act, commonly known as TADA, was an Indian law active between 1985 and 1995 (modified in 1987) for the prevention of terrorist activities in Punjab.
- It came into effect on 23rd May, 1985. It was renewed in 1989, 1991 and 1993 before being allowed to lapse in 1995 due to increasing unpopularity due to widespread allegations of abuse.

- The law gave wide powers to law enforcement agencies for dealing with terrorist and 'socially disruptive' activities.
- The police were not obliged to produce a detainee before a judicial magistrate within 24 hours. The accused person could be remanded upto 1 year in police custody, as opposed to the maximum of 90 days detainment for the accused of other crimes.
- Confessions made to police officers were admissible as evidence in the court of law, with the burden of proof being on the accused to prove his innocence.
- Special court known as TADA court was set up to hear the cases and deliver judgements pertaining to 1993 Bombay bomblast case. The trials could be held in camera with the identities of the witnesses kept hidden.
- The legislation was ultimately succeeded by the controversial Prevention of Terrorist Activities Act (2002-04) which was scrapped by the UPA government.

The Prevention of Corruption Act, 1988

- The Prevention of Corruption Act, 1988 is a federal law enacted by the Parliament of India to combat corruption in government agencies and public sector businesses in India.
- This law defines who a public servant is and punishes public servants involved in corruption or bribery. It also punishes anyone who helps him/her commit the crime corruption or bribery.

The Arbitration and Conciliation Act, 1996

- The Arbitration and Conciliation Act, 1996 is the prime legislation relating to domestic arbitration, international commercial arbitration and enforcement of foreign arbitral awards and also to define the law relating to conciliation and for matters connected therewith or incidental thereto.
- It repealed the three statutory provisions for arbitration (i) the Arbitration Act, 1940; (ii) the Arbitration (Protocol and Convention) Act, 1937; (iii) the Foreign Awards (Recognition and Enforcement) Act, 1961.
- The Act was amended in 2015, that came into force in 2016 on 1st January. This amendment to Arbitration and Conciliation Act additional grounds to set aside an award *viz.* those awards contravention with the fundamental policy of Indian Law. The amendment also limits the jurisdiction of courts for passing interim orders.

The Benami Transaction (Prohibition) Act, 1988

The Act is concered to prohibit certain types of financial transactions. Such transactions were a feature of the Indian Economy, usually relating to the purchase of property (real estate), and were thought to contribute to the Indian black money problem.

The Act bans all benami transactions and gives the government the right to recover property held benami without paying any compensation.

In 2016, amendment in Benami Transaction (Prohibition) Act took place. This amendment seeks to give more teeth to the authorities to curb benami transactions. The new law also provides for an appellate mechanism in the form of an adjudicating authority and appellate tribunal.

The Juvenile Justice (Care and Protection of Children) Act, 2000

- The Juvenile Justice (Care and Protection of Children) Act, 2000 is the primary legal framework for juvenile justice in India.
- The Act provides for a special approach towards the prevention and treatment of juvenile delinquency and provides a framework for the protection, treatment and rehabilitation of children in the purview of the juvenile justice system.

- In 2015, Parliament of India has passed the Juvenile Justice (Care and Protection of Children) Act, 2015. It aims to replace the Existing Act, 2000, so that Juveniles in conflict with law in the age group of 16-18, involved in Heinous offences, can be tried as adults. The Act come into force from 15th January, 2016.

The Competition Act, 2002

- The Competition Act, 2002 is an anti-trust legislation enacted by the Parliament of India. It replaced the archaic Monopoly and Restrictive Trade Practices Act.
- Under this act, the Competition Commission of India was established to prevent activities that have an adverse effect on competition in India. The Competition Act, 2002 was amended by the Competition (Amendment) Act, 2007 and again by the Competition (Amendment) Act, 2009.

The Prevention of Money Laundering Act, 2002

The Prevention of Money Laundering Act is Indian law passed by the Parliament in 2002 to prevent money-laundering and to provide for confiscation of property derived from money- laundering.

This Act is further amended in 2005, 2009, 2012 and apeal in 2016. The Act and Rules no notified there under impose obligation on banking companies, financial institutions and intermediaries to verify identity of clients, maintain records and furnish information in prescribed borm to Financial Intelligence unit-India.

The Prevention of Terrorist Activities Act (POTA), 2002

- The Prevention of Terrorist Activities Act (POTA) was an anti-terrorism legislation enacted by the Parliament of India in 2002.
- The act replaced the Prevention of Terrorism Ordinance (POTO) of 2001 and the Terrorist and Disruptive Activities (Prevention) Act (TADA) (1985-95) and was supported by the governing National Democratic Alliance.
- The Act was repaled in 2004.

The Fiscal Responsibility and Budget Management Act, 2003

- The Fiscal Responsibility and Budget Management Act, 2003 (FRBMA) was enacted by the Parliament of India to institutionalise financial discipline, reduce India's fiscal deficit, improve macro-economic management and the overall management of the public funds by moving towards a balanced budget.
- The main purpose was to eliminate revenue deficit of the country (building revenue surplus thereafter) and bring down the fiscal deficit to a manageable 3% of the GDP by March 2008. However, due to the 2007 international financial crisis, the deadlines for the implementation of the targets in the act was initially postponed and subsequently suspended in 2009.
- In 2011, given the process of ongoing recovery, Economic Advisory Council publicly advised the Government of India to reconsider reinstating the provisions of the FRBMA.

The Electricity Act, 2003

- The Electricity Act, 2003 is a revolutionary piece of legislation enforced in India that aims to transform the power sector in India.
- The act covers major issues involving generation, distribution, transmission and trading in power.

The main features of the act are as follows

(i) Generation has been de-licensed and captive generation freely permitted.

(ii) No person shall

(a) transmit electricity; or

(b) distribute electricity; or

(c) undertake trading in electricity, unless he is authorised to do so by a license issued, exceptions informed by authorised commissions through notifications.

(iii) No license required for generation and distribution in rural India.

(iv) Setting up State Electricity Regulatory Commission (SERC) made mandatory.

(v) An appellate tribunal to hear appeals against the decision of (CERC's) and SERC's.

(vi) Metering of electricity supplied made mandatory.

(vii) Provisions related to thefts of electricity made more stringent.

(viii) For rural and remote areas stand-alone system for generation and distribution permitted.

(ix) Thrust to complete rural electrification and provide for management of rural distribution by panchayat, co-operative societies, NGOs, franchises etc.

(x) Central Government to prepare National Electricity policy and Tariff policy.

(xi) Central electricity authority to prepare National Electricity plan.

The Right to Information Act, 2005 (RTI)

- This law was passed by Parliament on 15th June, 2005 and came fully into force on 13th October, 2005.
- The Right to Information Act, 2005 (RTI) is an Act of the Parliament of India "to provide for setting out the practical regime of right to information for citizens".
- The Act applies to all States and Union Territories of India, except the State of Jammu and Kashmir-which is covered under a state-level law.
- Under the provisions of the Act, any citizen (excluding the citizens within J&K) may request information from a 'public authority' (a body of government or 'instrumentality of state') which is required to reply expeditiously or within thirty days.
- The Act also requires every public authority to computerise their records for wide dissemination and to pro-actively publish certain categories of information so that the citizens need minimum recourse to request for information formally.
- The formal recognition of a legal right to information in India occurred more than two decades before legislation was finally enacted, when the Supreme Court of India ruled in State of UP v Raj Narain that the right to information is implicit in the right to freedom of speech and expression explicitly guaranteed in Article 19 of the Indian Constitution.

Protection of Women from Domestic Violence Act, 2005

- The Protection of Women from Domestic Violence Act, 2005 was brought into force by the Indian Government from 26th October, 2006.
- The Act was passed by the Parliament in August 2005 and assented to by the President on 13th September, 2005. As of November, 2007 it has been ratified by four of twenty eight state governments in India.
- Domestic violence for the purposes of this Act, any conduct of the respondent shall constitute domestic violence if,
  - anyone habitually assaults or makes the life of the aggrieved person miserable by cruelty of conduct even if such conduct does not amount to physical ill- treatment.
  - anyone forces the aggrieved person to lead an immoral life.
  - anyone otherwise injures or harms the aggrieved person.

- nothing shall amount to domestic violence if the pursuit of course of conduct by the respondent was reasonable for his own protection or for the protection of his or another's property.

The Information Technology (Amendment) Act, 2008

- The Government of India has brought major amendments to ITA-2000 in form of the Information Technology Amendment Act, 2008.
- ITAA 2008 (Information Technology Amendment Act, 2008) as the new version of Information Technology Act, 2000 is often referred has provided additional focus on information security.
- It has added several new sections on offences including cyber terrorism and data protection.

Right of Children to Free and Compulsory Education Act, 2009

- The Right of Children to Free and Compulsory Education Act or Right to Education Act (RTE), which was passed by the Indian Parliament on 4th August, 2009, describes the modalities of the provision of free and compulsory education for children between 6 and 14 in India under Article 21A of the Indian Constitution making education a Fundamental Right.
- The law came into effect in the whole of India except the State of Jammu and Kashmir from 1st April, 2010, the first time in the history of India a law was brought into force by a speech by the Prime Minister.
- The Act makes education a Fundamental Right of every child between the ages of 6 and 14 and specifies minimum norms in elementary schools.
- It requires all private schools to reserve 25% of seats to children from poor families (to be reimbursed by the state as part of the Public-Private Partnership plan).
- It also prohibits all unrecognised schools from practice, and makes provisions for no donation or capitation fees and no interview of the child or parent for admission.
- The Act also provides that no child shall be held back, expelled or required to pass a board examination until the completion of elementary education.
- There is also a provision for special training of school drop-outs to bring them up to par with students of the same age.
- The RTE Act requires surveys that will monitor all neighbourhoods, identify children requiring education and set-up facilities for providing it.
- The World Bank education specialist for India, Sam Carlson.
- The RTE Act is the first legislation in the world that puts the responsibility of ensuring enrollment, attendance and completion on the government. It is the parents' responsibility to send the children to schools in the US and other countries.
- The Right to Education of persons with disabilities until 18 years of age has also been made a Fundamental Right. A number of other provisions regarding improvement of school infrastructure, teacher-student ratio and faculty are made in the Act.
- The Act provides for a special organisation the National Commission for the Protection of Child Right, an autonomous body set-up in 2007, to monitor the implementation of the act, together with commission to be set-up by the states.

Practice Exercise

1. Relevancy and admissibility under the Indian Evidence Act are
(a) synonymous
(b) co-extensive
(c) Neither (a) nor (b)
(d) Both (a) and (b)

2. What is correct as regards the admissibility of self-regarding statements?
(a) Self-harming statement is admissible, but a self-serving statement is not generally admissible
(b) Self-serving statement is admissible, but a self-harming statement is not generally admissible
(c) Self-serving and self-harming statements both are generally admissible
(d) Self-serving and self-harming statements both are generally inadmissible

3. Motives of preparation and conduct are under which section of Evidence Act?
(a) Under Section 6 of Evidence Act
(b) Under Section 7 of Evidence Act
(c) Under Section 8 of Evidence Act
(d) Under Section 9 of Evidence Act

4. Contractual rights and duties are created by
(a) state (b) statute
(c) parties (d) custom or usage

5. Voidable contract is one
(a) which is lawful
(b) which is invalid
(c) which is valid as long as it is not avoided by the party entitled to do so
(d) which is unlawful

6. A contract creates
(a) rights in personam
(b) rights in rem
(c) no obligations
(d) only obligations and no rights

7. The Negotiable Instruments Act, 1881 applies to
(a) the whole of India
(b) the whole of India except the State of Jammu and Kashmir
(c) those states as notified by the Union Government from time to time in the Official Gazette
(d) the whole of India except the State of Jammu and Kashmir and the North-Eastern states

8. The Negotiable Instruments Act, 1881 came into force on
(a) 9th December, 1881 (b) 19th December, 1881
(c) 1st March, 1882 (d) None of these

9. The undertaking contained in a promissory note, to pay a certain sum of money is
(a) conditional
(b) unconditional
(c) may be conditional or unconditional depending upon the circumstances
(d) None of the above

10. A bill of exchange contains a/an
(a) unconditional undertaking
(b) unconditional order
(c) conditional undertaking
(d) conditional order

11. Which Act provides for the provision of medical benefit to the insured employees?
(a) Workmen Compensation Act, 1923
(b) Employees State Insurance Act, 1948
(c) Maternity Benefit Act, 1961
(d) Contract Labour (Regulation and Abolition Act), 1970

12. The performance appraisal method which rates the appraisee on various parameters on a point scale is
(a) Critical Incident Method
(b) MBO Method
(c) Graphic Rating Sheet
(d) Bell Curve Appraisal

13. Contract Labour (Regulation and Abolition Act), 1970 can be classified into the category of
(a) Social Security Act
(b) Industrial Relations Act
(c) Welfare Act
(d) Commercial Act

14. The provisions of environmental protection in the Constitution were made under
(a) Article 5-A
(b) Article 21-B
(c) Article 27-B (h)
(d) Article 48-A and Article 51-A (g)

15. The first of the major environmental protection act to be promulgated in India was
(a) Water Act (b) Air Act
(c) Environmental Act (d) Noise Pollution Rule

16. Penalty for conservation of the provisions of the Forest Act is under
(a) Section 3A (b) Section 4A
(c) Section 12A (d) Section 8A

17. The present Arbitration and Conciliation Act of 1996 is based on
(a) Constitution of India
(b) Guidelines of Supreme Court of India
(c) European Commercial Arbitration Procedure
(d) UNCITRAL, 1985

18. The power of court to refer parties for arbitration would and must necessarily include, imply and inhere in it
(a) the power and jurisdiction to advise the parties
(b) the power and jurisdiction to review the award
(c) the power and jurisdiction to appoint the arbitrator
(d) the power and jurisdiction to call for another arbitrator

19. Part I of the Arbitration and Conciliation Act, 1996 applies where
(a) the place of arbitration is in India
(b) the place of arbitration is outside India, but is in Asia
(c) the place of arbitration is outside India, but is in Europe
(d) the place of arbitration is anywhere in the world

20. An arbitral award made under Part I of the Arbitration and Conciliation Act, 1996, shall be considered as a
(a) Domestic Award Conciliation Act, 1996
(b) Foreign award
(c) General award
(d) International award

21. Section 58 (a) of the TP Act defines
(a) mortgage, mortgagor, mortgagee and mortgage money.
(b) mortgage, mortgagor, mortgagee and mortgage deed
(c) mortgage, mortgagor, mortgagee, mortgage money and mortgage deed
(d) mortgage, mortgagor, mortgage money and mortgage deed

22. Under the Hindu Adoption and Maintenance Act, a mother is
(a) entitled to live along with her son's family
(b) not entitled to live along with her son's family
(c) morally entitled to her son's care
(d) entitled to have separate accommodation from her son

23. A boy of 17 years marries a girl of 15 years. The marriage is
(a) void
(b) voidable
(c) valid and not punishable
(d) valid and punishable

24. 'A' marries 'B', the widow of his elder brother. The marriage is
(a) valid (b) void
(c) voidable (d) All of these

25. Right to Work is guarantee under
(a) MGNREGA Act
(b) Right to Information Act
(c) Right to Education Act
(d) Ajeevika Yojana

26. Central Bureau of Investigation was set-up under
(a) Prevention of Corruption Act, 1988
(b) Special Police Establishment Act, 1941
(c) TADA Act, 1987
(d) Juvenile Justice Act, 2000

27. MGNREGA (Mahatma Gandhi National Rural Employment Guarantee Act, 2005) provide employment to
(a) all the below poverty line households
(b) all the rural households
(c) all the resident of rural area
(d) all the men above the age of 18 years

Previous Year's Questions

28. The Environment Protection Act was passed by the Parliament of India in the year **[CLAT 2013]**

(a) 1976 (b) 1986 (c) 1996 (d) 2006

29. Principle Where a person fraudulently or erroneously represents that he is authorised to transfer certain immovable property and professes to transfer such property for consideration, such transfer shall, at the option of the transferee, operate on any interest which the transferor may acquire in such property at anytime during which the contract of transfer subsists.

Facts 'A', a Hindu who has separated from his father 'B', sells to 'C' three fields, X, Y and Z representing that 'A' is authorised to transfer the same. Of these fields Z does not belong to 'A', it having been retained by 'B' on the partition; but on B's dying 'A' as successor obtains Z and at that time 'C' had not cancelled the contract of sale. **[CLAT 2014]**

(a) 'A' can sell Z to a third party
(b) 'A' is not required to deliver Z to 'C'
(c) 'A' is required to deliver Z to 'C'
(d) None of the above statements

30. Principle Where there is transfer of ownership of one thing for the ownership of some other thing it is called exchange, while transfer of ownership for consideration of money is called sale, whereas without consideration it becomes gift.

Facts 'A' transfers his house worth ₹ 50 lakh to 'B' for a shopping building worth the same amount, as consideration from 'B'. **[CLAT 2014]**

(a) The transaction is a gift
(b) The transaction is a sale
(c) The transaction is an exchange
(d) The transaction is a mortgage

31. Principle One of the essential conditions for a marriage between any two persons to be solemnised under the Special Marriage Act, 1954 is that at the time of the marriage the male has completed the age of twenty-one years and the female the age of eighteen years. If the said condition is not fulfilled such a marriage is null and void.

Facts 'A', a male aged twenty-two years, proposes to marry 'B', a female aged sixteen years, at Delhi in the month of June 2014 under the Special Marriage Act, 1954. **[CLAT 2014]**

(a) Marriage between 'A' and 'B' can be legally solemnised under the Special Marriage Act, 1954
(b) Marriage between 'A' and 'B' cannot be legally solemnised under the Special Marriage Act, 1954
(c) Marriage between 'A' and 'B' can remain valid for A under the Special Marriage Act, 1954
(d) None of the above is correct

32. Principle Under the Transfer of Property Act, 1882 a property must be transferred, by one living person to another living person. The Act deals only with transfer of property between living persons.

Facts 'X' wants to transfer his property to the presiding deity in a temple situated within the estate of 'A'. **[CLAT 2014]**

(a) Transfer of property by 'X' will be valid
(b) Transfer of property by 'X' will be invalid
(c) Transfer of property by 'X' to the presiding deity will become a valid transfer to 'A'
(d) None of the above

33. Principle Under copyright law copyright subsists in original literary works also. A literary work need not be of literary quality. Even so prosaic a work as an index of railway stations or a railway guide or a list of stock exchange quotations qualifies as a literary work if sufficient work has been expended in compiling it to give it a new and original character.

Facts Michael works hard enough, walking down the streets, taking down the names of people who live at houses and makes a street directory as a result of that labour. **[CLAT 2014]**

(a) Michael's exercise in making a street directory is sufficient to justify in making claim to copyright in that work which is ultimately produced
(b) Michael's exercise in making a street directory is not enough to justify in making claim to copyright in that work
(c) A street directory cannot be enough to be considered as a literary work
(d) None of the above statement is correct

34. Principle Under the Hindu Adoptions and Maintenance Act, 1956, no person shall be capable of being taken in adoption unless he or she is a Hindu, he or she not already been adopted, he or she has not been married, unless there is a custom or usage applicable to the parties which permits persons who are married being taken in adoption, and he or she has not completed the age of fifteen years, unless there is a custom or usage applicable to the parties which permits persons who have completed the age of fifteen years being take in adoption.

Facts Vijay being natural father had given Tarun, a boy aged 10 years, in adoption to Manoj in March 2010 in accordance with the Hindu Adoptions and Maintenance Act, 1956. In May 2012 Manoj gave Tarun in adoption to Sanjay. Subsequently in December 2013, Sanjay gave Tarun in adoption to Vijay. **[CLAT 2014]**

(a) Adoption of Tarun by Sanjay is valid
(b) Adoption of Tarun by Vijay is valid
(c) Adoption of Tarun by Manoj is valid
(d) None of the above adoptions is valid

35. Principle Under the Hindu Marriage Act, 1955 either the husband or the wife can move a petition for a decree of divorce on the ground of desertion. The term 'desertion' means desertion of the petitioner by the other party to the marriage for a continuous period of not less than two years immediately preceding the presentation of the petition, without reasonable cause and without the consent or against the wish of such party and includes the willful neglect of the petitioner by the other party to the marriage and its grammatical variations and cognate expressions shall be construed accordingly. It is also said that desertion is withdrawal not from a, place but from a state of things.

Facts Rohan, a technocrat, went to US in January 2011 for pursuing his higher studies for a period of three years. In fact, Rohan went to US with the consent of his wife Basanti, who stayed at her parents' home, and with a promise of his return to India upon the completion of his studies. From US he has quite often been in touch with his wife. Subsequently, Rohan has got a job there in US and he wishes to take his wife. She refuses to go to US and, in the meanwhile, she files a petition for a decree, of divorce on the ground of desertion by her husband. **[CLAT 2014]**

(a) Rohan's three year stay in US in the above context can amount to a ground of desertion for divorce
(b) Rohan's three year stay in US in the above context cannot amount to a ground of desertion for divorce
(c) Rohan's continued stay after three years can amount to a ground of desertion for divorce
(d) Basanti's refusal can amount to a ground of desertion for divorce

36. Principle According to Section 2 of the Industrial Disputes Act, 1947, 'Industrial dispute means any dispute or difference between employers and employers or between employers and workmen or between work men and workmen, which is connected with the employment of non-employment or the terms of employment or with the conditions of labour of any person'.

Facts The employees of DK Enterprises met the management and requested half a day leave to allow them to celebrate a lunar eclipse, which was going to happen two days later. The management refused the request. Does this situation amount to an 'Industrial dispute'? **[CLAT 2017]**

(a) Yes, because there is some difference of opinion it would be an industrial dispute
(b) No as declaring holidays is a prerogative of the employer. So no industrial dispute
(c) As the difference of opinion between the emloyees and employer is on declaration of holiday it amounts to an issue connected with employment or with the terms of employment and hence, an industrial dispute
(d) No as Lunar eclipse is unconnected with employment

37. Principle Under the Employees Compensation Act, 1923, an employer is liable to pay compensation to his workmen for injuries sustained by them by an accident arising out of and in the course of employment.

Facts M, the Manager of SRK Industries asked his secretary S to submit a report at the Government Labour Office. 'S' submitted the reports as directed. On his way back S met one of his class mates. He then decided to have a cup of tea together on a way side restaurant. Some time later, 'S' got a message from his office to report back as it was long time since he left the office. 'S' rushed back on his Motor Cycle. On his way back a Truck which was coming from side road hit 'S'. He was admitted in a nearby hospital with multiple injuries. He claims compensation under the Employees Compensation Act from his employer. **[CLAT 2017]**

(a) The employer is not liable as the truck driver was negligent
(b) The employer is liable to pay compensation as the accident took place arising out of and in the course of employment
(c) The employer is not liable as he was admitted in a private hospital and not a Government Hospital
(d) The employer is liable as S had to rush back to the office, because of the message from the office

Answers

1	*c*	2	*a*	3	*c*	4	*c*	5	*c*	6	*d*	7	*a*	8	*c*	9	*b*	10	*b*
11	*b*	12	*c*	13	*c*	14	*a*	15	*a*	16	*a*	17	*d*	18	*c*	19	*c*	20	*a*
21	*c*	22	*d*	23	*d*	24	*b*	25	*a*	26	*a*	27	*a*	28	*b*	29	*c*	30	*c*
31	*b*	32	*b*	33	*a*	34	*c*	35	*b*	36	*c*	37	*b*						

CHAPTER 05

LAW OF TORT

The social norms, cultural practices and etiquette are the guiding force for individual behaviour in our society. There is a expected human actions on par with socially accepted norms. When someone does not confirm to these norms, or acts in a twisted or abnormal manner, we say that he/she commits a 'tort'.

MEANING AND DEFINITION OF TORT

- The word 'tort' has been derived from the Latin term 'torturn', which means to 'twist'.
- It includes that conduct which is not straight or lawful, but on the other hand, twisted, crooked or unlawful.
- Salmond defined tort as, "It is a civil wrong for which the remedy is a common law action for unliquidated damages and which is not exclusively the breach of a contract or the breach of a trust or other merely equitable obligation".

Characteristics of Tort

The main characteristics of tort are as follows

1. **Civil Wrong** Tort is a civil wrong in the sense that it is a wrong against the person and not the society at large. However, tort is different from other civil wrongs such as breach of contract or breach of trust. Remedy under law of torts is based on common law and not on any specific statue. In case, wrongful act of a person results in tort as well as criminal wrongs then both remedies would be available to the victim.
2. **Infringement of a Legal Right** It is essential that there should be a violation of a legally protected right. Social and moral wrongs do not constitute a tort. Thus, if there is a violation of legally protected right then the aggrieved party can put the legal machinery in motion to claim compensation from the wrong doer.

3. **Remedy** It is the gist of tort and it is available in the form of unliquidated damages. Except that it's remedy in the form of injunction and restitution is also available in suitable cases.

Nature of Tort

The nature of a tort can be understood by distinguishing between the following

1. Tort and Crime

- Tort is a private wrong and crime is a public wrong.
- In the case of tort, the ends of justice are met by awarding compensation to the injured party. But in the case of crime, the wrong doer is punished.

e.g. 'A' digs a ditch on the public road resulting in inconvenience to the public at large. Here 'A' has committed the crime of public nuisance. If a passerby falls into the ditch, 'A' will be deemed to have committed the tort of private nuisance as well. Thus, here 'A' will be liable under civil as well as criminal law.

2. Tort and Breach of Contract

- A breach of contract results from the breach of a duty undertaken by the parties themselves with their free consent. A tort on the other hand, results from the breach of such duties which are not undertaken by the parties themselves but which are imposed by law.
- In a contract the duty is based on the privity of contract and each party owes duty only to the other contracting party.
  e.g. If 'A' and 'B' make a contract. A's duty is towards 'B' and 'B' only, similarly 'B' does not owe any duty in respect of this contract, to any person other than 'A'. But duties imposed by law under law of torts are not towards any specific individual, but they are towards the world at large.

3. Tort and Breach of Trust

- In the case of breach of trust by the trustee, the beneficiary can claim such compensation which depends upon the loss that the trust property has suffered.
- The damages in the case of breach of trust are liquidated while on the other hand damages in a tort are unliquidated.

Essentials of a Tort

- There must be some act or omission on the part of the defendant.
- In order to make a person liable for a tort, he must have done some act which he was not expected to do or he must have omitted to do something which he was supposed to do.

e.g. A commits the act of trespass or publishes a statement defaming another person or wrongfully detains another person he can be made liable.

- The act or omission should result in legal damage. In order to be successful in an action for tort, the plaintiff has to prove that there has been a legal damage caused to him.

Following are the two important maxims to explain this concept

1. **Injuria Sine Demnum** It means violation of a legal right without causing any harm, loss or damage to the plaintiff.
2. **Damnum Sine Injuria** It means damage which is not coupled with an unauthorised interference with the plaintiff's lawful right. Gloucester Grammar School case explains this maxim. According to the facts of the case; A the defendant set-up a rival school to that of plaintiff's. Because of competition the plaintiff had to reduce their fees. It was held that the plaintiff's had no remedy for the loss thus, suffered by them.

GENERAL DEFENCES

Volenti Non Fit Injuria Which means, no man can enforce a right which he has voluntarily weired or abondoned. If a person voluntarily agrees to suffer some harm, he is not allowed to complain for that and his consent serves as a good defence against him. The consent of the person may be implied or expressed, but it must be free. e.g.

- If you invite somebody to your house you can't sue him for trespass.
- No action for defamation can be brought by a person who agrees to the publication of a matter defamatory of himself.

In both of above examples, the consent is expressed.

It must be noted that for the defence to be available, it is necessary to show that the plaintiff's consent to the act done by the defendant was free and not obtained by fraud or under any compulsion.

Scope of Rescue Doctrine

- The Rescue Doctrine recognises that a danger to an individual often results in a rescue attempt by others. Therefore, the negligence of the defendant in creating a dangerous situation threatens not only the imperiled individual, but also wrongfully threatens any potential rescuer.
- Absent the Rescue Doctrine, a plaintiff would not be able to knowingly and voluntarily place himself or herself in a position where he or she might sustain serious injury, or death, without being found personally negligent in doing so.
- It follows then, that the Rescue Doctrine is not applicable to cases in which the danger is only to property. The Rescue Doctrine concept typically involves a voluntary act by a rescuer who acts spontaneously in the heat of the moment in an emergency situation, with a humane motive and without any legal duty to act, in order to prevent serious injury and loss of life.

Elements of Rescue Doctrine

- Defendant's negligence created a condition that endangered the safety of either the defendant or other person.
- Plaintiff attempted or completed a rescue of the endangered person.
- Plaintiff, as a result of the rescue effort, sustained injuries or died. The rescuer died in the rescue attempt and an action for wrongful death was brought by his survivors.

Limitations on the Scope of the Doctrine

Rescue Cases When the plaintiff voluntarily encounters a risk to rescue somebody from an imminent danger created by the wrongful act of the defendant he cannot be met with the defence of volenti non fit injuria.

e.g. A's servant left a two horses van unattended in a street. A boy threw stone on the houses and they bolted. Causing grave danger to women and children on the road. A police constable on seeing the same, managed to stop the horses, but in doing so, he himself suffered serious personal injuries. It being a rescue case, the defence of 'volenti non fit injuria' was not accepted and 'A' were held liable.

Vicarious Liability

Generally, a person is liable for his own wrongful acts and one does not incur any liability for the act done by others. However, vicarious liability that is the liability of one person for the act done by another person may arise. *The common examples of such a liability are as follows*

- Liability of the principal for the tort of his agent.
- Liability of partners of each other's tort.
- Liability of the master for the tort of his servant.

1. Principal and Agent

It is based on the principle 'Oui Facit Per Alium Facit Per Se' which means that the act of an agent is the act of the principal. Where one person authorises another to commit a tort, the liability for that will be not only of that person, who has committed it but also of that who authorised it. The authority to do the act may be expressed or implied.

e.g. If the owner of a car asked his friend to drive his car and while driving, car was collided with a bus. The owner of the car was held liable.

2. Partners

For the tort committed by any partner in the ordinary course of the business of the firm all the other partners are liable therefore to the same extent as the guilty partner. The liability of each partner is joint and several.

3. Master and Servant

If a servant does a wrongful act in the course of his employment, the master is liable for it. The servant of course is also liable. The wrongful act of the servant is deemed to be the act of the master as well.

e.g.

(i) 'A' is car driver and servant of 'B'. If he negligently knocks down 'X', 'B' is liable for that.

(ii) If 'B' hires a taxi for going to railway station and the taxi driver negligently hits 'X', 'B' will not be liable towards 'X' because the driver is not his servant but an independent contractor.

Absolute Liability

If an industry or enterprise is engaged in some inherently dangerous activity from which it is deriving commercial gain and that activity is capable of causing catastrophic damage then the industry officials are absolutely liable to pay compensation to the aggrieved parties. The industry cannot plead that all safety measures were taken care of by them and that there was negligence on their part. They will not be allowed any exceptions neither can they take up any defence like that of 'Act of God' of 'Act of Stranger.'

Act of God

'Act of God' is a defence. Because it is a kind of inevitable accident with the difference that in the case of Act of God the resulting loss arises out of the working of natural forces.

Essentials for this defence are as follows

- There must be working of natural forces.
- The occurance must be extraordinary. e.g. Extraordinary heavy rainfall, storms, tempests, tides and volcanic eruptions, which cannot be anticipated and reasonably guarded against.

Vicarious Liability of State

- In India, Article 300 of the Constitution of India governs the suability of the state.
- It states that the Union and State Government can be sued subject to the provisions of the law made by the Parliament and the State Legislature respectively.
- The state for the tortious acts of its servants, can be sued only in case of its non-sovereign functions but not in case of its sovereign functions.

NEGLIGENCE

There are two theories of the meaning of term negligence, one is subjective and other is objective. *And based upon these two theories, negligence has two meanings in law of torts*

(i) Negligence as a state of mind (subjective view).

(ii) Negligence as a type of conduct (objective view).

Essentials of Negligence

The defendant owed duty of care to the plaintiff. The defendant made a breach of the duty i.e. he failed to exercise due to care and skill. *Plaintiff suffered damage as a consequence thereof*

1. **Duty of Care** The idea of negligence and dry are strictly correlative. Negligence is simply neglect of some care which one is bound by law or duty or of an obligation to exercise towards another.

   e.g. If a man is driving on a barren plain and no other person is near him, he is at liberty to drive as fast as he pleases. But if he sees another carriage coming near to him. Immediately a duty arises not to drive in such a way as is likely to cause an injury to that other carriage.
2. **Breach of Duty** It means not taking due to care which is required in a particular case. *The law requires taking of two points into consideration, which are as follows*
   (i) **The Importance of the Object to be Attained** The law does not require greatest possible care, but the care required is that of a reasonable man under certain circumstances.
   (ii) **The Magnitude of the Riot** The degree of care varies according to the livelihood of harm and seriousness. A person handing a loaded gun is expected to take more care than a person carrying an ordinary stick.
3. **Damages** It is also necessary that the defendant's breach of duty must cause damage to the plaintiff. No action shall lie for negligence if no damage is caused. Damage must be reasonably foreseeable and a direct result of defendant's breach of duty of care.

Strict Liability

Strict liability applies when a defendant places another person in danger, even in the absence of negligence, simply because he is in possession of a dangerous product, animal or weapon. The plaintiff need not prove negligence.

Types of Strict Liability Torts

There are instances when a person becomes responsible for things that may go wrong even if the person did not intend for the wrong to occur. In other words, some actions hold a person strictly liable regardless of the circumstances. Say you owned an exotic Python. If the snake creeps out of the house and bites your neighbour, you will be held responsible even though you did not let the snake out. Ownership is enough to hold you responsible. In other words, strict liability tort means a defendant is held fully liable for any injury sustained by another party regardless of whether the injury was intended. Dangerous animals are just one of three major strict liability categories. *Strict liability categories include*

1. Animals, Owned or Possessed

The owner or person in possession of certain types of animals is liable for injuries if the animal causes injury to another person or animal. This may include livestock, like cows, horses, bulls or goats. Abnormally dangerous animals also fall under this category and may include snakes, tigers, monkeys or bears. You may think wild animals are not included because, well, they live in the wild. But that is not true. If a person is in possession of a wild animal or has wild animals on their land, like animals that are housed at a zoo and the animal causes injury, liability is assumed.

2. Abnormally Dangerous Acts

Another form of strict liability comes with engaging in abnormally dangerous acts. An Abnormally Dangerous Act can be defined as an act that carries a substantial risk to oneself and others personal property and physical being. That's plenty of legal mumbo jumbo, think pyrotechnics nuclear power plants and blasting rock with dynamite.

3. Product Liability

To be successful in making a products liability claim under strict liability, the plaintiff must prove that there was a defect in the product when it left the defendant's possession. He must also prove that he was a logical and foreseeable user of the product who used the product as it was intended. Additionally, the plaintiff must prove that he was injured by use of the product and that it was caused by the product's defective nature.

There are three primary types of defect in products liability cases

(i) **Manufacturing Defects** An irregularity or flaw in a product that was mass produced, the defect or which makes it more dangerous. When a manufacturer sells a product in defective condition, it is strictly liable for any damages or injuries that the product causes. Having used reasonable care to prevent defects is not a valid defense in such cases.

(ii) **Design Defects** At times an entire product line is defective as a result of faulty design. The manufacturer of such products is absolutely liable for injuries or damages caused by the products. In addition, it may be held liable for any foreseeable injuries that could occur due to the design defect, if there is a cost-effective way to reconstruct the product to make it safe, but the manufacturer continues to produce and sell the defective items.

(iii) **Failure to Warn** A product manufacturer is responsible for warning consumers if there is an inherent, but not obvious, danger in using the product. For instance, the manufacturer of chocolate raisin bars makes the bars in a plant that also processes peanuts. Because it is common for some residue to remain in the equipment, which has the potential to cause serious injury or death to some people, the manufacturer must warn consumers about the possible presence of peanuts.

Res Ipsa Loquitur

- As a rule the onus of proving negligence is on the plaintiff. He must not merely establish the facts of the defendant's negligence and of his own damage, but must show that the one was the effect of the other. But in certain cases when plaintiff need not prove that and inference of negligence is drown from the facts. Thus, direct evidence of negligence is not always necessary and the same may be inferred from the circumstances of the case.
- There is a presumption of negligence according to this maxim, which means the thing speaks for itself.

e.g. If a brick falls from a building and injures a passer-by on the highway or the goods while in the possession of a bailee are lost, or death of a person is caused by live broken electric wire in a street a presumption of negligence is raised in the above examples.

Defences to Negligence

If the negligence of the plaintiff is partially responsible for his harm, his recovery from the defendant may be reduced or barred. This is called contributory or comparative negligence. In a small minority of states, the common law contributory negligence rule is followed which states that if the plaintiff contributes to his harm, he cannot recover from the defendant. In most states, this rule has been rejected because it has been regarded as unjust in situations where the plaintiff's negligence was slight in comparison to the defendant's negligence.

It can be classified into following types

- Vis major (Act of God)
- Inevitable accident
- Contributory negligence of the plaintiff
- Volenti non fit injuria (Defence of Consent)
- Express contract
- Judicial acts, executive acts and statutory authority in very exceptional and appropriate cases.

e.g.

(i) Acts which are occasioned by the elementary force of nature, unconnected with the agency of man or other cause, will come under the category of acts of God e.g. storm, tempest, lightning, severe frost etc.

(ii) 'A' is lying drunk on a roadway. 'B' approaches in a motor car round a bend in the road, but just before he reaches the point at which under ordinary circumstances, he would first see 'A', a sheet of newspaper is blown by wind against his windscreen and materially obscures his view. He runs over 'A', and injures him. Here, 'A' cannot held 'B' liable for accident because it being a case of inevitable accident or misfortune.

Nuisance as a tort means an unlawful interference with a person's use or enjoyment of land, or some right over, or in connection with it. Nuisance includes any act, omission, injury, damage, annoyance, or offence to the sense of sight, smell, hearing or which is or may be dangerous to life or injurious to health or property.

Nuisance is of two kinds

(a) Public or Common nuisance (crime under Section 268 of IPC)

(b) Private nuisance (tort or civil wrong)

Damages in Nuisance

In an action for nuisance, actual damage is required to be proved. In the case of public nuisance, the plaintiff can bring an action in tort only when he proves a special damage to him. In private nuisance, although damage is one of the essentials, the law will often presume it.

Defamation

- Defamation is a tort which injures reputation by exposing a person to hatred, contempt or ridicule, and is therefore actionable.
- If a person injures the reputation of another he does so at his own risk. Defamation is both a civil and a criminal wrong.
- Defamation is a reasonable restriction on the Fundamental Right of freedom of speech and expression.

Essentials of Defamation

Some essentials of defamation are as follows

- The words must be false and defamatory.
- The said words must refers to the plaintiff.
- The words must be published.

Defences to Defamation

The defences to an action for defamation are as follows

- Justification or truth
- Fair comment
- Privilege (absolute or qualified)

e.g. 'Z' is not having good relations with his mother-in-law. He tells his wife, "There is hardly a day when your mother does not indulge in adultery." The statement made by 'Z' is false. 'Z' is liable for the tort of defamation.

Nervous Shock

- The nervous shock may be caused by words or act of the defendant. It may be induced by some accident due to the defendant's negligence or on account of a false statement willfully made or due to intimidation (intentional wrong doing).

- The plaintiff could suffer nervous shock by witnessing (seeing or hearing) personal injury (or an accident) or destruction of his property caused by the defendant's wrongful act.

e.g. 'A' by way of practical joke, falsely represented to 'P' that her husband had met with a serious accident whereby both his legs were broken. By reason of this mis-representation 'P' suffered with a serious nervous shock and was made seriously ill.

'P's husband who had to incur expenses for-medical treatment can claim damage from 'A' for shock cause by his false news.

Practice Exercise

1. Tort is a ....
(a) Criminal wrong (b) Civil wrong
(c) Both (a) and (b) (d) None of these

2. Injuria sine demnum stands for
(a) Injury with damage
(b) Injury without damage
(c) Wrongful act
(d) Actionable claim

3. Unliquidated damage stands for
(a) Not pre-estimated
(b) Pre-estimated
(c) According to the rule
(d) According to the IPC

4. Consent defines as
(a) given by words (b) given by conduct
(c) Both (a) and (b) (d) None of these

5. Defamation means
(a) Attack on the persons reputation
(b) Attack on the person self respect
(c) All of the above
(d) None of the above

6. Qui facit per alium facit per se stands for
(a) To act for another (b) To act independently
(c) Let the principle liable (d) None of these

7. Public nuisance include
(a) digging trench on a highway
(b) Brother keeping
(c) All of the above
(d) None of the above

8. Defence under nuisance are
(a) Statutory action (b) Prescription
(c) Both (a) and (b) (d) None of these

9. **PRINCIPLE** Where the plaintiff himself is in fault, the defendant shall not be answerable for the harm brought on by the plaintiff's own actions.

FACTS Jimmy had put up a board in his house warning all trespassers of 'Beware of Dogs'. Jimmy arrived home using a cab and since he did not have wallet asked the driver to stay outside. He received a long distance phone call and spoke for 20 straight minutes. The cab driver outside was getting very restless and was ringing the bell which turned out to be broken. Left with no other alternative the driver came in only to be bitten black and blue by Jimmy's Rottweiler. In a suit brought by the cab driver
(a) Jimmy shall succeed as the cab driver came inside despite the warning
(b) Jimmy shall succeed as the cab driver was a trespasser
(c) Cab driver shall succeed because he did not read the board
(d) Cab driver shall succeed because he was not a trespasser

10. **PRINCIPLE** Whoever by words either spoken or intended to be read or by signs or by visible representations, makes or publishes any imputation concerning any person intending to harm, or knowing or having reason to believe that such imputation will harm, the reputation of such person, is to defame that person.

FACTS In a community, there is a custom of stealing shoes of the bridegroom during the marriage ceremony. The shoes of the bridegroom were stolen by 'Y'. 'A' announced that 'Z' has stolen the shoes. Everyone present in the marriage party started staring at 'Z' with great surprise. 'Z' felt very ashamed.

(a) A defamed Z
(b) A did not defame Z
(c) A defamed Z for Z felt very ashamed
(d) A defamed the whole marriage party

11. PRINCIPLES

I. A master is liable for the wrongful acts of his servant.

II. A person can be called a servant only if there is a relation of employment and he acts under the order and on behalf of his master.

FACTS X bank launched a saving scheme for poor sections of the society and the customer can deposit ₹ 10 per day. Y, an unemployed youth, collected money from several customers, and on behalf of them deposited the money at the bank every day. The bank gave to Y a small commission. After sometime , Y disappeared without depositing the money given by the customers. The customers bring a suit alleging that the bank is liable. Decide

(a) the bank is liable because it paid commission to Y
(b) the bank is liable because Y was their servant
(c) the bank is not liable because Y was not their servant
(d) No one is liable

12. The railway authorities negligently allowed a train to be over crowded. In consequence, a legitimate passenger Mr X got his pocket picked. Choose the appropriate answer.

(a) Mr X can sue the railway authorities for the loss suffered
(b) Mr X ran sue because he had given consent to travel in a over crowded train
(c) Mr X cannot sue railway authorities because there was no infringement of his legal right and mere fact that the loss was caused does not give rise to a cause of action
(d) None of the above

13. PRINCIPLE An unlawful interference with a person's use or enjoyment of land, or some right over, or in connection with it, is a nuisance in law of tort.

FACTS During the scarcity of onions, long queues were made outside the defendant's shop who having a licence to sell fruits and vegetables used to sell only 1 kg of onion per ration card. The queues extended on to the highway and also caused some obstruction to the neighbouring shops. The shopkeepers filed a suit for nuisance against the defendant.

Which one of the following decisions will be correct on this suit?

(a) The defendant is liable for nuisance
(b) The defendant is not liable for nuisance
(c) The defendant is liable under the principle of strict liability
(d) The plaintiff's suit should be decreed in favour of the neighbouring shopkeeper

14. PRINCIPLE An owner of land has the right to use the land in any manner he or she desires. The owner of land also owns the space above and the depths below it.

FACTS Ramesh owns an acre of land on the outskirts of Sullurpeta, Andhra Pradesh. The Government of India launches its satellites into space frequently from Sriharikota, near Sullurpeta. The Government of India does not deny that once the satellite launch has travelled the distance of almost 7000 kilometres it passes over Ramesh's property. Ramesh files a case claiming that the Government of India has violated his property rights by routing its satellite over his property, albeit 7000 kilometre directly above it.

Applying the principle to the case you would decide

(a) In favour of the Government of India because the transgression was at a height at which Ramesh could not possibly have any use
(b) That ownership of land does not mean that the owner's right extends infinitely into space above the land
(c) In favour of Ramesh because he has the right to infinite space above the land he owns

(d) In favour of the Government of India because it would lead to the absurd result that Ramesh and most other property owners would have a claim against airline companies and other countries of the world whose satellites orbit the Earth

15. PRINCIPLE Trespass is the unauthorised entry through person or tangible object into the property of another. The rights of property exist on the surface, aerially and in the subterrain.

FACTS Kumari and Shravan lived in houses interspersed by plot of Shantanu. Kumari and Shravan set-up a walkie talkie connection by setting up their transmitters facing each other. When Shantanu came to know about the arrangement, he filed a suit of trespass stating that the same was a case of trespass as signals could reach each other only by crossing his plot.

(a) Shantanu shall succeed as the signals transmit through his property
(b) Shantanu shall not succeed as the transmitters do not belong to him
(c) Shantanu shall succeed as the signals transmit aerially
(d) Shantanu shall not succeed as signals are not tangible

16. PRINCIPLE Assault is the use of words or gestures inducing a threat of force or danger to person.

FACTS X and Y being friends were comparing stalwarts of their favourite football teams. X egged Y to go on and without realising it converted into a verbal sling fest and reduced to angry expletives. X and Y decided to file suits of verbal assault against each other.

(a) X and Y shall be able to sue each other as the expletives amount to assault on senses
(b) Y shall be able to sue X as X provoked Y
(c) X shall be able to sue Y as Y should not have been provoked
(d) No one will be able to sue as one

17. PRINCIPLE Nuisance is the interference in the enjoyment of property.

FACTS Pizzeria, a small cafeteria selling namesake used to run a wood fired oven. The resulting smoke caused a lot of smoke in the neighbourhood and there were a number of complaints from the locals who had not witnessed such an oven. The food inspector taking cognizance of these reports asked the restaurant to shut down the oven. The owner who had earlier ran a similar establishment in Italy did not comply. Is Pizzeria committing nuisance?

(a) It shall not be nuisance as the oven was a common occurrence in Italy
(b) It shall be nuisance as the oven was emitting smoke continuously in the neighbourhood
(c) There shall be no nuisance as there were no complaints from customers
(d) There shall be nuisance as there were a large number of complaints

18. PRINCIPLE The use of force with the intent to cause harm, or annoy or induce fear is termed as the tort of battery.

FACTS A group of construction workers were negligently handling bricks by catch and throw. Simmons was passing by the site where one such brick fell on Simmons and he brought a case of battery against the contractor under whose employment the workmen were carrying out the construction.

(a) The case cannot be described as battery as the requisite intention was not present
(b) The case cannot be described as battery as Simmons should have been more careful
(c) The case can be described as battery as Simmons was injured
(d) The case can be described as battery as the workers ought to have been more careful

19. PRINCIPLE A master is liable for the acts of his servant, a principal is liable for the acts of the agent, but a hirer of services is not liable for the acts of the independent contractor.

FACTS While implementing the request of Mr Sampat, the confectioner at Ghantewali and Co. made the oil extra hot to make him a batch of extra crispy banana fritters, the oil sizzled on impact and burnt Dadabhoy who was standing nearby. He wants to know as to whom he should sue

(a) The confectioner as he made the oil extra hot
(b) Mr Sampat as the confectioner was under the control of Mr Sampat and had made the oil extra hot at his request for extra crispy fritters

(c) Ghantewali and Co. under whose employment the confectioner worked
(d) None of the above as it was a case of damnum sine injuria

20. PRINCIPLE Res ipsa loquitur reverses the burden of proof, creating a rebuttable presumption of the guilt of the defendant in situations where the default of the defendant seems apparent.

FACTS X, a truck driver, crashed into Y for no fault of his while trying to save Z, a student who was loitering in school uniform. Based on the facts above, Y inquires the presumption of negligence shall be in favour of

(a) X as X crashed into Y
(b) the parents as the crash happened due to their child
(c) the school if it is apparent that the parents left the child at school
(d) None of the above

21. PRINCIPLE A master is liable for the acts of servant done in the course of employment.

FACTS A nurse was deployed for the care of an old invalid suffering a very painful and terminal illness in a hospice. A visiting doctor used to come in every week and prescribe certain medications. In order to alleviate the pain she used to slip in certain narcotic drug to the patient with whom she had developed a friendly relationship. The narcotics eventually reacted with the drugs of the doctor's prescription thereby inducing a fatal cardiac arrest in the patient. In a suit brought by the legal heirs of the patient, the suit shall

(a) not succeed as the drugs were given in personal capacity
(b) not succeed as the nurse was carrying an unauthorised act
(c) succeed against the hospice in whose employ the nurse was
(d) succeed against the doctor as the nurse was under his direction and control

22. PRINCIPLE A person is not liable for every harm which comes of the act but is only liable for those harms which can be reasonably foreseen at the time of the injury.

FACTS Sumati, who was being threatened of armed robbery pulled the railway chain. The engine driver recorded the chain pulling, but did not stop thinking it to be the work of mischievous passengers wishing to alight before the station. As a result no help came to Sumati, who was robbed and injured. The suit brought by her was resisted by the railways. As judge you would

(a) award damages to Sumati for the negligence of the engine driver
(b) award partial damages to Sumati as the driver was negligent, but could not have foreseen the extent of harm
(c) not award damages to Sumati as the driver was under a genuine mistaken belief
(d) None of the above

23. PRINCIPLE Mere delegation does not transfer authority unless there is an actual transference of the power to control the actions of the servant.

FACTS The Delhi Metro Rail Corporation set-up a link transport service permitting passengers to use buses to the end destinations. These buses and drivers were provided on contract to the Metro Corporation by the Delhi Bus Company and the drivers were trained, supervised and instructed into the routes and manner of driving by employees of the corporation. When a passenger X, had boarded one such bus and was involved in an accident on account of the bus driver; he wants to know against whom should he file the suit under the principle of vicarious liability.

(a) The bus driver
(b) Delhi Bus Company
(c) Delhi Metro Rail Corporation
(d) All of the above

24. PRINCIPLE Where a dangerous article escapes, the owner shall be strictly liable for the harm which comes without being at fault.

FACTS Bhopal Gas Co. was in business of manufacturing chemicals which produced a large amount of toxic residue. As per procedure they used to store the waste in insulated boxes and hand it over to the collecting van of the municipal corporation once a week. After one such collection, the van driver drove negligently resulting in the escape and spilling of the contents of one of the waste barrels. Is Bhopal Gas Co. liable?

(a) Bhopal Gas Co. is strictly liable for the spill
(b) Bhopal Gas Co. is not liable for the spill
(c) Municipal Corporation is not liable for the spill
(d) Both Bhopal Gas Co. and Municipal Corporation are liable for the spill

25. PRINCIPLE Right to private defence entitles you the licence of force in the failure of other options to the extent of harm faced and proportionate resistance likewise.

FACTS X had a snake farm where he used to extract venom from the snakes and sell them for medicinal uses. One such neutralised snake entered into Y's property and into his child's nursery. On bein tried to be removed the snake got aggravated and was therefore killed by Y's servant. In a suit brought by X against Y.

(a) Y is to compensate for the action of X on account of vicarious liability
(b) Y is to compensate X for not taking steps to determine as to whether the snake was venomous or not and as such the force was disproportionate
(c) Y is not to compensate X as X should have ensured his snake did not leave X's premises
(d) X is not to compensate as the act was one not proportional with the threat at hand

26. PRINCIPLE A principal is liable for such acts as committed in the course of agency, but is not liable for such acts as committed outside the course of agency.

FACTS ABC, a partnership between A, B and C maintained a bank account with XYZ. As per the standing arrangement with the bank, signatures of at least two partners were required for withdrawal of the money from the partnership account. B forged the signatures of A, which were exactly alike and withdrew a large amount of money and disappeared. In a suit brought by A and C

(a) The bank will succeed as A committed wrong in the course of agency
(b) The bank will succeed as A committed a wrong outside the course of agency
(c) A and C shall succeed as the bank honoured a forged cheque
(d) A and C shall succeed because they had not authorised B to withdraw money

27. PRINCIPLE The test as to whether the act done by an officer or agency of state is a sovereign function or a function done ordinarily, is dependent on the fact that an alternative person may also carry out the latter, but the former may only be carried out by the state.

FACTS In a boundary settlement dispute between India and Bangladesh, certain territory was exchanged in pursuit of a treaty agreement. X's land which lay in the Indian enclave thus got transferred to Bangladesh, which did not recognise his proprietary rights. In a suit against the Indian Government, the likely outcome is

(a) the Indian Government must compensate by way of money giving fair price of the land to X
(b) the Indian Government need not compensate X
(c) the Bangladeshi Government should compensate X
(d) the Indian Government should give him property in the land received from Bangladesh

28. PRINCIPLE Vis major or an act of God entails a sudden manoeuvre by elements of nature over which we have no control.

FACTS In a bus accident where the driver died of a sudden cardiac arrest, the legal heirs of the deceased brought a suit against the bus company for not making the driver undergo the mandatory health and fitness test before giving employment. The bus company claims a defence of 'vis major'. The defence of vis major in this case shall

(a) sustain as death is an act of nature
(b) not sustain as the act may have been preventable
(c) sustain as a general fitness test does not guarantee detecting a possible cardiac arrest
(d) not sustain as the defence of inevitable accident shall be applicable

29. PRINCIPLE An unlawful action is sufficient to establish an actionable claim under the law of torts and the court need not go into the motivations behind such unlawful action.

FACTS Z, a reporter, had approached A, a famous politician, several times for an interview. Z knew that A was having an affair with his secretary. Frustrated and vengeful, Z ran a cover story about the affair disclosing all the information and evidence of the affair. A in turn sued Z for defamation, stating the action was based on vendetta and malice on account of his refusal to give Z an interview. The suit against Z shall

(a) succeed as the action of Z was unlawful
(b) not succeed as the action of Z was lawful
(c) succeed as the action of Z was malicious
(d) not succeed as the action of Z was not malicious

30. The act of unlawful entering into another's property constitutes

(a) trespass (b) restraint
(c) appropriation (d) encroachment

31. When the master is held liable for the wrongful acts of his servant, the liability is

(a) strict liability
(b) vicarious liability
(c) tortuous liability
(d) absolute liability

32. 'No-fault liability' means

(a) liability for damage caused through negligence
(b) liability for damage caused through fault
(c) absolute liability even without any negligence or fault
(d) freedom from liability

33. LEGAL PRINCIPLE 'Consent' defined as - Two or more persons are said to consent when they agree upon the same thing in the same sense.

What does 'consent' include?

(a) Agreement
(b) Two or more person
(c) They agree upon the same thing in the same sense
(d) All of the above

34. LEGAL PRINCIPLE 'Free consent' defined as - Consent is said free when it is not caused by

I. coercion as defined in Section 15
II. under influence, as defined in Section 16
III. fraud, as defined in Section 17, or
IV. misrepresentation, as defined in Section 18
V. mistake, subject to the provisions of Sections 20, 21 and 22

Consent is said to be so caused when it would not have been given but for the existence of such coercion, under influence, fraud, misrepresentation or mistake. 'Fraud' is defined in which Section?

(a) Section 18 (b) Section 19
(c) Section 17 (d) Section 20

Previous Year's Questions

Instructions to Candidates

This section consists of 2 problems (with 10 **questions**) in total. Each problem consists of a set of rules and facts. Apply the **specified rules** to the set of **facts** and answer the questions.

In answering the following questions, you should **not** rely on any rule(s) except the rule(s) that are supplied for every problem. Further, you should not assume any fact other than those stated in the problem. The aim is to test your ability to properly apply a rule to a given set of facts, even when the result is absurd or unacceptable for any other reason. It is **not** the aim to test any knowledge of law you may already possess. **[CLAT 2011]**

Problem 1 (Q. Nos. 35 to 39)

Principle

A. Whoever intending to take any moveable property out of the possession of any person, without that person's consent, moves that property out of his or her possession, is said to commit theft.

B. A person who, without lawful excuse, damages any property belonging to another intending to damage any such property shall be guilty of causing criminal damage.

C. Damage means any impairment of the value of a property.

Facts Veena, an old lady of 78 yr, used to live with her granddaughter Indira. Veena was ill and therefore bed-ridden for several months. In those months, she could not tolerate any noise and it became quite difficult to clean her room. After she aied, Indira hired a cleaner, Lucky, to clean the room and throw away any rubbish that may be there.

There was a pile of old newspapers which Veena had stacked in a corner of her room. Lucky asked Indira if he should clear away the pile of old newspapers, to which she said yes. Lucky took the pile to a municipality rubbish dump. While Lucky was sorting and throwing away the newspapers, he was very surprised to find a beautiful painting in between two sheets of paper. He thought that Indira probably wouldn't want this old painting back, especially because it was torn in several places and the colour was fading. He took the painting home, mounted it on a wooden frame and hung it on the wall of his bedroom. Unknown to him, the painting was an old masterpiece, and worth twenty thousand rupees. Before mounting the painting, Lucky pasted it on a plain sheet of paper so that it does not tear any more. By doing so, he made its professional restoration very difficult and thereby reduced its value by half.

Lucky's neighbour Kamala discovered that the painting belonged to Indira. With the motive of returning the painting to Indira, Kamala climbed through an open window into Lucky's room when he was away one afternoon and removed the painting from his house.

35. Has Lucky committed theft?

(a) Yes, Lucky has committed theft of the newspapers and the painting
(b) No, Lucky has not committed theft because he had Veena's consent
(c) Yes, Lucky has committeed theft of the painting, but not of the newspapers
(d) No, Lucky has not committed theft because he has not moved the painting out of Veena's possession

36. Is Lucky guilty of criminal damage?

(a) No, Lucky is not guilty of criminal damage as he did not intentionally impair the value of the painting
(b) Yes, Lucky is guilty of criminal damage as he intentionally stuck the paper on to the painting
(c) No, Lucky is not guilty of criminal damage as he does not have the painting in his possession anymore
(d) No, Lucky is not guilty of criminal damage as he has not destroyed the painting

37. If Lucky had discovered the painting before leaving Indira's house rather than at the rubbish dump, would he have been guilty of theft in this case?

(a) Yes, he would be guilty of theft of the newspapers and the paintings
(b) No, he would not be guilty of theft
(c) Yes, he would be guilty of theft of the painting
(d) None of the above

38. Is Kamala guilty of theft?

(a) No, Kamala is not guilty of theft since the person she took the painting from (Lucky) was not its lawful owner
(b) No, Kamala is not guilty of theft since she took the painting only with the motive of returning it to Indira
(c) Yes, Kamala is guilty of theft as she took the painting out of Lucky's possession without his consent
(d) None of the above

39. Which of the following propositions could be inferred from the facts and the rules specified?

(a) Kamala is guilty of criminal damage as the person she took the painting from (Lucky) was not its lawful owner
(b) Kamala is guilty of criminal damage as she took the painting without Lucky's consent
(c) Kamala is not guilty of criminal damage as the painting has not been completely destroyed
(d) None of the above

Problem 2 (Q. Nos. 40 to 44)

40. Principle

A. An owner of land has the right to use the land in any manner he or she desires. The owner of land also owns the space above and the depths below it

B. Rights above the land extend only to the point they are essential to any use or enjoyment of land

C. An owner cannot claim infringement of her property right if the space above his or her land is put to reasonable use by someone else at a height at which the owner would have no reasonable use of it and it does not affect the reasonable enjoyment of his or her land

Ramesh's case Ramesh owns an acre of land on the outskirts of Sullurpeta, Andhra Pradesh. The Government of India launches its satellites into space frequently from Sriharikota, near Sullurpeta. The Government of India does not deny that once the satellite launch has travelled the distance of almost 7000 km it passes over Ramesh's property. Ramesh files a case claiming that the Government of India has violated his property rights by routing its satellite over his property, albeit 7000 km directly above it.

40. Applying **only** Principle A to Ramesh's case, as a judge you would decide
(a) In favour of the Government of India because the transgression was at a height at which Ramesh could not possibly have any use for
(b) That ownership of land does not mean that the owner's right extends infinitely into space above the land
(c) In favour of Ramesh because he has the right to infinite space above the land he owns
(d) In favour of the Government of India because it would lead to the absurd result that Ramesh and most other property owners would have a claim against airline companies and other countries of the world whose satellites orbit the earth

Shazia's case Shazia owns a single storeyed house in Ahmedabad which has been in her family for more than 75 yr. The foundation of the house cannot support another floor and Shazia has no intention of demolishing her family home to construct a bigger building. Javed and Sandeep are business partners and own three storey houses on either side of Shazia's house. Javed and Sandeep are also Ahmedabad's main distributors for a major soft drinks company. They have erected a huge hoarding advertising their products, with the ends supported on their roofs but the hoarding also passes over Shazia's house at 70 feet and casts a permanent shadow on her terrace. Shazia decides to hoist a huge Indian flag, going up to 75 feet, on her roof. She files a case, asking the court to order Javed and Sandeep to remove the hoarding for all these reasons

41. Applying **only** Principle B to Shazia's case, you would decide in favour of
(a) Javed and Sandeep because Shazia can easily hoist a flag below 70 ft
(b) Shazia because she has the right to put her land to any use and the court cannot go into her intentions for hoisting a flag at 75 ft
(c) Shazia because she has the absolute right to the space above her land
(d) Javed and Sandeep because hoisting a flag 75 ft above one's roof is not essential to the use and enjoyment of the land

42. Applying **only** Principle A and B to Shazia's case, you would decide
(a) in favour of Shazia only under Rule A
(b) in favour of Shazia under Rule A as well as B
(c) against Shazia under Rule B
(d) against Shazia under Rule A as well as B

43. Applying **only** Principle B and C to Ramesh's case, you would decide
(a) in favour of Ramesh only under Rule B
(b) in favour of Ramesh under Rule B as well as C
(c) against Ramesh under Rule C
(d) against Ramesh under Rule B as well as C

44. Applying Principle C to Shazia's case, you would decide
(a) in her favour because hoisting a 75 ft high flag is reasonable
(b) against her because hoisting a 75 ft high flag is not reasonable
(c) against her because the hoarding is a reasonable use of the space above her land
(d) in her favour because the permanent shadow cast by the hoarding affects the reasonable enjoyment of her land

45. Principle A careless person becomes liable for his negligence when he owed a duty of care to others.

Factual Situation As the bus was leaving the platform, Kashish rushed and boarded the bus keeping the door open. Ashish, who was standing at the edge of the platform, was hit by the door of the moving bus and injured. Aashish claims compensation from Kashish. **[CLAT 2011]**

(a) Kashish is liable to Aashish for not having taken care to close the door of the moving bus
(b) Kashish is not liable to Aashish as it was the duty of the conductor of the bus to close the door
(c) Kashish is not liable to Aashish, as it was the duty of the latter, to take sufficient care, while standing on the platform, as not to expose oneself to such accidental harm
(d) None of the above

46. Principle Whoever by words, either spoken or written brings or attempts to bring into hatred or contempt or excites or attempts to excite disaffection towards the government established by law in India shall be punished. However, comments expressing disapprobation of the administrative or other action of the government without exciting or attempting to excite hatred, contempt or disaffection, do not constitute an offence.

Facts A renowned professor of Economics wrote a critical comment on the economic policies of the Government of India in a National Daily. This piece of writing generated academic debate not only in the print media but also on television and internet. A student of law asked the fellow Indians on a social networking website to assemble at a particular place for peaceful and silent demonstration against the said economic policies on a stipulated date and time. The crowd assembled at that venue and started shouting anti-government slogans. Police arrested the professor. **[CLAT 2013]**

(a) The professor has committed the offence
(b) The professor has not committed any offence
(c) The student of law has committed the offence
(d) The crowd has committed an offence

47. Principle Whenever there is an invasion of a legal right, the person in whom the right is vested, is entitled to bring an action though he has suffered no actual loss or harm and may recover damages (compensation).

Facts 'A' was a qualified voter for the Lok Sabha election. However, a returning officer wrongfully refused to take A's vote. Inspite of such wrongful refusal, the candidate, for whom 'A' wanted to vote, won the election. But, 'A' brought an action for damages.

Which of the following derivations is correct? **[CLAT 2014]**

(a) Since, no legal right of 'A' had been violated, therefore, as such no compensation could be granted
(b) Since, legal right of 'A' had been violated, therefore, compensation should be granted
(c) No, compensation could be granted, as 'A' had suffered no loss as his candidate won the election.
(d) Since, no fundamental right of 'A' had been violated, therefore, as such no compensation could be granted

48. Principle In a civil action for defamation, truth of the defamatory matter is an absolute defence. However, the burden of proving truth is on the defendant; and he is liable if he does not successfully discharge this burden.

Facts 'D', who was the editor of a local weekly, published a series of articles mentioning that 'P', who was a government servant, issued false certificates, accepted bribe, adopted corrupt and illegal means to mint money and was a 'mischief monger'. 'P' brought a civil action against 'D', who could not prove the facts published by him.

Under the circumstances, which of the following derivations is correct? **[CLAT 2014]**

(a) 'D' would be liable, since he could not prove the facts published by him
(b) 'D' would not be liable, as such an action could curtail the right of expression and speech of press
(c) 'D' would not be liable, as media could publish anything
(d) None of the above

49. Principle Damage without the violation of a legal right is not actionable in a court of law. If the interference with the rights of another person is not unlawful or unauthorised, but a necessary consequence of the exercise of defendant's own lawful rights, no action should lie.

Facts There was an Established School ('ES') in a particular locality. Subsequently, a New School ('NS') was set up in the same locality, which charged lower fees, on account of which people started patronising the new school. Because of the competition, 'ES' had to reduce its fees. 'ES' filed a case against 'NS' saying that 'NS' had caused it ('ES') financial loss and thus claimed compensation. **[CLAT 2014]**

Which of the following derivations is correct?

(a) Since no legal right of 'ES' had been violated, therefore, as such no compensation could be granted
(b) Since, damage is caused to 'ES', therefore, it should be awarded compensation
(c) 'ES' should be awarded compensation, as opening of school in competition is not good
(d) No compensation could be granted, as reduction in fees is good for the public

50. Principle Vicarious liability is the liability of the Master or Principal for the tort committed by his servant or agent, provided the tort is committed in the course of employment. The Master or Principal is not liable for private wrongs of the servant/agent.

Facts 'X' hands over some cash money at his house to 'Y', who is his (X's) neighbour and is also cashier in a bank, to be deposited in A's account in the bank. Instead of depositing the money, 'Y' misappropriates it. **[CLAT 2014]**

Which of the following statements depicts correct legal position in this given situation?

(a) The bank would not be liable because 'Y' did not do any wrong in the course of his employment
(b) The bank would be vicariously liable because 'Y' was the employee of the bank
(c) The bank would not be liable because 'Y' did not do any wrong
(d) The bank would be liable because 'Y' acted as bank's agent

51. Principle Master is liable for the wrongful acts committed by his servant; provided the acts are committed during the course of employment. However, the master is not liable if the wrongful act committed by his servant has no connection, whatsoever, with the servant's contract of employment.

Facts 'D' is a driver employed by 'M', who is the owner of a company. During the lunch time, 'D' goes to a closeby tea shop to have a cup of tea. There he ('D') picks up fight with the tea shop owner ('T'), which resulted in some damage to his shop. 'T' wants to sue 'M' for claiming compensation for the damage caused by the fight. **[CLAT 2014]**

Which of the following derivations is correct?

(a) 'M' will be liable because 'D' is his servant
(b) Both 'M' and 'D' will be liable
(c) 'M' will not be liable because the wrongful act (picking up fight) was not committed in the course of D's employment
(d) 'M' will be liable albeit the wrongful act (picking up fight) was not committed in the course of D's employment

52. Principle Nuisance is an unlawful interference with a person's use or enjoyment of land or some right over or in connection with it. If the interference is 'direct', the wrong is trespass; whereas, if the interference is 'consequential', it amounts to nuisance.

Facts 'A' plants a tree on his land. However, he allows its branches to project over the land of 'B'.

Which of the following derivations is correct? **[CLAT 2014]**

(a) 'A' has committed trespass
(b) 'A' has committed nuisance
(c) 'A' has not committed nuisance
(d) None of the above

53. Principle Interference with another's goods in such a way as to deny the latter's title to the goods amounts to conversion, and thus it is a civil wrong. It is an act intentionally done inconsistent with the owner's right, though the doer may not know of, or intend to challenge, the property or possession of the true owner.

Facts 'R' went to a cycle-stand to park his bicycle. Seeing the stand fully occupied, he removed a few bicycles in order to rearrange a portion of the stand and make some space for his bicycle. He parked his bicycle properly, and put back all the bicycles except the one belonging to 'S', In fact, 'R' was in a hurry, and therefore, he could not put back S's bicycle. Somebody came on the way and took away S's bicycle. The watchman of the stand did not take care of it assuming that the bicycle was not parked inside the stand. 'S' filed a suit against 'R' for conversion. **[CLAT 2014]**

Which of the following derivations is correct?

(a) 'R' could not be held liable for the negligence of the watchman
(b) 'S' would succeed because R's act led to the stealing of his bicycle
(c) 'S' would not succeed because 'R' did not take away the bicycle himself
(d) 'S' would not succeed because R's intention was not bad

54. Principle Whoever, unlawfully or negligently does any act which is, and which he knows or has reason to believe to he, likely to spread the infection of any disease dangerous to life, shall be guilty of a negligent act likely to spread infection of disease dangerous to life.

Facts 'K', a person, knowing that he is suffering from Cholera, travels by a train without informing the railway officers of his condition. **[CLAT 2014]**

(a) 'K' has committed an unlawful and negligent act, which is likely to spread the infection of Cholera disease dangerous to the life of fellow-passengers.
(b) Railway officers are guilty of an unlawful and negligent act, as 'K' who is suffering from Cholera disease has travelled by the train
(c) 'K' has not committed an unlawful and negligent act, which is likely to Spread the infection of Cholera disease dangerous to the life of fellow-passengers
(d) Both 'K' and Railway officers are guilty of an unlawful and negligent act, which is likely to spread the infection of Cholera disease dangerous to the life of fellow-passengers.

55. Principle When a person represents to another something as a true fact knowing well truly that it is not true, he is guilty of fraud. The person subjected to fraud may avoid an agreement.

Factual Situation A presents a horse for sale. The horse is kept on display, so that anyone interested could examine it. The horse has a cracked hoof and it is cleverly concealed by the owner. B tells "if you do not deny it, I shall assume that the horse is sound." A keeps silent. B purchases the horse. **[CLAT 2015]**

Decision

(a) B can avoid the agreement on discovery of the defect.
(b) B cannot avoid the agreement, as the horse was on display and he could have satisfied himself of its soundless by personal examination.
(c) B cannot avoid the agreement as A did not make any representation to mislead him. He merely kept silent so that B could find things by himself.
(d) None of the above

56. Assertion (A) In the event of violation of any legal right (tort), the aggrieved party is entitled to recover unliquidated damages.

Reason (R) The object of awarding damages to the aggrieved party is to put him in the same position in which he would have been if the wrong would not have been committed. Damages, are therefore, assessed on that basis. **[CLAT 2015]**

Codes

(a) Both (A) and (R) are true and (R) is the correct explanation of (A)
(b) Both (A) and (R) are true, but (R) is not the correct explanation of (A)
(c) (A) is true, but (R) is false
(d) (A) is false, but (R) is true

57. Define 'Vicarious Liability'. **[CLAT 2015]**
(a) Liability of the principle for the tort of his agent.
(b) Liability of partners for each other.
(c) Liability of the master for the tort of his servant.
(d) All of the above

58. X went to Y's house and forgot his bag which contained 1 kg sweets. Y's children consumed the sweets. Decide the liability of Y. **[CLAT 2015]**
(a) Y is bound to pay the price of sweets to X.
(b) Y is not bound to pay anything.
(c) Y is bound to pay half the price of sweets.
(d) Y would not have to pay anything because X loves Y's children.

59. Principle False imprisonment is a tort (wrong) which means the total restraint of a person's liberty without lawful justification.

Fact A part of a public road had been closed for spectators of a boat race. 'P' wanted to enter but he was prevented by 'D' and other policeman because he had not paid the admission fee. 'P' was able to enter the enclosure by other means, but was unable to go where he wanted to go. The policeman refused access to where he wanted to go but allowed him to remain where he was or to go back. 'P' remained within the enclosure and refused to leave. Subsequently, 'P' sued 'D' for false imprisonment. **[CLAT 2015]**
(a) It was a case of false imprisonment, but 'D' could not be made liable for it
(b) 'D' could not be made liable for false imprisonment as he has not touched him
(c) 'D' could not be made liable for false imprisonment, as he did restrict P's movements
(d) 'D' could not be made liable for false imprisonment, as he did not totally restrict P's movements

60. Principle Whoever by words or writing conveys to others any imputation concerning any person's reputation is said to defame that person.

Fact During a marriage ceremony, 'A' circulated a pamphlet saying that 'S', sister of the bride, is a thief, she has stolen the shoes of the bridegroom.
(a) 'A' has defamed 'S' **[CLAT 2016]**
(b) 'A' did not defame 'S' as he never intended it
(c) 'A' defamed the bride
(d) 'A' has defamed the bridegroom.

61. Principle Defamation of the publication of a statement which tends to lower reputation of a person in the intimation of other members of the society generally.

Fact 'A' writes a highly offensive and derogatory letter about 'B', and sends it directly to 'B' in a sealed cover. **[CLAT 2016]**
(a) 'A' is liable to 'B' for defamation, as the letter is highly offensive and is derogatory and is directly sent to 'B'
(b) 'A' is not liable to 'B' for defamation, since there is no publication to any other person in whose estimation the reputation of 'B' could be brought down
(c) 'A' is liable to 'B' for defamation, as it has hurt his 'B's self-esteem
(d) 'A' is liable for defamation, as the letter is highly offensive and derogatory

62. Principle It is a case of fraud where a party to a contract knows or believes a fact to be true, but conceals it actively from the other party with a view to induce that person to enter into the contract.

Facts While taking a life insurance policy, in reply to questions by the insurance company during the inquiry into his proposal, Zameer deliberately concealed the fact of his medical treatment for a serious ailment, which he had undergone only a few weeks ago. **[CLAT 2017]**
(a) The act of Zameer amounted to innocent misrepresentation.
(b) The act of Zameer did not amount to fraud, as disclosing the fact would have resulted in exposure of his privacy.
(c) The act of Zameer did not amount to any misrepresentation.
(d) The concealment of fact by Zameer amounted to fraud.

63. Principle When a person makes such a statement which lowers other person's reputation in the estimation of other persons, is liable for committing defamation.

Facts 'A' writes a letter to 'B' in which he use abusive language against 'B' and also states that 'B' is a dishonest person. 'A' put the letter in a sealed envelope and delivered it to 'B'. **[CLAT 2017]**

(a) 'A' has not committed defamation
(b) 'A' has committed a moral wrong
(c) 'A' has not committed moral wrong
(d) 'A' has committed defamation

64. Principle Negligence is actionable in law. In simple terms, negligence is the failure to take proper care over something.

Facts A, a doctor, conducted a hysterectomy sincerely on B and left a small cotton swab inside the abdomen. As a consequence of which B developed some medical problems and had to undergo another surgery. Is A liable? **[CLAT 2017]**

(a) Liability for negligence does not arise here as A performed the operation sincerely
(b) A is liable for the negligence as he failed to take proper care during the surgery.
(c) A is not liable as he did not foresee any consequences at the time of surgery.
(d) As only a small swab was left in the abdomen, there was no negligence.

65. Principle According to the law of trade unions in India, no suit or other legal proceeding shall be maintainable in any civil court against any registered trade union or any officer or member there of in respect of any act done in contemplation or in furtherance of a trade dispute.

Facts Soloman, the Secretary of a registered Trade Union took a loan from a Bank for the higher education of his daughter. Soon after completing the course she was married to an NRI Engineer. Solomon did not repay the loan. The Bank demanded the payments form Soloman and warned him that the Bank will take suitable legal action against him. Identify the legal position in this regard. **[CLAT 2017]**

(a) As Soloman did not use the loan amount for his use and hence, no action can be initiated against him.
(b) The Bank can file a suit for recovery of the loan amount against Soloman as he took the loan for a personal purpose and in such case no immunity will work.
(c) The Bank can recover the loan amount from the Trade Union as Soloman is the Secretary of the Union.
(d) The Bank cannot initiate any action against Soloman as he is the Secretary of a Registered Trade Union.

Answers

1	*b*	2	*b*	3	*a*	4	*c*	5	*c*	6	*b*	7	*c*	8	*c*	9	*d*	10	*b*
11	*b*	12	*c*	13	*b*	14	*c*	15	*d*	16	*d*	17	*b*	18	*a*	19	*c*	20	*c*
21	*c*	22	*a*	23	*c*	24	*b*	25	*d*	26	*a*	27	*b*	28	*b*	29	*b*	30	*a*
31	*c*	32	*c*	33	*c*	34	*c*	35	*b*	36	*a*	37	*c*	38	*c*	39	*b*	40	*c*
41	*b*	42	*b*	43	*d*	44	*d*	45	*a*	46	*b*	47	*b*	48	*a*	49	*a*	50	*a*
51	*c*	52	*b*	53	*b*	54	*a*	55	*a*	56	*a*	57	*d*	58	*b*	59	*d*	60	*a*
61	*b*	62	*d*	63	*a*	64	*b*	65	*b*										

CHAPTER 06

LEGAL MAXIMS

Legal maxims and legal phrases are sometimes compared to axioms in geometry. These are the established universal principles of law and moral philosophy, usually well known to people in the legal profession. However, it must be said that these pages can in no circumstances be used as a source of legal advice, legal counselling and/or simple recommendation on any matter, including but not limited to judicial proceedings of criminal, civil, family, common law and court etc.

A

- **A vinculo matrimonii** From the bond of matrimony.
- **Ab extra** From outside.
- **Ab initio** From the beginning.
- **Absoluta sententia expositore non-indiget** An absolute judgement needs no expositor.
- **Abundans cautela non nocet** Abundant caution does no harm.
- **Accessorium non ducit sed sequitur suum principale** An accessory does not draw, but follows its principal.
- **Acta exteriora iudicant interiora secreta** Outward acts indicate the inward intent.
- **Actio non accrevit infra sex annos** The action has not accrued within six years.
- **Acton non datur non damnificato** An action is not given to one who is not injured.
- **Actio personalis moritur cum persona** A personal action dies with the person.
- **Actiones legis** Law suits.

- **Actus non facit reum nisi mens sit rea** The act dies not make one guilty unless there be a criminal intent.
- **Actus reus** A guilty deed or act.
- **Ad ea quae frequentius acciduunt jura adaptantur** The laws are adapted to those cases which occur more frequently.
- **Ad hoc** For this purpose.
- **Ad infinitum** Forever, without limit, to infinity.
- **Ad perpetuam rei memoriam** For a perpetual memorial of the matter.
- **Aequitas legem sequitur** Equity follows the law.
- **Alibi** At another place, elsewhere.
- **Alienatio rei praefertur juri accrescendi** Alienation is preferred by law rather than accumulation.
- **Aliunde** From elsewhere, or, from a different source.
- **Allegans contraria non est audiendus** One making contradictory statements is not to be heard.
- **Ambiguitas verborum patens nulla verificatione excluditur** A patent ambiguity is never helped by averment.
- **Amicus curiae** A friend of the court.
- **Animo furandi** With an intention of stealing.
- **Animo testandi** With an intention of making a will.
- **Arbitrium est judicium** An award is a judgement.
- **Arbor dum crescit; lignum cum crescere nescit** A tree while it grows, wood when it cannot grow.
- **Argumentum ab auctoritate fortissimum est in lege** An argument drawn from authority is the strongest in law.
- **Assentio mentium** The meeting of minds, i.e. mutual assent.

B

- **Bis dat qui cito dat** He gives (pays) twice who pays promptly.
- **Bona fide** Sincere, in good faith.
- **Bona vacantia** Goods without an owner.
- **Boni judicis lites dirimere est** It is the duty of a good judge to prevent litigation.
- **Breve judiciale non cadit pro defectu formae** A judicial writing does not fail through defect of form.

C

- **Cadit quaestio** The matter admits of no further argument.
- **Casus fortuitus non est spectandus; et nemo tenetur divinare** A fortuitous event is not to be foreseen and no person is bound to divine it.
- **Catalla reputantur inter minima in lege** Chattels are considered in law among the minor things.
- **Causa proxima, non remota spectatur** The immediate, and not the remote cause is to be considered.
- **Consuetudo loci observanda est** The custom of the place is to be observed.
- **Contra** To the contrary.
- **Contra bonos mores** Against good morals.
- **Contractus est quasi actus contra actum** A contract is an act as it were against an act.
- **Conventio est modus vincunt legem** A contract and agreement overcome the law.
- **Coram non judice** Before one who is not a judge.
- **Corpus** Body.
- **Corpus delicti** The body, i.e. the gist of crime.
- **Crescente malitia crescere debet et poena** Vice increasing, punishment ought also to increase.

- **Crimen omnia ex se nata vitiat** Crime vitiates every thing, which springs from it.
- **Cujus est dare, ejus est disponere** He who has a right to give has the right to dispose of the gift.
- **Cujus est solum, ejus est usque ad coelam; et ad inferos** He, who owns the soil owns it upto the sky; and to its depth.
- **Cursus curiae est lex curiae** The practice of the court is the law to the court.
- **Custos morum** A guardian of morals.

D

- **Damnum sine injuria** Damage without legal injury.
- **De bonis asportatis** Of goods carried away.
- **De bonis non administratis** Of goods not administered.
- **De die in diem** From day-to-day.
- **De facto** In fact.
- **De futuro** In the future.
- **De integro** As regards the whole.
- **De jure** Rightful, by right.
- **De novo** Starting afresh.
- **Dubitante** Doubting the correctness of the decision.

E

- **Ei incumbit probatio qui** The onus of proving a fact rests upon the man.
- **Ei incumbit probatio qui dicit, non qui negat** The burden of the proof lies upon him who affirms, not he who denies.
- **Error, qui non resistitur approbatur** An error not resisted is approved.
- **Et cetera** Other things of that type.
- **Ex cathedra** With official authority.
- **Ex concessis** In view of what has already been accepted.
- **Ex facie** On the fact of it.
- **Ex gratia** By favour.
- **Ex nihilo nil fit** From nothing comes.
- **Ex nudo pacto actio non oritur** No action arises on a contract without a consideration.
- **Ex parte** Proceeding brought by one person in the absence of another.
- **Ex post facto** By reason of a subsequent act.
- **Ex praecedentibus et consequentibus optima fit interpretatio** The best interpretation is made from things preceding and following.
- **Ex turpi causa non oritur actio** No action arises on immoral contract.
- **Exception probat regulam** An exception proves the rule.
- **Executio est executio juris secundum judicium** Execution is the fulfilment of the law in accordance with the judgement.
- **Executio est finis et fructus legis** An execution is the end and the fruit of the law.
- **Executio legis non habet injuriam** Execution of the law does not injury.

F

- **Faciendum** Something which is to be done.
- **Factum** An act or deed.
- **Facultas probationum non est angustanda** The right of offering proof is not to be narrowed.
- **Falsa demonstratio non nocet** A false description does not vitiate.

G

- **Generale nihil certum implicat** A general expression implies nothing certain.
- **Generalia praecedunt, specialia sequuntur** Things general precede, things special follow.
- **Generalia specialibus non derogant** Things general do not derogate from things special.
- **Generalis regula generaliter est intelligenda** A general rule is to be generally understood.

- **Gravius est divinam quam temporalem laedere majestatem** It is more serious to hurt divine than temporal majesty.

H

- **Habeas corpus** That you have the body.
- **Habemus optimum testem confitentem reum** We have the best witness, a confessing defendant.
- **Haeredem est nomen collectum** Heir is a collective name.
- **Haeres est nomen juris, filius est nomen naturae** Heir is a term of law, son, one of nature.
- **Haeres legitimus est quem nuptiae demonstrant** He is the lawful heir whom the marriage indicates.
- **Homo vocabulum est naturae; persona juris civilis** Man is term of nature, person of the civil law.

I

- **Id est** (i.e.) That is.
- **Idem** The same person or thing.
- **Idem nihil dicere et insufficienter dicere est** It is the same to say nothing as not to say enough.
- **Ignorantia facti excusat, ignorantia juris non excusat** Ignorance of fact excuses, ignorance of law does not excuse.
- **Impotentia excusat legem** Impossibility is an excuse in the law.
- **Impunitas semper ad deteriora invitat** Impunity always leads to greater crimes.
- **In alta proditone nullus potest esse acessorius; sed principalis solum modo** In high treason no one can be an accessory; but a principal only.
- **In camera** In private.
- **In delicto** At fault.
- **In esse** In existence.
- **In extenso** At full length.
- **In fictione legis aequitas existit** A legal fiction is consistent with equity.
- **In foro conscientiae** In the forum of conscience.
- **In futoro** In the future.
- **In limine** At the outset, on the threshold.
- **In loco parentis** In place of the parent.
- **In mortua manu** In dead hand.
- **In omnibus** In every respect.
- **In personam** Against the person.
- **In pleno** In full.
- **In situ** In its place.
- **In terrorem** As a warning or deterrent.
- **In verbis, non verba sed res et ratio quaerenda est** In words, not words, but the thing and the meaning are to be inquired into.
- **Indicia** Marks, signs.
- **Injuria non excusat injuriam** A wrong does not excuse a wrong.
- **Intentio inservire debet legibus, non leges intentioni** Intention ought to be subservient to the laws, not the laws to the intention.
- **Inter alia** Amongst other things.
- **Ira furor brevis est** Anger is brief insanity.
- **Iter arma leges silent** In war, the laws are silent.

J

- **Judes est loquens** A judge is the law speaking.
- **Judex non potest esse testis in propira causa** A judge cannot be witness in his own cause.
- **Judex non potest injuriam sibi datam punire** A judge cannot punish a wrong done to himself.
- **Jura naturae sunt immutabilia** The laws of nature are immutable.

- **Jura publica antreferenda privatis juribus** Public right are to be preferred to private rights.
- **Jus naturale** Natural justice.
- **Justitia nemini neganda est** Justice is to be denied to no one.

L

- **Leges posteriores priores contrarias abrogant** Subsequent laws repeal prior conflicting ones.
- **Legibus sumptis desinentibus legibus naturae utendum est** When laws imposed by the state fail, we must use the laws of nature.
- **Lex aliquando sequitur aequitatem** The law sometimes follows equity.
- **Lex citius tolerare vult privatum damnum quam publicum malum** The law would rather tolerate a private injury than a public evil.
- **Lex dabit remedium** The law will give a remedy.
- **Lex dilationes abhorret** The law abhors delays.
- **Lex est judicum tutissimus ductor** The law is the safest guide for judges.
- **Lex est sanctio sancta jubens honesta et prohibens contraria** The law is a sacred sanction, commanding what is right and prohibiting the contrary.
- **Lex indendit vicinum vicini facta scire** The law presumes that one neighbour knows the acts of another.
- **Lex necessitatis est lex temporis, ie, instanits** The law of necessary is the law of time, that is time present.
- **Lex neminem cogit ad vana seu impossiblia** The law compels no one to do vain or impossible things.
- **Lex nil frustra facit** The law does nothing in vain.
- **Lex non a rege est violanda** The law must not be violated even by the King.
- **Lex non deficere potest in justitia exhibenda** The law cannot fail in dispensing justice.
- **Lex non novit paterm, nec materm; solam veritatem** The law does not know neither father nor mother, only the truth.
- **Lex non requirit verificari quod apparet curiae** The law does not require that to be proved which is apparent to the court.
- **Lex non favet delicatorum votis** The law does not favour the wishes of the dainty.
- **Lex plus laudatur quando ratione probatur** The law is the more praised when it is supported by reson.
- **Lex prospicit not respicit** The law looks forward, not backward.
- **Lex punit mendaciam** The law punishes falsehood.
- **Lex succurrit ignoranti** The law succors the ignotant.
- **Lex tutissima cassis, sub clypeo legis nemo decipitur** Law is the safest helmet; under the shield of the law no one is deceived.
- **Lex uno ore omnes alloquitur** The law speaks to all through one mouth.
- **Longa possessio parit jus possidendi et tollit actionem vero domino** Long possession produces the right of possession and takes away from the true owner his action.

M

- **Magister rerum usus; magistra rerum experientia** Use is the master of things; experience is the mistress of things.
- **Major continet in se minus** The greater contains the less.
- **Majus est delictum se ipsum occidere quam alium** It is a greater crime to kill oneselves than another.

- **Mala fide** In bad faith.
- **Mala grammatica non vitiat chartam** Bad grammar does not vitiate a deed.
- **Mala prohibita** Crimes prohibited.
- **Mala animo** With evil intent.
- **Mandamus** We command.
- **Maximus magister erroris populus est** The people are the greatest master of error.
- **Melior est conditio possidentis, ubi neuter jus habet** Better is the condition of the possessor where neither of the two has the right.
- **Mens rea** Guilty state of mind.
- **Mentiri est contra menten ire** To lie is to act against the mind.
- **Miseta est servitus, ubi jus est vagum aut incertum** It is a miserable slavery where the law is vague or uncertain.
- **Mors dicitur ultimum supplicium** Death is called the extreme penalty.
- **Muita exercitatione facilius quam regulis percipies** You will perceive many things more easily by experience than by rules.

N

- **Nam nemo haeres viventis** For no one is an heir of a living person.
- **Nemo potest esse tenens et dominus** No one can at the same time be a tenant and a landlord (of the same tenement).
- **Nemo se accusare debet, nisi coram deo** No one should accuse himself except in the presence of God.
- **Nemo tenetur armare adversarium contra se** No one is bound to arm his adversary against himself.
- **Nexus** Connection
- **Nil facit error nominis cum de corpore constat** An error of name makes not difference when it appears from the body of the instrument.
- **Nisi** Unless.
- **Non compus mentis** Not of sound mind and understanding.
- **Non constat** It is not certain.
- **Non decipitur qui scit se decipi** He is not deceived who knows that he is deceived.
- **Non est arctius vinculum inter homines quam jusjurandum** There is no stronger link among men than an oath.
- **Non est factum** It is not his deed.
- **Non est informatus** He is not informed.
- **Non facias malum ut inde veniat bonum** You shall not be evil that good may come of it.

O

- **Omnis innovatio plus novitate perturbat quam utilitate prodeat** Every innovation disturbs more by its novelty than it benefits by its utility.
- **Optima legum interpres est consuetudo** The best interpreter of laws is custom.
- **Optimus interpres rerum est usus** The best interpreter of things is usage.

P

- **Pacta privata juri publico non derogare possunt** Private contracts cannot derogate from public law.
- **Par delictum** Equal fault.
- **Pari passu** On an equal footing.
- **Pater est quem nuptiae demonstrant** The father is he whom the marriage points out.
- **Peccata contra naturam sunt gravissima** Wrongs against nature are the most serious.
- **Per curiam** In the opinion of the court.
- **Post mortem** After death.
- **Prima facie** On the face of it.
- **Prima impressionis** On first impression.
- **Pro hac vice** For this occasion.
- **Pro rata** In proportion.
- **Pro tanto** So far, to that extent.
- **Pro tempore** For the time being.

Q

- **Quaeitur** The question is raised.
- **Quantum** How much, an amount.
- **Qui facit per alium, facit per se** He who acts through another acts himself.
- **Qui haeret in litera, haeret in cortice** He who stices to the letter, sticks to the bark.
- **Qui in utero est, pro jam nato habetur, quoties de ejus commodo quaeritur** He who is in the womb is considered as already born as far as his benefit is considered more true; and what is prior in time is stronger in law.
- **Quod vanum et inutile est, lex non requirit** The law does not require what is vain and useless.
- **Quinon habet, ille non dat** He who has not, does not give.
- **Qui non improbat, approbat** He who does not disapprove, approves.
- **Qui peccat evrius, luat sobrius** He who does wrong when drunk must be punished when sober.
- **Qui potest et debet vetare et non vetat jubet** He who is able and ought to forbit and does not, commands.
- **Qui prior est tempore potior est jure** He who is prior in time is stronger in right.
- **Qui sentit commodum, debet et sentire onus** He who derives a benefit ought also to bear a burden.
- **Qui tacet consentire videtur** He who is silent appears to consent.
- **Quid pro quo** Consideration, something for something.
- **Quod constat curiae opere testium non indiget** What appears to the court needs not the help of witnesses.
- **Quod nccessarie intelligitur, id non deest** What is necessarily understood is not wanting.
- **Quod necessitas cogit, defendit** What necessity forces it justifies.
- **Quod non apparet, non est** What does not appear, is not.
- **Quod non habet principium non habet finem** What has no beginning has no end.
- **Quod per me non possum, nec per alium** What I cannot do through myself I cannot do through another.

R

- **Reprobata pecunia leberat solventem** Money refused releases the debtor.
- **Res** Matter, affair, thing, circumstance.
- **Res gestae** Things done.
- **Res integra** A matter untouched (by decision).
- **Res inter alios acta alteri nocere non debet** Things done between strangers ought not to affect a third person, who is a stranger to the transaction.
- **Res judicata accipitur pro veritate** A thing adjudged is accepted for the truth.
- **Res nuilius** Nobodys property.
- **Respondeat superior** Let the principal answer.
- **Rex est major singulis, minor universis** The King is greater than individuals, less than all the people.
- **Rex quod injustum est facere non potest** The King cannot do what is unjust.

S

- **Semper pro matriomonio praesumitur** It is always presumed in favour of marriage.
- **Servitia personalia sequuntur personam** Personal services follow the person.
- **Sic utere tuo ut alienum non laedas** So, use your own as not to injure anothers property.
- **Simplex commendatio non obligat** A simple recommendation does not bind.

- **Stare decisis** To stand by decisions (precedents).
- **Stet** Do not delete, let it stand.
- **Sub modo** Within limits.
- **Sub nomine** Under the name of.
- **Sub silentio** In silence.
- **Sublato fundamento, cadit opus** The foundation being removed, the structure falls.
- **Suggestio falsi** The suggestion of something which is untrue.
- **Sui generis** Unique.
- **Summa ratio est quae pro religione facit** The highest reason is that which makes for religion, i.e. religion dictates.
- **Supperssio veri expressio falsi** A suppression of truth is equivalent to an expression of falsehood.

T

- **Talis qualis** Such as it is.
- **Terra firma** Solid ground.
- **Traditio loqui chartam facit** Delivery makes a deed speak.
- **Transit terra cum onere** The land passes with its burden.

U

- **Ubi eadem ratio ibi idem jus, et de similibus idem est judicium** When there is the same reason, then the law is the same, and the same judgement should be rendered as to similar things.
- **Ut poena ad paucos, metus ad omnes, perveniat** That punishment come to a few, the fear of it should affect all.
- **Utile per inutile non vitiatur** What is useful is not vitiated by the useless.

V

- **Vacate** To set aside.
- **Venue** Authority of a court to hear a matter based on geographical location.
- **Verdict** A conclusion, as to fact or law that forms the basis for the court's judgement. (See Directed verdict.)
- **Visa** An official endorsement on a document or passport denoting that the bearer may proceed.
- **Void** Invalid; a void agreement is one for which there is no remedy.
- **Voidable** Capable of being declared invalid; a voidable contract is one were a person may avoid his obligation, as a contract between an adult and a minor.
- **Voir Dire** The preliminary examination made in court of a witness or juror to determine his competency or interest in a matter. Literally, to speak the truth.
- **Verba debent intelligi cum effectu** Words ought to be understood with effect.
- **Verba intentioni, non e contra, debent inservire** Words ought to serve the intention, not the reverse.
- **Vigilantibus non dormientibus jura subveniunt** The laws serve the vigilant, not those who sleep.
- **Vir et uxor consentur in lege una persona** A husband and wife are regarded in law as one person.
- **Volens** Willing
- **Volenti non fit injuria** An injury is not done to one consenting to it.
- **Voluntas in delictis non exitus spectatur** In offences the intent and not the result is looked at.
- **Voluntas reputatur pro facto** The will is taken for the deed.

W

- **Waiver** Intentionally given up a right.
- **Waiver of Immunity** A means authorised by statute by which a witness, before testifying or producing evidence, may relinquish the right to refuse to

testify against himself or herself, thereby making it possible for his or her testimony to be used against him or her in future proceedings.

- **Warrant** Most commonly, a court order authorising law enforcement officers to make an arrest or conduct a search. An application seeking a warrant must be accompanied by an affidavit which facts upon which the request is based.
- **Warranty** A promise that a proposition of fact is true.
- **Warranty Deed** A deed which guarantees that the title conveyed is good and its transfer rightful.
- **Water Rights** The rights to use water.
- **Will** A legal declaration that disposes of a person's property when that person dies.
- **Withholding** A tax dedcuted from a salary, wage or other income on behalf of the government at the time of payment of wages to the person who pays it.
- **Witness** One who personally sees or perceives a thing; one who testifies as to what he has seen, heard or otherwise observed.
- **Words and Phrases Legally Defined** A set of book in dictionary form which lists judicial determinations of a word or phrase.
- **Worker's Compensation** A state agency which handles claims of workers injured on their jobs.
- **Writ** A judicial order directing a person to do something.
- **Writ of Certiorari** An order issued by the Supreme Court directing the lower court to transmit records for a case for which it will hear on appeal.
- **Writ of Execution** An order of the court evidencing debt of one party to another and commanding the court officer to take property in satisfaction of the debt.
- **Writ of Garnishment** An order of the court whereby property, money or credits in the possession of another person may be seized and applied to pay a debtor's debt. It is used as an incident to or auxiliary of a judgement rendered in a principal action.

Z

- **Zoning Commission** Local agencies with jurisdiction to regulate use of properties within their geographic area.

Practice Exercise

1. An 'encumbrance' in legal parlance is a
(a) liability on property (b) grant of property
(c) gift of property (d) restriction on property

2. The maxim 'Ubi jus ibi remedium' means
(a) justice should not be done but should be seen also
(b) law provides remedy for every wrong
(c) justice is to be according to law
(d) None of the above

3. Intra vires means
(a) a within the powers
(b) outside the powers
(c) within the scope of Fundamental Rights
(d) regular

4. Inter vivos
(a) between the living
(b) among the living and the dead
(c) between the dead
(d) among the (lead and the living)

5. Corpus juris
(a) body of judges (b) group of jurists
(c) body of law (d) knowledge of law

6. A right available against world at large is
(a) in pleno (b) in situ
(c) in rem (d) in personam

7. Ab ...... non fit injuria.
(a) abnsu (b) assuetis
(c) esse (d) usque

8. Nemo debet ...... pro una ...... Causa.
(a) vinculo, non (b) bis vexari, eadem
(c) mensa, et (d) debet, et

9. Actus non facit reum .... sit rea.
(a) nisi mens (b) rem cantelam
(c) ad quem (d) ligitimi non

10. Interest republicae ...... Litium.
(a) uexari pro (b) nemo debet
(c) ut sit finis (d) executio non

11. Administrator ..... .
(a) bonis (b) litem (c) ancillary (d) uitam

12. One of the basic tenets of criminal liability is "actus non facit reum nisi mens sit rea". What does this mean in English?
(a) A guilty act is not required in criminal law
(b) If a person does a criminal act, he will be found guilty
(c) The act is not guilty unless the mind is guilty
(d) The guilty mind and guilty act are the same thing

13. What is the 'actus reus'?
(a) The guilty act (b) A feeling of guilt
(c) The guilty mind (d) Moral guilt

14. This is a maxim of tort law: "Ex turpi causa non oritur actio".
(a) A person cannot pursue a cause of action if it arises out of his own guilty act
(b) A person cannot be guilty if he has no reason to commit the crime
(c) The victim of a crime has a right to sue the perpetrator in tort
(d) Friends who commit crimes together cannot be tried together

15. What is the 'ratio decidendi' in a judgement?
(a) The non-binding part of the decision
(b) The part of the judgement in which the judge recites the facts of the case
(c) The irrelevant part of the decision
(d) The reasoning behind the decision

16. What does the 'sine qua non' rule, in terms of causation, mean?
(a) Legal causation
(b) The 'but for' rule or factual causation
(c) A break in the chain of causation
(d) Causation does not apply to some crimes

17. The doctrine of 'stare decisis' underpins the common law system. What is 'stare decisis'?
(a) Courts must adhere to statues in all of their decisions
(b) The reasoning behind the decision
(c) To stand by what has gone before
(d) Parliament can overturn decided cases

18. Textbooks are always referring to 'obiter dicta' (sometimes shortened to just dicta). What are 'obiter dicta'?
(a) The binding part of a judgement
(b) Things said by the way
(c) The discussion between judges in court
(d) The arguments made by counsel in court

19. Oops, the House of Lords has stated that a case heard in the Court of Appeal is 'per incuriam'. What did they mean?
(a) A case settled with a lack of care so that the decision is wrong
(b) A case decided on facts alone as no law exist in the area
(c) To stand by what has gone before
(d) To bind all other courts

20. Tort seems to be full of catchy Latin phrases-what does this one mean? 'Volenti non fit injuria'.
(a) No injury is done to a willing victim
(b) Consent is never a defence
(c) Violence is never the answer
(d) A person must do an act willingly

21. I love the phrase 'doli incapax'. What does it means?
(a) An overruled decision
(b) Incapable of crime
(c) A new judge
(d) New law

22. Who is amicus curiae?
(a) A friend of the court of tribunal i.e. a non-party who gives evidence before the court, so as to assist it with research, argument or submissions
(b) He is party to the case
(c) He is a public prosecutor otherwise designated as advocate general
(d) None of the above

23. Res Judicata known as
(a) action of estoppel
(b) it is same as ratio decendie
(c) Neither (a) nor (b)
(d) Both (a) and (b)

24. Ignorantia Juris Nemineam exusal stands for
(a) ignorance of law is no excuse
(b) ignorance of fact is no excuse
(c) laws are universally known
(d) None of the above

25. Res inspa loquitur means
(a) no one should be condemned unheard
(b) when the thing speaks for itself
(c) it is a principle of extradition law
(d) None of the above

26. Delegates non protest delegate means
(a) delegated legislation cannot be further delegated
(b) delegated legislation is meant to be further delegated
(c) Neither (a) nor (b)
(d) Both (a) and (b)

27. A ratio decidendi means
(a) the proportion of justice in a case
(b) the principle upon which a case was decided
(c) the decisive facts of the case
(d) None of the above

28. The doctrine of res judicata means that
(a) justice has resulted
(b) residual justice
(c) the final judgement of a competent court may not be disputed by the parties or their heirs in any subsequent legal proceedings
(d) None of the above

29. Stare decisis means
(a) it is necessary to abide by former precedents when the same points arise again in litigation
(b) it is not necessary to abide by former precedents when the same point arise again in litigation
(c) Neither (a) nor (b)
(d) Both (a) and (b)

30. Ubi jus ibi remedium means
(a) where there is a wrong there is a remedy
(b) to every wrong there is no remedy
(c) wrong the remedy have no relation
(d) None of the above

Previous Year's Questions

31. Principle Res ipsa loquiturie i.e. the thing speaks for itself.

Facts Seema got herself operated for the removal of her uterus in the defendant's hospital, as there was diagnosed to be a cyst in one of her ovaries. Due the negligence of the surgeon, who performed the operation, abdominal pack was left in her abdomen. The same was removed by a second surgery. **[CLAT 2013]**
(a) Surgeon cannot be held responsible because it is merely a human error
(b) Surgeon can be held responsible but Seema will have to prove in the court of law that the surgeon was grossly negligent
(c) Surgeon will be responsible and Seema need not to prove surgeon's negligence because presence of abdominal pack in her abdomen is sufficient proof therefor
(d) None of the above

32. Qui facit per alium facit per se, i.e. he who does things through others does it himself.

Facts Nisha, the owner of a car, asked her friend Saurabh to take her car and drive the same to her office. As the car was near her office, it hit a pedestrian Srikant on account of Saurabh's negligent driving and injured him seriously. Now, Srikant files a suit for damages against Nisha. **[CLAT 2013]**
(a) Nisha is not liable as it was the negligence of Saurabh
(b) Saurabh is solely liable as Nisha was not driving the car
(c) Nisha is liable as Saurabh was driving under her authority and for her purpose
(d) Saurabh will be exempted from liability under the principle of inevitable accident

33. 'Alibi' means a plea by an accused person that he **[CLAT 2016]**
(a) was present elsewhere
(b) underwent preventive detention
(c) was facing trial
(d) remained in judicial custody

34. 'Obiter dicta' means **[CLAT 2016]**
(a) judgement of a court in the case before it
(b) basis of judicial decision
(c) direction by a judge

(d) an opinion given by the court not necessary for the decision

35. 'Persona non grata' means **[CLAT 2016]**

(a) non-person
(b) ungrateful person
(c) non-performance of promise
(d) an unacceptable person

36. 'Audi alteram partem' means **[CLAT 2016]**

(a) giving opportunity of hearing of the other side
(b) following the substantive law
(c) a transferee cannot retransfer
(d) not connected to facts

37. 'Tis pendens' means **[CLAT 2016]**

(a) decision awaited
(b) on the basis of evidence
(c) awaited information
(d) a pending suit

38. Faux pas **[CLAT 2017]**

(a) Pausing for a while (b) Passage of time
(c) Tactless mistake (d) Cheating

39. Per incuriam **[CLAT 2017]**

(a) Supremacy of law
(b) Mistaken identity
(c) Mistaken decision
(d) Supreme of the Constitution

40. 'Punctum Temporis' means **[CLAT 2017]**

(a) Functional authority
(b) Point of time
(c) Timely assistance
(d) Temporary position

41. Caveat venditor **[CLAT 2017]**

(a) Buyer beware (b) Seller beware
(c) Transporter beware (d) Manufacturer beware

42. 'Turpis arbiter' means **[CLAT 2017]**

(a) Corrupt judge
(b) Inefficient lawyer
(c) Corrupt prosecutor
(d) Inefficient judge

43. In pari delicto **[CLAT 2017]**

(a) Where the lawyer is at fault
(b) Where the judge is at fault
(c) Where both parties to a dispute are equally at fault
(d) Where the petitioner is at fault

44. Bona vacantia **[CLAT 2017]**

(a) Goods that have no owner
(b) Vacant building
(c) Vacant land
(d) Order of the court for eviction

Answers

1	*a*	2	*b*	3	*b*	4	*a*	5	*c*	6	*d*	7	*b*	8	*b*	9	*a*	10	*c*
11	*b*	12	*c*	13	*a*	14	*a*	15	*d*	16	*b*	17	*c*	18	*b*	19	*a*	20	*a*
21	*b*	22	*a*	23	*a*	24	*a*	25	*b*	26	*a*	27	*b*	28	*c*	29	*a*	30	*a*
31	*c*	32	*c*	33	*a*	34	*c*	35	*d*	36	*a*	37	*d*	38	*c*	39	*c*	40	*b*
41	*b*	42	*a*	43	*c*	44	*a*												

CHAPTER 07

LEGAL TERMS

When dealing with legal matters or starting an education in law, there are basic terms that can help you understand court-room and legal documents. Legal wording can be very complex and almost inaccessible if you do not have a basic knowledge of the important terms. Many people consider legalese a separate language of its own, requiring specific training just to understand. Much like learning a foreign language, developing a basic understanding of some of the essential terms can help you navigate legal documents.

A

- **Abrogate** To repeal, cancel or annul an agreement.
- **Abefance** The condition of an inheritance which has no present owner or a state of suspension.
- **Abstract of Title** A chronological summary of all official records and recorded documents affecting the title to a parcel of real property.
- **Acceptance** The taking and receiving of anything in good faith with the intention of retaining it.
- **Accomplice** A partner in a crime, a person who knowingly and voluntarily participates with another in a criminal activity.
- **Accretion** The increase or accumulation of land by natural causes, as out of a lake or river.
- **Acquittal** A release, absolution or discharge of an obligation or liability. In criminal law the finding of not guilty.
- **Administrative Agencies** Agencies created by the legislative branch of government to administer laws pertaining to specific areas such as taxes, transportation and labour.
- **Admiralty Law** Also, maritime law. That body of law relating to ships, shipping, marine commerce and navigation, transportation of persons or property by sea, etc.

- **Admissible Evidence** Evidence that can be legally and properly introduced in a civil or criminal trial.
- **Adverse Possession** Method of acquiring real property under certain conditions by possession for a statutory period.
- **Affirmation** A solemn and formal declaration that an affidavit is true. This is substituted for an oath in certain cases.
- **Aid and Aabet** To actively, knowingly or intentionally assist another person in the commission or attempted commission of a crime.
- **Allegation** A statement of the issues in a written document (a pleading) which a person is prepared to prove in court.
- **Alternative Dispute Resolution** Settling a dispute without a full, formal trial. Methods include mediation, conciliation, arbitration and settlement, among others.
- **Answers to Interrogatories** A formal written statement by a party to a lawsuit which answers each question or interrogatory propounded by the other party. These answers must be acknowledged before a notary public or other person authorised to take acknowledgments.
- **Antitrust Acts** Federal and state statutes to protect trade and commerce from unlawful restraints, price discriminations, price fixing and monopolies.
- **Appeal** A proceeding brought to a higher court to review a lower court decision.
- **Appeal Bond** A guarantee by the appealing party insuring that court costs will be paid.
- **Appearance** The act of coming into court as a party to a suit either in person or through an attorney.
- **Appellate Court** A court having jurisdiction to hear appeals and review a trial court's procedure.
- **Arbitration** The hearing of a dispute by an impartial third person or persons (chosen by the parties), whose award the parties agree to accept.
- **Arbitrator** A private, disinterested person chosen by the parties in arbitration to hear evidence concerning the dispute and to make an award based on the evidence.
- **Arrest** To take into custody by legal authority.
- **Assault** Threat to inflict injury with an apparent ability to do so. Also, any intentional display of force that would give the victim reason to fear or expect immediate bodily harm.
- **Assumption of Risk** A doctrine under which a person may not recover for an injury received when he has voluntarily exposed himself to a known danger.
- **Attachment** Taking a person's property to satisfy a court-ordered debt.

B

- **Bail** Money or other security (such as a bail bond) provided to the court to temporarily allow a person's release from jail and assure their appearance in court. 'Bail' and 'Bond' are often used interchangeably. (applies mainly to state courts.)
- **Bail Bond** An obligation signed by the accused to secure his or her presence at the trial. This obligation means that the accused may lose money by not properly appearing for the trial. Often referred to simply as 'bond'.
- **Bailee** Person who accepts property through a contract of bailment, from a Bailor and who has certain denties of care while the property remains in this possession.
- **Bar** 1. Historically, the partition separating the general public from the space occupied by the judges, lawyers and other participants in a trial. 2. More commonly, the term means the who body of lawyers.
- **Bar Examination** A state examination taken by prospective lawyers in order to be admitted and licensed to practice law.
- **Bench** The seat occupied by the judge. More broadly, the court itself.

- **Bench Trial** (Also known as court trial.) Trial without a jury in which a judge decides the facts.
- **Bench Warrant** An order issued by a judge for the arrest of a person.
- **Beneficiary** Someone named to receive property or benefits in a will. In a trust, a person who is to receive benefits from the trust.
- **Best Evidence** Primary evidence; the best evidence available. Evidence short of this is 'secondary'. i.e. an original letter is 'best evidence', and a photocopy is 'secondary evidence'.
- **Bill of Particulars** A statement of the details of the charge made against the defendant.
- **Blasphemy** It consistently attacking religion, God and religions tenets for the purpose of imposing the doctrines to contempt and redicule.
- **Bond** A written agreement by which a person insures he will pay a certain sum of money if he does not perform certain duties property.
- **Breach** The breaking or violating of a law, right, or duty, either by commission or omission. The failure of one part to carry out any condition of a contract.
- **Breach of Contract** An unjustified failure to perform when performance is due.
- **Burglary** The act of illegal entry with the intent to steal.
- **Business Bankruptcy** A proceeding under the bankruptcy code filed by a business entity.
- **Bylaws** Rules or laws adopted by an association or corporation to govern its actions.

C

- **Capital Crime** A crime punishable by death.
- **Case Law** Law established by previous decisions of appellate courts, particularly the United States Supreme Court.
- **Cases** General term for an action, cause, suit or controversy, at law or in equity; questions contested before a court of justice.
- **Cause** A lawsuit, litigation or action. Any question, civil or criminal, litigated or contested before a court of justice.
- **Cause of Action** The fact or facts which give a person a right to relief in court.
- **Censure** An official reprimand or condemnation of an attorney.
- **Certification** Written attestation, authorised declaration verifying that an instrument is a true and correct copy of the original.
- **Certiorari** A writ of review issued by a higher court to a lower court. A means of getting an appellate court to review a lower court's decision. If an appellate court grants a writ of certiorari, it agrees to take the appeal.
- **Challenge** An objection, such as when an attorney objects at a hearing to the seating of a particular person on a civil or criminal jury.
- **Challenge for Cause** A request from a party to a judge that a certain prospective juror not be allowed to be a member of a jury because of specified causes or reasons.
- **Change of Venue** Moving a lawsuit or criminal trial to another place for trial.
- **Charge to the Jury** The judge's instructions to the jury concerning the law that applies to the facts of the case on trial.
- **Chief Judge** Presiding or administrative judge in a court.
- **Civil** Relating to private rights and remedies sought by civil actions as contrasted with criminal proceedings.
- **Civil Law** Law based on a series of written codes or laws.
- **Civil Procedure** The rules and process by which a civil case is tried and appealed, including the preparations for trial, the rules of evidence and trial conduct, and the procedure for pursuing appeals.

- **Clerk of Court** Administrator or chief clerical officer of the court.
- **Code of Federal Regulations** An annual publication which contains the cumulative executive agency regulations.
- **Code of Professional** The rules of conduct that govern the legal profession responsibility.
- **Collective Mark** Trademark or service mark used by members of a cooperative, an association, or other collective group or organisation.
- **Commit** To send a person to prison, asylum or reformatory by a court order.
- **Common Law** Also case law. Law established by subject matter heard in earlier cases.
- **Complainant** The party who complains or sues; one who applies to the court for legal redress.
- **Complaint** The legal document that usually begins a civil lawsuit. It states the facts and identifies the action the court is asked to take, formal written charge that a person has committed a criminal offense.
- **Concurrent Sentences** Sentences for more than one crime that are to be served at the same time, rather than one after the other.
- **Consecutive Sentences** Successive sentences, one beginning at the expiration of another, imposed against a person convicted of two or more violations.
- **Consent** Agreement; voluntary acceptance of the wish of another.
- **Consideration** The price bargained for and paid for a promise, goods or real estate.
- **Constitutional Law** Law set forth in the Constitution of the United States and the State Constitutions.
- **Consumer Bankruptcy** A proceeding under the bankruptcy code filed by an individual (or husband and wife) who is not in business.
- **Contempt of Court** Willful disobedience of a judge's command or of an official court order.
- **Continuance** Postponement of a legal proceeding to a later date.
- **Contract** An agreement between two or more persons which creates an obligation to do or not to do a particular thing. A legally enforceable agreement between two or more competent parties made either orally or in writing.
- **Conviction** A judgement of guilt against a criminal defendant.
- **Corroborating Evidence** Supplementary evidence that tends to strengthen or confirm the initial evidence.
- **Counterclaim** A claim made by the defendant in a civil lawsuit against the plaintiff. In essence, a counter lawsuit within a lawsuit.
- **Court of Original Jurisdiction** A court where a matter is initiated and heard in the first instance; a trial court.
- **Cross-Examination** The questioning of a witness produced by the other side.
- **Cumulative Sentences** Sentences for two or more crimes to run consecutively, rather than concurrently.

D

- **Damages** Money awarded by a court to a person injured by the unlawful actor negligence of another person.
- **Declaratory Judgement** A statutory remedy for judicial determination of a controversy where plaintiff is in doubt about his legal rights.
- **Decree** An order of the court. A final decree is one that fully and finally disposes of the litigation.
- **Defamation** That which tends to injure a person's reputation.

- **Default Judgement** A judgement entered against a party who fails to appear in court or respond to the charges.
- **Defendant** The person defending or denying a suit.
- **Deficient** Incomplete; defective; not sufficient in quantity or force.
- **Dependent** One who derives existence and support from another.
- **Deposition** Testimony of a witness or a party taken under oath outside the courtroom, the transcript of which becomes a part of the court's file.
- **Direct Evidence** Proof of facts by witnesses who saw acts done or heard words spoken.
- **Direct Examination** The first questioning of witnesses by the party on whose behalf they are called.
- **Discharge** The name given to the bankruptcy court's formal discharge of a debtor's debts. In probate, the release of the estate's representative from fiduciary responsibility.
- **Dissent to Disagree** An appellate court opinion setting forth the minority view and outlining the disagreement of one or more judges with the decision of the majority.
- **Dissolution** The termination; process of dissolving or winding up something.
- **Diversity of Citizenship** The condition when the party on one side of a lawsuit is a citizen of one state and the other party is a citizen of another state; such cases are under the jurisdiction of federal courts.
- **Docket Control** A system for keeping track of deadlines and court dates for both litigation and non-litigation matters.
- **Domicile** The place where a person has his permanent home to which he intends to return.
- **Double Jeopardy** Putting a person on trial more than once for the same crime. It is forbidden by the Fifth Amendment to the United States Constitution.

E

- **Entity** A person or legally recognised organisation.
- **Entry** A statement of conclusion reached by the court and placed in the court record.
- **Environment** The conditions, influences or forces which affect the desirability and value of property, as well as the effect on people's lives.
- **Equal Protection of the Law** The guarantee in the Fourteenth Amendment to the US Constitution that all persons be treated equally by the law.
- **Escheat** The process by which a deceased person's property goes to the state if no heir can be found.
- **Ethics** Of on relating to moral action and conduct; professionally right; conforming to professional standards.
- **Evidence** Information presented in testimony or in documents that is used to persuade the fact finder (judge or jury) to decide the case for one side or the other.
- **Exceptions** Declarations by either side in a civil or criminal case reserving the right to appeal a judge's ruling upon a motion. Also, in regulatory cases, objections by either side to points made by the other side or to rulings by the agency or one of its hearing officers.
- **Exclusionary Rule** The rule preventing illegally obtained evidence to be used in any trial.
- **Execute** To complete; to sign; to carry out according to its terms.
- **Exempt Property** All the property of a debtor which is not attachable under the bankruptcy code or the state statute.
- **Exhibit** A document or other item introduced as evidence during a trial or hearing.

- **Ex Parte** On behalf of only one party, without notice to any other party. e.g. a request for a search warrant is an ex parte proceeding, since the person subject to the search is not notified of the proceeding and is not present at the hearing.

F

- **Family Law** Those areas of the law pertaining to families, i.e. marriage, divorce, child custody, juvenile, paternity etc.
- **Finding** Formal conclusion by a judge or regulatory agency on issues of fact. Also, a conclusion by a jury regarding a fact.
- **Food and Drug Agency** (FDA) A federal agency which sets safety and quality standards for administration food, drugs, cosmetics and household substances.
- **Foreclosure** A court proceeding upon default in a mortgage to vest title in the mortgagee.
- **Forfeiture** A cancellation. A legal action whereby a contract purchaser following default loses all his interest in the property.
- **Fraud** A false representation of a matter of fact which is intended to deceive another.

G

- **General Jurisdiction** Refers to courts that have no limit on the types of criminal and civil cases they may hear.
- **Good Time** A reduction in sentenced time in prison as a reward for good behaviour. It usually is one third to one half of the maximum sentence.
- **Grievance** In labour law a complaint filed by an employee regarding working conditions to be resolved by procedural machinery provided in the union contract. An injury, injustice or wrong which gives ground for complaint.
- **Guardian** A person appointed by will or by law to assume responsibility for incompetent adults or minor children. If a parent dies, this will usually be the other parent. If both die, it probably will be a close relative.
- **Guardianship** Legal right given to a person to be responsible for the food, housing, health care and other necessities of a person deemed incapable of providing these necessities for himself or herself.

H

- **Habeas Corpus** The name of a writ having for its object to bring a person before a court.
- **Harmless Error** An error committed during a trial that was corrected or was not serious enough to affect the outcome of a trial and therefore was not sufficiently harmful (prejudicial) to be reversed on appeal.
- **Hearing** A formal proceeding (generally less formal than a trial) with definite issues of law or of fact to be heard. Hearings are used extensively by legislative and administrative agencies.
- **Hearsay** Statements by a witness who did not see or hear the incident in question but heard about it from someone else. Hearsay is usually not admissible as evidence in court.
- **Hostile Witness** A witness whose testimony is not favourable to the party who calls him or her as a witness. A hostile witness may be asked leading questions and may be cross-examined by the party who calls him or her to the stand.
- **Hung Jury** A jury whose members cannot agree upon a verdict.

I

- **Immigrants** Persons who come into a foreign country or region to live.
- **Immunity** Grant by the court, which assures someone will not face prosecution in return for providing criminal evidence.
- **Impeachment** A criminal proceeding against a public official.

- **Impeachment of a Witness** An attack on the credibility (believability) of a witness, through evidence introduced for that purpose.
- **Implied Contract** A contract not created or evidenced by the explicit agreement of the parties but one inferred by law; as the use of electric power in your home implies a contract with the light company.
- **Inadmissible** That which, under the rules of evidence, cannot be admitted or received as evidence.
- **Incapacity** Lack of legal ability to act; disability, incompetence; lack of adequate power.
- **Incompetent** One who lacks ability, legal qualification, or fitness to manage his own affairs.
- **Information** Accusatory document, filed by the prosecutor, detailing the charges against the defendant. An alternative to an indictment, it serves to bring a defendant to trial.
- **Instructions** Judge's explanation to the jury before it begins deliberations of the question it must answer and the applicable law governing the case.
- **Intangible Assets** Non-physical items such as stock certificates, bonds, bank accounts, and pension benefits that have value and must be taken into account in estate planning.
- **Intentional Tort** Wrong perpetrated by one who intends to break the law.
- **Interlocutory** Temporary; provisional; interim; not final.
- **Interrogatories** A set or series of written questions propounded to a party, witness, or other person having information or interest in a case; a discovery device.
- **Intervention** An action by which a third person who may be affected by a lawsuit is permitted to become a party to the suit.

J

- **Joint Tenancy** A form of legal co-ownership of property (also known as survivorship). At the death of one co-owner, the surviving co-owner becomes sole owner of the property. Tenancy by the entirety is a special form of joint tenancy between a husband and wife.
- **Judge** A presiding officer of the court.
- **Judgement** The official and authentic decision of a court of justice upon the rights and claims of parties to an action or suit submitted to the court for determination.
- **Judiciary** The branch of government invested with judicial power to interpret and apply the law; the court system; the body of judges; then bench.
- **Jurisdiction** The power or authority of a court to hear and try a case; the geographic area in which a court has power or the types of cases it has power to hear.
- **Jurisprudence** The study of law and the structure of the legal system.
- **Jury** A certain number of men and women selected according to law and sworn to try a question of fact or indict a person for public offense.
- **Justiciable** Issues and claims capable of being properly examined in court.

L

- **Lapsed Gift** A gift made in a will to a person who has died prior to the will- makers death.
- **Larceny** Obtaining property by fraud or deceit.
- **Law** The combination of those rules and principles of conduct promulgated by legislative authority, derived from court decisions and established by local custom.
- **Leading Question** A question that suggests the answer desired of the witness. Leading questions may be asked only of hostile witnesses and on cross-examination.

- **Legal Aid** Professional legal services available usually to persons or organisations unable to afford such services.
- **Legal Process** A formal paper that is legally valid; something issuing from the court, usually a command such as a writ or mandate.
- **Legislation** The act of giving or enacting laws; the power to make laws *via* legislation in contrast to court-made laws.
- **Legitimate** That which is legal, lawful, recognised by law or according to law.
- **Letters Testamentary** Legal document issued by a court that shows an executor's legal right to take control of assets in the deceased person's name.
- **Lien** An encumbrance or legal burden upon property.
- **Limited Jurisdiction** Refers to courts that are limited in the types of criminal and civil cases they may hear. e.g. traffic violations generally are heard by limited jurisdiction courts.
- **Litigant** A party to a lawsuit.
- **Litigation** A lawsuit; a legal action, including all proceedings therein.

M

- **Manslaughter** The unlawful killing of another without intent to kill; either voluntary (upon a sudden impulse); or involuntary (during the commission of an unlawful act not ordinarily expected to result in great bodily harm).
- **Marshal** The executive officer of the federal court.
- **Mediation** A form of alternative dispute resolution in which the parties bring their dispute to a neutral third party, who helps them agree on a settlement.
- **Memorandum** An informal note or instrument embodying something the parties desire to have in written evidence.
- **Memorialised** In writing.
- **Merger** The absorption of one thing or right into another.
- **Minor** A person under the age of legal competence.
- **Mistrial** An invalid trial, caused by fundamental error. When a mistrial is declared, the trial must start again from the selection of the jury.
- **Mitigating Circumstances** Those which do not constitute a justification or excuse for an offense but which may be considered as reasons for reducing the degree of blame.
- **Mitigation** A reduction, abatement, or diminution of a penalty or punishment imposed by law.
- **Murder** The unlawful killing of a human being with deliberate intent to kill: (1) murder in the first degree is characterised by premeditation; (2) murder in the second degree is characterised by a sudden and instantaneous intent to kill or to cause injury without caring whether the injury kills or not.
- **Mutual Assent** A meeting of the minds; agreement.

N

- **National Labour Relations Board** (NLRB) A federal agency which prevents and remedies unfair labour practices by employers and labour organisations.
- **Naturalisation** Process by which a person acquires nationality after birth and becomes entitled to privileges of citizenship.
- **Negligence** Failure to use care which a reasonable and prudent person would use under similar circumstances.
- **Negotiation** The process of submission and consideration of offers until an acceptable offer is made and accepted.
- **Next Friend** One acting without formal appointment as guardian for the benefit of an infant, a person of unsound mind not judicially declared incompetent, or other person under some disability.

- **No-Contest Clause** Language in a will that provides that a person who makes a legal challenge to the will's validity will be disinherited.
- **No-Fault Proceedings** A civil case in which parties may resolve their dispute without a formal finding of error or fault.
- **Nonfeasance** Non-performance of an act which should be performed; omission to perform a required duty or total neglect of duty.
- **Nonjury Trial** Trial before the court but without a jury.
- **Notary Public** A public officer whose function it is to administer oaths, to attest and certify documents and to take acknowledgements.
- **Notice** Formal notification to the party that has been sued in a civil case of the fact that the lawsuit has been filed. Also, any form of notification of a legal proceeding.
- **Notice to Creditors** A notice given by the bankruptcy court to all creditors of a meeting of creditors.
- **Nuncupative Will** An oral (unwritten) will.

O

- **Oath** A solemn pledge made under a sense of responsibility in attestation of the truth of a statement or in verification of a statement made.
- **Objection** The process by which one party takes exception to some statement or procedure. An objection is either sustained (allowed) or overruled by the judge.
- **Official Reports** The publication of cumulated court decisions of state or federal courts in advance sheets and bound volumes as provided by statutory authority.
- **Order** A mandate, command, or direction authoritatively given. Direction of a court or judge made in writing.
- **Ordinance** A rule established by authority; may be a municipal statute of a city council, regulating such matters as zoning, building, safety, matters of municipality etc.
- **Overrule** A judge's decision not to allow an objection. Also, a decision by a higher court finding that a lower court decision was in error.

P

- **Paralegal** Also, legal assistant. A person with legal skills who works under the supervision of a lawyer.
- **Pardon** An act of grace from governing power which mitigates punishment and restores rights and privileges forfeited on account of the offense.
- **Parol Evidence** Oral or verbal evidence; evidence given by word of mouth in court.
- **Parole** Supervised release of a prisoner from imprisonment on certain prescribed conditions which entitle him to termination of his sentence.
- **Patent and Trademark Office** The federal agency which examines and issues patents and registers trademarks.
- **Permanent Injunction** A court order requiring that some action be taken or that some party refrain from taking action. It differs from forms of temporary relief, such as a temporary restraining order or preliminary injunction.
- **Per Se Doctrine** Under this doctrine, an activity such as price fixing can be declared as a violation of the antitrust laws without necessity of a court inquiring into the reasonableness of the activity.
- **Plea Bargaining** Process where the accused and the prosecutor in a criminal case work out a satisfactory disposition of the case, usually by the accused agreeing to plead guilty to a lesser offense. Such bargains are not binding on the court. Also referred to as plea negotiating.
- **Pleadings** The written statements of fact and law filed by the parties to a lawsuit.
- **Post-Trial** Refers to items happening after the trial, i.e. post-trial motions or post-trial discovery.

- **Power** Authority to do. One has the power to do something if he is of legal age. Also, used as 'powers', the term refers to authority granted by one person to another, i.e. powers given an executor in a will or an agent in a power of attorney.
- **Power of Attorney** An formal instrument authorising another to act as one's agent or attorney.
- **Precedent** Laws established by previous cases which must be followed in cases involving identical circumstances.
- **Preinjunction** Court order requiring action or forbidding action until a decision can be made whether to issue a permanent injunction. It differs from a temporary restraining order.
- **Preliminary Hearing** Also, preliminary examination. A hearing by a judge to determine whether a person charged with a crime should be held for trial.
- **Preponderance of the Proof** Greater weight of the evidence, the common standard of evidence in civil cases.
- **Presentment** Declaration or document issued by a grand jury that either makes a neutral report or notes misdeeds by officials charged with specified public duties. It ordinarily does not include a formal charge of crime. A presentment differs from an indictment.
- **Pretermitted Child** A child born after a will is executed, who is not provided for by the will. Most states have laws that provide for a share of estate property to go to such children.
- **Prima Facie Case** A case that is sufficient and has the minimum amount of evidence necessary to allow it to continue in the judicial process.
- **Probable Cause** A reasonable belief that a crime has or is being committed; the basis for all lawful searches, seizures and arrests.
- **Probation** An alternative to imprisonment allowing a person found guilty of an offense to stay in the community, usually under conditions and under the supervision of a probation officer. A violation of probation can lead to its revocation and to imprisonment.
- **Product Liability** Legal responsibility of manufacturers and sellers to buyers, users and bystanders for damages or injuries suffered because of defects in goods.
- **Promissory Estoppel** A promise which estops the promisee from asserting or taking certain action.
- **Property Tax** A tax levied on land and buildings (real estate) and on personal property.
- **Public Law** That law such as traffic ordinances or zoning ordinances which applies to the public.
- **Public Defender** Government lawyer who provides free legal defense services to a poor person accused of a crime.
- **Public Service Commission** Also, Public Utilities Commission. A State Agency which regulates utilities.
- **Punitive Damages** Money award given to punish the defendant or wrongdoer.
- **Purchase Agreement or Purchase Offer** Also, sales agreement and earnest money contract. Agreement between buyer and seller of property which sets forth in general the price and terms of a proposed sale.

Q

- **Quash** To vacate or void a summons, subpoena etc.
- **Quasi-Contract** An obligation created by the law in the absence of an agreement or contract; not based upon the intentions or expressions of the parties.
- **Quitclaim Deed** A deed without warranty of title which passes whatever title the grantor has to another.

R

- **Real Property** Land, buildings, and whatever is attached or affixed to the land. Generally, synonymous with the words 'real estate'.
- **Rebut** Evidence disproving other evidence previously given or re-establishing the credibility of challenged evidence.
- **Recognizance** An obligation entered into before a court whereby the recognisor acknowledges that he will do a specific act required by law.
- **Rehearing** Another hearing of a civil or criminal case by the same court in which the case was originally heard.
- **Rejoinder** Opportunity for the side that opened the case to offer limited response to evidence presented during the rebuttal by the opposing side.
- **Replevin** An action for the recovery of a possession that has been wrongfully taken.
- **Rescission** The unmaking or undoing of a contract; repeal.
- **Resolution** The formal adoption of a motion.
- **Respondent** The person against whom an appeal is taken.
- **Restitution** Act of restoring anything to its rightful owner; the act of restoring someone to an economic position he enjoyed before he suffered a loss.
- **Retainer** Act of the client in employing the attorney or counsel and also denotes the fee which the client pays when he or she retains the attorney to act for them.
- **Return** A report to a judge by police on the implementation of an arrest or search warrant. Also, a report to a judge in reply to a subpoena, civil or criminal.
- **Reverse** An action of a higher court in setting aside or revoking a lower court decision.
- **Reversible Error** A procedural error during a trial or hearing sufficiently harmful to justify reversing the judgement of a lower court.
- **Revocable Trust** A trust that the grantor may change or revoke.
- **Rules Established** Standards, guides or regulations set-up by authority.
- **Rules of Evidence** Standards governing whether evidence in a civil or criminal case is admissible.

S

- **Search Warrant** A written order issued by a judge that directs a law enforcement officer to search a specific area for a particular piece of evidence.
- **Secondary Authority** Legal encyclopaedias, treatises, legal texts, law review articles, and citators. Writings which set forth the opinion of the writer as to the law.
- **Secured Debts** In bankruptcy, a debt is secured if the debtor gave the creditor a right to repossess the property or goods used as collateral.
- **Self-Defense** The claim that an act otherwise criminal was legally justifiable because it was necessary to protect a person or property from the threat or action of another.
- **Sentence** The punishment ordered by a court for a defendant convicted of a crime.
- **Sequester** To separate. Sometimes juries are separated from outside influences during their deliberations. e.g. this may occur during a highly publicised trial.
- **Service of Process** The delivering of writs, summonses and subpoenas by delivering them to the party named in the document. Also referred to as 'service'.
- **Settlor** The person who sets-up a trust. Also referred to as 'grantor'.
- **Sidebar** A conference between the judge and lawyers, usually in the courtroom, out of earshot of the jury and spectators.
- **Slander** Spoken defamation which tends to injure a person's reputation.

- **Small Claims Court** A State Court that handles civil claims for small amounts of money. People often represent themselves rather than hire an attorney.
- **Social Security** A system of federal old-age pensions for employed persons begun in 1935. A portion of the payment is deducted from the employee's salary and an equal portion is contributed by the employer.
- **Sovereign Immunity** The doctrine that the Government, State or Federal, is immune to lawsuit unless it give its consent.
- **Status Offenders** Youths charged with the status of being beyond the control of their legal guardian or are habitually disobedient, truant from school or having committed other acts that would not be a crime if committed by an adult, i.e. smoking. Also referred to as minors or children in need of supervision.
- **Statute** Legislative enactment; it may be a single act of a legislature or a body of acts which are collected and arranged for a session of a legislature.
- **Statute of Frauds** A statutory requirement that certain contracts must be in writing.
- **Statutory** Relating to a statute; created or defined by a law.
- **Statutory Law** Laws promulgated by Congress and State Legislatures.
- **Stay** A court order halting a judicial proceeding.
- **Stipulation** An agreement between the parties involved in a suit regulating matters incidental to trial.
- **Subpoena** A command to appear at a certain time and place to give testimony upon a certain matter.
- **Subpoena Duces Tecum** A court order commanding a witness to bring certain documents or records to court.
- **Substantive Law** The statutory or written law that governs rights and obligations of those who are subject to it.
- **Surety Bond** A bond purchased at the expense of the estate to insure the executor's proper performance. Also referred to as 'fidelity bond.'
- **Suspension** A temporary loss of the right to practice law by an attorney.

T

- **Taxable Income** The income against which tax rates are applied to compute tax paid; gross income of businesses or adjusted gross income of individuals less deductions and exemptions.
- **Temporary Relief** Any form of action by a court granting one of the parties an order to protect its interest pending further action by the court.
- **Temporary Restraining Order** An emergency remedy of brief duration issued by a court only in exceptional circumstances, usually when immediate or irreparable damages or loss might result before the opposition could take action.
- **Tender of Performance** An offer or attempt to do what is required under a contract or under the law.
- **Testamentary Capacity** The legal ability to make a will.
- **Testamentary Trust** A trust set-up by a will.
- **Testator** Person who makes a will (Female: testatrix).
- **Testimony** The evidence given by a witness under oath. It does not include evidence from documents and other physical evidence.
- **Third Party Complaint** A petition filed by a defendant against a third party (not presently a party to the suit) which alleges that the third party is liable for all or part of the damages plaintiff may win from defendant.
- **Title** Legal ownership of property, usually real property or automobiles.

- **Tort** A private or civil wrong or injury for which the court provides a remedy through an action for damages.
- **Trademark** A word, name, symbol or devise used by a manufacturer to distinguish his goods from those sold by others.
- **Transcript** A written, word-for-word record of what was said. Usually refers to a record of a trial, hearing or other proceeding which has been transcribed from a recording or from shorthand.
- **Transmittal Form** Form required in certain courts for transmitting documents for filing.
- **Trial** A judicial examination of issues between parties to an action.
- **Trust** A legal device used to manage real or personal property, established by one person (grantor or settlor) for the benefit of another (beneficiary).
- **Trustee** The person or institution that manages the property put in trust.

U

- **Unfair Labour Practice** Actions by the employer which interfere with, restrain, coerce, or threaten employees with respect to their rights.
- **Uniform Commercial Code** (UCC) A uniform law governing commercial transactions. The UCC has been adopted by all states except Louisiana.
- **Uniform Laws** Annotated uniform and model acts approved by the National Conference of Commissioners on Uniform State Laws.
- **Unilateral Contract** An agreement by which one undertakes an express performance without receiving any express promise of performance from the other.
- **Union** An organisation of workers formed for the purpose of collective bargaining.
- **United States Court of Appeals** Courts which hear appeals from federal district courts, bankruptcy courts and tax courts.
- **United States Court of Claims** Court which hears actions against the US Government.
- **United States Court of Customs and Patent Appeals** Court which hears appeals from all US customs courts.
- **United States Court of International Trade** Court which hears cases concerning federal tariff laws.
- **United States Reports** Publication of court decisions of the United States Supreme Court.
- **United States Supreme Court** The highest court in the land, established by US Constitution.
- **Unlawful Detainer** A detention of real estate without the consent of the owner or other person entitled to its possession.
- **Unliquidated Debt** Remaining not determined; unassessed or unsettled; in dispute as to the proper amount.
- **Unsecured Debts** In bankruptcy, debts such as open accounts at department stores for which the debtor has not pledged collateral to guarantee payment.

V

- **Vagrancy** Moving about without a means to support oneself, without a permanent home and relying on begging. The same is true of 'loitering'.
- **Valuable Consideration** A necessary element of a contract, which confers a benefit on the other party. Valuable consideration can include money, work, performance, assets, a promise or abstaining from an act.
- **Vendee** A buyer, particularly of real property.
- **Vendor** A seller, particularly of real property.
- **Venire** (ven-eer-ay) The list from which jurors may be selected.

- **Venue** The proper or most convenint location for trial of a case.
- **Verdict** The decision of a jury after a trial, which must be accepted by the trail judge to be final. A judgement by a judge sitting without a jury is not a verdict.
- **Verification** The declaration under oath or upon penalty of perjury that a statement or pleading is true, located at the end of a document.
- **Vest** To give an absolute right to title or ownership, including real property and pension right.
- **Vested** Referring to having an absolute right or title, when previously the holder of the right or title only had an expectation. e.g. after 20 years of employment Akbar Khan's pension rights are now vested.
- **Vested Remainder** The absolute right to receive title after a presently existing interest in real property terminates. A 'vested remainder' is created by deed or by a decree of distribution of an estate given by will.
- **Vexatious Litigation** Filing a lawsuit with the knowledge that it has no legal basis, with its purpose to bother, annoy, embarrass and cause legal expenses to the defendant.
- **Vicarious Liability** Sometimes called 'imputed liability,' attachment of responsibility to a person for harm or damages caused by another person in either a negligence lawsuit or criminal prosecution.
- **Vigilante** Someone who takes the law into his/her own hands by trying and/or punishing another person without any legal authority. A mother who shoots the alleged molester of her child is a vigilante.
- **Void** Referring to a statute, contract, ruling or anything which is null and of no effect. A law or judgement found by an appeals court to be unconstitutional is void, a rescinded (mutually cancelled) contract is void, and a marriage which has been annulled by court judgement is void.
- **Void for Vagueness** Referring to a statute defining a crime which is so vague that a reasonable person of atleast average intelligence could not determine what elements constitute the crime.
- **Voidable** Capable of being made void. e.g. a contract entered into by a minor under 18 is voidable upon his/her reaching majority, but the minor may also affirm the contract at the time. 'Voidable' is distinguished from 'void' in that it means only that a thing can become void, but is not necessarily void.
- **Voluntary Bankruptcy** The filing for bankruptcy by a debtor who believes he/she/it cannot pay bills and has more debts than assets. Voluntary bankruptcy differs from 'involuntary bankruptcy' filed by creditors money to bring the debtor before the bankruptcy court.
- **Voting Trust** A trust which solicits vote proxies of shareholders of a corporation to elect a board of directors and vote on other matters at a shareholders, meeting.
- **Victim (Impact) Statement** Information provided to a court by victims for the purpose of helping to determine the proper punishment to be imposed on a convicted criminal.
- **Voir Dire** Old French and Latin term for a special hearing to decide whether evidence is admissible.

W

- **Witness** Person who provides information as evidence in a hearing.
- **Written Submissions (or Written Argument)** Document containing arguments of law or fact submitted to a legal decision-maker.
- **Waive** To voluntarily give up something, including not enforcing a term of a contract (such as insisting on payment on a exact date) or knowingly/giving up a legal right such as a speedy trial, a jury trial or a hearing on extradition.

- **Waiver** The intentional and voluntary giving up of something, such as a right, either by an express statement or by conduct (such as not enforcing a right).
- **Wanton** 1. Grossly negligent to the extent of being recklessly unconcerned with the safety of people or property. e.g. speeding by a school while it is letting out students of firing a shotgun in a public park. 2. Sexually immoral and unrestrained.
- **Ward** A person (usually a minor) who has a guardian appointed by the court to care for and take responsibility for that person.
- **Warrant** An order (writ) of a court which directs a law enforcement officer, to arrest and bring a person before the judge, such as a person who is charged with a crime, convicted of a crime but failed to appear for sentencing, owes a fine or is in contempt of court.
- **Warranty** A written statement of good quality of merchandise, clear title to real estate or that a fact stated in a contract is true. An 'express warranty' is a definite written statement and 'implied warranty' is based on the circumstances surrounding the sale or the creation of the contract.
- **Warranty Deed** A deed to real property which guarantees that the seller owns clear title which can be transferred (conveyed). A 'grant deed' generally is a warranty deed, while a 'quitclaim deed' is not.
- **Waste** 1. Any damage to real property by a tenant which lessens its value to the landlord, owner or future owner. An owner can sue for damages for waste, terminate a lease of one committing waste and/or obtain an injunction against further waste.
  2. Garbage, which may include poisonous effluents.
- **Watered Stock** Shares of stock of a corporation which have been issued at a price far greater than true value. In this case, the actual value of all shares is less than the value carried on the books of the corporation.
- **Weight of Evidence** The strength, value and believability of evidence presented on a factual issue by one side as compared to evidence introduced by the other side.
- **Wet Reckless** A plea to a reckless driving which was 'alcohol related'.
- **Whiplash** A common neck and/or back injury suffered in automobile accidents.
- **White Collar Crime** A generic term for crimes involving commercial fraud, cheating consumers, swindles, insider trading on the stock market, embezzlement and other forms of dishonest business schemes.
- **Widow** A woman whose husband died while she was married to him and who has not since remarried.
- **Widow's Election** The choice a widow makes between accepting what her husband left her in his will and what she would receive by the laws of succession.
- **Widower** A man whose wife died while he was married to her and who has not remarried.
- **Will** A written document which leaves the estate of the person who signed the will to named persons or entities (beneficiaries, legatees, divisees) including portions or percentages of the estate, specific gifts, creation of trusts for management and future distribution of all or a portion of the estate (a testamentary trust).
- **Will Contest** A lawsuit challenging the validity of a will and/or its terms.
- **Willfully** Referring to doing something intentionally, purposefully and stubbornly. e.g. "He drove the car willfully into the crowd on the sidewalk." "She willfully left the dangerous substances on the property."
- **Witness Stand** A chair at the end of the judge's bench on the jury box side, usually with a low 'modesty screen', where a witness sits and gives testimony after he/she has sworn to tell the truth.

- **Words of Art** 1. specialised language with meaning peculiar to a particular profession, art, technical work, science or other field of endeavor. 2. Jargon known only to people who specialise in a particular occupation.
- **Writ of Coram Nobis** (writ of core-uhm noh-bis) from Latin for 'in our presence', an order by a court of appeals to a court which rendered judgment requiring that trial court to consider facts not on the trial record which might have resulted in a different judgement if known at the time of trial.
- **Writ of Execution** A court order to a law enforcement officer to enforce a judgement by levying on real or personal property of a judgement debtor to obtain funds to satisfy the judgement amount (pay the winning plaintiff)
- **Writ of Mandate** (mandamus) A court order to a government agency, including another court, to follow the law by correcting its prior actions or ceasing illegal acts.
- **Wrongful Death** The death of a human being as the result to a wrongful act of another person. Such wrongful acts include: negligence (like careless driving), an intentional attack such as assault and/or battery, a death in the course of another crime, vehicular manslaughter, manslaughter or murder.
- **Wrongful Termination** A right of an employee to sue his/her employer for damages (loss of wage and 'Fringe' benefits and if against 'public policy', for punitive damages).

Y

- **Your Honor** The proper way to address a judge in court.
- **Youthful Offenders** Under-age people accused of crimes who are processed through a juvenile court and juvenile detention or prison facilities. A youthful offender is under the age of 18.

Z

Zoning A system of developing a city or country plan in which various geographic areas (zones) are restricted to certain uses and development, such as industrial, light industrial, commercial, light-commercial, agricultural, single-family residential, multi-unit residential, parks, schools and other purposes.

CHAPTER 08

IMPORTANT TREATIES AND CONVENTIONS

A treaty is an agreement under International law entered into by actors in International law, namely sovereign states and international organisations.

A treaty may also be known as an (international) agreement, protocol, covenant, convention, pact or exchange of letters, among other terms. Regardless of terminology, all of these forms of agreements are, under International law, equally considered treaties and the rules are the same. Treaties can be loosely compared to contracts both are means of willing parties assuming obligations among themselves, and a party to either that fails to live upto their obligations can be held liable under International law.

Following are various treaty and conventions of international importance

- **Magna Carta** (Great Charter of Liberty) 1215 Magna Carta required King John of England to proclaim certain rights, respect certain legal procedures and accept that his will could be bound by the law.
- **Strasbourg Agreement** (1675) It is the first international agreement banning the use of chemical weapons. The treaty was signed between France and holy Roman Empire.
- **First Geneva Convention** (For the Amelioration of the Condition of the Wounded in Armies in the Field) 1864. This convention provide for immunity from capture and destruction of all establishments for the treatment of wounded and sick soldiers, impartial reception and treatment of all combatants, protection of civilian as providing aid to the wounded and recognition of the Red Cross symbol as a means of identifying persons and equipment covered by the agreement.

- **Paris Convention** (For the Protection of Industrial Property) 1883. The 'convention of priority right', also called 'Paris convention priority right' or 'Union priority right', was established by this treaty. It provides that an applicant from one contracting state shall be able to use its first filing date (in one of the contracting state) as the effective filing date in another contracting state, provided that the applicant files another application within 6 months (for designs and trademarks) or 12 months (for patents from the first filing.
- **Berne Convention** (For Protection of Literary and Artistic Works) 1886. This convention requires its signatories to recognise the copyright of works of authors from other signatory countries (known as members of the Berne Union) in the same way as it recognises the copyright of its own nationals.
- **Hague Conventions** The Hague conventions are international treaties negotiated at the First and Second Peace Conferences at the Hague, Netherlands in 1899 and 1907. The main effect of the convention was to ban the use of certain types of modern technology in war: bombing from the air, chemical warfare and hollow point bullets. The convention also set-up the Permanent Court of Arbitration.
- **Second Geneva Convention** (For the Amelioration of the Condition of Wounded Sick and Shipwrecked Members of Armed Forces at Sea) 1906.
- **Washington Naval Treaty** 1922 (Five Power Treaty). This treaty limited the naval armaments of its five signatories: the United States of America, the British Empire, the Empire of Japan, the French Third Republic and the Kingdom of Italy.
- **General Treaty for the Renunciation of War** (Pact of Paris) (Kellog-Briand Pact) 1928. The pact renounced aggressive war, prohibiting the use of war as 'an instrument of national policy' except in matters of self-defense.
- **London Naval Treaty** (Treaty for the Limitation and Reduction of Naval Armament) 1930. The terms of the treaty were seen as an extension of the conditions agreed in the Washington Naval Treaty.
- **Second London Naval Treaty** (1936) Extended the earlier treaty to submarines.
- **Bretton Woods Agreement** (1944) Outcome of Bretton Woods Conference (United Nations Monetary and Financial Conference) held at Carroll, New Hampshire, USA. This agreement led to the establishment of International Monetary Fund (IMF) and International Bank for Reconstruction and Development (also known as World Bank). It provided rules for commercial and financial relations among the major industrial states.
- **The Charter of United Nations** (1945) It is the foundational treaty of United Nations signed in San Francisco on 26th June, 1945 by 50 out of 51 founding members (Poland joined later). It entered into force on 24th October, 1945, after being ratified by the five permanent members of the Security Council the Republic of China (later replaced by the People's Republic of China), France, the USSR (later replaced by the Russian Federation), the UK and the USA and a majority of the other signatories.
- **General Agreement on Tariffs and Trade** (GATT) It was negotiated during the UN Conference on Trade and Employment (held at Geneva) and was the outcome to the failure of negotiating governments to create the International Trade Organisation (ITO). GATT was formed in 1947 and lasted until 1993. The World Trade Organisation replaced it in 1995. The original GATT text (GATT 1947) is still in effect under the WTO framework.
- **North Atlantic Treaty** (1949) It is the treaty that brought North Atlantic Treaty Organisation into existence, signed in Washington DC on 4th April, 1949 by twelve countries including USA, UK, Canada, France and Italy.

- **Fourth Geneva Convention** 1949 (The Protection of Civilian Persons in Time of War). This Convention established rules for the protection of civilians during wartime.
- **Treaty of London** 1949 (Statute of the Council of Europe). This treaty created the Council of Europe (different form European Union). The original signatories include UK, France and Italy.
- **Convention on the Prevention and Punishment of the Crime of Genocide** (1948) It was adopted by the United National General Assembly on 9th December, 1948 as General Assembly Resolution 260. The Convention entered into force on 12th January, 1951.
- **Indus Water Treaty** (1960) Its water sharing treaty between India and Pakistan (at the behest of the World Bank). The treaty was signed in Karachi on 19th September, 1960 by Indian Prime Minister Jawahar Lal Nehru and President of Pakistan Mohammad Ayub Khan. This treaty gives India exclusive use of all of the water of the Eastern Rivers (Sutlej, Beas and Ravi and their tributaries before the point when the rivers enter into the Pakistan. Similarly, Pakistan has exclusive use of the Western Rivers (Indus, Jhelum and Chenab).
- **Vienna Convention on Diplomatic Relations** (1961) It is an international treaty that defines a framework in diplomatic relations between independent countries. It specifies the privileges of diplomatic mission that enable diplomatic countries. It specifies the privileges of a diplomatic mission that enable diplomats to perform their function without fear of coercion of harassment by the host country. This forms the legal basis for diplomatic immunity.
- **WIPO Convention** (1967) It was signed in 1967 at Stockholm and entered in force in 1970. It established the World Intellectual Property Organisation and has 184 contracting parties.
- **Nuclear Non-Proliferation Treaty** (NPT or NNPT) 1968. NPT is commonly described as having three main 'pillars' non-proliferation, disarmament, and peaceful use. It was signed in 1968 at New York and came into force in 1970. As of now there are 189 parties to it India, Israel, Pakistan and North Korea (no longer recognises this treaty) being exceptions.
- **Vienna Convention on the Law of Treaties** (1969) This treaty (as the name indicates) covers international law of treaties and is widely recognised as the authoritative guide vis-a-vis the formation and effects of treaties.
- **Maastricht Treaty** (1922) It was signed in 1992 and upon its entry into force in 1993, it created the European Union and led to the creation of Euro.
- **The United Nations Framework Convention on Climate Change** (UNFCCC or FCCC) It is an international environmental treaty produced at the Earth Summit (UN Conference on Earth and Development) held in Rio de Janerio in June 1992. The objective of the treaty is to stabilise greenhouse gas concentrations in the atmosphere at a sustainable level.
- **CIS Collective Security Treaty** (Tashkent Treaty) 1992. This treaty was signed in 1992 by Armenia, Kazakhstan, Kyrgyzstan, Russia, Tajikistan, Uzbekistan (joined later by Azerbaijan, Georgia and Belarus) and entered into force in 1994 to create CSTO a NATO like organisation.
- **Rome Statute of the International Criminal Court** (often referred to as the International Criminal Court Statute or the Rome Statute). It is the treaty that established the International Criminal Court (ICC). It was adopted at a diplomatic conference in Rome in 1998 and it entered into force in 2002. This treaty (statute) provides for the court's functions, jurisdiction and structure.

INDIAN CONSTITUTION

CHAPTER 01

CONSTITUTIONAL DEVELOPMENT OF INDIA

CONSTITUTION OF INDIA

The Constitution of India was drafted by the Constituent Assembly of India and was declared as passed on 26th November, 1949. It was enacted on 26th January, 1950 and laid the foundations for establishment of the democratic republic of India.

Background

- The British came to India in 1600 as traders, in form of East India Company with exclusive right of trading in India. But in 1765 Company obtained the Diwani of Bengal, Bihar and Odisha.
- In 1858, in the wake of 'sepoy mutiny' the British Crown assumed direct responsibility for the governance in India and continued till 1947.
- It was in 1934 when MN Roy put forward the idea for the Constitution of a Constituent Assembly which was finally formed in 1946 and on 26th January, 1950 the Constitution came into being.

IMPORTANT ACTS BEFORE 1947

Regulating Act, 1773

- Under this act, central administration was established in India.
- Initiative to regulate the affairs of East India Company by British Government.

- Recognised both the administrative and political functions of company.
- It made the Governors of Bombay and Madras presidencies subordinate to the Governor-General of Bengal.
- It established a Supreme Court in Calcutta in 1774 comprising one chief justice and three other judges.
- It strengthened the control of the British Government over the company by requiring the Court of Directors (governing body of the company) to report on its revenue, civil and military affairs in India.

Pitt's India Act, 1784

After the Regulating act, the British Parliament passed the Pitt's India Act (on the name of Prime Minister William Pitt) in 1784. *Some of the important provisions of the act are as follows*

- It completely distinguished the commercial and political functions of the company and allowed the Court of Directors to manage the commercial affairs.
- Under this act, for the first time the company's territories were called as the **British Possessions in India**.
- It created a new body called Board of Control to manage the civil and military government or revenues of the government. Thus, it established a system of dual government.

Charter Act, 1833

This act was the final step towards centralisation of administration in British India. *Some of the important provisions of the act are as follows*

- It made the Governor-General of Bengal as the Governor-General of India (First Governor-General was Lord William Bentinck) and vested in him all civil and military powers.
- End of company's monopoly even in tea and trade with China. Company was asked to close its commercial business at the earliest.
- It ended the activities of the East India Company as a commercial body, which became a purely administrative body.
- It attempted to introduce a system of open competition for selection of civil servants and stated that the Indians should not be debarred from holding any place, office and employment under the company.

Charter Act, 1853

It was last Charter Act of British. It laid down parliamentary form of government and extended the terms of company for an indefinite period.

Some of the important provisions of the act are as follows

- It separated the legislative and executive functions of the Governor-General's Council and provided for addition of six new members called legislative councillors to the council (Indian Legislative Council).
- It introduced an open competition system of selection and recruitment of civil servants. The covenanted civil service was thus thrown open to the Indians also.
- It introduced local representation in the Indian (Central) Legislative Council. Of the six new legislative members of the Governor-General's Council, four members were appointed by the local (provincial) governments of Madras, Bombay, Bengal and Agra.

Government of India Act, 1858

This act was enacted in the wake of the Revolt of 1857. *Some of the important provisions of the act are as follows*

- It abolished the East India Company and transferred the powers of government, territories and revenues to the British Crown.
- It changed the designation of the Governor-General of India to that of Viceroy of India, who was direct representative of the British Crown in India. **Lord Canning** became the first Viceroy of India.

- It ended the system of dual government by abolishing the Board of Control and Court of Directors.
- It created a new office of secretary of state for India. The secretary of state was a member of the British cabinet and was responsible ultimately to the British Parliament. He was assisted by 15 members council (called Indian Council).

Indian Councils Act, 1861

The Indian Councils Act of 1861 is an important landmark in the constitutional and political history of India. *Some of the important provisions of the act are as follows*

- A fifth member, who was to be a jurist, was added to the Viceroy's Executive Council.
- It provided that the Viceroy should nominate some Indians as non-official members of his expanded council.
- It initiated the process of decentralisation by restoring the legislative powers to the Bombay and Madras Presidencies.
- It also provided for the establishment of new legislative councils for Bengal, North- Western Frontier Province (NWFP) and Punjab, which were established in 1862, 1866 and 1897, respectively.
- It gave recognition to the 'portfolio' system, introduced by Lord Canning in 1859.
- It empowered the Viceroy to issue ordinances, without the concurrence of the legislative council, during an emergency. *The life of such an ordinance was six months.*

Indian Councils Act, 1892

The act allowed the limited and indirect use of election in filling up some of non-Official seats. *Some of the important provisions of the act are as follows*

- It increased the functions of legislative councils and gave them the power of discussing the budget and addressing questions to the executive.
- It provided for the nomination of some non-official members of the Central Legislative Council by the Viceroy and the provincial legislative councils by the Governors. Indian leaders, like GK Gokhale, Ashuthosh Mukherji, Rasbihari Ghosh, SN Banerjee found their way in the Legislative Council.

Indian Councils Act, 1909

This act is also known as **Morley-Minto Reforms** (Lord Morley was the Secretary of State for India and Lord Minto was the Viceroy of India). *Some of the important provisions of the act are as follows*

- It considerably increased the size of the legislative councils, both central and provincial from 16 to 60 and provincial councils allowed to have non-official majority.
- It enlarged the deliberative functions of the legislative councils at both the levels.
- It provided for the association of Indians with the Executive Councils of the Viceroy and Governors. **Satyendra Prasad Sinha** became the first Indian to join the Viceroy's Executive Council. He was appointed as the law member.
- It introduced a system of communal representation for Muslims by accepting the concept of separate electorate. Thus, Lord Minto came to be known as the **Father of Communal Electorate**.

Government of India Act, 1919

On 20th August, 1917, the British Government declared that its objective was the gradual introduction of responsible government in India. Hence, the Government of India Act of 1919 was enacted which came into force in 1921. This act is also known as **Montague-Chelmsford Reforms** (Montague was the Secretary of State for India and Lord Chelmsford was the Viceroy of India).

Some of the important provisions of the act are as follows

- It relaxed the central control over the provinces by demarcating and separating the central and provincial subjects.
- It further divided the provincial subjects into two parts namely transferred and reserved. This dual scheme of governance was known as dyarchy.
- It introduced for the first time, bicameralism and direct elections in the country. The legislature consisting of an Upper House (Council of State) and a Lower House (Legislative Assembly).
- It extended the principle of communal representation by providing separate electorates for Sikhs, Indian Christians, Anglo-Indians and Europeans.
- It created a new office of the High Commissioner for India in London and transferred to him some of the functions hitherto performed by the Secretary of State for India.
- It provided for the establishment of a Public Service Commission. Hence, a Central Public Service Commission was set-up in 1926 for recruiting civil servants.
- Principle of separate electorate was extended to include Anglo-Indians, Indian Christians and Europeans.
- Appointment of Statutory Commission to inquire into and report on its working after ten years of its coming into force. (In 1927, seven member Statutory Commission appointed under Chairmanship of Sir John Simon).

Government of India Act, 1935

The act marked a second milestone towards a completely responsible government in India. It was a lengthy and detailed document having 321 Sections and 10 Schedules. *Some of the important provisions of the act are as follows*

- It provided for the establishment of an All India Federation consisting of provinces and Princely states as units.
- The act divided the powers between the centre and units in terms of three lists namely; Federal List (for centre, with 59 items) Provincial List (for provinces, with 54 items) and the Concurrent List (for both, with 36 items). Residuary powers were given to the Viceroy.
- It abolished dyarchy in the provinces and introduced 'provincial autonomy' in its place.
- It introduced bicameralism in six out of eleven provinces. Thus, the legislatures of Bengal, Bombay, Madras, Bihar, Asom and the United Provinces.
- It further extended the principle of communal representation by providing separate electorates for depressed classes (scheduled castes), women and labour (workers).
- It provided for the establishment of not only a Federal Public Service Commission but also a Provincial Public Service Commission and Joint Public Service Commission for two or more provinces.
- It provided for the establishment of a Federal Court, which was set-up in 1937.
- Burma (Myanmar) and Aden were separated from India and two new provinces Orissa (Odisha) and Sindh were created.

Indian Independence Act, 1947

The act ended the British rule in India and declared India as an independent and sovereign state from 15th August, 1947. The act was based on Mountbatten plan. *Some of the important provisions of the act are as follows*

- It provided for the partition of India and creation of two independent dominions of India and Pakistan with the right to secede from the British Commonwealth.
- It empowered the Constituent Assemblies of the two dominions to frame and adopt any

Constitution for their respective nations and to repeal any act of the British Parliament, including the Independence Act itself.

- It empowered the Constituent Assemblies of both the dominions to legislate for their respective territories till the new constitutions were drafted.
- It granted freedom to the Indian Princely States either to join the Dominion of India or Dominion of Pakistan or to remain independent.

Thus, at the stroke of midnight of 14-15th August, 1947, the British rule came to an end and power was transferred to the two newly independent Dominions of India and Pakistan. **Lord Mountbatten** became the first Governor-General of the new Dominion of India. He sworne in **Jawaharlal Nehru** as the first Prime Minister of independent India. The Constituent Assembly of India formed in 1946 became the Parliament of the Indian Dominion.

MAKING OF THE CONSTITUTION

In 1938, Indian National Congress declared that the Constitution of free India must be framed, without outside interference, by a Constituent Assembly (the idea of Constituent Assembly was put forward by MN Roy in 1934) elected on the basis of adult franchise.

The demand of Constituent Assembly was accepted by the British Government. In 1946, finally Cabinet Mission (three members named Lord Pethick Lawrence, Sir Stafford Cripps and AV Alexander) was sent and they arrived in India on 24th March, 1946.

The Constituent Assembly

- The Constituent Assembly was constituted in November 1946 under the scheme formulated by the Cabinet Mission Plan. The total strength of the Constituent Assembly was to be 389. Of these, 296 seats were to be allotted to British India and 93 seats to the Princely States.
- The Constituent Assembly held its first meeting on 9th December, 1946. The Muslim League boycotted the meeting and insisted on a separate state of Pakistan.
- The meeting was thus attended by only 211 members.
- Dr Sachchidanand Sinha was elected as the temporary President of the Assembly.
- Later, on 11th December, 1946, Dr Rajendra Prasad and HC Mukherjee were elected as the President and Vice-President of the Assembly respectively. Sir BN Rau was appointed as the Constitutional Advisor to the Assembly.
- On 13th December, 1946, Jawaharlal Nehru moved the historic 'Objectives Resolution' in the Assembly. It laid down the fundamentals and philosophy of the constitutional structure.
- This Resolution was unanimously adopted by the Assembly on 22nd January, 1947. It influenced the eventual shaping of the Constitution through all its subsequent stages. Its modified version forms the Preamble of the present Constitution.
- The representatives of the Princely states, who had stayed away from the Constituent Assembly, gradually joined it. On 28th April, 1947, representatives of the six states were part of the Assembly. The members of the Muslim League from the Indian Dominion also entered the Assembly.
- The last session of the Constituent Assembly was held on 24th January, 1950.

Enactment of the Constitution

In all, the Constituent Assembly had 11 sessions over 2 years, 11 months and 18 days.

Dr BR Ambedkar introduced the final draft of the Constitution in the Assembly on 4th November, 1948. The Constitution enacted on 26th November, 1949, contained a Preamble, 395 Articles and 8 Schedules.

The remaining provisions (the major part) of the Constitution came into force on 26th January, 1950. This day is referred to in the Constitution as the 'date of its commencement', and celebrated as the Republic Day.

In addition to the making of the Constitution and enacting of ordinary laws, *the Constituent Assembly also performed the following functions*

- It ratified the India's membership of the Commonwealth in May 1949.
- It adopted the National Flag on 22nd July, 1947.
- It adopted the National Anthem on 24th January, 1950.
- It adopted the National Song on 24th January, 1950.
- It elected Dr Rajendra Prasad as the first President of India on 24th January, 1950.

First Cabinet of Free India (1947)

Members	Portfolios Held
Pt Jawaharlal Nehru	Prime Minister, External Affairs & Commonwealth Relation; Scientific Research
Sardar Vallabhbhai Patel	Home, Information and Broadcasting; States
Dr Rajendra Prasad	Food and Agriculture
Maulana Abul Kalam Azad	Education
Dr John Mathai	Railways and Transport
RK Shanmugham Chetty	Finance
Dr BR Ambedkar	Law
Jagjivan Ram	Labour
Sardar Baldev Singh	Defence
Rajkumari Amrit Kaur	Health
CH Bhabha	Commerce
Rafi Ahmed Kidwai	Communication
Dr Shyam Prasad Mukherji	Industries and Supplies
VN Gadgil	Works, Mines and Power

Interim Government (1946)

Members	Portfolios Held
Pt Jawaharlal Nehru	External Affairs & Commonwealth Relations
Sardar Vallabhbhai Patel	Home, Information and Broadcasting
Dr Rajendra Prasad	Food and Agriculture
Dr John Mathai	Industries and Supplies
Jagjivan Ram	Labour
Sardar Baldev Singh	Defence
CH Bhabha	Works, Mines & Power
Liaquat Ali Khan	Finance
Abdur Rab Nishtar	Posts and Air
Asaf Ali	Railways & Transport
C Rajagopalachari	Education and Arts
Ibrahim Ismail Chundrigar	Commerce
Ghaznafar Ali Khan	Health
Joginder Nath Mandal	Law

Evolution of States and Union Territories

- In 1956, there were fourteen States and six Union Territories.
- In 1953, Andhra Pradesh and in 1956 Kerala was created.
- In 1956, Karnataka was created.
- In 1960, Bombay was bifurcated into Gujarat and Maharashtra.
- In 1963, Nagaland was created as separate state.
- In 1966, Haryana was created out of Punjab and Chandigarh became a Union Territory.
- In 1970, the Union Territory of Himachal Pradesh was elevated to the status of state.
- In 1971, Manipur, Tripura and Meghalaya were granted statehood.
- In 1974, Sikkim became an associate state of the Indian Union. By the 36th Constitutional Amendment Act (1975), Sikkim became a full fledged state of the Indian Union.

Practice Exercise

1. Which of the following act established the Supreme Court at Calcutta?
(a) Regulating Act, 1773
(b) Pitt's India Act, 1784
(c) Government of India Act, 1858
(d) Charter Act, 1833

2. Which of the following was first Governor-General of Bengal?
(a) Lord Canning
(b) Lord Warren Hastings
(c) Lord Dalhousie
(d) Lord William Bentinck

3. Which of the following act completely distinguished the commercial and political function of the company?
(a) Charter Act, 1853
(b) Pitt's India Act, 1784
(c) Charter Act, 1833
(d) Regulating Act, 1773

4. By which of the following act, the Indian (Central) Legislative Council was set-up?
(a) Charter Act, 1853
(b) Charter Act, 1833
(c) Charter Act, 1856
(d) Indian Council Act, 1861

5. For the first time, British Parliament enacted which law for the British Government to Government of India?
(a) Government of India Act, 1857
(b) Government of India Act, 1858
(c) Government of India Act, 1891
(d) Government of India Act, 1935

6. Which of the following became the first Viceroy of India by Government of India Act, 1858?
(a) Lord William Bentinck
(b) Lord Wellesley
(c) Lord Canning
(d) Lord Chelmsford

7. During the British period under which act direct election was introduced in India?
(a) Indian Council Act, 1909
(b) Government of India Act, 1919
(c) Charter Act, 1853
(d) Indian Council Act, 1861

8. Which of the following act, provided for the establishment of Public Service Commission first time?
(a) Government of India Act, 1919
(b) Charter Act, 1892
(c) Government of India Act, 1935
(d) Indian Council Act, 1861

9. Under the Government of India Act, 1935, which communities were provided separate representation in the electorate system?
(a) Sikh, Europeans (b) Indian Christians
(c) Anglo-Indians (d) All of the above

10. Under which Government of India Act, Federation and Provincial Autonomy were introduced in India?
(a) Government of India Act, 1935
(b) Government of India Act, 1909
(c) Government of India Act, 1919
(d) Government of India Act, 1937

11. Under the Government of India Act, 1935, the Indian Federation worked through which kind of list?
(a) Federal list (b) Provincial list
(c) Concurrent list (d) All of the above

12. Which act provided for the establishment of not only a Federal Public Service Commission but also a Provincial Public Service Commission and Joint Public Service Commission?
(a) Indian Independence Act, 1947
(b) Indian Councils Act, 1909
(c) Indian Councils Act, 1919
(d) Government of India Act, 1935

13. Who of the following was the first Governor-General of new Dominion of India?
(a) Lord Mountbatten
(b) Warren Hastings
(c) Chakrawarti Rajagopalachari
(d) Lord Macauley

14. The 1946, Constituent Assembly became the Parliament of which of the following?
(a) Pakistan (b) India
(c) Both 'a' and 'b' (d) None of these

15. Who one of the following put forward the idea of Constituent Assembly for India?
(a) Jawaharlal Nehru (b) MN Roy
(c) Mahatma Gandhi (d) C Rajagopalachari

16. Which of the following is not a member of Cabinet Mission?
(a) Lord Clement (b) Lord P Lawrence
(c) Sir Cripps (d) AV Alexander

17. When did the Constituent Assembly pass a resolution for translation of the Constitution of India into Hindi and other many languages of India?
(a) 17th September, 1949
(b) 17th October, 1949
(c) 17th November, 1949
(d) 17th December, 1949

18. When was the last session of the Constituent Assembly held?
(a) 24th January, 1950 (b) 24th February, 1950
(c) 24th April, 1950 (d) 24th December, 1950

19. For how long did the Constituent Assembly work on the Constitution of India?
(a) 2 years, 11 months and 18 days
(b) 3 years, 12 months and 16 days
(c) 4 years, 18 months and 6 days
(d) None of the above

20. In the final form of the Constitution adopted by the Constituent Assembly how many Articles and Schedules were there?
(a) 397 Articles and 9 Schedules
(b) 395 Articles and 4 Schedules
(c) 396 Articles and 7 Schedules
(d) 395 Articles and 8 Schedules

21. Who presented the objective resolution in the Constituent Assembly?
(a) Jawaharlal Nehru (b) Mahatma Gandhi
(c) MN Roy (d) C Rajagopalachari

Directions (Q. Nos 22-24) *In the questions given below are two statements labelled as Assertion (A) and Reason (R). In the context of the two statements, which of the following is correct?*

Codes
(a) Both (A) and (R) are true and (R) is the correct explanation of (A)
(b) Both (A) and (R) are true, but (R) is not the correct explanation of (A)
(c) (A) is true, but (R) is false
(d) (A) is false, but (R) is true

22. **Assertion** (A) The Government of India Act, 1919 was passed by British Parliament to introduce Dyarchy in provincial government.
Reason (R) Montague-Chelmsford Reform has recommended the introduction of Dyarchy in the provincial government.

23. **Assertion** (A) The Government of India Act, 1935 and the Constitution of India both are lengthy documents.
Reason (R) The Government of India Act, 1935 was taken as a model and substantially incorporated in the Constitution of India.

24. **Assertion** (A) The Government of India Act, 1858 transferred the Governance of India from the East India Company to the Crown.
Reason (R) The East India Company was unwilling to administer India any more.

25. When did Constituent Assembly adopt a National Flag?
(a) 22nd August, 1947
(b) 22nd July, 1947
(c) 22nd January, 1947
(d) 22nd October, 1947

26. Morley-Minto Reform was associated with which of the following act?
(a) Government of India Act, 1858
(b) Indian Council Act, 1861
(c) Indian Council Act, 1919
(d) Indian Council Act, 1909

27. Who was the last British Governor-General, who addressed the Constituent Assembly?

(a) Lord Attlee (b) Lord Mountbatten
(c) Lord Bentinck (d) None of the above

28. Which of the following act empowered the Constituent Assemblies of both the dominions to legislate for their respective territories?

(a) Government of India Act, 1947
(b) Government of India Act, 1935
(c) Indian Independence Act, 1947
(d) Cabinet Mission, 1946

29. Which of the following act gave the recognition to the portfolio system?

(a) Charter Act, 1853
(b) Charter Act, 1858
(c) Indian Council Act, 1861
(d) Indian Council Act, 1892

30. From the Constitution of which country, the procedure for amendment of the Constitution has been borrowed by India?

(a) Constitution of France
(b) Constitution of United Stares
(c) Constitution of Germany
(d) Constitution of South Africa

Previous Year's Question

31. Which of the following acts formally introduced the principle of elections for the first time? **[CLAT 2015]**

(a) Indian Councils Act, 1909
(b) Govenment of India Act, 1919
(c) Government of India Act, 1935
(d) India's Independence Act, 1947

Answers

1	*a*	2	*b*	3	*b*	4	*a*	5	*b*	6	*c*	7	*b*	8	*a*	9	*d*	10	*a*
11	*d*	12	*d*	13	*a*	14	*b*	15	*b*	16	*a*	17	*a*	18	*a*	19	*a*	20	*d*
21	*d*	22	*a*	23	*a*	24	*c*	25	*b*	26	*d*	27	*b*	28	*c*	29	*c*	30	*d*
31	*a*																		

CHAPTER 02

FEATURES OF THE INDIAN CONSTITUTION

The Constitution of India is the supreme law of India. Though it borrowed from many Constitution of the world, the Constitution of India has several salient features that distinguish it from the constitutions of other countries.

SALIENT FEATURES OF THE CONSTITUTION

The salient features of the Constitution, as it stands today, are as follows

1. **Written Constitution** In a federation, there should be a written Constitution. The written Constitution is very essential for a federal so that whenever there is any dispute between the federal government and the federating units, it can be used as an evidence.
2. **Largest Constitution** In sheer physical terms, our Constitution is definitely the largest, bulkiest and most detailed Constitution in the world. As originally passed, it contained 395 Articles and 8 Schedules. Presently, it consists of a Preamble, about 395 Articles (divided into 22 Parts) and 12 Schedules.
3. **Sovereign, Democratic and Republic** A sovereign nation is initially supreme and independent of any outside control. The word 'socialist' aims at the establishment of an egalitarian society in India. The term 'secular' means a state which has no official religion.

4. **Parliamentary Type of Government** In a parliamentary type of government, the head of the state is nominal, whereas the Prime Minister who is the leader of the majority in the Parliament is the real executive. The Indian Constitution establishes in India a parliamentary type of government on the British model.
5. **Partly Rigid and Partly Flexible** There are certain provisions which can be amended by a simple majority in the Parliament. While there are certain provisions whose amendment requires, not only a special majority in Parliament, but also ratification by atleast one-half of the State Legislature.
6. **Fundamental Rights** Under Indian Constitution as originally enacted, the citizen of India had been granted the seven Fundamental Rights (currently six). These rights are mentioned in Part III of the Constitution and are justiciable. Fundamental Rights are the claim of citizen against the state.
7. **Fundamental Duties** The 42nd Constitutional Amendment added a new part to the Constitution i.e. under the heading Fundamental Duties lays down a code of ten currently (eleven) duties for all the citizens of India.
8. **Directive Principles of State Policy** The Directive Principle of State Policy concept has been borrowed from the Constitution of Ireland. These principles are contained in Part IV of our Constitution. The aim of these principles is to establish a welfare state in India on the socialistic pattern of society.
9. **Independent Judiciary** The Indian Constitution provides for an independent judiciary. The Constitution made the Supreme Court as the custodian and protector of the Constitution. The judgements of the Supreme Court are legally binding and there is no appeal against the judgement of the Supreme Court.
10. **A Secular State** Under the 42nd Constitutional Amendment, the word 'Secular' has been included in the Preamble of the Constitution. Thus, India has been now officially become a secular state.
11. **Single Citizenship** The Constitution of India grants one citizenship to all citizens. In a federation, sometimes a citizen gets double citizenship, one for the Union and the other for the State in which a person lives.
12. **Universal Adult Franchise** The Indian Constitution originally granted universal adult franchise to all those men and women, who attained the age of 21 years. Under the 61st Constitutional Amendment, the age of voting has been reduced from 21 to 18 years.
13. **Official Language of India** A provision was made in our Constitution to declare Hindi in the Devanagiri script as the official language of India (Article 343). Till that time English was to continue as the official language.

Parts of Indian Constitution

Part - I (Articles 1-4)	• Deals with territory of India, formation of new states, alterations, names of existing states.
Part - II (Articles 5-11)	• Deals with the citizenship.
Part - III (Articles 12-35)	• Deals with Fundamental Rights of Indian citizens. (Article 31 - dealing with the Right to Property was deleted by 44th Amendment).

Part - IV (Articles 36-51)	• Deals with Directive Principles of State Policy.
Part - IV A (Article 51A)	• Added by 42nd Amendment in 1976. Contains the Fundamental Duties of the citizens.
Part - V (Articles 52-151)	• Deals with Government at the Union Level.
Part - VI (Articles 152-237)	• Deals with Government at the State Level.
Part - VII (Articles 238)	• Deals with states, was replaced in 1956 by the 7th Amendment.
Part - VIII (Articles 239-242)	• Deals with Union Territories.
Part-IX (Articles 243 -243 O)	• Added by 73rd Amendment in 1992. Contains a new 'Schedule Eleven'. It contains 29 subjects related to Panchayati Raj. (They have been given administrative powers).
Part - IX A (Articles 243B -243-ZG)	• Added by 74th Amendment in 1992. Contains a new 'Schedule Twelve'. It contains 18 subjects related to Municipalities. (They have been give administrative powers).
Part - IX B (Articles 243 ZH -243 ZG)	• Deals with the cooperative societies added by 97th Constitutional Amendment Act.
Part - X (Articles 244, 244 A)	• Deals with Scheduled and Tribal Areas.
Part - XI (Articles 245 -263)	• Deals with relation between Union and States.
Part - XII (Articles 264 - 300A)	• Deals with distribution of revenue between Union and States, appointment of Finance Commission (Article 280), contracts, liabilities etc.
Part - XIII (Articles 301-307)	• Relates to trade, commerce and intercourse within the Territory of India.
Part - XIV (Articles 308-323)	• Deals with UPSC and Public Service Commissions.
Part - XIV A (Articles 323A-323 B)	• Deals with tribunals added by 42nd Constitutional Amendment, 1976.
Part - XV (Articles 324-329 A)	• Deals with elections (also Election Commission)
Part - XVI (Articles 330-342)	• Deals with special provisions for Scheduled Castes and Scheduled Tribes and Anglo - Indian Representatives.
Part - XVII (Articles 343-351)	• Relates to official language.
Part -XVIII (Articles 352-360)	• Deals with emergency provisions.
Part - XIX (Articles 361-367)	• Exemption of criminal proceedings for their official acts as President and Governors.
Part - XX (Articles 368)	• Deals with Amendment of Constitution.
Part - XXI (Articles 369-392)	• (Article-369 gives temporary powers to the Parliament to make laws for State list). (Article 370 contains temporary provisions of Jammu and Kashmir restricts the Parliament to make laws for that state).
Part - XXII (Articles 393 - 395)	• Concerns the short title, commencement and repeal of the Constitution.

→ Till November 2016, total article is 449 and all the newly added articles are in between Articles 1 to 395. Total parts are 25, but the newly added parts are in between Parts 1 to 22. e.g. Part IX A and Part XIV A.

Schedules of Indian Constitution

First Schedule	• List of States and Union Territories.
Second Schedule	• Salary of President, Governors, Chief Judges, Judges of High Court and Supreme Court, Comptroller and Auditor General.
Third Schedule	• Forms of oaths and affirmations.
Fourth Schedule	• Allocate seats for each State and Union Territories of India in Rajya Sabha.
Fifth Schedule	• Administration and control of Scheduled Areas and Tribes.
Sixth Schedule	• Provisions for administration of tribal area in Asom, Meghalaya, Tripura, Mizoram and Arunachal Pradesh.
Seventh Schedule	• Gives allocation of powers and functions between Union and States. *It contains three lists* 1. Union List (for Central Government) 100 subjects. 2. State List (powers of State Government) 61 subjects. 3. Concurrent List (both Union and States) 52 subjects.
Eighth Schedule	*List of 22 languages of India recognised by Constitution* 1. Assamese 2. Bengali 3. Gujarati 4. Hindi 5. Kannada 6. Kashmiri 7. Manipuri 8. Malayalam 9. Konkani 10. Marathi 11. Nepali 12. Oriya 13. Punjabi 14. Sanskrit 15. Sindhi 16. Tamil 17. Telugu 18. Urdu 19. Santhali 20. Bodo 21. Maithili 22. Dogri • Sindhi was added in 1967 by 21st Constitutional Amendment. • Konkani, Manipuri and Nepali were added in 1992 by 71st Constitutional Amendment and Santhali, Maithili, Bodo and Dogri were added in 2003 by 92nd Constitutional Amendment.
Ninth Schedule	• Added by 1st Amendment in 1951. Contains acts and orders related to land tenure, land tax, railway, industries.(Right of Property not a Fundamental Right now).
Tenth Schedule	• Added by 52nd Constitutional Amendment in 1985. Contains provisions of disqualification on grounds of defection.
Eleventh Schedule	• Specifies the powers, authority and responsibilities of Panchayats. This schedule was added by the 73rd Constitutional Amendment Act, 1992.
Twelfth Schedule	• By 74th Constitutional Amendment in 1992 contains provisions of Municipal Corporation.

Borrowed Features of the Indian Constitution

From UK	Nominal Head - President (like Queen) • Cabinet System of Ministers • Post of Prime Minister • Parliamentary Type of Government • Bicameral Parliament • Lower House more powerful • Council of Ministers responsible to Lower House • Speaker in Lok Sabha

From US	• Written Constitution • Executive head of state known as President and he is being the Supreme Commander of the Armed Forces • Vice- President as the ex-officio Chairman of Rajya Sabha • Fundamental Rights • Supreme Court • Provision of States • Independence of Judiciary and Judicial review • Preamble • Removal of Supreme Court and High Court Judges
From USSR	• Fundamental Duties • Five Year Plan
From Australia	• Concurrent List • Language of the Preamble • Provision regarding trade, commerce and intercourse
From Japan	• Procedure established by law
From Weimar Constitution of Germany	• Suspension of Fundamental Rights during the emergency
From Canada	• Scheme of federation with a strong centre • Distribution of powers between centre and the states and placing Residuary powers with the centre
From Ireland	• Concept of Directive Principles of States Policy (Ireland borrowed it from Spain) • Method of election of President • Nomination of members in the Rajya Sabha by the President
From France	• Republic and the ideals of liberty, equality and fraternity in the preamble.
Government of India Act, 1935	• Federal Scheme, Office of Governor, Judiciary Public Service Commissions, Emergency provisions and administrative details
From South Africa	• Procedure for Amendment of the Constitution and election of members of Rajya Sabha.

PREAMBLE OF THE CONSTITUTION

The Preamble of the Indian Constitution is fully inspired by Objective Resolution, which is drafted and moved by Pandit Jawaharlal Nehru, and adopted by the Constituent Assembly. It has been amended by the **42nd Constitutional Amendment Act, 1976**, which added three new words namely; Socialist, Secular and Integrity.

The Preamble of Indian Constitution reflects the basic structure and the spirit of the Constitution. The Preamble acts as the preface of the Constitution of India and lays down the fundamental value and philosophical ideas.

It contains the basic features of the Constitution and thus, considered to be a vital part.

PREAMBLE

"WE, THE PEOPLE OF INDIA, having solemnly resolved to constitute India into a SOVEREIGN, SOCIALIST, SECULAR, DEMOCRATIC, REPUBLIC and to secure all its citizens."

Justice, Social, Economic and Political.

Liberty of thought, expression, belief, faith and worship.

Equality of status and of opportunity to promote among them all.

Fraternity assuring the dignity of the individual and unity and integrity of the nation.

In our Constituent Assembly, this 26th of November, 1949, **do hereby adopt, "enact and give to ourselves this Constitution".**

The Preamble keeps an important place in the Constitution of India because it highlights the type of society and government.

However, the Preamble does not contain laws enforceable in a court but, no law can be enacted or amended in a manner that violates the spirit of the Preamble. Thus, the Preamble of the Constitution of India is unamendable or unalterable.

Idea of Preamble borrowed from Constitution of US and the Preamble is not justifiable.

Important Words in the Preamble

The Preamble contains the words such as Sovereign, Socialist, Secular, Democratic, Republic, Justice, Liberty, Equality and Fraternity are the important for the society as well as for the well development of the nation. *These words are explained as follows*

1. Sovereign

The word 'sovereign' says that India is neither a dependency nor a dominion of any other nation, but an independent state. There is no authority above it and it is free to conduct its both internal and external affairs.

2. Socialist

The word 'socialist' has been added by the 42nd Constitutional Amendment, 1976 to the Preamble. The Constitution has a socialist content in the form of certain Directive Principles of State Policy. Notably, the Indian brand of socialism is a democratic socialism and not a communistic socialism (also known as state socialism).

3. Secular

The term 'secular' was also added by the 42nd Constitutional Amendment, 1976. The Indian Constitution embodies the positive concept of secularism i.e. all religions in our country (irrespective of their strength) have the same status and support from the state.

4. Democratic

The word 'democratic' in the Preamble is based on the doctrine of popular sovereignty i.e. possession of supreme power by the people. The Constitution of India adopted representative democracy under which the executive is responsible to the legislature for all its policies and actions.

The term 'democratic' is used in the Preamble in the broader sense embracing not only political democracy but also social and economic democracy.

5. Republic

The word 'republic' in our Preamble indicates that India has an elected (indirect election) head called the President. *A republic also means two more things, which are as follows*

(i) Vesting of political sovereignty in the people and not in a single individual like a king.

(ii) The absence of any privileged class and hence all public offices being opened to every citizen without any discrimination.

6. Justice

The word 'Justice' in the Preamble has been taken from the Russian Revolution (1917), that embraces three distinct forms namely; social, economic and political which are secured through various provisions of Fundamental Rights and Directive Principles.

7. Liberty

The word 'liberty' means the absence of restraints on the activities of individuals and at the same time, providing opportunities for the development of individual personalities.

8. Equality

The word 'equality' implies that there are no any special privileges to any section of the society and the provision of adequate opportunities for all individuals without any discrimination.

The Preamble secures to all citizens of India equality of status and opportunity. This provision embraces three dimensions of equality namely; civil, political and economic. Parts III, IV and XV of the Constitution secure all three dimensions of the equality.

9. Fraternity

The word *fraternity* means a sense of brotherhood is promoted by the Constitution with the feeling of fraternity by the system of single citizenship. The term 'fraternity' implies in the Fundamental Duties (Article 51-A).

The Preamble declares that fraternity has to assure two things namely

(i) **The Dignity of the Individual** It signifies that the Constitution not only ensures material betterment and maintains a democratic set-up, but it also recognises that, the personality of every individual is sacred.

(ii) **The Unity and Integrity of the Nation** It embraces both the psychological and territorial dimensions of national integration (the word 'integrity' has been added to the Preamble by the 42nd Constitutional Amendment, 1976). Article 1 of the Constitution describes India as a 'Union of States' to make it clear that the states have no right to secede from the Union, implying the indestructible nature of the Indian Union.

It aims at overcoming hindrances to national integration like communalism, regionalism, casteism, linguism and secessionism.

Practice Exercise

1. How many Articles consists presently in the Indian Constitution?
(a) 448 Articles
(b) 395 Articles
(c) 750 Articles
(d) 495 Articles

2. Which one of the following is a basic feature of the Presidential Government?
(a) Rigid Constitution
(b) Single Executive
(c) Supremacy of the Legislature
(d) Residual Powers of the States

3. The most essential feature of the parliamentary form of the government is
(a) Sovereignty of the Parliament
(b) Written Constitution
(c) Accountability of the executive to the Legislature
(d) Independent Judiciary

4. The cardinal features of the political system in India are

I. It is a democratic republic.
II. It has a parliamentary form of government.
III. The Supreme power vests in the people of India.

Select the correct answer using the codes given below.

(a) Only I (b) I and III
(c) I and II (d) All of these

5. Which of the following consisting in Part IV A of the Constitution?

(a) Fundamental Rights (b) Fundamental Duties
(c) Directive Principles (d) The Executive

6. How many are schedules are there in our Indian Constitution?

(a) 80 Schedules (b) 15 Schedules
(c) 12 Schedules (d) 9 Schedules

7. The 97th Constitutional Amendment Act, 2011 added a new part to the Constitution. Which of the following is that part?

(a) Part XII (b) Part IX A
(c) Part IX B (d) Part XI A

8. How many contents are there in Panchayati Raj System?

(a) 18 subjects (b) 21 subjects
(c) 29 subjects (d) 23 subjects

9. Power, authority and responsibility of Municipalities are listed in which one of the following Schedule of the Constitution?

(a) Ninth (b) Tenth
(c) Eleventh (d) Twelfth

10. Schedule Ninth of the Indian Constitution deals with

(a) subjects contained in the Union List, State List and Concurrent List
(b) the recognition of languages
(c) certain acts and regulations of State Legislatures dealing with land reforms and abolition of Zamindari System
(d) the territories of States and Union Territories

11. The Concept of Judicial Review is our Constitution has taken from

(a) Britain (b) USA (c) Canada (d) Australia

12. The idea of including the emergency provisions in the Constitution of India has been borrowed from the

(a) Constitution of Canada
(b) Weimar Constitution of Germany
(c) Constitution of Ireland
(d) Constitution of USA

13. Which of the following was the biggest source for the Constitution of India?

(a) The Government of India Act, 1919
(b) The Government of India Act, 1935
(c) The Indian Independence Act, 1947
(d) None of the above

14. Which of the following Article requires ratification by the legislatures of one-half of the states?

(a) Article 54 (b) Article 84
(c) Article 51 (d) Article 173

15. At the time of enactment of the Constitution, which one of the following ideals was not included in the Preamble?

(a) Liberty
(b) Equality
(c) Socialist
(d) Justice

16. Which Amendment Act introduced changes in the Preamble to the Indian Constitution?

(a) 38th Constitutional Amendment Act, 1975
(b) 40th Constitutional Amendment Act, 1976
(c) 42nd Constitutional Amendment Act, 1976
(d) 44th Constitutional Amendment Act, 1978

17. Which among the following is the correct expression of the term secular in India?

(a) India has many religions
(b) Indians have religious freedom
(c) To follow the religion depends upon the will of an individual
(d) There is no religion of the state in India

18. Which one of the following describe India a Secular State?

(a) Fundamental Rights
(b) Preamble of the Constitution
(c) Ninth Schedule
(d) Directive Principles

19. Consider the following words

I. Socialist II. Democratic
III. Sovereign IV. Secular

Choose the response that gives the correct sequence in the Preamble.

(a) III, I, IV and II
(b) III, IV, I and II
(c) III, IV, II and I
(d) IV, I, III and II

20. Supreme Court of India propounded sequence basic doctrine in which of the following case?
(a) Golaknath Case
(b) Kesavananda Bharati Case
(c) Maneka Gandhi Case
(d) Gopalan Case

Directions (Q. Nos. 21-24) *In the questions given below are two statements labelled as Assertion (A) and Reason (R). In the context of the two statements, which of the following is correct?*

Codes
(a) Both (A) and (R) are true and (R) is the correct explanation of (A)
(b) Both (A) and (R) are true, but (R) is not the correct explanation of (A)
(c) (A) is true, but (R) is false
(d) (A) is false, but (R) is true

21. Assertion (A) If the Constitution is flexible, it may be playing at the whims and caprices of the ruling party.
Reason (R) The framers of the Indian Constitution were keen to avoid excessive rigidity.

22. Assertion (A) Indian Constitution is quasi federal.
Reason (R) Indian Constitution is neither federal nor unitary.

23. Assertion (A) The basic features of the Constitution cannot be amended by exercising the power of Amendment under Article 368.
Reason (R) Though Fundamental Rights, as such are not immune from Amendment enbloc, particular rights or parts there of may be held as basic feature.

24. Assertion (A) The framers of the Indian Constitution were keen to preserve the democratic value to which Indians had attached the highest importance in their struggle for freedom.
Reason (R) The Constitution describes India as a Union of States, thereby implying the indestructible natural of its unity.

25. The basic features of the Indian Constitution which are not amendable under Article 368 are
(a) sovereignty, territorial integrity, federal system and judicial review
(b) sovereignty, territorial integrity and parliamentary system of government
(c) judicial review and the federal system
(d) sovereignty, territorial integrity, federal system, judicial review and parliamentary form of government

26. By which of the following amendment the voting age has been reduced from 21 to 18 years?
(a) 42nd Constitutional Amendment
(b) 61st Constitutional Amendment
(c) 63rd Constitutional Amendment
(d) 44th Constitutional Amendment

27. Which of the following amendment added Tenth Schedule to the Constitution?
(a) 51st Amendment (b) 52nd Amendment
(c) 94th Amendment (d) 72nd Amendment

28. Which of the following Article deals with the Finance Commission?
(a) Article 281 (b) Article 280
(c) Article 301 (d) Article 281

29. The Constitutional Amendment with 2/3rd majority in Parliament and election of the members of Rajya Sabha on the basis of proportional representation has been derived from
(a) South Africa (b) Britain
(c) Canada (d) Germany

30. Justice social, economic and political is ....
(a) A Directive Principle of states policy taken into account while making law
(b) An ideal enshrined in the Preamble to the Constitution of India
(c) Guaranteed by Fundamental Rights in the Constitution of India
(d) Guaranteed by Supreme Court though its writ jurisdiction

31. Which of the following amendments, amended the preamble to the constitution of India 1950?
(a) 42nd Amendment (b) 43rd Amendment
(c) 44th Amendment (d) 24th Amendment

32. How many language are there in the English Schedule of the Constitution of India?

(a) 17 (b) 18 (c) 20 (d) 22

33. In United States, the residuary power lies with ....

(a) States
(b) Federal Government
(c) States and federal government depending upon the subject matter as the Constitution did not define it in clear and cogent terms
(d) Local Government

Previous Years' Questions

34. Identify the correct statement. [CLAT 2012]

(a) Federalism implies a system of Government which embodies a division of powers between a central and a number of regional authorities
(b) Federalism implies a system of government which embodies a division of powers between Legislature, Executive and Judiciary
(c) Federalism implies a system of Government which embodies Parliamentary supremacy
(d) None of the above

35. The following are enshrined in the Preamble of the Constitution of India.

I. Equality of status and of opportunity.
II. Liberty of thought, expression, belief, faith and worship.
III. Justice-social, economic and political.
IV. Fraternity assuring the dignity of the individual.
V. Unity and integrity of the nation.

Which of the following is the correct order in which they appear in the Preamble? [CLAT 2012]

(a) V, I, II, IV, III (b) III, II, I, IV, V
(c) III, I, II, V, IV (d) I, II, IV, III, V

36. Match schedule one and two and choose the appropriate answer [CLAT 2012]

Schedule I	Schedule II
A. Concurrent list	1. Constitution of Japan
B. Rule of Law	2. Constitution of Ireland
C. Directive Principle of State Policy	3. British Constitution
D. Procedure Established by Law	4. Constitution of Australia

Codes

	A	B	C	D
(a)	1	2	3	4
(b)	2	4	3	1
(c)	1	3	4	2
(d)	4	3	2	1

37. Affirmative action cannotes [CLAT 2012]

I. measures taken by the state to help the socially disadvantaged groups.
II. positive discrimination.
III. Strict quotas for the socially and educationally backward class in school/college admissions and jobs.

Which of the above mentioned is true?

(a) I and II
(b) Only II
(c) All of the above
(d) II and III

38. **Assertion** (A) All minorities, whether based on religion or language, shall have the right to establish and administer educational institution of their choice.

Reason (R) Institutions established by the minorities are not entitled to governmental aid and government is not under an obligation to give aid. [CLAT 2012]

Codes

(a) Both (A) and (R) are true and (R) is the correct explanation of (A)
(b) Both (A) and (R) are true, but (R) is not the correct explanation of (A)
(c) (A) is true, but (R) is false
(d) (A) is false, but (R) is true

39. The Constitution (One Hundred Seventeenth Amendment) Bill, 2012 makes provisions regarding [CLAT 2013]

(a) reservation in matters of promotions for Scheduled Castes and Scheduled Tribes
(b) reservation in matters of appointments for Scheduled Castes and Scheduled Tribes
(c) reservation in matters of appointments and promotions for Scheduled Castes and Scheduled Tribes
(d) None of the above

40. **Assertion** (A) All minorities, whether based on religion or language, shall have the right to establish or administer educational institutions of their choice.

Reason (R) Institutions established by the minorities are not entitled to governmental aid and government is not under an obligation to give aid. **[CLAT 2015]**

Codes

(a) Both (A) and (R) are true and (R) is the correct explanation of (A)
(b) Both (A) and (R) are true, but (R) is not the correct explanation of (A)
(c) (A) is true, but (R) is false
(d) (A) is false, but (R) is true

41. Which of the following statements is correct? **[CLAT 2015]**

(a) Federalism implies a system of government which embodies a division of powers between a central and a number of regional authorities
(b) Federalism implies a system of government which embodies a division of powers between Legislature, Executive and Judiciary
(c) Federalism implies a system of government which embodies parliamentary supremacy
(d) None of the above

42. Who was the Constitutional Advisor to the Constituent Assembly in framing the Indian Constitution? **[CLAT 2016]**

(a) Dr BR Ambedkar
(b) BN Rau
(c) Dr Rajendra Prasad
(d) Pandit Jawaharlal Nehru

43. Which among the following was described by Dr BR Ambedkar as the 'Heart and Soul of the Constitution of India'? **[CLAT 2016]**

(a) Right to Move Throughout the Territory of India
(b) Right to Constitutional Remedies
(c) Right to Equality
(d) Freedom of Religion

44. Under the Constitution of India, the official language of the Union is **[CLAT 2016]**

(a) Hindi in Devanagari script
(b) Hindi
(c) English
(d) English and Hindi

Answers

1	*b*	2	*b*	3	*a*	4	*d*	5	*b*	6	*c*	7	*c*	8	*c*	9	*d*	10	*c*
11	*b*	12	*c*	13	*b*	14	*a*	15	*c*	16	*c*	17	*d*	18	*b*	19	*a*	20	*b*
21	*b*	22	*c*	23	*a*	24	*b*	25	*d*	26	*b*	27	*b*	28	*b*	29	*a*	30	*b*
31	*a*	32	*d*	33	*a*	34	*a*	35	*b*	36	*d*	37	*c*	38	*c*	39	*a*	40	*c*
41	*a*	42	*b*	43	*b*	44	*d*												

CHAPTER 03

UNION AND ITS TERRITORY

A Union Territory is a type of administrative division in the Republic of India. Part I of Indian Constitution is titled as 'the Union and its Territory'. It includes Articles from 1-4, Part I which is a compilation of laws pertaining to the Constitution of India as a country and the Union of States that it is a made of.

India, i.e., Bharat is a 'Union of States' rather than a 'Federation of States' (Article 1). This provision deals with two things namely; the name of the country and the type of polity. Articles 1 to 4 under Part I of the Constitution of India deal with the union and its territory.

Articles Related to Union and its Territory

Article No.	Subject Matter
1	Name and territory of the union.
2	Admission or establishment of new states.
2A	Sikkim to be associated with the union (Repealed).
3	Formation of new states and alteration of areas, boundaries or names of existing states.
4	Laws of made under Articles 2 and 3 to provide for the Amendment of the First and the Fourth Schedules and supplemental, incidental and consequential matters.

EVOLUTION OF STATES AND UNION TERRITORIES

At the time of independence, India comprised two categories of political units, namely, the British Provinces (under the direct rule of British Government) and the Princely States (under the rule of native princes, but subject to the paramountcy of the British Crown).

The Indian Independence Act, 1947 created two independent and separate dominions of India and Pakistan and gave three options to the Princely States either join India or join Pakistan or remaining independent.

However, all the Princely States situated within the geographical boundaries of India joined India through integration or instrument of accession.

- In 1950, the Constitution contained a four-fold classification of the states of the Indian Union, i.e. Part A, Part B, Part C and Part D State (in all their numbers are 29).
- The integration of Princely States with the rest of India has purely an ad hoc arrangement. There has been a demand from different regions, particularly South India, for reorganisation of states on linguistic basis. Thus, Government of India has appointed committees and commissions to resolve the issues.

The important commissions and committees are as follows

1. Dhar Commission

In June 1948, the Government of India appointed the Linguistic Provinces Commission under the Chairmanship of SK Dhar to examine the feasibility of reorganisation on linguistic line. The Commission submitted its report in December 1948 and recommended the reorganisation of states on the basis of administrative convenience rather than linguistic factor.

2. JVP Committee

The recommendation of Dhar Commission created much resentment and led to the appointment of another Linguistic Provinces Committee by the Congress in December 1948. It consisted of Jawaharlal Nehru, Vallabhbhai Patel and Pattabhi Sitaramayya (popularly known as **JVP Committee**). It submitted its report in April 1949 and formally rejected language as the basis for reorganisation of states.

However, in October 1953, the Government of India was forced to create the first linguistic state, known as Andhra state, by separating the Telugu speaking areas from the Madras state. This followed a prolonged popular agitation and the death of Potti Sriramulu after a 56 days hunger strike for the cause.

3. Fazl Ali Commission

The creation of Andhra state intensified the demand from other regions for creation of states on linguistic basis. This forced the Government of India to appoint (in December 1953) a three-member States Reorganisation Commission under the Chairmanship of Fazl Ali.

The Commission had other two members named as KM Panikkar and HN Kunzru. It submitted its report in September 1955 and broadly accepted language as the basis of reorganisation of states. But it rejected the Theory of 'One Language One State'. On the recommendation of the Fazl Ali Commission, 14 States and 6 Union Territories were created on 1st November, 1956.

States and UTs of India in 1956

States

1. Andhra Pradesh, 2. Assam (Asom), 3. Bihar, 4. Bombay, 5. Jammu and Kashmir, 6. Kerala,
7. Madhya Pradesh, 8. Madras (Tamil Nadu),
9. Mysore (Karnataka), 10. Orissa (Odisha),
11. Punjab, 12. Rajasthan, 13. Uttar Pradesh and
14. West Bengal

Union Territories

1. Andaman and Nicobar Islands,
2. Delhi (now, NCT of Delhi),
3. Himachal Pradesh,
4. Laccadive, Minicoy and Amindivi Islands (now, Lakshadweep),
5. Manipur and
6. Tripura

New States and Union Territories Created After 1956

The demand for the creation of some more states on the basis of language or cultural homogeneity resulted in the bifurcation of existing states.
These states are as follows

1. **Maharashtra and Gujarat** In 1960, the bilingual State of Bombay was divided into two separate states namely Maharashtra for Marathi-speaking people and Gujarat for Gujarati-speaking people. Gujarat was established as the 15th State of the Indian Union.
2. **Dadra and Nagar Haveli** The Portuguese ruled this territory until its liberation in 1954. Subsequently, the administration was carried until 1961 by an administrator chosen by the people themselves. It was converted into a Union Territory of India by the 10th Constitutional Amendment Act, 1961.
3. **Goa, Daman and Diu** India acquired these three territories from the Portuguese by means of a police action in 1961. They were constituted as a Union Territory by the 12th Constitutional Amendment Act, 1962. Later, in 1987, Goa was conferred a statehood (25th State of Indian Union).
4. **Puducherry** The territory of Puducherry comprises the former French establishments in India known as Puducherry, Karaikal, Mahe and Yanam. The French handed over this territory to India in 1954. Later, it became a Union Territory by the 14th Constitutional Amendment Act, 1962 .
5. **Nagaland** In 1963, the State of Nagaland was formed by taking the Naga Hills and Tuensang area out of the State of Asom. This was done to satisfy the movement of the hostile Nagas. It became the 16th State of the Indian Union.
6. **Haryana, Chandigarh and Himachal Pradesh** In 1966, the State of Punjab was bifurcated to create Haryana, the 17th State of the Indian Union and the Union Territory of Chandigarh. This followed the demand for a separate 'Sikh Homeland' (Punjabi Subha) raised by the Akali Dal.

   Finally, on the recommendation of Shah Commission (1966) Punjabi-speaking areas were constituted into the unilingual state of Punjab, the Hindi-speaking areas were constituted into the State of Haryana and the hill areas were merged with the adjoining Union Territory of Himachal Pradesh. In 1971, the Union Territory of Himachal Pradesh was elevated to the status of a state (18th State of the Indian Union).

7. **Manipur, Tripura and Meghalaya** In 1972, the two Union Territories of Manipur and Tripura and the sub-State of Meghalaya got statehood of 19th, 20th and 21st respectively and the two Union Territories of Mizoram and Arunachal Pradesh came into being.
8. **Sikkim** Till 1947, Sikkim was an Indian Princely State ruled by Chogyal. After British, Sikkim became a 'protectorate' of India. But the 36th Constitutional Amendment Act (1975) was made Sikkim a full-fledged State of the Indian Union (the 22nd state).
9. **Mizoram, Arunachal Pradesh** In 1987, new States of Mizoram and Arunachal Pradesh came into being as the 23rd and 24th States of the Indian Union respectively.
10. **Chhattisgarh, Uttarakhand and Jharkhand** In 2000, three more new States of Chhattisgarh, Uttarakhand and Jharkhand were created out of the territories of Madhya Pradesh, Uttar Pradesh and Bihar respectively. These became the 26th, 27th and 28th States of the Indian Union respectively.
11. **Telangana** In 2014, the new State of Telangana came into existence as 29th State of Indian Union. It was carved out of the territories of Andhra Pradesh. Thus, the number of states and Union Territories increased from 14 and 6 in 1956 to 29 and 7 in 2014 respectively.

States and UTs of India in 2017

States

Andhra Pradesh, Arunachal Pradesh, Assam (Asom), Bihar, Chhattisgarh, Goa, Gujarat, Haryana, Himachal Pradesh, Jammu and Kashmir, Jharkhand, Karnataka, Kerala, Madhya Pradesh, Maharashtra, Manipur, Meghalaya, Mizoram, Nagaland, Orissa (Odisha), Punjab, Rajasthan, Sikkim, Tamil Nadu, Telangana, Tripura, Uttar Pradesh and West Bengal.

Union Territories

Andaman and Nicobar Islands, Chandigarh, Dadra and Nagar Haveli, Daman and Diu, Delhi (National Capital Territory), Lakshadweep and Puducherry.

Practice Exercise

1. Which of the following Article states that India as a Union of States rather than a Federation of States?

(a) Article 3 (b) Article 2
(c) Article 370 (d) Article 1

2. Which of the following Article states that Sikkim to be associated with the Union which is repealed?

(a) Article 2
(b) Article 2A
(c) Article 1
(d) Article 1A

3. In 1950, the Constitution of India contain how many classification of States of Indian Union?

(a) Three-fold classification
(b) Five-fold classification
(c) Four-fold classification
(d) Six-fold classification

4. Which of the following is not a member of JVP Committee?

(a) Jawaharlal Nehru
(b) Vallabhbhai Patel
(c) Potti Sriramulu
(d) Pattabhi Sitaramayya

5. Fazl Ali Commission was appointed by Government of India in which of the following year?

(a) 1953 (b) 1954
(c) 1955 (d) 1956

6. Which of the following is not a member of Fazl Ali Commission?

(a) KM Panikkar
(b) HN Kunzru
(c) Vallabhbhai Patel
(d) All of the above

7. On the recommendation of the Fazl Ali Commission, how many States and Union Territories were created on 1st November, 1956?

(a) 15 States and 7 Union Territories
(b) 14 States and 6 Union Territories
(c) 14 States and 7 Union Territories
(d) 15 States and 6 Union Territories

8. Which of the following became the 15th State of Indian Union?

(a) Maharashtra (b) Gujarat
(c) Madras (d) Mysore

9. Which of the following were constituted as a Union Territory by 12th Constitutional Amendment Act, 1962?

(a) Goa, Daman and Diu
(b) Dadra and Nagar Haveli
(c) Manipur, Arunachal Pradesh and Tripura
(d) Andaman and Nicobar Islands

10. Which of the following state was formed by taking the Naga Hills and Tuensang area out of the State of Asom?

(a) Meghalaya (b) Mizoram
(c) Nagaland (d) Manipur

11. Among the following states, which one was formed as a State of Indian Union at last?

(a) Andhra Pradesh (b) Gujarat
(c) Karnataka (d) Punjab

12. Which of the following became the 22nd State of Indian Union?

(a) Sikkim (b) Meghalaya
(c) Tripura (d) Manipur

13. Which of the following states became the 28th State of Union India?

(a) Odisha
(b) Jharkhand
(c) Uttarakhand
(d) Chhattisgarh

14. Which one of the following is the correct chronological order of the formation of the following states as full statehood?

(a) Nagaland - Haryana - Sikkim - Arunachal Pradesh
(b) Sikkim - Arunachal Pradesh - Nagaland - Haryana
(c) Haryana - Sikkim - Nagaland - Arunachal Pradesh
(d) Haryana - Nagaland - Sikkim - Arunachal Pradesh

15. Arrange the following Indian States in a chronological order, according to their formation?

I. Chhattisgarh II. Arunachal Pradesh
III. Jharkhand IV. Sikkim

Codes

(a) IV, I, III, II (b) IV, II, I, III
(c) III, II, I, IV (d) I, IV, II, III

16. The States of the Indian Union can be reorganised on their boundaries altered by

(a) an executive order of the Union Government with consent of the concerned State Government
(b) the Union Parliament by a simple majority in the ordinary process of legislation
(c) two - third majority of both the Houses of the Parliament
(d) two - third majority of both the Houses of the Parliament and the consent of the concerned State Legislature

17. What is the correct chronological order in which the following States of the Indian Union were created as granted full statehood?

I. Andhra Pradesh II. Maharashtra
III. Nagaland IV. Haryana

Codes

(a) I, II, III, IV (b) II, I, III, IV
(c) I, II, IV, III (d) II, I, IV, III

18. The creation of a new state in India from an existing state involves the consent of the

I. Supreme Court
II. Legislature of the state concerned
III. President
IV. Parliament

Select the correct answer using the codes given below

(a) I, II and III (b) II, III and IV
(c) I and IV (d) I, II, III and IV

19. The boundary of a state in India can be altered through the procedure laid down in the Article

(a) 368 (b) 130
(c) 3 (d) 4

Directions (Q. Nos. 20-23) *In the questions given below are two statements labelled as Assertion (A) and Reason (R). In the context of the two statements, which of the following is correct?*

Codes

(a) Both (A) and (R) are true and R is the correct explanation of (A)
(b) Both (A) and (R) are true, but (R) is not the correct explanation of (A)
(c) (A) is true, but (R) is false
(d) (A) is false, but (R) is true

20. Assertion (A) Through the 35th Constitutional Amendment Act, 1974 Government of India inserted a new Article 2A.
Reason (R) Sikkim expressed its desire for greater association with India and India conferring on Sikkim the status of an associate state.

21. Assertion (A) India and Bangladesh have a common land boundary of approximately 4096.7 km.
Reason (R) The 100th Constitutional Amendment Act provided the transfer of III enclaves to Bangladesh by India and Bangladesh transferred 51 enclaves to India.

22. Assertion (A) The first linguistic state known as Andhra State was formed by separating the Telugu speaking areas from the Madras State.
Reason (R) A prolonged agitation and death of Potti Sriramulu after a 56 days hunger strike for the cause.

23. Which of the following is the first state to have been formed on linguistic basis?

(a) Andhra Pradesh
(b) Gujarat
(c) Punjab
(d) Tamil Nadu

24. Which of the following Commission/Committee was first time set-up for reorganisation of the state on linguistic line?

(a) Dhar Commission
(b) Potti Sriramulu Committee
(c) JVP Committee
(d) Fazl Ali Commission

25. By which one of the following constitutional amendments Delhi has become National Capital Region (NCR)?

(a) 61st Constitutional Amendment
(b) 69th Constitutional Amendment
(c) 71st Constitutional Amendment
(d) 79th Constitutional Amendment

26. Which among the following state is a member of the Seven Sister?

(a) West Bengal (b) Tripura
(c) Odisha (d) Bihar

27. Which Commission made the recommendation which formed the basis for the Punjab Reorganisation Act, which created the States of Punjab and Haryana?

(a) Dhar Commission (b) Dass Commission
(c) Mahajan Commission (d) Shah Commission

28. The secession of a state from the Indian Union has been barred by the

(a) 16th Constitutional Amendment Act, 1963
(b) 22nd Constitutional Amendment Act, 1969
(c) 29th Constitutional Amendment Act, 1972
(d) 35th Constitutional Amendment Act, 1974

Privious Year's Question

29. The Constitution (100th Amendment) Act, 2015 was enacted to give effect to **[CLAT 2016]**

(a) National Judicial Appointment Commission
(b) transfer of certain territories by India to Bangladesh
(c) the acquiring of territories by India from Bangladesh
(d) the transfer of certain territories by India to Bangladesh and transfer of certain territories from Bangladesh to India

Answers

1	*d*	2	*b*	3	*c*	4	*c*	5	*a*	6	*c*	7	*b*	8	*b*	9	*a*	10	*c*
11	*c*	12	*a*	13	*b*	14	*a*	15	*b*	16	*b*	17	*a*	18	*b*	19	*c*	20	*a*
21	*b*	22	*a*	23	*a*	24	*a*	25	*b*	26	*b*	27	*d*	28	*a*	29	*d*		

CHAPTER 04

CITIZENSHIP

Citizenship is the status of a person recognised under the sovereign state or part of a nation.

Part II under Articles 5 to 11 of the Constitution of India deal with the Citizenship. It identifies the persons who became citizens of India after the commencement of the Constitution (i.e. on 26th January, 1950).

The Constitution empowers the Parliament to enact a law to provide for such matters like acquisition or loss and any other matter relating to citizenship. Accordingly, the Parliament has enacted the Citizenship Act, 1955, which has been amended in 1986, 1992, 2003, 2005 and 2015.

Articles Related to Citizenship at a Glance

Article No.	Subject-Matter
5	Citizenship at the commencement of the Constitution
6	Rights of citizenship of certain persons who have migrated to India from Pakistan
7	Rights of citizenship of certain migrants to Pakistan
8	Rights of citizenship of certain persons of Indian origin residing outside India
9	Persons voluntarily acquiring citizenship of a foreign state not to be citizens
10	Continuance of the rights of citizenship
11	Parliament to regulate the right of citizenship by law

CITIZENSHIP ACT, 1955

The Citizenship Act, 1955 provides for acquisition and loss of citizenship after the commencement of the Constitution. This act has been amended so far five times, i.e. 1955, 1992, 2003, 2005 and 2015.

Originally, the Citizenship Act (1955) also provided for the Commonwealth Citizenship. But, this provision was replaced by the Citizenship (Amendment) Act, 2003.

Acquisition of Citizenship

- A citizen is a person who enjoys full membership of the country in which he lives, Indian Constitution provides a single and uniform citizenship for the entire country.
- The Citizenship Act of 1955, prescribes five ways of acquiring citizenship *viz* birth descent, registration, naturalisation and incorporation of territory.

1. By Birth

- Every person born in India on or after 26th January, 1950, but before 1st July, 1987 is a citizen of India by birth irrespective of nationalities of his/her parents.
- A person born in India on or after 1st July, 1987 is citizen only if either of his/her parents is a citizen of India at the time of his/her birth shall be a citizen of India by birth, irrespective of the nationality of his parents. The children of foreign diplomats posted in India and enemy aliens cannot acquire Indian citizenship.

2. By Descent

Persons born outside India on or after 26th January, 1950, but before 10th December, 1952 are citizens of India by descent if their father was a citizen of India at the time of their birth.

3. By Registration

The Central Government may, on an application, register as a citizen of India. Any person, if he belongs to any of the following categories

(i) A person of Indian origin, residing in India for 7 years.

(ii) A person of Indian origin, who is ordinarily resident in any country or place outside undivided India.

(iii) Women, who are married to citizen of India and resident of India for 7 years.

(iv) Minor children of persons, who are citizen of India.

(v) A person of full age and capacity, whose parents are registered as citizen of India.

4. By Naturalisation

It can be acquired by foreigner, who has resided in India for 12 years.

5. By Incorporation of Territory

If any new foreign territory become a part of India, the Government of India specifies the persons who among the people or the territory shall be the citizens of India. Such persons become the citizens of India from the notified date.

6. Special Provisions as to Citizenship of Person Covered by Asom Accord

- According to the Accord, all the persons of Indian origin who came to Asom before the 1st January, 1966 from Bangladesh and who have ordinarily residents in Asom since the date of his/her entry into Asom and who was been detected to be foreigner shall register himself.
- Such a registered person shall be deemed to be a citizen of India for all purposes as from the date of expiry of a period of 10 years from the date of detection as be a foreigner. But, in the intervening period of 10 years, he/she shall have the same rights and obligations as a citizens of India, excepting the right to vote.

Loss of Citizenship

The Citizenship Act, 1955, prescribes three ways of losing citizenship namely : renunciation, termination and deprivation. These are explained as follows

1. By Renunciation

- Any citizen of India of full age and capacity can make a declaration renouncing his/her Indian citizenship.

- Upon the registration of that declaration, that person ceases to be a citizen of India. However, if such a declaration is made during a war in which India is engaged, its registration shall be withheld by the Central Government.
- Further, when a person renounces his/her Indian citizenship, every minor child of that person also loses Indian citizenship. However, when such a child attains the age or 18 years, he/she may resume Indian citizenship.

2. By Termination

When an Indian citizen voluntarily (consciously, knowingly and without duress undue influence or compulsion) acquires the citizenship of another country, his Indian citizenship automatically terminates. This provision, however does not apply during a war in which India is engaged .

3. By Deprivation

It is a compulsory termination of Indian citizenship by the Government of India, if

(i) the citizen has obtained the citizenship by fraud.

(ii) the citizen has shown disloyalty to the Constitution of India.

(iii) the citizen has unlawfully traded or communicated with the enemy during a war.

(iv) the citizen has, within 5 years after registration or naturalisation, been imprisoned in any country for 2 years.

(v) the citizen has been ordinarily resident out of India for 7 years continuously.

Overseas Citizen of India (OCI)

- In September 2000, the Government of India had set-up a high-level committee on Indian Diaspora under the Chairmanship of LM Singhavi.
- The Committee submitted its report in January 2002 and recommended to amend the Citizenship Act, 1955, to provide for grant of dual citizenship to the Persons of Indian Origin (PIOs) belonging to certain specified countries.
- Accordingly, the Citizenship (Amendment) Act, 2003, made provision for acquisition of OCI by the PIOs or 16 specified countries other than Pakistan and Bangladesh.
- Later, the Citizenship (Amendment) Act, 2005, expanded the scope of grant of OCI for PIOs of all countries all except Pakistan and Bangladesh as long as their home countries all dual citizenship under their local laws.
- Again Citizenship (Amendment) Act, 2015, has modified the provisions pertaining to the OCI in the Principal Act (Citizenship Act, 1955).
- It has introduced a new scheme called Overseas Citizen of India Cardholder by merging the PIO Card Scheme and OCI Card Scheme.

The Citizenship (Amendment) Act, 2019

- It amends the Citizenship Act, 1955.
- The Amended Act provides that the Hindus, Sikhs, Buddhists, Jains, Parsis & Christians from Afghnistan, Bangladesh and Pakistan, who entered India on or before 31st December, 2014 will not be treated as illegal migrants and will be eligible for grant of citizenship.
- It also reduce the period of naturalisation for such group of persons from 11 years to 5 years.

Practice Exercise

1. With what subject do the Articles 5 to 11 of the Constitution of India deal?

(a) Indian Union and its Territory
(b) Citizenship
(c) Fundamental Duties
(d) Features of the Constitution

2. Which of the following Article provides the Right of Citizenship of certain migrants to Pakistan?

(a) Article 5 (b) Article 6
(c) Article 7 (d) Article 8

3. By which of the following Article Parliament has power to regulate the Right of Citizenship by law?

(a) Article 8 (b) Article 9
(c) Article 10 (d) Article 11

4. By how many times the Citizen Act, 1955 has been amended?

(a) Only four times (b) Only five times
(c) Only six times (d) Only two times

5. By which of the following Amendment act, special provisions as to citizenship of person covered by Asom Accord?

(a) By Citizenship (Amendment) Act, 1985
(b) By Citizenship (Amendment) Act, 1986
(c) By Citizenship (Amendment) Act, 1992
(d) By Citizenship (Amendment) Act, 2003

6. Those who born in India on or after which of the following date are considered citizens of India only if both of their parents are citizens of India or one of whose parents is a citizen of India?

(a) 1st July, 2003
(b) 17th August, 2003
(c) 3rd December, 2003
(d) 17th December, 2003

7. Which of the following cannot acquire Indian citizenship by birth?

(a) Foreign diplomats children during their posting in India
(b) Enemy aliens of India
(c) Both 'a' and 'b'
(d) None of the above

8. Which of the following person is eligible for the citizen of India by descent?

(a) Born on or after 26th January, 1950 but before 10th December, 1992
(b) Born on or after 26th January, 1950 but before 10th December, 2003
(c) Born only on or after 26th January, 1950
(d) Born before 10th December, 1992

9. A person of India origin who is ordinarily resident in India for seven years before making is eligible for

(a) descent
(b) registration
(c) naturalisation
(d) an application for registration

10. Which of the following become citizen of India by registration?

(a) A person who is married to a citizen of India and is ordinarily resident in India for seven years before making an application for registration
(b) Minor children of persons who are citizen of India
(c) A person of full age and capacity whose parents are registered as citizens of India
(d) All of the above

11. Under which of the following conditions can citizenship be provided in India?

I. One should be born in India.
II. Either of whose parents was born in India.
III. Who was been ordinary resident of India for not less than five years.

Select the correct answer using the codes given below.

(a) I and II (b) II and III
(c) I and III (d) All of these

12. If a person has an adequate knowledge of a language specified in the Eighth Schedule to the Constitution is eligible for Indian citizenship by

(a) descent
(b) registration
(c) naturalisation
(d) incorporation of territory

13. By which of the following date a person from Bangladesh is deemed to be an Indian citizen?
(a) Before 1st January, 1971
(b) Before 1st January, 1966
(c) Before 1st December, 1922
(d) Before 1st January, 1992

14. If any new territory become a part of India the Government of India specifies the persons of the territory who shall be
(a) citizens of India
(b) citizen of Bhutan
(c) citizen of Bangladesh
(d) All of these

15. Who among the following has the power to regulate the right of citizenship in India?
(a) The Union Cabinet (b) The Parliament
(c) The Supreme Court (d) The Law Commission

16. If a person resources his/her citizenship his/her child attains the Indian citizenship.
(a) His/Her child loses Indian citizenship automatically
(b) His/Her child never attains the Indian citizenship
(c) His/Her child attains the Indian citizenship after attaing the age of 18 years
(d) His/Her child never loses the Indian citizenship

17. It is compulsory termination of Indian citizenship by Central Government if one
I. has obtained the citizenship by fraud.
II. has shown disloyalty to the Constitution of India.
III. has been ordinarily resident out of India for 7 years continuously.

Which of the statements given above are correct?
(a) I and II (b) II and III
(c) I and III (d) All of these

18. Which of the following countries have no right to acquire the Overseas Citizen of India by the persons of Indian origin?
(a) Nepal and Bhutan
(b) Pakistan and Sri Lanka
(c) Pakistan and Bangladesh
(d) Nepal and Bangladesh

19. Which one of the following changes has not been made to the Citizenship Act of India by the Amendment in 2015?
(a) The Overseas Citizen of India will now be called the Overseas Citizens of India Cardholders
(b) The NRIs are entitled to vote in election in India
(c) The PIOs have been placed at par with the OCI
(d) The PIOs are now entitled to lifelong visa to visit India

20. Which of the following is not an Article given to the OCIs?
(a) Article 16
(b) Article 14
(c) Article 58
(d) Article 124

21. The Indian citizenship cannot be terminated
(a) when there is an emergency
(b) when there is a war
(c) when there are elections
(d) when there can be terminated regardless of the conditions

Directions (Q. Nos. 22-25) *In the questions given below are two statements labelled as Assertion (A) and Reason (R). In the context of the two statements, which of the following is correct?*

Codes
(a) Both (A) and (R) are true and (R) is the correct explanation of (A)
(b) Both (A) and (R) are true, but (R) is not the correct explanation of (A)
(c) (A) is true, but (R) is false
(d) (A) is false, but (R) is true

22. **Assertion** (A) A person born outside India on or after 26th January, 1950, but before 10th December, 1992 is a citizen of India by descent.
Reason (R) If his/her father was a citizen of India at the time of his/her birth.

23. **Assertion** (A) If a person of Indian origin ordinarily reside in India for 7 years before making an application for registration.
Reason (R) The Government of India may on an application register him/her as a citizen of India.

24. Assertion (A) The Government of India may on an application grants a certificate of naturalisation to any person.

Reason (R) He/She possesses the good character with knowledge of all language which are specified in Eighth Schedule to the Constitution.

25. Assertion (A) Home Ministry is the nodal agency for citizenship of any person.

Reason (R) Home Ministry has to maintain the internal security, census, law and order and other safety concerns for India.

26. The Citizenship Act, 1955 provides for the acquisition of Indian citizenship.

(a) Right to freedom of religion
(b) No right to vote
(c) After January 1950 shall be a citizen of India is his parents is citizen of India at the time by birth
(d) All of the above

27. If a person of any country undertakes to renounce the citizenship of that country in the event of his/her application for Indian citizenship being accepted, by which of the following process he/she get Indian citizenship?

(a) By descent
(b) By registration
(c) By naturalisation
(d) All of these

28. By which of the following amendment the Citizenship Act, 1955 provided for the Commonwealth Citizenship has been repealed?

(a) By Citizenship (Amendment) Act, 1986
(b) By Citizenship (Amendment) Act, 1992
(c) By Citizenship (Amendment) Act, 2003
(d) By Citizenship (Amendment) Act, 2005

29. Which of the following committee was set-up by Government of India on Indian Diaspora?

(a) LM Singhavi Committee
(b) M Rajamouly Committee
(c) Rajmannar Committee
(d) Balwant Rai Mehta Committee

30. Under which of the following section of Citizenship (Amendment) Act, 2015, cancellation of registration as Overseas Citizenship?

(a) Section 8 (b) Section 7
(c) Section 7A (d) Section 8A

Answers

1	*b*	2	*c*	3	*d*	4	*b*	5	*a*	6	*c*	7	*c*	8	*a*	9	*d*	10	*d*
11	*a*	12	*c*	13	*b*	14	*a*	15	*b*	16	*c*	17	*d*	18	*c*	19	*b*	20	*b*
21	*d*	22	*a*	23	*b*	24	*a*	25	*a*	26	*c*	27	*c*	28	*c*	29	*a*	30	*c*

CHAPTER 05

FUNDAMENTAL RIGHTS

The Fundamental Rights in Indian Constitution acts as a guarantee that all Indian citizens can and will live their lives in peace as long as they live in Indian democracy.

FUNDAMENTAL RIGHTS IN INDIA

The Fundamental Rights are enshrined in Part III of the Constitution from Articles 12 to 35. In this regard, the framers of the Constitution derived inspiration from the Constitution of USA (i.e. Bill of Right).

- They include individual rights common to most liberal democracies, such as equality before the law, freedom of speech and expression, freedom of association and peaceful assembly, freedom of religion and the right to constitutional remedies for the protection of civil right.
- Originally, the Right to Property was also included in the Fundamental Rights, however, the 44th Constitutional Amendment Act, 1978, revised the status of property rights by stating that "No person shall be deprived of his property saved by authority of law."
- Part III of the Constitution is rightly described as the **Magna Carta** of India. It contains a very long and comprehensive list of justiciable Fundamental Rights.
- Fundamental Rights are essential human rights that are offered to every citizen irrespective of caste, race, creed, place of birth, religion or gender. Fundamental Rights are subjected to specific restrictions and enforceable by courts.
- These are equal to freedoms and these rights are essential for personal good and the society at large.

Fundamental Rights at a Glance

Right to Equality (Articles 14-18)	• Article 14 Equality before law and equal protection of laws. • Article 15 Prohibition of discrimination on grounds only of religion, race, caste, sex or place of birth. • Article 16 Equality of opportunity in matters of public employment. • Article 17 Abolition of untouchability and prohibition of its practices. • Article 18 Abolition of titles, military and academic distinctions are, however, exempted.
Right to Freedom (Articles 19-22)	• Article 19 guarantees the citizens of India the following six fundamentals freedom (i) Freedom of Speech and Expression (ii) Freedom of Assembly (iii) Freedom to form Associations (iv) Freedom of Movement (v) Freedom of Residence and Settlement (vi) Freedom of Profession, Occupation, Trade and Business • Article 20 Protection in respect of conviction for offences • Article 21 Protection of life and personal liberty • Article 22 Protection against arrest and detention in certain cases
Right against Exploitation (Articles 23-24)	• Article 23 Traffic in human beings prohibited and forced labour is prohibited. • Article 24 Prohibition of employment of children in factories etc.
Right to Freedom of Religion (Articles 25-28)	• Article 25 Freedom of conscience and free profession, practice and propagation of religion. • Article 26 Freedom to manage religious affairs. • Article 27 Freedom from payment of taxes for promotion of any religion. • Article 28 Freedom as to attendance the religious instruction or worship in certain educational institutions.

- The Fundamental Rights are named so because they are guaranteed and protected by the Constitution, which is fundamental law of land.
- They are fundamental also in the sense that they are most essential for the all round development such as, material, intellectual, moral and spiritual of the individuals.

The Constitution of India guarantees six Fundamental Rights to the citizens. They are discussed below

1. Right to Equality

- Right to Equality is the foremost right guaranteed to the citizens of India.
- It is provided in Articles 14, 15, 16, 17 and 18 of the Constitution. This right is regarded as the principal foundation of all other rights and liberties.
- The Right to Equality guarantees equality before law as per which citizens shall be equally protected by the laws of the country.
- Article 15 of the Constitution states that there will be social equality and equal accessibility to public areas and no person shall be discriminated on the basis of caste, religion gender and language.
- Equality in matters of public employment is provided in Article 16 of the Constitution of India that defines that all citizens can apply for government opportunities.

- Article 17 puts forth abolition of untouchability. The practice of untouchability is an offense and anyone found doing so is punishable by law.
- Abolition of titles is another right to equality described by the Article 18 of the Constitution. It forbids the state from conferring any titles to the citizens of India.

2. Right to Freedom

- Among the Fundamental Right, Right to Freedom is included in the Articles 19, 20, 21 and 22.
- Right to Freedom includes freedom of speech and expression, freedom to assemble peacefully without arms, freedom to form associations or unions and freedom to move freely throughout the territory of India.
- Furthermore, Right to freedom also states that citizens have the freedom to reside and settle in any part of the territory of India and also have the freedom to practice any profession or to carry on any occupation, trade or business. However, subject to reasonable restrictions by the state in the interest of the general public.

> **Article 21A** declares that state shall provide free and compulsory education to all children of the age of 6 to 14 years in such a manner as the state may determine. Thus, this provision makes only elementary education a Fundamental Right and not higher or professional education. This provision was added by the 86th Constitutional Amendment Act, 2002.

- Furthermore the Constitution of India provides certain rights against protection to persons who are arrested or detained under Article 22. Detention is of two types namely
  (i) **Punitive Detention** It is to punish a person for an offence committed by him/her after trial and conviction in a court.
  (ii) **Preventive Detention** It is not to punish a person for a past offence but to prevent him/her from committing an offence in the near future. Thus, preventive detention is only a precautionary measure and based on suspicion.

3. Right Against Exploitation

- Right against Exploitation is another essential among the Fundamental Rights. This right is given in the Articles 23 and 24.
- It provides for two provisions such as abolition of trafficking in human beings and forced labour.
- The right also lays down abolition of employment of children below the age of 14 years in dangerous jobs like factories and mines.

4. Right to Freedom of Religion

- Right to Freedom of Religion is included under Articles 25, 26, 27 and 28.
- It provides religious freedom to all citizens of India and sustains the principle of secularism in India.
- The Constitution provides that all religions are equal before the state and no religion shall be given preference over the other. Citizens are free to preach, practice and propagate any religion of their choice.

5. Cultural and Educational Rights

- Fundamental Rights also provided cultural and educational rights to its citizens and it is covered in Articles 29 and 30.
- According to this right, any community which has a language and a script of its own has the right to conserve and develop them.

No citizen can be discriminated against for admission in state aided institutions.

- All minorities, religious or linguistic, can set-up their own educational institutions in order to preserve and develop their own culture.

6. Right to Constitutional Remedies

- Right to Constitutional Remedies is also provided in the Constitution under Article 32. This right authorises the citizens to move a court of law in case of any denial of the Fundamental Rights.
- The courts can issue various kinds of writs such as habeas corpus, mandamus, prohibition, quo-warranto and certiorari.
- These writs help preserving and safeguarding the Fundamental Rights of the citizens of India.
- Right guaranteed under Article 32 is in itself a Fundamental Right that available of alternate remedy and is not bar to relief under this article.

Writs : Types and Scope

The Supreme Court and High Courts can issue the writs of habeas corpus, mandamus, prohibition, certiorari and quo-warranto. *Further, the Parliament (under Article 32) can empower any other court to issue to these writs.*

1. **Habeas Corpus** It literally means *'to have the body of'*. It is an order issued by the court to a person who has detained another person, to produce the body of the arrested person before it. It would set the detained person free, if the detention is found to be illegal. Thus, this writ is a bulwark of individual liberty against arbitrary detention.
2. **Mandamus** It literally means *we command*. It is a command issued by the court to a public official asking him to perform his official duties that he has failed or refused to perform. It can also be issued against any public body, a corporation, an inferior court, a tribunal or government for the same purpose.

   The writ of mandamus cannot be issued against

- the President of India or the Governors.
- the Chief Justice of High Court acting in judicial capacity.

3. **Prohibition** It literally means to *'forbid'*. The writ or prohibition can be issued only against judicial and quasi-judicial authorities. It is not available against administrative authorities, legislative bodies and private individuals or bodies.
4. **Certiorari** It literally means *to be 'certified or to be informed'*. It is issued by a higher court to a lower court or tribunal either to transfer a case pending with the latter to itself or to squash the order or the latter in a case.

   The writ of certiorari could be issued against judicial and quasi-judicial authorities and not against administrative authorities. But, in 1991, the Supreme Court ruled that the certiorari can be issued even against administrative authorities if its decision affecting the rights or individuals.
5. **Quo-Warranto** It literally means *by 'what authority or warrant'*. It is issued by the court to enquire into the legality of claim of a person to a public office. Hence, it prevent illegal usurpation of public office by a person.

   The writ can be issued only in case of a substantive public office of a permanent character created by a statute or by the Constitution. It cannot be issued in cases of ministerial office or private office.

Armed Forces and Martial Law

Article 33 of the Constitution of India empowers the Parliament to restrict or abrogate the Fundamental Rights of the members or armed forces, para-military forces, police forces, intelligence agencies and analogous forces.

Hence, they all have no right to freedom of speech, form associations, be members of trade unions or political associations, communicate with the press, attend public meetings or demonstrations etc.

Further, Article 33 can also exclude the Court Martial (tribunals established under the military law) from the writ jurisdiction of the Supreme Court and the High Courts, so far as the enforcement of Fundamental Rights is concerned.

Article 34 of the Constitution provides for the restrictions on Fundamental Rights while martial law (military rule) is in force in any area within the territory of India.

The martial law is imposed under the extraordinary circumstances like war, invasion, insurrection, rebellion, riot or any violent resistance to law. Its justification is to repel force by force for maintaining or restoring order in the society.

The Supreme Court held that the declaration of martial law does not ipso facto result in the suspension of the writ of habeas corpus.

Significance of Fundamental Rights

Fundamental Rights are significant in the following respects

- They constitute the bedrock of democratic system in the country.
- They provide necessary conditions for the material and moral protection or man.
- They serve as a formidable bulwark of individual liberty.
- They facilitate the establishment of rule of law in the country.
- They protect the interests of minorities and weaker sections of society.
- They strengthen the secular fabric of the Indian State.
- They check the absoluteness of the authority of the government.
- They lay down the foundation stone of social equality and social justice.
- They ensure the dignity and respect of individuals.
- They facilitate the participation of people in the political and administrative process.

Fundamental Rights (FR) Available for Non-Citizen (Foreigners) of India

FR available only to citizens and not to foreigners	FR available to both citizens and foreigners (except enemy aliens)
• Prohibition of discrimination on grounds of religions race, caste, sex or place of birth (Article 15).	• Equality before law and equal protection of laws (Article 14).
• Equality of opportunity in matters of public employment (Article 16).	• Protection in respect of conviction for offences (Article 20).
• Protection of six rights that is Right to Freedom (Article 19).	• Protection of life and personal liberty (Article 21).
• Protection of language, script and culture of minorities (Article 29).	• Right to elementary education (Article 21A).
• Right of minorities to establish and administer education institutions (Article 30).2	• Protection against arrest and detention in certain cases (Article 22).
	• Prohibition of traffic in human beings and force labour (Article 23).
	• Prohibition of employment of children in factories etc. (Article 24).
	• Freedom of conscience and free profession, practice and propagation of religion (Article 25).
	• Freedom to manage religious affairs (Article 26).
	• Freedom from payment of taxes for promotion of any religion (Article 27).
	• Freedom from attending religious instruction or worship in certain education institutions (Article 28).

Practice Exercise

1. The Fundamental Rights to the Constitution are inspired from which of the following Constitution of the world?
(a) Constitution of USA
(b) Constitution of Ireland
(c) Constitution of Germany
(d) Constitution of Russia

2. Fundamental Rights Resolution was adopted in
(a) Karachi session (b) Tripura session
(c) Madras session (d) Nagpur session

3. Which of the following amendment Right to Property was deleted from Fundamental Right?
(a) 42nd Constitutional Amendment Act
(b) 44th Constitutional Amendment Act
(c) 46th Constitutional Amendment Act
(d) 61st Constitutional Amendment Act

4. Which among the following in the Constitution of India is called Magna Carta?
(a) DPSP (b) Preamble
(c) Fundamental Duties (d) Fundamental Rights

5. In the Indian Constitution, which of the following is not a Fundamental Right?
(a) Right to Freedom
(b) Right to Equality
(c) Right to Property
(d) Right to Constitutional Remedy

6. In the Indian Constitution, the Right to Equality is granted by which of the following Articles?
(a) Articles 13 to 17
(b) Articles 14 to 18
(c) Articles 15 to 19
(d) Articles 16 to 20

7. Which of the following have no guaranteed right to effective bargaining or right to strike?
(a) Armed force (b) Trade union
(c) Political parties (d) Student union

8. The founder member of the movement for Right to Information is
(a) Anna Hazare (b) Aruna Roy
(c) Arvind Kejriwal (d) Arundhati Roy

9. Which of the following Article protects against the arbitrary and excessive punishment to an accused person?
(a) Article 19 (b) Article 20
(c) Article 21 (d) Article 22

10. In which of the following case the Supreme Court has taken a narrow interpretation of the Article 21?
(a) Keshvananda Bharti case
(b) Berubari case
(c) Gopalan case
(d) Golakhnath case

11. In which of the following case the Supreme Court ruled that the right to life and personal liberty of a person can be deprived by a law provided the procedure prescribed by that law is reasonable, fair and just?
(a) Gopalan case
(b) Vesheshika case
(c) Shah Bano case
(d) Menaka case

12. Which of the following comes under the arrest or detention (Article 22) under an ordinary law?
I. Right to be produced before a magistrate within 24 hours, excluding the journey time.
II. The detenu should be afforded an opportunity to make a representation against the detention order.
Select the correct answer using the codes given below.
(a) Only I (b) Only II
(c) Both I and II (d) Neither I nor II

13. The first Anti-terror legislation in India was....
(a) POTA (b) TADA
(c) FERA (d) NIA Act

14. The word begar has been listed in which of the following Article?
(a) Article 22 (b) Article 23
(c) Article 24 (d) Article 25

15. Which of the following article permits the state to impose compulsory services for public purposes?
(a) Article 19 (b) Article 20
(c) Article 21 (d) Article 23

16. Rights relating to freedom of religion are contained in
(a) Articles 25 to 30 (b) Articles 26 to 30
(c) Articles 25 to 28 (d) Articles 25 to 31

17. Find the odd out
(a) Right to Equality
(b) Right to Property
(c) Right against Exploitation
(d) Cultural and Educational Rights

18. Which of the following Article lays down that no person shall be compelled to pay any taxes for the promotion or maintenance of any particular religion or religious denomination?
(a) Article 25 (b) Article 26
(c) Article 27 (d) Article 28

19. Which of the following Article lays down no religious instruction shall be provided in any educational institution wholly maintained out of state funds?
(a) Article 26 (b) Article 27
(c) Article 28 (d) Article 29

20. Which one of the following Article grants protection to both religious minorities as well as linguistic minorities?
(a) Article 28 (b) Article 29
(c) Article 30 (d) Article 31

21. Which of the following courts is responsible for the enforcement of Fundamental Rights?
(a) Supreme Court
(b) High Court
(c) Sub-ordinate Court
(d) Both 'a' and 'b'

22. Which of the following means 'to be certified'?
(a) Certiorari (b) Mandamus
(c) Prohibition (d) Quo-warranto

23. Choose the Fundamental Rights available only to Indian citizens but not to aliens

I. Freedom of speech and expression.

II. Equality before the law.

III. Right of minorities.

IV. Protection of life and liberty.

Select the correct answer using the codes given below.

(a) I and II (b) I and III
(c) II and IV (d) II and III

Directions (Q. Nos. 24-27) *In the questions given below are two statements labelled as Assertion (A) and Reason (R). In the context of the two statements, which of the following is correct?*

Codes

(a) Both (A) and (R) are true and (R) is the correct explanation of (A)
(b) Both (A) and (R) are true, but R is not the correct explanation of (A)
(c) (A) is true, but (R) is false
(d) (A) is false, but (R) is true

24. Assertion (A) Legislations which gives as wide power to the executive to select cases for special treatment, without indicating the policy, may be set aside as violative of equality.

Reason (R) Article 14 of the Constitution provides the state shall not deny to any person equality before law or equal protection of laws within the territory of India.

25. Assertion (A) The Right to Property in the constitution of India ceased to be a Fundamental Right, but it continues to exist as a constitutional right.

Reason (R) 44th Amendment deleted Article 19 (f) and 31 from Part III and added a new Article 300 in Part XII of the Constitution.

26. Assertion (A) The Writ of Quo-warranto is issued by the court to enquire into the legality of claim of a person to a public office.

Reason (R) It prevents illegal usurpation of public office by a person. Hence, it literally a means 'by what authority or warrant'.

27. Assertion (A) A person suffering from AIDS can be restricted in his movements by law.

Reason (R) Where policy is laid down discretion is not of reasonableness.

28. Which of the following rights has declared as a part of Article 21 by the Supreme Court?

I. Right to livelihood

II. Right to shelter

III. Right to health

IV. Right to free legal aid

Select the correct answer using the codes given below.

(a) I, II and III (b) II, III and IV
(c) II and IV (d) All of these

29. Which of the following is not a writ issued by Supreme Court?

(a) Mandamus (b) Quo-warranto
(c) Habeas Corpus (d) Suo Motto

30. Under Section 141 of the Indian Penal Code, as assembly of five or more persons becomes unlawful if, which of the following is/are objectives?

(a) To reset the execution of any law or legal process
(b) To forcibly occupy the property of some person
(c) To commit any mischief or criminal treespass
(d) All of the above

31. Right to Education is added as Article 21A in the Constitution of India by

(a) 86th Constitutional Amendment, 2002
(b) 88th Constitutional Amendment, 2002
(c) 89th Constitutional Amendment, 2003
(d) 90th Constitutional Amendment, 2004

32. Which of the following writ issued by the court to a public official asking him to perform his official duties that he has failed or refused to perform?

(a) Habeas Corpus (b) Mandamus
(c) Certiorari (d) Quo-warranto

33. Which of the following includes the freedom of speech and expression?

I. Freedom of press.

II. Right against tapping of telephonic conversation.

III. Right to known about government activities.

IV. Freedom of silence.

Select the correct answer using the codes given below.

(a) I, II and III
(b) II, III and IV
(c) I, III and IV
(d) All of the above

34. Under which Article of the Constitution has untouchability been abolished and its practice prohibited?

(a) Article 17
(b) Article 19
(c) Article 20
(d) Article 21

35. When was Article 21A (Right to Education) inserted in part of the Constitution?

(a) 2000 (b) 2002
(c) 2003 (d) 2005

Previous Year's Questions

36. The Right of Children to Full and Compulsory Education Act, 2009 requires private schools to ensure that _____ per cent of their students come from weaker sections and disadvantaged groups? **[CLAT 2011]**

(a) 2 (b) 15
(c) 25 (d) 40

Directions (Q. Nos. 37) *In the questions given below are two statements labelled as Assertion (A) and Reason (R). In the context of the two statements, which of the following is correct?*

Codes

(a) Both (A) and (R) are true and (R) is the correct explanation of (A)
(b) Both (A) and (R) are true, but R is not the correct explanation of (A)
(c) (A) is true, but (R) is false
(d) (A) is false, but (R) is true

37. Assertion (A) The state shall not make any law, which takes away or abridges the rights conferred by Part III (Fundamental Rights) and any law made in contravention of this clause shall, to the extent of the contravention, be void.

Reason (R) The Fundamental Rights are the rights reserved by the people and for this reason they are eternal and sacrosanct. **[CLAT 2012]**

38. Which one of the following statements is correct?
Right to free and compulsory education for all children of the age of 6 to 14 yr is **[CLAT 2012]**

(a) a fundamental right enforceable in law
(b) a fundamental duty
(c) a directive principle of State Policy
(d) a Fundamental Right which, however can be enforced only if the state makes an enabling legislation

39. Principle Only the Parliament or the State Legislatures have the authority to enact laws on their own. No law made by State can take away a person's fundamental right.

Facts Parliament enacted a law, which according to a group of lawyers is violating the Fundamental Rights of traders. The group of lawyers filed a writ petition against the Parliament for enacting such law and requests the court to quash the law and to direct the Parliament to make a new law. **[CLAT 2013]**

(a) No writ would lie against the Parliament, as the Court has no authority to direct the Parliament to enact or re-enact a law
(b) The Court can quash the existing law, if it violates Fundamental Right and can direct to make a new law
(c) The Court can quash the existing law, if it violates Fundamental Right but cannot direct the Parliament to make a new law
(d) None of the above

40. The chairman of Fundamental Rights sub-committee of the Constituent Assembly was **[CLAT 2013]**

(a) Dr Rajendra Prasad (b) Dr BR Ambedkar
(c) Pt Jawaharlal Nehru (d) JB Kripalani

41. Principle All citizens shall have the Fundamental Right to carry on any occupation, trade or business. But reasonable restrictions on the exercise of such rights can be imposed by law in the interest of the general public.

Facts A large number of persons had been carrying on the business of dyeing and printing in Rajkot area for the last 25 yr providing employment to about 30000 families. From these business places untreated dirty water was being discharged on the roads thereby causing damage to the public health. A notice, therefore, was given to close this business till necessary measures to protect public health as provided under the environmental statutes were taken by those businessmen. **[CLAT 2013]**

(a) Notice cannot be justified as it will cause loss of employment to 30000 families
(b) Notice cannot be justified as it amounts to violation of the Fundamental Right of the persons who have been carrying on the business for the last 25 yr
(c) The notice cannot be justified on the ground of damage to public health as the persons in that area have been voluntarily residing for long and have become used to that environment
(d) The notice can be justified as the right to business is not absolute and reasonable restriction can be imposed by law in the interest of the public

42. Double jeopardy is **[CLAT 2015]**

(a) a two-edged weapon
(b) a dilemma
(c) a confusing expression
(d) second prosecution after the first trial for the same offense

Directions (Q. Nos. 43) *In the questions given below are two statements labelled as Assertion (A) and Reason (R). In the context of the two statements, which of the following is correct?*

Codes

(a) Both (A) and (R) are true and (R) is the correct explanation of (A)
(b) Both (A) and (R) are true, but R is not the correct explanation of (A)
(c) (A) is true, but (R) is false
(d) (A) is false, but (R) is true

43. Assertion (A) The State shall not make any law, which takes away or abridges the rights conferred by Part-III (Fundamental Rights) and any law made in contravention of this clause shall, to the extent of the contravention, be void.

Reason (R) The Fundamental Rights are the rights reserved by the people and for this reason they are eternal and sacrosanct. **[CLAT 2015]**

44. Under the Constitution of India, 'Right to Pollution Free Environment' has emerged as a Fundamental Right from the Right to **[CLAT 2016]**

(a) Life and Personal Liberty under Article 21
(b) Freedom of Movement under Article 19
(c) Conserve Culture under Article 29
(d) Equality under Article 14

45. Which among the following does not belong to the 'Right to Freedom of Religion'? **[CLAT 2016]**

(a) Freedom of conscience and free profession, practice and propagation of religion
(b) Freedom from attending religious instruction or religious worship in certain educational institutions
(c) Freedom from payment of taxes for promotion of any particular religion
(d) Freedom of speech and expression

Answers

1	*a*	2	*a*	3	*b*	4	*d*	5	*c*	6	*b*	7	*b*	8	*b*	9	*b*	10	*c*
11	*d*	12	*a*	13	*b*	14	*b*	15	*d*	16	*c*	17	*b*	18	*c*	19	*c*	20	*b*
21	*d*	22	*a*	23	*b*	24	*d*	25	*a*	26	*a*	27	*d*	28	*d*	29	*c*	30	*d*
31	*a*	32	*b*	33	*d*	34	*a*	35	*b*	36	*c*	37	*a*	38	*d*	39	*c*	40	*d*
41	*b*	42	*d*	43	*a*	44	*a*	45	*a*										

CHAPTER 06

DIRECTIVE PRINCIPLES & FUNDAMENTAL DUTIES

The Directive Principles of State Policy and Fundamental Duties are the sections of the Constitution of India that prescribe the fundamental obligations of the state to its citizens and the duties of the citizens to the state. These sections comprise a constitutional bill of rights for government policy-making and the behaviour and conduct of citizens. These sections are considered vital elements of the Constitution.

THE DIRECTIVE PRINCIPLES OF STATE POLICY (DPSP)

The Directive Principles of State Policy (DPSP) are in the form of instructions or guidelines to the governments at the center as well as in the states. These are enumerated in Part IV of the Constitution from Articles 36 to 51. The framers or the Constitution borrowed this idea from the **Irish Constitution of 1937**.

Articles of the Constitution which are related to the Directive Principles of State Policy are elaborated below

- **Article 38** To secure and protect a social order which stands for the welfare of the people.

- **Article 39** The state will in particular, direct its policy towards securing.
  - Adequate means of livelihood to all citizens.
  - A proper distribution of the material resources of the community for the common good.
  - Prevention of concentration of wealth to common detriment.
  - Equal pay for equal work for both men and women.
  - The protection of the strength and health of the workers and avoiding circumstances that force citizens to enter avocations unsuited to their age or strength.
  - The protection of childhood and youth against exploitation or moral and material abandonment.
- **Article 40** To organise village panchayats as units of self-government.
- **Article 41** To secure the right to work, education and public assistance in cases of unemployment, old, age, sickness etc.
- **Article 42** To secure just and humane conditions of work and maternity relief.
- **Article 43** To secure work, a living wage, a decent standard of life, leisure and social and cultural opportunities for people and in particular to promote cottage industries.
- **Article 44** To secure a uniform civil code applicable to the entire country.
- **Article 45** To provide within 10 years from the commencement of the Constitution, free and compulsory education for all children until they complete the age of 14 years.
- **Article 46** To promote with special care the educational and economic interests of the weaker sections of the people, especially the Scheduled Castes and Scheduled Tribes.
- **Article 47** To secure the improvement of public health and the prohibition of intoxicating drinks and drugs.
- **Article 48** To organise cultural and animal husbandry on scientific lines and preserve and improve the breeds and prohibit the slaughter of cows, calves and other milch and draught cattle.
- **Article 49** To protect all monuments of historic interest and national importance.
- **Article 50** To bring about the separation of the judiciary from the executive.
- **Article 51** To endeavour to secure
  - The promotion of international peace and security.
  - The maintenance of just and honourable relations between nations.
  - The settlement of international disputes by arbitration.

New Added Directive Principles of the State Policy

The 42nd Constitutional Amendment Act, 1976 added four new Directive Principles to the original list. *They require the state*

- to secure opportunities for healthy development of children (Article 39).
- to promote equal justice and to provide free legal aid to the poor (Article 39A).
- to take steps to secure the participation of workers in the management or industries (Article 43 A).
- to protect and improve the environment and to safeguard forests and wildlife (Article 48 A).

The 44th Amendment Act of 1978 added one more Directive Principle, which requires the state

- to minimise inequalities in income, status, facilities and opportunities (Article 38).
- Again, the 86th Amendment Act of 2002 changed the subject-matter of Article 45 and made elementary education a Fundamental Right under Article 21 A.

The amended directive requires the state

- To provide early childhood care and education for all children until they complete the age of 14 years (Article 45).
- The 97th Amendment Act of 2011 added a new Directive Principle relating to co-operative societies. *It requires the state*
- To promote voluntary formation, autonomous functioning, democratic control and professional management of co-operative societies (Article 43 B).

Directive Principles Outside Part IV

Apart from the Directive Principles included in Part IV, there are some other directive contained in other parts of the Constitution. *They are as follows*

- **Article 335 in Part XVI** The claims of the members of the Scheduled Castes and the Scheduled Tribes shall be taken into consideration, consistently with the maintenance of efficiency of administration, in the making of appointments to services and posts in connection with the affairs of the union or a state.
- **Article 350 A in Part XVII** It shall be the endeavour of every state and every local authority within the state to provide adequate facilities for instruction in the mother-tongue at the primary stage of education to children belonging to linguistic minority groups.
- **Article 351 in Part XVII** It shall be the duty of the union to promote and the spread the Hindi language and to develop it so that it may serve as a medium of expression for all the elements of the composite culture of India.

Difference between Fundamental rights and Directive Principles

Fundamental Rights	Directive Principles
These are negative as they prohibit the State from doing certain things.	These are positive as they require the State to do certain things.
These are justiciable.	These are non-justiciable.
They aim at establishing political democracy in the country.	They aim at establishing social and economic democracy in the country.
These have legal sanctions.	These have moral and political sanctions.
They promote the welfare of the individual.	They promote the welfare of the community.
They do not require any legislation for their implementation.	They require legislation for their implementation.
They are automatically enforced.	They are not automatically enforced.
The courts are bound to declare a law violative of any of the Fundamental Rights as unconstitutional and invalid.	The courts cannot declare a law violative of any of the Directive Principles as unconstitutional and invalid. However, they can upheld the validity of a law on the ground that it was enacted to give effect to a directive.

FUNDAMENTAL DUTIES

Fundamental duties for citizens are in nature of a code of conduct. They are inspired by the Constitution of erstwhile USSR (Russia) and added to the Constitution by the 42nd Constitutional Amendment in 1976, upon the recommendations of the Swaran Singh Committee.

This amendment added a new part, namely Part IV A to the Constitution. This new part consists of only one Article, i.e. **Article 51A** which for the first time specified a code of ten fundamental duties of the citizens.

Though the Swaran Singh Committee suggested the incorporation of eight fundamental duties in the Constitution, but, the 42nd Constitutional Amendment Act included ten fundamental duties. Further the fundamental duties were increased to eleven by the 86th Constitutional Amendment Act, 2002 which added a duty on every parent or guardian to ensure that their child or ward was provided opportunities for education between the ages of six and fourteen years.

The fundamental duties under Article 51A noted in the Constitution are as follows

- It shall be the duty of every citizen of India to abide by the Constitution and respect its ideals and institutions, the National Flag and the National Anthem.
- To cherish and follow the noble ideals which inspired our national struggle for freedom.
- To uphold and protect the sovereignty, unity and integrity of India.
- To defend the country and render national service when called upon to do so.
- To promote harmony and the spirit of common brotherhood amongst all the people of India transcending religious, linguistic and regional or sectional diversities and to renounce practices derogatory to the dignity of women.
- To value and preserve the rich heritage of our composite culture.
- To protect and improve the natural environment including forests, lakes, rivers, wildlife and to have compassion for living creatures.
- To develop the scientific temper, humanism and the spirit of inquiry and reform.
- To safeguard public property and to abjure violence.
- To strive towards excellence in all spheres of individual and collective activity, so that the nation constantly rises to higher levels of endeavour and achievement.
- To provide opportunities for education to his child or ward between the age of six and fourteen years.

The Verma Committee on fundamental duties of the citizens identified the existence of legal provisions for the implementation of some of the fundamental duties.

Practice Exercise

1. The Concept of Welfare State is included in which part of Indian Constitution?
(a) Preamble of the Constitution
(b) The Fundamental Rights
(c) The Directive Principles of State Policy
(d) The Fundamental Duties

2. By which of the following Constitution the Directive Principles of State Policy are borrowed?
(a) USA Constitution (b) Spain Constitution
(c) England Constitution (d) Irish Constitution

3. Which of the following Articles contain the Directive Principles of State Policy?
(a) Articles 15 to 31 (b) Articles 35 to 39
(c) Articles 36 to 51 (d) Articles 36 to 52

4. Which of the following Article lays down to secure and protect a social order which stands for the welfare of the people?
(a) Article 38 (b) Article 36
(c) Article 35 (d) Article 37

5. To secure just and humane conditions of work and maternity relief is enumerated in which of the following Articles?
(a) Article 40 (b) Article 39
(c) Article 42 (d) Article 43

6. Which of the following is not included in the Directive Principles of State Policy?
(a) Prohibition of liquor
(b) Right to work
(c) Equal wage for equal work
(d) Right to information

7. By which of the following Article free and compulsory education for all children until they complete the age of 14 years?

(a) Article 21A (b) Article 45
(c) Article 45A (d) Article 46

8. By which of the following Article prohibit the slaughter of cows, calves and other milch and draught cattle?

(a) Article 46
(b) Article 47
(c) Article 48
(d) Article 49

9. The purpose of the inclusion of DPSP in the Indian Constitution is to establish

(a) political democracy
(b) social democracy
(c) Gandhian democracy
(d) social and economical democracy

10. Separation of the judiciary from the executive has been provided in one of the following parts of the Indian Constitution.

(a) The Preamble
(b) The Fundamental Rights
(c) The DPSP
(d) The Fundamental Duties

11. Which Directive Principle bears the direct impact of Gandhian moral philosophy?

(a) Equal pay for equal work
(b) Provision of free legal aid and advice
(c) Prohibit the slaughter of cows, calves
(d) Protection of the moments of historical importance

12. In which one of the following is promotion of international peace and security mentioned to the Constitution of India?

(a) The Preamble
(b) Union and its Territory
(c) Directive Principle of State Policy
(d) The Fundamental Duties

13. Which of the following are stated as DPSP by Article 51 of the Constitution?

(a) Promote international peace and security
(b) Maintain just and honourable relation between nations
(c) Encourage settlement of international disputes by arbitration
(d) All of the above

14. By which of the following amendment Article 43A has been added to the Directive Principle of State Policy?

(a) 42nd Constitutional Amendment
(b) 44th Constitutional Amendment
(c) 86th Constitutional Amendment
(d) 97th Constitutional Amendment

15. The 97th Constitutional Amendment Act, 2011 added which of the following Article?

(a) Article 45A (b) Article 43B
(c) Article 43A (d) Article 48A

16. Who among the following pointed out that Directive Principles lays down the goals of Indian polity is economic democracy as distinguished from political democracy?

(a) Dr BR Ambedkar
(b) Verma Committee
(c) Jawaharlal Nehru
(d) Dr Rajendra Prasad

17. Directive Principle of State Policy as enunciated in the Constitution of India do not include

(a) legal aid to poor
(b) compulsory primary education
(c) minimum wages for workers
(d) adult education

18. Which of the following serve as a guide, philosopher and friend in its legislative and executive acts to ruling party?

(a) Fundamental Duties
(b) Directive Principles
(c) Fundamental Rights
(d) Part V

19. By which Amendment Act, the fundamental duties of citizen are included in Indian Constitution?

(a) 42nd Amendment Act
(b) 44th Amendment Act
(c) 56th Amendment Act
(d) 73rd Amendment Act

20. How many fundamental duties are in the Indian Constitution?

(a) Nine (b) Eight
(c) Eleven (d) Twelve

21. Which of the following statements regarding the fundamental duties contained in the Constitution of India are correct?

I. Fundamental duties can be enforced through writ jurisdiction of Supreme and High Courts.

II. Fundamental duties are applicable only to citizens of India.

Select the correct answer using the codes given below.

(a) Only I (b) Only II
(c) Both I and II (d) Neither I nor II

22. Which one of the following is not a fundamental duty?

(a) To respect the National Anthem
(b) To safeguard public property
(c) To protect monuments and places of public importance
(d) To protect and improve the natural environment

Directions (Q. Nos. 23-25) *In the questions given below are two statements labelled as Assertion (A) and Reason (R). In the context of the two statements, which of the following is correct?*

Codes

(a) Both (A) and (R) are true and (R) is the correct explanation of (A)
(b) Both (A) and (R) are true, but (R) is not the correct explanation of (A)
(c) (A) is true, but (R) is false
(d) (A) is false, but (R) is true

23. Assertion (A) The Directive Principles are relevant for determining the reasonableness of restrictions under Article 19.

Reason (R) The Directive Principles have been declared superior to Fundamental Rights.

24. Assertion (A) The Directive Principles enshrined in the Constitution aim at providing the social and economic base of a genuine democracy.

Reason (R) The Directive Principles are merely directives which the government has to keep in mind while framing policy and are not enforceable through the court.

25. Assertion (A) The fundamental duties are included into the Constitution by 42nd Constitution Amendment Act, 1976.

Reason (R) The inclusion of fundamental duties in the Constitution would help to strengthen the democracy and making the people conscious of their duties equally as they are conscious of their rights.

26. The Directive Principles of State Policy is a cheque which is paid on bank's convenience who said the statement?

(a) Dr BR Ambedkar
(b) KM Munshi
(c) Dr Rajendra Prasad
(d) KT Seth

27. The main purpose of including Directive Principles of State Policy in the Constitution is

(a) to establish a welfare state
(b) to provide best opportunities of development
(c) to check the arbitrary actions of government
(d) to establish a secular state

28. Under the Constitution of India, which one of the following is not a fundamental duty?

(a) To vote in public elections
(b) To develop the scientific temper
(c) To safeguard public property
(d) To abide by the Constitution and respect its ideals

29. Which one of the following Articles of DPSP deals with the promotion of International peace and security?

(a) 51 (b) 51A
(c) 43A (d) 48A

30. To organise village panchayats is enumerated in which of the following Article?

(a) Article 38 (b) Article 39
(c) Article 40 (d) Article 42

31. "To provide free local aid to an accused" is covered under ....

(a) Directive Principles of State Policy
(b) Fundamental of the rights
(c) Discretion of the state
(d) Moral rights

Previous Year's Questions

32. Assertion (A) Directive Principles of State Policy contained in Part IV shall not be enforceable by any court, but the principles therein laid down are nevertheless fundamental in the governance of the country and it shall be the duty of the State to apply these principles in making laws.

Reason (R) Directive Principles of State Policy and Fundamental Rights are both complementary to each other but in case of any controversy Fundamental Rights will prevail. **[CLAT 2012]**

Codes

(a) Both (A) and (R) are true and (R) is the correct explanation of (A)
(b) Both (A) and (R) are true, but (R) is not the correct explanation of (A)
(c) (A) is true, but (R) is false
(d) (A) is false, but (R) is true

33. Which of the following statements is incorrect about Fundamental Duties under the Constitution of India?

It shall be the duty of every citizen of India **[CLAT 2014]**

(a) to uphold and protect the sovereignty, unity and integrity of India.
(b) to strive towards excellence in all spheres of individual and collective activity, so that the nation constantly rises to higher levels of endeavour and achievement.
(c) who is a parent or guardian to provide opportunities for education to his child or as the case may ho, ward between the age of 6 and 14 yrs.
(d) To vote in public elections.

34. Which one of the following is not a Directive Principles of State Policy under Part-IV of the Constitution of India? **[CLAT 2016]**

(a) Organisation of village panchayats
(b) Promotion of adult education
(c) Provision for just and humane conditions of work and maternity relief
(d) Promotion of international peace and security

Answers

1	*c*	2	*d*	3	*b*	4	*a*	5	*c*	6	*d*	7	*b*	8	*c*	9	*d*	10	*c*
11	*c*	12	*c*	13	*d*	14	*a*	15	*b*	16	*a*	17	*d*	18	*b*	19	*a*	20	*c*
21	*a*	22	*c*	23	*c*	24	*b*	25	*a*	26	*a*	27	*a*	28	*a*	29	*a*	30	*c*
31	*a*	32	*c*	33	*d*	34	*b*												

CHAPTER 07

THE EXECUTIVE

The executive is the branch of government that is responsible for the day-to-day management of the state. The executive is led by the head or government. Under the doctrine of the separation of powers, the executive is neither supposed to make laws nor to interpret them. The executive is supposed to put the laws into action. On the other hand, the executive is the organ exercising authority in and holding responsibility for the governance of the state.

UNION EXECUTIVE

Part V under Articles 52 to 78 of the Constitution deal with the Union Executive. The Union Executive consists of the President, the Vice-President, Prime Minister along with his council ministers who advise to the President and the Attorney General of India.

The President

- The President is the head of the Indian State. He is the first citizen of India and acts as the symbol of unity, integrity and solidarity of the nation. He is the supreme commander of the defence forces of India.
- The President is elected by members of an electoral college consisting of elected members or both Houses of Parliament and Legislative Assemblies of the states in accordance with the system of proportional representation, by means of single transferable vote.

- The President must be a citizen of India (either by birth or naturalisation only) not less than 35 years of age and qualified for election as member of the Lok Sabha.
- His term of office is for five years and he is eligible for re-election. His removal from office is to be in accordance with procedure prescribed in Article 61 of the Constitution.
- He may, by writing addressed to the Vice-President, resign his office.
- Executive power of the union is vested in the President and is exercised by him either directly or through officers subordinates to him in accordance with the Constitution.

Powers and Functions of the President

The powers enjoyed and the functions performed by the President can be studied under the following heads

1. Executive Powers

- All executive actions of the Government of India are formally taken in his name.
- He appoints the Prime Minister and the other ministers, the Attorney General of India, the Comptroller and Auditor General of India, the Chief Election Commissioner and other Election Commissioners, the Chairman and members of the Union Public Service Commission, the Governors of states, the Chairman and members of Finance Commission, an Inter-State Council and so on.
- He can declare any area as scheduled area and has powers with respect to the administration of scheduled areas and tribal areas.
- He can directly administers the union territories through administrator appointed by him.

2. Legislative Powers

The President is an integral part of the Parliament of India and enjoys the following legislative powers

- He can summon or prorogue the Parliament and dissolve the Lok Sabha. He can also summon a joint sitting of both the Houses of Parliament.
- He can address the Parliament at the commencement of the first session after each general election and the first session of each year.
- He can appoint any member of the Lok Sabha to preside over its proceedings when the offices of both the Speaker and the Deputy Speaker fall vacant. Similarly, he can also appoint any member of the Rajya Sabha to preside over its proceedings when the offices of both the Chairman and the Deputy Chairman fall vacant.
- He nominates 12 members of the Rajya Sabha from amongst persons having special knowledge or practical experience in literature, science, art and social service and also nominates two members to the Lok Sabha from the Anglo-Indian Community.
- His prior recommendation or permission is needed to introduce certain types of bills in the Parliament. When a bill is sent to the President after it has been passed by the Parliament, he can : (i) give his assent to the bill, or (ii) withhold his assent to the bill, or (iii) return the bill (if it is not a Money bill) for reconsideration of the Parliament. However, if the bill is passed again by the Parliament, with or without amendments, the President has to give his assent to the bill.

3. Financial Powers

- He constitute a Finance Commission after every five year.
- Money bill can be introduced in the Parliament only with his prior recommendation.
- He causes to be laid before the Parliament the annual financial statement (i.e. the Union Budget). He can make advances out of the Contingency fund of India to meet any unforeseen expenditure.

4. Judicial Powers

- He appoints the Chief Justice and the judges of Supreme Court and High Court.
- He can grant pardon, reprieve, respite and remission of punishment, or suspend, remit or commute the sentence or any person convicted of any offence.

5. Emergency Powers

The Constitution confers extraordinary powers on the President to deal with the following three types of emergencies

(i) **National Emergency** (Article 352) The President can declare a national emergency when the security of India or a part of it is threatened by war or external aggression or armed rebellion. A proclamation of national emergency may be applicable to the entire country or only a part or it. The 42nd Constitutional Amendment Act of 1976 enabled the President to limit the operation of a national emergency to a specified part of India.

(ii) **President's Rule** (Articles 356 and 365) The President rule also known as state emergency or constitutional emergency (notably, the President can act either on a report of the Governor of the state or otherwise too) can be proclaimed under Article 356 on two grounds one mentioned in Article 356 itself and another in Article 365.

Article 356 empowers the President to issue a proclamation, if he is satisfied that a situation has arisen in which the government of a state cannot be carried on in accordance with the provisions of the Constitution.

Article 365 says that whenever a state fails to comply with or to give effect to any direction from the centre. The President may proclaim emergency.

(iii) **Financial Emergency** (Article 360) Article 360 empowers the President to proclaim a financial emergency if he is satisfied that a situation has arisen due to which the financial stability or credit of India or any part of its territory is threatened. During the operation of a financial emergency, the centre acquires full control over the states in financial matters.

6. Veto Power

The veto power enjoyed by the President are of three types

(i) **Absolute Veto** It means withholding of assent to the bill passed by the legislature.

(ii) **Suspensive Veto** When the legislature send the bill for consideration it can be over ridden by the legislature with an ordinary majority.

(iii) **Pocket Veto** It means taking no action on the bill passed by the legislature.

7. Ordinance Making Power

Article 123 of the Indian Constitution empowers the President to promulgate ordinances during the recess of Parliament. These ordinances have the same force and effect as an act of Parliament, but are in the nature of temporary laws.

Vice-President of India

Article 63 of the Constitution of India provides for the office of a Vice-President who shall be elected indirectly in accordance with the system of proportional representation by means of a single transferable vote. The Vice-President will be elected by an electoral college consisting of the members of both Houses of Parliament.

The legislature of states participate in the election process of the President whereas the President have no participation in the election of the Vice-President of India.

Election	• Elected by both the houses (Electoral College) in accordance with the system of proportional representation by means of single transferable vote and the vote being secret. Nominated members also participate in his election. • The Supreme Court has the final and exclusive jurisdiction for resolving disputes and doubts relating to the election of the Vice-President of India.
Criteria	• Citizen of India. • More than 35 years of Age. • Passes the qualification of membership of Rajya Sabha. • Not hold any office of profit under union, state of local authority. However, for this purpose, the President, Vice-President, Governor of a state and a Minister of the union or a state, are not held to be holding an office of profit.
Other Points	• Holds office for 5 years. Can be re-elected. • Term can be cut short if he resigns or by a resolution of the Rajya Sabha passed by a majority of all the members of the Rajya Sabha and agreed to by the Lok Sabha. • He is the ex-officio Chairman of Rajya Sabha. Since he is not a member of Rajya Sabha, he has no right to vote. • Being the Vice-President of India, he is not entitled for any salary, but he is entitled to the salary and allowances payable to the Chairman of the Rajya Sabha. • All bills, resolution, motion can be taken in Rajya Sabha after his consent. • Can discharge the function of the President, the Vice-President shall not perform the duties of the office of the Chairman of Rajya Sabha and shall not be entitled to receive the salary of the Chairman. During this period, he is entitled for the salary and privileges of the President of India.

Prime Minister

- The Prime Minister of India is the Chief of Government, head of the Council of Ministers and the leader of the majority party in Parliament. The Prime Minister leads the executive branch of the Government of India.
- The Prime Minister selects and can dismiss other members of the cabinet; allocates posts to members within the government; is the presiding member and Chairman of the Cabinet and responsible for bringing proposal of legislation.
- The Prime Minister is appointed by the President to assist the latter in the administration of the affairs of the executive.

Constitutional Framework and Position of Prime Minister

The Constitution envisages a scheme of affairs in which the President of India is the head of the executive in terms of Article 53 with office of the Prime Minister as heading the Council of Ministers to assist and advise the President in the discharge of the executive power. [Article 53 (1) and Article 74 (1)]

Role and Powers of the Prime Minister

- The Prime Minister leads the functioning and exercise of authority of the Government of India.
- He is invited by the President of India in the Parliament of India as leader of the majority party to form a government at the federal level (known as Central or Union Government in India) and exercise its powers.
- In practice, the Prime Minister nominates the members of the Council of Ministers to the President. They also work upon to decide a core group of Ministers (known as the Cabinet) as in-charge of the important functions and ministries of the Government of India.

- The Prime Minister is responsible for aiding and advising the President in distribution of work of the Government to various ministries and offices and in terms of the Government of India (Allocation of Business) Rules, 1961 .
- The co-ordinating work is generally allocated to the Cabinet Secretariat which in turn acts as a nodal agency for the functioning of the various ministries. Generally, the work of the Government is divided into various ministries, the Prime Minister may retain certain portfolios.
- The Prime Minister is also the ex-officio chairman of the NITI Ayog of India. He also appoint the Deputy Chairman of the Commission, who is responsible for the functioning of the commission and reports to the Prime Minister.
- He also has exclusive jurisdiction over disposal of two national funds, (i) the PM's National Relief Fund, and (ii) the PM's National Defence Fund, which he uses at his discretion to attain the objectives behind the establishment of these funds.

Eligibility

- Article 84 Eligibility of the Constitution sets the principal qualifications one must meet to be eligible to the office of the Prime Minister. A Prime Minister must be a citizen of India.
- He should be a member of the Lok Sabha or Rajya Sabha. If a person elected Prime Minister is neither a member of the Lok Sabha nor Rajya Sabha, then he must become a member of the Lok Sabha or Rajya Sabha within six months.
- He must be of above 25 years of age (in the case of a seat in the Lok Sabha) or above 30 years of age (in the case of a seat in the Rajya Sabha).
- A person shall not be eligible for election as Prime Minister if he holds any office of profit under the Government of India or the Government of any state or under any local or other authority subject to the control of any of the said governments.

Remuneration

Article 75 of the Constitution of India deals with the remuneration of the Prime Minister as well as other ministers is to be decided by the Parliament and is renewed from time to time.

Council of Ministers of India

- Article 74 of the Constitution deals with Council of Ministers to aid and advise the President, headed by the Prime Minister.
- Council of Ministers of India are mandated by the Constitution to be the members of either House of the Parliament of India.
- This council comprises the Cabinet Ministers, Ministers of State and the Deputy Ministers.
- The number of the members of the Council of Ministers has specified by the Constitution of India. It shall not exceed fifteen per cent of total member of House of People.
- The Union Council of Ministers remains collectively responsible to the Lok Sabha. In addition to the collective responsibility, the ministers are also individually responsible for the functioning of their respective departments.
- The Council of Ministers is responsible for preparing and introducing bills in the Parliament, to aid and advise the President in the exercise of his functions, to determine the policy and administer them and to implement all the decisions adopted by the Parliament of India.
- The Union Council of Ministers carries out their functions with the help of the government officials.

Attorney General of India

- In Article 76 of the constitution of India mentioned that Attorney General of India shall be appointed by President.

- He shall be qualified to be a judge of the Supreme Court.
- He advise the government on legal matter and such other duty assigned to him by President.
- He holds office during the pleasure of President and receive renumeration as President may determine.
- He has the right to speak and to take part in the proceedings of both the House of Parliament or their joint sitting and any committee of Parliament of which he may be named as member, but without a right to vote.

State Executive

The Constitution of India envisages the same pattern of government in the states as that for the centre, i.e. a parliamentary system. Part VI under Articles 153 to 167 of the Constitution deal with the state executive. The state executive consists of the Governor, the Council of Ministers headed by the Chief Minister and the Advocate General of the state.

Governor

- The Governor is the Constitutional Head of the state and the same Governor can act as Governor of more than one state (Article 153).
- The Governor is appointed by the President (Article 155) Article 156 states that the Governor holds office during the pleasure of the President.

Qualification

Under **Article 157** and **158**, the Constitution lays down the following conditions for the Governor's office

- Must be citizen of India.
- Completed 35 years of age.
- Shouldn't be a member of either House of Parliament or State Legislature.

Tenure

Under Article 156,

(i) the Governor shall hold office during the pleasure of the President;

(ii) may resign by writing under his hand addressed to the President;

(iii) hold office for a period of 5 years. Governor shall hold office until his successor enters upon his office.

Powers and Functions of Governor Executive Powers

The executive power of the state shall be vested with the Governor and shall be exercised by him either directly or through officers subordinate to him in accordance with the Constitution. *These powers are as follows*

- All executive actions of the Government of a State are formally taken in his name. He can make rules for more convenient transaction of the business of a State Government.
- Appoints the **Advocate General** of a State, State Election Commissioners, Chairman and Members of the State Public Service Commission, VCs of Universities.
- He can seek any information relating to the administration of the affairs of the state and proposals for legislation from the Chief Minister.

Legislative Powers

Governor is an integral part of the State Legislature. He has the right of addressing and sending messages and of summoning, proroguing and dissolving the State Assembly. He has the power to nominate one member of Anglo-Indian Community to the Legislative Assembly of the state. He appoints 1/6 members of Legislative Council.

Financial Powers

- State budget is laid before the State Legislature. He constitutes a Finance Commission after every 5 years to review the financial position of the Panchayats and the municipalities.
- Shall not be a member of both the Houses of Parliament or of a House of Legislative Assembly or Legislative Council (if any).
- Shall not hold office of profit.
- Use his official residence (Raj Bhawan) without payment.
- When same person is appointed as the Governor of two or more states, the emoluments and allowances payable to him are shared by states as determined by the President.

Oath

His oath is administered by the Chief Justice of the concerned State High Court and in his absence, the seniormost judge of that court.

Judicial Powers

He can grant pardons, reprives, respites and remissions of punishment or suspend, remit and commute the sentence of any person convicted of any offence against any law relating to a matter to which the executive power of the state extends. He cannot pardon a death sentence.

Emergency Powers

The Governor has no emergency power to counter external aggression or armed rebellion. He reports to the President if the State Government is not running constitutionally and recommends to the Union Government for President's (Article 356) rule. When President's rule comes into force in any state, the Governor runs the state with the help of advisers on behalf of the President.

Chief Minister

Chief Minister is the real Executive, Head of the State Government. His position at the state level is analogous to the position of the Prime Minister at the centre.

Appointment

Article 164, says that Chief Minister shall be appointed by the Governor. This does not mean that the Governor is free to appoint anyone as a Chief Minister.

Oath, Term and Salary

- Oath of the office of Chief Minister is administered by the Governor or person appointed by him for this purpose.
- A person, who is not a member of State Legislature can be appointed but he has to get himself elected within 6 months otherwise he is removed.
- The term of the CM is not fixed and he holds office during the pleasure of the Governor. However, this does not mean that the Governor can dismiss him at any time. He cannot be dismissed by the Governor as long as he enjoys the majority support in the Legislative Assembly. But, if he loses the confidence of the assembly, he must resign or the Governor can dismiss him. The salary and allowances of the Chief Minister are determined by the State Legislature.

Practice Exercise

1. Which of the following Articles deal with the Union executive in the Constitution?
(a) Articles 74 to 152 (b) Articles 52 to 78
(c) Articles 51 to 80 (d) Articles 52 to 80

2. Under which Article of the Constitution of India can the President of India be impeached?
(a) Article 62 (b) Article 61
(c) Article 52 (d) Article 60

3. The President is elected in India by
(a) direct election
(b) single transferable vote
(c) proportional vote system
(d) open ballot system

4. The President of India is elected by the
(a) members of the Lok Sabha
(b) members of both the Houses of the Parliament
(c) members of electoral college consisting of the elected members of both the Houses of the Parliament and State Assemblies
(d) members of the State Assemblies

5. What is the maximum age limit prescribed for the post of the President of India?
(a) 58 years
(b) 60 years
(c) 62 years
(d) There is no maximum age limit

6. Who can initiate impeachment of the President?
(a) 1/4th members of either House of the Parliament
(b) Half of the members of either House of the Parliament
(c) Half of the State Legislature
(d) 1/3rd members of any State Legislature

7. Who among the following is appointed by the President?
(a) Attorney General of India
(b) Comptroller General of India
(c) Governor of State
(d) All of the above

8. Which of the following has power of decide on question as to disqualifications of members of the Parliament?
(a) The Election Commissioner
(b) The Speaker
(c) The President
(d) The Prime Minister

9. How many members from Anglo-Indian Communities have been nominated by President in the Lok Sabha?
(a) 2 members (b) 4 members
(c) 10 members (d) 12 members

10. Money bill can be introduced in the Parliament only with the prior recommendation of whom?
(a) The leader of Lok Sabha
(b) The President
(c) The Speaker
(d) The Vice-President

11. Judges of the High Courts are appointed by which of the following?
(a) The Governor of that State
(b) The Chief Justice of India
(c) The President of India
(d) The Prime Minister

12. Which Indian State came under President's rule for maximum number of time?
(a) Punjab (b) Himachal Pradesh
(c) Kerala (d) Karnataka

13. Which one of the following Articles of the Indian Constitution provides that, it shall be the duty to union to protect every state against external aggression and internal distribution?
(a) Article 352
(b) Article 355
(c) Article 356
(d) Article 365

14. How many times the Financial Emergency has been proclaimed in India so far?
(a) Two times (b) Three times
(c) One time (d) Never

15. The single instance of the unanimous election of the President of India so far, was the election of
(a) Dr Rajendra Prasad
(b) Dr Radhakrishnan
(c) Dr Zakir Hussain
(d) Neelam Sanjeeva Reddy

16. Who was the President of India at the time of proclamation of emergency in the year of 1975?
(a) VV Giri
(b) Giani Zail Singh
(c) Fakhruddin Ali Ahmad
(d) Sankardayal Sharma

17. Which one of the following statements regarding the Vice-President of India officiating as President is correct?
(a) He shall continue to be Chairman of the Council of States
(b) He shall cease to be the Chairman of the Council of States
(c) He shall nominate the next seniormost member of the house to be the Chairman of the Council of States
(d) None of the above

18. Which of the following statements is true?
I. The resignation of the Prime Minister means the resignation of whole Cabinet.
II. It is on the advice of Prime Minister that the President summons and prorogues Parliament and dissolve the Lok Sabha.
Select the correct answer using the codes given below.
(a) Only I (b) Only II
(c) Both I and II (d) Neither I nor II

19. Who exercises the actual executive power under the parliamentary form of Government?
(a) The President
(b) The Vice-President
(c) The Prime Minister
(d) The Parliament

20. Who recommends person who can be appointed as minister by the President?
(a) The Prime Minister
(b) The Speaker
(c) Chairman of Rajya Sabha
(d) Council of Minister

21. Who one of the following is the Chairman of Inter-State Council?
(a) The Inter-State Commissioner
(b) The President of India
(c) The Prime Minister of India
(d) Defence Minister

22. Which of the following Article lays down the appointed of Prime Minister by the President?
(a) Article 74 (b) Article 75
(c) Article 84 (d) Article 78

23. By which of the following Article the Prime Minister has to furnish such information relating to the administration of the affairs of the union and proposals for legislation as the President may call for?
(a) Article 78 (b) Article 77
(c) Article 76 (d) Article 75

24. Which of the following Article deal with the status of the Council of Minister?
(a) Article 74 (b) Article 75
(c) Article 76 (d) Article 77

25. The Council of Minister is collectively responsible for whom?
(a) The President of India
(b) The Prime Minister
(c) The Rajya Sabha
(d) The Lok Sabha

26. Which of the following Article deals with the State Executive in the Constitution of India?
(a) Articles 153 to 167
(b) Articles 152 to 161
(c) Articles 153 to 160
(d) Articles 150 to 167

27. By which of the following Constitutional Amendment same person as a Governor for two or more states?
(a) 70th Constitutional Amendment Act
(b) 7th Constitutional Amendment Act
(c) 9th Constitutional Amendment Act
(d) 11th Constitutional Amendment Act

28. By which of the following warrant under his hand and seal Governor is appointed?
(a) Chief Justice of India
(b) The Central Government
(c) The President of India
(d) Prime Minister

29. Which of the following is appointed by the Governor?
(a) Tribal Welfare Minister for Jharkhand
(b) State Election Commission
(c) Chief Minister
(d) All of the above

Directions (Q. Nos. 30-32) *In the questions given below are two statements labelled as Assertion (A) and Reason (R). In the context of the two statements, which of the following is correct?*

Codes
(a) Both (A) and (R) are true and (R) is the correct explanation of (A)
(b) Both (A) and (R) are true, but (R) is not the correct explanation of (A)
(c) (A) is true, but (R) is false
(d) (A) is false, but (R) is true

30. **Assertion** (A) During the term of office no litigation can be instituted in any court of law against the President of India.
Reason (R) President's office is above the Constitution.

31. **Assertion** (A) The Council of Ministers in India collectively responsible to the Lok Sabha and Rajya Sabha.
Reason (R) The members of both the Houses of Parliament are eligible to be the members in Council of Ministers.

32. **Assertion** (A) The Governor is the Chief Executive Head of the state.
Reason (R) All the executive actions of the Government of a State are formally taken in his name.

33. Who is the crisis manager-in-chief at the political level during emergencies?
(a) The President of India
(b) The Prime Minister of India
(c) The Vice-President of India
(d) Home Minister

Previous Year's Questions

34. Who is the Union Finance Minister of India? **[CLAT 2016]**
(a) Arun Jaitley
(b) Rajnath Singh
(c) DV Sadananda Gowda
(d) Sushma Swaraj

35. President Pranab Mukherjee on 6th, January 2015 signed the ordinance to amend Citizenship Act, 1995. Which of the statements in the regard is/are correct? **[CLAT 2016]**
I. The ordinance exempts Person of Indian Origin (PIO) from appearing before the local police station on every visit.
II. It replaced the clause that says foreigners marrying Indians must continuously stay in the country for a period of six months before they get an Indian citizenship.
(a) Only I (b) Only II
(c) Both I and II (d) Neither I nor II

36. Power to summon the Houses of the Parliament is vested with **[CLAT 2016]**
(a) President
(b) Vice-President
(c) Prime Minister
(d) Speaker and Vice-President

37. In case, the President of India wants to resign, he shall address his resignation to the **[CLAT 2016]**
(a) Chief Election Commissioner
(b) Prime Minister
(c) Chief Justice of India
(d) Vice-President

38. Who is the Chairperson of NITI Aayog? **[CLAT 2016]**
(a) Sushmita Mahajan (b) Arun Jaitley
(c) Sushma Swaraj (d) Narendra Modi

39. In January, 2016, at the first stage, the Union Ministry of Urban Development, unveiled the list of .... cities for Smart Cities Mission out of 98 shortlisted cities. **[CLAT 2016]**
(a) 30 (b) 15 (c) 20 (d) 25

Answers

1	*b*	2	*b*	3	*b*	4	*c*	5	*d*	6	*a*	7	*d*	8	*c*	9	*a*	10	*b*
11	*c*	12	*a*	13	*b*	14	*d*	15	*d*	16	*c*	17	*b*	18	*c*	19	*c*	20	*a*
21	*c*	22	*b*	23	*a*	24	*a*	25	*d*	26	*a*	27	*b*	28	*c*	29	*d*	30	*c*
31	*d*	32	*a*	33	*b*	34	*a*	35	*a*	36	*a*	37	*d*	38	*d*	39	*c*		

CHAPTER 08

LEGISLATURE (UNION & STATES)

India adopted parliamentary form of government in which representative of people functions at Lok Sabha and representative of states functions at Rajya Sabha. Unlike in US, Indian executive i.e. Council of Ministers, are collective responsible to Lok Sabha in particular and Parliament in general.

PARLIAMENT (UNION LEGISLATURE)

- The Constitution of India provides a parliamentary form of government both at the centre and in the states.
- The Parliament of India consists of the President, the Lok Sabha and the Rajya Sabha (Article 79).
- Although, President is not a member of either House. He is an integral part of Parliament.
- Out of seven UTs, only two (Delhi and Puducherry) have representation in the Rajya Sabha.
- The population of other five are too small to have any representative in the Rajya Sabha.

Rajya Sabha (Article 80)

Rajya Sabha is a permanent body and not subject to dissolution. Its maximum strength is 250 (12 members nominated by the President having special knowledge or practical experience in the fields of science, literature, art and social service).

The total membership of the present Rajya Sabha is 245 however, one-third members retire every second year. Their seats are filled up by fresh elections and presidential nomination at the beginning of every third year.

- There are no seats reserved for SCs and STs in Rajya Sabha.
- Constitution has not fixed the term of office of members of the Rajya Sabha and left it to the Parliament.
- Representation of People Act (1951) provided the term of office of a member of the Rajya Sabha shall be 6 years.

Lok Sabha (Article 81)

Lok Sabha is not a permanent body and subject to dissolution. Its maximum strength is 552, which includes 2 nominated members of Anglo-Indian Community, 530 members from States and 20 from Union Territories. Present strength of Lok Sabha is 545.

- Its normal term is 5 years from the date of its first meeting after the general elections, after which it automatically dissolves.
- The President is authorised to dissolve Lok Sabha at any time even before the completion of five years and this cannot be challenged in the Court of Law.
- Lok Sabha can be extended during the National Emergency by a law of Parliament for one year at a time for any length of time. But this extension cannot go beyond a period of 6 months after the emergency has ceased to operate.

Difference between Powers of Lok Sabha and the Rajya Sabha

- A Money bill can be introduced only in the Lok Sabha and not in the Rajya Sabha. The final power to decide whether a particular bill is a Money bill or not is vested in the Speaker of the Lok Sabha.
- The Speaker of Lok Sabha presides over the joint sitting of both the Houses of Parliament.
- A resolution for the discontinuance of the National Emergency can be passed only by the Lok Sabha and not by the Rajya Sabha.
- The Rajya Sabha cannot remove the Council of Ministers by passing a no-confidence motion.
- This is because the Council of Ministers is collectively responsible only to the Lok Sabha. But, the Rajya Sabha can discuss and criticise the policies and activities of the government.

Membership of Parliament

Member of Parliament is a representative of people of a particular constituency in the Lok Sabha. MP is selected on the basis of first-post the post system meaning thereby those securing the majority of vote will be elected.

Qualification (Article 84)

The Constitution lays down the following qualifications for a person to be chosen as a member of the Parliament.

- He must be a citizen of India.
- He must make and subscribe before the person authorised by the Election Commission an oath or affirmation according to, the form prescribed in the Third Schedule. And must not be less than 30 years of age in the case of Rajya Sabha and not less than 25 years of age in the case of the Lok Sabha.
- He must possess other qualifications as prescribed by Parliament.

Disqualification (Article 102)

Under the Constitution, a person shall be disqualified for being elected as a member of Parliament.

- If he/she holds any office of profit under the Union or State Government (except that of a minister or any other office exempted by the Parliament).

- If he/she is of unsound mind and stands so declared by court.
- If he/she declared by court and stands so is undischarged insolvent.
- If he/she is not a citizen of India or has voluntarily acquired the citizenship of a foreign state or is under any acknowledgement of allegiance to a foreign state; and if he is so, disqualified under any law made by the Parliament.

Under the following conditions, a member of Parliament vacates his seat (Article 101)

- Double membership (both Rajya Sabha and Lok Sabha).
- Disqualification, resignation.
- Absence (more than 60 days without permission).
- If his election is declared void by the court.
- If he/she is expelled by the House.
- If he/she is elected to the office of the President or Vice-President.
- If he/she is appointed as a Governor of a State.

Oath and Salary (Article 99)

- Every member has to make and subscribe to an oath or affirmation before the President or some other person appointed by him for this purpose.
- Salaries and allowances are determined by Parliament.

Speaker of Lok Sabha (Article 93)

- He/She is elected by Lok Sabha from amongst its members, as soon as, after the first meeting.
- The date of election is fixed by the President. Usually, the speaker remains in his office during the life of the Lok Sabha. *He/She vacates office earlier in any of the following cases.*
  - If he/she ceases to be member of Lok Sabha; if he/she resigns by writing to the Deputy Speaker.
  - If he/she is removed by a resolution passed by a majority of all the members of the Lok Sabha. Such a resolution can be moved only after giving 14 days advance notice.
- Under resolution of removal, the Speaker cannot preside at the sitting of the House (he may be present). (Article 96)
- Whenever the Lok Sabha is dissolved, the Speaker does not vacate his office and continues till the newly elected Lok Sabha meets.

Role, Powers and Functions of Speakers

- He is the principal spokesman of the House, and his decision in all parliamentary matters is final.
- He maintains order and decorum in the House for conducting its business.
- He adjourns the House to suspend the meeting in the absence of quorum (presence of only 1/10th of the total strength of the House). He does not vote in the first instance, but he can exercise a casting vote in the case of a tie (deadlock).
- He presides over a joint sitting of two Houses of the Parliament.
- He can allow a 'secret' sitting of the House.
- He certifies a Bill as Money bill and his decision cannot be challenged.
- He appoints the Chairman of all the Parliamentary Committees of Lok Sabha.
- The speaker acts as the ex-officio Chairman of the Indian Parliamentary group of the Inter Parliamentary Union.

Deputy Speaker

- While the office of the Speaker is vacant due to any reason, the Deputy Speaker presides. (Article 95)
- M Ananthasayanam Ayyangar was the First Deputy Speaker of Lok Sabha.
- At present, Mr M Thambidurai is Deputy Speaker of Lok Sabha.

Chairman of Rajya Sabha

- The Vice-President is the ex-officio Chairman of Rajya Sabha. (Article 89).
- As a presiding officer, the powers and functions of the Chairman of Rajya Sabha are similar to those of Speaker of Lok Sabha.

Deputy Chairman

Elected by Rajya Sabha itself from amongst its members. Deputy Chairman is not subordinate to the Chairman. He is directly responsible to the Rajya Sabha.

Joint Session (Article 108)

Joint sessions take place on the order of the President if

(i) a Bill passed by one House, is rejected by another.

(ii) the amendments made by the other House are not acceptable to the House where the Bill originated.

- Joint session is presided over by the Speaker of the Lok Sabha. The deadlock over a Bill is resolved by a majority of the total numbers of the members of both the Houses present and voting.
- So far, joint sittings have been held thrice in the history of Indian Parliament (1961, 1978 and 2002).
- Provision of joint sitting is applicable to Ordinary bills or Financial bills only and not to Money bills or Constitutional Amendment bills.

Sessions of Parliament

- The Parliament generally meets in three sessions in a year i.e. Budget session (February-May) (longest session), Monsoon session (July-September), Winter session (November - December) (shortest session).
- There should not be a gap of more than 6 months between two sessions of Parliament.

Legislative Proceedings

All legislative proposals are initiated in the Parliament in the terms of bills. The bill is a proposed legislation. It becomes a law when it is asserted by the President. *The bill can broadly be categorised as*

1. Ordinary Bills

- All the bills other than Financial bills, Money bills and the Constitutional Amendment bills are Ordinary bills.
- Such bills can be introduced in either House of the Parliament (in Lok Sabha or the Rajya Sabha) without the recommendation of the President.
- These bills are passed by a simple majority by both the Houses. Both the Houses enjoy equal jurisdiction over such bills and in case of a deadlock due to any reason, the tie is resolved by a joint sitting. The President has the right to return such bills for reconsideration to the Parliament once.

2. Money Bill

According to Article 110, A Bill shall be deemed to be a Money bill if it contains only provisions dealing with all or *any of the following matters, namely*

- The imposition, abolition, remission, alteration or regulation of any tax;
- The regulation of the borrowing of money or the giving of any guarantee by the Government of India or the amendment of the law with respect to any financial obligations undertaken or to be undertaken by the Government of India;
- The declaring of any expenditure to be expenditure charged on the Consolidated Fund of India or the increasing of the amount of any such expenditure;

24. **Assertion** (A) Vice-President is the member of Rajya Sabha.
Reason (R) Constitution mention the position of Vice-President election.

25. Elections to fill up one third seats of Rajya Sabha are held
(a) every year (b) once in two years
(c) once in five years (d) once in six years

26. Who among the following is the first woman Speaker of Lok Sabha?
(a) Vijaya Lakshmi Pandit
(b) Meera Kumar
(c) Girija Vyas
(d) Sucheta Kripalani

27. Who is the Deputy Speaker of Lok Sabha?
(a) Rahman Khan (b) Karia Munda
(c) MH Ansari (d) Sushma Swaraj

28. Parliament or a State Legislature in India can declare a seat vacant, if a member absents himself without notice from the session for more than
(a) 30 days (b) 60 days
(c) 90 days (d) 120 days

29. Who decides whether a member of Parliament is subject to any disqualification?
(a) President
(b) Speaker
(c) Election Commissioner
(d) None of the above

30. Parliament of India consists of
(a) Lok Sabha and Rajya Sabha
(b) Lok Sabha, Rajya Sabha, Speaker and Deputy Speaker
(c) President, Lok Sabha and Rajya Sabha
(d) None of the above

31. Indian Parliament is based on the Principle of
(a) Bicameralism
(b) Universal Adult Franchise
(c) Diarchy
(d) Federalism

32. Who was the first Speaker of Lok Sabha?
(a) MA Ayyangar
(b) GV Mavalankar
(c) Sardar Hukum Singh
(d) Bali Ram Bhagat

33. How many members the President can nominate to the Rajya Sabha?
(a) 10 (b) 12 (c) 14 (d) 16

34. Who decide on issue whether a Bill is a Money Bill or not?
(a) President of India
(b) Speaker of Lok Sabha
(c) Chairman of Rajya Sabha
(d) Finance Minister

35. Who was the first leader of opposition on Lok Sabha?
(a) Jagjivan Ram
(b) Ram Suhag Singh
(c) B Y Chavan
(d) Sharad Pawar

36. Which of the following statement is incorrect about Money Bill?
(a) On the question weather a bill is Money bills or not, the decision of the President final
(b) A bill is not to be deemed a Money bill by reason only that it provides for the imposition, abolition, temission, alternation or regulation of many tax by any local authority or body
(c) A Money bill shall not be introduced in a Legisative Council
(d) If the Legislative Assembly does not accept any of the recommendations of the Legislative Council, the Money bill shall be deemed have been passed by both house in the form in which it was passed by Legislative Assembly

37. Who preside over joint sitting of both houses of Parliament?
(a) President
(b) Prime Minister
(c) Chairman of Raja Sabha
(d) Speaker of Lok Sabha

38. The Legislative Assembly of each states shall consists of ....
(a) not more than five hundred fifty and not less than fifty members
(b) not more than fifty hundred and not less than sixty members
(c) not more than four hundred and not less than seventy members
(d) not more than and not less than as many members as decided by Parliament

Previous Year's Questions

39. Who is chairing the Joint Parliamentary Committee (JPC) on the 2G Spectrum allocation issue? **[CLAT 2011]**

(a) Murli Manohar Joshi
(b) A Raja
(c) M Thambi Durai
(d) PC Chacko

40. Under whose premiership was the Women's Reservations Bill (to secure quotas for women in Parliament and State Legislative Assemblies) first introduced in Parliament? **[CLAT 2011]**

(a) Rajiv Gandhi
(b) HD Deve Gowda
(c) Atal Bihari Vajpayee
(d) Manmohan Singh

41. Who presides over the joint sitting of both Houses of the Parliament? **[CLAT 2012]**

(a) Speaker of Lok Sabha
(b) President
(c) Chairman of Rajya Sabha
(d) Prime Minister

42. As per the Indian Union Budget of 2012-13, the income tax exemption limit for persons below 65 years of age is **[CLAT 2012]**

(a) ₹ 175000 (b) ₹ 200000
(c) ₹ 250000 (d) ₹ 190000

43. Assertion (A) If the budget presented to the Rajya Sabha is not passed in the stipulated period, the budget proposals are not affected.
Reason (R) The Lok Sabha is more powerful, in financial matters, than the Rajya Sabha. **[CLAT 2014]**

Codes

(a) Both (A) and (R) are individually true and (R) is the correct explanation of (A)
(b) Both (A) and (R) are individually true, but (R) is not the correct explanation of (A)
(c) (A) is true, but (R) is false
(d) (A) is false, but (R) is true

44. General election is being held in India from 7th April to 12th May, 2014 to constitute **[CLAT 2014]**

(a) 14th Lok Sabha (b) 15th Lok Sabha
(c) 16th Lok Sabha (d) 17th Lok Sabha

45. Consider the following statements about Money bill **[CLAT 2015]**

1. It cannot be introduced in the Council of States.
2. It needs to be certified as such by the President.
3. It can be amended by the Council of States.
4. President has to assent it without delay.

Which of the statements given above are correct?

(a) 2 and 4 (b) 1, 2 and 4
(c) 2, 3 and 4 (d) All of these

Answers

1	*b*	2	*a*	3	*c*	4	*d*	5	*a*	6	*c*	7	*b*	8	*b*	9	*c*	10	*b*
11	*c*	12	*d*	13	*c*	14	*a*	15	*d*	16	*a*	17	*b*	18	*b*	19	*a*	20	*d*
21	*a*	22	*a*	23	*c*	24	*c*	25	*b*	26	*b*	27	*b*	28	*d*	29	*a*	30	*d*
31	*b*	32	*b*	33	*b*	34	*b*	35	*b*	36	*a*	37	*d*	38	*d*	39.	*d*	40.	*b*
41	*a*	42	*b*	43	*a*	44	*c*	45	*b*										

CHAPTER 09

CENTRE-STATE RELATIONS

Centre-State relations means the relations between centre and its's units where there exist federal system. It is of great importance in a country like India constrained by regionalism, religion, uneven developments demand for autonomy, identity politics, competing political interests, caste and race.

In the federal set-up of India, the centre and the states derive the power independently from Constitution of India. Each have their own sphere of political authority. Nevertheless in terms of power distribution, the union has been vested with disproportionately greater powers. The centre-state relations are comprehensive in nature as they cover the entire range of administrative, legislative and financial powers.

The Constitution of India contains detail provisions to regulate the various dimensions of the relations between the centre and the states. *The centre-state relations can be broadly studied under three heads*

LEGISLATIVE RELATIONS

The legislative relations between the centre and states governments are discussed in Part XI from Articles 245 to 255 of the Constitution of India.

Centre's Control over the State Legislation

- In addition to the Parliament's power to legislate directly on the state subjects, the Constitution also provides for the centre's consent before a Bill passed by a State Legislature can become a law. Although, the state enjoys authority to legislate on the subjects of the State List, the centre has power to direct the State Legislature to have conformity with the Union Laws.

- Any legislation passed by the State Legislature for acquisition of private property for public purposes will not become a law, unless it has the assent of the President.
- Under **Article 200**, the Governor is empowered to reserve a Bill for the President's consideration. Further, under the same article, the Governor has been directed to reserve any Bill affecting the dignity and functioning of the High Court for the President's consideration.
- Under **Article 288(2)**, a state is authorised to impose taxes on water, electricity-stored, generated, consumed or distributed by the central authority e.g. National Thermal Power Corporation (NTPC), National Hydel Power Operation etc. But any such law is effective only after the President's assent.
- Under **Article 304(b)**, the State Legislature is authorised to pass Bills regarding the imposition of reasonable restrictions on the freedom of trade, commerce and intercourse within the state in public interest. But any such Bill needs the President's prior approval for its introduction in the House.

Taxes Levied and Collected by the Centre, but Assigned to the States (Article 269)

The following duties and taxes shall be levied and collected by the Government of India, but shall be assigned to the States in accordance with such principles of distribution as may be formulated by Parliament by law. They are as follow

- Duties in respect of succession to property other than agricultural land.
- Estate duty in respect to property other than agricultural land.
- Terminal taxes on goods or passengers carried by railway, sea or air.
- Taxes on railway fares and freights.
- Taxes other than stamp duties on transactions in stock exchanges and future markets.
- Taxes on the sale or purchase of goods other than newspapers, where such sale or purchase takes place in the course of inter-state trade or commerce.

ADMINISTRATIVE RELATIONS

- Articles 256 to 263 in Part XI of the Constitution deal with the administrative relations between the centre and the states.
- The administrative relations corresponds to coordination aspects between the states and the centre. The Constitution directs the states to oblige by the directions given by the centre.
- This includes actions that should be taken for implementation of Union Laws and policies as determined by the Union Government.
- If the states refuse to comply with the directions given so, the President may declare a situation has arisen in the state of breakdown of constitutional machinery and may invoke President's rule in that state.

Centre-State Administrative Relations during Emergencies

- During National Emergency under Article 352, the centre becomes empowered to give directions to the state on any matter.
- During State Emergency under Article 356, the President assumes to himself the functions vested in the State Government.
- Also during Financial Emergency under Article 360, the centre can direct the states to observe Cannons of financial propriety, even President can give directions regarding the reductions of salaries of persons serving in the state including High Court Judges.
- Apart from other provisions, there are extra constitutional devices like NITI Aayog, National Development Council, Zonal Councils, Central Welfare Council etc to promote cooperation and coordination between the centre and states.

Financial Relations

- The financial relations between the Union Government and the states are discussed in Part XII from Articles 268 to 293 of the Constitution of India.
- In a federation, the centre and the units are given their separate sources of revenues, so that they can stand on their feet. The Constitution provides the distribution of finances between the centre and states.
- These provisions have undergone several amendments with the latest being the Alternative Scheme of Devolution developed by the 88th Constitutional Amendment Act.
- The recent initiative of goods and services tax is further expected to refine the financial relations between the centre and the states.
- Duties levied by the centre, but collected and appropriated by the states.
- Article 268 of the Constitution lays down that the stamp duties and such duties of excise on medicinal and toilet preparations as are mentioned in the Union List shall be levied by the Government of India, but shall be collected by the states.
- The proceeds in any financial year of any such duty leviable within any state shall not form part of the Consolidated Fund of India, but shall be assigned to that state.

Important Sources of Union Revenue

- Corporation tax.
- Currency, coinage and legal tender, foreign exchange.
- Duties of customs included export duties.
- Duties of excise on tobacco and certain goods manufactured or produced in India.
- Estate duty in respect of property other than agricultural land.
- Fees in respect of any of the matters in the Union List, but not including any fees taken in any court.
- Foreign loans-lotteries organised by the Government of India or the Government of a State.
- Post Office Savings Bank.
- Post and telegraphs, telephones, wireless broadcasting and other like forms of communications.
- Property of the union, public debt of the union railways.
- Rates of stamp duty in respect of Bills of Exchange, Cheques, Promissory Notes etc.
- Reserve Bank of India.
- Taxes on income-other than agricultural income.
- Taxes on the capital value of the assets exclusive of agricultural land of individuals and companies.
- Taxes other than stamp duties on transactions in stock exchanges and future markets.
- Taxes on the sale or purchase of newspapers and on advertisements published therein.
- Terminal taxes on goods or passengers, carried by railways, sea or rail.

Important Sources of the State Revenue

- Capitation tax.
- Duties in respect of succession to agricultural land.
- Duties of exchange on certain goods produced or manufactured in the states, such as alcoholic liquids, opium etc.
- Estate duty in respect of agricultural land.
- Fees in respect of any of the matters in the State List, but not including fees taken in any court.
- Land revenue.
- Rates of stamp duty in respect of documents other than those specified in the Union List.
- Taxes on agricultural income.
- Taxes on land and buildings.
- Taxes on mineral rights, subject to limitations imposed by Parliament relating to mineral development.

- Taxes on the consumption or sale of electricity.
- Taxes on the entry of goods into a local area for consumption, use or sale therein.
- Taxes on the sale and purchase of goods other than newspapers.
- Taxes on advertisement other than those published in newspapers.
- Taxes on goods and passengers carried by road or on inland waterways, Taxes on vehicles.
- Taxes on animals and boats.
- Taxes on professions, traders, callings and employments.
- Taxes on luxuries, including taxes on entertainments, amusements, betting and gambling.
- Taxes on tools.

Finance Commission

- The Finance Commission is constituted by the President under **Article 280** of the Constitution, mainly to give its recommendations on distribution of tax revenues between the centre and the states and amongst the states themselves. It is a quasi-judicial body.
- Two distinctive features of the commission's work involve redressing the vertical imbalances between the taxation powers and expenditure responsibilities of the centre and the states respectively and equalisation of all public services across the states.

Functions of Finance Commission

It is the duty of the commission to make recommendations to the President as to

- the distribution between the centre and the states of the net proceeds of taxes which are to be or may be, divided between them and the allocation between the states of the respective shares of such proceeds.
- the principles which should govern the grants in aid of the revenues of the states out of the Consolidated Fund of India.
- the measures needed to augment the Consolidated Fund of a State to supplement the resources of the panchayats in the state on the basis of the recommendations made by the Finance Commission of the state.
- the measures needed to augment the Consolidated Fund of a State to supplement the resources of the municipalities in the state on the basis of the recommendations made by the Finance Commission of the state.
- any other matter referred to the commission by the President in the interests of sound finance.

Goods and Services Tax (GST)

- The GST is an **indirect tax** that would replace existing levies such as excise duty, service tax and Value Added Tax (VAT). The states and the Union Government will impose the tax on almost all goods and services produced in India or imported.
- Producers will receive credits for tax paid earlier, which will eliminate multiple taxation on the same product or service. Direct taxes, such as income tax, corporate tax and capital gains tax will not be affected.
- Eliminating a multiplicity of existing indirect taxes will simplify the tax structure, broaden the tax base and create a common market across states and federally administered districts.
- At the same time, GST will lower the average tax burden for goods and services companies that now pay 'cascading' taxes on top of taxes through the production process. Reducing production costs will make exporters more competitive.

Practice Exercise

1. The centre and states derive the power independently from the
(a) the Parliament (b) the Constitution
(c) State Government (d) Union Government

2. Which of the following articles concerned with the legislative relations between the centre and the states?
(a) Articles 215-225 (b) Articles 226-236
(c) Articles 235-244 (d) Articles 245-255

3. Which of the provision in Constitution deals with the distribution of items of legislation?
(a) Article 236 (b) Article 246
(c) Article 256 (d) Article 266

4. The State List, Union List and Concurrent List are contained in the
(a) Fourth Schedule (b) Fifth Schedule
(c) Sixth Schedule (d) Seventh Schedule

5. Which among these are the principles used when interpreting the three lists of Seventh Schedule?
I. Predominance of the Union List.
II. Each entry to be interpreted broadly.
III. Doctrine of pith and substance.
IV. Doctrine of colourable legislation.
Select the correct answer using the codes given below.
(a) II and III (b) II, III and IV
(c) I, II and III (d) All of these

6. How many items contained in the Union List?
(a) 100 (b) 101 (c) 103 (d) 110

7. How many items contained in the State List?
(a) 55 (b) 61 (c) 51 (d) 71

8. How many items contained in the Concurrent List?
(a) 50 (b) 51 (c) 52 (d) 53

9. Which of the following items are not in the Concurrent List?
(a) Education
(b) Forests
(c) Protection of wild animals and birds
(d) Defence

10. According to which article, the Parliament can make any law with respect to any matter not enumerated in the Concurrent List or State List?
(a) Article 246 (b) Article 248
(c) Article 280 (d) Article 368

11. Which of the following items in the Seventh Schedule deals with defence matter?
(a) Union List (b) State List
(c) Concurrent List (d) Residue List

12. Which one of the following is in the Concurrent List in the Constitution of India?
(a) Population Control and Family Planning
(b) Public Health and Sanitation
(c) Capitation Taxes
(d) Cardington

13. The Parliament can legislate on any subject in the State List
I. If the Rajya Sabha declares by a two-third majority resolution that it is expedient to do so in national interest.
II. For the implementation of international treaties or agreements.
III. If two or more states make a request to Parliament to do so.
IV. When Article 356 is imposed in the state.
Which of the statements given above are correct?
(a) I, II and III (b) I, III and IV
(c) I, II and IV (d) All of these

14. Which of the following subjects comes under the Concurrent List?
(a) Citizenship (b) Inter-State rivers
(c) Trade Union (d) Local Government

15. The Union Parliament has the power to legislate on the subjects of all three lists in respect of
(a) scheduled areas
(b) hill areas
(c) backward areas
(d) union territories

16. The Union Territories are administered by
(a) the Prime Minister
(b) the Union Cabinet
(c) the Parliament
(d) the President through administrators appointed by him

17. A change in distribution of powers between the centre and the states can be done by
(a) the Central Government
(b) the federating units by themselves
(c) amending the Constitution
(d) None of the above

18. The Central Government can issue directions to the states with regard to the
I. Union List
II. State List
III. Concurrent List
Select the correct answer using the codes given below.
(a) II and III
(b) Only I
(c) I and III
(d) All of these

19. Which article authorises the state to impose taxes on water, electricity etc?
(a) Article 288 (1)
(b) Article 288 (2)
(c) Article 288 (3)
(d) Article 288 (4)

20. Which of the following taxes is/are levied by the Union and collected and appropriated by the States?
(a) Stamp Duties
(b) Passenger and Goods Tax
(c) Estate Duty
(d) Taxes on Newspapers

21. Agricultural Income Tax is assigned to the State Government by
(a) the Constitution of India
(b) the National Development Council
(c) the Finance Commission
(d) the Inter-State Council

22. The Union Legislature cannot legislate on a subject in the State List unless
(a) the President calls upon it to do so
(b) the Rajya Sabha passes a resolution that it is necessary in national interest to do so
(c) the Speaker certifies that it is necessary
(d) there is a National Emergency

23. Which of the following is not included the State List in the Constitution of India?
(a) Law and order
(b) Prison
(c) Criminal procedure code
(d) Police

24. In the case of a conflict between the centre and a state in respect of a subject included in the Concurrent List
(a) the Union law prevails
(b) the State law prevails
(c) the matter is resolved by the Supreme Court
(d) the law which had been passed first would prevail

25. Which Article of the Indian Constitution discusses the financial relations between the centre and the states?
(a) Articles 268 to 281
(b) Articles 289 to 295
(c) Articles 278 to 291
(d) Articles 168 to 171

26. Under which of the following Article the Governor can reserve a Bill for the President's Constitution?
(a) Article 198
(b) Article 199
(c) Article 200
(d) Article 201

Directions (Q. Nos. 27 *and* 28) *In the questions given below are two statements labelled as Assertion (A) and Reason (R). In the context of the two statements, which of the following is correct?*

Codes
(a) Both (A) and (R) are true and (R) is the correct explanation of (A)
(b) Both (A) and (R) are true, but (R) is not the correct explanation of (A)
(c) (A) is true, but (R) is false
(d) (A) is false, but (R) is false

27. **Assertion** (A) The fiscal stimulus is an intense affirmative action of the government to boost economic activity in the country.

Reason (R) It affirmative action by the Government to pursue its policy of financial inclusion.

28. Assertion (A) The State Finance Commission is responsible of the distribution of taxes between State and Panchayat.

Reason (R) To run all the allocation of taxes between the State and Panchayat Governor appoints the State Finance Commission.

29. The executive power relating to concurrent subjects remain with

(a) the Centre (b) the States

(c) the President (d) the Constitution

30. Which of the following constitutional amendment transfered five subjects to Concurrent List from State List?

(a) 42nd Amendment (b) 44th Amendment

(c) 86th Amendment (d) 73rd Amendment

31. Which of the following statements are true regarding the Constitution (One Hundred and First Amendment) Act, 2016?

I. GST Act is a comprehensive direct tax on manufacture, sale and consumption of goods and services throughout India.

II. The Act will transform India into a common market, harmonising myriads of State and Central levies into a national goods and services tax which is expected to boost manufacturing and reduce corruption.

III. It provides for Constitution of a Goods and Services Tax Council by inserting Article 297A in the Constitution.

IV. GST will be based on input tax credit method.

Select the correct answer using the codes given below.

(a) I, II and III

(b) II, III and IV

(c) I, II and V

(d) All of these

Previous Year's Questions

32. Who is the Chairman of the 14th Finance Commission? **[CLAT 2014]**

(a) Dr M Govinda Rao

(b) Dr Vijay Kelkar

(c) Dr YV Reddy

(d) Dr Raghuram Rajan

33. The Chairperson of the Seventh Pay Commission is **[CLAT 2014]**

(a) Justice BN Srikrishna

(b) Justice DK Jain

(c) Justice AP Shah

(d) Justice AK Mathur

Answers

1	*b*	2	*d*	3	*b*	4	*d*	5	*d*	6	*a*	7	*b*	8	*c*	9	*d*	10	*b*
11	*a*	12	*a*	13	*d*	14	*c*	15	*d*	16	*d*	17	*c*	18	*d*	19	*b*	20	*a*
21	*a*	22	*b*	23	*c*	24	*a*	25	*a*	26	*c*	27	*c*	28	*a*	29	*a*	30	*a*
31	*b*	32	*c*	33	*d*														

CHAPTER 10

JUDICIARY

The judiciary (also known as the judicial system or court system) is the system of courts that interprets and applies the law in the name of the state. The judiciary also provides a mechanism for the resolution of disputes.

There is a single integrated judicial system in India. It is organised in pyramidal form. At the apex of the entire judicial system stands the Supreme Court of India.

Immediately below the Supreme Court are the various High Courts and below them are the subordinate courts in each state.

All the courts in the Union of India are under the control of the Supreme Court. And the decisions of the Supreme Court are binding on all other courts within the territory of India.

SUPREME COURT

- Supreme Court stands at the apex of the Judicial System of India. It is the ultimate interpreter of the Constitution and the laws of the land.
- Article 124 states the establishment and Constitution of Supreme Court.
- Supreme Court was inaugurated on 28th January, 1950.
- At present, the Supreme Court consists of 34 Judges (1 Chief Justice of India (CJI) and 33 Judges).

Appointment of Chief Justice

Only seniormost Judge of the Supreme Court is appointed by the President as CJI. Other judges of the Supreme Court are appointed by the President in consultation with the Chief Justice. He may also consult other judges of the Supreme Court and High Court while appointing a Judge of the Supreme Court.

Acting Chief Justice

Under **Article 126**, the President can appoint a Judge of the Supreme Court as an acting CJI, when

- office of CJI is vacant; or
- the CJI is temporarily absent; or
- the CJI is unable to perform the duties of his office.

Qualifications

Under **Article 124** (3), a person to be appointed as a Judge of the Supreme Court should have the following qualifications

- He should be a citizen of India.
- He should have been a Judge of a High Court (or High Courts in succession) for five years.
- He should have been an advocate of a High Court (or High Courts in succession) for ten years.

Or

- He should be a distinguished jurist in the opinion of the President.
- The Constitution does not prescribe a minimum age for appointment as a Judge of the Supreme Court.

Oath or Affirmation

Administered by the President or some person appointed by him for this purpose.

Tenure of Judges

The Constitution has not fixed the tenure of a Judge of the Supreme Court. *It makes the following provisions*

- Holds office until he attains the age of 65 years.
- Resign his office by writing to the President.
- Removed from his office by the President on the recommendation of the Parliament.

Removal of Judges or Impeachment

Under **Article 124 (4)**, a Judge of the Supreme Court shall not be removed from his office except by an order of the President passed after an address by each House of the Parliament by special majority. Judges can be removed only on the grounds of proved misbehaviour or incapacity.

Under **Article 124 (5)** Parliament may by law regulate the procedure relating to the removal of a Judge of the Supreme Court. Under this Article, Parliament provides the procedure for removal by the Judges Enquiry Act (1968).

- No Judge of the Supreme Court has been impeached so far. The first such case of impeachment is that of Justice V Ramaswami of the Supreme Court in Lok Sabha (1991-93). But, finally he could not be impeached.
- The second case of impeachment is that of Justice Saumitra Sen of the Calcutta High Court (became the first Judge in Indian History, against whom an impeachment motion was passed in the Rajya Sabha). The BSP was the only party to oppose the motion to remove the judge. After this, he resigned and there was no need for impeachment.

Under Article 217 (a), a Judge of the High Court "may by writing under his hand addressed to the President" resign his office.

Under **Article 124(2) (a),** a Judge of the Supreme Court "may by writing under his hand addressed to the President, resign his office".

Salaries and Allowances

Under **Article 125**, the salaries, allowances, privileges, leave and pension of the Judges of the Supreme Court are determined from time to time by the Parliament.

- Salary of Chief Justice of India is ₹ 1 lakh per month. Salary of other Judges of Supreme Court is ₹ 90000 per month.
- The retired Chief Justice and Judges are entitled to 50% of their last drawn salary as monthly pension.

Ad hoc Judges

Under **Article 127**, if at any time there is not a quorum of the Judges of the Supreme Court to hold or continue any session, CJI can appoint a Judge of the High Court as an Ad hoc Judge of the Supreme Court for a temporary period.

- He can do so only after consultation with, Chief Justice of the High Court concerned and with previous consent of the President.
- The Judge appointed as a Ad hoc Judges should be qualified for be appointment as the Judge of the Supreme Court.

Retired Judges

Under Article 128, at any time, the Chief Justice of India can request a retired Judge of the Supreme Court or a retired Judge of the High Court (who is duly qualified for appointment as a Judge of the Supreme Court) to act as a Judge of the Supreme Court for a temporary period.

> **SEAT OF SUPREME COURT**
>
> Under **Article 130**, the Constitution declares Delhi as the seat of the Supreme Court. But, it authorises the CJI to appoint any other place or places as seat of the Supreme Court. He can take this decision only with the approval of the President.

Procedure of the Court

The Supreme Court can, with the approval of the President, make rules for regulating generally the practice and procedure of the court.

Constitutional Bench A bench consisting of at least 5 Judges. Constituted by the CJI to hear a case involving a substantial question of law.

Independence of the Judges

Various organs of the polity is based on doctrine of check and balance, and independence from arbitrary encroachment of legislature.

Independence of judges is ensured by following provisions

- Mode of appointment of CJI and Judges of the Supreme Court.
- Security of tenure (removed only by the President).
- Fixed service conditions (salary charged from Consolidated Fund of India).
- Conduct of Judges cannot be discussed in Parliament or State Legislature.
- Ban on practice after retirement.
- Power to punish its contempt.
- Freedom to appoint its staff.
- Its jurisdiction cannot be curtailed.
- Difficult removal procedure .
- Separation from executive.

Jurisdiction and Powers of Supreme Court

Jurisdiction and powers of Supreme Court are as follows

Original Jurisdiction (Article 131)

The Supreme Court decides the dispute between the centre and one or more states; the centre and any state or states on one side and one or more states on the other; or between two or more states.

In the above disputes, the Supreme Court has exclusive original jurisdiction. They lie directly and exclusively with the Supreme Court.

Writ Jurisdiction (Article 32)

Every individual has the right to move the Supreme Court directly by appropriate proceedings for the enforcement of his Fundamental Rights through the issuance of writs.

Appellate Jurisdiction (Article 132)

The Supreme Court is primarily a court of appeal and hears appeals against the judgements of the lower courts. *It enjoys a wide appellate jurisdiction, which can be classified under four heads*

(i) Appeals in constitutional matters
(ii) Appeals in civil matters (Article 133)
(iii) Appeals in criminal matters (Article 134)
(iv) Appeal by special leave (Article 136)

Advisory Jurisdiction

The Constitution (Article 143) authorises the President to seek the opinion of the Supreme Court. It is duty bound to give its opinion, which is not binding on President.

Court of Record

As a Court of Record, Supreme Court has two powers

- Judgements, proceedings and acts of Supreme Court are recorded for perpetual memory and testimony.
- It can punish for contempt of court.

Power of Judicial Review (Article 137)

- Judicial review is the power of the Supreme Court to examine the constitutionality of legislative enactments and executive order of both Central and State Governments.
- On examination, if they are found to be violative of the Constitution, they can be declared as illegal, unconstitutional and invalid and they cannot be enforced by any authority.
- Judicial review is needed for various reasons i.e. to uphold the supremacy of the Constitution, maintain federal equilibrium, protect the Fundamental Rights of the citizens.

Some famous cases, in which the Supreme Court used the power of judicial review are as follows

- Golakanath Case (1967)
- Bank Nationalisation Case (1970)
- Privy Purse Abolition Case (1971)
- Kesavananda Bharati Case (1973)
- Minerva Mills Case (1980)

- **Article 141** Law declared by Supreme Court to be binding on all courts, within the territory of India.
- **Article 144** All authorities, civil and judicial in the territory of India to act in aid of the Supreme Court.
- **Public Interest Litigation** (PIL) Any person can now initiate a proceeding on behalf of the aggrieved person (if the aggrieved persons cannot do so on their own) is either the High Court or the Supreme Court for the protection of greater public interest.

HIGH COURT

- Every High Court (whether exclusive or common) consists of a Chief Justice and such other Judges as the President may from time to time deem necessary to appoint. Thus, the Constitution does not specify the strength of a High Court and leaves it to the discretion of the President.
- Accordingly, the President determines the strength of a High Court from time to time depending upon its workload.
- The Constitution of India provides a High Court for each state, but the 7th Amendment Act of 1956, authorised the Parliament to establish a common High Court for two or more states or a State and a Union Territory.
- The territorial jurisdiction of a High Court is co-terminus with the territory of a state.

Jurisdiction and Seats of High Courts

Name	Established in the Year	Territorial Jurisdiction	Seat
Madhya Pradesh	1956	Madhya Pradesh	Jabalpur (Benches at Gwalior and Indore)
Bombay	1862	Maharashtra, Dadar and Nagar Haveli, Goa, Daman and Diu	Mumbai (Benches at Nagpur, Panaji and Aurangabad)
Calcutta	1862	West Bengal and Andaman and Nicobar islands	Kolkata (Circuit Bench at Port Blair)
Madras	1862	Tamil Nadu and Puducherry	Chennai
Allahabad	1866	Uttar Pradesh	Allahabad (Bench at Lucknow)
Karnataka	1884	Karnataka	Bengaluru
Patna	1916	Bihar	Patna
Orissa	1948	Odisha	Cuttack
Guwahati	1948	Assam, Nagaland, Mizoram and Arunachal Pradesh	Guwahati (Benches at Kohima and Aizawl and Itanagar)
Rajasthan	1949	Rajasthan	Jodhpur (Bench at Jaipur)
Andhra Pradesh	1954	Andhra Pradesh	Amrawati
Kerala	1958	Kerala and Lakshadweep	Ernakulam
Jammu and Kashmir	1928	Jammu and Kashmir	Srinagar and Jammu
Gujarat	1960	Gujarat	Ahmedabad
Delhi	1966	Delhi	Delhi
Punjab and Haryana	1875	Punjab, Haryana and Chandigarh	Chandigarh
Himachal Pradesh	1971	Himachal Pradesh	Shimla
Sikkim	1975	Sikkim	Gangtok
Uttarakhand	2000	Uttarakhand	Nainital
Jharkhand	2000	Jharkhand	Ranchi
Chhattisgarh	2000	Chhattisgarh	Bilaspur
Manipur	2013	Manipur	Imphal
Meghalaya	2013	Meghalaya	Shillog
Tripura	2013	Tripura	Agartala
Telengana	2019	Telengana	Hyderabad

- At present, there are 25 High Courts in the country. Out of them, three and seven are common High Courts for states and for both states and union territories respectively, Delhi is the only union territory that has a High Court of its own (since 1966).
- The Union Territory of Andaman and Nicobar islands comes under the jurisdiction of circuit bench of Kolkata High Court at Port Blair.

Appointment of Judges

- Under Article 217, the Judges of the High Court are appointed by the President.
- The Chief Justice of the High Court is appointed by the President after consultation with the Chief Justice of Supreme Court and Governor of the concerned state.

Qualification Oath/Removal of Judges

- He should have held a judicial office in the territory of India for 10 year or he should have been an advocate of a High Court (or High Courts in succession) for 10 years. He should be a citizen of India.
- Oath is administered by Governor or person appointed by him for this purpose.
- He holds office until he attains the age of 62 years. Any questions regarding his age is to be decided by the President and is considered as final.
- He can resign his office by writing to the President.
- He can be removed from his office on the recommendation of the Parliament (same as Judge of Supreme Court).
- He vacates his office when he is appointed as a Judge of the Supreme Court or when he is transfered to another High Court.
- Determined by Parliament from time to time.

Independence of High Court

Following provisions are made to safeguard and ensure the independence of High Court

- Mode of appointment.
- Security of tenure.
- Fixed service conditions.
- Expenses charged on the Consolidated Fund of State.
- Conduct of judge cannot be discussed.
- Ban on practice after retirement.
- Power to punish for its contempt.
- Freedom to appoint its staff.
- Its jurisdiction cannot be curtailed.
- Separation from executive.

Jurisdiction and Power of High Court

At present, a High Court enjoys the following jurisdiction and powers

- Original jurisdiction
- Writ jurisdiction (Article 226)
- Appellate jurisdiction
- Supervisory jurisdiction
- Control over subordinate courts
- A court of record
- Power of judicial review

The Supreme Court can issue writ jurisdiction, only where a Fundamental Right has been infringed. High Court can issue these writs under Article 226 not only in such cases, but also where an ordinary legal right has been infringed. High Court does not have advisory power as in case of Supreme Court.

Subordinate Courts

Articles 233 to 237 in Part VI of the constitutions make the provisions to regulate the organisation of subordinate courts and an ensure their independence from the executive.

Appointment of District Judges

The appointment, posting and promotion of district judges in a state are made in Governor of the State in consultation and the High Court.

A person to be appointed as district should have the following qualifications

- He should not already be in the Central or the State Government.
- He should have been an advocate or a pleader for seven years.
- He should be recommended by the High Court.

Appointment of Other Judges

Appointment of person (other than district judges) to the judicial services of a state are made by the Governor of the State after consultation with the State Public Service Commission and the High Court.

Lok Adalat

- Lok Adalat (People's Courts), established by the government, settles disputes through conciliation and compromise. The first Lok Adalat was held in Gujarat on 14th March, 1982.
- The Lok Adalat is presided over by a sitting or retired judicial officer as Chairman, with two other member, usually a lawyer and a social worker. There is no court fee.
- If the case is already filed in a regular court, the fee paid is refunded if the dispute is settled at the Lok Adalat.
- Lok Adalat is very effective in settlement of money claims. Disputes, like partition suits, damages and matrimonial cases, can also be easily settled in Lok Adalat, as chances of compromise, through give and take approach stand high in such cases.
- Lok Adalat is a boon to the litigant public, where they can get their disputes settled fast and free of cost.
- Lok Adalats have been given the status of a Civil Court and every award made by the Lok Adalat is final and binding on all parties and no appeals lies to any court against its award.

Practice Exercise

1. After independence the Supreme Court of India came into existence in the year?
(a) 1953 (b) 1952
(c) 1951 (d) 1950

2. Which of the following is the ultimate interpreter of the Constitution in India?
(a) The President
(b) The Parliament
(c) The Supreme Court of India
(d) The Chief Justice of India

3. Which article deals with the establishment of the Supreme Court?
(a) Article 124 (b) Article 134
(c) Article 104 (d) Article 114

4. Who among the following appoints the Chief Justice of India?
(a) The Parliament (b) The President
(c) The Prime Minister (d) None of these

5. Which article concerned with the appointment of Acting Judge by the President?
(a) Article 124 (b) Article 125
(c) Article 126 (d) Article 127

6. The qualification of appointment of Judges is falls under the
(a) Article 124 (1) (b) Article 124 (2)
(c) Article 124 (3) (d) Article 124 (4)

7. What is the tenure of a Judge of the Supreme Court?
(a) 2 years (b) 3 years
(c) 4 years (d) Not fixed

8. Which article of the Constitution of India provides the procedure for removal of the Judges Enquiry Act, 1968?
(a) Article 124 (3) (b) Article 124 (4)
(c) Article 124 (5) (d) Article 124 (6)

9. Who among the following judges faced the impeachment process in the Lok Sabha?
(a) V Ramaswami (b) Altamas Kabir
(c) HL Dattu (d) None of these

10. Under which article falls the salaries and allowances of the Judges of the Supreme Court?
(a) Article 124 (b) Article 125
(c) Article 126 (d) Article 127

11. Who was the first Chief Justice of the Supreme Court of India?
(a) M Patanjali Shastri (b) Hiralal J Kania
(c) S Mukherjee (d) SR Das

12. Who is the Chief Justice of India presently?
(a) HL Dattu (b) TS Thakur
(c) P Sathasivam (d) Deepak Mishra

13. At which of the following place the first Lok Adalat was held on 14th March, 1982?
(a) Gujarat (b) Mumbai
(c) Bihar (d) Kolkata

Directions (Q. Nos. 14-18) *In the questions given below are two statements labelled as Assertion (A) and Reason (R). In the context of the two statements, which of the following is correct?*

Codes
(a) Both (A) and (R) are true and (R) is the correct explanation of (A)
(b) Both (A) and (R) are true, but (R) is not the correct explanation of (A)
(c) (A) is true, but (R) is false
(d) (A) is false, but (R) is true

14. Assertion (A) The Indian Constitution recognises the supremacy of judiciary.
Reason (R) The question as to what constitutes a reasonable restriction on Fundamental Rights is to be determined by the Court of Law.

15. Assertion (A) An award made by Lok Adalat is deemed to be a decree of a Civil Court.
Reason (R) Award of Lok Adalat is final and binding on all parties and no appeal lies against there to before any court.

16. Assertion (A) The circuit bench of Andaman and Nicobar rest in Kolkata High Court.
Reason (R) The Constitution specify the strength of a Supreme Court.

17. Assertion (A) Special leave petition is the prerogative of Supreme Court only.
Reason (R) Special leave petition involves the substantive question of law is involved.

18. Assertion (A) United judiciary is the function of unitary feature.
Reason (R) USA judiciary is the example of strong federation.

19. A Judge of the Supreme Court retires at the age of
(a) 65 years (b) 62 years
(c) 60 years (d) 68 years

20. A Judge of the Supreme Court can be removed from office only on the ground of
(a) senility
(b) proven misbehaviour or incapacity
(c) imbecile conduct
(d) gross-inefficiency

21. The minimum number of judges to sit on the constitutional bench or a bench which gives its advisory opinion on a reference by the President must be
(a) One-third of the total strength of the Court
(b) 3
(c) 7
(d) 5

22. The High Court of a State is under the direct supervision of
(a) Governor (b) President
(c) Parliament (d) Supreme Court

23. How many High Courts are there in India?
(a) 28 (b) 25
(c) 24 (d) 22

24. Which High Court has the highest number of benches in India?
(a) Allahabad High Court
(b) Punjab and Haryana High Court
(c) Mumbai High Court
(d) Guwahati High Court

25. A Judge of a High Court retires at the age of
(a) 58 years (b) 65 years
(c) 62 years (d) 60 years

26. A retired Judge of a High Court cannot
(a) practice in any Court in India
(b) practice in the High Court from where he has retired
(c) practice in any High Court in India
(d) practice in the Supreme Court

27. The oldest High Court in India
(a) Bombay High Court
(b) Calcutta High Court
(c) Madras High Court
(d) Allahabad High Court

28. A sentence of death by a lower court
(a) must be confirmed by High Court
(b) must be confirmed by Supreme Court
(c) is operational if no appeal is made to higher courts
(d) must be confirmed by the President

29. Supreme Court's advisory jurisdiction is provided under .... of the Constitution.
(a) Article 123 (b) Article 124
(c) Article 143 (d) Article 226

30. Which of the following is a Court of Record?
(a) Supreme Court (b) High Court
(c) District Court (d) Both 'a' and 'b'

31. The 39th Constitutional Amendment laid that election of any person to Lok Sabha holding the office of Prime Minister cannot be challenged before a Court of Law, but only before an authority established by Parliament. This was declared unconstitutional by the Supreme Court in
(a) Keshavananda Bharati case
(b) Maneka Gandhi case
(c) Indira Gandhi *v/s* Raj Narain case
(d) None of the above

32. The Concept of Public Interest Litigation originated in
(a) Canada
(b) The United States of America
(c) Australia
(d) The United Kingdom

33. Under which of the following provision of the constitution of India 1950, the Supreme Court may grant special leave to appeal from any judgement, decree, determination, sentence or order?
(a) Article 131
(b) Article 134
(c) Article 136
(d) Article 143

34. Who amongest the following was not a Chief Justice of India?
(a) Justice PN Bhagwati
(b) Justice RM Lodha
(c) Justice Krishna Lyer
(d) Justice JS Verma

35. The 'Collegium system' is ....
(a) a process to appoint judges in the High Court and the Supreme Court of India
(b) a process to elect the speaker of the Lok Sabha
(c) a process to elect President and Vice-President of India
(d) a process to elect Leader of the Opposition party in the Lok Sabha

36. The Delhi High Court has asked Facebook to ban children below .... years of age
(a) 10 (b) 13 (c) 16 (d) 18

37. Which of the following Articles of the Constitution of India authorise the Chief Justice of India to request a retired Judge to Join the Supreme Court?
(a) 129 (b) 128 (c) 127 (d) 126

Previous Year's Questions

38. In which case did the Nagpur Bench of the Bombay High Court on 14 July, 2010 commute the death sentence of six accused to rigorous life imprisonment? **[CLAT 2011]**
(a) Khairlanji Case
(b) Bhopal Gas Leak Case
(c) Bhagalpur Case
(d) Nithari Case

39. The Supreme Court in 2010 upheld an order of the Bombay High Court to lift a four year old ban imposed by the Maharashtra Government on publication and circulation of a controversial book, authored by American scholar James Laine. Identify the book from the following. **[CLAT 2011]**
(a) Chhatrapati Shivaji
(b) Shivaji–The Warrior King
(c) Shivaji–The Hindu King in Muslim India
(d) None of the above

40. Which one of the following was not awarded a portion of the contested land by the judgment of the Allahabad High Court in 2010 pertaining to the Ayodhya dispute? **[CLAT 2011]**
(a) Nirmohi Akhada
(b) Sunni Central Board of Waqf
(c) Rashtriya Swayamsevak Sangh
(d) Bhagwan Sri Ram Lala Virajman

41. Consider the following statement(s) **[CLAT 2012]**

I. In a recent Supreme Court verdict pronounced by Justice Markandeya Katju and Justice Gyan Sudha Mishra, the court upheld the constitutionality of the Haj subsidy.

II. Muslims are not the only beneficiaries of the secular state's generosity. Hindus have also received substantial financial support from the Government.

With reference to the statement are mentioned above, which of the following is correct?

(a) Only I
(b) Only II
(c) Both I and II
(d) Neither I nor II

42. The two Supreme Court Judges, who delivered the famous (2G) judgement in February, 2012 were **[CLAT 2012]**

(a) Justice GS Singhvi and Justice Gyan Sudha Mishra
(b) Justice GS Singhvi and Justice AK Ganguly
(c) Justice SH Kapadia and Justice AK Ganguly
(d) Justice Chandramauli Kumar Prasad and Justice HL Gokhale

43. Supreme Court recently declared 'Salva Judum' unconstitutional. What is 'Salwa Judum'? **[CLAT 2012]**

(a) A terrorist outfit
(b) An armed civilian group formed to combat Maoists
(c) A money-chain business
(d) Custom of killing a girl for inter-caste marriage in the name of honour

44. **Assertion** (A) The right to move the Supreme Court under Article 32 of the Constitution by appropriate proceedings for the enforcement of the Fundamental Rights is guaranteed as a Fundamental Rights.

Reason (R) The Supreme Court of India has been appointed as the guardian of the Constitution. **[CLAT 2012]**

Codes

(a) Both (A) and (R) are true and (R) is the correct explanation of (A)
(b) Both (A) and (R) are true, but (R) is not the correct explanation of (A)
(c) (A) is true, but (R) is false
(d) (A) is false, but (R) is true

45. In the month of March, 2013 the Supreme Court of India issued a notice that the ambassador of the following country shall not leave India without the permission of the Supreme Court. **[CLAT 2013]**

(a) Germany (b) Maldives
(c) Italy (d) Nepal

46. The number of High Courts in India is **[CLAT 2013]**

(a) 18 (b) 24 (c) 21 (d) 28

47. Mention the name of the current Chief Justice of India. **[CLAT 2013]**

(a) Justice Altamas Kabir
(b) Justice P Sathasivam
(c) Justice RM Lodha
(d) Justice HL Dattu

48. Which of the following Judges of the Supreme Court of India is famously known as the 'Green Judge'? **[CLAT 2014]**

(a) Justice VR Krishna Iyyar
(b) Justice PN Bhagwati
(c) Justice KuldeepSingh
(d) Justice BN Kirpal

49. Match List I with List II and select the correct answer using the codes given below the lists **[CLAT 2014]**

	List I (Person)		List II (Position)
A.	Nagendra Singh	1.	Chief Election Commissioner of India
B.	SH Kapadia	2.	President of the International Court of Justice
C.	NR Madhava Menon	3.	Former Chief Justice of India
D.	VS Sampath	4.	Legal educator and Founder-Director of National Law School of India University

Codes

	A	B	C	D
(a)	2	3	1	4
(b)	4	3	2	1
(c)	1	2	4	3
(d)	2	3	4	1

50. Who is the present Chief Justice of Supreme Court of India? **[CLAT 2015]**

(a) Rajendra Mal
(b) Harilal Jekisundas Kania
(c) HL Dattu
(d) Mohammad Hidayatullah

51. The Supreme Court of India has struck down the institution (99th-ninth Amendment) Act, 2014 as unconstitutional. It is related to **[CLAT 2016]**

(a) religious rights
(b) National Judicial Appointment Commission
(c) land exchange between India and Bangladesh
(d) Jallikattu

52. The object of which one of the following writs is to prevent a person to hold public office which he is not legally entitled to hold? **[CLAT 2016]**

(a) Quo warranto
(b) Prohibition
(c) Mandamus
(d) Certiorari

Answers

1	*d*	2	*c*	3	*a*	4	*b*	5	*c*	6	*c*	7	*d*	8	*c*	9	*a*	10	*b*
11	*b*	12	*d*	13	*a*	14	*a*	15	*c*	16	*d*	17	*a*	18	*c*	19	*a*	20	*b*
21	*d*	22	*d*	23	*c*	24	*a*	25	*c*	26	*c*	27	*a*	28	*a*	29	*c*	30	*a*
31	*c*	32	*b*	33	*c*	34	*c*	35	*a*	36	*b*	37	*b*	38	*a*	39	*c*	40	*c*
41	*d*	42	*b*	43	*b*	44	*b*	45	*c*	46	*b*	47	*c*	48	*d*	49	*d*	50	*c*
51	*b*	52	*a*																

CHAPTER 11

CONSTITUTIONAL & NON- CONSTITUTIONAL BODIES OF INDIA

Constitutional bodies in India are the bodies or institutions that have its name mentioned in the Indian Constitution. It derives power directly from the Constitution.

CONSTITUTIONAL BODIES OF INDIA

Comptroller and Auditor General of India

The Constitution of India (Article 148) provides for an independent office of the Comptroller and Auditor General of India (CAG). He is the guardian of the public purse and audits the accounts of the government at both the levels the centre and the state.

- His duty is to uphold the Constitution of India and laws of Parliament in the field of financial administration.
- **Articles 148 to 151** of the Constitution deals with CAG's appointment, powers and audit reports.
- The CAG of India is appointed by the President for six years or till sixty five years, of age whichever is earlier.
- His removal process is similar to that of a Judge of the Supreme Court.
- Shri V Narahari Rao, was the first Comptroller and Auditor General of India (1948-1954).

Independence of CAG (Article 148)

Following points show that the Constitution ensures the independence of the CAG

- He is provided with the security of tenure. He can be removed by the President only in accordance with the procedure mentioned in the Constitution. Thus, he does not hold his office till the pleasure of the President, though he is appointed by him. He is not eligible for further office, after he ceases to hold his office.
- By charging his salary and other expenses for the maintenance of his office upon the Consolidated Fund of India.
- By providing that, the salary and other service conditions of the CAG shall not be changed to his disadvantage during his tenures.
- By giving him complete control over administrative staff.

Articles Related to CAG

Article 148	Comptroller and Auditor General of India.
Article 149	Duties and Powers of the Comptroller and Auditor General.
Article 150	Form of accounts of the Union and of the States.
Article 151	Audit Reports.

Duties and Responsibilities of CAG (Article 149)

- Audit of receipts and expenditure of Consolidated Funds of the Union and the States and UTs having a Legislative Assembly.
- Audit of the Contingency Fund of India and the public accounts.
- Audit of the transactions related to authorities, developmental bodies, welfare boards etc substantially funded by the government.
- Accounts of bodies receiving loans and grants from the government. Audit of stocks, shares of government organisations and corporations as enacted in the statues constituting them.
- Submits his audit reports relating to the accounts of the centre and of a state to the President and Governor respectively.
- Assertions and certifies the net proceeds of any tax or duty. His certificate is final.
- Acts as a guide, friend and philosopher of the Public Accounts Committee of Parliament.
- Regulatory agencies like Telecom Regulatory Authority of India (TRAI), Public-Private Partnerships (PPP). Panchayats and Municipalities should be audited by the Comptroller and Auditor General (CAG) of India.
  - Reports of CAG to be tabled in the Parliament timely.
  - Enabled to perform concurrent audit instead of post-mortem audit.

Removal of CAG

- The procedure of removing the CAG is similar to that of a Judge of the Supreme Court.
- The CAG can be removed by the President after an address by each of the House of the Parliament supported by a majority of the total membership of that House and by majority of not less than two-third of the members of that House present and voting, on the ground of proved misbehaviour or incapacity.

Election Commission of India

The Election Commission of India is an autonomous, quasi-judicial constitutional body of India. Its mission is to conduct free and fair elections in India. It was established on 25th January, 1950 under Article 324 of the Constitution of India.

Structure of Election Commission

- The Commission presently consists of a Chief Election Commissioner and two Election Commissioners, appointed by the President.
- The Chief Election Commissioner can be removed from his office by Parliament with two-thirds majority in Lok Sabha and Rajya Sabha on the ground of proved misbehaviour or incapacity.
- Other Election Commissioner can be removed by the President on the recommendation of the Chief Election Commissioner.
- Salary of Chief Election Commissioner is same as of Justice of Supreme Court of India. All three commissioner have same right of taking a decision. Tenure of Election Commissioners are 6 years or upto 65 years of age whichever is earlier.
- The Election Commission shall have the power superintendence, direction and control of all elections to Parliament and the State Legislatures and of elections to the office of the President and Vice-President.

Powers and Duties of Election Commission

- The Election Commission enjoys complete autonomy and is insulated from any kind of executive interference.
- The body also functions as a quasi-judicial body in matters of electoral disputes and other matters involving the conduct of elections.
- Its recommendations and opinions are binding on the President of India. However, the decisions of the body are liable for independent judiciary reviews by courts acting on electoral petitions.
- The Election Commission is responsible for planning and executing a whole amount of complex operations that go into the conduct of elections. However, Election forces and the Police is deemed to be on deputation to the Election Commission, which takes effective control of personnel, movable and immovable Government properties it deems necessary for successful completion of the electoral process.

Union Public Service Commission (UPSC)

- UPSC is an independent recruiting agency of union and performs other functions as provided by the Constitution.
- Chairman and other members of UPSC shall be appointed by President of India.
- A member of UPSC shall hold office for a term of 6 years from date on which he enters into the office or until he attains age of 65 years whichever is earlier.
- UPSC members can resign by addressing their letter of resignation to the President.
- President can remove them by issuing orders under the circumstances provided in the Constitution.
- To conduct exams for appointment to services under the union. Advise the President (not obligatory on him) in matters relating to appointment, promotions and transfers from one service to another of civil servants.
- All disciplinary matters affecting person in the service of union.
- Matters regarding award of pension and awards in respect to injuries sustained during service under the government.

National Commission for SCs and STs

- The National Commission for SCs and STs have been established under the Article 338 and 338-A respectively as a constitutional body.
- They investigate all matter related to constitutional and other legal safeguards for SCs and STs and report to the President on their working. It also advice on the planning process for socio-economic development of SCs and STs.

Finance Commission of India

- It has all the powers of the Civil Court as per the Code of Civil Procedure, 1908. It can call any witness, or can ask for the production of any public record or document from any court or office.
- It can ask any person to give information or document on matters as it may feel to be useful or relevant. It can function as a civil court in discharging its duties.

NON-CONSTITUTIONAL BODIES

There are certain bodies enacted from legislative procedure, which are essential for maintaining democratic society. *These bodies are as follows*

Lokpal and Lokayuktas

The Lokpal and Lokayuktas Act, 2013 was made by the Parliament to provide for the establishment of body of Lokpal for the Union and Lokayukta for State to inquire into allegations of corruptions against certain public functionaries and for matters concerning them.

Some salient features of Lokpal and Lokayukta Act are given as under

- Lokpal bill consists of a chairperson and a maximum of eight members, of which 50% shall be judicial members, 50% of members of Lokpal shall be from SC/ST/OBCs, minorities and women.
- The selection of chairperson and members of Lokpal shall be through a selection committee consist of
  - Prime Minister.
  - Speaker of Lok Sabha.
  - Leader of opposition in Lok Sabha.
  - Chief Justice of India or a sitting Judge of Supreme Court nominated by CJI.
  - Eminent jurist on the basis of recommendations of the first four members of the selection committee. Prime Minister has been brought under the purview of the Lokpal.

National Human Rights Commission

- The National Human Rights Commission is a statutory body, constituted in 1993 under the protection of Human Right Act, 1993.
- The Commission acts a watchdog of human rights in the country. It is a multi-member body consisting of a chairman and four members. The chairman should be a retired Chief Justice of India and members should be serving or retired Judges of Supreme Court and person having special knowledge or practical experience with respect to human rights.
- The commission has also four ex-officio members : the Chairman of the National Commission for minorities, the National Commission for SCs, the National Commission for STs and National Commission for Women.

Functions of National Human Rights Commission

- Inquire on its initiative or on a petition presented to it by a victim or any person on his behalf, into complaint of violation of human rights or abetment or negligence in the prevention of such violation, by a public servant.
- Intervene in any proceeding involving any allegation of violation of human rights pending before a court with the approval of such court.
- Visit, under intimation to the State Government, any jail or any other institution under the control of the State Government, where persons are detained or lodged for purposes of treatment, reformation or protection to study the living condition of the inmates and make recommendations thereon.

- Review the safeguards by or under the Constitution or any law for the time being in force for the protection of human rights and recommend measures for their effective implementation.
- Review the factors, including acts of terrorism that inhibit the enjoyment of human rights and recommend appropriate remedial measures.

National Commission for Backward Classes

- The Government of India enacted the National Commission for Backward Classes Act, 1993 (Act No. 27 of 1993) for setting up a National Commission for Backward Classes as a permanent body.
- The Act provides that the Commission shall consist of five members, comprising of a Chairperson who is or has been a judge of the Supreme Court of India or of High Courts of India; a social scientist; two persons, who have special knowledge in matters relating to backward classes; and a member-secretary, who is or has been an officer of the Central Government in the rank of Secretary to the Government of India.
- Article 340 of the Constitution provides for the appointment of a Commission to investigate the conditions of and the difficulties faced by the socially and educationally backward classes and to make appropriate recommendations.

National Commission for Women

- National Commission for Women is the apex national body which was formed with the mandate of promoting and protecting the interests of women.
- The National Commission for Women was set-up as a statutory body in January 1992 under the National Commission for Women Act, 1990 (Act No. 20 of 1990) of Government of India, to review the constitutional and legal safeguards for women; recommend remedial legislative measures, facilitate redressal of grievances and advice the government on all policy matters affecting women.

Central Vigilance Commission (CVC)

- CVC was set-up by the Government of India in February 1964 on the recommendations of the Committee on Prevention of Corruption, headed by K Santhanam, to advise and guide Central Government agencies in the field of vigilance.
- CVC is conceived to be the apex vigilance institution, free of control from any executive authority, monitoring all vigilance activity under the Central Government and advising various authorities in Central Government organisations in planning, executing, reviewing and reforming their vigilance work.
- Consequent upon promulgation of an ordinance by the President, the Central Vigilance Commission has been made a multi member commission with 'statutory' status with effect from 25th August, 1998.
- The CVC bill was passed by both the Houses of Parliament in 2003 and the President gave his assent on 11th September, 2003. Thus, the Central Vigilance Commission Act, 2003 (No 45 of 2003) came into effect from that date.
- Central Vigilance Commissioner is provided by Chairperson; and not more than two Vigilance Commissioners should be members.

Powers and Functions of Central Vigilance Commission

To exercise superintendence over the functioning of the Delhi Special Police Establishment (DSPE) with respect to investigation under the Prevention of Corruption Act, 1988 or offence under CRPC for certain categories of public servants and to give directions to the DSPE for purpose of discharging this responsibility.

Commission's Jurisdiction under CVC Act

- Members of All India Services serving in connection with the affairs of the Union and Group A officers of the Central Government.
- Board level appointees and other senior officers upto two grades below the Board level, in the Public Sector Undertakings of the Central Government.
- Officers of the rank of Scale V and above in the Public Sector Banks.
- Officers of the rank of Assistant Manager and above in the Insurance Sector (covered by LIC and GIC and four non-life insurance companies in the Public sector).
- Officers drawing basic pay of ` 8700 per month and above in autonomous bodies/local authorities or societies owned or controlled by the Central Government.

Central Information Commission (CIC)

- Right to Information became an act in 2005. The aim is to make the governments more transparent in its working. It came into operation on 12th October, 2005.
- Under the act, a Central Information Commission and State Information Commissions shall be constituted.
- The Central Information Commission and State Information Commission hear complaints from any person, who has been denied information by any government authority.
- The Chief Information Commissioner and other Information Commissioners shall be appointed by the President on the recommendation of a committee consisting of the Prime Minister, the leader of opposition in Lok Sabha and a Union Cabinet Minister to be nominated by the PM.
- In its 12 years of working, the RTI Act has given citizens the power to make its government accountable. Increasingly citizens are using RTI Act to get access to information.

NITI Aayog (National Institution for Transforming India)

- The institution will serve as 'Think Tank' of the government, a directional and policy dynamo.
- NITI Aayog will provide governments and the Central and State levels with relevant strategic and technical advice across the spectrum of key elements of policy. This includes matters of national and international importance. PM is the ex-officio Chairman of NITI Aayog.

Functions of NITI Aayog

- To foster cooperative federalism through structured support, initiatives and mechanisms with the states on a continuous basis, recognising that strong states make a strong nation.
- To develop mechanism to formulate credible plans at the village level and aggregate these progressively at higher levels of government.
- To ensure, on areas that are specifically referred to it, that the interest national security are incorporated in economic strategy and policy.
- To pay special attention to the sections of our society that may be at risk of not benefitting adequately from economic progress.
- To provide advice and encourage partnerships between key stakeholders and national and international like minded 'Think Tanks' as well as educational and policy research institutions.

- To create a knowledge, innovation and entrepreneurial support system through a collaborative community of national and international experts, practitioners and other partners.
- To offer a platform for resolution of inter-sectional and inter-departmental issues in order to accelerate the implementation of the development agenda.
- To actively monitor and evaluate the implementation of programmes and initiatives, including the identification of the needed resources so as to strengthen the probability of success and scope of delivery.

Practice Exercise

1. Which of the following Article provides for the independent office of the Comptroller and Auditor General of India (CAG)?
(a) Article 148 (b) Article 149
(c) Article 150 (d) Article 151

2. The retirement age of the Comptroller and Auditor General is
(a) 60 years (b) 62 years
(c) 65 years (d) 55 years

3. Who among the following undertake the special audit at the request of the government?
(a) The Election Commission of India
(b) Comptroller and Auditor General
(c) The Attorney-General
(d) Chairman of UPSC

4. In which year the Election Commission of India was established?
(a) 25th January, 1950
(b) 26th January, 1950
(c) 24th January, 1947
(d) 26th January, 1952

5. Who was the first election commissioner of India?
(a) KVK Sundaram (b) RK Trivedi
(c) Sukumar Sen (d) MS Gill

6. Who can remove the members of the Union Public Service Commission by issuing order under the circumstances provided by the Constitution?
(a) The President
(b) The Speaker of the Lok Sabha
(c) The Prime Minister
(d) The Home Minister

7. Which Article provides for the office of the Attorney General of India?
(a) Article 74 (b) Article 75
(c) Article 76 (d) Article 77

8. Who among the following is the highest law officer of the Government of India?
(a) Advocate General
(b) Attorney General
(c) Chief Justice of India
(d) Solicitor General

9. Who among the following advice the Government of India upon the legal matters?
(a) Advocate General
(b) Solicitor General
(c) Attorney General
(d) Chief Justice of India

10. The Attorney General of India hold office during the pleasure of
(a) President (b) Law Minister
(c) Home Minister (d) Prime Minister

11. The National Commission of Scheduled Caste has been established under the
(a) Article 367 (b) Article 366
(c) Article 338 (d) Article 336

12. The National Commission of Scheduled Tribes has been established under the
(a) Article 335 (b) Article 338
(c) Article 338 A (d) Article 338 B

13. In which year the Finance Commission of India was formed?
(a) 1947 (b) 1948 (c) 1950 (d) 1951

14. The Lokpal and Lokayuktas Act was passed by the Parliament in the year
(a) 2011 (b) 2012
(c) 2013 (d) 2014

15. In which year the National Human Rights Commission was formed?
(a) 1992 (b) 1993
(c) 1994 (d) 1995

16. Who becomes the Chairman of the National Human Rights Commission?
(a) Retired Chief Justice of India
(b) Chief Justice of India
(c) Chief Justice of High Courts
(d) Attorney-General

17. Who is the ex-officio Chairman of the NITI Aayog?
(a) The President
(b) The Vice-President
(c) The Prime Minister
(d) Speaker of the Lok Sabha

Directions (Q. Nos. 18-20) *In the questions given below are two statements labelled as Assertion (A) and Reason (R). In the context of the two statements, which of the following is correct?*

Codes
(a) Both (A) and (R) are true and (R) is the correct explanation of (A)
(b) Both (A) and (R) are true, but (R) is not the correct explanation of (A)
(c) (A) is true, but (R) is false
(d) (A) is false, but (R) is true

18. **Assertion** (A) Power for conducting elections to the Parliament and State Legislature in a free and fair manner have been given to an independent body called Election Commissioner.

Reason (R) Power of removal of Election Commissioners is with Executive.

19. **Assertion** (A) The salaries of the members of the UPSC cannot be changed to their disadvantage during their tenure.

Reason (R) The independence of the Public Service Commission has to be maintained by itself.

20. **Assertion** (A) CAG is the guardian of public purse in India.

Reason (R) In democracy, doctrine of check and balance is necessary to maintain just society.

21. Who among the following does not hold his/her office at the pleasure of the President of India?
(a) Chairman of UPSC **[DU 2015]**
(b) Attorney General for India
(c) Speaker of Lok Sabha
(d) Comptroller and Auditor General of India

22. Planning Commission has been scrapped and replaced by a new 'Think Tank' called **[DU 2015]**
(a) National Institution for Transforming India Aayog
(b) National Rural Development Commission
(c) National Commission for Progress and Development
(d) National Research and Development Commission

23. Which officer of the Government of India has the right to take part in the proceeding of Parliament of India even though he is not a member?
(a) Vice-President
(b) Attorney General of India
(c) Comptroller and Auditor General
(d) Election Commissioner

24. Who among the following is the guardian of the public purse?
(a) Parliament
(b) Public Account Committee
(c) President
(d) Comptroller and Auditor General

25. Election Commission is a
(a) constitutional body
(b) political body
(c) quasi-judicial and quasi-political body
(d) judicial body

26. The power to direct, control the elections to the Panchayat is vested in
(a) State Election Commission
(b) Election Commission at the Centre
(c) Delimitation Commission at State Level
(d) Governor

27. The retirement age of Chief Information Commissioner of India is
(a) 65 years (b) 62 years
(c) 60 years (d) 55 years

28. Central Vigilance Commissioner shall hold office for a term of .... years from the date on which he enters upon his office.
(a) 4 (b) 3 (c) 2 (d) 1

Previous Year's Questions

29. With which of the following do you associate the name PJ Thomas? **[CLAT 2011]**
(a) Central Vigilance Commission
(b) Lokpal
(c) Anti-corruption Ombudsman
(d) Banking Ombudsman

30. Who is the Chairperson of National Human Rights Commission? **[CLAT 2016]**
(a) Justice DK Jain (b) Justice BS Chauhan
(c) Justice HL Dattu (d) Justice Balakrishnan

31. Who is the Chairman of National Green Tribunal? **[CLAT 2016]**
(a) Justice RC Lahoti
(b) Justice Balakrishna Reddy
(c) Justice Bhandari
(d) Justice Swatanter Kumar

32. If an authority is holding information about another in a 'fiduciary capacity', the information under the Right to Information Act, 2005 may not be obtainable. 'Fiduciary relationship' is based on **[CLAT 2016]**
(a) contract
(b) authority
(c) law
(d) trust

Answers

1	*a*	2	*c*	3	*b*	4	*a*	5	*c*	6	*a*	7	*c*	8	*b*	9	*c*	10	*a*
11	*c*	12	*c*	13	*d*	14	*c*	15	*b*	16	*a*	17	*c*	18	*b*	19	*a*	20	*a*
21	*d*	22	*a*	23	*b*	24	*d*	25	*a*	26	*a*	27	*a*	28	*a*	29	*a*	30	*c*
21	*d*	32	*d*																

CHAPTER 12

LOCAL SELF GOVERNMENT

The Local Self Government is administrated by a body insisting of the representatives of the local people. Points of its total revenue is collected by imposing some taxes locally. The services are quite different from the services of the control on the State Government.

Panchayati Raj

- The idea of Panchayati Raj forms a basic tenet of the Gandhian philosophy that envisions village councils as the units of self-governance.
- Panchayati Raj Institutions serve as steering instruments for people's empowerment in so far as they enhance people's capacities to bring tangible progress in their socio-economic life through direct participation in routine administration.

Heads of Panchayats

Traditionally, Panchayats have been headed by five elderly wise men, whose acumen in administration served a useful purpose in local administration. The Panchayats earned legitimacy not only by the consent and approval of the village or town residents, but also of the central political power reigning the entire territory.

Three-tier System

It consists of Panchayats at village, block and the district level.

Village Level

- Gram Panchayat is the basic unit of the Panchayati Raj.
- Functions of the Gram Panchayats are of very primary nature concerning the basic aspects of the rural life confined to the geographical areas of village.

Block Level

- Block Panchayat or Panchayat Samiti, constituted for a host of villages representing the population of about 15000 to 20000.
- Panchayat Samiti consists of a chief called Block Pramukh and around fifteen to twenty members in additon to a number of ex-officio members.

District Level

Consisting of members directly elected by the people and headed by a member from amongst themselves elected for the purpose and known as the **Zila Pramukh**.

State and Committees for Development of Local Self Government Institution

State	Committee for Development of Local Self Government Institution	Year
Maharashtra	Naik Committee	1961
	Bongiwar Committee	1963
Karnataka	Basappa Committee	1963
Andhra Pradesh	Purushottam Rai Committee	1964
	Ramachandra Reddy Committee	1965
	Narasimham Committee	1972
Rajasthan	Mathur Committee	1963
	Sadiq Ali Committee	1964
	GL Vyas Committee	1973
Uttar Pradesh	Govind Sahai Committee	1959

The Municipalities

According to **Article 243 R**, of the Constitution of India all the seats in a Municipality shall be filled by persons chosen by direct election from the territorial constituencies in the Municipal area and for this purpose each Municipal area shall be divided into territorial constituencies to be known as wards.

Constitutional Status for Municipalities

It emerged as the 74th Constitutional Amendment Act of 1992 and came into force on 1st June, 1993. This Act contains Part IX A of the Constitution of India. The Act also added the Twelfth Schedule to the Constitution. It contains 18 functional items of the Municipalities and deals with **Article 243**. The Act brought them under the purview of justiciable part of the Constitution.

Powers and Responsibilities of Municipalities

Under Article 243W, subject to the provisions of this Constitution, the Legislature of a state may, by law, endow

1. The Municipalities with such powers and authority as may be necessary to enable them to function as institutions of self-government and such law may contain provisions for the devolution of powers and responsibilities upon municipalities, subject to such conditions as may be specified therein, with respect to
   (a) the preparation of plans for economic development and social justice.

(b) the performance of functions and the implementation of schemes as may be entrusted to them including those in conferred upon them including these in relation to the matters listed in the Twelfth Schedule.

2. The committees with such powers and authority as may be necessary to enable them to carry out the responsibilities conferred upon them including those in relation to the matters listed in the Twelfth Schedule.

Practice Exercise

1. Which of the following Amendment act of the Constitution added provisions regarding Municipalities?
(a) The Constitution (Seventy-Second Amendment) Act, 1992
(b) The Constitution (Seventy-Third Amendment) Act, 1993
(c) The Constitution (Seventy-Fourth Amendment) Act, 1993
(d) The Constitution (Seventy-Sixth Amendment) Act, 1994

2. Which of the following articles Contains provisions regarding Municipalities?
(a) 243 to 243 L (b) 243 B to 243M
(c) 243P to 243ZG (d) 243S to 243ZA

3. Which of the following part of the Constitution contains provisions regarding Municipalities?
(a) Part XII (b) Part IXA
(c) Part X (d) part XI

4. Which of the following Article of the Constitution dealt with the establishment of the Nagar Panchayats, Municipal Councils and Municipal Corporations?
(a) Article 243Q (b) Article 243R
(c) Article 243S (d) Article 243T

5. Which of the following Article of the Constitution dealt with the reservation of seats to SCs and STs?
(a) Article 243R (b) Article 243S
(c) Article 243T (d) Article 243U

6. Which of the following Amendment Act of the Constitution added provisions regarding Panchayats?
(a) The Constitution (Seventy-Second Amendment) Act, 1992
(b) The Constitution (Seventy-Third Amendment) Act, 1993
(c) The Constitution (Seventy-Fourth Amendment) Act, 1993
(d) The Constitution (Seventy-Sixth Amendment) Act, 1994

7. Which of the following Articles contain provisions regarding Panchayats?
(a) 243 to 243L (b) 243 to 243M
(c) 243 to 243N (d) 243 to 243O

8. Which of the following part of the Constitution contains provisions regarding Panchayats?
(a) Part IX (b) Part IXA (c) Part X (d) Part XI

9. As per Article 243B of the Constitution Panchayats shall be constituted at
(a) Village level (b) Intermediate level
(c) District level (d) All of these

10. Panchayats may not be constituted in a state having a population of not exceeding
(a) 20 lakhs (b) 30 lakhs (c) 40 lakhs (d) 50 lakhs

Previous Year's Question

11. Which Indian State has prescribed minimum education qualification for candidates contesting Panchayat polls? **[CLAT 2016]**
(a) Kerala (b) Haryana (c) Punjab (d) Gujarat

Answers

1	c	2	c	3	b	4	a	5	c	6	b	7	d	8	a	9	d	10	a
11	b																		

CHAPTER 13

SPECIAL PROVISION FOR INDIAN STATES

The Constitution of India provides special provision for some states through Article 370 and 371, which is enshrined in the Part XXI of the Constitution of India. The special provision granted to some states to protect their cultural identities, customs, economics and political interests of the original inhabitants of these areas.

Jammu and Kashmir

Jammu and Kashmir is a constituent State of the Indian Union. It is included in the list of the States in the First Schedule of the Constitution of India. Also, under **Article 1** of the Indian Constitution, the State of Jammu and Kashmir has been mentioned as an integral part of the territory of India. The state was acceded to the Dominion of India by **Maharaja Hari Singh**, who was the ruler of the State in 1947.

Jammu and Kashmir is the only State in the Indian Union which has a separate Constitution. **Article 370** of the **Part XXI** of our Constitution has given a special status to it. Certain other Indian States have also been given special provisions.

Constitution of Jammu and Kashmir

The Constitution of Jammu and Kashmir was enacted by a separate Constituent Assembly set-up by the State and it came into force on 26th January, 1957. Jammu and Kashmir is the only State in India which has a Constitution of its own.

For Nagaland

Article 371(A) *makes the following special provisions for Nagaland*

The Acts of Parliament relating to the following matters would not apply to Nagaland unless the State Legislative Assembly so decides

- Religious or social practices of the Nagas.
- Naga customary law and procedure.
- Administration of Civil and Criminal Justice involving decisions according to Naga customary law.
- Ownership and transfer of land and its resources.

For Manipur

Article 371(C) *makes the following special provisions for Manipur*

- The President is authorised to provide for the creation of a Committee of the Manipur Legislative Assembly consisting of the members elected from the hill areas of the State.
- The President can also direct that the governor shall have special responsibility to secure the proper functioning of that committee.
- The Governor should submit an annual report to the President regarding the administration of the hill areas.
- The Central Government can give directions to the State Government as to the administration of the hill areas.

For Asom

As per **Article 371(B),** the President is empowered to constitute a Committee of the Assam Legislative Assembly, consisting of the members elected from the tribal areas of the State and such other members as he may specify.

For Sikkim

Article 371(F), which was added by the **36th Constitutional Amendment Act 1975**, deals with the special provisions with respect to Sikkim. *The provisions related to this article are given below*

- The Legislative Assembly of the State of Sikkim is to consist of not less than 30 members.
- One seat is allotted to Sikkim in the Lok Sabha.

For Mizoram

Article 371(G) *specifies the following special provisions for Mizoram*

- Laws enacted by Parliament, on below matters, are not extended to Mizoram unless the State Legislative Assembly so decides
  - religious or social practices of the Mizos,
  - customary law and procedures of the Mizos,
  - administration of civil and criminal justice involving decisions according to customary laws of Mizos; and
  - ownership and transfer of land.
- The Legislative Assembly of Mizoram shall consist of not less than 40 members.

For Arunachal Pradesh

Article 371(H) *deals with the following special provisions for the State of Arunachal Pradesh*

- The Governor of Arunachal Pradesh shall have special responsibility for law and order in the State.
- The strength of Arunachal Pradesh Legislative Assembly should not be less than 30 members.

Practice Exercise

1. Under which Article of the Constitution of India the State of Jammu and Kashmir has been mentioned?
(a) Article 1 (b) Article 2 (c) Article 3 (d) Article 4

2. Which of the following State has its own Constitution?
(a) Nagaland (b) Meghalaya
(c) Manipur (d) Jammu and Kashmir

3. Which part of the Constitution of India contains Article 370?
(a) Part XV (b) Part XVII
(c) Part XXI (d) Part XX

4. The Constitution of Jammu and Kashmir came into force on
(a) 26th, January, 1950 (b) 26th, January, 1957
(c) 15th, August, 1947 (d) 15th, August, 1957

5. Which Article provides special provisions to the State of Nagaland?
(a) Tripura (b) Nagaland
(c) Mizoram (d) Manipur

6. Which of the following matters should be only decided by the State Assembly of Nagaland?
(a) Naga customary law and precedence
(b) Religions or social practices of the nagar
(c) Ownership and transfer and land and its resources
(d) All of the above

7. 73rd Amendment does not apply to the State of
I. Nagaland II. Mizoram
III. Jammu and Kashmir IV. Meghalaya
Select the correct answer using the codes given below
(a) I and II (b) I, II and III
(c) I, II, III and IV (d) II and III

8. Which of the following Article empowers the President to constitute a Committee of the Asom Legislative Assembly?
(a) Article 371 B (b) Article 371 D
(c) Article 371 E (d) Article 371 F

9. Which Article provides special provisions for the State of Mizoram?
(a) Article 371 E (b) Article 371 F
(c) Article 371 G (d) Article 371 H

10. How many members are allowed to be elected in the Legislative Assembly of Mizoram?
(a) Less than 40
(b) More than 40
(c) Not less than 40
(d) Not more than 40

11. Who among the following conferred with the special responsibility law and order in the State of Arunachal Pradesh?
(a) Governor
(b) President
(c) Chief Minister
(d) Home Minister of the State

12. Which Article of the Constitution of India deals with the special provisions to the State of Arunachal Pradesh?
(a) Article 371 E (b) Article 371 F
(c) Article 371 G (d) Article 371 H

13. What is the strength of the Legislative Assembly of Arunachal Pradesh?
(a) 20 (b) 30
(c) 40 (d) 50

14. The Residuary Powers of legislation in case of Jammu and Kashmir belong to
(a) Parliament (b) the State Legislature
(c) Governor (d) Both (a) and (b)

Answers

1	*a*	2	*d*	3	*c*	4	*b*	5	*b*	6	*d*	7	*c*	8	*a*	9	*c*	10	*c*
11	*a*	12	*d*	13	*b*	14	*b*												

ENGLISH LANGUAGE

CHAPTER 01

SPOTTING ERRORS

The spotting of errors forms an indispensable part of any competitive exam. In this section, a number of sentences are given and each of them is divided into three parts (a), (b) and (c). You are required to spot the part which has an error. If there is no error, then your answer is (d).

Such kind of questions are usually based on different grammatical rules and their correct usage. A sound knowledge of grammatical rules and regular practice will enable you to solve these questions.

ARTICLES

The adjectives a, an and the are called Articles. *There are two kinds of articles*

(I) Indefinite article—A/An

(II) Definite article—The

Use of Indefinite Article–A/An

1. The article **An** is used before a word beginning with a vowel sound. e.g.

(i) She is *an* intelligent girl.

(ii) He is *an* MP.

2. The article **A** is used before a word beginning with a consonant sound. e.g.

(i) He is *a* University student.

(ii) He is *a* European.

3. **A/An** is used before a singular countable noun when it is mentioned for the first time representing no particular person or thing. e.g.
   (i) He has *an* axe.
   (ii) She is *a* lawyer.
4. **A/An** is used before a singular countable noun which is used as the representative of a class of things or persons. e.g.
   (i) *A* lion is a fierce animal.
   (ii) *A* pupil should obey his teacher.
5. **A/An** is used to make a common noun of a proper noun. e.g.
   (i) My neighbour is *a* Daniel.
   (ii) He is *an* androcles when it comes to dealing with animals.
6. **A/An** is used in exclamations before singular countable nouns. e.g.
   (i) What *an* interesting movie!
   (ii) What *a* pretty girl!
7. **A/An** is used in its original sense of one or any. e.g.
   (i) She wants *a* car.
   (ii) There are twelve inches in *a* foot.

Use of Definite Article—The

The definite article **The** is used

1. When we talk about a particular person or thing or one already mentioned. e.g.
   (i) Give me the book which you bought yesterday.
   (ii) The dress you want is out of stock.
2. When a singular noun represents a whole class. e.g.
   (i) The lotus is a beautiful flower.
   (ii) The cat loves comfort.
3. Before the first noun in 'noun + preposition + noun' construction. e.g.
   (i) The Bharat of Ramayana is an ideal brother.
   (ii) The gold of India is famous.
4. Before names of mountain-ranges. e.g.
   The Alps, The Himalayas, The Vindhyas
5. Before names of groups of islands. e.g.
   The Andamans, The Hebrides, The West Indies
6. Before names of rivers, oceans, gulfs, deserts and forests. e.g.
   The Ganges, The Amazon, The Nile, The Arabian Sea, The Pacific Ocean, The Indian Ocean, The Persian Gulf, The Gulf of Mexico, The Sahara, The Black Forest
7. Before names of religious and mythological books. e.g.
   The Veda, The Ramayana, The Bible
8. Before names of newspapers and magazines. e.g.
   The Hindustan Times, The Times of India, The Statesman
9. Before names of heavenly bodies, directions and things unique of their kind. e.g.
   The Earth, The Sun, The Moon, The East, The North, The Equator

> 'The' is not used before the words 'Heaven, Hell, God, Parliament'.

10. Before names of historical buildings, places and events. e.g.
    The Taj Mahal, The Red Fort, The Pyramids, The Kaba, The Kurukshetra, The French Revolution
11. Before musical instruments. e.g.
    (i) He can play the guitar.
    (ii) She is fond of playing on the piano.

> When musical instruments are used as countable nouns, **A/An** is used. e.g.

12. Before religious communities and political parties. e.g.
    The Hindus, The Muslims, The Sikhs, The BJP, The Congress Party, The Janata Dal
13. Before names of ships, aeroplanes and trains. e.g.
    The Virat, The Vikrant, The Meghdoot
    The Shatabdi Express, The Punjab Mail, The Rajdhani Express

14. Before the words denoting physical positions. e.g.
    The top, The bottom, The centre
    The inside, The front, The back
15. Before parts of body. e.g.
    (i) He was hit on the head.
    (ii) She pulled the cat by the tail.
16. Before names of government departments and armed forces. e.g.
    The Judiciary, The Legislative, The Executive, The Army, The Navy, The Air Force
17. Before the dates of months. e.g.
    The 6th of February, The 21st of December
18. Before the superlative degree. e.g.
    (i) Honesty is the best policy.
    (ii) She is the tallest girl in the class.
19. Before the names of a few countries and provinces. e.g.
    The USA, The USSR, The Netherlands, The Sudan, The Punjab
20. Before comparative degree in case of a choice. e.g.
    (i) She is the prettier of the two sisters.
    (ii) He is the stronger of the two.
21. Before the ordinals. e.g.
    The first, The third, The ninth

Omission of Articles

The articles **a, an, the** are omitted

1. Before names of days and months. e.g.
   (i) She will go on Monday.
   (ii) They are getting married in January.
2. Before names of languages. e.g.
   (i) He cannot speak French.
   (ii) She is learning Marathi.
3. Before names of subjects. e.g.
   (i) She has no interest in mathematics.
   (ii) Biology is his favourite subject.
4. Before names of diseases. e.g.
   (i) AIDS is spreading like wild fire.
   (ii) He died of cancer.

> But 'The' is used before the names of a few diseases. e.g. the measles, the plague, the gout, the mumps

5. Before names of festivals and seasons. e.g.
   (i) He will go to Canada in winter.
   (ii) She celebrated Christmas with her friends.

   But,
   (i) He will go to Canada in the winter season.
   (ii) She went to Delhi in the Diwali holidays.
6. Before names of sports. e.g.
   (i) She plays tennis. (ii) We like cricket.
7. Before the names of persons, villages, cities, districts, states and countries. e.g.
   (i) Anjali is a beautiful girl.
   (ii) London is a big city.
8. Before names of meals. e.g.
   (i) They take lunch at 2 pm.
   (ii) Breakfast is ready.

> 'A' is used when there is an adjective before names of meals. We use 'the' when we specify. e.g.
> (i) We had a late breakfast today.
> (ii) The lunch I had at the Rajmahal was nice.

9. After possessive adjectives (my, our, your, his, her, their, its) and nouns in possessive case (Ram's, lion's). e.g.
   (i) This is Rahul's car.
   (ii) That is my book.
10. Before school, college, church, prison, hospital, bed, market, when these places are visited or used for their primary purpose. e.g.
    (i) She goes to church on Sunday.
    (ii) The criminal was sent to prison.

11. Before man, life, death, art, science, when these words are used in the widest sense. e.g.
    (i) Man is mortal.
    (ii) Science has developed much in the past fifty years.
12. Before the nouns used after rank of / title of. e.g.
    (i) He was promoted to the rank of Colonel.
    (ii) He was given the title of Nawab.

Uses of Tense and Verbs

Simple Present Tense

1. **Simple Present Tense** is used to express universal truth, principle and proverb. e.g.
   (i) The Earth moves round the Sun.
   (ii) Oil floats on water.
2. This tense is used to express habitual, regular and repeated actions. e.g.
   (i) She drinks tea every morning.
   (ii) He often gets late for school.
3. This tense is used to express human feelings, emotions and mental activity. e.g.
   (i) I love my family.
   (ii) She thinks he is the best.
4. This tense is used to show possession. e.g.
   (i) She has a piano.
   (ii) This car belongs to him.
5. This tense is used to express a future event that is part of fixed time table or fixed programme. e.g.
   (i) The next train is at 6.00 am tomorrow morning.
   (ii) The show starts at 12 o'clock.
6. This tense is used, instead of the Simple Future Tense, in clauses of time and of condition. e.g.
   (i) She will not come if it rains.
   (ii) I shall wait till he comes.

Present Continuous Tense

1. **Present Continuous Tense** is used for an action going on at the time of speaking. e.g.
   (i) The boys are playing cricket.
   (ii) It is raining heavily.
2. This tense is used for a temporary action which may not be actually happening at the time of speaking. e.g.
   (i) He is reading the Bible.
   (ii) She is learning French.
3. This tense is used for an action that is planned or arranged to take place in the near future. e.g.
   (i) Her brother is arriving tomorrow.
   (ii) We are going to the cinema tonight.
4. This tense is used to express intention or likelihood and it indicates future time. e.g.
   (i) He is going to meet her.
   (ii) Dhoni is playing to score runs.

Present Perfect Tense

1. **Present Perfect Tense** is used to indicate completed activities in the immediate past. e.g.
   (i) He has just arrived.
   (ii) They have left for Delhi.
2. This tense is used to denote an action beginning at some time in the past and continuing up to the present moment (often with since/for phrases). e.g.
   (i) I have worked here for five years.
   (ii) She has known him for a long time.
3. This tense is used to express past actions whose time is not given and not definite. e.g.
   (i) Have you been to Agra?
   (ii) She has read 'Geetanjali'.

Present Perfect Continuous Tense

1. **Present Perfect Continuous Tense** is used to express an action which began at some time in the past and is still continuing. e.g.
   (i) She has been sleeping for four hours.
   (ii) They have been living here for ten years.
2. This tense is also sometimes used for an action already finished. In such cases, the continuity of the activity is emphasised as an explanation of something. e.g.
   (i) She has been waiting for you.
   (ii) He has been playing.

Simple Past Tense

1. **Simple Past Tense** is used to indicate an action completed in the past. e.g.
   (i) I met her a week ago.
   (ii) We left school last year.
2. This tense is used to indicate a situation related to past. e.g.
   (i) She was a good teacher.
   (ii) We were very poor.
3. This tense is also used to express past habits. e.g.
   (i) He always carried a stick.
   (ii) She never came late.

Past Continuous Tense

1. **Past Continuous Tense** is used to denote an action going on at sometime in the past. e.g.
   (i) She was playing chess.
   (ii) We were talking loudly.
2. This tense is used to denote actions going on at the same time in the past. e.g.
   (i) While you were sleeping, she was reading.
   (ii) While he was laughing, Sonu was weeping.
3. This tense is also used for persistent habits in the past. e.g.
   (i) She was always complaining.
   (ii) He was always chewing tobacco.

Past Perfect Tense

1. **Past Perfect Tense** is used to describe an action completed before a certain moment in the past. e.g.
   (i) She had written a poem even before she was eight years old.
   (ii) I had seen him last five years before.
2. If two actions happened in the past, the earlier one is denoted by past perfect while the latter one is denoted by simple past. e.g.
   (i) The train had left before I reached the station.
   (ii) She took dinner after they had gone.

Past Perfect Continuous Tense

Past Perfect Continuous Tense is used to express an action that had begun before a certain point in the past and continued up to that time. e.g.
   (i) At that time she had been living there for two years.
   (ii) We had been playing football since 2000.

Simple Future Tense

1. **Simple Future Tense** is used to express an action that is yet to take place. e.g.
   (i) He will come here tomorrow.
   (ii) We shall meet her on Monday.
2. This tense is also used to express intention, will, threat and determination. e.g.
   (i) I will never tell a lie.
   (ii) He shall not come here again.

Future Continuous Tense

1. **Future Continuous Tense** is used to talk about actions which will be in progress at a time in the future. e.g.
   (i) She will be sleeping in the room.
   (ii) They will be watching the match on TV.
2. This tense is also used to express future events that are planned. e.g.
   (i) She will be coming here for your marriage.
   (ii) I shall be staying here till Monday.

Future Perfect Tense

1. **Future Perfect Tense** is used to indicate the completion of an action by a certain future time. e.g.
   (i) We shall have reached there by evening.
   (ii) She will have written the letter by then.
2. This tense is used when there are two actions and it is necessary to emphasise that the preceding action will be completely finished before the next action starts. e.g.
   (i) She will have left before you go to see her.
   (ii) I shall have come before she sleeps.

Future Perfect Continuous Tense

Future Perfect Continuous Tense is used for actions which will be in progress over a period of time that will end in the future. e.g.

(i) We shall have been living here for ten years by next August.
(ii) She will have been reading for three hours.

> When sentence is in Indirect Narration and the 'reporting verb' is in the past tense, all present tense of the 'reported speech' are changed into the corresponding past tenses and the Simple past is changed into Past perfect.
> - He said that he does not wish to see any of them and orders them to go away. (*Incorrect*)
> - He said that he did not wish to see any of them and ordered them to go away. (*Correct*)

SUBJECT-VERB AGREEMENT

The subject and the verb are the essential parts of a sentence. A verb must agree with its subject in number and person.

> - If the subject is singular, verb must be singular.
> - If the subject is plural, verb must be plural.

Some Important Rules

Rule 1 Two or more singular nouns or pronouns joined by 'and' take a plural verb. e.g.
(i) He and his sister were playing.
(ii) Gold and silver are precious metals.

Rule 2 If two singular nouns refer to the same person or thing, the verb must be singular. e.g.
(i) The magistrate and collector has come.
(ii) The poet and critic has been honoured.

> When the **article** is used before only one noun, one person/thing is intended and hence the verb must be singular.

When the **article** is used before both the nouns, two different, persons/things are intended and hence, the verb must be plural. e.g.
(i) The magistrate and the collector have come.
(ii) The poet and the critic have been honoured.

Rule 3 When two or more subjects are joined by as well as, like, besides, with, in addition to, together with, along with, but, except etc, the verb is used according to the first subject. e.g.
(i) The leader with all his followers was arrested.
(ii) The ship along with its crew was lost.

Rule 4 Either, neither, each, every, anyone, someone, nobody must be followed by a singular verb. e.g.

(i) Neither of your friends is intelligent.
(ii) Each of these substances is found in India.

Rule 5 When the subjects joined by or, nor, either ....or, neither ....nor are of different persons, the verb agrees with the nearer. e.g.

(i) Either you or I am going.
(ii) Neither Rekha nor her friends were present at the party.

Rule 6 If two subjects together express one idea, the verb is singular. e.g.

(i) Honour and glory is his reward.
(ii) Whisky and soda was served in the party.

Rule 7 If the subject of a clause is a relative pronoun (who, which, that), the verb is used according to the antecedent of the relative pronoun. e.g.

(i) The boys who are playing are my friends.
(ii) It is I who am helping you.

Rule 8 When plural nouns explain specific amount, distance, quantity, time or period as a whole, the verb should be singular. e.g.

(i) Fifty rupees was the amount given to her.
(ii) Three hours is too short a time to judge one's character.

Rule 9 When nouns like glasses, shoes, scissors, pants, trousers, spectacles etc are used as subject, the verb is plural. e.g.

(i) His trousers are very loose.
(ii) My scissors are sharp.

> If a pair of is used before these nouns, the verb must be singular. e.g.
> (i) A pair of scissors has been bought.
> (ii) A pair of shoes was presented to him.

Rule 10 Furniture, luggage, scenery, information, poetry, percentage, knowledge, advice, news, music etc are always singular and take a singular verb. e.g.

(i) All his luggage was thrown out.
(ii) Wordsworth's poetry is immortal.

Rule 11 If given nouns look like plurals (i.e. they end in '*s*') but they are, in fact, singular nouns, then we use a singular verb.
e.g. Economics is my favourite subject.

Rule 12 Words such as audience, congregation, crowd, group and family take a singular or plural verb depending upon the sentence, but it is always safe to use a plural verb with these nouns.
e.g. The family are our strongest support.

Rule 13 The title of a book, play, story or a musical composition even though plural takes a singular verb. e.g.

(i) The Arabian Nights is worth reading.
(ii) The Gulliver's Travels is an interesting book.

Rule 14 Words joined to a singular subject by with, as well as, etc are parenthetical. The verb should therefore be put in the singular.
e.g. The Prime Minister, with his cabinet colleagues, is to be present.

Rule 15 The verb must agree with the first subject, irrespective of whether it is singular or plural. When the two are joined by as well as together with and along with. e.g.

(i) My friends as well as I are going abroad.
(ii) Mr Sinha along with his friends is going to Pune.

Rule 16 Two nouns qualified by each or every, even though connected by 'and', require a singular verb.
e.g. very boy and each girl was given vaccination.

Rule 17 None is singular, but takes a plural/ singular if verb according to the sense involved in the sentence. e.g.

(i) None are so deaf as those who will not hear.

(ii) I asked for a maid, but none was there.

Rule 18 When the plural noun is a proper name for some single object or some collective unit, it must be followed by a singular verb.

e.g. The United Nations is not an effective body for world peace.

Rule 19 Uncountable nouns like advice, news, media stationary, weather, progress are singular and take a singular verb. e.g.

(i) The weather is pleasant today.

(ii) Advice is valued when it is asked for.

Rule 20 A collective noun takes a singular verb when the collection is thought of as one whole. It takes a plural verb when the stress is on the individuals. e.g.

(i) The cartel of oil supplying countries has submitted its report.

(ii) The cartel of oil supplying countries are divided over the issue.

Rule 21 Unfulfilled wishes are a kind of imaginary conditionals. These types of conditionals take "if/as if/as though/ it is time/I wish/ it is high time" as the expression. It uses 'were'. e.g.

(i) I wish I were a mermaid.

(ii) He talks to me as if he were my boss.

Rule 22 If 'wh words like which, who, whom are used as a relative pronoun then the verb follows the antecedent's number and person. e. g.

(i) Rita, who is a doctor, lives here

(ii) The students. who are absent today, have gone to stadium.

Rule 23 'There' and 'It' used as introductory subjects. When these two words come as the subject then the verb agrees to the number and person of the noun that comes after 'there'.

e.g.

(i) There <u>are</u> <u>trees</u> in the forest

↓ ↓

Plural verb Plural noun

(ii) There <u>is</u> a <u>pen</u> lying on the table

↓ ↓

Singular verb Singular noun

Rule 24 When the expression 'more than one' is used the sentence, noun and verb both are used singular.

e.g.

(i) More than one <u>book</u>

↓

Singular noun

<u>is to be bought</u>

↓

Singular verb

(ii) More than one <u>computer</u>

↓

Singular noun

<u>is not working</u>

↓

Singular verb

Rule 25 When 'more than one' comes as parts, verb plural.

e.g.

Structure More + Plural noun + than one plural verb

<u>More</u> <u>parents</u> <u>than one</u> <u>are</u>

↓ ↓ ↓ ↓

More + Plural noun + than one + Plural verb

Rule 26 Expression having 'Half of/ two thirds of/ on, fourth of' etc takes plural verb when the noun is countable, but if the noun is uncountable then verb is singular.

e.g.

(i) Three fourths of the work is done.

(ii) Half of the boys from the class were absent.

Rule 27 Statements having "many of/ both of/ few of/ a few of" in it takes a plural noun or pronoun followed by a plural verb

e.g.

(i) Many of the boys are playing.

(ii) Both of the girls have danced.

Rule 28 Statements that contain "some/some of/ plenty of/ lots of/ a lot of/ all/ all of/ most/ most of/ enough/ a great deal of" take both singular and plural verb depending upon the verb. e.g.

(i) All girls are beautiful.

(ii) A lot of energy has been saved.

Rule 29 Statements that have "many/ a great many/ a good many" take plural nouns along with plural verb. e.g.

(i) A great many farmers are working.

(ii) Many boys were accused.

Rule 30 Statements that contain "a number of/a large number of", etc takes plural noun and plural verb. e.g.

(i) A number of people have gone to fair.

(ii) A large number of candidates have appeared in the examination.

NOUNS

Nouns are naming words. The names can be of person, place, thing, an abstract idea or that of a feeling. Rules related to noun play an important role in error detection assignment.

Some Important Rules

Rule 1 Some nouns like furniture, information, poetry, scenery, machinery, work, wood, paper, glass, dust, traffic, electricity, food, grass, luggage, advice etc are always singular.

> These are Uncountable Nouns. Neither a/an is used before them nor their plural is formed. e.g.
>
> (i) Young persons dislike the advice of elderly people.
>
> (ii) He gave me information.

Rule 2 Some nouns have the singular and the plural alike. As, sheep, deer, swine, species etc. e.g.

(i) A sheep is grazing in the field.
Sheep are grazing in the field.

(ii) It is a rare species.
There are many species of dogs.

Rule 3 Nouns expressing number like dozen, score, hundred, thousand etc are used in singular with numerical adjectives. e.g.

(i) She bought three dozen oranges.

(ii) There are two score books in this almirah.

Rule 4 Some nouns like cattle, poultry, people, police, gentry, peasantry, electorate etc are always plural. e.g.

(i) Cattle are not allowed to enter this ground.

(ii) These poultry are mine.

Rule 5 These collective nouns may be used singularly as well as plurally. If they are shown as a body or group then they are singular, but if they are shown as individual members then they are plural. Public, Board, Team, Mob, Audience, Ministry, Jury, Staff, Police, Number, Crowd, House and Committee. e.g.

(i) The public was angry. *(Public used as a whole)*
The public were reading different books. *(Public used individuals)*

(ii) Family is on a holiday. *(Family used as a whole)*
Family are working in the houses. *(Family used as individual members)*

Rule 6 If same noun is to come after a preposition and before the preposition then the noun remains singular. e.g.

(i) I want word to word copied.

(ii) He went door to door to sell things.

Rule 7 Some nouns that end with's' or 'es' look like a plural one but used with singular verb
Physics, Economics, Mathematics, Mechanics, Politics, Stastistics, Statics, Summons, News, Series, Innings, Mumps, Measles, Rickets, Atheletics, Billiards, United States, Aquatics, Gymnastics and United Arab Emirates. e.g.

(i) Physics is an interesting subject.

(ii) He wants to study economics as it is his favourite subject.

Rule 8 Name of the books that reflect plurality is used as a singular noun with singular verb. e.g.

(i) War and peace is loved by people.
(ii) The Arabian Nights has a bulk sale.

Rule 9 Some nouns are always used in plural number with plural verb
Jeans, Trousers, Pants, Breeches, Scales, Shears, Scissors, Spectacles, Alms, Thanks, Proceeds, Riches, Contents, Surroundings, Orders, Ashes, Credentials, Auspices, Refreshments, Savings, Requirements, Outskirts, Customs, Rations, Annals, Archives, Manners, Earnings, Quarters, Assets, Arrears, Spirits and Stairs. e.g.

(i) His trousers are dirty.
(ii) Scissors are used widely.

Rule 10 In a compound noun, if a noun qualified by a quantitative adjective is used as an adjective of another noun then it is kept in singular form since adjectives are never used in plural forms. e.g.

(i) We are planning a ten-day tour. (*not days*).
(ii) She rail a forty-mile race. (*not miles*).

Rule 11 Avoid using apostrophe with 's' if the noun is a non-living thing, but it can be used with living thing, Time, Weight, Distance, Amount or with personified nouns. e.g.

(i) Car's tyre is old now. (*wrong*)
Tyre of the car is old now. (*right*)
(ii) None can change nature's laws. (*wrong*)
The laws of nature cannot be changed by anyone. (*right*)

Rule 12 If a singular noun is qualified by two different adjectives then it is considered plural and used with a plural verb. e.g.

(i) Social and political value in India are changing these days.
(ii) Summer and winter sale are in vogue these days.

PRONOUNS

Pronouns are the words used in place of a noun. They perform all the functions of a noun. Pronouns can have different cases and therefore, they add beauty to the writing.

Rules related to different types of pronouns

1. Personal Pronouns

I, we, you, he, me, her, them etc.

1. If a pronoun acts as the subject of a verb, it is in nominative/subjective case and if it acts as an object of a verb, it is in objective case.
Nominative case I, we, you, he, she, it, they.
Objective case me, us, you, him, her, it, them. e.g.
(i) She is doing the work.
⇓
Subject
⇓
Subjective case
(ii) Ram was playing with me
⇓
object
⇓
Objective case
2. A pronoun is used in objective case after **let**. e.g.
(i) Let him and me do this .
(ii) Let her and us go.
3. A pronoun is used in objective case after a **preposition**. e.g.
(i) She was angry with you and him.
(ii) They laughed at her and me.
4. Nominative case is used after **than** if the comparison is between two nominatives. e.g.
(i) As a student of science you are far better than he.
(ii) She drives faster than I do.
5. Objective case is used after **than** if the comparison is between two objects. e.g.
(i) She loves you more than me.
(ii) I know her better than him.

6. Good manners require that the order of personal pronouns in a sentence should be 231 i.e. the second person should come before the third and the third person before the first. e.g.
(i) You and I must work together.
(ii) You and he will follow it.

> While referring to unpleasant acts or accepting guilt/mistake, the order of personal pronouns in a sentence should be 123. e.g.
> (i) I, you and he have stolen the money.
> (ii) I and you will be punished.

2. Distributive Pronouns

Each, either, neither

1. Either and **Neither** are used for two persons or things. e.g.
(i) Either of them can do this.
(ii) Neither of you will go there.

2. Each is used for two or more than two persons/things. e.g.
(i) Each of the students contributed fifty rupees.
(ii) Each of the two boys is doing his work.

3. Demonstrative Pronouns

This, that, these, those, such.

1. This and **these** are used for the persons / things which are near the speaker.

This is used for one person/thing and **these** is used for more than one person/ thing. e.g.
(i) This computer is a present for you.
(ii) These flowers are beautiful.

2. That and **those** are used for the persons/ things which are away from the speaker.

That is used for one person/thing and **those** is used for more than one person/thing. e.g.
(i) That boy is my friend.
(ii) Those shirts are mine.

4. Indefinite Pronouns

One, some, any, everybody, somebody, anybody, everyone, someone, anyone, no one, everything, something, anything, nothing etc.

1. In referring to anybody, everybody, everyone, anyone, each etc, the pronoun **he** or **she** is used according to the context. e.g.
(i) I shall be glad to help everyone of my boys in his studies.
(ii) Everyone of the Miss India contestants tried to improve herself through rigorous training.

2. The indefinite pronoun *one* should be used throughout, if used at all, i.e. its nominative —one, objective—one, possessive—one's and reflexive—oneself should be used. e.g.
(i) One should take care of one's house .
(ii) One should help oneself.

5. Reflexive Pronouns

Myself, yourself, himself, herself, ourselves, itself etc.

1. A reflexive pronoun or an object must be put after **acquit, absent, avail, resign, revenge, enjoy, exert, apply, adopt, adjust, avenge, pride**. e.g.
(i) I absented myself from the class.
(ii) You should avail yourself of every chance in life.

2. Verbs such as **bathe, break, burst, feed, gather, hide, keep, make, move, open, qualify, rest, roll, speed, steal, stop, turn,** are usually not followed by a reflexive pronoun. e.g.
(i) He has qualified for the post.
(ii) You should keep from bad boys.

3. A reflexive pronoun cannot be used as a substitute for the subject. e.g.

Bunti and myself decided to join the army. (*Incorrect*)

Bunti and I decided to join the army. (*Correct*)

6. Emphatic Pronouns

When myself, yourself, ourselves, herself, itself, themselves etc are used for the sake of emphasis they are called emphatic pronouns.

e.g. (i) I myself went to finalise the deal.
(ii) They themselves admitted their guilt .

7. Relative Pronouns

Who, whom, whose, which, that

1. **Who** is used for persons only and **which** is used for things without life and for animals. e.g.
   (i) This is the man who brought the news.
   (ii) The horse which I recently bought is an Arab.
2. **That** is used for persons and things. e.g.
   (i) This is the man that brought the news.
   (ii) The horse that I recently bought is an Arab.
3. **Who/Which** is used in both defining and non-defining cases **that** is used in defining case. e.g.
   (i) The horse which she has bought is black.
   (ii) I have bought a dog which is white.
   Here, in the first sentence **that** can be used in place of **which** but in the second sentence it can't be used.
4. **That** is used after superlative degree, all, same, only, none, nothing. e.g.
   (i) He was the most eloquent speaker that I ever heard.
   (ii) It is only donkeys that bray.
5. **Who** is used in nominative case i.e. it is followed by a verb while **whom** is used in objective case i,e. it is not followed by a verb. e.g.
   (i) This is the boy who broke the glass.
   (ii) The girl whom I met today was his friend.

8. Interrogative Pronouns

Who, whom, whose, which, what

1. **Who** is used for person. e.g
   (i) Who was knocking at the door?
   (ii) Who called you here?
2. **Which** is used for both persons and things. It implies selection. e.g.
   (i) Which of these boys will win the prize?
   (ii) Which of them has said so?
3. After preposition **whom** is used instead of **who**. e.g.
   (i) By whom was the flower plucked?
   (ii) About whom are you talking?

9. Exclamatory Pronouns

When the interrogative word *what* is used to express surprise it is called exclamatory pronoun.

e.g. What! you don't know Amitabh?

10. Reciprocal Pronouns

Each other, one another

Each other is used for two persons/ things and **one another** is used for more than two persons/things. to refer to some kind of exchange.

But, in modern use there is no difference in the use of **each other** and **one another**. e.g.

(i) They all loved one another.
(ii) The four friends quarrelled with each other.

ADJECTIVES

An **Adjective** is a word which qualifies a noun or a pronoun.

Some Important Rules Related to Adjective

1. Senior, superior, junior, prior, inferior, posterior are followed by *to* instead of *than*.
   All his colleagues are senior than him. *(Incorrect)*
   All his colleagues are senior to him. *(Correct)*

2. **Interior, exterior, minor, major** etc are the adjectives of positive degree.

   Neither more / most is used before them nor than / to is used after them. e.g.

   (i) His age is a matter of minor importance.

   (ii) The interior decoration of his office is excellent.

3. After **comparatively** or **relatively** positive degree is used. e.g.

   The wind is comparatively colder today. *(Incorrect)*

   The wind is comparatively cold today. *(Correct)*

4. Before **enough** positive degree is used. e.g.

   He is smarter enough to get selected for this prestigious post. *(Incorrect)*

   He is smart enough to get selected for this prestigious post. *(Correct)*

5. **To** is used after **prefer** if the comparison is between two nouns. e.g.

   He prefers milk to tea.

   But, 'rather than' is used after prefer if the comparison is between two infinitives.
   e.g. She prefers to sleep *rather than* to play.

6. **To** is used after preferable.
   e.g. Fish is preferable to chicken.

7. Perfect, complete, full, excellent, unique, circular, extreme, universal, chief, golden etc. are used neither in comparative degree nor in superlative degree. e.g.

   Money is the chiefest aim of his life. *(Incorrect)*

   Money is the chief aim of his life. *(Correct)*

8. **Positive degree** and **as** are used with **so/as**. e.g.

   Dhoni's performance in the match was as better as Yuvraj's. *(Incorrect)*

   Dhoni's performance in the match was as good as Yuvraj's. *(Correct)*

ADVERBS

An **Adverb** is a word which modifies the meaning of a verb, an adjective or another adverb.

Some Important Adverbs

1. Too and Very

Too means 'more than required' and it is usually used before unpleasant adjectives.

Very means 'in a great degree' and it is used before pleasant/ unpleasant adjectives.

If the sentence is not based on **too ...... to** structure, very should be used in place of too. e.g.

(i) I am too happy today. *(Incorrect)*
I am very happy today. *(Correct)*

(ii) My son's health has been too good. *(Incorrect)*
My son's health has been good. *(Correct)*

2. Too Much and Much Too

After **too much** a noun is used.

After **much too** an adjective is used. e.g.

His wife's rude behaviour gives him much too pain. *(Incorrect)*

His wife's rude behaviour gives him too much pain. *(Correct)*

3. Much and Very

(a) **Very** is used with positive degree and **much** is used with comparative degree. e.g.

   (i) The air is very hot today.

   (ii) The air is much hotter today than yesterday.

(b) **Very** is used with present participle and **much** is used with past participle. e.g.

   (i) It is very surprising for me.

   (ii) I was much surprised at hearing the news.

4. Fairly and Rather

(a) **Fairly** is used with positive degree while **rather** is used with both positive degree and comparative degree.

(b) **Fairly** is used with pleasant objectives while **rather** is usually used with unpleasant adjectives. e.g.

(i) She is fairly wise.

(ii) This job is rather difficult.

But, rather good, rather clever, rather pretty are used.

5. Hard and Hardly

Hard means 'difficult' or 'solid'. It is used as an adjective as well as an adverb.

Hardly means 'almost not' and it is used as an adverb. e.g.

(i) It is hard to believe that he is guilty.

(ii) There is hardly any tea left.

6. Late and Lately

Late means 'near the end of a period of time' and **lately** means 'recently'. e.g.

(i) She married in her late twenties.

(ii) He had lately returned from Australia.

7. Ago

Ago is always used in past indefinite tense. e.g.

(i) I met her a year ago.

(ii) This had happened a week ago. *(Incorrect)*

This happened a week ago. *(Correct)*

8. Enough

(i) Enough is used just after the word that it qualifies.

(ii) Always use positive degree of adjective/ adverb before **enough.** e.g.

(a) He is now strong enough to leave his bed.

(b) She is enough wise to allow her son to go. *(Incorrect)*

She is wise enough to allow her son to go. *(Correct)*

9. Else

Else should always be followed by **but** and never by than.

e.g. It is nothing else but love.

10. Still and Yet

Still is usually used in affirmative sentences and **yet** in negative sentences. e.g.

He has not still returned the money. *(Incorrect)*

He has not yet returned the money. *(Correct)*

Position of Adverbs

1. Always, often, seldom, never, just, ever, usually, hardly, already, nearly etc are used before the main verb. e.g.

(i) I have told often him to write neatly. *(Incorrect)*

I have often told him to write neatly. *(Correct)*

(ii) He never talks ill of his friends. *(Correct)*

2. Adverbs of time/ place/manner if there is one are generally placed after the verb or after the object. e.g.

(i) He does his work carefully.

(ii) She looked everywhere.

> Adverb of manner is used before the object if a clause starting with who/ which/ that is used after the object. e.g. She received all those who had come in time warmly.

3. If adverbs of time/place/manner all are to be used in a sentence, the normal order is— adverb of manner, adverb of place, adverb of time. e.g.

He danced in the city hall well last night. *(Incorrect)*

He danced well in the city hall last night. *(Correct)*

4. Adverbs of quantity are usually used before the word that they qualify. e.g.

(i) The party was too dull.

(ii) She is quite cool.

5. **Only** should be placed immediately before the word it qualifies. e.g.
   (i) We solved only four sums.
   (ii) She has slept only two hours.
6. Preposition is not used before an adverb. e.g.
   My sister asked me to go to market with quickly. *(Incorrect)*
   My sister asked me to go to market quickly. *(Correct)*
7. The adverbs of frequency and quantity should be placed before the auxiliaries **have to** and **used to.** e.g.
   I used to often take a break from my packed schedule. *(Incorrect)*
   I often used to take a break from my packed schedule. *(Correct)*
8. An adverb is not used by splitting an infinitive. e.g.
   She asked him to carefully write the answer. *(Incorrect)*
   She asked him to write the answer carefully. *(Correct)*
9. No adverb is used before **quite.** e.g.
   Raman is absolutely quite alone. *(Incorrect)*
   Raman is quite alone. *(Correct)*
10. 'Inverted form of verb' is used in the sentences starting with seldom, never, hardly, scarcely, rarely, **no sooner.** e.g.
   (i) No sooner had he entered the class than the bell rang.
   (ii) Seldom she meets her friends. *(Incorrect)*
   Seldom does she meet her friends. *(Correct)*

CONJUNCTIONS

Conjunction are the words that join two words, phrases or sentences. These are also called 'Linkers' or 'Joining words'.

Some Important Rules

Rule 1 Scarcely/hardly is always followed by **when/before.** e.g.

Scarcely had he gone out of the office then he came. *(Incorrect)*

Scarcely had he gone out of the office when he came. *(Correct)*

Rule 2 Lest is followed by **should.**

Not is not used with it. e.g.

Be careful lest you will fall. *(Incorrect)*

Be careful lest you should fall. *(Correct)*

Rule 3 Although/though must always be followed by **yet** or comma 'yet' is not necessary (,). e.g.

Although he worked hard but he failed. *(Incorrect)*

Although he worked hard, yet he failed. *(Correct)*

Rule 4 Both is followed by *and* and not by *else*, but or as well as. e.g.

Both Sonu as well as Pawan have done their work. *(Incorrect)*

Both Sonu and Pawan have done their work. *(Correct)*

Rule 5 Rather and **other** are always followed by **than.** e.g.

I have no other choice but to do it. *(Incorrect)*

I have no other choice than to do it. *(Correct)*

Rule 6 Neither .... **nor** and **Either** .... **or** are used in pairs. These are followed by the same part of speech. e.g.

(i) He has invited neither him not her. *(Incorrect)*
   He has invited neither him nor her. *(Correct)*
(ii) Either the step taken was right or wrong . *(Incorrect)*
   The step taken was either right or wrong. *(Correct)*

Rule 7 Not only is followed by **but also.** These always join the same parts of speech. e.g.

He is going not only to open a hospital but also an inn. *(Incorrect)*

He is going to open not only a hospital but also an inn. *(Correct)*

Rule 8 **Whether** is always followed by **or.** e.g.

We don't care that you pass or fail. *(Incorrect)*

We don't care whether you pass or fail. *(Correct)*

Rule 9 **The same** is followed by relative pronoun **that** or **as.** e.g.

He is the same boy who broke the glass. *(Incorrect)*

He is the same boy that broke the glass. *(Correct)*

> 'As' is used if the verb is not clear in the sentence. e.g. This is the same dress as mine.

Rule 10 **Because, since, as, as soon as** are not followed by therefore, thus, etc. e.g.

As he came late, therefore he was punished. *(Incorrect)*

As he came late, he was punished. *(Correct)*

RULES RELATED TO PREPOSITION

Prepositions are the words that are used to show the positional relations of nouns or pronouns.

Rule 1 When the object in the interrogative pronoun is understood then preposition is placed after the object. e.g.

(i) Whom are you talking to?
(ii) What are you looking for?

Rule 2 When the object of a preposition is relative pronoun 'that' then preposition is placed afterwards. e.g.

(i) He is the boy that everybody talks of.
(ii) This is the book that I was looking for.

Rule 3 When an infinitive qualifies a noun then the preposition should be placed after the infinitive. e.g.

(i) This is a better place to live in.
(ii) He gave me a pen to write with.

Rule 4 These verbs are not used with a preposition Stress, Emphasise, Discuss, Investigate, Comprise, Accompany, Consider, Violate, Demand, Pervade, Resemble, Precede, Resign, Concern, Regret, Await, Lack, Describe, Ensure and Join. e.g.

(i) He has ordered his transfer.
(ii) She is accompanying me.

Rule 5 'Than' and 'But' are generally conjunction but they can be used as prepositions. e.g.

(i) There was none other than Rakhi.
(ii) There was no one else but Rakhi.

Rule 6 Words take certain preposition with them. *See the list below*

- Assent to (a proposal)
- Avail ourselves of (an opportunity)
- Addicted to (drinking, something)
- Abstain from (food, indulgence etc)
- Afraid of (a ghost)
- Accession to (throne)
- Absorbed in (study)
- Acquaintance with (a person)
- Abundance of (wealth)
- Accustomed to (work)
- Attain to (a position)
- Accede to (a request)
- Absolved from (a promise, a sin)
- Adhere to (principles)
- Abhorrent to (good nature)
- Assure of (a thing)
- Acquit (someone) of a charge
- Beware of (cheating)
- Comply with (one's wishes)
- Cured of (a disease)
- Conducive to (health)
- Condemn to (death)
- Comply with (wishes)
- Desirous of (doing something)
- Devoid of (quality)
- Despair of (success)
- Deprive of (something)
- Duty of (the country)
- Eligible for (a post)
- Excuse for (a fault)

- Exchange a thing (with a person)
- Exception to (a rule)
- Envious of (a person or a thing)
- Elder to (some family member)
- Fatal to (one's cause)
- Furnish with (clothes)
- Fearful of (death)
- Greedy for (wealth)
- Heir to (ancestral property)
- Hopeful of (success)
- Healed of (a disease)
- Hostile to (a person)
- Intimate with (a person)
- Insist on a (thing)
- Impertinent to (elders)
- Innocent of (a crime)
- Invite to (dinner)
- Intimate with (person)
- Insight into (a matter or thing)
- Keep to (the left, the point)
- Match for (a person)
- Mourn for (the dead)
- Mad with (anger)
- Need for (help)
- Notorious for (drinking, doing)
- Overwhelmed with (sorrow, grief)
- Passion for (study)
- Persist in (doing)
- Pleased with (a person)
- Proud of (a thing)
- Prefer to (a thing)
- Repent of (a mistake)
- Rob (a person) of (a thing)
- Short of (money)
- Shocked at (a loss)
- Sure of (some fact)
- Sacred to (a cause)
- Invite to (dinner)
- Jealous of (a person)
- Knock at (the door)
- Key to (success)
- Match for (a person)
- Motive for (an action)
- Need of (a thing)
- Occur to (mind)
- Pay for (One's mistakes)
- Peculiar to (a person or a thing)
- Pity for (poor, downtrodden)
- Preface to (a book)
- Pride (on a thing)
- Refrain from (doing some wrong)
- Respectful to (a person)
- Sentence to (punishment)
- Side with (a person)
- Superior to (a thing)
- Search for (a thing)

Practice Exercise

Exercise 1

Directions (Q. Nos. 1-50) *In these questions, read each sentence to find out whether there is any error in it. If there is no error; the answer is (d). (Ignore errors of Punctuation, if any.)*

1. My father is (a) / in bad mood (b) / today. (c) / No error (d)
2. If a man diligently seeks to come into the contact (a) / with the best that has been thought and said in this world (b) / he will become simple and selfish. (c) / No error (d)
3. With little patience (a) / you will be able to (b) / cross this hurdle. (c) / No error (d)
4. This town isn't very well known (a) / and there isn't much to see, (b) / so a few tourists come here. (c) / No error (d)
5. The accelerating pace of life in our metropolitan city (a) / has had the tremendous effect (b) / on the culture and life-style of the people. (c) / No error (d)
6. Both the civilians (a) / and army men (b) / joined the Second World War. (c) / No error (d)
7. The hospital is (a) / within hundred meters (b) / from my house. (c) / No error (d)
8. The famous Dr. Narayana (a) / is only Orthopedist (b) / in our village. (c) / No error (d)
9. This incumbent lacks (a) / an experience (b) otherwise he is well qualified. (c) / No error (d)
10. A person I met (a) / in the theatre (b) / was the actor himself. (c) / No error (d)
11. Celebrating his ten long years in the film industry (a) / the actor announce that he would be doing a new show (b) / on television which would be done completely free of cost. (c) / No error (d)
12. After you will return (a) / from Mumbai (b) / I will come to meet you. (c) / No error (d)
13. My father (a) / has left (b) / for Mumbai last Saturday. (c) / No error (d)
14. I used to study (a) / till 10 pm and (b) / and then I go to bed. (c) / No error (d)
15. The Judge asked the man (a) / if the bag he had lost (b) / contain five thousand rupees. (c) / No error (d)
16. As you can see (a) / by my visiting card (b) / that now I am in Mumbai. (c) / No error (d)
17. The ministry was considered several proposals (a) / for the development of small and medium enterprises (b) / during budget discussions. (c) / No error (d)
18. Having work (a) / in both public and private sector banks (b) / she is the most suitable person to take over the post of the chairman. (c) / No error (d)
19. He started a very small business two years ago (a) / but it grew very fast (b) / as the country is experiencing a boom at that time. (c) / No error (d)
20. Her goal is to win gold medal (a) / in the Asian games and (b) / made her country proud. (c) / No error (d)
21. Order has been issued (a) / for his transfer to another district (b) / but he has not received them so far. (c) / No error (d)
22. Although she has studied (a) / English for almost a year (b) / she is yet to learn the alphabets. (c) / No error (d)
23. There are two scores of books (a) / which are lying (b) / unused in the library. (c) / No error (d)
24. Children are prone (a) / to making mischiefs (b) if they have nothing to do. (c) No error (d)
25. Sheeps are economically useful (a) / and so they are reared (b) / in the hills. (c) / No error (d)

26. Do you know (a) / whom all (b) / are inside the room ? (c) / No error (d)

27. They that run (a) / after frame and money (b) / are likely to be disappointed. (c) / No error (d)

28. One should (a) / take care of one's belongings (b) / himself. (c) / No error (d)

29. God helps those (a)/ who helps (b) / themselves. (c) / No error (d)

30. He and her (a) / went to the party (b) / in the hotel. (c) / No error (d)

31. There were (a)/ no less than fifty persons (b) / present in the room. (c) / No error (d)

32. Few remarks (a) / that he made were (b) / offensive to my friend. (c) / No error (d)

33. It is a (a) / worth watching documentary (b)/ and you must not miss it. (c) / No error (d)

34. Of all the students (a)/ Rita was less worried (b) / when the date for the annual examination was announced. (c) / No error (d)

35. Even the most perfect person (a) / in the world is said to have erred (b)/ when there was time to perform. (c) / No error (d)

36. He looks full of energy (a) / today because he (b) / soundly slept last night. (c) / No error (d)

37. She had barely nothing (a) / to eat when she came (b) / to me last month. (c) / No error (d)

38. It had been too cold (a) / the whole month and we preferred (b) / to stay in the plains. (c) / No error (d)

39. The quickly brown fox (a) / jumped over (b) / the lazy dog. (c) / No error (d)

40. He slowly (a) / went to open (b) / the lock. (c) / No error (d)

41. Although they listen to me (a) / but their actions (b) / prove otherwise. (c) / No error (d)

42. He treats (a) / us as (b) / slaves. (c) / No error (d)

43. Most of the girls are doing (a) / their post graduation because (b) / they may get good husbands. (c) / No error (d)

44. Such was his pronunciation (a) / as (b) / I could not understand him. (c) / No error (d)

45. He asked (a) / that who (b) / I was. (c) / No error (d)

46. He knows very well (a) / what is expected from him (b) / but he is not able to fulfil all the expectations. (c) / No error (d)

47. My brother has (a) / ordered for (b) / a new book. (c) /No error (d)

48. That Brutus, who was his trusted friend (a) / had attacked on him (b) / caused heart break to Julius Caesar. (c) / No error (d)

49. Bhuvan was (a) / blind with (b) / one eye. (c) / No error (d)

50. The doctor attended (a) / to (b) / the patient very quietly. (c) / No error (d)

Exercise 2

Directions (Q. Nos. 1 to 100) *Find out the part which has an error in the following sentences. If there is no error, your answer is* (d).

1. You can not withdraw (a)/ all your money until (b)/ you give a prior notice. (c)/ No error (d)

2. You should behave with others (a)/ the same way which you (b)/ would expect them to behave with you. (c)/ No error (d)

3. Either he nor his brother (a)/ was informed about the venue (b)/ of the meeting of our society. (c)/ No error (d)

4. He not only believes (a)/ in hard work but also (b)/ in honesty of the highest order. (c)/ No error (d)

5. No sooner did she (a)/ reach the station then (b)/ it started raining. (c)/ No error (d)

6. The captain and his wife (a)/ were invited for the (b)/ cultural function at my home. (c)/ No error (d)

7. He tried (a)/ to open the can (b)/ by a can opener. (c)/ No error (d)

8. Let no one (a)/ remain with doubt that (b)/ India is getting stronger and stronger. (c)/ No error (d)

9. When the students reached late (a)/ the teacher objected their entering the class (b)/ without his permission. (c)/ No error (d)

10. Sheela advised to her (a)/ child not to play (b)/ with the ball on the road. (c)/ No error (d)

11. The expert mason reported (a)/ to the owner of the hotel that (b)/ there was no question of the wall's falling down. (c)/ No error (d)

12. This blade's edge is sharper (a)/ than any other blades's (b)/ said the representative of the company. (c)/ No error (d)

13. Your son's-in law's friend is seriolusy ill and (a)/ he wants you (b)/ to see him as soon as possible. (c)/ No error (d)

14. You know it well that your success in life (a)/ depends not on my advice (b)/ but on somebody's else. (c)/ No error (d)

15. He suggested to me (a)/ that I should go to nursery (b)/ to bring some beautiful summer's flowers. (c)/ No error (d)

16. No sooner we entered (a)/ than he got up (b)/ and left the room. (c)/ No error (d)

17. He ultimately decided (a)/ to willingly and cheerfully accept (b)/ the responsibility entrusted to him. (c)/ No error (d)

18. Harish is (a)/ very much willing (b)/to come with you. (c)/ No error (d)

19. Mahesh thought that he would pass (a)/ in the examination although he did not (b)/ answer most of the questions correct. (c)/ No error (d)

20. Kunal's father advised him (a)/ not to ride the motorcycle (b)/ lately at night. (c)/ No error (d)

21. Looking into the situation (a)/ that prevailed a few years ago (b)/ he was taken that decision. (c)/ No error (d)

22. If you had not come in time (a)/ the child would have taken (b)/ by the dacoits. (c)/ No error (d)

23. I knew our college library was run chaotically (a)/ but only recently did I discover (b)/ how bad the situation is. (c)/ No error (d)

24. They talked for a while (a)/ and then they will continue to play (b)/ the game till tomorrow morning. (c)/ No error (d)

25. We got everything ready (a)/ for all of them (b)/ long before they arrived. (c)/ No error (d)

26. He looks more depressed (a)/ than her but I don't (b)/ know the reason. (c)/ No error (d)

27. The person which was (a)/ recommended for the position (b)/ did not fulfil the prescribed qualifications. (c)/ No error (d)

28. Between you and I (a)/ he probably (b)/ won't come at all. (c)/ No error (d)

29. If all of you quarrel (a)/ among yourself we shall not (b)/ be able to solve your problems. (c)/ No error (d)

30. They have invited Ramesh and I (a)/ to the function (b)/ to be held in the next month. (c)/ No error (d)

31. We should drink several glasses (a)/ of the water daily (b)/ if we want to remain healthy. (c)/ No error (d)

32. Children who have had (a)/ good Pre-School Education are most likely (b)/ to outdo other children at school. (c)/ No error (d)

33. On my request Jatin (a)/ introduced me to his friend (b)/ who is singer and scientist. (c)/ No error (d)

34. The burglars were caught just as (a)/ they were about to (b)/ escape from the jail. (c)/ No error (d)

35. The teacher drew (a)/ and attention of the boys (b)/ to the importance of regular practice. (c)/ No error (d)

36. He has brought (a)/ four breads (b)/ for lunch today. (c)/ No error (d)

37. This data are (a)/ very useful to arrive (b)/ at correct conclusion. (c)/ No error (d)

38. I have never seen (a)/ such a lovely spectacles in my life," (b)/said the passer by. (c)/ No error (d)

39. When you see his offsprings (a)/ you can't (b)/ believe that he is above seventy. (c)/ No error (d)

40. An earthquake (a)/ is a natural phenomena (b)/ and nobody can check it, be sure. (c)/ No error (d)

41. The Secretary of the worker's union remarked that (a)/ the present Government is so selfish that (b)/ it cared very little about solving anyone else's problem. (c)/ No error (d)

42. Please explain to me (a)/ how is a digital computer different (b)/ from an analogue computer. (c)/ No error (d)

43. We had swam (a)/ across the river (b)/ before the sunset. (c)/ No error (d)

44. The Secretary and Treasurer (a)/ were not present (b)/ at today's meeting. (c)/ No error (d)

45. Neither Rakesh nor I (a)/ are leaving (b)/ for Hyderabad. (c)/ No error (d)

46. My book is superior (a)/ than yours although it has (b)/ cost me much less. (c)/ No error (d)

47. When Charles was in hospital (a)/ his sister sent (b)/ much fruit than his uncle. (c)/ No error (d)

48. Dilip's performance in the film (a)/ was worst than Amit's (b)/ but was not as bad as Vinod's. (c)/ No error (d)

49. The teacher said that (a)/ Ajay was capable of (b)/ doing more better work. (c)/ No error (d)

50. A severe cold (a)/ Prevented the President (b)/ being present (c)/ at the function (d)

51. After he had read the two first chapters (a)/ of the novel, he felt like (b)/ reading the book at one sitting. (c)/ No error (d)

52. The girl said that (a)/ she preferred the blue gown (b)/ than the black one. (c)/ No error (d)

53. Raju cannot walk (a)/ much than two miles (b)/ at a stretch. (c)/ No error (d)

54. I often give him money (a)/ and I gave him few (b)/ yesterday also. (c)/ No error (d)

55. It is always easy (a)/ to talk about a thing (b)/ than to do it ourselves. (c)/ No error (d)

56. The doctor advised him (a)/ to give off smoking (b)/ but he did not pay any heed. (c)/ No error (d)

57. Their father has left (a)/ behind a huge sum to be (b)/ destributed among the two brothers. (c)/ No error (d)

58. No effort has been made (a)/ at all to cash on (b)/ the refurnished image of Indian tennis. (c)/ No error (d)

59. The elegantly designed collection (a)/ for ladies has an emphasis (b)/ with style, variety and colour. (c)/ No error (d)

60. As soon as he reached the venue (a)/ he enquired from the supervisor (b)/ about the closing time of the examinaiton. (c)/ No error (d)

61. The table's wood (a)/ is infested with mite (b)/ and I am likely to dispose it of. (c)/ No error (d)

62. The finance Minister (a)/ boasts of improving (b)/ the economic condition of the country's. (c)/ No error (d)

63. He told her that (a)/ he had ever seen her (b)/ with his mind's eye. (c)/ No error (d)

64. Unfortunately for me (a)/ the root cause of my frustration (b)/ lies in the Government dubious policy. (c)/ No error (d)

65. I have read (a)/ many plays of Shaw's (b)/ who is called the Shakespeare of our age. (c)/ No error (d)

66. We have carefully considered (a)/ the importance of issues (b)/ raised in the report. (c)/ No error (d)

67. Every man, woman and Child (a)/ is now aware of the terrible consequences (b)/ of habit of smoking. (c)/ No error (d)

68. Ravi prefers self-employment (a)/ to job in (b)/ any office. (c)/ No error (d)

69. In a fit of temper (a)/ he tore up a sweet letter (b)/ which his wife had written to him. (c)/ No error (d)

70. He used very inaccurate (a)/ language for (b)/ he knew no better. (c)/ No error (d)

71. The gentleman (a)/ together with his wife (b)/ and daughter were drowned. (c)/ No error (d)

72. It is in 1929 (a)/ that we first (b)/ flew to the United States. (c)/ No error (d)

73. Our country need (a)/ a number of self sacrificing (b)/ devoted political leaders. (c)/ No error (d)

74. The issues are complex (a)/ and has been obscured (b)/ by other factors. (c)/ No error (d)

75. He reminded me that (a)/ he has often told me (b)/ not to play with fire. (c)/ No error (d)

76. The taxi driver who had come (a)/ to receive us at the airport (b)/ was speaking fluently French. (c)/ No error (d)

77. The only criteria (a)/ to judge (b)/ a person. (c)/ is to observe his behaviour (d)

78. We are confident enough (a)/ to earn our livelihood (b)/ by toiling hardly. (c)/ No error (d)

79. The observers feel that the stronger team (a)/ has to face defeat because (b)/ the players don't play whole hearted. (c)/ No error (d)

80. You seem to be (a)/ enough rich to buy (b)/ anything you like. (c)/ No error (d)

81. Radha came (a)/ to the meeting much later (b)/ than I expect. (c)/ No error (d)

82. I have been working (a)/ for this organisation (b)/ for the last ten years. (c)/ No error (d)

83. I know he is having (a)/ a lot of books on (b)/ how to improve English. (c)/ No error (d)

84. If it snowed (a)/ tomorrow we'll (b)/ go for skating. (c)/ No error (d)

85. He told me that (a)/ he wrote a letter (b)/ to his superior for a certain reason. (c)/ No error (d)

86. Cattles were (a)/ grazing in the meadows (b)/ near our farm. (c)/ No error (d)

87. The infromation supplied to us (a)/ were not as useful as (b)/ we first thought it would be. (c)/ No error (d)

88. It was evident (a)/ to me that there (b)/ was any mistake. (c)/ in that account (d)

89. The audience (a)/ are requested (b)/ to be in its seats. (c)/ No error (d)

90. He says that (a)/ a two miles walk (b)/ always keeps him healthy and fresh. (c)/ No error (d)

91. The guide told us that (a)/ where the island was (b)/ and went on narrating its history. (c)/ No error (d)

92. How do you say that (a)/ neither he or Ramesh (b)/ has qualified in the examinaion. (c)/ No error (d)

93. Unless you return (a)/ his book he will (b)/ not talk to you. (c)/ No error (d)

94. He neither gave satisfaction (a)/ as a cook (b)/ nor as a chauffeur. (c)/ No error (d)

95. Hardly had I reached (a)/ the airport where I learnt (b)/ about the powerful bomb explosion. (c)/ No error (d)

96. If you are good to people (a)/ you will be treated (b)/ well by themselves. (c)/ No error (d)

97. This is one company who not only sells (a)/ its products but also gives (b)/ good after sales service. (c)/ No error (d)

98. I asked him (a)/ whom he thought would be (b)/ able to get the first prize. (c)/ No error (d)

99. They visited the place (a)/ because they wanted to see for themself (b)/ the damage caused by the floods. (c)/ No error (d)

100. There should be (a)/ no misunderstanding (b)/ between your father and she. (c)/ No error (d)

Previous Year's Questions

Directions (Q. Nos. 101-103) *In the following questions, identify the incorrect sentence/sentences.* **[CLAT 2015]**

101. A. The letter was posted to the address.

B. Your stand is beyond all reason.

C. How do you deal with friend who doesn't listen to a reason?

D. My wife runs profitable business in this suburb.

Codes

(a) Only A (b) Only D

(c) B and C (d) C and D

102. A. I want to do an MBA before going into business.

B. Priti's husband has been on active service for 3 months.

C. The horse suddenly broke into a buckle.

D. I need to file an insurance claim.

Codes

(a) A and B (b) Only C

(c) B and C (d) B, C and D

103. A. I must run fast to catch up with him.
B. The newly released book is enjoying a popular run.
C. The doctor is on a hospital round.
D. You can't run over him like that.

Codes
(a) A and C
(b) Only D
(c) A, C and D
(d) Only A

Directions (Q. Nos. 104-113) *In each of the following sentences four words or phrases are underlined. If there is any mistake with regard to grammar or usage, it is in the underlined part only. Identify the incorrect part.* **[CLAT 2017]**

104. Evidently (A) our product is the most (B) unique in (C) the market (D).
(a) D (b) C
(c) A (d) B

105. The most (A) difficult job is to bend (B) and then lifting (C) the weight (D).
(a) B (b) C
(c) A (d) D

106. The hope (A) to go through (B) the book today I have (C) already read (D) half of it.
(a) B (b) D
(c) A (d) C

107. Our boss always (A) asks us to pay (B) full (C) attention to the work at hand (D).
(a) D (b) A (c) C (d) B

108. After being finished (A) the (B) last chapter of the book, return it (C) to me (D).
(a) D (b) A (c) C (d) B

109. The officer asked if (A) the report (B) be submitted (C) immediately (D).
(a) A (b) D (c) C (d) B

110. Since (A) I have forgotten (B) all the equations I will have (C) to start from the scratch (D).
(a) C (b) A (c) D (d) B

111. He gave me (A) a ticket so that (B) I may visit (C) the (D) book fair.
(a) D (b) B (c) A (d) C

112. On listening (A) to the confession of love (B) she blushed until (C) she was purple (D).
(a) B (b) A (c) C (d) D

113. Five gallons of (A) petrol are (B) not enough (C) to cover the distance (D).
(a) B (b) D (c) C (d) A

Answers

Exercise 1

1	*b*	2	*a*	3	*a*	4	*c*	5	*b*	6	*b*	7	*b*	8	*b*	9	*b*	10	*a*
11	*b*	12	*a*	13	*b*	14	*c*	15	*c*	16	*d*	17	*a*	18	*a*	19	*c*	20	*b*
21	*a*	22	*c*	23	*a*	24	*b*	25	*a*	26	*b*	27	*a*	28	*c*	29	*b*	30	*a*
31	*b*	32	*a*	33	*b*	34	*b*	35	*a*	36	*c*	37	*a*	38	*a*	39	*a*	40	*d*
41	*b*	42	*d*	43	*b*	44	*b*	45	*b*	46	*b*	47	*b*	48	*b*	49	*b*	50	*d*

Exercise 2

1	*b*	2	*b*	3	*a*	4	*a*	5	*b*	6	*b*	7	*c*	8	*b*	9	*b*	10	*a*
11	*c*	12	*d*	13	*a*	14	*c*	15	*c*	16	*a*	17	*b*	18	*b*	19	*c*	20	*c*
21	*c*	22	*b*	23	*c*	24	*a*	25	*a*	26	*b*	27	*a*	28	*a*	29	*b*	30	*a*
31	*b*	32	*b*	33	*c*	34	*c*	35	*b*	36	*b*	37	*a*	38	*b*	39	*a*	40	*b*
41	*b*	42	*b*	43	*a*	44	*b*	45	*b*	46	*b*	47	*c*	48	*b*	49	*c*	50	*c*
51	*a*	52	*c*	53	*b*	54	*b*	55	*a*	56	*b*	57	*c*	58	*b*	59	*c*	60	*b*
61	*a*	62	*c*	63	*d*	64	*c*	65	*b*	66	*b*	67	*c*	68	*b*	69	*b*	70	*a*
71	*c*	72	*a*	73	*a*	74	*b*	75	*b*	76	*c*	77	*a*	78	*c*	79	*c*	80	*b*
81	*c*	82	*d*	83	*a*	84	*a*	85	*b*	86	*a*	87	*b*	88	*c*	89	*c*	90	*b*
91	*a*	92	*b*	93	*a*	94	*a*	95	*b*	96	*c*	97	*a*	98	*b*	99	*b*	100	*c*
101	*d*	102	*b*	103	*b*	104	*d*	105	*b*	106	*c*	107	*a*	108	*b*	109	*c*	110	*c*
111	*d*	112	*d*	113	*a*														

EXPLANATIONS

Exercise 1

1. Add 'a' before 'bad mood'.

2. Remove 'the'

3. Add 'a' before 'little'

4. Remove 'a'

5. Replace 'the' by 'a'

6. Add 'the' before 'army men'.

7. Add 'a' before 'hundred'. Here, 'a' is used for 'one'.

8. Add 'the' before 'only'.

9. Remove 'an'.

10. Replace 'A' by 'The' as 'The' is used before specified objects.

11. Replace 'announce' by 'announced' as the sentence is in past tense.

12. Remove 'will'. Do not use 'will' after time clause.

13. It is clearly mentioned that the activity is of last Saturday therefore, use simple past in part (b). So remove 'has'.

14. 'Used to' is used for past habitual action. In part (c) replace 'go' by 'went'.

15. Replace 'contain' by 'contained' as the sentence is in past tense.

16. No error

17. Use simple past tense. Using 'was' is indicative of passive mode which is not needed here.

18. Replace 'work' by 'worked' as the sentence is in past tense.

19. The sentence is in past tense. So use 'was experiencing'.

20. Replace 'made' by 'make'.

21. When a person is assigned to a new station, he receives his 'orders'.

This is a set of instructions,including where to be, when to be there etc. So, the correct sentence would be 'Orders have been issued'.

22. 'Alphabet' is the set of letters in a language. English alphabet has 26 letters from A-Z. In the given sentence, we will use 'alphabet' instead of 'alphabets'.

23. When a quantity is given before 'score' like '2' or '5' etc, 'score' is not used in the plural form. Hence, we would use 'score' in place of 'scores' in the given sentence.

24. The word 'mischief' does not have a plural form. Hence, 'mischief' would be used.

25. The plural of 'sheep' is 'sheep'. In the given sentence, the word 'Sheeps' would be replaced by 'Sheep'.

26. 'Whom' should be replaced by 'who'.

27. 'They' needs to be replaced by 'Those'.

28. 'Himself' should be replaced by 'oneself'.

29. 'Helps' should be replaced by 'help' to make the sentence grammatically correct.

30. 'Her' would be replaced by 'she' to make the sentence error free.

31. 'No fewer than ' should be replaced by 'no less than' to make the sentence meaningful.

32. 'A few' would be used in the sentence instead of 'Few'.

33. The usage of 'worth watching documentary' is incorrect. The correct usage will be 'doumentary worth watching.'

34. 'Least worried' should be replaced by 'less worried' to make the sentence meaningful.

35. 'Most perfect' should be replaced by 'perfect' to make the sentence meaningful .

36. 'Soundly slept' needs to be changed to 'slept soundly' to make the sentence meaningful.

37. As per the rule, two negative words cannot be used together in a sentence. In the given sentence, 'barely' and 'nothing' are negative words. So, we would replace 'nothing' by 'anything'.

38. 'Too' needs to be replaced by 'very' to make the sentence grammatically correct.

39. 'Quickly' does not make sense. So, we should replace it by its adjective form i.e. 'quick'.

40. No error

41. The correlative of 'Although' is 'yet' and not 'but'. Hence, we should remove 'but' and use 'yet' in place of it.

42. No error

43. As the sentence starts with 'Most of', 'because' will not be used. We would replace it by 'so that'.

44. As per the rule, 'such.... that' is used for mentioning consequences. Hence, we would use 'that' in place of 'as'.

45. As per the rule, 'that' is not used in Indirect speech if the sentence is interrogative. Hence, we would remove 'that' from the sentence.

46. The preposition 'of' should be used instead of 'from' in the given sentence.

47. 'For' in part (b) of the sentence is not needed. It should be deleted.

48. The preposition 'on' in the sentence is not needed. We need to delete it to convey the correct meaning of the sentence.

49. 'Blind in one eye' is the correct usage. Hence, we should replace 'with' by 'in'.

50. No error.

Exercise 2

1. Use 'unless' for 'until'

2. Use 'as' in place of 'which'

3. Neither he nor his

4. Say 'he believes not only'

5. Use 'than' for 'then'

6. Use 'to' in place of 'for'

7. Say 'with a can opener'

8. Use 'in' for 'with'

9. Insert 'to' after 'objected'

10. Remove 'to'

11. Say ' the falling down of the wall'

12. No error

13. Say 'son-in-law's'

14. Say 'somebody else's'

15. Say 'summer flower's'

16. Insert 'had' after 'sooner'

17. Place 'accept' before 'willingly'

18. Remove 'much'

19. Say 'correctly'

20. Use 'late' for 'lately'

21. Use 'took' for 'was taken'

22. Use 'have been' in place of 'have'
23. Say 'the situation was'
24. Use 'will talk' for 'talked'
25. Say 'we had got'
26. Use 'she' for 'her'
27. Use 'who' in place of 'which'
28. Use 'me' for 'I'
29. Use 'yourselves' in place of 'yourself'
30. Say 'Ramesh and me'
31. Remove 'the'
32. Insert 'a' before 'good'
33. Insert 'a' before 'singer'
34. Remove 'the'
35. Say 'the attention'
36. Say 'four pieces of bread'
37. Use 'These' for 'This'
38. Say 'a pain of spectacles'
39. Use 'offspring' for 'offsprings'
40. Say 'a natural phenomenon'
41. Use 'was' in place of 'is'
42. Place 'is' after 'computer'
43. Use 'swum' for 'swam'
44. Use 'was' in place of 'were'
45. Say 'am leaving'
46. Use 'to' for 'than'
47. Use 'more' in place of 'much'
48. Say 'was worse'
49. Remove 'more'
50. Put 'from' before being
51. Say 'the first two'
52. Use 'to' for 'than'.
53. Say 'more than'
54. Use 'a little/ some' in place of 'few'
55. Say 'easier'
56. Say 'to give up'
57. Use 'between' for 'among'
58. Say 'cash in on'
59. Use 'on' in place of 'with'
60. Say 'enquired of'
61. Say 'The wood of the table'
62. Say 'country'
63. No error
64. Say 'Government's dubious policy'
65. Say 'many plays of Shaw'
66. Insert 'the' before 'issues'
67. Say 'of the habit of smoking'
68. Insert 'a' before 'job'
69. Say 'the sweet letter'
70. Insert 'a' before 'very'

Previous Year's Solutions

101. Sentences C and D both are incorrect. In sentence C, we should use Article 'a' after 'with' and in sentence D we should use article 'a' after 'runs', so that the syntax is rectified.

As no option was there for three incorrect sentences. B sentences has been corrected.

Your stand is beyond reason should be the correct sentence.

102. In this question, sentence A has error of use of an MBA. It should be I want to do MBA before going into business.

In sentence B, this use of preposition 'on' is wrong. 'In' is the correct preposition to be used here.

103. Sentence D has an error in its syntax. One should write 'run him over' in place of 'run over him'. Hence, (b) is correct option.

104. Part 'B' has the error as most cannot be used with 'unique' as it makes it superflous use of the degree of adjectives.

105. Part 'C' has the error as 'to lift' (infinitive) will be used in place of lifting (gerund) to make it correct as the objective case should be used in same form (gerund or infinitive) and second object follows the first object.

106. Part 'A' has the error as 'the hope' should be proceeded by 'with' to make it meaningful.

107. Part 'D' has the error of preposition as 'in' should be used in place of 'at'.

108. Part 'A' has the error as being finished should be replaced by finishing to make it correct.

109. Part 'C' has the error as there must be a helping verb (was) before be to make the sentence meaningful.

110. Part 'D' has the error as idiom 'start from scratch' means to begin from the beginning, so remove article 'the'.

111. Part 'C' has the error as the main clause is in past tense, so the subordinate should also be in past. Replace 'may' with 'might' here.

112. Part 'D' has the error as replace 'was' with became to make the sentence meaningful.

113. Part 'B' has the error. Replace 'are' with 'is' as the subject of the verb is singular.

CHAPTER 02

COMPREHENSION

Reading comprehension is an indispensable part in CLAT Entrance exam. If a candidate is well-versed with the topic then a handsome score can be made upon. A careful and intensive reading of the passage and quick glance on the questions help the students in solving these questions easily.

Comprehension is the ability to understand completely and be familiar with the situation, facts etc. There are a number of approaches to improve reading comprehension, including improving one's vocabulary and reading strategies.

Directions *Read the given passages and answer the questions with the help of information provided in the passage.*

Passage 1

Rural development in India has witnessed several changes over the years in its emphasis, approaches, strategies and programmes. It has assumed a new dimension and perspectives as a consequence. Rural development can be richer and more meaningful only through the participation of clienteles of development. Just as **implementation** is the touchstone for planning, people's participation is the centre-piece in rural development.

People's participation is one of the foremost **pre-requisites** of development process both from procedural and philosophical perspectives. For the development planners and administrators, it is important to solicit the participation of different groups of rural people, to make the plans participatory.

Rural development aims at improving rural people's livelihoods in an equitable and sustainable manner, both socially and environmentally, through better access to assets and services and control over productive capital. The basic objectives of Rural Development Programmes have been alleviation of poverty and unemployment through creation of basic social and economic infrastructure, provision of training to rural unemployed youth and providing employment to marginal farmers/labourers to discourage seasonal and permanent migration to urban areas.

Rural development is the main pillar of our nation's development. In spite of rapid urbanisation, a large section of our population still lives in the villages. Secondly, rural India has lagged behind in development because of many historical sectors. Though, the 11th Plan began in very behaviourable circumstances with the economy having grown at the rate of 7.7% per year in the 10th Plan period, there still existed a big challenge to correct the development imbalances and to accord due priority to development in rural areas.

Ministry of Rural Development is implementing a number of programmes aimed at sustainable **holistic** development in rural areas. The thrust of these programmes is on all round economic and social transformation in rural areas, though a multi-pronged strategy aiming to reach out to the most disadvantaged sections of the society.

Although, concrete efforts have been initiated by the Government of India through several plans and measures to alleviate poverty in rural India, there still remains much more to be done to bring prosperity in the lives of the people in rural areas. At present, technology **dissemination** is uneven and slow in the rural areas.

1. According to the passage, which of the following are the objectives of most Rural Development Programmes?

I. To promote urbanisation
II. Provide training to youth
III. Reducing unemployment

Codes

(a) I and III (b) Only III
(c) II and III (d) All of these

2. As per the passage, the basic objective of Rural Development Programmes have been alleviation of poverty and through creation of basic social and economic ....

(a) dissemination
(b) unemployment
(c) attention
(d) infrastructure

3. According to the passage, experiences of many countries suggest that technological development fuelled by demand has a higher............ rate.

(a) dissemination (b) promulgation
(c) promotion (d) circulation

4. Which of the following is true according to the passage?

I. Urbanisation has resulted in a majority of Indian population living in urban areas.
II. The economic growth of the 10th Five Year Plan did not translate into proportionate rural development.
III. The efforts of the Government of India for poverty alleviation have been met with complete failure.

Codes

(a) I and II (b) Only III
(c) I and III (d) Only II

Directions (Q. Nos. 5-6) *Choose the word that is most similar to the meaning of the given word.*

5. Implementation

(a) Exercise (b) Suggestion
(c) Play (d) Use

6. Holistic

(a) Covered (b) Healthy
(c) Full (d) Integrated

Directions (Q. Nos. 7-8) *Choose the word that is opposite in the meaning to the given word.*

7. Pre-requisite

(a) Essential (b) Required
(c) Unnecessary (d) Advantage

8. Dissemination

(a) Distribution (b) Spread
(c) Diffusion (d) Collection

Passage 2

A large number of branches of banks have been set-up in the villages. The main purpose of setting up these banks is to develop the habit of saving among the villagers and also to give loans to farmers for boosting production in one way or the other. So, far banks had been concentrated in the bigger cities and Indian villagers had no faith in them.

The new banks also intend to re-channel bank credit -from the big industries to the small sectors. With the **intention** of promoting rural banking, regional rural banks were established. These aligned the local field with the rural problems. These banks are not to replace the other credit-giving bodies but to supplement them.

The Steering Committee of the Regional Rural Banks considered some structural changes. First of all, they gave thought to the staffing spectrum, then to effective **coordination** among banks rural cooperatives and commercial and the possibility of bringing credit within the access to weaker sections. They wanted to recruit staff for the rural banks at lower salaries. But, this type of **discrimination** would have been unfruitful. So, it was given up.

A problem with regard to the rural banks is the creditworthiness of the poor. The Indian farmers are so poor that they cannot pay back their loans. The rural Indian surveys make it quite clear that practically rural farmers have no credit worthiness. Their socio-economic mobility is almost zero. That is why, banks fear that their credit will never be paid back.

Another difficulty for the rural banks is that loans cannot be processed so easily. Processing loans also entails heavy expenditure. This was also going to affect their financial position. Still the establishment of the rural banks was decided because the social advantages were more important than the commercial consideration.

Rural banks definitely encourage saving. No doubt the villagers do not have to pay income tax and they get many other **concessions**, yet their saving is not significant. Despite all the hurdles, the rural banking system will boost up the economy of villages and thereby the economy of the country.

1. Which of the following is/are the purpose of setting up banks in rural areas?

I. Replacing other credit-giving bodies.

II. Giving loans to farmers.

III. Increasing the amount of savings of villager.

Codes

(a) Only II (b) I and II

(c) II and III (d) Only I

2. Which of the following is not true according to the passage?

(a) Processing of loans by rural banks is difficult

(b) Staff of the rural banks is paid a lower salary as compared to urban banks

(c) Rural banks may not make as much profit as their urban counterparts

(d) Processing of loans by bank is not cheap

3. The structural changes made by the steering committee were in respect of

(a) staffing, co-ordinating and providing access to weaker sections

(b) building smaller buildings to house the banks

(c) investing very little in terms of infrastructure required to start a bank

(d) discriminating between urban bank staff and rural bank staff

4. Which of the following is one of the benefits of living in the village, as mentioned in the passage?

(a) People living in the villages enjoy a higher income than urban counterparts

(b) People living in villages do not have to pay income tax and they also get other concessions

(c) People living in villages have a better quality of life

(d) Villages are self-sufficient; hence they do not need outside help for any activity

5. Which of the following is possibly the most appropriate title for the passage?

(a) Regional Rural Banks

(b) The Rural Consumer

(c) Microfinance in Rural India

(d) Characteristics of Indian Villages

Directions (Q. Nos. 6-7) *Choose the word that is most similar in the meaning to the given word.*

6. Intention

(a) Struggle (b) Center

(c) Motive (d) Last

7. Discrimination

(a) Injustice (b) Separation

(c) Wrong (d) Cleverness

Directions (Q. Nos. 8-9) *Choose the word that is most opposite in the meaning to the given word.*

8. Coordination

(a) Non-cooperation (b) Teamwork

(c) Community (d) Symbiosis

9. Concession

(a) Accommodation (b) Agreement

(c) Repudiation (d) Claim

Passage 3

A new analysis has determined that the threat of global warming can still be greatly **diminished** if nations cut emissions of heat-trapping greenhouse gases by 70% this century. The analysis was done by scientists at the National Centre for Atmospheric Research (NCAR). While global temperatures- would rise, the most dangerous potential aspects of climate change, including massive losses of Arctic sea ice and **permafrost** and significant sea-level rise, could be partially avoided.

This research indicates that we can no longer avoid significant warming during this century, said NCAR scientist Warren Washington, the study paper's lead author. But, if the world were to implement this level of mission cuts, we could stabilise the threat of climate change, he added. Average global temperatures have armed by close to 1° C since the pre-industrial era.

Much of the warming is due to human- produced emissions of greenhouse gases, **predominantly** carbon dioxide. This heat-trapping gas has increased from a pre-industrial level of about 284 parts per million (ppm) in the atmosphere to more than 380 ppm today. With research showing that additional warming of about 1°C may be the **threshold** for dangerous climate change, the European Union has called for dramatic cuts in emissions of carbon dioxide and other greenhouse gases.

To examine the impact of such cuts on the world's climate. Washington and his colleagues ran a series of global studies with the NCAR based Community Climate System Model (CCSM). They assumed that carbon dioxide levels could be held to 450 ppm at the end of this century. In contrast, emissions are now on track to reach about 750 ppm by 2100 if unchecked.

The team's results showed that If carbon dioxide were held to 450 ppm, global temperatures would increase by 0.6° C above current readings by the end of the century.

1. What would not be one of the impacts of cutting greenhouse gas emission?
(a) Temperatures will stop soaring
(b) Ice in the Arctic sea would melt at a slower pace
(c) The rise in sea level would be lesser
(d) All of the above

2. What would be the impact of unchecked greenhouse gas and carbon dioxide emissions?
(a) The temperature would rise from the current temperature by 2.2°C
(b) The sea level would rise by about 5.5 inches
(c) The Arctic ice would stabilise by 2100
(d) The Arctic ice would reduce by one-fourth

3. Why has the European Union called for dramatic cuts in carbon dioxide and greenhouse gas emissions?
(a) As global warming is not an issue of concern
(b) As the temperatures may rise almost by an additional one degree and this may lead to severe climate change
(c) As the NCAR has forced the European Union to announce the cuts
(d) As all the nations have decided to cut emissions of carbon dioxide

4. What can be the most appropriate title for the above passage?
(a) A study of the rise in water level
(b) A study of rise in temperature
(c) A study of the effects of greenhouse gas emissions
(d) A study of the Arctic region

Directions (Q. Nos. 5-6) *Choose the word that is most similar to the meaning of the given word.*

5. Diminish
(a) Lower (b) Increase
(c) Contract (d) Worse

6. Permafrost
(a) Crystal (b) Water
(c) Last (d) Vapour

Directions (Q. Nos. 7-8) *Choose the word that is most opposite in the meaning to the given word.*

7. Predominantly
(a) Partly (b) Largely
(c) Completely (d) Chiefly

8. Threshold
(a) Verge
(b) Edge
(c) Cradle
(d) Close

Passage 4

Today, with a Noble Prize to its credit, Grameen is one of the largest micro-finance organisations in the world. It started out lending small sums to poor entrepreneurs in Bangladesh to help them grow from a **subsistence** living to a livelihood. The great discovery its founders made was that even with few assets, these entrepreneurs repaid on time.

Grameen and micro-finance have since become financial staples of the developing world. Grameen's approach, unlike other micro-financers, uses the group-lending model. Costs are kept down by having borrowers vet one another, tying together their financial fates and eliminating expensive loan offices entirely. The ultimate promise of Grameen is to use business lending as a way of people to lift themselves out of poverty.

Recently, Grameen has taken on a different challenge by setting up operations in the US Money may be tight in the waning recession but it is still a nation of 100000 bank branches. Globally, the working micro-finance equation consists of, borrowing funds cheaply and keeping loan defaults and overhead expenses sufficiently low. Microlenders, including Grameen, do this by charging **colossal** interest rates-as high as 60% or 70% which is necessary to compensate for the risk and attract bank funding. But, loans at rates much above the standard 15% would most likely be attacked as usurious in America.

So, the question is whether there is a role for a third world lender in the world's largest economy? Grameen America believes that in a few years it will be successful and turn a profit thanks to 9 million US households untouched by mainstream banks and 21 million using the likes of payday loans and pawn shops for financing. But **enticing** the unbanked won't be easy.

After all, profit has long eluded micro-financiers and if it is not lucrative, it is not mlcrolending, but charity. When Grameen first went to the US, in the late 1980s. it tripped up. Under Grameen's futelage, banks started micro loans to entrepreneurs with a shocking 30% loss. But, Grameen America says that this time results will be different because Grameen employees themselves will be making the loans, not training an American bank to do it.

More often than not, the borrowers, Grameen finds, in the US already have jobs (as factory workers e.g.) or side businesses-selling toys. cleaning houses, etc. The loans from Grameen, by and large, provide a **steadier** source of funding, but they don't create businesses out of nothing. But, money isn't everything. More importantly, for many entrepreneurs, group members are tremendous sources of support to one another. So, even if studies are yet to determine if Grameen is a clear-cut pathway out of poverty it still achieves something useful.

1. What has adversely affected the success of micro-finance institutions in the US?

(a) The focus of these institutions is on making a profit at any cost instead of being charitable to the needy

(b) American banks engaged in micro-lending were the most severely hit during the recession

(c) Widespread perception among bankers that these institutions are better suited to developing countries

(d) Their failure to attract those outside the formal banking system as customers

2. What is the central theme of the passage?

(a) The contention that Grameen is doomed to fail in developed countries

(b) A comprehensive evaluation of the current status of the American economy

(c) A discussion about the prospects of Grameen and micro-finance in the US

(d) The role of banks in facilitating micro-lending efforts in developed nations

3. Why has Grameen made a second attempt to launch itself in the US?

(a) The willingness of US banks to provide the necessary staff and funds to facilitate the spread of micro-finance

(b) The rates of interest on loans in the US are exorbitant making it easier to recover capital

(c) The realisation that a large percentage of the American population not reached by mainstream banks can be tapped

(d) Recognition of the fact that disbursing credit in developing countries during the recession is too risky

4. Which of the following can be inferred from the passage?
(a) Micro-finance has been successful only in Asian countries
(b) Micro-finance makes individual borrowers dependent rather than independent
(c) America has the largest number of banks in the world
(d) There is a scope for micro-finance institutions to be profitable in developed countries

Directions (Q. Nos. 5-6) *Choose the word that is most similar to the meaning of given word.*

5. Subsistence
(a) Livelihood (b) Close
(c) Absence (d) Substitute

6. Enticing
(a) Attention (b) Grand
(c) Energy (d) Attractive

Directions (Q. Nos. 7-8) *Choose the word that is opposite to the meaning of the given word.*

7. Colossal
(a) Epic (b) Super
(c) Enormous (d) Tiny

8. Steadier
(a) Even (b) Sure
(c) Unstable (d) Fast

Previous Year's Questions

Directions *Read the following question carefully and answer the questions following that.*

Passage 5

The work which Gandhiji had taken up was not only regarding the achievement of political freedom but also the establishment of a new social order based on truth and non-violence, unity and peace, equality and universal brotherhood and maximum freedom for all. This unfinished part of his experiment was perhaps even more difficult to achieve than the achievement of political freedom. In the political struggle, the fight was against a foreign power and all one could do was either join it or wish it success and give it his/her moral support. In establishing a social order on this pattern, there was a strong possibility of a conflict arising between diverse groups and classes of our own people. Experience shows that man values his possessions even more than his life because in the former he sees the means for perpetuation and survival of his descendants even after his body is reduced to ashes. A new order cannot be established without radically changing the mind and attitude of men toward property and at some stage or the other, the 'haves' have to yield place to the 'have-nots'. We have seen, in our time, attempts to achieve a kind of egalitarian society and the picture of it after it was achieved. But, this was done, by and large, through the use of physical force.

In the ultimate analysis, it is difficult, if not impossible, to say that the instinct to possess has been rooted out or that it will not reappear in an even worse form under a different guise. It may even be that, like a gas kept confined within containers under great pressure or water held back by a big dam, once the barrier breaks, the reaction will one day sweep back with a violence equal in extent and intensity to what was used to establish and maintain the outward egalitarian form. This enforced egalitarianism contains, in its bosom, the seed of its own destruction.

The root cause of class conflict is possessiveness or the acquisitive instinct. So, long as the ideal that is to be achieved is one of securing the maximum material satisfaction, possessiveness is neither suppressed nor eliminated but grows, on what it feeds. Nor does it cease to be possessiveness, whether it is confined to only a or is shared by many.

If egalitarianism is to endure, it has to be based not on the possession of the maximum material goods by a few or by all but on voluntary, enlightened renunciation of those goods which cannot be shared by others or can be enjoyed only at the expense of others. This calls for substitution of material values by purely spiritual ones. The paradise of material satisfaction, which is sometimes equated with progress these days, neither spells peace nor progress. Mahatma Gandhi has shown us how the acquisitive instinct inherent in man can be transmuted by the adoption of the ideal of trusteeship by those who 'have' for the benefit of all those who 'have not' so that, instead of leading to exploitation and conflict, it would become a means and incentive for the amelioration and progress of society, respectively. **[CLAT 2012]**

1. According to the passage, egalitarianism will not survive if
   (a) it is not based on voluntary renunciation
   (b) it is achieved by resorting to physical force
   (c) underprivileged people are not involved in its establishment
   (d) people's outlook towards it is not radically changed
2. According to the passage, why does man value his possessions more than his life?
   (a) He has inherent desire to share his possession with others
   (b) He is endowed with the possessive instinct
   (c) Only his possession helps him earn love and respect from his descendants
   (d) Through his possessions he can preserve his name even after his death
3. According to the passage, which was the unfinished part of Gandhi's experiment?
   (a) Educating people to avoid class conflict
   (b) Achieving total political freedom for the country
   (c) Establishment of an egalitarian society
   (d) Radically changing the mind and attitude of men towards truth and non-violence
4. Which of the following statements is 'not true' in the context of the passage?
   (a) True egalitarianism can be achieved by giving up one's possessions under compulsion
   (b) Man values his life more than his possessions
   (c) Possessive instinct is a natural desire of human beings
   (d) In the political struggle, the fight was against alien rule
5. According to the passage, true egalitarianism will last only if
   (a) it is thrust upon people
   (b) it is based on truth and non-violence
   (c) people inculcate spiritual values instead of material values
   (d) 'haves' and 'have-nots' live together peacefully
6. According to the passage, people ultimately overturn a social order
   (a) which is based on coercion and oppression
   (b) which does not satisfy their basic needs
   (c) which is based upon conciliation and reapprochement
   (d) which is not congenital to the spiritual values of the people
7. According to the passage, the root cause of class conflict is
   (a) the paradise of material satisfaction
   (b) dominant inherent acquisitive instinct in man
   (c) exploitation of the 'have-nots' by the 'haves'
   (d) a social order where the unprivileged are not a part of the establishment
8. Which of the following statements is 'not true' in the context of the passage?
   (a) A new order can be established by radically changing the outlook of people towards it
   (b) Adoption of the ideal of trusteeship can minimise possessive instinct
   (c) Enforced egalitarianism can be the cause of its own destruction
   (d) Ideal of new order is to secure maximum material satisfaction
9. Which of the following conclusions can be deduced from the passage?
   (a) A social order based on truth and non-violence alone can help the achievement of political freedom
   (b) After establishing the social order of Gandhiji's pattern, the possibility of a conflict between different classes of society will hardly exist
   (c) It is difficult to change the mind and attitude of men towards property
   (d) In an egalitarian society, material satisfaction can be enjoyed only at the expense of others
10. According to the passage, what does 'adoption of the ideal of trusteeship' mean?
   (a) Equating peace and progress with material satisfaction
   (b) Adoption of the ideal by 'haves' for the benefit of 'have-nots'
   (c) Voluntary enlightened remuneration of the possessive instinct by the privileged class
   (d) Substitution of spiritual values by material ones by those who live in the paradise of material satisfaction

Passage 6

It is an old saying that knowledge is power. Education is an instrument, which imparts knowledge and therefore, indirectly controls power. Therefore, ever since the dawn of our civilisation, persons in power have always tried to supervise or control education. It has been handmaid of the ruling class. During the Christian Era, the ecclesiastics controlled the institution of education and diffused among the people the gospel of the Bible and religious teachings. These gospels and teachings were no other than a philosophy for the maintenance of the existing society. It taught the poor man to be meek and to earn his bread with the sweat of his brow, while the priests and the landlords lived in luxury and fought duels for the slightest offence. During the Renaissance, education passed more from the clutches of the priest into the hands of the prince. In other words, it became more secular. Under the control of the monarch, education began to devise and preach the infallibility of its masters, the monarch or king. It also invented and supported fantastic theories like 'The Divine Right Theory' and that the king can do no wrong etc. With the advent of the industrial revolution, education took a different turn and had to please the new masters. It now no longer remained the privilege of the baron class, but was thrown open to the new rich merchant class of the society. The philosophy, which was in vogue during this period was that of 'Laissez Faire' restricting the function of the state to a mere keeping of laws and order while on the other hand, in practice the law of the jungle prevailed in the form of free competition and the survival of the fittest. **[CLAT 2013]**

1. What does the theory 'Divine Right of King' stipulate?

(a) The kings are God
(b) That the right of governing is conferred upon the kings by God
(c) They have the right to be worshipped like Gods by their subjects
(d) That the right of kings are divine and therefore sacred

2. Who controlled education during the Renaissance?

(a) The common people
(b) The prince
(c) The church and the priests
(d) None of the above

3. What did the ruling class in the Christian Era think of the poor man?

(a) That he is the beloved of God
(b) That he deserves all sympathy of the rich
(c) That he should be strong and lord over others
(d) That he is meant for serving the rich

4. Who controlled the institution of education during the Christian Era?

(a) The secular leaders of society
(b) The church and the priests
(c) The monarchs
(d) The common people

5. What does the word 'fallibility' mean?

(a) That every man is open to error
(b) Sensitivity
(c) The virtue of not making mistake
(d) That some divine power is responsible for determining the fate of the man

6. What do you mean by the 'sweat of his brow'?

(a) Very hard work
(b) The tiny droplets of sweat on the forehead
(c) The wrinkles visible on the forehead
(d) The sign of innocence

7. What does the policy of 'Laissez Faire' stand for ?

(a) Individual freedom in the economic field
(b) State control over law and order in society
(c) Joint control of the means of production by the state and private enterprise
(d) Decontrol over law and order by the ruling class

8. Which of the following describes the writer?

(a) Concerned
(b) Unconcerned
(c) Aggressive
(d) Frustrated

9. Choose the correct synonym out of the four choices given.
Gospel

(a) Chit chat
(b) A teaching or doctrine of a religious teacher
(c) Rumour
(d) Guidance

10. Choose the correct synonym out of the four choices given.

Vogue

(a) Uncertain
(b) Out-dated
(c) The prevailing fashion or style
(d) Journey

Passage 7

The spread of education in society is at the foundation of success in countries that are latecomers to development. In the quest for development, primary education is absolutely essential because it creates the base. But higher education is just as important for it, provides the cutting edge. And universities are the life-blood of higher education. Islands of excellence in professional education, such as Indian Institutes of Technology (IITs) and Indian Institutes of Management (IIMs), are valuable complements but cannot be substitutes for universities which provide educational opportunities for people at large.

There can be no doubt that higher education has made a significant contribution to economic development, social progress and political democracy in independent India. It is a source of dynamism for the economy. It has created social opportunities for people. It has fostered the vibrant democracy in our polity. It has provided a beginning for the creation of a knowledge society. But it would be a mistake to focus on its strengths alone. It has weaknesses that are a cause for serious concern.

There is, in fact, a quiet crisis in higher education in India that runs deep. It is not yet discernible simply because there are pockets of excellence, an enormous reservoir of talented young people and an intense competition in the admissions process. And, in some important spheres, we continue to reap the benefits of what was sown in higher education 50 years ago by the founding fathers of the republic. The reality is that we have miles to go. The proportion of our population, in the age group 18-24, that enters the world of higher education is around 7%, which is only one-half the average for Asia. The opportunities for higher education, in terms of the number of places in universities, are simply not enough in relation to our needs. What is more, the quality of higher education in most of our universities requires substantial improvement.

It is clear that the system of higher education in India faces serious challenges. It needs a systematic overhaul, so that we can educate much larger numbers without diluting academic standards. This is imperative because the transformation of economy and society in the 21st century would depend, in significant part, on the spread and the quality of education among our people, particularly in the sphere of higher education. It is only an inclusive society that can provide the foundations for a knowledge society. The challenges that confront higher education in India are clear. It needs a massive expansion of opportunities for higher education, to 1500 universities nationwide, that would enable India to attain a gross enrolment ratio of atleast 15% by 2015. It is just as important to raise the average quality of higher education in every sphere. At the same time, it is essential to create institutions that are exemplars of excellence at par with the best in the world. In the pursuit of these objectives, providing people with access to higher education in a socially inclusive manner is imperative. The realisation of these objectives, combined with access, would not only develop the skills and capabilities we need for the economy but would also help transform India into a knowledge economy and society. **[CLAT 2014]**

1. The principle focus of the passage is
(a) primary education
(b) intermediate education
(c) higher education
(d) entire education system

2. The style of the passage can be best described as
(a) academic (b) critical and analytical
(c) comparative (d) None of these

3. What kind of society can provide the foundation for a knowledge society?
(a) Elite society
(b) Contracted society
(c) Exclusive society
(d) Inclusive society

4. According to the passage, which one of the following is incorrect?
(a) There are no quality institutes providing excellent professional education in India
(b) Not many people go for higher education in India
(c) Education is the basis of success
(d) All the above options are correct

5. According to the passage, the current state of affairs of higher education in India is
(a) satisfactory
(b) excellent and there is no need of any expansion of opportunities for higher education
(c) not good enough and there is a need of expansion of opportunities for highe education, besides creating institutions and universities that are models of excellence
(d) not explained in the passage

6. According to the passage, which of the following is not a challenge that confronts higher education in India?
(a) Expanding opportunities for higher education
(b) Creating institutions and universities that are exemplars of excellence
(c) Substantial improvement in the quality of higher education in most of our universities
(d) Getting into World University Rankings

7. According to the passage, which of the following is correct?
(a) Primary education is very important
(b) Universities are the life-blood of higher education
(c) Transformation of economy and society in the 21st century would depend, in significant part, on the spread and the quality of education among our people, particularly in the sphere of higher education
(d) All the above propositions are correct

8. Should the entire university system in India be modelled on premier institutes, such as, IITs and IIMs, providing professional education?
(a) Yes
(b) For sure
(c) No
(d) The passage is silent on this question

9. What is the antonym of the expression 'cutting edge'?
(a) conventional
(b) avant-garde
(c) advanced
(d) contemporary

10. What is the meaning of the word 'discernible'?
(a) unobtrusive (b) noticeable
(c) unremarkable (d) inconspicuous

Passage 8

Unreasonableness is a tendency to do socially permissible things at the wrong time. The unreasonable man is the sort of person, who comes to confide in you when you are busy. He serenades his beloved when she is ill. He asks a man, who has just lost money by paying a bill for a friend to pay a bill for him.

He invites a friends to go for a ride just after the friend has finished a long car trip.

He is eager to offer services which are not wanted, but which cannot be politely refused. If he is present at an arbitration, he stirs up dissension between the two parties, who were really anxious to agree. Such is the unreasonable man. **[CLAT 2015]**

1. The unreasonable man tends to
(a) bring a higher bidder to a salesman, who has just closed a deal
(b) disclose confidential information to others
(c) sing the praise of the bride when he goes to a wedding
(d) sleep late and rise early

2. The unreasonable man tends to
(a) entertain women
(b) be helpful when solicited
(c) tell a long story to people, who have heard it many times before
(d) be a successful arbitrator when dissenting parties are anxious to agree

Passage 9

1. Often, we passionately pursue matters that in the future appear to be contradictory to our real intention of nature, and triumph is followed by remorse or regret. There are numerous examples of such a trend in the annals of history and contemporary life.

2. Alfred Nobel was the son of Immanuel Nobel, an inventor who experimented extensively with explosives. Alfred too carried out research and experiments with a large range of chemicals; he found new methods to blast rocks for the construction of roads and bridges; he was engaged in the development of technology and different weapons; his life revolved around rockets and cannons and gun powder. The ingenuity of the scientist bought him enough

wealth to buy the Botors armament plant in Sweden.

3. Paradoxically, Nobel's life was a busy one yet he was lonely; and as he grew older, he began suffering from guilt of having invented the dynamite that was purposes. He set aside a huge part of his wealth to institute Nobel Prizes. Men and women for their extraordinary achievements in physics, chemistry, medicine literature, he wished to honour people who work for the promotion of peace.

4. It's strange that the very name whose name was closely connected with explosives and inventions that helped in waging wars willed a large part of his earnings for the people who work for the promotion of peace and the benefit of mankind. The Nobel Peace Prize is intended for a person who has accomplished the best work for fraternity among nations, for abolition or reduction of war and for promotion of peace.

5. Another example that comes to one's mind is that of Albert Einstein. In 1939, learning that the Nazis would win the race to build the world's first atomic bomb, Einstein urged President Franklin (d) Roosevelt to launch an American programme on nuclear research. The matter was considered and a project called the Manhattan Project was initiated. The project involved intense nuclear research, the construction of the world's first atomic bomb. All this while, Einstein had the impressions that the bomb would be used to protect the world from the Nazis. But in 1945, when Hiroshima was bombed to end World War II, Einstein was deeply grieved and he regretted his endorsement of the need for nuclear research.

6. He also stated that had he known that the Germans would be unsuccessful in making the atomic bomb, he would have probably never recommended making one. In 1947, Einstein began working for the cause of disarmament. But, Einstein's name still continues to be linked with the bomb. Man's fluctuating thoughts, changing opinions, varying opportunities keep the mind in a state of flux. Hence, the paradox of life, it's certain that nothing is certain in life. **[CLAT 2016]**

1. Alfred established the Nobel Prize to
(a) use his wealth for hard working people
(b) honour only those people who are intelligent
(c) remind people of his achievements
(d) ease his guilt and promote work for the betterment of mankind

2. In the fifth paragraph, the word 'endorsement' means
(a) expressing one's regret
(b) making a promise to do something
(c) expressing one's approval or support
(d) expressing one's opposition

3. The paradox, 'It's certain that nothing is certain in life', indicates the writer's
(a) analytic mind
(b) scientific mind
(c) persuasive nature
(d) hatred for scientists

4. Working with arms and ammunition helped Alfred to amass
(a) popularity (b) intelligence
(c) enemies (d) wealth

5. Immanuel's interest in dynamite influenced Alfred's inclination for working
(a) for the Nobel Peace Prize
(b) with contradiction
(c) with explosives
(d) for humanity

6. One of the paradoxes in Alfred's life was that he was
(a) intelligent yet lonely
(b) occupied yet lonely
(c) lonely yet rich
(d) hard working but a failure

7. Einstein had the impression that the Germans would
(a) bomb Hiroshima
(b) be successful in making the world's first atomic bomb
(c) be unsuccessful in making the atomic bomb
(d) work for humanity

8. The Manhattan Project was initiated
(a) to protect the Nazis
(b) in honour of Einstein
(c) to bomb Hiroshima
(d) to carry out nuclear research

9. The passage is
(a) a process essay
(b) an argumentative essay
(c) an expository essay
(d) a descriptive essay

10. In paragraph 4, the word 'accomplished' means
(a) worked hard
(b) completed successfully
(c) won awards
(d) made an effort to do something

Passage 10

The World Trade Organisation (WTO) was created in the early 1990s as a component of the Uruguay Round negotiation. However, it could have been negotiated as part of the Tokyo Round of the 1970s, since negotiation was an attempt at a 'constitutional reform' of the General Agreement of Tariffs and Trade (GATT). Or it could have been put off to the future, as the US Government wanted. What factors led to the creation of the WTO in the early 1990s?

One factor was the pattern of multilateral bargaining that developed late in the Uruguay Round. Like all complex international agreements, the WTO was a product of a series of trade-offs between principal actors and groups. For the United States, which did not want a new organisation, the disputed settlement part of the WTO package achieved its longstanding goal of a more effective and more legal dispute settlement system. For the Europeans, who by the 1990s had come to view GATT dispute settlement less in political terms add more as a regime of legal obligations, the WTO package was acceptable as a means to discipline the resort to unilateral measures by the United States. Countries like Canada and other middle and smaller trading partners were attracted by the expansion of a rule-based system and by the symbolic value of a trade organisation, both of which inherently support the weak against the strong. The developing countries were attracted due to the provisions banning unilateral measures. Finally, and perhaps most important, many countries at the Uruguay Round came to put a higher priority on the export gains than on the import losses that the negotiation would produce, and they came to associated the WTO and a rule-based system with those gains. This reasoning—replicated in many countries—was contained in US Ambassador Kantor's defence of the WTO, and it announced to a recognition that international trade and its benefits cannot be enjoyed unless trading nations accept the discipline of a negotiated rule-based environment.

A second factor in the creation of the WTO was pressure from lawyers and the legal process. The dispute settlement system of the WTO was seen as a victory of legalists but the matter went deeper than that. The GATT, and the WTO, are contract organisations based on rules and it is inevitable that an organisation creating a further rule will in turn be influenced by legal process. Robert Hudee has written of the 'momentum of legal development', but what is this precisely? Legal development can be defined as promotion of the technical legal values of consistency, clarity (or certainty) and effectiveness; these are values that those responsible for administering any legal system will seek to maximise. As it played out in the WTO, consistency meant integrating under one roof the whole lot of separate agreements signed under GATT auspices; clarity meant removing ambiguities about the powers of contracting parties to make certain decisions or to undertake waivers; and effectiveness meant eliminating exceptions arising out of grandfather-rights and resolving defects in dispute settlement procedures and institutional provisions. Concern for these values is inherent in any rule-based system of co-operation, since without these value rules would be meaningless in the first place, therefore, create their own incentive for fulfilment.

The moment of legal development has occurred in other institutions besides the GATT, most notably in the European Union (EU). Over the past two decades the European Court of Justice (ECJ) has consistently rendered decisions that have expanded incrementally the EU's internal market, in which the doctrine of 'mutual recognition' handed down in Cassis de Dijon case in 1979 was a key turning point. The court is now widely recognised as a major player in European integration, even though arguably such a strong role was not originally envisaged in the Treaty of Rome, which initiated the current European Union. One means the Court used to expand integration was the 'teleological method of interpretation', whereby the actions of member states were evaluated against 'the accomplishment of the most elementary goals set forth in the Preamble to the (Rome) treaty. The teleological method represents an effort to keep current policies consistent with stated goals and it is analogous to the effort in GATT to keep contracting party trade practices consistent with stated rules. In both cases, legal concerns and procedures are an independent force for further co-operation.

In the large part, the WTO was an exercise in consolidation. In the context of a trade negotiation that created a near-revolutionary expansion of international trade rules, the formation of the WTO was a deeply conservative act needed to ensure that the benefits of the new rules would not be lost. The WTO was all about institutional structure and dispute settlement: these are the concerns of conservatives and not revolutionaries, that is why lawyers and legalists took the lead on these issues. The WTO codified the GATT institutional practice that had developed by custom over three decades, and it incorporated a new dispute settlement system that was necessary to keep both old and new rules from becoming a sham. Both the international structure and the dispute settlement system were necessary to preserve and enhance the integrity of the multilateral trade regime that had been built incrementally from the 1940s to the 1990s.

[CLAT 2017]

1. In the statement "... it amounted to a recognition that international trade and its benefits cannot be enjoyed unless trading nations accept the discipline of a negotiated rule-based environment", it refers to
   (a) Ambassador Kantor's defence of the WTO
   (b) the export gains many countries came to associated with a rule-based system
   (c) the higher priority on export gains placed by many countries at the Uruguay Round
   (d) the provision of a rule-based system by the WTO

2. What would be the closest reason why WTO was not formed in 1970s?
   (a) The Tokyo Round negotiations was an attempt at constitutional reform
   (b) Lawyers did not work for the dispute settlement system
   (c) The US Government did not like it
   (d) Important players did not find it in their best interest to do so

3. The most likely reason for the acceptance of the WTO package by nations was that
   (a) its rule-based system leads to export gains
   (b) it has the means to prevent the US from taking unilateral measures
   (c) they recognised the need for a rule-based environment to protect the benefits of increased trade
   (d) it settles disputes more legally and more effectively

4. In the method of interpretation of the European Court of Justice
   (a) enunciation of the most elementary community goals needed to be emphasised
   (b) contracting party trade practices need to be consistent with stated rules
   (c) current policies need to be consistent with stated goals
   (d) actions against member states needed to be evaluated against the said community goals

5. According to the passage, WTO promoted the technical legal values partly through
   (a) ambiguities about the powers of contracting parties to make certain decisions
   (b) grandfather-rights exceptions and defects in dispute settlement procedures
   (c) rules that create their own incentive for fulfilment
   (d) integrating under one roof the agreements signed under GATT

Answers

Passage 1

1	*c*	2	*b*	3	*a*	4	*c*	5	*a*	6	*d*	7	*c*	8	*d*

Passage 2

1	*a*	2	*b*	3	*a*	4	*b*	5	*a*	6	*c*	7	*a*	8	*a*	9	*c*

Passage 3

1	*d*	2	*a*	3	*b*	4	*c*	5	*a*	6	*a*	7	*a*	8	*d*

Passage 4

1	*d*	2	*c*	3	*c*	4	*d*	5	*a*	6	*d*	7	*c*	8	*c*

Passage 5

1	*d*	2	*d*	3	*c*	4	*b*	5	*c*	6	*a*	7	*b*	8	*d*	9	*b*	10	*b*

Passage 6

1	*d*	2	*b*	3	*d*	4	*b*	5	*c*	6	*a*	7	*d*	8	*a*	9	*b*	10	*c*

Passage 7

1	*c*	2	*b*	3	*d*	4	*c*	5	*c*	6	*a*	7	*d*	8	*a*	9	*c*	10	*b*

Passage 8

1	*a*	2	*d*

Passage 9

1	*d*	2	*c*	3	*a*	4	*d*	5	*c*	6	*b*	7	*b*	8	*d*	9	*c*	10	*b*

Passage 10

1	*a*	2	*b*	3	*a*	4	*a*	5	*d*

CHAPTER 03

SYNONYMS AND ANTONYMS

A language lies in its words. Therefore, a sound vocabulary is always desired. If candidates have a good vocabulary then language becomes easy to master questions based on synonyms and antonyms are asked in most of the entrance exams. A candidate should keep a good vocabulary to score good.
Synonyms are words that have the same or nearly the same meanings while antonyms are words that have opposite meanings.
In competitive exams, 2-4 questions based on this section are asked.
Students are required to study the words given in the list carefully.

A

Words	Synonyms	Antonyms
Allure (V)	entice, fascinate, tempt, seduce	repulse, repel, deter, distaste
Abortive (Adj)	vain, useless, fruitless, unproductive	effectual, productive, successful, progressive
Abominable (Adj)	odious, detestable, repugnant, aversion	likable, pleasant, affectionate, enjoyable
Assiduous (Adj)	constant, diligent, attentive, persevering	indifferent, careless, indolent, lethargic
Aversion (N)	dislike, hatred, indifference, apathy	affection, fondness, niceness, kindness
Audacity (Adj)	boldness, arrogance, insolence, haughtiness	mildness, humility, cowardice, submission
Abate (V)	moderate, mitigate, lessen, decrease	aggravate, intensify, augment, supplement
Apathy (N)	unconcern, indifference, insensitivity, aloofness	concern, care, anxiety, eagerness

Words	Synonyms	Antonyms
Affront (N/V)	provoke, exasperate, indignity, irreverence	conciliate, appease, mollify, assuage
Antique (N)	ancient, old-fashioned, primitive	modern, recent, novelty, vogue
Antipathy (N)	hostility, aversion, disillusion, dislike	admiration, approval, fascination, devotion

B

Word	Synonyms	Antonyms
Bustle (N/V)	haste, tumult, stir, flurry	slowness, sluggishness, quiet, inertness
Blemish (N/V)	fault, smirch, stigma, stain	purity, impeccable, spotless, stainless
Bleak (Adj)	dismal, gloomy, chilly, dreary	bright, pleasant, balmy, cheerful
Blame (V)	reprove, upbraid, reproach, censure	commend, applaud, laud, praise
Benevolence (N)	humanity, generosity, charity, liberality	malevolence, inhumanity, malignity, unkindness
Barbarous (Adj)	uncivilised, savage, untamed, brutal	cultured, humane, refined, gentle

C

Words	Synonyms	Antonyms
Covetous (N)	cupidity, avarice, greed, voracity	liberality, benevolence, selfless, magnanimous
Convenient (Adj)	handy, suited, comfortable, advantageous,	unsuitable, tedious, impractical, fatiguing
Contrary (N)	dissimilar, conflicting, contradictory, opposite	similar, alike, homogeneous, resembling
Contradict (V)	impugn, deny, oppose, confront	approve, confirm, sanction, endorse
Contempt (N)	scorn, disregard, disdain, despicable	regard, approval, praise, recommend
Consequence (N)	effect, outcome, repercussion, result	origin, incipient
Conscious (N)	aware, apprised,	unaware, ignorant, unfeeling
Compassion (N)	kindness, sympathy, clemency, commiseration	cruelty, barbarity, persecution, apathy
Cherish (V)	nurture, treasure, foster, encourage	abandon, forsake, renounce, discard
Chastise (V)	punish, admonish, scold, reprove	cheer, comfort, encourage, stimulate
Chaste (Adj)	virtuous, pure, honourable, immaculate	defiled, licentious, sullied, lustful
Catastrophe (N)	disaster, calamity, misfortune, mishap	prosperity, blessing, restoration, resurgence

D

Words	Synonyms	Antonyms
Despicable (Adj)	contemptible, worthless, shameless, base	worthy, decent, honourable, respectable
Disdain (V)	detest, despise, loathe, scorn	approve, praise, laud
Deride (V)	mock, taunt, ridicule, jeer	inspire, encourage, stimulate, comfort
Deplore (V)	lament, bemoan, complain, regret	rejoice, applaud
Denounce (V)	indict, condemn, derogate, reprimand	praise, commend, flatter, compliment
Delusion (N)	deception, hallucination, illusion, fallacy	certainty, veracity, reality, surety
Deliberate (V)	ponder, intentional, mediate, consider	rash, sudden, indifferent, discard

Words	Synonyms	Antonyms
Degradation (V)	disgrace, dishonour, humiliation, debase	exaltation, praise, triumphant, honour
Deficient (Adj)	scanty, inadequate, lacking, wanting	adequate, ample, sufficient, abundant
Default (N/V)	failure, omission, negligence, lapse	perfection, vigilance, attentive, observance

E

Words	Synonyms	Antonyms
Exalt (V)	extol, dignify, glorify, elevate	dishonour, disgrace, degrade, denounce
Evident (Adj)	obvious, apparent, distinct, conspicuous	obscure, concealed, hidden, unnoticeable
Esteem (N)	regards, reverence, admiration	ridicule, spurn, despise, humiliate
Equivocal (Adj)	uncertain, hazy, ambiguous, vague	obvious, lucid, clear
Epitome (N)	precise, miniature, exemplar, essence	increment, expansion, lengthen, enlargement
Enormous (Adj)	colossal, mammoth, immense, spacious	insignificant, diminutive, trivial, negligible
Enjoin (V)	direct, counsel, exhort, command	prohibit, forbid, revolt, dissuade
Endeavour (V)	undertake, aspire, venture, effort	cease, quit, shun, idle
Embrace (V)	cling, hug, adopt, caress	reject, neglect, shun, slight

F

Words	Synonyms	Antonyms
Frivolous (Adj)	petty, worthless, capricious, volatile	solemn, significant, pertinent, sensible
Forsake (V)	desert, renounce, relinquish, disown	maintain, retain, claim
Forerunner (N)	precursor, predecessor, ancestor, pioneer	descendant, follower, heir, successor
Fluctuate (V)	deflect, vacillate, vary, deviate	stable, resolute, inalterable
Flimsy (Adj)	trifling, transparent, brittle, unsubstantial	firm, tenacious, durable, retentive
Fleeting (Adj)	transient, temporary, ephemeral, transitory	enduring, eternal, perpetual, unceasing

G

Words	Synonyms	Antonyms
Grudge (N)	hatred, aversion, unwilling, objection	benevolence, affection, goodwill
Gracious (Adj)	courteous, beneficent, magnificient, dignified	rude, unforgiving, discourteous, uncourtly
Gigantic (Adj)	huge, enormous, immense, monstrous	diminutive, miniature, slight
Garrulous (Adj)	loquacious, talkative, communicative, informative	reserved, quiet, taciturn, reticent
Gallant (Adj)	heroic, intrepid, valorous, chivalrous	coward, timid, craven, base

H

Words	Synonyms	Antonyms
Hustle (N)	hurry, haste, bustle, activity	lull, quiet, idle, motionless
Hypocrisy (N)	deception, affectation, trickery, illusion	sincerity, integrity, righteousness, frankness

Words	Synonyms	Antonyms
Hideous (Adj)	frightful, shocking, abominable, monstrous	attractive, alluring, splendid, appealing
Harass (V)	irritable, molest, suppress, tyranny	assist, comfort, tolerant, console

I

Words	Synonyms	Antonyms
Invincible (Adj)	unconquerable, impregnable, unsubdued, unbeatable	effeminate, languid, crippled, fragile
Intimidate (N)	frighten, dictate, hopeless, irresolute	console, encourage, appease, hearten
Intricate (Adj)	tangled, complicated, formidable, arduous	regulated, orderly, manageable, ductile
Intrigue (N)	scheme, conspiracy, manipulation, counterplot	candour, sincerity, bluntness
Intrinsic (Adj)	genuine, fundamental, inherent, congenital	extraneous, incidental, extrinsic, derived
Instil (V)	inculcate, inject, infuse, implant	eradicate, extract, eliminate, expel
Insipid (Adj)	tasteless, vapid, savourless, unflavoured	delicious, luscious, pungent, piquant
Inquisitive (Adj)	inquiring, curious, searching, studious	distracted, negligent, indifferent, impassive
Innocuous (Adj)	salutary, wholesome, innocent, harmless	deleterious, baneful, insanitary, injurious

J

Words	Synonyms	Antonyms
Juvenile (Adj)	young, tender, youthful, adolescent	dotage, antiquated, senile, grown up
Judicious (Adj)	thoughtful, prudent, discerning, discriminating	irrational, misconception, fatuous
Jubilant (Adj)	rejoicing, triumphant, gay, cheerful	melancholy, depressing, gloomy, despondent
Jovial (Adj)	frolicsome, cheerful, merry, exultant	solemn, morose, malcontent

K

Words	Synonyms	Antonyms
Knave (Adj)	dishonest, scoundrel, vagabond, rogue	paragon, benefactor, idealist
Knotty (Adj)	complicated, difficult, arduous, onerous	manageable, tractable, flexible

L

Words	Synonyms	Antonyms
Luscious (Adj)	palatable, delicious, delectable, delightful	unsavoury, tart, sharp, sour
Lure (V)	attract, entice, tempt, induce	repel, dissuade, confute, threaten
Lunacy (N)	delusion, insanity, madness, imbecility	normalcy, sanity, sagacity, shrewdness
Linger (V)	loiter, prolong, hesitate, delay	hasten, quicken, dart, hurry
Liberate (V)	emancipate, rescue, unshackle, absolve	suppress, menacle, obstruct, detain
Liable (N)	accountable, bound, responsible, likely	unaccountable, apt to, irresponsible, exempt
Lenient (Adj)	compassionate, merciful, moderate, tolerant	cruel, severe, violent, vehement

Words	Synonyms	Antonyms
Lavish (Adj)	abundant, excessive, profuse, extravagant	scarce, deficient, frugal, conserve
Laudable (Adj)	deserving, honourable, approvable, acceptable	vicious, blame-worthy, venomous, condemnable
Lament (V)	grieve, deplore, regret, bemoan	amuse, entertain, enliven, solace

M

Words	Synonyms	Antonyms
Multitude (N)	throng, mass, swarm, profusion	minority, handful, paucity, scarcity
Morose (Adj)	surly, sulky, sullen, depressed	buoyant, blithe, sprightly, animated
Molest (V)	pester, harass, vex, misbehave	console, soothe, cheer, protect
Miraculous (Adj)	marvellous, extraordinary, astounding, amazing	ordinary, trivial, familiar, plausible
Mettle (N)	courage, determination, stamina, spirit	timidity, fear, cowardice, diffident
Melodious (Adj)	dulcet, musical, harmonious, sweet	grating, dissonant, discordant, rancour

N

Words	Synonyms	Antonyms
Nullify (V)	annul, obliterate, invalidate, neutralise	uphold, empower, endorse
Nourish (V)	sustain, nurture, tend, foster	exhaust, starve, weaken, enervate
Negligent (Adj)	inattentive, heedless, perfunctory	vigilant, considerate, attentive, caring
Nasty (Adj)	offensive, defiled, malevolent, malignant	pleasing, gratifying, benevolent, attractive

O

Words	Synonyms	Antonyms
Oversight (N)	omission, error, fault, slip	precision, observance, circumspection, caution
Overbearing (Adj)	oppressive, domineering, intimidating, despotic	submissive, humble, lenient, forbearing
Outrage (N/V)	offence, maltreatment, assault, irreverent	praise, favour, esteem, reverence
Outbreak (V)	eruption, insurrection, explosion, outburst	compliance, subjection, passivity, harmony
Ominous (Adj)	threatening, inauspicious, forebode, menacing	consoling, auspicious, propitious, comforting
Occult (Adj)	latent, ambiguous, esoteric, elusive	intelligible, transparent, fathomable, scrutable

P

Words	Synonyms	Antonyms
Pungent (Adj)	acute, penetrating, sharp, pervasive	mild, soothing, pleasant, palatable
Prudent (Adj)	cautious, discreet, judicious, circumspect	impetuous, unwise, reckless, rash

Words	Synonyms	Antonyms
Propitiate (V)	appease, soothe, pacify, placate	aggravate, annoy, scorn, displease
Profuse (Adj)	lavish, abundant, generous, plentiful	scarce, scanty, meagre, paucity
Presumptuous (Adj)	presuming, arrogant, affected, insolent	unassuming, modest, bashful, unobtrusive

Q

Words	Synonyms	Antonyms
Quell (V)	subdue, reduce, suppress, extinguish	exacerbate, agitate, foment, instigate
Quack (N)	impostor, deceiver, dissembler, knave	upright, unfeigned, trained, genuine
Quash (V)	abrogate, annul, revoke, repudiate	uphold, empower, authorise, encourage

R

Words	Synonyms	Antonyms
Rustic (Adj)	pastoral, bucolic, uncivilised, unsophisticated	cultured, refined, urban, urbane
Reverence (N)	esteem, regards, veneration, acclaim	disrespect, dishonour, affront, offence
Resentment (N)	displeasure, wrath, ire, bitterness	content, pleasure, agreement
Repulsive (Adj)	repellent, forbidding, hideous, detestable	agreeable, enticing, attractive, alluring
Repugnant (Adj)	hostile, offensive, disagreeable, distasteful	agreeable, pleasant, friendly, tasteful
Relinquish (V)	forsake, abandon, surrender, abdicate	persist, continue, occupy, hold
Redress (N/V)	relief, restoration, remedy, repair, recover, liberate,	retribution, forfeiture, degenerate, barter

S

Words	Synonyms	Antonyms
Subvert (V)	overthrow, suppress, demolish, sabotage	accomplish, sustain, generate organise
Substantial (Adj)	durable, lasting, concrete, tangible	tenuous, abstract, fragile, immaterial
Subsequent (Adj)	consequent, following, later, ensuing	preceding, prior, former, earlier
Stern (Adj)	harsh, severe, austere, rigorous	lenient, considerate, benevolent, generous
Sporadic (Adj)	intermittent, scattered, isolated, infrequent	incessant, frequent, constant, continuous
Solicit (V)	entreat, implore, approach, accost	protest, oppose, prohibit, disapprove

T

Words	Synonyms	Antonyms
Tumultuous (Adj)	uproarious, violent, disorderly, riotous	peaceful, passive, orderly, harmonious
Treacherous (Adj)	faithless, deceitful, disloyal, unreliable	faithful, reliable, dependable, trustworthy
Transient (Adj)	temporal, transitory, fleeting, passing	lasting, enduring, perpetual, immortal
Tranquil (Adj)	peaceful, composed, placid	violent, furious, restless, distracting
Throng (N)	assembly, gathering, congregation	dispersion, scattering, handful, sparsity

U

Words	Synonyms	Antonyms
Utterly (AdV)	completely, entirely, extremely, wholly	deficient, incomplete, insufficient, partial
Usurp (V)	seize, wrest, encroach, coup	restore, compensate, grant, reinstate
Unseemly (Adj)	undesirable, inappropriate, uncouth, awkward	becoming, acceptable, decorous, admirable
Uncouth (Adj)	awkward, ungraceful, inelegant, vulgar	elegant, graceful, distinguished, shapely

V

Words	Synonyms	Antonyms
Volatile (Adj)	light, changing, transient, temporal	heavy, ponderous, perpetual, stable
Vigilant (Adj)	cautious, alert, wary, circumspect	careless, negligent, inattentive, casual
Vicious (Adj)	corrupt, obnoxious, degraded, demoralised	noble, virtuous, innocent, undefiled
Venerable (Adj)	esteemed, honoured, respectable, worthy	unwortahy, immature, degrade, degenerate

W

Words	Synonyms	Antonyms
Waive (V)	relinquish, remove, abjure, renounce	impose, clamp, grasp, retain
Wary (Adj)	cautious, circumspect, prudent, chary	heedless, negligent, impulsive, reckless
Withhold (V)	reserve, restrain, hamper, retard	emancipate, liberate, dispense, release

Y

Words	Synonyms	Antonyms
Yoke (N/V)	connect, harness, hitch, shackle	liberate, release, detach, disconnect
Yell (V)	shout, shriek, exclaim, gesticulate	suppress, whisper, muffled, muted
Yearn (V)	languish, crave, require, pine	content, unwanted, satisfied, gratified

Z

Words	Synonyms	Antonyms
Zigzag (Adj)	oblique, crooked, winding, wayward	straight, even, direct, unbent
Zest (N)	delight, enthusiasm, vigorous, energetic	disgust, passive, detriment, languid
Zenith (N)	summit, apex, maximum, pinnacle	nadir, floor, bottom, unimportance

Practice Exercise

Exercise 1

Directions (Q. Nos. 1-35) *In each of the following sentences, a word or phrase is written in italicised letter. For each italicised part, four words/phrases are listed below each sentence. Choose the word nearest in meaning to the italicised part.*

1. A million cinemas a year bring the same *stale bladerdash.*
(a) adventure (b) nonsense
(c) thriller (d) romance

2. There must be lively discussion of Indian authors if we are to *foster* our knowledge.
(a) promote (b) cherish (c) nourish (d) nurture

3. Buoyed by these visions of the future of his son, the artist *soldiered on.*
(a) continued bravely (b) stopped further
(c) struggled hard (d) fought on

4. Last fortnight, the rains came to the parched soils of India after the merciless drought had already *sapped* the vitality and livelihood of millions of peasants.
(a) decreased (b) demolished
(c) destroyed (d) drained away

5. The boy gave a *vivid description* of all that happened.
(a) brilliant (b) fresh
(c) explanatory (d) picturesque

6. It is *compulsory* for all the students to join this tour.
(a) regular (b) necessary
(c) dutiful (d) obligatory

7. Some of the discoveries of modern science are simply *marvellous.*
(a) praiseworthy (b) commendable
(c) amazing (d) admirable

8. The teacher felt that the student *lacked discrimination* in the study of his data.
(a) imagination (b) good taste
(c) objectivity (d) good judgement

9. We don't know how we are to *recompense* you for the trouble you have taken.
(a) reward (b) help (c) praise (d) thank

10. John Milton wrote 'Paradise Lost' to *vindicate* the ways of God to man.
(a) explain (b) support
(c) justify (d) criticise

11. When youngsters do not have good role-models to *emulate,* they start searching for them among sportsmen or filmstars.
(a) inhabit (b) imitate
(c) mollify (d) modify

12. The eyewitness testimony was *incontrovertible.*
(a) debatable (b) unquestionable
(c) unacceptable (d) disputable

13. The invasion forces had no artillery and were completely *annihilated.*
(a) reduced (b) destroyed
(c) dismembered (d) split

14. The novel was so interesting that I was *oblivious* of my surroundings.
(a) indifferent (b) watchful
(c) unmindful (d) precarious

15. Elsie is seventy years old and a *fanatical* gardener.
(a) crazy
(b) fantastic
(c) excessively enthusiastic
(d) obsessed

16. The courage shown by the soldiers at this moment of crisis is *exemplary.*
(a) admirable (b) clear
(c) elementary (d) suitable

17. Grandfather has been getting *feeble* of late.
(a) tall (b) weak
(c) diseased (d) small

18. Even though Akshay does not study hard, he always *comes* first in his class.
(a) scores (b) stands
(c) arrives (d) completes

19. The arguments of the lawyer of the accused were so *persuasive* that the judge acquitted him.
(a) convincing (b) clever
(c) eloquent (d) logical

20. Your master will like you if you are *diligent*.
(a) conscientious (b) obedient
(c) meticulous (d) hard working

21. We should always try to maintain and promote communal *amity*.
(a) understanding (b) bondage
(c) friendship (d) contention

22. Before I could *make out* anything, he had spoken again.
(a) find out (b) comprehend
(c) explain (d) reveal

23. It is amazing how such a *motley* group could get along so well.
(a) heterogenous (b) assorted
(c) promiscuous (d) confused

24. His speech was nothing but *a string of platitudes*.
(a) grand statements
(b) stereo-typed statements
(c) noble sentiments
(d) humorous anecdotes

25. He wrote a *scathing* review of the prize-winning novel.
(a) biased (b) scornful
(c) unbalanced (d) subjective

26. India has made *spectacular* progress in Science and technology.
(a) remarkable (b) great
(c) formidable (d) super

27. The opposition criticised the ruling party for the *deteriorating* law and order situation in the state.
(a) disrupting (b) worsening
(c) crumbling (d) eroding

28. The flat has been *refurbished* recently.
(a) white-washed (b) painted
(c) renovated (d) repaired

29. Even the most careful researcher cannot predict the possible future *ramifications* of his findings.
(a) uses (b) developments
(c) consequences (d) conclusions

30. He ended his speech on a *supercilious* note which was quite unexpected of a person of balanced and stable temperament.
(a) defamatory (b) contemptuous
(c) superfluous (d) irrelevant

31. Graduation day is a *momentous* day for most students.
(a) memorable (b) melancholy
(c) important (d) hectic

32. The two opposing parties have *reached a stalemate*.
(a) dilemma (b) deadlock
(c) exhaustion (d) settlement

33. The Prime Minister delivered an *impromptu* speech to the students.
(a) important (b) impressive
(c) inspiring (d) offhand

34. This is a *lucrative* business.
(a) profitable (b) dangerous
(c) challenging (d) questionable

35. *Forthrightness* in speech may not always be a desirable quality.
(a) outspokenness (b) obliqueness
(c) mendacity (d) equivocation

Directions (Q. Nos. 36-50) *In each of the following questions, out of the given alternatives, choose the one which best expresses the meaning of the given word.*

36. Garnish
(a) Dirty (b) Paint (c) Decorate (d) Abuse

37. Inebriated
(a) Inexperienced (b) Tired
(c) Befuddled (d) Intoxicated

38. Imposture
(a) Claim (b) Status
(c) Destruction (d) Deception

39. Parley
(a) Discuss (b) Deliver
(c) Sweeten (d) Race

40. Aphorism
(a) Prune (b) Wither (c) Aphis (d) Proverb

41. Passe
(a) Rude (b) Old-fashioned
(c) Modern (d) Chic

42. Vituperation
(a) Moisture (b) Parallel
(c) Malediction (d) Recover

43. Qualm
(a) Concavity (b) Amplitude
(c) Misgiving (d) Repute

44. Exaggerate
(a) Earthly (b) Understate
(c) Overstate (d) Luxurious

45. Languish
(a) To become strong (b) To gain vitality
(c) To elevate (d) To become dispirited

46. Rapport
(a) Ambiguity (b) Clarity
(c) Harmonious relation (d) Cooperation

47. Rebate
(a) Gift (b) Interest
(c) Commission (d) Discount

48. Unabated
(a) Unsympathetic (b) Unaltered
(c) Unparalleled (d) Uncompromising

49. Reinforced
(a) Strengthened (b) Reconstructed
(c) Replaced (d) Restructured

50. Colossal
(a) Evil (b) Colourful (c) Gigantic (d) Atheletic

Exercise 2

Directions (Q. Nos. 1-36) *The following sentences consist of a word or a phrase which is written in italicised letters. Each of them is followed by four words or phrases. Select the word or the phrase which is closest to the opposite in meaning of the italicised word or phrase.*

1. Self reliance has been *adopted* as an important objective of economic planning in modern India.
(a) refused (b) forsaken
(c) denied (d) discarded

2. His *appointment* was confirmed last month.
(a) disappointment (b) suspension
(c) dismissal (d) discharge

3. He has a passion for *indigenous* goods.
(a) native (b) foreign (c) silly (d) cheap

4. He made an *exhaustive* list of the items his secretary should attend to
(a) short (b) incomplete
(c) interesting (d) meticulous

5. I like his *friendly* attitude.
(a) jealous (b) envious
(c) hostile (d) vicious

6. He appears to be a *phony* person.
(a) beautiful (b) unread
(c) genuine (d) ugly

7. He was in a *dejected* mood.
(a) jubilant (b) rejected
(c) irritable (d) romantic

8. Philosophers say that the world is an *illusion*.
(a) a fact (b) a reality
(c) an actuality (d) a truth

9. There was a marked *deterioration* in his condition.
(a) improvement (b) revision
(c) reformation (d) amendment

10. This offer has come as a great *boon* to me.
(a) curse (b) blemish
(c) trouble (d) misfortune

11. I liked the poem for its *literal* meaning.
(a) deep (b) complex
(c) fictitious (d) figurative

12. His book has a short but useful *introduction*.
(a) end (b) conclusion
(c) termination (d) deduction

13. The Principal hardly managed to give the papers a *cursory* glance.
(a) curious (b) thorough
(c) through (d) superficial

14. The attack on the freedom of the press is a *retrograde* step.
(a) progressive (b) stubborn
(c) punitive (d) aggressive

15. We received a *cordial* welcome from our host.
(a) indifferent (b) distrustful
(c) cold (d) official

16. We should not *belittle* the value of small things.
(a) extol (b) praise (c) inflate (d) expand

17. It used to be said that travel *broadens* ones outlook.
(a) narrows (b) shrinks
(c) contracts (d) restricts

18. The criminal was *detained* by the police.
(a) deterred (b) released
(c) dismissed (d) protected

19. It is *obligatory* for a common citizen to follow the rules.
(a) advisable (b) unnecessary
(c) superfluous (d) optional

20. The government empowered itself to *attach* the assets of all the scam suspects.
(a) release (b) return (c) donate (d) detach

21. His *urbane* attitude won him many friends.
(a) indifferent (b) violent
(c) rustic (d) rude

22. The leader might have had some *covert* reason for the change of his political affiliations.
(a) unjustifiable (b) obvious
(c) inexplicable (d) flimsy

23. Lucy is a *smart* girl.
(a) lazy (b) active (c) indecent (d) casual

24. The room was filled with a *delicious* odour.
(a) bitter (b) repulsive
(c) strange (d) unpalatable

25. That man is known for his *elegance*.
(a) awkwardness (b) indelicacy
(c) clumsiness (d) savagery

26. Unsettled conditions in the land led to the *exodus* of hundreds of its citizens.
(a) invasion (b) intrusion
(c) arrival (d) expulsion

27. In the interest of one's own reputation, one should avoid *ostentation* while entertaining friends.
(a) miserliness (b) simplicity
(c) purity (d) innocence

28. Every thing about him especially his talkative nature proclaims his *effeminacy*.
(a) aggressiveness (b) attractiveness
(c) manliness (d) boorishness

29. The leader was *pragmatic* in his approach to the problems facing the country.
(a) indefinite (b) vague
(c) idealistic (d) optimistic

30. She used to *disparage* her neighbours every now and then.
(a) please (b) praise
(c) belittle (d) denigrate

31. The plantation workers were on a *collision* course before the labour officer intervened.
(a) retaliatory (b) perfunctory
(c) conciliatory (d) circuitous

32. Every self-respecting circus needs at least one *dwarf*.
(a) pigmy (b) undersized
(c) giant (d) human

33. Of all the companions of our joyous *ascent*, there were only the two of us left.
(a) descant (b) descendant
(c) descent (d) decent

34. Our knowledge of the past is still largely a matter of *conjecture*.
(a) certainty (b) guess (c) position (d) form

35. In all places and at all times, there is a *profusion* of talents.
(a) plenty (b) scarcity
(c) aversion (d) generosity

36. It was *altercation* throughout and there was no discussion.
(a) consonance (b) alternative
(c) inconsistency (d) resonance

Directions (Q. Nos. 37-50) ***Choose the most appropriate word that is nearly opposite in meaning to the given word.***

37. Union
(a) Separation (b) Merger
(c) Combination (d) Mixture

38. Magnify
(a) Produce (b) Attract (c) Reduce (d) Enlarge

39. Protean
(a) Versatile (b) Amateur
(c) Dull (d) Cautious

40. Predilection
(a) Antipathy (b) Ignorance
(c) Dissonance (d) Disharmony

41. Impalpable
(a) Visible (b) Audible
(c) Tangible (d) Fearless

42. Parochial
(a) Dogmatic (b) Dominant
(c) Cosmopolitan (d) Niggardly

43. Ambiguity
(a) Lucidity (b) Basal
(c) Dull (d) Necessity

44. Antidote
(a) Medicine (b) Poison
(c) Anodyne (d) Amity

45. Folly
(a) Right (b) Exact
(c) Action (d) Wisdom

46. Heighten
(a) Widen (b) Decrease
(c) Increase (d) Strengthen

47. Lavish
(a) Grand (b) Penny wise
(c) Frugal (d) Dull

48. Subvert
(a) Strengthen (b) Create
(c) Conquer (d) Escalate

49. Deliberately
(a) Unintentionally (b) Reluctantly
(c) Wrongly (d) Notoriously

50. Despise
(a) Detest (b) Hate (c) Relieve (d) Love

Previous Year's Questions

Directions (Q. Nos. 51-55) *Choose the correct synonym out of the four choices given.* **[CLAT 2012]**

51. Lethargy
(a) Serenity (b) Listlessness
(c) Impassivity (d) Laxity

52. Emaciated
(a) Tall (b) Languid
(c) Very thin (d) Wise

53. Latent
(a) Concealed (b) Apparent
(c) Lethargic (d) Prompt

54. Sporadic
(a) Epidemic (b) Whirling
(c) Occasional (d) Stagnant

55. Compendium
(a) Summary (b) Index
(c) Reference (d) Collection

Directions (Q. Nos. 56-60) *For the word, a contextual sentence is given. Pick the word from the alternatives given, that is most inappropriate in the given context.* **[CLAT 2015]**

56. SPECIOUS : A specious argument is not simply a fast one but one that has the ring of truth.
(a) Deceitful (b) Fallacious
(c) Credible (d) Deceptive

57. DISUSE : Some words fall into disuse as technology makes objects obsolete.
(a) Prevalent (b) Discarded
(c) Obliterated (d) Unfashionable

58. PARSIMONIOUS : The evidence was constructed parsimonious scraps of information.
(a) Prevalent (b) Penurious
(c) Thrifty (d) Altruistic

59. OBVIATE : The new mass transit system may obviate the need for the use of personal cars.
(a) Prevent (b) Forestall
(c) Preclude (d) Bolster

60. FACETIOUS : When I suggested that war is a method of controlling population, my father remarked that I was being facetious.
(a) Jovian (b) Jovial (c) Jocular (d) Joking

Answers

Exercise 1

1	*b*	2	*d*	3	*a*	4	*d*	5	*d*	6	*d*	7	*c*	8	*d*	9	*a*	10	*c*
11	*b*	12	*b*	13	*b*	14	*c*	15	*c*	16	*a*	17	*b*	18	*b*	19	*a*	20	*d*
21	*c*	22	*b*	23	*b*	24	*b*	25	*b*	26	*a*	27	*b*	28	*c*	29	*c*	30	*b*
31	*c*	32	*b*	33	*d*	34	*a*	35	*a*	36	*c*	37	*d*	38	*d*	39	*a*	40	*d*
41	*b*	42	*c*	43	*c*	44	*c*	45	*d*	46	*c*	47	*d*	48	*a*	49	*a*	50	*c*

Exercise 2

1	*d*	2	*c*	3	*b*	4	*b*	5	*c*	6	*c*	7	*a*	8	*b*	9	*a*	10	*a*
11	*d*	12	*b*	13	*b*	14	*a*	15	*a*	16	*b*	17	*a*	18	*b*	19	*d*	20	*a*
21	*d*	22	*b*	23	*a*	24	*d*	25	*a*	26	*c*	27	*b*	28	*c*	29	*c*	30	*b*
31	*c*	32	*c*	33	*c*	34	*a*	35	*b*	36	*a*	37	*a*	38	*c*	39	*c*	40	*a*
41	*c*	42	*c*	43	*a*	44	*b*	45	*d*	46	*b*	47	*c*	48	*b*	49	*a*	50	*d*
51	*c*	52	*c*	53	*a*	54	*c*	55	*d*	56	*c*	57	*a*	58	*d*	59	*d*	60	*a*

CHAPTER 04

IDIOMS AND PHRASES

Idioms and phrases are important from the scoring point of view. If a candidate has ample number of idioms and phrases to himself then he can score better in the exam. Moreover, a constant practice will enable the candidate to master this topic.

An idiom is a common word or phrase with a culturally understood meaning that differs from what its composite words denotions would suggest. e.g. 'kick the bucket' means 'to die' and also to actually kick a bucket. Here are some frequently used Phrasal verbs (phrases) with the following verbs—'break, carry, cast, catch, come, cut, do, fall, get, give, go, have, hold, keep, lay, make, play, put, set, stand, take, throw, turn.

IDIOMS

Break

- **To *break* cover** is used when you leave a place where you have been hiding or sheltering to save yourself from attack, usually in order to run to another place.
- **To *break* the heart** means to afflict grievously, to cause to suffer seriously from grief.
- **To *break* the ice** means to start conversations by getting over the feeling of restraint.

Carry

- **To *carry* one's point** means to achieve the desired goal, to overcome obstacles placed in the way to defeat the opposition in a public debate.
- **To *carry* away captive** means to take away into captivity, as prisoners of war.
- **To *carry* a thing too far** means to continue it beyond what is logical or safe.

Cast

- **To *cast* or throw light upon** means to illuminate or to describe in detail.
- **To *cast* into the shade** means to separate the earlier effect of something on someone.

Catch

- **To *catch* one's eye** means to attract one's notice by being seen or to come under one's notice.
- **To *catch* it** means to achieve the most continued goal.
- **To *catch* a Tartar** means to seize or encounter an adversary who proves too strong for him.

Come

- **To *come* to close quarters** means to tackle an enemy closely.
- **To *come* to grief** is said of a person who meets with disaster or a scheme that proves abortive.
- **To *come* to hand** is idiomatic for, to reach one.
- **To *come* to be** means generally, to become important.
- **To *come* to no good** means to come to a bad end.
- **To *come* to age** means to become adult.

Cut

- **To *cut* short** means to shorten or abridge what is likely to lengthen out.
- **To *cut* or sting, to the quick**. The quick is the sensitive flesh, that which is susceptible of keen feeling. The phrase means to cause acute pain.
- **To *cut* off in its prime** means to destroy a fair thing when in its prime.

Do

- **To *do* good** means to act in a manner that others are benefited.
- **To *do* well out of something** means to derive profit from the activity.

Fall

- **To *fall* foul of** means to come into collision with.
- **To *fall* out** means to quarrel.
- **To *fall* into abeyance** means to cease to be exerted or used.
- **To *fall* to work or set to work** means to begin to do work.
- **To *fall* a prey to** means to be the victim of.
- **To *fall* for something** means to yield to its charms.

Get

- **To *get* clear of** means to become free from difficulty or annoyance.
- **To *get* one's back up** means to become irritated.
- **To *get* rid of; to be deprived** of means quitting of a thing or to get free from a thing.
- **To *get* into a scrape** means to find oneself in an awkward position.

Give

- **To be *given* to understand** means to be led to believe.
- **To *give* or show a person cold shoulder** means to treat him coldly, to receive him in cold manner.
- **To *give* someone the slip** means to avoid someone who is looking for you.
- **To *give* a thing a wide berth** means to keep at a distance from it.
- **To *give* good measure** means to give rather more than full, correct measure.
- **To *give* chapter and verse for a thing** means to produce the proof of it.

Go

- **To *go* a long way** means to go far, to go to a great length.
- **To *go* to law** means to litigate, to seek redressal through a court of law.

- **To *go* hard with** means to press heavily upon.
- **To *go* on a fool's errand** means to go on an expedition which leads to a foolish end.

Have

- **To *have* clean hands** means to be perfectly innocent, to be a person of honesty and integrity.
- **To *have* to do a thing** means to be forced to do it.
- **To *have* a difference with a person** means to have mild quarrel (or difference of opinion) with him.

Hold

- **To *hold* one's tongue** means to be silent, not to speak.
- **To *hold* oneself ready or in readiness** means to be ready, to be in a state of preparedness.
- **To *hold* up one's head** means to be able to look at every man in the face.
- **To *hold* one's head high** means to bear oneself proudly.
- **To *hold* true** means to regard as true, to continue to be true.

Keep

- **To *keep* within bounds** means to keep within due limits.
- **To *keep* a thing dark** means to keep it hidden or concealed, not to disclose it or make it known to others.
- **To *keep* company with a person** means to associate with him as a companion.
- **To *keep* house** means to manage the business of a household.
- **To *keep* open house** means to be ready to entertain all guests.
- **To *keep* a sharp look-out** means to maintain a keen watch.
- **To *keep* pace with** means to keep abreast of the development, to advance or progress equally fast with.

Lay

- **To *lay* waste** means to make desolate.
- **To *lay* bare, *lay* open** means to disclose or reveal a secret thing.
- **To *lay* someone under an obligation** means to do a favour so that he feels indebted.
- **To *lay* oneself open to** means to expose oneself to.
- **To *lay* down the law** means to speak in tones of authority.

Make

- **To *make* a will** means to make a testamentary disposal of his property.
- **To *make* love to** means to make love with a woman.
- **He *makes* a good soldier** means he possesses qualities of a good soldier.
- **To *make* a point of** means doing a thing, to set it before you as a thing to be certainly done.
- **To *make* a clean breast of something** means to disclose fully and without reserve.
- **To *make* (both) ends meet** means to be able to supply the necessaries of life while keeping expenditure within income.

Play

- **To *play* a truant** means to stay away without permission.
- **To *play* into the hands of other** means to act as to be of advantage to another.
- **To *play* fast and loose with** means to disregard one's promises or engagements.
- **To *play* a double game or act as a double part** means to do one thing openly and a different thing in secrecy.

Put

- **To *put* to the sword** means to slay with the sword.
- **To *put* to shame** means to make someone ashamed or to disgrace.
- **To *put* a thing to the vote** means to take a vote upon a proposal.
- **To *put* (or get) things ship-shape** means to settle them in an appropriate order.
- **To *put* to sea** means to start on a voyage.
- **To *put* one's oar in** means to interfere in something.

Set

- **To *set* a scheme on foot** is to start it, to set it going.
- **To *set* store by** is to value highly.

Stand

- **To *stand* in another man's shoes** means to occupy another man's place.
- **To *stand* in good stead** means to be of great advantage to one in a time of difficulty.
- **To *stand* one's ground** means to maintain one's position.

Take

- **To *take* into account** means to regard, to consider.
- **To *take* to task, call to account** means to reprove and require explanation.
- **To *take* advantage of** means to use any benefit offered by; also, to get benefit by cunning means.
- **To *take* a thing in hand** means to undertake to do it, to attempt, to accomplish it.
- **To *take* a city by storm** means to capture it through a fierce and surprised attack.
- **To *take* people by storm** means to captivate them unexpectedly.
- **To *take* to one's heels** means to run away.

Throw

- **To *throw* cold water upon a project** means to discourage it, to disparage the project.
- **To *throw* dust in one's eyes** means to deceive one.
- **To *throw* off the mask** is said of one who, having acted a deceitful part for a time, suddenly declares his real intentions.
- **To *throw* up the sponge** means to give up a contest, to surrender.

Turn

- **To *turn* one's back upon** means to abandon, to reject or refuse unceremoniously, to change to a directly opposite course.
- **To *turn* a matter over in one's mind** means to consider it carefully and look at it from all sides.
- **To *turn* one's hand to** means to engage oneself in.
- **To *turn* tail** means to retreat ignominiously. It is said when a person behaves like a coward.

PHRASES

To read between the lines (to understand the hidden meaning)

If her essay is *read between the lines*, we will find that she has made comments against the government.

To see eye to eye (to agree)

Neema could never *see eye to eye* with her elder brother.

To have blue blood (aristocratic blood)

Though my friend *has blue blood* yet her conduct is very mean and vulgar.

The halcyon days (peaceful days)

The days we spend in our school are *the halcyon days* of our life.

The swan song (last creation)

'Lament' was *the swan song* of Shelley.

Uphill task (difficult task) The problem of holding exams on time is an *uphill task* for the VC of CCS University.

A wet blanket (any person that dampens enthusiasm)

The Principal proved to be ***a** wet blanket* while the students were on picnic

A wild goose chase (unprofitable)

All the efforts of the government to remove illiteracy in India is like ***a** wild goose chase.*

Bird's eye view (concise view)

We had a *bird's eye view* of the whole fair from top of the giant-wheel.

To live in a fool's paradise (false hope)

My brother is *living in a fool's* ***paradise***, if he thinks that he can be a rich man without working hard.

To have feet of clay (full of faults)

The CBI enquiry has revealed that many ministers *have feet of clay.*

Over and above (moreover, besides)

I shall lend you books *over and above* what I have promised to give you in cash.

Apple-pie order (in perfect order)

On the eve of inspection, everything was kept in *apple-pie order.*

A fair weather friend (selfish friend)

A ***fair weather friend*** will never stand by you in difficulty.

To take up arms (to fight)

The tribals of this region have *taken up arms* against the government.

To bite the dust (to be defeated)

Pakistan had *to bite the dust* in the finals of the World Cup.

Off colour (not in usual form)

Once a glamorous actress, she is *off colour* these days.

A dare devil (a fearless person)

Only *a dare devil* can challenge the city mafia and bring them to their knees.

A die-hard (persistent in struggle)

He is *a die-hard* person and will not easily surrender.

To be born with a silver spoon in one's mouth (to be born in a rich family)

My friend does not have to worry about spending any amount of money as she is *born with a silver spoon in her mouth.*

Snake in the grass (a secret enemy)

The country is always betrayed by the *snakes in the grass.*

By fits and starts (irregularly)

If we study *by fits and starts*, we can never be successful in our exams.

The ins and outs (secrets)

The servants are generally familiar with *the ins and outs* of the family.

Tooth and nail (violently)

All the students revolted *tooth and nail* for the partiality of the teachers towards some students.

Hard and fast (strict)

No *hard and fast* rule is laid down about being regular in the college.

To meet one's Waterloo (to face final defeat)

Tipu Sultan *met his Waterloo* in the fourth battle of Mysore.

To hang fire (remain unsolved)

Kashmir problem has been *hanging fire* for the last fifty years.

An eye-wash (a pretence) My friend's promise to help me proved just *an eye-wash.*

Out of question (not possible)

His success is *out of question* because he is not studying these days.

Herculean task (very difficult)

It is a *Herculean task* to root out corruption in India.

To throw cold water (to discourage)

Instead of encouraging me, my business partner *threw cold water* on my plans.

Practice Exercise

Exercise 1

Directions (Q. Nos. 1-37) *In the following questions, four alternatives are given for the idioms/phrases. Choose the one which best expresses the meaning of the given idioms/phrases.*

1. Take exception to
(a) different (b) to take with difficulty
(c) object to (d) difficult

2. Through thick and thin
(a) big and small (b) large object
(c) under all conditions (d) thin and fat

3. Sitting on the fence
(a) unbalanced
(b) uncomfortable
(c) coward
(d) between two opinions

4. An axe to grind
(a) difficult job (b) hard labour
(c) private ends to serve (d) punishment

5. His wit's end
(a) finished (b) confused
(c) comedy (d) very intelligent

6. To be born with a silver spoon in one's mouth
(a) to be born in a rich home
(b) to be born in a jeweller's home
(c) to be fed milk with a silver spoon
(d) to be a first born child

7. A hard nut to crack
(a) difficult things require extra effort
(b) a difficult problem to solve
(c) a difficult problem solved effortlessly
(d) costly things need careful handling

8. From hand to mouth
(a) something repeated often
(b) consuming food
(c) to survive without saving
(d) hitting someone by hand on the mouth

9. To beat about the bush
(a) not to come to the point
(b) vigorous search for the culprit
(c) easily achieved success without much effort
(d) working hard to achieve the goal

10. To burn one's fingers
(a) to get injured in an accident
(b) to pay a heavy price
(c) to suffer from meddling in something
(d) to get a burn injury on the hands

11. To make mince meat
(a) copy the appearance of somebody
(b) take care of something
(c) refute utterly
(d) have the same opinion

12. To carry all before one
(a) finish quickly
(b) make a promise
(c) be free from danger
(d) be completely successful

13. To run riot
(a) befool other
(b) be violent in action
(c) criticise other
(d) behave in an undisciplined way

14. To carry the conviction
(a) be extremely fond of anything
(b) bear the proof of the truth
(c) feel displeasure
(d) make overtures of reconciliation

15. To hold
(a) show unwillingness
(b) keep at a distance
(c) stop by threats of violence
(d) endure hardship or danger

16. To come round
(a) to get well (b) to reach a roundabout
(c) to succeed (d) to complete a circle

17. A white elephant
(a) an elephant with white skin
(b) a costly thing
(c) a costly and useful thing
(d) a costly but useless thing

18. Merry as a cricket
(a) to enjoy a game of cricket
(b) to be carefree
(c) to dance and sing
(d) to be good at sports

19. To show white feather
(a) to meet a strong adversary
(b) to run away
(c) to show cowardice
(d) to die an iganoble death

20. To set the Thames on fire
(a) to wreak evil on something
(b) to destroy with fire
(c) to do a heroic deed
(d) to try to do the impossible

21. To smell a rat
(a) to see hidden meaning
(b) to smell bad odour
(c) to misunderstand
(d) to suspect a trick or deceit

22. On the spur of the moment
(a) at once or without any kind of deliberation
(b) in accordance with the prevailing style
(c) open to blame
(d) on the side of something undesirable

23. To go hard with one
(a) to remain neutral
(b) to be busy over trifles
(c) to be unreliable
(d) to prove a serious matter

24. To keep house
(a) to keep pace with
(b) to be silent about one's own purpose
(c) to waste time
(d) to manage the business of the household

25. To talk over
(a) to consider (b) to discuss
(c) to understand (d) to think over

26. To rule the roost
(a) to domineer (b) to surrender
(c) to run away (d) to fight

27. To turn down
(a) give up (b) reject (c) follow (d) throw

28. The term 'sine die' means
(a) indefinitely
(b) inadequate
(c) signature by a person on death bed
(d) continuously

29. Modus Operandi
(a) way of doing something
(b) manner of theft
(c) way of doing theft
(d) way of worship

30. 'To play second fiddle' means
(a) to support the role and view of another person
(b) to act like a minor criminal
(c) to deceive your superior
(d) to play the second musical instrument

31. 'Hanging fire' means
(a) going to be sacrificed
(b) going on slowly
(c) being hotly debated
(d) going to be burnt soon

32. 'Go out on a limb' means
(a) being at two places at the same time
(b) put oneself in an isolated or disadvantageous position
(c) going somewhere without being noticed
(d) fracturing one's limb

33. Ab initio
(a) from the very beginning
(b) high initiative
(c) thing done later
(d) without initiative

34. Pell-mell
(a) in hurried disorder (b) gaiety and excitement
(c) extremely worried (d) None of these

35. To have one's heart in one's boots
(a) to get angry
(b) to be deeply depressed
(c) to be frightened
(d) to keep a secret

36. To give one's ears
(a) to listen carefully
(b) to act in a foolish way
(c) to make a guess
(d) to make almost any sacrifice

37. To fight tooth and nail
(a) making every possible effort to win
(b) to fight fiercely with great effort
(c) to fight heroically
(d) to fight a losing battle

Exercise 2

Directions (Q. Nos. 1-40) *In each of the following questions, some alternatives are given or suggested for the idiom/phrase in italics in the sentence. Choose the one which best expresses the meaning of the idiom/phrase in italics.*

1. The girls *hit it off right away.*
(a) got along very well (b) clobbered
(c) became agitated (d) cracked the plan

2. You *have a hustle* to get there on time.
(a) jostle (b) catch a bus
(c) get ready (d) get a move on

3. At Christmas, even the elderly fathers *paint the town red.*
(a) indulge in rioting (b) paint the houses red
(c) spill red wine (d) have a lively time

4. The members of the group were *at odds* over the selection procedure.
(a) acting foolishly (b) in dispute
(c) unanimous (d) behaving childishly

5. There is no *love lost* between the two neighbours.
(a) close friendship
(b) intense dislike
(c) a love-hate relationship
(d) cool indifference

6. I did not mind what he was saying, he was only *talking through his hat.*
(a) talking insultingly (b) talking irresponsibly
(c) talking ignorantly (d) talking nonsence

7. If you pass this difficult examination, it will *be a feather in your cap.*
(a) you will get a very good job
(b) additional achievement
(c) your parents will be very happy
(d) you will get a scholarship for higher studies

8. He is in the habit of *chewing the cuds.*
(a) accusing others (b) crying over spilt milk
(c) forgetting things (d) to muse on

9. If you *rub him the wrong way,* he is bound to react.
(a) annoy him (b) abuse him
(c) flatter him (d) encourage him

10. There was opposition to the new policy by the *rank and file* of the government.
(a) the majority
(b) the ordinary members
(c) the cabinet members
(d) the official machinery

11. Dowry is a *burning question* of the day.
(a) a dying issue
(b) a relevant problem
(c) an irrelevant problem
(d) a widely debated issue

12. His voice *gets on my nerves.*
(a) makes me sad (b) irritates me
(c) makes me ill (d) pierces my eardrums

13. The hero of Naipaul's novel 'A House for Mr. Biswas', like modern young men, wishes *to paddle his own canoe.*
(a) lead an independent life
(b) depend on others
(c) make the best of his life
(d) have his own means of livelihood

14. Our school is *within a stone's throw* of the railway station.
(a) within a certain radius
(b) at a short distance
(c) within a definite circumference
(d) very far off

15. Some people have a habit of *wearing their heart on their sleeve.*
(a) avoiding being friendly with others
(b) saying something which is not to be taken seriously
(c) exposing their innermost feelings to others
(d) wasting their time on unnecessary details

16. The sight of the accident *made my flesh creep.*
(a) worried me
(b) frightened me
(c) confused me
(d) drew my attention

17. Komal was *left high and dry* by her friends when she lost all her money.
(a) isolated (b) rejected
(c) wounded (d) depressed

18. I just *paid him a left handed compliment.*
(a) an honest (b) a well deserved
(c) an insincere (d) a flattering

19. The party stalwarts have advised the President *to take it lying down for a while.*
(a) to show no reaction (b) to take rest
(c) to be on the defensive (d) to be cautious

20. A movement for the world unity is *in the offing.*
(a) at the end (b) about to start
(c) on decline (d) in the air

21. He is *a queer fish,* I have failed to understand him.
(a) funny person (b) sensitive person
(c) strange person (d) quarrelsome person

22. No caring for the family, Devendra wanted to *gather roses* only.
(a) wanted to paint a rosy picture of past
(b) wanted to start business of roses
(c) wanted to make safe investment
(d) wanted to seek all the enjoyments of life

23. His most trusted friend proved to be *a snake in the grass.*
(a) cowardly and brutal
(b) an unreliable and deceitful person
(c) a hidden enemy
(d) low and mean

24. The new CM *stuck his neck out* today and promised 10 kg free wheat a month for all rural families.
(a) extended help
(b) took an oath
(c) caused embarrassment
(d) took a risk

25. The involvement of teachers in the scheme of education proves *to be a mare's nest.*
(a) a false invention (b) a noble thing
(c) a successful idea (d) a timely step

26. Pt Nehru was *born with a silver spoon in his mouth.*
(a) born in a royal family
(b) born in a middle class family
(c) born in a family of nationalists
(d) born in a wealthy family

27. He *burnt his fingers* by interfering in his neighbour's affairs.
(a) got rebuked
(b) got himself insulted
(c) burnt himself
(d) got himself into trouble

28. When the police came, the thieves *took to their heels.*
(a) were taken by surprise
(b) took to flight
(c) took shelter in a tall building
(d) unconditionally surrendered

29. He is a strange fellow. It is very difficult to deal with him; it seems that he has *a bee in his bonnet.*
(a) an achievement to be proud of
(b) an obsession about something
(c) to face problems as a result of his senseless actions
(d) peculiar habit of confusing others

30. The politician was able to sway the mob *with his gift of the gab.*
(a) fluency of speech
(b) flattering words
(c) abundance of promises
(d) political foresight

31. The speaker gave *a bird's eye view* of the political conditions in the country.
(a) a detailed presentation
(b) a biased view
(c) a general view
(d) a personal view

32. The detective *left no stone unturned* to trace the culprit.
(a) did very irrelevant things
(b) used all available means
(c) took no pains
(d) resorted to illegitimate practices

33. They sold their house because it was *a real white elephant.*
(a) an expensive one (b) a big one
(c) a useless one (d) a rare find

34. It will be wise on your part to let the *bygones be bygones.*
(a) resist the past (b) ignore the past
(c) recollect the past (d) revive the past

35. She was ***in a brown study*** and did not notice any entrance.
(a) reverie (b) sleep (c) fear (d) dream

36. Prohibition is *gall and wormwood* to distillers.
(a) opportunity (b) mayhem
(c) abominable (d) heaven

37. The co-operation and *esprit de corps* between the soldiers and the officers was directly responsible for their victory.
(a) bravery (b) loyalty
(c) subordination (d) unity

38. She exhibited remarkable *sang froid* during the crisis.
(a) temper (b) irritation
(c) composure (d) anger

39. Professor Giri said, "We will have to *cover a lot of ground* in this course". What did he men by "cover a lot of ground"?
(a) We have to skip a large of syllabus
(b) We have to complete a lot of material
(c) We have to start from basics
(d) We have to travel a lot

40. Ramesh said to me, *You have the floor*. What does this mean?
(a) You have practically won
(b) You have full right to disagree
(c) You have full permission to speak your mind now
(d) You have tenancy rights over the property's floor

Previous Year's Questions

Directions (Q. Nos. 41-45) *Select the correct meaning of the italicized idioms and phrases out of the four choices given.* **[CLAT 2012]**

41. He *burnt his fingers* by interfering in his neighbour's affair.
(a) got himself into trouble
(b) burnt himself
(c) got himself insulted
(d) got rebuked

42. Mr Gupta, who is one of the trustees of a big charity, is suspected of *feathering his own nest.*
(a) being lazy in doing his work
(b) being too generous
(c) neglecting his job
(d) making money unfairly

43. Mrs Hashmi has been *in the blues* for the last several weeks.
(a) abroad (b) unwell
(c) depressed (d) penniless

44. For the first week, the apprentice felt like a *fish out of water.*
(a) frustrated (b) homeless
(c) disappointed (d) uncomfortable

45. His friends failed to see why he should *ride the high horse* just because he had won an election.
(a) become abnormal (b) appear arrogant
(c) indulge in dreams (d) hate others

Directions (Q. Nos. 46-50) *Choose the explanation that catches the spirit of the idiom given in each question.* **[CLAT 2013]**

46. To blaze a trail
(a) to set on fire
(b) to blow the trumpet
(c) to initiate work in a movement
(d) to be hopeful

47. A snake in the grass
(a) a secret or hidden enemy
(b) an unreliable person
(c) unforeseen happening
(d) a dangerous enemy

48. Have too many irons in the fire
(a) engaged in too many enterprises at the same time
(b) facing too many problems at the same time
(c) said or done too many things at the same time
(d) to incite the feeling amongst the people

49. A fair weather friend
(a) a friend who is fair to us at all the times
(b) a friend who deserts us in difficulties
(c) a friend whom we love the most
(d) a friend who loves us the most

50. A panacea
(a) an injection that serves as a life line
(b) a lecture full of precepts
(c) a strong drug that induces sleep
(d) a single cure for all diseases or troubles

Directions (Q. Nos. 51-55) *Choose the explanation that best reflects the spirit of the idiom/proverb/ phrase given in each question.* **[CLAT 2014]**

51. To make clean breast of
(a) to tell the truth about something
(b) to gain prominence
(c) to destroy before it blooms
(d) to praise oneself

52. A man of straw
(a) a creditable man
(b) a very active man
(c) a man of no or little substance
(d) an unreasonable man

53. A wild-goose chase
(a) a wise search (b) a fruitful search
(c) a worthwhile hunt (d) a futile pursuit

54. Put on the market
(a) to offer for sale
(b) alongside the market
(c) already purchased
(d) None of the above

55. To meet someone halfway
(a) to show that you are prepared to strain your relationship with someone
(b) to compromise with someone
(c) confrontation
(d) incongruity

Directions (Q. Nos. 56-58) *Complete the proverb in the following questions.* **[CLAT 2016]**

56. 'To bury the hatchet' means
(a) to end a feud with an enemy
(b) to hide some treasure
(c) to plant grass in the field
(d) to cremate carcass of an animal

57. When .... is bliss, it is .... to be wise.
(a) romance; boring
(b) bachelorhood; single
(c) knowledge; better
(d) ignorance; folly

58. .... waters run ....
(a) Muddy; slow
(b) Still; deep
(c) Hot; fast
(d) Stagnant; leisurely

Answers

Exercise 1

1	*c*	2	*c*	3	*d*	4	*c*	5	*b*	6	*a*	7	*b*	8	*c*	9	*a*	10	*c*
11	*c*	12	*d*	13	*d*	14	*b*	15	*d*	16	*d*	17	*d*	18	*b*	19	*c*	20	*c*
21	*d*	22	*a*	23	*d*	24	*d*	25	*b*	26	*a*	27	*b*	28	*a*	29	*a*	30	*a*
31	*b*	32	*b*	33	*a*	34	*a*	35	*b*	36	*a*	37	*a*						

Exercise 2

1	*a*	2	*a*	3	*d*	4	*b*	5	*b*	6	*d*	7	*b*	8	*d*	9	*a*	10	*b*
11	*d*	12	*c*	13	*a*	14	*b*	15	*c*	16	*b*	17	*b*	18	*c*	19	*a*	20	*b*
21	*c*	22	*d*	23	*c*	24	*d*	25	*a*	26	*d*	27	*d*	28	*b*	29	*b*	30	*a*
31	*a*	32	*b*	33	*c*	34	*b*	35	*a*	36	*c*	37	*d*	38	*c*	39	*b*	40	*c*
41	*a*	42	*d*	43	*c*	44	*d*	45	*b*	46	*d*	47	*a*	48	*c*	49	*b*	50	*d*
51	*a*	52	*c*	53	*d*	54	*a*	55	*b*	56	*a*	57	*d*	58	*b*				

CHAPTER

05

SENTENCE IMPROVEMENT

Sentence improvement type questions test the grammatical acumen of the candidates as in common errors. Learn all the fundamentals of the grammar and syntax so that these types of questions can be dealt with well. This type has a usual frequency of about four questions in the exams.

In sentence improvement questions, a sentence is given with a word or phrase in bold letters or underlined. Four substitutes are given as alternatives the candidate has to find the error in the past that is in the bold or underlined then find the correct answer from among the alternatives. Sound knowledge of grammatical rules and constant practice can make you able to solve such questions.

e.g.

(i) I and you are using the same computer in the office. (*Incorrect*)

You and I are using the same computer in the office. (*Correct*)

(ii) none of the two brothers has broken the glass. (*Incorrect*)

Neither of the two brothers has broken the glass. (*Correct*)

Practice Exercise

Directions (Q. Nos. 1-90) *In the questions given below, a part of the sentence is underlined. Below are given alternatives to the underlined part which may improve the sentence. Choose the correct alternative. In case, no improvement is needed, option (d) is the answer.*

1. When the examinations were over Anil and me went to our native town.
(a) me and Anil (b) Anil and I
(c) I and Anil (d) No improvement

2. Will you kindly open the knot?
(a) untie (b) break
(c) loose (d) No improvement

3. Realising is the significance of technical education for developing country, the government laid aside a large sum on it during the last plan-period.
(a) laid up (b) set aside
(c) laid out (d) No improvement

4. Other countries have eradicated this disease ten years ago.
(a) eradicateda (b) had eradicated
(c) did eradicated (d) No improvement

5. We were not the wiser for all this effort to explain the case to us.
(a) none (b) neither
(c) nevertheless (d) No improvement

6. The logic of Berlin wall already had been undetermined but when the news came through that the wall itself had been opened, I jumped into a car.
(a) had been undetermined already
(b) had already been undetermined
(c) had been already undetermined
(d) No improvement

7. Taxpayers are to be conscious of their privileges.
(a) have to (b) need
(c) ought to (d) No improvement

8. I would have waited for you at the station if I knew that you would come.
(a) had known (b) was knowing
(c) have known (d) No improvement

9. If I stood alone in defence of truth and the whole world is banded against me and against truth. I would fight them all.
(a) was be banded (b) was banded
(c) banded (d) No improvement

10. During his long discourse, he did not touch that point.
(a) touch upon (b) touch on
(c) touch of (d) No improvement

11. He has not and can never be in the good books of his employer because he lacks honesty.
(a) has not and cannot be
(b) has not and can never been
(c) has not been and can never be
(d) No improvement

12. This matter admits of no excuse.
(a) admits to (b) admits from
(c) admits (d) No improvement

13. You have come here with a view to insult me.
(a) to insulting me (b) of insulting me
(c) for insulting me (d) No improvement

14. For all powers of reason and understanding, we know a little of life's secrets.
(a) a little of love secrets
(b) little about life's secrets
(c) nothing about life's secrets
(d) No improvement

15. My sister-in-law has a house for letting.
(a) for letting out (b) to rent out
(c) to let (d) No improvement

16. More than one person was killed in accident.
(a) were killed (b) are killed
(c) have been killed (d) No improvement

17. If he had time he will call you.
(a) would have (b) would have had
(c) has (d) No improvement

18. His powerful desire brought about his downfall.
(a) His intense desire (b) His desire for power
(c) His fatal desire (d) No improvement

19. All, but her had made an attempt.
(a) All, but she (b) An, but herself
(c) All, but her (d) No improvement

20. Hope you vividly remember the premier of the film when, my wife and you were present in the hall.
(a) my wife, I and you (b) you, I and my wife
(c) my wife, you and I (d) No improvement

21. With a thundering roar, the huge rocket soared up from the launching pad.
(a) flew up (b) went upwards
(c) took off (d) No improvement

22. My opinion for the film is that it will bag the national award.
(a) opinion to (b) opinion about
(c) opinion on (d) No improvement

23. He sent a word to me that he would be coming late.
(a) sent word (b) had sent a word
(c) sent words (d) No improvement

24. It became dear that the strangers were heading into serious disaster.
(a) along (b) towards
(c) for (d) No improvement

25. Fifty km are not a great distance in these days of fast moving vehicles.
(a) is not a great distance
(b) is no distance
(c) aren't a great distance
(d) No improvement

26. I am used to hard work.
(a) work hard (b) work hardly
(c) hard working (d) No improvement

27. It was indeed a shock for her, but she has later recovered from it.
(a) since
(b) then
(c) afterwards
(d) No improvement

28. There is dearth of woman doctor in our state. We shall have to recruit some from the other states.
(a) women doctor (b) woman doctors
(c) women doctors (d) No improvement

29. The poor villagers have waited in the bitter cold for more than 4 hours now.
(a) have been waiting (b) have waited
(c) has been waiting (d) No improvement

30. Most donors would seriously protest any effort to extrapolate from such limited data.
(a) protest against (b) protest at
(c) protest to (d) No improvement

31. The greatest thing in style is to have a use of metaphor.
(a) knowledge (b) command
(c) need (d) No improvement

32. In fact, if it hadn't been for his invaluable advice on so many occasions I wouldn't have achieved anything in life.
(a) remarkable advice
(b) valuable advices
(c) priceless suggestion
(d) No improvement

33. To get one's name in the Rowland Ward's book of hunting records was the hot ambition of every serious hunter.
(a) extreme (b) burning
(c) high (d) No improvement

34. I have lived in Delhi since I was four.
(a) am living (b) lived
(c) had lived (d) No improvement

35. My friend was in hospital for a week after an accident.
(a) through (b) following
(c) for (d) No improvement

36. I want you to clearly understand that matter.
(a) you clearly to understand
(b) you to understand clearly
(c) to clearly understand you
(d) No improvement

37. If you cross the line you will be disqualified.
(a) cross upon the line (b) cross on the line
(c) cross out the line (d) No improvement

38. No sooner he had returned home then his mother felt happy.
(a) had he returned home when
(b) he had returned home than
(c) did he return home than
(d) No improvement

39. There is no more room for you in this compartment.
(a) There is no more seat
(b) There is no more space
(c) There is no more accommodation
(d) No improvement

40. Young men and women should get habituated to reading and writing about current affairs.
(a) used (b) prepared
(c) trained (d) No improvement

41. While crossing the highway, a five years old child was knocked out by a passing car.
(a) away (b) up
(c) down (d) No improvement

42. Every time I go in a lift to my sixth floor apartment, I remember the calm and serenity of my ancestral home in the village.
(a) move in a lift (b) ascend in a lift
(c) take a lift (d) No improvement

43. He found a wooden broken chair in the room.
(a) wooden and broken chair
(b) broken wooden chair
(c) broken and wooden chair
(d) No improvement

44. If the room had been brighter, I would have been able to read for a while before bed time.
(a) If the room was brighter
(b) If the room are brighter
(c) Had the room been brighter
(d) No improvement

45. Practically every part of the banana tree is used by man.
(a) each part (b) any part
(c) most part (d) No improvement

46. Hoping not to be disturbed, I sat down in my easy chair to read the book I won as a prize.
(a) I had won as a prize (b) I have won as prize
(c) I had to win as a prize (d) No improvement

47. His father won't be able to leave for Varanasi until they have arrived.
(a) until they arrive
(b) until they will have arrived
(c) until they will arrive
(d) No improvement

48. The company goes to great length to ensure that employees can be comfortable in their work environment.
(a) are comfortable (b) will be comfortable
(c) should be comfortable (d) No improvement

49. The reason why he wrote the leatter was because he could not contact him over the phone.
(a) why he wrote the letter was since
(b) for which he wrote the letter because
(c) why he wrote the letter was that
(d) No improvement

50. I shall be grateful to you if you are of help to me now.
(a) help (b) would help
(c) helped (d) No improvement

51. Will you lend me few rupees in this hour of need?
(a) lend me any rupees
(b) borrow me a few rupees
(c) lend me a few rupees
(d) No improvement

52. He should move on to the next point and not harp one string only.
(a) harp on string only
(b) harp only one string
(c) harp upon one string only
(d) No improvement

53. Please make it a point to send your letter at my address.
(a) on my address (b) to my address
(c) in my address (d) No improvement

54. The demonstration passed off peacefully.
(a) passed out (b) passed away
(c) passed on (d) No improvement

55. This telephone number is not existing.
(a) has not existed (b) does not exist
(c) has not been existing (d) No improvement

56. Whenever my students come across new words, I ask them to look for them in the dictionary.
(a) to look it up (b) to look them up
(c) to look at them (d) No improvement

57. Please remind me of posting these letters to my relatives.
(a) by posting (b) to post
(c) for posting (d) No improvement

58. If you are living near a market place, you should be ready to bear the disturbances caused by traffic.
(a) to bear upon (b) to bear with
(c) to bear away (d) No improvement

59. I shall not go until I am invited.
(a) till I am invited (b) unless I am invited
(c) if not I am invited (d) No improvement

60. I, took the cycle which he bought yesterday.
(a) that he bought yesterday
(b) that which he had bought yesterday
(c) that he had bought the previous day
(d) No improvement

61. If you had attended the meeting, you would have benefited a great deal.
(a) could benefit (b) would benefit
(c) benefited (d) No improvement

62. The cloud of misfortunes appears to have blown out.
(a) over (b) up
(c) away (d) No improvement

63. We had nothing to eat since 8'o clock, this morning.
(a) have had nothing (b) has had nothing
(c) did have nothing (d) No improvement

64. If you are not clear about the meaning of a word, it is wise to look to this in a dictionary.
(a) look for (b) look at
(c) look up (d) No improvement

65. They are social insects, living in communities, regulated by definite laws, each member of society bearing well-defined and separate part in the work of a colony.
(a) who are living in communities
(b) living among a community
(c) who lives with a community
(d) No improvement

66. The dissidents hold a great problem in every political party.
(a) cause (b) give
(c) pose (d) No improvement

67. Not long back, in Japan, a mysterious nerve gas affected a large number of people.
(a) effected (b) infected
(c) infested (d) No improvement

68. As she was suffering from high fever, she could not face the examination.
(a) bear (b) suffer
(c) take (d) No improvement

69. As he is past his teens now, he can look for himself.
(a) after (b) to
(c) around (d) No improvement

70. Either he or I am going.
(a) he or I are going (b) he is going or I am
(c) I or he is going (d) No improvement

71. It will be no good trying to find an excuse next time.
(a) to try to find (b) to try finding
(c) trying finding (d) No improvement

72. We did not see this movie yet.
(a) have seen (b) have not seen
(c) had seen (d) No improvement

73. She says she's already paid me back, but I can't remember, so I'll have to take her word.
(a) to take her word true
(b) to take her to her word
(c) to take her word for it
(d) No improvement

74. When it was feared that the serfs might go too far and gain their freedom from serfdom, the protestant leaders joined the princes at crushing them.
(a) into crushing (b) in crushing
(c) without crushing (d) No improvement

75. In India, today many of our intellectuals still talk in terms of the French Revolution and the Rights of Man, not appreciating that much has happened since then.
(a) much has been happening
(b) much had happened
(c) much might happen
(d) No improvement

76. The end of the examinations is a/an opportunity for celebrating.
(a) change (b) moment
(c) occasion (d) No improvement

77. Our office clock is not so correct as it should be. It is usually five minutes fast.
(a) right (b) regular
(c) accurate (d) No improvement

78. You cannot forbid him leaving.
(a) he leaving (b) his leaving
(c) him to leave (d) No improvement

79. I hope you won't object to me watching while you work.
(a) against me watching (b) me to watch
(c) to my watching (d) No improvement

80. But in all these cases, conversion from scale have well-formulated.
(a) can be well-formulated
(b) are well-formulated
(c) well-formulated
(d) No improvement

81. The more they earn, more they spend.
(a) More they earn, more they spend
(b) More they earn, the more they spend
(c) The more they earn, the more they spend
(d) No improvement

82. Although, India is still by far a poor country, it can become rich if its natural and human resources are fully utilised.
(a) few and far between
(b) by and large
(c) by and by
(d) No improvement

83. Due to these reason, we are all in favour of universal compulsory education.
(a) Out of these reasons (b) For these reasons
(c) By these reasons (d) No improvement

84. While we would like that all Indian children to go to school, we need to ponder why they do not.
(a) that all the Indian children
(b) if all the children of India
(c) all Indian children
(d) No improvement

85. You are warned against committing the same mistake again.
(a) to commit (b) for committing
(c) against to commit (d) No improvement

86. The workers are hell bent at getting what is due to them.
(a) hell bent on getting (b) hell bent for getting
(c) hell bent upon getting (d) No improvement

87. He died in the year 1960 at 11 pm on 14th July.
(a) on 14th July in the year 1960 at 11 pm
(b) in the year 1960 on 14th July at 11 pm
(c) at 11 pm on 14th July in the year 1960
(d) No improvement

88. Because of the patient's ill health, losing weight was advised him by the doctor.
(a) to lose weight was advised to him by the doctor
(b) he was advised by the doctor to lose weight
(c) the doctor's advice to him was losing weight
(d) No improvement

89. I was telling a lie if I ever said that I liked you.
(a) have been telling
(b) would have told
(c) would have been telling
(d) No improvement

90. There is nothing quite miserable than property in youth.
(a) as miserable (b) very miserable
(c) more miserable (d) No improvement

Previous Year's Questions

Directions (Q. Nos. 91-93) *In the following sentences, a part of the sentence is underlined. Beneath each sentence, four different ways of paraphrasing the underlined part are indicated. Choose the best alternative among the four options.* **[CLAT 2015]**

91. This government has given subsidies to the Navratnas, but there is no telling whether the subsequent one will do.
(a) whether the subsequent government will do so
(b) if the government to follow will accept the policy
(c) if the government to follow will adhere to the policy
(d) no telling whether the subsequent one will do so

92. The management can still hire freely but cannot scold freely.
(a) cannot scold at will
(b) cannot give umbrage
(c) cannot take decision to scold
(d) cannot scold wilfully

93. The Romanians may be restive under Soviet direction, but they are tied to Moscow by ideological and military links.
(a) they are close to Moscow from ideological and military perspective
(b) they are preparing for a greater revolution
(c) secretly they rather enjoy the prestige of being protected by the mighty Soviets
(d) there is nothing they can do about it

Directions (Q. Nos. 94-97) *Choose the correct option for each of the following questions.* **[CLAT 2016]**

94. (a) Your grammar is very good, but you need to work on modifying your pronunciation
(b) Your grammar is very good but you need to work on managing your pronunciation
(c) Your grammar is very good, but you need to work on repairing your pronunciation
(d) Your grammar is very good, but you need to work on correcting your pronunciation

95. (a) The Titanic did not reach their destination
(b) The Titanic did not reach her destination
(c) The Titanic did not reach his destination
(d) The Titanic did not reach its destination

96. (a) Please stop interfering into my romantic life
(b) Please stop interfering for my romantic life
(c) Please stop interfering in my romantic life
(d) Please stop interfering with my romantic life

97. (a) The Film Star come out of the car and smiled at the people
(b) The Film Star got off the car and smiled at the people
(c) The Film Star got out of the car and smiled at the people
(d) The Film Star climbed off the car and smiled at the people

Direction (Q. Nos. 98-102) *In each of the following sentences, some part of the sentence or the entire sentence is underlined. Beneath each sentences, you will find four ways of phrasing the underlined part. Choose the most appropriate option given in each of the sentences given below that is the best version than the underlined part of the sentence.* **[CLAT 2017]**

98. Plausible though it sounds, the weakness of the hypothesis is that it does not incorporate all relevant facts.
(a) Though plausible, the hypothesis weakness
(b) The weakness of the hypothesis which sounds plausible.
(c) Even though it sounds plausible, the weakness of the hypothesis
(d) Though the hypothesis sounds plausible, its weakness

99. Many of them chiselled from a solid rock centuries ago the mountainous regions are dotted with hundreds of monasteries
(a) The mountainous regions are dotted with hundreds of monasteries, many of which are chiselled from solid rock centuries ago.
(b) The mountainous regions are dotted with hundreds of monasteries, many of them chiselled from solid rock centuries ago.
(c) Chiselled from solid rock centuries ago, the mountainous regions are dotted with many hundreds of monasteries.
(d) Hundreds of monasteries, many of them chiselled from solid rock centuries ago, are dotting the mountainous regions.

100. Two valence states of uranium, one with a deficit of four electrons and the other one with a deficit of six occurs in nature and contributes to the diversity of uranium's behaviour.
(a) the other with a deficit of six, occurs in Nature and contributes
(b) one with six occurs in Nature and contributes
(c) the other one a deficit of six, occur in Nature and contribute
(d) the other with a deficit of six, occur in Nature and contribute

101. Initiative and referendum, is a procedure that allows voters to propose and pass law as well as to repeal them.

(a) allow voters to propose to pass, and repeal laws

(b) allows voters to propose, pass and to repeal laws

(c) will allow voter to propose, pass, as well as to repeal laws.

(d) will allow laws on be proposed, passed, as well as repeated by voters

102. During her lecture, the speaker tried to clarify directional terms, for not everyone in attendance was knowledgeable that winds are designed by the direction from which they come.

(a) for everyone in attendance did not known.

(b) for not everyone attending knew.

(c) with everyone attending not knowledgeable.

(d) with everyone in attendance not knowing.

Answers

1	*b*	2	*a*	3	*b*	4	*a*	5	*a*	6	*b*	7	*a*	8	*a*	9	*b*	10	*b*
11	*c*	12	*d*	13	*d*	14	*b*	15	*c*	16	*a*	17	*c*	18	*b*	19	*a*	20	*c*
21	*c*	22	*b*	23	*a*	24	*b*	25	*a*	26	*d*	27	*a*	28	*c*	29	*a*	30	*a*
31	*a*	32	*d*	33	*c*	34	*d*	35	*b*	36	*b*	37	*d*	38	*c*	39	*b*	40	*d*
41	*c*	42	*c*	43	*b*	44	*c*	45	*d*	46	*a*	47	*a*	48	*a*	49	*c*	50	*b*
51	*c*	52	*c*	53	*b*	54	*d*	55	*b*	56	*b*	57	*b*	58	*b*	59	*b*	60	*c*
61	*d*	62	*a*	63	*a*	64	*c*	65	*d*	66	*a*	67	*b*	68	*c*	69	*a*	70	*d*
71	*d*	72	*b*	73	*b*	74	*b*	75	*d*	76	*b*	77	*c*	78	*b*	79	*c*	80	*b*
81	*c*	82	*b*	83	*b*	84	*c*	85	*d*	86	*c*	87	*c*	88	*b*	89	*c*	90	*c*
91	*d*	92	*a*	93	*a*	94	*d*	95	*b*	96	*c*	97	*c*	98	*b*	99	*b*	100	*b*
101	*a*	102	*d*																

CHAPTER 06

FILL IN THE BLANKS & CLOZE TEST

Fillers are the application of vocabulary. If a student has sound vocabulary then he can crack these question very easily. There is no hard and fast rules for this type of question. Also, the same applies with the cloze tests. Sentences with blanks are receptive to the words in their context.

A **Fill in the Blank** question consists of a phrase, sentence or paragraph with a blank space indicating where a student should provide the missing word or words while a **Cloze Test** is an exercise where the candidates are provided with a passage which has certain words missing from it. It follows logically that to ace such an assessment, candidates must have a strong command over English language along with a flair for grammar and a good vocabulary.

In terms of the general preparation you can do, read and read as much as you can. The more you read, the more proficient you will become to see which word would fit the blank. It will also help build up your vocabulary. Both these things will go a long way in helping you ace the Cloze Test. *e.g.*

He will come .... 7 O' clock in the moring.

(a) at (b) in (c) by (d) on

Solution Option (a) at, for the fixed time preposition 'at' is used.

Practice Exercise

Exercise 1

Directions (Q. Nos. 1-20) *In each of the following sentences, there is a blank space in the given sentences. Below each sentence there are four words denoted by letters (a), (b), (c) and (d). Choose the correct word to fill in the blank.*

1. They even passed .... without any untoward incident.
(a) of (b) on (c) off (d) away

2. Please give me .... to drink.
(a) little water (b) a little water
(c) any water (d) some water

3. Everybody was drunk ....
(a) wasn't he? (b) weren't they?
(c) wasn't she? (d) are they?

4. In his address to the senior managers, the managing director .... certain measures being taken for improving the office discipline.
(a) claimed (b) imposed
(c) instructed (d) highlighted

5. Leadership defines what the future should be like and .... people with that vision.
(a) aligns (b) trains
(c) encourages (d) develops

6. You currently have all the newest software programmes. The reason your computer is running so slow is that you have old .... You may have to buy more physical memory, perhaps, a bigger hard drive if you want your computer to run faster.
(a) warehouses (b) software
(c) wires (d) hardware

7. The new teacher loves poems and makes us......... .
(a) heartily learn them (b) learn them heartily
(c) learn them by heart (d) learning by heart them

8. Retirement can either be a .... to age or an opportunity for new adventure.
(a) surrender (b) defeat
(c) setback (d) victory

9. Your treatment of your servant is .... mean.
(a) golden (b) nobly
(c) flexibly (d) notoriously

10. Gangotri is .... by mountains on three sides.
(a) hidden (b) kept
(c) flanked (d) located

11. Good boys do not quarrel with ....
(a) each other (b) another
(c) one another (d) other

12. Everyone .... to clear their dues.
(a) are required (b) required
(c) were required (d) is required

13. After hours of acrimonious arguments the negotiations reached a(n) .... neither side was willing to compromise.
(a) solution (b) resolution
(c) end (d) impasse

14. Punishment for transgressions of the law ceases to have a deterrent effect if the punishment is frequently ....
(a) Changed (b) Arbitrary
(c) Lenient (d) Commuted

15. The injured security guard was first .... to a small private hospital from where he was shifted to a bigger civil hospital as his .... deteriorated.
(a) rushed, condition (b) hurried, status
(c) taken, life (d) admitted, form

16. Hundred rupees .... too much for the job.
(a) seem (b) are seen
(c) seems (d) is seeming

17. An overdose of chloroform is .... to a plant as to a man.
(a) enough fatal (b) too fatal
(c) as fatal (d) so fatal

18. My friend feels as though nothing .... to him.
(a) has happened (b) happened
(c) had happened (d) will have happened

19. The lease of our premises has .... and we have to vacate it.
(a) run out (b) run off
(c) run over (d) run down

20. His boss .... an explanation of his conduct with his colleagues.
(a) called up (b) called upon
(c) called for (d) called off

Directions (Q.Nos. 21-49) *In each of the following sentences, there are two blank spaces in the given sentences. Below each sentence there are four pair of words denoted by letters (a), (b), (c) and (d). Find out which pair of words can be filled up in the blanks in the sentence in the same sequence to make the sentence meaningfully complete.*

21. Somesh .... me coming to his table, he smiled and .... me a chair.
(a) found, signalled (b) met, sat
(c) looked, gave (d) saw, offered

22. The leaders were .... needed by those to .... they addressed.
(a) angrily, who (b) readily, which
(c) scarcely, whom (d) rarely, where

23. I am not .... to sell you my house unless you offer a more .... price,
(a) agree, better (b) prepared, realistic
(c) ready, correct (d) having , actual

24. Due to .... rainfall this year, there will be .... cut in water supply.
(a) scanty, substantial (b) meagre, least
(c) sufficient, no (d) surplus, abundant

25. In a changing and .... unstructured business environment, creativity and innovation are being .... demanded of executives.
(a) excessively, rapidly
(b) highly, extremely
(c) increasingly, moderately
(d) progressively, increasingly

26. The interest has .... innovation related to several sectors of......... pharmaceutical and industry.
(a) accepted, skeletal
(b) insured, fateful
(c) affected, plummeting
(d) accelerated, burgeoning

27. The new policy seeks to .... a process of widespread participation of people .... the way for more effective implementation.
(a) amend, opening
(b) halt, propelling
(c) generate, paving
(d) diagnose, resulting

28. Journalism is a .... for truth, a crusade to .... injustice and wrong doing.
(a) product, limit (b) boon, justify
(c) travesty, attack (d) quest, expose

29. This book is readable, clear and .... researched with .... detailed references.
(a) fabulously, intricate
(b) meticulously, extensive
(c) leisurely , complete
(d) hardly, notional

30. Part of the confusion in our societies .... from our pursuit of efficiency and economic growth, in the .... that these are the necessary ingredients of progress.
(a) stems, conviction
(b) derives, evaluation
(c) emerges, consideration
(d) obtains, exploration

31. Four officials of a rural cooperative bank .... the institution of ₹ 1.56 crore, by .... of loan through fake Self Help Groups (SHGs).
(a) swindled, availing
(b) arrested, seeking
(c) cheated, taking
(d) duped, recommending

32. Handicrafts constitute an important .... of the decentralised sector of India's economy and .... employment to over six million artisans.
(a) factors, aims (b) extension, plans
(c) segment, provides (d) supplier, gives

33. The Indian hospitality industry which has been .... a prolonged slump is now entering a new .... phase ready to enhance profitability.
(a) witnessing, ambitious
(b) observing, listless
(c) demonstrating, efficient
(d) recovering, debt

34. French Government has said it will conduct a fourth search for the flight recorders of an Air France jetliner that .... into the Atlantic ocean while flying from Rio de Janeiro to Paris 18 months ....

(a) crashed, ago (b) plunged, later
(c) dove, before (d) fell, prior

35. After .... pursuing it for nearly twenty one months, the city police .... the case of the triple murder of professor and his family.

(a) relentless, solved
(b) doggedly, cracked
(c) constantly, handed
(d) persistently, found

36. It's not just the .... reggae and dance hall music that sets their party experience apart, the group has a Disc Jockey who .... the crowd to dance, interacts with them and also raps to the music.

(a) regular, extols (b) groovy, exhorts
(c) morose, compels (d) upbeat, beats

37. The problem of housing shortage .... with the population explosion has also been .... by this policy.

(a) coped, highlighted
(b) dispensed, acknowledged
(c) compounded, addressed
(d) threatened, manifested

38. The quality of .... between individuals and the organisation for which they work can be .... to the benefit of both the parties.

(a) services, evaluated
(b) interaction, improved
(c) sophistication, developed
(d) work, appreciated

39. Among a number of hobbies that one can .... the hobby of reading is the most useful and ....

(a) develops, accumulative
(b) cultivate, enlightened
(c) nourish, cumulative
(d) absorbs, durable

40. When you are living with your .... values and principles, you can be straight forward, honest and ....

(a) inherited, distinct (b) core, upfront
(c) innate, durable (d) cultural, perceptive

41. The quality of .... between individuals and the organisation for which they work can be .... to the benefit of both parties.

(a) life, conceptualised (b) interactions, improved
(c) service, evaluated (d) work, better

42. Genetic engineering in humans should be used to .... diseases, not to .... genetic uniformity.

(a) treat, foster (b) eradicate, cater
(c) cure, generate (d) avoid, promote

43. Stating that the ATM operations are .... losses, the nation's largest bank, the State Bank plans to .... the management of some of its ATMs.

(a) generating, resource (b) generating, close
(c) incurring, outsource (d) reporting, tighten

44. Most journalistic writing could do with .... of paragraphs to make the prose more ....

(a) suppression, legible
(b) removal, argumentative
(c) simplification, abstruse
(d) deletion, succinct

45. Angered by bureaucrat's .... comments, the reporter insisted for a more .... response.

(a) redundant, repetitive
(b) tactless, immediate
(c) circumlocutions, beneficial
(d) sarcastic, direct

46. One of the most productive research .... in contemporary neurosciences is devoted to .... maps of human consciousness.

(a) trajectories, reconnoitring
(b) designs, enunciating
(c) paradigms, elucidating
(d) declensions, obfuscating

47. But .... are now regularly written not just for tools but well-established practices, organisations and institutions not all of which seem to be .... away.

(a) reports, withering (b) stories, trading
(c) books, dying (d) obituaries, fading

48. In this context, the .... of the British Labour Movement is particularly ....

(a) affair, weird (b) activity, moving
(c) experience, significant (d) atmosphere, gloomy

49. The film's hero, a Pearl Diver, naively expects that the purchasers will compete amongst themselves to pay him the best price for his pearl, but instead they ..... to ..... him.

(a) work.....help (b) plan .....incentives
(c) refuse..... deceive (d) collude....swindle

Directions (Q.Nos. 50-53) *Choose the most appropriate option to fill in the blanks.*

50. A lyre was played in ancient Rome. The lyre is a ....

(a) stringed instrument in the harp classes
(b) wind instrument in the wind class
(c) percussion instrument in the leap class
(d) a combination of wind and percussion instruments

51. The President has a .... of .... Around him where make public appearances.

(a) catalyst, individuals (b) barrier, catalyst
(c) hedge, protection (d) derrick, limits

52. .... the green room now?

(a) Whos in (b) Whose in
(c) Who's in (d) Whos' in

53. The rumors were .... and she welcomed the opportunity .... them.

(a) appealing, demystify (b) fabricated, demystify
(c) fabricated, refute (d) pertinent, enjoy

Exercise 2

Directions *Read the following passages carefully and answer the questions that follow.*

Passage 1

Can we see ...(1)... the Earth is a globe? Yes, we can, when we watch a ship that sails out to sea. If we watch closely, we see that the ship begins ...(2)... The bottom of the ship disappears first and then the ship seems to sink lower and lower, ...(3)... we can only see the top of the ship and then we see nothing at all. What is hiding the ship from us? It is the Earth. Stick a pin most of the way into an orange and ...(4)... turn the orange away from you. You will see the pin disappear, ...(5)... a ship does on the Earth.

1. (a) if (b) where
(c) that (d) whether

2. (a) being disappeared (b) to be disappeared
(c) to have disappeared (d) to disappear

3. (a) until (b) since
(c) after (d) by the time

4. (a) reluctantly (b) accidentally
(c) slowly (d) passionately

5. (a) the same (b) alike
(c) just as (d) by the way

Passage 2

After months of colder weather, the days get longer, the buds ...(1)... in the trees, birds sing and the world ...(2)... a green dress. Spring passes ...(3)... summer. Everyone knows that summer will not ...(4)... . The power of all the wisest men and women in the world cannot keep it for us. The corn becomes ripe, the leaves turn brown and then drop to the ground, ...(5)... the world changes its green dress for a dress of autumn colours.

1. (a) fall off (b) take up
(c) put off (d) come out

2. (a) looks after (b) puts on
(c) carries on (d) comes round

3. (a) into (b) by
(c) from (d) on

4. (a) forego (b) evaluate
(c) succumb (d) last

5. (a) yet (b) therefore
(c) since (d) whereas

Passage 3

...(1)... people breathe, pollutants in the air ...(2)... in the lungs or absorbed into the body. And polluted air can harm animals and plants ...(3)... people. For this reason, our air supply should be ...(4)... watched and managed to assure ...(5)... good quality.

1. (a) When (b) Until
(c) During (d) If

2. (a) have deposited
(b) are depositing
(c) had to be deposited
(d) may be deposited

3. (a) as well as (b) in addition
(c) even if (d) in spite of

4. (a) alternately (b) previously
(c) hastily (d) closely

5. (a) them (b) its
(c) his (d) their

Passage 4

It ...(1)... that policing in the future will be ...(2)... more different than it is today. Advances in technology— ...(3)... in computers, television and communication—will assist the police in solving and preventing crimes. Advances in forensic science ...(4)... evidence more reliable and meaningful. All of these changes will be for the better if they help ...(5)... the quality of police service.

1. (a) predicted (b) has predicted
(c) is predicted (d) was predicting
2. (a) any (b) some (c) such (d) much
3. (a) particularly (b) placidly
(c) roughly (d) widely
4. (a) had to make (b) would be made
(c) has made (d) should make
5. (a) improving (b) be improved
(c) to improve (d) have improved

Passage 5

A century ago, the process of choosing a career was a much simpler matter than it is today. A boy often followed in his father's footsteps. His sister learned the household skills that ...(1)... her to become a wife and mother. Now-a-days, young people grow up in a much freer society ...(2)... they enjoy almost unlimited career opportunities. In recent years, there ...(3)... an enormous increase in the kinds of vocations from which it is possible to choose. In addition, many of the barriers to career, opportunity that existed only a few decades ago, such as ...(4)... based on sex or religion or ethnic origins, are ...(5)... disappearing.

1. (a) had prepared (b) may prepare
(c) was prepared (d) would prepare
2. (a) where (b) when
(c) why (d) whom
3. (a) had been (b) has been
(c) will be (d) would have
4. (a) judgement (b) perception
(c) goodwill (d) discrimination
5. (a) rapidly (b) incessantly
(c) categorically (d) vigilantly

Passage 6

King Mongkut ...(1)... the King of Siam (Thailand) in the year 1851. Mongkut ...(2)... Siam for seventeen years. Mongkut was a ...(3)... . A dynast is a ...(4)... ruler. This means that Mongkut became King because his family had been ruling Siam before him. Mongkut was the fourth member of his family to be king of Siam and so he was ...(5)... . Rama IV. How did Mongkut's family become the rulers of Siam?

In the previous century, Taksin had been the King of Siam and for a number of years he had slowly gone ...(6)... . Many of the King's advisers turned against him and asked a powerful. General (Chakri) to ...(7)... Taksin and become the new King of Siam. General Chakri overthrew Taksin and ...(8)... himself King of Siam. He was known as Rama I and was the first ruler of the Chakri Dynasty. The Chakri Dynasty was ...(9)... and it has ...(10)... to the present day.

1. (a) became (b) insane
(c) overthrow (d) called
2. (a) made (b) ruled
(c) dynasty (d) became
3. (a) hereditary (b) insane
(c) dynasty (d) called
4. (a) became (b) ruled
(c) dynasty (d) hereditary
5. (a) hereditary (b) called
(c) overthrow (d) insane
6. (a) hereditary (b) insane
(c) overthrow (d) called
7. (a) overthrow (b) ruled
(c) dynasty (d) made
8. (a) before (b) ruined (c) dynamic (d) made
9. (a) hereditary (b) established
(c) overthrow (d) called
10. (a) survived (b) insane
(c) overthrow (d) called

Passage 7

Around the world, forests are being destroyed at a rate of about thirteen million hectares a year and deforestation accounts for an estimated 17% - 20% of all global emissions.

In addition, forests and other terrestrial carbon sinks play a ...(1)... role in preventing runaway climate change soaking up a full 2.6 Gt of atmospheric carbon every year. The destruction of forests, therefore not only emits carbon, a staggering 1.6 Gt a year, which severely ...(2)... forests' capacity to absorb emissions from other sources, but also drastically ...(3)... the amount of forested land available to act as a carbon sink in the future.

However, the effects of deforestation extend beyond carbon.

Rainforests ...(4)... a wide variety of ecosystems services, from regulating rainfall to purifying groundwater and keeping fertile soil from ...(5)... deforestation in one area can seriously damage food production and ...(6)... to clean water in an entire region. The value of global ecosystem services has been estimated at 33 trillion USD each year (almost half of global GDP) but these services have been taken for granted without a mechanism to make the market reflect their value.

Rainforests are also a home and ...(7)... of income for a huge number of people in Africa, Asia, and South America ...(8)... this, economic pressures frequently drive both local communities and national governments in the developing world to ...(9)... these forests in ways that are unsustainable, clear-cutting vast areas for fuel, timber, mining, or agricultural land.

1. (a) Tough (b) Important (c) Vital (d) Biggest

2. (a) Affect (b) Diminish (c) Increases (d) Impairs

3. (a) Plagues (b) Develops (c) Reduces (d) Shortens

4. (a) Sell (b) Offer (c) Give (d) Provide

5. (a) Transforming (b) Decoding (c) Erupting (d) Eroding

6. (a) Handiness (b) Excess (c) Availability (d) Access

7. (a) Beginning (b) Source (c) Ways (d) Reference

8. (a) Despite (b) Also (c) In spite (d) Apart

9. (a) Exploit (b) Encompass (c) Nurture (d) Work

Passage 8

Under a zero-hour contract, a party described as a 'casual worker' has a contract with an employer, but the contract may be of little benefit as Its provisions do not (1)........ any obligation upon the employer to offer work, and similarly, there is no obligation for the worker to accept it. A 'casual worker' is the correct term to define workers who do not have ...(2) ... hours of work but instead supply services on an irregular, flexible basis when the employer needs them. A 'worker' is not, therefore, an 'employee'. This is an important distinction, as employees enjoy significantly better protection under the law.

Although workers do have basic rights, for example, the right to a national minimum ...(3)..., the right not to be unlawfully discriminated against and the right to sick pay, but they are denied other important rights. For example, casual workers do not have the same rights when it comes to issues such as maternity or paternity pay, ...(4)... pay in the event that there is not enough work available and the, right not to be unfairly ...(5)... . These contracts are very unpopular with trade unions, who argue that employers are using this type of contract as a way of denying workers the benefits which they would otherwise be entitled to under current employment ...(6)....

As a result of public criticism, the Eurona government held an independent review to analyse the use of these contracts. In June 2016, Eurona Business Secretary, Zoro, concluded that zero-hour contracts were not to be declared ...(7)..., as he considered that many groups of people benefited from them. However, he did change the law in order to prevent employers from banning casual workers from working elsewhere when bound by a zero-hour contract. This is not the end of the story, however. The use of zero-hour contracts is extremely popular in the food and retail ...(8)... of the Eurona economy. For example, McDonald's and Burger King have recently disclosed that they use this type of contract for over 80% of their workers in the Eurona and another high-street gaint, Sports Direct, has admitted that 90% of its workers are under this type of contract. However, the latter ...(9)... a legal challenge in November 2016 when Tara Phera filed a claim against the company in a Eurona Employment Tribunal. Tara Phera claimed that although she was contracted as a casual worker for Sports Direct, she had the same responsibilities and duties as an employee but without receiving the benefits of an employee. A ...(10)... was reached according to which Sports direct is now required at the time of advertising for future zero-hours staff to expressly state that the role does not ...(11)... work. The company must also produce clear written policies setting out what sick pay and paid holiday their zero-hours staff are entitled to.

1. (a) impose (b) compel
(c) force (d) impress

2. (a) fixed (b) secure
(c) firm (d) stable

3. (a) salary (b) wage
(c) earnings (d) remuneration

4. (a) let go (b) reduncancy
(c) termination (d) laid off

5. (a) dismissed (b) discharged
(c) terminated (d) release

6. (a) statutes (b) codes
(c) legislations (d) acts

7. (a) unlawful (b) illegal
(c) illegitimate (d) felonious

8. (a) zones (b) regions
(c) sectors (d) areas

9. (a) suffered (b) bore
(c) endured (d) faced

10. (a) agreement (b) settlement
(c) deal (d) decision

11. (a) provide (b) entitle
(c) guarantee (d) offer

Previous Years' Questions

Directions (Q. Nos. 1- 10) *Choose the correct option out of the four choices given.* **[CLAT 2012]**

1. Give an example pertinent________ the case.
(a) with (b) on
(c) for (d) to

2. My voice reverberated ________the walls of the castle.
(a) with (b) from
(c) in (d) on

3. The reward was not commensurate ______ the work done by us.
(a) for (b) on
(c)with (d) order

4. Our tragic experience in the recent past provides an index ______ the state of lawlessness in the region.
(a) of (b) in (c) at (d) by

5. Your conduct smacks _____ recklessness.
(a) of (b) with (c) from (d) in

6. A good judge never gropes ________ the conclusion.
(a) to (b) at (c) on (d) for

7. Nobody in our group is a genius ______ winning friends and in convincing people.
(a) for (b) in (c) of (d) at

8. If you are averse ______ recommending my name, you should not hesitate to admit it.
(a) about (b) for
(c) to (d) against

9. Religious leaders should not delve _____ politics.
(a) in (b) with (c) at (d) into

10. What you say has hardly any bearing ____ the lives of tribals.
(a) about (b) for
(c) on (d) with

Directions (Q. Nos. 11-20) *Select the best option from the four alternatives given below.* **[CLAT 2013]**

11. Unless he .... this office, I will not say anything.
(a) left (b) did not leave
(c) leaves (d) had left

12. .... I would help all the poor people.
(a) If I am rich (b) If I was rich
(c) If I were rich (d) In case I am rich

13. I .... the news an hour ago.
(a) have heard (b) heard
(c) was hearing (d) have been hearing

14. He spoke .... about his prospects.
(a) consciously (b) conscientiously
(c) confidentially (d) confidently

15. The boy is not interested in playing, ...?
(a) doesn't he (b) isn't he
(c) didn't he (d) is he

16. He told us that we should never live beyond .... means.
(a) his (b) their (c) our (d) her

17. May I request .... you again to consider my case favourably.
(a) to
(b) onto
(c) of
(d) no preposition required

18. Known as devout and serious person, she also has .... sense of humour.
(a) better (b) quick
(c) good (d) beautiful

19. Galileo said, 'The Earth .... around the Sun'.
(a) revolved (b) is revolving
(c) revolves (d) is revolved

20. We .... our work before the guests arrived at our house.
(a) shall finish (b) have finished
(c) had finished (d) shall have finished

Directions (Q. Nos. 21-30) *Fill in the blank by choosing the most appropriate option.* **[CLAT 2014]**

21. A vote of .... proposed at the end of the meeting.
(a) thanks were (b) thank was
(c) thanks had been (d) thanks was

22. During the recession many companies will .... lay off workers.
(a) be forced to (b) have the force to
(c) forcefully (d) be forced into

23. She has good .... over the famous foreign languages.
(a) expertise (b) command
(c) control (d) authority

24. The chairman pointed out in favour of the manager that the profitability of the industrial plant had .... since he took over the administration.
(a) arisen (b) declined
(c) added (d) increased

25. When the examinations were over,............ went to Paris.
(a) me and Rohan (b) I and Rohan
(c) Rohan and me (d) Rohan and I

26. Let's go for a walk,............?
(a) can we (b) shall we
(c) can't we (d) shouldn't we

27. Had Anil been on time, he .... missed the train.
(a) would not have been (c) will not have
(b) had not (d) would not have

28. The most alarming fact is that infection is spreading .... the state and reaching villages and small towns.
(a) over (b) across (c) far (d) from

29. In big cities, people are cut .... from nature.
(a) off (b) down (c) away (d) out

30. The dissidents .... a great problem in every political party.
(a) give (b) cause
(c) pose (d) hold

Directions (Q. Nos. 31-40) *Fill in the blanks by choosing the most appropriate option.* **[CLAT 2016]**

31. A fire broke .... in the neighbourhood.
(a) out (b) off (c) away (d) from

32. The method and practice of teaching is called ....
(a) philately (b) pedagogy
(c) paediatrics (d) training

33. There is a lot of work .... hand. Let's cancel .... picnic.
(a) on, a (b) in, the
(c) in, a (d) upon, the

34. There isn't .... water in the overhead tank.
(a) some (b) any (c) lot of (d) little

35. Professor Ahmed .... teaching us .... August, 2012.
(a) was, for (b) had been, since
(c) has been, since (d) has been, for

36. It's unfortunate that he died .... cancer.
(a) by (b) of (c) with (d) from

37. A thief does not .... the door.
(a) knock at (b) knock to
(c) knock on (d) knock

38. I like reading journals .... novels.
(a) the best (b) most than
(c) more than (d) the less than

39. If you promise .... angry with me, I'll tell you what I broke.
(a) not getting (b) not to get
(c) get not (d) not get

40. They always give the available seats to .... comes first.
(a) whichever (b) whomever
(c) whom (d) whoever

Directions (Q. Nos. 41-45) *Complete the sentences with the correct options.* **[CLAT 2016]**

41. Her parents have arrived .... the airport.
(a) on (b) in
(c) to (d) at

42. I have never come .... anyone as rude as him.
(a) across (b) at
(c) around (d) to

43. Mani, along with his friends, ... for basketball practice every morning.
(a) were going (b) are going
(c) goes (d) go

44. I can't bear .... late.
(a) be (b) been
(c) to (d) being

45. They returned home .... a taxi.
(a) on (b) with
(c) in (d) from

Directions (Q. Nos. 46-55) *Fill in the blanks by choosing the most appropriate option.* **[CLAT 2017]**

46. If they want to succeed, they .... have to work very hard.
(a) must (b) ought
(c) should (d) will

47. The minister flew .... the flooded areas in a helicopter.
(a) about (b) over (c) along (d) in

48. You have played a great role, for .... your help I possibly would have landed my self into a problem.
(a) without (b) despite
(c) after (d) although

49. Would anybody .... a mother have risked her life for the baby?
(a) rather (b) but
(c) than (d) however

50. Kanak is endowed .... many great qualities.
(a) of (b) by (c) in (d) with

51. The passengers were very happy .... the friendly and warm treatment.
(a) from (b) by (c) about (d) to

52. Sunita decided to set .... some time every day for prayers.
(a) aside (b) on (c) up (d) in

53. She stood .... Amit, but could not utter a single word for quite so me time.
(a) for (b) before
(c) about (d) to

54. We shall fail .... we are industrious.
(a) until (b) unless
(c) though (d) whether

55. The doctor advised him to go .... several medical tests.
(a) through (b) into
(c) about (d) under

Answers

Exercise 1

1	*c*	2	*d*	3	*b*	4	*d*	5	*d*	6	*d*	7	*c*	8	*a*	9	*d*	10	*c*
11	*c*	12	*d*	13	*d*	14	*d*	15	*a*	16	*c*	17	*c*	18	*a*	19	*a*	20	*c*
21	*d*	22	*c*	23	*b*	24	*a*	25	*d*	26	*d*	27	*c*	28	*d*	29	*b*	30	*c*
31	*a*	32	*c*	33	*a*	34	*a*	35	*b*	36	*b*	37	*c*	38	*b*	39	*a*	40	*b*
41	*b*	42	*a*	43	*c*	44	*d*	45	*d*	46	*c*	47	*d*	48	*c*	49	*d*	50	*a*
51	*c*	52	*c*	53	*c*														

Exercise 2

Passage 1

1	*c*	2	*d*	3	*a*	4	*c*	5	*c*

Passage 2

1	*d*	2	*b*	3	*a*	4	*d*	5	*d*

Passage 3

1	*a*	2	*d*	3	*a*	4	*d*	5	*b*

Passage 4

1	*c*	2	*d*	3	*a*	4	*d*	5	*c*

Passage 5

1	*d*	2	*a*	3	*b*	4	*d*	5	*a*

Passage 6

1	*a*	2	*b*	3	*c*	4	*d*	5	*b*	6	*b*	7	*a*	8	*d*	9	*b*	10	*a*

Passage 7

1	*c*	2	*d*	3	*c*	4	*b*	5	*d*	6	*d*	7	*b*	8	*a*	9	*a*

Passage 8

1	*a*	2	*a*	3	*b*	4	*b*	5	*d*	6	*d*	7	*b*	8	*c*	9	*d*	10	*d*
11	*c*																		

Previous Year's Answers

1	*d*	2	*b*	3	*c*	4	*a*	5	*a*	6	*d*	7	*d*	8	*c*	9	*d*	10	*c*
11	*c*	12	*c*	13	*a*	14	*d*	15	*d*	16	*c*	17	*d*	18	*c*	19	*c*	20	*c*
21	*d*	22	*a*	23	*b*	24	*d*	25	*d*	26	*b*	27	*d*	28	*b*	29	*a*	30	*b*
31	*a*	32	*b*	33	*b*	34	*b*	35	*c*	36	*d*	37	*d*	38	*c*	39	*b*	40	*d*
41	*d*	42	*a*	43	*c*	44	*d*	45	*c*	46	*d*	47	*b*	48	*a*	49	*c*	50	*d*
51	*c*	52	*a*	53	*b*	54	*b*	55	*a*										

CHAPTER 07

SPELLING TEST

"Questions based on spelling test are important part of the English language test of Hotel Management. Usually 5-8 questions are asked in entrance examinations in two forms–correctly spelt word or wrongly spelt word. It is designed to test a candidate's vocabulary and his ability to choose words with their correct spellings. Sound knowledge of prefix, suffix and root words gives an advantage while attempting this section."

Spelling test is designed to test a candidate's vocabulary and his ability to write words with their correct spellings. In this test, questions are asked in two different ways— *to choose the correctly spelt word and to choose the wrongly spelt word.*

Actually, English spelling does follow specific rules. Knowing some basic rules of English spelling can eleminate many common errors even though there are some exceptions. *Here are a few rules to spell words.*

Final Consonant

Rule 1 When one-syllable word ending in single vowel + single consonant, double the consonant before a suffix beginning with a vowel.

e.g.

(i) beg + ed = begged (ii) big + er = bigger

(iii) swim + ing = swimming (iv) sad + est = saddest

Rule 2 Words of two or three syllables ending in single vowel + single consonant, double the final consonant if the last syllable is stressed.

e.g.

(i) permit + ed = permitted

(ii) occur + ing = occurring

(iii) control + er = controller

(iv) begin + ing = beginning

Rule 3 Consonant 'l' is doubled if the words ending in single vowel + 'l' before a suffix beginning with a vowel.

e.g.

(i) signal	+	ing	=	signalling
(ii) repel	+	ent	=	repellent
(iii) quarrel	+	ed	=	quarrelled
(iv) travel	+	er	=	traveller

Rule 4 When the suffix 'full' is added to a word, one 'l' is removed.

e.g.

(i) faith	+	full	=	faithful
(ii) use	+	full	=	useful
(iii) harm	+	full	=	harmful

If the word to which the suffix 'full' is added ends in 'll', one 'l' is removed from the word also.

e.g.

(i) skill	+	full	=	skilful
(ii) will	+	full	=	wilful

Final 'e'

Rule 5 Words ending in silent 'e', drop the 'e' before a suffix beginning with a vowel.

e.g.

(i) hope	+	ing	=	hoping
(ii) live	+	ed	=	lived
(iii) drive	+	er	=	driver
(iv) tire	+	ing	=	tiring

If the suffix begins with a consonant, 'e' is not dropped.

e.g.

(i) hope	+	full	=	hopeful
(ii) sincere	+	ly	=	sincerely

Exceptions

(i) true	+	ly	=	truly
(ii) nine	+	th	=	ninth
(iii) argue	+	ment	=	argument

Rule 6 When the suffix 'ous' is added to a word ending in 'ce', 'e' is changed to 'i'.

e.g.

(i) space	+	ous	=	spacious
(ii) vice	+	ous	=	vicious
(iii) malice	+	ous	=	malicious
(iv) grace	+	ous	=	gracious

Rule 7 Words ending in 'ee', do not drop an 'e' before a suffix.

e.g.

(i) see	+	ing	=	seeing
(ii) agree	+	ment	=	agreement
(iii) foresee	+	ing	=	foreseeing
(iv) agree	+	ed	=	agreed

Rule 8 If the suffix 'ing' is added to a word ending in 'ie', then 'ie' is changed to 'y'.

e.g.

(i) lie	+	ing	=	lying
(ii) die	+	ing	=	dying
(iii) tie	+	ing	=	tying

Final 'y'

Rule 9 Final 'y' following a consonant changes to 'i' before a suffix except 'ing'.

e.g.

(i) carry	+	ed	=	carried
(ii) happy	+	ly	=	happily
(iii) marry	+	age	=	marriage
(iv) beauty	+	full	=	beautiful

Exceptions

(i) marry	+	ing	=	marrying
(ii) carry	+	ing	=	carrying

Rule 10 A final 'y' following a vowel does not change before a suffix.

e.g.

(i) obey	+	ed	=	obeyed
(ii) play	+	er	=	player
(iii) pray	+	ed	=	prayed

'ie' or 'ei'

Rule 11 In a word 'ei' is generally used after 'c' and 'ie' is used after any other letter.

e.g.

conceive	achieve	conceit
relieve	deceive	believe
receive	field	

Exceptions

seize	protein
counterfeit	weird
surfeit	

Practice Exercise

Exercise 1

Directions (Q. Nos. 1-50) *In each of the following questions, choose the correctly spelt word.*

1. (a) Efflorascence (b) Efflorescence (c) Effloresçence (d) Eflorescence

2. (a) Exemple (b) Exampel (c) Example (d) Exampal

3. (a) Argumant (b) Arguemant (c) Argument (d) Arguement

4. (a) Aproched (b) Aproached (c) Approched (d) Approached

5. (a) Scripture (b) Scriptur (c) Skripture (d) Scripcher

6. (a) Pasanger (b) Pessenger (c) Pesanger (d) Passenger

7. (a) Sattellite (b) Satellite (c) Sattelite (d) Satelite

8. (a) Commettee (b) Committe (c) Comittee (d) Committee

9. (a) Corupt (b) Curropt (c) Corrupt (d) Currupt

10. (a) Achievement (b) Acheivment (c) Achievment (d) Achevement

11. (a) Bouquete (b) Bouquet (c) Boquet (d) Bouquette

12. (a) Foreigner (b) Forienor (c) Foriegnor (d) Foreiner

13. (a) Exagerate (b) Exadgerate (c) Exaggerate (d) Exeggerate

14. (a) Acurrate (b) Accurate (c) Acurate (d) Accuratte

15. (a) Forecast (b) Forcaust (c) Forcast (d) Forecaste

16. (a) Puerille (b) Puerrile (c) Puerile (d) Purrile

17. (a) Entreprenuer (b) Entrepraneur (c) Entrapreneur (d) Entrepreneur

18. (a) Commission (b) Commisson (c) Commision (d) Comission

19. (a) Preservarance (b) Perseverance (c) Perseverence (d) Preserverence

20. (a) Illusteous (b) Illistrious (c) Ilustrious (d) Illustrious

21. (a) Pitiaeble (b) Pitiable (c) Pitiabale (d) Pitiebale

22. (a) Paralelled (b) Parallelled (c) Paralleled (d) Parralleled

23. (a) Vetniary (b) Vetarinary (c) Veteninary (d) Veterinary

24. (a) Tranquility (b) Trenquillity (c) Trenquility (d) Traanquility

25. (a) Fullfil (b) Fulfil (c) Fulfill (d) Fullfill

26. (a) Recommand (b) Recommend (c) Reccomend (d) Recomend

27. (a) Omenous (b) Ominous (c) Omineous (d) Ommineous

28. (a) Tempereture (b) Temparature (c) Temperature (d) Tamperature

29. (a) Overlapped (b) Overlaped (c) Overleped (d) Overlaped

30. (a) Necessary (b) Necessarry (c) Necesary (d) Neccessary

31. (a) Benefeted (b) Benifited (c) Benefitted (d) Benifitted

32. (a) Sacrilegeous (b) Sacrilegious (c) Sacriligious (d) Sacreligious

33. (a) Giraf (b) Gerraffe (c) Geraff (d) Giraffe

34. (a) Forein (b) Fariegn (c) Foriegn (d) Foreign

35. (a) Lackadaisical (b) Lackadisical (c) Lackadaisicle (d) Lackdaisical

36. (a) Sepulchral (b) Sepalchrle (c) Sepalchral (d) Sepulchrle

37. (a) Acomodation (b) Accomodation (c) Acommodation (d) Accommodation

38. (a) Inimitable (b) Innimatible (c) Inimitible (d) Inimmitable

39. (a) Refrigerator (b) Refriderater (c) Refridgerator (d) Referigerator

40. (a) Obssesion (b) Obssession (c) Obsession (d) Obsessien

41. (a) Hindrence (b) Hindrance (c) Hinderence (d) Hinderance

42. (a) Conesceintious (b) Conscientous
(c) Conscintous (d) Conscientious

43. (a) Cancelation (b) Cancelletion
(c) Cancellation (d) Cancellasion

44. (a) Equannimity (b) Equinimity
(c) Equanimity (d) Equanimmity

45. (a) Accomplish (b) Ackmplesh
(c) Accompalish (d) Acomplush

46. (a) Occurrance (b) Occurrence
(c) Occurance (d) Occurence

47. (a) Gaurantee (b) Guarantee
(c) Garuntee (d) Guaruntee

48. (a) Parlamentry
(b) Parliamentary
(c) Parlimentry
(d) Parliamentry

49. (a) Itinarary (b) Itenerary
(c) Itinerary (d) Itinarery

50. (a) Tentaitive (b) Tentative
(c) Tentitive (d) Tantitive

Exercise 2

Directions (Q. Nos. 1-50) *In each question below, some words are given, one of which may be wrongly spelt. Find out that word the spelling of which is wrong.*

1. (a) Designation (b) Amature
(c) Controversy (d) Burglar

2. (a) Kitten (b) Cumulative
(c) Justified (d) Inediable

3. (a) Hillock (b) Vilify
(c) Mileage (d) Hillarious

4. (a) Neice (b) Neither
(c) Neigh (d) Rein

5. (a) Adhesive (b) Abusive
(c) Applauce (d) Accomplice

6. (a) Breakage (b) Brevity
(c) Breathless (d) Briliance

7. (a) Explaination (b) Extermination
(c) Exaggeration (d) Expectation

8. (a) Utility (b) Vitality
(c) Specaility (d) Casualty

9. (a) Cruise (b) Deduse
(c) Truce (d) Bruise

10. (a) Believe (b) Relieve
(c) Grieve (d) Decieve

11. (a) Democracy (b) Beaureaucracy
(c) Prophecy (d) Aristocracy

12. (a) Ballistic (b) Baloon
(c) Bulletin (d) Bullock

13. (a) Bearer (b) Governor
(c) Conquerer (d) Admirer

14. (a) Careful (b) Untill
(c) Fulfil (d) Final

15. (a) Knack (b) Knee
(c) Kneed (d) Kneel

16. (a) Adulteration (b) Adulation
(c) Advancement (d) Admittance

17. (a) Perpendicular (b) Boundry
(c) Exaggerate (d) Flourish

18. (a) Hack (b) Hawl
(c) Halve (d) Hark

19. (a) Deficient (b) Efficient
(c) Magnificient (d) Reticent

20. (a) Deep (b) Heap
(c) Sleep (d) Weap

21. (a) Impression (b) Competition
(c) Miscelleneous (d) Reproach

22. (a) Instructor (b) Grammer
(c) Carrier (d) Organiser

23. (a) Conquer (b) Passenger
(c) Variety (d) Retalitate

24. (a) Homogenious (b) Honorarium
(c) Honourable (d) Hooligan

25. (a) Imperative (b) Ilicit
(c) Imminent (d) Immature

26. (a) Teaser (b) Teething
(c) Tedious (d) Teatoteler

27. (a) Indefinite (b) Courteous
(c) Advurtise (d) Periphery

28. (a) Lovible (b) Manageable
(c) Usable (d) Soluble

29. (a) Illegal (b) Illitrate
(c) Illegitimate (d) Illegible

30. (a) Secretry (b) Enunciate
(c) Controversy (d) Campaign

31. (a) Kin (b) Masculine
(c) Muslim (d) Disciplin

32. (a) Conceit (b) Deceit
(c) Receive (d) Percieve

33. (a) Seige (b) Solemn
(c) Syllable (d) Seize

34. (a) Proprietor (b) Personl
(c) Personal (d) Proposal

35. (a) Slight (b) Shoote
(c) Thrift (d) Subtle

36. (a) Beetle (b) Beautician
(c) Bearable (d) Beautifull

37. (a) Anxiety (b) Ankel
(c) Accommodation (d) Allergy

38. (a) Lonesome (b) Lovely
(c) Ludicruous (d) Logical

39. (a) Dairy (b) Dafodil
(c) Dainty (d) Damage

40. (a) Allottee (b) Almighty
(c) Allright (d) Altogether

41. (a) Coupious (b) Cautious
(c) Captious (d) Capricious

42. (a) Birth (b) Beginer
(c) Benefit (d) Banana

43. (a) Weighty (b) Piety
(c) Height (d) Gaeity

44. (a) Magnanimous (b) Magnetism
(c) Manifeasto (d) Magnify

45. (a) Municpality (b) Restaurant
(c) Compartment (d) Approach

46. (a) Jewellry (b) Beneficiary
(c) Military (d) Literary

47. (a) Miscellaneous (b) Precarious
(c) Mischeivous (d) Licentious

48. (a) Referring (b) Openning
(c) Beginning (d) Stopping

49. (a) Handicraft (b) Handbar
(c) Handkerchef (d) Handicap

50. (a) Impediment (b) Judgment
(c) Merriment (d) Embarrassment

Previous Year's Questions

Directions (Q. Nos. 51-55) *Select the word that is spelt correctly.* **[CLAT 2013]**

51. (a) Paraphernalia (b) Paraphrenalia
(c) Parapherenalia (d) Paraphrennalia

52. (a) Enterprenuer (b) Entrepreneur
(c) Entrepenur (d) Enteruepeur

53. (a) Onomaetopoeia (b) Onomoatopoeia
(c) Onomatopoeia (d) Onomatapoeia

54. (a) Hemorhage (b) Haemorhhage
(c) Haemorrhage (d) Hemoorhage

55. (a) Dylexsia (b) Dyslexia
(c) Dislexia (d) Dislecsia

Directions (Q. Nos. 56-60) *Select the word that is spelt correctly.* **[CLAT 2014]**

56. Which of the following spellings is correct?
(a) Concensus (b) Consencus
(c) Consenssus (d) Consensus

57. Which of the following spellings is correct?
(a) Procede (b) Proceed
(c) Proceede (d) Proced

58. Which of the following spellings is correct?
(a) Accommodate (b) Acommodate
(c) Accomodate (d) Acomodate

59. Which of the following spellings is correct 'for a page at the beginning of a book'?
(a) Foreward (b) Forword
(c) Forworde (d) Foreword

60. Which of the following spellings is correct?
(a) Arguement (b) Argument
(c) Arguemant (d) Arguemint

Directions (Q. Nos. 61-65) *In the following questions, find the correctly spelt word.* **[CLAT 2016]**

61. (a) Decieve (b) Diecieve
(c) Deceeve (d) Deceive

62. (a) Inetgereity (b) Integrity
(c) Integerity (d) Intigerity

63. (a) Barisster (b) Berister
(c) Barrister (d) Berrister

64. (a) Sacribegous (b) Sacrilegious
(c) Sacreligious (d) Sacrileguos

65. (a) Collaborate (b) Collaborat
(c) Colaborate (d) Collaborrate

Directions (Q. Nos. 66-75) *Choose the correct spelling from the options given below.* **[CLAT 2017]**

66. (a) Accomedation (b) Accomodation
(c) Acconmodation (d) Accomodation

67. (a) Blashphemy (b) Bleshphemy
(c) Blasphamy (d) Blasphemy

68. (a) Renumaration (b) Remuneration
(c) Remunaration (d) Renumeration

69. (a) Ghallows (b) Gallows
(c) Ghellows (d) Gellows

70. (a) Interrogation (b) Interogation
(c) Interagation (d) Interogetion

71. (a) Gratutious (b) Gratuitus
(c) Gratetious (d) Gratitious

72. (a) Annulmant (b) Annulment
(c) Anulment (d) Annulement

73. (a) Hypothecation (b) Hypthacation
(c) Hyphothecation (d) Hypathecation

74. (a) Abheyance (b) Abeyence
(c) Abhayence (d) Abeyance

75. (a) Moretorium (b) Maratorium
(c) Moratorium (d) Moratarium

Answers

Exercise 1

1	*b*	2	*c*	3	*c*	4	*d*	5	*a*	6	*d*	7	*b*	8	*d*	9	*c*	10	*a*
11	*b*	12	*a*	13	*c*	14	*b*	15	*a*	16	*c*	17	*d*	18	*a*	19	*b*	20	*d*
21	*b*	22	*c*	23	*d*	24	*a*	25	*b*	26	*b*	27	*b*	28	*c*	29	*a*	30	*a*
31	*c*	32	*b*	33	*d*	34	*d*	35	*a*	36	*a*	37	*d*	38	*a*	39	*a*	40	*c*
41	*b*	42	*d*	43	*c*	44	*c*	45	*a*	46	*b*	47	*b*	48	*b*	49	*c*	50	*b*

Exercise 2

1	*b*	2	*d*	3	*d*	4	*a*	5	*c*	6	*d*	7	*a*	8	*c*	9	*b*	10	*d*
11	*b*	12	*b*	13	*c*	14	*b*	15	*c*	16	*a*	17	*b*	18	*b*	19	*c*	20	*d*
21	*c*	22	*b*	23	*d*	24	*a*	25	*b*	26	*d*	27	*c*	28	*a*	29	*b*	30	*a*
31	*d*	32	*d*	33	*a*	34	*b*	35	*b*	36	*d*	37	*b*	38	*c*	39	*b*	40	*c*
41	*a*	42	*b*	43	*d*	44	*c*	45	*a*	46	*a*	47	*c*	48	*b*	49	*c*	50	*b*
51	*a*	52	*a*	53	*c*	54	*c*	55	*b*	56	*d*	57	*b*	58	*a*	59	*d*	60	*b*
61	*d*	62	*b*	63	*c*	64	*b*	65	*a*	66	*b*	67	*d*	68	*b*	69	*b*	70	*a*
71	*a*	72	*c*	73	*c*	74	*c*	75	*d*										

CHAPTER 08

FOREIGN LANGUAGE PHRASES

It order to crack some competitive exams like CLAT and other law entrance exam, a good vocabulary of some foreign language words is essential. CLAT loves challenging you with words of a different origin to test your knowledge

A

Ab Antiquo	From ancient times
Ab Intitio	From the very beginning
Abjure	To renounce on oath or affirmation
Acta Extoriora Indicant Interiora Secreta	Acts indicate the intention
Actus Legis Nemini Facit Injuriam	Law holds no man responsible for the act of god
Actus Non Facit Renum Nisi Mens Sit Rea	A guilt mind is necessary to constitute a crime
Actus Reus	Wrongful act, the physical act of involving in the crime
Ad Hoc	For a particular purpose
Ad Idem	Of the same mind
Ad Referendum	For further consideration
Ad Rem	To the point

B

Bailiff	A subordiante officer of the court who executes writ other court orders
Bona Fide	In good faith, honestly
Bona Vacantia	Goods that do not have an owner. Generally they go to the finder
Boni Judici Est Ansliare Jurisdictioness	It is the part of a good judge to enlarge his jurisdiction

C

Carte Fide	In good faith, honesty
Causa Sine Qua Non	Factor essential to the occurring of event
Caveat	An order given to officers may 'let him beware'
Caveat Emptor	Let the buyer beware
Caveat Venditor	Let the seller beware
Caveat Viator	Let the traveller beware
Certiorari	An order of a higher court which quashes the decision of lower court
Compos Mentis	Of sound mind
Consensus, Non Concubitus, Facit Matrimonium	It is the consent of the parties, not their cohabitation which constitutes a valid marriage

D

De Facto	In fact
De Jure	In law
De Novo	New
Decree	Order of court pronounced after hearing the case
Decree Nisi	A conditional decree
Defeasible Right	Right which can be defeated
Doli Capax	Capable of crime
Doli Incapax	Incapable of crime

E

En Bloc	All at the same time
En Masse	In a body
Ex Aequo Et Bono	In justice and good faith
Ex Contractu	Arising out of contract
Ex Curia	Out of court
Ex Delicto	Arising out of wrong
Ex Gratia	As a favour
Ex Nudo Pacto-Non Oitur Actio	An action does not arise from a bare promise

F

Factum Probantia	Facts which are given in evidence to prove other facts in crime
Faux Pas	Tactless mistake
Flagrante Delicto	In the commission of the offence
Force Majeure	Beyond one's control

G

Generale dictum generaliter est inter pretandum	A general expression is to be construed generally
Generalia specialibus non derogant	General statements/provisions do not derogate from special statements/provisions
Generalibus specialia derogant	Special things derogate from general
Grammatica falsa non vitial chartam	Grammatical error does not vitiate a writing

H

Habeas Corpus	A court order that directs the person to be produced before a court who has been illegally detained beyond twenty four hours before
Honoris Causa	As mark of esteem

I

Ignoratia Juris Non Excusat	Ignorance of law has no excuse
Impasse	An insoluble difficulty
In Curia	In open court
In Loco Parentis	In the place of a parent
In Memoriam	In memory of
In Pari Delicto	Where both parties are equally at fault
In Pari Materia	Where two enactments have a common purpose in an analogous case
In Personam	Proceeding directed against or reference to a specific person

In Re	In the matter of
In Rem	Right available against the world at large
In Situ	In its original situation
In Toto	Wholly
Infra	Below
Injuria Sine Damunum	Legal injury without actual damage

J

Jus	Right
Jus Naturale	Law of nature, natural justice
Judecas Dati	Judges given or appointed
Judex tenetur impertiri judicium suum	A judge is bound to communicate his decision
Judicandum est legibus non exemplis	Judgement must be given by the laws, not by the laws, not by examples
Judicia posteriora sunt in lege fortiora	Later judgments are stronger in law
Jus respicit aequitatem	The law pays regard to equity
Justo tempore	At the right time

L

Laissez Faire	Doctrine of non-interference by state in economy
Lex	Statute
Lex Fori	The law of the court in which the case is tried
Lex Loci	The law of a place

M

Male Fide	With bad faith
Mandamus	We command
Manifesta Probatione Non Indiget	Things manifest do not require proof
Mens Rea	Guilty mind
Mesne	Intermediate
Mesne Profits	Damage payable by trespassers who have stayed in possession after their right to occupy land has ended
Modus Operandi	Mode of operating
Mutatis Mutandis	With necessary changes being made

N

Nemo Tenetur Seipsum Accusore	No man can be compelled to incriminate himself
Nisi	Ineffective unless person affected fails to show cause
Non Assumpsit	He did not promise
Non Compos Mentis	Not of sound mind
Non Obstante	Notwithstanding
Noscitur A Sociis	Meaning of word can be gathered from context
Noscitur A Socvis	Meaning of a doubtful word may be ascertained by reference to the meaning of words associated with it

O

Obiter Dicta	Remark of a judge
Obiter Dictum	Judge's opinion
Ob contingentiam	On account of similarity
Occupantis fiunt derelicta	Things abandoned become the property of the occupier
Omne verbum de ore fideli cadit in debitum	Every word sincerely spoken will constitute obligation
Omnia praesumuntur contra spoliatorem	Every presumption is made against a wrong doer
Optimus interpres rerum usus	Usage is the best interpreter of things
Ore tenus	By word of mouth

P

Par Excellence	Eminently
Pendente Lite	Pending litigation
Per	As stated by
Per Annum	By the year
Per Capita	Individually

Per Curiam	By the court
Per Incuriam	Wrong decision by court, by oversight

Q

Quantum Merit	As a person earned
Quash	Making null or invalid or making end to a legal proceeding
Quasi Contract	A contract between a party comes
Quasi Judicial	Sharing of qualities of and approximating to what is judicial
Qui Facit Per Alium Facit Per Se	He who acts through another is deemed to act in person
Qui Per Alium Facit Per Seipsum Facere Videtur	He who does an act through another is deemed in law to do it himself
Quid Pro Quo	Something for something
Quo Warranto	Order of a court in the form of writ directing the person in authority to show by what right he claims it
Quorum	Minimum number of persons necessary for conduct of proceeding of Parliament
Quo Jure	By what right

R

Raison D'etre	Reason for the existence of a thing
Rapprochement	Restoration of harmonious relations
Ratio Decidendi	Principal laid down by the court in deciding a case
Rebus Sic Stantibus	Binding bill circumstances remain the same
Res Gestae	The facts so connected with a fact in issue so as to explain its nature
Res Judicata	A case already decided

S

Salus Populi Est Suprema Lex	The welfare of the people is the paramount law
Sine Die	Indefinitely
Sine Qua Non	Indispensable condition
Spes Successionis	Mere hope of succeeding to property
Stare Decisis	The principle that decision of courts in previous cases must be followed in subsequent cases of similar nature
Status Quo	To maintain the present state of affairs
Statute	An act of Parliament
Sub Judice	Under judicial consideration or in course of trial
Subpoena	An order of a court to a person to appear and give evidence before it
Sui Generis	The only one of its kind
Suo Moto	On its own
Supra	Above

T

Tort	Civil wrong
Trespass	To pass beyond
Turpis Causa	A base on which no action can be founded, the maxim being *ex turpi causa non oritur actis*

U

Uberrinae Fide	Of the utmost good faith
Ubi Jus Remedium	Where there is a right there is a remedy
Ultra Vires	Beyond the power

V

Vide	Refer to
Vigilantibus, Non Dormientibus, Jura Suveniunt	The law assists those who are vigilant, not those who sleep over their rights
Vis Major	Irresistible force
Void	Have no legal effect
Void Ab Initio	Void from very beginning

Practice Exercise

Directions (Q.Nos. 1-20) *A few foreign language phrases, which are commonly used, are given below. Select the correct meaning of each phrase.*

1. Raison d'etre
(a) Logical conclusion (b) Reason for existence
(c) Free choice (d) Dubious argument

2. Quantum ramifactus
(a) The amount of damage suffered
(b) The amount of damage caused
(c) The amount of damage paid
(d) The amount of damage received

3. Vis-a-vis
(a) Direct (b) Opposite
(c) Face-to-face (d) Agree

4. Ex aquo et bono
(a) In equity and good conscience
(b) For the public good
(c) The thing speaks for itself
(d) In good faith

5. Lex est norma recti
(a) Law is rule of right (b) Law rules the right
(c) Law is a rule of State (d) Law follow equity

6. Ultra vires
(a) Beyond the powers (b) Within the powers
(c) According to law (d) None of these

7. Per jure
(a) To confess (b) To deny
(c) To hide (d) To lie

8. Fait Accompli
(a) Co-accused (b) Co-conspirator
(c) Accomplished fact (d) Supplicable

9. Quid pro quo
(a) Evidence (b) Favourable opinion
(c) Revenge (d) Something in return

10. De facto
(a) Actual (b) Factual (c) Initial (d) Beginning

11. Pro rata
(a) At the rate of (b) At quoted rate
(c) In proportion (d) Beyond all proportion

12. Sine die
(a) Without setting a fixed day
(b) By voice vote
(c) Applying mathematical concepts to solve a difficult problem
(d) Signing legal documents before death

13. Res subjudice
(a) The case has been decided by a court
(b) The case decided by a lower court could be appealed to a higher court
(c) A case has been dismissed by a court
(d) The case is pending before a court

14. Ratio decidendi
(a) A judicial decision
(b) Part of the judgement which possesses authority
(c) Any observation made by the court which goes beyond the requirement of the case
(d) An observation made by a judge

15. Vice versa
(a) In verse (b) Bersatile verse
(c) In consonance with round (d) The other way

16. Status quo
(a) Legally valid (b) Present condition
(c) Social position (d) Side remarks

17. Alibi
(a) Every where (b) Else where
(c) No where (d) Without any excuse

18. Vox populi
(a) A famous personality (b) Popular opinion
(c) A very popular drama (d) Group of people

19. Volte face
(a) To not face (b) To face about
(c) To remain absent (d) To remain present

20. Coup d'etat
(a) A change of government
(b) An abrupt change of government by force
(c) Attack on a country
(d) Formation of a new government

Previous Year's Questions

Directions (Q. Nos. 21-25) *Given below are a few commonly used foreign language phrases, select the correct answer from the four options given below.* **[CLAT 2012]**

21. Mala fide
(a) Generous (b) Bad intention
(c) Trustworthy (d) Genuine

22. Tabula rasa
(a) Clean slate (b) Agitated
(c) Deprived (d) Creative

23. Carte blanche
(a) Slavery (b) Complete discretion
(c) Anarchy (d) Cependent

24. De jure
(a) Illegal (b) Heir
(c) Concerning law (d) Forbidden

25. Raison d'etre
(a) Logical conclusion (b) Reason for existence
(c) Free choice (d) Dubious argument

Directions (Q. Nos. 26-30) *Given below are a few foreign language phrases, which are commonly used. Choose the correct meaning for each of the phrases.* **[CLAT 2013]**

26. El-Dorado
(a) An imaginary place
(b) High altitude
(c) A literary man
(d) A country full of gold and precious stones

27. Quantum ramifactus
(a) The amount of damage suffered
(b) The amount of damage caused
(c) The amount of damage paid
(d) The amount of damage received

28. Corpus delicti
(a) Fake evidence of an offence
(b) Hearsay evidence of an offence
(c) Lack of evidence of an offence
(d) An evidence which constitute an offence

29. Vis-a-vis
(a) Direct (b) Opposite
(c) Face-to-Face (d) Agree

30. Carte blanche
(a) Complete authority
(b) Issue the warrant
(c) No authority
(d) Lack of authority

Directions (Q. Nos. 31-35) *Given below are a few foreign language phrases which are commonly used. Choose the correct meaning for each of the phrases.* **[CLAT 2014]**

31. Ex officio
(a) By virtue of previously held position
(b) Former official
(c) By virtue of office
(d) Outside the office

32. Ultra Vires
(a) Within powers (b) Full powers
(c) Near powers (d) Beyond powers

33. Quid pro quo
(a) Something for nothing
(b) Something for something
(c) Everything for something
(d) Something for everything

34. Corpus juris
(a) Body of judges (b) Group of jurists
(c) Body of law (d) Knowledge of law

Directions (Q. Nos. 35-37) *Given below are a few foreign language phrases, which are commonly used. Choose the correct meaning for each of the phrases.* **[CLAT 2015]**

35. Pro rata
(a) At the rate of (b) At quoted rate
(c) In proportion (d) Beyond all proportion

36. Mala fide
(a) In good faith (b) In bad faith
(c) Without any faith (d) With full faith

37. Alibi
(a) Everywhere (b) Elsewhere
(c) Nowhere (d) Without any excuse

Directions (Q. Nos. 38-39) *Choose the most appropriate option for each of the following questions.* **[CLAT 2016]**

38. 'Amicus curiae' means
(a) one of the judges of the court
(b) a friend of the court
(c) one among the parties to the dispute
(d) one among the expert witnesses in a case

39. 'Ab initio' means
(a) from the beginning
(b) in connection with the future
(c) in continuation with
(d) in defence of a comment

Answers

1	*b*	2	*a*	3	*c*	4	*a*	5	*a*	6	*a*	7	*d*	8	*c*	9	*d*	10	*a*
11	*c*	12	*a*	13	*d*	14	*b*	15	*d*	16	*b*	17	*b*	18	*b*	19	*b*	20	*b*
21	*b*	22	*a*	23	*b*	24	*c*	25	*b*	26	*d*	27	*d*	28	*d*	29	*c*	30	*c*
31	*c*	32	*d*	33	*b*	34	*c*	35	*a*	36	*b*	37	*b*	38	*b*	39	*a*		

MATHEMATICS

CHAPTER 01

NUMBER SYSTEM AND SIMPLIFICATION

A system in which we study different types of numbers, the relationship governing them is called as number system. In the Hindu-Arabic system, we use the symbols 0, 1, 2, 3, 4, 5, 6, 7, 8 and 9, these symbols are called digits. Out of these ten digits, 0 is called an insignificant digit whereas the others are called significant digits.

NUMERALS

A mathematical symbol representing a number in a systematic manner is called a numeral represented by a set of digits.

How to Write a Number To write a number, we put digits from right to left at the places designated as units, tens, hundreds, thousands, ten thousands, lakhs, ten lakhs, crores and ten crores.

Let us see how the number 308761436 is denoted.

Ten crores	Crores	Ten lakhs	Lakhs	Ten thousands	Thousands	Hundreds	Tens	Units
10^8	10^7	10^6	10^5	10^4	10^3	10^2	10^1	10^0
3	0	8	7	6	1	4	3	6

It is read as "Thirty crore eighty seven lakh sixty one thousand four hundred and thirty six."

Face value and Place value of the Digits in a Number.

1. **Face Value** In a numeral, the face value of a digit is the value of the digit itself irrespective of its place in the numeral.
   e.g. In the numeral 486729, the face value of 8 is 8, the face value of 7 is 7, the face value of 6 is 6, the face value of 4 is 4 and so on.
2. **Place Value** In a numeral, the place value of a digit changes according to the change of its place. Look at the following to get the idea of place value of digits in 72843016.
   Place value of $7 \rightarrow 7 \times 10000000 = 70000000$
   Place value of $2 \rightarrow 2 \times 1000000 = 2000000$

Classification of Numbers

1. **Natural numbers** All counting numbers are called natural numbers and it is denoted by N.
   e.g. $N = \{1, 2, 3, 4, 5, ...\}$
2. **Whole numbers** The set of all natural numbers with zero is called the set of whole numbers and it is denoted by W.
   e.g. $W = \{0, 1, 2, 3, ...\}$
3. **Even numbers** The numbers which are divisible by 2 are called even numbers.
   e.g. 2, 4, 6, 8, 10, 12, ... and so on.
4. **Odd numbers** The numbers which are not divisible by 2 are called odd numbers.
   e.g. 1, 3, 5, 7, 9, 11, ... and so on.
5. **Prime numbers** The numbers which have only two factors, 1 and itself are called prime numbers.
   e.g. 2, 3, 5, 7, 11 and so on.
   - 2 is the only even number, which is prime.
   - A prime number is always greater than 1.
6. **Composite numbers** The Numbers which have more than two factors are called composite numbers.
   e.g. 4, 6, 8, 9 and so on.

   1 is neither prime nor composite number.
7. **Integers** Whole numbers and negative numbers together form a set of integers. They are denoted by I.
   e.g.
   $I = \{........, -4, -3, -2, -1, 0, 1, 2, ...\}$
   - {1, 2, 3, 4 ......} are called positive integers.
   - $\{... -4, -3, -2, -1\}$ are called negative integers.
   - 0 is neither positive nor negative integer.
8. **Rational numbers** Numbers which can be expressed in the form of p/q, where $q \neq 0$ and p and q are integers are called rational numbers.
   e.g. $-\frac{9}{25}, \frac{16}{7}, \frac{8}{1}, -\frac{27}{51}$, etc.
9. **Irrational numbers** Numbers which cannot be expressed in the form of p/q, where $q \neq 0$ are called irrational numbers.
   e.g. $\sqrt{2}, 3\sqrt{4} ..., 4.965896, ...$
10. **Real numbers** All rational and irrational numbers together form a set of real numbers.
    e.g. $\frac{7}{9}, \sqrt{2}, \pi, \frac{8}{9}$ etc.

Operations on Numbers

There are four operations performed on numbers *viz*. Addition, Subtraction, Multiplication and Division.

1. Addition

When two or more numbers are combined together, then it is called addition. Addition is denoted by '+' sign.

e.g. $24 + 25 + 30 = 79$

2. Subtraction

When two or more numbers are taken out from a larger number, then it is called subtraction. Subtraction is denoted by '–' sign.

e.g. $400 - 223 = 177$

3. Multiplication

When x is multiplied by 'y', then 'x' is added 'y' times or 'y' is added 'x' times. It is denoted by '$\times$' sign.

e.g. $2 \times 4 = 8$ or $(2+2+2+2) = 8$

or $(4+4) = 8$

4. Division

In the problems of division, we have four quantities, or terms which are

(i) **Dividend** The number which is being divided is known as the dividend.

(ii) **Divisor** The number which is dividing the other number is known as the divisor.

(iii) **Quotient** The answer that comes after dividing the number is known as the quotient.

(iv) **Remainder** The value which is left undivided is known as the remainder.

The relation between the above four terms is expressed in the following way
Dividend = (Divisor × Quotient) + Remainder.

$\frac{\text{Dividend}}{\text{Divisor}}$ is called the operation of division and is denoted by '÷' sign. e.g. $225 \div 25 = \frac{225}{25} = 9$

EXAMPLE 1 On dividing a number by 357, we get 39 as remainder. On dividing the same number by 17, what will be the remainder?

(a) 0 (b) 3 (c) 5 (d) 11

Solution *(c)* Let x be the number and y be the quotient. Then, by using, Dividend = Divisor × Quotient + Remainder

We have, $x = 357 \times y + 39$

$= (17 \times 21 \times y) + (17 \times 2) + 5$

$= 17 \times (21y + 2) + 5$

$\therefore$ Required remainder = 5

Divisibility Rules

A number is said to be divisible by another number, if the quotient obtained is an integer and remainder obtained is zero.

Divisibility Tests	Examples
A number is divisible by 2, if the last digit is 0, 2, 4, 6 or 8.	168 is divisible by 2, since the last digit is 8.
A number is divisible by 3, if the sum of the digits is divisible by 3.	168 is divisible by 3, since the sum of the digits is 15, i.e. (1+ 6+ 8), and 15 is divisible by 3.
A number is divisible by 4, if the number formed by the last two digits is divisible by 4.	316 is divisible by 4, since 16 is divisible by 4.
A number is divisible by 5, if the last digit is either 0 or 5.	195 is divisible by 5, since the last digit is 5.
A number is divisible by 6, if it is divisible by 2 and 3.	168 is divisible by 6, since it is divisible by 2 and it is divisible by 3.
A number is divisible by 8, if the number formed by the last three digits is divisible by 8.	7120 is divisible by 8, since 120 is divisible by 8.
A number is divisible by 9, if the sum of the digits is divisible by 9.	549 is divisible by 9, since the sum of the digits is 18, i.e. (5+ 4+ 9), and 18 is divisible by 9.
A number is divisible by 10, if the last digit is 0.	1470 is divisible by 10, since the last digit is 0.
A number is divisible by 11, if the difference of the sum of its digits at odd places and the sum of its digits at even places is either 0 or divisible by 11.	30426 is divisible by 11, since $(3 + 4 + 6) - (0 + 2)$ $= 13 - 2 = 11$ is divisible by 11.

EXAMPLE 2 If the number 481 * 673 is completely divisible by 9, then the smallest whole number in place of * will be

(a) 2 (b) 5 (c) 6 (d) 7

Solution *(d)* If the number is completely divisible by 9, then sum of its digits must be divisible by 9.

Sum of digits $= (4 + 8 + 1 + * + 6 + 7 + 3)$

$= (29 + *)$,

which must be divisible by 9.

$\therefore$ $* = 7$

EXAMPLE 3 Which one of the following numbers is exactly divisible by 11?

(a) 235641 (b) 245642 (c) 315624 (d) 415624

Solution *(d)* For a number to be divisible by 11, the difference of the sum of its digits at odd places and the sum of its digits at even places must be either 0 or divisible by 11.

Now, $(4 + 5 + 2) - (1 + 6 + 3) = 1$, not divisible by 11.

$(2 + 6 + 4) - (4 + 5 + 2) = 1$, not divisible by 11.

$(4 + 6 + 1) - (2 + 5 + 3) = 1$, not divisible by 11.

$(4 + 6 + 1) - (2 + 5 + 4) = 0$. So, 415624 is divisible by 11.

Finding Unit's Digit

(i) **When number is given in the form of product of number** To find the unit's digit in the product of two or more numbers, we take unit's digit of every number and then multiply them. Then, the unit's digit of the resultant product is the unit's digit of the product of original numbers.

(ii) **When number is given in the form of a^b**, we have two cases

Case I When b is a multiple of 4.

- If a is an even number i.e. 2, 4, 6 or 8, then the unit's place digit is 6.
- If a is an odd number i.e. 1, 3, 7 or 9, then the unit's place digit is 1.

Case II When b is not a multiple of 4.

- Let r be the remainder when b is divided by 4, then unit's place digit of a^b will be equal to unit's place digit of a^r.

EXAMPLE 4 The unit digit in the product $(784 \times 618 \times 917 \times 463)$ is

(a) 6 (b) 2 (c) 4 (d) 8

Solution *(b)* Unit digit in the given product

$= \text{Unit digit in } (4 \times 8 \times 7 \times 3)$

$= \text{Unit digit in } (672) = 2$

EXAMPLE 5 What is the unit in $(4137)^{756}$?

(a) 1 (b) 3 (c) 7 (d) 9

Solution *(a)* Here, 756 is divisible by 4 and 4137 is odd.

Hence, Unit digit in $(4137)^{756}$ is 1.

FACTOR AND MULTIPLE

1. **Factor** A number which can divide a given number exactly, is called a factor of that number.
2. **Multiple** A number which is divisible by a given number is called multiple of that number.

HCF (Highest Common Factor)

The HCF of two or more than two numbers is the greatest number which divides each of them without any remainder.

There are two methods to find out the HCF of the given numbers. There are as follow

Method I Prime Factorisation Method

Express each one of the given numbers as the product of the prime factors. The product of least powers of common prime factors gives HCF.

e.g. $24 = 2 \times 2 \times 2 \times 3$

$36 = 2 \times 2 \times 3 \times 3$

and $72 = 2 \times 2 \times 2 \times 3 \times 3$

HCF = Product of common factors with least power $= 2 \times 2 \times 3 = 12$

Method II Division Method

Step I Divide the larger number by smaller number.

Step II Take remainder (as obtained in step I) as divisor and the last divisor as the dividend.

Step III Repeat step II until 0 is obtained as remainder. The last divisor will be the required HCF.

e.g.

$$\begin{array}{l} 24)84(3 \\ \quad\ \ 72 \\ \hline 12)24(2 \\ \quad\ \ 24 \\ \hline \quad\ \ \times \end{array}$$

So, HCF of 24 and 84 is 12.

To find HCF of more than two numbers, first find the HCF of first two numbers by any of two methods.

Next, find HCF of the third number and previously found HCF. Similarly, it can be done for any number of numbers.

LCM (Least Common Multiple)

The least number which is exactly divisible by two or more given numbers is called LCM of those numbers.

Prime Factorisation Method

***Step* I** Find prime factors of each of the given number.

***Step* II** Find the product of all the prime factors which appears greatest number of times in the prime factorisation of any given numbers. The product is the required LCM.

e.g $72 = 2 \times 2 \times 2 \times 3 \times 3$

$240 = 2 \times 2 \times 2 \times 2 \times 3 \times 5$

$\therefore$ $\text{LCM} = 2 \times 2 \times 2 \times 2 \times 3 \times 3 \times 5 = 720$

Product of numbers = LCM × HCF

EXAMPLE 6 The HCF of two numbers is 11 and their LCM is 7700. If one of the numbers is 275, then the other is

(a) 279 (b) 283
(c) 308 (d) 318

Solution *(c)* Other number $= \left(\dfrac{11 \times 7700}{275}\right) = 308$

EXAMPLE 7 Five bells first begin to toll together and then at intervals of 3, 5, 7, 8 and 10 s. Find after what interval they will again tall together. How many times do they toll together in one hour?

(a) 14 min; 3 times
(b) 12 min; 4 times
(c) 14 min; 4 times
(d) 12 min; 3 times

Solution *(b)* Required time interval = LCM of 3, 5, 7, 8 and 10 = 840 s = 14 min

$\therefore$ Number of times they will together in one hour

$= \dfrac{60}{14} = 4$ time

[ignoring the fraction part]

Arithmetic Series

Arithmetic series or arithmetic progression is a sequence of numbers such that the difference between the consecutive terms is constant.

e.g. The sequence of 5, 7, 9, 11, 13, 15, ... is an arithmetic series with common difference of 2. The general form of an arithmetic series is $a, a+d, a+2d, a+3d, \ldots$, where a = First term and d = Common difference = Second term – First term

- nth term, $T_n = a + (n-1)d$
- Sum of n terms, $S_n = \dfrac{n}{2}[2a + (n-1)d]$

$= \dfrac{n}{2}[a + l]$, where l is the last term.

EXAMPLE 8 Find the sum of all positive multiples of 3 less than 50.

(a) 400 (b) 404 (c) 408 (d) 412

Solution *(c)* Multiples of 3 upto 50 are

3, 6, 9, 12, ..., 42, 45, 48

The terms form an AP consisting of 16 terms, then

We have, $n = 16, a = 3, l = 48$

$\therefore$ Sum of AP $= \dfrac{n}{2}(a + l) = \dfrac{16}{2}(3 + 48) = 8 \times 51$

$= 408$

EXAMPLE 9 Which term of the sequence $\dfrac{1}{2}, -\dfrac{1}{4}, \dfrac{1}{8}, -\dfrac{1}{16}, \ldots$ is $-\dfrac{1}{256}$?

(a) 9th (b) 8th (c) 7th (d) 5th

Solution *(b)* The sequence is

$$\frac{1}{2}, -\frac{1}{2^2}, \frac{1}{2^3}, -\frac{1}{2^4}, \ldots, \frac{1}{-2^8}$$

It is a GP, where first term, $a = \dfrac{1}{2}$

and common ratio, $r = -\dfrac{1}{2}$

Let T_n term be $\dfrac{-1}{256}$.

$\because$ nth term of GP is given by $T_n = ar^{n-1}$

$\therefore$ $\dfrac{-1}{256} = \dfrac{1}{2} \cdot \left(\dfrac{-1}{2}\right)^{n-1}$

$\Rightarrow$ $\dfrac{1}{-2^7} = \dfrac{1}{(-2)^{n-1}} \Rightarrow n - 1 = 7 \Rightarrow n = 8$

EXAMPLE 10 The nth term of the sequence $\frac{1}{n}, \frac{n+1}{n}, \frac{2n+1}{n}, \ldots$ is

(a) $\frac{n^2+1}{n}$ (b) $\frac{n^2-n+1}{n}$

(c) $n+1$ (d) 2

Solution *(b)* The sequence is $\frac{1}{n}, \frac{n+1}{n}, \frac{2n+1}{n}, \ldots$ in AP, where first term, $a = \frac{1}{n}$ and common difference,

$$d = \frac{n+1}{n} - \frac{1}{n} = \frac{n+1-1}{n} = 1$$

$\therefore$ nth term of the sequence,

$$T_n = a + (n-1)d$$

$$= \frac{1}{n} + (n-1) \cdot 1 = \frac{1+n^2-n}{n} = \frac{n^2-n+1}{n}$$

Some Important Results

- Sum of first n natural numbers $= \frac{n(n+1)}{2}$
- Sum of first n odd natural numbers $= n^2$
- Sum of first n even natural numbers $= n(n+1)$
- Sum of square of first n natural numbers $= \frac{n(n+1)(2n+1)}{6}$
- Sum of cubes of first n natural numbers $= \left[\frac{n(n+1)}{2}\right]^2$

EXAMPLE 11 The sum of all the natural numbers from 51 to 100 is

(a) 5050 (b) 4275 (c) 4025 (d) 3775

Solution *(d)* Required sum = (Sum of natural numbers from 1 to 100) − (Sum of natural numbers from 1 to 50)

$\because$ Sum of $[1+2+3+4+\ldots+100] = \frac{n(n+1)}{2}$

$$= \frac{100(101)}{2} = 5050$$

and sum of $[1+2+3+4+\ldots+50] = \frac{n(n+1)}{2}$

$$= \frac{50(51)}{2} = 1275$$

Hence, sum of $[51+52+53+\ldots+100]$
$= 5050 - 1275 = 3775$

EXAMPLE 12 The sum of first 20 odd natural numbers is equal to

(a) 210 (b) 300 (c) 400 (d) 420

Solution *(c)* Sum of first n odd numbers $= n^2$

Here, $n = 20$

$\therefore$ Required sum $= (20)^2 = 400$

EXAMPLE 13 $1^2 + 2^2 + 3^2 + \ldots + 10^2$ is equal to

(a) 380 (b) 385 (c) 390 (d) 392

Solution *(b)* By the formula,

Sum of squares of first n natural numbers

$$= \frac{n(n+1)(2n+1)}{6}$$

$$= \frac{10(10+1)(20+1)}{6} = 385$$

EXAMPLE 14 $(1^3 + 2^3 + 3^3 + \ldots + 9^3 + 10^3)$ is equal to

(a) 3575 (b) 2525 (c) 5075 (d) 3025

Solution *(d)* Sum of cubes of first n natural numbers

$$= \left[\frac{n(n+1)}{2}\right]^2$$

$\therefore 1^3 + 2^3 + 3^3 + \ldots + 9^3 + 10^3$

$$= \left[\frac{10 \times (10+1)}{2}\right]^2 \quad [\because n = 10]$$

$$= \left[\frac{10 \times 11}{2}\right]^2 = (55)^2 = 55 \times 55 = 3025$$

VBODMAS RULE

VBODMAS is a rule which helps us to know the correct order to perform operations within complex sums.

The meaning of 'VBODMAS' is

V → Vinculum or line bar
B → Bracket
O → Of
D → Division
M → Multiplication
A → Addition
S → Subtraction

(i) Order of the letters which is used in this rule, is always fixed and absence of any operation or more than the one operation does not change the order of the rule.

(ii) There can be more than one bracket present in a problem. If these brackets are to be given one inside the other, we use different brackets in a fixed order. If all the brackets are used in a problem, then they will be placed as [{(–)}]. We start from solving inside brackets.

EXAMPLE 15 Simplify $240 \div 8 \times 512 + \frac{1}{2}$ of $\{1800 \div (11 \times 24 \div 8 \times 3 - 69)^2\}$.

(a) 15361 (b) 15360
(c) 12695 (d) 28492

Solution *(a)* We will apply 'VBODMAS' rule step-by-step

$240 \div 8 \times 512 + \frac{1}{2}$ of $\{1800 \div (11 \times 24 \div 8 \times 3 - 69)^2\}$

$= 240 \div 8 \times 512 + \frac{1}{2}$ of $\{1800 \div (11 \times 3 \times 3 - 69)^2\}$ (solving circular brackets first)

$= 240 \div 8 \times 512 + \frac{1}{2}$ of $\{1800 \div (99 - 69)^2\}$

$= 240 \div 8 \times 512 + \frac{1}{2}$ of $\{1800 \div 900\}$

$= 240 \div 8 \times 512 + \frac{1}{2}$ of 2 (solve curly brackets)

$= 240 \div 8 \times 512 + \frac{1}{2} \times 2$ (solve 'of')

$= 240 \div 8 \times 512 + 1$

$= 30 \times 512 + 1$ (solve 'division')

$= 15360 + 1$ (solve 'multiplication')

$= 15361$ (solve 'addition')

EXAMPLE 16 Simplify $108 \div 36$ of $\frac{1}{4} + \frac{2}{5} \times 3\frac{1}{4}$.

(a) $2\frac{6}{5}$ (b) $\frac{18}{23}$ (c) $13\frac{3}{10}$ (d) $\frac{11}{10}$

Solution *(c)* We have $108 \div 36$ of $\frac{1}{4} + \frac{2}{5} \times 3\frac{1}{4}$

$= 108 \div 9 + \frac{2}{5} \times \frac{13}{4}$

$= \frac{108}{9} + \frac{13}{10} = 12 + \frac{13}{10}$

$= \frac{133}{10} = 13\frac{3}{10}$

Important Formulae

(i) $(a + b)^2 = a^2 + 2ab + b^2$
(ii) $(a - b)^2 = aa^2 - 2ab + b^2$
(iii) $(a + b)^2 - (a - b)^2 = 4ab$
(iv) $(a + b)^2 + (a - b)^2 = 2(a^2 + b^2)$
(v) $(a^2 - b^2) = (a + b)(a - b)$
(vi) $(a + b)^3 = a^3 + b^3 + 3ab(a + b)$
(vii) $(a - b)^3 = a^3 - b^3 - 3ab(a - b)$
(viii) $(a^3 + b^3) = (a + b)(a^2 - ab + b^2)$
(ix) $(a^3 - b^3) = (a - b)(a^2 + ab + b^2)$
(x) $(a + b + c)^2 = a^2 + b^2 + c^2 + 2(ab + bc + ca)$
(xi) $(a^3 + b^3 + c^3 - 3abc) = (a + b + c)(a^2 + b^2 + bc^2 - ab - bc - ca)$

EXAMPLE 17 Simplify

$$\frac{0.3 \times 0.3 + 0.03 \times 0.03 - 0.6 \times 0.03}{0.54}.$$

(a) 0.03 (b) 9.37 (c) 0.982 (d) 0.135

Solution *(d)* We have,

$0.3 \times 0.3 + 0.03 \times 0.03 - 0.6 \times 0.03$
$= 0.3 \times 0.3 + 0.03 \times 0.03 - 2 \times 0.3 \times 0.03$

is of the form $(a^2 + b^2 - 2ab) = (a - b)^2$

where, $a = 0.3$ and $b = 0.03$

$\Rightarrow (0.3 - 0.03)^2 = (0.27)^2$

$\therefore$ Given expression $= \frac{0.27 \times 0.27}{0.54} = 0.135$

EXAMPLE 18 Simplify

$$\left(\frac{2.75 \times 2.75 \times 2.75 - 2.25 \times 2.25 \times 2.25}{2.75 \times 2.75 + 2.75 \times 2.25 + 2.25 \times 2.25}\right).$$

(a) 0.30 (b) 0.50 (c) 3 (d) 5

Solution *(b)* We have, $\frac{(2.75)^3 - (2.25)^3}{(2.75)^2 + 2.75 \times 2.25 + (2.25)^2}$

$= \frac{a^3 - b^3}{a^2 + ab + b^2}$,

where $a = 2.75$ and $b = 2.25$

$= \frac{(a - b)(a^2 + ab + b^2)}{a^2 + ab + b^2} = (2.75 - 2.25) = 0.50$

EXAMPLE 19 Simplify

$$\frac{(2.697 - 0.498)^2 + (2.697 + 0.498)^2}{2.697 \times 2.697 + 0.498 \times 0.498}.$$

(a) 2.199 (b) 2.195 (c) 2 (d) $\frac{1}{2}$

Solution *(c)* Take, $a = 2.697$ and $b = 0.498$, then

$$= \frac{(a-b)^2 + (a+b)^2}{a^2 + b^2} = \frac{2(a^2 + b^2)}{a^2 + b^2} = 2$$

INDICES

An index is the power or exponent of a number. In the expression x^n, n is called the exponent or index and x is called the base and x^n is read as 'x to the power of n' or 'x raised to the power n'.

Laws of Indices

1. $a^m \times a^n = a^{m+n}$
2. $\frac{a^m}{a^n} = a^{m-n}$ where $a \neq 0$
3. $(a^m)^n = a^{mn}$
4. $(ab)^m = a^m b^m$
5. $\left(\frac{a}{b}\right)^m = \frac{a^m}{b^m}$, where $b \neq 0$
6. $a^0 = 1$, where $a \neq 0$
7. $a^{-n} = \frac{1}{a^n}$, where $a \neq 0$
8. $a^{m^n} \neq (a^m)^n$
9. When the base of two numbers are equal, then their powers are also equal and *vice-versa*.
   e.g. (i) If $3^a = 3^2$, then $a = 2$
   (ii) If $b^3 = 4^3$, then $b = 4$
   where, b is a positive real number.

EXAMPLE 20 Simplify $2^{25} \times 2^{35} - 2^{20} \times 2^{40}$.

(a) 0 (b) 1 (c) 2 (d) 3

Solution *(a)* $2^{25} \times 2^{35} - 2^{20} \times 2^{40} = 2^{25+35} - 2^{20+40}$

$(\because a^m \times a^n = a^{m+n})$

$= 2^{60} - 2^{60} = 0$

EXAMPLE 21 If $2^{x-7} \cdot 5^{x-4} = 1250$, then find x.

(a) 9 (b) 10 (c) 8 (d) 11

Solution *(c)* We have, $2^{x-7} \cdot 5^{x-4} = 1250$

$\Rightarrow \quad 2^{x-7} \cdot 5^{x-4} = 1250 = 2^1 \times 5^4$

$\Rightarrow \quad x - 7 = 1$ and $x - 4 = 4$

(by comparing on both sides)

$\Rightarrow \quad x = 8$ and $x = 8$

Hence, $x = 8$

SURDS

If n is a positive integer and a is a positive rational number ($a > 0$), then $\sqrt[n]{a}$ is called a surd of order n or nth order surd if $\sqrt[n]{a}$ is an irrational number. Here, the symbol '$\sqrt{\ }$' is called radical sign and a is called the radicand.

e.g. $\sqrt{2}, 3\sqrt{8}, a - \sqrt{b}$, etc.

All surds are irrational numbers.

Laws of Surds

1. $a^{\frac{1}{n}} = \sqrt[n]{a}$ is called the nth root of a
2. $\sqrt[n]{a} \times \sqrt[n]{b} = \sqrt[n]{ab}$
3. $\frac{\sqrt[n]{a}}{\sqrt[n]{b}} = \sqrt[n]{\frac{a}{b}}$
4. $\sqrt[m]{\sqrt[n]{a}} = \sqrt[mn]{a} = \sqrt[n]{\sqrt[m]{a}}$
5. $\sqrt[n]{a^p} = a^{\frac{p}{n}} = \sqrt[mn]{a^{pm}}$
6. $(\sqrt[n]{a})^n = a$

EXAMPLE 22 The value of $\sqrt[3]{512} + \sqrt[4]{16} - \sqrt{576}$, is

(a) 6 (b) −14 (c) −12 (d) 18

Solution *(b)* We have, $\sqrt[3]{512} + \sqrt[4]{16} - \sqrt{576}$

$= (512)^{1/3} + (16)^{1/4} - (576)^{1/2}$

$= (8)^{3\times1/3} + (2)^{4\times1/4} - (24)^{2\times1/2}$

$= 8 + 2 - 24 = -14$

EXAMPLE 23 Simplify $\left(\sqrt[3]{\sqrt[6]{2^9}}\right)^4 \times \left(\sqrt[6]{\sqrt[3]{2^9}}\right)^4$.

(a) 32 (b) 20 (c) 16 (d) 14

Solution *(c)* We have, $\left(\sqrt[3]{\sqrt[6]{2^9}}\right)^4 \times \left(\sqrt[6]{\sqrt[3]{2^9}}\right)^4$

$= \left(2^{9\times\frac{1}{6}\times\frac{1}{3}\times4}\right) \times \left(2^{9\times\frac{1}{3}\times\frac{1}{6}\times4}\right)$

$= (2)^2 \times (2)^2$

$= 2^{2+2} = 2^4 = 16$

Rationalisation of a Surd

The process of reducing a given surd to a rational form after multiplying it by a suitable 'surd' is known as 'Rationalisation'.

If the product of two surds is rational, then each of the two surds is called a rationalising factor of the another. In general, if the surd is of type $a+\sqrt{b}$, then its rationalising factor is $a-\sqrt{b}$. The rationalising factor of a surd is not unique.

Rationalising Factors of a Given Surd

(i) Rationalising factor of $\frac{1}{\sqrt{a}} = \sqrt{a}$

(ii) Rationalising factor of $\frac{1}{a \pm \sqrt{b}} = a \mp \sqrt{b}$

(iii) Rationalising factor of $\frac{1}{\sqrt{a} \pm \sqrt{b}} = \sqrt{a} \mp \sqrt{b}$

EXAMPLE 24 Rationalise the denominator of $\left(\frac{\sqrt{5}+\sqrt{3}}{\sqrt{5}-\sqrt{3}}\right)$.

(a) $4+\sqrt{15}$ (b) $4-\sqrt{15}$
(c) $2\sqrt{5}+2\sqrt{3}$ (d) $2\sqrt{5}-2\sqrt{3}$

Solution *(a)* We have,

$$\frac{\sqrt{5}+\sqrt{3}}{\sqrt{5}-\sqrt{3}} = \frac{\sqrt{5}+\sqrt{3}}{\sqrt{5}-\sqrt{3}} \times \frac{\sqrt{5}+\sqrt{3}}{\sqrt{5}+\sqrt{3}}$$

$$= \frac{(\sqrt{5}+\sqrt{3})^2}{(\sqrt{5})^2-(\sqrt{3})^2} = \frac{5+3+2\sqrt{15}}{5-3}$$

$$= \frac{8+2\sqrt{15}}{2} = 4+\sqrt{15}$$

SQUARE ROOT

The square root of a number is a number which when multiplied with itself gives the original number. e.g. The square root of 400 is 20, the square root of 625 is 25. The square root of a number is denoted by the symbol '$\sqrt{\ }$' called the radical sign. The expression '$\sqrt{9}$' is read as 'root nine', 'radical nine' or 'the square root of nine'.

To find the square root, there are two methods which are given below

1. **By the method of prime factorisation** When a given number is a perfect square, we resolve it into prime factors and take the product of prime factors, choosing one out of every two.
2. **By the method of long division** This method can be used when the number is large and the factors cannot be determined easily. This method can also be used when we want to add a least number or to subtract a least number from a given number, so that the resulting number may give a perfect square.

Steps of Long Division Method

***Step* I** Group the digits in pairs, starting with the digit in the unit place. Each pair and the remaining digit (if any) is called a period.

***Step* II** Think of the largest number whose square is equal to or just less than the first period. Take this number as the divisor and also as the quotient.

***Step* III** Subtract the product of the divisor and the quotient from the first period and bring down the next period to the right of the remainder. This becomes the new dividend.

***Step* IV** Now, the new divisor is obtained by taking two times the quotient and annexing with it a suitable digit which is also taken as the next digit of the quotient, chosen in such a way that the product of the new divisor and this digit is equal to or just less than the new dividend.

***Step* V** Repeat steps (II), (III) and (IV) till all the periods have been taken up. Now, the quotient so obtained is the required square root of the given number.

EXAMPLE 25 Find the square root of 156816.

(a) 396 (b) 287 (c) 284 (d) 354

Solution *(a)* ***Step* I** Group the digits in pairs, starting with the digit in the unit place.

$\overline{15}\,\overline{68}\,\overline{16}$

***Step* II** Find the largest square number less than or equal to 15.

Since, $3^2 < 15$ and $4^2 > 15$

$\therefore$ 3 is the number.

So, our divisor and quotient are 3.

	3
3	156816
	9
	6

Step **III** Now, bring down the next period and take it as the new dividend.

	3
3	156816
	9 ↓
	668

Step **IV** Now, obtain a new divisor by doubling the quotient (i.e. $2 \times 3 = 6$) and annexing with it a suitable digit.

Here, $69 \times 9 = 621 < 668$

	39
3	156816
	9
69	668
	621
	4716

Step **V** Now, new dividend is 4716 and new divisor is 786 as $786 \times 6 = 4716$

13	1568169	396
69	668	
	621	
786	4716	
	4716	
	×	

So, $\sqrt{156816} = 396$

EXAMPLE 26 Find the square root of 4356.

(a) 34 (b) 66 (c) 11 (d) 26

Solution (*b*) Resolving 4356 as the product of primes, we get

2	4356
2	2178
3	1089
3	363
11	121
	11

$\Rightarrow \quad 4356 = 2 \times 2 \times 3 \times 3 \times 11 \times 11$

Now, choose one factor from each pair and take the product of these factors.

$\therefore \quad \sqrt{4356} = 2 \times 3 \times 11 = 66$

CUBE ROOT

The cube root of a number is a number which when multiplied with itself twice gives the original number, i.e. the cube root of 64 is 4. The cube root of a number is denoted by the symbol $\sqrt[3]{\ }$. The expression $\sqrt[3]{8}$ is read as the 'cube root of eight'. To find the cube root, the following method is used

By the method of prime factors When a given number is a perfect cube, we resolve it into prime factors and then write the factors in a group of three of same prime numbers. Then, take the product of a prime number from each group. It will give the cube root of the original number.

EXAMPLE 27 Find the cube root of 74088.

(a) 3 (b) 6 (c) 42 (d) 11

Solution (*c*) Resolving 74088 as the product of primes, we get

2	74088
2	37044
2	18522
3	9261
3	3087
3	1029
7	343
7	49
7	7

$\Rightarrow \quad 74088 = 2 \times 2 \times 2 \times 3 \times 3 \times 3 \times 7 \times 7 \times 7$

Now, choose one factor from each pair and take the product of these factors.

$\therefore \quad \sqrt[3]{74088} = 2 \times 7 \times 3 = 42$

EXAMPLE 28 Find the smallest number by which 2400 should be divided to make it a perfect cube.

(a) 220 (b) 300 (c) 385 (d) 260

Solution (*b*) By prime factorisation,

$$2400 = 2^5 \times 5^2 \times 3$$

To make it a perfect cube, it must be divided by $2^2 \times 5^2 \times 3 = 300$

Practice Exercise

1. The difference between the place values of two 7s in the numeral 69758472 is
(a) 0 (b) 6993
(c) 699930 (d) None of these

2. Which one of the following is not a prime number?
(a) 31 (b) 61 (c) 71 (d) 91

3. The smallest 6-digit number exactly divisible by 111 is
(a) 111111 (b) 110011
(c) 100011 (d) 110101

4. The largest 5-digit number exactly divisible by 91 is
(a) 99921 (b) 99918
(c) 99981 (d) 99971

5. Which one of the following numbers is completely divisible by 99?
(a) 3572404 (b) 135792
(c) 913464 (d) 114345

6. Which natural number is nearest to 9217 which is completely divisible by 88?
(a) 9152 (b) 9240
(c) 9064 (d) 9184

7. n is a whole number which when divided by 4 gives 3 as remainder. What will be the remainder when $2n$ is divided by 4?
(a) 3 (b) 2
(c) 1 (d) 0

8. 476** 0 is divisible by both 3 and 11. The non-zero digits in the hundred's and ten's places are respectively
(a) 7 and 4 (b) 7 and 5
(c) 8 and 5 (d) None of these

9. Which of the following numbers will completely divide $(49^{15} - 1)$?
(a) 8 (b) 14 (c) 48 (d) 50

10. A number divided by 56 gives 29 as remainder. If the same number is divided by 8, the remainder will be
(a) 4 (b) 5 (c) 6 (d) 7

11. When a number is divided by 779, we get a remainder of 47. What remainder will be obtained by dividing the same number by 19?
(a) 6 (b) 7 (c) 9 (d) 11

12. What smallest number should be added to 4456, so that the sum is completely divisible by 6?
(a) 4 (b) 3 (c) 2 (d) 1

13. Which of the following numbers should be added to 11158 to make it exactly divisible by 77?
(a) 9 (b) 8 (c) 7 (d) 5

14. The greatest number which on dividing 1657 and 2037 leaves remainders 6 and 5 respectively, is
(a) 123 (b) 127 (c) 235 (d) 305

15. Three numbers which are coprimes to each other are such that the product of the first two is 551 and that of the last two is 1073. The sum of the three numbers is
(a) 75 (b) 81
(c) 85 (d) 89

16. The smallest number which is divided by 9, 12 and 16, each time 5 remains. The number is
(a) 149 (b) 144
(c) 197 (d) 113

17. Three consecutive positive even numbers are such that thrice the first number exceeds double the third by 2, the third number is
(a) 10 (b) 14
(c) 16 (d) 12

18. If x and y are positive integers such that $(3x + 7y)$ is a multiple of 11, then which of the following will be divisible by 11?
(a) $4x + 6y$ (b) $x + y + 4$
(c) $9x + 4y$ (d) $4x - 9y$

19. The sum of three numbers is 132. If the first number be twice the second and third number be one-third of the first, then the second number is
(a) 32 (b) 34 (c) 36 (d) 24

20. Number of students who have opted for the subjects A, B and C are 60, 84 and 108 respectively.The examination is to be conducted for these students such that only the students of the same subject are allowed in one room. Also the number of students in each room must be same. What is the minimum number of rooms that should be arranged to meet all these conditions?

(a) 28 (b) 60 (c) 12 (d) 21

21. The unit digit in the product $(784 \times 618 \times 917 \times 463)$ is

(a) 2 (b) 3 (c) 4 (d) 5

22. Unit's place digit in $(122)^{173}$ is

(a) 2 (b) 4 (c) 6 (d) 8

23. On dividing a number by 68, we get 269 as quotient and 0 as remainder. On dividing the same number by 67, what will the remainder?

(a) 0 (b) 1 (c) 2 (d) 3

24. LCM of 22, 54, 108, 135, 198 is

(a) 330 (b) 1980 (c) 5940 (d) 11880

25. Three numbers are in the ratio of 3:4:5 and their LCM is 2400. Then, their HCF is

(a) 40 (b) 80 (c) 120 (d) 200

26. Six bells commence tolling together and toll at intervals of 2, 4, 6,8, 10 and 12s respectively. In 30 min, how many times do they toll together?

(a) 4 (b)10 (c) 15 (d) 16

27. The product of two numbers is 4107. If the HCF of these numbers is 37, then the greater number is

(a) 101 (b) 107 (c) 111 (d) 185

28. The ratio then, of two numbers is 3:4 and their HCF is 4 their LCM is

(a) 12 (b) 16 (c) 24 (d) 48

29. The sum of the three numbers in AP is 21 and the product of the first and third number of the sequence is 45. What are the three numbers?

(a) 5, 7 and 9 (b) 9, 7 and 5
(c) 3, 7 and 11 (d) Both (a) and (b)

30. In AP find 4 + 7 + 10 + 13 + 16 + ... upto 20 terms

(a) 750 (b) 854 (c) 650 (d) 740

31. In GP find $1 + \frac{1}{2} + \frac{1}{4} + \ldots$ up to 5 terms.

(a) $1\frac{16}{15}$ (b) $2\frac{15}{16}$ (c) $1\frac{15}{16}$ (d) $2\frac{16}{15}$

32. Simplify $\frac{23}{19} \times \frac{19}{17} \times 85$.

(a) 110 (b) 125
(c) 115 (d) 120

33. $\left(\frac{1}{2} - \frac{1}{3}\right) + \left(\frac{1}{3} - \frac{1}{4}\right) + \left(\frac{1}{4} + \frac{1}{2}\right)$ is equal to

(a) 0 (b) $\frac{1}{4}$ (c) $\frac{1}{2}$ (d) 1

34. Simplify $\left(\sqrt{\frac{625}{784}} - \sqrt{\frac{16}{49}}\right) \div \left(\sqrt{\frac{81}{144}}\right)$.

(a) $\frac{2}{7}$ (b) $\frac{3}{7}$ (c) $\frac{6}{7}$ (d) $\frac{5}{7}$

35. Simplify $15.876 - (2.49 + 4.056) \div \frac{1}{2}$.

(a) 2.784 (b) 3.052
(c) 2.984 (d) 3.152

36. Simplify $\frac{0.48 \div 0.12 + 0.04 \times 25}{0.05}$.

(a) 100 (b) 110 (c) 90 (d) 105

37. Find P in the expression, if $\frac{P}{1 + \frac{1}{1 + \frac{P}{1-P}}} = 1$.

(a) 2 (b) $\frac{1}{4}$ (c) 1 (d) $\frac{1}{2}$

38. Simplify $\frac{\frac{3}{2} \div \frac{1}{2} \times \frac{3}{2}}{\frac{3}{2} \div \frac{1}{2} \text{ of } \frac{3}{2}} \div \frac{1}{8}$.

(a) 18 (b) 21 (c) 16 (d) 24

39. The value of $\frac{2125 \times 2125 \times 2125 + 875 \times 875 \times 875}{2125 \times 2125 - 2125 \times 875 + 875 \times 875}$ is

(a) 2×10^3 (b) 3×10^3 (c) 1×10^3 (d) 4×10^3

40. The value of $\frac{(4.256 - 1.744)^2 + (4.256 + 1.744)^2}{4.256 \times 4.256 + 1.744 \times 1.744}$ is

(a) 8 (b) 2
(c) 4 (d) 6

41. If $27^x = \frac{9}{3^x}$, then the value of x is

(a) $\frac{1}{2}$ (b) 1
(c) $\frac{3}{2}$ (d) None of these

42. The value of $\frac{5^n + 5^{n-1}}{5^{n+1} - 5^n}$ is equal to

(a) 0.1 (b) 0.2
(c) 0.3 (d) None of these

43. If $2^{x-7} \times 5^{x-4} = 1250$, then x is equal to

(a) 2 (b) 4 (c) 6 (d) 8

44. $\frac{x^{a(b-c)}}{x^{b(a-c)}} \div \left(\frac{x^b}{x^a}\right)^c$ is equal to

(a) 1 (b) 2
(c) 3 (d) None of these

45. $\frac{(x^{a+b})^2 (x^{b+c})^2 (x^{c+a})^2}{(x^a x^b x^c)^4}$ is equal to

(a) 1 (b) 2
(c) 3 (d) None of these

46. $8^{\frac{2}{3}} - 16^{\frac{1}{4}} + 9^{\frac{1}{2}}$ is equal to

(a) 3 (b) 5 (c) $\sqrt{2}$ (d) $\sqrt{2} + \sqrt{3}$

47. If $9^{2x-1} = 27^{x+2}$, then x is equal to

(a) 2 (b) 4 (c) 8 (d) 16

48. $\left(\sqrt{2}^{\sqrt{2}}\right)^{\sqrt{2}} = 2^x$, then x is equal to

(a) 4 (b) 2 (c) 1 (d) $\sqrt{2}$

49. $\frac{5^{2/3} \times \sqrt[3]{5^8}}{\sqrt[3]{5^7}}$ is equal to

(a) 5 (b) 25 (c) $\sqrt[3]{5}$ (d) 1

50. The square root of 104976 is

(a) 322 (b) 324 (c) 326 (d) 328

51. The square root of 906.01 is

(a) 30.1 (b) 31.1 (c) 30.11 (d) 31.11

52. The value of $\sqrt{17 + \sqrt{51 + \sqrt{152 + \sqrt{289}}}}$ is

(a) 11 (b) 5 (c) 7 (d) 9

53. $\left(\frac{\sqrt{1296}}{13} \times \frac{14}{\sqrt{36}} \times \frac{13}{\sqrt{49}}\right)$ is equal to

(a) 16 (b) 12 (c) 14 (d) 18

54. Evaluate $\sqrt{234 - \sqrt{73 + \sqrt{69 - \sqrt{25}}}}$.

(a) 15 (b) 18 (c) 12 (d) 17

55. Find the value of

$\sqrt{0.09} + \sqrt{0.81} + \sqrt{1.44} + \sqrt{0.0004}$.

(a) 0.26 (b) 2.42 (c) 0.28 (d) 0.22

56. Square root of $15 + 4\sqrt{14}$ is

(a) $\sqrt{6} + \sqrt{9}$ (b) $\sqrt{7} + \sqrt{8}$
(c) $\sqrt{10} + \sqrt{5}$ (d) None of these

57. $\left(\frac{1.5}{2.5}\right)^2$ is equal to

(a) 0.06 (b) 0.36 (c) 0.21 (d) 0.41

58. $\left(\frac{64}{25}\right)^{-\frac{3}{2}}$ is equal to

(a) $\frac{125}{215}$ (b) $\frac{125}{512}$
(c) $\frac{125}{72}$ (d) None of these

59. $(0.001)^{\frac{1}{3}}$ is equal to

(a) 0.1 (b) 0.01
(c) 1.1 (d) None of these

60. Find the value of x, if $5^{x-3} . 3^{2x-8} = 225$.

(a) 3 (b) 4
(c) 5 (d) None of these

61. If $K = \sqrt[3]{54} + \sqrt[3]{128} + \sqrt[3]{250} - \sqrt[3]{16}$, the value of K is

(a) 10 (b) $10(3)^{\frac{1}{3}}$
(c) $10(2)^{\frac{1}{3}}$ (d) None of these

Previous Year's Questions

62. The 10th term of the series

5, 8, 11, 14, ... is **[CLAT 2011]**

(a) 32 (b) 35
(c) 38 (d) 185

63. Difference between two numbers is 9 and difference between their squares is 981. Lowest of the two numbers is **[CLAT 2011]**

(a) 40 (b) 50
(c) 55 (d) 59

64. Arun can climb a Coconut tree by 1.5 ft by each lift; however he slips 0.5 ft every time he makes the next lift. How many individual lifts he will have to reach the top of the Coconut tree of 18.5 ft? **[CLAT 2011]**
(a) 20 (b) 19 (c) 18 (d) 17

65. In a staff room of 25 teachers, 13 drink black coffee, 7 milk coffee, 9 drink both tea and either type of coffee and everyone drinks either of the beverages. How many teachers drink only tea? **[CLAT 2011]**
(a) insufficient information
(b) 5
(c) 6
(d) 9

66. If $(9/7)^3 \times (49/81)^{2x-6} = (7/9)^9$, then the value of x is **[CLAT 2011]**
(a) 12 (b) 9 (c) 8 (d) 6

67. In the number series 4, 10, 23, 50, 104, 216, 439 the wrong number is **[CLAT 2012]**
(a) 10 (b) 23 (c) 104 (d) 50

68. One-third of one-fourth of a number is 12. Then, the number is **[CLAT 2012]**
(a) 96 (b) 144 (c) 108 (d) 36

69. The least value of x, for which the expression $x^2 + x + 17$ will not give a prime number, is **[CLAT 2012]**
(a) 7 (b) 11 (c) 13 (d) 17

70. The value of $\frac{1}{x^2} + \frac{1}{y^2}$, where $x = 2+\sqrt{3}$ and $y = 2-\sqrt{3}$, is **[CLAT 2012]**
(a) 12 (b) 16 (c) 14 (d) 10

71. If $x + \frac{1}{x} = 3$, then $x^2 + \frac{1}{x^2}$ will be **[CLAT 2012]**
(a) 9 (b)10 (c) 27 (d) 7

72. If $x = \left(\frac{3}{2}\right)^2 \left(\frac{2}{3}\right)^{-4}$, the value of x^{-2} is **[CLAT 2012]**
(a) $\left(\frac{2}{3}\right)^{12}$ (b) $\left(\frac{3}{2}\right)^{12}$ (c) $\left(\frac{6}{5}\right)^{-12}$ (d) $\left(\frac{5}{6}\right)^{-12}$

73. In a school of 500 students, 102 students can read Hindi and Tamil both, 200 students can read only Hindi. The students who can read only Tamil are **[CLAT 2013]**
(a) 198 (b) 402 (c) 302 (d) 300

74. Sum of first 15 multiples of 8 is **[CLAT 2013]**
(a) 960 (b) 660 (c) 1200 (d) 1060

75. 2/3 is a rational number whereas $\sqrt{2}/\sqrt{3}$ is **[CLAT 2013]**
(a) also a rational number
(b) an irrational number
(c) not a number
(d) a natural periodic number

76. Greatest number which divides 926 and 2313, leaving 2 and 3 remainders, respectively, is **[CLAT 2013]**
(a) 52 (b) 54 (c) 152 (d) 154

77. The Least Common Multiple (LCM) of 0.12,9.60 and 0.60 is **[CLAT 2014]**
(a) 9.60 (b) 0.12
(c) 0.6 (d) None of these

78. The next number in the following sequence is 19, 29, 37, 43, ... **[CLAT 2014]**
(a) 45 (b) 47 (c) 50 (d) 53

79. The value of A in the expression,
$5 + 12 \times 10 \div \frac{120}{240} = A \times 10$, is **[CLAT 2014]**
(a) 11 (b) 24.5 (c) 34 (d) 6.5

80. The sum of all the natural numbers from 200 to 600 (both inclusive) which are neither divisible by 8 nor by 12 is **[CLAT 2015]**
(a) 123968 (b) 133068
(c) 133268 (d) 187332

81. In a tournament, there are n teams, $T_1, T_2, T_3, \cdots, T_n$, with $n > 5$. Each team consist of K players, $K > 3$. The following pairs of teams have one player in common T_1 and T_2, T_2 and T_3, ..., T_{n-1} and T_n and T_n and T_1. No other pair of teams has any player in common. How many players are participating in the tournament, considering all the n teams together? **[CLAT 2015]**
(a) $K(n-1)$ (b) $n(K-2)$
(c) $K(n-2)$ (d) $n(K-1)$

82. If $x = (16^3 + 17^3 + 18^3 + 19^3)$, then x divided by 70 leaves a remainder of **[CLAT 2015]**
(a) 0 (b) 1 (c) 69 (d) 35

83. What are the last two digits of 7^{2008}? **[CLAT 2015]**
(a) 01 (b) 21 (c) 61 (d) 71

84. A group of 630 children is arranged in rows for a group photograph session. Each row contains three fewer children than the row in front of it. What number of rows is not possible? **[CLAT 2015]**

(a) 3 (b) 4 (c) 5 (d) 6

85. Along a road lie on odd number of stones placed at intervals of 10 m. These stones have to be assembled around the middle stone. A person can carry only one stone at a time.

A man carried out the job starting with the stone in the middle, carrying stones in succession, thereby covering a distance of 4.8 km. Then, the number of stones is **[CLAT 2015]**

(a) 35 (b) 15 (c) 31 (d) 29

86. What is the value of (x) in the following equation?

$$x^{0.4} \div 16 = 32 \div x^{2.6}$$ **[CLAT 2015]**

(a) 8 (b) 9
(c) 6 (d) 7

87. Simplify $\left[\frac{(0.333)^3}{(0.111)^2} - \frac{(0.222)^4}{(0.111)^3}\right]$ **[CLAT 2015]**

(a) 1.331 (b) 1.221
(c) 1.484 (d) 1.551

88. If $n^2 = 12345678987654321$, then what is n? **[CLAT 2015]**

(a) 12344321 (b) 1235789
(c) 111111111 (d) 11111111

89. What is the sum of all the natural numbers from 1 to 100? **[CLAT 2016]**

(a) 6000 (b) 5000 (c) 5050 (d) 5052

90. The traffic lights at three different signal points change after every 45 s, 75 s and 90s, respectively. If all change simultaneously at 7 : 20 : 15 h, then they will change again simultaneously at **[CLAT 2016]**

(a) 7 : 28 : 00 h (b) 7 : 27 : 45 h
(c) 7 : 27 : 30 h (d) 7 : 27 : 50 h

91. The number of 'three-digit numbers' which are multiples of 9 are **[CLAT 2016]**

(a) 100 (b) 99
(c) 98 (d) 101

92. A piece of cloth costs ₹ 75. If the piece in ₹ 4 meters longer and each meter costs ₹ 5 less, the cost remains unchanged what in the length of piece? **[CLAT 2017]**

(a) 12 m (b) 8 m
(c) 6 m (d) 10 m

Answers

1	c	2	d	3	c	4	b	5	d	6	b	7	b	8	d	9	a	10	b
11	c	12	c	13	c	14	b	15	c	16	a	17	b	18	d	19	c	20	d
21	a	22	a	23	b	24	c	25	a	26	d	27	c	28	d	29	d	30	c
31	c	32	c	33	d	34	b	35	a	36	a	37	c	38	a	39	b	40	b
41	a	42	c	43	d	44	a	45	a	46	b	47	c	48	c	49	a	50	b
51	a	52	b	53	b	54	a	55	b	56	b	57	b	58	b	59	a	60	c
61	c	62	a	63	b	64	c	65	a	66	d	67	c	68	b	69	d	70	c
71	d	72	a	73	a	74	a	75	b	76	d	77	a	78	b	79	b	80	c
81	b	82	a	83	a	84	b	85	c	86	a	87	b	88	c	89	c	90	b
91	a	92	c																

SOLUTIONS

1. Required difference

$= (700000 - 70)$

$= 699930$

2. 91 is divisible by 7. So, it is not a prime number.

3. The smallest 6-digit number is 100000.

111)100000(900
999
100

$\therefore$ Required number

$= 100000 + (111 - 100)$

$= 100011$

4. Largest 5-digit number $= 99999$

91)99999(1098
91
899
819
809
728
81

$\therefore$ Required number

$= (99999 - 81) = 99918$

5. $99 = 11 \times 9$, where 11 and 9 are coprimes.

By hit and trial, we find that 114345 is divisible by 11 as well as 9. So, it is divisible by 99.

6. On dividing, we get

88)9217(104
88
417
352
65

Therefore, required number

$= 9217 + (88 - 65)$

$= 9217 + 23 = 9240$

7. Let $n = 4q + 3$

Then, $2n = 8q + 6 = 4(2q + 1) + 2$

Thus, when $2n$ is divided by 4, the remainder is 2.

8. Let the given number be 476 xy 0.

Then, $(4 + 7 + 6 + x + y + 0)$ $= (17 + x + y)$ must be divisible by 3 and

$(0 + x + 7) - (y + 6 + 4) = (x - y - 3)$ must be either 0 or multiple of 11.

$x - y - 3 = 0$

$\Rightarrow \quad y = x - 3$

Then,

$(17 + x + y) = (17 + x + x - 3)$

$= (2x + 14)$

$\Rightarrow x = 2$ or $x = 8$ or $x = 5$

$\therefore\ x = 8$ and $y = 5$ or $x = 5$ and $y = 2$

Hence, option (d) is correct.

9. $(x^n - 1)$ will be divisible by $(x + 1)$ only,

When n is even.

$(49^{15} - 1) = \{(7^2)^{15} - 1\}\ (7^{30} - 1)$, which is divisible by $(7 + 1)$, i.e. 8.

10. Let x be the number and y be the quotient.

Then, $x = 56 \times y + 29$

$= (8 \times 7y) + 8 \times 3 + 5$

$= 8(7y + 3) + 5$

$\therefore$ Required remainder $= 5$

11. Let x be the number and y be the quotient.

Then, $x = 779y + 47$

$= 19 \times 41y + 19 \times 2 + 9$

$= 19(41y + 2) + 9$

$\therefore$ Required remainder $= 9$

12. 4456 is divisible by 2. For it, to be divisible by 6, it should be divisible by 3 also. Therefore,

required number $= 2$

13. 77)11158(144
77
345
308
378
308
70

$\therefore$ Required number $= 77 - 70 = 7$

14. Required number

$=$ HCF of $(1657 - 6)$

and

$(2037 - 5) =$ HCF of 1651 and $2032 = 127$

15. Since, the numbers are coprimes, they contain only 1 as the common factor. Also, the given two products have the middle number in common.

So, middle number

$=$ HCF of 551 and $1073 = 29$

First number $= \left(\frac{551}{29}\right) = 19$

Third number $= \left(\frac{1073}{29}\right) = 37$

$\therefore$ Required sum

$= 19 + 29 + 37 = 85$

16. LCM of 9, 12 and $16 = 144$

So, required number $= 144 + 5 = 149$

17. Let three consecutive positive even numbers are x, $x + 2$, $x + 4$.

According to the question,

$$3x = 2(x + 4) + 2$$

$$\Rightarrow \quad 3x = 2x + 8 + 2$$

$$\Rightarrow \quad x = 10$$

Hence, third number $= 10 + 4 = 14$

18. By hit and trial, we put $x = 5$ and $y = 1$, so that $(3x + 7y) = (3 \times 5 + 7 \times 1)$ $= 22$, which is divisible by 11.

$\therefore \quad (4x + 6y) = (4 \times 5 + 6 \times 1) = 26.$ which is not divisible by 11;

$(x + y + 4) = (5 + 1 + 4) = 10.$ which is not divisible by 11'

$(9x + 4y) = (9 \times 5 + 4 \times 1) = 49.$ which is not divisible by 11

$(4x - 9y) = (4 \times 5 - 9 \times 1) = 11.$ which is divisible by 11

19. Let, second number $= x$

then, first number $= 2x$

and third number $= \frac{1}{3} \times 2x$

Now, sum $= 132$

$$\Rightarrow \quad x + 2x + \frac{2x}{3} = 132$$

$$\Rightarrow \quad \frac{9x + 2x}{3} = 132$$

$$\Rightarrow \quad x = 132 \times \frac{3}{11} = 36$$

$\therefore$ The second number is 36

20. HCF of 60, 84 and 108 $= 12$

So, number of students in such room $= 12$

$\therefore$ Minimum number of rooms

$$= \frac{60}{12} + \frac{84}{12} + \frac{108}{12}$$

$$= 5 + 7 + 9 = 21$$

21. Unit digit in the given product $=$ unit digit in $(4 \times 8 \times 7 \times 3) = (672)$, i.e. unit digit is 2.

22. By dividing 173 by 4, we get 1 as a remainder.

So, unit's place digit in $(122)^{173} = 2^1 = 2$

23. Number $= 269 \times 68 + 0 = 18292$

Therefore, required remainder $= 1$

24. $22 = 2 \times 11$

$54 = 2 \times 3 \times 3 \times 3$

$108 = 2 \times 2 \times 3 \times 3 \times 3$

$135 = 5 \times 3 \times 3 \times 3$

$198 = 2 \times 3 \times 3 \times 11$

$\therefore$ LCM $= 2 \times 2 \times 3 \times 3 \times 3 \times 5 \times 11$ $= 5940$

25. Let the numbers be $3x, 4x$ and $5x$.

Then, their LCM $= 60x$

So, $60x = 2400$ or $x = 40$

$\therefore$ The numbers are $(3 \times 40), (4 \times 40)$ and (5×40).

Hence, required HCF $= 40$

26. LCM, of 2, 4, 6, 8, 10, 12, is 120.

So, the bells will toll together after every 120 s (2 min).

In 30 min, they will toll together

$$\frac{30}{2} + 1 = 16 \text{ times}$$

27. Let the numbers be $37a$ and $37b$.

Then, $37a \times 37b = 4107$

$$\Rightarrow \quad ab = 3$$

Now, coprimes with product 3 are (1, 3).

So, the required numbers are $(37 \times 1, 37 \times 3)$ i.e. (37, 111).

$\therefore$ Greater number $= 111$

28. Let the numbers be 3x and 4x.Then, their HCF $= x$. So, $x = 4$. So, the numbers are 12 and 16.

LCM of 12 and 16 $= 48$

29. Let the numbers be $a - d, a, a + d$

Then, $a - d + a + a + d = 21$

$\Rightarrow \quad 3a = 21$

$\Rightarrow \quad a = 7$ and $(a - d)(a + d) = 45$

$\Rightarrow \quad a^2 - d^2 = 45$

$\Rightarrow \quad 49 - d^2 = 45$

$\Rightarrow \quad d^2 = 4 \Rightarrow d = \pm 2$

Hence, the numbers are 5, 7 and 9 when $d = 2$ and 9, 7 and 5 when $d = -2$. In both the cases numbers are the same.

30. $a = 4$

$d = 7 - 4 = 3$

Sum of first 20 terms,

$$S_{20} = \frac{n}{20}[2a + (n - 1)d]$$

$$= \frac{20}{2}[(2 \times 4) + (20 - 1)3]$$

$$= 10[8 + (19 \times 3)]$$

$$= 10(8 + 57) = 650$$

31. $a = 1, r = \frac{\left(\frac{1}{2}\right)}{1} = \frac{1}{2}, n = 5$

Here $r < 1$.

Hence,

$$S_6 = \frac{a(1 - r^n)}{1 - r} = \frac{1\left[1 - \left(\frac{1}{2}\right)^5\right]}{\left(1 - \frac{1}{2}\right)}$$

$$= \frac{\left(1 - \frac{1}{32}\right)}{\left(\frac{1}{2}\right)} = \frac{\left(\frac{31}{32}\right)}{\left(\frac{1}{2}\right)}$$

$$= \frac{31}{16} = 1\frac{15}{16}$$

32. $\frac{23}{19}\times\frac{19}{17}\times 85 = 23\times 5 = 115$

33. $\left(\frac{1}{2}-\frac{1}{3}\right)+\left(\frac{1}{3}-\frac{1}{4}\right)+\left(\frac{1}{4}+\frac{1}{2}\right)$

$=\frac{1}{2}-\frac{1}{3}+\frac{1}{3}-\frac{1}{4}+\frac{1}{4}+\frac{1}{2}$

$=\frac{1}{2}+\frac{1}{2}=1$

34. Given expression,

$=\left(\sqrt{\frac{625}{784}}-\sqrt{\frac{16}{49}}\right)\div\left(\sqrt{\frac{81}{144}}\right)$

$=\left(\frac{25}{28}-\frac{4}{7}\right)\div\left(\frac{9}{12}\right)$

$=\frac{9}{28}\times\frac{12}{9}=\frac{3}{7}$

35. Given expression,

$=15.876-(2.49+4.056)\div\frac{1}{2}$

$=15.876-(6.546)\div\frac{1}{2}$

$=15.876-6.546\times 2$

$=15.876-13.092=2.784$

36. We have,

$\frac{0.48\div 0.12+0.04\times 25}{0.05}$

$=\frac{4+0.04\times 25}{0.05}=\frac{4+1}{0.05}$

$=\frac{5}{0.05}=100$

37. Given expression,

$\frac{P}{1+\frac{1}{1+\frac{P}{1-P}}}=1$

$\Rightarrow \frac{P}{1+\frac{1}{\frac{(1-P)+P}{1-P}}}=1$

$\Rightarrow \frac{P}{1+\frac{1}{\frac{1}{1-P}}}=1$

$\Rightarrow \frac{P}{1+(1-P)}=1$

$\Rightarrow \frac{P}{2-P}=1$

$\Rightarrow P=2-P$

$\Rightarrow P=1$

38. Given expression,

$\frac{\frac{3}{2}\div\frac{1}{2}\times\frac{3}{2}}{\frac{3}{2}\div\frac{1}{2}\text{ of }\frac{3}{2}}\div\frac{1}{8}=\frac{\frac{3}{2}\times\frac{2}{1}\times\frac{3}{2}}{\frac{3}{2}\div\frac{3}{4}}\div\frac{1}{8}$

$=\frac{\frac{9}{2}}{\frac{3}{2}\times\frac{4}{3}}\div\frac{1}{8}=\frac{\frac{9}{2}}{2}\div\frac{1}{8}$

$=\frac{9}{4}\times\frac{8}{1}=18$

39. Put $2125=a$ and $875=b$, then given expression is of the form $\frac{a^3+b^3}{a^2-ab+b^2}$

$=\frac{(a+b)(a^2-ab+b^2)}{a^2-ab+b^2}=a+b$

$=2125+875$

$=3000=3\times 10^3$

40. Put $4.256=a, 1.744=b$, then given expression is of the form, $\frac{(a-b)^2+(a+b)^2}{a^2+b^2}$.

$=\frac{2(a^2+b^2)}{(a^2+b^2)}=2$

41. Given expression, $27^x=\frac{9}{3^x}$

$\Rightarrow (3^3)^x\times 3^x=9$

$\Rightarrow (3)^{3x}\times(3)^x=9$

$\Rightarrow (3)^{3x+x}=9$

$\Rightarrow 3^{4x}=3^2$

$\Rightarrow 4x=2$

$\therefore x=\frac{1}{2}$

42. $\frac{5^n+5^{n-1}}{5^{n+1}-5^n}=\frac{5^{n-1}(5+1)}{5^n(5-1)}$

$=\frac{5^{n-1}\times 6}{5^n\times 4}$

$=\frac{5^n\times 5^{-1}\times 6}{5^n\times 4}$

$=\frac{6}{5\times 4}=\frac{3}{10}=0.3$

43. Given expression,

$2^{x-7}\times 5^{x-4}=1250$

$\Rightarrow \frac{2^x}{2^7}\times\frac{5^x}{5^4}=1250$

$\Rightarrow \frac{(10)^x}{(10)^4\times 2^3}=1250$

$\Rightarrow \frac{(10)^x}{(10)^4}=10000$

$\Rightarrow (10)^{x-4}=(10)^4$

$\Rightarrow x-4=4$

$\therefore x=8$

44. $\frac{x^{a(b-c)}}{x^{b(a-c)}}\div\left(\frac{x^{bc}}{x^{ac}}\right)=x^{ab-ac-ab+bc}\times\frac{x^{ac}}{x^{bc}}$

$=\frac{x^{bc}}{x^{ac}}\times\frac{x^{ac}}{x^{bc}}=1$

45. Given expression,

$\frac{(x^{2a+2b})(x^{2b+2c})(x^{2c+2a})}{x^{4a}\times x^{4b}\times x^{4c}}$

$=\frac{x^{4a}x^{4b}x^{4c}}{x^{4a}x^{4b}x^{4c}}=1$

46. $8^{\frac{2}{3}}-16^{\frac{1}{4}}+9^{\frac{1}{2}}=2^{3\times\frac{2}{3}}-2^{4\times\frac{1}{4}}+3^{2\times\frac{1}{2}}$

$=4-2+3=5$

47. $9^{2x-1}=27^{x+2}$

$\Rightarrow 3^{4x-2}=3^{3x+6}$

$\Rightarrow 4x-2=3x+6$

$\therefore x=8$

48. $\left(\sqrt{2}^{\sqrt{2}}\right)^{\sqrt{2}}=2^x$

$\Rightarrow \sqrt{2}^{\sqrt{2}\times\sqrt{2}}=2^x$

$\Rightarrow (\sqrt{2})^2=2^x$

$\Rightarrow 2=2^x$

$\Rightarrow x=1$

49. $\frac{5^{2/3}\times\sqrt[3]{5^8}}{\sqrt[3]{5^7}}=\frac{5^{2/3}\times 5^{8/3}}{5^{7/3}}$

$=5^{\frac{2}{3}+\frac{8}{3}-\frac{7}{3}}=5$

50.

3	$\overline{10}\,\overline{49}\,\overline{76}$	324
	9	
62	149	
	124	
644	2576	
	2576	
	×	

$\therefore \quad \sqrt{104976} = 324$

51.

3	$\overline{9}\,\overline{06}.\overline{01}$	30.1
	9	
601	601	
	601	
	×	

$\therefore \quad \sqrt{906.01} = 30.1$

52. Given expression,

$$\sqrt{17+\sqrt{51+\sqrt{152+\sqrt{289}}}}$$
$$= \sqrt{17+\sqrt{51+\sqrt{152+17}}}$$
$$= \sqrt{17+\sqrt{51+\sqrt{169}}}$$
$$= \sqrt{17+\sqrt{51+13}}$$
$$= \sqrt{17+\sqrt{64}}$$
$$= \sqrt{17+8} = \sqrt{25} = 5$$

53. Given expression,

$$\frac{\sqrt{1296}}{13} \times \frac{14}{\sqrt{36}} \times \frac{13}{\sqrt{49}}$$
$$= \frac{\sqrt{36 \times 36}}{13} \times \frac{14}{\sqrt{36}} \times \frac{13}{\sqrt{7}}$$
$$= \frac{\sqrt{36} \times \sqrt{36} \times 14 \times 13}{13 \times \sqrt{36} \times 7}$$
$$= 6 \times 2 = 12$$

54. Given expression,

$$\sqrt{234-\sqrt{73+\sqrt{69-\sqrt{25}}}}$$
$$= \sqrt{234-\sqrt{73+\sqrt{69-5}}}$$
$$= \sqrt{234-\sqrt{73+\sqrt{64}}}$$
$$= \sqrt{234-\sqrt{73+8}}$$
$$= \sqrt{234-\sqrt{81}}$$
$$= \sqrt{234-9} = \sqrt{225} = 15$$

55. Given expression,

$$= \sqrt{\frac{9}{100}} + \sqrt{\frac{81}{100}} + \sqrt{\frac{144}{100}} + \sqrt{\frac{4}{10000}}$$
$$= \frac{3}{10} + \frac{9}{10} + \frac{12}{10} + \frac{2}{100}$$
$$= \frac{24}{10} + \frac{2}{100}$$
$$= 2.4 + 0.02 = 2.42$$

56. $\sqrt{15+4\sqrt{14}} = \sqrt{15+2\sqrt{56}}$
$$= \sqrt{15+2\sqrt{8 \times 7}}$$
$$= \sqrt{(\sqrt{7})^2 + (\sqrt{8})^2 + 2\sqrt{8 \times 7}}$$
$$= \sqrt{(\sqrt{7}+\sqrt{8})^2}$$
$$= \sqrt{7} + \sqrt{8}$$

57. $\left(\frac{1.5}{2.5}\right)^2 = \left(\frac{3}{5}\right)^2$
$$= (0.6)^2 = 0.36$$

58. $\left(\frac{64}{25}\right)^{-3/2} = \frac{1}{\left(\frac{64}{25}\right)^{3/2}} = \left(\frac{25}{64}\right)^{3/2}$
$$= \left[\left(\frac{5}{8}\right)^2\right]^{3/2}$$
$$= \left(\frac{5}{8}\right)^3 = \frac{125}{512}$$

59. $(0.001)^{\frac{1}{3}} = \left(\frac{1}{1000}\right)^{\frac{1}{3}} = \left[\left(\frac{1}{10}\right)^3\right]^{\frac{1}{3}}$
$$= \frac{1}{10} = 0.1$$

60. We have, $5^{x-3} \cdot 3^{2x-8} = 225$

$\Rightarrow \quad 5^{x-3} \cdot 3^{2x-8} = 5^2 \times 3^2$

$\Rightarrow \quad x - 3 = 2$ and $2x - 8 = 2$

In both cases, $x = 5$

61. $K = \sqrt[3]{2}[\sqrt[3]{27} + \sqrt[3]{64} + \sqrt[3]{125} - \sqrt[3]{8}]$
$$= \sqrt[3]{2}[(27)^{\frac{1}{3}} + (64)^{\frac{1}{3}} + (125)^{\frac{1}{3}} - (8)^{\frac{1}{3}}]$$
$$= \sqrt[3]{2}[3 + 4 + 5 - 2]$$
$$= \sqrt[3]{2}[10] = 10(2)^{\frac{1}{3}}$$

Previous Year's Solutions

62. Ist terms $(a) = 5$

Common difference $(r) = 3$
$$T_n = a + (n-1)\,d$$
$$= 5 + (10-1)\,3$$
$$= 5 + 27 = 32$$

63. Let the I (lowest) number be x.

Then, II number will be $(x + 9)$

According to the question,
$$(x+9)^2 - x^2 = 981$$
$$\{(x+9+x)\}\,\{(x+9)-x\} = 981$$
$$9\,\{2x+9\} = 981$$
$$18x = 900$$
$$\therefore \quad x = 50$$

64. First time he climb 1.5 ft second and onward he climb 1 ft every lift.

In 18th lift he will reach
$$= 1 \times 17 + 1.5 \times 1 = 18.5 \text{ ft}$$

65. On the given information we cannot be determined the required number of teachers drink only tea.

66. $\left(\frac{9}{7}\right)^3 \times \left(\frac{49}{81}\right)^{2x-6} = \left(\frac{7}{9}\right)^9$

$$\Rightarrow \left(\frac{9}{7}\right)^3 \times \left(\frac{9}{7}\right)^{-2(2x-6)} = \left(\frac{9}{7}\right)^{-9}$$
$$\Rightarrow \quad 3 - 4x + 12 = -9$$
$$\Rightarrow \quad -4x = -9 - 15$$
$$\therefore \quad x = 6$$

67.

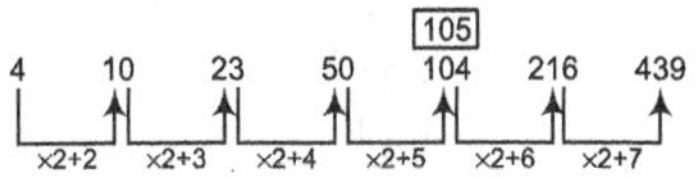

68. Let the number be x. Then,
$$\frac{1}{3} \text{ of } \frac{1}{4} \text{ of } x = 12 \Rightarrow \frac{1}{3} \times \frac{1}{4} \times x = 12$$
$$\Rightarrow \quad x = 12 \times 12 = 144$$

69. Let $f(x) = x^2 + x + 17$

Here, we will check each option one-by-one

(A) $f(7) = 7^2 + 7 + 17 = 73$

(B) $f(11)=11^2+11+17=149$
(C) $f(13)=13^2+13+17=199$
(D) $f(17)=17^2+17+17=323$
Here, 323 is not a prime number.
Thus, required number is 17.

70. $x=2+\sqrt{3},\ y=2-\sqrt{3}$

$x+y=2+\sqrt{3}+2-\sqrt{3}=4$

$xy=(2+\sqrt{3})(2-\sqrt{3})=4-3=1$

Now, $\frac{1}{x^2}+\frac{1}{y^2}=\frac{x^2+y^2}{(xy)^2}$

$=\frac{(x+y)^2-2xy}{(xy)^2}$

$=\frac{(4)^2-2(1)}{(1)^2}$

$=\frac{16-2}{1}=14$

71. $x+\frac{1}{x}=3$

$\Rightarrow \left(x+\frac{1}{x}\right)^2=(3)^2$

$\Rightarrow x^2+\frac{1}{x^2}+2x\cdot\frac{1}{x}=9$

$\Rightarrow x^2+\frac{1}{x^2}+2=9$

$\Rightarrow x^2+\frac{1}{x^2}=7$

72. $x=\left(\frac{3}{2}\right)^2\left(\frac{2}{3}\right)^{-4}$

$=\left(\frac{3}{2}\right)^2\left(\frac{3}{2}\right)^4=\left(\frac{3}{2}\right)^6$

$\Rightarrow x^2=\left(\frac{3}{2}\right)^{12} \Rightarrow x^{-2}=\left(\frac{3}{2}\right)^{-12}$

$=\left(\frac{2}{3}\right)^{12}$

73. Total students = 500
Students read Hindi and Tamil both = 102
Students read Hindi only = 200
$\therefore$ Students read Tamil only = 500 − 102 − 200
= 198

74. First 15 multiple of 8 are
8, 16, 24, ..., 120
So, 8(1, 2, 3, 4,....,15)

Their sum $= 8\left[\frac{n(n+1)}{2}\right]$

$= 8\left[\frac{15(15+1)}{2}\right] = 8\times15\times8$

$= 960$

75. $\sqrt{2}$ is an irrational and $\sqrt{3}$ is also an irrational number.
So, $\frac{\sqrt{2}}{\sqrt{3}}$ is an irrational number.

76. Required number is HCF of (926-2) and (2313-3).

So,
```
924) 2310 (2
     1848
      462) 924 (2
           924
             0
```

Hence, 462 is the greatest number but it is not in the options, so the greatest among option should be factor of 462.
So, the required number is 154.

77. Consider the numbers given
0.12, 9.60, 0.60

LCM$\left(\frac{12}{100},\frac{96}{10},\frac{6}{10}\right)$;

$=\frac{\text{LCM of Numerator}}{\text{HCF of Denominator}}$

$=\frac{\text{LCM (12, 96, 6)}}{\text{HCF (100, 10, 10)}}$

$=\frac{96}{10}=9.60$

78.

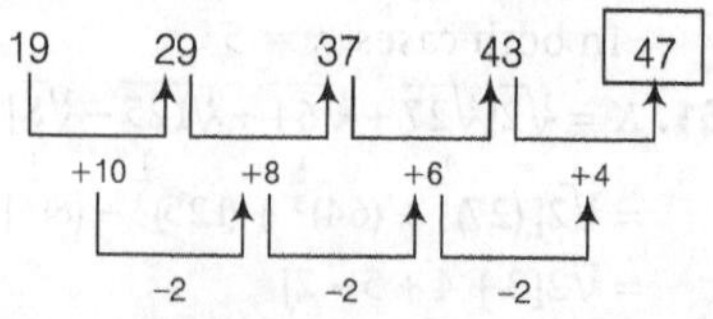

Hence, 47 will be the next number in sequence.

79. Given expression,

$5+12\times10\div\frac{120}{240}=A\times10$

Taking LHS and applying VBODMAS,

$=5+12\times10\div\frac{120}{240}$

$=5+120\div\frac{1}{2}$

$=5+120\times2 \quad =245$

RHS, $A\times10=245 \Rightarrow A=\frac{245}{10}$

$\therefore \quad A=24.5$

80. Total numbers which are divisible by both 8 and 12
$n(8)+n(12)-n$ (LCM of 8 and 12)
$n(8)$ = Numbers which are divisible by 8
$n(12)$ = Numbers which are divisible by 12
n (LCM of 8 and 12 i.e. 24) = Numbers which are divisible by 24.
Sum of all the numbers divisible by 8
Total numbers divisible by 8

$=\frac{51}{2}(\underset{\text{13th term}}{200}+\underset{\text{Last term}}{600})$

$=51\times400=20400$

Sum of all the numbers divisible by 12
Total numbers divisible by 12

$=\frac{34}{2}(\underset{\text{First term}}{204}+\underset{\text{Last term}}{600})$

$=\frac{34}{2}\times804=2\times17\times402$

$=13668$

Sum of all the terms divisible by 24
Total numbers divisible by 24

$=\frac{17}{2}(\underset{\text{First term}}{216}+\underset{\text{Last term}}{600})$

$=\frac{17}{2}\times816$

$=17\times408=6936$

Total sum of all the numbers between 200 and 600 (both inclusive)

$=\frac{401}{2}(\underset{\text{First term}}{200}+\underset{\text{Last term}}{600})$

$=\frac{401\times800}{2}$

$=401\times400=160400$

∴ Sum of all the numbers which are neither divisible by 8 nor divisible by 12

$=160400-(20400+13668-6936)$

$=160400-27132=133268$

82. $x=(16^3+17^3+18^3+19^3)$

$=(4096+4913+5832+6859)$

$\therefore x=21700$

According to the question, when x divided by 70, $(\because x=21700)$

$\Rightarrow \quad \frac{21700}{70}=310$

So, there is no remainder. Then, answer is '0'.

Alternative Method

$x=\{(16)^3+(17)^3+(18)^3+(19)^3\}\div7$

$=6+3+2+9$

(Sum of digit at unit place)

$=0$

Here, at unit place, it is 0. Hence, we have to check divisibility of 7.

$\therefore 2^3+3^3+4^3+5^3$

(Remainder theorem)

$\Rightarrow \quad 8+27+64+125$

$\Rightarrow$ 224 and it is divisible by 7. Hence, there is no remainder.

83. Here, $(7)^{2008}$

or $(7)^{4\times502}$ or $(24\underline{01})^{502}$

Hence, last two digits will be 01.

84. Total number of children $=630$

The number of rows should be the factor of 630. So, from the given option it is clear that 4 is not the factor of 630.

So, 4 rows are not possible.

85. Let the number of stones $=n$

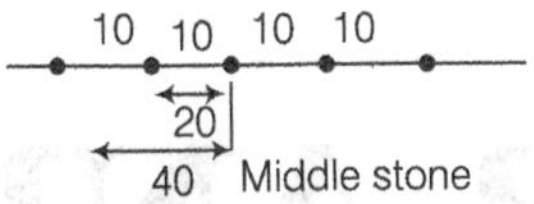

The distance between every stone = 10 m

So, here an AP is formed, $a=20, d=20$

So, the distance covered in one side,

$=\frac{n}{2}[2a+(n-1)d]$

Distance covered in both side,

$\Rightarrow \quad 4800=2\left(\frac{n}{2}(2a+(n-1)d\right)$

$\Rightarrow 4800=n[2\times20+(n-1)20]$

$\therefore \quad n=15$ (on one side)

Then, number of stones on both side

$=2\times15=30$

∴ Total number of stones

$=30+1$ (middle stone) $=31$

86. $\frac{x^{0.4}}{16}=\frac{32}{x^{2.6}}$

$\Rightarrow \quad x^{0.4}\times x^{2.6}=16\times32$

$\Rightarrow \quad x^3=512$

$\Rightarrow \quad x^3=(8)^3$

On comparing both sides,

$\therefore \quad x=8$

87. Here, let $0.111=a$

Then, $0.222=2a$

and $0.333=3a$

We can also write the above expression as

$\left[\frac{(3a)^2}{(a)^2}-\frac{(2a)^4}{(a)^3}\right]$

$\Rightarrow \quad \frac{27a^3}{a^2}-\frac{16a^4}{a^3}$

$\Rightarrow 27a-16a=11a \quad \ldots(i)$

Putting the value of a in Eq. (i),

$11\times0.111=1.221$

88. We know that,

$\Rightarrow \quad 11^2=121$

$\Rightarrow \quad (111)^2=12321$

$\Rightarrow \quad (1111)^2=1234321$

$\Rightarrow \quad (11111)^2=123454321$

$\vdots \quad \vdots$

$\Rightarrow (111111111)^2$

$=12345678987654321$

Given that,

$n^2=12345678987654321$

Then, $\quad n=111111111$

89. Required sum $=\frac{100}{2}[1+100]$

$=101\times50=5050$

90. LCM (45, 75, 90) = 450

∴ Traffic lights will change simultaneously after 7 min 30 s i.e. at 7 : 27 : 45 h.

91. The first three-digit numbers divisible by 9 is 108 and last is 999.

So, we have an AP with $a=108, d=9$ and $l_n=999$

$\therefore \quad l_n=a+(n-1)d$

$\Rightarrow \quad 999=108+(n-1)9$

$\Rightarrow \quad 999-108=(n-1)9$

$\Rightarrow \quad 891=(n-1)9$

$\Rightarrow \quad (n-1)=\frac{891}{9}=99$

$\Rightarrow \quad n=99+1=100$

So, there are 100 three-digit numbers, which are multiples of 9.

92. Let the piece of both be x m and cost be ₹ y per m.

Then, $xy=75 \quad \ldots(i)$

$(x+4)(y-5)=75 \quad \ldots(ii)$

$\Rightarrow x=6$ m and $y=12.5$ per m

CHAPTER 02

LINEAR AND QUADRATIC EQUATIONS

POLYNOMIAL

Let $a_0, a_1, a_2, \ldots, a_n$ are real numbers, then $f(x) = a_0 + a_1x + a_2x^2 + \ldots + a_nx^n$ is known as polynomial of degree n.

Polynomial Equation

If $f(x)$ is a real or complex polynomial, then $f(x) = 0$ is known as a polynomial equation.

If $f(x)$ is a polynomial of degree 2, then $f(x) = 0$ is known as quadratic equation.

General equation of quadratic equation is $ax^2 + bx + c = 0$ where $a, b, c \in R$ or C.

The quadratic equation of the form $ax^2 + c = 0$ is known as pure quadratic equation.

Linear Equations in One Variable

These are first degree equations in one unknown. An equation of the form $ax + b = 0$ where $a, b \in R$ and $a \neq 0$ and x is the variable, is called a linear equation in one variable.

The value of x which satisfies the given equation, is called its solution.

EXAMPLE 1 Solve $3x + 8 = x + 9$.

(a) 1/2 (b) 3/2 (c) 4/5 (d) 1/3

Solution *(a)* $3x + 8 = x + 9 \Rightarrow 3x - x = 9 - 8$

$$2x = 1 \Rightarrow x = \frac{1}{2}$$

EXAMPLE 2 Solve $\frac{2x-3}{2x-1}=\frac{3x-1}{3x+5}$.

(a) $2\frac{3}{5}$ (b) $2\frac{2}{3}$ (c) $3\frac{4}{5}$ (d) $2\frac{3}{2}$

Solution *(b)* $\frac{2x-3}{2x-1}=\frac{3x-1}{3x+5}$

$\Rightarrow$ $(2x-3)(3x+5)=(2x-1)(3x-1)$

$\Rightarrow$ $6x^2+10x-9x-15=6x^2-2x-3x+1$

$\Rightarrow$ $6x^2+x-15=6x^2-5x+1$

$\Rightarrow$ $6x^2-6x^2+x+5x=1+15 \Rightarrow 6x=16$

$\Rightarrow$ $x=\frac{16}{6}=\frac{8}{3}=2\frac{2}{3}$

Linear Equations in Two Variables

These are first degree equations in two unknowns. An equation of the form $ax+by+c=0$, where $a, b, c \in R$ and $a \neq 0, b \neq 0$ and x, y are variables is called linear equation in two variables.

Any pair of values of x and y which satisfy the equation $ax+by+c=0$, is called its solution.

EXAMPLE 3 What is the solution of the equations

$$\frac{2}{x}+\frac{2}{3y}=\frac{1}{6}; \frac{3}{x}+\frac{2}{y}=0?$$

(a) 6, – 4 (b) 5, 6 (c) – 3, 2 (d) 1, 1

Solution *(a)* Let $\frac{1}{x}=a, \frac{1}{y}=b$

We get, $2a+\frac{2b}{3}=\frac{1}{6}$ ...(i)

$3a+2b=0$ ...(ii)

Multiplying Eq. (i) by 3, we get

$6a+2b=\frac{1}{2}$

Multiplying Eq. (ii) by 2, we get

$6a+4b=0$

On subtracting, $-2b=\frac{1}{2} \Rightarrow b=-\frac{1}{4}$

Substituting the value of b in Eq. (ii), we get

$3a+2\left(-\frac{1}{4}\right)=0$

$\Rightarrow$ $3a=\frac{1}{2} \Rightarrow a=\frac{1}{6}$

$\Rightarrow$ $a=\frac{1}{x}=\frac{1}{6} \Rightarrow x=6$ $b=\frac{1}{y}=-\frac{1}{4} \Rightarrow y=-4$

The solution is $x=6, y=-4$.

Consistency of a System of Linear Equations

Let the system of equations is

$$a_1x+b_1y+c_1=0 \text{ and } a_2x+b_2y+c_2=0$$

We have

(i) a unique solution, if $\frac{a_1}{a_2} \neq \frac{b_1}{b_2}$

(ii) an infinite number of solutions, if

$$\frac{a_1}{a_2}=\frac{b_1}{b_2}=\frac{c_1}{c_2}$$

(iii) no solution, if $\frac{a_1}{a_2}=\frac{b_1}{b_2} \neq \frac{c_1}{c_2}$

EXAMPLE 4 Find the value of m for which the system of linear equations $x+2y-3=0$, $5x+my+7=0$ have no solution.

(a) 20 (b) 10 (c) 5 (d) 15

Solution *(b)* We have, $x+2y-3=0$

and $5x+my+7=0$

Here, $a_1=1, b_1=2, c_1=-3$,

$a_2=5, b_2=m, c_2=7$

For no solution $\frac{a_1}{a_2}=\frac{b_1}{b_2} \neq \frac{c_1}{c_2}$

$\Rightarrow$ $\frac{1}{5}=\frac{2}{m} \neq \frac{-3}{7} \Rightarrow m=10$

Quadratic Equation

These are second degree equations in one unknown. An equation of the form $ax^2+bx+c=0$, where $a, b, c \in R$ and $a \neq 0$ is called quadratic equation.

Like a first degree equation in x has one value of x satisfying the equation, a quadratic equation in x will have two values of x that satisfy the equation. The values of x that satisfy the equation are called the roots of the equation. These roots may be real or imaginary.

$x^2+5x+6=0$ has roots $x=-2, -3$

$15x^2-x-28=0$ has roots $x=\frac{7}{5}, -\frac{4}{3}$

$x^2-8=0$ has roots $x=2\sqrt{2}, -2\sqrt{2}$

To Find the Roots of a Quadratic Equation

In general, the roots of a quadratic equation can be found out in two ways

Method 1 By Factorisation

If the quadratic equation $ax^2+bx+c=0$ can be expressed in the form $(x-\alpha)(x-\beta)=0$, then the roots of the equation are α and β.

EXAMPLE 5 Find the roots of

$$3x^2-x+10=2x^2+4x+4.$$

(a) 3 or 5 (b) 4 or 2 (c) 2 or 3 (d) 1 or 5

Solution *(c)* $3x^2-x+10=2x^2+4x+4$

$$\Rightarrow 3x^2-2x^2-x-4x+10-4=0$$
$$\Rightarrow x^2-5x+6=0$$
$$\Rightarrow x^2-2x-3x+6=0$$
$$\Rightarrow x(x-2)-3(x-2)=0$$
$$\Rightarrow (x-2)(x-3)=0$$
$$\Rightarrow x-2=0 \text{ or } x-3=0$$
$$\Rightarrow x=2 \text{ or } 3$$

Method 2 Using Formula

If the quadratic equation is $ax^2+bx+c=0$, then we can use the standard formula given below to find out the roots of the equation. If α and β are the roots of the quadratic equation, then

$$\alpha=\frac{-b+\sqrt{b^2-4ac}}{2a} \text{ and } \beta=\frac{-b-\sqrt{b^2-4ac}}{2a}$$

EXAMPLE 6 Find the roots of $9x^2-3x-2=0$.

(a) $\frac{2}{3},-\frac{1}{3}$ (b) $\frac{3}{2},-\frac{1}{3}$ (c) $\frac{2}{3},-\frac{1}{2}$ (d) $\frac{3}{2},-\frac{4}{5}$

Solution *(c)* Here, $a=9$, $b=-3$ and $c=-2$

$$\alpha=\frac{-b+\sqrt{b^2-4ac}}{2a}$$
$$=\frac{-(-3)+\sqrt{(-3)^2-(4\times9\times-2)}}{2\times9}$$
$$=\frac{3+\sqrt{9+72}}{18}=\frac{3+\sqrt{81}}{18}=\frac{3+9}{18}=\frac{12}{18}=\frac{2}{3}$$
$$\beta=\frac{-b-\sqrt{b^2-4ac}}{2a}$$
$$=\frac{-(-3)-\sqrt{(-3)^2-(4\times9\times-2)}}{2\times9}$$
$$=\frac{3-\sqrt{9+72}}{18}=\frac{3-\sqrt{81}}{18}=\frac{3-9}{18}=-\frac{6}{18}=-\frac{1}{3}$$

$\therefore$ The roots are $\frac{2}{3},-\frac{1}{3}$.

FACTOR THEOREM

Let $f(x)$ be a polynomial of degree greater than or equal to 1 and a be any real number such that $f(a)=0$, then $(x-a)$ is a factor of $f(x)$. Conversely, if $(x-a)$ is a factor of $f(x)$, then $f(a)=0$.

Sum and Product of Roots of a Quadratic Equation

If α and β are the roots of the quadratic equation $ax^2+bx+c=0$, then

Sum of the roots $=\alpha+\beta=-\frac{b}{a}$

Product of the roots $=\alpha\beta=\frac{c}{a}$

EXAMPLE 7 Find the sum and product of the roots for the equation $x^2-5x-300=0$.

(a) 5, − 300 (b) 6, − 400 (c) 5, − 400 (d) 6, − 300

Solution *(a)* $a=1$, $b=-5$ and $c=-300$

Sum of the roots $=-\frac{b}{a}=-\frac{(-5)}{1}=5$

Product of the roots $=\frac{c}{a}=\frac{-300}{1}=-300$

$\therefore$ The sum of the roots is 5 and the product of the roots is −300.

Formation of Quadratic Equation

If the roots of the quadratic equation are given as α and β, the equation can be written as $(x-\alpha)(x-\beta)=0$, i.e $x^2-x(\alpha+\beta)+\alpha\beta=0$. So, if we know the sum of the roots and the product of roots, we can frame the quadratic equation as

$$x^2-x\,(\text{sum of the roots}) + \text{product of the roots}=0$$

EXAMPLE 8 Form the quadratic equation whose roots are 2 and 12.

(a) $x^2 - 17x + 24 = 0$ (b) $x^2 - 14x + 24 = 0$
(c) $x^{2-} 25x + 23$ (d) $x^2 - 17x + 2y$

Solution ***(b)*** Sum of the roots

$$= (\alpha + \beta) = (2 + 12) = 14$$

Product of the roots $= \alpha\beta = 2 \times 12 = 24$

Quadratic equation is given by

$$x^2 - x(\alpha + \beta) + \alpha\beta = 0$$

where, α and β are the two roots of the equation.

$\therefore$ The required equation is

$$x^2 - x(14) + 24 = 0$$

$$\Rightarrow \quad x^2 - 14x + 24 = 0$$

Nature of the Roots

The discriminate given by $b^2 - 4ac$ determines the nature of roots of the quadratic equation $ax^2 + bx + c = 0$. It is represented as D.

(i) If $b^2 - 4ac > 0$ and is a perfect square, then the roots are real, rational and unequal.

(ii) If $b^2 - 4ac > 0$ and is not a perfect square, then the roots are real, irrational and unequal.

(iii) If $b^2 - 4ac = 0$, then the roots are real, rational and equal.

(iv) If $b^2 - 4ac < 0$, then the roots are distinct conjugate complex number or imaginary.

Example 9 Determine the nature of the roots of the equation $x^2 - 6x + 9 = 0$.

(a) rational, unequal (b) rational, equal
(c) equal, real (d) real, unequal

Solution ***(b)*** $a = 1, b = -6$ and $c = 9$

$$D = b^2 - 4ac = (-6)^2 - 4(1)(9)$$

$$= 36 - 36 = 0$$

Since, D = 0 the roots are real rational and equal

Practice Exercise

1. Find y, if $\frac{1}{2}(3y + 1) - \frac{1}{3}(5y + 2) = y - 1$.

(a) 5 (b) 7 (c) $\frac{5}{7}$ (d) $\frac{7}{5}$

2. Solve $0.4x + 0.2y = 2.4$ and $0.3x - 0.2y = 1.1$.

(a) $x = 5, y = 2$ (b) $x = -5, y = 2$
(c) $x = 5, y = -2$ (d) $x = -5, y = -2$

3. Solve $\frac{26}{x + y} + \frac{9}{x - y} = 5$ and $\frac{65}{x + y} + \frac{15}{x - y} = 10$.

(a) $x = 10, y = -5$ (b) $x = 8, y = 5$
(c) $x = -8, y = 5$ (d) $x = -10, y = 5$

4. If $2x - y = 3$ and $4x + y = 3$, what is the value of $(x + y)$?

(a) 0 (b) -1
(c) 1 (d) $\frac{1}{2}$

5. If $\left(k, -\frac{1}{2}\right)$ is a solution of $\frac{x}{2} + 4y - 1 = 0$, then $k = ?$

(a) -3 (b) -6 (c) 3 (d) 6

6. The system of equations $2x + ky = 5$ and $3x + y = 8$ has a unique solution when

(a) $k \neq \frac{2}{3}$ (b) $k \neq \frac{3}{2}$ (c) $k \neq \frac{2}{5}$ (d) $k \neq \frac{5}{2}$

7. The system of equations $3x - y = 5$ and $kx - 2y = 10$ has infinite number of solutions when

(a) $k = 6$ (b) $k = -6$ (c) $k = \frac{1}{6}$ (d) $k = -\frac{1}{6}$

8. The system of equations $5x + 4y = 3$ and $kx + 8y = 7$ has no solution when

(a) $k = 10$ (b) $k = 8$ (c) $k = 4$ (d) $k = 12$

9. The sum of two consecutive odd numbers is 152. Find the bigger number.

(a) 74 (b) 77 (c) 72 (d) 79

10. *A* has 5 more pencils than *B* and *B* has 5 more pencils than *C*. What is the least number of pencils which must change hands in order that *A*, *B* and *C* now have equal pencils?
(a) 5 (b) 4 (c) 6 (d) 2

11. Three numbers are in the ratio 5 : 6 : 9 and the sum of their squares is 2272. Find the smallest of these numbers.
(a) 24 (b) 20 (c) 36 (d) 32

12. A two-digit number is such that the tens digit exceeds twice the units digit by 2 and the number obtained by interchanging the digits is 5 more than three times the sum of the digits. Find the two-digit number.
(a) 83 (b) 38 (c) 56 (d) 65

13. Ramesh and Ganesh had some oranges initially. If Ramesh gave 5 oranges to Ganesh, then Ganesh will have thrice as many as Ramesh. Instead of that, if Ganesh gave 5 oranges to Ramesh, then they will both have the same number of oranges. Find the ratio of oranges of Ramesh and Ganesh.
(a) 3 : 5 (b) 1 : 3 (c) 5 : 7 (d) 7 : 9

14. In a class of x boys and y girls, 3 girls leave the class, the number of boys and girls become equal. Now, five boys leave the class and the number of boys is two-third the number of girls present in the class, find y.
(a) 18 (b) 15 (c) 21 (d) 27

15. In a farm, there are some hens and horses. If their legs are counted, these are 294, if the heads are counted, these are 111. Find the number of horses.
(a) 75 (b) 36 (c) 48 (d) 64

16. A sum of ₹ 13.50 is made of 38 coins which are either 50 paise or 25 paise. Find the number of 25 paise coins.
(a) 16 (b) 24
(c) 18 (d) 22

17. In an examination consisting of 60 questions, three marks are given for every correct answer and one mark deducted for every wrong answer. A student attempts all the questions and gets 120 marks. How many questions he marked were right?
(a) 45 (b) 42 (c) 15 (d) 18

18. If the cost of 2 apples, 3 oranges and a pear is ₹ 62 and the cost of 5 apples, 6 oranges and 4 pears is ₹ 120. Find the cost of 3 apples, 3 oranges and 3 pears.
(a) ₹ 39 (b) ₹ 46 (c) ₹ 58 (d) ₹ 24

19. A student was asked to find $\frac{2}{5}$th of a number and he instead multiplied it by $\frac{5}{2}$. As a result, he got an answer which was more than the correct answer by 5208. What was the original number?
(a) 2485 (b) 2456 (c) 2480 (d) 2455

20. The following system,
$3x+\frac{5}{2}y=7, 9x+\frac{15}{2}y-21=0$, has
(a) unique solution
(b) infinite number of solutions
(c) no solution
(d) Cannot say

21. A girl is now x yr old and her father is $5x$ yr old. How old will the father be when the girl is $3x$ yr old?
(a) $15x$ (b) $7x$ (c) $8x$ (d) $10x$

22. The roots of the equation $2\sqrt{5}\,x^2-3x-\sqrt{5}=0$ are
(a) $\frac{-\sqrt{5}}{2}, \frac{1}{\sqrt{5}}$ (b) $\frac{\sqrt{5}}{2}, \frac{1}{\sqrt{5}}$
(c) $\frac{\sqrt{5}}{2}, \frac{-1}{\sqrt{5}}$ (d) $\frac{-\sqrt{5}}{2}, -\frac{1}{\sqrt{5}}$

23. The roots of the equation $4x^2-2(a^2+b^2)x+a^2b^2=0$, are
(a) $\frac{a^2}{b}, \frac{b^2}{a}$ (b) $\frac{a^2}{2}, \frac{b^2}{2}$
(c) $\frac{a^2}{b^2}, \frac{a}{b}$ (d) ab, a^2b^2

24. The roots of the equation $\frac{x+3}{x-2}-\frac{1-x}{x}=\frac{17}{4}$, are

(a) $4, -\frac{2}{9}$ (b) $3, -\frac{5}{7}$ (c) $4, \frac{2}{9}$ (d) $3, \frac{5}{7}$

25. If $x=2$ and $x=-\frac{3}{2}$ are the roots of the equation $2x^2-kx-m=0$, find the values of k and m.

(a) –3, 5 (b) 2, 4
(c) 1, 6 (d) –1, 5

26. Find the sum and product of the roots of the equation $\frac{2}{x^2}-\frac{5}{x}+2=0$.

(a) $\frac{3}{4}, 2$ (b) $\frac{1}{4}, -2$ (c) $\frac{5}{2}, 1$ (d) $\frac{2}{3}, -1$

27. If $6+\sqrt{5}$ is a root of the equation $x^2+mx+n=0$, where m and n are real, then (m, n) is

(a) 12, 31 (b) – 12, 31
(c) 12, – 31 (d) – 12, – 31

28. Find the value of k so that the roots of $kx^2+5x-2=0$ are reciprocal of each other.

(a) –1 (b) –2 (c) 2 (d) 1

29. Find the quadratic equation for which the sum of the roots is 5 and the sum of the squares of the root is 13.

(a) $x^2-5x+6=0$ (b) $x^2+5x+6=0$
(c) $x^2-5x-6=0$ (d) $x^2+5x-6=0$

30. The roots of $2x^2+2x+5=0$ are

(a) real and equal
(b) real, unequal and rational
(c) real, unequal and irrational
(d) imaginary

31. Find the two consecutive positive even integers, the sum of whose squares is 884.

(a) 22, 24 (b) 16, 18 (c) 20, 22 (d) 18, 20

32. Find a negative number which when increased by 17 is equal to sixty times the reciprocal of the number.

(a) – 17 (b) – 18 (c) – 20 (d) – 25

33. Divide 45 into two parts so that the sum of the squares is 1157.

(a) 14, 31 (b) 16, 29
(c) 15, 30 (d) 18, 27

34. The sum of a number and its positive square root is $\frac{8}{49}$. Find the number.

(a) $\frac{5}{49}$ (b) $\frac{1}{49}$ (c) $\frac{3}{49}$ (d) $\frac{6}{49}$

Previous Year's Questions

35. The denominator of a fraction is greater than its numerator by 11. If 8 is added to both its numerator and denominator, then it becomes 3/4. The fraction is **[CLAT 2012]**

(a) 25/26 (b) 35/26
(c) 26/35 (d) 25/36

36. A sum was divided among *P*, *Q* and *R*. *R* got double than *P* who got double than *Q*. If the difference between the shares of *Q* and *R* is ₹ 3675.00, then the sum in rupees is **[CLAT 2012]**

(a) 4900 (b) 8575
(c) 11025 (d) 7350

37. When $16x^4+12x^3-10x^2+8x+20$ is divided by $4x-3$, the quotient and the remainder are, respectively **[CLAT 2012]**

(a) $4x^3+6x^2+2x$ and $\frac{61}{2}$

(b) $4x^3+6x^2+\frac{7}{2}$ and $\frac{51}{2}$

(c) $6x^2+2x+\frac{2}{7}$ and $\frac{61}{2}$

(d) $4x^3+6x^2+2x+\frac{7}{2}$ and $\frac{61}{2}$

38. The price of 2 trousers and 4 shirts is ₹ 1600 with the same amount one can buy 1 trouser and 6 shirts. If one wants to buy 12 shirts he has to pay **[CLAT 2012]**

(a) ₹ 2400 (b) ₹ 4800
(c) ₹ 1200 (d) ₹ 3700

39. The value of k or which $kx+3y-k+3=0$ and $12x+ky=k$, have infinite solutions, is **[CLAT 2013]**

(a) 0 (b) – 6 (c) 6 (d) 1

40. A farmer has some hens and some goats. If the total number of animal heads is 80 and the total number of animal feet is 200, what is the tolal number of goats? **[CLAT 2014]**
(a) 40
(b) 60
(c) 20
(d) Cannot be determined

41. A man went to the Reserve Bank of India with ₹ 2000. He asked the cashier to give him ₹ 10 and ₹ 20 notes only in return. The man got 150 notes in all. How many notes of ₹ 10 did he receive? **[CLAT 2014]**
(a) 100 (b) 150 (c) 50 (d) 70

42. A person spends 1/3 part of his income on food, 1/4 part on house rent and remaining ₹ 630 on other items. The house rent is **[CLAT 2014]**
(a) ₹ 504 (b) ₹ 1512
(c) ₹ 378 (d) None of these

43. Two consecutive even positive integers, sum of the squares of which is 1060, are **[CLAT 2016]**
(a) 12 and 14 (b) 20 and 22
(c) 22 and 24 (d) 15 and 18

44. If the product of zeroes of the polynomial $ax^2 - 6x - 6$ is 4, then find the value of 'a'. **[CLAT 2016]**
(a) $-\frac{3}{2}$ (b) $\frac{1}{2}$ (c) $-\frac{1}{2}$ (d) $\frac{3}{2}$

45. Keerthi's father gave him some money to buy books. He spent half of the money equally to buy books and entertaining his friends. whateveve amount left with him, he deposited half in his savings account and gave ₹ 5 to a poor person as charity. Finally, Keerthi was left with ₹ 20 which he returned to his father. What amount did his father give him initially. **[CLAT 2017]**
(a) ₹ 160 (b) ₹ 100
(c) ₹ 200 (d) ₹ 120

Answers

1	c	2	a	3	b	4	a	5	d	6	a	7	a	8	d	9	a	10	b
11	b	12	a	13	a	14	a	15	b	16	d	17	a	18	d	19	c	20	d
21	b	22	c	23	b	24	a	25	c	26	c	27	b	28	c	29	d	30	d
31	c	32	c	33	a	34	b	35	d	36	b	37	d	38	a	39	c	40	c
41	a	42	c	43	c	44	a	45	b										

SOLUTIONS

1. $\frac{1}{2}(3y+1) - \frac{1}{3}(5y+2) = y - 1$
$\Rightarrow (9y+3) - (10y+4) = 6y - 6$
$\Rightarrow -y - 1 = 6y - 6$
$\Rightarrow 7y = 5$
$\Rightarrow y = \frac{5}{7}$

2. $0.4x + 0.2y = 2.4$ ...(i)
$0.3x - 0.2y = 1.1$ ...(ii)
On adding Eqs. (i) and (ii), we get $x = 5$
On substituting the value of x in Eq. (i), we get $y = 2$
$\therefore \quad x = 5$
and $\quad y = 2$

3. Let $\frac{1}{x+y} = u$ and $\frac{1}{x-y} = v$
Then, we get
$26u + 9v = 5$ ...(i)
$65u + 15v = 10$ ...(ii)
On multiplying Eq. (i) by 5 and Eq. (ii) by 3 and On subtracting it from Eq. (i), we get $u = \frac{1}{13}$
On Substituting the value of u in Eq. (i), we get
$v = \frac{1}{3}$
$u = \frac{1}{x+y} = \frac{1}{13}$
$\Rightarrow \quad x + y = 13$ ...(iii)
$v = \frac{1}{x-y} = \frac{1}{3}$

$\Rightarrow \quad x - y = 3 \qquad \ldots(\text{iv})$

On solving Eqs. (iii) and (iv), we get

$$x = 8 \text{ and } y = 5$$

4. Given, $2x - y = 3 \qquad \ldots(\text{i})$

$$4x + y = 3 \qquad \ldots(\text{ii})$$

On adding Eqs. (i) and (ii), we get $x = 1$

On substituting the value of x in Eq. (i), we get

$$y = -1$$

Now,

$x + y = 1 + (-1) = 1 - 1 = 0$

5. Clearly, $x = k$ and $y = -\frac{1}{2}$

satisfy

$$\frac{x}{2} + 4y - 1 = 0$$

$$\Rightarrow \quad \frac{k}{2} + 4\left(-\frac{1}{2}\right) - 1 = 0$$

$$\Rightarrow \quad \frac{k}{2} - 2 - 1 = 0$$

$$\Rightarrow \quad \frac{k}{2} = 3$$

$$\Rightarrow \quad k = 6$$

6. For a unique solution,

$$\frac{a_1}{a_2} \neq \frac{b_1}{b_2}$$

$$\Rightarrow \quad \frac{2}{3} \neq \frac{k}{1}$$

$$\Rightarrow \quad k \neq \frac{2}{3}$$

7. For infinite number of solutions

$$\frac{a_1}{a_2} = \frac{b_1}{b_2} = \frac{c_1}{c_2}$$

$$\Rightarrow \quad \frac{3}{k} = \frac{-1}{-2} = \frac{5}{10}$$

$$\Rightarrow \quad \frac{3}{k} = \frac{1}{2} = \frac{1}{2}$$

$$\Rightarrow \quad k = 6$$

8. For a system of equations to have no solutions

$$\frac{a_1}{a_2} = \frac{b_1}{b_2} \neq \frac{c_1}{c_2}$$

$$\Rightarrow \quad \frac{5}{k} = \frac{4}{8} \neq \frac{3}{7} \Rightarrow \frac{5}{k} = \frac{4}{8} = \frac{1}{2}$$

$$\Rightarrow \quad k = 10$$

9. Let the two numbers be $(2x + 1)$ and $(2x + 3)$.

Given, $(2x + 1) + (2x + 3) = 152$

$\Rightarrow \quad 4x + 4 = 152$

$\Rightarrow \quad 4x = 148 \Rightarrow x = 37$

The bigger number

$= (2x + 3) = (2 \times 37 + 3) = 77$

10. Let the number of pencils C has x.

The number of pencils B has $(x + 5)$.

The number of pencils A has

$$(x + 5) + 5 = (x + 10)$$

Clearly, if A gives 5 pencils to C, then each of the three will have $(x + 5)$ pencils.

$\Rightarrow$ 5 pencils should change hands.

11. Let the required numbers be $5x$, $6x$ and $9x$. Then,

$$25x^2 + 36x^2 + 81x^2 = 2272$$

$$\Rightarrow \quad 142x^2 = 2272$$

$$\Rightarrow \quad x^2 = \frac{2272}{142} = 16$$

$$\Rightarrow \quad x = 4$$

Smallest of the given numbers

$$= 5x = 5 \times 4 = 20$$

12. Let the digit in the units place be y and digit in the tens place be x.

$\therefore \quad$ Number $= 10x + y$

Then, $\quad x = 2y + 2$

$\Rightarrow \quad x - 2y - 2 = 0 \qquad \ldots(\text{i})$

Number obtained by reversing the digits

$$= 10y + x$$

Then, $\quad 10y + x = 5 + 3(x + y)$

$\Rightarrow \quad 2x - 7y + 5 = 0 \qquad \ldots(\text{ii})$

On multiplying Eq. (i) by 2 and subtracting it from Eq. (ii), we get $y = 3$

On substituting the value of y in Eq. (i), we get

$$x = 8$$

So, the two-digit number is 83.

13. Let the number of oranges Ramesh has be x and the number of oranges Ganesh has be y.

According to first condition,

$\Rightarrow \quad y + 5 = 3(x - 5)$

$\Rightarrow \quad 3x - y - 20 = 0 \qquad \ldots(\text{i})$

According to second condition,

$\Rightarrow \quad x + 5 = y - 5$

$\Rightarrow \quad x - y + 10 = 0 \qquad \ldots(\text{ii})$

On subtracting Eq. (ii) from Eq. (i), we get

$$x = 15$$

On substituting the value of x in Eq. (ii), we get

$$y = 25$$

$\therefore$ The ratio of oranges between Ramesh and Ganesh $= 15 : 25 = 3 : 5$

14. The number of girls in the class is y and the number of boys is x.

When 3 girls leave the class, then

$$y - 3 = x$$

$\Rightarrow \quad x - y + 3 = 0 \qquad \ldots(\text{i})$

When 5 boys leave the class, then

$$x - 5 = \frac{2(y - 3)}{3}$$

$\Rightarrow \quad 3x - 2y - 9 = 0 \quad \ldots(\text{ii})$

Multiplying Eq. (i) by 3 and subtracting from Eq. (ii), we get $y = 18$

So, the number of girls in the class is 18.

15. Let the number of hens be x and the number of horses be y. Then,

$$2x + 4y = 294 \qquad \ldots(\text{i})$$

and $\quad x + y = 111 \qquad \ldots(\text{ii})$

On multiplying Eq. (ii) by 2 and subtracting it from Eq. (i), we get $y = 36$

So, the number of horses are 36.

16. Let the number of 25 paise coins be x.

Let the number of 50 paise coins be y.

$$x + y = 38 \quad \ldots(i)$$

Also, $25x + 50y = 1350 \quad \ldots(ii)$

multiplying Eq. (i) by 25 and subtracting from Eq. (ii), we get $y = 16$

On substituting the value of y in Eq. (i), we get

$$x = 22$$

So, the number of 25 paise coins is 22.

17. Let the number of correct answers marked be c and the number of wrong answers marked be w.

$$c + w = 60 \quad \ldots(i)$$

Also, $3c - w = 120 \quad \ldots(ii)$

Adding Eqs. (i) and (ii), we get $c = 45$

$\therefore$ The questions marked right are 45.

18. Let the cost of each apple, orange and pear be ₹ x, ₹ y and ₹ z respectively. Then,

$$2x + 3y + z = 62 \quad \ldots(i)$$

$$5x + 6y + 4z = 120 \quad \ldots(ii)$$

On subtracting Eq. (i) from Eq. (ii), we get

$$3x + 3y + 3z = 58$$

So, the cost of 3 apples, 3 oranges and 3 pears is ₹ 58.

19. Let the number be x. Then,

$$\frac{5x}{2} - \frac{2x}{5} = 5208$$

$$\Rightarrow \frac{25x - 4x}{10} = 5208$$

$$\Rightarrow \frac{21x}{10} = 5208$$

$$\Rightarrow 21x = 5208 \times 10$$

$$\Rightarrow x = \frac{5208 \times 10}{21}$$

$$\Rightarrow x = 2480$$

So, the original number was 2480.

20. Here, $\frac{a_1}{a_2} = \frac{3}{9} = \frac{1}{3}, \frac{b_1}{b_2} = \frac{\frac{5}{2}}{\frac{15}{2}} = \frac{1}{3},$

$$\frac{c_1}{c_2} = \frac{-7}{-21} = \frac{1}{3} \quad \therefore \frac{a_1}{a_2} = \frac{b_1}{b_2} = \frac{c_1}{c_2}$$

Hence, equations have infinite number of solutions.

21. Age of girl = x yr and age of father = $5x$ yr

After $2x$ yr,

Age of girl = $x + 2x = 3x$ yr and age of father

$= 5x + 2x = 7x$ yr

Hence, age of father is $7x$ yr when age of girl is $3x$ yr.

22. $2\sqrt{5}x^2 - 3x - \sqrt{5} = 0$

$$\Rightarrow 2\sqrt{5}x^2 - 5x + 2x - \sqrt{5} = 0$$

$$\Rightarrow \sqrt{5}x\,(2x - \sqrt{5}) + 1\,(2x - \sqrt{5}) = 0$$

$$\Rightarrow (2x - \sqrt{5})(\sqrt{5}x + 1) = 0$$

$$\Rightarrow 2x - \sqrt{5} = 0 \text{ or } \sqrt{5}x + 1 = 0$$

$$\Rightarrow x = \frac{\sqrt{5}}{2} \text{ or } x = -\frac{1}{\sqrt{5}}$$

23. $4x^2 - 2(a^2 + b^2)x + a^2 b^2 = 0$

$$\Rightarrow (4x^2 - 2a^2x) - (2b^2x - a^2 b^2) = 0$$

$$\Rightarrow 2x\,(2x - a^2) - b^2(2x - a^2) = 0$$

$$\Rightarrow (2x - a^2)(2x - b^2) = 0$$

$$\Rightarrow 2x - a^2 = 0 \text{ or } 2x - b^2 = 0$$

$$\Rightarrow x = \frac{a^2}{2} \text{ or } \frac{b^2}{2}$$

24. $\frac{x+3}{x-2} - \frac{1-x}{x} = \frac{17}{4}$

$$\Rightarrow \frac{x(x+3) - (x-2)(1-x)}{x(x-2)} = \frac{17}{4}$$

$$\Rightarrow \frac{x^2 + 3x - x + x^2 + 2 - 2x}{x(x-2)} = \frac{17}{4}$$

$$\Rightarrow \frac{2x^2 + 2}{x(x-2)} = \frac{17}{4}$$

$$\Rightarrow 4\,(2x^2 + 2) = 17x(x-2)$$

$$\Rightarrow 8x^2 + 8 = 17x^2 - 34x$$

$$\Rightarrow 9x^2 - 34x - 8 = 0$$

$$\Rightarrow 9x^2 - 36x + 2x - 8 = 0$$

$$\Rightarrow 9x(x-4) + 2(x-4) = 0$$

$$\Rightarrow (x-4)(9x+2) = 0$$

$$\Rightarrow x - 4 = 0 \text{ or } 9x + 2 = 0$$

$$\Rightarrow x = 4 \text{ or } x = -\frac{2}{9}$$

25. Since, $x = 2$ is a root of

$$2x^2 - kx - m = 0$$

$$\therefore \quad 2\,(2)^2 - k(2) - m = 0$$

$$\Rightarrow \quad -2k - m + 8 = 0$$

$$\Rightarrow \quad 2k + m - 8 = 0 \quad \ldots(i)$$

Also, $x = -\frac{3}{2}$ is a root of

$2x^2 - kx - m = 0$

$$\therefore \quad 2\left(-\frac{3}{2}\right)^2 - k\left(-\frac{3}{2}\right) - m = 0$$

$$\Rightarrow \quad 2 \times \frac{9}{4} + \frac{3k}{2} - m = 0$$

$$\Rightarrow \quad \frac{3k}{2} - m + \frac{9}{2} = 0$$

$$\Rightarrow \quad 3k - 2m + 9 = 0 \quad \ldots(ii)$$

Multiplying Eq. (i) by 2 and adding to Eq. (ii), we get

$$k = 1$$

Substituting the value of k in Eq. (i), we get

$$m = 6$$

$$\therefore \quad k = 1 \text{ and } m = 6$$

26. Given, $\frac{2}{x^2} - \frac{5}{x} + 2 = 0$

$$\Rightarrow \quad 2x^2 - 5x + 2 = 0$$

Here, $a = 2, b = -5$ and $c = 2$

Sum of the roots

$$= -\frac{b}{a} = -\frac{(-5)}{2} = \frac{5}{2}$$

Product of the roots

$$= \frac{c}{a} = \frac{2}{2} = 1$$

27. If $(6+\sqrt{5})$ is one root, then the other root is $(6-\sqrt{5})$ as m and n are real.
Sum of the roots
$$=(6+\sqrt{5})+(6-\sqrt{5})=12$$
Product of the roots
$$=(6+\sqrt{5})(6-\sqrt{5})=31$$
Thus, the required equation is
$$x^2-12x+31=0$$
$$\Rightarrow \quad m=-12 \text{ and } n=31$$

28. If the roots of the equation are reciprocals of each other, then the product of the roots should be equal to 1.
Here, $a=k, b=5$ and $c=-2$
Product of the roots
$$=\frac{c}{a}=-\frac{2}{k}=1$$
$$\Rightarrow \quad k=-2$$

29. Let α and β be the roots of the equation. Then,
$$\alpha+\beta=5 \quad \ldots\text{(i)}$$
$$\alpha^2+\beta^2=13 \quad \ldots\text{(ii)}$$
$$(\alpha+\beta)^2=\alpha^2+\beta^2+2\alpha\beta$$
$$5^2=13+2\alpha\beta$$
$$\Rightarrow \quad 2\alpha\beta=25-13=12$$
$$\Rightarrow \quad \alpha\beta=6$$
$\therefore$ The required equation is
$$x^2-5x+6=0$$

30. Here, $a=2, b=2$ and $c=5$
$$b^2-4ac=(2)^2-4\times2\times5$$
$$=4-40=-36$$
As $-36<0$, the roots are imaginary.

31. Let the two consecutive even integers be
$2n$ and $2n+2$.
Then, $(2n)^2+(2n+2)^2=884$
$$\Rightarrow 4n^2+4n^2+8n+4=884$$
$$\Rightarrow \quad 8n^2+8n-880=0$$
$$\Rightarrow \quad n^2+n-110=0$$
$$\Rightarrow \quad n^2+11n-10n-110=0$$
$$\Rightarrow \quad n(n+11)-10(n+11)=0$$
$$\Rightarrow \quad (n+11)(n-10)=0$$
$$\Rightarrow \quad n+10=0 \text{ or } n-10=0$$
$$\Rightarrow \quad n=-11 \text{ or } 10$$
$$\Rightarrow \quad n=10$$
[$\because$ n cannot be negative]
Then, the required numbers are $2n$ and $(2n+2)$, i.e, 20 and 22.

32. Let the number be x.
$$\Rightarrow \quad x+17=60\times\frac{1}{x}$$
$$\Rightarrow \quad x+17=\frac{60}{x}$$
$$\Rightarrow \quad x^2+17x-60=0$$
$$\Rightarrow \quad x^2+20x-3x-60=0$$
$$\Rightarrow x(x+20)-3(x+20)=0$$
$$\Rightarrow \quad (x+20)(x-3)=0$$
$$\Rightarrow \quad x+20=0$$
$$\text{or} \quad x-3=0$$
$$\Rightarrow \quad x=-20 \text{ or } 3$$
$$\Rightarrow \quad x=-20$$
as x cannot be positive

33. Let the two parts be x and $(45-x)$.
Then, $x^2+(45-x)^2=1157$
$$\Rightarrow x^2+2025+x^2-90x=1157$$
$$\Rightarrow \quad 2x^2-90x+868=0$$
$$\Rightarrow \quad x^2-45x+434=0$$
$$\Rightarrow \quad x^2-31x-14x+434=0$$
$$\Rightarrow x(x-31)-14(x-31)=0$$
$$\Rightarrow \quad (x-31)(x-14)=0$$
$$\Rightarrow \quad x=31 \text{ or } x=14$$
If $x=31, (45-x)=14$
and if $x=14$ $(45-x)=31$
So, the two parts are 14 and 31.

34. Let the number be x. Then,
$$x+\sqrt{x}=\frac{8}{49}$$
Let $\sqrt{x}=y$.
Then, $y^2+y=\frac{8}{49}$
$$\Rightarrow 49y^2+49y-8=0$$
$$\Rightarrow \quad 49y^2+56y-7y-8=0$$
$$\Rightarrow 7y(7y+8)-1(7y+8)=0$$
$$\Rightarrow \quad (7y+8)(7y-1)=0$$
$$\Rightarrow \quad 7y+8=0 \text{ or } 7y-1=0$$
$$\Rightarrow \quad y=\frac{-8}{7} \text{ or } \frac{1}{7}$$
$$\Rightarrow \quad y=\frac{1}{7}$$
[$\because y$ cannot be negative]
Now, $\sqrt{x}=y=\frac{1}{7}$
$$\Rightarrow \quad x=\frac{1}{49}$$
So, the required number is $\frac{1}{49}$.

Previous Year's Solutions

35. Let numerator of the fraction $=x$
Then, denominator of the fraction $=x+11$
According to the question,
$$\frac{x+8}{(x+11)+8}=\frac{3}{4}$$
$$\Rightarrow \quad 4(x+8)=3(x+19)$$
$$\Rightarrow \quad 4x+32=3x+57$$
$$\Rightarrow \quad x=25$$
Thus, fraction $=\frac{x}{x+11}=\frac{25}{36}$

36. Let amount given to $Q=x$
Then, amount given to $P=2x$
And amount given to $R=4x$
Given, difference between the shares of Q and $R=3675$
$$\Rightarrow \quad 4x-x=3675$$
$$\Rightarrow \quad 3x=3675$$
$$\Rightarrow \quad x=1225$$
Thus, total sum
$$=x+2x+4x=7x$$
$$=7\times1225=₹8575$$

37. $4x^3 + 6x^2 + 2x + \frac{7}{2}$

$4x-3)16x^4+12x^3-10x^2+8x+20($

$16x^4-12x^3$

$- \quad +$

$24x^3-10x^2$

$24x^3-18x^2$

$- \quad +$

$8x^2+8x$

$8x^2-6x$

$- \quad +$

$14x+20$

$14x-\frac{21}{2}$

$- \quad +$

$\frac{61}{2}$

Thus, quotient

$=4x^3+6x^2+2x+\frac{7}{2}$

Remainder $=\frac{61}{2}$

38. Let the prices of 1 trouser and 1 shirt are ₹ x and ₹ y, respectively.

Therefore, according to the question,

$2x+4y=1600$

$\Rightarrow \quad x+2y=800$ ...(i)

and $\quad x+6y=1600$ ...(ii)

On subtracting Eq. (i) from Eq. (ii), we get

$4y=800 \Rightarrow y=200$

Thus, price of 12 shirts

$=12\times200=$₹2400

39. For infinite solutions

$\frac{a_1}{a_2}=\frac{b_1}{b_2}=\frac{c_1}{c_2}$

Here,

$a_1=K, b_1=3,$

$a_2=12, b_2=K$

$c_1=-K+3$ and $c_2=-K$

$\Rightarrow \frac{K}{12}=\frac{3}{K}=\frac{-K+3}{-K}$

$\Rightarrow K^2=36$

$\therefore \quad K=\sqrt{36}=6$

40. Let the number of hens be x and that of goats be y.

According to the question,

$x+y=80$ (number of total heads) ...(i)

and $2x+4y=200$ (number of total feet) ...(ii)

On multiplying Eq. (i) by 2 and subtracting it from Eq. (ii), we get

$2y=200-160=40$

$\Rightarrow \quad y=\frac{40}{2}=20$

$\therefore \quad x=80-20=60$

(x, y) or (hens, goats) $=(60, 20)$

So, the number of total goats are 20.

41. Let the ₹10 notes be x.

Then, notes of ₹ 20 = $(150-x)$

$\Rightarrow 10\times x+(150-x)\,20=2000$

$\Rightarrow 10x+3000-20x=2000$

$\Rightarrow \quad -10x=2000-3000$

$\Rightarrow \quad 10x=1000$

$\therefore \quad x=100$

42. Let the total income be x.

Part spent on food $=\frac{1}{3}$ of total income

Part spent on house rent $=\frac{1}{4}$ of total income.

Then, remaining part spent on other items

$=x-\left(\frac{x}{4}+\frac{x}{3}\right)=x-\left(\frac{7x}{12}\right)$

$=\frac{12x-7x}{12}=\frac{5x}{12}$

According to the question,

$\frac{5x}{12}=630$

(part spent on other item)

$\therefore \quad x=\frac{630\times12}{5}=$₹ 1512

To find hourrent we Know it is $\frac{x}{4}$

$\therefore$ House rent $=\frac{x}{4}=1512\times\frac{1}{4}$

$=$₹378

43. Let the two consecutive even numbers be x and $(x+2)$, respectively.

According to the question,

$x^2+(x+2)^2=1060$

$\Rightarrow x^2+x^2+4+4x=1060$

$\Rightarrow 2x^2+4x-1056=0$

$\Rightarrow x^2+2x-528=0$

$\Rightarrow x^2+24x-22x-528=0$

$\Rightarrow x(x+24)-22(x+24)=0$

$\Rightarrow (x-22)(x+24)=0$

$\Rightarrow x=-24, 22$

Since, the numbers are positive.

So, the required numbers are 22 and 24.

44. Given, polynomial $=ax^2-6x-6$

Let α and β be the zeroes of above polynomial.

$\therefore \quad \alpha\beta=4 \Rightarrow \frac{c}{a}=4$

$\Rightarrow \frac{-6}{a}=4$

$\Rightarrow \quad a=\frac{-6}{4}=\frac{-3}{2}$

45. Let Keerthi's father gives amount be x amount be Then,

$\frac{x}{2}+\frac{x}{4}+5+20=x$

$\Rightarrow \frac{3x}{4}+25=x$

$\Rightarrow \frac{x}{4}=25$

$\Rightarrow \quad x=$₹100

CHAPTER 03

PERCENTAGE

The meaning of term per cent is per hundred or hundredth part.

"Per cent is a fraction whose denominator is 100 and numerator of the fraction is called the rate per cent". Per cent is denoted by the symbol '%'.

e.g. Meaning of 35% is $\frac{35}{100}$, i.e. parts out of 100 parts.

Important Formulae

(i) $y\,\%$ of $x = \frac{x \times y}{100} = \frac{xy}{100}$.

(ii) To convert a fraction into per cent, multiply the fraction by 100 and then put the sign '%'.

e.g. $\frac{5}{35} = \frac{5}{35} \times 100\% = 14\frac{2}{7}\%$

(iii) To convert the given percentage into fraction, remove the sign % and divide the quantity by 100.

e.g. $24\% = \frac{24}{100} = 0.24$

(iv) The per cent of one quantity to another $= \frac{\text{First quantity}}{\text{Second quantity}} \times 100\%$

e.g. Percentage of 30 kg to 120 kg $= \frac{30}{120} \times 100\% = 25\%$

To use this formula, both the quantities must be in same unit.

(v) Percentage increase/decrease $= \frac{\text{Increase / decrease}}{\text{Base value}} \times 100$

EXAMPLE 1. Which of the following numbers represents 30% of 450? **[BHU 2015]**

(a) 150 (b) 135 (c) 180 (d) 1350

Solution *(b)* 30% of 450 $= 450 \times \frac{30}{100} = 135$

EXAMPLE 2. A basket contains 250 eggs. 150 were not broken. What percentage of the eggs were broken?

(a) 40% (b) 50% (c) 60% (d) 66.6%

Solution *(a)* Total Number of eggs = 250

Number of eggs not broken = 150

∴ Number of eggs broken = 250 − 150 = 100

Broken egg's percentage $= \frac{100}{250} \times 100\% = 40\%$

Useful Tricks

(i) If the price of a commodity is increased (or decreased) by x%, then the decrease (or increase) in consumption so as not to increase (or decrease) the expenditure is $\left(\frac{x}{100 \pm x} \times 100\right)\%$.

> (i) If price of a commodity is increased then take '+' sign.
>
> (ii) If price of a commodity is decreased then take '−' sign.

(ii) If the value of a number is first increased (or decreased) by x_1% and then decreased (or increased) by x_2%, then

$$\text{Net effect} = \left[\pm x_1 \pm x_2 + \frac{(\pm x_1) \times (\pm x_2)}{100}\right]\%$$

+ ve sign for increase

− ve sign for decrease

Net effect is a increase or a decrease according to the + ve or − ve sign, respectively of the final result.

(iii) If the population of a town is P and population increases or decreases by annually, then the population of town after n year will be A.

Then, $A = P\left(1 \pm \frac{x}{100}\right)^n$

Also, population of town n year ago,

$$A = \frac{P}{\left[1 \pm \frac{x}{100}\right]^n}$$

Use '+' sign for increment and '−' sign for decrement.

EXAMPLE 3. Price of a commodity is decreased by 45 %. By how much per cent can the consumption be increased so that the expense remains the same?

(a) 80% (b) 45%

(c) 70% (d) None of these

Solution *(d)* Here, $x = 45$

∴ Required percentage $= \frac{x}{(100 - x)} \times 100$

$= \frac{45}{(100 - 45)} \times 100$

$= \frac{45 \times 100}{55} = \frac{900}{11}$

$= 81\frac{9}{11}\%$

EXAMPLE 4. When the price of an article was reduced by 20% and its sale increased by 80%. What was the net effect on the sale?

(a) 80% decrease (b) 20% increase

(c) 70% decrease (d) 44% increase

Solution *(d)* Given, $x = 80\%$ and $y = 20\%$

∴ Required effect $= \left(x - y - \frac{xy}{100}\right)$

$= \left(80 - 20 - \frac{80 \times 20}{100}\right)\%$

$= (60 - 16)\% = 44\%$

Practice Exercise

1. Three candidates contested an election and received 1136, 7636 and 11628 votes, respectively. What percentage of the total votes did the winning candidate get?

(a) 57% (b) 60%
(c) 65% (d) 90%

2. Two tailors *X* and *Y* are paid a total of ₹ 550 per week by their employer. If *X* is paid 120% of the sum paid to *Y*. Then, how much is *Y* paid per week?

(a) ₹ 200 (b) ₹ 250
(c) ₹ 300 (d) None of these

3. A has some mangoes. He sold 40% more than he ate. If he sold 70 mangoes, how many did he eat?

(a) 50 (b) 90
(c) 18 (d) 42

4. Rajeev buys goods worth ₹ 6650. He gets a rebate of 6% on it. After getting the rebate, he pays sales tax @ 10%. Find the amount he will have to pay for the goods.

(a) ₹ 6876.10 (b) ₹ 6999.20
(c) ₹ 6654 (d) ₹ 7000

5. The population of a town increased from 175000 to 262500 in a decade. The average per cent increase of population per year is

(a) 4.37% (b) 5%
(c) 6% (d) 8.75 %

6. If each of the dimensions of a rectangle is increased by 200%, the area is increased by

(a) 300% (b) 200%
(c) 800% (d) 600%

7. What percentage of numbers from 1 to 70 have 1 or 9 as the unit's digit?

(a) 1% (b) 14%
(c) 20% (d) 21%

8. A fruit seller had some apples. He sells 40% apples and still has 420 apples. Originally, he had

(a) 588 apples (b) 600 apples
(c) 672 apples (d) 700 apples

9. Two students appeared at an examination. One of them secured 9 marks more than the other and his marks was 56% of the sum of their marks. The marks obtained by them are

(a) 39, 30 (b) 41, 32
(c) 42, 33 (d) 43, 34

10. A batsman scored 110 runs which included 3 boundaries and 8 sixes. What per cent of his total score did he make by running between the wickets?

(a) 45% (b) $45\frac{5}{11}\%$ (c) $54\frac{6}{11}\%$ (d) 55%

11. A student multiplied a number by $\frac{3}{5}$ instead of $\frac{5}{3}$. Find the error percentage.

(a) 34% (b) 44%
(c) 54% (d) 64%

12. Two numbers *A* and *B* are such that the sum of 5% of *A* and 4% of *B* is two-third of the sum of 6% of *A* and 8% of *B*. Find the ratio of *A* : *B*.

(a) 2 : 3 (b) 1 : 1
(c) 3 : 4 (d) 4 : 3

13. Population of a city is 2,96,000 out which 1,66,000 are males. 50% population is literate. If 70% males are literate, then the number of women who are literate is

(a) 48,000 (b) 66,400
(c) 32,000 (d) 31,800

14. If 20% of $a = b$, then b% of 20 is same as

(a) 4% of *a* (b) 5% of *a*
(c) 20% of *a* (d) None of these

15. In a test, a candidate secured 336 marks out of maximum marks *x*. If the maximum marks *x* had been converted into 400 marks, he would have secured 192 marks. What was the maximum marks of the test?

(a) 700 (b) 750 (b) 500 (d) 650

16. In a factory, 60% of the workers are above 30 yr and of these 75% are males and the rest are females. If there are 1350 male workers above 30 yr, the total number of workers in the factory is

(a) 3000 (b) 2000
(c) 1800 (d) 1500

17. Twelve per cent of Kaushal's monthly salary is equal to sixteen per cent of Nandini's monthly salary. Suresh's monthly salary is half that of Nandini's monthly salary. If Suresh's annual salary is ₹ 1.08 lakh, what is Kaushal's monthly salary?

(a) ₹ 20000 (b) ₹ 18000
(c) ₹ 26000 (d) ₹ 24000

18. Fresh grapes contain 90% water by weight while dried grapes contain 20% water by weight. What is the weight of dry grapes available from 20 kg of fresh grapes?

(a) 2 kg (b) 2.4 kg
(c) 2.5 kg (d) 2.6 kg

Previous Year's Questions

19. If 0.06% of a number is 84, then 30% of that number is **[CLAT 2012]**

(a) 25.2 (b) 420
(c) 42000 (d) 2520

20. Out of the total income, X spends 20% on house rent and 70% of the remaining amount on household expenditure. If X saves ₹ 1800, the total income is **[CLAT 2012]**

(a) ₹ 8000 (b) ₹ 9500
(c) ₹ 7500 (d) ₹ 8500

21. The sum of two numbers is 2490. If 6.5% of one number is equal to 8.5% of the other, the numbers are **[CLAT 2012]**

(a) 1411 and 1079 (b) 1412 and 1080
(c) 1141 and 1709 (d) 1214 and 1800

22. A mixture of 40 L of alcohol and water contains 10% water. How much water should be added to this mixture, so that the new mixture contains 20% water? **[CLAT 2014]**

(a) 9 L (b) 5 L
(c) 7 L (d) 6 L

23. If 80% of A = 20% of B and B = $5x$% of A, then the value of x is **[CLAT 2014]**

(a) 75 (b) 80 (c) 90 (d) 85

24. In a company, 60% workders are males. If the number of female workers in the company is 800, what is the number of male workers in the company? **[CLAT 2017]**

(a) 16000 (b) 14000
(c) 1900 (d) 1200

Answers

1	*a*	2	*b*	3	*a*	4	*a*	5	*b*	6	*c*	7	*c*	8	*d*	9	*c*	10	*b*
11	*d*	12	*d*	13	*d*	14	*a*	15	*a*	16	*a*	17	*d*	18	*c*	19	*c*	20	*c*
21	*a*	22	*b*	23	*b*	24	*d*												

SOLUTIONS

1. Total number of votes

$= (1136 + 7636 + 11628)$

$= 20400$

$\therefore$ Required percentage

$= \left(\frac{11628}{20400} \times 100\right)\%$

$= 57\%$

2. Let the sum paid to Y per week be ₹ z.

Then, $z + 120\%$ of $z = 550$

$\Rightarrow \quad z + z\frac{120}{100} = 550$

$\Rightarrow \quad \frac{11}{5}z = 550$

$\Rightarrow \quad z = \left(\frac{550 \times 5}{11}\right) =$ ₹ 250

3. Let he ate x mangoes.

Then, sold mangoes

$= x + 40\%$ of x

But given sold mangoes $= 70$

$\therefore \quad x + 40\%$ of $x = 70$

$\Rightarrow \quad x + \frac{40}{100}x = 70$

$\Rightarrow \quad \frac{14x}{10} = 70$

$\Rightarrow \quad x = 70 \times \frac{10}{14} = 50$

Hence, he ate 50 mangoes.

4. Rebate $= 6\%$ of ₹ 6650

$=$ ₹ $\left(6650 \times \frac{6}{100}\right) =$ ₹ 399

Sales tax $= 10\%$ of ₹ $(6650 - 399)$

$=$ ₹ $\left(6251 \times \frac{10}{100}\right) =$ ₹ 625.10

$\therefore$ Final amount

$=$ ₹ $(6251 + 625.10)$

$=$ ₹ 6876.10

5. Increase in 10 yr

$= (262500 - 175000)$

$= 87500$

Per cent increase

$= \left(\frac{87500}{175000} \times 100\right)\% = 50\%$

$\therefore$ Required average

$= \left(\frac{50}{10}\right)\% = 5\%$

6. Let dimensions of rectangle are x and y respectively.

Then, Area $= xy$

After increment dimensions

$= (x + 200\%$ of $x)$

and $(y + 200\%$ of $y)$

$= \left(x + \frac{200}{100}x\right)$

and $\left(y + \frac{200}{100}y\right)$

$= 3x$ and $3y$

Then, new area

$= (3x)(3y) = 9xy$

Increment in area

$= 9xy - xy = 8xy$

$\therefore$ Required percentage

$= \frac{8xy}{xy} \times 100\% = 800\%$

7. Such numbers from 1 to 70 are 1, 9, 11, 19, 21, 29, 31, 39, 41, 49, 51, 59, 61, 69.

Total such number $= 14$

$\therefore$ Required percentage

$= \left(\frac{14}{70} \times 100\right)\% = 20\%$

8. Suppose originally he had x apples.

Then, $(100 - 40)\%$ of $x = 420$

$\Rightarrow \quad \frac{60}{100} \times x = 420$

$\Rightarrow \quad x = \left(\frac{420 \times 100}{60}\right) = 700$

9. Let their marks be $(x + 9)$ and x.

Then, $x + 9 = \frac{56}{100}(x + 9 + x)$

$\Rightarrow 25(x + 9) = 14(2x + 9)$

$\Rightarrow \quad 3x = 99$

$\Rightarrow \quad x = 33$

So, their marks are 42 and 33.

10. Number of runs made by running

$= 110 - (3 \times 4 + 8 \times 6)$

$= 110 - 60 = 50$

$\therefore$ Required percentage

$= \left(\frac{50}{110} \times 100\right)\% = 45\frac{5}{11}\%$

11. Let the number be x.

Then, error $= \frac{5}{3}x - \frac{3}{5}x = \frac{16}{15}x$

Error percentage

$= \left(\frac{16x}{15} \times \frac{3}{5x} \times 100\right)\% = 64\%$

12. 5% of $A + 4\%$ of $B = \frac{2}{3}$ $(6\%$ of $A + 8\%$ of $B)$

$\Rightarrow \frac{5}{100}A + \frac{4}{100}B$

$= \frac{2}{3}\left(\frac{6}{100}A + \frac{8}{100}B\right)$

$\Rightarrow \frac{1}{20}A + \frac{1}{25}B = \frac{1}{25}A + \frac{4}{75}B$

$\Rightarrow \left(\frac{1}{20} - \frac{1}{25}\right)A = \left(\frac{4}{75} - \frac{1}{25}\right)B$

$\Rightarrow \quad \frac{1}{100}A = \frac{1}{75}B$

$\Rightarrow \quad \frac{A}{B} = \frac{100}{75} = \frac{4}{3}$

$\therefore$ Required ratio $= 4 : 3$

13. Total literate population

$= 50\%$ of 296000

$= \frac{50}{100} \times 296000$

$= 148000$

Number of literate males

$= 70\%$ of 166000

$= \frac{70}{100} \times 166000 = 1,16,200$

∴ Number of literate women $= 148000 - 116200 = 31,800$

14. 20% of $a = b$

$\Rightarrow \frac{20}{100} a = b$

∴ b% of $20 = \frac{20}{100} a \times \frac{1}{100} \times 20$

$= \frac{4}{100} a = 4\%$ of a

15. ∵ Percentage of marks scored by the candidates

$= \frac{192}{400} \times 100\% = 48\%$

∴ 48% of $x = 336$

$\Rightarrow x = \frac{336 \times 100}{48} = 700$

16. Let the total number of workers be x.

∴ $x \times \frac{60}{100} \times \frac{75}{100} = 1350$

$\Rightarrow x = \frac{1350 \times 100 \times 100}{60 \times 75}$

$= 3000$

17. ∵ Suresh's annual salary

= ₹ 1.08 lakh

∴ Suresh's monthly salary

$= \frac{108000}{12} =$ ₹ 9000

⇒ Nandini's monthly salary

$= 9000 \times 2$

Now, 12% of Kaushal's monthly salary

$= 16\%$ of $18000 = \frac{16 \times 18000}{100}$

⇒ Kaushal's monthly salary

$= \frac{16 \times 18000}{100} \times \frac{100}{12}$

= ₹ 24000

18. Weight of fresh grapes = 20 kg

Quantity of water in it

= 90% of

$20 = \frac{90}{100} \times 20 = 18$ kg

Quantity of pulp in it

$= (20 - 18) = 2$ kg

Let weight of dry grapes

$= y$ kg

Then, quantity of water in it = 20% of

$y = \frac{20}{100} \times y = \frac{1}{5} y$

Quantity of pulp in it

$= y - \frac{1}{5} y = \frac{4}{5} y$

∴ $\frac{4}{5} y = 2$

$\Rightarrow y = \frac{2 \times 5}{4} = 2.5$ kg

Previous Year's Solutions

19. Let the required number be x.

Then, 0.06% of $x = 84$

$\Rightarrow x = \frac{84}{0.06\%} = \frac{84}{0.06} \times 100$

$x = 140000$

Now, 30% of $x = \frac{30}{100} \times 140000$

$= 42000$

20. If total income = ₹ x

Expenditure on house rent = 20% of x

Remaining amount $= x - 20\%$ of $x = 80\%$ of $x = 0.80x$

Expenditure on household

$= 70\%$ of $0.80x$

$= 56\%$ of x

Total expenditure

$= (20 + 565\%)$ of x

$= 76\%$ of x

Remaining amount

$= (100 - 76)\%$ of $x = 24\%$ of x

$\Rightarrow x = \frac{1800 \times 100}{24} =$ ₹ 7500

21. Let the two numbers are x and y.

Then, $x + y = 2490$ ...(i)

and 6.5% of $x = 8.5\%$ of y

$\Rightarrow 6.5x = 8.5y$

$\Rightarrow 13x = 17y$

$\Rightarrow x = \frac{17}{13} y$

On putting this value in Eq. (i), we get

$\frac{17}{13} y + y = 2490$

$\frac{30}{13} y = 2490$

$\Rightarrow y = 2490 \times \frac{13}{30} = 1079$

∴ $x = \frac{17}{13} y = \frac{17}{13} \times 1079 = 1411$

22. In 40 L of mixture (alcohol and water) 10% is water.

Quantity of water in mixture at present

$= \frac{40 \times 10}{100} = 4$ L

Now, if mixture contains 20% water after mixing x L of water, then

$\frac{20}{100}(40 + x) = 4 + x$

$\Rightarrow 40 + x = 20 + 5x$

$\Rightarrow 5x - x = 40 - 20$

$\Rightarrow 4x = 20$

∴ $x = 5$ L

23. Given, 80% of $A = 20\%$ of B

$\Rightarrow \frac{80}{100}$ of $A = \frac{20}{100}$ of B

$\Rightarrow 4A = B$ ...(i)

Also given, $B = \frac{5x}{100}$ of A

Now, using Eq. (i),

$4A = \frac{5x}{100} A \Rightarrow x = \frac{400}{5}$

∴ $x = 80$

24. Let total number of worker be x.

The according to given condition.

40% of $x = 800$

$\Rightarrow \frac{40}{100} \times x = 800$

$\Rightarrow x = 2000$

∴ Number of male workers

$= 60\%$ of x

$= \frac{60}{100} \times 2000 = 1200$

CHAPTER 04

RATIO AND PROPORTION

Concept of ratio and proportion is broadly used in the problem solving and data interpretation problems where percentage increase/decrease is compared.

RATIO

Ratio is the relation between one quantity and another quantity, given that both quantity must be of the same kind and same unit, denoted by symbol ':' i.e. the ratio of A and B is written as $A : B$, where A is called the antecedent and B is called the consequent, i.e. $\frac{A}{B}$ or $A : B$.

Types of Ratio

The different types of ratio are explained as below

1. **Duplicate Ratio** If $a : b$ is a ratio, then its duplicate ratio is $a^2 : b^2$.

   e.g. Duplicate ratio of $4 : 5 = 16 : 25$
2. **Sub-duplicate Ratio** If $a : b$ is a ratio, then its sub-duplicate ratio will be $\sqrt{a} : \sqrt{b}$.

   e.g. Sub-duplicate ratio of $25 : 36 = \sqrt{25} : \sqrt{36} = 5 : 6$.
3. **Triplicate Ratio** If $a : b$ is a ratio, then its triplicate ratio will be $a^3 : b^3$.

   e.g. Triplicate ratio of $8 : 3 = 8^3 : 3^3 = 512 : 27$
4. **Sub-triplicate Ratio** If $a : b$ is a ratio, then its sub-triplicate ratio will be $\sqrt[3]{a} : \sqrt[3]{b}$.

   e.g. Sub-triplicate ratio of $4 : 3 = \sqrt[3]{4} : \sqrt[3]{3}$

5. **Inverse Ratio or Reciprocal Ratio** If $y:x$ is a given ratio, then inverse ratio of y and x will be $x:y$.
e.g. Inverse ratio of 9 : 5 = 5 : 9
6. **Compound Ratio** Ratio obtained by multiplying together the **antecedents** of different ratios to get a new antecedent and consequents to get a new consequents is called compound ratio.

e.g. Compound ratio of $\frac{2}{3}, \frac{4}{7}$ and

$$\frac{1}{3} = \frac{2 \times 4 \times 1}{3 \times 7 \times 3} = \frac{8}{63}$$

Comparison of Ratios

Let $a:b$ and $c:d$ be two ratios, then

(i) $a:b > c:d$, if $ad > bc$

(ii) $a:b < c:d$, if $ad < bc$

(iii) $a:b = c:d$, if $ad = bc$

EXAMPLE 1 Two numbers are respectively 20% and 50% more than a third number. What is the ratio of the two numbers?

(a) 5 : 2 (b) 4 : 5 (c) 2 : 5 (d) 5 : 4

Solution *(b)* Let the third number be x.

Then, first number = 120% of $x = \frac{120x}{100} = \frac{6x}{5}$

Second number = 150% of $x = \frac{150x}{100} = \frac{3x}{2}$

Ratio of first two numbers $= \frac{6x}{5} : \frac{3x}{2}$

$= 12x : 15x$

$= 4 : 5$

EXAMPLE 2 Salaries of Ravi and Sumit are in the ratio 2 : 3. If the salary of each is increased by ₹ 4000, then new ratio becomes 40 : 57. What is Sumit's present salary?

(a) 34000 (b) 36000
(c) 38000 (d) 40000

Solution *(c)* Let the original salaries of Ravi and Sumit be ₹ $2x$ and ₹ $3x$, respectively.

Then, $(2x + 4000) / (3x + 4000) = 40 / 57$

$\Rightarrow 57 \times (2x + 4000) = 40 \times (3x + 4000)$

$\Rightarrow 6x = 68000$

$\Rightarrow 3x = 34000$

$\therefore$ Sumit's present salary $= (3x + 4000)$

$= (34000 + 4000)$

$=$ ₹ 38000

Important Tricks

If $A : B = a : b$ and $B : C = m : n$, then $A : C = am : bn$ and $A : B : C = am : mb : nb$.

If $A : B = a : b$, $B : C = c : d$ and $C : D = e : f$, then $A : B : C : D = ace : bce : bde : bdf$.

If x is divided in $a : b$, then 1st part $= \frac{ax}{a+b}$ and 2nd part $= \frac{bx}{a+b}$

PROPORTION

Proportion is an expression in which two ratios are equal. It is denoted by symbol '::'. If a, b, c and d are in proportion, then $a:b::c:d$.

Here, a and d are known as extreme terms and b and c are known as mean terms.

Note The product of extremes is equal to the product of means, i.e. $a \times d = b \times c$.

Continued Proportion Quantities a, b and c are called continued proportion, if $a:b = b:c$, i.e.

$$\frac{a}{b} = \frac{b}{c} \Rightarrow b^2 = ac \text{ or } c = \frac{b^2}{a}$$

Then, b is known as mean proportional and c is known as the third proportional.

Note If $a : b :: c : d$, then d is called the 4th proportional to a, b and c, d will be calculated as $d = \frac{bc}{a}$.

Results on Proportion

1. **Invertendo** If $a:b::c:d$, then $b:a::d:c$.
2. **Alternendo** If $a:b::c:d$, then $a:c::b:d$.
3. **Componendo** If $a:b::c:d$, then $(a + b):b::(c + d):d$.

4. **Dividendo** If $a:b::c:d$, then $(a-b):b::(c-d):d$.
5. **Componendo and dividend** If $a:b::c:d$, then $(a+b):(a-b)::(c+d):(c-d)$.

EXAMPLE 3 What must be added to each of 6, 17, 27 and 59, so that the sums are in proportion?

(a) 3 (b) 4
(c) 5 (d) 6

Solution *(c)* Let x be the number to be added. Then,

$$(6+x):(17+x)::(27+x):(59+x)$$

$$\Rightarrow \frac{6+x}{17+x} = \frac{27+x}{59+x}$$

Using dividendo, we get

$$\frac{6+x-(17+x)}{17+x} = \frac{27+x-(59+x)}{59+x}$$

$$\Rightarrow \frac{-11}{17+x} = \frac{-32}{59+x}$$

$$\Rightarrow -11(59+x) = -32(17+x)$$

$$\Rightarrow -649-11x = -544-32x$$

$$\Rightarrow 32x-11x = -544+649$$

$$\Rightarrow 21x = 105$$

$$\therefore x = 5$$

APPLICATIONS OF RATIO AND PROPORTION

Partnership

Partnership is an association of two or more persons who put their money together to carry out on a certain business. These persons are called partners.

The different types of partnership are explained as below

1. **Simple Partnership** In simple partnership, capitals of partners are invested for the same period of time. In simple partnership, Capital of A : Capital of B = Profit or loss of A : Profit or loss of B.
2. **Compound Partnership** In compound partnership, capitals of partners are invested for the different period of time. In compound partnership, Capital of $A \times$ Time period of A: Capital of $B \times$ Time period of B = Profit or loss of A : Profit or loss of B.

EXAMPLE 4 A starts a business with ₹ 2000. B joins him after 3 months with ₹ 4000. C invests a sum of ₹ 10000 in the business for 2 months only. At the end of yr, the business gave a profit of ₹ 112000. How should the profit be divided amongst A, B and C respectively?

(a) ₹ 30000, ₹ 43000, ₹ 39000
(b) ₹ 33600, ₹ 50400, ₹ 28000
(c) ₹ 25200, ₹ 46800, ₹ 40000
(d) ₹ 28300, ₹ 35700, ₹ 48000

Solution *(b)* Ratio of profit of A, B and C

= capital invested × Time period of investment

A's share : B's share : C's share

$= 2000\times12 : 4000\times(12-3) : 10000\times2$

$= 2\times12 : 4\times9 : 10\times2 = 6:9:5$

Now, let A's share = $6x$,

B's share = $9x$,

C's share = $5x$

According to the question,

$$6x+9x+5x = 112000$$

$$\Rightarrow 20x = 112000$$

$$\therefore x = ₹\ 5600$$

Now, A's share = $6x = 6\times5600 =$ ₹ 33600

B's share = $9x = 9\times5600 =$ ₹ 50400

C's share = $5x = 5\times5600 =$ ₹ 28000

Mixture and Alligation

1. Mixture

The new product obtained by mixing two or more ingredients in a certain ratio is called a mixture.

Mean Price The cost price of a unit quantity of the mixture is called the mean price. It will always be higher than cost price of cheaper quantity and lower than cost price of dearer quantity.

EXAMPLE 5 Two bottles contain mixture of milk and water in the ratios of 8 : 3 and 5 : 1. In what ratio must liquid be drawn from each bottle to give a mixture in the ratio of 4 : 1?

(a) 11 : 24 (b) 11 : 23
(c) 18 : 13 (d) 7 : 11

Solution *(a)* Suppose, we take x units from bottle 1 and y units from bottle 2 to make a mixture of 4 : 1. Bottle with ratio, 8 : 3 will contribute $\frac{8}{11}x$ milk and $\frac{3}{11}x$ water. Similarly, other bottle will contribute $5/6y$ milk and $1/6y$ water.

$$\text{Total milk} = \frac{8}{11}x + \frac{5}{6}y$$

$$\text{Total water} = \frac{3}{11}x + \frac{1}{6}y$$

Now, total milk/total water = 4 / 1

So, $$\left[\frac{8}{11}x + \frac{5}{6}y\right] / \left[\frac{3}{11}x + \frac{1}{6}y\right] = 4/1$$

On solving, we get $x/y = 11/24$

So, $$x : y = 11 : 24$$

2. Alligation

Alligation is the rule that enables us to find the ratio in which two or more ingredients at the given price must be mixed to produce a mixture of the desired price.

When two elements are mixed to make a mixture and one of the elements is cheaper and other one is dearer, then

$$\frac{\text{Quantity of cheaper}}{\text{Quantity of dearer}} = \frac{\text{Price of dearer} - \text{Mean price}}{\text{Mean Price} - \text{Price of cheaper}}$$

Above rule is written as

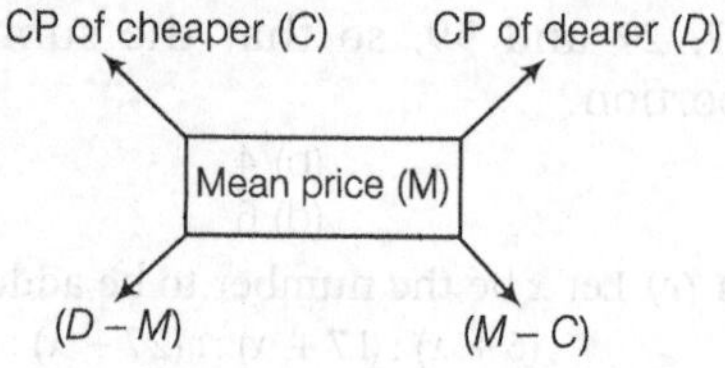

Then, cheaper quantity : dearer quantity
$= (D - M) : (M - C)$

> If a container initially contains a unit of liquid and b unit of liquid is taken out and it is filled with b unit of another liquid, then after n operations, the final quantity of the original liquid in the container is given as $\left[a\left(1 - \frac{b}{a}\right)^n\right]$ units.

EXAMPLE 6 In what ratio should tea at the rate ₹ 40 per kg be mixed with tea at the rate ₹ 27 per kg, so that mixture may cost ₹ 30 per kg?

(a) 4 : 7 (b) 3 : 10
(c) 10 : 11 (d) 7 : 5

Solution *(b)* Using the given formula,

Quantity of cheaper/Quantity of dearere

$= (40 - 30)/(30 - 27)$
$= 10/3$

So, the two should be mixed in the ratio 3 : 10.

Practice Exercise

1. In a bag, there are coins of 25 paise, 10 paise and 5 paise in the ratio of 1 : 2 : 3. If there is ₹ 30 in all, how many 5 paise coins are there?
(a) 50 (b) 100
(c) 150 (d) 200

2. The ratio between two numbers is 2 : 3. If the consequent is 24, the antecedent is
a) 36 (b) 16 (c) 48 (d) 72

3. The fourth proportional to 5, 8, 15 is
(a) 18 (b) 24 (c) 19 (d) 20

4. Seats for Mathematics, Physics and Biology in a school are in the ratio 5 : 7 : 8. There is a proposal to increase these seats by 40%, 50% and 75%, respectively. What will be the ratio of increased seats?
(a) 2 : 3 : 4 (b) 6 : 7 : 8
(c) 6 : 8 : 9 (d) None of these

5. The ratio of ages of Ram and Gopal is 2 : 5 and the ratio of the ages of Gopal and Vishnu is 3 : 4. What would be the ratio of the ages of Ram, Gopal and Vishnu?
(a) 2 : 3 : 4 (b) 3 : 4 : 5
(c) 6 : 10 : 15 (d) 6 : 15 : 20

6. The sum of three numbers is 98. If the ratio of the first to the second is 2 : 3 and that of the second to the third is 5 : 8, then the second number is
(a) 20 (b) 30 (c) 48 (d) 58

7. A sum of money is to be distributed among *A*, *B*, *C* and *D* in the proportion of 5 : 2 : 4 : 3. If *C* gets ₹ 1000 more than *D*, what is *B*'s share?
(a) ₹ 500 (b) ₹ 1500
(c) ₹ 2000 (d) None of these

8. Simran started a software business by investing ₹ 50000. After six months, Nanda joined her with a capital of ₹ 80000. After 3 yr, they earned a profit of ₹ 24500. What was Simran's share in the profit?
(a) ₹ 9423 (b) ₹ 10250
(c) ₹ 12500 (d) ₹ 10500

9. *A*, *B*, *C* subscribe ₹ 50000 for a business. *A* subscribes ₹ 4000 more than *B* and *B* ₹ 5000 more than *C*. Out of a total profit of ₹ 35000, *A* receives
(a) ₹ 8400 (b) ₹ 11900 (c) ₹ 13600 (d) ₹ 14700

10. *A*, *B* and *C* enter into a partnership in the ratio $\frac{7}{2}:\frac{4}{3}:\frac{6}{5}$. After 4 months, *A* increases his share 50%. If the total profit at the end of one year be ₹ 21600, then *B*'s share in the profit is
(a) ₹ 2100 (b) ₹ 2400 (c) ₹ 3600 (d) ₹ 4000

11. At the beginning of a partnership business, the capital of *B* was $\frac{3}{2}$ times that of *A*. After 8 months *B* withdrew $\frac{1}{2}$ of his capital and after 10 months *A* withdrew $\frac{1}{4}$ of his capital. At the end of the year, if the profit incurred is ₹ 53000 find the amount received by *A*.
(a) ₹ 30000 (b) ₹ 23000
(c) ₹ 30800 (d) ₹ 32000

12. Two partners invest ₹ 125000 and ₹ 85000, respectively in a business and agree that 60% of the profit should be divided equally between them and the remaining profit is to be treated as interest on capital. If one partner gets ₹ 600 more than the other, find the total profit made in the business.
(a) ₹ 8800 (b) ₹ 8885 (c) ₹ 8995 (d) ₹ 7875

13. In a mixture of 60 L, the ratio of milk and water 2 : 1. If this ratio is to be 1 : 2, then the quantity of water to be further added is
(a) 20 L (b) 30 L (c) 40 L (d) 60 L

14. 4 L are drawn from a container full of milk and then is filled with water. This operation is performed three more times. The ratio of the quantity of milk left in the container and that of water is 16 : 65. How much milk did the container hold initially?
(a) 24 L (b) 12 L (c) 15 L (d) 25 L

15. A merchant has 1000 kg of sugar, part of which he sells at 8% profit and the rest at 18% profit. He gains 14% on the whole. The quantity sold at 18% profit is

(a) 400 kg (b) 560 kg (c) 600 kg (d) 640 kg

16. A can contains a mixture of two liquids *A* and *B* in the ratio 7 : 5. When 9 L of mixture are drawn off and the can is filled with *B*, the ratio of *A* and *B* becomes 7 : 9. How many litres of liquid *A* was contained by the can initially?

(a) 10 (b) 20 (c) 21 (d) 25

17. Tea worth ₹ 126 per kg and ₹ 135 per kg are mixed with a third variety in the ratio 1 : 1 : 2. If the mixture is worth ₹ 153 per kg, the price of the third variety per kg will be

(a) ₹ 169.50 (b) ₹ 170 (c) ₹ 175.50 (d) ₹ 180

18. How many kilogram of sugar costing ₹ 9 per kg must be mixed with 27 kg of sugar costing ₹ 7 per kg so that there may be a gain of 10% by selling the mixture at ₹ 9.24 per kg?

(a) 36 kg (b) 42 kg (c) 54 kg (d) 63 kg

19. Find the ratio in which rice at ₹ 7.20 per kg, be mixed with rice at ₹ 5.70 per kg to produce a mixture worth ₹ 6.30 per kg.

(a) 1 : 3 (b) 2 : 3 (c) 3 : 4 (d) 4 : 5

Previous Year's Questions

20. During the academic session 2009-10, in Banaras Hindu University, Varanasi, the number of students studying Arts, Law and Commerce was in the ratio of 5 : 6 : 7. If during the academic session 2010-11 the number of students studying Arts, Law and Commerce increased by 20%, 30% and 40% respectively, what will be new ratio? **[CLAT 2011]**

(a) 26 : 42 : 63 (b) 36 : 44 : 73
(c) 26 : 39 : 49 (d) 30 : 39 : 49

21. The ratio of two numbers is 4 : 5. But, if each number is increased by 20, the ratio becomes 6 : 7. The sum of such numbers is **[CLAT 2011]**

(a) 90 (b) 95 (c) 100 (d) 60

22. *A* starts a business with ₹ 5000 and *B* joins the business 5 months later with an investment of ₹ 6000. After a year, they earn a profit of ₹ 34000. Find the shares of *A* and *B* in the profit amount depending on their individual investment. **[CLAT 2014]**

(a) ₹ 20000, ₹ 14000 (b) ₹ 16000, ₹ 16000
(c) ₹ 14000, ₹ 20000 (d) None of these

23. An employer reduces the number of employees in the ratio 8 : 5 and increases their wages in the ratio 7 : 9. Therefore, the overall wages bill is **[CLAT 2016]**

(a) increased in the ratio 45 : 56
(b) decreased in the ratio 56 : 45
(c) increased in the ratio 13 : 17
(d) decreased in the ratio 72 : 35

24. 60 kg of an alloy *X* is mixed with 100 kg of an alloy *Y*. If alloy *X* has lead and tin in the ratio of 3 : 2 and alloy *Y* has tin and copper in the ratio of 1: 4, then the amount of tin in the new alloy is **[CLAT 2016]**

(a) 44 kg (b) 80 kg
(c) 53 kg (d) 36 kg

25. Gold and copper are as heavy as water by 19 and 9 times respectively. The ratio in which these two metals be mixed so that the mixture is 17 times as heavy as water is **[CLAT 2017]**

(a) 3 : 2 (b) 4 : 1
(c) 2 : 3 (d) 3 : 4

26. Praveen has ₹ 4,662 in the form of 2, 5 and 10 rupees notes. If these notes are in the ratio of 3:5:8, the number of five rupees notes with him is **[CLAT 2017]**

(a) 250 (b) 210
(c) 336 (d) 84

27. A vessel contains a mixture of milk and water in the ratio of 5 : 3 respectively. How much of the mixture must be siphoned off and replaced with water, so that the mixture may be half milk and half water? **[CLAT 2017]**

(a) 1/4 (b) 1/7 (c) 1/5 (d) 1/3

Answers

1	*c*	2	*b*	3	*b*	4	*a*	5	*d*	6	*b*	7	*c*	8	*d*	9	*d*	10	*d*
11	*b*	12	*d*	13	*d*	14	*b*	15	*c*	16	*c*	17	*c*	18	*d*	19	*b*	20	*d*
21	*a*	22	*a*	23	*b*	24	*a*	25	*b*	26	*b*	27	*c*						

SOLUTIONS

1. Let the numbers of 25 paise, 10 paise and 5 paise coins be x, $2x$ and $3x$, respectively.

Then, sum of their values

$= ₹\left(\frac{25x}{100} + \frac{10 \times 2x}{100} + \frac{5 \times 3x}{100}\right)$

$= ₹\frac{60x}{100}$

$\therefore \quad \frac{60x}{100} = 30$

$\Rightarrow \quad x = \frac{30 \times 100}{60} = 50$

Hence, the number of 5 paise coins

$= (3 \times 50) = 150$

2. Let antecedent = x

Then, $2:3 :: x:24$

$\Rightarrow 3 \times x = 2 \times 24$

$\Rightarrow \quad x = \frac{2 \times 24}{3}$

$= 16$

3. Let the fourth proportional to 5, 8, 15 be x.

Then, $5 : 8 : : 15 : x$

$\Rightarrow \quad 5x = (8 \times 15)$

$\Rightarrow \quad x = \frac{(8 \times 15)}{5} = 24$

4. Originally, let the numbers of seats for Mathematics, Physics and Biology be $5x$, $7x$ and $8x$, respectively.

$\therefore$ The required ratio

$= \left(\frac{140}{100} \times 5x\right) : \left(\frac{150}{100} \times 7x\right) :$

$\left(\frac{175}{100} \times 8x\right) = 7x : \frac{21x}{2} : 14x$

$= 14x : 21x : 28x = 2 : 3 : 4$

5. Given, Ram : Gopal = 2:5

Gopal : Vishnu = 3:4

$\therefore$ Ram : Gopal : Vishnu

$= 2 \times 3 : 3 \times 5 : 4 \times 5$

$= 6 : 15 : 20$

6. Let the three parts be A, B, C. Then,

$A : B = 2 : 3$

and $\quad B : C = 5 : 8$

$\Rightarrow \quad A : B : C = 10 : 15 : 24$

$\Rightarrow \quad B = \left(98 \times \frac{15}{49}\right) = 30$

7. Let the shares of A, B, C and D be ₹ $5x$, ₹ $2x$, ₹ $4x$ and ₹ $3x$, respectively.

Then, $\quad ₹ 4x - 3x = ₹ 1000$

$\Rightarrow \quad x = ₹ 1000$

$\therefore B$'s share $= 2 \times 1000$

$= ₹ 2000$

8. Simran : Nanda

$= (50000 \times 36)$

$: (80000 \times 30) = 3 : 4$

$\therefore$ Simran's share

$= ₹\left(24500 \times \frac{3}{7}\right) = ₹ 10500$

9. Let $\quad C = x$

Then, $\quad B = x + 5000$

and $\quad A = x + 5000 + 4000$

$= x + 9000$

So, $x + x + 5000 + x + 9000$

$= 50000$

$\Rightarrow \quad 3x = 36000$

$\Rightarrow \quad x = 12000$

$A : B : C$

$= 21000 : 17000 : 12000$

$= 21 : 17 : 12$

$\therefore A$'s share $= ₹\left(35000 \times \frac{21}{50}\right)$

$= ₹ 14700$

10. Let the initial investments be $105x$, $40x$ and $36x$.

$\therefore A : B : C$

$= \left[105x \times 4 + 105x \times \frac{150}{100} \times 8\right]$

$: (40x \times 12) : (36x \times 12)$

$= 1680x : 480x : 432x$

$= 35 : 10 : 9$

Hence, B's share = ₹

$\left(21600 \times \frac{10}{54}\right) = ₹ 4000$

11. Let A invested ₹ x at the beginning of the partnership business, then

Ratio of the profit A and B

$= \left(x \times 10 + \frac{3x}{4} \times 2\right)$

$: \left(\frac{3x}{2} \times 8 + \frac{3x}{4} \times 4\right)$

$= \frac{23}{2} x : 15x = 23 : 30$

$\therefore$ Amount received by A in the profit

$= \frac{23}{53} \times 53000$

$= ₹ 23000$

12. The difference counts only due to 40% of the profit which was distributed according to their investments.

Let total profit = x.

40% of x is distributed in the ratio,

$125000 : 85000 = 25 : 17$

Share of 1st partner

$= 40\% \text{ of } x\left(\frac{25}{25 + 17}\right)$

= 40% of

$\frac{25x}{42} = \frac{40}{100} \times \frac{25x}{42} = \frac{5x}{21}$

Share of 2nd partner

= 40% of

$\frac{17x}{42} = \frac{40}{100} \times \frac{17x}{42} = \frac{17x}{105}$

Now, according to the question

$\frac{5x}{21} - \frac{17x}{105} = 600$

⇒ $\frac{x(25-17)}{105} = 600$

⇒ $x = \frac{600 \times 105}{8} = ₹\ 7875$

13. Quantity of milk = $60 \times \frac{2}{3}$ L

= 40 L

Quantity of water

= (60 − 40) L = 20 L

Let quantity of water to be added further be x litres.

Then, milk : water = $\left(\frac{40}{20+x}\right)$

Now, $\left(\frac{40}{20+x}\right) = \frac{1}{2}$

⇒ 20 + x = 80 ∴ x = 60 L

14. According to the formula,

After *n* operations, quantity of pure liquid

$= \left[a\left(1-\frac{b}{a}\right)^n\right]$ units

Here, $b = 4, n = 4, a = ?$

Quantity of milk left in the container after four operations $= \left[a\left(1-\frac{4}{a}\right)^4\right]$ L

Then, according to the question,

⇒ $\frac{a\left[\left(1-\frac{4}{a}\right)^4\right]}{a} = \frac{16}{65+16} = \frac{16}{81}$

⇒ $\frac{81}{85}$

$\left(1-\frac{4}{a}\right)^4 = \frac{16}{65} - \frac{16}{55}\left(1-\frac{4}{a}\right)^4$

⇒ $\left(1-\frac{4}{a}\right)^4 = \frac{16}{81}$

⇒ $1-\frac{4}{a} = \frac{2}{3} \Rightarrow \frac{4}{a} = \frac{1}{3}$

∴ $a = 12$ L

15. By the rule of alligation, we have

8% 18%
Mean Profit
14%
4 6

Ratio of 1st and 2nd parts

= 4 : 6 = 2 : 3

∴ Quantity of 2nd kind

$= \left(\frac{3}{5} \times 1000\right)$ kg

= 600 kg

16. Let the quantity of liquid *A* and *B* be 7*x* and 5*x*, respectively.

Then, as per question

$\frac{7x - 9 \times \frac{7}{12}}{5x - 9 \times \frac{5}{12} + 9} = \frac{7}{9}$

⇒ $\frac{7x - \frac{21}{4}}{5x - \frac{15}{4} + 9} = \frac{7}{9}$

⇒ $\frac{28x - 21}{20x - 15 + 36} = \frac{7}{9}$

⇒ $252x - 189 = 140x + 147$

⇒ $112x = 336 \Rightarrow x = 3$

∴ Initial amount of liquid $A = 7x = 7 \times 3 = 21$ L

17. Since, first and second varieties are mixed in equal proportions.

So, their average price

$= ₹\left(\frac{126+135}{2}\right) = ₹\ 130.50$

So, the mixture is formed by mixing two varieties, one at ₹ 130.50 per kg and the other at say, ₹ *x* per kg in the ratio 2 : 2, i.e. 1 : 1. We have to find *x*. By the rule of alligation, we have

₹ 130.50 ₹ x
Mean Price
₹ 153
(x−153) 22.50

∴ $\frac{x - 153}{22.50} = \frac{1}{1}$

⇒ x − 153 = 22.50

∴ x = ₹ 175.50

18. SP of 1 kg of mixture

= ₹ 9.24 Gain = 10%

∴ CP of 1 kg of mixture

$= ₹\left(\frac{100}{110} \times 9.24\right)$

= ₹ 8.40

By the rule of alligation, we have

₹ 9 ₹ 7
Mean Price
₹ 8.40
₹ 1.40 ₹ 0.60

∴ Ratio of quantities of 1st and 2nd kind

= 14 : 6 = 7 : 3

Let *x* kg of sugar of 1st be mixed with 27 kg of 2nd kind.

Then, 7 : 3 = *x* : 27

⇒ $x = \left(\frac{7 \times 27}{3}\right)$

= 63 kg

19. By the rule of alligation,

720 paise 570 paise
Mean Price
630 paise
60 paise 90 paise

∴ Required ratio

= 60 : 90 = 2 : 3

Previous Year's Solutions

20. According to question,

New ratio

$= \frac{5 \times 120}{100} : \frac{6 \times 130}{100} : \frac{7 \times 140}{100}$

$= 30 : 39 : 49$

21. Let the numbers be $4x$ and $5x$.

According to the question,
$$\frac{4x+20}{5x+20}=\frac{6}{7}$$
$$\Rightarrow \quad 28x+140=30x+120$$
$$\Rightarrow \quad x=10$$
∴ Sum of numbers
$$=10\times 4+10\times 5=90$$

22. Ratio of shares of A and B = Ratio of investment of A and B
$$\Rightarrow \frac{A\text{'s investment}}{B\text{'s investment}}=\frac{A\text{'s share}}{B\text{'s share}}$$
$$\Rightarrow \frac{5000\times 12}{6000\times(12-5)}=\frac{A\text{'s share}}{B\text{'s share}}$$
$$\Rightarrow \frac{60}{42}=\frac{A\text{'s share}}{B\text{'s share}}$$
$\Rightarrow$

$10:7=A$'s share : B's share

i.e. A's share : B's share $=10:7$
$$\therefore A\text{'s share}=\frac{\text{Total earning}}{\text{Total ratio}}\times A\text{'s ratio}$$
$$=\frac{34000}{17}\times 10=₹\,20000$$
and B's share $=34000-20000$ = ₹ 14000

23. Let the number of employees before and after reduction be $8x$ and $5x$ respectively and let their respective wages (per employee) be $7y$ and $9y$.

∴ Wage bill before reduction
$$=8x\times 7y=56xy$$
and wage bill after reduction
$$=5x\times 9y=45xy$$
Hence, over all wage bill has decreased in the ratio 56 : 45.

24. Quantity of tin in alloy
$$X=60\times\frac{2}{5}=24\text{ kg}$$
Quantity of tin in alloy
$$Y=100\times\frac{1}{5}=20\text{ kg}$$
∴ Quantity of tin in new alloy $=24+20=44$ kg

25. Let 1 gm of gold be mixed with y gm of copper to give $(1+y)$ gm of mixture.

Now 1 G = 19W, 1C = 9W and mixture = 17W

Now, 1 gm gold + y gm copper $=(1+y)$ gm mix
$$\Rightarrow 19w+9wy=(1+y)\times 17w$$
$$\Rightarrow \quad 19w-17w=17wy-9wy$$
$$\Rightarrow 2w=8wy\Rightarrow y=\frac{1}{4}$$

26. Let the number of 2, 5 and 10 rupees notes be x, y and z respectively.
$$\therefore 2x+5y+10z=4662$$
Also, $x:y:z=3:5:8$

$\Rightarrow x=3k, y=5k$ and $z=8k$

$\Rightarrow$ From Eq. (ii)
$$2(3k)+5(5k)+10(8k)=4662$$
$$\Rightarrow \quad 6k+25k+80k=4662$$
$$\Rightarrow 111k=4662$$
∴ Number of ₹5 notes $=5k$
$$=5\times 42=210$$

27. Final fraction of milk

= initial fraction of milk × (1 − fraction of mixture taken out)^n

∴ Where 'n' is the number of times process is done

Thus, $\frac{1}{2}=\frac{5}{8}\times(1-x)^1$
$$\Rightarrow \quad \frac{1}{2}=\frac{5}{8}-\frac{5x}{8}$$
$$\Rightarrow \quad \frac{5x}{8}=\frac{5}{8}-\frac{1}{2}=\frac{5-4}{8}$$
$$\therefore \quad x=\frac{1}{5}$$

CHAPTER 05

AVERAGE

The average of given numbers is obtained on dividing the sum of the given observations by the total number of observations.

i.e. $$\text{Average} = \frac{\text{Sum of observations}}{\text{Number of observations}}$$

Let $a_1, a_2, \ldots, a_n$ be n observations, then

$$\text{Average} = \frac{a_1 + a_2 + a_3 + \ldots + a_n}{n}$$

Example 1 A person wrote down the time he spent on doing exercise in a week. These readings are as follow

Day	Exercise time
Monday	20 min
Tuesday	30 min
Wednesday	20 min
Thursday	35 min
Friday	25 min

Find the average time spent on exercise each day.

(a) 25 min (b) 26 min (c) 28 min (d) 30 min

Solution *(b)* Average = Sum of the reading time/Number of days

$$= \frac{20+30+20+35+25}{5} = 130/5 = 26 \text{ min}$$

Weighted Average

If the average on n_1 quantitites is x and that of n_2 quantities is y, then the average of total $(n_1 + n_2)$ quantities is given by $\frac{n_1 x + n_2 y}{n_1 + n_2}$.

EXAMPLE 2 In a class, there are 2 students of 20 yr, 3 students of 21 yr, 4 students of 22 yr and 5 students of 23 yr. Find their average age.

(a) 380/7 yr (b) 426/9 yr
(c) 306/14 yr (d) 295/32 yr

Solution *(c)* Required average age

$$= \frac{(2 \times 20) + (3 \times 21) + (4 \times 22) + (5 \times 23)}{2 + 3 + 4 + 5}$$

$$= \frac{2}{14} \times 20 + \frac{3}{14} \times 21 + \frac{4}{14} \times 22 + \frac{5}{14} \times 23$$

$$= \frac{306}{14} \text{ yr}$$

Properties of Average

- Average of a given data is less than the greatest observation and greater than the smallest observation of the given data.
- If all the observations of a given data are equal, then the average will also be the same as the observations.
- If 0 (zero) is one of the observations of a given data, then that 0 (zero) will also be included while calculating average.

Important Facts

- If numbers get increased by 'a', then their average also gets increased by 'a'.
- If all the numbers get decreased by 'a', then their average also gets decreased by 'a'.
- If all the numbers are multiplied by 'a', then their average also gets multiplied by 'a'.
- If all the numbers are divided by 'a', then their average also gets divided by 'a'.

Some Important Formulae

- Average of first n natural numbers is $\frac{n+1}{2}$.
- Average of first n natural even numbers is $(n+1)$.
- Average of first n natural odd numbers is n.
- If the average of n_1 and n_2 observations is x_1 and x_2, respectively, then the average of $(n_1 + n_2)$ observations will be $\frac{n_1 x_1 + n_2 x_2}{n_1 + n_2}$.

Example 3 The average weight of 14 students was calculated as 71. But it was later found that the weight of one student had been wrongly entered as 42 instead of 56 and of another as 74 instead of 32. The correct average is

(a) 75 (b) 80 (c) 68 (d) 69

Solution *(d)* Total weight of 14 students $= 71 \times 14$

$= 994$

Correct total weight of 14 students

$= 994 - (42 + 74) + (56 + 32)$

$= 966$

$\therefore$ Correct average $= \frac{966}{14} = 69$

PROBLEM BASED ON AGES

Age is defined as a period of time that a person has lived or a thing has existed. Age is measured in months, years, decades and so on.

In 'problem based on ages' usually relationships between the ages of two or more persons at two different time are given and we are required to find the ages of these persons.

- If ratio of present ages of A and B is $x : y$ and n yr ago, the ratio of their ages was $p : q$, then $\frac{x - n}{y - n} = \frac{p}{q}$.
- If ratio of present ages of A and B in $x : y$ and after n yr, the ratio of their ages will be $p : q$, then $\frac{x + n}{y + n} = \frac{p}{q}$.

EXAMPLE 4 The present age of A is 9 times the present age of B. 3 yr hence A's age will be 5 times that of B. Find their present ages.

(a) 3 yr, 27 yr (b) 3 yr, 3 yr
(c) 3 yr, 24 yr (d) None of these

Solution *(a)* Let the present age of B be x yr.

Then, the present age of $A = 9x$ yr.

3 yr hence,

B's age $= (x + 3)$ yr

A's age $= (9x + 3)$ yr

But it is given that 3 yr hence A's age will be 5 times the age of B.

$\therefore \quad 9x + 3 = 5(x + 3)$

$\Rightarrow \quad 9x + 3 = 5x + 15$

$\Rightarrow \quad 4x = 12 \Rightarrow x = 3$

B's present age $= 3$ yr

A's present age $= 9 \times 3 = 27$ yr

Practice Exercise

1. The average weight of A, B and C is 45 kg. If the average weight of A and B be 40 kg and that of B and C be 43 kg, then the weight of B is
(a) 17 kg (b) 20 kg
(c) 26 kg (d) 31 kg

2. If the average marks of three batches of 55, 60 and 45 students are respectively 50, 55 and 60, then the average marks of all the students is
(a) 53.33 (b) 54.68
(c) 55 (d) None of these

3. A library has an average of 510 visitors on Sunday and 240 on the other days. The average number of visitors per day in a month of 30 days beginning with a Sunday is
(a) 250 (b) 276
(c) 280 (d) 285

4. The average weight of 8 persons increases by 2.5 kg when a new person comes in place of one of them weighing 65 kg. What must be the weight of the new person?
(a) 76 kg
(b) 75.5 kg
(c) 85 kg
(d) 49.25 kg

5. The average weight of 5 men is 67.5 kg, and the average weight is diminished by 7.5 kg, when the weight of a boy is included. What is the weight of the boy?
(a) 22.5 kg (b) 30 kg
(c) 25 kg (d) 20 kg

6. A grocer has a sale of ₹ 6435, ₹ 6927, ₹ 6855, ₹ 7230 and ₹ 6562 for 5 consecutive months. How much sale must he have in the sixth month, so that he gets an average sale of ₹ 6500?
(a) ₹ 4991 (b) ₹ 5991
(c) ₹ 6001 (d) ₹ 6991

7. A family consists of grandparents, parents and three grandchildren. The average age of the grandparents is 67 yr, that of the parents is 35 yr and that of the grandchildren is 6 yr. What is the average age of the family?
(a) $28\frac{4}{7}$ yr (b) $31\frac{5}{7}$ yr
(c) $32\frac{1}{7}$ yr (d) None of these

8. In the first 10 overs of a cricket game, the run rate was only 3.2. What should be the run rate in the remaining 40 overs to reach the target of 282 runs?
(a) 6.25 (b) 6.5 (c) 6.75 (d) 7

9. The captain of a cricket team of 11 players is 26 yr old and the wicket keeper is 3 yr older. If the ages of these two are excluded, the average age of the remaining players is one year less than the average age of the whole team. What is the average age of the team?
(a) 23 yr (b) 24 yr
(c) 25 yr (d) None of these

10. A man bought 5 shirts at ₹ 450 each, 4 trousers at ₹ 750 each and 12 pairs of shoes at ₹ 750 each. What is the average expenditure per article?
(a) ₹ 1000 (b) ₹ 900
(c) ₹ 800 (d) ₹ 678.50

11. If the sum of a few number is 450 and their mean is 50 if another number 100 is included, the mean would become
(a) 55 (b) 60
(c) 75 (d) None of these

12. The mean of 100 items was found to be 30. If at the time of calculation, two items were wrongly taken as 32 and 12 instead of 23 and 11, correct mean is
(a) 29.4 (b) 29.5
(c) 29.8 (d) 29.9

13. The average of three numbers is 28. The first numbers is half of the second and the third number is twice the second. The third number is

(a) 18 (b) 24 (c) 36 (d) 48

14. A car owner buys petrol at ₹ 7.50, ₹ 8 and ₹ 8.50 per litre for three successive years. What approximately is the average cost per litre of petrol, if he spends ₹ 4000 each year?

(a) ₹ 7.98 (b) ₹ 8 (c) ₹ 8.50 (d) ₹ 9

15. In Arun's opinion, his weight is greater than 65 kg but less than 72 kg. His brother does not agree with Arun and he thinks that Arun's weight is greater than 60 kg but less than 70 kg. His mother's view is that his weight cannot be greater than 68 kg. If all of them are correct in their estimation, what is the average of different probable weights of Arun?

(a) 67 kg (b) 68 kg
(c) 69 kg (d) Data inadequate

16. The average of 12 results is 15. The average of the first 5 results is 13.7 and that of the last 5 is 16.3. The average of the other two is

(a) 15 (b) 15.2 (c) 14.8 (d) 15.5

17. There were 35 students in a hostel. Due to the admission of 7 new students the expenses of the mess were increased by ₹ 42 per day while the average expenditure per head diminished by ₹ 1.
What was the original expenditure of the mess?

(a) ₹ 450 (b) ₹ 320 (c) ₹ 550 (d) ₹ 420

18. The sum of the ages of six children born at interval of 5 yr each is 93 yr. What is the age of the youngest child?

(a) 3 yr (b) 2 yr (c) 4 yr (d) 5 yr

19. Amita gave birth to twins, when she was thirty years old. After x yr, the sum of the ages of Amita and her children is 60 yr. What is the value of x?

(a) 11 yr (b) 10 yr (c) 12 yr (d) 9 yr

20. The average of three prime numbers lying between 47 and 74 is 191/3. The greatest possible sum between any two out of the 3 prime numbers is

(a) 120 (b) 138 (c) 132 (d) 136

21. Four years ago, the ages of Ritu and Reena were in the ratio 5 : 6 respectively. Eight years from now the respective ratio of their ages will be 8 : 9. What is the sum of their ages at present?

(a) 52 yr (b) 50 yr
(c) 60 yr (d) 62 yr

22. In a family, father is 5 years older than mother and mother's age now is thrice the age of the daughter. The daughter is now 10 years old. What was the age of the father when daughter was born?

(a) 25 yr (b) 30 yr
(c) 35 yr (d) 40 yr

23. The average age of 5 members of a family is 20 yr. The youngest member of the family is 4 yr old. Average age of all the members of the family excluding the youngest member is

(a) 24 (b) 30
(c) 32 (d) 40

24. At present Meena is eight times her daughter's age. Eight years from now, the ratio of the ages of Meena and her daughter will be 10 : 3, respectively. What is Meena's present age?

(a) 32 yr
(b) 40 yr
(c) 36 yr
(d) Cannot be determined

Previous Year's Questions

25. Father is 3 yr older than the mother and the mother's age is now twice the daughter's age. If the daughter is 20 yr old now, then the father's age when the daughter was born **[CLAT 2011]**

(a) 20 yr (b) 40 yr
(c) 43 yr (d) 23 yr

26. Ms Jhulan Goswami scores 102 runs in the 18th innings of her career and thus increases her average by 5. After the 18th inning, her average is **[CLAT 2011]**

(a) 17 (b) 12
(c) 26 (d) 28

27. Akbar will turn 50 when his son Jehangir turns 18. What will be Akbar's age when it will be exactly 5 times that of Jehangir? **[CLAT 2011]**

(a) 36 yr (b) 40 yr
(c) 44 yr (d) 48 yr

28. There are 30 boys and 40 girls in a class. If the average age of boys is 10 yr and average age of girls is 8 yr, then the average age of the whole class is **[CLAT 2014]**

(a) 8 yr (b) 8.86 yr
(c) 8.2 yr (d) 9 yr

29. The mean of 72 items was found to be 63. If two of the items were mis-recorded as 27 and 9 instead of 72 and 90 respectively, then find the correct mean. **[CLAT 2016]**

(a) 64.75 (b) 65.75
(c) 64.25 (d) 63.25

30. A library has an average of 510 visitors on Sundays and 240 on other days. What is the average number of visitors per day in the month of June beginning with a Sunday? **[CLAT 2016]**

(a) 276 (b) 280
(c) 285 (d) 250

31. Age of father 10 year ago was three ago was three times the age of his son. After 10 years, father's age is twice that of his son. The ratio of their present ages is **[CLAT 2017]**

(a) 7 : 4 (b) 9 : 5
(c) 7 : 3 (d) 11 : 7

32. The average weight of 3 man '*X*', '*Y*' and '*Z*' is 75 kgs. Another man '*A*' joins the group and the average weight now becomes 80 kgs. If another person '*B*' whose weight is 5 kgs more than '*A*' replaces '*X*' then the average weight of '*X*', '*Z*' '*A*' and *B* will be 85 kgs. What is the weight of '*X*'? **[CLAT 2017]**

(a) 78 kgs (b) 82 kgs
(c) 80 kgs (d) 84 kgs

Answers

1	d	2	b	3	d	4	c	5	a	6	a	7	b	8	a	9	a	10	d
11	a	12	d	13	d	14	a	15	a	16	a	17	d	18	a	19	b	20	b
21	a	22	a	23	a	24	a	25	d	26	a	27	b	28	b	29	a	30	c
31	c	32	c																

SOLUTIONS

1. Let *A*, *B* and *C* represent their respective weights. Then, we have

$$A+B+C=(45\times 3)=135 \quad ...(i)$$
$$A+B=(40\times 2)=80 \quad ...(ii)$$
$$B+C=(43\times 2)=86 \quad ...(iii)$$

On adding Eqs. (ii) and (iii), we get

$$A+2B+C=166 \quad ...(iv)$$

On subtracting Eq. (i) from Eq. (iv), we get

$$B=31$$

$\therefore$ *B*'s weight = 31 kg

2. Required average

$$=\left(\frac{55\times 50+60\times 55+45\times 60}{55+60+45}\right)$$
$$=\left(\frac{2750+3300+2700}{160}\right)=\frac{8750}{160}=54.68$$

3. Since, the month begins with a Sunday. So, there will be five Sunday in the month.

$\therefore$ Required average

$$=\left(\frac{510\times 5+240\times 25}{30}\right)$$

$= \frac{8550}{30} = 285$

4. Total weight increased

$= (8 \times 2.5)$ kg $= 20$ kg

Weight of new person

$= (65 + 20)$ kg $= 85$ kg

5. Total weight of 5 men = 67.5 kg × 5 = 337.5 kg

New average weight

$= 67.5 - 7.5 = 60$ kg

Total new weight

$= 60 \times 6 = 360$ kg

∴ Weight of new boy

$= 360 - 337.5$

$= 22.5$ kg

6. Total sale for 5 months

= ₹ (6435 + 6927 + 6855 + 7230 + 6562)

= ₹ 34009

∴ Required sale

= ₹ [(6500 × 6) − 34009]

= ₹ (39000 − 34009)

= ₹ 4991

7. Required average

$= \left(\frac{67 \times 2 + 35 \times 2 + 6 \times 3}{2 + 2 + 3}\right)$

$= \left(\frac{134 + 70 + 18}{7}\right)$

$= \frac{222}{7} = 31\frac{5}{7}$ yr

8. Required run rate

$= \left(\frac{282 - (3.2 \times 10)}{40}\right)$

$= \frac{250}{40} = 6.25$

9. Let the average age of the whole team be x yr.

$\therefore\ 11x - (26 + 29) = 9(x - 1)$

$\Rightarrow\ 11x - 9x = 46$

$\Rightarrow\ 2x = 46 \Rightarrow x = 23$

So, average age of the team is 23 yr.

10. Average expenditure

$= \frac{5 \times 450 + 4 \times 750 + 12 \times 750}{5 + 4 + 12}$

$= \frac{2250 + 3000 + 9000}{21}$

$= \frac{14250}{21} = 678.5$

11. Let number of numbers = x

Then, $50 = \frac{450}{x}$

$\Rightarrow\ x = \frac{450}{50} = 9$

New mean

$= \frac{9 \times 50 + 100}{10} = \frac{550}{10} = 55$

12. Sum of 100 items

$= 30 \times 100 = 3000$

New sum

$= 3000 - (32 + 12) + (23 + 11)$

$= 2990$

∴ Correct mean

$= \frac{2990}{100} = 29.90$

13. Let second number = x

Then, first number $= \frac{x}{2}$ and third number $= 2x$

$\therefore\ \frac{x + \frac{x}{2} + 2x}{3} = 28$

$\Rightarrow\ 3x + \frac{x}{2} = 84$

$\Rightarrow\ 7x = 168 \Rightarrow x = 24$

Hence, third number

$= 2 \times 24 = 48$

14. Total quantity of petrol

$= \left(\frac{4000}{7.50} + \frac{4000}{8} + \frac{4000}{8.50}\right)$ L

$= 4000\left(\frac{2}{15} + \frac{1}{8} + \frac{2}{17}\right)$ L

$= \left(\frac{76700}{51}\right)$ L

Total amount spent

= ₹ (3 × 4000) = ₹ 12000

∴ Average cost

$= ₹\left(\frac{12000 \times 51}{76700}\right) = ₹\,\frac{6120}{767}$

= ₹ 7.98

15. Let Arun's weight be x kg.

According to Arun,

$65 < x < 72$

According to Arun's brother,

$60 < x < 70$.

According to Arun's mother,

$x \le 68$.

The values satisfying all the above conditions are 66, 67 and 68.

∴ Required average

$= \left(\frac{66 + 67 + 68}{3}\right)$

$= \left(\frac{201}{3}\right) = 67$ kg

16. Total of 12 results $= 12 \times 15 = 180$

Sum of the first five and last five results

$= 5 \times (13.7 + 16.3) = 150$

Sum of the remaining two results

$= 180 - 150 = 30$

∴ Average of two results = 15

17. Let the original average expenditure be ₹ x. Then,

$42(x - 1) - 35x = 42$

$\Rightarrow\ 7x = 84 \Rightarrow x = 12$

Therefore, original expenditure

= ₹ (35 × 12) = ₹ 420

18. Let the age of the youngest child be x yr. Then,

$x + (x + 5) + (x + 10) + (x + 15) + (x + 20) + (x + 25) = 93$

$\Rightarrow\ 6x + 75 = 93$

$\Rightarrow\ 6x = 18 \Rightarrow x = 3$

19. Given present age of Amita = 30 yr

After x yr, Amita's age $= (30 + x)$ yr

After x yr sum of the ages of twins

$= (x + x)$ yr $= 2x$

Now, $(30 + x) + 2x = 60$

$\Rightarrow\ 3x = 60 - 30 = 30$

$\Rightarrow\ x = 10$ yr

20. Three prime numbers lying between 47 and 74 are 53, 67 and 71.

whose mean

$= \frac{53+67+71}{3} = \frac{191}{3}$

$\therefore$ Greatest possible sum

$= 67 + 71 = 138$

21. Let four years ago, age of Ritu and Reena $= 5x$ and $6x$

Then, according to question,

$\frac{5x+4+8}{6x+4+8} = \frac{8}{9}$

$\Rightarrow \quad 9(5x+12) = 8(6x+12)$

$\Rightarrow \quad 45x + 108 = 48x + 96$

$\Rightarrow \quad 3x = 12$

$\Rightarrow \quad x = 4$

Sum of present ages

$= (5x+4) + (6x+4)$

$= 11x + 8 = 11 \times 4 + 8$

$= 52$ years

22. Given age of daughter $= 10$ yr

$\therefore$ Age of mother

$= 3 \times 10 = 30$ yr

and age of father

$= 30 + 5 = 35$ yr

Hence, the required age of father

$= 35 - 10 = 25$ yr

23. Total age of 5 members

$= 5 \times 20 = 100$ yr

$\therefore$ New average

$= \frac{100-4}{4} = \frac{96}{4} = 24$

24. Let age of daughter $= x$ yr

$\therefore$ Age of Meena $= 8x$ yr

According to the question,

$\frac{8x+8}{x+8} = \frac{10}{3}$

$\Rightarrow 24x + 24 = 10x + 80$

$\Rightarrow \quad 14x = 56 \Rightarrow x = 4$

Hence, Meena's present age $= 4 \times 8 = 32$ yr

Previous Year's Solutions

25. Given that mother is twice the age of her daughter, way back 20 yr, when daughter took birth, her mother should be 20 yr old. Father's age is 3 yr more than mother's age hence father's age at the time of birth of his daughter would be 23 yr.

26. Before 18th inning her average

$= 102 - 18 \times 5 = 12$

After 18th inning her average $= 12 + 5 = 17$

27. Only option (b) is divisible by 5. Here, answer will be 40 yr.

28. Total number of boys in the class $= 30$

Total number of girls in the class $= 40$

Given that, Average age of boys $= 10$ yr

and Average age of girls $= 8$ yr

$\therefore$ Total of ages of all boys

$= 30 \times 10 = 300$ yr

Similarly,

Total of ages of all girls $= 40 \times 8 = 320$ yr

Sum of ages of boys + Sum of ages of girls = Total age of the class, i.e. $300 + 320 = 620$

Total students $= 30 + 40 = 70$

Hence, average age of class

$= \frac{\text{Total age of class}}{\text{Number of students}}$

$= \frac{620}{70}$

Average age $= 8.857 \approx 8.86$ yr

29. Given, mean of 72 items $= 63$

$\therefore$ Sum of 72 items

$= 63 \times 72 = 4536$

$\because$ Two items were mis-recorded as 27 and 9 instead of 72 and 90 respectively.

$\because$ New sum of 72 items

$= 4536 - 27 - 9 + 72 + 90$

$= 4662$

Now, correct mean of 72 items

$= 4662 \div 72 = 64.75$

30. If a month begins with Sunday, then there are 5 Sundays in that month.

$\therefore$ Average number of visitors per day

$= \frac{510 \times 5 + 240 \times 25}{30}$

$= \frac{2550 + 6000}{30}$

$= \frac{8550}{30} = 285$

31. Let the present age of father and son be x and y, respectively.

According to the given condition

$x - 10 = 3(y - 10)$

and $\quad x + 10 = 2(y + 10)$

$\Rightarrow x - 3y = -20 \quad \ldots$(i)

and $x - 2y = 10 \quad \ldots$(ii)

On solving, we get

$x = 70, y = 30$

$\therefore$ Required ration $= \frac{x}{y} = \frac{70}{30}$

$= \frac{7}{3}$

32. Total weights of three men X, Y and Z

$= 3 \times 75 = 225$ kg $\quad \ldots$(i)

Total weight of four men X, Y, Z and A

$= 4 \times 80$

$\Rightarrow 225 + A = 320$

$\Rightarrow \quad A = 95$ kg

Now, total weight of four men, Y, Z, A and B

$= 4 \times 85$

$\Rightarrow (Y + Z) + 95 + (95 + 5) = 340$

$\Rightarrow \quad (Y + Z) = 340 - 195$

$\Rightarrow \quad (Y + Z) = 145$

From Eq. (i), we get

$X + (Y + Z) = 225$

$\Rightarrow \quad x = 80$ Kg

CHAPTER

06

PROFIT AND LOSS

Profit and loss is an easy and scoring chapter in the numerical ability and analytical aptitude.

In our daily life, we buy goods from the shopkeepers in the market which they buy either directly from the manufacturers or through the sellers. In order to earn money the shopkeeper sells goods at higher price than which they bought.

The price at which a person buys a product, is called the **Cost Price** (CP) of the product and the price at which a person sells a product, is called the **Selling Price** (SP) of the product. In a transaction, if the selling price is more than the cost price, it gives a profit i.e. Profit = Selling price – Cost price

On the other hand, if the selling price is less than the cost price, the transaction results into loss i.e. Loss = Cost price – Selling price

It should be noted that the selling price of the seller is the cost price of the buyer.

Important Formulae

(i) $\text{Profit per cent} = \frac{\text{Profit}}{\text{CP}} \times 100\%$

(ii) $\text{SP} = \left(\frac{100 + \text{Gain\%}}{100}\right) \times \text{CP}$

(iii) $\text{CP} = \frac{100}{(100 + \text{Gain\%})} \times \text{SP}$

(iv) $\text{Loss per cent} = \frac{\text{Loss}}{\text{CP}} \times 100\%$

(v) $\text{SP} = \left(\frac{100 - \text{Loss\%}}{100}\right) \times \text{CP}$

(vi) $\text{CP} = \left(\frac{100}{100 - \text{Loss\%}}\right) \times \text{SP}$

Note Profit and loss are always calculated on CP unless otherwise stated.

EXAMPLE 1 A person sells an article for a price which gives him a profit of 20% on cost price of ₹ 500. Calculate the selling price of the article.

(a) ₹ 400 (b) ₹ 500 (c) ₹ 600 (d) ₹ 680

Solution ***(c)*** Here, CP = 500, Gain% = 20

$$\because \quad SP = \left(\frac{100 + \text{Gain\%}}{100}\right) \times CP$$

$$\therefore \quad SP = 500\left(\frac{100+20}{100}\right) = \frac{500 \times 120}{100} = ₹\,600$$

Hence, the selling price of the article is ₹ 600.

EXAMPLE 2 A person buys an article for ₹ 600 and sells the same at a loss of 30%. Find the selling price of the article.

(a) ₹ 500 (b) ₹ 380 (c) ₹ 450 (d) ₹ 420

Solution ***(d)*** Here, CP = 600, loss% = 30

$$\because \quad SP = \left(\frac{100 - \text{Loss\%}}{100}\right) \times CP$$

$$\therefore \quad SP = \left(\frac{100-30}{100}\right) \times 600$$

$$= \frac{70}{100} \times 600 = ₹\,420$$

Therefore, the selling price of the article is ₹ 420.

EXAMPLE 3 When a commodity is sold for ₹ 34.80 there is a loss of 25%. The cost price of the commodity is

(a) ₹ 46.40 (b) ₹ 26.10 (c) ₹ 43 (d) ₹ 43.20

Solution ***(a)*** $CP = \left(\frac{100}{100 - \text{Loss\%}}\right) \times SP$

$$\therefore \quad CP = \left(\frac{100}{100-25}\right) \times 34.80 = \frac{3480}{75} = ₹\,46.40$$

MARKED PRICE

The printed price or original price of an article is called **Marked Price** (MP). It is the price without any discount or rebate.

DISCOUNT

Discount means reducing the price or value of an object or item.

Discount = Market Price – Selling Price

Important formulae

(i) $\text{Discount\%} = \frac{\text{Discount}}{\text{Marked Price}} \times 100$

(ii) Selling Price = Marked Price $\times \left(1 - \frac{\text{Discount\%}}{100}\right)$

(iii) Single discount equivalent to two successive discounts r_1 % and r_2 %

$$= \left(r_1 + r_2 - \frac{r_1 r_2}{100}\right)\%$$

> Discount percentage is always calculated on marked price unless specified.

EXAMPLE 4 A person marks his goods 20% more than the cost price and allows some discount on it. He still makes a profit of 10%. Find the discount percentage.

(a) 3.33% (b) 8.33% (c) 6.66% (d) 10%

Solution ***(b)*** Let the CP of the article be ₹ 100.

Then, MP of the article = ₹ 120; Profit = 10%

∴ SP = CP + Profit = 100 + 10 = ₹ 110

Since, the difference between marked price and selling price is the discount.

∴ Discount = MP – SP = 120 – 110 = ₹ 10

$$\therefore \text{ Discount percentage} = \frac{\text{Discount}}{\text{Marked Price}} \times 100\,\%$$

$$= \frac{10}{120} \times 100\% = 8.33\%$$

EXAMPLE 5 On a 20% discount sale, an article costs ₹ 596. What was the original price of the article?

(a) ₹ 720 (b) ₹ 735 (c) ₹ 745 (d) ₹ 775

Solution ***(c)*** Let the original price be x.

At discount of 20%, article costs ₹ 596.

We have, Selling Price = Marked Price $\times \left(\frac{100 - \text{Discount\%}}{100}\right)$

$$\Rightarrow \quad 596 = \frac{80}{100} \times x \Rightarrow x = \frac{596 \times 100}{80} = 745$$

Hence, the original price is ₹ 745.

EXAMPLE 6 Calculate a single discount equivalent to a series discounts of 20% and 10%.

(a) 28% (b) 30% (c) 25% (d) 10%

Solution *(a)* Here, $r_1 = 20, r_2 = 10\%$

$\therefore$ Single discount $= \left(r_1 + r_2 - \frac{r_1 r_2}{100}\right)\%$

$= \left(20 + 10 - \frac{20 \times 10}{100}\right)\% = (30 - 2)\% = 28\%$

Hence, single discount is 28%.

Some Important Formulae

(i) If a dishonest dealer sells his goods at CP but uses false weight, then

$$\text{Gain per cent} = \frac{\text{Error}}{\text{True value} - \text{Error}} \times 100\%$$

(ii) If a person sells two commodities at same prices. On one, he gains x% and on other, he loses x%, then as a whole he will be in loss and the loss percentage will be equal to

$$\left(\frac{\text{Common gain or loss\%}}{10}\right)^2 \text{ i.e. } \frac{x^2}{100}.$$

(iii) If CP of m articles is equal to the SP of n articles, then gain or loss per cent

$$= \left(\frac{m-n}{n}\right) \times 100\%$$

(iv) By selling x number of articles, a person loses or gains the selling price of y number of articles, then

$$\text{Gain per cent} = \frac{y}{x-y} \times 100\%$$

$$\text{Loss per cent} = \frac{y}{x+y} \times 100\%$$

(v) By selling x number of articles, a person gains the cost price of y number of articles, then

$$\text{Gain per cent} = \frac{y-x}{x} \times 100\%$$

EXAMPLE 7 A dishonest dealer professes to sell his goods at cost price but uses a weight of 960 g for a kg weight. Find his gain per cent.

(a) 5% (b) 4% (c) $3\frac{1}{3}\%$ (d) $4\frac{1}{6}\%$

Solution *(d)* Here, error $= 1000 - 960 = 40$ g and true value $= 1000$ g

$\therefore$ Gain per cent $= \left[\frac{\text{Error}}{\text{True value} - \text{Error}} \times 100\right]\%$

$= \left(\frac{40}{960} \times 100\right)\% = 4\frac{1}{6}\%$

EXAMPLE 8 By selling two articles for ₹ 180 each a shopkeeper gains profit of 20% on one and loses 20% on the other, find the profit/loss percentage.

(a) 4% loss (b) 4% profit (c) 1% loss (d) 1% profit

Solution *(a)* We know that, shopkeeper incurs a loss and loss per cent

$= \left(\frac{x}{10}\right)^2 = \left(\frac{20}{10}\right)^2 = 4\%$

EXAMPLE 9 If CP of 15 articles is equal to the SP of 12 articles, then find the gain per cent.

(a) 40% (b) 30% (c) 25% (d) 20%

Solution *(c)* Gain per cent $= \left(\frac{m-n}{n}\right) \times 100\%$

$= \left(\frac{15-12}{12}\right) \times 100\%$ [here, $m = 15$, $n = 12$]

$= \frac{100}{4}\% = 25\%$

EXAMPLE 10 By selling 18 chocolates, a vendor loses the selling price of 2 chocolates. Find his loss per cent.

(a) 12% (b) 10% (c) 15% (d) 6%

Solution *(b)* Here, $y = 2$, $x = 18$

We know that, loss per cent $= \frac{y}{x+y} \times 100\%$

$\therefore$ Required loss per cent $= \frac{2}{18+2} \times 100\%$

$= \frac{2}{20} \times 100\% = 10\%$

EXAMPLE 11 Find the gain per cent when Ram gains the SP of 10 articles after selling 50 articles.

(a) 15% (b) 20% (c) 30% (d) 25%

Solution *(d)* Here, $y = 10$ and $x = 50$

We know that, gain per cent $= \frac{y}{x-y} \times 100\%$

$\therefore$ Required gain per cent $= \frac{10}{40} \times 100\%$

$= \frac{10}{50-10} \times 100\% = 25\%$

Practice Exercise

1. By selling 33 m of cloth, one gains the selling price of 11 m. Find the gain per cent.

(a) 20% (b) 40% (c) 50% (d) 22%

2. A man sold 250 chairs and had a gain equal to the selling price of 50 chairs. His profit per cent is

(a) 5% (b) 10% (c) 25% (d) 50%

3. By selling 110 mangoes, the CP of 120 mangoes is realised. What is the gain percentage?

(a) $11\frac{1}{9}\%$ (b) $9\frac{1}{9}\%$ (c) $10\frac{10}{11}\%$ (d) $9\frac{1}{11}\%$

4. A cloth merchant claims to sell his material at cost price but uses a scale which reads 1 m for 95 cm. Find his gain percentage.

(a) 5.26% (b) 6.2% (c) 6.5% (d) 7.5%

5. The cost price of 9 articles is equal to the selling price of 11 articles. Find the loss percentage.

(a) $18\frac{2}{11}\%$ (b) $2\frac{9}{11}\%$ (c) $15\frac{1}{2}\%$ (d) $16\frac{1}{2}\%$

6. Sunanda is making a profit of 25% on her selling, price, what is her actual profit percentage?

(a) $\frac{100}{3}\%$ (b) 20% (c) 25% (d) 30%

7. The cost price of an article is 40% of the selling price. The per cent that the selling price is of cost price is

(a) 250% (b) 240% (c) 60% (d) 40%

8. A trader marks his goods 20% above the cost price and allows a discount of 15% on it. Find his gain per cent.

(a) 4% (b) 5% (c) 1% (d) 2%

9. A reduction of 25% in the price of eggs enables a man to buy 4 dozen eggs for ₹ 96. What is the price per dozen?

(a) ₹ 6 (b) ₹ 8 (c) ₹ 8.50 (d) ₹ 9

10. If an article is sold at 5% gain instead of 5% loss, the seller gets ₹ 6.72 more. The cost price of the article is

(a) ₹ 67.20 (b) ₹ 120
(c) ₹ 134.40 (d) ₹ 240

11. A man bought an article and sold it at a gain of 5%. If he had bought it at 5% less and sold it for ₹ 1 less, he would have made a profit of 10%. The cost price of the article was

(a) ₹ 100 (b) ₹ 150
(c) ₹ 200 (d) ₹ 500

12. An article when sold at a gain of 5% yields ₹ 15 more than when sold at a loss of 5%. What is the cost price?

(a) ₹ 64 (b) ₹ 80
(c) ₹ 150 (d) ₹ 200

13. A seller blends two varieties of tea one costing ₹ 18 per kg and another ₹ 20 per kg in the ratio 5 : 3. If he sells the blended variety at ₹ 21 per kg, then his gain per cent is

(a) 10 (b) 12
(c) 22 (d) 19

14. A man buys oranges at ₹ 5 a dozen and an equal number at ₹ 4 a dozen. He sells them at ₹ 5.50 a dozen and makes a profit of ₹ 50. How many oranges does he buy?

(a) 30 dozen (b) 40 dozen
(c) 50 dozen (d) 60 dozen

15. If a man reduces the selling price of a fan from ₹ 400 to ₹ 380, his loss increases from x% to $(x + 4)$%. What is the cost price of the fan?

(a) ₹ 420 (b) ₹ 550
(c) ₹ 500 (d) ₹ 400

16. If an article is sold at 8% profit instead of 8% loss, it would have brought ₹ 12 more. Find the cost price of the article.

(a) ₹ 75 (b) ₹ 72
(c) ₹ 70 (d) ₹ 60

17. A man sells two articles for the same price for ₹ 640. He earns 20% profit on the first and 10% profit on second. Find the over all profit per cent.

(a) 14.78% (b) 14.08%
(c) 14.58% (d) None of these

18. When the selling price of an article is ₹ 280, the loss percentage is 20%. What is the loss or gain percentage, if the selling price is increased to ₹ 380?

(a) $8\frac{4}{7}$% profit (b) $4\frac{5}{7}$% loss
(c) $\frac{50}{3}$% profit (d) $4\frac{9}{11}$% profit

19. Ajeet calculates his profit percentage as a percentage of selling price. He sells an item for ₹ 150 and calculates his profit percentage to be 20%. What is the true profit percentage?

(a) 20% (b) 25% (c) 22.5% (d) 15%

20. Profit earned by selling an article for ₹ 1060 is 20% more than the loss incurred by selling the article for ₹ 950. At what price should the article be sold to earn 20% profit?

(a) ₹ 1000 (b) ₹ 1150 (c) ₹ 1250 (d) ₹ 1200

21. A man buys 25 chairs for ₹ 375 and sells them at a profit equal to the selling price of 5 chairs. What is the selling price of one chair?

(a) ₹ 18.75 (b) ₹ 14.50 (c) ₹ 15.20 (d) ₹ 17.20

22. A grocer purchased 80 kg of rice at ₹ 13.50 per kg and mixed it with 120 kg of rice at ₹ 16 per kg. At what rate per kilogram should he sell the mixture to gain 16%?

(a) ₹ 14.50 (b) ₹ 17.40
(c) ₹ 11.50 (d) ₹ 9.50

23. A person incurs a loss of 10% by selling a toy for ₹ 10.80. At what price he should sell the same to earn a profit of 20%?

(a) ₹ 12 (b) ₹ 12.96
(c) ₹ 14.40 (d) None of these

24. A person bought 20 L of milk at the rate of ₹ 8 per L. He got it churned after spending ₹ 10 and got 5 kg of cream and 20 L of toned milk. If he sold the cream at ₹ 30 per kg and toned milk at ₹ 4 per L, his profit in the transaction is

(a) 37.5% (b) 42.5%
(c) 35.3% (d) 25%

25. *A* bought an article and spent ₹ 110 on its repair. He sold it to *B* at 20% profit, *B* sold it to *C* at a loss of 10% and *C* sold it for ₹ 1188 at a profit of 10%. What is the amount for which *A* bought the article?

(a) ₹ 850 (b) ₹ 950 (c) ₹ 930 (d) ₹ 890

26. A man sells two commodities for ₹ 4000 each, neither losing nor gaining in the deal. If he sold one commodity at a gain of 25%, the other commodity is sold at a loss of

(a) $16\frac{2}{3}$% (b) $18\frac{2}{9}$%
(c) 25% (d) None of these

27. What price should a shopkeeper mark on an article, costing ₹ 153 to gain 20%, after allowing a discount of 15%?

(a) ₹ 224 (b) ₹ 216 (c) ₹ 154 (d) ₹ 132

28. A dealer marks his goods 20% above cost price. He then allows some discount on it and makes a profit of 8%. The rate of discount is

(a) 4% (b) 6% (c) 10% (d) 12%

29. If a selling price of ₹ 24 results in a 20% discount of the list price, the selling price that would result in a 30% discount of the list price is

(a) ₹ 16 (b) ₹ 21 (c) ₹ 25 (d) ₹ 31

30. A trade man marks his goods at 20% above the CP and gives a discount of 10% for cash payments. What profit percentage does he make?

(a) 8% (b) 6%
(c) 10% (d) 12%

31. A business man marked the price of his goods 30% more than his cost price. He then sells $\frac{1}{4}$ of his stock at a discount of 15%, and half of the stock at the marked price and rest at a discount of 30%. Find his gain percentage.

(a) 16.5% (b) $15\frac{3}{8}$% (c) 14.20% (d) 13.37%

32. If a commission of 10% is given on the marked price of an article, then the gain is 25%. Find the gain per cent, if commission is increased to 20%.

(a) $11\frac{1}{9}$% (b) 12% (c) $\frac{100}{3}$% (d) $\frac{50}{3}$%

33. An article is listed at ₹ 900 and two successive discounts of 8% and 8% are given on it. How much would the seller gain or lose, if he gives a single discount of 16%, instead of two discounts?

(a) Gain of ₹ 4.76 (b) Loss of ₹ 5.76
(c) Gain of ₹ 5.76 (d) Loss of ₹ 4.76

34. A trader marked the selling price of an article at 20% above the cost price. At the time of selling he allows certain discount and suffer a loss of 4%. He allowed the discount of

(a) 20% (b) 25% (c) 24% (d) 22%

35. The marked price of a radio set is ₹ 480. The shopkeeper allows a discount of 10% and gains 8%. If no discount is allowed, his gain per cent would be

(a) 18% (b) 18.5% (c) 20% (d) 25%

Previous Year's Questions

36. Francis has 18 eggs out of which 12 eggs were sold at 10% loss than the cost price. At what mark up should he sell the remaining eggs to cover his losses? **[CLAT 2011]**

(a) 5% (b) 10%
(c) 15% (d) 20%

37. A customised jewellery was sold at ₹ 1000 with 90% discount on the 'making charges'. If the payment made for making charges was ₹ 100, what is the approximate rate of discount on the product? **[CLAT 2011]**

(a) 35% (b) 45% (c) 47% (d) 90%

38. A dealer buys an article for ₹ 380.00. What price should he mark so that after allowing a discount of 5% he still makes a profit of 25% on the article? **[CLAT 2012]**

(a) ₹ 500 (b) ₹ 475 (c) ₹ 95 (d) ₹ 465

39. P sells a table to Q at a profit of 10% and Q sells it to R at a profit of 12%. If R pays ₹ 246.40 for it, then how much had P paid for it? **[CLAT 2012]**

(a) ₹ 200.00 (b) ₹ 300.00
(c) ₹ 248.00 (d) ₹ 346.00

40. A single discount equivalent to a discount series 15% and 5% is **[CLAT 2013]**

(a) 32% (b) 20% (c) 10% (d) 8.5%

41. If selling price of 10 articles is equal to cost price of 11 articles, then gain is **[CLAT 2013]**

(a) 8% (b) 9% (c) 8.5% (d) 10%

42. By selling a cycle for ₹ 2345, a student losses 19%. His cost price is nearly **[CLAT 2013]**

(a) ₹ 4000 (b) ₹ 5000 (c) ₹ 3000 (d) ₹ 3500

43. A dealer marked his goods 20% above the cost price and allows a discount of 10%. Then, the gain per cent is **[CLAT 2014]**

(a) 2% (b) 4% (c) 6% (d) 8%

44. A part of monthly hostel charges is fixed and the remaining depends on the number of days one has taken food in the mess. When a student A takes food for 20 days, she has to pay ₹ 1000 as hostel charges whereas a student B, who takes food for 26 days, pays ₹ 1180 as hostel charges. Find the fixed charges and the cost of food per day. **[CLAT 2016]**

(a) ₹ 400, ₹ 30 (b) ₹ 400, ₹ 40
(c) ₹ 300, ₹ 20 (d) ₹ 200, ₹ 20

45. A shop gives 15% discount on the purchase of a TV. If paid in cash immediately, a further discount of 12% is given. If the marked price is ₹ 15000, what is the price of the TV if cash purchase is made? **[CLAT 2016]**

(a) ₹ 10950 (b) ₹ 12750 (c) ₹ 11220 (d) ₹ 11475

46. A trader sells rice at a profit of 20% and uses weights which are 10% less than the correct weight. The total gain earned by him is **[CLAT 2017]**

(a) 35% (b) $22\frac{2}{9}\%$

(c) 30% (d) $33\frac{1}{3}\%$

Answers

1	c	2	c	3	d	4	a	5	a	6	a	7	a	8	d	9	a	10	a
11	c	12	c	13	b	14	c	15	c	16	a	17	a	18	a	19	b	20	d
21	a	22	b	23	c	24	c	25	d	26	a	27	b	28	c	29	b	30	a
31	b	32	a	33	b	34	a	35	c	36	d	37	c	38	a	39	a	40	b
41	d	42	c	43	d	44	a	45	c	46	d								

SOLUTIONS

1. Gain percentage

$$= \frac{11}{33-11} \times 100\% = 50\%$$

2. Profit per cent

$$= \frac{50}{250-50} \times 100\%$$

$$= \frac{50}{200} \times 100\% = 25\%$$

3. Gain per cent

$$= \frac{120-110}{110} \times 100\% = 9\frac{1}{11}\%$$

4. Gain percentage in using false weight

$$= \left(\frac{\text{Error}}{\text{True value} - \text{Error}} \times 100\right)\%$$

$$= \frac{5}{100-5} \times 100\% = \frac{500}{95}\%$$

$= 5.26\%$

5. CP of m articles is equal to the SP of n articles, then loss percentage is

$$= \frac{m-n}{n} \times 100 = \frac{9-11}{11} \times 100\%$$

$$= -18\frac{2}{11}\%$$

[here '–' represent loss]

6. Let the selling price = ₹ 100, if profit is ₹ 25 on SP, then cost price = ₹ 75

Actual profit percentage

$$= \frac{\text{Profit}}{\text{CP}} \times 100\%$$

$$= \frac{25}{75} \times 100\% = \frac{100}{3}\%$$

7. The CP will be ₹ 40, if the SP is ₹ 100.

Percentage of SP to CP

$$= \frac{100}{40} \times 100\% = 250\%$$

8. Let the CP of the goods be ₹ 100.

Then, marked price of the goods = ₹ 120.

Selling price of the goods at a discount of 15% = ₹ 120 × 0.85 = ₹ 102

∴ Gain per cent = 2%

9. Reduction of 25% means that due to reduction of ₹ 24 (25% of 96) a man buys 4 dozen more.

Therefore, reduced price per dozen $= \frac{24}{4} =$ ₹ 6

10. CP of the article be ₹ x.

Then, $1.05x - 0.95x = 6.72$

⇒ $0.1x = 6.72$

∴ $x =$ ₹ 67.20

11. Let the CP of the article be ₹ x.

Then, SP $= 1.05x$

New CP $= 0.95x$

New SP $= 1.1 \times 0.95x =$ ₹ $1.045x$

Now, it is given that difference between two SP's is ₹ 1.

∴ $0.005x =$ ₹ 1 or $x =$ ₹ 200

12. Let CP be ₹ 100.

When gain = 5%, SP = 105%

When loss = 5%, SP = 95%

⇒ 105% – 95% = 15

⇒ 10% = 15

∴ 100% = ₹ 150

13. Let the quantity of each type of tea be $5x$ and $3x$.

Cost price of $8x$ kg of tea

= ₹ $(5x \times 18 + 3x \times 20) =$ ₹ $150x$

SP of $8x$ kg of tea

= ₹ $21 \times 8x =$ ₹ $168x$

Profit = ₹18x

$\therefore$ Profit per cent $= \frac{\text{Profit}}{\text{CP}} \times 100$

$= \frac{18x}{150x} \times 100 = 12\%$

14. Let he buys x dozen of oranges of each type.

Then, CP of $2x$ dozen of oranges

$= ₹(5x + 4x) = ₹9x$

and SP of $2x$ dozen of oranges

$= ₹5.5 \times 2x = ₹11x$

Now, profit $= 11x - 9x = 2x$

$\Rightarrow \quad 2x = 50$

Hence, he purchased 50 dozens oranges.

15. Difference of SPs = Difference of loss/profit

$\Rightarrow 400 - 380 = [(x + 4) - (x)]\%$

$\Rightarrow \quad 20 = 4\%$

$\therefore \quad 100\% = ₹\frac{20}{4} \times 100 = ₹500$

16. Let the CP of the article be ₹x.

Then, SP at 8% profit = ₹$1.08x$

and SP at 8% loss = $0.92x$

Given, $1.08x - 0.92x = ₹12$

$\Rightarrow \quad 0.16x = ₹12$

$\therefore \quad x = ₹\frac{12}{0.16} = ₹75$

17. CP of item sold at a profit of 20%

$= ₹\frac{640}{1.2} = ₹533.33$

CP of the item sold at a profit of 10%

$= ₹\frac{640}{1.1} = ₹581.81$

Total CP = ₹1115.14

Total SP = ₹1280

$\therefore$ Profit per cent

$= \frac{164.86}{1115.14} \times 100 = 14.78\%$

18. The cost of an article at a loss of 20%

$= \frac{280 \times 100}{80} = ₹350$

New SP of an article = ₹380

$\therefore \quad$ Profit $= 380 - 350 = ₹30$

Hence, profit per cent

$= \frac{30}{350} \times 100\% = 8\frac{4}{7}\%$

19. Selling price = ₹150

Profit calculated = ₹30 (given 20% of SP)

$\therefore$ Cost price = (150 – 30)

= ₹120

True profit percentage

$= \frac{\text{Profit}}{\text{CP}} \times 100$

$= \frac{30}{120} \times 100\%$

$= 25\%$

20. Let the cost price of the article be ₹x.

If SP = ₹1060,

then profit = ₹$(x - 1060)$

If SP = ₹950,

then loss = ₹$(950 - x)$

Now, it is given that profit $= 1.2 \times$ Loss

$\therefore \quad (x - 1060) = 1.2\,(950 - x)$

$\Rightarrow \quad x - 1060 = 1140 - 1.2x$

$\Rightarrow \quad x = 1000$

Therefore, selling price to earn a profit of 20%

$= 1.2 \times 1000 = ₹1200$

21. $\because$ SP of 25 chairs = CP of 25 chairs + profit

SP of 25 chairs = CP of 25 chairs + SP of 5 chairs

($\because$ profit = SP of 5 chairs)

$\Rightarrow$ SP of 20 chairs

= CP of 25 chairs

$\Rightarrow$ SP of 20 chairs = ₹375

$\therefore$ SP of one chair = ₹18.75

22. CP of 200 kg of rice

$= ₹(80 \times 13.5 + 120 \times 16)$

= ₹3000

CP of 1 kg of rice

$= ₹\frac{3000}{200} = ₹15$

$\therefore$ SP of rice per kg to earn a profit of 16%

$= ₹1.16 \times 15 = ₹17.40$

23. SP = ₹10.80, Loss = 10%

Then, CP $= ₹\frac{10.80}{0.9} = ₹12$

$\therefore$ SP at a gain of 20%

$= ₹1.2 \times 12 = ₹14.40$

24. CP of 20 L of milk with other expense = ₹$(20 \times 8 + 10)$

= ₹170

SP of 5 kg cream and 20 L toned milk

$= ₹(5 \times 30 + 20 \times 4) = ₹230$

$\therefore$ Profit per cent

$= \frac{60}{170} \times 100 = 35.29\%$

or 35.3%

25. Let the CP of the article for A is ₹x.

$\therefore (x + 110)\left(\frac{100 + 20}{100}\right)\left(\frac{100 - 10}{100}\right)\left(\frac{100 + 10}{100}\right) = 1188$

$\Rightarrow (x + 110) \times \frac{6}{5} \times \frac{9}{10} \times \frac{11}{10} = 1188$

$\Rightarrow x + 110 = 1000$

$\therefore x = 1000 - 110 = ₹890$

26. CP for the commodity sold at gain of 25%

$= ₹\frac{4000}{1.25} = ₹3200$

Since, CP and SP are the same.

Hence, CP for other commodity

$= ₹(8000 - 3200) = ₹4800$

Loss $= ₹(4800 - 4000) = ₹800$

$\therefore$ Loss per cent $= \frac{800}{4800} \times 100$

$= \frac{100}{6} = 16\frac{2}{3}\%$

27. SP of the article $= ₹\,153 \times 1.2$
$= ₹\,183.60$

Therefore, if we suppose marked price be x, then it results into a selling price of ₹ 183.60 after giving a discount of 15%.

$\Rightarrow \quad x \times 0.85 = 183.60$

$\therefore \quad x = ₹\,216$

28. Let the CP of the goods be ₹ x.

Then, marked price $= ₹\,1.2\,x$

SP of the goods $= ₹\,1.08x$

Discount = MP − SP $= ₹\,0.12x$

So, discount per cent

$$= \frac{0.12x \times 100}{1.2x} = 10\%$$

29. Let the list price of the article be ₹ x.

Then, $x \times 0.8 = 24 \Rightarrow x = ₹\,30$

$\therefore$ Required selling price

$= ₹\,0.7 \times 30 = ₹\,21$

30. Let the CP of the goods be ₹ x.

Therefore, marked price

$= ₹\,1.2\,x$

Selling price $= ₹\,0.9 \times 1.2x$

$= ₹\,1.08\,x$

Profit $= ₹\,(1.08x - x) = ₹\,0.08\,x$

$\therefore$ Profit per cent

$$= \frac{0.08x}{x} \times 100 = 8\%$$

31. Let the cost price of 100 items be ₹ 100.

Marked price of the same

$= ₹\,130$

SP of 25 items $\left(\frac{1}{4}\text{th}\right)$ at a discount of 15%

$$= ₹\,\frac{130}{100} \times 25 \times 0.85 = ₹\,27.62$$

SP of 50 items $\left(\frac{1}{2}\right)$ at the marked price

$$= ₹\,\frac{130}{100} \times 50 = ₹\,65$$

SP of 25 items $\left(\frac{1}{4}\right)$ at the discount of 30%

$$= ₹\,\frac{130}{100} \times 25 \times 0.7 = ₹\,22.75$$

Total selling price $= ₹\,115.37$

$\therefore$ Profit per cent

$$= \frac{15.37}{100} \times 100\% = 15\frac{3}{8}\%$$

32. Let MP $= ₹\,100$,

then after 10% commission

SP $= ₹\,90$

and CP $= \frac{90}{1.25} = ₹\,72$

If SP = 80, then

$$\therefore \text{Gain } \% = \frac{80-72}{72} \times 100$$

$$= \frac{100}{9} = 11\frac{1}{9}\%$$

33. Equivalent discount for two successive discounts of 8% and 8%,

$$= \left(x + y - \frac{xy}{100}\right)\%$$

$$= \left(8 + 8 - \frac{8 \times 8}{100}\right)\%$$

[here, $x = 8$; $y = 8$]

$= (16 - 0.64)\% = 15.36\%$

$\therefore$ SP $= (100 - 15.36)\%$ of ₹ 900

$$= ₹\left(\frac{84.64 \times 900}{100}\right) = ₹\,761.76$$

For a single discount of 16%

SP = 84% of 900

$$= ₹\left(\frac{84 \times 900}{100}\right) = ₹\,756$$

Certainly seller will loss in this case.

$\therefore$ Loss $= ₹\,(761.76 - 756)$

$= ₹\,5.76$

34. Let cost price of the article

$= ₹\,x$

$\therefore$ Marked price of the article

$$= 120\% \text{ of } x = \frac{x \times 120}{100} = 1.2x$$

and selling price of the article = 96% of $x = 0.96x$

Let the trader allows the discount of d%.

Then, according to question

$(100 - d)\%$ of $1.2x = 0.96x$

$$\Rightarrow \quad \frac{100-d}{100} = \frac{0.96}{1.2}$$

$\Rightarrow \quad 100 - d = 80$

$\therefore \quad d = 20\%$

35. Given, marked price $= ₹\,480$

So, cost after discount

$$= \frac{480 \times 90}{100}$$

$= ₹\,432$

Let actual cost of the ratio set be x.

According to the question,

$$\frac{108 \times x}{100} = 432$$

$$\Rightarrow \quad x = \frac{432 \times 100}{108} = 400$$

If discount is not allowed, then

$$\text{Gain } \% = \frac{480-400}{400} \times 100$$

$$= \frac{80}{400} \times 100 = 20\%$$

Previous Year's Solutions

36. Let cost price of 18 eggs be ₹ x.

Then, cost price of 12 eggs

$$= \frac{x}{18} \times 12$$

Selling price of 12 eggs

$$= \frac{x}{18} \times 12 \times \frac{90}{100} = 0.6\,x$$

and selling price of remaining eggs

$= x - 0.6x$

$= 0.4\,x$

Profit in remaining eggs

$$= 0.4x - \frac{x}{18} \times 6$$

$= 0.4\,x - 0.33x$

$= 0.07x$

Profit percentage on remaining eggs

$= \frac{0.07 \times 100}{0.33} \approx 20\%$

37. Total making charge

$= 100 \times 10 = ₹1000$

Cost of jewellery

$= 1000 - 100 = ₹ 900$

Total cost $= 1000 + 900$

$= ₹1900$

Discount

$= 1900 - 1000 = ₹ 900$

Percentage discount

$= \frac{900 \times 100}{1900}$

$\approx 47\%$

38. CP $= ₹380$, Profit $= 25\%$

$\therefore$ SP $= 125\%$ of $380 = \frac{125}{100} \times 380$

$= ₹475$

Now, 95% of MP $= 475$

$\text{MP} = 475 \times \frac{100}{95}$

$= ₹ 500$

39. Let P paid ₹ x for the table.

Then, $x \times \frac{110}{100} \times \frac{112}{100} = 246.40$

$\Rightarrow \quad x = \frac{246.40 \times 100 \times 100}{110 \times 112}$

$= ₹200$

40. Single discount equivalent to series discount of 15% and 5% is

$\left[a + b + \frac{a \times b}{100}\right]\%$

Here, $a = 15$ and $b = 15$

$= \left\{\left[\left(-15 - 5 + \frac{-15 \times (-5)}{100}\right)\right]\right\}\%$

(–ve for discount)

$= (-20 + 0.75)\ \%$

$\Rightarrow -19.25\ \% \simeq 20\%$

So, equivalent discount $= 20\%$

41. Total gain $= \frac{11 - 10}{10} \times 100$

$= 10\%$

42. Let cost price $= ₹ x$

Selling price = 2345

Loss $= 19\%$

$\text{Cost price} = \frac{\text{SP} \times 100}{(100 - \text{Loss}\%)}$

$= \frac{2345 \times 100}{(100 - 19)}$

$= \frac{234500}{81}$

$= ₹ 2895 \simeq ₹ 3000$

43. Let the cost price $= ₹100$

Marked price $= ₹ 120$

(given in question that MP is 20% more than CP)

Allowing a discount of 10%.

$\therefore \text{Discount} = \frac{120 \times 10}{100} = ₹12$

$\Rightarrow \quad \text{SP} = 120 - 12 = 108$

Hence, if CP is 100, then SP is 108.

Gain = (SP – CP)

$= 108 - 100 = ₹ 8$

$\therefore$ Gain percentage $= 8\%$

44. Let fixed charges be ₹ x and cost of food per day be ₹ y.

As per question,

$x + 20y = 1000 \quad \ldots(i)$

$x + 26y = 1180 \quad \ldots(ii)$

On solving Eqs. (i) and (ii), we get

$x = ₹ 400,\ y = ₹ 30$

45. Single discount equivalent to two successive discounts

$= 15 + 12 - \frac{15 \times 12}{100}$

$= 27 - 1.8$

$= 25.2\%$

$\therefore$ Price of TV

$= \frac{100 - 25.2}{100} \times 15000$

$= \frac{74.8}{100} \times 15000$

$= 74.8 \times 150$

$= ₹ 11220$

46. Let the actual price of rice per kg $= ₹100$

Then, selling price $= 120\%$ of $100 = ₹120$

Now, trader sells 10% less than actual weight So, cost price to trader will be = 90% of 100 = ₹ 90

$\therefore$ Required profit gained by trader

$= \frac{(120 - 90)}{90} \times 100$

$= \frac{30}{90} \times 100 = 33\frac{1}{3}\%$

CHAPTER 07

WORK, TIME, DISTANCE AND SPEED

In this chapter, we will study techniques to solve problems based on work and its completion time as well as number of persons required to finish the given work in stipulated time.

Also we study, the concept of time, distance and speed is related to a particular object in motion. Time, distance and speed problems are asked to solve for one of the three variables given certain information. In these problems, objects are moving at either constant or average speeds

In time and work conceptual clarification of relationship between working efficiency and time is very important.

IMPORTANT RELATIONS

1. **Work and Person** Directly proportional (more work, more men and conversely less work, less men).
2. **Time and Person** Inversely proportional (more men, less time and conversely less men, more time).
3. **Work and Time** Directly proportional (more work, more time and conversely less work, less time).

Basic Rules Related to Work and Time

(i) If a person can do a piece of work in n days (hours), then person's 1 day's (hour) work $= \frac{1}{n}$.

(ii) If a person's 1 day's (hour) work $= \frac{1}{n}$, then the person will complete the work in n days (hours).

WAGES

Money received by a person for a certain work is called wages of the person for that particular work. Wages are directly proportional to the work done and indirectly proportional to the time taken.

Important Formulae

- Consider M_1 men can do W_1 work in D_1 days working H_1 hours per day and M_2 men can do W_2 work in D_2 days working H_2 hours per day, then
$$\frac{M_1 \times D_1 \times H_1}{W_1} = \frac{M_2 \times D_2 \times H_2}{W_2}$$
- If A can do a work in D_1 days and B can do the same work in D_2 days, then A and B can together do the same work in $\frac{D_1 \times D_2}{D_1 + D_2}$ days.
- If A and B can do a piece of work in x and y days, respectively and they received ₹ z as wages by working together, then
$$\text{Share of } A = ₹\,\frac{y}{x+y} \times z$$
$$\text{Share of } B = ₹\,\frac{x}{x+y} \times z$$
- If A, B and C can do a piece of work in x, y and z days, respectively. The contract for the work is ₹ a and all of them work together, then
$$\text{Share of } A = ₹\left(\frac{ayz}{xy + yz + zx}\right)$$
$$\text{Share of } B = ₹\left(\frac{azx}{xy + yz + zx}\right)$$
$$\text{Share of } C = ₹\left(\frac{axy}{xy + yz + zx}\right)$$

EXAMPLE 1 If A can do a piece of work in 10 days and B can do the same work in 15 days, then how long will they take if they both work together?

(a) 5 days
(b) 6 days
(c) 7 days
(d) 8 days

Solution *(b)* A can finish the work in $D_1 = 10$ days

B can finish the work in $D_2 = 15$ days

$$A \text{ and } B \text{ working together} = \frac{D_1 \times D_2}{D_1 + D_2} = \frac{10 \times 15}{10 + 15}$$
$$= \frac{150}{25} = 6 \text{ days}$$

EXAMPLE 2 5 men can prepare 10 cycles in 6 days working 6h a day. Then, in how many days can 12 men prepare 16 cycles working 8h a day?

(a) 1 days (b) 2 days (c) 3 days (d) 4 days

Solution *(c)* Here, $M_1 = 5, W_1 = 10, D_1 = 6, H_1 = 6$ and $M_2 = 12, W_2 = 16, H_2 = 8, D_2 = ?$

So, from the above rule

$$M_1 D_1 H_1 W_2 = M_2 D_2 H_2 W_1$$
$$5 \times 6 \times 6 \times 16 = 12 \times D_2 \times 8 \times 10$$
$$D_2 = 3 \text{ days}$$

So, they will complete the work in 3 days.

EXAMPLE 3 A, B and C can do a work in 6, 8 and 12 days, respectively. Doing that work together they get an amount of ₹ 1350. What is the share of B in that amount?

(a) ₹ 350 (b) ₹ 450 (c) ₹ 550 (d) ₹ 650

Solution *(b)* Here, $x = 6, y = 8$

$z = 12$ and $a = 1350$

$$\therefore \text{ Share of } B = ₹\left(\frac{azx}{xy + yz + zx}\right)$$
$$= ₹\left(\frac{1350 \times 12 \times 6}{6 \times 8 + 8 \times 12 + 6 \times 12}\right)$$
$$= ₹\left(\frac{97200}{48 + 96 + 72}\right)$$
$$= ₹\left(\frac{97200}{216}\right) = ₹\,450$$

PIPES AND CISTERNS

Pipes and Cisterns problems are similar to time and work problems. A pipe is used to fill or empty the tank or cistern.

1. **Inlet Pipe** A pipe used to fill the tank or cistern is known as inlet pipe.

2. **Outlet Pipe** A pipe used to empty the tank or cistern is known as outlet pipe.

Basic Concept

(i) If a pipe can fill/empty the tank in x hours, then the part filled/emptied in 1 hour $= \frac{1}{x}$.

(ii) If a pipe can fill a tank in x hours and another pipe can empty the full tank in y hour ($y > x$), then on opening both the pipes, the net part filled in 1 h $= \left(\frac{1}{x}\right) - \left(\frac{1}{y}\right)$, if $y > x$.

EXAMPLE 4 A tap can fill an empty tank in 12 h and another tap can empty half the tank in 10 h. If both the taps are opened simultaneously, then how long would it take to be filled to half its capacity?

(a) 10 h (b) 15 h (c) 20 h (d) 30 h

Solution *(b)* Part of tank filled by first tap in 1 h

$$= \frac{1}{12}$$

and part of tank emptied by second tap in 1 h

$$= \frac{1}{10 \times 2} = \frac{1}{20}$$

$\therefore$ Part of tank filled by both tap in 1 h $= \frac{1}{12} - \frac{1}{20}$

$$= \frac{5-3}{60} = \frac{2}{60} = \frac{1}{30}$$

Hence, tank will be filled to its full capacity in 30 h. Thus, to fill the half tank it will take 15 h.

Time, Distance and Speed

1. **Time** The duration in hours, minutes or second spent to cover a certain distance is called the time.
2. **Distance** The length of the path travelled by any object or a person between two places is known as distance. It is usually measured in m or km.
3. **Speed** The distance travelled by any object or a person in unit time is known as speed.

   The unit of speed is m/s or km/h.

Relation between Speed, Time and Distance

- Speed $= \frac{\text{Distance}}{\text{Time}}$
- Distnace = Speed × Time
- Time $= \frac{\text{Distance}}{\text{Speed}}$

(i) 1 km/h $= \frac{5}{18}$ m/s. (ii) 1 m/s $= \frac{18}{5}$ km/h.

(iii) If a man covers certain distance at x km/h, and an equal distance at y km/h, then the average speed during the whole journey is $\frac{2xy}{x+y}$

EXAMPLE 5 A man covers a distance with speed 45 km/h in 6h. To cover the same distance in 5h, what should be the speed of his car?

(a) 45 km/h (b) 50 km/h
(c) 54 km/h (d) 60 km/h

Solution *(c)* Distance covered in 6h with speed 45 km/h

$$= 45 \times 6 = 270 \text{ km}.$$

$\therefore$ Speed of car to cover 270 km in 5h

$$= \frac{270}{5} = 54 \text{ km/h}$$

Problems Based on Trains

Problems based on trains are same as the problems related to speed, time and distance. The only difference is we have to consider the length of the moving train while solving problems based on trains.

Some Important Points

- Time taken by a train of length L m to pass a stationary pole is equal to the time taken by train to cover L m.
- Time taken by a train of length of L meters to pass a stationary object of length P m is equal to the time taken by train to cover ($L + P$) m.
- If two trains are moving in same direction and their speeds are x km/h and y km/h ($x > y$), then their relative speed is ($x - y$) km/h.
- If two trains are moving in opposite direction and their speeds are x km/h and y km/h, then their relative speed is ($x + y$) km/h.

EXAMPLE 6 If the speed of a train is 92.4 km/h, how much distance would be covered by it in 20 minutes?

(a) 30800 meters (b) 31800 meters
(c) 32200 meters (d) 32800 meters

Solution *(a)* Given speed = 92.4 km/h

Then, distance covered in 1 hr or 60 min

$= 92.4$ km

$\therefore$ Distance covered in 20 min $= \frac{92.4}{60} \times 20$

$= 30.8 \text{ km} = 30800 \text{ m}$

EXAMPLE 7 A train running at a rate of 40 km/h passes a man riding parallel to the railway line in the same direction at 25 km/h in 48 seconds. Find the length of the train in metres.

(a) 100 m (b) 200 m
(c) 150 m (d) 250 m

Solution *(b)* Speed of train relative to man

$= 40 - 25 = 15 \text{ km/h} = 15 \times \frac{5}{18} \text{ m/s}$

Then, length of train = speed × time

$= 15 \times \frac{5}{18} \times 48 = 200 \text{ m}$

BOATS AND STREAMS

Boats and streams is an application of concepts of speed, time and distance. It is based on the speed of boat (or swimmer) in still water or flowing water.

Some important terms used here are as follows

1. **Still Water** If the water is not moving, Then it is called still water.
2. **Stream** Moving water of the river is called stream.
3. **Upstream** If a boat or a swimmer moves in the opposite direction of the stream, then it is called upstream.
4. **Downstream** If a boat or a swimmer moves in the same direction of the stream, then it is called downstream.
5. **Speed of Boat** If the speed of a boat is given, then that particular speed is the speed in still water.

Basic Formulae Related to Boats and Streams

1. If the speed of a boat in still water be x km/h and that of stream be y km/h, the
   (i) Speed of the boat downstream $= (x + y)$ is v km/h
   (ii) Speed of the boat upstream $= (x - y)$ is u km/h
2. If the speed of a boat downstream is u km/h and speed upstream is v km/h, then
   (i) Speed of the boat in still water $= \frac{1}{2}(u + v)$ km/h
   (ii) Speed of the stream $= \frac{1}{2}(u - v)$ km/h

EXAMPLE 8 A man takes twice as long to row a distance against the stream as to row the same distance in favour of the stream. Find the ratio of the speed of the boat (in still water) and the stream

(a) 1:1 (b) 2:1 (c) 3:1 (d) 1:3

Solution *(c)* Let man's rate upstream be x km/h.

Then, his rate downstream = $2x$ km/h.

(Speed in still water) : (Speed of stream)

$= \frac{(2x + x)}{2} : \frac{(2x - x)}{2}$

$= \frac{3x}{2} : \frac{x}{2} = 3:1$

Practice Exercise

1. *A* can complete a piece of work in 18 days and *B* can complete the same work in half time taken by *A*. Then, working together, what part of the same work they can complete in a day?

(a) $\frac{1}{6}$ (b) $\frac{1}{9}$ (c) $\frac{2}{5}$ (d) $\frac{2}{9}$

2. *A* and *B* together can do a piece of work in 12 days, while *B* alone can finish it in 30 days. *A* alone can finish the work in

(a) 15 days (b) 18 days
(c) 20 days (d) 25 days

3. Aarti can do a piece of work in 6 days. In how many days will she complete the three time of work of same type?

(a) 18 days (b) 21 days
(c) 3 days (d) 6 days

4. *A* and *B* can do a piece of work in 6 and 12 days, respectively. They (both) will complete the work in how many days?

(a) 9 days (b) 18 days
(c) 6 days (d) 4 days

5. 15 men can do a work in 20 days. If there are 25 men, how many days will it take to complete the work?

(a) 20 (b) 15
(c) 12 (d) 35

6. *A* is 30% more efficient than *B*. How much time will they, working together, take to complete a job which *A* alone could have done in 23 days?

(a) 11 days (b) 13 days
(c) 203 days (d) None of these

7. *A* does 80% of a work in 20 days. He then calls in *B* and they together finish the remaining work in 3 days. How long *B* alone would take to do the whole work?

(a) 23 days (b) 37 days
(c) $37\frac{1}{2}$ days (d) 40 days

8. If 6 men and 8 boys can do a piece of work in 10 days while 26 men and 48 boys can do the same work in 2 days, the time taken by 15 men and 20 boys in doing the same type of work will be

(a) 4 days (b) 5 days
(c) 6 days (d) 7 days

9. Twenty women can do a piece of work in sixteen days. Sixteen men can complete the same work in fifteen days. What is the ratio between the capacity of a man and a woman?

(a) 3 : 4 (b) 4 : 3
(c) 5 : 3 (d) Data inadequate

10. 4 men and 6 women can complete a work in 8 days, while 3 men and 7 women can complete it in 10 days. In how many days, will 10 women complete it?

(a) 35 days (b) 40 days
(c) 45 days (d) 50 days

11. *A* and *B* can together finish a work in 30 days. They worked together for 20 days and then *B* left. After another 20 days, *A* finished the remaining work. In how many days, *A* alone can finish the work?

(a) 40 days (b) 50 days
(c) 54 days (d) 60 days

12. *A*, *B* and *C* can do a piece of work in 20, 30 and 60 days, respectively. In how many days can *A* do the work, if he is assisted by *B* and *C* on every third day?

(a) 12 days (b) 15 days
(c) 16 days (d) 18 days

13. *A* alone can do a piece of work in 6 days and *B* alone in 8 days. *A* and *B* undertook to do it for ₹ 3200. With the help of *C*, they completed the work in 3 days. How much is to be paid to *C*?

(a) ₹ 375 (b) ₹ 400
(c) ₹ 6004 (d) ₹ 800

14. Pipes P and Q can fill a tank in 5 and 6 h respectively. Pipe R can empty it in 12 h. If all the three pipes are opened together, then the tank will be filled in :

(a) $4\frac{5}{13}$ h (b) $1\frac{9}{17}$ h (c) $3\frac{5}{13}$ h (d) $3\frac{9}{17}$ h

15. Two pipes P and Q can fill a tank in 15 min and 20 min, respectively. Both the pipes are opened together but after 4 min, pipe P is turned off. What is the total time required to fill the tank?

(a) 15 min 10 sec (b) 12 min 20 sec
(c) 12 min 30 sec (d) 14 min 40 sec

16. A tank is filled is 5 by three pipes P, Q and R. The pipe R is twice as fast as Q and Q is twice as fast as P. How much time will pipe P alone take to fill the tank?

(a) 35 h (b) 55 h (c) 20 h (d) 10 h

17. A person crosses a 600 m long street in 5 min. What is his speed in km per hour?

(a) 3.6 (b) 7.2 (c) 8.4 (d) 10

18. A man covers half of his journey as 6 km/h and the remaining half at 3 km/h. His average speed is

(a) 9 km/h (b) 4.5 km/h
(c) 4 km/h (d) 3 km/h

19. A car completes a certain journey in 8 h. It covers half the distance at 40 km/h and the rest at 60 km/h. The length of the journey is

(a) 350 km (b) 420 km
(c) 384 km (d) 400 km

20. If a person walks at 14 km/h instead of 10 km/h, he would have walked 20 km more. The actual distance travelled by him is

(a) 50 km (b) 56 km (c) 70 km (d) 80 km

21. In covering a distance of 30 km, Abhay takes 2 h more than Sameer. If Abhay doubles his speed, then he would take 1 h less than Sameer. Abhay's speed is

(a) 5 km/h (b) 6 km/h
(c) 6.25 km/h (d) 7.5 km/h

22. A man covered a certain distance at some speed. Had he moved 3 km/h faster, he would have taken 40 min less. If he had moved 2 km/h slower, he would have taken 40 min more. The distance (in km) is

(a) 35 (b) $36\frac{2}{3}$ (c) 371 (d) 40

23. In a flight of 600 km, an aircraft was slowed down due to bad weather. Its average speed for the trip was reduced by 200 km/h and the time of flight increased by 30 min. The duration of the flight is

(a) 1 h (b) 2 h
(c) 3 h (d) 4 h

24. Robert is travelling on his cycle and has calculated to reach point A at 2 pm if he travels at 10 km/h, he will reach there at 12 noon if he travels at 15 km/h. At what speed must he travel to reach A at 1 pm?

(a) 8 km/h (b) 11 km/h
(c) 12 km/h (d) 14 km/h

25. Mr. X drives to his office at an average speed of 48 km per hour. The time taken to cover the first 60% of the distance is 10 minutes more than the time taken to cover the remaining distance. How far is his office?

(a) 30 km (b) 40 km
(c) 45 km (d) 48 km

26. The length of the bridge, which a train 130 m long on travelling at 45 km/h can cross in 30 s, is

(a) 200 m (b) 225 m
(c) 245 m (d) 250 m

27. A train passes a 110 m long platform in 40 s and a boy standing on the platform in 30 s. The length of the train is

(a) 100 m (b) 110 m
(c) 200 m (d) 330 m

28. A train moving with uniform speed crosses a pole in 2 s and a 250 m long bridge in 7 s. Find the length of the train.

(a) 150 m (b) 120 m
(c) 100 m (d) 80 m

29. Two trains, each 100 m long, moving in opposite directions, cross each other in 8 s. If one is moving twice as fast the other, then the speed of the faster train is

(a) 30 km/h (b) 45 km/h
(c) 60 km/h (d) 75 km/h

30. Two trains of equal length are running on parallel lines in the same direction at 46 km/h and 36 km/h. The faster train passes the slower train in 36 s. The length of each train is

(a) 50 m (b) 72 m
(c) 80 m (d) 82 m

31. Two trains running in opposite directions cross a man standing on the platform in 27 sec and 17 sec, respectively and they cross each other in 23 sec. The ratio of their speeds is

(a) 1 : 3 (b) 3 : 2
(c) 3 : 4 (d) None of these

32. A streamer goes downstream from one port to another in 4 h. It covers the same distance upstream in 5 h. If the speed of stream is 2 km/h, the distance between the two ports is

(a) 80 km (b) 81 km
(c) 70 km (d) 71 km

33. A boat takes 90 min less to travel 36 miles downstream than to travel the same distance upstream. If the speed of the boat in still water is 10 min/h, the speed of the stream is

(a) 2 min/h
(b) 2.5 min/h
(c) 3 min/h
(d) 4 min/h

34. A man rows to a place 48 km distance and come back in 14 h. He finds that he can row 4 km with the stream in the same time as 3 km against the stream. The rate of the stream is

(a) 1 km/h (b) 1.5 km/h
(c) 2 km/h (d) 2.5 km/h

Previous Year's Questions

35. A man walks from his house to the Railway station to catch a train, which is running as per schedule. If he walks at 6 km/h, he misses the train by 9 min. However, if he walks at 7 km/h, he reaches the station 6 min before the departure of train. The distance of his home to the Railway station is **[CLAT 2011]**

(a) 2 km (b) 1.5 km
(c) 10.5 km (d) 1.25 km

36. A train 300 m long is running at a speed of 25 m/s , it will cross a bridge 200 m long in? **[CLAT 2012]**

(a) 5 s (b) 10 s
(c) 20 s (d) 25 s

37. 120 men had food provision for 200 days. After 5 days, 30 men died of an epidemic. The food will last for further **[CLAT 2012]**

(a) 280 days (b) 260 days
(c) 290 days (d) 252 days

38. Pipe *A* can fill a tank in 10 h and pipe *B* can fill the same tank in 12 h. Both the pipes are opened to fill the tank and after 3 h pipe *A* is closed. Pipe *B* will fill the remaining part of the tank in **[CLAT 2013]**

(a) 5 h (b) 4 h
(c) 5 h 24 min (d) 3 h

39. In a school for mid-day meal food is sufficient for 250 students for 33 days, if each student is given 125 g meal. 80 more students joined the school. If same amount of meal is given to each student, then the food will last for **[CLAT 2013]**

(a) 20 days (b) 40 days
(c) 30 days (d) 25 days

40. A man can row 5 km/h in still water. If the speed of the current is 1 km/h, it takes 3 h more in upstream than in the downstream for the same distance. The distance is **[CLAT 2014]**

(a) 36 km (b) 24 km
(c) 20 km (d) 32 km

41. *A* can do a piece of work in 20 days and *B* can do the same work in 15 days. How long will they take to finish the work, if both work together? **[CLAT 2014]**

(a) $13\frac{1}{2}$ days (b) 10 days

(c) $8\frac{4}{7}$ days (d) $17\frac{1}{2}$ days

42. A person covers a certain distance by car at a speed of 30 km/h and comes back at a speed of 40 km/h. The average speed during the travel is **[CLAT 2014]**

(a) 34.3 km/h (b) 35 km/h

(c) 37.5 km/h (d) 32.8 km/h

43. Two trains, one from Howrah to Patna, and other from Patna to Howrah, start simultaneously. After they meet, the trains reach their destinations after 9 h and 16 h, respectively. The ratio of their speed is **[CLAT 2015]**

(a) 2 : 3 (b) 4 : 3

(c) 6 : 7 (d) 9 : 6

44. A man earns ₹ 20 on the first day and spends ₹ 15 on the next day. He again earns ₹ 20 on the third day and spends ₹ 15 on the fourth day. If he continues to save in this way, then how soon will he have ₹ 60 in hand? **[CLAT 2016]**

(a) On 17th day (b) On 24th day

(c) On 27th day (d) On 12th day

45. A train which is moving at an average speed of 40 km/h reaches its destination on time. When its average speed reduces to 35 km/h, then it reaches its destination 15 min late. The distance travelled by the train, is **[CLAT 2016]**

(a) 70 km (b) 80 km (c) 40 km (d) 30 km

46. A man rows to a place 45 k.ms distant and back in 12 hours. He realises that he can row 5 k.ms downstream in the same time as 3 k.ms against the stream. The velocity of the stream is **[CLAT 2017]**

(a) 4 k m/h (b) 1.5 k m/h

(c) 3.2 k m/h (d) 4.1 k m/h

47. '*A*' and '*B*' complete a work in 12 days, '*B*' and '*C*' in 8 days and '*C*' and '*A*' in 16 days. '*A*' left after working for 3 days. In how many days more will '*B*' and '*C*' finish the remaining work? **[CLAT 2017]**

(a) $6\frac{5}{6}$ (b) $7\frac{3}{4}$ (c) $4\frac{3}{4}$ (d) $3\frac{3}{4}$

48. *A* can do a piece of work in 8 days and *B* alone can do the same work in 10 days. *A* and *B* agreed to do the work together for ₹ 720. With the help of *C*, they finished the work in 4 days. How much *C* is to be paid? **[CLAT 2017]**

(a) ₹ 80 (b) ₹ 70

(c) ₹ 72 (d) ₹ 82

49. A train '*X*' leaves station '*A*' at 3 p.m and reaches station '*B*' at 4.30 p.m., while another train '*Y*' leaves station '*B*' at 3.00 p.m and reaches station '*A*' at 4.00 p.m. These two trains cross each other at **[CLAT 2017]**

(a) 3.36 p.m. (b) 3.30 p.m.

(c) 3.20 p.m. (d) 3.40 p.m.

50. Taps '*A*' and '*B*' can fill a tank is $37\frac{1}{2}$ minutes and 45 minutes respectively. Both taps are opened and after some time tap '*B*' is turned off. The tank is filled completely in exactly 30 minutes, if tap '*B*' is turned off after **[CLAT 2017]**

(a) 12 minutes (b) 9 minutes

(c) 10 minutes (d) 15 minutes

51. Two men and seven boys can do a work in 14 days. Three men and eight boys can do the same work in 11 days. Further eight men and six boys can do three times the amount of this work in **[CLAT 2017]**

(a) 24 days (b) 30 days (c) 21 days (d) 18 days

52. A boat travels upstream from *A* to *B* and back from *B* to *A* in 5 h. The speed of the boat in still water is 8 km/h and the speed of the current is 4 km/h. Then, the distance from *A* to *B* is **[CLAT 2017]**

(a) 10 kms (b) 9 kms

(c) 12 kms (d) 15 kms

Answers

1	a	2	c	3	a	4	d	5	c	6	b	7	c	8	a	9	b	10	b
11	d	12	b	13	b	14	d	15	d	16	a	17	b	18	c	19	c	20	a
21	a	22	d	23	a	24	c	25	b	26	c	27	d	28	c	29	c	30	a
31	b	32	a	33	a	34	a	35	c	36	c	37	b	38	c	39	d	40	a
41	c	42	a	43	b	44	a	45	a	46	c	47	c	48	c	49	a	50	b
51	c	52	d																

SOLUTIONS

1. A's 1 day's work $= \frac{1}{18}$

B's 1 day's work $= \frac{1}{9}$

$(A + B)$'s 1 day's work

$= \frac{1}{9} + \frac{1}{18} = \frac{3}{18} = \frac{1}{6}$

2. $A + B)$'s 1 day's work $= \frac{1}{12}$

B's 1 day's work $= \frac{1}{30}$

$\therefore$ A's 1 day's work $= \frac{1}{12} - \frac{1}{30}$

$= \frac{5-2}{60} = \frac{1}{20}$

$\therefore$A alone can finish the work in 20 days.

Second Method

Here, $x = 12$ and $y = 30$

$\therefore$ Required number of days

$= \frac{xy}{y-x} = \frac{12 \times 30}{30-12}$

$= \frac{12 \times 30}{18} = 20$ days

$\therefore$ A alone can finish the work in 20 days.

3. We have the important relation,

More work, More time (days)

$\because$ A piece of work can be done in 6 days.

$\therefore$ Three times of work of same type can be done in $6 \times 3 = 18$ days.

4. A's 1 day's work $= \frac{1}{6}$

B's 1 day's work $= \frac{1}{12}$

$(A + B)$'s 1 day's work

$= \frac{1}{6} + \frac{1}{12} = \frac{2+1}{12} = \frac{3}{12} = \frac{1}{4}$

Hence, both will complete the work in 4 days.

Second Method

Here, $x = 6$

and $y = 12$

$\therefore$Time taken by $(A + B)$

$= \frac{xy}{x+y} = \frac{6 \times 12}{12+6} = 4$ days.

5. Here, $M_1 = 15, D_1 = 20$

$M_2 = 25, D_2 = ?$

$M_1 D_1 = M_2 D_2$

$15 \times 20 = 25 \times D_2$

$D_2 = \frac{15 \times 20}{25}$

$\Rightarrow \quad D_2 = 12$

6. Ratio of times taken by A and B

$= 100 : 130 = 10 : 13$

Suppose, B takes x days to do the work.

Then, $10 : 13 :: 23 : x$

$\Rightarrow x = \left(\frac{23 \times 13}{10}\right) \Rightarrow x = \frac{299}{10}$

A's 1 day's work $= \frac{1}{23}$

B's 1 day's work $= \frac{10}{299}$

$(A + B)$'s 1 day's work

$= \left(\frac{1}{23} + \frac{10}{299}\right) = \frac{23}{299} = \frac{1}{13}$

Therefore, A and B together can complete the work in 13 days.

7. Whole work is done by A in $\left(20 \times \frac{5}{4}\right) = 25$ days.

Remaining work $\frac{1}{5}$ is done by A and B in 3 days.

Whole work will be done by A and B in

$(3 \times 5) = 15$ days

A's 1 day's work $= \frac{1}{25}$

$(A + B)$'s 1 day's work $= \frac{1}{15}$

$\therefore B$'s 1 day's work

$= \left(\frac{1}{15} - \frac{1}{25}\right) = \frac{4}{150} = \frac{2}{75}$

So, B alone would do the work in

$\frac{75}{2} = 37\frac{1}{2}$ days

8. Let 1 man's 1 day's work = x and 1 boy's 1 day's work = y

Then, $6x + 8y = \frac{1}{10}$

and $26x + 48y = \frac{1}{2}$

Solving these two equations, we get

$$x = \frac{1}{100} \text{ and } y = \frac{1}{200}$$

(15 men + 20 boy)'s 1 day's work

$$= \left(\frac{15}{100} + \frac{20}{200}\right) = \frac{1}{4}$$

∴ 15 men and 20 boys can do the work in 4 days.

9. (20 × 16) women can complete the work in 1 day.

∴ 1 woman's 1 day's work

$$= \frac{1}{320}$$

(16 × 15) men can complete the work in 1 day.

∴ 1 man's 1 day's work $= \frac{1}{240}$

So, required ratio $= \frac{1}{240} : \frac{1}{320}$

$$= \frac{1}{3} : \frac{1}{4} = 4 : 3$$

10. Let 1 man's 1 day's work = x

1 woman's 1 day's work = y

Then, $4x + 6y = \frac{1}{8}$ and $3x + 7y = \frac{1}{10}$

On solving these two equations, we get

$$x = \frac{11}{400} \text{ and } y = \frac{1}{400}$$

∴ 1 woman's 1 day's work

$$= \frac{1}{400}$$

⇒ 10 women's 1 day's work

$$= \left(\frac{1}{400} \times 10\right) = \frac{1}{40}$$

Hence, 10 women will complete the work in 40 days.

11. $(A + B)$'s 20 day's work

$$= \left(\frac{1}{30} \times 20\right) = \frac{2}{3}$$

Remaining work

$$= \left(1 - \frac{2}{3}\right) = \frac{1}{3}$$

Now, $\frac{1}{3}$ work is done by A in 20 days.

Therefore, the whole work will be done by A in

(20 × 3) = 60 days

12. A's 2 day's work

$$= \left(\frac{1}{20} \times 2\right) = \frac{1}{10}$$

$(A + B + C)$'s 1 day's work

$$= \left(\frac{1}{20} + \frac{1}{30} + \frac{1}{60}\right) = \frac{6}{60} = \frac{1}{10}$$

Work done in 3 days

$$= \left(\frac{1}{10} + \frac{1}{10}\right) = \frac{1}{5}$$

Whole work will be done in (3 × 5) = 15 days

13. C's 1 day's work

$$= \frac{1}{3} - \left(\frac{1}{6} + \frac{1}{8}\right) = \frac{1}{3} - \frac{7}{24} = \frac{1}{24}$$

A's wages : B's wages : C's wages

$$= \frac{1}{6} : \frac{1}{8} : \frac{1}{24} = 4 : 3 : 1$$

∴ C's share (for 3 days)

$$= ₹\left(\frac{1}{8} \times 3200\right) = ₹\,400$$

14. Net part fill in 1 h

$$\left[\frac{1}{5} + \frac{1}{6} - \frac{1}{12}\right] = \frac{17}{60}$$

⇒ The tank will be full in $\frac{60}{17}$ h, i.e. $3\frac{9}{17}$ h.

15. Part filled in 4 min

$$= 4\left(\frac{1}{15} + \frac{1}{20}\right) = \frac{7}{15}$$

Remaining part

$$= \left(1 - \frac{7}{15}\right) = \frac{8}{15}$$

Part filled by Q in 1 min

$$= \left(\frac{1}{20}\right)$$

Therefore, $\left(\frac{1}{20}\right) : \left(\frac{8}{15}\right) :: 1 : x$

$$\Rightarrow \quad x = \left(\frac{8}{15}\right) \times 1 \times 20 = \frac{32}{3} = 10$$

mim 40 sec.

Therefore, the tank will be full in total (4 min + 10 min 40 sec)

= 14 min 40 sec.

16. Suppose, pipe P alone takes x h to fill the tank

Then, pipes Q and$R$ will take $\frac{x}{2}$ and $\frac{x}{4}$ h respectvely to fill the tank.

$$\therefore \frac{1}{x} + \frac{2}{x} + \frac{4}{x} = \frac{1}{5}$$

$$\Rightarrow \quad x = 35\text{ h}$$

17. Speed $= \left(\frac{600}{5 \times 60}\right)$ m/s = 2 m/s

$$= \left(2 \times \frac{18}{5}\right) \text{ km/h} = 7.2 \text{ km/h}$$

18. Required average speed

$$= \frac{2 \times 6 \times 3}{6 + 3}$$

$$= \frac{2 \times 6 \times 3}{9} = 4 \text{ km/h}$$

19. Let the length of journey = x

Then, $\frac{\frac{x}{2}}{40} + \frac{\frac{x}{2}}{60} = 8$

$$\Rightarrow \frac{x}{80} + \frac{x}{120} = 8$$

$$\Rightarrow 120x + 80x = 8 \times 80 \times 120$$

$\Rightarrow \quad x = \dfrac{8 \times 80 \times 120}{200}$

$\therefore \quad x = 384$ km

20. Let the actual distance travelled by a person is x km.

Then, $\dfrac{x}{10} = \dfrac{x+20}{14}$

$\Rightarrow \quad 14x = 10x + 200$

$\Rightarrow \quad 4x = 200$

$\therefore \quad x = 50$ km

21. Let Abhay's speed be x km/h.

Then, $\dfrac{30}{x} - \dfrac{30}{2x} = 3$

$\Rightarrow \quad 6x = 30$

$x = 5$ km/h

22. Let distance $= x$ km and usual rate $= y$ km/h

Then, $\dfrac{x}{y} - \dfrac{x}{y+3} = \dfrac{40}{60}$

$\Rightarrow \quad 2y(y+3) = 9x \quad \ldots$(i)

and $\dfrac{x}{y-2} - \dfrac{x}{y} = \dfrac{40}{60}$

$\Rightarrow \quad y(y-2) = 3x \quad \ldots$(ii)

On solving Eqs. (i) and (ii), we get

$y = 12, \ x = 40$

23. Let the duration of the flight be x h.

Then,

$\dfrac{600}{x} - \dfrac{600}{x + (1/2)} = 200$

$\Rightarrow \dfrac{600}{x} - \dfrac{1200}{2x+1} = 200$

$\Rightarrow \dfrac{3}{x} - \dfrac{6}{2x+1} = 1$

$\Rightarrow 3(2x+1) - 6x = x(2x+1)$

$\Rightarrow \quad x(2x+1) = 3$

$\Rightarrow \quad 2x^2 + x - 3 = 0$

$\Rightarrow (2x+3)(x-1) = 0$

$\therefore \ x = 1$ h [leaving the –ve value of x]

24. Let the distance travelled be x km.

Then, $\dfrac{x}{10} - \dfrac{x}{15} = 2$

$\Rightarrow \quad 3x - 2x = 60$

$\Rightarrow \quad x = 60$ km

Time taken to travel 60 km at 10 km/h

$= \left(\dfrac{60}{10}\right)$ h $= 6$ h

So, Robert started 6 h before 2 pm, i.e. at 8 am.

$\therefore$ Required speed

$= \left(\dfrac{60}{5}\right)$ km/h $= 12$ km/h

25. Let the distance of office $= x$

Then,

$\dfrac{60\% \text{ of } x}{48} - \dfrac{40\% \text{ of } x}{48} = \dfrac{10}{60}$

$\Rightarrow \dfrac{60 \times x}{100 \times 48} - \dfrac{40 \times x}{100 \times 48} = \dfrac{1}{6}$

$\Rightarrow \dfrac{6x - 4x}{10 \times 48} = \dfrac{1}{6}$

$\Rightarrow 2x = \dfrac{10 \times 48}{6} = 80$

$\Rightarrow \ x = 40$ km

26. Speed $= \left(45 \times \dfrac{5}{18}\right)$ m/s

$= \left(\dfrac{25}{2}\right)$ m/s

Time $= 30$ s.

Let, the length of bridge be x m

Then, $\dfrac{130 + x}{30} = \dfrac{25}{2}$

$\Rightarrow \quad 2(130 + x) = 750$

$\therefore \quad x = 245$ m

27. Let the length of train $= x$ m

$\therefore$ Speed of train while crossing a platform

$= \dfrac{110 + x}{40}$ m/s

and speed of train while crossing a boy $= \dfrac{x}{30}$

$\therefore \quad \dfrac{x}{30} = \dfrac{110 + x}{40}$

$\Rightarrow \quad 4x = 330 + 3x$

$\therefore \quad x = 330$ m

28. Let length of the train be L m.

According to the question,

$\dfrac{L}{2} = \dfrac{L + 250}{7}$

$\Rightarrow 7L - 2L = 500 \Rightarrow L = 100$ m

29. Let the speed of the slower train be x m/s.

Then, speed of the faster train $= 2x$ m/s.

Relative speed $= (x + 2x)$ m/s $= 3x$ m/s.

$\therefore \quad \dfrac{(100 + 100)}{8} = 3x$

$\Rightarrow \quad 24x = 200$

$\Rightarrow \quad x = \dfrac{25}{3}$ m/s

So, speed of the faster train

$= \dfrac{50}{3}$ m/s

$= \left(\dfrac{50}{3} \times \dfrac{18}{5}\right)_{\text{km/h}} = 60$ km/h

30. Let the length of each train be x m.

Then, distance covered $= 2x$ m

Relative speed $= (46 - 36)$ km/h

$= \left(10 \times \dfrac{5}{18}\right)$ m/s $= \left(\dfrac{25}{9}\right)$ m/s

$\Rightarrow \quad \dfrac{2x}{36} = \dfrac{25}{9}$

$\Rightarrow \quad 2x = 100$

$\therefore \quad x = 50$ m

31. Let, the speeds of the two trains be x m/s and y m/s, respectively.

Then, length of the first train $= 27x$ m

and length of the second train $= 17y$ m

$\therefore \quad \dfrac{27x + 17y}{x + y} = 23$

$\Rightarrow \quad 27x + 17y = 23x + 23y$

$\Rightarrow \quad 4x = 6y$

$\therefore \quad \dfrac{x}{y} = \dfrac{3}{2}$

32. Let speed of streamer = y

Then, according to the question,

$$4(y+2)=5(y-2)$$

$$\Rightarrow \quad 4y+8=5y-10$$

$$\Rightarrow \quad y=18 \text{ km/h}$$

Now, let distance between the two ports = x

Then, $\frac{x}{18+2}=4$

$$\Rightarrow \quad x=4\times 20=80 \text{ km}$$

33. Let the speed of the stream x m/h. Then,

speed downstream = $(10+x)$ min/h,

Speed upstream = $(10-x)$ min/h.

$$\therefore \quad \frac{36}{(10-x)}-\frac{36}{(10+x)}=\frac{90}{60}$$

$$\Rightarrow \quad 72x\times 60=90\,(100-x^2)$$

$$\Rightarrow \quad x^2+48x-100=0$$

$$\Rightarrow \quad (x+50)\,(x-2)=0$$

$$\therefore \quad x=2 \text{ min/h}$$

[∵ –ve value neglecting]

34. Suppose, man move 4 km downstream in x hours. Then,

Speed downstream = $\left(\frac{4}{x}\right)$ km/h.

Speed upstream = $\left(\frac{3}{x}\right)$ km/h.

$$\therefore \quad \frac{48}{\left(\frac{4}{x}\right)}+\frac{48}{\left(\frac{3}{x}\right)}=14\Rightarrow x=\frac{1}{2}$$

So, speed downstream = 8 km/h,

speed upstream = 6 km/h.

Rate of the stream = $\frac{1}{2}(8-6)$ km/h = 1 km/h.

Previous Year's Solutions

35. Let the distance be x km.

According to the question,

$$\frac{x}{6}-\frac{9}{60}=\frac{x}{7}+\frac{6}{60}$$

$$\frac{x}{6}-\frac{x}{7}=\frac{6}{60}+\frac{9}{60}$$

$$\Rightarrow \quad \frac{x}{42}=\frac{1}{4}$$

$$\therefore \quad x=\frac{42}{4}=10.5 \text{ km}$$

36. Required time taken by the train

$$=\frac{\text{Total distance covered by train}}{\text{Speed of train}}$$

$$=\frac{(300+200)}{25}=\frac{500}{25}=20 \text{ s}$$

37. $M_1=120,\ D_1=200-5=195$

$M_2=120-30=90,\ D_2=?$

Using $\quad M_1D_1=M_2D_2$

$$120\times 195=90\times D_2$$

$$\Rightarrow \quad \frac{120\times 195}{90}=D_2$$

$$\therefore \quad D_2=260$$

Thus, the food will last for 260 days.

38. Part filled by pipe A in 1 h $=\frac{1}{10}$

Part filled by pipe B in 1 h $=\frac{1}{12}$

∴ Total part filled by pipe A and B in 3 h

$$=3\left(\frac{1}{10}+\frac{1}{12}\right)$$

$$=3\left(\frac{6+5}{60}\right)=\frac{11}{20}$$

$$\therefore \quad \text{Part left}=1-\frac{11}{20}=\frac{9}{20}$$

Now, $\frac{9}{20}$ part is filled by pipe B in

$$=\frac{9}{20}\times 12$$

$$=5 \text{ h } 24 \text{ min}$$

39. $M_1=250,\ D_1=33$ days, Per day meal $=125$ g

$M_2=(250+80)=330,$

$D_2=x$ dau s, Per day meal $=125$ g

$$\therefore \frac{M_1D_1}{\text{Per day meal}}=\frac{M_2D_2}{\text{Per day meal}}$$

$$\Rightarrow \quad \frac{250\times 33}{330}=x$$

$$\therefore \quad x=25 \text{ days}$$

40. Let us consider that man travelled the distance of d.

Given, speed of man in still water = 5 km/h

and speed of current = 1 km/h

Case I When, man is going downstream,

$$t_1=\frac{d}{5+1}$$

$$t_2=\frac{d}{6} \quad \text{...(i)}$$

Case II When, man is going upstream,

$$t_2=\frac{d}{5-1}$$

$$\Rightarrow \quad t_2=\frac{d}{4} \quad \text{...(ii)}$$

Also given,

$$t_1+3=t_2 \quad \text{...(iii)}$$

Taking value of t_1 and t_2 from Eqs. (i) and (ii) and putting in Eq. (iii), we get

$$\frac{d}{6}+3=\frac{d}{4}\Rightarrow \frac{d}{6}-\frac{d}{4}=-3$$

$$\Rightarrow d\left(\frac{4-6}{24}\right)=-3\Rightarrow \frac{d}{12}=3$$

$$\therefore \quad d=36 \text{ km}$$

41. Time taken to complete the work by $A=20$ days

Time taken to complete the work by $B=15$ days

Total work units = LCM of 20, 15 = 60 units

One day's work of A

$$=\frac{\text{Total unit}}{\text{Total time}}=\frac{60}{20}=3 \text{ units}$$

One day's work of B

$$=\frac{\text{Total unit}}{\text{Total time}}$$

$= \frac{60}{15} = 4$ units

If A and B work together, then time taken by both

$= \frac{\text{Total unit of work}}{\text{One day's work of } A \text{ and } B}$

$= \frac{60}{7} = 8\frac{4}{7}$ days

42. From question it is clear that distance is same hence applying formula for average speed when a person covers the same distance with different speeds of going for (v_1) and coming back (v_2).

So, Average Speed $= \frac{2v_1v_2}{v_1 + v_2}$

$\therefore \quad = \frac{2 \times 30 \times 40}{30 + 40}$

$= \frac{2 \times 30 \times 40}{70} = \frac{240}{7}$

$= 34.28 \approx 34.3$ km/h

43. 

The train from Howrah to Patna reach the destination after 9 h and the train from Patna to Howrah reach the destination after 16 h.

Then,

$\frac{\text{Speed of train I}}{\text{Speed of train II}} = \sqrt{\frac{16}{9}} = \frac{4}{3}$

$= 4:3$

44. Money saved in 2 days $= 20 - 15 = ₹\,5$

Money saved in 16 days $= 8 \times 5 = ₹\,40$

So, next day the man will earn ₹ 20 and hence he will have ₹ 60 in his hand on 17th day.

45. Distance travelled

$= \frac{40 \times 35}{40 - 35} \times \frac{15}{60}$

$= \frac{40 \times 35}{5} \times \frac{15}{60} = 70$ km

48. C's 1 day's work

$= \frac{1}{4} - \left(\frac{1}{8} + \frac{1}{10}\right)$

$= \frac{10 - (5 + 4)}{40} = \frac{1}{40}$

$\therefore A$'s wages : B's wages : C's wages

$= \frac{1}{8} : \frac{1}{10} : \frac{1}{24} = 15:12:5$

$\therefore C$'s shares (For 4 day's)

$= ₹\left(\frac{1}{10} \times 720\right) = ₹\,72$

50. Let both taps are open for x min.

Now, both taps filled in x min

$= x\left(\frac{1}{37.5} + \frac{1}{45}\right)$

$= x\left(\frac{2}{75} + \frac{1}{45}\right)$

$= x\left(\frac{6 + 5}{225}\right)$

$= \frac{11x}{225}$

Remaning part left

$= \left(1 - \frac{11x}{225}\right) = \frac{225 - 11x}{225}$

Part filled by A is 1 min

$= \frac{1}{37.5}$

$\therefore \frac{1}{37.5} : \frac{225 - 11x}{225} = 1 : 30 - x$

$\Rightarrow \frac{225}{37.5 \times (225 - 11x)} = \frac{1}{30 - x}$

$\Rightarrow \frac{6}{225 - 11x} = \frac{1}{30 - x}$

$\Rightarrow 180 - 6x = 225 - 11x$

$\Rightarrow 5x = 45$

$\Rightarrow x = 9$ min

51. Let 1 man's 1 day's work $= x$ and 1 boys's 1 day's work $= y$

Then, $2x + 7y = \frac{1}{14}$

and $3x + 8y = \frac{1}{11}$

On solving, we get

$x = \frac{2}{154,}\ y = \frac{1}{154}$

$\therefore\ 8x + 6y = 8 \times \frac{2}{154} + 6 \times \frac{1}{54}$

$= \frac{22}{154} = 7$

$\therefore$ 3 times the amount of above work

$= 3\,(8x + 6y)$

$= 3 \times 7 = 21$ day

52. Let the distance from A to B is x km

Then, $\frac{x}{8 + 4} + \frac{xy}{8 - 4} = 5$

$\Rightarrow \frac{x}{12} + \frac{xy}{4} = 5$

$\Rightarrow \frac{4x}{12} = 5$

$\Rightarrow x = 15$ km

CHAPTER

08

SIMPLE AND COMPOUND INTERESTS

Simple interest and Compound interest is the basic chapter based on day-to-day calculations. In every competitive exam you may find problems based on this chapter.

Interest is the extra sum which is paid by the borrower to the lender for using the money for a specific time period. The money borrowed is called Principal. The rate at which the interest is calculated on the principal is called Rate of Interest. The period for which money is borrowed is called Time and the total sum of principal value and interest is called an Amount.

Interest is calculated in two ways

1. Simple Interest

When the interest is calculated only on the principal value at the beginning for the given period, then interest is called simple interest.

$$\text{SI} = \frac{PRT}{100}$$

where, SI = Simple Interest

T = Time

P = Principal on which interest is calculated

R = Rate of interest and amount $(A) = P + \text{SI}$

EXAMPLE 1 Calculate the simple interest on ₹ 7200 at $12\frac{3}{4}\%$ per annum for 9 months.

(a) ₹ 962 (b) ₹ 800 (c) ₹ 784.2 (d) ₹ 688.5

Solution *(d)* Here, $P = ₹\,7200, T = 9 \text{ months} = \frac{9}{12}$ yr

and $R = 12\frac{3}{4}\% = \frac{51}{4}\%$

$\therefore \quad SI = \frac{PRT}{100} = \frac{7200 \times 51 \times 9}{100 \times 4 \times 12} = ₹\,688.5$

EXAMPLE 2 A sum of ₹ 2668 amounts to ₹ 4669 in 5 yr at the rate of simple interest. Find the rate per cent.

(a) 12 % (b) 15 %
(c) 20 % (d) 18 %

Solution *(b)* Here, $P = ₹\,2668$

$T = 5$ yr

$A = ₹\,4669$

We know that, $A = P + SI$

$4669 - 2668 = SI$

$\Rightarrow \quad SI = 2001$

Again, $SI = \frac{PRT}{100}$

$\Rightarrow \; 2001 = \frac{2668 \times 5 \times R}{100} \Rightarrow R = \frac{2001 \times 100}{2668 \times 5}$

$\Rightarrow \quad R = 15\%$

2. Compound Interest

When the interest is calculated on the amount of previous year, then it is known as compound interest. In this method, the principle grows as the interest is added to it.

(i) When interest is compounded annually

$$\text{Amount} = P\left(1 + \frac{R}{100}\right)^n, \text{ where } P = \text{Principal}$$

$R =$ Rate of interest per annum, $n =$ Time period

(ii) When interest is compounded half-yearly

$$\text{Amount} = P\left(1 + \frac{R/2}{100}\right)^{2n}$$

(iii) When interest is compounded quarterly

$$\text{Amount} = P\left(1 + \frac{R/4}{100}\right)^{4n}$$

(iv) When interest is compounded annually but time is in fraction, say $n\frac{b}{c}$ yr. Then,

$$\text{Amount} = P\left(1 + \frac{R}{100}\right)^n \times \left(1 + \frac{\frac{b}{c}R}{100}\right)$$

(v) When rate of interests are $R_1\%, R_2\%$ and $R_3\%$ for first, second and third year, respectively, then

$$\text{Amount} = P\left(1 + \frac{R_1}{100}\right)\left(1 + \frac{R_2}{100}\right)\left(1 + \frac{R_3}{100}\right)$$

(vi) $A = P + CI$

(vii) $CI = P\left\{\left(1 + \frac{r}{100}\right)^n - 1\right\}$

(viii) If the difference between simple interest and compound interest on a certain sum of money at $R\%$ rate is given, then

(a) for 2 year : Sum = Difference $\left(\frac{100}{R}\right)^2$

(b) for 3 year : Sum $= \frac{\text{Difference} \times 100^3}{R^2(300 + R)}$

EXAMPLE 3 Find the compound interest on ₹ 30500 at 15% per annum for 2 yr compounded annually.

(a) ₹ 9836.25 (b) ₹ 9486.58
(c) ₹ 8862.25 (d) ₹ 8953.2

Solution *(a)* When interest is compounded annually, then amount,

$$A = P\left(1 + \frac{R}{100}\right)^n$$

Here $P = 30500$,

$R = 15\%, \quad n = 2$

$\therefore \quad A = 30500\left(1 + \frac{15}{100}\right)^2$

$= 30500 \times 1.15 \times 1.15 = 40336.25$

$\therefore$ Compound Interest $= A - P$

$= (40336.25 - 30500) = ₹\,9836.25$

EXAMPLE 4 Find the compound interest on ₹ 5000 in 2 yr at 4%, if the interest being compounded half-yearly.

(a) ₹ 486.7 (b) ₹ 412.2 (c) ₹ 515.2 (d) ₹ 854.3

Solution *(b)* Given, principal = ₹ 5000, rate = 4% and time = 2 yr

$$\therefore \quad \text{Amount} = P\left(1+\frac{R/2}{100}\right)^{2n} = 5000\left(1+\frac{2}{100}\right)^4$$

$$\left[\because \frac{R}{2}=\frac{4}{2}=2\% \text{ and } n = 2 \text{ yr}\right]$$

$$= 5000\left(\frac{51}{50}\right)^4 = 5412.2$$

Compound interest = $A - P$

$$= 5412.2 - 5000 = ₹412.2$$

EXAMPLE 5 Find the compound interest on ₹ 2000 at 15 % per annum for 2 yr 4 months compounded annually.

(a) ₹ 553.3 (b) ₹ 789.28
(c) ₹ 682.35 (d) ₹ 777.25

Solution *(d)* Given, $P =$ ₹ 2000, $R = 15\%$ and

$$n = 2\frac{4}{12} = 2\frac{1}{3} \text{ yr}$$

$$\therefore \text{ Amount} = P\left(1+\frac{R}{100}\right)^n \times \left(1+\frac{\frac{a}{b}R}{100}\right)$$

$$= \left[2000\left(1+\frac{15}{100}\right)^2 \times \left(1+\frac{\frac{1}{3}\times 15}{100}\right)\right] \left[\text{here, } \frac{a}{b}=\frac{1}{3}\right]$$

$$= 2000 \times \frac{23}{20} \times \frac{23}{20} \times \frac{21}{20} = \frac{11109}{4} = 2777.25$$

$$\therefore \quad CI = A - P = 2777.25 - 2000 = 777.25$$

EXAMPLE 6 The compound interest on ₹ 16000 at 20% per annum for 9 months, compounded quarterly is

(a) ₹ 2450 (b) ₹ 2500 (c) ₹ 2522 (d) ₹ 2544

Solution *(c)* Given, $P =$ ₹ 16000, $R = 20\%$, $n = 9$ months $= \frac{9}{12}$ yr

$$\therefore \quad A = P\left(1+\frac{R/4}{100}\right)^{4n}$$

$$= 16000\left(1+\frac{20/4}{100}\right)^{4\times 9/12}$$

$$= 16000\left(\frac{21}{20}\right)^3 = ₹18522$$

$$\therefore \quad CI = A - P = 18522 - 16000 = ₹\ 2522$$

EXAMPLE 7 ₹ 25000 is borrowed at CI at the rate of 3% for the first year, 4% for the second year and 5% for the third year. Find the amount to be paid after 3 yr.

(a) ₹ 27523 (b) ₹ 38250 (c) ₹ 28119 (d) ₹ 46928

Solution *(c)* Given, $P =$ ₹25000, $R_1 = 3\%$, $R_2 = 4\%$, $R_3 = 5\%$

$$\therefore \text{Amount} = P\left(1+\frac{R_1}{100}\right)\left(1+\frac{R_2}{100}\right)\left(1+\frac{R_3}{100}\right)$$

$$= 25000\left(1+\frac{3}{100}\right)\left(1+\frac{4}{100}\right)\left(1+\frac{5}{100}\right)$$

$$= 25000 \times 1.03 \times 1.04 \times 1.05$$

$$= ₹\ 28119$$

EXAMPLE 8 On a certain sum of money, the simple interest for 2 yr is ₹ 50 at the rate of 5% per annum. Find the difference in CI and SI.

(a) ₹ 1.75 (b) ₹ 1.50
(c) ₹ 1.25 (d) ₹ 1.65

Solution *(c)* Given, SI = 50, $R = 5\%$, $T = 2$ yr

$$\text{Difference} = \text{Sum} \times R^2/100^2 = \frac{\text{SI}\times 100}{R \times T} \times \frac{R^2}{100^2}$$

$$= \frac{\text{SI} \times R}{T \times 100}$$

$$\therefore \text{Difference in CI and SI} = \frac{50 \times 5}{200} = ₹1.25$$

EXAMPLE 9 The difference between the compound interest and the simple interest on a certain sum of money at 5% per annum for 2 yr is ₹ 1.50. Find the sum.

(a) ₹ 600 (b) ₹ 625 (c) ₹ 2700 (d) ₹ 610

Solution *(a)* Given, difference = ₹1.50

$T = 2$ yr

$R = 5\%$

$$\therefore \quad \text{Sum} = \text{Difference}\left(\frac{100}{R}\right)^2$$

$$= 1.5\left(\frac{100}{5}\right)^2 = 1.5 \times 400 = ₹\ 600$$

EXAMPLE 10 The difference between the compound interest and the simple interest on a sum of money for 3 yr at 10% per annum is ₹ 620. The sum is

(a) ₹ 4000 (b) ₹ 12000
(c) ₹ 10000 (d) ₹ 20000

Solution *(d)* Given, difference = ₹ 620, $R = 10\%$, $T = 3$ yr

By the formula,

$$\text{Sum} = \frac{\text{Difference} \times 100^3}{R^2(300+R)} = \frac{620 \times 100^3}{10^2(300+10)} = ₹\ 20000$$

Applications of Compound Interest

Growth/Appreciation

We know that, certain things like the tree, population, the weight etc., increase over a period of time. This increment in things is called growth, while the growth per unit time is called the rate of growth. If the rate of growth is constant, then $V = V_0\left(1 + \frac{R}{100}\right)^n$ where, R % is the rate of growth per year, n is the number of years, V_0 is the present measure of the quantity and V is the measure of the quantity after n years.

> If the rate of growth is R_1% during the first year and R_2% during the second year and so on, then $V = V_0\left(1 + \frac{R_1}{100}\right)\left(1 + \frac{R_2}{100}\right)\ldots$

Depreciation

We know that, certain things like the machine, vehicle etc., decrease over a period of time. The decrement in the things is called depreciation, while the depreciation per unit time is called the rate of depreciation. If the rate of depreciation is constant, then $V = V_0\left(1 - \frac{R}{100}\right)^n$ where, R % is the rate of depreciation per year, n is the number of years, V_0 is the present value and V is the value after n years.

> - The difference between growth and depreciation formula is only the sign of coefficient of R.
> - The number of years, a machine can be effectively used is called its **life span**, after which it is sold as **waste** or **scrap**.
> - For the case of growth always positive is used in formula and negative sign in case of depreciation.

EXAMPLE 11 The value of a vehicle depreciates by 12.5% every year. By what per cent will the value of the vehicle decrease after two years?

(a) 23.8 (b) 22%
(c) 23.44% (d) None of these

Solution *(c)* Let the present value of vehicle be ₹ V_0. Given, rate of depreciation = 12.5% and time = 2 yr

Value of the vehicle after 2 yr

$$= V_0\left(1 - \frac{12.5}{100}\right)^2$$

$$= V_0\left(1 - \frac{1}{8}\right)^2 = V_0\left(\frac{7}{8}\right)^2$$

∴ Decrease in the value of vehicle

$$= V_0 - V_0\left(\frac{7}{8}\right)^2$$

$$= V_0\left(1 - \frac{49}{64}\right)$$

$$= V_0\left(\frac{64-49}{64}\right)$$

$$= V_0\left(\frac{15}{64}\right)$$

Now, the per cent decrease in the value of vehicle $= \left(\frac{\frac{15V_0}{64}}{V_0} \times 100\right)\% = \frac{15}{64} \times 100\%$

$= 23.44\%$

Practice Exercise

1. Find the SI on ₹ 7200 at 8% per annum for 10 months.
(a) ₹ 400 (b) ₹ 420 (c) ₹ 460 (d) ₹ 480

2. A sum is lent at 10% per annum. Simple interest will get doubled in how many year?
(a) 8 yr (b) 10 yr
(c) 12 yr (d) None of these

3. If the simple interest on ₹ 1500 increases by ₹ 30, when the time increases by 8 yr. The rate per cent per annum is
(a) 0.5% (b) 0.25% (c) 0.75% (d) 1.25%

4. The simple interest on a sum of money is 1/25 of the principal and the number of year is equal to the rate per cent per annum. The rate per cent is
(a) 3% (b) 4% (c) 2% (d) 2.5%

5. The simple interest on a sum of money is equal to the principal and the number of year is equal to the rate per cent per annum. The rate per cent is
(a) 25% (b) 100% (c) 10% (d) 12%

6. A certain sum is invested for certain time at simple interest. It amounts to ₹ 400 at 10% per annum. But when invested at 4% per annum, it amounts to ₹ 200. The time is
(a) 100 yr (b) 75 yr
(c) 50 yr (d) 60 yr

7. A certain sum is invested for certain time at simple interest. It amounts to ₹ 450 at 7% per annum. But when invested at 5% per annum, it amounts to ₹ 350. The time is
(a) 50 yr (b) 60 yr
(c) 45 yr (d) 40 yr

8. A sum was put at SI at a certain rate for 6 yr. Had it been put at 4% higher rate, it would have fetched ₹ 960 more. The sum was
(a) ₹ 3000 (b) ₹ 3500
(c) ₹ 4000 (d) ₹ 4500

9. Ajay deposited two parts of sum of ₹ 25000 in different banks at the rates of 15% per annum and 18% per annum, respectively. In one year, he got ₹ 4050 as the total interest. What was the amount deposited at the rate of 18% per annum?
(a) ₹ 9000 (b) ₹ 18000
(c) ₹ 15000 (d) None of these

10. At a certain rate of simple interest, ₹ 900 amounted to ₹ 1260 in 4 yr. If the rate of interest be decreased by 2%, what will be the amount after 4 yr?
(a) ₹ 1338 (b) ₹ 1188 (c) ₹ 1378 (d) ₹ 1128

11. The simple interest on a sum of money will be ₹ 190 after 7 yr. In the next 7 yr, principal becomes 3 times. What will be the total interest at the end of the 14th yr?
(a) ₹ 760 (b) ₹ 850 (c) ₹ 750 (d) ₹ 780

12. A sum of money becomes five times at simple interest of 8% per annum. At what rate per cent will it become seven fold?
(a) 6% (b) 10% (c) 12% (d) 14%

13. The sum of money that will amount to ₹ 5105 in $6\frac{1}{2}$ yr at $4\frac{1}{4}$% per annum at simple interest is
(a) ₹ 3600 (b) ₹ 4500
(c) ₹ 4000 (d) ₹ 4400

14. A person lent a certain sum of money at 4% simple interest and in 5 yr the interest amounted to ₹ 520 less than the sum lent. The sum lent was
(a) ₹ 600 (b) ₹ 650
(c) ₹ 700 (d) ₹ 750

15. The simple interest on a sum of money will be ₹ 600 after 10 yr. If the principal is tripled after 5 yr, the total interest at the end of 10 yr will be
(a) ₹ 600 (b) ₹ 900
(c) ₹ 1200 (d) Data inadequate

16. Find the compound interest on ₹5500 at 9% per annum for 2 yr, if the interest is compounded annually?
(a) ₹ 1020 (b) ₹ 1034.55
(c) ₹ 1050.50 (d) ₹ 1055.35

17. Find compound interest on ₹15000 at 10% per annum for $2\frac{1}{2}$ yr. If the interest is compounded annually?
(a) ₹ 4057.50 (b) ₹ 4092.50
(c) ₹ 4040.30 (d) None of these

18. Find compound interest on ₹12000 for 3 yr, if the rate of interest for first year is 5%, second year is 6% and third year is 7%.
(a) ₹ 2290.92 (b) ₹ 2200.47
(c) ₹ 2878.50 (d) None of these

19. The difference between the interest received from two different banks on ₹ 750 for 2 yr is ₹ 90. The difference between their rates is
(a) 4% (b) 6%
(c) 8% (d) None of these

20. Sita deposited ₹ 5000 at 10% simple interest for 2 yr. How much more money will Sita have in her account at the end of 2 yr, if it is compounded semi-annually.
(a) ₹ 50 (b) ₹ 40 (c) ₹ 77.50 (d) ₹ 85.50

21. A sum of money at compound interest amounts to thrice itself in 3 yr. In how many years will it be 9 times itself?
(a) 9 yr (b) 27 yr (c) 6 yr (d) 3 yr

22. If the rate of interest be 4% per annum for first year, 5% per annum for second year and 6% per annum for third year, then the compound interest of ₹ 10000 for 3 yr will be
(a) ₹ 1600 (b) ₹ 1625.80
(c) ₹ 11575.20 (d) ₹ 2000

23. On what sum does the difference between the compound interest and the simple interest for 3yr at 10% is ₹ 31?
(a) ₹ 1500 (b) ₹ 1200 (c) ₹ 1100 (d) ₹ 1000

24. A sum becomes ₹ 4500 after 2 yr and ₹ 6750 after 4 yr at compound interest. The sum is
(a) ₹ 4000 (b) ₹ 2500 (c) ₹ 3000 (d) ₹ 3050

25. A man borrows money at 3% per annum interest payable yearly and lend it immediately at 5% interest (compound) payable half-yearly and thereby gains ₹ 330 at the end of the year. The sum borrowed is
(a) ₹ 17000 (b) ₹ 16500 (c) ₹ 15000 (d) ₹ 16000

26. The present population of a village is 10816. If it has increased at the rate of 4% every year, then what was the population two years ago?
(a) 10000 (b) 12000 (c) 11000 (d) 12500

27. The cash price of a new machine is ₹ 90000. If its price depreciates at the rate of 5% per year during the first two years and at the rate of 10% per year thereafter, what will be the price of the machine after 2 years?
(a) ₹ 81500 (b) ₹ 81225
(c) ₹ 81200 (d) None of these

28. The bacteria in a culture grows by 7%, 8% and 6%, respectively for 3 successive hours. Their number in the beginning was 150500. Find their count at the end of 3 h.
(a) 184352.87 (b) 184360
(c) 184357 (d) None of these

29. A charitable society started with its members equal to 2000. If the membership increases successively for three years at the rate of 10%, 20% and 30%, respectively, then find the total number of members of the society. Also, find total amount of subscription, if membership fee be ₹ 1100 per members.
(a) ₹ 3775600 (b) ₹ 3775200
(c) ₹ 387560 (d) ₹ 3775600

30. The value of a machine worth ₹ 500000 is depreciating at the rate of 10% every year. In how many years will it be reduced to 364500?
(a) 3 yr (b) 4yr (c) 5yr (d) 7yr

31. A factory increases its production of cars from 80000 to 92610 in three successive years. Find the annual rate of growth of production.
(a) 4% (b) 5% (c) 3% (d) 2%

Previous Year's Questions

32. In a factory, the production of scooters rose to 48400 from 40000 in 2 yr. The rate of growth per annum is **[CLAT 2012]**

(a) 20% (b) 10% (c) 30% (d) 8%

33. The population of a city is 250 thousand. It is increasing at the rate of 2% every year. The growth in the population after 2 yr is **[CLAT 2013]**

(a) 2500 (b) 10000 (c) 252000 (d) 10100

34. The difference between the simple interest and the compound interest (compounded annually) on ₹ 2000 for 2 yr at 8% per annum will be **[CLAT 2014]**

(a) ₹ 10 (b) ₹ 20 (c) ₹ 13 (d) ₹ 25

35. The value of a machine depreciates every year at the rate of 10% on its value at the beginning of that year. If the present value of the machine is ₹ 729, its worth three years ago was **[CLAT 2016]**

(a) ₹ 947.70 (b) ₹ 1000
(c) ₹ 750.87 (d) ₹ 800

36. The difference between simple interest and compound interest at the same rate for ₹ 5,000 for two years is ₹ 98. The rate of interest is **[CLAT 2017]**

(a) 14% (b) 10%
(c) $10\frac{1}{2}\%$ (d) 12%

Answers

1	d	2	b	3	b	4	c	5	c	6	c	7	a	8	c	9	d	10	b
11	a	12	c	13	c	14	b	15	c	16	b	17	a	18	a	19	b	20	c
21	c	22	c	23	d	24	c	25	d	26	a	27	b	28	a	29	b	30	a
31	b	32	b	33	d	34	c	35	b	36	a								

SOLUTIONS

1. Here, $P = ₹\,7200, R = 8\%$ per annum and

$$T = \frac{10}{12}\text{ yr} = \frac{5}{6}\text{ yr}$$

$$\therefore \text{SI} = \left(\frac{P \times R \times T}{100}\right)$$

$$= ₹\left(7200 \times 8 \times \frac{5}{6} \times \frac{1}{100}\right)$$

$$= ₹\,480$$

2. Sum will be doubled, when SI = P

$$\because \text{SI} = \frac{PRT}{100}$$

$$\therefore P = \frac{PRT}{100} \Rightarrow RT = 100$$

$$\Rightarrow T = \frac{100}{R} = \frac{100}{10} = 10\text{ yr}$$

3. $T = 8$ yr

SI increase by ₹ 30 in 8 yr

$$\therefore \text{SI increase in 1 yr} = \frac{30}{8} = 3.75$$

Let the rate be $x\%$ per annum.

$$\therefore 3.75 = \frac{1500 \times 1 \times x}{100}$$

$$x = 0.25\%$$

4. Given, $\text{SI} = \frac{P}{25}$ and $T = R$

$$\therefore \frac{P}{25} = \frac{PR^2}{100} \quad \left(\because \text{SI} = \frac{PRT}{100}\right)$$

$$\Rightarrow R^2 = 4$$

$$\Rightarrow R = 2\%$$

5. Given, SI = P, T = R

$$\therefore P = \frac{P \times R \times R}{100}$$

$$\Rightarrow R^2 = 100$$

$$\therefore R = 10\%$$

6. Let the principal be ₹ P and time be T yr.

Then,

$$(400 - P) = \frac{P \times 10 \times T}{100}$$

$$\Rightarrow 4000 - 10P = P \times T \quad \text{...(i)}$$

Again,

$$(200 - P) = \frac{P \times 4 \times T}{100}$$

$$\Rightarrow 5000 - 25P = P \times T \quad \text{...(ii)}$$

From Eqs. (i) and (ii), we get

$$4000 - 10P = 5000 - 25P$$

$$\Rightarrow P = \frac{1000}{15}$$

From Eq. (i), we get

$$= 4000 - \frac{10 \times 1000}{15}$$

$$= \frac{1000}{15} \times T$$

$$\therefore T = 50\text{ yr}$$

7. Let the principal be ₹P and time be T yr.

$(450 - P) = \frac{P \times 7 \times T}{100}$

$\Rightarrow \frac{45000 - 100P}{7} = PT$ ...(i)

Again, $(350 - P) = \frac{P \times 5 \times T}{100}$

$\Rightarrow \frac{35000 - 100P}{5} = PT$ ...(ii)

From Eqs. (i) and (ii), we get

$\frac{45000 - 100P}{7} = \frac{35000 - 100P}{5}$

$\Rightarrow P = 100$

From Eq. (i), we get

$\frac{45000 - 100 \times 100}{7 \times 100} = T$

$\therefore T = 50$ yr

8. $\because \frac{P \times (R + 4) \times 6}{100} - \frac{P \times R \times 6}{100} = 960$

$\Rightarrow \frac{24P}{100} = 960 \therefore P =$ ₹ 4000

9. Let the amount deposited at 18% interest be ₹ x.

Then,

$\frac{x \times 18}{100} + \frac{(25000 - x) \times 15}{100} = 4050$

$\Rightarrow 18x + 375000 - 15x = 405000$

$\Rightarrow 3x = 405000 - 375000$

$\Rightarrow 3x = 30000$

$\therefore x =$ ₹10000

10. SI = (1260 − 900) = ₹ 360

$\Rightarrow 360 = \frac{900 \times R \times 4}{100}$

$\therefore R = 10\%$

New rate = (10 − 2) = 8%

$\therefore$ New SI $= \frac{900 \times 8 \times 4}{100} = 288$

$\therefore$ Amount after 4 yr = ₹ (900 + 288) = ₹1188

11. Simple interest for the next 7 yr

= 3 × 190 = ₹ 570

Therefore, simple interest after 14 yr

= (190 + 570) = ₹ 760

12. Let the sum be ₹ P.

Then, $5P = \frac{P \times R \times T}{100} + P$

$\Rightarrow 1 + \frac{RT}{100} = 5 \Rightarrow \frac{8 \times T}{100} = 5 - 1$

$\Rightarrow T = \frac{400}{8} = 50$

$\therefore 7P = \frac{P \times R \times 50}{100} + P$

$\Rightarrow 7 = \frac{R \times 50}{100} + 1$

$\Rightarrow R = 12\%$

13. $(5105 - P) = \frac{P \times 17 \times 13}{4 \times 2 \times 100}$

$\Rightarrow 5105 - P = P \times 0.27625$

$\Rightarrow P = \frac{5105}{1.27625} =$ ₹ 4000

14. $(P - 520) = \frac{P \times 4 \times 5}{100}$

$\Rightarrow 100P - 52000 = 20P$

$\Rightarrow 80P = 52000 \Rightarrow P =$ ₹ 650

15. If the simple interest for 10 yr is ₹ 600, then simple interest for 5 yr will be ₹ 300. Now, since the principal is tripled after 5 yr, the interest will also be tripled for the next 5 yr i.e. 900.

Therefore, total interest at the end of 10 yr

= (300 + 900) = ₹1200

16. $P =$ ₹ 5500, $R = 9\%$ per annum and $n = 2$ yr

Amount $= P\left(1 + \frac{R}{100}\right)^n$

= ₹ $5500\left(1 + \frac{9}{100}\right)^2$

= ₹ $\left(5500 \times \frac{109}{100} \times \frac{109}{100}\right)$

= ₹ 6534.55

CI = ₹ (6534.55 − 5500)

= ₹1034.55

17. $P =$ ₹15000, $R = 10\%$ per annum,

$n = 2\frac{1}{2}$ yr

$A = P\left(1 + \frac{R}{100}\right)^2 \left(1 + \frac{\frac{R}{2}}{100}\right)$

= ₹ $\left[15000\left(1 + \frac{10}{100}\right)^2\left(1 + \frac{5}{100}\right)\right]$

(the rate for the third year is halved)

= ₹ $\left[15000\left(\frac{11}{10}\right)^2\left(\frac{21}{20}\right)\right]$

= ₹19057.50

Compound interest

= ₹ (19057.50 − 15000)

= ₹ 4057.50

18. $P =$ ₹12000, $R_1 = 5\%$, $R_2 = 6\%$ and $R_3 = 7\%$

Amount

$= P\left(1 + \frac{R_1}{100}\right)\left(1 + \frac{R_2}{100}\right)\left(1 + \frac{R_3}{100}\right)$

= ₹ $\left[12000\left(1 + \frac{5}{100}\right)\left(1 + \frac{6}{100}\right)\left(1 + \frac{7}{100}\right)\right]$

= ₹ $\left[12000 \times \frac{105}{100} \times \frac{106}{100} \times \frac{107}{100}\right]$

= ₹14290.92

Compound interest

= ₹ (14290.92 − 12000)

= ₹ 2290.92

19. $\frac{750 \times 2}{100}(R_1 - R_2) = 90$

$\Rightarrow (R_1 - R_2) = \frac{90 \times 100}{750 \times 2} = 6\%$

20. Rate = 5%, Time = 4 half-years

$CI = P\left[\left(1 + \frac{r}{100}\right)^n - 1\right]$

$= 5000\left[\left(1 + \frac{5}{100}\right)^4 - 1\right]$

$= 5000\left[\left(\frac{194481}{160000}\right)^4 - 1\right]$

$$= \frac{5000 \times 34481}{160000} = ₹\ 1077.5$$

$$SI = \frac{5000 \times 10 \times 2}{100} = ₹\ 1000$$

Difference $= 1077.5 - 1000$
$= ₹\ 77.5$

21. Let $A = ₹\ 3x$, $P = ₹x$

By the formula

$$A = P\left(1 + \frac{r}{100}\right)^n$$

Then, $3x = x\left(1 + \frac{r}{100}\right)^3$

$$\Rightarrow \quad 3 = 1\left(1 + \frac{r}{100}\right)^3$$

On squaring both sides, we get

$$9 = 1\left(1 + \frac{r}{100}\right)^6$$

It will becomes 9 times itself in 6 yr.

22. Amount

$$= P\left(1 + \frac{R_1}{100}\right)\left(1 + \frac{R_2}{100}\right)\left(1 + \frac{R_3}{100}\right)$$

$$= 10000\left(1 + \frac{4}{100}\right)\left(1 + \frac{5}{100}\right)\left(1 + \frac{6}{100}\right)$$

$$= 10000 \times \frac{26}{25} \times \frac{21}{20} \times \frac{53}{50}$$

$= ₹\ 11575.2$

23. When difference between the CI and SI on certain sum of money for 3 yr at r% rate is ₹x, then difference between SI and CI

$$= \frac{Pr^2(300 + r)}{(100)^3}$$

$$\Rightarrow \quad 31 = \frac{P \times (10)^2 (300 + 10)}{1000000}$$

$$\Rightarrow \quad 31 = \frac{P \times 100 \times 310}{1000000}$$

$$\Rightarrow \quad 31 = \frac{31P}{1000}$$

$$\Rightarrow \quad P = 1000$$

24. $P\left(1 + \frac{r}{100}\right)^2 = 4500 \quad \ldots(i)$

$P\left(1 + \frac{r}{100}\right)^4 = 6750 \quad \ldots(ii)$

On dividing Eq. (ii) by Eq. (i), we get

$$\left(1 + \frac{r}{100}\right)^2 = \frac{6750}{4500}$$

From Eq. (i), we get

$$P \times \frac{6750}{4500} = 4500$$

$$\Rightarrow P = \frac{4500 \times 4500}{6750} = ₹\ 3000$$

25. Here, $R = 3$ and $T = 1$

Let the sum borrowed be ₹x.

Then, $SI = \frac{P \times R \times T}{100}$

$$= \frac{x \times 3 \times 1}{100} = ₹\ \frac{3x}{100}$$

$\therefore$ CI on the sum when compound half-yearly

$$= \left[P\left(1 + \frac{R/2}{100}\right)^{2n} - P\right]$$

$(\because R = 5$ and $n = 1)$

$$= x\left[\left(1 + \frac{5}{2 \times 100}\right)^2 - 1\right]$$

$$= x\left[\left(1 + \frac{1}{40}\right)^2 - 1\right] = x\left[\left(\frac{41}{40}\right)^2 - 1\right]$$

$$= x\left[\frac{1681}{1600} - 1\right] = x\left[\frac{81}{1600}\right]$$

Man's gain $=$ CI $-$ SI

$$330 = \frac{81x}{1600} - \frac{3x}{100}$$

$$\Rightarrow 330 = \frac{81x - 48x}{1600}$$

$$\Rightarrow \quad x = \frac{330 \times 1600}{33} = ₹\ 16000$$

26. Given, present population, $V = 10816$, rate of interest, $R = 4\%$ and time, $n = 2$ yr

Let the population 2 yr ago be V_0.

$$\because \quad V = V_0\left(1 + \frac{R}{100}\right)^n$$

$$\therefore \quad 10816 = V_0\left(1 + \frac{4}{100}\right)^2$$

$$\Rightarrow \quad 10816 = V_0\left(1 + \frac{1}{25}\right)^2$$

$$\Rightarrow \quad 10816 = V_0\left(\frac{26}{25}\right)^2$$

$$\Rightarrow V_0 = \frac{10816 \times 25 \times 25}{26 \times 26} = 10000$$

27. Given, initial cost of a machine,

$V_0 = ₹\ 90000$, rate of depreciation,

R_1 (for1st two years) $= 5\%$

and R_2 (for later years) $= 10\%$

Here, $n = 2$yr, $R_1 = 5\%$

$$\because \quad V = V_0\left(1 - \frac{R_1}{100}\right)^n$$

$$\therefore \quad V = 90000\left(1 - \frac{5}{100}\right)^2$$

$$= 90000\left(1 - \frac{1}{20}\right)^2$$

$$= 90000 \times \left(\frac{19}{20}\right)^2$$

$$= 90000 \times \frac{19 \times 19}{20 \times 20} = ₹\ 81225$$

28. Given different rates of increment successively are $R_1 = 7\%$, $R_2 = 8\%$ and $R_3 = 6\%$ and number of bacteria in the beginning, $V_0 = 150500$.

Now, number of bacteria after 3 h,

$$V = V_0\left(1 + \frac{R_1}{100}\right)\left(1 + \frac{R_2}{100}\right)\left(1 + \frac{R_3}{100}\right)$$

$$= 150500\left(1 + \frac{7}{100}\right)\left(1 + \frac{8}{100}\right)\left(1 + \frac{6}{100}\right)$$

$$= 150500\left(\frac{107}{100}\right)\left(\frac{108}{100}\right)\left(\frac{106}{100}\right)$$

$$= \frac{184352868000}{1000000} = 18435287$$

29. Given, total members in the beginning $(M_0) = 2000$ and successive rates of increase, $R_1, R_2, R_3 = 10\%$, 20% and 30%,

$\therefore$ Total members

$$= M_0\left(1+\frac{R_1}{100}\right)\left(1+\frac{R_2}{100}\right)\left(1+\frac{R_3}{100}\right)$$

$$= 2000\left(1+\frac{1}{10}\right)\left(1+\frac{2}{10}\right)\left(1+\frac{3}{10}\right)$$

$$= 2000 \times \frac{11}{10} \times \frac{12}{10} \times \frac{13}{10}$$

$$= 3432$$

Total amount of subscription

$= 3432 \times 1100$

$= ₹3775200$

30. Given, initial value V_0 of the machine $= ₹\,500000$,

rate of depreciation,

$R = 10\%$ per year

Let 'n' be number of years in which machine reduced to ₹ 364500.

Using $V = V_0\left(1-\frac{R}{100}\right)^n$, we have

$$364500 = 500000\left(1-\frac{10}{100}\right)^n$$

$$\Rightarrow \quad 3645 = 5000 \times \left(\frac{9}{10}\right)^n$$

$$\Rightarrow \quad \frac{3645}{5000} = \left(\frac{9}{10}\right)^n$$

$$\Rightarrow \quad \left(\frac{9}{10}\right)^n = \frac{729}{1000}$$

$$\Rightarrow \left(\frac{9}{10}\right)^n = \left(\frac{9}{10}\right)^3$$

On comparing,

we get $n = 3$ yr

31. Given, initial production of cars,

$$P_0 = 80000$$

After 3 yr, the final production,

$$P = 92610$$

Using $\quad P = P_0\left(1+\frac{R}{100}\right)^n$,

we have

$$92610 = 80000\left(\frac{100+R}{100}\right)^3$$

$$\Rightarrow \quad \frac{92610}{80000} = \left(\frac{100+R}{100}\right)^3$$

$$\Rightarrow \quad \left(\frac{21}{20}\right)^3 = \left(\frac{100+R}{100}\right)^3$$

Taking cube root on both sides, we get

$$\frac{21}{20} = \frac{100+R}{100}$$

$$\Rightarrow \quad 2000 + 20R = 2100$$

$$\Rightarrow \quad 20R = 2100 - 2000$$

$$\Rightarrow \quad R = \frac{100}{20}$$

$$\Rightarrow \quad R = 5\,\%$$

Previous Year's Solutions

32. From the formula,

$$A = P\left(1+\frac{r}{100}\right)^n, \text{ we have}$$

$$48400 = 40000\left(1+\frac{r}{100}\right)^2$$

$$\Rightarrow \quad \frac{484}{400} = \left(1+\frac{r}{100}\right)^2$$

$$\Rightarrow \quad \left(1+\frac{r}{100}\right)^2 = \left(\frac{22}{20}\right)^2$$

$$\Rightarrow \quad 1+\frac{r}{100} = \frac{22}{20}$$

$$\Rightarrow \quad 1+\frac{r}{100} = \frac{11}{10}$$

$$\Rightarrow \quad \frac{r}{100} = \frac{1}{10}$$

$$\Rightarrow \quad r = 10\%$$

33. Population after 2 yr

$$= P\left(1+\frac{R}{100}\right)^2$$

(where, R = Rate of increase)

$$= 250000\left(1+\frac{2}{100}\right)^2$$

$$= 250000 \times \frac{51}{50} \times \frac{51}{50}$$

$$= 260100$$

$\therefore$ Growth $= 260100 - 250000$

$= 10100$

34. For a 2yr duration we use the difference formula,

$$CI - SI = P\left(\frac{R}{100}\right)^2$$

where,

$P = ₹\ 2000$ = Principal

$R = 8\%$ = Rate of interest

$$\therefore\ CI - SI = 2000\left(\frac{8}{100}\right)\left(\frac{8}{100}\right)$$

$$= \frac{128}{10} = ₹\ 12.8 \approx ₹13$$

35. Given, present value of machine $= ₹\ 729$

and rate of depreciation $= 10\%$

$\therefore$ Worth three years ago

$$= \frac{729}{\left(1-\frac{10}{100}\right)^3} = \frac{729}{\left(\frac{9}{10}\right)^3}$$

$$= \frac{729 \times 10 \times 10 \times 10}{9 \times 9 \times 9}$$

$$= ₹\ 1000$$

36. $\therefore$ Sum = Difference $\left(\frac{100}{R}\right)^n$

$$\therefore \quad 500 = 98\left(\frac{100}{R}\right)^2$$

$$\Rightarrow \quad \left(\frac{R}{100}\right)^2 = \frac{98}{5000}$$

$$\Rightarrow \quad \frac{R}{100} = \frac{9.899}{70.71}$$

$$\Rightarrow R = \frac{989.9}{70.71} = 13.999\%$$

$\therefore \quad R = 14\%$ (approx)

CHAPTER 09

MENSURATION

Mensuration is a branch of mathematics that deals with the measurement of areas, perimeters and volumes of various geometrical figures. Here, we will study about different types of plane and solid geometrical figures.

Plane Figures

Plane figures are two-dimensional figures. They are made up of straight lines, curved lines or both.

Name	Definition	Figure	Formulae	Nomenclature
Scalene triangle	A figure enclosed by three sides of unequal lengths is known as a scalene triangle.	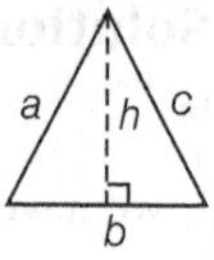	Area $= \frac{1}{2}bh$ $= \sqrt{s(s-a)(s-b)(s-c)}$ Perimeter $= a + b + c = 2s$	b = Base h = Altitude s = Semiperimeter a, c = Side
Isosceles right triangle	A triangle in which two sides are equal and one angle is equal to 90° is called isosceles right triangle.	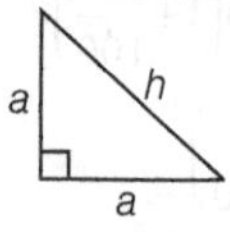	Area $= \frac{1}{2}a^2$ Perimeter $= 2a + h$ Hypotenuse $= a\sqrt{2}$	a = Equal sides h = Hypotenuse
Equilateral triangle	A triangle in which all three sides are equal and each angle is equal to 60° is an equilateral triangle.	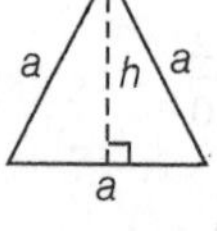	Area $= \frac{1}{2}ah = \frac{\sqrt{3}}{4}a^2$ Perimeter $= 3a$ Altitude $= \frac{\sqrt{3}}{2}a$	a = Side h = Altitude
Right triangle	A triangle in which one angle is 90° is a right triangle.	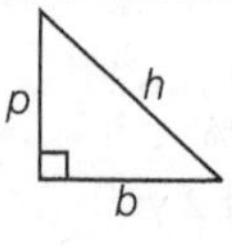	Area $= \frac{1}{2}bp$ Perimeter $= b + h + p$ Hypotenuse $= \sqrt{b^2 + p^2}$	b = Base p = Perpendicular h = Hypotenuse
Quadrilateral	A figure enclosed by four sides is called a quadrilateral.	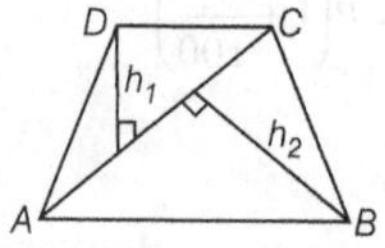	Area $= \frac{1}{2}(AC)(h_1 + h_2)$ Perimeter = Sum of four sides	h_1 and h_2 = Altitude AC = Diagonal

Name	Definition	Figure	Formulae	Nomenclature
Parallelogram	A parallelogram is a quadrilateral which has both pairs of opposite sides parallel.	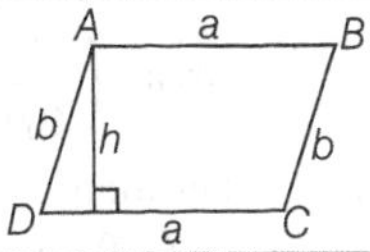	Area = $a \times h = 2$. Area of ΔABC Perimeter = $2(a + b)$	a, b = sides h = Altitude
Rectangle	It is a quadrilateral with opposite sides equal and each angle is equal to 90°. Diagonals are also equal.	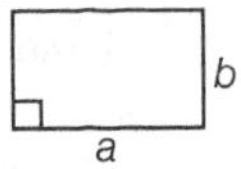	Area = ab Perimeter = $2(a + b)$ Diagonal = $\sqrt{a^2 + b^2}$	a = Length b = Breadth
Square	A square is a rectangle with a pair of adjacent sides equal. Diagonals are also equal.	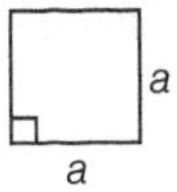	Area = a^2 Perimeter = $4a$ Diagonal = $a\sqrt{2}$	a = Side
Rhombus	A parallelogram having all sides equal is called a rhombus. It's opposite angles are also equal and diagonals bisect each other at 90°.	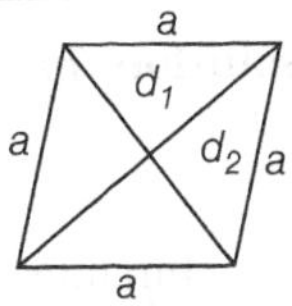	Area = $\frac{1}{2} d_1 d_2$ Perimeter = $4a$ side = $\frac{1}{2}\sqrt{d_1^2 + d_2^2}$	d_1 and d_2 = Diagonals a = Side
Trapezium	A quadrilateral having exactly one pair of parallel sides is called a trapezium.	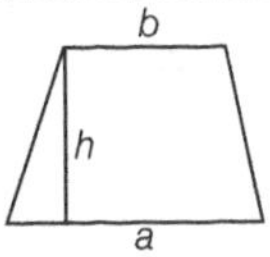	Area = $\frac{1}{2} h(a + b)$ Perimeter = Sum of its four sides	a, b = Parallel sides h = Altitude
Circle	It is a plane figure enclosed by a curve in which every point is equidistant from a fixed point (centre) inside the curve.	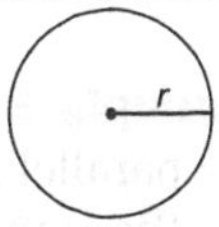	Area = πr^2 Circumference = $2\pi r$ Diameter = $2r$	r = Radius of circle $\pi = \frac{22}{7}$ or 3.14
Semi-circle	A diameter of a circle divides it into two equal parts which are arcs. Each of these two arcs is called a semi-circle.	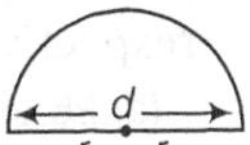	Area = $\frac{1}{2} \pi r^2$ Circumference = $\pi r + 2r$	r = Radius of circle d = Diameter
Ring (shaded region)	It is a part enclosed by two concentric circles.	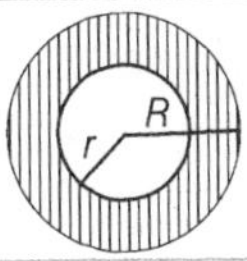	Area = $\pi(R^2 - r^2)$	R = Outer radius r = Inner radius

Name	Definition	Figure	Formulae	Nomenclature
Sector of a circle	It is a portion of a circle enclosed by two equal radii and an arc.	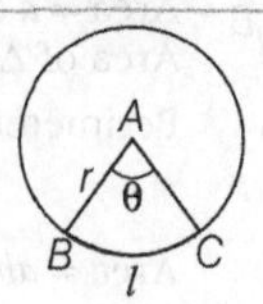	Area $=\left(\frac{\theta}{360°}\right)\times \pi r^2$ Perimeter $= l + 2r$, where l = Length of arc $l=\left(\frac{\theta}{360°}\right)\times 2\pi r$	θ = Central angle r = Radius of sector
Segment of a circle	It is the region bounded by a chord and the arc subtended by the chord.	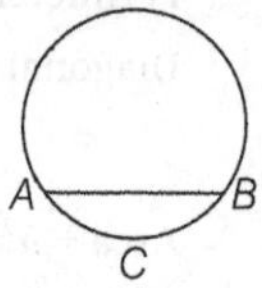	Area of segment ACB $= r^2\left[\frac{\pi\theta}{360°}-\frac{\sin\theta}{2}\right]$ Perimeter $=\left(\frac{\theta}{360°}\right)\times 2\pi r + 2r\sin\frac{\theta}{2}$	r = Radius of circle θ = Central angle

> Circumference represents the perimeter of circle.
> In an equilateral triangle
> Circumradius
> $$=\frac{2}{3}\times \text{height}$$
> $\Rightarrow$ In radius $=\frac{1}{3}\times$ height

Example 1 A rectangle has 20 cm as its length and 200 sq cm as its area. If the area is increased by $1\frac{1}{5}$ times the original area by increasing its length only, then what will be the perimeter of the rectangle, so formed?

(a) 70 cm (b) 45 cm (c) 68 cm (d) 32 cm

Solution *(c)* Here, length (l_1) = 20 cm, area (A_1) = 200 sq cm

Now, area = length × breadth

$\therefore$ breadth $(b_1)=\frac{200}{20}=10$ cm,

Now, new area $(A_2)=200\times\frac{6}{5}=240$ sq cm

$\because$ $b_2=b_1=10$ cm, then $l_2=\frac{240}{10}=24$ cm

$\therefore$ Perimeter of new rectangle

$$=2(l_2+b_2)=2(24+10)$$
$$=2\times 34=68 \text{ cm}$$

Example 2 The height of an equilateral triangle is $4\sqrt{3}$ cm. The ratio of the area of its circumcircle to that of its incircle is

(a) 2 : 1 (b) 4 : 1 (c) 4 : 3 (d) 3 : 2

Solution *(b)* Circumradius of equilateral triangle

$$=\frac{2}{3}\times \text{height}=\frac{2}{3}\times 4\sqrt{3}$$

Inradius of equilateral triangle $=\frac{1}{3}\times 4\sqrt{3}$

$$\therefore \quad \text{Required ratio}=\frac{\pi\times\left(\frac{2}{3}\times 4\sqrt{3}\right)^2}{\pi\times\left(\frac{1}{3}\times 4\sqrt{3}\right)^2}$$

$$=\frac{4}{1}=4:1$$

Example 3 Find the distance between the two parallel sides of a trapezium. If the area of the trapezium is 500 sq m and the two parallel sides are equal to 30 m and 20 m, respectively.

(a) 25 cm (b) 28 cm (c) 30 cm (d) 20 cm

Solution *(d)* Let the distance between two parallel sides = h

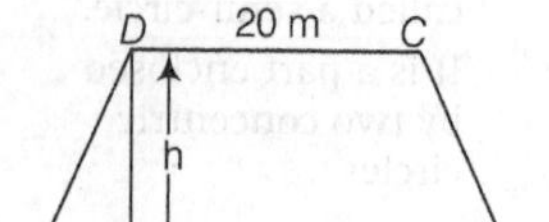

Given, area = 500 sq m

$$\Rightarrow \quad \frac{1}{2}(\text{Sum of parallel sides})\times h=500$$

$$\Rightarrow \quad \frac{1}{2}(20+30)h=500$$

$$\Rightarrow \quad 50h=500\times 2 \Rightarrow h=20 \text{ cm}$$

Example 4 Sides of a parallelogram are in the ratio 5 : 4. Its area is 1000 sq units. Altitude on the greater side is 20 units. Altitude on the smaller side is

(a) 30 units (b) 25 units (c) 10 units (d) 15 units

Solution *(b)* Let the sides of parallelogram be $5x$ and $4x$ and altitude on the smaller side be h.

Base × Height = Area of parallelogram

$$\therefore \quad 5x \times 20 = 1000 \Rightarrow x = \frac{1000}{5\times 20} = 10$$

∴ Sides of parallelogram are 50 and 40.

Now, again $40 \times h = 1000$

$$\Rightarrow \quad h = \frac{1000}{40} = 25 \text{ units}$$

Example 5 The inner circumference of a circular path around a circular lawn is 440 m. What is the radius of the outer circumference of the path, if the path is 14 m wide?

(a) 80 cm (b) 84 cm
(c) 70 cm (d) 76 cm

Solution *(b)* Let inner radius = r

and outer radius = R

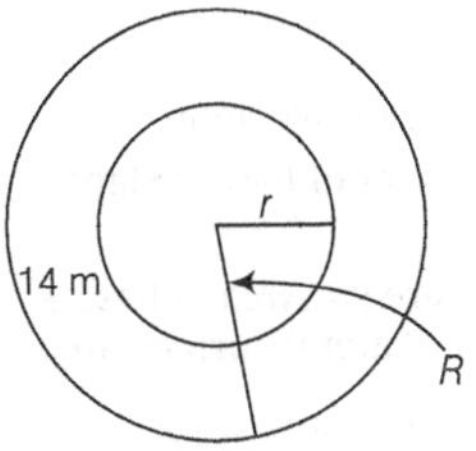

Given, the circumference of inner circle = 440 m

$$\Rightarrow \quad 2\pi r = 440 \Rightarrow r = \frac{440}{2\pi}$$

$$\Rightarrow \quad r = 70\,\text{m}$$

We have width of path = 14 m

∴ Outer radius $R = r + 14$

$= 70 + 14 = 84$ m

Example 6 The perimeter of a rhombus is 100 cm. If one of its diagonals is 14 cm, then the area of the rhombus is

(a) 144 cm² (b) 225 cm²
(c) 336 cm² (d) 400 cm²

Solution *(c)* Side of rhombus is given by

$$= \frac{1}{2}\sqrt{d_1^2 + d_2^2}$$

Perimeter of rhombus $= 4 \times \frac{1}{2}\sqrt{d_1^2 + d_2^2}$

$$\therefore \quad 2\sqrt{d_1^2 + d_2^2} = 100$$

$$\Rightarrow \quad \sqrt{d_1^2 + d_2^2} = 50$$

$$\Rightarrow \quad d_1^2 + d_2^2 = 2500$$

$$\Rightarrow \quad (14)^2 + d_2^2 = 2500$$

$$\Rightarrow \quad d_2^2 = 2500 - 196 = 2304$$

$$\therefore \quad d_2 = \sqrt{2304} = 48$$

Area of the rhombus

$$= \frac{1}{2} d_1 \times d_2$$

$$= \frac{1}{2} \times 14 \times 48$$

$$= 336\,\text{cm}^2$$

Example 7 A parallelogram has sides 15 cm and 7 cm long. The length of one of the diagonals is 20 cm. The area of the parallelogram is

(a) 42 cm² (b) 60 cm²
(c) 84 cm² (d) 96 cm²

Solution *(c)* Area of parallelogram $ABCD$

$= 2 \times$ Area of ΔABC

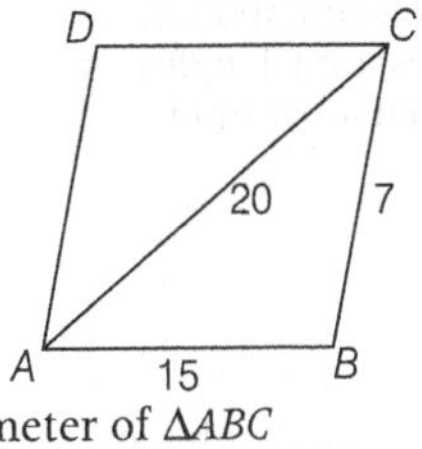

Semi-perimeter of ΔABC

$$s = \frac{20 + 7 + 15}{2}$$

$$= \frac{42}{2} = 21\,\text{cm}$$

Area of $\Delta ABC = \sqrt{s(s-a)(s-b)(s-c)}$

$$= \sqrt{21(21-7)(21-20)(21-15)}$$

$$= \sqrt{21 \times 14 \times 6}$$

$= 42$ sq cm

∴ Area of parallelogram $= 2 \times 42 = 84$ sq cm

Solid Figures

Solid figures are three dimensional figures. These three dimensions are length, breadth and height.

Name	Definition	Figure	Formulae	Nomenclature
Cuboid	A rectangular solid body having 6 rectangular faces is called a cuboid.	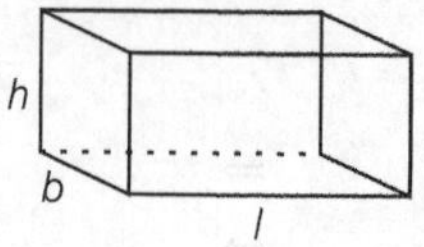	Lateral curved surface area $= 2h(l + b)$ Total surface area $= 2(lb + bh + lh)$ Volume $= lbh$ Diagonal $= \sqrt{l^2 + b^2 + h^2}$	l = Length b = Breadth h = Height
Cube	It is a solid body having 6 equal faces with equal length, breadth and height.	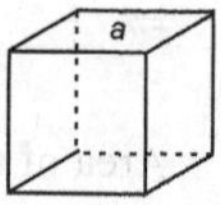	Lateral/curved surface area $= 4a^2$ Total surface area $= 6a^2$ Volume $= a^3$ Diagonal $= a\sqrt{3}$	a = Edge
Right prism	It is a solid whose top and bottom faces are identical polygons that are parallel.	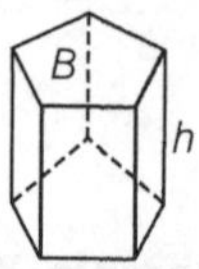	Lateral/Curved surface area = (Perimeter of base × Height) Total surface area = 2(Area of base) + Lateral surface area Volume = Area of base × Height	
Right circular cylinder	It is a solid or hollow body that is formed by keeping circles of equal radii one on another.	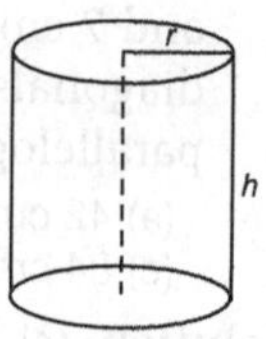	Lateral/curved surface area $= 2\pi rh$ Total surface area $= 2\pi rh + 2\pi r^2$ or $2\pi r(r + h)$ Volume $= \pi r^2 h$	r = Radius of base h = Height of cylinder
Right pyramid	A solid whose base is a polygon and whose faces are triangles, is called a pyramid.	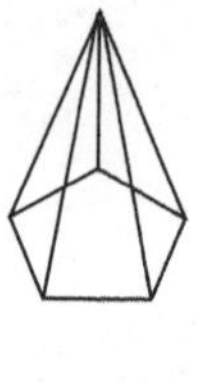	Lateral/curved surface area = (1/2 × Perimeter of base × Slant height) Total surface area = Area of base + Lateral surface area Volume $= \frac{1}{3}$ (Area of base) × Height	
Right circular cone	It is a solid or hollow body with a round base and pointed top. It is formed by the rotation of a triangle along any of the side.	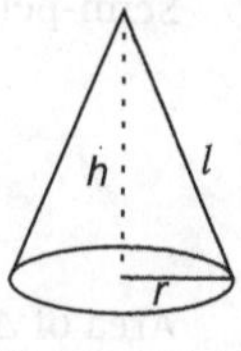	Lateral/curved surface area $= \pi rl$ Total surface area $= \pi r(l + r)$ Volume $= \frac{1}{3}\pi r^2 h$ Slant height, $l = \sqrt{h^2 + r^2}$	h = Height r = Radius l = Slant height

Name	Definition	Figure	Formulae	Nomenclature
Sphere	It is a three-dimensional solid figure, which is made up of all points in the space, which lie at a constant distance from a fixed point.	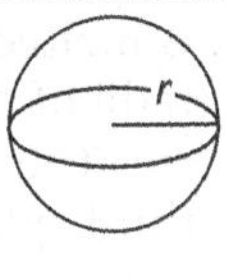	Total surface area = $4\pi r^2$ Volume = $\frac{4}{3}\pi r^3$	r = Radius
Hemisphere	It is the half part of a sphere.	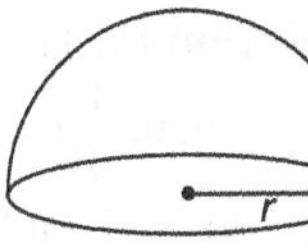	Lateral/curved surface area = $2\pi r^2$ Total surface area = $3\pi r^2$ Volume = $\frac{2}{3}\pi r^3$	r = Radius
Frustum of cone	A cone with some of its top portion cut off is called the frustum of original cone.	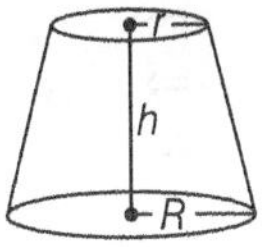	Lateral/curved surface area = $\pi(R+r)l$ Total surface area = $\pi\{l(r+R)+r^2+R^2\}$ Slant height = $\sqrt{h^2+(R-r)^2}$ Volume = $\frac{\pi h}{3}(r^2+R^2+rR)$	R = Radius of base r = Radius of top h = Height l = Slant height

Example 8 Internal length, breadth and height of a rectangular box are 10 cm, 8 cm and 6 cm, respectively. How many boxes are needed which can be packed in a cube whose volume is 6240 cu cm?

(a) 15 (b) 13
(c) 12 (d) 14

Solution *(b)* Volume of rectangular box

$= \text{Length} \times \text{Breadth} \times \text{Height}$

$= 10 \times 8 \times 6 = 480 \text{ cm}^3$

Volume of cube $= 6240 \text{ cm}^3$

$\therefore \text{Required boxes} = \frac{\text{Volume of cube}}{\text{Volume of rectangular box}}$

$= \frac{6240}{480} = 13$

Hence, 13 boxes are needed.

Example 9 A prism has the base of a right angled triangle whose sides adjacent to the right angle are 10 cm and 12 cm long. The height of the prism is 20 cm. The density of the material of the prism is 6 g/cu cm. The weight of the prism is

(a) 7.2 kg (b) 7.3 kg
(c) 7.1 kg (d) 7.4 kg

Solution *(a)* Volume of prism = Area of base × Height

$= \frac{1}{2} \times 10 \times 12 \times 20 = 1200 \text{ cm}^2$

$\therefore$ Weight of prism $= 1200 \times 6 = 7200 \text{ g} = 7.2 \text{ kg}$

Example 10 The curved surface area of a cylindrical pillar is 264 sq m and its volume is 924 m^3. What will be the ratio of its diameter to its height.

(a) 3 : 2 (b) 7 : 6
(c) 3 : 4 (d) 7 : 3

Solution *(d)* Given that, $2\pi rh = 264$

and $\pi r^2 h = 924$

$\therefore \frac{\pi r^2 h}{2\pi rh} = \frac{924}{264} = \frac{7}{2}$

$\Rightarrow \frac{r}{2} = \frac{7}{2} \Rightarrow r = 7 \text{m}$

$\therefore$ Diameter $= 2r = 14$ m

Also, $2\pi rh = 264$

$\Rightarrow 2 \times \frac{22}{7} \times 7 \times h = 264$

$\Rightarrow h = 6$

$\therefore \frac{\text{Diameter}}{\text{Height}} = \frac{14}{6} = \frac{7}{3} = 7:3$

Example 11 A sphere has the same curved surface as a cone of height 12 cm and base radius 5 cm. Find the radius to the nearest cm.

(a) 7 cm (b) 5 cm (c) 4 cm (d) 3cm

Solution *(c)* Given, for cone,

$$h = 12 \text{ cm}, r = 5 \text{ cm}$$

$\therefore$ $l = \sqrt{12^2 + 5^2} = 13 \text{ cm}$

$\because$ Curved surface area of sphere = Curved surface area of cone

$\Rightarrow$ $4\pi r^2 = \pi rl$

$\Rightarrow$ $4\pi r^2 = \pi \times 5 \times 13$

$\Rightarrow$ $r^2 = \dfrac{65}{4}$

$\Rightarrow$ $r = 4$ cm (approx.)

Example 12 A metallic sphere of radius 12 cm is melted into three smaller spheres. If the radii of two smaller spheres are 6 cm and 8 cm. Then, what will be the radius of the third sphere.

(a) 12 cm (b) 10 cm
(c) 13 cm (d) 14 cm

Solution *(b)* Let radius of the third sphere be r.

Then, $\dfrac{4}{3}\pi \times (12)^3 = \dfrac{4}{3}\pi \times (6)^3 + \dfrac{4}{3}\pi \times (8)^3 + \dfrac{4}{3}\pi r^3$

$\Rightarrow$ $(12)^3 = (6)^3 + (8)^3 + r^3$

$\Rightarrow$ $r^3 = 1728 - 216 - 512$

$\Rightarrow$ $r^3 = 1000$

$\therefore$ $r = 10$ cm

Practice Exercise

1. Find the area of an equilateral triangle whose side is $4\sqrt{3}$ cm.

(a) $\dfrac{12}{\sqrt{3}}$ cm^2 (b) $12\sqrt{3}$ cm^2
(c) 12 cm^2 (d) None of these

2. Diagonals of a rhombus are 1 m and 1.5 m in lengths. The area of the rhombus is

(a) 0.75 m^2 (b) 1.5 m^2
(c) 1.5 m^2 (d) 0.375 m^2

3. The diagonal of a square is $4\sqrt{2}$ cm. The diagonal of another square whose area is double that of the first square is

(a) 8 cm (b) $8\sqrt{2}$ cm
(c) $4\sqrt{2}$ cm (d) 6 cm

4. The area of a circle is increased by 22 sq cm when its radius is increased by 1 cm. Find the original radius of the circle.

(a) 6 cm (b) 3.2 cm (c) 3 cm (d) 3.5 cm

5. A man riding a bicycle, completes one lap of a circular field along its circumference at the speed of 14.4 km/h in 1 min 28 s. What is the area of the field?

(a) 7958 sq m
(b) 9856 sq m
(c) 8842 sq m
(d) Cannot be determined

6. A person observed that he required 30 s time to cross a circular ground along its diameter than to cover it once along the boundary. If his speed was 30 m/min, then the radius of the circular ground is (take $\pi = 22/7$)

(a) 10.5 m (b) 3.5 m
(c) 5.5 m (d) 7.5 m

7. Four horses are tethered at four corners of a square plot of side 14 m , so that the adjacent horses can just reach one another. There is a small circular pond of area 20 m^2 at the centre. Find the ungrazed area.

(a) 22 m^2 (b) 42 m^2
(c) 84 m^2 (d) 168 m^2

8. A certain city has a circular wall around it and this wall has four gates pointing North, South, East and West. A house stands outside the city, three kilometres North of the North gate and it can just be seen from a point nine kilometres East of the South gate. What is the diameter of the wall that surrounds the city?

(a) 6 km (b) 9 km
(c) 12 km (d) None of these

9. What is the number of distinct triangles with integral valued sides and perimeter as 14?
(a) 6 (b) 5 (c) 4 (d) 3

10. A cow is tethered at point A by a rope. Neither the rope nor the cow is allowed to enter the ΔABC, in which $\angle BAC = 30°$, $AB = AC = 10$ m.

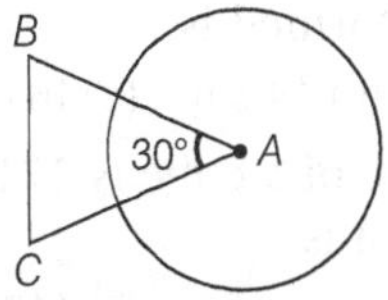

What is the area that can be grazed by the cow, if the length of the rope is 8 m?
(a) $134\pi \frac{1}{3}$ sq m (b) 121π sq m
(c) 132π sq m (d) $\frac{176\pi}{3}$ sq m

11. AB is the diameter of the given circle, while points C and D lie on the circumference as shown. If AB is 15 cm, AC is 12 cm and BD is 9 cm, find the area of the quadrilateral $ACBD$.

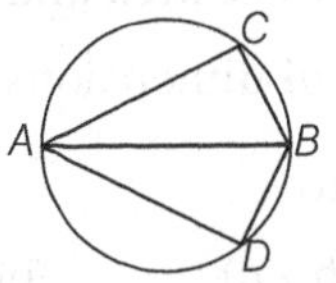

(a) 54 sq cm (b) 216 sq cm
(c) 162 sq cm (d) None of these

12. In this figure, the total surface area is

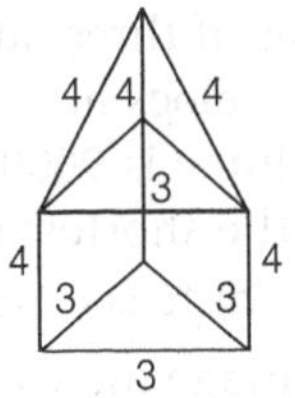

(a) $(54 + \sqrt{3})$ cm^2 (b) $(54 + 9\sqrt{3})$ cm^2
(c) $\left(54 + \frac{9\sqrt{3}}{4}\right)$ cm^2 (d) $\left(54 + \frac{4\sqrt{3}}{9}\right)$ cm^2

13. The area of a sector of a circle of radius 36 cm is 72π cm^2. The length of the corresponding arc of the sector, is
(a) π cm (b) 2π cm (c) 3π cm (d) 4π cm

14. The inner circumference of a circular race track 7 m wide is 440 m. Find the radius of the outer circle.
(a) 57 m (b) 68 m (c) 77 m (d) 69 m

15. In a trapezium, the two non-parallel sides are equal in length, each being of 5 cm. The parallel sides are at a distance of 3 cm apart. If the smaller side of the parallel sides is of length 2 cm, then the sum of the diagonals of the trapezium, is
(a) $10\sqrt{5}$ cm (b) $6\sqrt{5}$ cm (c) $5\sqrt{5}$ cm (d) $3\sqrt{5}$ cm

16. A square park has each side 50 m. At each corner of the park, there is a flower bed in the form of a quadrant of radius 7 m, as shown in the figure. Find the area of remaining part of the park.

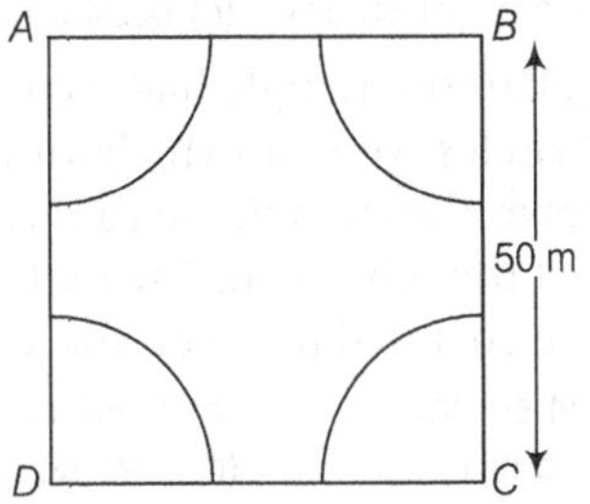

(a) 2346 sq m (b) 2340 sq m
(c) 2250 sq m (d) 2155 sq m

17. A rectangular grassy plot 160 m × 45 m has a gravel path 3 m wide around all the four sides inside it. Find the cost of gravelling the path at ₹ 5 per sq m.
(a) ₹ 5970 (b) ₹ 4970 (c) ₹ 6490 (d) ₹ 4970

18. The difference between two parallel sides of a trapezium is 8 cm. The perpendicular distance between them is 19 cm while the area of trapezium is 760 sq cm. What will be the lengths of the parallel sides?
(a) 44 cm and 36 cm (b) 44 cm and 38 cm
(c) 36 cm and 25 cm (d) 39 cm and 26 cm

19. The perimeter of a square whose area is equal to that of a circle with perimeter $2\pi x$, is
(a) $2\pi x$ (b) $\sqrt{\pi x}$
(c) $4\sqrt{\pi}$ (d) $4x\sqrt{\pi}$

20. Four equal circles are described about the four corners of a square, so that each touches two of the others. If each side of the square is 14 cm, then the area enclosed between the circumferences of the circles, is

(a) 24 sq cm (b) 42 sq cm
(c) 154 sq cm (d) 196 sq cm

21. *ABCD* is a rectangle. The points *P* and *Q* lie on *AD* and *AB*, respectively. If the triangles *PAQ*, *QBC* and *PCD* all have the same areas and $BQ = 2$ then *AQ* is equal to

(a) $1+\sqrt{5}$ (b) $1-\sqrt{5}$ (c) $2+\sqrt{5}$ (d) $\sqrt{7}$

22. Find the perimeter (in centimetres) of a square which is symmetrically inscribed in a semicircle of radius 10 cm.

(a) $\sqrt{80}$ cm (b) 80 cm (c) $8\sqrt{24}$ cm (d) $16\sqrt{5}$ cm

23. An equilateral triangle had 7 cm long sides. Equal circles were drawn about the three vertices of the triangle, so that each circle touched the other two. Calculate the area of space enclosed between these circles.

(a) 3.934 sq cm (b) 1.967 sq cm
(c) 3.9 sq cm (d) 1.95 sq cm

24. An equilateral triangle is inscribed in a circle of radius 4 cm. Find the possible dimensions of a rectangle having its area equal to that of the triangle.

(a) $4\sqrt{3}$, $\sqrt{3}$ (b) $3\sqrt{3}$, $2\sqrt{2}$
(c) $\sqrt{24}$, $3\sqrt{2}$ (d) $\sqrt{12\sqrt{3}}$, $\sqrt{12\sqrt{3}}$

25. If the height of a triangle is decreased by 40% and its base is increased by 40%, what will be the effect on its area?

(a) No change (b) 8% decrease
(c) 16% decrease (d) 16% increase

26. A brick measures 20 cm × 10 cm × 7.5 cm. How many bricks will be required for a wall 20 m × 2 m × 0.75 m?

(a) 10000 (b) 15000 (c) 20000 (d) 25000

27. A beam 9 m long, 40 cm wide and 20 cm high is made up of iron which weighs 50 kg/m^3. The weight of the beam, is

(a) 56 kg (b) 48 kg (c) 36 kg (d) 27 kg

28. The length of the longest rod that can be placed in a room 30 m long, 24 m broad and 18 m high, is

(a) 30 m (b) $15\sqrt{2}$ m (c) $30\sqrt{2}$ m (d) 60 m

29. Three cubes of iron whose edges are 6 cm, 8 cm and 10 cm respectively are melted and formed into a single cube. The edge of new cube formed is

(a) 12 cm (b) 14 cm (c) 16 cm (d) 18 cm

30. The volume of a cube is 2744 cm^3. Its surface area is

(a) 196 cm^2 (b) 1176 cm^2
(c) 784 cm^2 (d) 588 cm^2

31. A metal sheet 27 cm long, 8 cm broad and 1 cm thick is melted into a cube. The difference between surface areas of two solids is

(a) 284 cm^2 (b) 286 cm^2 (c) 296 cm^2 (d) 300 cm^2

32. If the areas of three adjacent faces of a cuboid are *x*, *y*, *z* respectively, then the volume of the cuboid is

(a) xyz (b) $2xyz$ (c) $\sqrt{xyz}$ (d) $3\sqrt{xyz}$

33. If *S* be surface area and *V* be the volume of a cuboid of dimensions *a*, *b* and *c*, then $\frac{1}{V}$ is equal to

(a) $\frac{S}{2}(a+b+c)$ (b) $\frac{2}{S}\left(\frac{1}{a}+\frac{1}{b}+\frac{1}{c}\right)$
(c) $\frac{2S}{a+b+c}$ (d) $2S(a+b+c)$

34. If the areas of three adjacent faces of a rectangular block are in the ratio of 2 : 3 : 4 and its volume is 9000 cm^3, then the length of the shortest side is

(a) 10 cm (b) 15 cm (c) 20 cm (d) 30 cm

35. The percentage increase in the surface area of a cube when each side is doubled, is

(a) 25% (b) 50% (c) 150% (d) 300%

36. The curved surface area of a right circular cylinder of base radius *r* is obtained by multiplying its volume by

(a) $\frac{2}{r^2}$ (b) $2r^2$ (c) $\frac{2}{r}V$ (d) $2r$

37. Two circular cylinders of equal volume have their heights in the ratio 2 : 1. The ratio of their radii is

(a) 2 : 1 (b) 1 : 2 (c) $\sqrt{2}$: 1 (d) 1 : $\sqrt{2}$

38. The radius of a sphere is *r* and the radius of the base as well as the height of cylinder is *r*, the ratio of their volumes is

(a) 4 : 3 (b) 3 : 4 (c) 2 : 3 (d) 3 : 2

39. Three spherical metal balls of radii 6 cm, 8 cm and *R* cm are melted into a solid sphere of radius 12 cm, the value of *R*, is

(a) 8 cm (b) 10 cm (c) 14 cm (d) 18 cm

40. A cone and sphere have equal radii and volumes. The ratio of the diameter of sphere to the height of the cone is

(a) 3 : 1 (b) 1 : 3 (c) 6 : 1 (d) 1 : 2

41. A hemisphere of lead of radius 6 cm is cast into a right circular cone of height 75 cm. The radius of the base of the cone, is

(a) 1.4 cm (b) 2 cm (c) 2.4 cm (d) 4.2 cm

42. Find the total surface area of a pyramid having a slant height of 8 cm and a base which is a square of side 4 cm (in cm^2)?

(a) 80 (b) 64 (c) 72 (d) 84

43. A prism and a pyramid have the same base and the same height. Find the ratio of the volumes of the prism and the pyramid.

(a) 1 : 1
(b) 1 : 3
(c) 3 : 1
(d) Cannot be determined

44. What is the volume of a cone having a base of radius 10 cm and height 21 cm?

(a) 2200 cm^3 (b) 3000 cm^3
(c) 5600 cm^3 (d) 6600 cm^3

45. The height of a cone is 30 cm. *A* small cone is cut off at the top by a plane parallel to the base. If its volume is 1/27 of the given cone, then the height of the smaller cone, is

(a) 13.5 cm (b) 11 cm (c) 10 cm (d) 12 cm

46. A cylindrical tub of diameter 12 cm contains water to a depth of 20 cm. A spherical iron ball is dropped into the tub and thus the level of water is raised by 6.75 cm. What is the radius of the ball?

(a) 6 cm (b) 9 cm
(c) 8 cm (d) None of these

47. If the weight of spherical shell is seven-eighths of what it would be if it were a solid shell. The ratio of outer to inner radii of the shell, is

(a) 1:2 (b) 1:3
(c) 1:3 (d) 3:4

48. Find the smallest side of a prism of volume 3600 units if its edges are in the ratio 5 :12 :13 :15.

(a) 10 (b) 24
(c) 7.5 (d) None of these

Previous Year's Questions

49. If the length and height of a brick increases by 10% each respectively and the breadth reduces by 20%, what is the percentage change in the volume of the brick? **[CLAT 2011]**

(a) 28 % (b) 30 %
(c) 32 % (d) 36 %

50. A cylindrical tennis ball container can contain maximum three balls stacked on one another. The top and bottom balls also touch the lid and the base of the container respectively. If the volume of a tennis ball is 240 cm^3, then what is the volume of the container? **[CLAT 2011]**

(a) 1080 cm^3 (b) 840 cm^3
(c) 1440 cm^3 (d) 720 cm^3

51. Ranjeetha walks around the circular park in 15 min. If she walks at the rate of 5 km/h, how much distance would she have to travel, at the minimum, to reach the centre of the park from any point on its perimeter? **[CLAT 2011]**

(a) 100 m (b) 200 m
(c) 250 m (d) 300 m

52. If the ratio of the areas of two squares is 25 : 36, then the ratio of their perimeters is **[CLAT 2012]**

(a) 5 : 6 (b) 25 : 36 (c) 6 : 5 (d) 36 : 25

53. If the volume of a sphere is divided by its surface area, we obtain 27 cm. The radius of the sphere is **[CLAT 2012]**

(a) 9 cm (b) 81 cm (c) 27 cm (d) 24 cm

54. A rod of 2 cm diameter and 30 cm length is converted into a wire of 3 m length of uniform thickness. The diameter of the wire is **[CLAT 2013]**

(a) 2/10 cm (b) $2/\sqrt{10}$ cm
(c) $1/\sqrt{10}$ cm (d) 1/10 cm

55. A ground $100 \times 80\ m^2$ has, two cross roads in its middle. The road parallel to the length is 5 m wide and the other road is 4 m wide, both roads are perpendicular to each other. The cost of laying the bricks at the rate of ₹ 10 per m^2, on the roads, will be **[CLAT 2013]**

(a) ₹ 700 (b) ₹ 8000 (c) ₹ 900 (d) ₹ 1000

56. Diagonals of a rhombus are 1 m and 1.5 m in lengths. The area of the rhombus is **[CLAT 2013]**

(a) $0.75\ m^2$ (b) $1.5\ m^2$
(c) $1\ m^2$ (d) $0.375\ m^2$

57. Two straight poles of unequal length stand upright on a ground. The length of the shorter pole is 10 m. A pole joins the top of the two vertical poles. The distance between the two tops is 5 m. The distance between the poles along the ground is 4 m. The area thus formed by the three poles with the ground is **[CLAT 2013]**

(a) $52\ m^2$ (b) $46\ m^2$
(c) $20\ m^2$ (d) $50\ m^2$

58. If a square field has its area equal to $324\ m^2$, then the perimeter of the field is **[CLAT 2014]**

(a) 36m (b) 72m
(c) 18m (d) 6561m

59. A closed metal box measures $30\ cm \times 20\ cm \times 10\ cm$. Thickness of the metal is 1cm. The volume of the metal required to make the box is **[CLAT 2014]**

(a) $1041\ cm^3$ (b) $6000\ cm^3$
(c) $4536\ cm^3$ (d) $1968\ cm^3$

60. A patient in a hospital is given soup daily in a cylindrical bowl of diameter 7 cm. If the bowl is filled with soup to a height of 4 cm, how much soup the hospital has to prepare daily to serve 250 patients? **[CLAT 2016]**

(a) 38 L (b) 40 L
(c) 39.5 L (d) 38.5 L

61. A circular park, 42 m in diameter, has a path 3.5 m wide running around it on the outside. Find the cost of gravelling the path at ₹ 4 per sq m. **[CLAT 2016]**

(a) ₹ 2048 (b) ₹ 1652
(c) ₹ 1672 (d) ₹ 2002

Answers

1	b	2	a	3	a	4	c	5	b	6	b	7	a	8	b	9	c	10	d
11	d	12	c	13	d	14	c	15	b	16	a	17	a	18	a	19	d	20	b
21	a	22	d	23	b	24	d	25	c	26	c	27	c	28	c	29	a	30	b
31	b	32	c	33	b	34	b	35	d	36	c	37	d	38	a	39	b	40	d
41	c	42	a	43	c	44	a	45	c	46	d	47	a	48	a	49	c	50	a
51	b	52	a	53	b	54	c	55	b	56	a	57	b	58	b	59	d	60	d
61	d																		

SOLUTIONS

1. Area of an equilateral triangle

$$=\frac{\sqrt{3}}{4}\times(\text{side})^2=\frac{\sqrt{3}}{4}\times(4\sqrt{3})^2$$

$$=\frac{\sqrt{3}}{4}\times 48=12\sqrt{3}\text{ cm}^2$$

2. Area of rhombus $=\frac{1}{2}\times d_1\times d_2=\frac{1}{2}\times 1\times 1.5$

$$=0.75\text{ m}^2$$

3. Diagonal of square $=\sqrt{2}\,a$ (a = side)

$$4\sqrt{2}=\sqrt{2}\,a$$

$\Rightarrow$ $a=4$ cm

Now, area of square $=a^2=(4)^2=16$

Side of a square whose area is 2×16.

$$a_1^2=32$$

$\Rightarrow$ $a_1=\sqrt{32}$ $\Rightarrow$ $a_1=4\sqrt{2}$

Now, diagonal of new square

$$=\sqrt{2}a=\sqrt{2}\times 4\sqrt{2}=8\text{ cm}$$

4. Let original radius be r.

Then, according to the question,

$$\pi(r+1)^2-\pi r^2=22$$

$\Rightarrow$ $\pi\times[(r+1)^2-r^2]=22$

$\Rightarrow$ $\frac{22}{7}\times(r+1+r)(r+1-r)=22$

$\Rightarrow$ $2r+1=7$

$\Rightarrow$ $2r=6$

$\therefore$ $r=\frac{6}{2}=3$ cm

5. The man takes 3600 s for 14.4 km.

The man will takes 88 s for

$$\frac{14.4\times 88}{3600}=\frac{352}{1000}\text{ km}=352\text{ m}$$

Now, circumference of circular field = 352 m

$\Rightarrow$ $2\pi r=352$ m

$\Rightarrow$ $2\times\frac{22}{7}\times r=352$

$\Rightarrow$ $r=56$ m

Therefore, area of the field $=\pi r^2$

$$=\frac{22}{7}\times 56\times 56=8\times 22\times 56\text{ m}^2$$

$$=9856\text{ sq m}$$

6. Let the radius of circular field = r m

Speed of person in m/s $=\frac{30}{60}=\frac{1}{2}$ m/s

According to the question,

$$\frac{2\pi r}{1/2}-\frac{2r}{1/2}=30\Rightarrow 4\pi r-4r=30$$

$\Rightarrow$ $\left(4\times\frac{22}{7}-4\right)r=30$

$\Rightarrow$ $(12.5-4)\,r=30$

$\Rightarrow$ $(8.5)\,r=30\Rightarrow r=\frac{30}{8.5}=3.5$ m

7.

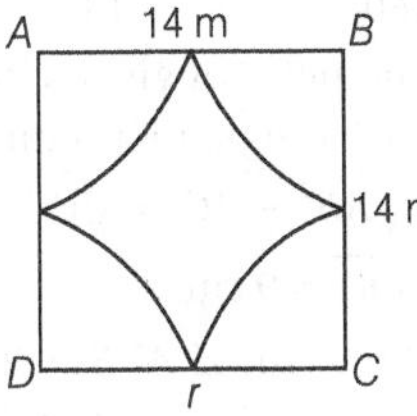

Total area $=14\times 14=196\text{ m}^2$

Grazed area $=\left(\frac{\pi\times r^2}{4}\right)\times 4$

$\left[\because \text{area a of a sector}=\frac{\pi r^2\theta}{360^\circ}\right]$

$$=\pi r^2=\frac{22}{7}\times 7\times 7=22\times 7=154\text{ m}^2$$

Ungrazed area $=(196-154-20)=22\text{ m}^2$

8.

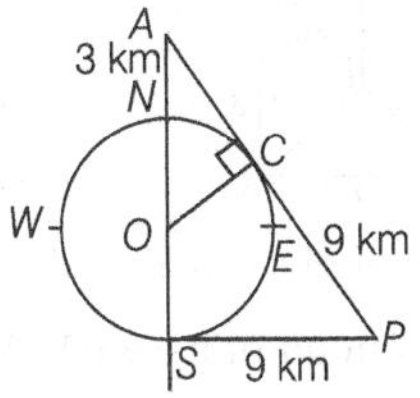

ΔAPS and ΔAOC are similar triangles.

Now, $\frac{OC}{AO}=\frac{SP}{AP}$

$\therefore$ $\frac{r}{r+3}=\frac{9}{\sqrt{81+(2r+3)^2}}$, where

$$ON=OS=r$$

Now, use the options. Hence, the diameter is 9 km.

9. If the sides of the triangle are a, b and c, then $a + b > c$. Given, $a + b + c = 14$.
Then, the sides of the triangle can be (4, 4, 6), (5, 5, 4), (6, 5, 3) and (6, 6, 2). Hence, 4 triangles are possible.

10.

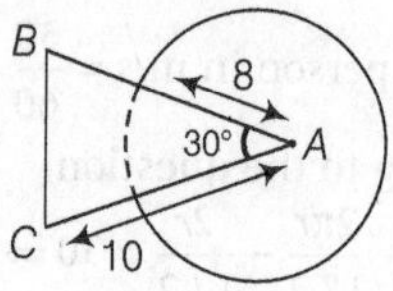

It can be seen that, if the length of the rope is 8m, then the cow will be able to graze an area of the sector of the circle with angle 330°.
Required area =

$$\pi \times 8^2 \times \frac{330^\circ}{360^\circ} = \pi \times 64 \times \frac{11}{12} = \frac{176\pi}{3} \text{ m}^2$$

11. AB is the diameter of given circle.
$\therefore \angle ACB = 90^\circ$ (angle in a semicircle)

$$CB = \sqrt{AB^2 - AC^2} = \sqrt{15^2 - 12^2}$$
$$= \sqrt{81} = 9 \text{ cm}$$

Given, $BD = 9$ cm, $\angle ADB = 90^\circ$
(angle in a semi-circle)

$\therefore$ $\Delta ABC \cong \Delta ABD$
$\therefore$ Area of the quadrilateral
$= 2 \times$ Area of ΔABC
$= 2 \times \frac{1}{2} \times 12 \times 9 = 108$ sq m

12.

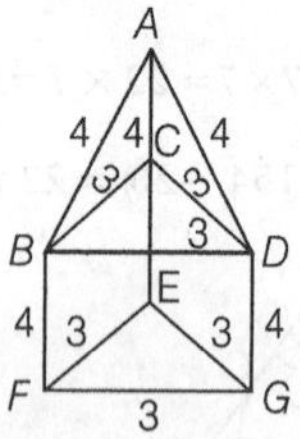

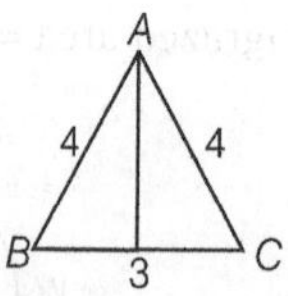

Lateral area of given pyramid
$= \frac{1}{2} \times$ Perimeter of base $\times$ Height
$= \frac{1}{2} \times 9 \times 4 = 18 \text{ cm}^2$

And lateral area of prism
$= 9 \times 4 = 36 \text{ cm}^2$

So, total area
$= 18 + 36 +$ Area of base

$$= 54 + \frac{(3)^2 \times \sqrt{3}}{4} = \left(54 + \frac{9\sqrt{3}}{4}\right) \text{cm}^2$$

13. Given, area of sector $= 72\pi \text{ cm}^2$

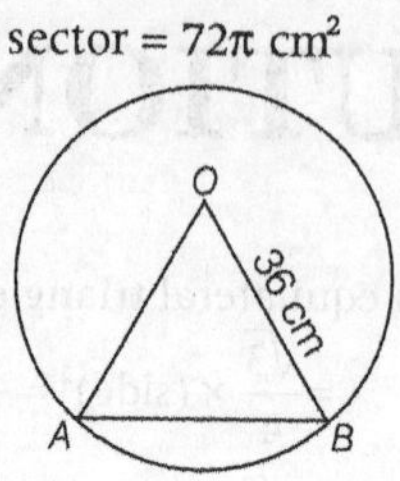

or $\frac{\pi r^2 \theta}{360^\circ} = 72\pi$

$\Rightarrow$ $\theta = \frac{72 \times 360^\circ}{36 \times 36}$

$\Rightarrow$ $\theta = 20^\circ$

Now, length of arc

$$= \frac{\pi r \theta}{180^\circ} = \frac{\pi \times 36 \times 20^\circ}{180^\circ} = 4\pi \text{ cm}$$

14.

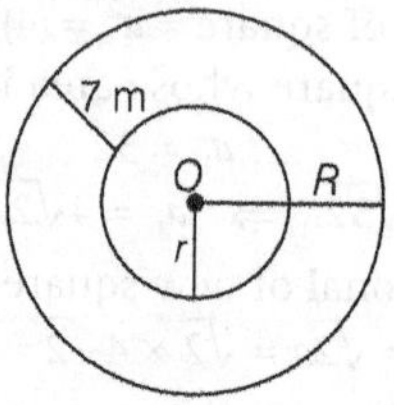

Let R = Radius of outer circle
and r = Radius of inner circle
According to the question,

$$2\pi r = 440 \Rightarrow r = \frac{440}{2\pi} = \frac{440}{2 \times \frac{22}{7}}$$
$$= \frac{440 \times 7}{44} = 70 \text{ m}$$

Clearly, $R - r = 7$
$\Rightarrow$ $R - 70 = 7$
$\therefore$ $R = 70 + 7 = 77$ m

15. In ΔBFC, by Pythagoras theorem,

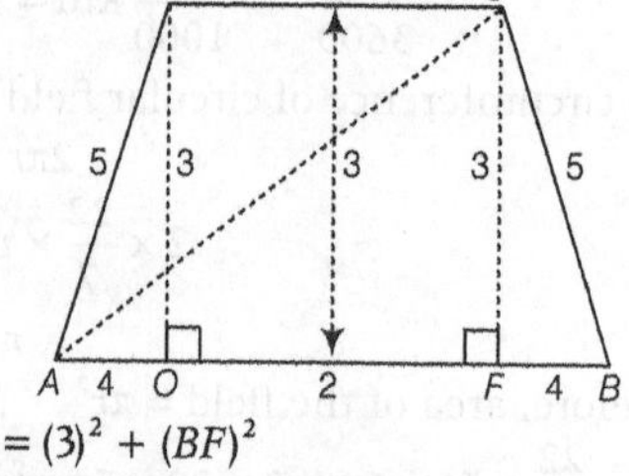

$(5)^2 = (3)^2 + (BF)^2$
$\Rightarrow$ $BF = 4$ cm
$\therefore$ $AB = 2 + 4 + 4 = 10$ cm
Now, in ΔACF, $AC^2 = CF^2 + FA^2$

$\Rightarrow AC^2 = 3^2 + 6^2 \Rightarrow AC = \sqrt{45}$ cm

Similarly, $BD = \sqrt{45}$ cm

$\therefore$ Sum of diagonals

$= AC + BD = \sqrt{45} + \sqrt{45}$

$= 2\sqrt{45} = 6\sqrt{5}$ cm

16. As four quadrants make a circle,

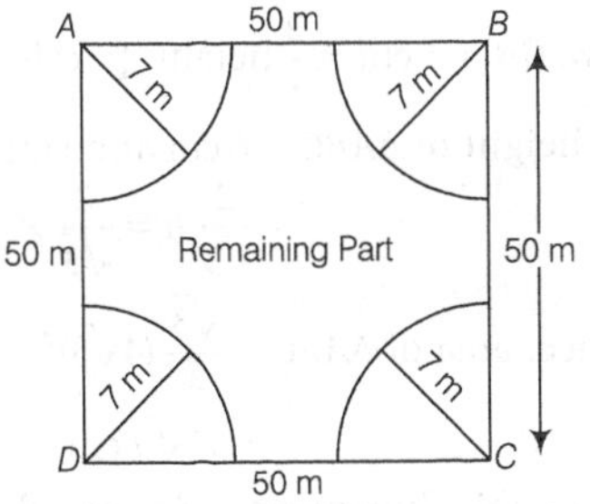

$\therefore$ Area of park without flower bed

= Area of square − Area of circle

$= \left[(50)^2 - \left(\frac{22}{7} \times 7 \times 7\right)\right]$

$= (2500 - 154) = 2346$ sq m

$\therefore$ Area of remaining part = 2346 sq m

17. Given that, $l = 160$ m, $b = 45$ m and $x = 3$ m

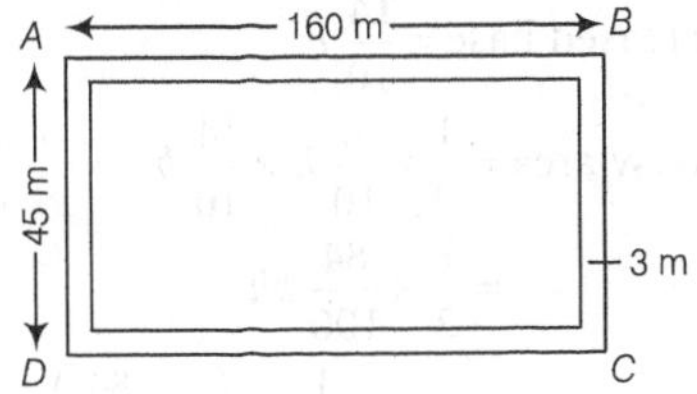

By the formula,

$\therefore$ Area of path $= 45 \times 160 - (45 - 6)(160 - 6)$

$= 1200 - 6006 = 1194$ sm^2

Required cost = (1194 × 5) = ₹ 5970

18.

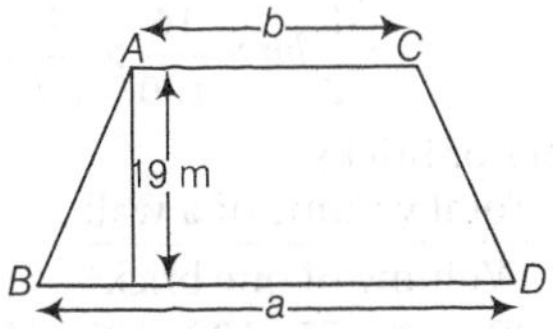

Let the two parallel sides be a and b.

According to the question,

$$a - b = 8 \quad \text{...(i)}$$

and $\frac{1}{2}(a + b) \times 19 = 760 \Rightarrow a + b = 40 \times 2$

$$\Rightarrow \quad a + b = 80 \quad \text{...(ii)}$$

From Eqs. (i) and (ii), we get

$$2a = 88 \therefore a = \frac{88}{2} = 44 \text{ cm}$$

From Eq. (i), we get

$a - b = 8 \Rightarrow b = a - 8 = 44 - 8 = 36$

$\therefore \quad a = 44$ cm and $b = 36$ cm

19. Perimeter of the circle $= 2\pi x$

$\therefore$ Radius of the circle $= x$

$\Rightarrow$ Area of the circle $= \pi x^2$

Let y be the side of the square

$\therefore \quad y^2 = \pi x^2$

$\Rightarrow \quad y = x\sqrt{\pi}$

$\therefore$ Perimeter of the square $= 4y$

$= 4 \times x\sqrt{\pi}$

20.

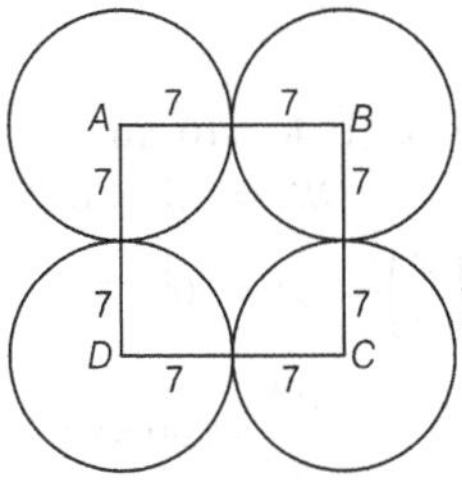

Area of the four quadrants

= Area of the circle with radius 7

$= \pi \times (7)^2 = 154$ sq cm.

$\therefore$ Required area = Area of square − Area of four quadrants

$= 196 - 154$

$= 42$ sq cm

21.

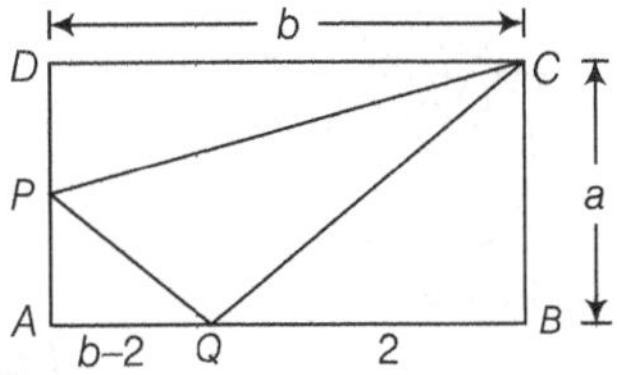

As, Area (ΔPAQ) = Area (ΔQCB) = Area (ΔPCD)

Now, Area (ΔQBC) $= \frac{1}{2} \times a \times 2 = a$ ...(i)

Area (ΔPAQ) $= \frac{1}{2} \times (b - 2) \times AP$

$\Rightarrow \quad AP = \frac{2a}{b - 2}$ [from Eq. (i)]

Area (ΔPCD) $= \frac{1}{2} \times DP \times b$

$\Rightarrow \quad DP = \dfrac{2a}{b}$ [from Eq. (i)]

We know, $AP + DP = a$

$\Rightarrow \quad \dfrac{2a}{b} + \dfrac{2a}{b-2} = a$

$\Rightarrow \quad b = 3 + \sqrt{5}$

$\therefore \quad AQ = 1 + \sqrt{5}$

22.

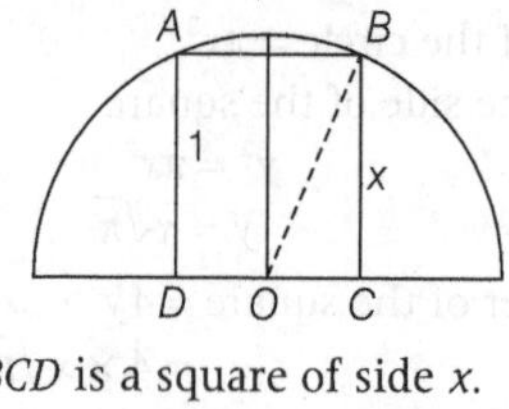

Here, $ABCD$ is a square of side x.

$\therefore OC = \dfrac{x}{2}$, [$\because$ square is symetrically inscribed]

$BC = x$

OB = radius of circle = 10 cm

In ΔOCB, $\quad OB^2 = OC^2 + BC^2$

$\Rightarrow \quad \left(\dfrac{x}{2}\right)^2 + x^2 = 10^2$

$\Rightarrow \quad \dfrac{5x^2}{4} = 100 \Rightarrow x^2 = 80$

$\therefore \quad x = 4\sqrt{5}$ cm

Hence, perimeter of the square $ABCD = 4x$

$= 4 \times 4\sqrt{5} = 16\sqrt{5}$ cm

23. Let side of the triangle = $2L$

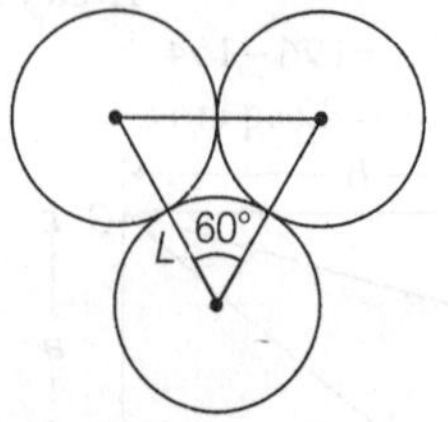

Radius of each circle $= L$

Required area = Area of the triangle $- 3\left(\dfrac{\pi L^2}{6}\right)$,

where $\dfrac{\pi L^2}{6}$ is the area of each circle inside the triangle

$= \sqrt{3}L^2 - \dfrac{\pi L^2}{2} = 1.967 \text{ cm}^2$

[area of the equilateral triangle $= \dfrac{\sqrt{3}}{4} a^2$, a being the side].

24.

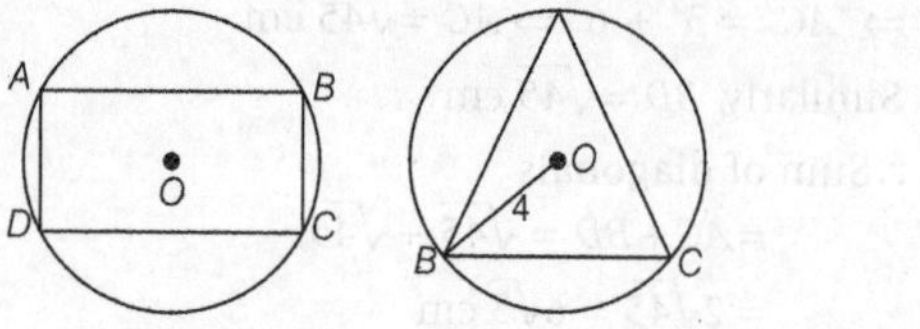

First of all calculate the area of an equilateral triangle inscribed in a circle of radius 4 cm.

Now, $OB = 4 \text{ cm} = \dfrac{2}{3}$ height. [$\because O$ is the centroid]

So, height of ΔABC = 6 cm and side of ΔABC

$= \dfrac{2}{\sqrt{3}} h = \dfrac{2}{\sqrt{3}} \times 6 = 4\sqrt{3}$

Hence, area of $\Delta ABC = \dfrac{\sqrt{3}}{4}(4\sqrt{3})^2$

$= 12\sqrt{3} \text{ cm}^2$

$\therefore$ Possible dimensions of rectangle

$= \sqrt{12\sqrt{3}}$ and $\sqrt{12\sqrt{3}}$

25. Let the height of the triangle be h and the base be b.

$\therefore$ Area $= \dfrac{1}{2} bh$

Decreased height $= \dfrac{6}{10} h$

Increased base $= \dfrac{14}{10} b$

$\therefore$ New area $= \dfrac{1}{2} \times \dfrac{6}{10} h \times \dfrac{14}{10} b$

$= \dfrac{1}{2} \times \dfrac{84}{100} bh$

Decreased in area $= \dfrac{1}{2} bh \left(1 - \dfrac{84}{100}\right)$

$= \dfrac{1}{2} bh \times \dfrac{16}{100}$

Percentage decrease

$= \dfrac{1}{2} bh \times \dfrac{16}{100} \times \dfrac{2}{bh} \times 100 = 16\%$

26. Number of bricks

$= \dfrac{\text{Total volume of a wall}}{\text{Volume of one brick}}$

$= \dfrac{20 \times 2 \times 0.75 \times 100 \times 100 \times 100}{20 \times 10 \times 7.5} = 20000$

27. Volume of beam $V = 9 \times 0.4 \times 0.2 = 0.72 \text{m}^3$

1 m^3 weight = 50 kg

$\therefore 0.72 \text{ m}^3$ weight $= 50 \times 0.72 = 36$ kg

28. The length of longest rod = Diagonal of a room

$= \sqrt{l^2 + b^2 + h^2}$

$= \sqrt{(30)^2 + (24)^2 + (18)^2}$

$= \sqrt{900 + 576 + 324}$

$= \sqrt{1800} = 30\sqrt{2}$ m

29. Volume of new cube $= 6^3 + 8^3 + 10^3$

$= 216 + 512 + 1000 = 1728 \text{ cm}^3$

So, the edge of new cube

$= \sqrt[3]{1728} = 12 \text{ cm}$

30. Volume, $a^3 = 2744$

$\Rightarrow \quad a = 14$

$\therefore$ Surface area $= 6a^2 = 6 \times (14)^2$

$= 1176 \text{ cm}^2$

31. Surface area of given cuboid

$= 2(27 \times 8 + 8 \times 1 + 27 \times 1) = 502 \text{ cm}^2$

Volume of cube = Volume of sheet

$= 27 \times 8 \times 1 \text{ cm}^3 = 216 \text{ cm}^3$

$\therefore$ Edge of the cube $= \sqrt[3]{216} = 6 \text{ cm}$

Surface area of this cube $= 6 \times (6)^2 = 216 \text{ cm}^2$

Hence, the difference between surface areas

$= 502 - 216 = 286 \text{ cm}^2$

32. Volume of cuboid $= l \times b \times h$

Given, $\quad l \times b = x,\ b \times h = y,\ l \times h = z$

$\therefore \quad xyz = (l \times b \times h)^2$

So, $\quad l \times b \times h = \sqrt{xyz}$

33. $S = 2(ab + bc + ca)$ and $V = abc$

Now, $\dfrac{S}{V} = 2\left(\dfrac{ab}{abc} + \dfrac{bc}{abc} + \dfrac{ca}{abc}\right)$

$= 2\left(\dfrac{1}{a} + \dfrac{1}{b} + \dfrac{1}{c}\right)$

$\therefore \quad \dfrac{1}{V} = \dfrac{2}{S}\left(\dfrac{1}{a} + \dfrac{1}{b} + \dfrac{1}{c}\right)$

34. Let dimensions of rectangular block are a, b and c.

Given $ab : bc : ca = 2 : 3 : 4$

and $abc = 9000 \text{ cm}^3$

Now, $\dfrac{ab}{abc} : \dfrac{bc}{abc} : \dfrac{ca}{abc} = \dfrac{2}{9000} : \dfrac{3}{9000} : \dfrac{4}{9000}$

$\Rightarrow \quad c : a : b = 4500 : 3000 : 2250 = 450 : 300 : 225$

$\Rightarrow \quad c : a : b = 30 : 20 : 15$

$\therefore \quad a = 20, b = 15, c = 30 \quad (\because 20 \times 15 \times 30 = 9000)$

Hence, shortest side is 15 cm.

35. Let original side be a. The original area $= 6a^2$

New side $= 2a$

New area $= 6(2a)^2 = 24a^2$

$\therefore$ Required percentage

$= \dfrac{24a^2 - 6a^2}{6a^2} \times 100 = 300\%$

36. Volume of circular cylinder $= \pi r^2 h$

Curved surface area $= 2\pi rh = \dfrac{2\pi r^2 h}{r} = \dfrac{2}{r} V$

37. $\pi r_1^2 h_1 = \pi r_2^2 h_2$, given $\dfrac{h_1}{h_2} = \dfrac{2}{1}$

$\left(\dfrac{r_1}{r_2}\right)^2 = \dfrac{h_2}{h_1} = \dfrac{1}{2}$

$\Rightarrow \quad \dfrac{r_1}{r_2} = \dfrac{1}{\sqrt{2}}$

$\therefore \quad r_1 : r_2 = 1 : \sqrt{2}$

38. Volume of the sphere $= \dfrac{4}{3}\pi r^3 = V_1$

and volume of the cylinder

$= \pi r^2 \times r = \pi r^3 = V_2$

So, $\quad \dfrac{V_1}{V_2} = \dfrac{(4/3)\pi r^3}{\pi r^3} = \dfrac{4}{3}$

$\therefore \quad V_1 : V_2 = 4 : 3$

39. $\dfrac{4}{3}\pi(6)^3 + \dfrac{4}{3}\pi(8)^3 + \dfrac{4}{3}\pi R^3 = \dfrac{4}{3}\pi(12)^3$

$\Rightarrow \quad 216 + 512 + R^3 = 1728$

$\Rightarrow \quad 728 + R^3 = 1728$

$\Rightarrow \quad R^3 = 1000$

$\therefore \quad R = 10 \text{ cm}$

40. Volume of sphere = Volume of cone

$\dfrac{4}{3}\pi r^3 = \dfrac{1}{3}\pi r^2 h$

$\Rightarrow \quad 4r = h$

$\Rightarrow \quad \dfrac{2r}{h} = \dfrac{1}{2}$

So, $\quad 2r : h = 1 : 2$

41. $\dfrac{2}{3}\pi \times 6^3 = \dfrac{1}{3}\pi R^2 \times 75$

$\therefore \quad R^2 = \dfrac{2 \times 6^3}{75} = \dfrac{144}{25}$

$\Rightarrow \quad R = \dfrac{12}{5} = 2.4 \text{ cm}$

42. Total surface area of the pyramid

$= \left[\frac{1}{2} \text{(Perimeter of the base) (Slant height)}\right]$ + Area of the base

$= \frac{1}{2}(4)(4)(8) + 4^2 = 80\text{ cm}^2$

43. Volume of the prism

$= \text{(Area of the base)} \times \text{(Height)} = A \times H$

Volume of the pyramid

$= \frac{1}{3}\text{(Area of the base)} \times \text{(Height)}$

$= \frac{1}{3} \times A \times H$

$\text{Required ratio} = \frac{A \times H}{\frac{1}{3} \times A \times H} = 3:1$

Therefore, ratio of the volumes of the prism and the pyramid = 3 : 1.

44. Given, $r = 10$ cm, $h = 21$ cm

$\therefore \text{Volume of cone} = \frac{1}{3}\pi r^2 h$

$= \frac{1}{3} \times \frac{22}{7} \times 10 \times 10 \times 21 = 2200\text{ cm}^3$

45. $AM = 30$ cm [given]

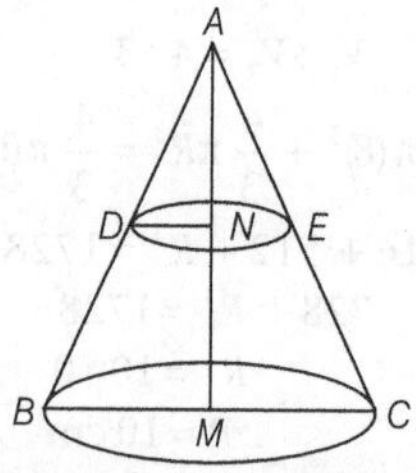

Let the cone ADE is cut off from the cone ABC.

Let DN = radius of the base of the cone $ADE = r_1$ cm.

Let MC = Radius of the base of cone $ABC = r$

Since, both the cones are similar.

$\therefore \quad \frac{h}{30} = \frac{r_1}{r} \Rightarrow r_1 = \frac{hr}{30}$ ...(i)

Also, volume of the cone ADE

$= \frac{1}{27} \times \text{Volume of the cone } ABC$

$\Rightarrow \quad \frac{1}{3}\pi r_1^2 h = \frac{1}{27} \times \frac{1}{3}\pi r^2 \times 30$

$\Rightarrow \quad r_1^2 h = \frac{1}{27} \times 30r^2$

$\Rightarrow \quad \frac{h^2 r^2}{(30)^2} \times h = \frac{30}{27} r^2$ [from Eq. (i)]

$\Rightarrow \quad h^3 = \frac{(30)^3}{(3)^3}$

$\Rightarrow \quad h = \frac{30}{3} = 10\text{ cm}$

46. Volume of the water in the cylinder before dropping the ball $= \pi \times (6)^2 \times 20 = 720\pi$ cu cm

Volume of water after dropping the ball

$= \pi \times (6)^2 \times 26.75$

$= 936\pi$ cu cm

$\therefore$ Volume of the spherical ball

$= 963\pi - 720\pi$

$\Rightarrow \quad \frac{4}{3}\pi r^3 = 243\pi$ cu cm

$\Rightarrow \quad r^3 = \frac{243\pi \times 3}{4\pi}$

$= \frac{729}{4} = 182.25$ cm

47. $\frac{\frac{4}{3}\pi(R^3 - r^3)}{\frac{4}{3}\pi R^3} = \frac{7}{8} \Rightarrow 8R^3 - 8r^3 = 7R^3$

$\Rightarrow \quad R^3 = 8r^3$

$\Rightarrow \quad \frac{R^3}{r^3} = \frac{1}{8}$

$\Rightarrow \quad \frac{R}{r} = \frac{1}{2}.$

48.

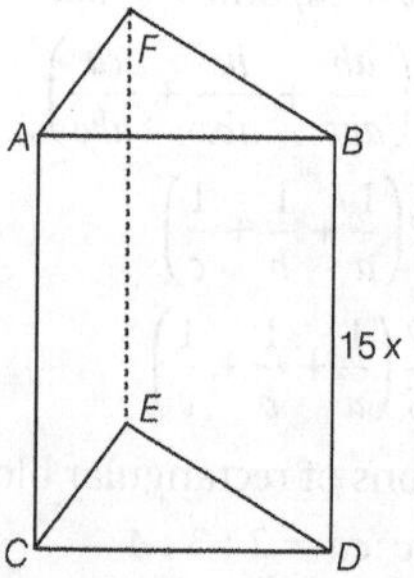

Here the ratio of edges of a prism is given, i.e. 5 : 12 : 13 : 15, in which 5 : 12 : 13 is the ratio of the sides of base. Since, $5x$, $12x$ and $13x$ form a Pythagorean triplet, so area of base

$= \frac{1}{2} \times 5x \times 12x$

$= 30x^2$

Volume of prism = Area of base × Height

$\Rightarrow \quad 3600 = 30x^2 \times 15x$

$\Rightarrow \quad x^3 = 8$

$\Rightarrow \quad x = 2$

Hence, the smallest side of prism

$= 5x = 5 \times 2$

$= 10$ units

Previous Year's Solutions

49. Let previous volume $= 1 \times 1 \times 1 = 1$

Then, present volume $= 1.1 \times 1.1 \times 0.8 = 0.968$

Change $= 0.032$

$\therefore$ Percentage change $= \dfrac{0.032 \times 100}{1} = 32\%$

50. According to the question,

$$\frac{4}{3}\pi r^3 = 240$$

$\therefore r$ (radius of ball) $= \sqrt[3]{57.27}$

We know, radius of ball = radius of container

$= \sqrt[3]{57.27}$

Height of container $= 6 \times \sqrt[3]{57.27}$

$\therefore$ Volume of container

$= \pi r^2 h = \pi (\sqrt[3]{57.27})^2 \times 6 \times \sqrt[3]{57.27}$

$= 6\pi\, (57.27)^{\frac{2}{3}} \times (57.27)^{\frac{1}{3}}$

$= 6\pi \times 57.27$

$\approx 1080 \text{ cm}^3$

51.

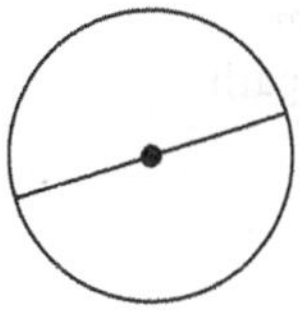

She would have to travel, at minimum, to reach the centre of the park = Radius of circular park

In 15 min, she travels equal distance of perimeter of circular park

Perimeter = Speed × Time

$= \dfrac{5 \times 1000}{60 \times 60} \times 15 \times 60$

$= \dfrac{5000}{4} = 1250$ m

According to the question,

$2\pi r = 1250$

$\Rightarrow \quad r = 198.86 \approx 200$ m

52. Let side of two squares be a_1 and a_2.

Then, $\quad \dfrac{a_1^2}{a_2^2} = \dfrac{25}{36}$

$\dfrac{a_1}{a_2} = \dfrac{5}{6}$

$\Rightarrow \quad \dfrac{4a_1}{4a_2} = \dfrac{4 \times 5}{4 \times 6} = \dfrac{5}{6}$

$\therefore$ Ratio of perimeters = 5 : 6

53. Let radius of the sphere is r.

Then, according to the question,

$$\frac{\frac{4}{3}\pi r^3}{4\pi r^2} = 27 \Rightarrow \frac{r}{3} = 27$$

$\therefore \quad r = 81$ cm

54. Volume of rod = Volume of wire

$\Rightarrow \quad \pi r^2 h = \pi r^2 h$

$\Rightarrow \quad \pi \times (1)^2 \times 30 = \pi \times r^2 \times 300$

$\Rightarrow \quad r^2 = \dfrac{30}{300}$

$\therefore \quad r = \dfrac{1}{\sqrt{10}}$ cm

55.

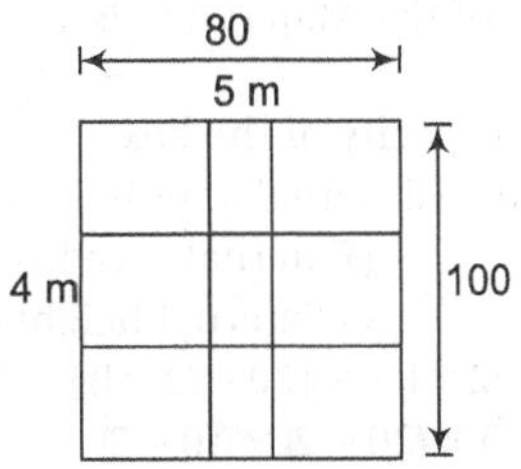

$\therefore$ Area to be paved with bricks

$= 5 \times 100 + 4 \times 80 - 4 \times 5 = 800 \text{ m}^2$

So, cost of lying bricks $= 800 \times 10 =$ ₹8000

56. Area of rhombus $= \dfrac{1}{2} \times d_1 \times d_2$

$= \dfrac{1}{2} \times 1 \times 1.5$

$= 0.75 \text{ m}^2$

57.

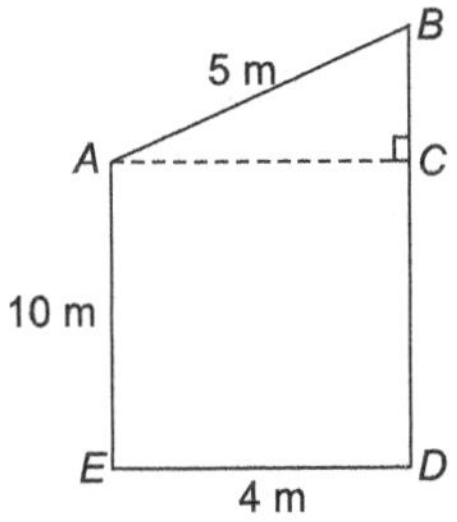

In ΔABC, $\angle ACB = 90°$

So, $\quad BC = \sqrt{AB^2 - AC^2}$

$= \sqrt{5^2 - 4^2}$ $(\because AC = ED)$

$= \sqrt{25 - 16} = 3$ cm

$\therefore$ Area of figure = Area of ΔABC + Area of rectangle $ACDE$

$= \frac{1}{2} \times 3 \times 4 + 4 \times 10$

$= 6 + 40 = 46 \text{ m}^2$

58. $\because$ Area of square field = 324 m^2

$\therefore$ Side of square field $= \sqrt{324} = 18$ m

$\therefore$ Perimeter = 4 × Side = 4 × 18 = 72 m

59.

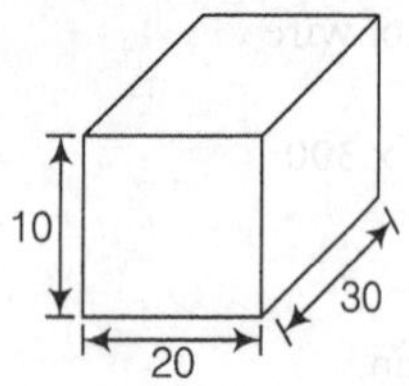

Given, thickness of metal = 1 cm

Volume of the Material = External Volume − Capacity of the box

To find capacity of the box

Capacity= (External length − 2 × Thickness) × (External breadth − 2 × Thickness) × (External height − 2 × Thickness)

$= \{30 - (2 \times 1)\} \times \{20 - (2 \times 1)\} \times \{10 - (2 \times 1)\}$

$= (30 - 2) \times (20 - 2) \times (10 - 2)$

$= 28 \times 18 \times 8 = 4032 \text{ cm}^3$

So, volume of the material required

$= \{10 \times 20 \times 30\} - \{4032\} = 1968 \text{ cm}^3$

60. Given, diameter of bowl = 7 cm

$\therefore$ Radius of bowl $= \frac{7}{2}$ cm

and height = 4 cm

$\therefore$ Volume of bowl $= \pi r^2 h = \frac{22}{7} \times \frac{7}{2} \times \frac{7}{2} \times 4$

$= 154$ cu cm

Hence, volume of soup for 250 patients

$= 154 \times 250 = 38500$ cu cm = 38.5 L

61.

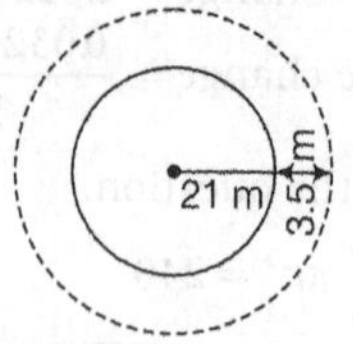

Given, diameter of park = 42 m

$\therefore$ Radius of park = 21 m

Radius of park along with path

$= 21 + 3.5 = 24.5$ m

$\therefore$ Area of path

= Area of park along with path − Area of park

$= \pi \times (24.5)^2 - \pi \times (21)^2$

$= \pi\,[(24.5)^2 - (21)^2]$

$= \pi\,[600.25 - 441]$

$= \pi\,[159.25] = 500.5$ sq m

Hence, cost of gravelling the path

$= 500.5 \times 4 =$ ₹ 2002

CHAPTER 10

STATISTICS AND PROBABILITY

Statistics is a Science, which deals with the collection, presentation, analysis and interpretation of numerical data.

SOME BASIC CONCEPTS

There are some basic concepts given below

Data

The word data means information or set of given facts in numerical figures or otherwise with definite purpose (i.e. observation/information collected).

(i) **Raw or Ungrouped Data** The data obtained in original form is called raw data or ungrouped data.

(ii) **Grouped Data** We may condense data into classes or groups, such a presentation is known as a grouped data.

Class-Intervals

Class-intervals are the groups in which all the observations are divided. Each class is bounded by two figures (numbers) which are called **class limits.** The figure on the left side of a class, is called its **lower limit** and that on the right side of a class, is called its **upper limit**.

The difference between the upper limit and the lower limit of a class is called its **class size**.

Class Mark

For each class-interval, we require a point which would serve as the representative of the whole class. It is assumed that the frequency of each class-interval is centred around its **mid-point**. This mid-point is called class mark and it can be chosen to represent the observations falling in the class.

Thus, Class mark

$$= \frac{\text{Upper class limit} + \text{Lower class limit}}{2}$$

Frequency

The number of times an observation occurs is called its frequency.

Frequency Distribution of an Ungrouped Data

The tabular arrangement of data, showing the frequency of each observation is called a frequency distribution.

Types of Frequency Distribution

1. **Exclusive form** (Continuous form) A frequency distribution in which upper limit of each class is excluded and lower limit is included, is called an exclusive form. e.g. We may consider the classes 0-10, 10-20 etc. In class 0-10, we include 0 and exclude 10. In class 10-20, we include 10 and exclude 20.
2. **Inclusive form** (Discontinuous form) A frequency distribution in which upper limit of each class as well as lower limit of each class is included, is called an inclusive form. Thus, we have classes of the form 0-10, 11-20, 21-30 etc. In 0-10, both 0 and 10 are included.

Cumulative Frequency

If the frequency of first class interval is added to the frequency of second class and this sum is added to third class and so on, then frequencies so obtained are known as cumulative frequency.

Grouped and Ungrouped Data

Grouped data is a data that has been organised into classes. Grouped data is classified and some data analysis have been done, i.e. this data is no longer raw. Ungrouped data is not organised into groups. It is just a list of numbers.

MEASURES OF CENTRAL TENDENCY

A certain value representative of the whole data and signifying its characteristics is called a measure of central tendency of that data or a numerical value which represents (approx.) the entire statistical data is known as measure of central tendency of that data. Mean, mediam and mode are the measures of central tendency.

MEAN

The mean (or arithmetic mean) of a set of observations is obtained by dividing the sum of the values of observations by the number of observations.

Direct Method for Calculating Mean

1. The mean of n observations $x_1, x_2, x_3, \ldots, x_n$ is

$$\text{Mean } (\bar{x}) = \frac{x_1 + x_2 + x_3 + \ldots + x_n}{n}$$

$$= \frac{\sum_{i=1}^{n} x_i}{n}$$

where, the Greek letter Σ (sigma) means summation.

2. Let $x_1, x_2, \ldots, x_n$ be n observations with respective frequencies $f_1, f_2, \ldots, f_n$. This means observation x_1 occurs f_1 times, x_2 occurs f_2 times and so on.

$\therefore$ Sum of the values of all the observations

$$= f_1 x_1 + f_2 x_2 + \ldots + f_n x_n = \sum_{i=1}^{n} f_i x_i$$

and number of observations

$$= f_1 + f_2 + \dots + f_n = \sum_{i=1}^{n} f_i$$

$$\therefore \quad \boxed{\text{Mean } (\bar{x}) = \frac{\sum_{i=1}^{n} f_i x_i}{\sum_{i=1}^{n} f_i}}$$

It can also be written as

$$\boxed{\bar{x} = \frac{\Sigma f_i x_i}{\Sigma f_i}}$$

It is understood that i varies from 1 to n.

Shortcut Method for Calculating Mean

Shortcut method is used in those cases, in which numerical values of x_i and f_i are large, since it becomes tedious and time consuming to find the products of x_i and f_i. So, in those cases, assumed mean method is used. In this method, first of all one among x_i's is chosen as the **assumed mean** and denoted by A. We may take A to be lies in the centre of $x_1, x_2, \dots, x_n$ to reduce our calculation work.

The steps used in shortcut method are given below

$$\boxed{\text{Mean} = A + \frac{\Sigma f_i d_i}{\Sigma f_i}} \quad \text{or} \quad A + \frac{\Sigma f_i d_i}{N}$$

Step Deviation Method for Calculating Mean

Step deviation method is used in those cases, in which the deviations from assumed mean are multiples of a common number.

$$\text{Mean} = \bar{x} = A + \left(\frac{\Sigma f_i u_i}{\Sigma f_i}\right) \times h = A + h \times \frac{1}{N} \Sigma f_i u_i$$

EXAMPLE 1 Find the mean of the following data.

x	10	30	50	70	89
f	7	8	10	15	10

(a) 56 (b) 55
(c) 57 (d) 58

Solution (*b*) Table for given data is

x_i	f_i	$f_i x_i$
10	7	70
30	8	240
50	10	500
70	15	1050
89	10	890
	$\Sigma f_i = 50$	$\Sigma f_i x_i = 2750$

Here, $\Sigma f_i = 50$ and $\Sigma f_i x_i = 2750$

$$\therefore \text{ Mean } (\bar{x}) = \frac{\Sigma f_i x_i}{\Sigma f_i}$$

$$= \frac{2750}{50} = 55$$

Hence, mean of the given data is 55.

EXAMPLE 2 Find the mean of the following frequency distribution.

Class	2-8	8-14	14-20	20-26	26-32
Frequency	6	3	12	11	8

(a) 18 (b) 18.5
(c) 18.8 (d) 19.2

Solution (*c*) Let the assumed mean, $a = 17$

Class	Frequency (f_i)	x_i	$d_i = x_i - a$	$f_i d_i$
2-8	6	5	$5 - 17 = -12$	$6(-12) = -72$
8-14	3	11	$11 - 17 = -6$	$3(-6) = -18$
14-20	12	$17 = a$	$17 - 17 = 0$	$12 \times 0 = 0$
20-26	11	23	$23 - 17 = 6$	$11 \times 6 = 66$
26-32	8	29	$29 - 17 = 12$	$8 \times 12 = 96$
	$\Sigma f_i = 40$			$\Sigma f_i d_i = 72$

Here, $\Sigma f_i = 40$ and $\Sigma f_i d_i = 72$

$$\therefore \quad \text{Mean } (\bar{x}) = a + \frac{\Sigma f_i d_i}{\Sigma f_i}$$

$$= 17 + \frac{72}{40}$$

$$= 17 + 1.8$$

$$= 18.8$$

MEDIAN

Median is defined as the middle most or the central value of the variable in a set of observations, when the observations are arranged either in ascending or descending order of their magnitudes. Median divides the arranged series into two equal parts i.e. 50% of the observations lie below the median and the remaining are above the median.

Let n be the number of observations. Then, arrange the data in ascending or descending order. Now,

***Case* I** If n is odd, then

$$\text{Median} = \text{Value of the } \left(\frac{n+1}{2}\right)\text{th observation}$$

***Case* II** If n is even, then

$$\text{Median} = \text{Mean of the} \left[\left(\frac{n}{2}\right)\text{th and } \left(\frac{n}{2}+1\right)\text{th}\right] \text{observation}$$

$$= \frac{1}{2} \times \text{Value of } \left[\left(\frac{n}{2}\right)\text{th} + \left(\frac{n}{2}+1\right)\text{th}\right] \text{observation}$$

Median Class

In a grouped continuous data, we may not find the middle observation by looking at the observations, since the middle observation will be some value in a class-interval, so it is necessary to find the value inside a class that divides the whole distribution into two halves. For this, we find the cumulative frequencies of all the classes and $\frac{n}{2}$, where n = number of observations.

Now, locate the class, whose cumulative frequency is greater than (and nearest to) $\frac{n}{2}$.

Median for Grouped Data

In a grouped data, we may not find the middle observation by looking at the cumulative frequencies, since the middle observation will be some value in a class interval, so it is necessary to find the value inside a class that divides the whole distribution into two halves.

For this, we find the cumulative frequencies of all the classes and $\frac{n}{2}$, where n = number of observations. Now, locate the class whose cumulative frequency is greater than (and nearest to) $\frac{n}{2}$ and this is called **median class**.

After finding the median class, use the following formula for calculating the median.

$$\text{Median} = l + \left\{\frac{\frac{n}{2} - cf}{f}\right\} \times h$$

where, l = lower limit of median class

n = number of observations

cf = cumulative frequency of the class preceding the median class

f = frequency of the median class

h = class width (assuming class sizes to be equal)

EXAMPLE 3 Find the median of the following data.

Marks obtained	20	29	28	42	19	35	51
Number of students	3	4	5	7	9	2	3

(a) 28 (b) 29

(c) 30 (d) 27

Solution **(*a*)** Arrange the data in ascending order of x_i and make a cumulative frequency table.

Marks obtained (x_i)	Number of students (f_i)	cf
19	9	9
20	3	9 + 3 = 12
28	5	12 + 5 = 17
29	4	17 + 4 = 21
35	2	21 + 2 = 23
42	7	23 + 7 = 30
51	3	30 + 3 = 33

Here, $n = 33$

$\therefore$ Median = Value of $\left(\frac{n+1}{2}\right)$th observation

= Value of $\left(\frac{33+1}{2}\right)$th observation

= Value of 17th observation

Corresponding value of 17th observation of cumulative frequency in x_i is 28.

Hence, Median is 28.

MODE

The observation which occurs most frequently among the given observations i.e. the value of the observation having maximum frequency is called mode. e.g. Mode of the numbers 2, 3, 4, 4, 6, 6, 6, 6, 7 and 9 is 6 because it is repeated the maximum number of times, i.e. 4 times.

(i) If the grouped data is discontinuous, i.e. the classes are not in the exclusive form. So, first we convert them in exclusive form by subtracting $\frac{h}{2}$ from the lower limit and adding $\frac{h}{2}$ to the upper limit of each class, where h is the difference of the lower limit of a class and the upper limit of the preceding class. Further, use the above method to determine the modal class

(ii) Mode can be less, equal or more than the mean of the data.

Mode of Grouped Data

In grouped data, mode is a value lies in the modal class and it is given by the formula,

$$\text{Mode} = l + \left\{\frac{f_1 - f_0}{2f_1 - f_0 - f_2}\right\} \times h$$

Here, l = lower limit of modal class

h = size of the class intervals (assuming all class sizes to be equal)

f_1 = frequency of the modal class

f_0 = frequency preceding to modal class

f_2 = frequency proceeding to modal class

EXAMPLE 4 If mode of the following series is 26, then find the value of f.

Class-interval	0-10	10-20	20-30	30-40	40-50	50-60	60-70
Frequency	8	10	f	16	12	6	7

(a) 17.14 (b) 18
(c) 19 (d) 17.60

Solution (*a*) Here, the maximum frequency is 16 and its corresponding class interval is 30-40. So, the modal class is 30-40.

Then, $f_1 = 16, f_0 = f, f_2 = 12, l = 30, h = 10$

Given, mode = 26 ...(i)

$$\therefore \quad \text{Mode} = l + \left\{\frac{f_1 - f_0}{2f_1 - f_0 - f_2}\right\} \times h$$

$$\Rightarrow \quad 26 = 30 + \left\{\frac{16 - f}{32 - f - 12}\right\} \times 10 \quad \text{...(ii)}$$

$[\because 2f_1 = 2 \times 16 = 32]$

$$26 = 30 + \frac{(16 - f)10}{20 - f}$$

$$\Rightarrow \quad 26 - 30 = \frac{160 - 10f}{20 - f}$$

$$\Rightarrow \quad -4 = \frac{160 - 10f}{20 - f}$$

$\Rightarrow -4(20 - f) = 160 - 10f$

$\Rightarrow -80 + 4f = 160 - 10f$

$\Rightarrow 4f + 10f = 160 + 80$

$\Rightarrow 14f = 240$

$\Rightarrow f = \frac{240}{14} \Rightarrow f = 17.14$

Some Basic Definitions used in Probability

Let us consider following definitions before proceeding chapter.

1. Random Experiment

If all the possible outcomes of an experiment are known but the exact output cannot be predicated in advance, then that experiment is called a random experiment.

e.g. When we toss a coin, the outcome will be either Head (H) or Tail (T).

2. Sample Space

Sample space is the set of all possible outcomes of an experiment. It is denoted by S.

e.g. When a dice is thrown, then sample space, $S = \{1, 2, 3, 4, 5, 6\}$

Event

A subset of the sample space associated with a random experiment is called event or case. e.g. Getting a head is an event related to tossing of a coin.

Types of Event

1. **Certain and Impossible Events** A certain event is certain to occur and an impossible event has no chance of occurring.
2. **Equally Likely Events** Events are said to be equally likely if none of them is expected to occur in preference to the other.

   e.g. When a die is thrown, all the six faces {1, 2, 3, 4, 5, 6} are equally likely to occur.
3. **Mutually Exclusive Events** Two or more than two events are said to be mutually exclusive if the occurrence of one of the events excludes the occurrence of the other.

   e.g. When a coin is tossed, we get either Head or Tail. Head and Tail cannot come simultaneously. Hence, occurrence of Head and Tail are mutually exclusive events.
4. **Dependent Events** Two events are called dependents if the outcome or occurrence of the first affects the outcome or occurrence of the second, so that the probability is changed.
5. **Independent Events** Two events A and B are called independent, if the occurrence or non-occurrence of one event does not influence the occurrence or non-occurrence of the other. If A and B are independent events, then

   $P(A)$ and $(B) = P(A \cap B) = P(A) \cdot P(B)$

   e.g. When a coin is tossed twice, the event of getting Tail (T) in the first toss and the event of getting Tail (T) in the second toss are independent events.

Algebra of Events

Let A and B are two events with sample space S. Then,

(i) $A \cup B$ is the event that atleast one of A or B occurs.

(ii) $A \cap B$ is the event that both A and B occur.

(iii) $\bar{A}$ is the event A does not occur. (compliment of A).

(iv) $\bar{A} \cap \bar{B}$ is the event that none of A and B occur.

PROBABILITY

If there are n elementary events associated with a random experiment and m of them are favourable to an event A, then the probability of happening or occurrence of A, denoted by $P(A)$, is given by

$$P(A) = \frac{m}{n}$$

$$= \frac{\text{Number of favourable events or cases}}{\text{Total number of possible events or cases}}$$

EXAMPLE 5 One card is drawn at random from a well shuffled pack of 52 cards. What is the probability that the card is either a red card or a king?

(a) $\frac{1}{2}$ (b) $\frac{8}{13}$ (c) $\frac{1}{13}$ (d) $\frac{7}{13}$

Solution (*d*) Total number of cards $= 52$

Total number of red cards or king $= 28$

$\therefore$ Required probability $= \frac{28}{52} = \frac{7}{13}$

Addition Rule of Probability

When two events A and B are mutually exclusive, then the probability that A or B will occur, is the sum of the probability of each event.

$$P(A \text{ or } B) = P(A) + P(B)$$

or $P(A \cup B) = P(A) + P(B)$

But when two events A and B are non-mutually exclusive events, then the probability that A or B will occur, is

$$P(A \text{ or } B) = P(A) + P(B) - P(A \text{ and } B)$$

or $P(A \cup B) = P(A) + P(B) - P(A \cap B)$

EXAMPLE 6 Eight persons A, B, C, D, E, F, G and H appeared for an interview. Find the probability that both A and D are selected in the interview?

(a) $\frac{1}{4}$ (b) $\frac{1}{8}$

(c) $\frac{1}{64}$ (d) None of these

Solution **(*c*)** Total number of persons = 8

Probability that A is selected $P(A) = \frac{1}{8}$

Probability that D is selected $P(D) = \frac{1}{8}$

∴ Required probability that both are selected

$$= \frac{1}{8} \times \frac{1}{8} = \frac{1}{64}$$

[since both are independent events]

EXAMPLE 7 From a well-shuffled pack of 52 cards, a card is drawn at random, find the probability that it is either a heart or a queen.

(a) $\frac{17}{52}$ (b) $\frac{6}{13}$ (c) $\frac{16}{13}$ (d) $\frac{4}{13}$

Solution **(*d*)** Let A be the probability of getting a heart and B be the probability of getting a queen

Then $P(A) = \frac{13}{52}, P(B) = \frac{4}{52}$

and $P(A \cap B) = \frac{1}{52}$

[∵ one heart card is a queen]

∴ Required probability = $P(A \cup B)$

$$= P(A) + P(B) - P(A \cap B)$$

$$= \frac{13}{52} + \frac{4}{52} - \frac{1}{52} = \frac{13 + 4 - 1}{52} = \frac{16}{52} = \frac{4}{13}$$

Important Results

Let S be the sample space and A, B and C be the three events, then

- $0 \le P(A) \le 1$
- $P(S) = 1$
- $P(\bar{A}) = 1 - P(A)$
- $P(A \cup B \cup C) = P(A) + P(B) + P(C) - P(A \cap B) - P(B \cap C) - P(A \cap C) + P(A \cap B \cap C)$
- $P(\bar{A} \cup \bar{B}) = 1 - P(A \cap B)$
- $P(\bar{A} \cap \bar{B}) = 1 - P(A \cup B)$

EXAMPLE 8 Three dice are thrown together. Find the probability of getting a total of atleast 6.

(a) $\frac{103}{108}$ (b) $\frac{105}{108}$

(c) $\frac{5}{108}$ (d) None of these

Solution **(*a*)** We know that one dice can be thrown in six ways to get any one of the six numbers marked on its six faces.

∴ Total number of possible events.

$$= 6 \times 6 \times 6 = 216$$

Let A be the event of getting a total less than 6. Then, A denotes the event of getting a total of 3, 4, 5.

∴ $A = \{(1, 1, 1,), (1, 1, 2), (1, 2, 1), (2, 1, 1), (1, 1, 3), (1, 3, 1), (3, 1, 1), (1, 2, 2), (2, 1, 2), (2, 2, 1)\}$

So, favourable number of cases =10

∴ $P(A) = \frac{10}{216}$

Now, probability of getting a total of atleast 6

$$= P(\bar{A}) = 1 - P(A)$$

$$= 1 - \frac{10}{216} = \frac{103}{108}$$

Practice Exercise

1. The numbers 6, 8, 10, 12, 13 and x are arranged in an ascending order. If the mean of the observations is equal to the median, find the value of x.

(a) 16 (b) 17
(c) 5 (d) 4

2. Find the mean of the distribution given below using the shortcut method.

Marks	11-20	21-30	31-40	41-50	51-60	61-70	71-80
Number of Students	2	6	10	12	9	7	4

(a) 48 (b) 46.9
(c) 45 (d) 43

3. Find the mode and median of the following frequency distribution.

x	10	11	12	13	14	15
f	1	4	7	5	9	3

(a) 14, 14 (b) 14, 13
(c) 14, 16 (d) 13, 15

4. Find the mean, median and mode of the following distribution.

8, 10, 7, 6, 10, 11, 6, 13, 10

(a) 9, 10, 10 (b) 9, 9, 10
(c) 10, 9, 9 (d) None of these

5. If the mean of the following distribution is 7.5, find the missing frequency f.

Variables	5	6	7	8	9	10	11	12
Frequency	20	17	f	10	8	6	7	6

(a) 15 (b) 16
(c) 14 (d) 13

6. The median of the observations 11, 12, 14, $(x-2)$, $(x+4)$, $(x+9)$, 32, 38 and 47 arranged in ascending order is 24. Find the value of x and hence find the mean.

(a) 18, 24 (b) 20, 25
(c) 20, 22 (d) None of these

7. Marks obtained by 40 students in a short assessment are given below, where a and b are missing data.

Marks	5	6	7	8	9
Number of Students	6	a	16	13	b

If the mean of the distribution is 7.2, find a and b.

(a) $a = 1, b = 4$ (b) $a = 4, b = 1$
(c) $a = 2, b = 4$ (d) None of these

8. The mean of the following distribution is 52 and the frequency of class-interval 30-40 is f. Find f.

Class-interval	Frequency
10-20	5
20-30	3
30-40	f
40-50	7
50-60	2
60-70	6
70-80	13

(a) 2 (b) 3 (c) 4 (d) 1

9. A student noted the number of cars passing through a spot on a road for 100 periods each of 3 min and summarised it in the table given below

Number of Cars	Frequency
0-10	7
10-20	14
20-30	13
30-40	12
40-50	20
50-60	11
60-70	15
70-80	8

Find the mode of the data.

(a) 40 (b) 45
(c) 44.7 (d) 38

10. 200 surnames were randomly picked up from a local telephone directory and the frequency distribution of the number of letters in English alphabets in the surnames was obtained as follows :

Number of letters	0-5	5-10	10-15	15-20	20-25
Number of surnames	20	60	80	32	8

Find the median of the above data

(a) 11.25 (b) 10
(c) 15 (d) 20

11. Tickets numbered 1 to 20 are mixed up and then a ticket is drawn at random. What is the probability that the ticket drawn has a number which is a multiple of 3 or 5?

(a) $\frac{1}{2}$ (b) $\frac{2}{5}$ (c) $\frac{8}{15}$ (d) $\frac{9}{20}$

12. A bag contains 6 black and 8 white balls. One ball is drawn at random. What is the probability that the ball drawn is white?

(a) $\frac{3}{4}$ (b) $\frac{4}{7}$
(c) $\frac{1}{8}$ (d) $\frac{3}{7}$

13. A coin is tossed 3 times. Find the probability of getting atleast 2 heads.

(a) 1/2 (b) 1/4
(c) 3/4 (d) 1/8

14. All the jacks, queens and kings are removed from a deck of 52 playing cards. The remaining cards are well shuffled and then one card is drawn at random. Giving ace a value 1 similar value for other cards, find the probability that the card has a value less than 7.

(a) 3/45 (b) 3/49
(c) 13/49 (d) 11/49

15. A letter of english alphabets is chosen at random. Find the probability that the letter is a consonant.

(a) 1 (b) 15/26
(c) 21/26 (d) 15/29

16. Two dice are thrown at the same time and the product of numbers appearing on them is noted. Find the probability that the product is less than 9.

(a) 4/7 (b) 4/9
(c) 3/8 (d) 5/9

17. A man and his wife appear in an interview for two vacancies in the same post. The probability of husband's selection is (1/7) and the probability of wife's selection is (1/5). What is the probability that only one of them is selected?

(a) $\frac{2}{7}$ (b) $\frac{1}{7}$ (c) $\frac{3}{4}$ (d) $\frac{4}{5}$

18. In a class, 30% of the students offered English, 20% offered Hindi and 10% offered both. If a student is selected at random, what is the probability that he has offered English or Hindi?

(a) $\frac{1}{2}$ (b) $\frac{3}{4}$ (c) $\frac{4}{5}$ (d) $\frac{2}{5}$

19. A speaks truth in 75% of cases and *B* in 80% of cases. In what percentage of cases are they likely to contradict each other, narrating the same incident?

(a) $\frac{30}{100}$ (b) $\frac{35}{100}$ (c) $\frac{45}{100}$ (d) $\frac{50}{100}$

20. A single letter is selected at random from the word 'PROBABILITY'. The probability that it is a vowel, is

(a) $\frac{3}{11}$ (b) $\frac{4}{11}$ (c) $\frac{2}{11}$ (d) 0

21. I forgot the last digit of a 7-digit telephone number. If I randomly dial the final 3 digits after correctly dialing the first four, then what is the chance of dialing the correct number?

(a) $\frac{1}{999}$ (b) $\frac{1}{1001}$ (c) $\frac{1}{1000}$ (d) $\frac{4}{1000}$

22. Two dices are thrown simultaneously. The probability of obtaining a total score of 8 is

(a) $\frac{5}{36}$ (b) $\frac{1}{6}$ (c) $\frac{1}{9}$ (d) $\frac{7}{36}$

23. The probability that a contractor will get a plumbing contract is $\frac{2}{3}$ and the probability that he will not get an electric contract is $\frac{5}{9}$. If the probability of getting atleast one contract is $\frac{4}{5}$, what is the probability that he will get both?

(a) $\frac{16}{45}$ (b) $\frac{13}{45}$ (c) $\frac{14}{45}$ (d) $\frac{15}{72}$

24. A Chartered accountant applied for a job in two firms X and Y. The probability of his being selected in firm X is 0.7 and being rejected at Y is 0.5 and the probability of atleast one of his applications being rejected is 0.6. What is the probability that he will be selected atleast one of the firms?

(a) 0.8 (b) 0.2 (c) 0.4 (d) 0.7

25. An instrument manufactured by a company consists of two parts A and B in manufacturing part A, 9 out of 100 are likely to be defective and in manufacturing part B, 5 out of 100 are likely to be defective. Calculate the probability that both the instruments will not be defective.

(a) 0.91 (b) 0.86
(c) 0.95 (d) 0.83

26. A dice is rolled three times and sum of three numbers appearing on the uppermost dice is 15. The chance that the first roll was four is

(a) $\frac{2}{5}$ (b) $\frac{1}{5}$
(c) $\frac{1}{6}$ (d) None of these

27. A card is drawn at random from a well-shuffled pack of 52 cards. What is the probability of getting a two of hearts or a two of diamonds?

(a) $\frac{3}{26}$ (b) $\frac{2}{17}$
(c) $\frac{1}{26}$ (d) $\frac{4}{13}$

28. Four boys and three girls stand in queue for an interview. The probability that they will stand in alternate positions is

(a) $\frac{1}{34}$ (b) $\frac{1}{35}$
(c) $\frac{1}{17}$ (d) $\frac{1}{68}$

29. The king, queen and jack of clubs are removed from a deck of 52 playing cards and then well shuffled. Now, one card is drawn at random from the remaining cards. Find the probability that the card is a king.

(a) 3/10 (b) 1/10
(c) 3/5 (d) 4/5

Previous Year's Questions

30. Two coins are tossed simultaneously. The probability of getting at the most one head is **[CLAT 2011]**

(a) 1/4 (b) 1/2
(c) 3/4 (d) 1

31. A box contains 90 discs which are numbered from 1 to 90. If one disc is drawn at random from the box, the probability that it bears a perfect square number is **[CLAT 2011]**

(a) 1/10 (b) 1/11
(c) 1/90 (d) 1/9

32. A bag contains 19 red balls, 37 blue balls and 27 green balls. If a ball is picked up from this bag at random, what is the probability of picking a blue ball? **[CLAT 2011]**

(a) 19/83 (b) 37/87
(c) 34/81 (d) None of these

33. Table shows the daily expenditure on food of 25 households arranged as followed

Locality ₹	100-150	150-200	200-250	250-300	250-350
Households	4	5	12	2	2

[CLAT 2013]

The mean daily expenditure on food is

(a) ₹ 11.1 (b) ₹ 161
(c) ₹ 211 (d) ₹ 261

34. A box contains 24 marbles, some are green and others are blue. If a marble is drawn at random from the jar, the probability that it is green is 2/3. The number of blue balls in the jar is **[CLAT 2013]**

(a) 13 (b) 12
(c) 16 (d) 8

35. An unknown man is found murdered. The corpse has one gold plated tooth, right ear is pierced and a healed fracture of left hand thumb. A man with these characteristics is reported missing. What are the chances (probability) of the corpse being the missing man? (Given the occurrence of the gold-plated teeth in the area, 1 in 5000, left hand thumb fractures 1 in 20000 and of right ear pierces 1 in 100). **[CLAT 2014]**

(a) 1 in 1000 (b) 1 in 1000000
(c) 1 in 1000000000 (d) 1 in 10000000000

36. *A* speaks truth in 75% cases and *B* in 80% of the cases. In what percentage of the cases are they likely to contradict each other, narrating the same incident?

(a) 5% (b) 15%
(c) 35% (d) 45%

37. A die is rolled twice. What is the probability that the sum of the numbers on the two faces is 5? **[CLAT 2015]**

(a) 3/13 (b) 4/13
(c) 6/13 (d) 1/9

38. 12 defectives pens are accidentally mixed with 132 good ones. It is not possible to just look at a pen and tell whether or not it is defective. One pen is taken out at random from this lot. Determine the probability that the pen taken out is a good one. **[CLAT 2016]**

(a) $\frac{7}{12}$ (b) $\frac{9}{12}$
(c) $\frac{10}{12}$ (d) $\frac{11}{12}$

39. There are two urns. One contains two white balls and four red balls, the other contains three white and nine red balls. All balls are of the same shape and size. From each urn, one ball is drawn. What is the probability of getting both the balls of the same colour? **[CLAT 2017]**

(a) $\frac{7}{12}$ (b) $\frac{1}{2}$
(c) $\frac{1}{24}$ (d) $\frac{1}{12}$

Answers

1	*b*	2	*b*	3	*b*	4	*a*	5	*b*	6	*b*	7	*a*	8	*c*	9	*c*	10	*a*
11	*d*	12	*b*	13	*a*	14	*b*	15	*c*	16	*b*	17	*a*	18	*d*	19	*b*	20	*b*
21	*c*	22	*a*	23	*c*	24	*a*	25	*b*	26	*b*	27	*b*	28	*b*	29	*c*	30	*c*
31	*a*	32	*d*	33	*c*	34	*d*	35	*d*	36	*c*	37	*d*	38	*d*	39	*a*		

SOLUTIONS

1. Given numbers in a scending order are 6, 8, 10, 12, 13 and x.

Here, the number of observations is $n = 6$.

$$\therefore \text{ Mean} = \frac{\text{Sum of observations}}{\text{Number of observations}}$$

$$= \frac{6+8+10+12+13+x}{6} = \frac{49+x}{6}$$

Here, $n = 6$ is even, so we use the formula,

Median

$$= \frac{\left(\frac{n}{2}\right)\text{th observation} + \left(\frac{n}{2}+1\right)\text{th observation}}{2}$$

$$= \frac{\left(\frac{6}{2}\right)\text{th observation} + \left(\frac{6}{2}+1\right)\text{th observation}}{2}$$ [put $n = 6$]

$$= \frac{\text{3rd observation} + \text{4th observation}}{2}$$

$$= \frac{10+12}{2} = \frac{22}{2} = 11$$

According to the question,

Mean = Median

$\Rightarrow \quad \frac{49+x}{6} = 11$

$\Rightarrow \quad 49 + x = 66$

$\Rightarrow \quad x = 66 - 49$

$\therefore \quad x = 17$

Hence, the value of x is 17.

2. Table for making product of frequency and deviation is shown below

Mark (CI)	Number of students (f_i)	Mid value (x_i)	$d_i = x_i - A$ $A = 45.5$	$f_i d_i$
11-20	2	15.5	−30	−60
21-30	6	25.5	−20	−120
31-40	10	35.5	−10	−100
41-50	12	45.5 = A	0	0
51-60	9	55.5	10	90
61-70	7	65.5	20	140
71-80	4	75.5	30	120
	$\Sigma f_i = 50$			$\Sigma f_i d_i = 70$

Here, $\Sigma f_i = 50$ and $\Sigma f_i d_i = 70$

Using shortcut method,

$$\text{Mean marks} = A + \frac{\Sigma f_i d_i}{\Sigma f_i} = 45.5 + \frac{70}{50}$$

$$= 45.5 + 1.4 = 46.9$$

Hence, the mean marks of the given distribution is 46.9.

3. Table for making continuous frequency is shown below

x	f	cf
10	1	1
11	4	5
12	7	12
13	5	17
14	9	26
15	3	29
	$n = 29$	

Here, $n = 29$, which is odd.

$$\therefore \text{ Median} = \left(\frac{n+1}{2}\right)\text{th observation}$$

$$= \frac{29+1}{2} = \frac{30}{2}\text{th observation}$$

$= 15$th observation $= 13$

[$\because$ all observations for 12 to 17 are equal = 13]

We know that, mode is the highest occurring frequency of an observation.

From table, we see that highest frequency is 9, so corresponding observation is 14.

$\therefore \quad$ Mode = 14

4. Given distribution is 8, 10, 7, 6, 10, 11, 6, 13, 10.

Here, number of observations, $n = 9$

$$\because \text{ Mean} = \frac{\text{Sum of all the observations}}{\text{Number of observations}}$$

$$= \frac{8+10+7+6+10+11+6+13+10}{9}$$

$$= \frac{81}{9} = 9$$

For the median, firstly arrange the given data in ascending order.

6, 6, 7, 8, 10, 10, 10, 11, 13

Here, $n = 9$ which is odd.

$\therefore$ Median $= \left(\frac{n+1}{2}\right)$th observation $= \left(\frac{9+1}{2}\right)$th observation [put $n = 9$]

$= \left(\frac{10}{2}\right)$th observation = 5th observation = 10

Mode is the observation which is repeated maximum number of times.

In the given distribution, 10 is repeated maximum number of times.

$\therefore$ Mode = 10

5. Table for making product of marks and frequency is shown below

Variable (x_i)	Frequency (f_i)	$f_i x_i$
5	20	100
6	17	102
7	f	$7f$
8	10	80
9	8	72
10	6	60
11	7	77
12	6	72
	$\Sigma f_i = 74 + f$	$\Sigma f_i x_i = 563 + 7f$

Here, $\Sigma f_i = 74 + f$, $\Sigma f_i x_i = 563 + 7f$

Given, $\bar{x} = 7.5$

$\because$ Mean, $\bar{x} = \frac{\Sigma f_i x_i}{\Sigma f_i}$

$\therefore$ $7.5 = \frac{563 + 7f}{74 + f}$

$\Rightarrow$ $7.5(74 + f) = 563 + 7f$

$\Rightarrow$ $555 + 7.5f = 563 + 7f$

$\Rightarrow$ $7.5f - 7f = 563 - 555$

$\Rightarrow$ $0.5f = 8$

$\therefore$ $f = \frac{8}{0.5} = \frac{8}{5} \times 10 = 16$

Hence, the missing frequency is 16.

6. Given observations in ascending order are 11, 12, 14, $(x - 2)$, $(x + 4)$, $(x + 9)$, 32, 38 and 47.

Here, number of observation, $n = 9$, which is odd.

So, we use the formula,

Median $= \left(\frac{n+1}{2}\right)$th observation

$= \left(\frac{9+1}{2}\right)$th observation [put $n = 9$]

$= \left(\frac{10}{2}\right)$th observation = 5th observation

$\Rightarrow$ $24 = x + 4$ [$\because$ median = 24, given]

$\Rightarrow$ $x = 24 - 4 = 20$ ...(i)

$\therefore$ Mean $= \frac{\text{Sum of observations}}{\text{Number of observations}}$

$= \frac{11+12+14+x-2+x+4+x+9+32+38+47}{9}$

$= \frac{165 + 3x}{9} = \frac{165 + 3 \times 20}{9}$ [from Eq. (i)]

$= \frac{165 + 60}{9} = \frac{225}{9} = 25$

Hence, the value of x is 20 and mean is 25.

7. Table for making product of marks and frequency is shown below

Marks (x_i)	Number of students (f_i)	$f_i x_i$
5	6	30
6	a	$6a$
7	16	112
8	13	104
9	b	$9b$
	$\Sigma f_i = 35 + a + b$	$\Sigma f_i x_i = 246 + 6a + 9b$

Here, $\Sigma f_i = 35 + a + b$,

$\Sigma f_i x_i = 246 + 6a + 9b$

Given, $\bar{x} = 7.2$, $\Sigma f_i = 40$

$\therefore$ $40 = 35 + a + b$

$\Rightarrow$ $a + b = 40 - 35$

$\Rightarrow$ $a + b = 5$ ...(i)

$\because$ Mean marks,

$\bar{x} = \frac{\Sigma f_i x_i}{\Sigma f_i}$

$\therefore$ $7.2 = \frac{246 + 6a + 9b}{40}$

$\Rightarrow$ $288 = 246 + 6a + 9b$

$\Rightarrow$ $6a + 9b = 288 - 246$

$\Rightarrow$ $6a + 9b = 42$

$\Rightarrow$ $2a + 3b = 14$

[dividing both sides by 3] ...(ii)

On multiplying Eq. (i) by 2 and then subtracting Eq. (ii) from Eq. (i), we get

$2a + 2b - (2a + 3b) = 10 - 14$

$\Rightarrow$ $-b = -4$

$\Rightarrow$ $b = 4$

On putting $b = 4$ in Eq. (i), we get

$$a + 4 = 5$$

$$\Rightarrow \quad a = 5 - 4 \Rightarrow a = 1$$

Hence, the value of a is 1 and b is 4.

8. Table for making product of frequency and mid value is shown below

Class-interval	Frequency (f_i)	Mid value (x_i)	$f_i x_i$
10-20	5	15	75
20-30	3	25	75
30-40	f	35	$35f$
40-50	7	45	315
50-60	2	55	110
60-70	6	65	390
70-80	13	75	975
	$\Sigma f_i = 36 + f$		$\Sigma f_i x_i = 1940 + 35f$

Here, $\Sigma f_i = 36 + f, \Sigma f_i x_i = 1940 + 35f$

Given, $\bar{x} = 52$

$\because \quad \text{Mean} = \dfrac{\Sigma f_i x_i}{\Sigma f_i}$

$\therefore \quad \bar{x} = \dfrac{1940 + 35f}{36 + f}$

$\Rightarrow \quad 52 = \dfrac{1940 + 35f}{36 + f}$

$\Rightarrow \quad 52(36 + f) = 1940 + 35f$

$\Rightarrow \quad 1872 + 52f = 1940 + 35f$

$\Rightarrow \quad 52f - 35f = 1940 - 1872$

$\Rightarrow \quad 17f = 68$

$\Rightarrow \quad f = \dfrac{68}{17} = 4$

Hence, the value of f is 4.

9. Here, modal class is 40-50, since it has maximum frequency which is 20.

So, $l = 40, f_1 = 20, f_0 = 12, f_2 = 11$ and $h = 10$

$\therefore \quad \text{Mode} = l + \left\{\dfrac{f_1 - f_0}{2f_1 - f_0 - f_2}\right\} \times h$

$= 40 + \left\{\dfrac{20 - 12}{40 - 12 - 11}\right\} \times 10 \quad [\because 2f_1 = 2 \times 20 = 40]$

$= 40 + \dfrac{18}{17}$

$= 40 + 4.7$

$= 44.7$ cars

10. The cumulative frequency table of given data is

Number of letters	Number of surnames (f)	Cumulative frequency (cf)
0-5	20	20
5-10	60	$20 + 60 = 80 (cf)$
10-15	$80 = f$	$80 + 80 = 160$
15-20	32	$160 + 32 = 192$
20-25	8	$192 + 8 = 200$
	$n = 200$	

Here, $n = 200$

$\therefore \quad \dfrac{n}{2} = \dfrac{200}{2} = 100$

Since, the cumulative frequency just greater than 100 is 160 and the corresponding class interval is 10-15.

Medianclass $10 - 15, l = 10$

$Cf = 80, h = 5$

$f = 80$

$\therefore \quad \text{Median} = l + \left\{\dfrac{\frac{n}{2} - cf}{f}\right\} \times h$

$= 10 + \left\{\dfrac{100 - 80}{80}\right\} \times 5$

$= 10 + \left\{\dfrac{20}{80}\right\} \times 5$

$= 10 + 1.25$

$= 11.25$

11. Here, $S = \{1, 2, 3, 4, \ldots\ldots, 19, 20\}$

Let $\quad E$ = event of getting a multiple of 3 or 5 = $\{3, 6, 9, 12, 15, 18, 5, 10, 20\}$

$\therefore \quad P(E) = \dfrac{n(E)}{n(S)} = \dfrac{9}{20}$

12. The number of balls = $(6 + 8) = 14$

Number of white balls = 8

P (drawing a white ball) $= \dfrac{8}{14} = \dfrac{4}{7}$

13. The possible outcomes if a coin is tossed 3 times is

$S = \{(HHH), (TTT), (HTT), (THT), (TTH), (THH), (HTH), (HHT)\}$

$\therefore \quad n(S) = 8$

Let $\quad E$ = Event of getting atlest 2 heads

$= \{(HHT), (HTH), (THH), (HHH)\}$

$\therefore\quad n(E) = 4$

$\therefore\quad P(E) = \dfrac{n(E_2)}{n(S)} = \dfrac{4}{8} = \dfrac{1}{2}$

14. If we remove one king, one queen and one jack of clubs from 52 cards, then the remaining cards left, $n(S) = 49$

Let E_1 = Event of getting a king

$n(E_1) = 3$ [since, out of 4 king, one club cards is already removed]

$\therefore\quad P(E_1) = \dfrac{n(E_1)}{n(S)} = \dfrac{3}{49}$

15. We know that, in english alphabets, there are (5 vowels + 21 consonants = 26 letters. So, total number of outcomes in english alphabets are,

$n(S) = 26$

Let E = Event of choosing a english alphabet, which is a consonant

$= \{b, c, d, f, g, h, j, k, l, m, n, p, q, r, s, t, v, w, x, y, z\}$

$\therefore\quad n(E) = 21$

Hence, required probability $= \dfrac{n(E)}{n(S)} = \dfrac{21}{26}$

16. Number of total outcomes = 36

When product of numbers appearing on them is less than 9, then possible ways are (1, 6), (1, 5), (1, 4), (1, 3), (1, 2), (1, 1), (2, 2), (2, 3), (2, 4), (3, 2), (4, 2), (3, 1), (5, 1), (6, 1) and (2, 1).

Number of possible ways = 16

$\therefore$ Required probability $= \dfrac{16}{36} = \dfrac{4}{9}$

17. Let A = Event that the husband is selected

and B = Event that the wife is selected.

Then, $P(A) = \dfrac{1}{7}$ and $P(B) = \dfrac{1}{5}$

$\therefore\quad P(\overline{A}) = \left(1 - \dfrac{1}{7}\right) = \dfrac{6}{7}$ and

$P(\overline{B}) = \left(1 - \dfrac{1}{5}\right) = \dfrac{4}{5}$

$\therefore$ Required probability $= P$ [(A and not B) or (B and not A)]

$= P[(A \text{ and } \overline{B}) \text{ or } (B \text{ and } \overline{A})]$

$= P(A \text{ and } \overline{B}) + P(B \text{ and } \overline{A})$

$= P(A) \,.\, P(\overline{B}) + P(B) \,.\, P(\overline{A})$

$= \left(\dfrac{1}{7} \times \dfrac{4}{5}\right) + \left(\dfrac{1}{5} \times \dfrac{6}{7}\right)$

$= \dfrac{10}{35} = \dfrac{2}{7}$

18. $P(E) = \dfrac{30}{100} = \dfrac{3}{10}$, $P(H) = \dfrac{20}{100} = \dfrac{1}{5}$

and $P(E \cap H) = \dfrac{10}{100} = \dfrac{1}{10}$

$P(E \text{ or } H) = P(E \cup H)$

$= P(E) + P(H) - P(E \cap H)$

$= \left(\dfrac{3}{10} + \dfrac{1}{5} - \dfrac{1}{10}\right)$

$= \dfrac{4}{10} = \dfrac{2}{5}$

19. Let A = Event the A speaks the truth

B = Event that B speaks the truth

Then, $P(A) = \dfrac{75}{100} = \dfrac{3}{4}$

$P(B) = \dfrac{80}{100} = \dfrac{4}{5}$

$P(\overline{A}) = 1 - \dfrac{3}{4} = \dfrac{1}{4}$

$P(\overline{B}) = 1 - \dfrac{4}{5} = \dfrac{1}{5}$

Now, A and B contradict each other = [A lies and B true] or [A true and B lies]

$\therefore$ Required probability $= P(A) \,.\, P(\overline{B}) + P(\overline{A}) . P(B)$

$= \left(\dfrac{3}{4} \times \dfrac{1}{5}\right) + \left(\dfrac{1}{4} \times \dfrac{4}{5}\right) = \dfrac{7}{20}$

$= \left(\dfrac{7}{20} \times 100\right) = 35\%$ or $\dfrac{35}{100}$

20. Total number of letters $= n(S) = 11$

Whereas, number of vowels $= n(E) = 4$

$\therefore$ Required probability $= \dfrac{n(E)}{n(S)} = \dfrac{4}{11}$

21. It is given that last three digits are randomly dialed.

Then each of the digit can be selected out of 10 digits in 10 ways.

Hence, required probability $= \left(\dfrac{1}{10}\right)^3 = \dfrac{1}{1000}$

22. $n(s) = 6 \times 6 = 36$

E = event of getting total score of 8

$= \{(2, 6)\ (6, 2)\ (3, 5)\ (5, 3)\ (4, 4)\}$

$\Rightarrow\ n(E) = 5$

$\therefore$ Required probability, $p(E) = \dfrac{n(E)}{n(s)} = \dfrac{5}{36}$

23. Let probability of getting plumbing contract $P(A) = \frac{2}{3}$ and probability of getting electric contract

$P(B) = 1 - P$ (not getting electric contract)

$= 1 - \frac{5}{9} = \frac{4}{9}$

Also, $P(A \cup B) = \frac{4}{5}$

$\therefore$ Required probability, $P(A \cap B)$

$= P(A) + P(B) - P(A \cup B)$

$= \frac{2}{3} + \frac{4}{9} - \frac{4}{5}$

$= \frac{30 + 20 - 36}{45} = \frac{14}{45}$

24. Given $P(X) = 0.7, P(\bar{Y}) = 0.5$

$\Rightarrow P(\bar{X}) = 0.3, P(Y) = 0.5$

Also, $P(\bar{X} \cup \bar{Y}) = 0.6$

$\Rightarrow 1 - P(X \cap Y) = 0.6$

$\Rightarrow P(X \cap Y) = 0.4$

$\therefore$ Required probability, $P(X \cup Y)$

$= P(X) + P(Y) - P(X \cap Y)$

$= 0.7 + 0.5 - 0.4 = 0.8$

25. Given, part A is not defective $P(A) = \frac{91}{100}$

and part B is not defective, $P(B) = \frac{95}{100}$

$\therefore$ Required probability $= P(A) \times P(B)$

$= \frac{91}{100} \times \frac{95}{100}$

$= 0.8645 = 0.86$

26. Total number of favourable outcomes

$n(S) = 6^3 = 216$

Combinations of outcomes for getting sum of 15 on uppermost face

= (4, 5, 6), (5, 4, 6), (6, 5, 4), (5, 6, 4), (4, 6, 5), (5, 5, 5), (6, 6, 3), (6, 3, 6), (3, 6, 6)

Now, outcomes on which first roll was a four,

$n(E)$ = (4, 5, 6), (4, 6, 5)

$\therefore P(E) = \frac{n(E)}{n(S)} = \frac{2}{10} = \frac{1}{5}$

27. Required probability $= \frac{^{13}C_2 + {^{13}C_2}}{^{52}C_2}$

$= \frac{78 + 78}{1326}$

$= \frac{156}{1326}$

$= \frac{6}{51} = \frac{2}{17}$

28. Total number of possible arrangement for 4 boys and 3 girls in a queue = 7!

When they occupy alternate position the arrangement would be like

B G B G B G B

Thus, total number of possible arrangements for boys = 4! and for girls = 3!

$\therefore$ Required probability $= \frac{4! \times 3!}{7}$

$= \frac{4 \times 3 \times 2 \times 3 \times 2}{7 \times 6 \times 5 \times 4 \times 3 \times 2}$

$= \frac{1}{35}$

29. In out of 52 playing cards, 4 jacks, 4 queens and 4 kings are removed, then the remaining cards are left, $n(S) = 52 - 3 \times 4 = 40$

Let E = Event of getting a card whose value is less than 7

= Event of getting a card whose value is 1, 2, 3, 4, 5 or 6

$\therefore n(E) = 6 \times 4 = 24$

$\therefore P(E) = \frac{n(E)}{n(S)} = \frac{24}{40} = \frac{3}{5}$

30. Possible outcomes are,

Head	Head	Head	Tail
Tail	Tail	Tail	Head

Hence, required probability $= \frac{3}{4}$

31. Perfect square number from 1 to 90 are

1, 4, 9, 16, 25, 36, 49, 64, 81.

Thus, there are 9 square numbers between 1 to 90.

Hence, required probability $= \frac{9}{90} = \frac{1}{10}$

32. Required probability $= \frac{\text{Total blue balls}}{\text{Total balls}}$

$= \frac{37}{19 + 37 + 27}$

$= \frac{37}{83}$

33.

Class interval	x_1	f_i	$d_i\ (x_1 - A_i)$	$d_i f_i$
100 – 150	125	4	–100	–400
150 – 200	175	5	–50	–250
200 – 250	225 = A	12	0	0
250 – 300	275	2	50	100
300 – 350	325	2	100	200

$$\therefore \text{ Mean} = A + \frac{\Sigma d_i f_i}{\Sigma f_i}$$

$$= 225 + \left(\frac{-400 - 250 + 0 + 100 + 200}{25}\right)$$

$$= 225 - \frac{350}{25} = 225 - 14 = ₹\,211$$

34. Let the number of green marble = x
Then, probability of getting a green marble

$$\Rightarrow \quad \frac{x}{24} = \frac{2}{3}$$

$$\therefore \quad x = 16$$

So, number of blue marble = 24 – 16 = 8

35. Probability of all the three characteristics occurring simultaneously,

$$P(E) = P(E_1 \cap E_2 \cap E_3)$$

Since, E_1, E_2 and E_3 are independent.

$$\therefore \quad P(E_1) \cdot P(E_2) \cdot P(E_3)$$

In question,

$P(E_1)$ = Gold plated teeth in Area = $\frac{1}{5000}$

$P(E_2)$ = Left hand thumb fractured = $\frac{1}{20000}$

$P(E_3)$ = Right ear piercing = $\frac{1}{100}$

Probability of found corpse being the missing man reported earlier $= \frac{1}{5000} \times \frac{1}{20000} \times \frac{1}{100}$

$$= \frac{1}{10000000000}$$

36. A speaks truth in 75% cases.

i.e. $P(A) = \frac{3}{4}$ and $P(\bar{A}) = \frac{1}{4}$

B speaks truth in 80% cases.

i.e. $P(B) = \frac{4}{5}$ and $P(\bar{B}) = \frac{1}{5}$

Percentage of the cases when they are likely to contradict each other, narrating the same incident = $P(A)\,(P\bar{B}) + P(\bar{A})P(B)$

$$= \frac{3}{4} \times \frac{1}{5} + \frac{1}{4} \times \frac{4}{5}$$

$$= \frac{7}{20} \times 100 = 35\%$$

37. $n(E) = (1,4)\ (4,1)\ (2,3)\ (3,2)$

$n(S) = 36$

$$P(E) = \frac{n(E)}{n(S)} = \frac{4}{36} = \frac{1}{9}$$

38. Required probability $= \frac{132}{132 + 12} = \frac{132}{144} = \frac{11}{12}$

39. Let event E_1 = Two white balls and four red balls
and E_2 = Three white balls and nine red balls

$\therefore$ Required probability = P (one white ball from each event)
+P (one red ball from each event)

$$= \frac{2}{6} \times \frac{3}{12} + \frac{4}{6} \times \frac{9}{12}$$

$$= \frac{1}{12} + \frac{6}{12} = \frac{7}{12}$$

CHAPTER 11

CLOCK

A clock is an instrument which displays time divided into hours, minutes and seconds.

A clock mainly consists of four components.

Dial

A clock is a circular dial. The periphery of the dial is numbered 1 through 12 indicating the hours in a 12 h cycle. The circumference of a dial is divided into 60 equal spaces called minute spaces or 12 equal spaces called hour spaces. Every clock has mainly two hands, one is smaller and other is bigger. The smaller hand is slower and the bigger hand is faster.

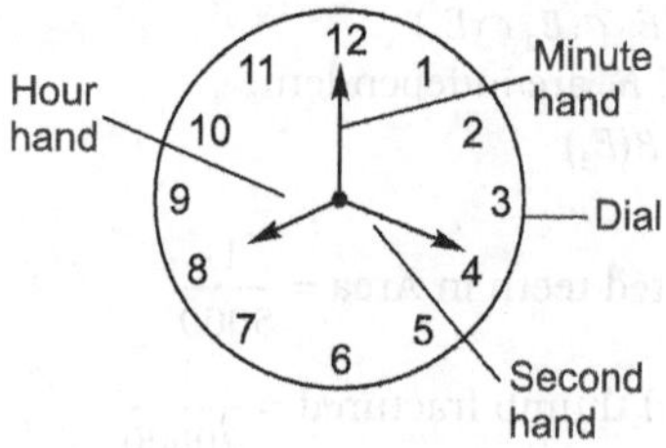

Hour Hand

The smaller or slower hand of a clock is called the hour hand. It makes two revolutions in a day.

Minute Hand

The bigger or faster hand of a clock is called the minute hand. It makes one revolution in every hour.

Second Hand

Second hand indicates seconds on a circular dial. It makes one revolution per minute.

Note In 1 h, minute hand covers 60 min spaces whereas the hour hand covers 5 min spaces. Therefore, minute hand gains (60 – 5) = 55 min in 1 h.

Important Points Related to Clock

1. In 1 h, both hands coincide once (i.e. 0° apart)
   e.g.
   Between 3 and 4'O clock, hands are together as shown in below figure.

2. In 12 h, both hands coincide 11 times (between 11 and 1'O clock they coincide once) and in a day both hands coincide 22 times.
   e.g.
   Between 11 and 1'O clock, hands are together as shown in below figure.

3. If two hands are at 90° they are 15 min spaces apart. This happens twice in 1 h. In a period of 12 h, the hands are at right angle 22 times (2 common positions) and in a day both hands are at right angle 44 times.

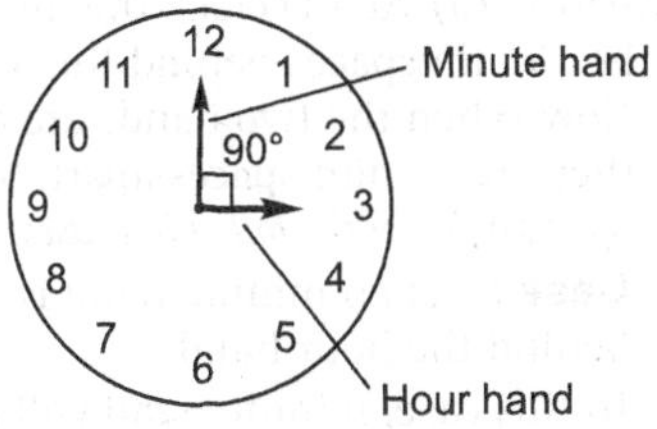

4. If two hands are in opposite direction. (i.e. 180° apart), then they are 30 min spaces apart. This happens once in 1 h. In a period of 12 h both hands are in opposite direction 11 times and in a day both hands are in opposite direction 22 times.

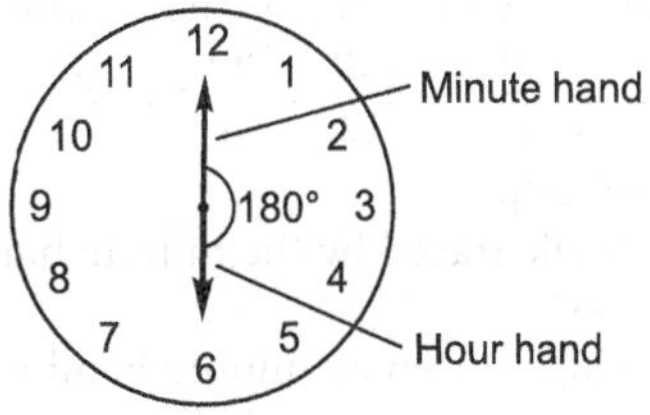

5. Angle covered by minute hand in 1 min
   $$= \frac{\text{Total angle}}{\text{Number of spaces}} = \frac{360°}{60} = 6° \text{in 1 min.}$$

6. As hour hand covers 360° in 12 h.
   Therefore, hour hand covers $\left(\frac{360°}{12}\right) = 30°$ in 1 h.
   Hence, hour hand covers $\left(\frac{30°}{60}\right) = \frac{1°}{2}$ in 1 min.
7. From points 5 and 6, we can say that the minute hand goes ahead by $5\frac{1°}{2}$ in comparison to hour hand, in 1 min.

Concept of Slow or Fast Clocks

Suppose a watch/clock indicates 9 : 15, when the correct time is 9, then it is said to be 15 min too fast. On the other hand, if the watch/clock indicates 6 : 45, when the correct time is 7, then it is said to be 15 min too slow.

EXAMPLE 1 What will be angle between the two hands of a clock at 9:50?

(a) 10° (b) 5° (c) 15° (d) 20°

Solutions *(b)* ∵ Angle traced by the hour hand in 12 h $= 360°$

∴ Angle traced by the hour hand in 1 h $= \frac{360°}{12}$

and angle traced by the hour hand in 9 h, 50 min

i.e. $\frac{59}{6}$ h $= \frac{360°}{12} \times \frac{59}{6} = 295°$

Similarly,

∵ Angle traced by the minute hand in 60 min $= 360°$

∴ Angle traced by minute hand in 50 min

$$= \frac{360°}{60} \times 50 = 300°$$

∴ Required angle $= 300° - 295° = 5°$

EXAMPLE 2 A clock gains 10 s in every 3 h. If the clock was set right at 4:00 am on Monday morning, then the time it will indicate on Tuesday evening at 7:00 pm is

(a) 7:05:15 pm (b) 7:25:00 pm

(a) 7:02:10 pm (b) 7:30:00 pm

Solution *(c)* Difference of time between 4:00 am on Monday to 7:00 pm Tuesday

$$24 + 12 + 3 = 39 \text{ h}$$

Now, time gained by clock in 3 h = 10 s

Time gained by clock in 1 h $= \frac{10}{3}$ s

∴ Time gained by clock in 39 h $= \frac{10 \times 39}{3} = 130$ s

∵ Correct time is 7:02:10 pm.

> Between n O'clock and $(n + 1)$ O'clock, the two hands of a clock will coincide at $\left(\frac{60n}{11}\right)$ min past n.

EXAMPLE 3 At what time between 4 O'clock and 5 O'clock, will the hands of a clock be together?

(a) $21\frac{9}{11}$ min past 5 (b) $21\frac{9}{11}$ min past 4

(c) $20\frac{9}{11}$ min past 5 (d) $21\frac{9}{11}$ min past 3

Solution *(b)* At 4 O'clock, the hour hand is at 4 and the minute hand is at 12. It means that they are 20 min spaces apart.

To be together, the minute hand must gain 20 min over the hour hand.

As we know,

55 min is gained by minute hand in 60 min.

∴ 20 min will be gained in $\left(\frac{60}{55} \times 20\right)$ min

$$= \frac{60 \times 4}{11} = \frac{240}{11} \text{ min} = 21\frac{9}{11} \text{ min}$$

Hence, the hands will coincide at $21\frac{9}{11}$ min past 4.

EXAMPLE 4 At what time between 1 O'clock and 2 O'clock, will the hands of a clock be together?

(a) $5\frac{5}{11}$ min past 1 (b) $5\frac{11}{5}$ min past 2

(c) $6\frac{5}{11}$ min past 1 (d) $6\frac{11}{5}$ min past 2

Solution *(a)* Given, $n = 1$ and $(n + 1) = 2$

∴ The two hands will coincide at $\left(\frac{60n}{11}\right)$ min past 1.

or $\frac{60 \times 1}{11}$ min past 1 or $5\frac{5}{11}$ min past 1.

> Between n O'clock and $(n + 1)$ O'clock, the two hands of a clock will mutually make right angle at $(5n \pm 15) \times \frac{12}{11}$ min past n.

EXAMPLE 5 At what time between 7 O'clock and 8 O'clock in the morning, will the both hands of a clock be at right angle?

(a) $5\frac{5}{11}$ min past 1 (b) $5\frac{11}{5}$ min past 2

(c) $6\frac{5}{11}$ min past 1 (d) $6\frac{11}{5}$ min past 2

Solution *(a)* At 7 O'clock the minute hand will be 35 min spaces behind the hour hand.

Now, when the two hands are at right angle, they are 15 min spaces apart. So, *they are at right angles in the following cases.*

Case I When minute hand is 15 min spaces behind the hour hand.

In this case, minute hand will have to gain $(35 - 15) = 20$ min spaces.

55 min spaces are gained by it in 60 min.

20 min spaces will be gained by it in $\left(\frac{60}{55} \times 20\right)$ min $= \frac{240}{11}$ min $= 21\frac{9}{11}$ min

Hence, they are at right angle at $21\frac{9}{11}$ min past 7.

Case II When the minute hand is 15 min spaces ahead of the hour hand.

To be in this position, the minute hand will have to gain $(35 + 15) = 50$ min spaces.

55 min spaces are gained in 60 min.

50 min spaces are gained in $\left(\frac{60}{55} \times 50\right)$ min

$= \left(\frac{60}{11} \times 10\right)$ min $= 54\frac{6}{11}$ min

Hence, they are at right angle at $54\frac{6}{11}$ min past 7.

> Between n O' clock and $(n + 1)$ O' clock, the hands of a clock will be in the same straight line (without being together) at
>
> (i) $(5n - 30) \times \frac{12}{11}$ min past n, when $n > 6$
>
> (ii) $(5n + 30) \times \frac{12}{11}$ min past n, when $n < 6$

EXAMPLE 6 At what time between 7 O' clock and 8 o'clock, will the hands of a clock be in the same straight line but not together?

(a) $5\frac{5}{11}$ min past 7 (b) $5\frac{5}{11}$ min past 8

(c) $5\frac{11}{5}$ min past 7 (d) $5\frac{11}{5}$ min past 8

Solution *(a)* At 7 O'clock, the hour hand is at 7 and the minute hand is at 12. It means that the two hands are 25 min spaces apart.

To be in the same straight line (but not together), they will be 30 min spaces apart.

∴ The minute hand will have to gain $(30 - 25) = 5$ min spaces over the hour hand. As we know, 55 min spaces are gained in 60 min.

∴ 5 min will be gained in $\left(\frac{60}{55} \times 5\right)$ min

$= 5\frac{5}{11}$ min

Hence, the hands will be in the same straight line but not together at $5\frac{5}{11}$ min past 7.

EXAMPLE 7 At what time between 3 O'clock and 4 O'clock, will the hands of a clock be in opposite directions?

(a) $49\frac{1}{11}$ past 3 (b) $49\frac{1}{11}$ past 2

(c) $50\frac{1}{11}$ past 3 (d) $50\frac{1}{11}$ past 2

Solution *(a)* At 3 O'clock, the hour hand is at 3 and the minute hand is at 12. It means that the two hands are 15 min spaces apart. But to be in opposite directions, the hands must be 30 min spaces apart. Therefore, the minute hand will have to gain $(30 + 15) = 45$ min spaces over the hour hand.

∵ 55 min spaces are gained in 60 min.

∴ 45 min spaces are gained in $\left(\frac{60}{55} \times 45\right)$ min $= \frac{60 \times 9}{11}$ min $= \frac{540}{11} = 49\frac{1}{11}$ min

Hence, required time $= 49\frac{1}{11}$ past 3.

> Between n O'clock and $(n + 1)$ O'clock, the hands of a clock are x min apart at $(5n \pm x) \times \frac{12}{11}$ min past n. If minute hand is ahead, then '+' sign is used and if hour hand is ahead, then '–' sign is used.

EXAMPLE 8 The minute hand of a clock overtakes the hour hand at intervals of 63 min of the correct time. How much does a clock gain or loss in a day?

(a) $56\frac{8}{77}$ min (b) $58\frac{8}{77}$ min

(c) $56\frac{9}{77}$ min (d) $58\frac{8}{76}$ min

Solution *(a)* As we know that in a correct clock, the min hand gains 55 min spaces over the hour hand in 60 min.

To be together again, the minute hand must gain 60 min over the hour hand.

∵ 55 min are gained in $\left(\frac{60}{55} \times 60\right)$ min

$= 65\frac{5}{11}$ min

But they are together after 63 min.

∴ Gain in 63 min

$$= \left(65\frac{5}{11} - 63\right) = 2\frac{5}{11}\text{ min} = \frac{27}{11}\text{min}$$

∴ Gain in 24 h (one day)

$$= \left(\frac{27}{11} \times \frac{60 \times 24}{63}\right)\text{min} = \frac{4320}{77}\text{min} = 56\frac{8}{77}\text{min}$$

As the result is positive, therefore the clock gains $56\frac{8}{77}$ min.

Practice Exercise

1. Number of hours and minutes from 6 : 14 am to 8 : 02 pm on the same days is
(a) 2 h and 12 min
(b) 12 h and 16 min
(c) 13 h and 48 min
(d) 14 h and 16 min

2. Find the angle between the hour hand and the minute hand of a clock when the time is 4 : 10.
(a) 65° (b) 35°
(c) 125° (d) 60°

3. At what time between 3 o'clock and 4 O'clock, will the hands of a clock be together?
(a) $16\frac{3}{11}$ min past 3 (b) $14\frac{3}{11}$ min past 3
(c) $13\frac{2}{11}$ min past 3 (d) $16\frac{4}{11}$ min past 3

4. At what point of time after 3 O' clock, hour hand and the minute hand are at right angles for the first time?
(a) 9 O' clock (b) 4 h $37\frac{1}{6}$ min
(c) 3 h $30\frac{8}{11}$ min (d) 3 h $32\frac{8}{11}$ min

5. At what time between 9 O'clock and 10 O'clock, will the hands of a clock be in the same straight line but not together?
(a) $16\frac{2}{11}$ min past 9
(b) $16\frac{2}{11}$ min past 10
(c) $16\frac{4}{11}$ min past 9
(d) $16\frac{4}{11}$ min past 10

6. At what time between 2 O'clock and 3 O'clock, will the hands of a clock point in opposite directions?
(a) $\frac{480}{11}$ min past 2 (b) $\frac{485}{11}$ min past 2
(c) $\frac{580}{11}$ min past 2 (d) $\frac{520}{11}$ min past 2

7. At what time between 5 O'clock and 6 O'clock in the morning, will the both hands of a clock be at right angle?
(a) $43\frac{7}{11}$ min past 5 and $1\frac{10}{11}$ min past 6
(b) $43\frac{7}{11}$ min past 5 and $10\frac{10}{11}$ min past 5
(c) $42\frac{7}{11}$ min past 5 and $11\frac{10}{11}$ min past 5
(d) $47\frac{7}{11}$ min past 5 and $1\frac{10}{11}$ min past 6

8. A watch which gains uniformly, is 5 min slow at 7 O'clock in the morning on Sunday and it is 5 min 48 s fast at 7 pm on following Sunday. Which day was it correct?
(a) Friday (b) Saturday
(c) Tuesday (d) Wednesday

9. A clock is set right at 6 am. The clock losses 16 min in 24 h. What will be true time, if the clock indicates 11 pm on 4th day?
(a) 12 o'clock (b) 11 pm (c) 9 pm (d) 2 pm

10. A clock is set right at 9 am. The clock gains 10 min in 24 h. What will be true time, when the clock indicates 2 pm on the following day?
(a) 48 min past 12 (b) 48 min past 11
(c) 48 min past 1 (d) 48 min past 2

11. The minute hand of a clock overtakes the hour hand at intervals of 70 min of the correct time. How much in a day does the clock gain or loss?

(a) $\frac{7200}{77}$ min gain (b) $\frac{7200}{77}$ min loss

(c) $\frac{7300}{77}$ min loss (d) $\frac{7300}{78}$ min gain

12. How much does a watch gain per day, if its hands coincide every 64 min?

(a) 37 min (b) $32\frac{8}{11}$

(c) 31 min (d) None of these

Previous Year's Questions

13. A watch which gains uniformly is 2 min slow at noon on Monday and is 4 min 48 s fast at 2 pm on the following Monday. When was it correct? **[CLAT 2015]**

(a) 2 pm on Tuesday (b) 2 pm on Wednesday

(c) 3 pm on Thursday (d) 1 pm on Friday

14. The angle between the hands of a clock when the time is 4 : 25 am, is **[CLAT 2016]**

(a) $13\frac{1}{2}^\circ$ (b) $17\frac{1}{2}^\circ$

(c) $14\frac{1}{2}^\circ$ (d) $12\frac{1}{2}^\circ$

15. A clock was set correct at 12 O' clock. It loses 10 minutes per hour. What will be the angle between the hour and minute hands of the clock after one hour? **[CLAT 2017]**

(a) 90° (b) 85° (c) 75° (d) 105°

16. How many times from 4 pm to 10 pm, the hands of a clock are at right angles? **[CLAT 2017]**

(a) 11 (b) 6 (c) 9 (d) 10

Answers

1	c	2	a	3	d	4	d	5	c	6	a	7	b	8	d	9	a	10	c
11	b	12	b	13	b	14	b	15	b	16	a								

SOLUTIONS

1. Total hours from 6:14 am morning to evening 6:14 pm = 12 h and total hours from 6:14 pm evening to 8:02 pm evening = 8:02 − 6:14 = 1:48 h

i.e. 1 h and 48 min

∴Total hours and minutes = 12 h + 1 h 48 min
= 13 h and 48 min

2. At 4:10, the hour hand is ahead of minute hand (see picture).

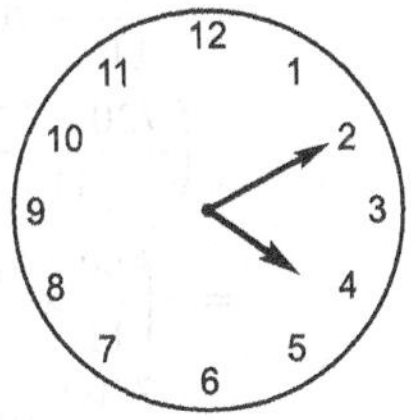

Angle traced by hour hand in 4 min and 10 min

$= \frac{360}{12} \times \frac{25}{6} = 125°$

Similarly, angle traced by minute hand in 10 min $= \frac{360}{60} \times 10 = 60°$

∴ Required angle = 125° − 60° = 65°

3. At 3 O' clock, the hour hand is at 3 and the minute hand is at 12. It means they are 15 min spaces apart.

To be together, the minute hand must gain 15 min over the hour hand.

As we know,

55 min is gained by minute hand in 60 min.

∴15 min will be gained in $\left(\frac{60}{55} \times 15\right)$ min

$= \frac{60 \times 3}{11} = \frac{180}{11} = 16\frac{4}{11}$ min

Hence, the hands will coincide at $16\frac{4}{11}$ min past 3.

4. Clock will make right angle at $(5n + 15) \times \frac{12}{11}$ min past n.

Given that, $n = 3$

$\therefore\ (5 \times 3 + 15) \times \frac{12}{11}$ min past 3.

$= 30 \times \frac{12}{11}$ min past 3.

$= 32\frac{8}{11}$ min past 3.

i.e. 3 h and $32\frac{8}{11}$ min.

5. At 9 O'clock, the hour hand is at 9 and the minute hand is at 12. It means that the two hands are 15 min spaces apart. To be in the same straight line (but not together), they will be 30 min space apart.

$\therefore$ The minute hand will have to gain $(30 - 15) = 15$ min spaces over the hour hand.

As we know,

55 min spaces are gained in 60 min.

$\therefore$ 15 min will be gained in

$\left(\frac{60}{55} \times 15\right)$ min

$= \frac{180}{11} = 16\frac{4}{11}$ min

Hence, the hands will be in the same straight line but not together at $16\frac{4}{11}$ min past 9.

6. Given that $n = 2$ and $(n + 1) = 3\ (n < 6)$

The hands will be at the same straight line at

$\Rightarrow (5n + 30) \times \frac{12}{11}$ min past n.

$\Rightarrow (5 \times 2 + 30) \times \frac{12}{11}$ min past 2.

$\Rightarrow (10 + 30) \times \frac{12}{11}$ min past 2.

$\Rightarrow \frac{40 \times 12}{11}$ min past 2.

$\Rightarrow \frac{480}{11}$ min past 2.

7. Given that, $n = 5$

and $n + 1 = 6$

The hands will make right angle at

$(5n \pm 15) \times \frac{12}{11}$ min past 5.

$\Rightarrow (5 \times 5 \pm 15) \times \frac{12}{11}$ min past 5.

$\Rightarrow (25 + 15) \times \frac{12}{11}$ min past 5 and

$(25 - 15) \times \frac{12}{11}$ min past 5.

$\Rightarrow 40 \times \frac{12}{11}$ min past 5

and $\frac{10 \times 12}{11}$ min past 5.

$\Rightarrow \frac{480}{11}$ min past 5 and

$\frac{120}{11}$ min past 5.

$\Rightarrow 43\frac{7}{11}$ min past 5 and

$10\frac{10}{11}$ min past 5

8. Time from 7 am on Sunday to 7 pm on following Sunday

$= 7$ days 12 h $= 180$ h

$\therefore$ Watch gains $\left(5 + 5\frac{4}{5}\right)$ min

or $\frac{54}{5}$ min in 180 h.

Now, $\frac{54}{5}$ min are gained in 180 h.

$\therefore$ 5 min are gained in

$\left(180 \times \frac{5}{54} \times 5\right)$ h

$= 83$ h 20 min

$= 3$ days 11 h and 20 min

$\therefore$ Watch is correct after 3 days 11 h and 20 min after 7 am of Sunday.

$\therefore$ It will be correct at 20 min past 6 pm on Wednesday.

9. Time from 6 am on a day to 11 pm on 4th day $= 89$ h

Now, 23 h 44 min of this clock $= 24$ h of correct clock

89 h of this clock

$= \left(24 \times \frac{15}{356} \times 89\right)$ h of correct clock $= 90$ h of correct clock

$\therefore$ Correct time will be 12 O'clock (mid-night).

10. Time from 9 am in a day to 2 pm on the following day $= 29$ h.

24 h 10 min of this clock $= 24$ h of the correct clock

or $\frac{145}{6}$ h of this clock $= 24$ h of the correct clock

29 h of this clock

$= \left(24 \times \frac{6}{145} \times 29\right)$ h of the correct clock

$= 28$ h 48 min of correct clock

$\therefore$ The correct time is 28 h 48 min after 9 am. This will be 48 min past 1.

11. Given that, $x = 70$ min

The required result

$= \left(\frac{720}{11} - x\right)\left(\frac{60 \times 24}{x}\right)$ min

$= \left(\frac{720}{11} - 70\right)\left(\frac{60 \times 24}{70}\right)$ min

$= \left(\frac{720 - 770}{11}\right)\left(\frac{60 \times 24}{70}\right)$ min

$= -\left(\frac{50}{11} \times \frac{6 \times 24}{7}\right)$ min

$= -\frac{7200}{77}$ min

[–ve sign indicates that there is a loss.]

12. If the minute hand of a clock overtakes the hour hand at interval x min of the correct time, then clock losses or gains by

$$\left(\frac{720}{11} - x\right) \times \left(\frac{60 \times 24}{x}\right) \text{min}$$

Positive for gain and negative for loss

Here, $x = 64$

putting the value of x in above formula, we get

$$\left(\frac{720}{11} - 64\right) \times \left(\frac{60 \times 24}{64}\right)$$

$$\left(\frac{720 - 704}{11}\right) \times \left(\frac{15 \times 24}{16}\right)$$

$$\frac{16 \times 15}{11} \times \frac{3}{2} = \frac{360}{11} = 32\frac{8}{11}\text{min}$$

13. Time from 12 pm on Monday to 2 pm on the following Monday = 7 days 2 h

$= 170$ h

So, the watch gains

$\left(2 + 4\frac{4}{5}\right)$ min or $\frac{34}{5}$ min in 170 h.

Now, $\frac{34}{5}$ min are gained in 170 h.

$\therefore$ 2 min are gained in

$$\left(170 \times \frac{5}{34} \times 2\right) \text{h} = 50 \text{ h}$$

So, watch is correct in 2 days 2 h after 12 pm on Monday i.e. it will be correct at 2 pm on Wednesday.

14. Required angle

$$= 30\left(\frac{M}{5} - H\right) - \frac{M}{2}$$

$$= 30\left(\frac{25}{5} - 4\right) - \frac{25}{2}$$

$$= 30 - \frac{25}{2}$$

$$= \frac{60 - 25}{2} = \frac{35}{2} = 17\frac{1}{2}^\circ$$

15. After one hour, actual position of a clock is shown in the below figure.

Now, angle traced by hour hand in 50 min

$$= \frac{1}{2} \times 50 = 25^\circ$$

and angle traced by minute hand in 50 min

$$= 6^\circ \times 50 = 300^\circ$$

Now, angle between hour and minute hand

$$= 360^\circ - 300^\circ + 25^\circ$$

$$= 60^\circ + 25^\circ = 85^\circ$$

16. We know that, if the difference between minute and hour hand is 15 min, then it will makes 90°. Between 4 pm to 5 pm, it will make two 90° angles (i.e. 4:05 pm and 4:36)

Similary, for 5 pm to 6 pm 6 pm to 7 pm, 7 pm to 8 pm, 8 pm to 9 pm each will makes two 90° angles. But in 9 pm to 10 pm, it will only makes one 90° angle

$\therefore$ Total number to 90° angles forwed between 4 pm to 10 pm is $(2 \times 5 + 1)$, i.e. 11

LOGICAL REASONING

CHAPTER 01

ANALOGY TEST

'Analogy' means similarity of one object to another in certain aspects. It aims to test the candidate's ability to determine the relationship existing between the two elements of a pair. In questions based on analogy, a pair of words/letters/numbers having a certain relation is given. Another pair is also given but an element of it, is missing. The candidate is required to find the missing element from the given alternatives that will complete the second pair having the same relationship as that of the first pair.

TYPES OF ANALOGY

Analogy may be broadly divided into the following types

1. Word Analogy

In word analogy, the two words are related to each other in some way.

The relationship can be based on following

Word and Synonym

e.g. Vacant : Empty

Vacant and Empty are synonym to each other.

Some more examples are given below

(i) Substitute : Replace	(ii) Brim : Edge	(iii) House : Home
(iv) Mend : Repair	(v) Sedate : Calm	(vi) Ban : Prohibition

Word and Antonym

e.g. Gentle : Harsh

Gentle and Harsh are antonym to each other.

Some more examples are given below.

(i) Chaos : Peace (ii) Cruel : Kind
(iii) Sink : Float (iv) Initial : Final
(v) Lend : Borrow (vi) Fresh : Stale

State and Capital

e.g. Madhya Pradesh : Bhopal

Bhopal is the capital of Madhya Pradesh.

Some more examples are given below

(i) Goa : Panaji
(ii) Sikkim : Gangtok
(iii) Uttar Pradesh : Lucknow
(iv) Karnataka : Bengaluru

Country and Capital

e.g. Iraq : Baghdad

Baghdad is the capital of Iraq.

Some more examples are given below

(i) Japan : Tokyo
(ii) France : Paris
(iii) Russia : Moscow
(iv) Bangladesh : Dhaka
(v) China : Beijing
(vi) S. Korea : Seoul

Country and Currency

e.g. Turkey : Lira

Lira is the currency of Turkey.

Some more examples are given below

(i) Kuwait : Dinar
(ii) Oman : Rial
(iii) Myanmar : Kyat
(iv) Japan : Yen

Male and Female

e.g. Dog : Bitch

Bitch is the female Dog.

Some more examples are given below

(i) Nephew : Niece (ii) Lion : Lioness
(iii) Drone : Bee (iv) Horse : Mare
(v) Son : Daughter (vi) Stag : Doe

Worker and Tool

e.g. Sculptor : Chisel

Chisel is the tool used by Sculptor.

Some more examples are given below

(i) Tailor : Needle
(ii) Carpenter : Saw
(iii) Chef : Knife
(iv) Soldier : Gun
(v) Surgeon : Scalpel
(vi) Woodcutter : Axe
(vii) Blacksmith : Anvil
(viii) Author : Pen

Product and Raw Material

e.g. Metal : Ore

Ore is the raw material for Metal.

Some more examples are given below

(i) Wall : Brick
(ii) Jewellery : Gold
(iii) Oil : Seed
(iv) Furniture : Wood
(v) Paper : Pulp
(vi) Shoes : Leather

Quantity and Unit

e.g. Pressure : Pascal

Pascal is the unit of Pressure.

Some more examples are given below

(i) Work : Joule (ii) Power : Watt
(iii) Time : Seconds (iv) Force : Newton
(v) Current : Ampere (vi) Length : Metre
(vii) Volume : Litre (viii) Area : Hectare

Instrument and Measurement

e.g. Ammeter : Current

Ammeter is an instrument used to measure Current.

Some more examples are given below

(i) Sphygmomanometer : Blood Pressure
(ii) Scale : Length
(iii) Hygrometer : Humidity
(iv) Odometer : Speed
(v) Barometer : Pressure
(vi) Anemometer : Wind Speed

Animal and Young One

e.g. Dog : Puppy

Puppy is the young one of Dog.

Some more examples are given below.

(i) Sheep : Lamb
(ii) Cat : Kitten
(iii) Lion : Cub
(iv) Horse : Colt/Filly/Foal
(v) Cow : Calf
(vi) Hen : Chick

Individual and Dwelling Place

e.g. Horse : Stable

Stable is the dwelling place of Horse.

Some more examples are given below.

(i) Birds : Nest (ii) Bee : Hive
(iii) Lion : Den (iv) Pig : Sty
(v) King : Palace (vi) Owl : Barn

Individual and Class

e.g. Whale : Mammal

Whale belongs to the class of Mammal.

Some more examples are given below.

(i) Rat : Rodent
(ii) Ostrich : Bird
(iii) Snake : Reptile
(iv) Man : Mammal

Study and Topic

e.g. Entomology : Insects

Entomology is the study of Insects.

Some more examples are given below.

(i) Oology : Eggs
(ii) Zoology : Animals
(iii) Ornithology : Birds
(iv) Botany : Plants
(v) Seismology : Earthquakes
(vi) Onomatology : Names

EXAMPLE 1 A 'Cow' is related to 'Calf' in the same way as 'Goat' is related to

(a) Puppy (b) Kid
(c) Lamb (d) Colt

Solution ***(b)*** Calf is the youngone of cow, similarly kid is the youngone of goat.

Directions (Ex. 2 - 4) *Find out the relationship between the first two words and choose the missing word from the given alternatives, which beass the same relationship to the third word, as the first two bear.*

EXAMPLE 2 King : Throne :: Judge : ?

(a) Lawyer (b) Bench (c) Court (d) Trial

Solution ***(b)*** As 'King' is related to the 'Throne', in the same way 'Judge' is related to 'Bench'.

EXAMPLE 3 Giant : Dwarf :: Genius : ?

(a) Wicked (b) Gentle (c) Idiot (d) Tiny

Solution ***(c)*** 'Dwarf' is antonym of 'Giant', in the same way 'Idiot' is antonym of 'Genius'.

EXAMPLE 4 Scientist : Laboratory :: Actor : ?

(a) Casino (b) Gallery
(c) Stage (d) Site

Solution ***(c)*** 'Laboratory' is the working place of 'Scientist', in the same way 'Stage' is the working place of 'Actor'.

EXAMPLE 5 Find the pair in which the words bear the same relationship to each other as similar to the words of the given pair bear.

Austria : Vienna

(a) Pakistan : Lahore (b) Egypt : Cairo
(c) USA : Orlando (d) Germany : London

Solution ***(b)*** 'Vienna' is the capital of 'Austria' and in the same way 'Cairo' is the capital of 'Egypt'.

EXAMPLE 6 Out of the four given alternatives choose that alternative as your answer which is similar to the given words.

Abandon : Forsake : Desert

(a) Down (b) Frown
(c) Prank (d) Leave

Solution ***(d)*** All the given words (Abandon, Forsake, Desert) are synonymous having meaning 'Leave'. Hence, the other synonymous word from the given alternatives will be 'Leave'.

EXAMPLE 7 Find out the relasionship among these words and choose another group with similar relationship from the options provided.

Furniture : Table : Almirah

(a) Building : Wall : Brick
(b) Fruit : Orange : Apple
(c) Mother : Father : Sister
(d) Sea : Road : City

Solution *(b)* Table and Almirah are both 'Furniture' and similarly 'Orange' and 'Apple' are both 'Fruits'. Clearly, both second and third belong to the class denoted by the first.

2. Alphabet Analogy

In alphabet analogy, there is a relationship between the letters or group of letters. The relationship can be based on increasing/decreasing position of letters in english alphabet, reverse order of position of letters and vowels or consonants etc.

The candidate must remember the position of letters in English alphabetical order to find the relationship between them.

Here, following table shows the letters' position in English alphabetical series.

Forward	1	2	3	4	5	6	7	8	9	10	11	12	13	14	15	16	17	18	19	20	21	22	23	24	25	26
Alphabet	A	B	C	D	E	F	G	H	I	J	K	L	M	N	O	P	Q	R	S	T	U	V	W	X	Y	Z
Backward	26	25	24	23	22	21	20	19	18	17	16	15	14	13	12	11	10	9	8	7	6	5	4	3	2	1

EXAMPLE 8 Complete the second pair in the same way as first pair.

N H P : O G Q : : T L J : ?

(a) U K L (b) V K K (c) U K K (d) K U K

Solution *(c)* As, Similarly,

N —(+1)→ O   T —(+1)→ U
H —(−1)→ G   L —(−1)→ K
P —(+1)→ Q   J —(+1)→ K

Directions (Ex. 9 and 10) *Complete the second pair in the same way as first pair.*

EXAMPLE 9 ACEG : DFHJ :: QSUW : ?

(a) TVNZ (b) TVZX (c) TVXZ (d) XVTZ

Solution *(c)*

As, A, C, E, G each +3 → D, F, H, J

Similarly, Q, S, U, W each +3 → T, V, X, Z

EXAMPLE 10 NEUROTIC : TICRONEU :: PSYCHOTIC : ?

(a) TICCOHPSY (b) TICOCHPSY
(c) TICCHOPSY (d) TICHCOPSY

Solution *(c)*

As, Similarly,

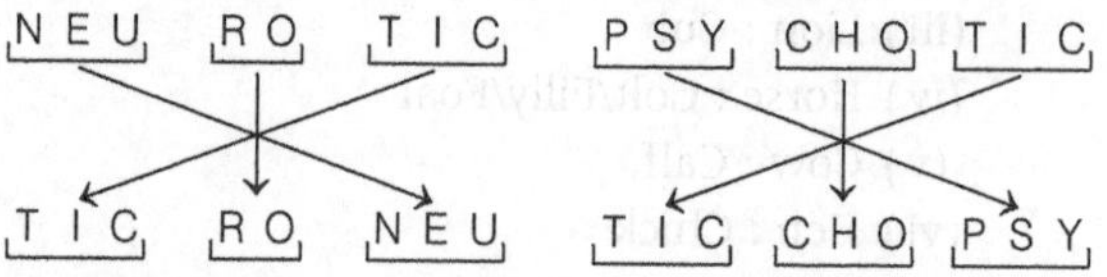

3. Number Analogy

In number analogy, the numbers in a pair are related to each other in a certain way. The relationship can be based on—even and odd numbers, square and cube of digits, addition and subtraction of numbers, multiplication and division of numbers etc.

Directions (Ex. 11-13) *Choose the term that will replace the question mark(?).*

EXAMPLE 11 36 : 18 : : 40 : ?

(a) 20 (b) 25 (c) 35 (d) 21

Solution *(a)* As, $36 \div 2 = 18$
Similarly, $40 \div 2 = 20$

EXAMPLE 12 11 : 121 : : ?

(a) 6 : 35 (b) 8 : 65
(c) 13 : 169 (d) 15 : 231

Solution *(c)* As, $11^2 = 121$
Similarly, $13^2 = 169$

EXAMPLE 13 6 : 10 : 16 : : ?

(a) 9, 12, 18 (b) 5, 10, 15
(c) 6, 11, 12 (d) 7, 11, 17

Solution *(d)* As, Similarly,

6 —(+4)→ 10 —(+6)→ 16   7 —(+4)→ 11 —(+6)→ 17

EXAMPLE 14 Find out the see among the four sets which is like the given set (13 : 20 :27).

(a) (3 : 11 : 18) (b) (18 : 25 : 32)
(c) (18 : 27 : 72) (d) (7 : 14 : 28)

Solution *(c)* As, $13 + 7 = 20$ and $20 + 7 = 27$
Similarly, $18 + 7 = 25$ and $25 + 7 = 32$

4. Mixed Analogy

In mixed analogy, the combination of letters and numbers are given in a pair. The letters and numbers are related to each other in a certain way. The relationship can be based on the position of the alphabets/letters, sum or product of the position of alphabet/letters etc.

Directions (Ex. 15-18) *What will come in place of question mark(?)?*

EXAMPLE 15 NEWS : 14, 5, 23, 19 :: PAPER : ?

(a) 16, 5, 16, 1, 18 (b) 18, 5, 16, 1, 16
(c) 16, 1, 16, 5, 18 (d) 32, 2, 32, 10, 36

Solution *(c)* Each letter is assigned its positional value in English alphabetical order.

∴ PAPER →16, 1, 16, 5, 18

EXAMPLE 16 NAME : 04 :: TRUMPET : ?

(a) 11 (b) 08 (c) 07 (d) 10

Solution *(c)* Here, 'NAME' has 4 letters and similarly TRUMPET has 7 letters.

EXAMPLE 17 TIME : 7, 18, 14, 22 :: CLOCK : ?

(a) 22, 15, 14, 24, 16
(b) 24, 15, 12, 24, 16
(c) 24, 14, 12, 15, 16
(d) 25, 15, 12, 16, 24

Solution *(b)* Each letter is assigned its positional value in backward order of English alphabet.

∴ CLOCK → 24, 15, 12, 24, 16

EXAMPLE 18 COME : 36 :: PRANK : ?

(a) 18 (b) 60
(c) 16 (d) 32

Solution *(b)* Here, in both the pairs, letters' positional value in forward order in English alphabet have been added to establish analogy.

As,

C	O	M	E	
↓	↓	↓	↓	
3 +	15 +	13 +	5	= 36

Similarly,

P	R	A	N	K	
↓	↓	↓	↓	↓	
16 +	18 +	1 +	14 +	11	= 60

Practice Exercise

1. 'Sports' is related to 'Logo' in the same way as 'Nation' is related to

(a) Emblem (b) Animal (c) Ruler (d) Anthem

2. 'Hour' is related to 'Second' in the same way as 'Tertiary' is related to

(a) Ordinary (b) Secondary
(c) Primary (d) Intermediary

Directions (Q. Nos. 3-5) *In each of the following questions, there is a certain relation between two given words on one side of (: :) and one word is given on another side of (: :) while another word is to be found from the given alternatives, having the same relation with this word as the words of the given pair bear. Choose the best alternative.*

3. White : Peace : : Red : ?

(a) Violence (b) Roses
(c) Hatred (d) Cleanliness

4. Electricity : Wire : : Water : ?

(a) Pipe (b) River (c) Jug (d) Bottle

5. Street : Lane : : Road : ?

(a) Avenue (b) Highway
(c) Footpath (d) Junction

Directions (Q. Nos. 6 and 7) *The following questions consist of two words each of that have certain relationship between each other, followed by four lettered pairs of words. Select the related pair that has the same relationship as the original pair of words.*

6. Numismatist : Coins

(a) Philatelist : Stamps
(b) Jeweller : Jewels
(c) Cartographer : Maps
(d) Geneticist : Chromosomes

7. Cells : Cytology

(a) Worms : Ornithology
(b) Insects : Entomology
(c) Diseases : Physiology
(d) Tissues : Morphology

Directions (Q. Nos. 8 and 9) *In each of the following questions, three words are given which have something in common among themselves. Out of three four given alternatives, choose that alternative as your answer which is similar to the given words.*

8. Bhopal, Panaji, Gandhinagar

(a) Amritsar (b) Allahabad (c) Patna (d) Baroda

9. Yuan, Kyat, Lira

(a) Dirham (b) Turkey (c) Madrid (d) Mass

Directions (Q. Nos. 10 and 11) *In each of the following questions, some words are given which are related in some way. The same relationship obtains among the words in one of the four alternatives given under it. Find the correct alternatives.*

10. School : College : University

(a) Transistor : Radio : Television
(b) Puppy : Dog : Bitch
(c) Village : City : Suburb
(d) Continent : Country : State

11. Green : Blue : Yellow

(a) Pink : Red : White
(b) Orange : Yellow : Black
(c) Brown : Black : Blue
(d) Yellow : Red : Green

Directions (Q. Nos. 12 and 15) *In each of the following questions, there is some relationship between the two terms to the left of (::) and the same relationship holds between the two terms to its right. Also, in each question, one term to the right of (::) is missing. This term is given as one of the alternatives, from the given alternatives below each question. Find out this term from the given alternatives.*

12. FJUL : BOQQ : : LHRX : ?

(a) BKPR (b) MNCC (c) HRYY (d) HMNC

13. EJOT : VQLG : : BGLQ : ?

(a) AEIM (b) AFKP (c) YTOJ (d) ZUPK

14. RH : 13 : : DP : ?

(a) 20 (b) 10
(c) 15 (d) 18

15. $\frac{M}{X} : \frac{31}{42} : : \frac{L}{O} : ?$

(a) $\frac{21}{32}$ (b) $\frac{15}{23}$ (c) $\frac{21}{51}$ (d) $\frac{11}{41}$

Directions (Q. Nos. 16 and 17) *In each of the following questions, there is a certain relationship between two given numbers on one side of (: :) and one number is given on the other side of (: :) while another number is to be found from the given alternatives having the same relationship with this number as the numbers of the given pair. Choose the best alternative.*

16. 20 : 11 : : 102 : ?

(a) 49 (b) 52 (c) 61 (d) 98

17. 7 : 50 : : 9 : ?

(a) 64 (b) 81 (c) 90 (d) 99

Directions (Q. Nos. 18 and 19) *In each of the following questions, choose that set of numbers from the four alternative sets, that is similar to the given set.*

18. Given set : (2, 14, 16)

(a) (2, 7, 8) (b) (2, 9, 16)
(c) (3, 21, 24) (d) (4, 16, 18)

19. Given set : (32, 24, 8)

(a) (26, 32, 42)
(b) (34, 24, 14)
(c) (24, 16, 0)
(d) (42, 34, 16)

Previous Year's Questions

Directions (Q. Nos. 20 and 24) *In each of the following questions a related pair of words is followed by four pairs of words or pharses. Select the pair that best expresses the a relationship similar to the one expressed in the question pair.* **[CLAT 2011]**

20. Action : Reaction

(a) Introvert : Extrovert
(b) Assail : Defend
(c) Diseased : Treatment
(d) Death : Rebirth

21. Sorrow : Misery

(a) Love : Obsession
(b) Amity : Harmony
(c) Happiness : Joy
(d) Enemy : Hatred

22. Drama : Audience

(a) Brawl : Vagabonds
(d) Game : Spectators
(c) Art : Critic
(d) Movie : Actors

23. Nuts : Bolts

(a) Nitty : Gritty (b) Bare : Feet
(c) Naked : Clothes (d) Hard : Soft

24. Book : Author

(a) Rain : Flood
(b) Light : Switch
(c) Symphony : Composer
(d) Song : Music

Directions (Q. Nos. 25-27) *In each of the following questions, a related pair of words is followed by four pairs of words or phrases. Select the pair that best expresses a relationship similar to the one expressed in the question pair.* **[CLAT 2014]**

25. India : Tricolour

(a) China: Sickle and Hammer
(b) UK: Red Cross
(c) USA : Stars and Stripes
(d) None of the above

26. Statute : Law

(a) Provision : Clause (b) Chapter : Exercise
(c) University : School (d) Section : Illustration

27. Buddhists: Pagoda

(a) Parsis : Temple (b) Christians: Cross
(c) Jains : Sun Temple (d) Jews: Synagogue

Directions (Q. Nos. 28-32) *Two words, which have a certain relation, are paired. Select a correct option to substitute the question mark so as to make a similar relational pair with the word given after double colon (::).* **[CLAT 2014]**

28. Bow : Arrow : : Pistol : ?

(a) Gun (b) Shoot
(c) Rifle (d) Bullet

29. Eye : Wink : : Heart : ?
(a) Throb (b) Move
(c) Pump (d) Respirate

30. Ocean : Water : : Glacier : ?
(a) Cooling (b) Cave
(c) Ice (d) Mountain

31. Prima facie : On the first view :: In pari delicto : ?
(a) Both parties equally at fault
(b) While litigation is pending
(c) A remedy for all disease
(d) Beyond powers

32. Delusion : hallucination :: Chagrin : ?
(a) Illusion
(b) Ordered
(c) Cogent
(d) Annoyance

Directions (Q. Nos. 33-34) *These questions consist of a related pair of words, followed by four pair of words. Choose the pair that best represents a similar relationship as the one expressed in the given pair of words.* **[CLAT 2016]**

33. SANDERLING : BIRD
(a) Cat : Mare (b) Mastiff : Dog
(c) Frog : Toad (d) Water : Fish

34. WAITER : RESTAURANT
(a) Driver : Car (b) Author : Book
(c) Teacher : School (d) Actor : Acting

35. If Oceans are Deserts, then Waves are
(a) Water (b) Powerful **[CLAT 2016]**
(c) Ripples (d) Sand Dunes

36. 9 : 72 : : 8 : ? **[CLAT 2017]**
(a) 43 (b) 18 (c) 34 (d) 64

Answers

1	*a*	2	*c*	3	*a*	4	*a*	5	*a*	6	*a*	7	*b*	8	*c*	9	*a*	10	*c*
11	*a*	12	*d*	13	*c*	14	*b*	15	*c*	16	*b*	17	*a*	18	*c*	19	*c*	20	*b*
21	*c*	22	*b*	23	*c*	24	*c*	25	*c*	26	*a*	27	*d*	28	*d*	29	*a*	30	*c*
31	*a*	32	*d*	33	*b*	34	*c*	35	*d*	36	*d*								

SOLUTIONS

1. The symbol 'Logo' is related to 'Sports'. Likewise 'Emblem' is related to a 'Nation'.

2. 'Hour' is 3rd position after 'Second' in time measurement, similarly 'Tertiary' is the 3rd position after 'Primary' in the order of raking.

3. 'White' is the symbol of 'Peace', in the same way 'Red' is the symbol of 'Violence'.

4. Second is used to transmit first.

5. Second is a smaller form of the first.

6. 'Numismatist' is the man who deals with 'Coins'. In the same way 'Philatelist' is the man who collects the 'Stamps'.

7. 'Cytology' is the science of study of 'Cells'. In the same way 'Entomology' is the science of study of 'Insects'.

8. All are the capitals of Indian states.

9. All are the currencies of different countries.

10. Second and third are bigger and more sophisticated forms than the first and second, respectively.

11. First is colour obtained by the combination of other two colours.

12. As,
$F \xrightarrow{-4} B$
$J \xrightarrow{+5} O$
$U \xrightarrow{-4} Q$
$L \xrightarrow{+5} Q$

Similarly,
$L \xrightarrow{-4} H$
$H \xrightarrow{+5} M$
$R \xrightarrow{-4} N$
$X \xrightarrow{+5} C$

13. Each letter of the first group occupies the same position from the beginning of the alphabet as the corresponding letter of the second group occupies from the end of the alphabet.

As,

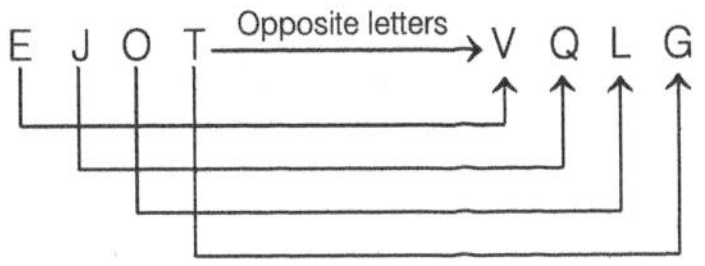

Similarly,

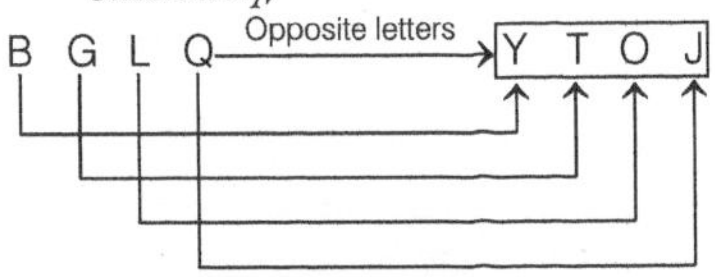

14. As, RH $\Rightarrow (18 + 8) \div 2$

$\Rightarrow \quad 26 \div 2 = 13$

Similarly, DP $\Rightarrow \quad (4 + 16) \div 2$

$\Rightarrow \quad 20 \div 2 = 10$

15. As, M ⟶ 13 ⟶ 31

X ⟶ 24 ⟶ 42

Similarly, L ⟶ 12 ⟶ 21

O ⟶ 15 ⟶ 51

16. As,

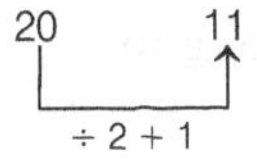

Similarly,

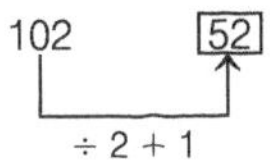

17. As,

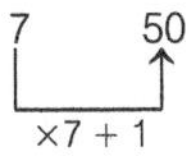

Similarly,

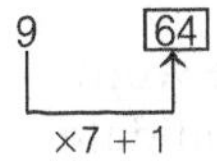

18. As,

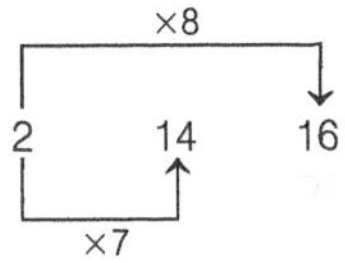

Similarly,

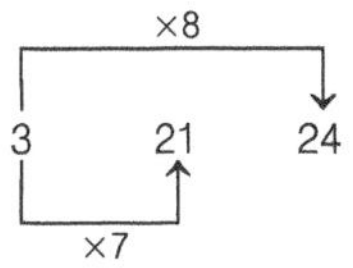

19. As,

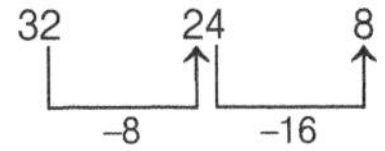

Similarly,

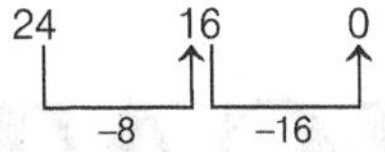

Previous Year's Solutions

20. Reaction is in response to an action just as a defence is in response to an assail.

21. Synonym pair

22. Drama is viewed by audience similarly game is viewed by spectators.

23. As nuts are covered with bolts in the same way a naked is covered with clothes.

24. Book is written by author in the same way symphony is composed by composer.

25. Given relation India: Tricolour is the relation of country and corresponding national flag.

26. Statute is a legislative body pass the law. Similarly provision has a clause.

27. As Buddhists are gathered in pagoda for worship similarly jews are gathered in synagogue.

28. A bow is a weapon for shooting arrows.
In the same way, pistol is used to fire the bullets.

29. Latter represents the movements of former.

30. As 'Ocean' is related to 'water'. In the same way 'glacier' is related to 'ice'.

31. Prima facie, is a latin expression and the meaning of this is 'On the first view'. In the same way the meaning of, In pari delicto is 'Both parties equally at fault'.

32. The words are synonyms of each other . So chagrin synonym is annoyance.

33. As, sanderling is a kind of a bird.
Similarly, mastiff is a kind of a dog.

34. As, the working place of waiter is restaurant, similarly, the working place of a teacher is school.

35. As, Waves are found in Oceans, similarly Sand Dunes are found in Deserts.

36. $9 \times 8 = 72$

$8 \times 8 = 64$

CHAPTER 02

CLASSIFICATION

Classification involves putting various objects/things into a class or group on the basis of certain common properties and then find out the odd object/thing from the group.

In this chapter, the questions are based on words, letters and numerals. In these questions, four elements are given, out of which one does not belong to the group. The candidate is required to find the 'odd one'.

TYPES OF CLASSIFICATION

Classification may be broadly divided into the following four types

1. Word Classification

In word classification, a group of four words is given in which all the words except one are related to one another in a particular manner. The candidate has to identify the odd word that does not belong to the group.

The relationship among the word classification is generally based on the following.

(i) Synonym of words (ii) Antonym of words (iii) Category of items etc

EXAMPLE 1 Choose the odd word.

(a) Car (b) Bus (c) Scooter (d) Jeep

Solution ***(c)*** All except 'Scooter' are four wheelers.

EXAMPLE 2 Find the odd pair of words

(a) Students : Scholar (b) Paddy : Rice (c) Soldier : Warrior (d) Politician : Leader

Solution ***(b)*** In all pair except (b), the first, when becomes an expert is known as second.

2. Number Classification

In number classification, there is a similarity among the numbers or group of numbers. The candidate has to identify the odd number or group of numbers which does not belong to the group.

The number classification is generally based on the following similarities

(i) Square and square root of a number
(ii) Cube and cube root of a number
(iii) Even and odd number
(iv) Prime number
(v) Divisibility test of a number, etc.

EXAMPLE 3 Choose the number which is difference from others.

(a) 25 (b) 9 (c) 16 (d) 18

Solution *(d)* Except 18, all others are square of natural numbers as $(5)^2 = 25$, $(3)^2 = 9$, $(4)^2 = 16$

EXAMPLE 4 Find the pair of numbers which is different from others.

(a) 4-16 (b) 3-12 (c) 7-28 (d) 5-15

Solution *(d)* All except '5-15' have the second number four times the first number.

3. Letter Classification

In letter classification, there is a similarity or pattern among the letters in the group and the candidate has to identify the pattern and select the one which does not follow the common pattern in the group.

The relationship among the letters is based on the following

(i) Position of letters in English alphabet
(ii) Vowel and consonant
(iii) Reverse order of letters, etc.

EXAMPLE 5 Choose the odd one.

(a) LNJ (b) RTP (c) NPK (d) FHD

Solution *(c)* As,

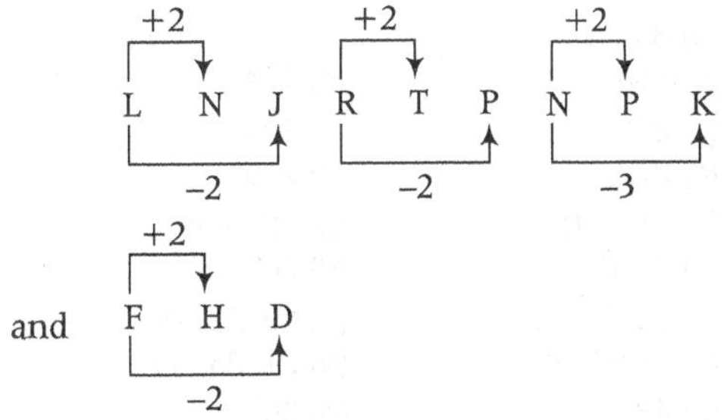

Clearly, letters group NPK follows different pattern from others.
Hence, 'NPK' does not belong to the group.

4. Mixed Classification

In mixed classification, the combination of both the letters and numbers are given as elements. All the elements, i.e. letters and numbers follow a certain common pattern but one element does not follow that common pattern.

The candidate has to find out the odd element on the basis of the common pattern.

The pattern can be based on positional values of letters in English alphabet.

EXAMPLE 6 Choose the odd one.

(a) C3 (b) H8
(c) T19 (d) N14

Solution *(c)* Here, the positional value of the given letters is given. So, T19 is odd one, since the positional value of T is 20.

Practice Exercise

Directions (Q. Nos 1-20) *In the following questions three out of the four alternatives are same in a certain way and so form a group. Find the odd one that does not belong to the group.*

1. (a) Huge (b) Tiny
(c) Heavy (d) Small

2. (a) Ring (b) Tyre
(c) Plate (d) Bangle

3. (a) Shimla (b) Ooty
(c) Darjeeling (d) Agra

4. (a) Swimming (b) Sailling
(c) Diving (d) Driving

5. (a) Blackmail (b) Smuggling
(c) Snobbery (d) Forgery

6. (a) Rigveda (b) Yajurveda
(c) Atharveda (d) Ayurveda

7. (a) Carpenter (b) Goldsmith (c) Blacksmith (d) Driver

8. (a) 68 (b) 85 (c) 153 (d) 174

9. (a) 240 (b) 304 (c) 272 (d) 210

10. (a) (29, 31) (b) (47, 49) (c) (5, 7) (d) (11, 13)

11. (a) 14, 17, 23 (b) 19, 22, 28 (c) 17, 20, 26 (d) 21, 23, 30

12. (a) 4867 (b) 5555 (c) 6243 (d) 6655

13. (a) 1625 (b) 3649 (c) 6481 (d) 5025

14. (a) 46, 57 (b) 38, 49 (c) 41, 52 (d) 64, 73

15. (a) TPLI (b) YUQM (c) RNJF (d) SOKJ

16. (a) MORV (b) CEHL (c) CENT (d) JLOS

17. (a) dcba (b) zyxw (c) srpq (d) hgfe

18. (a) DACB (b) EBCD (c) SPQR (d) XUVW

19. (a) A8C (b) D22G (c) H42M (d) F34J

20. (a) BdEg (b) PrSu (c) KmNp (d) TwXz

Directions (Q. Nos 21 and 22) *In each of the following questions, four pairs of words are given, out of which of words in all pairs except one, bear common relationship. Choose the odd pair.*

21. (a) Death : Disease (b) Milk : Butter (c) Grape : Wine (d) Water : Oxygen

22. (a) Oil : Lamp (b) Water : Tap (c) Oxygen : Life (d) Power : Machine

Directions (Q. Nos 23-25) *Choose the odd numbers pair/group in each of the following questions.*

23. (a) 80-9 (b) 64-8 (c) 36-6 (d) 49-7

24. (a) 1-1 (b) 9-729 (c) 7-343 (d) 1-100

25. (a) 547-563 (b) 71-55 (c) 517-523 (d) 248-231

Previous Year's Questions

Directions (Q. Nos 26-28) *Of the four alternatives given in each of the following questions, find the one which is different from the rest.* **[CLAT 2012]**

26. (a) Fast- Slow (b) Bright-Dark (c) Day-Night (d) Valley-Depth

27. (a) Body-Hand (b) Foot-Ankle (c) Eye-Ear (d) Wrist-Finger

28. (a) Snake-Frog (b) Goat-Hen (c) Dog-Cat (d) Tiger-Deer

29. Find the odd one out from the following group.
WINDSHIELD, SPARK PLUG, CLUTCH PEDAL, CAR, ENGINE **[CLAT 2016]**
(a) Car (b) Windshield (c) Engine (d) Spark plug

30. Which word in the following group does not belong to the others?
PROSPER, EXCITE, THRIVE, FLOURISH **[CLAT 2016]**
(a) Flourish (b) Prosper (c) Thrive (d) Excite

Directions (Q. Nos. 31 and 32) *Find the odd one out from the following alternatives.* **[CLAT 2017]**

31. (a) Exact estimate (b) Only choice (c) Clearly visible (d) Open secret

32. (a) Cruise (b) Crusade (c) Campaign (d) Explation

Answers

1	*c*	2	*c*	3	*d*	4	*d*	5	*c*	6	*d*	7	*d*	8	*d*	9	*d*	10	*b*
11	*d*	12	*d*	13	*d*	14	*d*	15	*c*	16	*c*	17	*c*	18	*a*	19	*d*	20	*d*
21	*a*	22	*b*	23	*a*	24	*d*	25	*d*	26	*d*	27	*c*	28	*b*	29	*a*	30	*d*
31	*d*	32	*a*																

SOLUTIONS

1. Except 'Heavy', all others are used to denote the size. But 'Heavy', denotes weight.
2. Except 'Plate' , all other things have hollow body.
3. Except Agra, all others are hill stations.
4. Except 'Driving', all other activities are related to water but Driving is related to road.
5. Except 'Snobbery', all other words are related to crime.
6. Ayurveda is the branch of medicine. All others are Vedas.
7. Except 'Driver', all three can made their specialization but only 'Driver' serves his work.
8. Except 174, all others are multiple of 17.
9. Except 210, in all other numbers, when we divide the number by 2, we get an even number.
10. Except (47, 49), all other options have prime numbers.
11. As,

$$14+3=17 \rightarrow 17+6=23$$
$$19+3=22 \rightarrow 22+6=28$$
$$17+3=20 \rightarrow 20+6=26$$
$$\boxed{21+2=23 \rightarrow 23+7=30}$$

So, (21, 23, 30) is different.

12. As, $4867 \rightarrow 4+8+6+7=25$
which is divisible by 5.
$5555 \rightarrow 5+5+5+5=20$
which is divisible by 5.
$6243 \rightarrow 6+2+4+3=15$
which is divisible by 5.
But $6655 \rightarrow 6+6+5+5=22$
which is not divisible by 5.

13.

16	25	36	49	64	81	and	50	25
↓	↓	↓	↓	↓	↓		↓	↓
4^2	5^2	6^2	7^2	8^2	9^2		$*^2$	5^2

50 is not a square of any natural number.
So, 5025 is different from others.

14. Except 64-73, all others are having difference of 11.
15. Except RNJF, all others contain one vowel.
16. Except option (c), all other options follow the similar pattern as.

$M \xrightarrow{+2} O \xrightarrow{+3} R \xrightarrow{+4} V$, $C \xrightarrow{+2} E \xrightarrow{+3} H \xrightarrow{+4} L$

$\boxed{C \xrightarrow{+2} E \xrightarrow{+9} N \xrightarrow{+6} T}$ and $J \xrightarrow{+2} L \xrightarrow{+3} O \xrightarrow{+4} S$

From the above, it is clear that letters group CENT is different from all others.

17. Except option (c), in all other options, the continuous letters in reverse order are given.
18. Option (a) shows different pattern from the rest others as

$$\boxed{D \xrightarrow{-3} A \xrightarrow{+2} C \xrightarrow{-1} B}$$

$$E \xrightarrow{-3} B \xrightarrow{+1} C \xrightarrow{+1} D$$
$$S \xrightarrow{-3} P \xrightarrow{+1} Q \xrightarrow{+1} R$$
$$X \xrightarrow{-3} U \xrightarrow{+1} V \xrightarrow{+1} W$$

Previous Year's Solutions

26. Except 'Valley-Depth', in all others both words are opposite to each other.
27. Except 'Eye-Ear', in all others, one is the past of other.
28. Except 'Goat-Hen', in all others first animal trace to second.
29. Except Car, all others are different parts of a car.
30. Except Excite, all other words mean 'to grow'.
31. Open secret is odd.
32. Cruise is a journey by ship.

CHAPTER 03

CODING DECODING

The method that is used to hide the actual meaning of a word or message is known as 'coding', while decoding is the method of breaking the code to understand the actual meaning of that message. In these questions, a basic word is given with its code. The candidates are required to understand the coding method/pattern/rule and find out the code for another word following the same method/pattern/rule.

To solve the questions based on coding-decoding, the candidate should remember the positional values of letters in English alphabetical order.

Note We have already discussed the letters positional values in English alphabetical order in chapter 1 Analogy Test.

TYPES OF CODING

There are 5 types of coding which are discussed below

1. Letter Coding

In letter coding, the letters of the word are replaced by certain other letters according to a specific pattern/rule. The candidate is required to detect the coding pattern/rule and answer the questions accordingly.

EXAMPLE 1 If 'ELCSUM' is the code for 'MUSCLE', then which of the following will be the code for 'LATIPAC'?

(a) CONFESS (b) CONDUCE (c) CAPITAL (d) CHAPRICE

Solution *(c)* Letters of the word have been reversed.

As, E L C S U M ⟶ M U S C L E

Similarly,

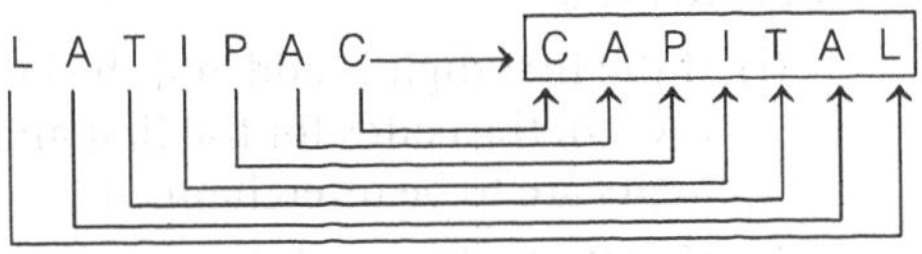

Example 2 In a certain code language, 'STRAIN' is written as 'UWTDKQ'. How will 'PLACES' be written in that code?

(a) RNDFGV (b) RODEGV
(c) ROCFHV (d) ROCFGV

Solution *(d)* As,

S $\xrightarrow{+2}$ U
T $\xrightarrow{+3}$ W
R $\xrightarrow{+2}$ T
A $\xrightarrow{+3}$ D
I $\xrightarrow{+2}$ K
N $\xrightarrow{+3}$ Q

Similarly,

P $\xrightarrow{+2}$ R
L $\xrightarrow{+3}$ O
A $\xrightarrow{+2}$ C
C $\xrightarrow{+3}$ F
E $\xrightarrow{+2}$ G
S $\xrightarrow{+3}$ V

Example 3 In a coding system, 'APPLE' is represented as 'ZKKOV'. In such system, 'COW' will be represented as

(a) XLD (b) XMD
(c) WLE (d) WDL

Solution *(a)* Here, each letter is coded by the letter of its opposite position.

As,

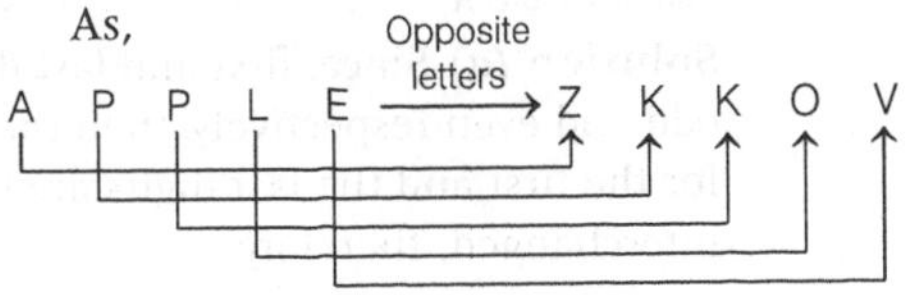

Similarly,

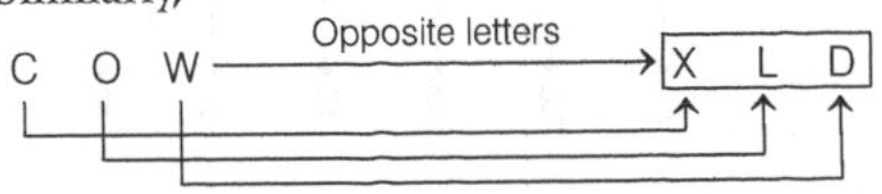

Example 4 If the word 'TABLECLOTH' is coded as 'XEMRANRIXT', then how can 'HOTEL' be coded?

(a) RIXAT (b) TIXAR
(c) TAXIR (d) RAXIT

Solution *(b)*

As,

T	A	B	L	E	C	L	O	T	H
↓	↓	↓	↓	↓	↓	↓	↓	↓	↓
X	E	M	R	A	N	R	I	X	T

Similarly,

H	O	T	E	L
↓	↓	↓	↓	↓
T	I	X	A	R

2. Number/Symbol Coding

In this type of coding, either numerical values or symbols or both are assigned to the letters of the word. And the same substitution helps to find out the code of the word given in the question.

Example 5 If 'HINDU' is coded as '61257' and 'MAN' is coded as '932', then 'INDIAN' will be written in the code language as

(a) 125312 (b) 125132 (c) 251312 (d) 121532

Solution *(b)* As

H ⟶ 6 and M ⟶ 9

I ⟶ 1 A ⟶ 3
N ⟶ 2 N ⟶ 2
D ⟶ 5
U ⟶ 7

Similarly,

I ⟶ 1
N ⟶ 2
D ⟶ 5
I ⟶ 1
A ⟶ 3
N ⟶ 2

Hence, INDIAN will be coded as 125132

Example 6 If B = 2, BAG = 10, then BOX = ?

(a) 36 (b) 39 (c) 41 (d) 52

Solution *(c)* Here, the positional values of letters in English alphabet are added to obtain the number.

As, B = 2 and BAG = 2 + 1 + 7 = 10

Similarly, BOX = 2 + 15 + 24 = 41

3. Substitution Coding

In this type of questions, some particular words are assigned certain substituted names. Then, a question is asked that is to be answered in the substituted code language.

Example 7 If 'CAR' is called 'BIKE', 'BIKE' is called 'BICYCLE', 'BICYCLE' is called 'SCOOTER', 'SCOOTER' is called 'TRAIN', 'TRAIN' is called 'AEROPLANE', then which one of the following options is associated with railways?

(a) BIKE (b) TRAIN
(c) AEROPLANE (d) SCOOTER

Solution *(c)* 'TRAIN' is associated with 'railways' but here train is called 'aeroplane'. Hence, in this case 'aeroplane' is associated with railways.

4. Deciphering Message Word Coding

In this type of questions, some messages are provided in the code language and some codes are assigned to each word of the messages. The candidates are required to decipher the code of each word by finding the common code for the common word and this process is followed to decipher the code for each word thereafter. Hence, the entire message is decoded.

Example 8 In a certain code language 'pul hir fin' means 'good sweet fruit', 'tie dip sig' means 'beautiful red rose', 'sig to fin' means 'rose and fruit'. Which of the following stands for 'and' in that language?

(a) pul (b) to (c) fin (d) sig

Solution *(b)* According to the question,

pul hir (fin) ⟶ good sweet (fruit)

tie dip △sig ⟶ beautiful red △rose

△sig to (fin) ⟶ △rose and (fruit)

Hence, and ⟶ to

5. Conditional Coding

In this type of questions, letters/numbers are given and their codes are given right under them. Candidate is required to find out code for a particular letter group/word/number according to the given conditions.

Directions (Ex. 9-11) *In each question below is given a group of digits followed by four combinations of letters/symbols numbered (a), (b), (c) and (d). You have to find out which of the combinations correctly represents the group of digits based on the coding system and the conditions given below and mark your answer accordingly.*

Digits	5	1	3	4	9	6	8	2	7
Letters/Symbols	P	A	K	%	R	@	D	©	M

Conditions

(i) If the first digit is odd and the last digit is even, the codes for the first and last digits are to be interchanged.

(ii) If both the first and the last digits are even, both are to be coded as ★.

(iii) If both the first and the last digits are odd, both are to be coded as $.

Example 9 794821

(a) MR%D©A
(b) AR%D©M
(c) M%RD©A
(d) $R%D©$

Solution *(d)* Since, first and last digits are odd, then both are to be coded as $, therefore

7 9 4 8 2 1
↓ ↓ ↓ ↓ ↓ ↓
$ R % D © $

Example 10 591426

(a) @RA%©P
(b) PRA%©@
(c) @AR%©P
(d) $RA%©★

Solution *(a)* Since, first and last digits are odd and even respectively, then the codes for the first and the last digits are to be interchanged, therefore

5 9 1 4 2 6
↓ ↓ ↓ ↓ ↓ ↓
@ R A % © P

Example 10 671254

(a) @MA©P%
(b) $MA©P$
(c) ★MA©P★
(d) %MA©P@

Solution *(c)* Since, first and last digits are even, then both are to be coded as ★,

therefore 6 7 1 2 5 4
★ M A © P ★

Practice Exercise

1. In a certain code, 'REFRIGERATOR' is coded as 'ROTAREGIRFER'. Which word from the following would be coded as 'NOITINUMMA'?

(a) ANMOMIUTMI (b) AMNTOMUIIN
(c) AMMUNITION (d) NMMUNITIOA

2. If 'VEHEMENT' is written as 'VEHETNEM', then how 'MOURNFUL' be written in that code language?

(a) MOURLUFN (b) MOUNULER
(c) OURMNFUL (d) URNFULMO

3. In a certain code, 'INACTIVE' is written as 'VITCANIE'. How would 'COMPUTER' be written in the same code?

(a) PMOCRETU (b) ETUPMOCR
(c) UTEPMOCR (d) MOCPETUR

4. In a certain code, 'INSTITUTION' is written as 'NOITUTITSNI'. How would 'PERFECTIONS' be written in that code?

(a) SNOICTEREP (b) SNOITCEFERP
(c) SNOITCEFRPE (d) SNOITCEFREP

5. In a certain language, 'EXECUTIVE' is coded as 'TCIEUXVEE', then how is 'MAUSOLEUM' coded in that same language?

(a) LSEUOAUMM (b) AUUCOSLMM
(c) AUEUOSEMM (d) SLUEOAUMM

6. If R is denoted by N, D is denoted by T, I by U, O by I, E by R, T by O, U by D, N by C and C by E, then how will the word INTRODUCE be written?

(a) UCONIDTER (b) UCONITDER
(c) UCONTIDER (d) UCOINTDER

7. If in a certain language, 'POPULAR' is coded as 'QPQVMBS', then which word from the following would be coded as 'GBNPVT'?

(a) FARMER (b) FAMOUS
(c) FRAMES (d) FAMOTH

8. If in a certain language, 'MIRACLE' is coded as 'NKUEHRL', then how is 'GAMBLE' coded in that same language?

(a) JDOCMF (b) CLEMNK
(c) HCPFQK (d) AELGMN

9. If in a certain code language, 'FRIEND' is written as 'ETKDPF', then how 'REVEAL' be coded in that language?

(a) LAEVER (b) VERQLM
(c) QXGCDN (d) QGXDCN

10. In a certain code, 'BELIEF' is written as 'AGKKDH'. How would 'SELDOM' be written in that code?

(a) RDKCHL (b) RFKENM
(c) RFKFNP (d) None of these

11. In a certain code language, 'CURATIVE' is written as 'BSVDDUHS'. How 'STEAMING' is to be written in the same code language?

(a) BFUTFMHL (b) TUFBFMHL
(c) BFUTLHMF (d) BFUTHOJN

12. In a certain code, 'BUILDER' is written as 'JVCKSFE'. How is 'SEALING' written in the same code?

(a) BTFKHOJ (b) JOHKBT
(c) TFBKHOJ (d) None of these

13. In a certain code language, 'COMPUTER' is written as 'RFUVQNPC'. How will 'MEDICINE' be written in the same code?

(a) EOJDEJFM (b) EOJDJEFM
(c) MFEDJJOE (d) MFFJDJOE

14. In a certain code, 'CAT' is written as 'SATC' and 'DEAR' is written as 'QEARD'. How would 'SING' be written in that code?

(a) BGINS (b) SGNIS
(c) SINGS (d) None of these

15. If 'RED' is coded as 2076, then how would 'GREEN' be coded?

(a) 16677199 (b) 1677209
(c) 16717209 (d) 9207716

16. In a certain code, 'CERTAIN' is coded as 'XVIGZRM', 'SEQUENCE' is coded as 'HVJFVMXV', then how would 'MUNDANE' be coded?

(a) NFMWZMX
(b) NFMWZMV
(c) NFMXZMV
(d) Cannot be determined

17. In a certain code language, 'ROUTINE' is written as 'VMRGFLI'. How will be 'CRUELTY' written in that code?

(a) VOCVZRL (b) VPCVZRL
(c) VPVCZRL (d) None of these

18. In a certain code, 'MIND' becomes 'KGLB' and 'ARGUE' becomes 'YPESC', then what will 'DIAGRAM' be in that code?

(a) BGYEPYK (b) BGYPYEK
(c) GYPRYKB (d) LKBGPK

19. In a certain code, 'RAIN' is written as '8$%6' and 'MORE' is written as '7#8@'. How would 'REMAIN' be written in that code?

(a) 8@7$86 (b) 8@$7%6
(c) 8@7$6% (d) 8@7$%6

20. If 'LINGER' is '123456' and 'FORCE' is '56789', then 'FIERCE' will be

(a) 345667
(b) 456678
(c) 345677
(d) Cannot be determined

21. If in a certain code language 'HACB' is written as '8132', then how will 'DEFA' be written in that language'?

(a) 4651 (b) 4561 (c) 4156 (d) 5641

22. If in a certain code language, 'PUT' is written as '57', then how will 'BAT' be written in that language?

(a) 25 (b) 60
(c) 55 (d) 23

23. If A =26, SUN =27, then CAT = ?

(a) 29 (b) 27
(c) 57 (d) 58

24. If GO = 32, SHE = 49, then 'SOME' will be equal to

(a) 56 (b) 57 (c) 58 (d) 62

25. If 'tree' means 'mountain', 'mountain' means 'water', 'water' means 'jungle', 'jungle' means 'bus', 'bus' means 'truck' and 'truck' means 'house', then where do fish live?

(a) Water (b) Jungle
(c) Mountain (d) Bus

26. On another planet the local terminology for 'earth', 'water', 'light', 'air' and 'sky' are 'sky', 'light', 'air', water and 'earth', respectively. If someone is thirsty there, what would he drink?

(a) Light (b) Air (c) Sky (d) Water

27. If the animals which can walk are called 'swimmers', animals who crawl are called 'flying', those living in water are called 'snakes' and those which fly in the sky are called 'hunters', then what will a lizard be called?

(a) Swimmers (b) Snakes
(c) Flying (d) Hunters

28. If 'orange' is called 'butter', 'butter' is called 'soap', 'soap' is called 'ink', 'ink' is called 'honey' and 'honey' is called 'orange', then which of the following will be used for washing clothes?

(a) Honey (b) Butter
(c) Orange (d) Ink

29. If 'Blue' means 'green', 'green' means 'white', 'white' means 'yellow', 'yellow' means 'black', 'black' means 'red' and 'red' means 'brown', then what is the colour of milk?

(a) Black (b) Brown
(c) Blue (d) Yellow

30. If 'REASON' is coded as 5 and 'BELIEVED' as 7, then what is the code number for 'GOVERNMENT'?

(a) 10 (b) 6 (c) 9 (d) 8

Directions (Q. Nos. 31-33) *In each of the questions below, a group of letters followed by four combinations of digits and symbols numbered (a), (b), (c) and (d) are given. You have to find out which of the combinations correctly represents the group of letters based on the digit/symbol. Code of each letter is given below and the conditions those follow and mark your answer correctly.*

Letters	P	K	A	R	E	T	I	M	N	U	J	F	V
Digits/Symbol Codes	6	1	★	$	8	©	3	@	4	#	7	5	9

Conditions

(i) If both the first and the last letters in the group are vowels both are to be coded as '?'.

(ii) If the first letter is vowel and the last letter is a consonant, the codes for these two letters are to be interchanged.

31. TMAPKI

(a) 32★61© (b) ©@★613
(c) ©$★613 (d) ©@★913

32. IJFNVE

(a) 375498 (b) 875493
(c) ?75498 (d) ?7549?

33. UATEMK

(a) 1★©8@#
(b) #★©8@1
(c) ?★©8@?
(d) #★8©@1

Directions (Q. Nos. 34-37) *Study the following information to answer the given questions.*

In a certain code, 'ze lo ka gi' is a code for 'must save some money', 'fe ka so ni' is a code for 'he made good money', 'ni lo da so' is a code for 'he must be good', and 'we so ze da' is a code for 'be good save grace'.

34. Which of the following is the code of 'must'?
(a) so (b) da (c) lo (d) ni

35. What does the code 'ze' stand for?
(a) some (b) must (c) be (d) save

36. Which of the following is the code of 'good'?
(a) so (b) we
(c) ze (d) lo

37. 'grace of money' may be coded as
(a) ka da fe (b) we ka so
(c) ja da we (d) ka we yo

38. Which of the following will be the changed form of the word 'OBLIQUE', when the word is written again by substituting each vowel by the 2nd letter following in English alphabet and each consonant is substituted by the 3rd letter following it in the English alphabet?
(a) M E D G T S D (b) R D N L S X H
(c) Q E O K T X G (d) Q E O K T W G

Directions (Q. Nos. 39-42) *Given below is a multiplication operation, where each alphabet represents a number, based on it.*

```
   Z Z
 × D F
 -----
  D 9 6
+P D C ×
 -------
 1 7 1 6
```

39. What is the value of Z?
(a) 3 (b) 4 (c) 2 (d) 1

40. What is the value of F?
(a) 3 (b) 4 (c) 2 (d) 9

41. What is the value of D?
(a) 3 (b) 4
(c) 2 (d) 1

42. What is the value of ZD + ZF – DF?
(a) 10 (b) 22
(c) 12 (d) 21

Directions (Q. Nos. 43-45) *These questions are to be answered using the coding and decoding of the letters in the English alphabet as given below.*

The rth letter is coded as $(r+1)$th letter if, r is odd and as $(r-1)$th letter if r is even. In decoding, the inverse process is followed:

43. What is the code letter for T ?
(a) S (b) U
(c) V (d) R

44. Which letter is coded as J ?
(a) H (b) I
(c) K (d) L

45. Which word is coded as FWOKBMS?
(a) EXPLOIT (b) EXPLORE
(c) EXPLODE (d) EXPLANT

Previous Year's Questions

46. In a certain code, SUCCESS is written as TWFGJYZ. How will the word MIRACLE be written in that language? **[CLAT 2015]**
(a) NKVEHRL (b) NKUEHRL
(c) NKTEHRL (d) NKUHHRL

47. In a certain code MAIL is written as ZNVY, then how will FILM be written in that code? **[CLAT 2016]**
(a) XLMP (b) NORY
(c) MLIF (d) SVYZ

48. If in a code language 'ABANDON' is written as 'areamoim' 'BORE' is written or 'rils' and 'BASIL' is written as "rabut', then what is the original word for the code : 'btiwo'? **[CLAT 2017]**
(a) SOFoIA (B) SOLID
(c) SOMAD (D) NASIA

Answers

1	c	2	a	3	b	4	d	5	a	6	b	7	b	8	c	9	d	10	d
11	a	12	d	13	b	14	d	15	d	16	b	17	d	18	a	19	d	20	d
21	b	22	d	23	c	24	a	25	b	26	a	27	c	28	d	29	d	30	c
31	b	32	d	33	a	34	c	35	a	36	a	37	d	38	d	39	b	40	d
41	a	42	d	43	a	44	b	45	d	46	b	47	d	48	b				

SOLUTIONS

1. As,

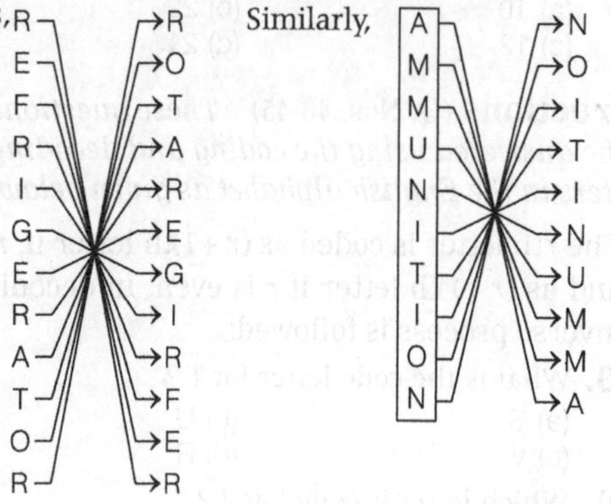

2. As,

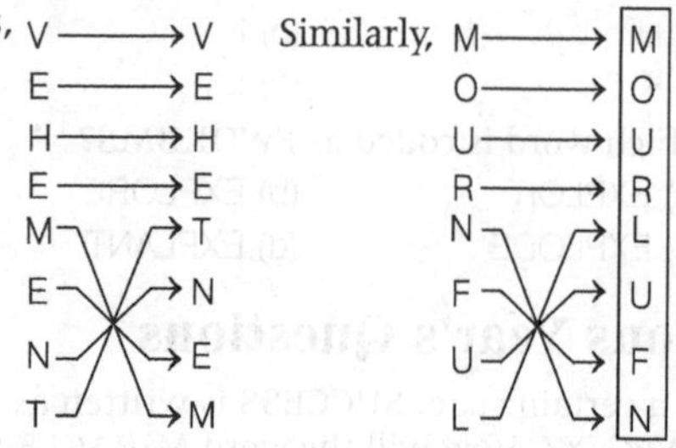

3. As,

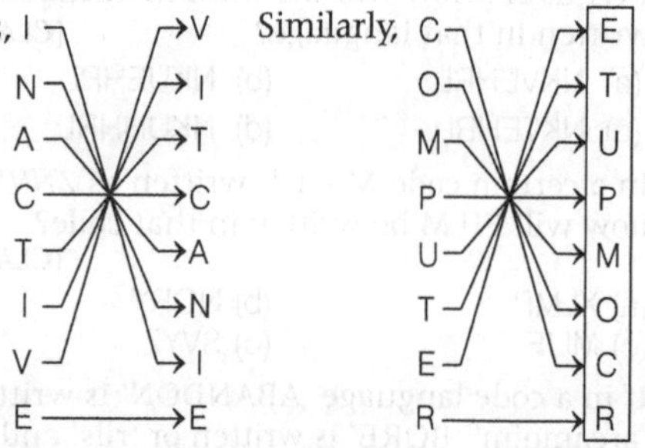

4. As, INSTITUTION —Reverse order→ NOITUTITSNI

Similarly,

PERFECTIONS —Reverse order→ SNOITCEFREP

5. E X E C U T I V E ⟶ T C I E U X V E E

1 2 3 4 5 6 7 8 9   6 4 7 3 5 2 8 1 9

Hence,

M A U S O L E U M ⟶ L S E U O A U M M

1 2 3 4 5 6 7 8 9   6 4 7 3 5 2 8 1 9

6. R→N, D→T, I→U, O→I, E→R, T→O, U→D, N→C, C→E

Hence,

I → U
N → C
T → O
R → N
O → I
D → T
U → D
C → E
E → R

7. As,

P —+1→ Q
O —+1→ P
P —+1→ Q
U —+1→ V
L —+1→ M
A —+1→ B
R —+1→ S

Similarly,

F —+1→ G
A —+1→ B
M —+1→ N
O —+1→ P
U —+1→ V
S —+1→ T

8. As,

M —+1→ N
I —+2→ K
R —+3→ U
A —+4→ E
C —+5→ H
L —+6→ R
E —+7→ L

Similarly,

G —+1→ H
A —+2→ C
M —+3→ P
B —+4→ F
L —+5→ Q
E —+6→ K

9. As,

F —−1→ E
R —+2→ T
I —+2→ K
E —−1→ D
N —+2→ P
D —+2→ F

Similarly,

R —−1→ Q
E —+2→ G
V —+2→ X
E —−1→ D
A —+2→ C
L —+2→ N

10. As,

B —−1→ A
E —+2→ G
L —−1→ K
I —+2→ K
E —−1→ D
F —+2→ H

Similarly,

S —−1→ R
E —+2→ G
L —−1→ K
D —+2→ F
O —−1→ N
M —+2→ O

11. As,

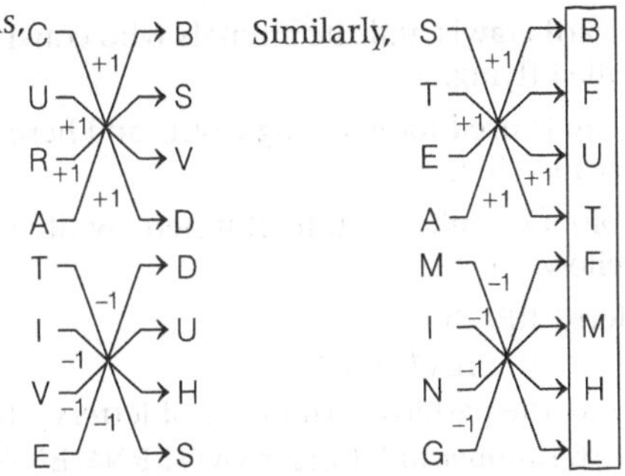

12. As,

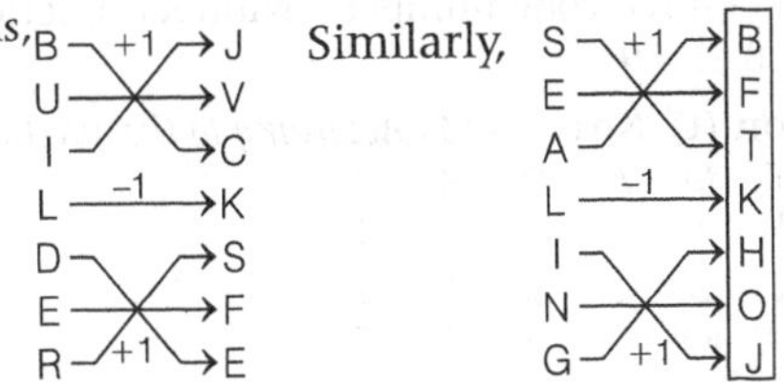

13. Each letter of the word, except the first and last letters, is moved one step forward and then the order of the letters so obtained, is reversed to get the code.

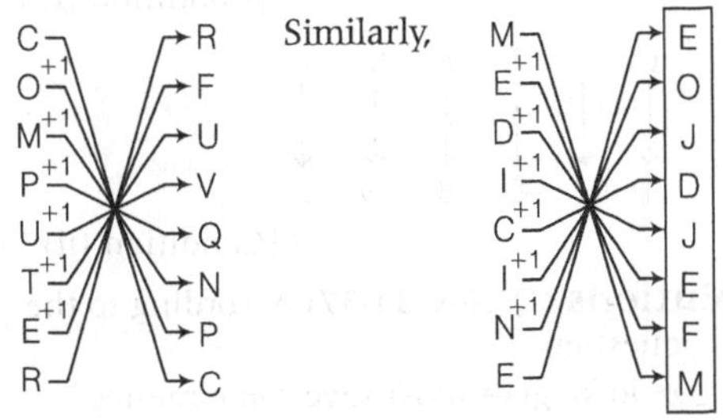

14. As,

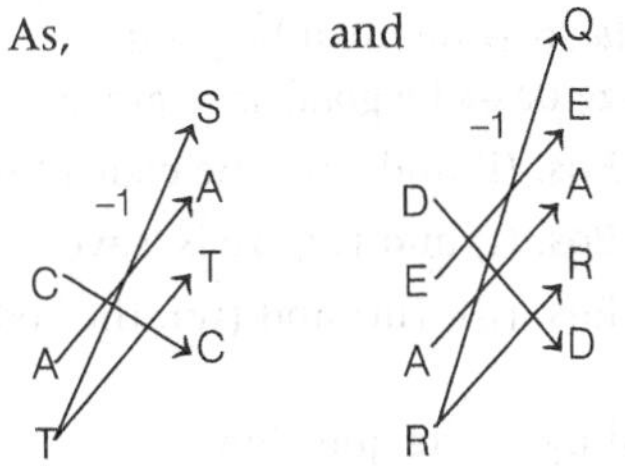

Similarly,

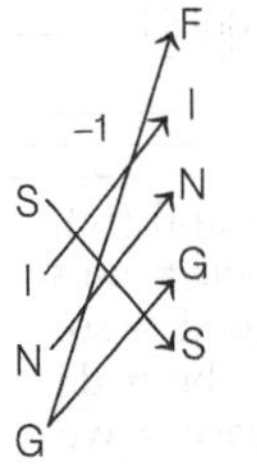

15. As,

R $\xrightarrow{+2}$ 20
E $\xrightarrow{+2}$ 7
D $\xrightarrow{+2}$ 6

Similarly,

G $\xrightarrow{+2}$ 9
R $\xrightarrow{+2}$ 20
E $\xrightarrow{+2}$ 7
E $\xrightarrow{+2}$ 7
N $\xrightarrow{+2}$ 16

16. Each letter in the word is replaced by its opposite letter in English alphabet, i.e. the letter, which occupies the same position from the other end of the alphabet, to obtain the code.

MUNDANE → NFMWZMV

17. Each letter in the word is replaced by its opposite letter in English alphabet, i.e. the letter which occupies the same position from the other end of the English alphabet and the group of letter, so obtained is then written in the reverse order to get the code. Hence,

CRUELTY ⟶ XIFVOGB ⟶ BGOVFIX

18. As M ⟶ K, I ⟶ G, N ⟶ L, D ⟶ B and A ⟶ Y, R ⟶ P, G ⟶ E, U ⟶ S, E ⟶ C

Similarly,
D ⟶ B
I ⟶ G
A ⟶ Y
G ⟶ E
R ⟶ P
A ⟶ Y
M ⟶ K

19. As, R ⟶ 8, A ⟶ $, I ⟶ %, N ⟶ 6 and M ⟶ 7, O ⟶ #, R ⟶ 8, E ⟶ @

Similarly,
R ⟶ 8
E ⟶ @
M ⟶ 7
A ⟶ $
I ⟶ %
N ⟶ 6

20. As,

L ⟶ 1	and	F ⟶ 5 (boxed)	
I ⟶ 2 (boxed)		O ⟶ 6	
N ⟶ 3		R ⟶ 7 (boxed)	
G ⟶ 4		C ⟶ 8 (boxed)	
E ⟶ 5 (boxed)		E ⟶ 9 (boxed)	
R ⟶ 6 (boxed)			

Similarly,
F ⟶ 5
I ⟶ 2
E ⟶ 5/9
R ⟶ 6/7
C ⟶ 8
E ⟶ 5/9

Hence, cannot be determined.

21. Here, the positional values of the given letters in English alphabet are given.

As, H A C B ⟶ 8 1 3 2   Similarly, D E F A ⟶ 4 5 6 1

22. Here, forward order letters positions are added

As, $\overset{16}{P}\overset{21}{U}\overset{20}{T} \rightarrow 16+21+20=57$

Similarly, $\overset{2}{B}\overset{1}{A}\overset{20}{T} \rightarrow 2+1+20=23$

23. Here, the backward order letters positional values are added.

As, A ⟶ 26
and S ⟶ 8
U ⟶ 6
N ⟶ 13

$8+6+13=27,$

Similarly, C ⟶ 24
A ⟶ 26
T ⟶ 7

$\therefore\ 24+26+7=57$

24. Mark 1, 2 ... for Z, Y ... Then,

GO ⟶ $20+12=32$

and SHE ⟶ $8+19+22=49$

Similarly, SOME

$=8+12+14+22=56$

25. We know that, fishes live in water and here, water means jungle. So, fishes live in jungle.

26. Water quenches thirst and here water is called light.

27. Lizard crawls and the animals who crawl are called flying.

28. Soap is used for washing cloths and here soap is called ink.

29. Colour of milk is white. But here, white means yellow.

30. Here, REASON = 5
BELIEVED = 7

Here, the pattern is (number of letters − 1)

Now, number of letters is GOVERNMENT = 10

∴ Required code number = Number of letters − 1
$=10-1=9$

Solution (Q. Nos. 31-33) *According to the question,*

31. T M A P K I ⟶ © @ 6 1 3

32. I J F N V E ⟶ ? 7 5 4 9 ?

[Condition (i) follows]

33. U A T E M K ⟶ 1 © 8 @ #

[Condition (ii) follows]

Solutions (Q. Nos. 34-37) According to the question,

ze lo ka gi ⟶ must save some money ...(i)
fe ka so ni ⟶ he made good money ...(ii)
ni lo da so ⟶ he must be good ...(iii)
we so ze da ⟶ be good save grace ...(iv)

34. From Eqs. (i) and (iii), the code of must is 'lo'.

35. From Eqs. (i) and (iv), ze is 'save'.

36. From Eqs. (ii), (iii) and (iv), the code of good is 'so'.

37. According to the question,

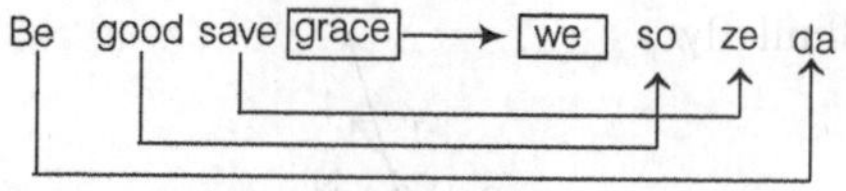

From Eqs. (iii) and (iv),
be good = da so
Since, good = so
∴ be = da
So, grace = we
From Eqs. (i) and (ii), money = ka

We cannot find the code for 'of'. But we can guess it with the help of answer options.

Grace of money ⟶ we yo ka

Accordingly, there will be two answer options—(b) we ka so and (d) ka we yo.
Since, the code of 'so' is 'good'. So, the correct code is 'ka we yo'.]

38. O $\xrightarrow{+2}$ Q B $\xrightarrow{+3}$ E
L $\xrightarrow{+3}$ O I $\xrightarrow{+2}$ K
Q $\xrightarrow{+3}$ T U $\xrightarrow{+2}$ W
E $\xrightarrow{+2}$ G

Solutions (Q. Nos. 39-42) *According to the question,*

$C + 9 = 1$ or 11 ...(i) means $C = 2$

Eq. (i) above indicate carrying 1 to next place, it means

$1 + D + D = 1 + 6 = 7$

$\therefore$ $D = 3$; So, $1 + 3 + 3 = 1 + 6 = 7$

This leads to the conclusion that P = 1

Now we know,

```
   Z Z
 × D F
 -----
   3 9 6
 +1 3 2 ×
 -------
  1 7 1 6
```

Now, Z and F can represent 4, 5, 7, 8 or 9.
6 is possible outcome of 7×8 or 4×9 fits into the equation and we come to know that Z = 4 and F = 9.

39. Z = 4

40. F = 9

41. D = 3

42. $ZD + ZF - DF = (4 \times 3) + (4 \times 9) - (3 \times 9) = 12 + 36 - 27 = 12 + 9 = 21$

Solutions (Q. Nos. 43-45) According to the question,
The rth letter is coded as $(r + 1)$th letter if r is odd and rth letter is coded as $(r - 1)$th letter if r is even.

Letter A B C D E F G H I J K L
Coded B A D C F E H G J I L K
Letter M N O P Q R S T U V W X Y Z
Coded N M P O R Q T S V U X W Z Y

43. Code for T is S.

44. I is coded as J.

45. F W O K B M S
↓ ↓ ↓ ↓ ↓ ↓ ↓
E X P L A N T

Previous Year's Solutions

46. As,
S U C C E S S
+1↓ +2↓ +3↓ +4↓ +5↓ +6↓ +7↓
T W F G J Y Z

Similarly,
M I R A C L E
+1↓ +2↓ +3↓ +4↓ +5↓ +6↓ +7↓
N K U E H R L

47. As, M A I L ⟶ Z N V Y (each letter +13)

Similarly, F I L M ⟶ S V Y Z (each letter +13)

48. A = a

B = r	B = r
A = e	O = i
N = m	R = l
D = o	E = s
O = i	
N = m	
and	Similarly,
B = r	b = S
A = a	t = O
S = b	i = L
I = u	w = I
L = t	o = D

CHAPTER 04

SERIES

Series is a sequential arrangement of numbers, letters or both and figures Each term in the series is obtained according to some specific rules. These rules can be based on mathematical operations, place of letters in alphabetical order etc.

TYPES OF SERIES

There are four types of series which are discussed below.

1. Number Series

Number series is a sequential order of numbers following a certain rule or pattern. The rule or pattern can be based on various mathematical operations.

The questions on number series are asked in two forms

(i) **To Find a Missing Term** In this type of questions, a series of numbers with one or more missing terms is given. The given series of numbers will be such that each number follows its preceding number in a particular way, i.e. according to a definite pattern. Candidates are required to analyse the pattern of the series and keeping this pattern in mind he/she has to find out the missing term(s).

Directions (Ex. 1-4) *In the following questions, find the number that will come in place of question mark (?).*

Example 1 67, 69, 72, 76, 81, ?

(a) 87 (b) 88 (c) 90 (d) 95

Solution *(a)* Here, the consecutive natural numbers starting from 2 are added respectively to each term of obtain the next term.

67 →(+2) 69 →(+3) 72 →(+4) 76 →(+5) 81 →(+6) [87]

∴ ? = 87

Example 2 2, 4, 8, 16, 32, ?

(a) 84 (b) 64 (c) 42 (d) 46

Solution *(b)* Here, each next term of the series is obtained by multiplying the previous term by 2.

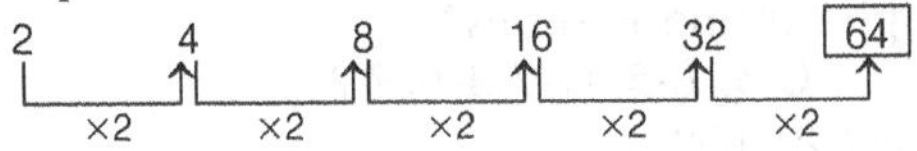

∴ ? = 64

Example 3 48, 43, 38, 33, 28, ?

(a) 24 (b) 18 (c) 23 (d) 19

Solution *(c)* Here, the difference between two consecutive elements is same, i.e. 5.

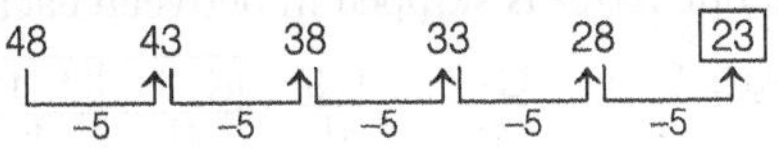

∴ ? = 23

Example 4 4, 8, 12, 16, 20, ?

(a) 18 (b) 21 (c) 19 (d) 24

Solution *(d)* Here, the difference between two consecutive elements is same, i.e. 4.

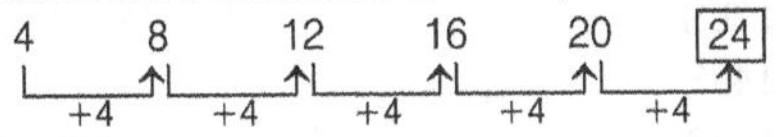

∴ ? = 24

(ii) **To Find the Wrong Number** In this type of questions, we are given a sequence of numbers. Whole sequence except one number follows a certain rule. Candidates have to find that number which does not follows the rule.

Directions (Ex. 5 and 6) *In each of the following questions, one number is wrong in the series. Find out the wrong number.*

Example 5 10, 14, 28, 32, 64, 68, 132

(a) 28 (b) 32 (c) 64 (d) 132

Solution *(d)* The correct pattern is +4, ×2, +4, ×2

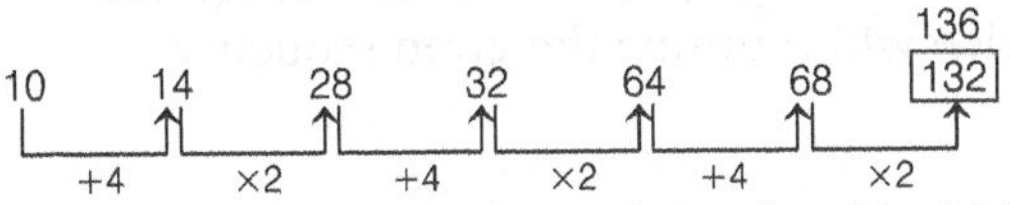

So, 132 is wrong and must be replaced by 136.

Example 6 2, 3, 12, 37, 86, 166, 288

(a) 2 (b) 3 (c) 166 (d) 86

Solution *(c)* Series moves with difference of squares of consecutive odd numbers, i.e. $(1)^2 = 1, (3)^2 = 9, (5)^2 = 25, \ldots\ldots$

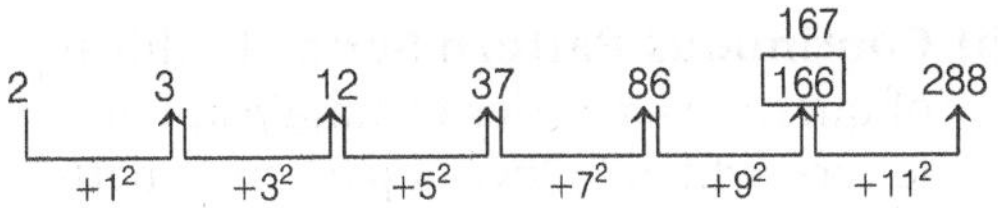

Hence, the number 166 should be replaced by 167.

> There is a large variety of patterns/logics that are possible and the candidates require a proper understanding of various patterns of number sequence to be able to do well in such problems.

2. Letter Series

Letter series is a logical order of letters of English alphabet arranged in specified pattern. There are two forms of questions on letter series that are asked in various examinations.

(i) **Alphabet Series** In this type of questions, the terms of the series form a particular pattern. The pattern can be based on reverse order of letters, skipping of letters, position of letters in English alphabetical order etc.

Example 7 Find out the next term in the following series.

R, O, L, I, F, ?

(a) C (b) A (c) E (d) I

Solution *(a)* The series follows below pattern

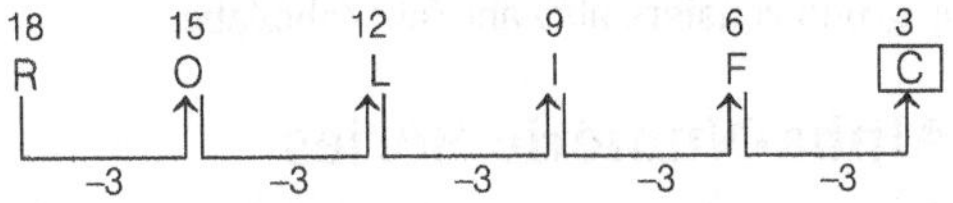

Here, each next term is obtained by moving 3 places backward in English alphabetical order from the preceding term.

Example 8 Find the next two terms of the given series.

Z, S, W, O, T, K, Q, G, ?, ?

(a) N, C (b) N, D (c) O, C (d) O, D

Solution *(a)* The given sequence is a combination of two series.

I. Z, W, T, Q, ? and II. S, O, K, G, ?

Now,

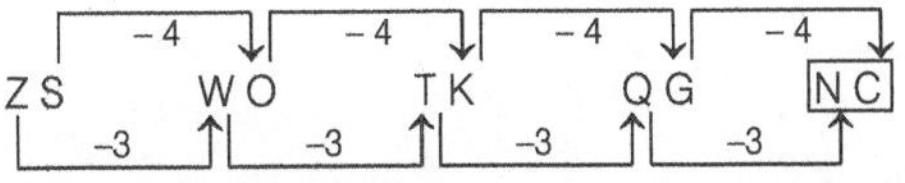

(ii) **Continuous Pattern Series** In this type of questions, a series of small/capital letters, which follows a particular pattern is given. However, some letters are missing from the series. In these questions, a set of letters is given four or five times with blank spaces, in between. The series follows a specific pattern and you are required to find letters which should come in place of the blank spaces.

Example 9 In the following series some letters are missing. Form the choices, select the choice that gives the letters that can fill the blanks in the given sequence.

a_c_b_ab_a_ca_c

(a) abaccb (b) accbab
(c) aabbcc (d) baccbb

Solution *(d)* The pattern of the series is

abc/abc/abc/abc/abc

So, the required letters = baccbb

In continuous pattern series, firstly, count the total given letters and blanks and secondly, find out how many multiple of numbers are exist, in the series. In above example there are 15 places having letters and blanks, so 15 could be the multiple of $5 \times 3 = 3 \times 5$.
Now, we will take 3×5 because the series is divided in 5 parts of 3 letters each and each part or group consists abc/abc/abc/abc/abc.

3. Alpha-Numeric Series

In this type of questions, the series consists of both, the letters and numbers. Each of the terms in the series follows a certain pattern based on either the alphabetical position of the letters or the numbers in different correlation. The candidates have to complete the series by inserting the missing number or letter or both.

Example 10 What should come in place of question mark (?) in the following alpha-numeric series?

C-3, E-5, G-7, I-9, ? ?

(a) X-24, M-21
(b) K-11, M-13
(c) O-15, X-24
(d) M-18, K-14

Solution *(b)* In this series, every letter is given its positional value in English alphabetical order and one letter is skipped in between each term.

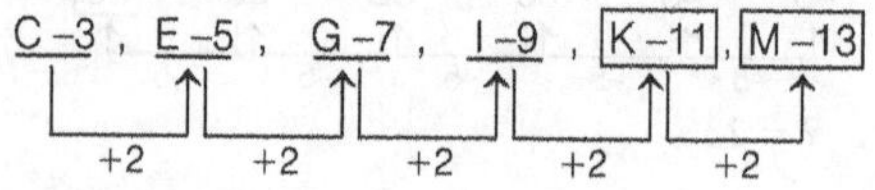

Example 11 Find the missing term in the following series.

1CV, 5FU, 9IT, ?, 17OR

(a) 11LS
(b) 14JS
(c) 15JS
(d) 13LS

Solution *(d)* The pattern of the given series is as follows

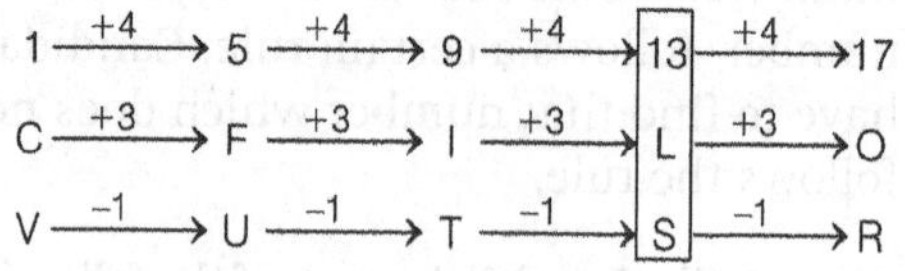

So, the missing term is 13LS.

4. Figure Series

A series of figures is given as problem figures and the candidate is required to select one figure from the given set of answer figures which will continue the given sequence.

Directions (Ex. 12-13) *Each of the following questions consists of five problem figures marked* 1, 2, 3, 4 *and* 5 *followed by four answer figures* (a), (b), (c) *and* (d). *Find out the figure from the answer figures which will continue the given series.*

Example 12 Problem Figures

1 2 3 4 5

Answer Figures

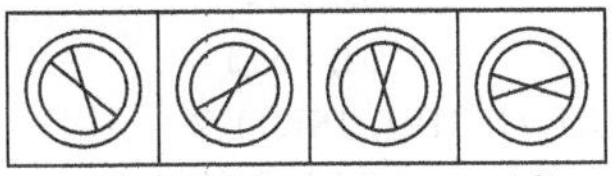

(a) (b) (c) (d)

Solution (*c*) The inner figure is rotating through 45° in clockwise direction in each subsequent block.

Example 13 Problem Figures

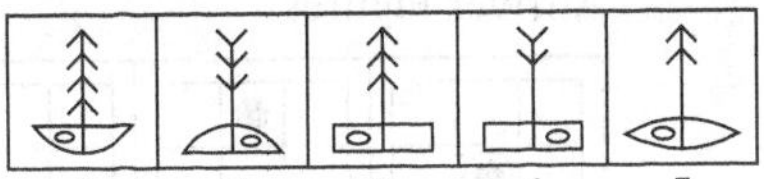

1 2 3 4 5

Answer Figures

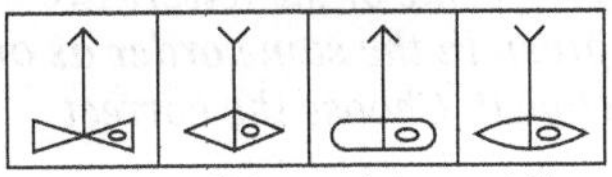

(a) (b) (c) (d)

Solution (*d*) Here, deletion of design in the figure takes place with the change in the figures. An arrow is deleted in each alternate block with the re-reversal in design. Similarly, base is also reversed with

Practice Exercise

Directions (Q. Nos. 1-5) *In each of the following questions, a number series is given with one of the terms missing. Choose the correct alternative that will continue the same pattern and replace the question mark (?) in the given series.*

1. 97, 90, 76, 55, ?
(a) 28 (b) 27 (c) 26 (d) 25

2. 4, 8, 16, 32, 64, ?, 256, 512
(a) 127 (b) 128 (c) 129 (d) 130

3. 01, 10, 12, 21, 13, 31, 14, ?, 15, 51
(a) 38 (b) 34 (c) 40 (d) 41

4. $33\frac{1}{3}, 20, 14\frac{2}{7}, ?, 9\frac{1}{11}$
(a) 14 (b) $5\frac{5}{17}$ (c) $5\frac{5}{19}$ (d) $11\frac{1}{9}$

5. 6, 13, 25, 51, 101, ?
(a) 201 (b) 202 (c) 203 (d) 205

Directions (Q. Nos. 6-11) *In the following number series, only one number is wrong. Find out the wrong number.*

6. 125, 126, 124, 127, 123, 129
(a) 126 (b) 124 (c) 123 (d) 129

7. 2, 10, 50, 500, 1000
(a) 2 (b) 10 (c) 50 (d) 1000

8. 8, 13, 21, 32, 47, 63, 83
(a) 13 (b) 32 (c) 47 (d) 63

9. 2, 6, 24, 96, 285, 568, 567
(a) 6 (b) 24 (c) 285 (d) 567

10. 888, 454, 237, 128.5, 76.25, 47.125
(a) 76.25 (b) 454 (c) 128.5 (d) 237

11. 146, 74, 40, 23, 19.5, 18.75
(a) 74 (b) 23 (c) 19.5 (d) 18.75

Directions (Q. Nos. 12-17) *In each of the following questions, various terms of an alphabet series are given with one term missing. Choose the missing term out of the given alternatives.*

12. W, T, Q, N, K, ..., E, B
(a) D (b) F (c) H (d) J

13. B, G, J, O, R, W, Z, ...
(a) D (b) I (c) E (d) L

14. VG, XI, ZK, BM,..., FQ
(a) DO (b) CM
(c) EL (d) None of these

15. GH, JL, NQ, SW, YD, ?
(a) EJ (b) FJ
(c) EL (d) FL

16. NOA, PQB, RSC, ?
(a) TUD (b) DTU
(c) ENO (d) FNQ

17. AYBZC, DWEXF, GUHVI, JSKTL,?
(a) MQORN (b) MQNRO
(c) NQMOR (d) QMONR

Directions (Q. Nos. 18-22) *In each of the following letter series, some of the letters are missing, they are given in the same order as one of the alternatives below it. Choose the correct alternative.*

18. mc_m_a_ca_ca_c_mc
(a) acmmma (b) camcam
(c) aaacmm (d) acmmca

19. _aa_ba_bb_ab_aab
(a) babab (b) aaabb
(c) bbaab (d) bbbaa

20. adb_ac_d_bcda_bcac_d
(a) bacbd (b) cbadb
(c) dbacb (d) acbda

21. B_CCABB_CABBC_AB_CCA
(a) BBBC (b) BBCC
(c) BCCB (d) BCBC

22. ac_ga_eg_ce_
(a) dbag (b) ecag
(c) deag (d) ebdg

Directions (Q. Nos. 23-26) *Complete the series by replacing the question mark (?).*

23. ABC = 6, EFG = 210, IJK = ?
(a) 1000 (b) 190 (c) 990 (d) 999

24. 2A11, 4D13, 12G17, ?
(a) 36J21 (b) 48J2l
(c) 88I19 (d) 48J23

25. 5G7, 7H10, 10I14, 14J19, ?
(a) 16K20 (b) 17K21
(c) 18K21 (d) 19K25

26. D23F, H19J, L17N, ?, T11V
(a) P15R (b) P14R
(c) P13R (d) P12R

Directions (Q. Nos. 27-31) *In each of the questions given below, which one of the four answer figures should come after the problem figures on the right, if the sequence were continued.*

27. Problem Figures

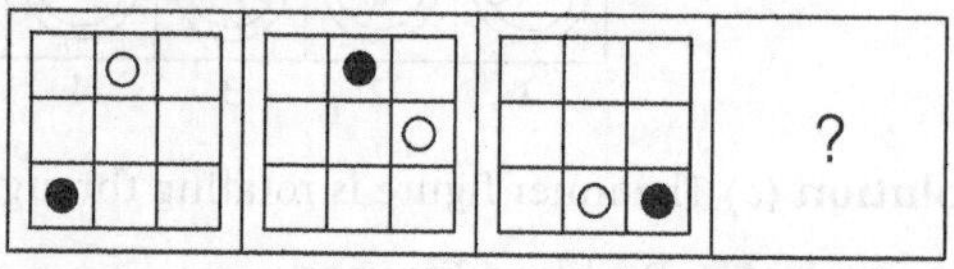

Answer Figures

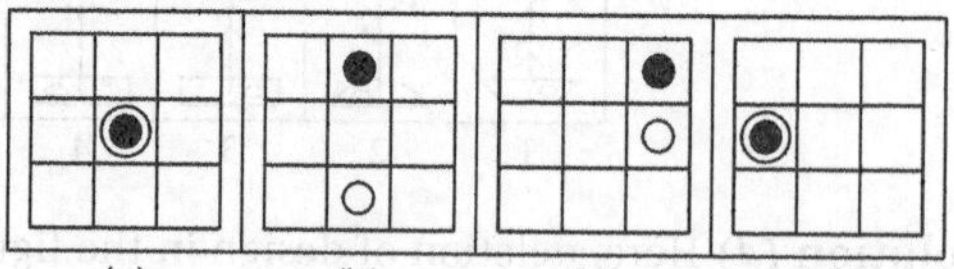

(a) (b) (c) (d)

28. Problem Figures

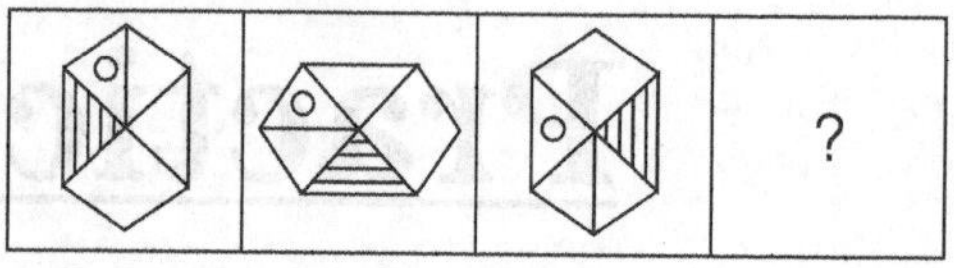

Answer Figures

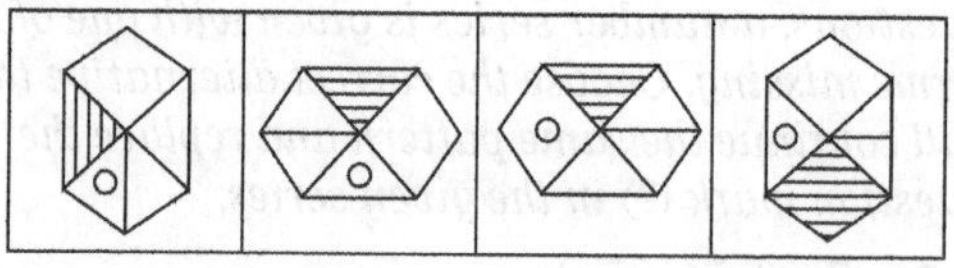

(a) (b) (c) (d)

29. Problem Figures

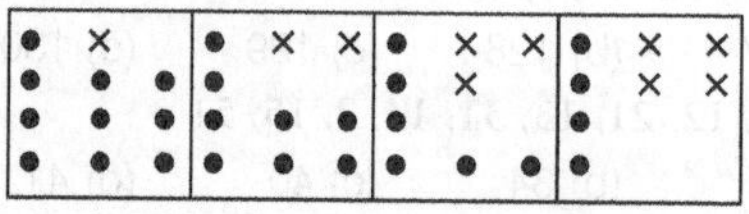

Answer Figures

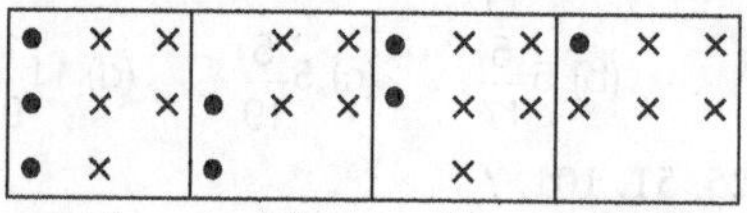

(a) (b) (c) (d)

30. Problem Figures

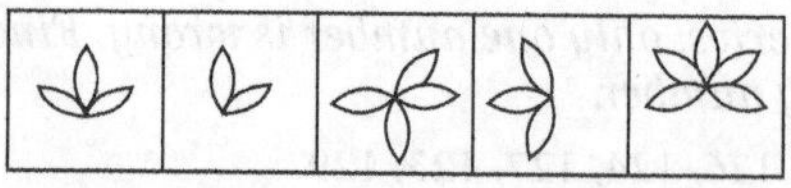

1 2 3 4 5

Answer Figures

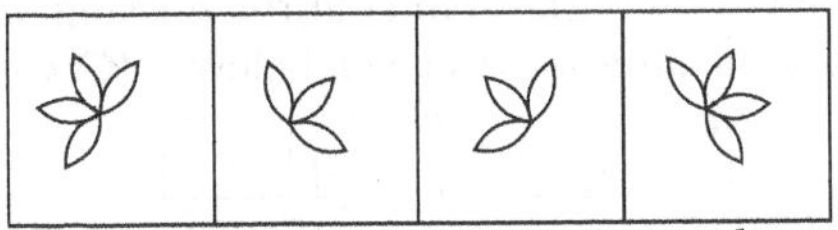

(a) (b) (c) (d)

31. Problem Figures

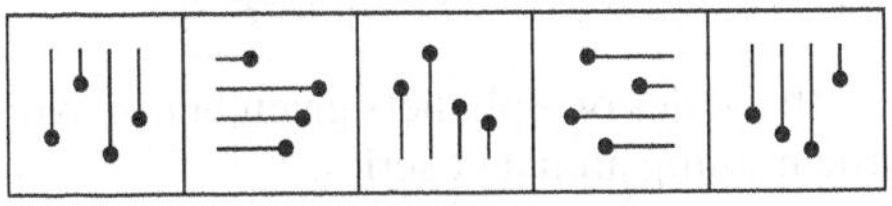

1 2 3 4 5

Answer Figures

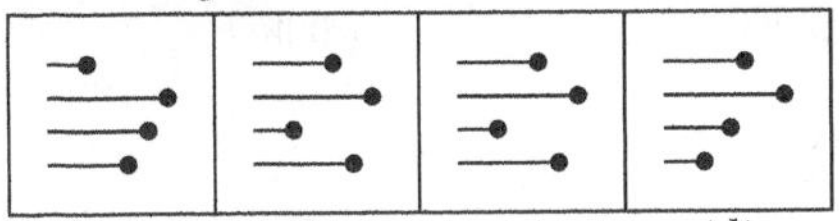

(a) (b) (c) (d)

Previous Year's Questions

Directions (Q. Nos. 32-34) *In each of the following questions, various terms of an alphabet series are given with one term missing. Choose the missing term out of the given alternatives.*

32. A, B, D, G, K, P, ...
What is the last alphabet in this above sequence? **[CLAT 2011]**
(a) Z (b) Y (c) V (d) X

33. B, C, E, G, K, M, Q, S, ...
What is the next alphabet in this above sequence? **[CLAT 2011]**
(a) T (b) U (c) V (d) W

34. Z, X, T, N, ...
What is the next alphabet in this above sequence? **[CLAT 2011]**
(a) E (b) F (c) G (d) H

35. 'Apple, application, ..., approval, apricot, April'
Which of the following best fits in the blank? **[CLAT 2011]**
(a) arrogant (b) April
(c) appropriate (d) apiary

36. 'Sunday, Monday, Wednesday, Saturday, Wednesday, Monday, Sunday, ...'
Which of the following best fits in the blank? **[CLAT 2011]**
(a) Sunday (b) Tuesday
(c) Saturday (d) Thursday

37. 'Gym, hymn, lynx, pygmy, rhythm'
Which of the following words does not belong to the above set? **[CLAT 2011]**
(a) Myrrh (b) Mythic (c) Flyby (d) Syzygy

38. Aadvark, Eerie, Iiwi, Oolong, ...
Which of the following words follows the pattern of this above series? **[CLAT 2011]**
(a) Uvula (b) Uulium (c) Uranium (d) Uranus

39. A-10, E-15, I-20, M-25, ... **[CLAT 2013]**
(a) Q-5 (b) Q-30
(c) P-30 (d) R - 30

40. A1, C3, F6, J10, O15, ?
(a) U21 (b) V21 (c) T20 (d) U20

41. POQ, SRT, VUW, ? **[CLAT 2014]**
(a) XYZ (b) XZY (c) YZY (d) YXZ

42. P3C, R5F, T8I, V12L, ? **[CLAT 2015]**
(a) Y17O (b) X16M
(c) X17O (d) X16O

43. ABP, CDQ, EFR, ? **[CLAT 2015]**
(a) GHS (b) GHT
(c) HGS (d) GHR

Directions (Q. Nos. 44-52) *In each of the following questions, a number series is given with one of the terms missing. Choose the correct alternative that will continue the same pattern and replace the question mark (?) in the given series.*

44. 387924, ? , 3724, 423, 32, 2 **[CLAT 2011]**
(a) 42978 (b) 42783
(c) 42983 (d) 42783

45. 0, 1, 1, 2, 3, 5, 8, 13, 21, ? **[CLAT 2013]**
(a) 34 (b) 35
(c) 33 (d) 36

46. 17,30,74,150, ?, 606 **[CLAT 2013]**
(a) 250 (b) 303
(c) 300 (d) 302

47. 2, 1, 4, 3, 6, 5, 8, ? **[CLAT 2013]**
(a) 9 (b) 10 (c) 7 (d) 8

48. 1, 4, 27, 256, ? **[CLAT 2013]**
(a) 625 (b)3125 (c) 3025 (d)1225

49. 0, 3, 8, 15, ? **[CLAT 2014]**
(a) 24 (b) 26
(c) 35 (d) None of these

50. 8, 16, 28, 44, ? **[CLAT 2014]**
(a) 60 (b) 64 (c) 62 (d) 66

51. 0, 6, 24, 60, 120, 210, ? **[CLAT 2014]**

(a) 290 (b) 240
(c) 336 (d) 504

52. 13, 25, 51, 101, 203, ?

(a) 405 (b) 406 (c) 407 (d) 411

53. Examine the series and identify the missing number **[CLAT 2016]**

46, 44, 40, 38, 34, ...

(a) 32 (b) 28 (c) 26 (d) 30

54. Examine the following numbers and identify the next number

45, 43, 40, 36, 31, 25,... **[CLAT 2016]**

(a) 17 (b) 23 (c) 29 (d) 18

55. There is some relationship between the figures given in the series. Find out the missing one from the alternatives given below. **[CLAT 2016]**

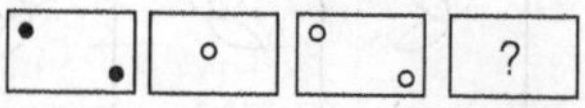

(a)  (b) 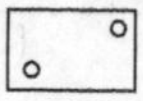

(c) 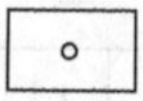 (d) 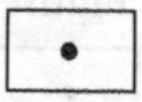

56. In the series of alphabets given below, which is the missing alphabet series.

AX, DU, GR, ..., ML **[CLAT 2017]**

(a) JO (b) HQ
(c) JN (d) IK

Answers

1	*b*	2	*b*	3	*d*	4	*d*	5	*c*	6	*d*	7	*d*	8	*c*	9	*b*	10	*a*
11	*b*	12	*c*	13	*c*	14	*a*	15	*d*	16	*a*	17	*b*	18	*a*	19	*c*	20	*c*
21	*c*	22	*b*	23	*c*	24	*d*	25	*d*	26	*c*	27	*d*	28	*c*	29	*c*	30	*d*
31	*d*	32	*c*	33	*d*	34	*d*	35	*c*	36	*a*	37	*b*	38	*c*	39	*a*	40	*a*
41	*d*	42	*c*	43	*a*	44	*b*	45	*a*	46	*d*	47	*c*	48	*b*	49	*b*	50	*b*
51	*c*	52	*a*	53	*a*	54	*d*	55	*d*	56	*a*								

SOLUTIONS

1. 97, 90, 76, 55, **27**

Differences: −7, −14, −21, −28

2. 4, 8, 16, 32, 64, **128**, 256, 512

×2, ×2, ×2, ×2, ×2, ×2, ×2

3. The series is pair series. The pairs are (01, 10), (12, 21), etc. ∴ 14 → 41

4. $33\frac{1}{3}, 20, 14\frac{2}{7}, ?, 9\frac{1}{11}$

It can be written as

$$\frac{100}{3} \xrightarrow{+2} \frac{100}{5} \xrightarrow{+2} \frac{100}{7} \xrightarrow{+2} \boxed{\frac{100}{9}} \xrightarrow{+2} \frac{100}{11}$$

Here, the denominator is increased by 2 in each step.

$$\therefore \frac{100}{9} = 11\frac{1}{9}$$

5. 6, 13, 25, 51, 101, **203**

(×2) + 1, (×2) − 1, (×2) + 1, (×2) − 1, (×2) + 1

6. 125, 126, 124, 127, 123, ~~128~~ **129**

+1, −2, +3, −4, +5

7. 2, 10, 50, 500, ~~5000~~ **1000**

×5, ×5, ×10, ×10

8. 8, 13, 21, 32, ~~46~~ **47**, 63, 83

+5, +8, +11, +14, +17, +20

9. 2 → 6 → [24] (25) → 96 → 285 → 568 → 567

(×6) − 6 (×5) − 5 (×4) − 4 (×3) − 3 (×2) − 2 (×1) − 1

10. 888 → 454 → 237 → 128.5 → [76.25] (74.25) → 47.125

(÷2)+10 (÷2)+10 (÷2)+10 (÷2)+10 (÷2)+10

11. 146 → 74 → 40 → [23] (25) → 19.5 → 18.75

(÷2) + 1 (÷2) + 3 (÷2) + 5 (÷2) + 7 (÷2) + 9

12. The sequence is –3 series. So, the next letters is

K – 3 = H.

13. The sequence is +5 and +3 alternately. So, the missing term is Z + 5 = E.

14. V —+2→ X —+2→ Z —+2→ B —+2→ [D] —+2→ F

G —+2→ I —+2→ K —+2→ M —+2→ [O] —+2→ Q

15. G —+3→ J —+4→ N —+5→ S —+6→ Y —+7→ [F]

H —+4→ L —+5→ Q —+6→ W —+7→ D —+8→ [L]

16. N —+2→ P —+2→ R —+2→ [T]

O —+2→ Q —+2→ S —+2→ [U]

A —+1→ B —+1→ C —+1→ [D]

17. AYBZC DWEXF GUHVI JSKTL [MQNRO]

−2 −2 −2 −2 −2 −2 −2 −2

+3 +3 +3 +3 +3 +3 +3 +3 +3 +3 +3 +3

18. mca/mca/mca/mca/mca/mc ⇒ acmmma

19. baab/baab/baab/baab ⇒ bbaab

20. adbc/acbd/abcd/adbc/acbd ⇒ cbadb

21. BBCCA/BBCCA/BBCCA/BBCCA ⇒ BCCB

22. aceg/aceg/aceg ⇒ ecag

23. The pattern is $ABC = 1\times2\times3 = 6$

$EFG = 5\times6\times7 = 210$

$IJK = 9\times10\times11 = 990$

24. 2 A 11 → 4 D 13 → 12 G 17 → [48 J 23]

+2 +4 +6

+3 +3 +3

×2 ×3 ×4

25. 5 G 7 → 7 H 10 → 10 I 14 → 14 J 19 → [19 K 25]

+1 +1 +1 +1

+2 +3 +4 +5 +6

26. D 23 F → H 19 J → L 17 N → [P 13 R] → T 11 V

−4 −2 −4 −2

+2 +2 +2 +2 +2 +2 +2 +2 +2 +2

27. In each successive problem figure, black dot moves three steps clockwise and white circle moves two steps clockwise.

28. Each time the figure is rotated by 90° in anti-clockwise direction and the small circle is moved one block in clockwise direction. So, the correct answer figure is (c).

29. The two dots are lost and one cross appears in each subsequent figure. So, in continuation with the given series of figures, the next figure would be (c).

30. From fig. (1) to (3), the figure is inverted and one leaf is added to one of its side. Also, from fig. (3) to (5), the figure is again inverted and one leaf is added to its other side. Same process follows from fig. (2) to (4) and from fig. (4) to (5).

31. Here, fig. (1) is similar to (4) while fig. (2) is similar to (5) except that the latter is 90° clockwise rotated.

Previous Year's Solutions

32. A → B → D → G → K → P → [V]

+1 +2 +3 +4 +5 +6

33. B → C → E → G → K → M → Q → S → [W]

+1 +2 +2 +4 +4 +4 +2 +2

34. Z → X → T → N → [F]

−2 −4 −6 −8

35. Words are arranged according to dictionary.

36. Sun Mon Wed Sat Wed Mon Sun Sun

+1 +2 +3 +4 +5 +6 +7

37. These are words without vowel in dictionary order.

38. First two letters of each word are same vowels.

39. A $\xrightarrow{+4}$ E $\xrightarrow{+4}$ I $\xrightarrow{+4}$ M $\xrightarrow{+4}$ [Q]

10 $\xrightarrow{+5}$ 15 $\xrightarrow{+5}$ 20 $\xrightarrow{+5}$ 25 $\xrightarrow{+5}$ [30]

So, next term is Q-30 .

40. The pattern is

A 1, C 3, F 6 J 10, O 15, [U 21]

+2 +3 +4 +5 +6

+2 +3 +4 +5 +6

41. The pattern is

+1 +1 +1 +1

P O Q, S R T, V U W, Y X Z

+1 +1 +1 +1

42. The pattern in the series is as follows

P $\xrightarrow{+2}$ R $\xrightarrow{+2}$ T $\xrightarrow{+2}$ V $\xrightarrow{+2}$ X

3 $\xrightarrow{+2}$ 5 $\xrightarrow{+3}$ 8 $\xrightarrow{+4}$ 12 $\xrightarrow{+5}$ 17

C $\xrightarrow{+3}$ F $\xrightarrow{+3}$ I $\xrightarrow{+3}$ L $\xrightarrow{+3}$ O

So, the next term be X17O.

43. The pattern in the letter series is as follows

+1 +1 +1 +1 +1 +1 +1

A B P C D Q E F R [G H S]

+1 +1 +1

So, the next term will be GHS.

44. Eliminate the largest digit.

387924, 42783, 3724, 423, 32, 2

45. $0+1=1$ $1+1=2$

$1+2=3$ $2+3=5$

$3+5=8$ $5+8=13$

$8+13=21$ $13+21=\boxed{34}$

46. Series is $X2+2, X2+2,...$

So, next term is $=150\times2+2 = 302$

47. 2 1 4 3 6 5 8 [7]

+2 +2 +2

+2 +2 +2

48. Series is as follows

$(1)^1 = 1$

$(2)^2 = 4$

$(3)^3 = 27$

$(4)^4 = 256$

$(5)^5 = 3125$

49. The pattern is

0 3 8 15 [26]

+3 +5 +7 +11

Addition of prime numbers.

50. The pattern is

8 16 28 44 [64]

8 12 16 20

+4 +4 +4

51. The series follows pattern is

$0^3-0=0$ $2^3-2=6$

$3^3-3=24$ $4^3-4=60$

$5^3-5=120$ $6^3-6=210$

$7^3-7=336$

52. The pattern is as follows

13 25 51 101 203 [405]

×2 − 1 ×2 + 1 ×2 − 1 ×2 + 1 ×2 − 1

So, the next term will be 405.

53. The pattern is as follows

46 44 40 38 34 [32]

−2 −4 −2 −4 −2

54. The pattern is as follows

45 43 40 36 31 25 [18]

−2 −3 −4 −5 −6 −7

55. From figure first to second the number of circles decreases by one and becomes unshaded.

Now, from figure third to fourth the number of circles decreases by one and becomes shaded from unshaded.

56. AX , DU , GR , [JO] , ML

+3 +3 +3 +3

−3 −3 −3 −3

CHAPTER 05

SITTING ARRANGEMENT

Sitting arrangement is a sequential arrangement of objects/persons according to the conditions given in the question. Questions of sitting arrangement are based on a set of information containing certain conditions. The candidate is required to form the proper sequence using the information and answer the given questions.

TYPES OF SITTING ARRANGEMENT

In examinations, questions are asked on the basis of two types of sitting arrangements.

1. Arrangement in Linear Pattern

In this type, we deal with questions where arrangement is required to be done in a linear format along a straight line. Before solving this type of questions, it is necessary to know the following facts.

(i) When it is not given in the question that in which direction the persons are facing, then we assume that they are facing in the North direction.

(ii) When A, B, C and D are facing to the South direction and P, Q, R and S are facing to the North direction in a line, then *positions to their right and left will be as follow*

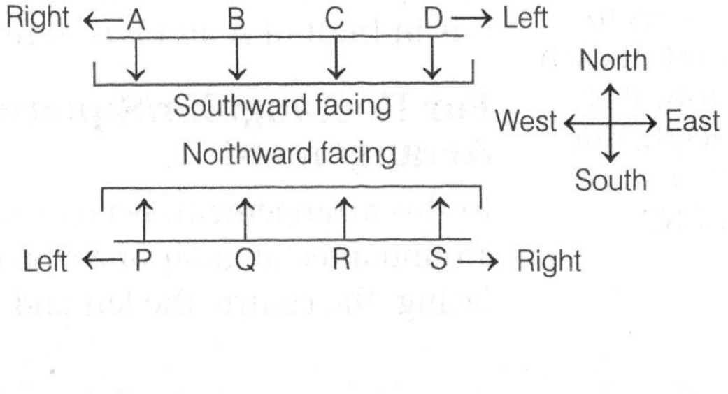

(iii) When A, B are in one line and P, Q in other, then diagonally opposite directions will be

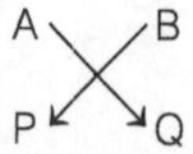

A is diagonally opposite to Q.

B is diagonally opposite to P.

Directions (Ex. 1-2) *These questions are based on the information given below.*

A group of seven singers, facing the audience, are standing in a line of the stage as follows :

I. D is to the right of C.

II. F is near G.

III. B is to the left of F.

IV. E is to the left of A.

V. C and B have one singer between them.

VI. A and D have one singer between them.

Example 1 Who is on the extreme right?

(a) D (b) F
(c) G (d) E

Example 2 If we start counting from the left, on which number is C?

(a) First
(b) Second
(c) Third
(d) Fifth

Solutions (Ex. 1-2) *According to the given information, we can arrange the singers as follows*

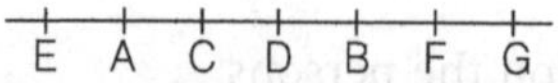

1. *(c)* Singer G is to the extreme right in the line.
2. *(c)* C is third from the left.

Example 3 Six persons M, N, O, P, Q and R are sitting in two rows with three persons in each row. Both the rows are in front of each other. Q is not at the end of any row. P is second to the left of R. O is the neighbour of Q and diagonally opposite to P. N is the neighbour of R. Who is in front of N?

(a) R (b) Q
(c) P (d) M

Solution *(b) According to the question, the arrangement is as follows*

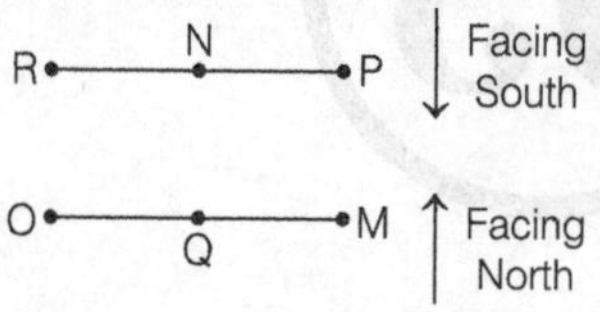

It is clear from the above diagram that Q is in front of N.

2. Arrangement Around a Closed Path

In this type of questions, we are given some clues regarding the sitting/placing arrangement. We have to apply these clues to arrange the persons/objects around a circle/square and then find the solutions of questions associated with them. Before solving the questions based on this type following facts are necessary to know.

For Circular Arrangement

In this arrangement, persons/objects are arranged around a circle facing towards the centre or outside the centre on the basis of the information provided.

Facing Towards the Centre

Suppose A, B, C and D are four persons facing towards the centre, then their right and left sides are shown by the arrows in the alongside diagram. B is on the right side of A and D is on the left side of A. C is in front of A and B is in front of D.

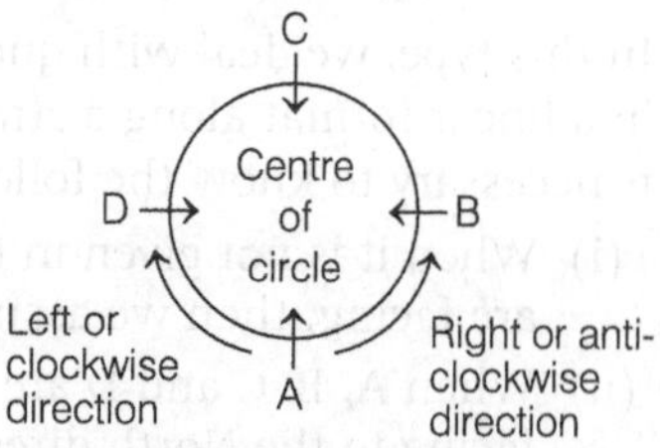

For Rectangular/Square Arrangement

In this arrangement, persons/objects are placed around a rectangular or a square shaped table facing the centre the left and right of each person can be understood with the help of following diagram.

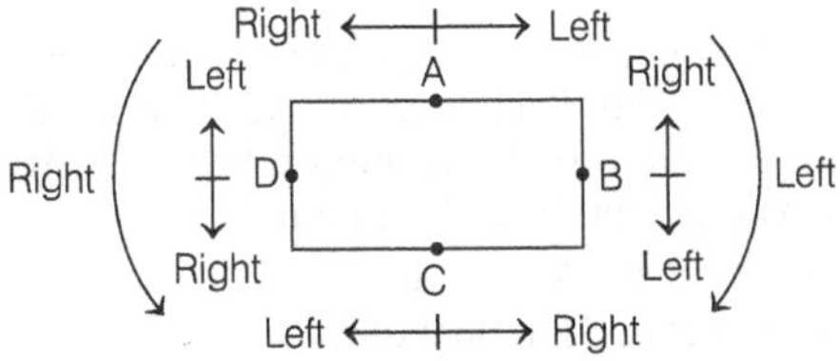

Facing the centre

Directions (Ex. 5-8) *Study the following information carefully and answer the questions given below.*

P, Q, R, S, T, V and W are sitting around a circle facing at the centre. V is second to the left of P and second to the right of W. T is third to the right of Q and is not an immediate neighbour of V. S is third to the right of R.

Example 5 Who is second to the right of Q?

(a) R (b) W (c) T (d) S

Example 6 Who is to the immediate left of S?

(a) V (b) T (c) Q (d) W

Example 7 Who is to the immediate right of R?

(a) W (b) T
(c) P (d) Data inadequate

Example 8 In which of the following groups is the first person sitting between the second and the third person?

(a) RPQ (b) TWS
(c) QPR (d) None of these

Solutions (Ex. 5-8) *According to the question, the arrangement is as follows*

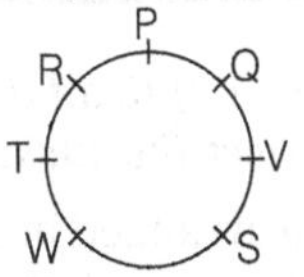

5. *(a)* R is second to the right of Q.
6. *(d)* W is to the immediate left of S.
7. *(b)* T is to the immediate right of R.
8. *(d)* None of the given alternatives follows such condition.

Example 9 Radha, Sheela, Mahima and Seeta are sitting around a rectangular table. Radha is to the right of Sheela. Mahima is to the left of Seeta. Which of the persons given in the options are sitting opposite to each other?

(a) Sheela-Seeta
(b) Radha-Seeta
(c) Radha-Sheela
(d) Mahima-Radha

Solutions *(b) Arrangement according to the question is as follows*

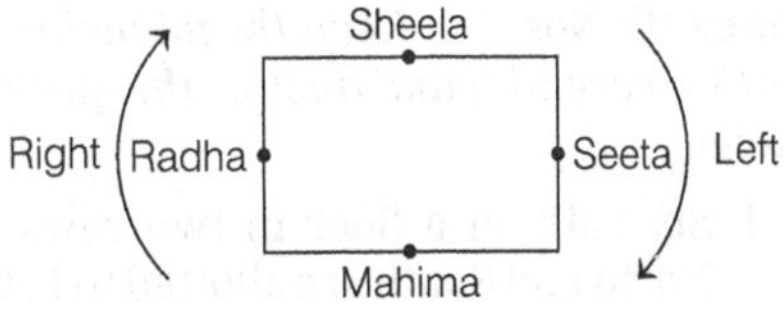

Clearly, Radha and Seeta are sitting opposite to each other.

Practice Exercise

Directions (Q. Nos. 1-3) *Read the following information to answer the questions based on it.*

Seven letters are arranged in a line as follows :

I. E and F have one letter between them.
II. G is to the right of A.
III. B is to the immediate left of F.
IV. There is one letter between D and A.
V. D is not G's neighbour.
VI. G and F have two letters between them.

1. Which letter is second to the left of letter A?
(a) C (b) B
(c) D (d) E

2. Which letter will be exactly in the middle of the letters series so obtained?
(a) D (b) A
(c) E (d) None of these

3. Which pair of the letters is adjacent to the letter B?
(a) A and C (b) G and E
(c) E and F (d) C and D

Directions (Q. Nos. 4-6) *Read the following information carefully and answer the questions that follow.*

I. Six flats on a floor in two rows facing North and South are allotted to P, Q, R, S, T and U.
II. Q gets a North facing flat and is not next to S.
III. S and U get diagonally opposite flats.
IV. R next to U gets a South facing flat and T gets a North facing flat.

4. Whose flat is between Q and S?
(a) T (b) U (c) R (d) P

5. The flats of which of the other pair, than SU, is diagonally opposite to each other?
(a) PT (b) QP (c) QR (d) TS

6. If the flats of T and P are interchanged, whose flat will be next to that of U?
(a) Q (b) T (c) P (d) R

7. There are six houses in a row. Mr. Lal has Mr. Bhasin and Mr. Sachdeva as neighbours. Mr. Bhatia has Mr. Gupta and Mr. Sharma as neighbours. Mr. Gupta's house is not next to Mr. Bhasin or Mr. Sachdeva and Mr. Sharma does not live next to Mr. Sachdeva. Who are Mr. Bhasin's next door neighbours?
(a) Mr. Lal and Mr. Bhasin
(b) Mr. Lal and Mr. Sachdeva
(c) Mr. Sharma and Mr. Lal
(d) Only Mr. Lal

Directions (Q. Nos. 8-10) *Read the following information and then answer the questions below.*

Ten students A, B, C, D, E, F, G, H, I and J are sitting in a row facing West.

I. B and F are not sitting on either of the edges.
II. G is sitting to the left of D and H is sitting to the right of J.
III. There are four persons between E and A.
IV. I is to the North of B and F is to the South of D.
V. J is in between A and D and G is in between E and F.
VI. There are two persons between H and C.

8. Who is sitting at the seventh place counting from the left?
(a) H (b) C
(c) J (d) Either H or C

9. Who among the following is definitely sitting at one of the ends?
(a) C (b) H
(c) E (d) Cannot be determined

10. Who are the immediate neighbours of I?
(a) B and C
(b) B and H
(c) A and H
(d) Cannot be determined

11. Five people are standing in a queue outside the ATM for cash withdrawal. The two persons standing at the extreme ends are Pankaj and Vijender. Anita is standing behind Rohit. Babita is in front of Vijender. Rohit is standing between Pankaj and Anita. Counting from the front, at which place is Anita?
(a) Fourth (b) Second (c) First (d) Third

Directions (Q. Nos. 12-14) *Study the following information carefully and answer the questions given below.*

M, D, P, K, R, T and W are sitting around a circle facing at the centre. D is second to the right of P who is third to the right of K. T is third to the right of W who is not an immediate neighbour of D. M is third to the left of R.

12. Who is second to the right of T?
(a) D (b) K
(c) M (d) Data inadequate

13. In which of the following pairs is second person sitting to the immediate right of the first person?
(a) DT (b) TP (c) PR (d) KW

14. Who is to the immediate left of R?
(a) W (b) P (c) K (d) T

Directions (Q. Nos. 15-17) *These questions are based on the information given below.*

Six girls are sitting in a circle. Sonia is sitting opposite to Radhika. Poonam is sitting right of Radhika but left of Deepti. Monika is sitting left of Radhika. Kamini is sitting right of Sonia and left of Monika. Now Deepti and Kamini, Monika and Radhika manually exchange their positions.

15. Who will be opposite to Sonia?
(a) Radhika (b) Monika (c) Kamini (d) Sonia

16. Who will be sitting left of Kamini?
(a) Poonam (b) Deepti (c) Radhika (d) Sonia

17. Who will be sitting left of Deepti?
(a) Sonia (b) Monika (c) Radhika (d) Poonam

18. Six friends P, Q, R, S, T and V are sitting around a circle. Q is between P and T. P is second right to R, who is immediate right of S. Which of the following is the position of T?
(a) Immediate left of S
(b) Immediate right of Q
(c) 4th right to R
(d) All of the above

Directions (Q. Nos. 19-21) *Study the following information to answer the given questions.*

L, M, N, O, P, Q and R are sitting around a circle facing the centre. O is sitting between L and R. Q is second to the right of R and P is second to the right of Q. N is not an immediate neighbour of R.

19. Which of the following is not correct?
(a) R is second to the right of L
(b) M is second to the left of N
(c) L sits exactly between O and P
(d) P sits to the opposite of N

20. How many persons are seated between L and Q, if we count anti-clockwise from L to Q?
(a) One (b) Two (c) Three (d) Four

21. Who is to the immediate left of P?
(a) L (b) N (c) M (d) O

Previous Year's Questions

Directions (Q. Nos. 22-26) *Read the information given below to answer the questions.* **[CLAT 2013]**

A, B, C, D, E, F, G and H want to have a dinner on a round table and they have worked out the following seating arrangements.

I. A will sit beside C.
II. H will sit beside A.
III. C will sit beside E.
IV. F will sit beside H.
V. E will sit beside G.
VI. D will sit beside F.
VII. G will beside B.
VIII. B will sit beside D.

22. Which of the following is wrong?
(a) A will be to the immediate right of C
(b) D will be to the immediate left of B
(c) E will be to the immediate right of A
(d) F will be to the immediate left of D

23. Which of the following is correct?
(a) B will be to the immediate left of D
(b) H will be to the immediate right of A
(c) C will be to the immediate right of F
(d) B will be to the immediate left of H

24. A and F will become neighbours if
(a) B agrees to change her sitting position
(b) C agrees to change her sitting position
(c) G agrees to change her sitting position
(d) H agrees to change her sitting position

25. During sitting
(a) A will be directly facing C
(b) B will be directly facing C
(c) A will be directly facing B
(d) B will be directly facing D

26. H will be sitting between
(a) C and B (b) A and F (c) D and G (d) E and G

27. G, H, I, J, K, L, M and N are sitting around a round table in the same order for group discussion at equal distances. Their positions are clock wise. If M sits in the North, then what will be the position of J? **[CLAT 2014]**
(a) East (b) South-East
(c) South (d) South-West

28. Roshan, Vaibhav, Vinay and Sumit are playing cards. Roshan and Vaibhav are partners. Sumit faces towards North. If Roshan faces towards West, then who faces towards South?
(a) Vinay (b) Vaibhav **[CLAT 2014]**
(c) Sumit (d) Data is inadequate

29. Five boys are standing in a row facing East. Pavan is to the left of Tavan, Vipin, Chavan. Tavan, Vipin and Chavan are to the left of Nakul. Chavan is between Tavan and Vipin. If Vipin is fourth from the left, then how far is Tavan from the right? **[CLAT 2014]**
(a) First (b) Second (c) Third (d) Fourth

Direction (Q. Nos. 30-33) *Read the following data and use it for answering the questions that follow:*

Six people A, B, C, D, E and F live on a six-storey building each on one floor. The following statements describe where they stay.

I. B lives on floor 6.
II. A is equally far from C and E.
III. F is an engineer.
IV. D is two floors above F.
V. C does not live next to an engineer.

30. Which of the following is true?
(a) C lives on floor number 4.
(b) A is exactly between D and F.
(c) E is on floor number 5.
(d) B is on floor number 5.

31. If statement (v) is disregarded, which floor does A stay on?
(a) 5 (b) 4 (c) 3 (d) 1

32. Which of the following is not true?
(a) F is not next to D.
(b) C lives between B and D.
(c) E lives on floor number 2.
(d) B is on floor number 6.

33. If 'C does not live next to an engineer' is invalid, then how many types of arrangements are possible?
(a) 2 (b) 3
(c) 1 (d) 5

Directions (Q. Nos. 34-36) *Read the following information carefully and choose the most approriate option in the questions given below:* **[CLAT 2017]**

I. Six flats on a floor in two row I facing North and Sourth are alloted to P, Q, R, S, T, and U.
II. Q gets a North-Facing flat and is not next to s.
III. S and U get diagonally opposite flats.
IV. R, next to U gets a South-Facing flat and the gets a North-Facing flat.

34. Whose flat is between Q and S?
(a) U (b) R
(c) P (d) T

35. If the flats of T and P are introchanged, who's flat will be next to that of U?
(a) T (b) P (c) Q (d) R

36. Which of the following combination gets-South-facing flats?
(a) U, R, P (b) U, P, T
(c) Data inadequate (d) Q, T, S

37. Two women and two men are playing bridge and seated at North. East, South and West of a table. No woman is facing East. Persons sitting opposite to each other are not of the same sex. One man is facing South. Which direction are the women facing to? **[CLAT 2017]**
(a) South and East (b) East and West
(c) North and West (d) None of these

Answers

1	c	2	d	3	c	4	a	5	b	6	d	7	c	8	d	9	c	10	d
11	d	12	c	13	d	14	a	15	b	16	a	17	a	18	d	19	d	20	c
21	b	22	c	23	b	24	d	25	c	26	b	27	d	28	d	29	d	30	b
31	c	32	c	33	a	34	d	35	d	36	a	37	c						

SOLUTIONS

Solutions (Q. Nos. 1-3) *The given figure shows the arrangement of given seven letters*

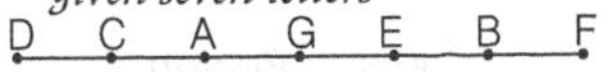

1. Letter D is second to the left of letter A.

2. It is clear from the diagram that letter G is in the middle of the letters arrangement.

3. Clearly, letters E and F are adjacent to B.

Solutions (Q. Nos. 4-6) *Below the figure shows the correct positions of persons.*

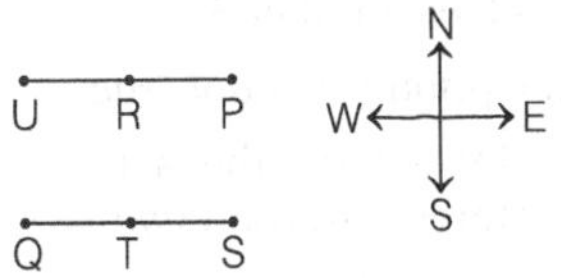

4. Clearly, T's flat is between Q and S.

5. As given in statement (iii), S and U are diagonally opposite. Similarly, from the figures we can say P and Q are also diagonally opposite.

6. Position after interchanging T and P.

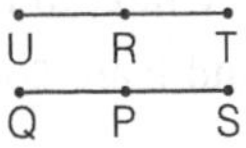

Next to U's flat is R's flat.

7. The given figure shows the correct positions of eight members

According to the question,

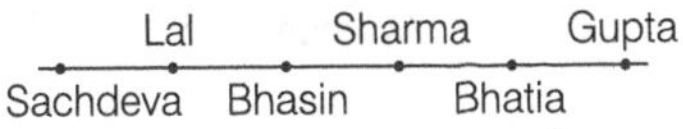

Hence, it is clear from the diagram that Mr. Bhasin's next door neighbours are Mr. Lal and Mr. Sharma.

Solutions (Q. Nos. 8-10) *Given figure shows the possible positions of all the ten students.* We kno the position of directions are as follows

If all directions move 90° clockwise, then it will be

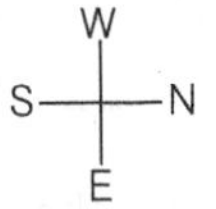

Now, apply this diagram in this solution.

Here, correct position of C and H cannot be determined.

8. It is clear from the diagram that either H or C is sitting at the seventh place counting from the left.

9. E is sitting at the left end.

10. Clearly, the immediate neighbours of I will be either H or C and B.

11. According to the given information, five people are standing in a queue as shown below

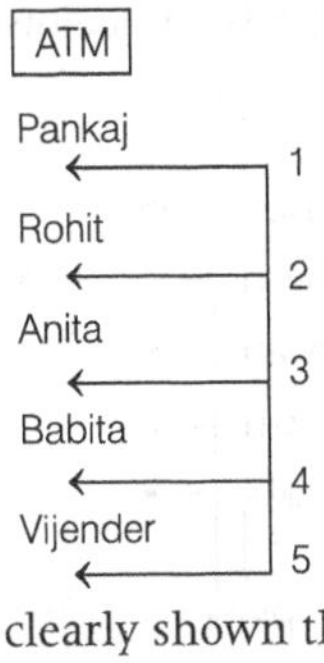

It is clearly shown that the position of Anita is third from the front.

Solutions (Q. Nos. 12-14) *According to the question, the arrangement is as follows*

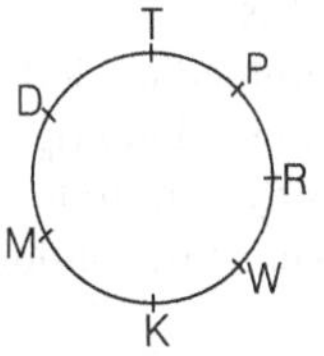

12. M is second to the right of T.

13. W is sitting to the to the immediate right of K.

14. W is to the immediate left of R.

Solutions (Q. Nos. 15-17) *According to the question, the sitting arrangement is as follows*

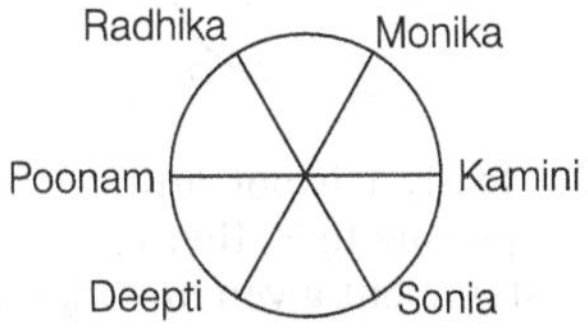

After interchanging the positions of Deepti with Kamini and Monika with Radhika as given in the question, we have the order of sitting of girls as given in the figure.

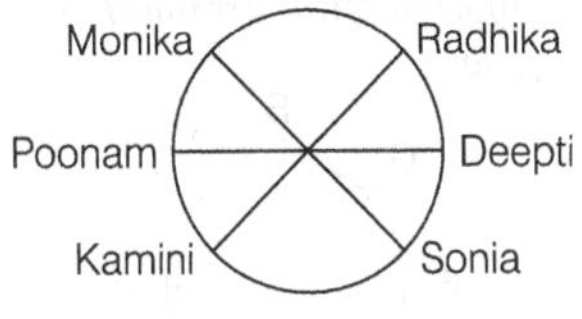

15. Monika will be at the opposite to Sonia.

16. Poonam will be sitting just left of Kamini.

17. Sonia will be sitting just left of Deepti.

18. Below the figure shows the correct position of persons sitting around the circle.

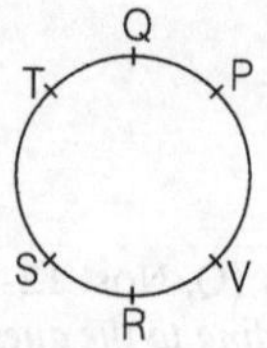

It is clear from the diagram that T is

(i) immediate left of S

(ii) immediate right of Q

(iii) 4th right to R

Hence, all the options are true.

Solutions (Q. Nos. 19-21) *According to the question, the seating arrangement is as shown below*

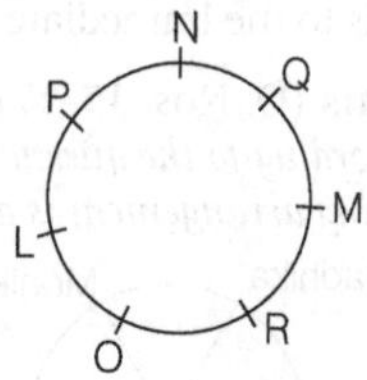

19. Clearly, P is not sitting opposite to N. Hence, statement given in option (d) is not correct.

20. Three persons—O, R and M are sitting between L and Q.

21. N is to the immediate left of P.

Previous Year's Solutions

Solutions (Q. Nos. 22-26) *Information is arranged as follows*

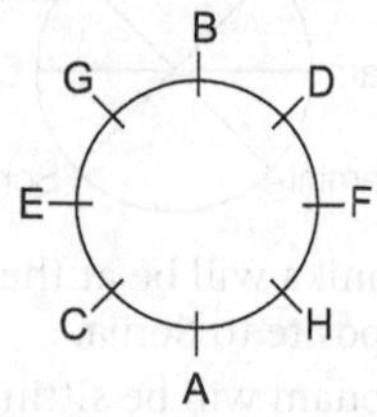

22. E is not to immediate right of A.

23. H will be on immediate right of A.

24. A and F will become neighbour on if H agrees to change her sitting position.

25. A will be directly facing B.

26. H is sitting between A and F.

27. Clearly the seating arrangement is as shown in the adjoining figure.

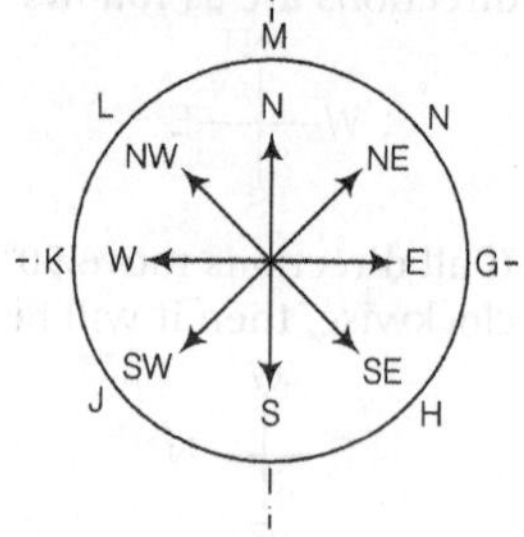

So, 'J' is at the South-West position

28.

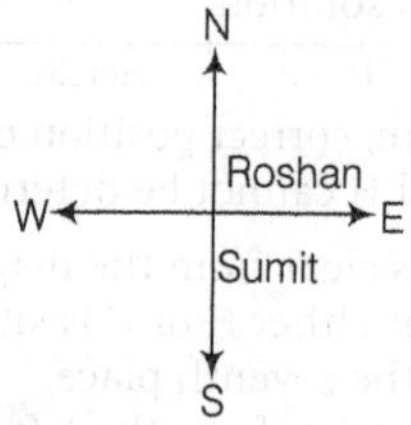

Here, it is not clear that the partners Roshan and Vaibhav sit opposite to each other or next to each other. So, can't give any answer.

29. According to the question. Five boys are Pavan, Tavan, Vipin, Chavan and Nakul standing in a row as shown in the figure below.

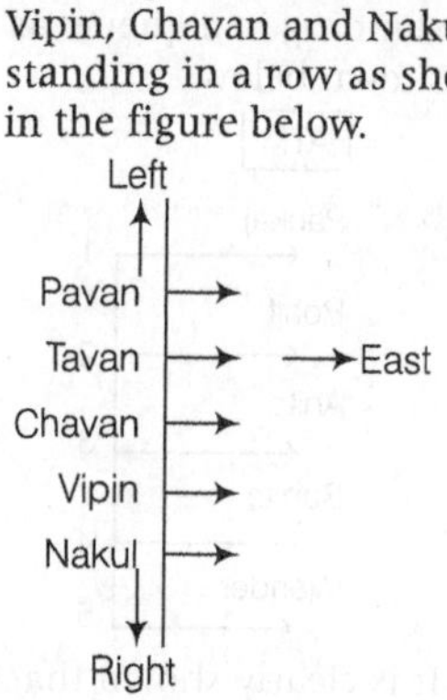

From above figure it is clear that Tavan is fourth from the right end.

Solutions (Q. Nos. 30-33) *According to the information given in the statements, we can draw an arrangement.*

Floor	Person
6	B
5	C
4	D
3	A
2	F
1	E

30. From the table, it is clear that A is exactly between D and F.

31. Floor number 3.

32. Option (c) is not true.

33. If we ignore the last statement, then two types of arrangements are possible.

Solution (Q. Nos. 34-36) *From the given information the arrangement is as*

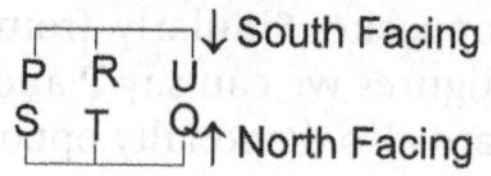

34. T flat is between Q and S.

35. R will be next to U.

36. U, R and P are South facing flats.

37. The sitting arrangement is as

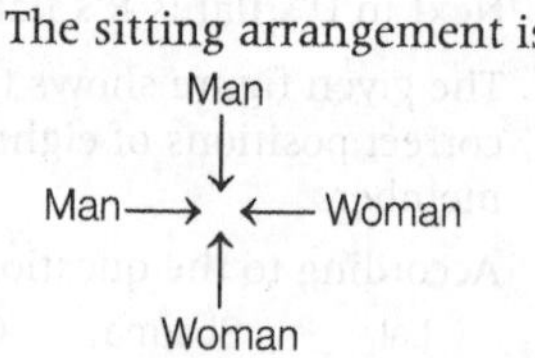

CHAPTER 06

NUMBER RANKING AND TIME SEQUENCE TEST

This chapter of reasoning deals with different type of questions which are based on Number, Ranking and Time Sequence. We have to find answers on the basis of given conditions. The importance of such type of questions cannot be denied as their presence in a test of reasoning is almost certain.

1. Number Test

In this type of questions, a number, a set of numbers, a series of digits is given and the candidates are asked to find out digits following certain given conditions.

EXAMPLE 1 How many even numbers are there in the following sequence of numbers, each of which is followed by an odd number as well as preceded by an even number?

8 6 7 6 8 9 3 2 7 5 3 4 2 2 3 5 5 2 2 8 1 1 9

(a) 1 (b) 3 (c) 5 (d) None of these

Solution *(d)* There are four such even numbers

8 $\boxed{6}$ 7 6 8 $\boxed{9}$ 3 2 7 5 3 4 2 2 $\boxed{3}$ 5 5 2 2 8 $\boxed{1}$ 1 9

EXAMPLE 2 The positions of how many digits in the number 5314687 will remain unchanged after the digits are rearranged in ascending order withing the number?

(a) One (b) Two (c) Three (d) None

Solution *(b)*

5	[3]	1	4	[6]	8	7
1	[3]	4	5	[6]	7	8

Hence, only two digits 3 and 6 will remain unchanged.

Directions (Ex. 3-4) *Following questions are based on the five three-digit numbers given below.*

519, 364, 287, 158, 835

EXAMPLE 3 If the positions of the first and the third digits within each number are interchanged, then which of the following will be the third digit of the second lowest number?

(a) 9 (b) 4 (c) 7 (d) 5

Solution *(d)* According to the question, after interchanging the positions of the first and third digits, new numbers are

$519 \Rightarrow 915$, $364 \Rightarrow 463$, $287 \Rightarrow 782$,

$158 \Rightarrow 851$, $835 \Rightarrow 538$

So, second lowest number $= 538$ and it is actually 835.

Hence, third digit of the second lowest number = 5

EXAMPLE 4 Which of the following is the difference between the second digit of the lowest and the highest of these numbers?

(a) 3 (b) 1
(c) 2 (d) 0

Solution *(c)* According to the question, difference between the second digit of the lowest and the highest number $= 5 - 3 = 2$

2. Ranking Test

In this type of questions generally, the ranks of a person both from the top and from the bottom are mentioned and the total number of persons are to be found out. In some questions, the total number of persons and the rank of a person from either of the ends of the row is given and the rank of that person from the other end is asked.

EXAMPLE 5 In a class, boys stand in a single line. One of the boys is nineteenth in order from both the ends. How many boys are there in the class?

(a) 27 (b) 37 (c) 38 (d) 39

Solution *(b)*

Clearly, the number of boys in the row

$= (18 + 18 + 1) = 37$

Alternate method

Total number of persons in a row or class = (Rank of a person from upper or left end) + (Rank of that person from lower or right end) – 1 (because the particular place counts two times)

$= 19 + 19 - 1 = 37$

EXAMPLE 6 Anu and Vinay are ranked seventh and eleventh respectively from the top in a class of 31 students. What will be their respective ranks from the bottom in the class?

(a) 20th and 24th (b) 24th and 20th
(c) 25th and 21st (d) None of these

Solution *(c)* Number of students after Anu in rank $= (31 - 7) = 24$

So, Anu is 25th from the bottom.

Number of students after Vinay in rank $= (31 - 11) = 20$

So, Vinay is 21st from the bottom.

Alternate method

Rank of a person from lower or right end = (Total number of persons in row) – (Rank of that person from upper or left end) + 1

Anu's rank from the bottom = 25th

Vinay's rank from the bottom $= 31 - 11 + 1 = 21$st

EXAMPLE 7 Nageena is taller than Pushpa but not as tall as Manish. Reena is taller than Namita but not as tall as Pushpa. Who among them is the tallest?

(a) Manish (b) Pushpa
(c) Namita (d) Nageena

Solution *(a)* Manish > Nageena > Pushpa

Pushpa > Reena > Namita

$\Rightarrow$ Manish > Nageena > Pushpa > Reena > Namita

Hence, Manish is the tallest one.

3. Time Sequence Test

Time sequence test further can be divided into two sub-types, i.e. clock and calendar.

(i) Clock

A clock has mainly 2 hands, the smaller one is called the hour hand while the larger one is called the minute hand. The dial of a clock is circular one, whose circumference is divided into 12 parts (12 equal big divisions) labelled as 1, 2, 3, 4 ... and 12. The space between every pair of two numbers is divided into 5 equal small divisions.

Points to be Remember

- In 60 min, the minute hand gains 55 min on the hour hand.
- In every hour, both the hands coincide once.
- The hands are in the same straight line, when they are opposite to each other.
- When the two hands are at right angles (90°), they are 15 min space apart.
- When the hands are in opposite directions, they are 30 min space apart.
- Both hands of a clock occurs at right angle twice in one hour, 22 times in 12 h and 44 times in 24 h.
- Both hands of a clock occurs in a straight line or are opposite once in one hour, 11 times in 12 h and 22 times in 24 h.

EXAMPLE 8 Reaching the place of meeting on Tuesday 15 min before 8:30 h, Anuj found himself half an hour earlier than the man who was 40 min late. What was the scheduled time of the meeting?

(a) 8:00 h (b) 8:05 h (c) 8:15 h (d) 8:45 h

Solution ***(b)*** Anuj reached the place of meeting at 8:15 h, he reached 30 min earlier than the man who was 40 min late, i.e. he reached 10 min late. Hence, the scheduled time of the meeting was 8:05 h.

EXAMPLE 9 A clock is set right at 5 am. The clock loss 16 min in 24 h. What will be the right time when the clock indicates 10 pm on the 4th day?

(a) 11:15 pm (b) 11:00 pm
(c) 12:00 pm (d) 12:30 pm

Solution ***(b)*** Time from 5 am of a particular day to 10 pm on the 4th day is 89 h. Now, the clock loses 16 min in 24 h or in other words, we can say that 23 h 44 min of this clock is equal to 24 h of the correct clock or $\left(23+\frac{44}{60}\right)=\frac{356}{15}$ h of this clock = 24 h of the correct clock

$\therefore$ 89 h of this clock $=\left(\frac{24\times15}{356}\times89\right)$ h of correct clock = 90 h of the correct clock

Therefore, it is clear that in 90 h this clock loses 1 h and hence the correct time is 11 pm when this clock shows 10 pm.

(ii) Calendar

The record of all the days of the year is given in the calendar. It shows the months, weeks and days in the year.

Days

There are seven days in a week. A week starts with Monday and ends at Sunday. After which again comes Monday. The same cycle goes on and on.

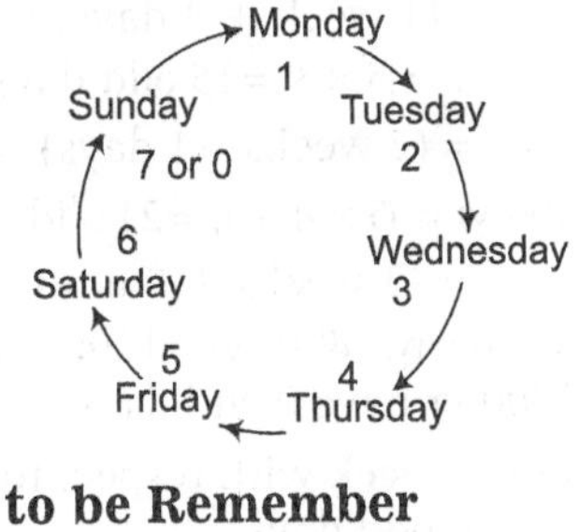

Points to be Remember

1. **Odd Days** The number of days more than the complete weeks for a given period called odd days.
2. **Ordinary Year** An ordinary year is a year which has 365 days (52 weeks + 1 odd day). Such years are not divisible by 4. e.g. 2001, 2002, 2003, 2005 etc.n Ordinary years in the form of century are not exactly divisible by 400. e.g. 100, 200 etc.

3. Leap Year

(i) A leap year has 366 days. (52 weeks + 2 odd days)

(ii) Any year (except a century) which is divisible by 4 is a leap year. e.g. 2004, 2008 etc.

(iii) However, every 4th century is a leap year, i.e. a century is a leap year when it is divisible by 400. e.g. 400, 1200 etc.

4. Counting of Odd Days

(i) 1 ordinary year = 365 days
= (52 weeks +1 day)
$\Rightarrow$ 1 ordinary year = 1 odd day

(ii) 1 leap year = 366 days
= (52 weeks + 2 days)
$\Rightarrow$ 1 leap year = 2 odd days

(iii) 100 yr
= 76 ordinary years + 24 leap years
$= (76 \times 1 + 24 \times 2)$ odd days
= 124 odd days = (17 weeks + 5 days)
= 5 odd days

(iv) 200 yr $= (5 \times 2) = 10$ odd days
= (1 week + 3 days) = 3 odd days

(v) 300 yr $= (5 \times 3) = 15$ odd days
= (2 weeks +1 days) = 1 odd day

(vi) 400 yr $= (5 \times 4 + 1) = 21$ odd days
= (3 weeks + 0 day) = 0 odd day

Similarly, 800 yr, 1200 yr, 1600 yr, 2000 yr have 0 odd days.

5. Day of the week with respect to the number of odd days.

Number of odd days	Day of the week
0	Sunday
1	Monday
2	Tuesday
3	Wednesday
4	Thursday
5	Friday
6	Saturday

6. The first day of century cannot be Wednesday, Friday and Sunday.

7. The last day of century cannot be Tuesday, Thursday and Saturday.

Month of the Year

We know that there are 12 months in a year. The months of the year with the number of days in that month are given below.

Name of the Month	Number of Days
January	31
February	28 or 29
March	31
April	30
May	31
June	30
July	31
August	31
September	30
October	31
November	30
December	31

February of an ordinary year has 28 days. There are 365 days in an ordinary year. Thus, 1 ordinary year = 365 days = 52 weeks and 1 day. February of a leap year has 29 days, so, there are 366 days in a leap year. Thus, 1 leap year = 366 days = 52 weeks and 2 days. A leap year comes after every 4 years.

EXAMPLE 10 Vinay remembers that his wife Anu's birthday falls after 20th June but before 28th June, while Shristi remembers that her mother Anu's birthday falls after 26th but before of 30th June, on what date Anu's birthday falls?

(a) 26th June (b) 27th June
(c) 28th June (d) 29th June

Solution *(b)*

According to	Anu's birthday
Vinay	21, 22, 23, 24, 25, 26, 27
Shristi	27, 28, 29

Here, 27th June is common date. So, Anu's birthday falls on 27th June.

EXAMPLE 11 If 8th February 2005, was a Tuesday, then what was the day on 8th February, 2004?

(a) Tuesday (b) Monday
(c) Sunday (d) Wednesday

Solution *(c)* The year 2004 is a leap year. It has 2 odd days. The day on 8th February, 2004 is 2 days before the day on 8th February, 2005. Hence, this day is Sunday.

Practice Exercise

Directions (Q. Nos. 1-2) *Study the number series given below and answer the questions that follow.*

7 8 9 7 6 5 3 4 2 8 9 7 2 4 5 9 2 9 7 6 4 7

1. How many 7's are preceded by 9 and followed by 6?

(a) 2 (b) 3 (c) 4 (d) 5

2. Which figures have equal frequency?

(a) 2, 5, 3 (b) 2, 4, 5
(c) 3, 7, 5 (d) 8, 6, 5

3. In the series, 6 4 1 2 2 8 7 4 2 1 5 3 8 6 2 1 7 1 4 1 3 2 8 6

How many pairs of alternate numbers have a difference of 2?

(a) 1 (b) 2 (c) 3 (d) 4

Directions (Q. Nos. 4-6) *Study the sets of numbers given below and answer the questions which follow*

972 682 189 298 751

4. If one is added to the lowest number and two is added to the highest number, then what will be the difference between the second digit of the smallest number and the third digit of the highest number?

(a) 5 (b) 7 (c) 9 (d) 8

5. If in each number, first and the last digit are interchanged, then which one of the following will be the third highest number?

(a) 972 (b) 682
(c) 189 (d) 298

6. If in each number, all the three digits are arranged in descending order, which of the following will be the third highest number?

(a) 972 (b) 682
(c) 189 (d) 298

7. The positions of how many digits in the number 837912 will remain unchanged after the digits within the number are rearranged in descending order (from left to right)?

(a) None (b) One (c) Two (d) Three

8. If in the number 3856490271, positions of the first and the second digits are interchanged, positions of the third and fourth digits are interchanged and so on till the positions of 9th and 10th digits are interchanged, then which digit will be fifth from the left end?

(a) 6 (b) 4 (c) 9 (d) 0

9. If it is possible to make only one such number with the first, the fourth and the sixth digits of the number 531697, which is the perfect square of a two-digit even number, which of the following will be the second digit of the two digit even number. If no such number can be made, give '@' as the answer and if more than one such numbers can be made, give © as the answer.

(a) 4 (b) 2 (c) @ (d) ©

10. Rashmi is 14th from the right end in a row of 40 girls. What is her position from the left end?

(a) 25th (b) 27th
(c) 21st (d) None of these

11. Surbhi ranks 18th in a class of 49 students. What is her rank from the last?

(a) 31st (b) 28th
(c) 35th (d) 32nd

12. Among P, Q, R, S, T and U, P is taller than R and S, but not shorter than T and U and Q is taller than R, S, T, and U but not as tall as P. Who amongst them is tallest?

(a) Data inadequate (b) T
(c) 4 (d) P

Directions (Q. Nos. 13 and 14) *Read the following information carefully and answer the questions.*

Among A, B, C, D and E. E is taller than D but not as fat as D. C is taller than A but shorter than B. A is fatter than D but not as fat as B. E is thinner than C who is thinner than D. E is shorter than A.

13. Who is the thinnest person?
(a) B (b) C
(c) D (d) E

14. Who is the big giant among them?
(a) A (b) B (c) C (d) D

15. Harish is taller than Manish but shorter than Suresh. Manish is shorter than Anil but taller than Raghu. Who among them is the shortest having regard to height?
(a) Anil
(b) Manish
(c) Raghu
(d) Cannot be determined

16. In a class of 60, where number of girls are twice that of boys, Kamal ranked seventeenth from the top. If there are 9 girls before of Kamal, how many boys are after him in rank?
(a) 3 (b) 7
(c) 12 (d) 23

17. N ranks fifth in a class. S is eighth from the last. If T is sixth after N and is in the middle of N and S, then how many students are there in the class?
(a) 23 (b) 24 (c) 25 (d) 26

18. In a row of boys Jeevan is 7th from the start and 11th from the end. In another row of boys Vikash is 10th from the start and 12th from the end. How many boys are there in both the rows together?
(a) Cannot be determined
(b) 37
(c) 36
(d) None of the above

19. In a row of 40 boys facing the North, Amar is 6th to the right of Sudeep and Sudeep is 11th to the left of Vijay. If Amar is 28th from the right end of the row, what is the position of Vijay from the left end of the row?
(a) 17th (b) 21st
(c) 20th (d) 18th

20. In a row of boys, Rajan is 10th from the right and Suraj is 10th from the left. When Rajan and Suraj interchange their positions, Suraj will be 27th from the left. Which of the following will be Rajan's position from the right?
(a) 10th (b) 26th
(c) 29th (d) None of these

21. Ashish leaves his house at 20 min to seven in the morning, reaches Kunal's house in 25 min, they finish their breakfast in another 15 min and leave for their office which takes another 35 min. At what time do they leave Kunal's house to reach their office?
(a) 7 : 40 am (b) 7 : 20 am
(c) 7 : 45 am (d) 18 : 15 am

22. It was 9 : 35 am in Rakhi's watch, which kept correct time, when Reena informed her that the last bus left the bus stop at 9 : 25 am Reena's watch is 5 min fast. The frequency of the bus is every 20 min. For how long must Rakhi wait to catch the next bus?
(a) 5 min (b) 10 min
(c) 15 min (d) 25 min

23. How many times are the hands of a clock is at right angle in a day?
(a) 22 (b) 24 (c) 44 (d) 48

24. Vinay remembers that his brother Anupam's birthday is after 20th of August but before 28th of August, while Rita remembers that Anupam's birthday is before 22nd of August but after 12th of August. On which date does Anupam's birthdays fall?
(a) 20th August
(b) 21st August
(c) 22nd August
(d) Cannot be determined

25. Ranjana correctly remembers that Kiran's birthday was after Tuesday but before Friday. Rajan correctly remembers that Kiran's birthday was after Wednesday but before Sunday. On which days of the week does Kiran's birthday definitely fall?
(a) Monday
(b) Thursday
(c) Saturday
(d) Cannot be determined

26. If a month in an year starts with Monday, then the date of the fourth day after the second Saturday in that month, will be

(a) 16 (b) 17 (c) 18 (d) 19

27. If 18th February, 1997 falls on Tuesday, then what will be the day on 18th February, 1999?

(a) Monday (b) Tuesday
(c) Thursday (d) Friday

28. Raju decided to marry 3 yr after he gets a job. He was 17 yr old when he passed class 12th. After passing class 12th, he had completed his graduation course in 3 yr and PG course in 2 yr. He got the job exactly 1 year after completing his PG course. At what age, will he get married?

(a) 27 yr (b) 26 yr (c) 28 yr (d) 23 yr

29. A clock is fast by 15 min in 24 h. It is made right at 12 noon, what time will it show at 4 am?

(a) 4 : 10 am (b) 4 : 15 am
(c) 3 : 45 am (d) 4 : 30 am

30. At what angle, the hands of a clock are inclined at 15 min past 5?

(a) $58\frac{1}{2}^\circ$ (b) 64° (c) $67\frac{1}{2}^\circ$ (d) $72\frac{1}{2}^\circ$

31. At what time between 7 and 8 O'clock, will the hands of a clock be in the same straight line but, not together?

(a) 5 min past 7 (b) $5\frac{2}{11}$ min past 7
(c) $5\frac{3}{11}$ min past 7 (d) $5\frac{5}{11}$ min past 7

Previous Year's Questions

32. If Monday falls on October 1, which day will fall 3 days after the 20th in that month? **[CLAT 2015]**

(a) Monday (b) Tuesday
(c) Saturday (d) Wednesday

33. In a class, student X has 8th position from the top and 84th from the bottom. How many students are there in the class? **[CLAT 2016]**

(a) 88 (b) 96 (c) 98 (d) 91

34. Vaishavi prefers Economics to Maths, English to Social science, and Political Science to History. If she prefers Maths to History, and Social science to maths, which is Vaishnavi's least preferred subject? **[CLAT 2017]**

(a) History (b) Economics
(c) Social science (d) Maths

35. The birthday of Mrs Y was celebrated sixs days before Mrs X, who was born on 4th October 1999. The independence day of that year fell on Sunday. On which day did Mrs Y celebrate her birthday, if it was not a leap year? **[CLAT 2017]**

(a) Wednesday (b) Tuesday
(c) Monday (d) Sunday

36. If 27th March, 2011 was Sunday, what was the day on 27th June, 2011? **[CLAT 2017]**

(a) Monday (b) Tuesday
(c) Sunday (d) Saturday

37. How many times from 4 pm to 10 pm, the hands of a clock are at right angles. **[CLAT 2017]**

(a) 11 (b) 6 (b) 9 (d) 10

Answers

1	*a*	2	*d*	3	*b*	4	*a*	5	*b*	6	*a*	7	*b*	8	*c*	9	*a*	10	*b*
11	*d*	12	*d*	13	*d*	14	*b*	15	*c*	16	*c*	17	*b*	18	*d*	19	*d*	20	*d*
21	*b*	22	*a*	23	*c*	24	*b*	25	*b*	26	*b*	27	*c*	28	*b*	29	*a*	30	*c*
31	*d*	32	*d*	33	*d*	34	*a*	35	*b*	36	*a*	37	*a*						

SOLUTIONS

1. There are two such 7's.

78 |976| 5342897245
92 |976| 47

2. Frequency of 2 = 3
Frequency of 3 = 1
Frequency of 4 = 3
Frequency of 5 = 2
Frequency of 6 = 2
Frequency of 7 = 5
Frequency of 8 = 2
Frequency of 9 = 4
Hence, 5, 6 and 8 have equal frequency.

3. There are two such pairs

6④1②2 8 7 4 2①5③8

6 2 1 7 1 4 1 3 2 8 6

4. 189 + 1 = 190; 972 + 2 = 974
Hence, required difference
= 9 − 4 = 5

5. After interchanging first and last digit, numbers are
→ 279, 286, 981, 892, 157
Hence, third highest number
= 286
⇒ 682

6. After arranging the digits in descending order, we get
972, 862, 981, 982, 751
Hence, third highest number
= 972

7. Given number 8 3 |7| 9 1 2
Descending order 9 8 |7| 3 2 1

Hence, the position of only one digit, i.e. 7, remain unchanged.

8.

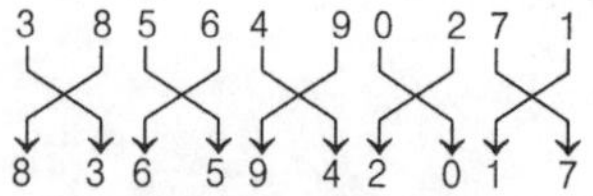

New arrangement
= 8365942017

Hence, fifth digit from the left end = 9

9. 5 3 1 6 9 7
1st 4th 6th
Perfect square = 576
Square root = $\sqrt{576}$ = 24
Hence, second digit = 4

10. Required position
= (40 + 1 − 14) = 27th

11. Surbhi's rank from last
= (49 + 1 − 18) = 32 th

12. P > R, S, T, U
P > Q > R, T, S, U
Hence, P is the tallest one.

Solutions (Q. Nos. 13 and 14)
According to the question,

Taller	Fatter
E > D	D > E
B > C > A	B > A > D
A > E	D > C > E
Finally,	Finally,
B > C > A > E > D	B > A > D > C > E

13. E is the thinnest person.

14. B is the big giant among them.

15. Suresh > Harish > Manish ...(i)
Anil > Manish > Raghu ...(ii)
⇒ From statement I, shortest is Manish and from statement II, Raghu is shorter than Manish. So, from both the statements Raghu is the shortest one.

16. Number of boys = 20
Number of girls = 40
Number of students behind Kamal in rank = (60 − 17) = 43
Number of girls ahead of Kamal in rank = 9
Number of girls behind Kamal in rank = (40 − 9) = 31
Number of boys behind Kamal in rank = (43 − 31) = 12

17. According to the question,

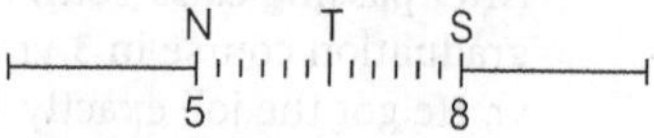

Number of students in the class
= (4 + 1 + 5 + 1 + 5 + 1 + 7)
= 24

18. Number of boys in the first row
= 7 + 11 − 1 = 17
Number of boys in the second row
= 10 + 12 − 1 = 21
Total number of boys
= 17 + 21 = 38

19. According to the question,

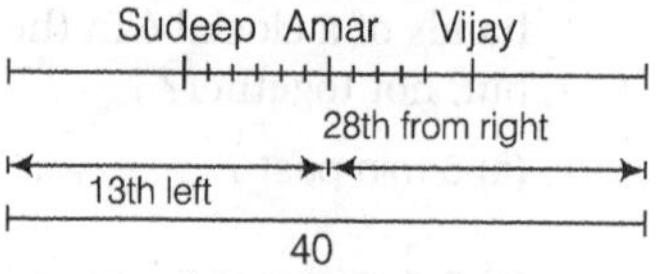

∴ Number of boys to the left of Sudeep = 40 − (28 + 6)
= 40 − 34 = 6
Position of Vijay from the left end
= 6 + 1 + 5 + 1 + 4 + 1 = 18 th

20. Total number of boys
= (10 + 27 − 1) = 37 − 1 = 36
So, Rajan's position from the right
= (36 − 10) + 1
= 26 + 1 = 27

21. According to the question, Ashish leaves his house at 6 : 40 am. And he reaches Kunal's house in 25 min i.e.

7 : 05 am. Hence, both leave for office 15 min after 7 : 05 am, i.e. 7 : 20 am.

22. The last but left at 9 : 25 am by Reena's watch.

$\therefore$ It left at $(9:25-0:05)$
$= 9:20$ am correct time.

$\therefore$ Next bus will leave at
$(9:20+0:20) = 9:40$ am

$\therefore$ Rakhi must wait for
$(9:40-9:35) = 5$ min

23. In 12 h, they are at right angles, 22 times. So, in 24 h, they are at right angles, 44 times.

24.

According to	Birth date
Vinay	21, 22, 23, 24, 25, 26, 27
Rita	13, 14, 15, 16, 17, 18, 19, 20, 21

Here, 21 is common to both. So, confirm date is 21st August.

25.

According to	Birthday
Ranjana	Wednesdya, Thursday
Rajan	Thursday, Friday, Saturday

Here, thursday is common to both. So, confirm day is thursday.

26. 1st day of month is Monday.
6th day of month is Saturday.
13th day of month is second Saturday.
$\therefore$ 17th day is the fourth day after second Saturday.

27. 18th February, 1997 is Tuesday. So, 17th February, 1998 will also Tuesday.

Again, 16th February, 1999 will also be Tuesday. Hence, 18th February, 1999 will be Thursday.

28. Age at the time of marriage of Raju $= 17+3+2+1+3$
$= 26$ yr

29. From 12 noon to next day 4 am.

$= (12+4) = 16$ h

$\because$ Clock gains in 24 h
$= 15$ min

$\therefore$ Clock will gain in 1 h
$= \frac{15}{24}$ min

So, clock will gain in 16 h
$= \frac{15}{24} \times 16 = 10$ min

Hence, time in the clock at 4 am
$= 4$ h, 10 min $= 4:10$ am

30. Angle traced by hour hand in
$5+\frac{15}{60} = \frac{21}{4}$ h
$= \left(\frac{360}{12} \times \frac{21}{4}\right)^\circ = 157\frac{1}{2}^\circ$

So, angle traced by minutes hand in 15 min
$= \left(\frac{360}{60} \times 15\right)^\circ = 90^\circ$

Hence, required angle
$= \left(157\frac{1}{2}\right)^\circ - 90^\circ = 67\frac{1}{2}^\circ$

31. We know that, when the hands of the clock are in the same straight line but not together, they are 30 min spaces apart.
At 7 O'clock they are 25 min spaces apart.
$\therefore$ Minute hand needs to gain only 5 min spaces.
5 min spaces are gained in
$\left(\frac{60}{55} \times 5\right)$ min $= 5\frac{5}{11}$ min

So, required time $= 5\frac{5}{11}$ min past 7

Previous Year's Solution

32. Given that,
1st October $\to$ Monday
then, 8th October $\to$ Monday
15th October $\to$ Monday
22nd October $\to$ Monday
So, 20th October
21st October
22nd October $\to$ Monday
23rd October $\to$ Tuesday
24th October $\to$ Wednesday
So, the day fall 3 days after the 20th October will be Wednesday.

33. Total number of students in the class
$= (8+84)-1$
$= 92-1 = 91$

34. The preference is as
Economics > Math
English > Social Science
Politcal Science > History
Math > Math
History is least preferred subject.

35. Birth date of X = 4th october
$\therefore$ Birth date Y = 28th September
Independence day = 15th August = Sunday
$\therefore$ 28th September
$= \frac{16+28}{7} = \frac{44}{7} = 2$ extra days
= Tuesday

36. Number of add days
$= \frac{4+30+31+27}{7} = \frac{92}{7} = 1$
$\therefore$ 27th June = Monday

37. Total number of rith angle
$= 6 \times 2 - 1 = 11$
(In each hour right angle is made trick)

CHAPTER 07

DIRECTION SENSE TEST

Direction is a measurement of position of one thing with respect to another thing and displacement is the measurement of distance between the starting and the final point. In the questions based on direction sense test, instructions regarding the movement of a person or an object from a starting point upto an end point are given. The candidates are required to ascertain the final direction or the distance between the starting and end points. These questions are designed to test the candidate's ability to sense the direction correctly.

TYPES OF DIRECTION

There are two types of directions

1. Main Directions

There are four main directions, *viz.*, East, West, North and South. Sun rises in the East and sets is the West. Just opposite of East is West and South is opposite to North.

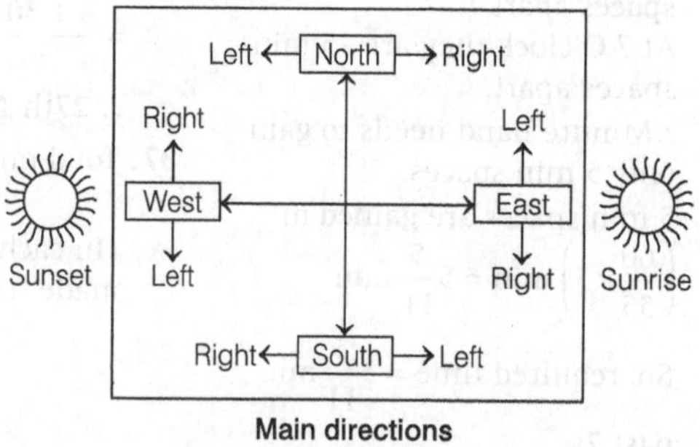

Main directions

Abbreviations for these directions are E (East), W(West), N(North) and S(South).

Example 1 A man started walking towards West. He turned right, then right again and finally turned left. Towards which direction was he walking finally?

(a) North (b) South (c) West (d) East

Solution *(a)* According to the question, the direction diagram can be drawn as

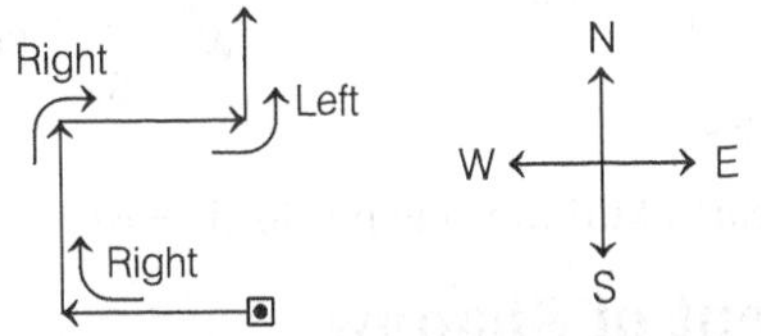

Finally, he was walking towards North.

2. Cardinal Directions/ Sub-directions

A direction between two adjacent main directions is called cardinal direction or sub-direction. There are four cardinal directions *viz.*, NE (North-East), NW (North-West), SE (South-East) and SW (South-West). Students are advised to use the following diagram for the purpose of sensing directions.

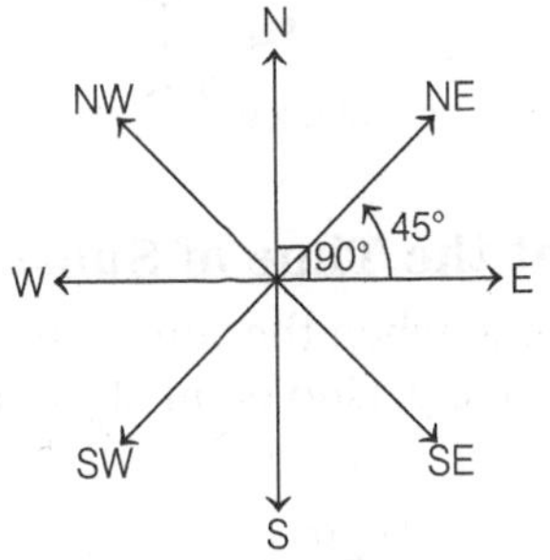

Standard Direction Diagram

Angle formed between two adjacent main directions or two adjacent cardinal directions is 90° and angle formed between a cardinal direction and adjacent main direction is 45°.

Example 2 If Ram's house is located to the South of Krishna's house and Govinda's house is to the East of Krishna's house, in what direction is Ram's house situated with respect to Govinda's house?

(a) North-East (b) North-West
(c) South-East (d) South-West

Solution *(d)* According to the question, the direction diagram is as follows

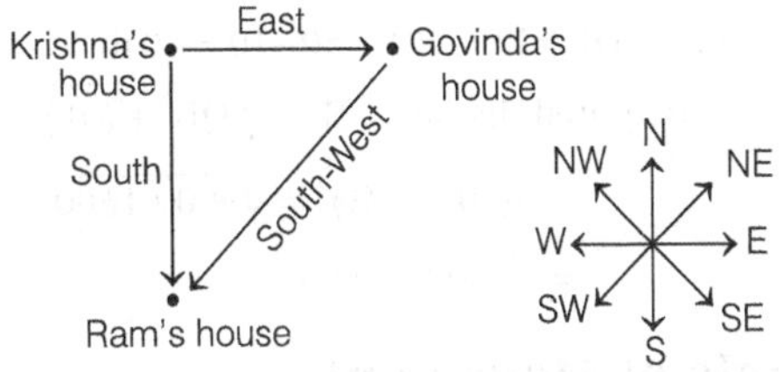

Clearly, Ram's house is to the South-West of Govinda's house.

TYPES OF QUESTIONS

The question based on direction since test can be divided into following types

Shortest Distance

For finding shortest distance, it is necessary to know Pythagoras theorem.

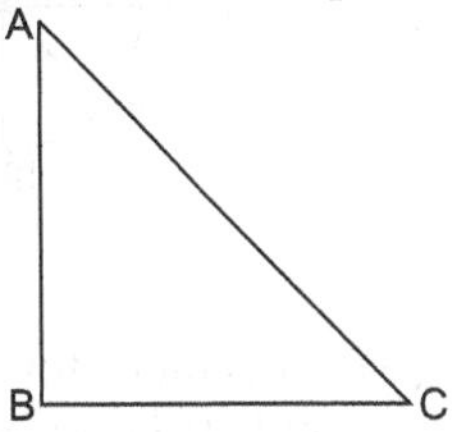

AB = Perpendicular

BC = Base

AC = hypotenuse

Hence, for shortest distance

$$AC = \sqrt{AB^2 + BC^2}$$

Example 3 Kavi walks Northward upto 10 m. He turns left and walks 30 m. Finally, he turns left and walks 50 m. At what distance Kavi is now from his starting position?

(a) 50 m (b) 10 m (c) 20 m (d) 90 m

Solution *(a)* According to the question, the direction diagram is drawn as shown in below figure

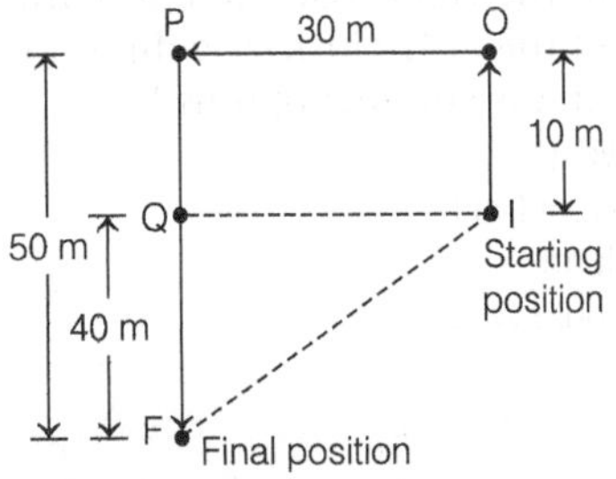

Here, $IO = 10\,m$, $OP = 30\,m$ and $PF = 50\,m$
$QI = PO = 30\,m$, $PQ = OI = 10\,m$

and $QF = PF - PQ = 50 - 10 = 40\,m$

$\therefore$ Required distance, $IF = \sqrt{(QI)^2 + (QF)^2}$

$= \sqrt{(30)^2 + (40)^2} = \sqrt{900 + 1600}$

$= \sqrt{2500} = 50\,m$

Angle of Movement

For solving questions based on angle of movement, it is necessary to know the rotations *which are given below*

(i) Movement towards the right is called the *clockwise* (CW) *movement*.

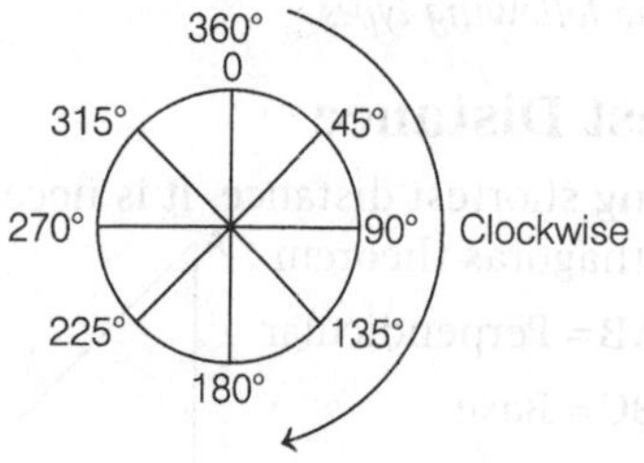

(ii) Movement towards the left is called *anti-clockwise* (ACW) *movement*.

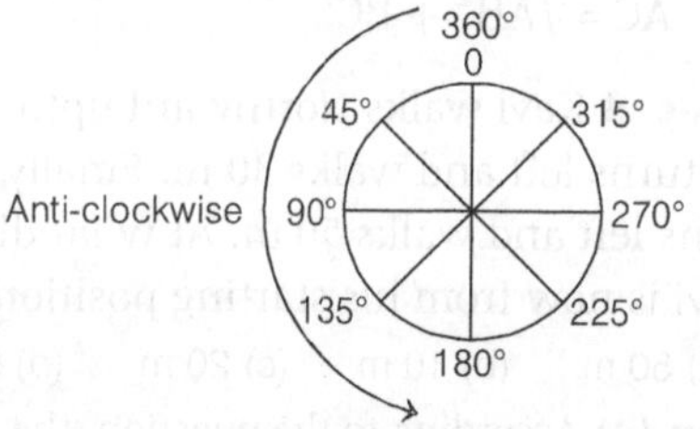

Example 4 Surbhi is facing East. She turns 100° in the clockwise direction and then 145° in the anti-clockwise direction. Which direction is she facing now?

(a) West
(b) North-East
(c) North
(d) South-West

Solution (*b*) According to the question, the direction diagram will be as follows

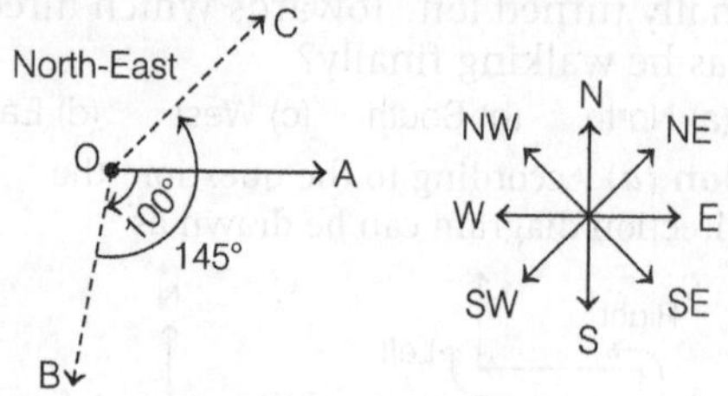

Clearly, Surbhi is facing North-East.

Concept of Shadow

When a person or object stand in sunlight, then his shadow is formed either towards his left or right or in any other direction. *It can be understood as follows*

Shadow at the Time of Sunrise

In the morning, sunrises in the East, the shadow of any person or object falls in the West.

Shadow at the Time of Sunset

In the evening, when the sunset in the West, the shadow of a person or an object falls in the East.

Example 5 One evening before sunset, two friends Raman and Arjun were talking to each other face to face. If Raman's shadow was exactly to his left side, then which direction was Arjun facing?

(a) West (b) East (c) North (d) South

Solution (*c*) According to the question,

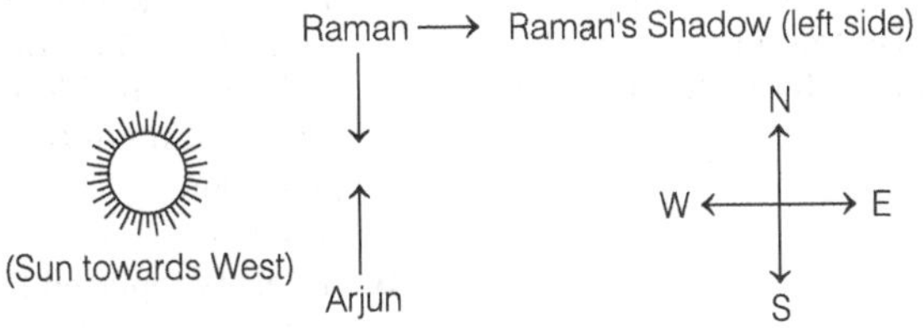

So, Arjun was facing North.

Practice Exercise

1. A girl walks Northward then turns left, then right and then left after walking some distance each time. In which direction is she from the starting point?
(a) North-East (b) North-West
(c) South-West (d) South-East

2. The clinic of doctor faces West. From the back side of his clinic, he walks straight 100 m, then turns to the left and walks 100 m again. Finally, he turns towards right and stops after walking 50 m. Now, in which direction is the doctor from the starting point?
(a) South-West (b) North-East
(c) South-East (d) North-West

3. Town D is to the West of town M. Town R is to the South of town D. Town K is to the East of town R. Town K is towards which direction of town D?
(a) South (b) East
(c) North-East (d) South-East

4. A rat runs 20 m towards East and turns to right, runs 10 m and turns to right, runs 9 m and again turns to left, runs 5 m and then turns to left, runs 12 m and finally turns to left and runs 6 m. Now, which direction is the rat facing?
(a) East (b) North
(c) West (d) South

5. Bharti travelled a distance of 85 m towards North, then turned to left and walked for 15 m. She turned left again and walked 60 m. Finally, she turned left at an angle of 45° and continued walking. In which direction was she moving ultimately?
(a) South-East (b) South
(c) South-West (d) West

6. Asha walks 3 km Southward and then turns right and walks 2 km. She again turns right and walks 3 km and tuns toward her left and starts walking straight. In which direction is she walking now?
(a) East (b) North
(c) South (d) West

7. Arun's office is situated at 5 km South from Bharat's office. Bharat starts from his office and walks 2 km towards Arun's office. He then turns left and walks 3 km and then turns right and walks 3 km. In which direction will he turn to reach Arun's office?
(a) East (b) West
(c) North (d) South

8. Ramesh walks 10 m Eastward, then turns right and walks 10 m. He then again turns right and walks 10 m. He takes a 45° turn leftwards and walks straight. In which direction is he walking now?
(a) North-West (b) South-East
(c) South-West (d) North-East

9. A clock is so placed that at 12 noon its minute hand points towards North-East. In which direction does its hour hand point at 1 : 30 pm?
(a) North (b) South
(c) East (d) West

10. A man is facing towards West and turns through 45° clockwise, again 180° clockwise and then turns through 270° anti-clockwise. In which direction is he facing now?
(a) West
(b) North-West
(c) North
(d) South-West

11. Mohan walked 30 m towards South, took a left turn and walked 15 m. He then took a right turn and walked 20 m. He again took a right turn and walked 15 m. How far is he from the starting point?
(a) 95 m
(b) 50 m
(c) 70 m
(d) Cannot be determined

12. A postman was returning to the post office which was in front of him to the North. When the post office was 100 m away from him, he turned to left and went 50 m to deliver the last letter at the Shanti Villa. He then went in the same direction for 40 m, turned to his right and went 100 m. How many metres was he away from the post office?
(a) 0 (b) 150 (c) 90 (d) 100

13. Maya starts from point P, walks straight to point Q which is 4 ft away. She turns left at 90° and walks to W which is 4 ft away, turns 90° right and goes 3 ft straight, turns 90° right and walks 1 ft to S, turns left at 90° and goes to U, which is 1 ft away and once again turns 90° right and goes to V, 3 ft away. What is the distance between P and V?
(a) 5 ft (b) 7 ft (c) 6 ft (d) 8 ft

14. Starting from a point M, Harish walked 18 m towards South. He turned to his left and walked 25 m. He then turned to his left and walked 18 m. He again turned to his left and walked 35 m and reached a point P. How far is Harish from the point M and in which direction?
(a) 10 m East (b) 10 m West
(c) 35 m West (d) 10 m South

15. I am facing South. I turn right and walk 20 m. Then, I turn right again and walk 10 m. Then, I turn left and walk 10 m and then turning right, walk 20 m. Then, turn right again and walk 60 m. In which direction am I from the starting point?
(a) North (b) North-East
(c) East (d) West

16. Madhuri travels 14 km Westwards and then turns left and travels 6 km and further turns left and travels 26 km. How far is Madhuri now from the starting point?
(a) $\sqrt{180}$ km (b) $\sqrt{80}$ km
(c) $\sqrt{100}$ km (d) None of these

17. Raj and Roy start walking in opposite directions. Raj walked 3 km and Roy walked 4 km. Then, Raj turned right and walked 4 km and Roy turned left and walked 3 km. How far is each of them from the starting point?
(a) 4.5 km (b) 6 km
(c) 5 km (d) 8 km

18. If East is replaced by South-East, then West will be replaced by which of the following directions?
(a) North-East (b) North
(c) East (d) North-West

Previous Year's Questions

19. One morning after sunrise, Suraj standing facing a pole. The shadow of the pole fell exactly to his right. Which direction was Suraj facing? **[CLAT 2014]**
(a) West (b) South
(c) East (d) Data is inadequant

20. Two buses start from the opposite points of a main road, 150 km apart. The first bus runs for 25 km and takes a right turn and then runs for 15 km. Then it turns left and runs for another 25 km and takes the direction back to reach the main road. In the meantime, due to a minor breakdown, the other bus has run only 35 km along the main road. What would be the distance between the two buses at this point? **[CLAT 2014]**
(a) 65 km (b) 75 km (c) 80 km (d) 85 km

21. John wants to go the university. He starts from his house which is in the East and comes to a crossing. The rood to his left ends in a Theatre, straight head is the hospital. In which direction is the university? **[CLAT 2014]**
(a) North (b) East
(c) West (d) South

22. If South-East becomes North, North-East become West and so on, what will West Become? **[CLAT 2017]**
(a) South-East (b) North
(c) East (d) North-West

23. Sunil's school bus is facing North when it reachers his school. After starting from Sunil's house, it turned right twice and then left before reaching the school. What direction the bus was facing when it left the bus stop in front of Sunil's house? **[CLAT 2017]**
(a) South (b) East
(c) West (d) North

24. A man walks 1 km towards East and then the turns to South and walks 5 km. Again he turns to East and walks 2 kms. After this he turns to North and walks 9 kms. Now how far is he from his starting point? **[CLAT 2017]**

(a) 5 km (b) 9 kms (c) 4 kms (d) 10 kms

25. In a millitary secret service map, South-East in shown as North, North-East as West and so on. What will West become? **[CLAT 2017]**

(a) South-West (b) North-West

(c) North-East (d) South-East

Answers

1	*b*	2	*b*	3	*d*	4	*b*	5	*a*	6	*d*	7	*b*	8	*c*	9	*c*	10	*d*
11	*b*	12	*c*	13	*d*	14	*b*	15	*b*	16	*a*	17	*c*	18	*d*	19	*b*	20	*a*
21	*a*	22	*a*	23	*c*	24	*a*	25	*d*										

SOLUTIONS

1.

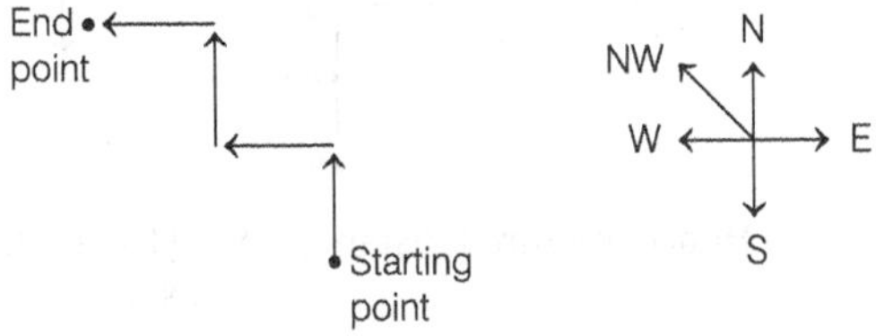

Clearly, she is in North-West direction from the starting point.

2.

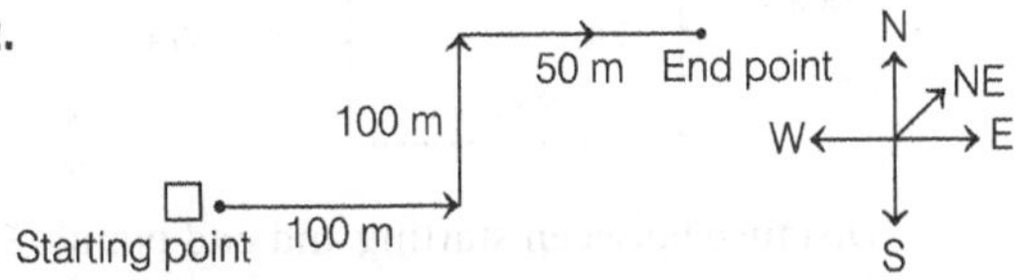

Clearly, the doctor is in North-East direction from the starting point.

3.

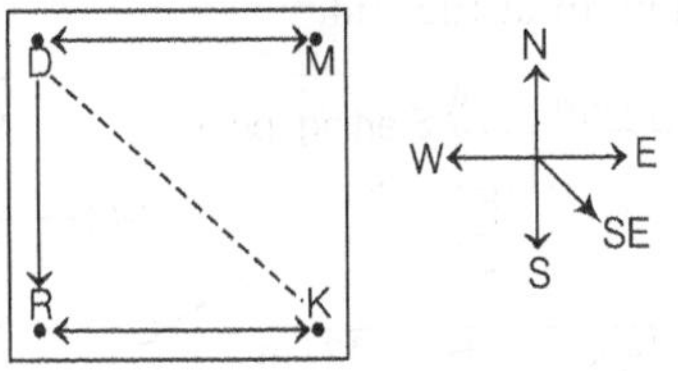

Hence, K is towards South-East of town D.

4.

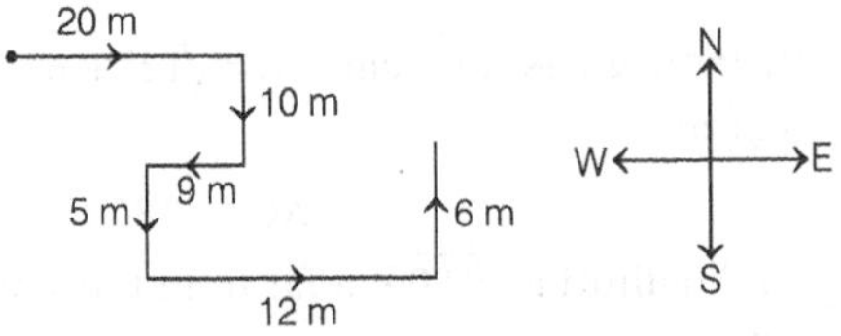

Hence, finally rat is facing North direction.

5.

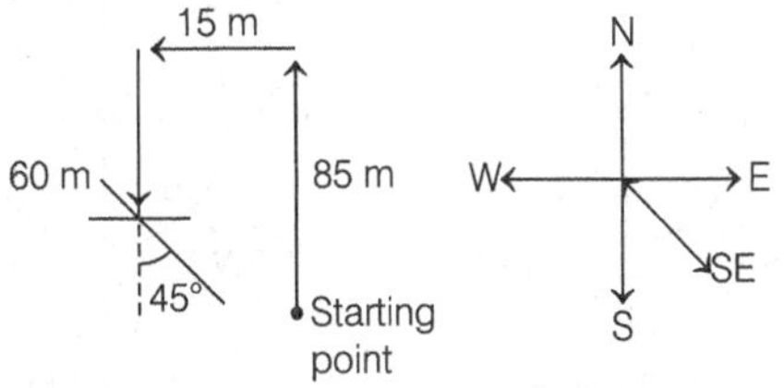

Finally, Bharti is moving in South-East direction..

6.

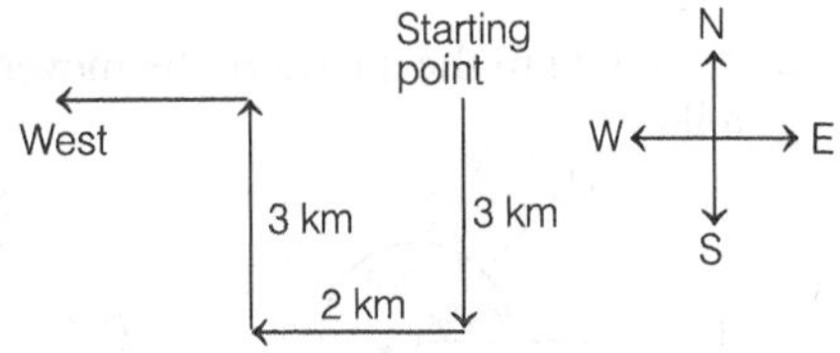

It is clear from the above diagram, that finally Asha is walking in West direction.

7.

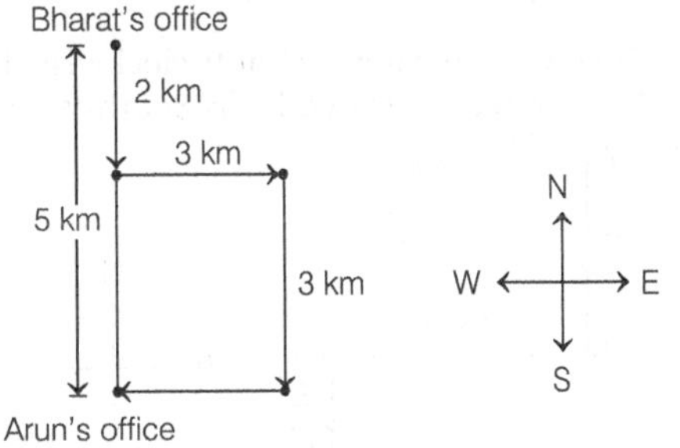

Clearly, he will have to turn in West direction to reach at Arun's office.

8.

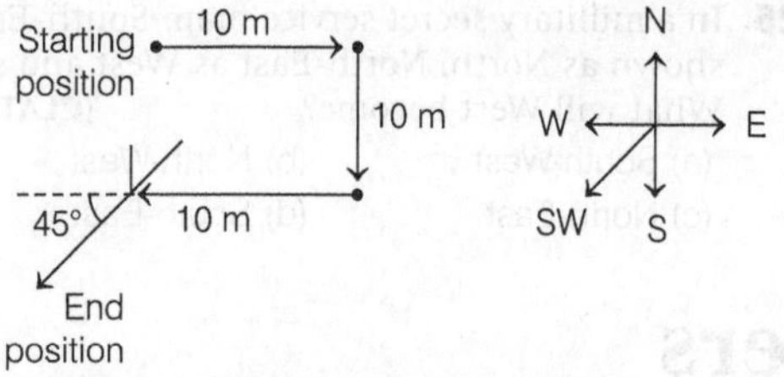

It is clear from the above diagram that finally he is walking towards South-West direction.

9. In this question, the clock is placed, so that at 12 noon its minute hand point towards North-East. We know that, minute and hour hand point in the same direction at 12 noon. Therefore, the clock will look some what like this

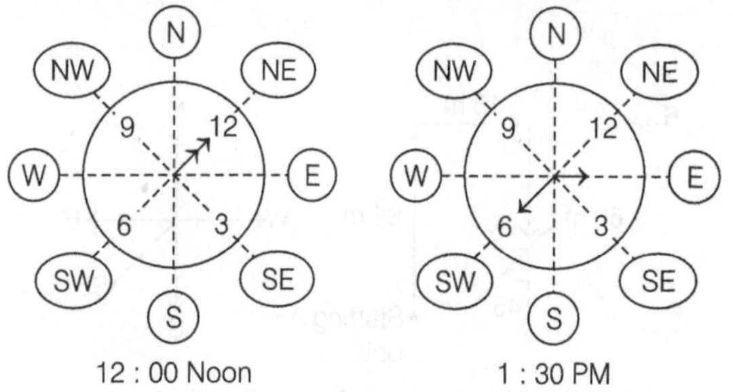

At 1 : 30 pm, the hour hand will point in the East direction.

10. According to the question, the movements are as follow

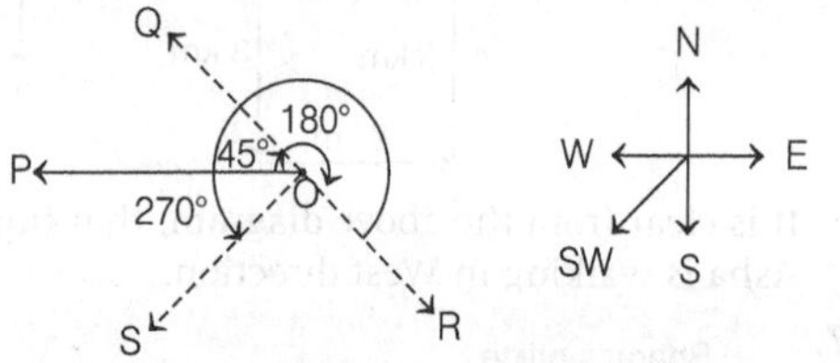

Finally, on moving 270° anti-clockwise, he faces in the direction OS which is South-West.

11.

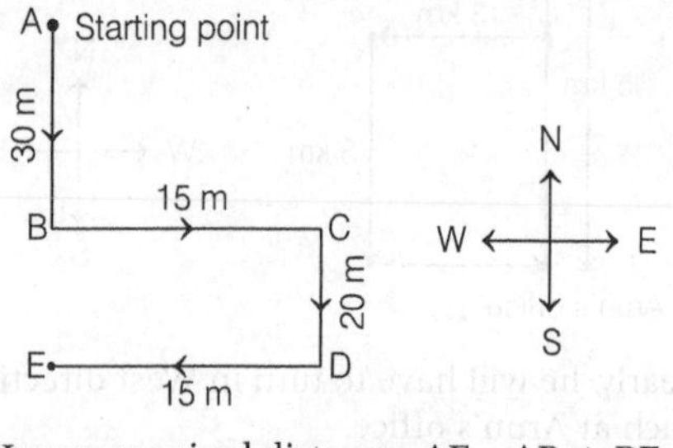

Hence, required distance, AE = AB + BE
= (30 + 20) m = 50 m

12.

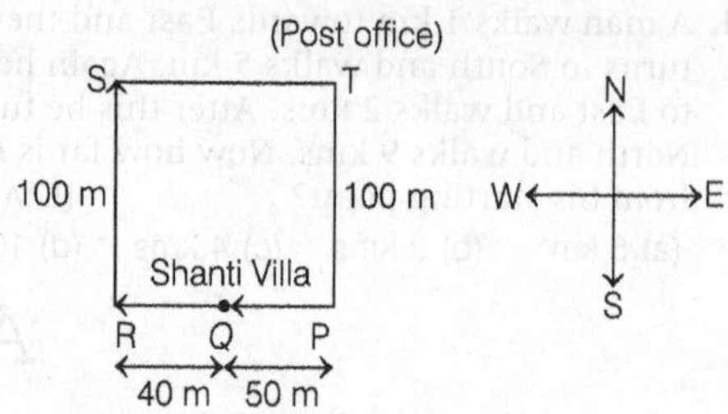

Clearly, required distance, ST
= (40 + 50) m = 90 m

13.

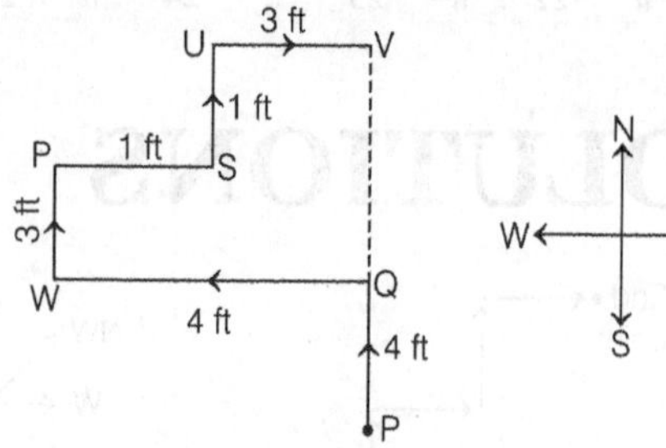

Hence, required distance, PV = (4 + 3 + 1) ft
= 8 ft

14.

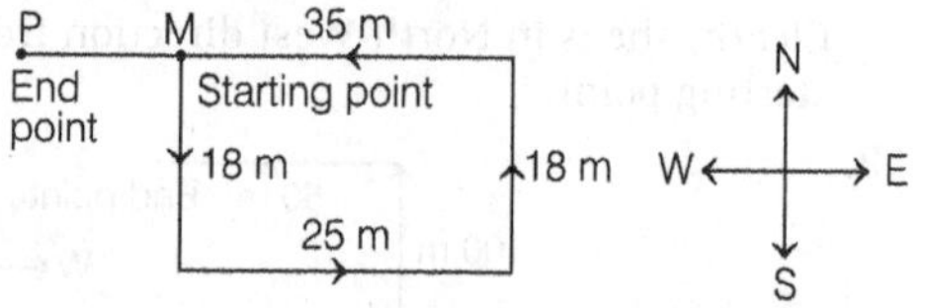

Distance between starting and end points, PM
= (35 − 25) m = 10 m and direction is West.

15. Clearly, I am in North-East direction from the starting point at the end.

16.

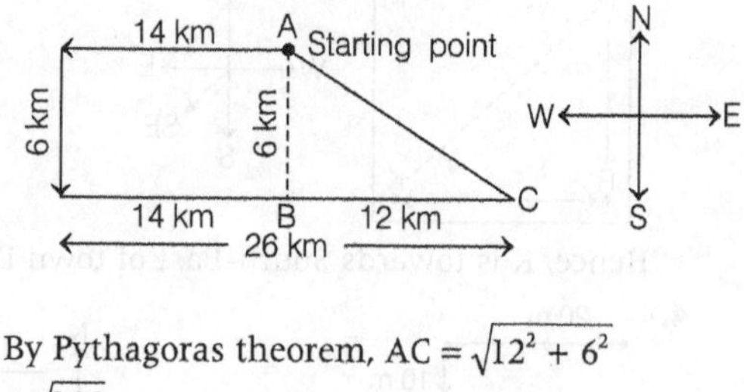

By Pythagoras theorem, $AC = \sqrt{12^2 + 6^2}$
$= \sqrt{180}$

$AC = \sqrt{180}$ km

So, Madhuri is $\sqrt{180}$ km far from the starting point.

17. Q→ Starting point

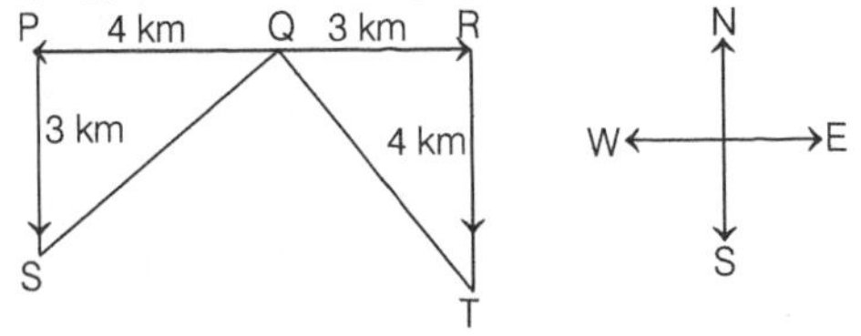

Hence, required distance

$$= QS = QT = \sqrt{4^2 + 3^2} = \sqrt{25} = 5\,\text{km}$$

18. According to the question, the diagram will be as follow

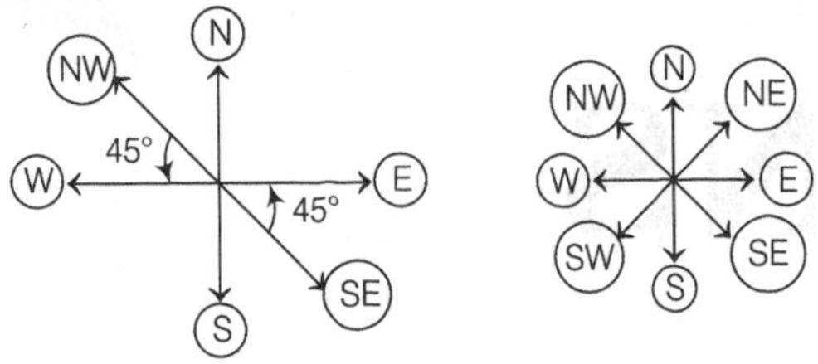

Clearly, West will be replaced by North-West.

Previous Year's Solutions

19. Sun rises in the East in the morning so in morning, the shadow falls towards the West. Now, Suraj's shadow falls to the right. So, he is standing facing South.

20. Let X and Y be two buses.

Bus X travels along the path

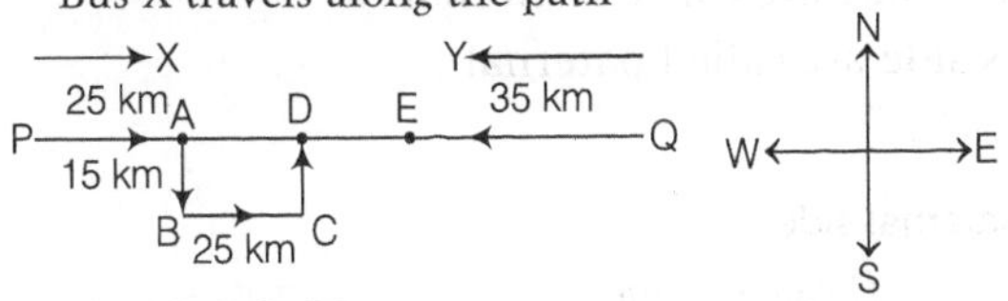

PA, AB, BC, CD

Now, AD = BC = 25 km

So, PD= PA + AD = 50 km

Bus Y travels 35 km upto E.

∵ Distance between two buses,

DE = PQ − (PD + QE) = [150 − (50 + 35)] = 65 km

21. So, University is in North-direction

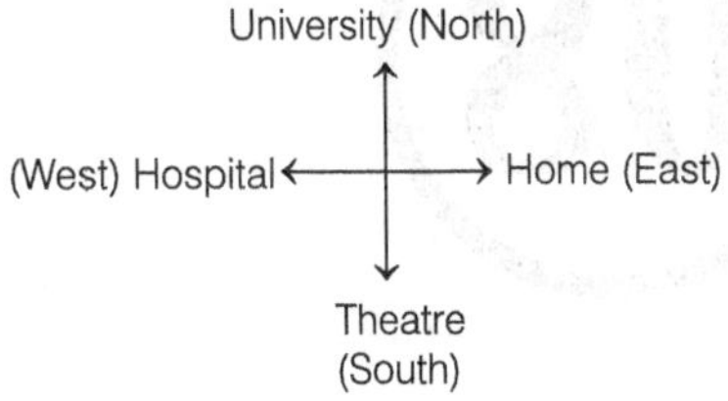

22. West will become South-East.

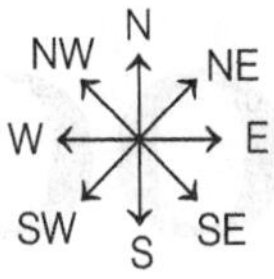

23.

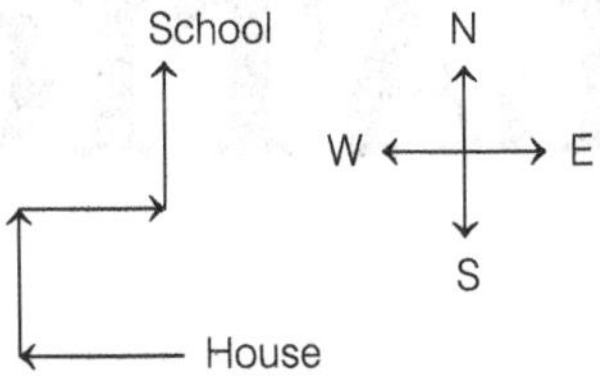

Hence, at stop bus was facing West.

24. Here, BC = 4 km

AC = 3 km

∴ $AB = \sqrt{4^2 + 3^2} = \sqrt{25} = 5\,\text{km}$

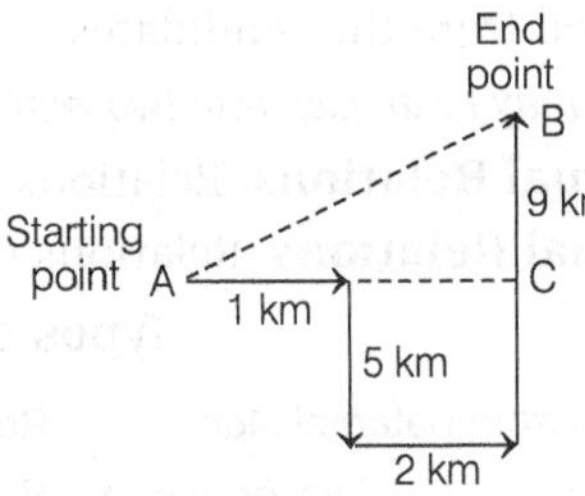

25. West will become South-East

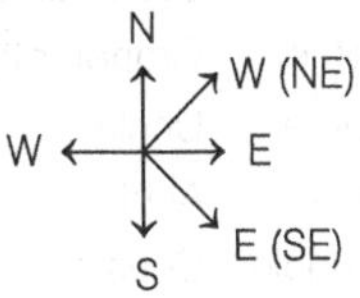

CHAPTER

08

BLOOD RELATIONS

Blood Relation is the relation in which a person is related to another person by birth. Blood relation problems arise through the particular relation among the family members. In these questions, a chain of relationship is given in the form of information and on its basis, relation between any two members of the chain is asked from the candidates.

The relations may be divided into two main categories

(i) **Maternal Relations** Relations on the mother's side are called maternal.

(ii) **Paternal Relations** Relations on the father's side are called paternal.

Types of Relations

Relations from paternal side		Relations from maternal side	
Relation	*Relation name*	*Relation*	*Relation name*
Father's father	Grandfather	Mother's father	Maternal grandfather
Father's mother	Grandmother	Mother's mother	Maternal grandmother
Father's brother	Uncle	Mother's brother	Maternal uncle
Father's sister	Aunt	Mother's sister	Aunt
Children of uncle or aunt	Cousin	Children of maternal uncle or aunt	Cousin
Wife of uncle	Aunt	Wife of maternal uncle	Maternal aunt
Husband of aunt	Uncle	Husband of maternal aunt	Uncle

Other Relations

Relation	Relation name
Grandfather's or Grandmother's son	Father or Uncle
Grandfather's or Grandmother' only son	Father
Grandfather's or Grandmother's daughter	Aunt
Mother's or father's son	Brother
Mother's or father's daughter	Sister
Son's wife	Daughter-in-law
Husband's or wife's sister	Sister-in-law
Daughter's husband	Son-in-law
Husband's or wife's brother	Brother-in-law
Brother's son	Nephew
Brother's daughter	Niece
Sister's husband	Brother-in-law
Brother's wife	Sister-in-law
Grandson's or Granddaughter's daughter or son	Great grand-daughter or son

Relations from One Generation to Next Generation

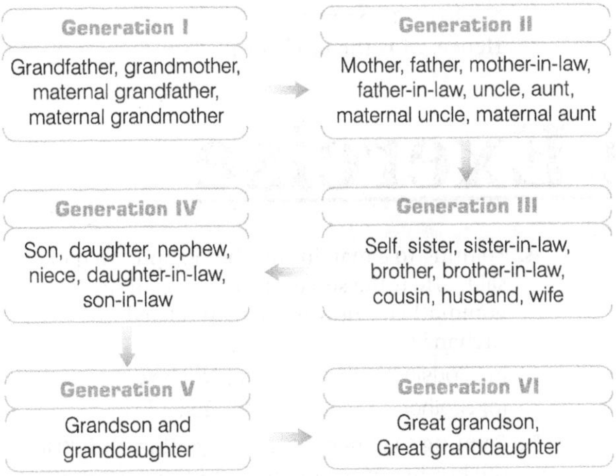

Important Notations

- ⊕ → Male
- ⊖ → Female
- ↔ → Married couple

TYPES OF QUESTIONS

There are mainly three types of questions based on blood relations which are generally asked in various competitive examinations.

1. Deciphering from Jumbled-Up Descriptions

In this type of questions, a person gives information to the another person either about a particular person in a photograph or a person present in front of him. Using this information, it is required to establish a relation between a given person and the person in the photograph/the person about which the information is provided.

Example 1 Introducing Asha to guests, Bhaskar said, "Her father is the only son of my father." How is Asha related to Bhaskar?

(a) Daughter (b) Mother
(c) Sister (d) Niece

Solution *(a)* The only son of Bhaskar's father is Bhaskar himself. This means that Bhaskar is the father of Asha. Hence, Asha is the daughter of Bhaskar.

By Relation Tree,

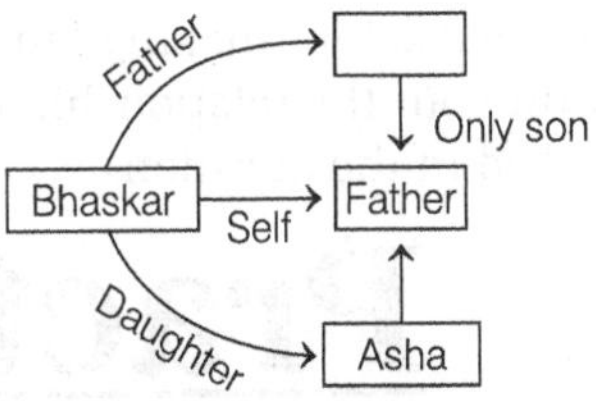

Hence, Asha is the daughter of Bhaskar.

2. Single Family Based Blood Relation

In this type of questions, more than one information in the form of some puzzle is given and based on the information, the candidate is required to deduce the relation between the two individuals.

Example 2 P is the brother of Q and R. S is R's mother. T is P's father. Which of the following statements cannot be definitely true?

(a) Q is T's son
(b) T is Q's father
(c) S is P's mother
(d) P is S's son

Solution *(a)* On the basis of the information given in the question, it is confirmed that S is the mother and T is the father of P, Q and R. Out of them P is male and the sex of Q and R is not determined. Hence, it cannot be definitely said that Q is T's son because may be daughter of T. By Relation Tree,

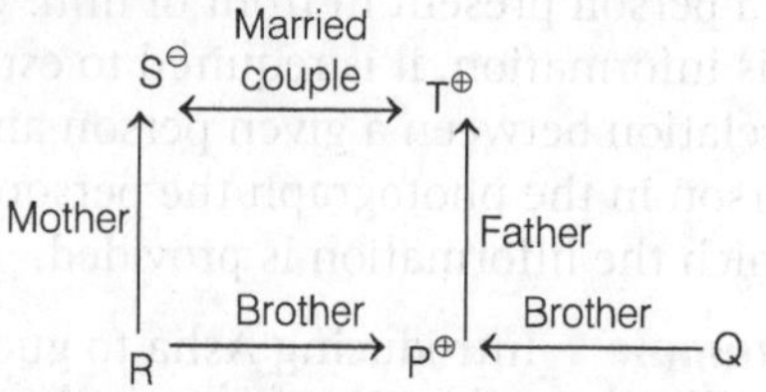

Here, the gender of Q is not known, so it cannot be conclude that Q is the son of T or daughter of T.

3. Coded Relations

In this type of questions, certain symbols and codes are used to represent the information in coded form. The candidate is required to decode the information with the help of symbols to be used for making family diagram and then find out the relationship between the persons asked in the question.

Example 3 If 'A + B' means that A is the brother of B, 'A ÷ B' means that A is the father of B and 'A × B' means that A is the sister of B. Which of the following means 'M' is the uncle of 'P'?

(a) M ÷ N × P (b) N × P ÷ M
(c) M + S ÷ R ÷ P (d) M + K ÷ T × P

Solution *(d)* Working on each of the options, we find that option M + K ÷ T × P shows the required relationship as explained below

(i) T × P means T is the sister of P.

(ii) K ÷ T means K is the father of T. Hence, from information (i), K is also the father of P.

(iii) M + K means M is the brother of K. Therefore using information (ii), we find that M is the uncle of P.

(iv) M + K ÷ T × P

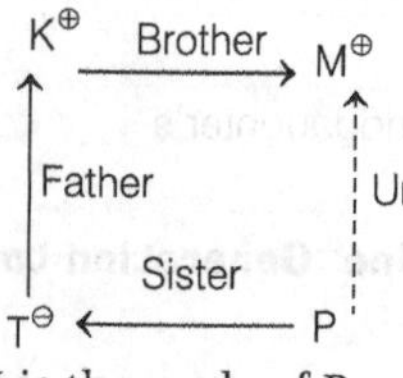

Hence, M is the uncle of P.

Practice Exercise

1. Introducing a man, Neeraj said, "His wife is the only daughter of my wife." How is Neeraj related to that man?

(a) Father (b) Grandfather
(c) Father-in-law (d) Son

2. Shyama says that father of Rajiv's father is my father. How is Shyama related to Rajiv?

(a) Sister
(b) Mother
(c) Aunt (Father's sister)
(d) Niece

3. Pointing to a lady, a man said, "The father of her brother is the only son of my grandfather." How is that lady related to that man?

(a) Sister
(b) Daughter
(c) Aunt (Father's sister)
(d) Mother-in-law

4. Pointing to a man in the photograph, Archana said, "He is the son of the only son of my grandfather". How is the man related to Archana?

(a) Cousin (b) Nephew
(c) Brother (d) Son

5. Pointing to a man on the stage, Rita said, "He is the brother of the daughter of the wife of my husband." How is the man on the stage related to Rita?

(a) Son (b) Husband
(c) Cousin (d) Nephew

6. A told B, "Yesterday I met the only brother of the daughter of my grandmother." Whom did A meet?

(a) Cousin (b) Brother
(c) Nephew (d) Father

7. A woman introduces a man as the son of the brother of her mother. How is that man related to the woman?
(a) Nephew (b) Son
(c) Cousin (d) Uncle

8. There are six members in a family A is the father of D, E is the grandfather of D. B is the daughter-in-law of C. F is the uncle of D. What is the relationship of C with F?
(a) Sister (b) Mother-in-law
(c) Nephew (d) Data inadequate

Directions (Q. Nos. 9 and 10) *Read the following information carefully to answer the questions given below it.*

I. 'P × Q' means 'P is the brother of Q'.
II. 'P + Q' means 'Q is mother of P'.
III. 'P − Q' means 'Q is sister of P'.
IV. 'P ÷ Q' means 'P is the father of Q'.

9. Which of the following means T is nephew of R?
(i) $R \times J \div T$
(ii) $R - M + T - J$
(iii) $R \times J \div T \times K$
(a) Only (i) (b) Only (ii)
(c) Only (iii) (d) Either (ii) or (iii)

10. If $T + L \div M \times J$, then how T is related to J?
(a) Mother (b) Grand father
(c) Grand mother (d) None of these

11. 'P + Q' means that P is the brother of Q, 'P − Q' means that P is the mother of Q and 'P × Q' means that P is the sister of Q. Which of the following means that M is the maternal uncle of R?
(a) $M - R + K$
(b) $M + K - R$
(c) $M + K \times Q$
(d) There is no such symbol

Previous Year's Questions

12. Moni is daughter of Sheela. Sheela is wife of my wife's brother. How Moni is related to my wife? **[CLAT 2013]**
(a) Cousin (b) Niece
(c) Sister (d) Sister-in-law

13. Annu is daughter of my mother's brother Abahi. Pari is granddaughter of my mother. Pari should call Annu as **[CLAT 2013]**
(a) maternal aunt (b) sister
(c) cousin (d) niece

14. Markandey is Rajiv's mother's father. Markandey has three brothers. One of them has grandson Abhi. Rajan is son of Abhi. Rajan is related to Rajiv as **[CLAT 2013]**
(a) brother (b) nephew
(c) cousin (d) uncle

15. Deepak said to Nitin, "That boy playing with the football is the younger of the two brothers of the daughter of my father's wife". How is the boy playing football related to Deepak? **[CLAT 2013]**
(a) Son (b) Brother
(c)Cousin (d) Brother-in-law

16. Pointing to a woman in the photograph, Rajesh said, 'The only daughter of her grandfather is my wife'. How is Rajesh related to that woman? **[CLAT 2013]**
(a) Uncle (b) Father
(c) Maternal Uncle (d) Brother

17. Pointing to a photograph, a man said, "I have no brother or sister but that man's father is my father's son". Whose photograph was that? **[CLAT 2014]**
(a) His father's (b) His own
(c) His son's (d) His nephew's

18. Ranjan introduces Abhay as the son of the only brother of his father's wife. How is Abhay related to Ranjan? **[CLAT 2014]**
(a) Son (b) Brother
(c) Cousin (d) Uncle

19. Pointing to a lady on the stage, Bhumika said, 'She is the sister of the son of the wife of my husband'. How is the lady related to Bhumika? **[CLAT 2014]**
(a) Cousin (b) Sister-in-law
(c) Sister (d) Daughter

20. Pinky, who is Victor's daughter, says to Lucy, "Your mother Rosy is the younger sister of my father, who is the third child of Joseph". How is Joseph related to Lucy? **[CLAT 2014]**
(a) Father-in-law (b) Father
(c) Maternal uncle (d) Grandfather

21. Pramod told Vinod, 'Yesterday I defeated the only brother of the daughter of my grandmother. Whom did Pramod defeat? **[CLAT 2014]**

(a) Father (b) Son
(c) Father-in-law (d) Cousin

Directions (Q. Nos. 22-24) *Read the following information and answer the questions given below.*

Anita is the niece of Prateek's mother. Anita's mother is Prateek's aunt. Rohan is Anita's mother's brother. Rohan's mother is Anita's grandmother. **[CLAT 2015]**

22. Rohan's mother is .... to Anita's mother.

(a) Aunt (b) Mother
(c) No relation (d) Sister

23. Prateek's and Anita's mother are

(a) Cousin sister (b) Sister-in-law
(c) Friends (d) Sisters

24. Rohan is Prateek's

(a) Brother (b) Brother-in-law
(c) Uncle (d) Cousin brothers

Directions (Q. No. 25) *Read the following information carefully to choose best option for the question:*

I. 'L % M' means that 'M is brother of L'.
II. 'L × M' means that 'L is mother of M'.
III. 'L ÷ M' means that 'L is the sister of M'.
IV. 'L = M' means that 'M is father of L'.
[CLAT 2015]

25. Which of the following means 'I is the nephew of Q'?

(i) Q % J = I (ii) Q ÷ M × B % I
(iii) C ÷ I = B % Q

(a) Only (iii) (b) Only (i)
(c) Only (ii) (d) None of these

26. If 'A $ B' means that 'A is the father of B'; 'A ✷ B' means that 'A is the mother of B', 'A @ B' means that 'A is the wife of B', then which of the following means that 'M is the grandmother of N'? **[CLAT 2015]**

(a) M ✷ R $ T @ N (b) M ✷ R @ T @ N
(c) M ✷ T $ N @ R (d) M ✷ T $ N @ R

27. Pointing to a boy in the photograph, Rajat said, "His mother is the only daughter of my grandfather's only son." How is the boy's mother related to Rajat's father? **[CLAT 2015]**

(a) Daughter (b) Sister
(c) Sister-in-law (d) Grand daughter

Directions (Q. Nos. 28 and 29) *Read the following information carefully and choose the most appropriate option.*

In a joint family, A, B, C, D, E and F are the members. B is the son of C. A and C are husband and wife. C is not the mother of B. E is the brother of C. D is the daughter of A and F is the brother of B. **[CLAT 2016]**

28. Who is the mother of B?

(a) F (b) D (c) A (d) E

29. Which of the following is a pair of females in the family?

(a) BD (b) AE (c) AD (d) DF

30. Pointing to a girl in the photograph, Ram said, 'Her Mother' s brother is the only son of my mother's father'. How is the girl's mother related to Ram? **[CLAT 2017]**

(a) Aunt (b) Grand mother
(c) Mother (d) Sister

31. A girl interoduced a boy as the son of the daughter of the father of her uncle. The boy is girl's **[CLAT 2017]**

(a) Uncle (b) Son
(c) Son-in-low (d) Brother

32. When Ravi saw Ramesh, he recalled, 'He is the son of the father of my daughter', Who is Ramesh? **[CLAT 2017]**

(a) Uncle (b) Brother-in-law
(c) Cousin (d) Son

33. Ravi was showing a photograph to his friend, Gopi. Pointing at a boy in the photograph, Ravi said, 'The boy sitting at the left is the son of the wife of the only son of the grand-mother of my younger brother'. What is the relation between the boy in the photograph and Ravi? **[CLAT 2017]**

(a) Nephew and uncle (b) Ravi's brother
(c) First cousins (d) Brothers

34. Pointing to a photograph, Prakash said, 'She is the daughter of my grandfather's only son'. How is Prakash related to the girl in the photograph? **[CLAT 2017]**

(a) Father (b) Brother
(c) Uncle (d) Cousing

Answers

1	*c*	2	*c*	3	*a*	4	*c*	5	*a*	6	*d*	7	*c*	8	*d*	9	*c*	10	*c*
11	*b*	12	*b*	13	*a*	14	*b*	15	*b*	16	*b*	17	*c*	18	*c*	19	*d*	20	*d*
21	*a*	22	*b*	23	*d*	24	*c*	25	*c*	26	*c*	27	*a*	28	*c*	29	*c*	30	*c*
31	*d*	32	*d*	33	*b*	34	*b*												

SOLUTIONS

1. The only daughter of Neeraj's wife is the daughter of Neeraj and her husband is the son-in-law of Neeraj.
Hence, Neeraj is the father-in-law of that man.

2. From the information given in the question, it is clear that Rajiv's father is the brother of Shyama. Therefore, Shyama is related as aunt (father's sister) to Rajiv.

3. The father of her brother means her father and the only son of my grandfather means my father. Therefore, lady's father is also the father of the man. Hence, the lady is related as sister to that man.

4. The only son of Archana's grandfather means Archana's father and his son is Archana's brother. Hence, the man is related as brother to Archana.

5. Wife of her husband means herself. And brother of her daughter means her son. Hence, the man on the stage is the son of Rita.

6. The daughter of A's grandmother is the sister of A's father and the only brother of A's father's sister is A's father himself. Hence, A met his father.

Solution (Q. Nos. 9 and 10)
According to the question,

9. (i)

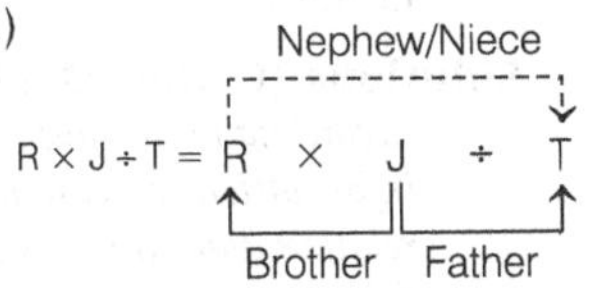

Here, T is either nephew or niece of R.

(ii)

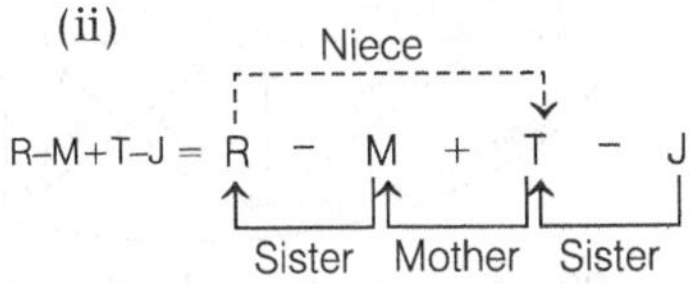

Here, T is niece of R.

(iii)

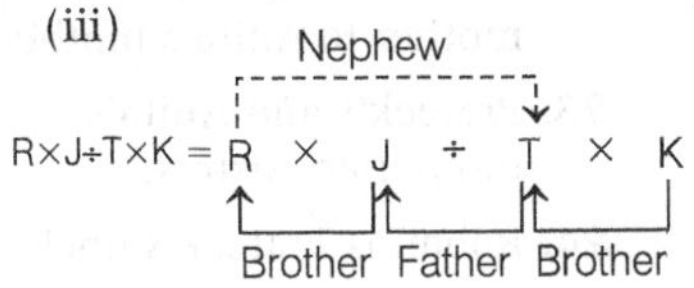

Hence, T is the nephew of R.

10.

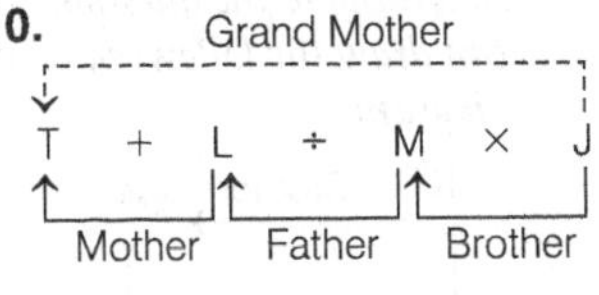

Hence, T is the Grand mother of J.

11.

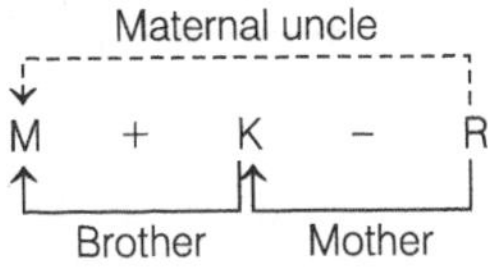

Clearly, M is the maternal uncle of R.

Previous Year's Solutions

12.

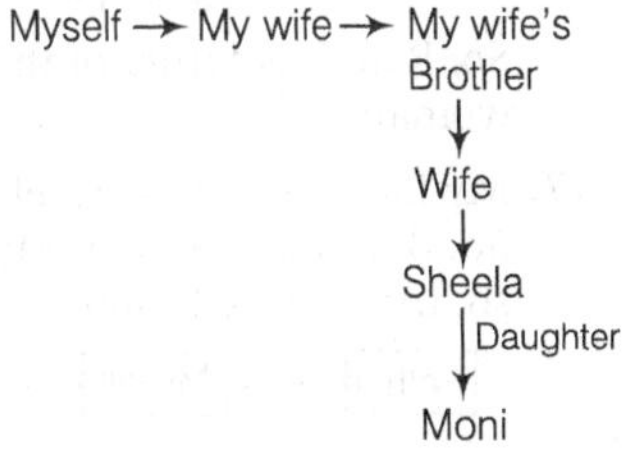

So, Moni is niece of my wife.

13.

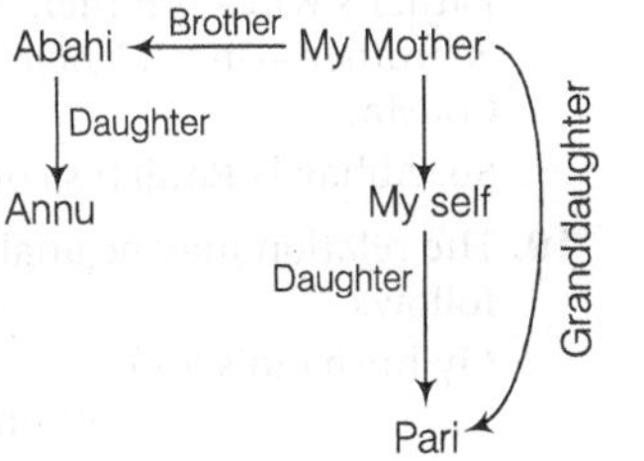

So, Pari should call Annu her maternal aunt.

14.

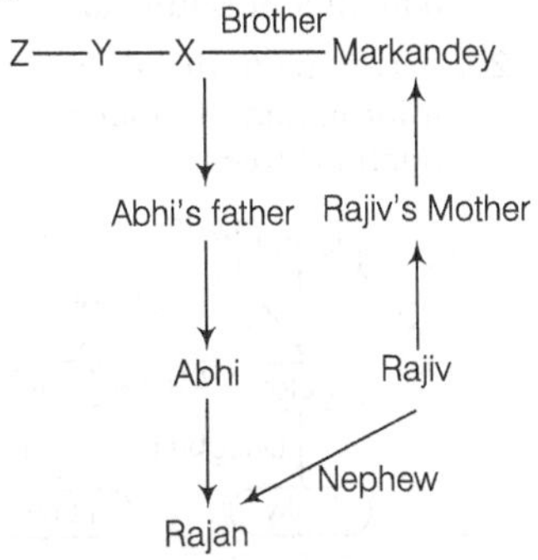

So, Rajan is nephew of Rajiv

15.

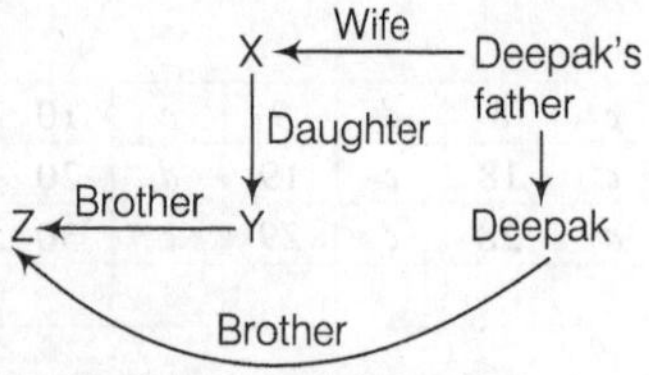

So, the boy is brother of Deepak.

16.

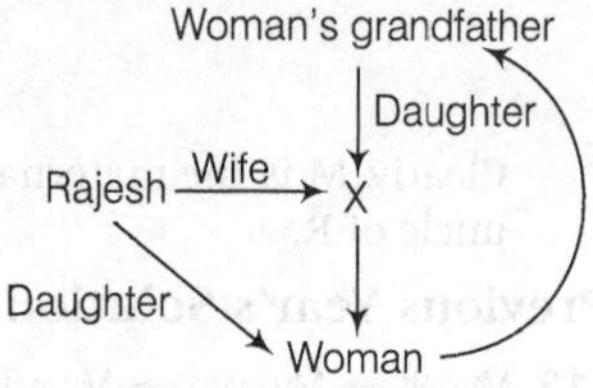

So, Rajesh is father of that woman.

17. My father's son —Myself
So, that man's father–Myself
so, that man–My son

18. The relation may be analysed as follows
Father's wife – Mother, Mother 's brother –Uncle, Uncle's son – Cousin.
So, Abhay is Ranjan's cousin.

19. The relation may be analysed as follows
My husband's wife – Bhumika
Sister of the son – Daughter of Bhumika
So, the lady on the stage is the daughter of Bhumika.

20. According to the given information, we make a relations tree

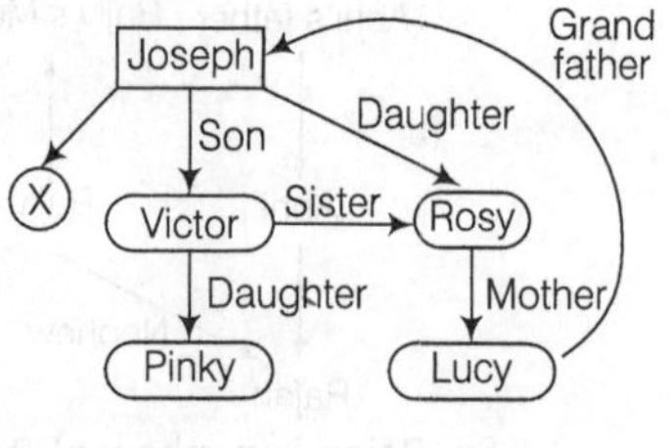

Joseph has three children, one is X, second is Victor and third is Rosy.
Here, it is not clear 'X' is male or female.
Rosy is the mother of Lucy.
So, Joseph is the grandfather of Lucy.

21. The relation may be analysed as follows
My grandmother's daughter – Aunt
My Aunt's only brother – Father
So, Pramod defeated his father.

Solutions (Q. Nos. 22-24)

According to the given information, we can draw a relation diagram is as shown below

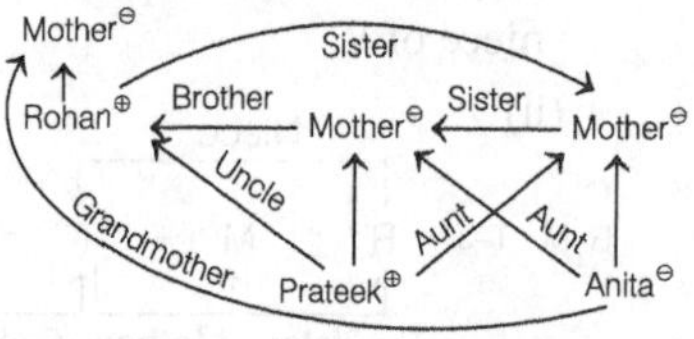

22. It is clear from the diagram, that Rohan's mother is mother to Anita's mother.

23. Prateek's and Anita's mother are sisters.

24. Rohan is Prateek's uncle.

Solutions (Q. Nos. 28-29)

According to the question, we can draw the following relation diagram

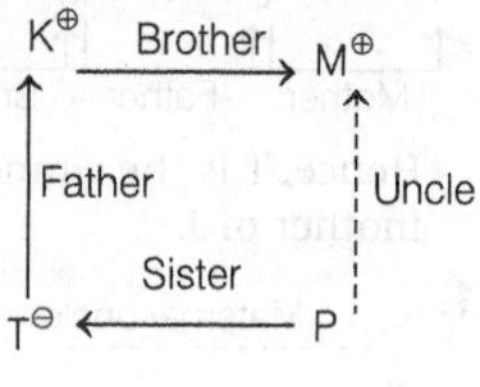

28. A is the mother of B.

29. A and D are female members in the family.

30. ∴ Hence, Girl's mother is Ram's mother.

31.

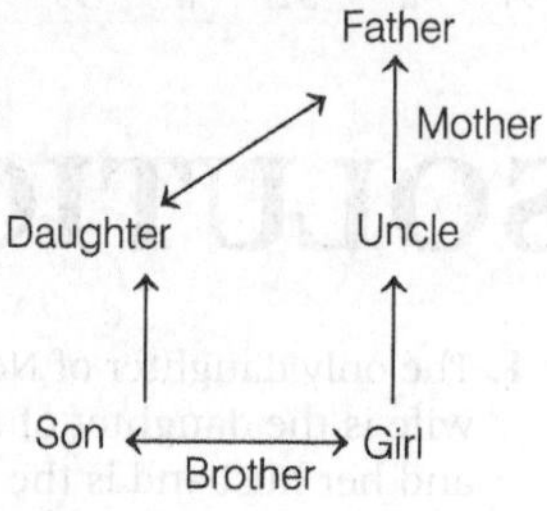

∴ Hence, Boy is girl's brother

32.

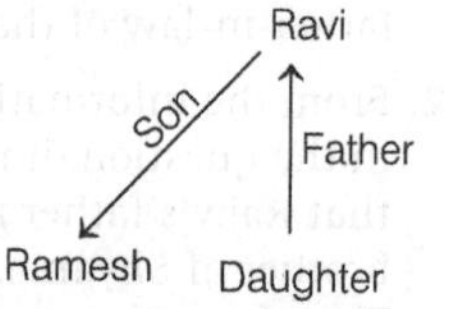

∴ Hence, Ramesh is son of Ravi

33.

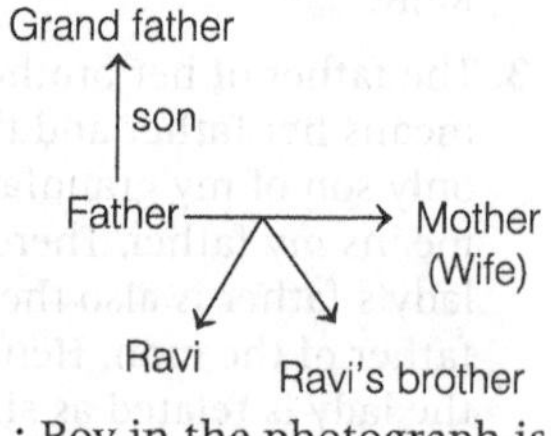

∴ Boy in the photograph is Ravi's brother.

34.

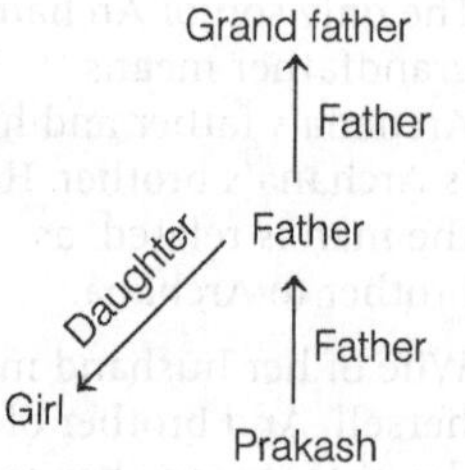

So, Prakash is brother of the girl.

CHAPTER 09

PUZZLE TEST

Puzzles are the problems in which the informations are given in jumbled form. These jumbled informations are need to be analysed and arranged in a proper way so that the answers to the questions can be found out accurately.

In this chapter, we deal with questions in which the informations are put in the form of puzzles involving certain number of items, it may be persons or objects. The students are required to analyse the given informations, condense it in a suitable form and answer the questions that are asked. These questions are generally based on placing arrangement, sequential order, based on family etc.

There are mainly four type of questions which are asked in examination.

1. Classification Based Problems

In this type of questions, certain items belonging to different groups or possessing different qualities are given along with some clues, with the help of which you are required to group and analyse the given items and answer the questions accordingly.

Directions (Ex. 1-3) *Read the following information carefully to answer these questions.*

Madhu and Shobha are good in Dramatics and Computer Science. Anjali and Madhu are good in Computer Science and Physics. Anjali, Poonam and Nisha are good in Physics and History. Nisha and Anjali are good in Physics and Mathematics. Poonam and Shobha are good in History and Dramatics.

Example 1 Who is good in Physics, History and Mathematics but not in Computer Science?

(a) Madhu (b) Poonam
(c) Nisha (d) Anjali

Example 2 Who is good in Physics, History and Dramatics?

(a) Poonam (b) Shobha
(c) Madhu (d) Anjali

Example 3 Who is good in History, Physics, Computer Science and Mathematics?

(a) Poonam (b) Nisha (c) Anjali (d) Madhu

Solutions (Ex. 1-3) From the given information, data is arranged as follows

People	Dramatics	Computer Science	Mathematics	Physics	History
Madhu	✓	✓		✓	
Shobha	✓	✓			✓
Anjali		✓	✓	✓	✓
Poonam	✓			✓	✓
Nisha			✓	✓	✓

1. *(c)* Nisha is good in Physics, History and Mathematics.
2. *(a)* Poonam is good in Physics, History and Dramatics
3. *(c)* Anjali is good in given four subjects.

2. Placing or Comparison Based Problems

In this type of questions, information regarding comparison or placing arrangement of some persons/objects along with additions (like their professions, favourite colour etc.) is given. The candidates are required to form the proper sequence and arrange the persons/objects using the given information and answer the questions accordingly.

Directions (Ex. 4-6) *Read the following information to answer the given questions.*

Five friends A, B, C, D and E are sitting on a bench and wearing different colours shirt, i.e. blue, red, yellow, white and green (not necessarily in this order).

I. A is sitting next to B and wearing red shirt.
II. C is sitting next to D and not wearing either blue or green shirt.
III. D is not sitting with E and E is wearing blue shirt.
IV. E is on the left end of the bench.
V. C is on the second position from the right.
VI. A is on the right of B and E.
VII. B is wearing green shirt.
VIII. A and C sitting together.
IX. D is not wearing white shirt.

Example 4 Where is A sitting?

(a) Between B and D (b) Between D and C
(c) Between E and D (d) Between B and C

Example 5 What is the colour of C's shirt?

(a) Blue (b) Red (c) White (d) Yellow

Example 6 Who is sitting in the centre?

(a) A (b) B (c) C (d) D

Solutions (Ex. 4-6) From the given information the arrangement can be drawn as follow

E	B	A	C	D
Blue	Green	Red	White	Yellow

4. *(d)* A is sitting between B and C.
5. *(c)* The colour of C's shirt is white.
6. *(a)* A is sitting in the centre.

3. Sequential Order of Things Based Problems

In this type of questions, the information regarding the order of occurrence of certain events is given. The candidates are required to analyse the given information, form the right sequence and then answer the questions accordingly.

Directions (Ex. 7-9) *Study the following information to answer the given questions.*

Six lectures are scheduled in a week starting from Monday and ending on Sunday of the same week. Computer Science is not on Tuesday or Saturday. Psychology is immediately after Organisational Behaviour. Statistics is not on Friday and there is one day gap between Statistics and Research Methods. One day prior to the schedule of Economics there is no lecture. And, Saturday is the off day.

Example 7 Which of the following is the last lecture scheduled?

(a) Statistic (b) Research Methods
(c) Psychology (d) None of these

Example 8 How many lectures were scheduled between Economics and Psychology?

(a) One (b) Two
(c) Three (d) None of these

Example 9 Which day is Computer Science sheduled?

(a) Monday (b) Wednesday
(c) Thursday (d) None of these

Solutions (Ex. 7-9) *The given information can be arranged as follow*

Days	Subjects
Monday	Organisational Behaviour
Tuesday	Psychology
Wednesday	Statistics
Thursday	Computer Science
Friday	Research Methods
Saturday	Off day
Sunday	Economics

7. *(d)* Last lecture is of Economics.

8. *(c)* Three lectures are scheduled between Economics and Psychology.

9. *(c)* Computer Science is scheduled on Thursday.

4. Family Based Problems

In this type of questions, some clues are provided regarding relationship amongst different members of a family, together with their professions, qualities, colours, dresses and others. You have to analyse the whole information and then answer the given questions accordingly.

Directions (Ex. 10-12) *Read the following information carefully to answer these questions.*

There is a family of six members A, B, C, D, E and F. They are lawyer, doctor, teacher, salesman, engineer and accountant not necessarily in that order. There are two married couples in the family. D, the salesman, is married to the lady teacher. The doctor is married to the lawyer. F, the accountant, is the son of B and brother of E. C, the Lawyer, is the daughter-in-law of A. E is the unmarried engineer. A is the grandmother of F.

Example 10 How is E related to F?

(a) Brother (b) Sister
(c) Cousin (d) None of these

Example 11 What is the profession of B?

(a) Teacher (b) Doctor
(c) Lawyer (d) Cannot be determined

Example 12 Which of the following is one of the couples?

(a) F and D (b) D and B
(c) E and A (d) None of these

Solutions (Ex. 10-12) *Following information is arranged as follows*

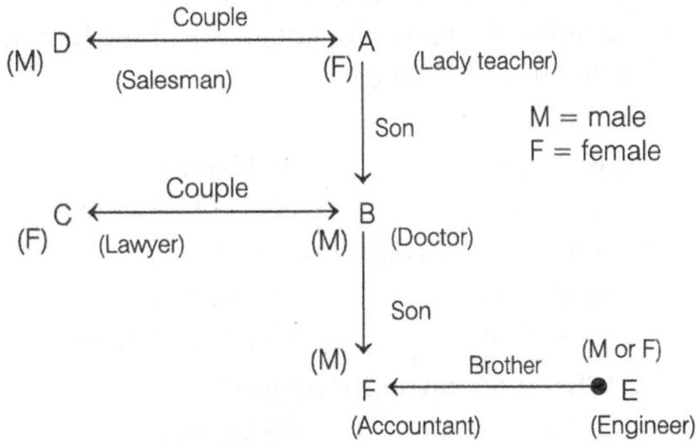

10. *(d)* As, it is not clear that E is male or female, so we cannot conclude that E is brother or sister of F.

11. *(b)* The profession of B is Doctor.

12. *(d)* D, A and C, B are married couples.

Practice Exercise

Directions (Ex. 1-5) *Study the following information carefully and answer the questions given below.*

A, B, C, D, E, F, G and H are eight students of a school. They study in Std. VI, VII and VIII with not more than three in any std. Each of them has a favourite subject from Physics, Geography, English, Marathi, Mathematics, Chemistry, Biology and Economics not necessarily in the same order. D likes Chemistry and studies in Std. VIII with only H. B does not study in Std. VII. E and A study in the same Std. but not with B. C and F study in the same Std. Those who study in Std. VI do not like Mathematics or Biology. F likes Physics. The one who studies in Std. VIII likes English. C does not like Geography. A's favourite subject is Marathi and G does not like Biology.

1. Which subject does H like?

(a) English (b) Marathi
(c) Science (d) Data inadequate

2. What is G's favourite subject?

(a) Biology (b) Physics
(c) English (d) None of these

3. What is C's favourite subject?

(a) Economics (b) Biology
(c) English (d) Geography

4. Which of the following combinations of Student-Std.- Subject is correct?

(a) C-VII-Economics (b) D-VI-Chemistry
(c) G-VII-Physics (d) None of these

5. Which of the following group of students study in VII Std?

(a) EAF (b) EGC
(c) EAG (d) Data inadequate

Directions (Q. Nos. 6-10) *Study the following given information and answer the given questions.*

A, B, C, D, E, F and G are standing in a straight line facing North with equal distances between them, not necessarily in the same order. Each one is pursuing a different profession—actor, reporter, doctor, engineer, lawyer, teacher and painter not necessarily in the same order.

G is fifth to the left of C. The reporter is third to the right of G. F is fifth to the right of A. E is second to the left of B. The engineer is second to the left of D. There are only three people between the engineer and the painter. The doctor is to the immediate left of the engineer. The lawyer is to the immediate right of the teacher.

6. What is A's profession?

(a) Painter (b) Doctor (c) Teacher (d) Actor

7. Which of the following statements is true according to the given arrangement?

(a) F is the teacher
(b) F is third to the left of E
(c) The painter is to the immediate left of B
(d) The lawyer is standing in the exact middle of the arrangement

8. Who among the following is an actor?

(a) E (b) F (c) C (d) B

9. What is D's position with respect to the painter?

(a) Third to the left (b) Second to the left
(c) Fourth to the right (d) Third to the right

10. Three of the following four are alike in a certain way based on the given standing arrangement and so form a group. Which of the following does not belong to the group?

(a) AED (b) DFC
(c) GDB (d) BFC

Directions (Q. Nos. 11-15) *Study the following information carefully and answer the questions given below.*

A, B, C, D, E, F and G are the seven members of a family. There are three females among them. There are two married couples in the family. Each of them has a different profession from Architect, Lawyer, Doctor, Teacher, Engineer, Manager and Musician, not necessarily in the same order.

B is the lawyer and he is married to F, the manager. A is brother of G, who is the architect. C is the doctor and is an unmarried lady. D is the teacher and the sister of G. E is not an engineer.

11. Which of the following combinations is definitely correct?
(a) B-Male-Manager
(b) B-Female-Lawyer
(c) C-Female-Musician
(d) E-Male-Musician

12. Which of the following combinations represents the husbands of the two married couples?
(a) B and G (b) A and F
(c) B and E (d) Data inadequate

13. What is E's profession?
(a) Doctor (b) Musician
(c) Teacher (d) Data inadequate

14. What is A's profession?
(a) Engineer
(b) Musician
(c) Engineer or Musician
(d) Data inadequate

15. Which of the following pairs represents a married couple?
(a) BG (b) AE
(c) AC (d) None of these

Directions (Q. Nos. 16-20) *Study the following information carefully and answer the questions given below.*

P, Q, R, S, T, V and W are seven students of a college. Each of them has a favourite subject from Physics, Chemistry, English, Biology, History, Geography and Philosophy, not necessarily in the same order. Each of them also has a favourite sport from Football, Cricket, Hockey, Volleyball, Badminton, Table-Tennis and Basketball, not necessarily in the same order.

R likes Philosophy and his favourite sport is Hockey. The one who likes Football likes English. T's favourite sport is not Badminton or Table-Tennis. V does not like either History or Biology. The one whose favourite sport is Basketball does not like Physics. W likes Chemistry and his favourite sport is Volleyball. S likes Geography. Q's favourite sport is Badminton. V does not like English and his favourite sport is not Basketball. P's favourite sport is Cricket. The one whose favourite sport is Badminton does not like Biology.

16. Which subject does P like?
(a) History (b) Biology
(c) Chemistry (d) Data inadequate

17. Who likes History?
(a) P (b) R
(c) Q (d) V

18. What is Q's favourite sport?
(a) Cricket (b) Table-Tennis
(c) Football (d) Badminton

19. Whose favourite sport is Basketball?
(a) S (b) W
(c) Q (d) Data inadequate

20. Which subject does T like?
(a) Biology (b) Physics
(c) Chemistry (d) None of these

Directions (Q. Nos. 21-25) *Read the following information and choose the right alternative for the questions given afterward.*

The sports week of an institute was organised from 19th to 26th of a month, 19th being a Wednesday. During that period six games, i.e. Cricket (C), Badminton (B), Table-Tennis (T), Kho-Kho (K), Hockey (H) and Football (F) were played, one game on each day. Further information is

I. Hockey was not played on the closing day, i.e. on 26th.
II. Table-Tennis was played on the previous day of Cricket.
III. Football was not played either on Wednesday or Saturday.
IV. No game was played on Thursday and Sunday.
V. Kho-Kho was played on Monday.
VI. There was a gap of two days between Cricket and Football.

21. The sports week started with which game?
(a) Table-Tennis (b) Cricket
(c) Kho-Kho (d) Hockey

22. How many day's gap is there between Hockey and Football?

(a) Three (b) Four
(c) Five (d) Two

23. Which pair of games was played on Wednesday?

(a) Hockey and Badminton
(b) Hockey and Cricket
(c) Cricket and Table-Tennis
(d) Cannot be determined

24. Which game exactly precedes Kho-Kho?

(a) Hockey
(b) Football
(c) Cricket
(d) Rest day, (i.e. No game)

25. Table-Tennis is followed by which game?

(a) Hockey (b) Cricket
(c) Table-Tennis (d) None of these

Previous Year's Questions

Directions (Q.Nos. 26-28) *Read the following information carefully and then answer the questions.*

Four friends W, X, Y and Z are students of class 10th. W and X are good in Hindi but poor in English. W and Y are good in Science but poor in Mathematics. Y and Z are good in English but poor in Social Studies. Z and X are good in Mathematics as well as in Science. **[CLAT 2012]**

26. Who amongst the following friends is not good in Mathematics but good in Hindi?

(a) W (b) Y
(c) X (d) Z

27. Which of the following pairs of friends are good, both in English and Science?

(a) W and Y (b) W and Z
(c) Y and Z (d) Z and X

28. Which of the following statements is definitely true?

(a) Y and Z are good in English as well as in Hindi
(b) All four friends are good in Science
(c) W is good in Social Studies, Hindi and Science
(d) Y is not good in Mathematics, Hindi and Social Studies

Directions (Q. Nos. 29-31) *Answer the following questions based on the statements given below.* **[CLAT 2013]**

I. There are 3 poles on each side of the road.
II. These six poles are labelled A, B, C, D, E and F.
III. The poles are of different colours namely Golden, Silver, Metallic, Black, Bronze and White.
IV. The poles are of different heights.
V. E, the tallest pole, is exactly opposite to the Golden coloured pole.
VI. The shortest pole is exactly opposite to the Metallic coloured pole.
VII. F, the Black coloured pole, is located between A and D.
VIII. C, the Bronze coloured pole, is exactly opposite to A.
IX. B, the Metallic coloured pole, is exactly opposite to F.
X. A, the White coloured pole, is taller than C but shorter than D and B.

29. What is the colour of the pole diagonally opposite to the Bronze coloured pole?

(a) White (b) Silver (c) Metallic (d) Golden

30. Which is the second tallest pole?

(a) A
(b) D
(c) B
(d) Cannot be determined

31. Which is the colour of the tallest pole?

(a) Golden (b) Silver
(c) Bronze (d) None of these

Directions (Q. Nos. 32 and 33) *Answer the questions on the basis of the information given below.*

The head of a newly formed Government desires to appoint five of the six elected ministers P, Q, R, S, T and U to portfolios of Foreign, Industry and Commerce, Agriculture, Rural Development and Human Resources. U does not want any portfolio if S gets one of the five. R wants either Foreign or Human Resources or no portfolio. Q says that if S gets industry and Commerce or Rural Development then she must get the other one. T insists on a portfolio if P gets one. **[CLAT 2013]**

32. Which of the following is a valid assignment?
(a) P-Foreign, Q-Industry and Commerce, R-Agriculture, S-Rural Development, T-Human Resources
(b) R-Foreign, S-Industry and Commerce, P-Agriculture, Q-Rural Development, T-Human Resources
(c) P-Foreign, Q-Industry and Commerce, T-Agriculture, S-Rural Development, U-Human Resources
(d) Q-Foreign, U-Industry and Commerce, T-Agriculture, R-Rural Development, P-Human Resources

33 If P gets Foreign and R gets Human Resources, then which is not a valid assignment of Agriculture and Rural Development?
(a) S-Agriculture, Q-Rural Development
(b) U-Agriculture, Q-Rural Development
(c) Q-Agriculture, T-Rural Development
(d) Q-Agriculture, S-Rural Development

Directions (Q. Nos. 34-38) *Read the information given below to answer the questions.* **[CLAT 2013]**

I. Kareena's dieting schedule consists of having only one fruit on a given day of the week.
II. Dietician has prescribed banana, papaya, pomegranate, apple and grape from Sunday to Friday, one day being a fasting day. Kareena cannot eat any fruit on Saturday.
III. Pomegranate day is neither on the first day nor on the last day but earlier than the papaya day.
IV. Apple day is on the immediate next day of papaya day.
V. Banana day is on the immediate previous day of the fasting day.
VI. Apple day and grape day must have a gap of two days between them.
VII. Grape day is the day immediately following the fasting day.

34. Which of the following is the fasting day?
(a) Monday
(b) Tuesday
(c) Wednesday
(d) Thursday

35. Banana day and apple day have a gap of how many days between them?
(a) One (b) Two
(c) Three (d) Four

36. Which day is grape day?
(a) Monday (b) Tuesday
(c) Thursday (d) Wednesday

37. Which day is pomegranate day?
(a) Sunday (b) Monday
(c) Thursday (d) Wednesday

38. Which of the following is the correct statement?
(a) Apple day is after papaya day
(b) Banana day is on Wednesday
(c) Fasting day is on Tuesday
(d) Papaya day is earlier than banana day

Directions (Q. Nos. 39-41) *Read the following information carefully and answer the questions given below*

Five friends Satish, Rajesh, Rehman, Rakesh and Vineet- each presents one paper to their class on Physics, Zoology, Botany, English or Geology - one day a week, Monday through Friday. **[CLAT 2014]**

I. Vineet does not present English and does not give his presentation on Tuesday.
II. Rajesh makes the Geology presentation and does not do it on Monday or Friday.
III. The Physics presentation is made on Thursday.
IV. Rehman makes his presentation, which is not on English, on Wednesday.
V. The Botany presentation is on Friday and not by Rakesh.
VI. Satish makes his presentation on Monday.

39. What day is the English presentation made?
(a) Friday (b) Monday
(c) Tuesday (d) Wednesday

40. What presentation does Vineet do?
(a) English (b) Geology
(c) Physics (d) Botany

41. What day does Rakesh make his presentation on?
(a) Monday (b) Tuesday
(c) Wednesday (d) Thursday

Directions (Q. Nos. 42-46) *Read the information given below to answer the questions.* **[CLAT 2014]**

I. In a family of six persons, there are people from three generations. Each person has separate profession and also each one likes different colours. There are two couples in the family.

II. Charan is a CA and his wife neither is a doctor nor likes green colour.

III. Engineer likes red colour and his wife is a teacher.

IV. Vanita is mother-in-law of Namita and she likes orange colour.

V. Mohan is grandfather of Raman and Raman, who is a principal, likes black colour.

VI. Sarita is grand daughter of Vanita and she likes blue colour. Sarita's mother likes white colour.

42. Who is an Engineer?

(a) Sarita (b) Vanita
(c) Namita (d) Mohan

43. What is the profession of Namita?

(a) Doctor
(b) Engineer
(c) Teacher
(d) Cannot be determined

44. Which of the following is the correct pair of two couples?

(a) Mohan — Vanita and Charan — Sarita
(b) Vanita — Mohan and Charan — Namita
(c) Charan — Namita and Raman — Sarita
(d) Cannot be determined

45. How many ladies are there in the family?

(a) Two (b) Three
(c) Four (d) None of these

46. Which colour is liked by CA?

(a) White (b) Blue
(c) Black (d) None of these

Directions (Q. Nos. 47-54) *Read the following information carefully and answer the questions that follow.*

W, X, Y and Z are four friends, who do not mind exchanging items. X has two chessboards each costing ₹ 500, and a record player. Z originally had a cycle and a walkman. Each cricket bat costs ₹ 700. Both W and Z got a cricket bat from Y. X gave his record player costing ₹ 2000 to Y. Z get a camera costing ₹1500 from W. The cycle of Z costs ₹1000 and the walkman is for ₹ 700. Y had three cricket bats at the beginning and W had two cameras, the total cost of which is ₹ 5000. X gave one of his chessboards to Z and took Z's cycle. Z gave his walkman to W. **[CLAT 2015]**

47. The person incurring the highest amount of financial loss through exchange lost an amount of

(a) ₹ 600 (b) ₹ 1000
(c) None of these (d) ₹ 500

48. Who did not have a cricket bat after the exchange of items was over?

(a) W (b) X
(c) Y (d) Z

49. Even after exchanges, an item of highest value remained in possession of

(a) W (b) X (c) Y (d) Z

50. Among the things exchanged, which one faced the highest exchange value in percentage term?

(a) Cricket bat (b) Record player
(c) Camera (d) Cycle

51. Total cost of materials Z had at the beginning was

(a) ₹ 1500 (b) ₹ 1700
(c) ₹ 1000 (d) ₹ 2000

52. Which became the gainer by highest amount through exchange?

(a) W (b) X
(c) Y (d) Z

53. At the beginning, who had the costliest items?

(a) W (b) X
(c) Y (d) Z

54. The amount of price of all the things remaining with the four persons lie between

(a) ₹ 800 – ₹ 900 (b) ₹ 10000 – ₹ 12000
(c) ₹ 9000 – ₹ 10000 (d) ₹ 10000 – ₹ 11000

Directions (Q. Nos. 55-59) *Read the following information and choose the best option.*

Recently, the answers of a test held nationwide were leaked to a group of unscrupulous people. The investigative agency has arrested the mastermind and nine other people A, B, C, D, E, F, G, H and I in this matter.

Interrogating them, the following facts have been obtained regarding their operation.

- Initially, the mastermind obtains the correct answer-key. All the others create their answer-key from one or two people who already possess the same. These people are called his/her 'sources'.
- If the person has two sources, then he/she compares the answer-keys obtained for both sources. If the key to a question from both sources is identical, it is copied, otherwise it is left blank.
- If the person has only one source, he/she copies the source's answer into his/her copy.
- Finally, each person compulsorily replaces one of the answers (not a blank one) with a wrong answer in his/her answer-key.

The paper contained 200 questions, so the investigative agency has ruled out the possibility of two or more of them introducing wrong answers to the same question.

The investigative agency has a copy of the correct answer-key and has tabulated the following data. This data represents question numbers.

Name	Wrong Answer(s)	Blank Answer(s)
A	46	—
B	96	46,90,25
C	27,56	17,46,90
D	17	—
E	46,90	—
F	14,46	92,90
G	25	—
H	46,92	—
I	27	17,26,90

[CLAT 2015]

55. Which of the following statement is true?
(a) C introduced the wrong answer to question 27
(b) E introduced the wrong answer to question 46
(c) F introduced the wrong answer to question 14
(d) H introduced the wrong answer to question 46

56. Which one of the following must have two sources?
(a) A (b) B (c) C (d) D

57. How many people (excluding the mastermind) needed to make answer-keys before C could make his answer-key?
(a) 2 (b) 3 (c) 4 (d) 5

58. Both G and H were sources to
(a) F (b) B
(c) A (d) None of these

59. Which of the following two groups of people has identical sources?
I. A, D and G II. E and H
(a) Only I (b) Only II
(c) Neither I nor II (d) Both I and II

Directions (Q. Nos. 60-62) *Read the following information carefully and choose the most appropriate option.*

A and B are good in driving bus and car. C and A are good in driving car and scooter. C, D and E are good in driving scooter and tractor. E and C are good in driving scooter and auto-rickshaw. D and B are good in driving bus and tractor. **[CLAT 2016]**

60. Who is good in driving tractor, scooter, car and auto-rickshaw but not bus?
(a) D (b) A (c) B (d) C

61. Who is good in driving scooter, tractor and auto-rickshaw but not good in driving car?
(a) D (b) C
(c) A (d) E

62. Who is good in driving scooter, tractor and bus?
(a) D (b) B
(c) C (d) A

Directions (Q. Nos. 63-65) *Read the following information carefully and choose the most appropriate option.*

I. There is a group of five persons-A, B, C, D and E
II. One of then is singer, one is a Sancer, one is a painter, one is a teacher and one is a Doctor.
III. There of them -A,C and Doctor prefer rice to chapati and two of them-B and the painter prefer chapati to rice.
IV. The Teacher S and A are friends to one another but two of these prefer chapati to rice.
V. The Singer is C' s brother. **[CLAT 2017]**

63. Who is a singer?
(a) S (b) C (c) B (d) A

64. Who is a dancer?
(a) C (b) A (c) E (d) S

65. Who is a Teacher?
(a) C (b) S (c) B (d) E

Answers

1	*a*	2	*d*	3	*a*	4	*d*	5	*c*	6	*b*	7	*d*	8	*c*	9	*b*	10	*d*
11	*d*	12	*c*	13	*b*	14	*d*	15	*d*	16	*b*	17	*c*	18	*d*	19	*a*	20	*d*
21	*d*	22	*c*	23	*a*	24	*d*	25	*b*	26	*a*	27	*c*	28	*b*	29	*d*	30	*d*
31	*b*	32	*a*	33	*a*	34	*a*	35	*b*	36	*c*	37	*d*	38	*a*	39	*a*	40	*d*
41	*d*	42	*d*	43	*d*	44	*b*	45	*b*	46	*d*	47	*c*	48	*b*	49	*a*	50	*c*
51	*b*	52	*d*	53	*a*	54	*b*	55	*c*	56	*b*	57	*c*	58	*d*	59	*a*	60	*d*
61	*d*	62	*a*	63	*d*	64	*a*	65	*c*										

SOLUTIONS

Solutions (Q. Nos. 1-5) *On the basis of given information, we can summarise the data in tabular form as given below.*

Subjects	Students	Std.s
Marathi	A	VII
Geography	B	VI
Economics	C	VI
Chemistry	D	VIII
Biology	E	VII
Physics	F	VI
Mathematics	G	VII
English	H	VIII

1. H likes English.

2. G's favourite subject is Mathematics.

3. C's favourite subject is Economics.

4. None is correct.

5. EAG study in VII Std.

Solutions (Q. Nos. 6-10) *From the given information, standing arrangement and profession of the persons are as follow*

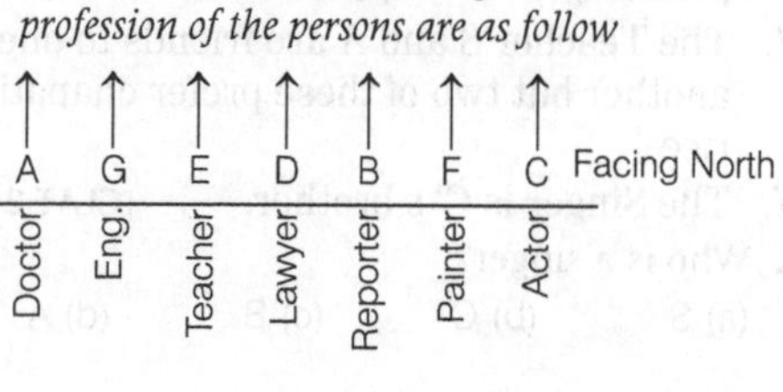

6. A is a doctor.

7. The lawyer is standing in the exact middle of the arrangement.

8. C is an actor.

9. D is second to the left of painter.

10. BFC, does not follow the group.

Solutions (Q. Nos.11-15) *Given informations can be summarised in the tabular form as*

Member	Profession	Male/Female	Married/ Unmarried	Relation
A	Engineer	Male	Unmarried	
B	Lawyer	Male	Married	F's husband
C	Doctor	Female	Unmarried	
D	Teacher	Female	Married	E's wife
E	Musician	Male	Married	D's husband
F	Manager	Female	Married	B's wife
G	Architect	Male	Unmarried	

11. E is a male-musician.

12. B and E are the husbands of two married couples.

13. E's profession is musician.

14. A's profession is engineer.

15. BF and ED are the married couples in the given question.

Solutions (Q. Nos. 16-20) *The given information can be represented as*

Students	Subjects	Sports
P	Biology	Cricket
Q	History	Badminton
R	Philosophy	Hockey
S	Geography	Basketball
T	English	Football
V	Physics	Table-Tennis
W	Chemistry	Volleyball

16. P likes Biology.

17. Q likes History.

18. Q's favourite sport is Badminton.

19. S's favourite sport is Basketball.

20. T likes English.

Solutions (Q. Nos. 21-25) *On the basis of given information, we can construct the following chart.*

Dates	Days	Game played
19	Wednesday	H
20	Thursday	–
21	Friday	T
22	Saturday	C
23	Sunday	–
24	Monday	K
25	Tuesday	F
26	Wednesday	B

21. The sports week was started with Hockey.

22. The gap between Hockey and Football is of 5 day.

23. Hockey and Badminton were played on Wednesday.

24. Kho-Kho will be preceded by the rest day on which no game is played.

25. Table-Tennis is followed by Cricket.

Previous Year's Solutions

Solutions (Q. Nos. 26-28)

Friends	Hindi	Eng	Sci	Math	Social Sci
W	✓	×	✓	×	
X	✓	×	✓	✓	
Y		✓	✓	×	×
Z		✓	✓	✓	×

26. W is not good in mathematics but good in Hindi.

27. Y and Z pair of friends are good both in English and Science.

28. From the given above diagram we clearly say that all four friends are good in Science.

Solutions (Q. Nos. 29-31) *Data is arranged in following way*

Also, $E > B, D > A > C > F$

29. Golden coloured pole diagonally opposite to the Bronze coloured pole.

30. As comparison between B and D is notgiven, so it can not determined who is second tallest.

31. Silver coloured pole is the tallest pole.

Solutions (Q. Nos. 34-38) *Following information is arranged as under*

Week days	Fruit
Sunday	Banana
Monday	Fast
Turusday	Grapes
Wednesday	Pomegranate
Thursday	Papaya
Friday	Apple
Saturday	No fruit day

34. Monday is the fasting day.

35. Four days.

36. Thursday is grape day.

37. Wednesday is pomegranate day.

38. Apple day is after papaya day.

Solutions (Q.No. 39-41) *As per the given information, we make table as follows*

Person	Days	Subject
Satish	Monday	English
Rajesh	Tuesday	Geology
Rehman	Wednesday	Zoology
Rakesh	Thursday	Physics
Vineet	Friday	Botany

39. Monday is the English presentation

40. Vineet makes the Botany presentation

41. Rakesh makes his presentation on Thursday.

Solutions (Q. Nos. 42-46) *According to given conditions, we can make a table follow all conditions*

Grandparents	Mohan (Engg) (Red)	Vanita (Teacher) (Orange)
Parents	Charan (CA)	Namita (White)
Children	Raman (Principal) (Black)	Sarita (Blue)

42. Mohan is an Engineer.

43. Namita's profession is not given

44. Pair of two couples are
Vanita – Mohan
Charan – Namita

45. There are three ladies in the family.

46. Charan is a CA and colour liked by him is not given.

Solutions (Q. Nos. 55-59) *According to the given information, the following results can be obtained. Initially mastermind obtained correct answer-key*

WA = Wrong Answer
BA = Blank Answer

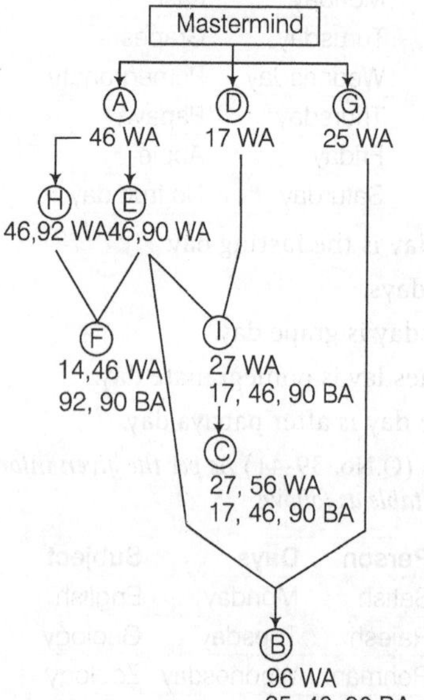

- The result shows that A, D and G obtained the answer-key from mastermind.
- E and H obtained the answer-key from A.
- F obtained the answer-key from both E and H.
- I obtained the answer-key from both E and D.
- C obtained the answer-key from I only.
- B obtained the answer-key from E and G.

And about the wrong answer

- A, D and G replaced the answer 46, 17 and 25 respectively.
- H replaced the answer 92
- E replaced the answer 90
- F replaced the answer 14
- I replaced the answer 27
- C replaced the answer 56
- B replaced the answer 96

55. F introduced the wrong answer to question 14 is the correct statement.

56. Only B have two sources. Because B obtained the answer-key from E and G.

57. Four persons I, E, A and D needed to make answer-keys before C could make his answer-key.

58. G was the source to B and H was the source to F separately.

59. A, D and G have identical sources.

Solutions (Q. Nos. 60-62) *According to the question, the given information can be represented as follows*

Person ↓	Bus	Car	Scooter	Tractor	Auto-rickshaw
A	✔	✔	✔		
B	✔	✔		✔	
C		✔	✔	✔	✔
D	✔		✔	✔	
E			✔	✔	✔

60. C is good in driving tractor, scooter, car and auto-rickshaw but not bus.

61. E is good in driving scooter, tractor and auto-rickshaw but not good in driving car.

62. D is good in driving scooter, tractor and bus.

Solutions (Q.No. 63-65) *From the given information the arrangement is as*

Person	Occupation	Farourite
A	Singer	Rice
B	Teacher	Chapati
C	Sancer	Rice
D	Painter	Chapati
E	Doctor	Rice

63. A is a singer.

64. C is a dancer.

65. B is a teacher.

CHAPTER 10

MATHEMATICAL REASONING

Now-a-days, in many competitive examinations various mathematical problems are asked in reasoning section. These problems can be called as Mathematical Reasoning. Mathematical reasoning test is designed to test the ability of a candidate to solve the various Mathematical problems which are encountered in day to day life. To solve the problems on Mathematical reasoning a candidate should have a knowledge of concepts of arithmetic or basic Mathematics.

Some examples are given below, which will give you a better idea about the types of questions asked in various examinations.

Example 1 If a number is multiplied by three-fourth of itself, then the value thus obtained is 10800. What is that number?

(a) 210 (b) 180 (c) 120 (d) 160

Solution *(c)* Let the number be x.

According to the question,

$$x \times \left(x \times \frac{3}{4}\right) = 10800 \Rightarrow \frac{3x^2}{4} = 10800$$

$$\Rightarrow \quad x^2 = \frac{10800 \times 4}{3} = 14400$$

$$\therefore \quad x = \sqrt{14400} = 120$$

Example 2 If cost of 15 eggs is ₹ 75, then find out the cost of 4 dozens eggs.

(a) ₹ 240 (b) ₹ 300 (c) ₹ 150 (d) ₹ 185

Solution *(a)* $\because$ Cost of 15 eggs = ₹ 75

$\therefore$ Cost of 1 egg = ₹ $\frac{75}{15}$ = ₹ 5

$\therefore$ Cost of 4 dozens $(4 \times 12 = 48)$ eggs $= 5 \times 48 =$ ₹ 240

Example 3 A person covers a distance of 12 km, while walking at a speed of 4 km/h. How much distance he would cover in same time, if he walks at a speed of 6 km/h?

(a) 10 km (b) 20 km
(c) 18 km (d) 16 km

Solution *(c)* Given, $D_1 = 12$ km, $S_1 = 4$ km/h, $D_2 = ?$

and $S_2 = 6$ km/h

Since, the time is kept constant. Therefore, according to the formula,

$$\frac{D_1}{S_1} = \frac{D_2}{S_2} \Rightarrow \frac{12}{4} = \frac{D_2}{6}$$

$$\Rightarrow D_2 = 18 \text{ km}$$

Therefore, the person will cover 18 km.

Example 4 In an examination, 78% of the total students who appeared were successful. If the total number of failures was 176 and 34% got first class, then how many students got first class?

(a) 272 (b) 112
(c) 210 (d) 254

Solution *(a)* Let total students appeared in an exam $= x$

Then, $22\% \text{ of } x = 176 \Rightarrow \frac{22}{100} \times x = 176$

$$\Rightarrow x = \frac{176 \times 100}{22} = 8 \times 100 \Rightarrow x = 800$$

Now, number of students who got first class

$$= 34\% \text{ of } 800 = \frac{34}{100} \times 800 = 34 \times 8 = 272$$

Example 5 The average expenditure of Chandan in four days is ₹ 90. If his expenditures for the first three days are ₹ 100, ₹ 125 and ₹ 85 respectively, then what is the expenditure of Chandan for the fourth day?

(a) ₹ 20 (b) ₹ 30 (c) ₹ 40 (d) ₹ 50

Solution *(d)* Let the expenditure for the fourth day $=$ ₹ x

Then, average expenditure

$$= \frac{\text{Sum of the expenditures of four days}}{4}$$

$$\therefore 90 = \frac{100 + 125 + 85 + x}{4}$$

$$\Rightarrow 310 + x = 360 \Rightarrow x = 360 - 310 = ₹\ 50$$

Practice Exercise

1. A man climbing up a wall of 24 m high. He climbs 16 m on one day but slipped back by 3 m 40 cm in the evening. How far had the man reached on that day?

(a) 11.4 m (b) 12.6 m
(c) 12 m 40 cm (d) 19 m 40 cm

2. Three persons walk some distance x along a street at the speed of 2 km, 3 km and 4 km per hour. Their average speed in km/h is

(a) $2\frac{1}{3}$ (b) $2\frac{3}{4}$
(c) $2\frac{10}{13}$ (d) $3\frac{1}{3}$

3. A box contains 10 green and 8 yellow balls. In how many ways, two balls of the same colour can be drawn?

(a) 73 (b) 36
(c) 28 (d) 54

4. If it takes two workers, working separately but at the same speed, 4 h and 40 min to complete a particular task, about how long will it take one worker, working at the same speed, to complete the same task alone?

(a) 1 h 20 min
(b) 4 h 40 min
(c) 5 h
(d) 5 h 20 min

5. There were a total of 10 bicycles and tricycles. If the total number of wheels was 24, how many tricycles were there?

(a) 2 (b) 6
(c) 18 (d) 4

6. How many odd numbered pages are there in a book of 1089 pages?

(a) 542 (b) 545
(c) 544 (d) 546

7. Jitendra says, "If Rajendra gives me ₹ 40, he will have half as much as Raja, but if Raja gives me ₹ 40, then the three of us will all have the same amount". What is the total amount of money that Jitendra, Rajendra and Raja have between them?

(a) ₹ 240 (b) ₹ 360
(c) ₹ 420 (d) ₹ 320

Previous Year's Questions

Directions (Q. Nos. 8 and 9) *Read the information given below to answer the questions.*

Diana is three times older than Jackson. Edward is half the age of Stephen. Jackson is older than Edward. **[CLAT 2014]**

8. Which one of the following can be inferred?

(a) Jackson is older than Stephen
(b) Diana is older than Stephen
(c) Diana may be younger than Stephen
(d) None of the above

9. Which one of the following information will be sufficient to estimate Diana's age?

(a) Edward is 10 year old
(b) Both Jackson and Stephen are older than Edward by the same number of years.
(c) Both A and B
(d) None of the above

10. Ram is half as old as Shyam, who is three times as old as Prakash. The sum of their ages is 55. How old is Ram? **[CLAT 2015]**

(a) 5 yr (b) 8 yr
(c) 10 yr (d) 15 yr

11. If it takes two workers, working separately but at the same speed, 2 h and 40 min to complete a particular task, about how long will it take one worker, working at the same speed, to complete the same task alone? **[CLAT 2015]**

(a) 1 h 20 min (b) 4 h 40 min
(c) 5 h (d) 5 h 20 min

12. You are given a 60 inch long ribbon, and you are instructed to cut 60, 1 inch long strips out of this ribbon. The time taken to cut one strip is one second. So, how long will it take to cut 60 strips? **[CLAT 2016]**

(a) 30 s
(b) 59 s
(c) 1 m
(d) 1 m and 1 s

13. A, B, C and D have got some money with them. If A gives ₹ 8 to B, B will have as much as C has and A will have ₹ 3 less than what C has. Also, if A takes ₹ 6 from C, A will have twice as much money as D. If B and D together have ₹ 50, how much money does A and B have, respectively? **[CLAT 2016]**

(a) 29, 32 (b) 40, 27 (c) 32, 29 (d) 27, 40

14. Mr X, the President of a club arrived in a meeting at 10 min to 1230 h. Mr X came earlier by 20 min than the other participating members in the meeting, who arrived late by 30 min. At what time was the meeting scheduled? **[CLAT 2016]**

(a) 1220 h (b) 1210 h (c) 1250 h (d) 1240 h

15. An old woman decided to divide her gold among her daughter and daughters-in-law. She first kept exactly half of the gold for her daughter. Then, she divided the rest of her gold among her daughters-in-law. The eldest one got 26 g more than the youngest daughter-in-law. The middle one got twice as the youngest one. If the eldest daughter-in-law got 66 g of gold, how much was received by the daughter? **[CLAT 2016]**

(a) 194 g (b) 172 g (c) 186 g (d) 192 g

16. A 2100 member team consisting of team leaders and athletes is attending a national athletic meet. For every 20 Athletes, there is one team leader. How many team leaders would be there in the team? **[CLAT 2016]**

(a) 100 (b) 110 (c) 105 (d) 95

17. Geeta is twice the present age of Seema. If age of Seema is 20 yr now, how many years ago Geeta was three times Seema's age? **[CLAT 2016]**

(a) 8 (b) 12 (c) 10 (d) 9

18. In a bag, there are some diamonds. In another bag, there is one-fourth the numbers more than the number of diamonds in the first bag. If the difference in the number of diamonds in the first and second bag is 3, how many diamonds are there in the first bag? **[CLAT 2016]**

(a) 16 (b) 8 (c) 10 (d) 12

19. In a company 60% workers are males. If the number of female workers in the company is 800, what is the number of male workers in the companay? **[CLAT 2017]**

(a) 1600 (b) 1400 (c) 1900 (d) 1200

Answers

1	*b*	2	*c*	3	*a*	4	*d*	5	*d*	6	*b*	7	*b*	8	*b*	9	*c*	10	*d*
11	*d*	12	*b*	13	*b*	14	*b*	15	*c*	16	*a*	17	*c*	18	*d*	19	*d*		

SOLUTIONS

1. Distance covered by man $= (16 - 3.4)\text{ m} = 12.6\text{ m}$

2. We know that average speed of 3 persons is $\dfrac{3xyz}{xy + yz + zx}$.

Hence, $x = 2$ km/h, $y = 3$ km/h and $z = 4$ km/h

∴ Average speed

$$= \frac{3 \times 2 \times 3 \times 4}{2 \times 3 + 3 \times 4 + 4 \times 2} = \frac{3 \times 2 \times 3 \times 4}{6 + 12 + 8} = \frac{72}{26} = \frac{36}{13} = 2\frac{10}{13}\text{ km/h}$$

3. Number of green balls in box = 10

Number of yellow balls in box = 8

∴ Total number ways, two balls of the same colour

$$= {}^{10}C_2 + {}^{8}C_2 = \frac{10!}{2!8!} + \frac{8!}{2!6!} = \frac{10 \times 9}{1 \times 2} + \frac{8 \times 7}{1 \times 2}$$

$$= 5 \times 9 + 4 \times 7 = 45 + 28 = 73$$

4. Given that the two workers, working separately but at the same speed takes 2 h and 40 min to complete a particular task. Then, one worker, working at the same speed, to complete the same task will take double time, i.e. 5 h 20 min.

5. Let the required number of tricycles $= x$

Then, the number of bicycles $= 10 - x$

According to the question,

$3x + 2(10 - x) = 24$ [∵ Tricycles = 3 wheels; Bicycle = 2 wheels]

$\Rightarrow x + 20 = 24$

$\Rightarrow x = 4$

Therefore, the required number of tricycles $= x = 4$

6. Required number of pages

$$= \frac{\text{Total number of pages} + 1}{2} = \frac{1089 + 1}{2} = \frac{1090}{2} = 545$$

7. Let money with Jitendra $= ₹\, x$

Money with Rajendra $= ₹\, y$

Money with Raja $= ₹\, z$

Then, according to the question

$y - 40 = \frac{1}{2}z$ ...(i)

$z - 40 = y$ ...(ii)

$z - 40 = x + 40$ ...(iii)

On putting the value of y from Eq. (ii) in Eq. (i), we get

$(z - 40) - 40 = \frac{1}{2}z$

$\Rightarrow z = 160$

So, $y = z - 40 = 160 - 40 = 120$

Then, putting the value of z in Eq. (iii), we get

$160 - 40 = x + 40$

$\Rightarrow x = 80$

Therefore, the total amount of money

$= ₹\,(x + y + z)$

$= ₹\,(80 + 120 + 160)$

$= ₹\,360$

Previous Year's Solutions

8. From the given information,

$\Rightarrow$ D = 3J ...(i)

$\Rightarrow$ 2E = S ...(ii)

$\Rightarrow$ J > E ...(iii)

where, D = Diana

J = Jackson

E = Edward

Since, D = 3J

∴ D > J > 2E [∵ J > E]

But 2E = S

∴ D > S

So, according to this, Diana is older than stephen.

9. Let the age of Jackson and Stephen both be $(10 + x)$ yr.

Now,

$2E = S \Rightarrow 2 \times 10 = 10 + x$

$\Rightarrow x = 10$ yr.

∴ Jackson's age $= 10 + x = 20$ yr

Hence, Diana's age $= 3 \times 20 = 60$ yr

10. Let the age of Prakash $= x$ yr

According to the question,

Age of Shyam $= 3x$ yr

Age of Ram $= \dfrac{3x}{2}$ yr

Now, given that the sum of their ages is 55.

$\therefore x + 3x + \frac{3x}{2} = 55$

$\Rightarrow \quad 8x + 3x = 110$

$\Rightarrow \quad 11x = 110$

$\therefore \quad x = 10$

Now, the age of Ram $= \frac{3x}{2}$

$= \frac{3 \times 10}{2} = 15$ yr

11. Given that the two workers, working separately but at the same speed, 2 h and 40 min to complete a particular task.
Then one worker, working at the same speed, to complete the same task will take double time, i.e. 5 h 20 min.

12. Time taken = 60 − 1 = 59 s

Since, last cut, i.e. 59th cut will produce 2 strips.

13. Let A, B, C and D have a, b, c and d rupees, respectively.
Now, A gives ₹ 8 to B, then B will have as much as C has and A will have ₹ 3 less than what C has.

So, $\quad b + 8 = c \quad$ ...(i)

$a - 8 = c - 3 \quad$ ...(ii)

Now, A takes ₹ 6 from C and A will have twice as much money as D.

$a + 6 = 2d \quad$ ...(iii)

Now, $\quad b = c - 8$

[from Eq. (i)] ...(iv)

$a = c + 5$

[from Eq. (ii)] ...(v)

$\Rightarrow \quad c + 5 + 6 = 2d$

[from Eqs. (iii) and (v)]

$d = \frac{c + 11}{2} \quad$ ...(vi)

Now, it is also given,

$b + d = 50$

$\Rightarrow \quad c - 8 + \frac{c + 11}{2} = 50$

[from Eqs. (iv), (v) and (vi)]

$\Rightarrow \frac{2c - 16 + c + 11}{2} = 50$

$\Rightarrow \quad 3c - 5 = 100$

$\Rightarrow \quad 3c = 105$

$\Rightarrow \quad c = 35$

Now, $\quad a = 35 + 5 \Rightarrow a = 40$

and $\quad b = 35 - 8 \Rightarrow b = 27$

Hence, A and B have ₹ 40 and ₹ 27, respectively.

14. Mr. X arrived in a meeting at 1230 h − 10 min = 1220 h
Now, the other participating members arrived at 1220 h + 20 min = 1240 h.
The other participating members arrived late by 30 min. So, the scheduled time of meeting was 1240 h − 30 min = 1210 h

15. Let the total quantity of gold be x g

Daughter's share $= \frac{x}{2}$ g

Daughters-in-law'sshare

$= \frac{x}{2}$ g

Now, it is given that the eldest daughter-in-law got 66 g of gold.
Also, the eldest daughter-in-law got 26 g more gold than the youngest daughter-in-law. So, the youngest daughter-in-law got the quantity of gold

$= 66 - 26 = 40$ g

Now, the middle daughter-in-law got

$= 40 \times 2 = 80$ g of gold

∴Total quantity of gold distributed among daughters-in-law

$= 66 + 40 + 80 = 186$ g.

Now, $\frac{x}{2} = 186 \Rightarrow x = 372$

Therefore, the daughter also received 186 g of gold.

16. Given, for every 20 Athletes, there is one team leader.
So, in a group of 20 + 1 = 21 members there is one team leader.
∴Number of team leaders in the team

$= \frac{2100}{21} = 100$

17. Given, age of Seema = 20 yr
∴ The age of Geeta

$= 2 \times 20 = 40$ yr

Let x yr ago Geeta was three times Seema's age.

Now, $\quad (40 - x) = 3(20 - x)$

$\Rightarrow \quad 40 - x = 60 - 3x$

$\Rightarrow \quad 20 = 2x \Rightarrow x = 10$

Hence, 10 yr ago Geeta was three times Seema's age.

18. Let the number of diamonds in first bag be x
∴ Number of diamonds in second bag

$= x + \frac{x}{4} = \frac{5x}{4}$

Now, according to the question,

$\frac{5x}{4} - x = 3$

$\Rightarrow \quad \frac{x}{4} = 3$

$\Rightarrow \quad x = 12$

∴Number of diamonds in first bag = 12

19. Total worker

$= \frac{800}{400} \times 100 = 2000$

∴ Number of Male worker

$= \frac{2000 \times 60}{100} = 1200$

CHAPTER

11

ANALYTICAL AND LOGICAL REASONING

"Analytical and Logical Reasoning section tests your decision making ability. This section measures your ability to understand, analyse and evaluate the arguments. Your strategy would consist in determining what has been specifically stated and drawing inferences on the basis of the facts stated. First of all, determine the assumptions made by the author when jumping from evidence to conclusion.

In this chapter we will discuss following types of problems

SYLLOGISM

Syllogism is a 'Greek' word that means 'Inference' or 'Deduction'. As such inferences are based on logic, so these inferences are called logical deduction. In this chapter, questions are based are based on some statements and their conclusions. We are not supposed to apply extra information except from the information given in statements, while drawing conclusions.

Proposition

A proposition, also known as a premise, is a grammatical sentence which comprises a subject, a predicate and a copula.

A proposition consists of three parts

1. **Subject** (S) A subject is that part of proposition about which something is said.
2. **Predicate** (P) A predicate is that part of proposition which is affirmed or denied about the subject.
3. **Copula** (C) A copula is that part of proposition which says about the relation between the subject and the predicate.

e.g. Dogs are black.
↓ ↓ ↓
Subject Copula Predicate

In the above example, the information is given about 'Dogs'. So, 'Dogs' are the subject. Black is the quality affirmed for this subject. So, it is the predicate. 'Are' shows the relation between the subject and the predicate. So, it is the copula.

Classification of Proposition

Propositions have been classified on the basis of quality and quantity of the propositions. Quality denotes whether the proposition is affirmative or negative in nature. Quantity denotes whether the proposition is universal or particular.

The four-fold proposition can be summarised as below

Symbols	Proposition	Quantity	Quality
A	All A are B	Universal	Affirmative
E	No A is B	Universal	Negative
I	Some A are B	Particular	Affirmative
O	Some A are not B	Particular	Negative

To draw valid inferences from the statements, the candidate is required to have a clear understanding of A, E, I, O relationships.

Venn Diagram Representation of Four Propositions

Types of Propositions	Venn Diagram
A : All S are P	Always 
E : No S are P	Always 
I : Some S are P	Either  Some S are P [Some S are not P]
	or  Some P are S [All S are P]
	or  Some S are not P [All P are S]
O : Some S are not P	Either  Some S are not P [Some S are P]
	or  Some S are not P [All P are S]
	or  Some S are not P [No S are P]

Complementary Pair of Conclusions ('Either or' Situation)

In this situation, neither of the conclusions is definitely true but a combination of both makes a complementary pair.

Example 1. Statements

Some chairs are tables.
Some tables are bed.

Conclusions

I. Some chairs are bed.
II. No chair is bed.

Solution Here, we will draw all possible Venn diagrams

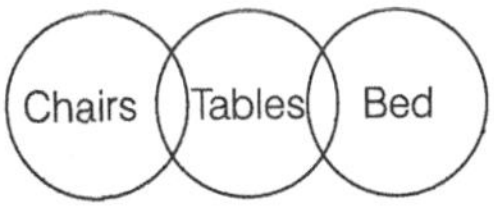

or

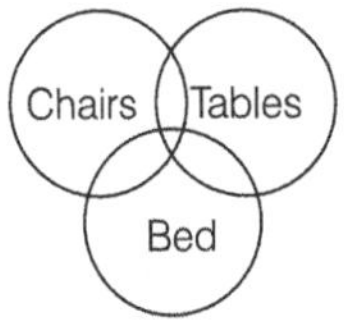

From the above diagrammatical representation we can conclude either 'Some chairs are bed' or 'No chair is bed'. Hence, atleast one of the conclusions must be true.

A complementary pair of conclusions must follow anyone of the three types of pairs

(i) I-O type

(ii) A-O type

(iii) I-E type

Example 2. Two statements are given in each of the following questions, followed by two Conclusions I and II. You have to take the given two statements to be true even if they seem to be at variance from commonly known facts. Read the conclusions and then decide which of the given conclusions logically follows from the two given statements, disregarding known facts.

Statements

Some schools are factories.

All factories are shops.

Conclusions

I. All shops are factories.

II. Some shops are schools.

(a) if only Conclusion I follows
(b) if only Conclusion II follows
(c) if neither I nor II follows
(d) if both Conclusions I and II follow

Solution *(b)*

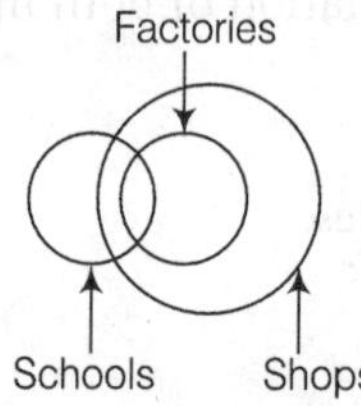

or

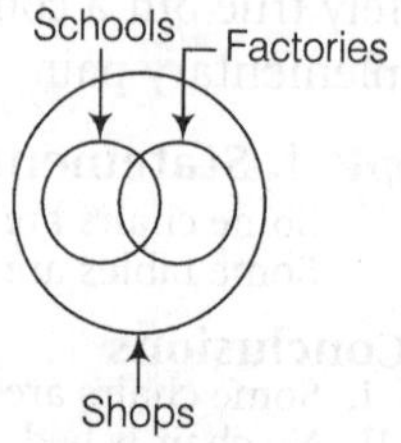

Conclusions I. All shops are factories. (✗)
II. Some shops are schools. (✓)

Hence, Conclusion II follows.

Example 3. In the following question, three statements and three Conclusions I, II and III are given. Select the correct answer from the options given.

Statements

All tables are mirrors.

Some mirrors are chairs.

All chairs are glasses.

Conclusion

I. Some glasses are mirrors.

II. Some chairs are tables.

III. Some mirrors are tables.

(a) I and II follow
(b) II and III follow
(c) I and III follow
(d) All I, II and III follow

Solution *(c)*

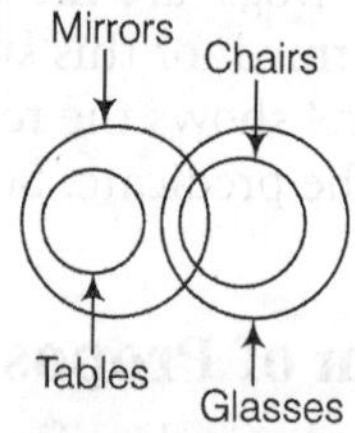

Conclusions I. Some glasses are mirrors. (✓)
II. Some chairs are tables. (✗)
III. Some mirrors are tables. (✓)

Hence, Conclusions I and III follow.

Practice Exercise

Directions (Q. Nos. 1-4) *In each of the questions below are given two statements followed by two Conclusions* I *and* II. *You have to take the two given statements to be true even if they seem to be at variance from commonly known facts and decide which of the given conclusion(s) logically follow(s) from the two given statements, disregarding commonly known facts.*

Give Answer

(a) if only Conclusion I follows
(b) if only Conclusion II follows
(c) if neither I nor II follows
(d) if Conclusions I and II follow

1. Statements All bottles are glasses.
No cup is a glass.

Conclusions

I. No bottle is a cup.
II. Atleast some glasses are bottles.

2. Statements No bangle is an earrings.
Some earrings are rings.

Conclusions

I. No ring is a bangle.
II. Some rings are definitely not earrings.

3. Statements All windows are doors.
No door is wall.

Conclusions

I. No window is wall.
II. No wall is door.

4. Statements Some banks are colleges.
All colleges are schools.

Conclusions

I. Atleast some banks are schools.
II. All schools are colleges.

Directions (Q. Nos. 5-7) *In each of the questions below are given three statements followed by three Conclusions* I, II *and* III. *You have to take the given statements to be true even, if they seems to be at variance with commonly known facts. Read all the conclusions and then decide which of the given conclusions logically follows from the given statements disregarding commonly known facts.*

5. Statements All keys are locks.
All locks are bangles.
All bangles are cars.

Conclusions

I. Some cars are locks.
II. Some bangles are keys.
III. Some cars are keys.

(a) Only I follows (b) I and II follow
(c) I and III follow (d) All I, II and III follow

6. Statements All calculators are boxes.
All boxes are taps.
Some taps are machines.

Conclusions

I. Some machines are boxes.
II. Some taps are calculators.
III. Some boxes are calculators.

(a) I and II follow (b) I and III follow
(c) II and III follow (d) All I, II and III follow

7. Statements Some books are papers.
Some papers are desks.
Some desks are chairs.

Conclusions

I. Some books are desks.
II. Some papers are chairs.
III. Some books are chairs.

(a) None follows (b) Only I follows
(c) Only II follows (d) Only III follows

Directions (Q. Nos. 8 and 9) *In each of the questions below are given three statements followed by four Conclusions* I, II, III *and* IV. *You have to take the given statements to be true even, if they seem to be at variance from commonly known facts. Read all the conclusions and then decide which of the given conclusion(s) logically follow(s) from the given statements disregarding commonly known facts.*

8. Statements Some dogs are rats.
All rats are trees.
Some trees are not dogs.

Conclusions

I. Some trees are dogs.
II. All dogs are trees.
III. All rats are dogs.
IV. No tree is dog.

(a) None follows (b) Only I follows
(c) I and II follow (d) II and III follow

9. Statements All books are papers.
All pencils are papers.
All tables are papers.

Conclusions

I. Some books are pencils.
II. Some pencils are tables.
III. Some tables are books.
IV. Some papers are tables.

(a) Only I follows (b) Only II follows
(c) Only III follows (d) Only IV follows

Previous Year's Questions

Directions (Q. Nos. 10-12) *Each question below has two statements followed by four Conclusions I, II, III and IV. You have to accept the given statements to be true, even if they appear to be at variance from commonly known facts. Read all the conclusions and then decide which of the given conclusions logically follows from the two statements.* **[CLAT 2012]**

10. Statement I. All girls are students.
II. All doctors are students.

Conclusions

I. All girls are students.
II. Some students are girls.
III. Some students are doctors.
IV. All doctors are girls.

(a) Only I follows (b) I and II follow
(c) II and IV follow (d) I, II and III follows

11. Statement I. All researchers are sociologists.
II. Some researchers are professors.

Conclusions

I. All researchers are professors.
II. Some researchers are professors.
III. Some professors are sociologists.
IV. Some sociologists are researchers.

(a) III and II follow
(b) II and IV follow
(c) Only III follows
(d) II, III and IV follow

12. Statement

I. Some democracies are dictatorship.
II. No dictatorship is a monarchy.

Conclusions

I. No democracy is a monarchy.
II. No dictatorship is a democracy.
III. Some democracies are monarchy.
IV. Some dictatorships are democracies.

(a) I and IV follow (b) Only IV follow
(c) I and III follow (d) None follow

Answers

1	*d*	2	*c*	3	*d*	4	*a*	5	*d*	6	*c*	7	*a*	8	*b*	9	*d*	10	*d*
11	*d*	12	*b*																

SOLUTIONS

1.

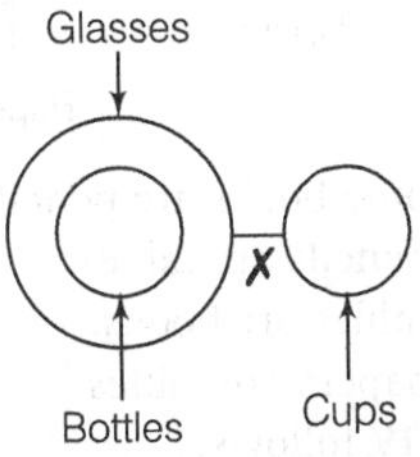

Conclusions I. No bottle is a cup. (✓)

II. Atleast some glasses are bottles. (✓)

Hence, Conclusions I and II follow.

2.

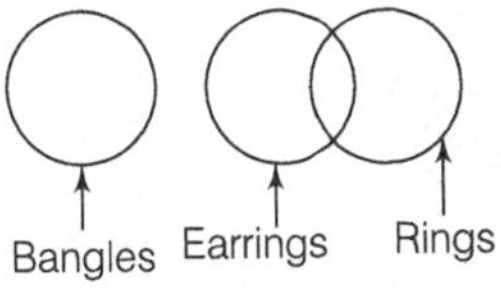

or

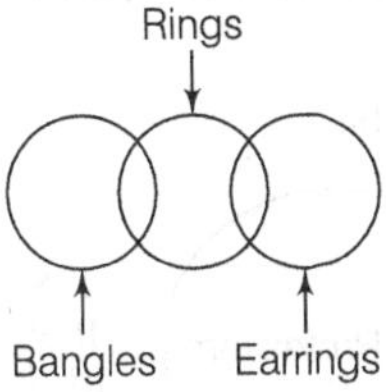

or

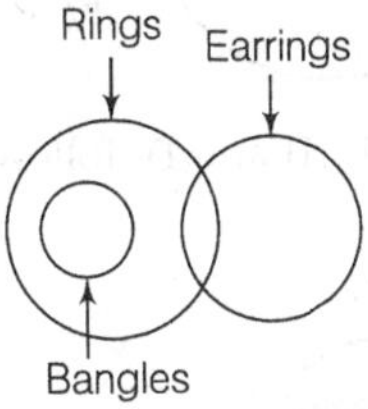

Conclusions I. No ring is a bangle. (✗)

II. Some rings are definitely not earrings. (✗)

Hence, neither I nor II follows.

3.

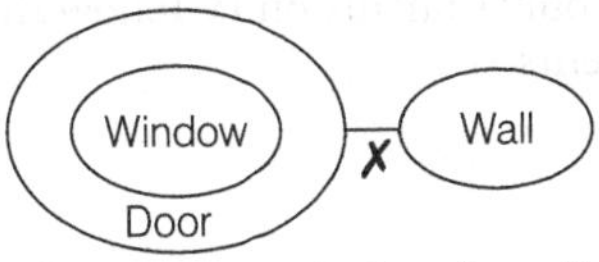

Conclusions I. No window is wall. (✓)

II. No wall is door. (✓)

Hence, Conclusions I and II follow.

4.

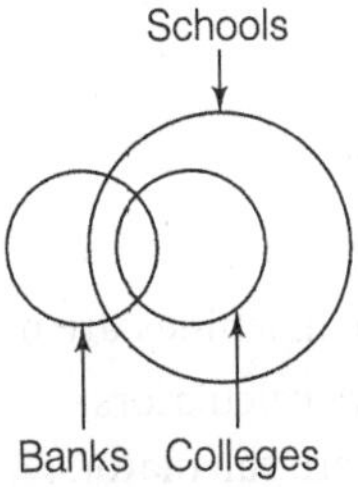

or

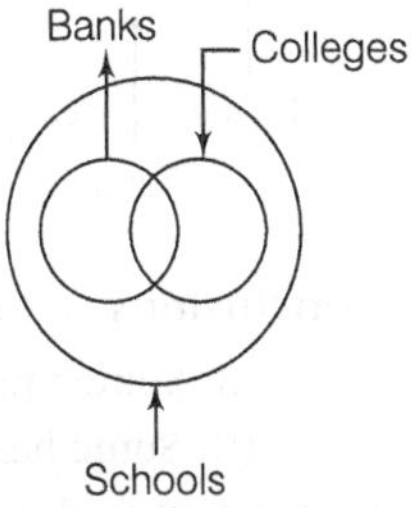

Conclusions

I. Atleast some banks are schools. (✓)

II. All schools are colleges. (✗)

Hence, Conclusion I follows.

5.

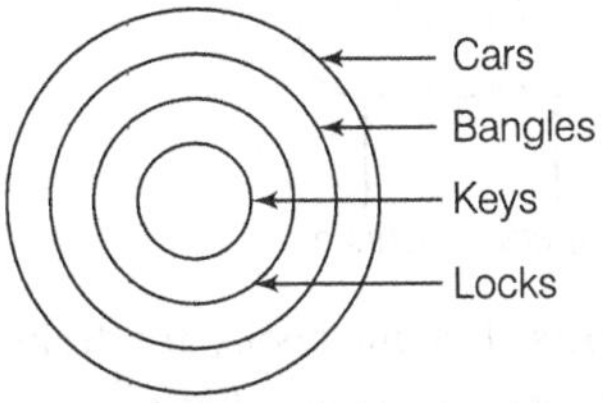

Conclusions I. Some cars are locks. (✓)

II. Some bangles are keys. (✓)

III. Some cars are keys. (✓)

Hence, Conclusions I, II and III follow.

6.

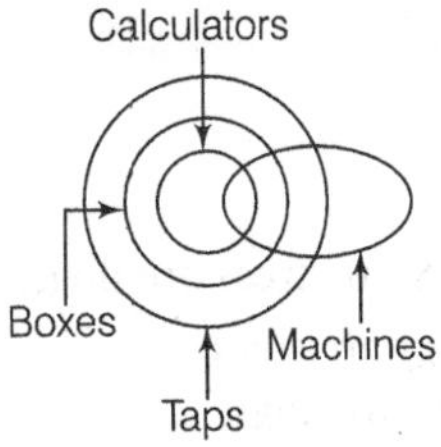

or

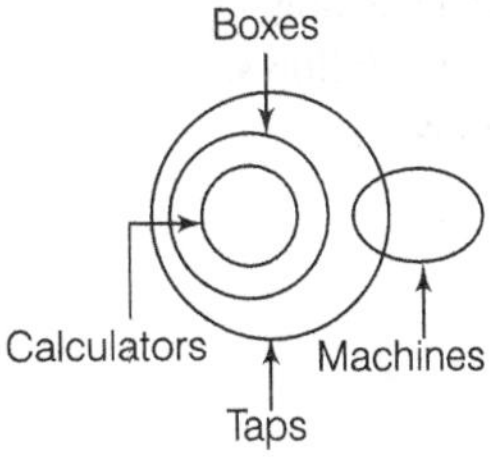

or

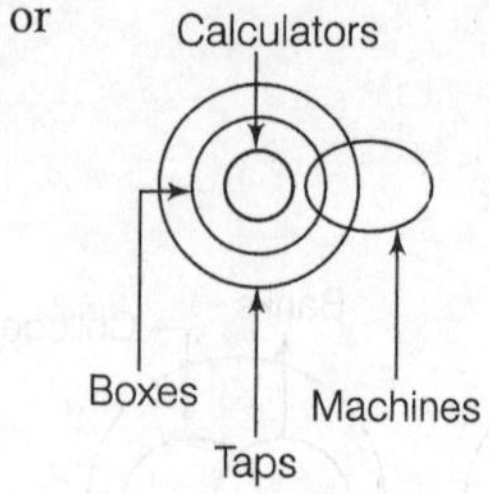

Conclusions I. Some machines are boxes. (✗)

II. Some taps are calculators. (✓)

III. Some boxes are calculators. (✓)

Hence, Conclusions II and III follow.

7.

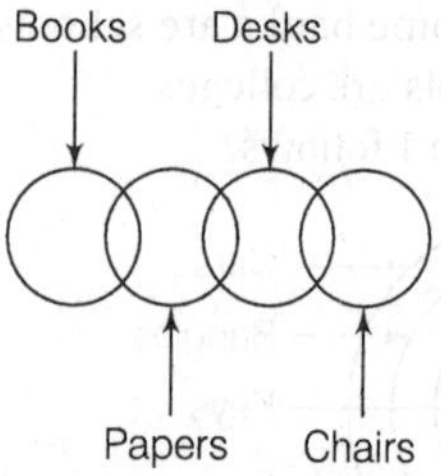

Conclusions I. Some books are desks. (✗)

II. Some papers are chairs. (✗)

III. Some books are chairs. (✗)

8.

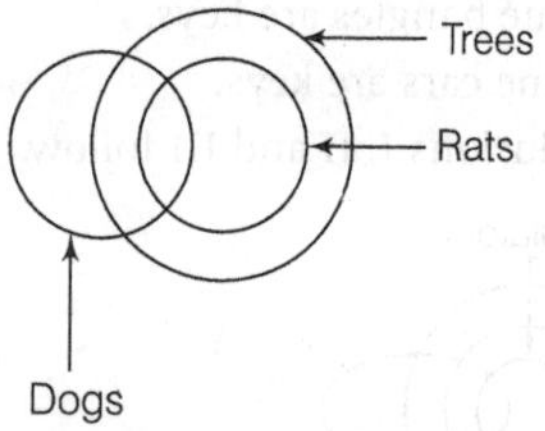

Conclusions I. Some trees are dogs. (✓)

II. All dogs are trees. (✗)

III. All rats are dogs. (✗)

IV. No tree is dog. (✗)

Hence, Conclusion I follows.

Hence, none follows.

9.

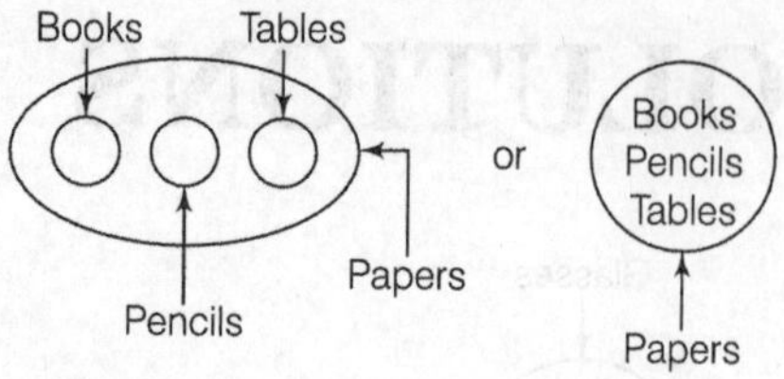

Conclusions I. Some books are pencils. (✗)

II. Some pencils are tables. (✗)

III. Some tables are books. (✗)

IV. Some papers are tables. (✓)

Hence, Conclusion IV follows.

Previous Year's Solutions

10. From both statements,

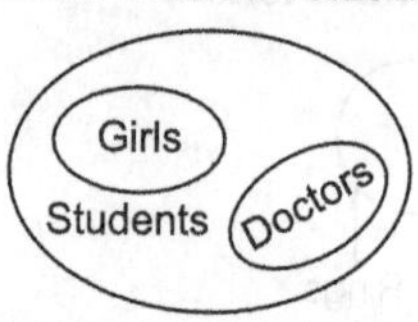

I. ✓
II. ✓
III. ✓
IV. ×

Hence, conclusions I, II and III follows the given statemsents.

11. From both statements,

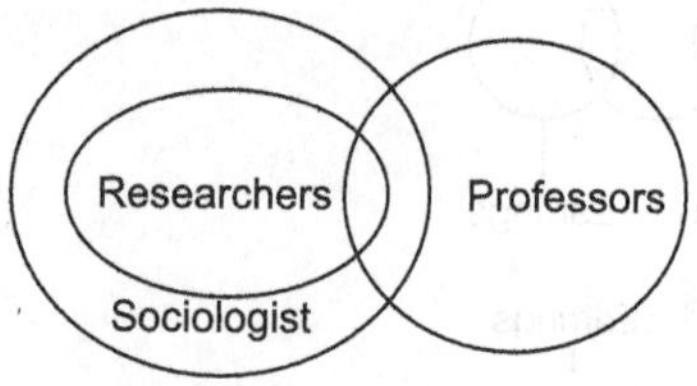

I. ×
II. ✓
III. ✓
IV. ✓

Hence, Conclusions II, III and IV follows the given statements.

12. From both statements,

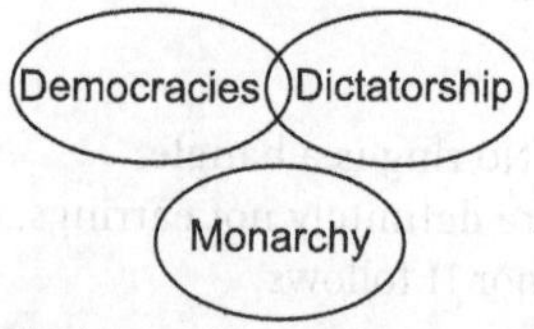

I. ×
II. ×
III. ×
IV. ✓

Hence, only Conclusion IV follow the given statements.

STATEMENT AND ARGUMENT

An argument is a fact or set of facts that is being given by a person to support an idea, statement or theory in its favour or against it.

In this chapter, a statement followed by certain arguments is given. The statement is concerned with an issue. These issues may be political, social or economical. The arguments are in favour or against the given statement. Generally, the two arguments are contrary to each other and refer to the positive and negative results of the action as mentioned in the statement issue.

Arguments can be of two types

1. Strong Argument

Touches the practical and real aspect of the situation as described in the statement.

Following points should be taken into consideration while choosing a strong argument

- A strong argument should give the realistic diagonosis of the situation described in the statement.
- A strong argument should give deep analysis of the topic dealing with the statement.
- A strong argument should relate with the statement and be supported up by facts or established thoughts.
- A strong argument should not be more reiteration of the situation given in the statement.

2. Weak Argument

An argument is called weak, if it is not directly related to the given statement and it does not address all the points put forward in the given statement.

Following points should be taken into consideration while choosing a weak argument

- Weak arguments are ambiguous in nature.
- Weak arguments are too simple and sometime superfluous in nature.
- Weak arguments are contrary to established facts.
- Weak arguments are those which contains the word 'only'.

Directions (Ex. Nos. 1 and 2) *Study the following instructions carefully and then answer the questions that follow.*

In making decisions about important questions, it is desirable to be able to distinguish between 'strong' and 'weak' arguments so far as they relate to the questions. 'Weak' arguments may not be directly related to the question and may be of minor importance or may be related to the trivial aspect of the question. Each question below is followed by two arguments numbered I and II. You have to decide which of the arguments is a 'strong' argument and which is a 'weak' argument?

Give Answer

(a) If only Argument I is strong
(b) If only Argument II is strong
(c) If neither I nor II is strong
(d) If both I and II are strong

Example 1. Statement Should luxury hotels be banned in India?

Arguments I. Yes, these are places from where international criminals operate.

II. No, affluent foreign tourists will have no place to stay.

Solution *(b)* The luxury hotels are symbols of country's development and a place for staying the affluent foreign tourists. So, Argument II is a strong one. Argument I is a weak argument because ban on luxury hotels is not a way to stop the international criminals.

Example 2. Statement Should there be no examination upto Std IX in all the schools in India?

Arguments I. No, students need to go through the process of giving examinations right from young age.

II. Yes, this will help students to think laterally and achieve their creative pursuits.

Solution *(d)* Argument I is strong as school is the ground where we prepare for the future battles of life. Argument II is strong as examinations kill our creativity, turning us all into more clerks.

Example 3. Below is followed by three arguments numbered I, II and III. You have to decide which of the arguments is a 'strong' argument and which is a 'weak' argument.

Statement Should road repair work in big cities be carried out only late at night?

Arguments I. No, this way the work will never get completed.

II. No, there will be unnecessary use of electricity.

III. Yes, the commuters will face a lot of problems due to repair work during the day.

(a) None is strong (b) Only I is strong
(c) Only III is strong (d) I and III are strong

Solution *(c)* Argument I is not true for all roads work is often done in phases and meets completion. Argument II is weak such use of electricity cannot be termed 'unnecessary.' Argument III is strong as it shows concern for commuters.

Practice Exercise

Directions (Q. Nos. 1 and 2) *Read the following passage carefully and answer the questions following that.*

Religions, like camel caravans, seem to avoid mountain passes. Buddhism spread quickly South from Buddha's birth-place in Southern Nepal across the flat Gangetic plain to Sri Lanka. But it took a millennium to reach China ... The religious belt stretched eventually to Mongolia and Japan but in Afghanistan Buddhism filled only a narrow belt that left pagans among the valleys to the East and West in Kailash and Ghor.

1. Which of the following best summarises the subject of this paragraph?
(a) The Afghan people were hostile to Buddhism
(b) Geography has considerable impact on the spread of religions
(c) Buddhism does not flourish in mountainous regions
(d) Religion has a considerable impact on geography

2. Which of the following, if true, would most *weaken* the conclusion to the above argument?
(a) Christianity took several centuries to cross the Atlantic Ocean to America
(b) The Hindukush mountains made no difference to the speed with which Islam spread
(c) Buddhism is strongest in mountainous regions
(d) Jainism is less popular in cold climates

Directions (Q. Nos. 3 and 4) *Read the following passage carefully and answer the questions following that.*

Friendship was indeed a value for the villagers, more for men than for women. Two good friends were said to be 'like brothers' (literally, 'like elder brother- younger brother', *annatammandirahage*). I heard this expression several times and I could not help recalling the statement of an elderly English colleague who had told me that he and his brother were very close and had written to each other every week. He had added, 'We are very good friends.' That is friendship connoted intimacy in England while in Rampura (as in rural India everywhere), brotherhood conveyed intimacy.

3. Which of the following best summarises the conclusion of the argument of this paragraph?
(a) Friendship has greater value for men than for women
(b) People in England have different attitudes to brotherhood and friendship than people in rural India
(c) Brotherhood has greater value in rural India than in England
(d) Friendship has greater value in England than in India

4. Which of the following, if true, would directly *contradict* the conclusion of the above argument?
(a) People are less likely to have large families in England
(b) People in England are no longer close to their family members
(c) People in England do not think that friendship connotes intimacy
(d) People in rural India think that sisters cannot be intimate

Directions (Q. Nos. 5 and 6) *Read the following passage carefully and answer the questions following that.*

A language is most easily learnt when it is in tune with the social context. To teach an Indian child in English at the primary stage .... strengthens distinctions of class and status and warps the mind. Failure to resort to regional languages in literacy campaigns also hampers their success.

5. Which of the following best summarises the argument of the passage above?
(a) Learning English warps the mind
(b) Language policy should be devised with an eye to social context
(c) Literacy campaigns in India have failed
(d) English should be taught at the secondary school level

6. Which of the following claims, if true, would *weaken* the argument in the passage above?
(a) Literacy campaigns are more successful when conducted in English
(b) Learning English at an early age has been found to weaken class distinctions
(c) Children who learn English at the primary school stage have been found to show greater intellectual ability than those who learn English only at the secondary level
(d) All of the above

Directions (Q.Nos. 7-9) *Read the given passage carefully and answer the questions that follow.*

Instead of being concerned with what actually happens in practice .... (economics) is increasingly preoccupied with developing pseudo-mathematical formulas. These provide models of behaviour which never quite fit what actually happens, in a way which resembles the physical sciences gone wrong instead of equations describing reality, economics produces equations describing ideal conditions and theoretical clarity of a type which never occurs in practice. **[CLAT 2011]**

7. Which of the following best summarises the argument of this passage?
(a) Economics ought to be more like the physical sciences
(b) Theoretical clarity is undesirable in economics
(c) The physical sciences are wrong to emphasise mathematic formulae
(d) The mathematical equations used by economists do not accurately describe the real world

8. Which of the following claims is *not* implied in the passage above?
(a) Economists should stop using mathematical models
(b) Equations describing ideal conditions should not be mistaken for equations describing reality
(c) Theoretical clarity should not come at the expense of accuracy
(c) Models of human behaviour should be true to the complexity of human nature

9. Which of the following, *if true*, would most *weaken* the argument of the passage above?
(a) The physical sciences are themselves reducing their reliance on mathematical formulae
(b) The real world in fact closely approximates ideal theoretical conditions
(c) We do not at present have the mathematical expertise to model the full complexity of the world economy
(d) Academic economists need to be more sensitive to human nature

Previous Year's Questions

10. An argument is given below, on the basis of that argument; find out the parallel argument from the given list of subsequent arguments

Argument Himalayan Sparrows are disappearing. This bird is an Indian bird, therefore Indian birds are disappearing.

Subsequent Arguments

(a) industrialists pay most of the taxes. 'Z' is a wealthy man, therefore 'Z' must pay most taxes

(b) a pineapple is a fruit, a mango is a fruit, therefore pineapple is a mango

(c) snow tigers are an endangered species; all endangered species must be protected; therefore snow tiger must be protected

(d) john is his father's favourite son and John knows this must be true because his father told him this and no father would lie to his favourite son

Directions (Q. Nos. 11-14) *Each question below is followed by arguments. Choose the most appropriate choice from the options given.* [CLAT 2012]

11. Statement Should Judicial Activism be discouraged?

Argument

I. No, it would lead to executive dictatorship.

II. Yes, Judiciary should stay in the constitutional limits.

(a) Argument I is strong

(b) Argument II is strong

(c) Both the arguments are strong

(d) Both the arguments are weak

12. Statement Should the Judiciary be independent of Executive and Legislature?

Argument

I. Yes, this is necessary to ensure impartiality in the administration of Justice.

II. No, it will develop inertia in Executive and Legislature

(a) Argument I is strong

(b) Argument II is strong

(c) Both the arguments are strong

(d) Both the arguments are weak

13. Statement Should E-Governance be introduced at every level of public administration?

Argument

I. Yes, it will reduce corruption.

II. No, it will lead to unemployment.

(a) Argument I is strong

(b) Argument II is strong

(c) Both the arguments are strong

(d) Both the arguments are weak

14. Statement Should there be a world Government?

Argument

I. Yes, it will eliminate inter state conflicts

II. No, Rich and Powerful countries will dominate it

(a) Argument I is strong

(b) Argument II is strong

(c) Both the arguments are strong

(d) Both the arguments are weak

15. "Some philosophers believe that a concept which cannot be verified can still be valid because of its inner logic which ennobles it."

In the light of the above statement, decide the status of the statement given below. [CLAT 2012]

Statement "Every person has certain inherent and inalienable rights which must be protected by Rule of Law."

(a) True

(b) False

(c) Difficult to determine

(d) Both true and false

Directions (Q. Nos. 16-22) *Given below are some statements followed by two arguments. Read carefully and decide which of the arguments strongly support the statement.* [CLAT 2012]

16. Statement Should the pay scale and conditions of service of government employees be made applicable to private sector employees?

Argument

I. No, this will develop inertia, inefficiency and would adversely affect spirit of competition.

II. Yes, this will enhance dedication to work and institutional loyalty.

(a) Argument I is strong

(b) Argument II is strong

(c) Both I and II are strong

(d) Neither I nor II is strong

17. Statement Should a strong institution of ombudsman be created in India?

Argument

I. Yes, this will bring transparency and accountability in the administration.

II. No, this will develop lack of initiative and flexibility in the administration.

(a) Argument I is strong
(b) Argument II is strong
(c) Both I and II are strong
(d) Neither I nor II is strong

18. Statement Should internal assessment in colleges and universities be abolished?

Argument

I. Yes, this will eliminate the possibility of favouritism

II. No, teaching faculty will lose control over the students and this would adversely affect their academic growth.

(a) Argument I is strong
(b) Argument II is strong
(c) Both I and II are strong
(d) Neither I nor II is strong

19. Statement Should military training be made compulsory for all college and university students?

Argument

I. Yes, this will develop in them a sense of punctuality and discipline.

II. No, military training should be given only to those students who are physically fit.

(a) Argument I is strong
(b) Argument II is strong
(c) Both I and II are strong
(d) Neither I nor II is strong

20. Statement Should students union in colleges and universities be abolished?

Argument

I. Yes, it detracts students from academic and career development.

II. No, all great leaders have been students union leaders.

(a) Argument I is strong
(b) Argument II is strong
(c) Both I and II are strong
(d) Neither I nor II is strong

21. Statement Should the age of marriage be raised to 25 yr for boys and 21 for girls?

Argument

I. No, it is difficult to change a social practice in Indian conditions.

II. Yes, by that age people develop a sense of responsibility and also complete their education.

(a) Argument I is strong
(b) Argument II is strong
(c) Both I and II are strong
(d) Neither I nor II is strong

22. Identify the argument which cannot be accepted.

(a) All rainy days are wet days. Therefore, all wet days are rainy days
(b) All equilateral triangles are equiangular. Therefore, all equilateral triangles are equilateral
(c) All unmarried woman are spinsters. Therefore, all spinsters are women
(d) All wives are married. Therefore, all married people are wives

Answers

1	*c*	2	*b*	3	*d*	4	*c*	5	*b*	6	*d*	7	*c*	8	*b*	9	*d*	10	*c*
11	*b*	12	*a*	13	*a*	14	*d*	15	*a*	16	*b*	17	*a*	18	*b*	19	*c*	20	*d*
21	*d*	22	*d*																

SOLUTIONS

Previous Year's Solutions

10. From the given argument the best subsequent argument is that 'Snow tigers are an endangered species; all endangered species must be protected; therefore snow tigers must be protected'.

11. **Argument I** is not strong because in this argument Judicial Activism lead to executive dictatorship which is totally wrong but **Argument II** is strong because it is necessary to any institution should stay in the constitutional limits.

12. **Only Argument I** is strong because without independence of judiciary from executive and legislature we cannot expect a true judgement, while **Argument II** is irrelevant.

14. Both arguments are weak because we cannot imagine or made a single world Government.

15. From the given light of statement. The status of the statement is definitely true and it is protected by Rule of Law.

16. Only **Argument II** is strong because if the pay scale and conditions of service of Government employees be made applicable to private sector employees, then this will enhance dedication to work and institutional loyalty, while **Argument I** is weak.

17. Only **Argument I** is strong because a strong institutional of ombudsman will bring transparency and accountability in the administration while **Argument II** is weak.

18. Only **Argument II** is strong because internal assessment in college and universities will help in academic growth of students, while **Argument I** is weak.

19. Both Arguments are strong because a military training develop a sense of punctuality and discipline among students and also military training should be given only these students who are physically fit.

20. Neither **Argument I** nor **II** is strong because students union in colleges and universities be abolished is not a permanent solution for students development.

21. Neither **Argument I** nor **II** is strong because increase marriage age is not a permanent solution for improvement conditions of people.

STATEMENT AND ASSUMPTIONS

Statement is an information or a fact related to any general subject and assumption is the hidden or unsaid part of the statement which a person assumes before stating some fact or statement.

In this chapter, one statement followed by two or more assumptions is given. The candidates are required to observe the given statement and assumptions and decide which of the assumptions is/are implicit.

The candidates must remember the following important points to decide whether the given assumption(s) is implicit or not.

- Assumption should be directly related to the statement.
- It should not be ambiguous.
- It should not be superfluous.
- It should not be merely repetition of the statement.
- It should not be the argument drawn from the statement.
- It should not include words like 'all', 'every', 'each', 'only', etc.
- It should not oppose government directions.
- It may include words related to any possibility, such as may be, possibly, etc.
- It can be many, in numbers, based on a single statement.

Directions (Ex. Nos. 1 and 2) *In each question below is given a statement followed by two assumptions numbered* I *and* II. *An assumption is something supposed or taken for granted. You have to consider the statement and the following assumptions and decide which of the assumption(s) is/are implicit in the statement.*

Give Answer

(a) If only Assumption I is implicit
(b) If only Assumption II is implicit
(c) If neither Assumption I nor II is implicit
(d) If both Assumptions I and II are implicit

Example 1. Statement It is surprising that India beat Australia even after follow on. It happens 2nd time in the history of test cricket.

Assumptions

I. Winning after follow on is possible.
II. India cannot repeat such victory again.

Solution *(a)* Assumption I is implicit as if it had not been possible India would not have won after follow on. Further, the word 'surprising' tells that winning after follow on is very difficult and this is the reason it happens only 2nd time. But if it is possible, then we cannot say that India will not repeat such victory again. Hence, Assumption II is invalid.

Example 2. Statement There has been a remarkable increase in the air traffic in India during the past few years.

Assumptions

I. Travelling by air has become a status symbol now.
II. Large number of people are able to afford air travel now.

Solution *(b)* The given statement hints that in recent years, the number of people travelling by air has increased. This implies that large number of travellers can now afford air travel. Hence, only Assumption II is a valid.

Example 3. A statement is given followed by several assumptions. Read the statement carefully and decide which of the assumptions are implicit in the statement.

Statement

Prabodh wrote a second letter to his mother after a month as he did not receive any reply to the first letter.

Assumptions

I. Prabodh's mother did not receive the letter.
II. The letter generally reaches within a fortnight.
III. His mother promptly sends reply to his letters.

(a) II and III are implicit (b) I and II are implicit
(c) Only III is implicit (d) I and III are implicit

Solution *(c)* Prabodh wrote the second letter to his mother only when he did not receive the reply from his mother. This fact implies that his mother promptly sends reply to his letters. Hence, only Assumption III is implicit.

Practice Exercise

Directions (Q. Nos. 1-3) *In each question below is given a statement followed by two assumptions numbered I and II. An assumption is something supposed or taken for granted. You have to consider the statement and the following assumptions and decide which of the assumption(s) is/are implicit in the statement.*

Give Answer

(a) If only Assumption I is implicit
(b) If only Assumption II is implicit
(c) If neither Assumption I nor II is implicit
(d) If both Assumptions I and II are implicit

1. Statement "We must appoint more subordinate officers on our office staff", the manager said to the chairman.

Assumptions

I. Subordinate officers are available.
II. The present office staff is inefficient.

2. Statement The state administration banned gathering of more than fifty people at any place during the visit of foreign dignitaries to the city.

Assumptions

I. People may avoid gathering at any place in the city during the period of visit of foreign dignitaries.
II. Many people may ignore the prohibitory orders and gather to get a glimpse of the dignitaries.

3. Statement The school authority decided to rent out the school premises during weekends and holidays for organising various functions to augment its resources.

Assumptions

I. The parents of the school students may protest against decision of the school authority.
II. There may not be enough demand for hiring the school premises for organising functions.

Directions (Q. Nos. 4 and 5) *In each question below, is given a statement followed by three assumptions numbered I, II and III. An assumption is something supposed or taken for granted, you have to consider the statement and the assumptions and decide which of the assumption(s) is/are implicit in the statement.*

4. Statement The situation of this area still continues to be tense and out of control. People are requested to be in their homes only.

Assumptions

I. There had been some serious incidents.
II. People will not go to the office.
III. Normality will be restored shortly.

(a) All are implicit
(b) None is implicit
(c) Only I is implicit
(d) I and II are implicit

5. Statement "The employees' association has appealed to the manager of company 'S' to introduce written examination for clerical cadre recruitment to prevent selection of incompetent persons."

Assumptions

I. So, far the company 'S' used to select candidates without conducting a written examination.
II. A written examination can help to identify competent persons.
III. At higher level, written examination may not be of much use.

(a) I and II are implicit
(b) Only I is implicit
(c) Only II is implicit
(d) All are implicit

Previous Year's Questions

Directions (Q. Nos. 6-8) *The following questions comprise of one or more statements. Answer the questions on the basis of the given statement(s). Accept the factual assumptions required by the question, even if you believe that the statements is false.* **[CLAT 2012]**

6. Statements

I. Cheese is bad for people with high-cholesterol.

II. Sumeet does not eat cheese.

Assuming that I and II are true, which of the following statement follows?

(a) Sumeet has high-cholesterol
(b) Cheese is bad for Sumeet
(c) People with high-cholesterol do not eat cheese
(d) None of the above

7. Statement Democrats are secularists.

Which of the following statements, if true would show that the above statement is false?

(a) My father is a secularist but he is not a democrat
(b) My father is a democrat but he is not secularist
(c) My father is a democrat and he is secularist
(d) My father is neither a democrat nor a secularist

8. Statement "Where there is a cloud, there is a rain." Which of the following statements if true, would, show that the above statement is false?

(a) Sometimes there is cloud but there is no rain
(b) Sometimes there is rain but there is no cloud
(c) There is no rain where there is no cloud
(d) Both (a) and (b)

Directions (Q. Nos. 9-11) *Read the following information carefully and choose the most appropriate option*

In each question, there is a statement and two assumptions numbered as I and II. Read the statement and find which of the given assumptions is implicit. **[CLAT 2016]**

9. Statement To attend a convocation ceremony scheduled to be held on Thursday at GM University, Chennai, Mr. X left for Chennai on Tuesday by Train.

Assumptions

I. Mr. X may reach home on Saturday.

II. Mr. X may reach the University on Wednesday.

(a) Neither assumption I nor assumption II is implicit
(b) Assumption II is implicit
(c) Assumption I is implicit
(d) Both assumptions I and II are implicit

10. Statement The next meeting of the executive board of a company will be held after six months.

Assumptions

I. Existing executive board will be dissolved before six months.

II. The company will remain in function after six months.

(a) Assumption II is implicit
(b) Both assumptions I and II are implicit
(c) Neither assumption I nor assumption II is implicit
(d) Assumption I is implicit

11. Statement In the State of Zuminisia, people prefer to travel by X airline instead of Y airline, as X airline has advanced German security system and 99% on time operations.

Assumptions

I. Airline X with advanced German security system and record on time operation is perceived better than airline Y.

III. Had advanced German security system and on time performance record of Y airline been implemented, it would have been preferred over airline X.

(a) Both assumptions I and II are implicit
(b) Neither assumption I nor assumption II is implicit
(c) Assumption II is implicit
(d) Assumption I is implicit

Directions (Q. Nos. 12 and 13) *Which alternative applies to the following Statements or Assumptions?*

12. Only ignorant people believe in withc raft' is equivalent to

(a) Som ignorant person are not those who believe in witchracft.
(b) All person who belive in withcraft are ignorant
(c) There is no link between ignorance and witchcraft
(d) No ignornat persons are those who do not believe in witchcraft

13. There is no man that is not naturally good' is equivalent to the proposetion

(a) No men are good.
(b) All men are naturally good
(c) Some men are not naturally good
(d) Some men are naturally good

Answers

1	*a*	2	*a*	3	*c*	4	*d*	5	*a*	6	*a*	7	*b*	8	*d*	9	*b*	10	*a*
11	*c*	12	*b*	13	*b*														

SOLUTIONS

Privous Year's Solutions

6. It is clear from the statements that 'Sumeet has high-cholesterol' because in the statements it is said that cheese is bad for people with high-cholesterol and Sumeet does not eat cheese, it means 'Sumeet has high-cholesterol.'

7.

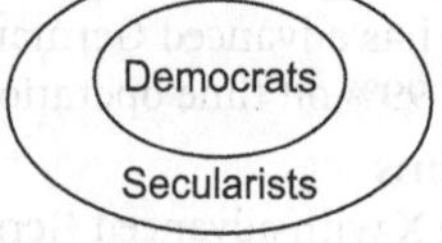

From the given above diagram we clearly say that all democrats are seaclarists means option (b) conclusion is definitely false because in this conclusion given that my father is a democrat but he is not secularist.

8. According to statement "where there is a cloud, there is a rain". It means that if there is cloud there must be rain and if there is rain, there must be cloud. So, both option (a) and (b) are false.

9. Assumption I does not follow because the given statement does not tell any thing about his returning to home. Assumption II is implicit for the same reason. He must planned to reach the convocation ceremony before Thursday, so he may reach on Wednesday.

10. Only assumption II is implicit.

If the next meeting of executive board of a company will be held after six months, then it clearly means that, the company will remain in function after six months.

11. Clearly, only assumption I is implicit.

12. The given statement is equivalent to -All persons who believe in withchcraft are ignornat

13. The given statement is equivalent to-All men are naturally goo.

STATEMENT AND CONCLUSIONS

A statement is a group of words arranged to form a meaningful sentence. A conclusion is an opinion or decision that is formed after a period of thought or research on some facts or sentence stated by someone. A consequent effect has always to be analysed before reaching to the final result or conclusion of a given statement. This requires a very systematic and logical approach.

> If definitive words like all, always, atleast, only, exactly and so on are used, then such words make the conclusion invalid or ambiguous.

Directions (Ex. Nos. 1 and 2) *Each of these questions has a statement followed by two Conclusions* I *and* II. *Consider the statement and the following conclusions. Decide which of the conclusion follows from the statement.*

Give Answer
(a) If Conclusion I follows
(b) If Conclusion II follows
(c) If either Conclusion I or II follows
(d) If neither Conclusion I nor II follows

Example 1. Statement Unemployment is one of the main reason for the poverty of the country.

Conclusions

I. To end poverty, it is required to create employment opportunities.

II. All the people in the country are unemployed.

Solution *(a)* Conclusion I is valid because if unemployment is the main reason behind poverty, then creating employment opportunities is the need of the hour. Conclusion II is invalid because of the presence of word 'all'.

Example 2. Statement Morning walks are good for health.

Conclusions

I. All healthy people go for morning walks.

II. Evening walks are harmful.

Solution *(d)* In the statement it is said that morning walks are good for health. But it does not mean that all the healthy persons go for morning walks. Hence, Conclusion I does not follow. Also, nothing is said about the evening walks in statement. Thus, Conclusion II also does not follow.

Example 3. Consider the following three statements.

I. Only students can participate in the race.

II. Some participants in the race are girls.

III. All girl participants in the race are invited for coaching.

Which one of the following conclusions can be drawn from the above statements?

(a) All participants in the race are invited for coaching
(b) All students are invited for coaching
(c) All participants in the race are students
(d) None of the above

Solution *(c)* From Statement I, it can be concluded that 'All participants in the race are students'. Since, it is given in Statement III that 'All girl participants in the race are invited for coaching'. So, options (a) and (b) cannot be concluded. Hence, answer is option (c).

Practice Exercise

Directions (Q. Nos. 1-3) *There are two or more statements along with four conclusions deduced from the statements. You are required to answer on the basis of the statements and the conclusions. Make the factual assumptions required by the question even, if you believe the statement is actually false.*

1. Statements Some aeroplanes are balloons.
Some balloons are rockets.

Conclusions
I. Some aeroplanes are rockets.
II. Some rockets are tables.
III. All the rockets are balloons.
IV. All the balloons are aeroplanes. Assuming that statements are true, which conclusions follow?

(a) II and IV (b) I and III
(c) Only IV (d) None of these

2. Statements All whales are fish.
Some fish are not amphibians.
All whales are amphibians.
Some amphibians are not fish.

Conclusions
I. Some fish are amphibians.
II. Some amphibians are fish.
II. Only whales are both fish and amphibians.
IV. All amphibians are fish.
Assuming only that statements are true, which of the above conclusions may be deduced?
(a) I and II (b) Only III
(c) Only IV (d) None of these

3. Statements All libraries are laboratories.
No laboratories are hostels.

Conclusions
I. All laboratories are libraries.
II. Some hostels are libraries.
III. Some libraries are hostels.
IV. No library is a hostel. Assuming that statements are true, which conclusions follow?

(a) I and II (b) II and III
(c) III and IV (d) Only IV

Directions (Q. Nos. 4-7) *Each question contains six statements followed by four sets of combination of three. Choose the set in which the statements are logically related.*

4. Statements
I. X and Y are siblings.
II. X and Y do not quarrel.
III. Siblings are known to quarrel often.
IV. X and Y quarrel often.
V. All those who quarrel are siblings.
VI. X and Y cannot be siblings.

(a) II, IV, V (b) I, IV, VI
(c) I, III, IV (d) I, II, V

5. Statements
I. All mangoes are fruits.
II. All mangoes are green.
III. All mangoes are oval shaped.
IV. All fruits are sweet.
V. All mangoes are sweet.
VI. AII fruits are expensive.

(a) I, II, III (b) I, IV, V
(c) II, III, IV (d) IV, V, VI

6. Statements
I. All frogs are amphibians.
II. All amphibians are not frogs.
III. All amphibians are cold blooded.
IV. All frogs lay eggs.
V. All amphibians lay eggs.
VI. Frogs are cold blooded.

(a) I, III, VI (b) I, IV, V
(c) I, II, V (d) II, V, IV

7. Statements
I. Some men are of short height.
II. Short heighted men are intelligent.
III. Sudhir is a man.
IV. Sudhir is of short height.
V. Sudhir is intelligent.
VI. AII men are intelligent.

(a) I, II, VI (b) II, III, IV
(c) II, IV, V (d) II, IV, VI

Directions (Q. Nos. 8-12) *In each question below are given two statements numbered I and II. You have to take the two given statements as true even, if they seem to be at variance with commonly known facts. Read all the conclusions and then decide which of the given conclusions logically follow from the given statements, disregarding commonly known facts.*

8. Statements I. All vegetables have gravy.
II. All lunch has vegetable.
(a) All lunch has gravy (b) All gravy has lunch
(c) Both (a) and (b) (d) None of these

9. Statements I. Karan Johar is a good director.
II. Directors are intelligent.
(a) All intelligent are directors
(b) Karan Johar is intelligent
(c) Both (a) and (b)
(d) None of the above

10. Statements I. Some blues are green.
II. Pink is green.
(a) Some blue is pink
(b) Some green is pink
(c) Either (a) or (b) follows
(d) Some pinks are blues

11. Statements I. All boys are tall.
II. All Punjabi are tall.
(a) All boys are Punjabi (b) Some boys are Punjabi
(c) Both of (a) and (b) (d) None of the above

12. Statements I. All girls go to the college.
II. Rina does not go to the college.
(a) Rina is not a girl
(b) Going to college is not essential to be a girl
(c) Rina is a girl
(d) None of the above

Privious Year's Questions

Directions (Q. Nos. 13-15) *Two statements are given below followed by two conclusions (I and II). You have to consider the two statements to be true even if they seem to be at variance with commonly known facts. You have to decide which of the conclusions, if any, follow from the given statements.* **[CLAT 2014]**

13. Statements
Some books are magazines.
Some magazines are novels.
Conclusions
I. Some books are novels.
II. Some novels are magazines.
(a) Only I follows
(b) Only II follows
(c) Both I and II follow
(d) Neither I nor II follows

14. Statements
All students like excursions.
Some students go for higher education.
Conclusions
I. Students who go for higher education also like excursions.
II. Some students do not go for higher education, but like excursions.
(a) Only I follows
(b) Only II follows
(c) Both I and II follow
(d) Neither I nor II follows

15. Statements
All good hockey players are in the Indian hockey team.
'X' is not a good hockey player.
Conclusions
I. 'X' is not in the Indian Hockey team.
II. 'X' wants to be in the Indian Hockey team.
(a) Only I follows
(b) Only II follows
(c) Both I and II follow
(d) Neither I nor II follows

Directions (Q. Nos. 16-17) *Each question comprises two statements (numbered as I and II). You have to take the statements as true even, if they seem to be at variance with commonly known facts. Read all the conclusions and then decide which of the given conclusions logically follow from the given statements, disregarding commonly known facts.* **[CLAT 2014]**

16. I. All contracts are agreements.
II. All agreements are accepted offers.
Which of the following derivations is correct?
(a) All accepted offers are contracts
(b) All agreements are contracts
(c) All contracts are accepted offers
(d) None of the above

17. I. Some beautiful women are actresses.
II. All actresses are good dancers.
Which of the following derivations is correct?
(a) Some beautiful women are good dancers.
(b) All good dancers are actresses.
(c) Both (a) and (b)
(d) None of the above

Direction (Q. Nos. 18 and 19) *Identify the answer which is the correct inference of the following questions. Assume the statement to be true.* **[CLAT 2015]**

18. If you are serious you must work.
You are not serious, you do not work.
(a) Inference is definitely true.
(b) Inference is definitely false.
(c) Inference is uncertain.
(d) Inference cannot be drawn.

19. All honest people are rogues. All rogues are politicians.
So, politicians are honest.
(a) Inference is definitely true.
(b) Inference is definitely false.
(c) Inference is uncertain.
(d) Inference cannot be drawn.

20. Statement Government has spoiled many top ranking financial institutions by appointing bureaucrats as directors of these institutions. **[CLAT 2015]**

Conclusions
I. Government should appoint directors of the financial institutes taking into consideration the expertise of the person in the area of finance.
II. The director of the financial institute should have expertise commensurate with the financial work carried out by the institute.
(a) Only I follows
(b) Only II follows
(c) Both I and II follow
(d) Neither I nor II follows

21. No porrots are black.
All cows are black.
From the above premises which one of the following conclusion is true? **[CLAT 2017]**
(a) Some cows are not parrots.
(b) No cows are parrots
(c) Some parrots are not cows.
(d) Now conclusion can be drawn.

Answers

1	*d*	2	*d*	3	*d*	4	*c*	5	*b*	6	*a*	7	*c*	8	*a*	9	*b*	10	*b*
11	*d*	12	*a*	13	*b*	14	*c*	15	*d*	16	*c*	17	*a*	18	*a*	19	*c*	20	*c*
21	*b*																		

SOLUTIONS

1. Same aeroplanes are balloons (I type)
Same balloons are rockets (I type)
Since,both statements are I type, therefore no mediate conclusion follows.

2. All whales are fish (A type)
Some fish are not amphibians (O type)
All whales are ammphibians (A type)
Some amphibians are not fish (O type)

Here, two A type prepositions have no common term, then no conclusion could be drawn.

3. All libraries are laboratories. (A type)
No laboratories are hostels. (E type)
A + E type →
No library is a hostel (this is conclusion D).

4. Statements (I), (III) and (IV) are true because they are logically related to each other.

5. Statements (I), (IV) and (V) are true because they are logically related to each other.

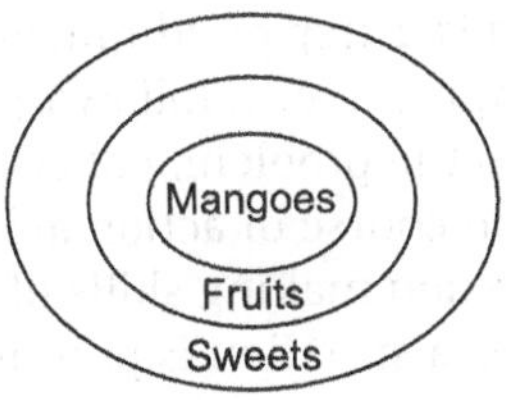

6. Statements (I), (III) and (VI) are true because they are logically related to each other.

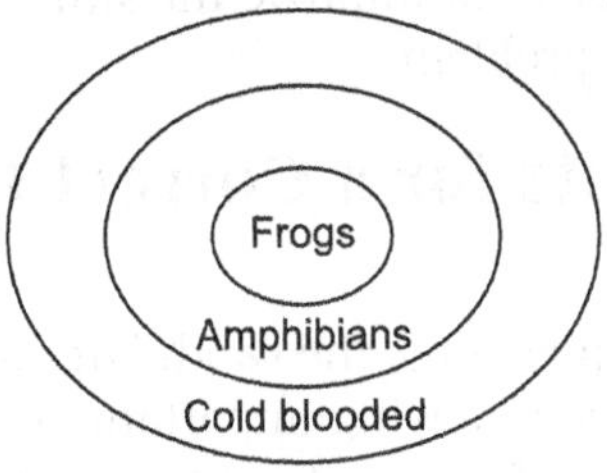

7. Statements (II), (IV) and (V) are true because they are logically related to each other.

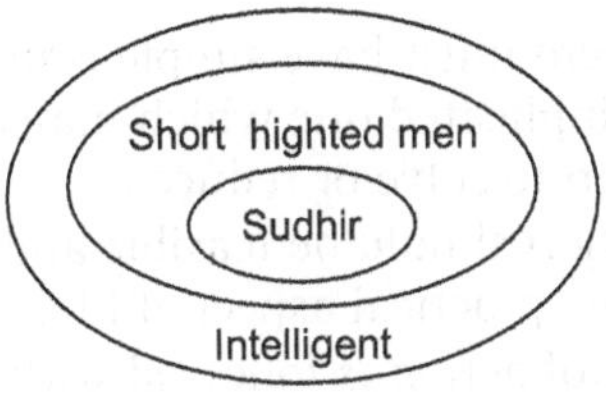

8.

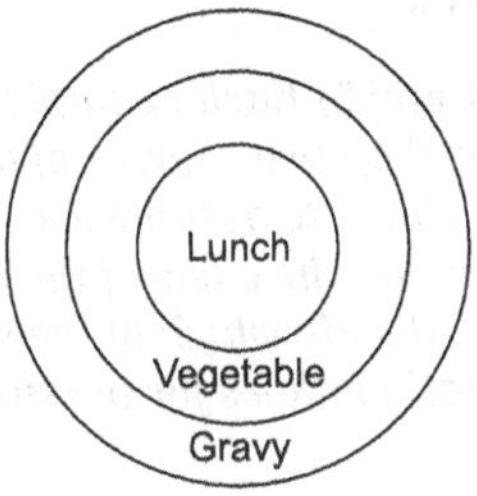

Only option (a), i.e. all lunch are gravy.

9. As directors are intelligent and Karan Johar is good director, so Karan Johar is intelligent.

10.

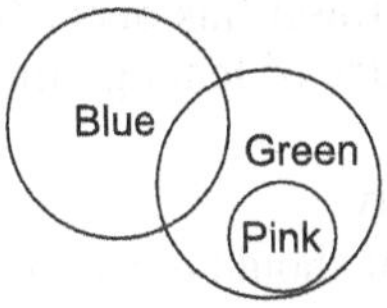

From above figure some green are definately pink.

11.

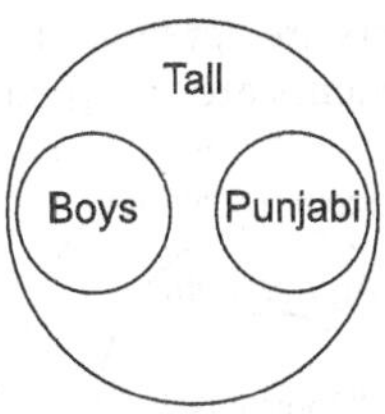

From above we cannot conclude the relation of boys and punjabi.

12.

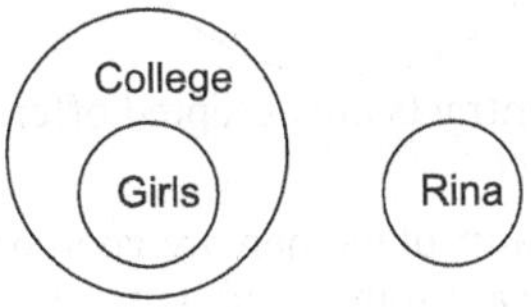

As all girls go to college and Rina does not go to college, so Rina is not a girl.

Previous Year's Solution

13.

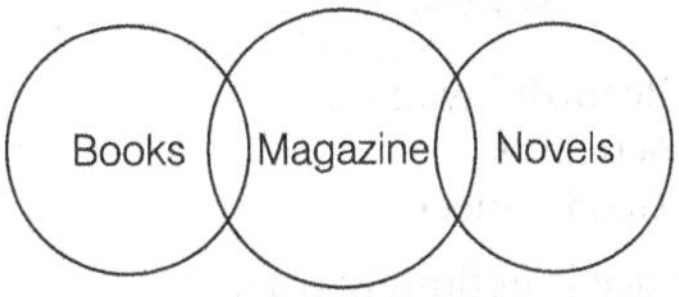

It is clear from the figure, only (II) follows from the given statements

14. Both I and II follow as is clear from the figure below

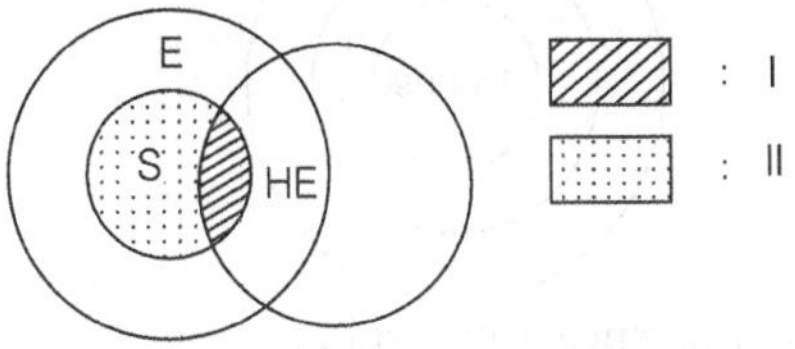

S : Students
E : People who like excursions
HE : People who go for higher education.

15. Neither of the two conclusions follows 'X' may or may not be inside the outer circle (representing people in the Indian Hockey team)

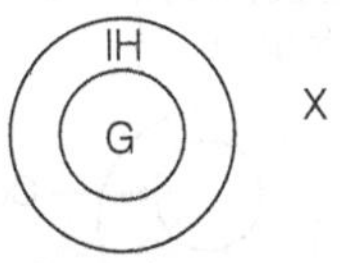

G : Good Hockey Players
IH : People in Indian Hockey Team

16. I. All contracts are agreements
II. All agreements are accepted offers.

So, all contracts are accepted offers, is the correct.

17. Some beautiful women are good dancers but there are some good dancers who are not actresses.

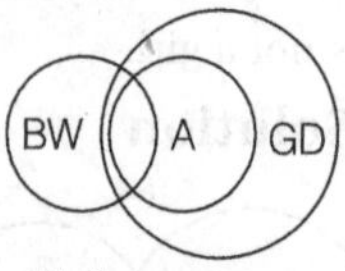

BW : Beautiful women
A : Actresses
GD : Good dancers

18. Inference is definitely true.

19. From the statements,

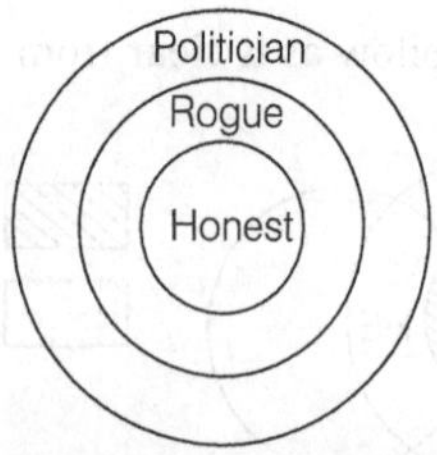

So, inference is uncertain.

20. According to the statement, government has spoiled financial institutions by appointing bureaucrats as directors. This means that only those persons should be appointed as directors who are experts in finance and are acquainted with the financial work of institute. So, both I and II follow.

21.

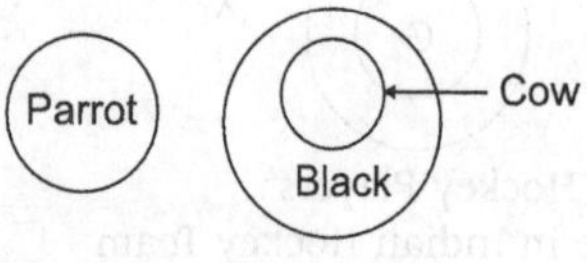

∴No cows are porrots.

COURSE OF ACTION

A course of action is a step or administrative decision to be taken for improvement, follow up or further action in regard to the problem, policy etc. The questions based on course of action are asked to test the analytical decision making skills of the candidate. In these questions, a situation is presented and some courses of action are suggested in the context of that situation. Correct course of action should either reduce the problem or improve the situation which is created by that problem.

Basic Points for a Correct Course of Action

To solve these questions, the candidates are advised to keep in mind the following important points

- Correct course of action should either lessen the problem or improve the situation created by the problem.
- Simple problem must have simple course of action and not a complicated one which may create more problems than to solve or reduce it.
- Course of action should be feasible and should relate with the practical aspect of life.
- If any course of action is followed with word 'only' it makes action weak.

Directions (Ex. Nos. 1 and 2) *Each example given below has a statement followed by two courses of action numbered* I *and* II. *You have to assume everything in the statement to be true and on the basis of the information given in the statement, decide which of the suggested courses of action logically follows for pursuing.*

Give Answer
(a) If only I follows (b) If only II follows
(c) If neither I nor II follow (d) If both I and II follow

Example 1. Statement Drinking water supply to many parts of the town has been disrupted due to loss of water because of leakage in pipes supplying water.

Courses of Action

I. The Government should order an enquiry into the matter.
II. The civic body should set up a fact finding team to assess the damage and take effective steps.

Solution *(b)* The first course of action does not match the scale of the problem. The problem is not so big as to merit a Government enquiry. It is enough that the civic body takes action and hence, II follows.

Example 2. Statement Heavy rains hit the state during October, just before the State Assembly elections and caused heavy damage to standing crops in most parts of the state.

Courses of Action

I. Elections should be postponed to give candidates the opportunity to campaign.

II. The Government should announce a relief package for those who are affected.

Solution *(d)* I follows because holding the elections at this juncture would render the exercise meaningless. II follows for 'heavy damage'.

Practice Exercise

Directions (Q. Nos. 1-5) *In each of the questions below is given a statement followed by two courses of action. Course of action is a step for administrative decision to be taken for improvement, follow-up or further action in regard to the problem, policy etc. On the basis of the information given in the statement, you have to assume everything in the statement to be true, then decide which of the given suggested courses of action is/are logically worth pursuing.*

Give Answer

(a) If only I follows

(b) If only II follows

(c) If neither I nor II follows

(d) If both I and II follow

1. Statement The number of people who die on the roads every year is so alarming that the numbers every year are close to the numbers which can be attributed to the major diseases of the world.

Course of Action

I. There should be an active campaign for sensitising people towards road safety norms.

II. There should be an increased emphasis on enforcing speed limits, road safety rules and traffic management on roads across the world.

2. Statement An unacceptable number of children die during the first year of their lives. The high incidence of infant death is a major cause for concern for the health ministry.

Course of Action

I. All government hospitals should be privatised to improve health care facilities.

II. Government should commit higher levels of their budget to health services.

3. Statement The cream of India's Cricket team is likely to retire in the next three years leaving a vacuum which the Indian Cricket team is going to struggle to overcome.

Course of Action

I. The BCCI should start to induct youngsters into the team and start to give them exposure to pressure situations.

II. There should be a rotation policy adopted for senior players in order to prolong their careers and keep them injury free.

4. Statement The lack of employment and income during economic depression leads to an increase in the crime rates.

Course of Action

I. The government should provide an unemployment compensation as done in advanced countries.

II. The government should encourage greater economic activity and increase the number of industries in order to reduce crime rates.

5. Statement The experts group on technical education has stressed that computer education should be provided to children from primary school itself. It should be implemented in urban and rural schools, simultaneously.

Courses of Action

I. Government should issue instructions to all schools for computer education.

II. Atleast one teacher of each school should be trained in computer operations for teaching children.

Directions (Q. Nos. 6-8) *Read the following case and answer the question.*

Sakshi is the Vice-President in an electrical equipment company in Delhi. One day, her subordinate Bhasker requested that Kishen, a project manager, be transferred to the Mumbai office from the Delhi office. In Mumbai, Kishen would work alone as a researcher. Bhaskar gave the following reasons for his request "Kishen is known for fighting frequently with colleagues of his team. He cannot accept criticism and feels rejected and get hostile. He is overbearing and is generally a bad influence on the team."

Sakshi called upon Samir, another project manager and sought further information on Kishen. Samir recalled that a former colleague Lalit (who was also Kishen's former boss) has made few remarks on Kishen in his appraisal report. In his opinion, Kishen was not fit for further promotion as he was emotionally unstable to work in groups in spite of the fact that he had seven years of work experience. Lalit has described Kishen as too authoritative to work under anyone. Lalit has further told Samir that Kishen had an ailing wife and an old mother, who does not want to stay with this wife.

Consider the following solutions to the problem mentioned above

I. Sakshi should transfer Kishen to Mumbai office.

II. Sakshi should try and verify the facts from other sources as well.

III. Kishen should be sacked.

IV. Kishen should be demoted.

V. Sakshi should suggest Kishen to visit a family counsellor.

6. Which of the following would be the most appropriate sequence of decisions in terms of immediacy starting from immediate to a long term solution?

(a) II, V, I (b) II, III, IV
(c) II, V, IV (d) II, I, V

7. Sakshi sought an appointment with Lalit to find out way to help Kishen. Lalit is of the view that the company's responsibility is restricted to the workplace and it should not try to address the personal problems of employees. If Sakshi has to agree to Lalit's view, then which of the solutions presented in the previous question would be weakened?

(a) Only III (b) Only IV
(c) Only V (d) Only II

8. Which of the following statements, if true would weaken the decision to sack Kishen the most?

(a) Another article published in the magazine, Caventers Quaterly, highlighted that employee's problem at home affect their performance at work.
(b) In the latest issue of a reputed Journal, Xanders Business Review, it was published that most top managers, find it difficult to work in a group.
(c) It was published is Santers Management Review, another reputed Journal that individuals who cannot work in teams find it difficult to adjust to a new location.
(d) Bhaskar was of the opinion that emotionally unstable persons, find it difficult to get back to normal working life.

Previous Year's Questions

Directions (Q. Nos. 9-13) *Each question contains one statement and two courses of action I and II. Assuming the statements to be true, decide which of the two courses of action most logically follows.* **[CLAT 2013]**

Give answer

(a) if only I follows
(b) if only II follows
(c) if either I or II follows
(d) if neither I nor II follows

9. Statement Indian children are very talented but are instead weak in Science and Mathematics.

Courses of Action

I. Teaching and textbooks are not available in mother language.

II. Education based on experiments in both the subjects is lacking.

10. Statement Despite of child labour laws, children can be seen working in hotels, shops, houses very frequently.

Courses of Action

I. The government should not make such laws which cannot be enforced.

II. A proper education system for the primary level particularly for lower caste community may eradicate this problem.

11. Statement Kyoto protocol on environment is signed by almost every country of the world.

Courses of Action

I. As a result air, water and soil pollution have come down.

II. Increasing production of automobiles, refrigerators and fertilisers do not affect our environment.

12. Statement School dropout rate is very high in the rural areas as children support their parents in income earning activities.

Courses of Action

I. Public awareness programme on primary education should be expanded immediately to educate parents.

II. Compensation is not a remedy.

13. Statement Smoking is one of those human weaknesses which tend to test the will power of the smoker of the edge.

Courses of Action

I. It is very difficult for the smoker to give up smoking even if they want to do so.

II. Human beings have other weaknesses as well.

Answers

1	*d*	2	*b*	3	*d*	4	*b*	5	*d*	6	*a*	7	*c*	8	*d*	9	*b*	10	*b*
11	*a*	12	*b*	13	*c*														

SOLUTIONS

1. Clearly, both the actions are strong.

2. The privatisation of all government hospitals is not the way to improve health care facilities. Government should invest higher levels of their budget to improve health services. They should place latest equipments and facility in hospital in order to give better treatment.

3. According to the given statement, both the actions are strong.

4. Clearly, the Statement II is the correct course of action. The unemployment compensation is not the permanent solution to the problem. It will only give temporary relief. The permanent solution will be the greater employment opportunities for the unemployed people.

5. Both are the right courses of action for effective implementation of computer education at primary level in urban and rural schools.

6. First of all, Sakshi should try to verify the facts from other sources as well. If Kishen has a family problem which is mentioned in the given passage, then Sakshi should suggest him to visit a family counsellor. Finally, if the positive results will not come from above step, then Sakshi should transfer Kishen to Mumbai office.

7. If Sakshi has to agree to Lalit's view that the company's resposibility is restricted to the workplace and it should not try to address the personal problem of employees, then the suggestion from Sakshi to Kishen to visit a family counsellor would be weakened.

8. Statement (d) if true should weaken the decision to sack Kishen the most.

Previous Year's Solution

9. Only Conclusion II can follow as text book must be available but lack of experiment may be the reason.

10. Only Conclusion II follow as primary education may eradicate the problem

11. Only Conclusion I can follow.

12. Only Conclusion I can follow.

13. None of the conclusion follows.

CAUSE AND EFFECT

An event does not occur automatically but there is a definite cause behind it. Causes are the conditions under which an event occurs and effects to these causes are the consequences of that event.

Usually, in such questions, the candidates are asked to determine whether a given event is the cause or the effect of some other event. Clearly, the cause must occur before the effect and the effect happens at some point of time, after the cause. This test is a step to test candidates ability to analyse a pair of given statements and to correlate them for cause and effect. There may be several necessary conditions for the occurrence of an event and that they all must be included in sufficient condition. Further going on practise first we should learn some rules. These are

- The cause will always occur before the effect. Hence, if two events are given then the effect that is chronologically antecedent to the other can only be regarded as a possible cause.
- A necessary condition for the occurrence of a specified event is a circumstance in whose absence the event cannot occur.
- A sufficient condition for the occurrence of an event is a circumstance in whose presence the event must occur.

Directions (Ex. 1-2) *In each of these questions, two statements I and I are given. These may have a cause and effect relationship or may have independent causes or be the effects of independent cause.*

Give answer

(a) Statement I is the cause and Statement II is its effect

(b) Statement II is the cause and Statement I is its effect

(c) Both the Statements are independent causes

(d) Both the Statements are independent effects

Example 1 Statement I Many vegetarians are suffering stomach ailments.

Statement II Many dead fish were found near the lake shor.

Solution *(d)* Statement I and Statement II are not related to each other and seem to be effects of different causes.

Example 2 Statement I School education has been made free for children of poor families.

Statement II Literacy rate among poor is steadily growing.

Solution *(a)* Clearly, Statement II is the effect of Statement I.

Practice Exercise

Directions (Q. Nos. 1-3) *Below in each question are given two Statements A and B. These statements may be effects of independent causes or may be effects of a common cause. One of these statements may be the effect of the other statement. Read both the statements and decide which of the following answer choices correctly depicts the relationship between these two statements.*

Give answer

(a) Statement A is the cause and Statement B is its effect
(b) Statement B is the cause and Statement A is its effect
(c) Both statements are independent causes
(d) Both statements are effects of independent causes

1. A.There has been mass recruitment of IT professionals by Indian IT companies.

B. Many developed countries are increasingly outsourcing IT related functions to India and China.

2. A.The Reserve Bank of India has recently put restrictions on few small banks in the country.

B. The small banks in the private and cooperative sector in India are not in a position to withstand the competitions of the bigger in the public sector.

3. A. The Government is considering changes in the Land Acquisition Act.

B. Several large infrastructure development projects have been stalled due to unavailability of land.

Directions (Q. Nos. 4-6) *Below in each questions are given two Statements A and B. These statements may be either independent causes or may be effects of independent causes or of a common cause. One of these statements may be the effect of the other statement. Read both the statements and decide which of the following answer choices correctly depicts the relationship between these two statements.*

Give answer

(a) Statement A is the cause and Statement B is its effect
(b) Statement B is the cause and Statement A is its effect
(c) Both statements are effects of independent causes
(d) Both statements are effects of some common cause

4. A. Most of the shopkeepers in the locality closed their shops for the second continuous day.

B. Two groups of people living in the locality have been fighting with each other with brick and stones, forcing people to stay indoors.

5. A. The Government has decided to increase the prices of LPG cylinders with immediate effect.

B. The Government has decided to increase the prices of Kerosine with immediate effect.

6. A. The prices of vegetables have been increased considerably during the summer.

B. There is tremendous increase in the temperature during this summer there by damaging crops greatly.

7. **Cause** Two wings of a building complex in a residential area collapsed.

Which of the following is the possible effect of the cause mentioned above?

I. Most of the flats of such residential wings were vacant from long time.
II. A flat owner got done some major repairing works and in this process a main part got collapsed.
III. Residents of the other wings in the complex were said to vacate their flats immediately.

(a) Only I (b) Only II
(c) Only III (d) Both II and III

8. **Effect** Cost of Petroleum products has been increased almost 20% in last two months.

Which of the following may be the possible cause of the effect mentioned above?

(a) The cost of vegetables and other food items has been increased by more than 30%.
(b) Union of truck owners has decided to increase carriage about 20% with immediate effect

(c) In last couple of weeks, the cost of crude oil in the international market has been increased immensely
(d) People have decided to protest against the inertia of government towards essential commodities

Previous Year's Questions

Directions (Q. Nos. 9-12) *Read the following information carefully and choose the most appropriate option.*

In each of the questions, two statements are numbered I and II. There may be a cause and effect relationship between the two statements. The statements may be the effect of the same cause or an independent cause. The statements may be independent causes without having any relationship. Read both the statements and mark your answer as. **[CLAT 2016]**

(a) If Statement I is the cause and Statement II is its effect
(b) If Statement II is the cause and Statement I is its effect
(c) If both Statements I and II are independent causes
(d) If both Statements I and II are effects of independent causes

9. Statement I In last two years, there is a considerable reduction in cancellation of flights due to fog in North India.

Statement II In last two years, there is a considerable improvement in passenger amenities on all airports of North India.

10. Statement I The Government, by legislation has decided to make all public information available to general public.

Statement II Before passing of legislation, general public did not have access to public information.

11. If it is false that 'Men always pray to God', then which one of the following statements is true? **[CLAT 2016]**

(a) Men seldom pray to God
(b) All men pray to God
(c) Men always pray to God
(d) Some men pray to God

12. Identify the statement which cannot be true. **[CLAT 2016]**

(a) Every natural number has a successor
(b) All bachelors are faithful to their wives
(c) Black body radiation is a physical phenomenon
(d) Snow is white

Answers

1	b	2	b	3	b	4	b	5	d	6	b	7	c	8	c	9	d	10	b
11	a	12	b																

SOLUTIONS

1. The outsourcing has led to creation of jobs in IT in India.

2. The inability of the small banks to complete with the bigger ones shall not ensure security and good service to the customers, which is an essential concomitant that has to be looked into by the RBI. It seems to be a remedial step for the same.

3. Since, the projects have been stalled, the Government is considering an amendment.

4. The fighting has led to the closure of the shops.

5. It seems the price of Petroleum has increased in general. Alternatively, subsidies may have been reduced, again a cause common to both the statements.

6. Clearly, damage to crops due to high temperature may have resulted in a short supply of vegetables and an increase in their prices.

7. Because of the collapse of certain wings, the residents of other wings may be said to vacate their flats, so that the residents of other wings could be safe from possible danger. Hence, option (c) is correct.

8. It is the obvious reason for the given effect.

Previous Year's Solution

9. Both the Statements I and II are effects of independent causes.

10. Clearly, Statement II is the cause and Statement I is its effect. The general public did not have access to public information that's why the government has decided to make all public information available to general public.

11. If it is false that 'Men always pray to God', then the true statement will be 'Men seldom pray to God'.

12. Bachelors are unmarried, so the statement 'all bechelors are faithful to their wives' cannot be ture.

ASSERTION AND REASON

Assertion is the statement which is made to state or claim something strongly and forcefully. Reason means a fact, event or statement that provides an explanation to the assertion.

This chapter is basically designed to judge the candidate's ability to reason out correctly. In these questions, two statements marked as Assertion (A) and Reason (R) are given. The candidates are required to analyse whether the reason is an optimum and correct explanation of the assertion. Sometimes both assertion and reason are correctly stated facts but the reason does not correctly explain the assertion. So, different possibilities can exist between given two statements.

Directions (Ex. Nos. 1-4) *Choose the correct alternative from the following options for the Assertion* (A) *and Reason* (R) *given below.*

Give Answer

(a) If both 'A' and 'R' are true and 'R' is the correct explanation of 'A'
(b) If both 'A' and 'R' are true but 'R' is not the correct explanation of 'A'
(c) If 'A' is true but 'R' is false
(d) If 'A' is false but 'R' is true

Example 1. Assertion (A) Pressure cookers are fitted with ebonite handles.

Reason (R) Ebonite is a strong conductor of heat.

Solution *(c)* Ebonite is a bad conductor of heat. It does not heat up. This is the reason why handles of pressure cookers are made of ebonite.

Example 2. Assertion (A) Earth is the only planet known to have life.

Reason (R) Earth has an atmosphere which is a mixture of oxygen, nitrogen and carbon dioxide.

Solution *(b)* Earth has presence of water which is the sustainer of life on it.

Practice Exercise

Directions (Q. Nos. 1-9) *In each of the following questions, there are two statements labelled as Assertion (A) and Reason (R).*

Give Answer

(a) If both 'A' and 'R' are true and 'R' is the correct explanation of 'A'
(b) If both 'A' and 'R' are true but 'R' is not the correct explanation of 'A'
(c) If 'A' is true but 'R' is false
(d) If 'A' is false but 'R' is true

1. Assertion (A) Leakages in household gas cylinders can be detected.
Reason (R) LPG has a strong smell.

2. Assertion (A) Mohammad-bin-Tughlaq is called the 'wisest fool'.
Reason (R) He had wise plans but implemented them foolishly.

3. Assertion (A) Too much work causes stress.
Reason (R) It disturbs the body balance between its capacity and the demand.

Directions (Q. Nos. 4-9) *Each of the next three questions consists two statements, one labeled as 'Assertion' (A) and other as 'Reason' (R). You are to examine these two statements carefully and select the correct answer.*

(a) Both A and R are individually true and R is the correct explanation of A
(b) Both A and R are individually true but R is not the correct explanation of A
(c) A is true but R is false
(d) A is false but R is true

4. Assertion (A) A void contract is not necessarily illegal.
Reason (R) Every illegal contract is void.

5. Assertion (A) Austin's concept of law is known as imperative theory.
Reason (R) Austin's emphasised on the commanding character of law.

6. Assertion (A) The essence of joint liability under section 149 of the IPC is that the criminal act must have been done with a view to fulfil the common object of an unlawful assembly.
Reason (R) Any sudden and provocative act done by an unlawful assembly would render the other members of that assembly liable.

7. Assertion (A) The constitution of India provides for the appointment of a Governor for a period of five years.
Reason (R) The Governor holds office during the pleasure of the president.

8. Assertion (A) X, because of unsound state of mind and not knowing the nature of the act, attack Y, who in self-defense and in order to ward off the attack hits him thereby injuring him. Y has not committed an offence.
Reason (R) Y had a right of private defense against X under the Indian Penal Code.

9. Assertion (A) In the event of violation of any legal right (tort) the aggrieved party is entitled to recover damages as determined by the court.
Reason (R) The object of awarding damages to the aggrieved party is to put him in the same position in which he would have been if the wrong would not have been committed. Damages are therefore, assessed on that basis.

Previous Year's Questions

Direction (Q. Nos. 10-12) *In the following three question assume that a 'fact' expresses something that can be proved by clear and objective data. An opinion expressses a judgement, view, attitude, or conclusion that is not backed by data* **[CLAT 2017]**

10. Which one of the following statements is best described as an assertion of opinion rather than an assertion of fact?
(a) Brazil, China and India are now among the largest emitters of greenhouse gases
(b) Scientists agree that human activity is an important cause of climate change
(c) The Indian government's policy on climate change is misguided
(d) The Indian governement's policy on climate change has changed significantly in the last five years

11. The Number of people migrating into Benguluru has increased significantly in recent years

I. This is beacuse Bengaluru provides more economics opportunities than the towns and villages from which these migrants come.

II. This sudden influx of migrants has made the city lessw pleasant to live in.

III. The success of the government's rural employment guarantee act might have the effect of stemming some rural-urban migration.

which one of the above statements is best described as an assertion of opinion rather than an assertion of fact?

(a) A (b) B

(c)C (d) D

12. Which one of the following statements, if true is best described as an assertion of opinion rather than an assertion of fact?

(a) Mumbai is larger than Pune

(b) Mumbai is smaller than Pune

(c) Mumbai is more cultured than Pune

(d) Mumbai is moree crowded than Pune.

Answers

1	*a*	2	*a*	3	*a*	4	*b*	5	*a*	6	*a*	7	*a*	8	*a*	9	*a*	10	*b*
11	*d*	12	*c*																

SOLUTIONS

1. (*a*) LPG contains ethyl merceptan which has strong smell. Because of this, smell leakages in household gas cylinders can be detected.

2. (*a*) R correctly explains A.

3. (*a*) Too much work causes stress because it disturbs the body balance between its capacity and the demand. Hence, both A and R are true and R is the correct explanation of A.

4. (*b*) Both A and R are individually true but R is not the correct explanation of A.

5. (*a*) Both A and R are individually true and R is the correct explanation of A.

6. (*a*) Both A and R are individually true and R is the correct explanation of A.

7. (*a*) Both A and R are true.

8. (*a*) Both A and R are individually true and R is the correct explanation of A.

9. (*a*) Both A and R are individually true and R is the correct explanation of A.

GENERAL KNOWLEDGE

CHAPTER 01

HISTORY

India is a land of ancient civilisation. Indian history begins with the birth of the Indus Valley Civilisation and the coming of the Aryans. These two phases are usually described as the pre-Vedic and Vedic age. Based on archeological findings, Indian history can be broadly divided into four phases i.e. Ancient History, Medieval History, Modern History and Indian National Movement.

ANCIENT INDIA

In Ancient India, before reading about Indus Valley civilisation, we need to study four ancient ages. These ancient ages are Paleolithic, Mesolithic, Neolithic and Chalcolithic Age.

Paleolithic Age

- People in Paleolithic age were hunters and gatherers. They were dependent on hunting for their livelihood and used to travel from one place to another depending on the availability of natural resources for survival.
- They developed sharp weapons of stone for hunting purpose. They survived on hunting wild animals and birds, fishing and collecting fruits and nuts.

Mesolithic Age

- It was the age between Paleolithic and Neolithic period. The main tools of this age i.e microliths were made of stone.
- During this period, people were still hunter-gatherers, but were possibly starting to stay in one place. Domestication of animals can be seen in this age.

Neolithic Age

- The Neolithic age contributed in the social and technological development. Stone tools and weapons were also further modified and were sharpened by fine shedding of the stones.

- Neolithic age also contributed greatly in the field of transportation by an important invention of the wheel.

Chalcolithic Age

- The people of Chalcolithic age practiced agriculture. They used tools made up of copper and stone.
- The people of this age worshiped mother goddess and the bull. Painted pottery was the most distinguishing feature of all Chalcolithic cultures.

The later Chalcolithic period saw an emergence of an ancient civilisation, which came to be known as the Indus Valley civilisation.

INDUS VALLEY CIVILISATION

It is one of the oldest civilisations of the world. It flourished along the banks of Indus river. Indus people produced wheat, barley, peas, seasum, rice and mustard and they were the first to produce cotton. The important sites of Indus Valley Civilisation are **Mohenjodaro** and **Harappa**.

Mohenjodaro

- The town planning was in a systematic manner based on grid system. Houses were made of burnt bricks. The towns were divided into two parts: Upper part or Citadel and Lower part.
- The most important feature at Mohenjodaro was the Great Bath which was used for religious bathing.
- Numerous objects were founded in excavation which include seated and standing figures, copper and stone tools, carved seals, balance-scales and weights, and children's toys.

Harappa

- Harappans were familiar with bronze age people and they were fond of ornaments and dressing up.
- Goddess of Earth and Pashupati Mahadeva were their main deity.
- Barter system was prevalent in the Harappan Civilisation.
- Animals known to Harappans were oxen, sheep, buffaloes, goats, pigs, elephants, dogs, cats, asses and camels.
- The Harappan culture flourished till about 1800 BC. There are many reasons for its decline like external aggression, epidemic, climate change, flood etc.

VEDIC PERIOD

- Vedic period came after the destruction of Indus Valley Civilisation. This period is called vedic because the four Vedas were composed during this time.
- In this period, it is believed that the Aryans came to India. There are many conflicts about the origin of Aryans.
- During this time, there were no big kingdoms. People lived in the tribal groups or small kingdoms.
- Four vedas are Rigveda, Samaveda, Yajurveda and Atharaveda
  - Rigveda is the oldest religious text. It contains the prayers of God and Gayatri mantra.
  - Samaveda deals with the music.
  - Yajurveda has the procedures for the performance of sacrifices.
  - Atharvaveda deals with medicines.
- Agriculture and cattle rearing were the main occupation of this period.
- Women had a respectable place in the society. They had the right to education and to participate in religious ceremonies.

Later Vedic Period

- In this period, Aryans expanded from Punjab over the whole of Western Uttar Pradesh covered by the Ganga-Yamuna Doab.
- Society was clearly divided into four varnas i.e Brahmana, Kshatriya, Vaishya and Shudra.

- The institution of Gotra appeared for the first time and Prajapati became the supreme God of this period. Sacrifices, rather than prayers, became more important in this period.

JAINISM AND BUDDHISM

Jainism and Buddhism came into existence around 600 BC. The main causes being the reaction against domination of Brahmanas and spread of agricultural economy.

Jainism

- There were 24 Tirthankaras in Jainism. Rishabhadeva was the first Tirthankara and Mahavira being the 24th.
- Mahavira was born in 540 BC in Kundagram near Vaishali. Mahavira rejected the authority of the vedas and did not believe in existence of God.
- He believed in the attainment of salvation by extreme penance and dying of starvation. He believed in universal brotherhood (equality) and non-belief in caste system.

Jain Councils

Council	Chairman	Development(s)
First (300 BC)	Sthulabhadra	Compilation of 12 angas to replace 14 purvas
Second (512 AD)	Devridhigani Kshmasramana	Final compilation of 12 angas and 12 upangas.

Buddhism

- Buddhism was founded by Gautam Buddha who was born in 563 BC at Lumbini (Sakya tribe of Kapilvastu).
- His father Suddhodana was a Saka ruler and his mother Mahamaya of Kosalan dynasty died early. Gautam Buddha brought up by stepmother Gautami.
- Gautam Buddha married to Yashodhara and had a son Rahul.
- He followed middle path for attainment of salvation and believed in the concept of non-violence.
- Kapilvastu relief (fragment of Lord Buddha's bone), for the second time in 114 years, recently travelled from India to Sri Lanka.
- Lord Buddha's image sometimes shown with the hard gesture is called 'Bhumisparsha Madra'. It signifies Buddha's calling of the Earth to watch over marr and to prevent mare from disturbing his meditation and Buddha calling of the Earth to witness his purity and chastity despite the temptations of marr.

Buddhist Councils

Council	Chairman	Royal Patron	Development (s)
First (483 BC)	Mahakassappa	Ajatashatru	Compilation of Sutta Pitaka by Ananda and Vinaya Pitaka by Upali
Second (383 BC)	Sabakami	Kalasoka	Monks split into Sthaviravada and Mahasanghika
Third (250 BC)	Mogaliputta Tissa	Ashoka	Compilation of Abhidhamma Pitaka
Fourth (AD 72)	Vasumitra (Chairman) and Ashwaghosha (Vice-Chairman)	Kanishka	Division of Buddhists into Hinayana and Mahayana

Phases of Buddha's Life

Phases of Buddha's Life	Known as
Left home at the age of 29	Mahabhinishkramana
Under Peepal tree at Bodh Gaya at the age of 35	Attained knowledge
First sermon	Dharmachakra-parivartana
Death	Mahaparinivana

Similarities between Buddhism and Jainism

- The source of both religions is vedic religion.
- Both Gautam Buddha and Mahavir belonged to princely families and not to priestly families.
- Both deny the existence of God.
- Both have accepted the theories of *karma*, *rebirth* and *moksha*.
- Later on both the religions were divided into two sects. Buddhism was divided into Mahayana and Hinayana. Jainism was divided into Svetambara and Digambara.

Dissimilarities between Jainism and Buddhism

- According to Buddhism, a man attains *moksha* when he ends all the desires and can attain it while living in the world. But according to Jainism, *moksha* is freedom from miseries and can be attained only after death.
- Buddhists do not believe in the existence of soul whereas Jainism believes the existence of soul in every living being.
- Buddhism emphasises the eight noble paths whereas Jainism emphasises Tri Ratna.
- Most of the Jain texts are in Sanskrit and Prakrit, whereas Buddhist texts are in Pali.
- Buddhism spread to foreign countries, whereas Jainism did not travel outside the boundaries of India.

DYNASTIES OF ANCIENT ERA

There were many important dynasties who ruled over India during the Ancient age.

Some important dynasties of ancient era are given below

Haryanka Dynasty

- Bimbisara was the founder of this dynasty. He expanded the Magdha kingdom by annexing Anga. The earliest capital of Magadha was Rajgir, which was called Girivraja at that time.
- Bimbisara was succeeded by his son Ajatasatru between 492-460 BC. Ajatasatru killed his father and seized the throne for himself.
- Ajatasatru was succeeded by Udayin (460-444 BC). Udayin temporarily shifted the capital to Vaishali.

Shishunaga Dynasty

- Shishunaga was the founder of this dynasty. He was succeeded by Kalashoka (Kakavarna), who transferred the capital from Vaishali to Pataliputra.
- The Shishunagas were succeeded by the Nandas.

Nanda Dynasty

- Nanda dynasty was founded by Mahapadma Nanda. The Nandas were the first Non-Kshatriya rulers in the history of India.
- Nanda's were also the first empire builders in the recorded history of India.
- The last ruler of this dynasty was Dhana Nanda. Alexander attacked during Dhana Nanda reign.
- Dhana Nanda was overthrown by Chandragupta Maurya, thus founding Mauryan Empire in 321 BC.

Mauryan Dynasty

Important rulers of Mauryan dynasty were

Chandragupta Maurya

- Chandragupta Maurya was the founder of the Mauryan empire and ascended the throne at the age of twenty-five.

- Chandragupta with the help of Chanakya, started building the famous Mauryan Empire.
- Chandragupta defeated Seleucus Nikator, the general of Alexander (304 BC). Later Seleucus sent his ambassador, Megasthenes, to the court of Chandragupta Maurya.
- Megasthenes wrote an elaborate account (*Indica*) of the army and power of the king.
- A drama called *Mudrarakshasa* was written by Vishakhadatta and describes about mechanisation of Chanakya against Chandragupta's enemy.
- Chandragupta adopted Jainism and went to Sravanabelgola with Bhadrabahu.

Bindusara

- Bindusara was the son of Chandragupta and was referred to as Amitraghata by Greek writers.
- Bindusara further expanded the Mauryan Dynasty to the South.
- Bindusara appointed his eldest son Susima or Sumana as Viceroy of Taxila and Ashoka at Ujjain.

Ashoka

- He was the son of king Bindusara and Maharani Dharma. In the early life as an emperor, he engaged in war with different states.
- Ashoka was the first king to maintain direct contact with people through inscriptions.
- The war of Kalinga (BC 261) was the turning point of Ashoka's life. The mass death of the war changed his mind and he became a follower of Buddhism.
- He made Buddhism his state religion.
- He build lion stambh's to spread Buddhism. These stambh's are now called Ashok Stambh.
- Ashok Stambh of Sarnath was adopted as national emblem of India.
- Besides Ashok stambh, Ashoka had build many constructions–Dhamek Stupa (Sarnath, Uttar Pradesh), Bharhut stupa (Madhya Pradesh), Mahabodhi Temple (Bihar).
- He died in the year 232 BC.

THE INDO-GREEKS

- The most famous king among the Indo-Greeks was Menander (165-145 BC) also called Milinda. His capital was Sakala (modern Sialkot) in Punjab.
- He was converted to Buddhism by Nagasena as per the *Milindapanho*.
- The Greeks were the first to issue coins attributable to the king.

The Sakas

- The Sakas are referred to as Scythians. The Sakas came to India through the Bolan pass and first settled in lower Indus region.
- The first Saka king in India was Maues or Moga, who established Saka power in Gandhara. The most famous ruler of this dynasty was Rudradaman I.

The Kushanas

- Kushanas were the nomadic people from the steppes. Kanishka was the greatest of the Kushanas who started the Saka Era in AD 78.
- Kushanas were the first rulers to issue gold coins on a wide scale known for metallic purity.
- Kanishka was the most known and greatest of all the Kushana kings.
- Kanishka ascended to throne in AD 78 and he founded the **Saka Era**.

The Sunga Dynasty

- The Sunga Dynasty was established by Pushyamitra Sunga. They were basically Brahmins.
- This period saw the revival of Bhagvatism. **Patanjali** wrote *Mahabhasya* at this time.
- Bharhut stupa is the most famous monument of the Sunga period.

The Kanva Dynasty

Devabhuti, the last ruler of the Sunga dynasty, was murdered by his minister **Vasudeva**. He illegally took over the throne and founded the Kanva dynasty. They were replaced by the Satavahanas.

The Satavahanas (or Andhras)

- Simuka (60-37 BC) was the founder of the Satavahana dynasty.
- Under the Satavahanas, many chaityas (worship halls) and viharas (monastries) were cut out from rocks.
- The official language of the Satavahanas was Prakrit.
- The Satavahanas issued coins of lead (mainly), copper, bronze and potin. Gautamiputra Satakarni was a famous king of this dynasty.

The Pandyas

The Pandyas were first mentioned by Megasthenese. Their capital was **Madurai** famous for pearls.

The Cholas

- The Chola kingdom, also called as Cholamandalam was situated to the North-East of Pandya kingdom between Pennar and Vellar rivers.
- The capital of Chola rulers was Kaveripattanam/ Puhar.

The Cheras

Their capital was *Vanji* (also called Kerala country). They had important trade relations with the Romans.

Sangam Age

- Sangam is the Tamil form of Sanskrit word 'Sangha'. Sangam was an academy of Tamil poets.
- According to tradition, the first Sangam was founded by sage Agasthya.

GUPTA PERIOD

The important rulers of Gupta period were

Chandragupta I

- He was the first Gupta ruler to acquire the title of Maharajadhiraja. He was married to Lichchhavi princess Kumaradevi.
- Chandragupta I was able to establish his authority over Magadha, Prayaga and Saketa.

Samudragupta

- Samudragupta succeeded his father Chandragupta I about AD 340.
- He earned a reputation as one of the greatest kings and conquerors. He was chosen by his father as his successor because of his qualities that would make him into a good king.
- The Allahabad pillar inscription gives a detailed account of the career and personality of Samudragupta. Harishena (one of the officials) composed the inscription and engraved on the Ashoka's pillar at Allahabad.
- Samudragupta was a great military general. He had a long list of the kings and rulers whom he defeated.
- Samudragupta assumed the titles of 'Kaviraj and Vikrama'.

Chandragupta II

- Chandragupta II was the son of Samudragupta and Dattadevi and he was chosen by his father as his successor.
- Under Chandragupta II, the Gupta Empire reached its highest glory, both in terms of territorial expansion and cultural excellence.
- After the victory over Sakas, Chandragupta II adopted the title of 'Vikramaditya.'

- He was the first ruler to issue the silver coins in the memory of victory over Sakas.
- Kalidas (the great Sanskrit poet) was a member of Chandragupta's II court.
- Fa-Hien (the Chinese Buddhist pilgrim) visited India during his reign.

Kumaragupta I

- Chandragupta II was succeeded by his son Kumaragupta I. He was the worshipper of God Kartikeya.
- He founded the Nalanda Mahavihara, which developed into a great centre of learning.

Skandagupta

- Skandagupta was the last great ruler of the Gupta dynasty.
- During his reign the Gupta empire was invaded by the Hunas.

Pushyabhuti Dynasty

- The Pushyabhuti dynasty is also known as the Vardhana dynasty. It ruled parts of northern India during 6th and 7th centuries.
- This dynasty reached its highest point under its last ruler Harsha Vardhana reign. Famous Chinese traveler Hieun Tsang visited India during Harsha Vardhana reign.
- Banabhata, who wrote *Harshacharita* and *Kadambari* was a member of Harsha Vardhana's court.

Other Dynasties of Ancient India

After the death of Harsha, a struggle for supremacy started between the **Palas**, the **Gurjara-Pratihara** and the **Rashtrakutas** for the possession of Kannauj. This is famous as the **Tripartite struggle**. Towards the South, there were many kingdoms who ruled over India. They were the **Cheras**, the **Cholas**, the **Pandyas**, the **Pallavas** and the **Rashtrakutas**.

MEDIEVAL HISTORY

Medieval history of India relates with the rise of Islam in India. It began with the conquest of Sindh, one of the provinces of the present day Pakistan. Among the Muslims, the first to conquer the territories of India were the Arabs. It was under the leadership of Mohammed-bin-Qasim, that Sindh was conquered. After Arabs, Turks conquered India.

Mahmud Ghaznavi was the founder of Turkish rule in India. He led as many as 17 expeditions into India. His expedition against the temple of Somnath was the most important as it gave Mahmud a vast treasure. He patronised Firdausi Al-Biruni (scholar), who wrote *Kitab-ul-Hind* and *Utbi* (court historian).

THE DELHI SULTANATE

The state set-up by the Turks towards the end of the 12th century in Northern India, gradually developed into a powerful and highly centralised state.

By the end of the 12th century, **Mohammed Ghori** was successful in occupying Delhi and started a dynasty of rulers which, together with some later dynasties, came to be called the Delhi Sultanate.

Five dynasties that ruled at Delhi from AD 1206 to 1526 were

(i) The Slave Dynasty AD 1206-1290
(ii) The Khilji Dynasty AD 1290-1320
(iii) The Tughlaq Dynasty AD 1320-1414
(iv) The Sayyid Dynasty AD 1414-1451
(v) The Lodhi Dynasty AD 1451-1526

Slave Dynasty

In 1206, Mohammed Ghori was killed and Qutub-ud-din Aibak became the ruler of Hindustan. This was the beginning of the slave dynasty in India.

The important rulers of slave dynasty were

- **Qutub-ud-din Aibak** He was the favourite slave of Mohammed Ghori. He was enthroned at Lahore in AD 1206. He laid the foundation of Qutub Minar. For his generosity, he was given the title of 'Lakh Baksh' (meaning, giver of lakhs). In AD 1210, while playing Chaugan (Polo) at Lahore, he fell down from his horse and died.
- **Iltutmish** Aram Shah, the son of Aibak became the ruler, but soon he was overthrown by Shamsuddin Iltutmish. He was son-in-law of Aibak. Iltutmish was the real founder of Delhi Sultanate. He made Delhi as his capital, in place of Lahore. He was the first Turkish ruler of Delhi who organised the army of the Sultanate as the king's army. He issued the Tanka (silver) and the Jital (copper) coins for the first time. He died in 1236.
- **Rukn-ud-din Firoz Shah** Though Iltutmish had nominated his daughter Raziya Sultan as the successor, but the nobles placed Rukn-ud-din Firoz Shah on the throne. However, Raziya got rid of Rukn-ud-din and his powerful mother, Shah Turkan and ascended the throne.
- **Raziya Sultan** She was the first and the last female ruler of Delhi or medieval India. She discarded the Purdah, adorned the male attire and held the open court. The proud Turkish nobles thought it beneath their dignity to be governed by a woman. Thus, in AD 1240, Raziya became a victim of a conspiracy and was assassinated near Kaithal.
- **Ghiyas-ud-din Balban** He ascended the throne in AD 1266. He was the consolidator of the Sultanate of Delhi as he broke the power of Chahalgani (Chalisa groups). He took many measures to establish good governance. He was the first sultan to put forward his Divine Theory of Kingship. The army establishment was separated from the rest of the civil department. Amir Khusrow, the Parrot of India (Tuti-e-Hind) adorned his court.

The Khilji Dynasty

The Khiljis were probably of Turkish origin, but had become Afghan in character. The replacement of Slave dynasty by Khilji dynasty is termed as Khilji Revolution because it marked the end of power by the Turkish nobility and racial dictatorship. *The important rulers of Khilji dynasty were*

- **Jalal-ud-din** He was the founder and first ruler of the Khilji dynasty. He was the first ruler of the Delhi Sultanate to clearly put forward the view that the state should be based on the willing support of the governed. As majority of people of India were Hindus, it could not be purely Islamic state. He followed mild and generous policies.
- **Ala-ud-din Khilji** He ascended the throne after getting his uncle Jalal-ud-din murdered. He was the first Sultan of Delhi who separated religion from politics. He captured Chittor, which was renamed Khizrabad, after the name of his son Khizr Khan. In Deccan, Ala-ud-din's army, led by Malik Kafur, defeated Yadavas of Devagiri, Kakatiyas of Warangal, Hoysalas of Dwarasamudram and Pandyas of Madurai. He called himself the Second Alexander (Sikander-i-Saini) in the Khutba and on his coins.
- **Qutb-ud-din Mubarak Shah Khilji** He was the third and last ruler of the Khilji dynasty. He started his rule by releasing all taxes and penalties imposed by his father. He launched an expedition to Devagiri and annexed it to the Delhi Sultanate. He was the only Delhi Sultan to call himself the Caliph. Qutb-ud-din Mubarak Shah was the weakest ruler of the dynasty. He was murdered by Khusro Khan.

The Tughlaq Dynasty (AD 1320-1414)

The Tughlaqs were Muslim family of Turkish origin. The Tughlaqs belonged to the 'Qarana Turk' tribe, which was a mixed tribe of the Turk and Mongol stock.

The important Tughlaq rulers were

- **Ghiyas-ud-din Tughlaq** He was the founder of the Tughlaq dynasty. He is the first Sultan to be credited with digging canals for the improvement of irrigation and agriculture. Ghiyas-ud-din strengthened the defense of North-Western frontier in order to check the Mongol invasion. He adopted a balanced policy known as Rasm-i-Miyana. He put down the revolt of Ghiyas-ud-din Bahadur in Bengal. Ghiyas-ud-din founded the city of Tughlaqabad and renamed Warangal as Sultanpur. On returning from Bengal, he died in 1325 due to the collapse of a wooden pavilion.
- **Muhammed-bin-Tughlaq** He tried to introduce many administrative reforms. He had five ambitious projects for which he had become particularly debatable. He was a great scholar of Persian and Arabic and was well-versed in various branches of learning, such as astronomy, philosophy, mathematics, medicine, logic etc. He transferred the capital from Delhi to Devagiri or Daulatabad. Muhammed Tughlaq introduced bronze coins, which had the same value as the silver ones.
- **Firoz Shah Tughlaq** He was the son of Malik Rajab who was the younger brother of Ghiyas-ud-din. After his accession, Firoz Shah Tughlaq faced the problem of the imminent break up of Delhi Sultanate. He adopted the policy of appeasing the nobles, the army and theologians. He also asserted his authority over only such areas, which could be easily administered from the centre. He was the first Sultan to impose irrigation tax (10%) known as Haq-i-Sharb.

The Sayyid Dynasty

The Sayyid dynasty was succeeded the Tughlaq dynasty and ruled the sultanate until they were displaced by the Lodi dynasty. *The important rulers of Sayyid dynasty were*

- **Khizr Khan** He founded the Sayyid (descendants of the Prophet) dynasty and ruled as a deputy of Timur's son and successor, Shah Rukh. His reign was marked by chaos and disorder. The empire's territory had shrunken to Delhi and adjoining areas. He died due to illness in AD 1421. Taj-ul-Mulk was his loyal minister.
- **Mubarak Shah** He was the son of Khizr Khan. Sultan conferred the title of 'Khan-i-Khana' on Bahlul Lodhi. He subdued the rebellions at Bhatinda and Doab and the revolt by the Khokhar Chief, Jasrat.

  However, he fell to a conspiracy by some Muslim and Hindu nobles, when he proceeded to superintend the construction of a newly planned town, called Mubarakabad, on the Jamuna. He patronised Yahiya bin Ahmed Sirhindi, author of *Tarikh-i- Mubarak Shahi*.
- **Mohammed Shah** His reign was characterised by court conspiracy. His real authority extended to mere forty miles around his capital as a result of intriguing nobility.
- **Ala-ud-din Alam Shah** Mohammed Shah was succeeded by his son Alam Shah, who had already established his residence at Badaun, resigned his era without operation. The betrayer Hamid Khan was later on asserted with the resignation of Ala-ud-din. The Sayyid dynasty came to an end in AD 1451 and Bahlul Lodhi ushered in the Lodhi dynasty.

The Lodhi Dynasty

It was the last Sultanate dynasty. *The important rulers of this dynasty were as follows*

- **Bahlul Lodhi** He was the founder of the Lodhi dynasty. During the reign of Mohammed Shah, he served as the Subedar of Lahore and Sirhind. He tried to restore the greatness of Delhi Sultanate and hence conquered territories around Delhi. He was succeeded by his able son Nizam Shah under the title of 'Sultan Sikandar Lodhi' in 1489.
- **Sikandar Lodhi** He was the intelligent among the three Lodhi rulers. He conquered Bihar and concluded a friendship treaty with

Ala-ud-din Hussain Shah of Bengal. He introduced the system of auditing the accounts. He relaxed restrictions on trade, which greatly promoted the economic prosperity of the people. He lacked religious tolerance and levied Jizya and pilgrim's tax on Hindus.

- **Ibrahim Lodhi** Sikandar Lodhi was succeeded simultaneously by his two sons–Ibrahim on the throne of Agra and Jalal on the throne of Jaunpur. Later, Ibrahim killed Jalal and became the ruler. In the First Battle of Panipat on (20th April, 1526), Ibrahim Lodhi was defeated by Babar, the ruler of Kabul. Ibrahim Lodhi was the first Sultan of Delhi, who was killed in battle ground. The Sultanate came to an end and a new dynasty, the Mughal dynasty began their rule in India.

PROVINCIAL KINGDOMS

Many provincial dynasties emerged in India in the 15th and 16th centuries due to weakening of the Delhi Sultanate.

Bengal

- Bengal was made a part of Delhi Sultanate by **Ikhtiyar-ud-din Muhammad bin Bakhtiyar Khilji AD 1204**. However, it remained a problem for the Sultans of Delhi due to its distance from the capital. A period of unrest was finally brought to an end when a noble of Arab origin named Sayyed Husain assumed power in (AD 1494) and entitled himself as Alauddin Hussain Shah.
- Thus, the **Hussain Shahi dynasty** was established. Alauddin Hussain Shah ruled from AD 1494-1519 and was the most popular ruler of Bengal. He was succeeded by **Nasiruddin-Nasrat-Shah**. After weak successor's of Nasrat Shah, Bengal occupied by Sher Shah Suri in 1538 AD.

Assam

- The Ahoms under Sukaphaa founded a kingdom in Assam in the first half of the 13th century. **Suhungmung** who reigned as Svarga Narayan, was the most powerful Ahom ruler. The kingdom was annexed to the Mughal empire in the 17th century.

Orissa

- The kingdom of Orissa was consolidated by Anantavarman Chodaganga Deva. The famous Jagannatha temple was built by him.
- After his death, his dynasty began to decline. Around AD 1434, this dynasty was supplanted by **Kapilendra**, who founded the **Gajapati dynasty**.
- In AD 1441-42, the Gajapati dynasty was replaced by the **Bhoi dynasty**, which was founded by Govinda **Vijayadhara**. Orissa was annexed to Bengal by Sulaiman in AD 1568.

Kashmir

- **Sultan Zainul Abidin** (AD 1420-70) was the greatest Muslim ruler of Kashmir. He abolished Jizya and withdrew Sati. He abolished cow slaughter. He had translated Mahabharata into Persian. He created Zaina Lanka, the artificial island on the Wular lake.
- After Zainul Abidin death, their ensued chaos and anarchy under the rule of the nominal kings who ascended the throne. Later, Akbar annexed Kashmir into the Mughal empire in AD 1588.

Gujarat

- After Timur's invasion in Delhi in AD 1398, Gujarat became independent under its Governor, Zafar Khan. He named himself Muzaffar Shah I.
- **Shihab-ud-din Ahmed** was another ruler of Gujarat who founded the city of Ahmedabad and shifted the capital from Patan to Ahmedabad. He also built the Jama Masjid and Teen Darwaja at Ahmedabad.

- **Mahmud Begarha** was considered the greatest Sultan of Gujarat and was called Begarha. He formed a naval alliance with the Sultans of Turkey and Egypt and defeated the Portuguese in the Battle of Chaul in (AD 1508), but got defeated in the next year in the Battle of Diu.
- The Italian traveller, Barthema and Portuguese traveller Barbosa visited his court.

Mewar

- Mewar was an old principality of minor importance under the rule of the **Guhilot dynasty**, with its capital Nagada. Although Ala-ud-din Khilji captured Chittor, the capital of Mewar, in AD 1303, it was soon restored by Rana Hamir, who established the rule of **Sisodiya dynasty**.
- **Rana Kumbha** was the greatest ruler of the Sisodiya dynasty, carried out continuous warfare against Gujarat and Malwa. He was murdered by his son, Uda, to gain the throne.
- **Rana Sanga** (AD 1509-28) was another popular ruler of Mewar who defeated Mahmud Khilji II of Malwa and also Ibrahim Lodhi of Delhi at Ghatoli. He was defeated by Babur in the Battle of Khanua in AD 1527.

THE VIJAYANAGARA EMPIRE

- Harihara I and Bukka I founded the Vijayanagara empire in 1336 on the advice of Vidyaranya, who converted them back to Hindu.
- The important dynasties of Vijayanagara empire were Sangama Dynasty, Saluva Dynasty, Tuluva Dynasty and Aravidu Dynasty.
- Harihara I and Bukka I belonged to **Sangama dynasty**.
- **Harihara I** made Anagundi his capital. He annexed the Hoysala state in AD 1346, when the Muslim ruler of Madurai defeated and killed the Hoysala ruler Vir Ballal III.
- **Bukka I** made Gutti his capital. The empire saw expansion under Bukka I. In AD 1374, he sent an embassy to the Emperor of China. Harihara laid the foundations of 'Vidyanagar'. Bukka I renamed it 'Vijayanagara'.
- Bukka I was succeeded by his son Harihara II. He was the first ruler to assume legal titles of Raja Parmeshwara, Maharajadhiraja. He embarked upon a policy of expansion towards the Eastern sea coast, led the Vijayanagara empire into fresh conflicts.
- After Sangama Dynasty, Vijayanagara witnessed chaos and disorder due to weak rulers. However, the situation was saved by the Governor of Chandragiri, Narasimha Saluva, who seized the throne in about 1485. He established **Saluva Dynasty**. In the history, he is known as the First Usurpation Dictator.
- Following the death of Narasa Nayak in AD 1505, his son Vira Narasimha, succeeded as the reagent. He deposed Imadi Narasimha and laid the foundation of the **Tuluva dynasty** by what is known in history as the Second Usurpation Dictator.
- **The Aravidu Dynasty** was founded by Tirumala II, the brother of Rama Raya, who ruled in the name of Sadasiva Raya. On his failure to repopulate Vijayanagara, he shifted the capital to Penugonda. During his rule, the Nayaks became independent.
- Tirumala then divided his empire into three practically linguistic sections and placed them under his sons. Ranga III was the last ruler of Vijayanagara.

THE BAHAMANI EMPIRE

- It was founded on 3rd August, 1347, by Turkish Governor Hasan Gangu or Ala-ud-din Hasan Bahman Shah or Ala-ud-din Hasan who revolted against the Delhi Sultanate Muhammed bin Tughlaq and proclaimed his independence from the Sultanate. He reigned under the titles of 'Ala-ud-din' Bahmani or Bahman Shah.

- Gulbarga was the capital of Bahmani kingdom. By the end of the 15th century, Bahmani kingdom had split into five independent kingdoms Bijapur, Ahmednagar, Barar, Bidar and Golconda.
- The important rulers of Bahmani empire were **Bahman Shah** (AD 1347-58). He was the founder of Bahmani kingdom. He was also known as Zafar Khan/ Hasan Gangu.
- **Muhammed Shah I** established a Council of Ministers having eight ministers (Ashta Pradhana). This concept was later borrowed by the Marathas. He is better known as the organiser of Bahmani kingdoms. He constructed 'Jama Masjid' in Gulbarga fort and Shah Bazar Masjid in Gulbarga town.
- **Aladdin Mujahid Shah** was son of Mohammad Shah. He was murdered by Masud Khan and Daud Khan.
- According to Ferishta, **Firoz Shah** was the greatest king of his dynasty. He fought a war with the Vijayanagara emperor, Dev Raya II, where the latter was defeated. He founded the city of Firozabad on the bank of the river Bhima. He was a good calligrapher and poet (poetic name Uruji and Firozi). 'Hazrat Khwaja Syed Muhammed Gesu Draz' was a sufi (saint) and was deeply related with the Bahmani kings and people of Gulbarga.
- **Ghiyath-ud-din Shah** is known as Ghiyas-ud-din Tahmatan Shah, son of Muhammad Shah II.

MUGHAL EMPIRE

The Mughal empire was one of the greatest empires that ruled over India for over 300 years. *Rulers of Mughal Empire are given below*

Babur

- The Mughal empire was founded by Babur after defeating Ibrahim Lodhi in the First Battle of Panipat in AD 1526.
- Babur defeated Rana Sanga in the Battle of Khanwa in (AD 1527), Medini Rai of Chanderi in the Battle of Chanderi in (AD 1528) and Mahmud Lodhi in the Battle of Ghagra in (AD 1529).

Humayun

- Humayun succeeded his father, Babur and became the next Mughal ruler. He built Dinpanah at Delhi as his second capital. Sher Shah Suri gradually gained power.
- He fought two battles with Humayun—**Battle of Chausa** (AD 1539) and another **Battle of Kannauj** (AD 1540) culminating into Humayun's defeat.
- Humayun passed 15 years in exile. He again invaded India in 1555 with the help of his officer Bairam Khan. He died in AD 1556 due to a fall from his library building's stairs. **Gulbadan Begum**, Humayun's half-sister wrote **Humayun-nama**.

Akbar

- Akbar was the greatest ruler of the Mughal empire. He defeated Hemu in the Second Battle of Panipat in AD 1556.
- Akbar captured many more states like Malwa, Chittor, Ranthambor and brought them under the control of Mughals.
- Akbar abolished Jaziya (AD 1564), built Ibadat Khana (Hall of prayer) at Fatehpur Sikri and formulated religious order Din-e-Illahi (AD 1582). Akbar introduced Mansabdari system (holder of rank) to organise mobility and army.

Jahangir

- Jahangir became the next Mughal ruler. He executed the fifth Sikh Guru, Guru Arjun Dev.
- He married with Mehr-un-Nisa in AD 1611 and conferred the title of 'Nurjahan' on her. He established **Zanjir-i-Adal** at Agra Fort for the seekers of royal justice. English merchants captain Hawkins and Sir Thomas Roy visited the court of Jahangir and East India Company was established in India during his reign.

Shah Jahan

- After Jahangir, Shah Jahan became the next Mughal ruler. Two French travellers Bernier and Tavernier and the Italian traveller **Nicolo Manucci** visited during his reign.
- He built Moti Masjid and Taj Mahal at Agra, Jama Masjid and Red Fort at Delhi. His reign is considered the Golden Age of the Mughal empire.

Aurangzeb

- Aurangzeb became the next emperor after defeating his brothers in the war of succession.
- Under him, the Mughal empire became the largest single state ever known in India. He ended the celebration of Navroz and reimposed Jaziya in 1679.
- Aurangzeb built Bibi Ka Maqbara on the tomb of his queen at Aurangabad, Moti Masjid within Red Fort at Delhi and the Jama or Badshahi Mosque at Lahore. He was called **Darvesh** or a **Zinda Pir**.

Mughal Rulers Who Built Famous Buildings

- **Babar** He built two mosques : one at Kabulibagh in Panipat and the other is Sambhal in Rohilkhand.
- **Humayun** He laid the foundation of the city Din Panah at Delhi. Built Jamali mosque and the Mosque of Isa Khan at Delhi. Humayun's tomb is called the prototype of Taj Mahal. It was built by his widow Haji Begum.
- **Akbar** He built Agra fort (in red sandstone). He also built Fatehpur Sikri (city of victory) near Agra. In Fatehpur Sikri — the Panch Mahal, Diwan-e-Khas, Diwan-e-Aam, Jodhabai's palace and Sheikh Salim Chishti's tomb are built. Buland Darwaza (53 m high) is located here, commemorating the emperor's conquest of Gujarat. He built his own tomb at Sikandra, near Agra. He built the temple of Govindadeva at Vrindavan.
- **Jahangir** With Jahangir's reign, the practice of putting up buildings in marble and decorating the walls with floral designs made of semi-precious stones. This method of decoration was known as Pietra Dura. Jahangir built Moti Masjid at Lahore and his own mausoleum at Shahdara (Lahore).
- **Nurjahan** She built the tomb of Itmad-ud-Daula at Agra.
- **Shahjahan** He built Taj Mahal, Moti Masjid at Agra, Jama Masjid and Red Fort at Delhi, Shalimar Bagh at Lahore and city of Shahjahanabad. He also built Mussaman Burz at Agra (where he spent his last years in captivity) Sheesh Mahal etc. He got the peacock throne built by Bebadal Khan or which Amir Khusrau's couplet–'If there is a paradise on Earth, it is here', inscribed on it.
- **Aurangzeb** He built Moti Masjid at Delhi and Badshahi Mosque at Lahore. He also built Bibi ka Makbara in Aurangabad.

LATER MUGHALS

- Bahadur Shah I ascended the Mughal throne after the death of Aurangzeb.
- Jahandar Shah became the next ruler with the help of Zulfikar Khan. He abolished the Jaziya system. After him, Farrukhsiyar ascended the throne with the help of Sayyid brothers.
- During the reign of Muhammad Shah, the next Mughal ruler, Nadir Shah invaded India and took away Peacock Throne and Kohinoor diamond.
- The last Mughal ruler was Bahadur Shah II who was made premier during the 1857 revolt.

MARATHAS

The Maratha empire was an Indian power who existed in India during the end of 17th and at the start of 19th century.

The rulers who ruled over Marathas were the following

Shivaji

- Shivaji belonged to the Bhonsle clan of Marathas. His father Shahji Bhonsle was a military commander under Nizam Shahi ruler of Ahmednagar.
- Shivaji conquered the fort of Torna and built forts at Raigarh and Pratapgarh in 1646. He also killed Afzal Khan, Ambassador of Ali Adil Shah (Sultan of Bijapur) in 1659.
- The Treaty of Purandhar (1665) was signed between Shivaji and Raja Jai Singh who was appointed by Aurangzeb. According to the treaty, Shivaji ceded some forts to the Mughals and paid a visit to the Mughal court at Agra.
- Shivaji very soon conquered the forts which he had surrendered to the Mughals. He defeated the Mughal forces in the Battle of Salher in 1672.
- Shivaji was coronated at Raigarh (AD 1674) and assumed the title of 'Haindava Dharmadharak' (Protector of Hinduism). He appointed Council of Ministers i.e. Ashtapradhan in the administration.
- Successors of Shivaji were Sambhaji, Rajaram and Shahu. It was during this period, Peshwas emerged as the virtual rulers of the state.

Peshwas

- Balaji Vishwanath became the first Peshwa. He became the functional head of the Maratha empire. He helped Sayyid brothers in overthrowing Farrukhsiyar.
- Balaji Vishwanath concluded an agreement with the Sayyid brothers by which the Mughal emperor (Farrukhsiyar) recognised Shahu as the King of Swarajya.
- The next Peshwa of the Maratha empire was Baji Rao. He was a bold and brilliant commander and was considered the greatest exponent in guerrilla tactics after Shivaji.
- Under him Maratha power reached its zenith. He compelled the Mughals first to give them the right to collect Chauth of the vast areas and then to cede those to the Maratha kingdom.
- Balaji Baji Rao became the next Peshwa. Under him, Maratha fought the third Battle of Panipat (AD 1761) with Ahmad Shah Abdali. The battle gave a big jolt to the Maratha empire.
- The later Peshwas include Madhav Rao I, Narayan Rao, Madhav Rao II and Baji Rao II.

Sikhism

Sikhism was established by Guru Nanak in Punjab. There were 10 Sikh gurus. *They are as follows*

- **Guru Nanak** was the first Sikh Guru and the founder of the Sikh religion.
- **Guru Angad** invented and introduced the Gurmukhi script.
  He also popularised and expanded the institution of 'Guru ka Langar' started by Guru Nanak.
- **Guru Amar Das** introduced the Anand Karaj marriage ceremony for the Sikhs, replacing the Hindu form.
- **Guru Ram Das** founded the city of Amritsar and started the construction of the famous Golden temple at Amritsar.
- **Guru Arjan Dev** compiled the Adi Granth, the scriptures of the Sikhs and wrote the Sukhmani Sahib.
- **Guru Hargobind** organised a small army and established the principles of Miri-Piri. He also erected Sri Akal Takhat at the Harmandar Sahib (Golden Temple).

- **Guru Har Rai** cautiously avoided conflict with emperor Aurangzeb and devoted his efforts to missionary work.
- **Guru Har Kishan** was the youngest of the Gurus.
- **Guru Tegh Bahadur** established the town of Anandpur.
- **Guru Gobind Singh** was the 10th and last Sikh Guru. He created the 'Khalsa' in 1699.

MODERN INDIA

Before the beginning, formal rule of British in India. There were five European companies which established their trading centres at various locations in India. *They are discussed below as follows*

Advent of The Europeans

Portuguese

- The Portuguese were the first to come to India for trade. Vasco-da-Gama reached the port of Calicut in 1498 during the reign of King Zamorin (Hindus ruler of Calicut).
- The Portuguese later established their settlements at Daman, Salsette, Chaul, Bombay, Santhome (near Madras) and at Hooghly.

Dutch

- Dutch East India Company was formed in AD 1602. Dutch were defeated by English at the Battle of Bedara in AD 1759. As per agreement, the Dutch gained the control over Indonesia and the British over India, Sri Lanka and Malaya.
- They set-up their first factory at Masulipatnam in 1605. Their other factories were at Pulicat, Chinsura, Patna, Balasore, Nagapattanam, Cochin, Surat, Karikal and Kasimbazar.

Britishers

- The English East India Company was formed in 1599 under a charter granted by Queen Elizabeth in 1600. Jahangir granted a *farman* to Captain William Hawkins permitting the English to erect a factory at Surat (1613).
- In 1615, Sir Thomas Roe succeeded in getting an imperial *farman* to trade and establish factory in all parts of the Mughal Empire by ruler Jahangir.
- In 1690, a factory was established at Suttanati by Jab Charnock. In 1698, zamindari of three villages of **Suttanati**, **Kalikata** and **Govindpur** was acquired which paved the foundation of the city of Calcutta. Fort William was set-up in 1700 in Calcutta. Shah Alam II granted Diwani of Bihar, Bengal and Orissa to the British.
- In 1717, John Surman obtained a *farman* from Farrukhsiyar, which gave large concessions to the company. This *farman* has been called the **Magna Carta** of the Company.
- **Battle of Plassey** (1757) was fought wherein English defeated Sirajuddaula, the nawab of Bengal.
- **Battle of Buxar** (1764) Captain Munro defeated joint forces of Mir Qasim (Bengal), Shujauddaula (Awadh) and Shah Alam II (Mughal).

Danes

The Danish East India Company was formed in 1616. The Danish colony 'Tranquebar' was established on Southern Coromondel coast of India.

French

The French East India Company was formed by Colbert under state patronage in 1664. The First French factory was established at Surat by Francois Caron in 1668. A factory at Masulipatnam was set-up in 1669. French were defeated by English in Battle of Wandiwash (1760).

GOVERNOR GENERALS OF BENGAL

During AD 1773-1828, there were Governor-Generals of Bengal. *Details of some main Governor-Generals of Bengal are given below*

Warren Hastings

He was the first Governor-General of Bengal from (1772 to 1985). Some of the important events that took place during his tenure were abolition of dual government (Regulating Act, 1773), introduction of quintessential settlement of land revenue in 1772, foundation of Asiatic Society of Bengal in 1784, by Charles Wilkins. He also translated Bhagwat Geeta which were published in 1785, started diwani and faujdari adalats at the district level, fought Rohilla War (1774), First Anglo-Maratha war (1776-82) and Second Anglo Maratha War (1780-84).

Lord Cornwallis

- He introduced Permanent Settlement in Bengal and Bihar. He is called the Father of Civil Services in India.
- He also introduced judicial reforms by separating revenue administration from judicial administration.

Sir John Shore

He played an important role in the introduction of Permanent Settlement. During his tenure, battle of Kharda took place between the Nizams and the Marathas (1795).

Lord Wellesley

He introduced of the **Subsidiary Alliance** (1798), first alliance with Nizam of Hyderabad followed by Mysore, Tanjore, Awadh, the Peshwa, the Bhonsle and the Scindia. During his tenure, **Treaty of Bassein** (1802) and the Second Maratha War took place.

Lord Minto I

He concluded the Treaty of Amritsar with Maharaja Ranjit Singh (1809). The Charter Act of 1813 was passed during his time.

Lord Hasting

- He became the Governor-General in AD 1813.
- His reign saw the establishment of Ryotwari system in 1820 by Thomas Munro.

GOVERNOR-GENERALS OF INDIA

Lord William Bentinck

- He was made the first Governor-General of India Charter Act of 1833. Before him, the designation given was Governor-General of Bengal.
- He carried out social reforms like prohibition of Sati (1829) and elimination of thugs (1830). On Macaulay's recommendations, English was made the medium of higher education. He suppressed female infanticide and child sacrifice.

Lord Hardinge

During his tenure, First Anglo-Sikh War (1845-46) and Treaty of Lahore (1846) took place. He gave preference to English educated persons in employment.

Lord Dalhousie

- He introduced **Doctrine of Lapse** and annexation of Satara (1848), Jaipur and Sambhalpur (1849), Udaipur (1852), Jhansi (1853), Nagpur (1854) and Awadh (annexed in 1856 on account of maladministration).
- He laid down the **first railway line** between Bombay and Thane (1853), Telegraph line between Calcutta and Agra and **Postal reforms**

(first issue of the Indian stamp in Karachi in 1854) with the Post Office Act.

- He passed **Widow Remarriage Act, 1856** (the main force being Ishwar Chand Vidyasagar). He started Public **Works Department**, Grand Trunk Road work and developed harbour of Karachi, Bombay and Calcutta.
- He passed Charter Act, 1853 which included selection to Civil Service through competitive examination. He started Engineering College at Roorkee and made Shimla, the summer capital.

VICEROYS OF INDIA

Lord Canning

He was the **last Governor-General** and the **first Viceroy**. He withdrew Doctrine of Lapse. During his tenure revolt of 1857 took place and Indian Penal Code 1860 was passed. He passed the Act, 1858, which ended the rule of the East India Company. During his tenure, the Universities of Calcutta, Bombay and Madras were established in 1857.

Lord Mayo

- He organised the Statistical Survey of India and for the first time in Indian history, a census was held in 1871.
- He started the process of financial decentralisation in India. He established the Department of Agriculture and Commerce.

Lord Lytton

- He was also known as the 'Viceroy of Reverse Character'. He passed **Royal Titles Act of 1876** and the assumption of the title of 'Empress of India' by Queen Victoria, the Delhi Durbar in January 1877.
- He also passed **Vernacular Press Act** (also called the 'Gagging Act' to restrain the circulation of printed matter) and the **Arms Act** (made it mandatory for Indians to acquire license in arms) of 1878.

Lord Ripon

- He passed First Factory Act of 1881 (prohibited labour) and introduced Local Self-Government in 1882. He repealed the Vernacular Press Act in 1882 and finances of the centre were divided.
- He is regarded as 'the founding father of local self governance' in India.

Lord Lansdowne

- During his tenure, **Factory Act of 1891** granted weekly holiday and stipulated working hours for women and children. In his tenure, Civil services were divided into Imperial, Provincial and Subordinate Services.
- He passsed **Indian Councils Act** of 1892. During his tenure, the **Durand Commission** defined the Durand Line between British India and Afghanistan (now between Pakistan and Afghanistan) in 1893.

Lord Curzon

- During his tenure, a Commission was appointed under **Sir Thomas Raleigh** in 1902, to suggest reforms regarding universities, the **Indian Universities Act of 1904** was passed on the basis of its recommendations.
- He passed Ancient Monuments Preservation Act of 1904. Thus, Archaeological Survey of India was established. Agricultural Research Institute was established at Pusa in Delhi. During his tenure, Bengal was partitioned in 1905.

Lord Minto

During the tenure of Lord Minto, many events took place such as foundation of Muslim League (1906), Surat split (1907) and Minto-Morley Reforms (1909).

Lord Hardinge

During his tenure several event took place such as Annulment of partition of Bengal (1911), Transfer capital from Calcutta to Delhi (1911), Delhi Darbar and coronation of King George V and Queen Mary, (1911).

Lord Chelmsford

The important events during his tenure included Lucknow Pact (1916), Khilafat movement, Emergence of Gandhiji as a National leader, passing of Rowlatt Act, Jallianwala Bagh Tragedy (1919) and Moutague-Chelmsford Reform (1919).

Lord Irwin

- During his tenure, Simon Commission visited India in 1927. Events that took place during his time were–Congress passed the Indian Resolution in 1929, Dandi March (12th March, 1930) and Civil Disobedience Movement (1930).
- During his tenure, **First Round Table Conference** was held in England in 1930, Gandhi-Irwin Pact was signed and Lahore Session of Congress and **Poorna Swaraj Declaration** (1925) took place.

Lord Willingdon

During his tenure, **Second Round Table Conference** in London in 1931 and Third Round Table Conference in 1932 took place. Government of India Act (1935) was passed, Communal Awards (16th August, 1932) assigned seats to different religious communities and Gandhiji went on a epic fast to protest against this division.

Lord Wavell

- Events that took place during his tenure were Cabinet Mission Plan (16th May, 1946), First meeting of the Constituent Assembly was held on 9th December, 1946.
- He arranged the Shimla Conference on 25th June, 1945 with the failure of the Indian National Congress and Muslim League. During his tenure, election to the Constituent Assembly were held and an interim government was appointed under Nehru.

Lord Mountbatten

- He was **Last Viceroy of British India** and the **first Governor-General of free India**. Partition of India decided by the 3rd June Plan or Mountbatten Plan. He retired in June, 1948 and was succeeded by C Rajagopalachari, the first and the last Indian Governor- General of Free India.
- **Indian Independence Act** was passed by the British Parliament on 4th July, 1947, by which India became independent on 15th August, 1947.
- At the time of independence of India, the British emperor was King George VI.

THE REVOLT OF 1857

- The revolt of 1857 was a product of the character and policies of British colonial rule. The causes of revolt emerged from all aspects like socio-cultural, economic and political.
- **Political causes** for the revolt include the policy of Doctrine of Lapse, refusal of pension to Nana Sahib, annexation of some states through the policy of subsidiary alliance.
- **Economic causes** include heavy taxation, evictions, destruction of traditional

handicrafts, discriminatory tariff policy against Indian products.

- Indian soldiers were paid low salaries, they could not rise above the rank of subedar and were racially insulted.
- The introduction of Enfield Rifle, the cartridge of which was greased with animal fat, provided the spark.
- British social reforms like widow remarriage, abolition of sati, education for girls, christians missionaries also led to the revolt by Indians.

Centre of Revolt and the Leaders

Centre of Revolt	Leader
Delhi	Bahadur Shah II, Bakht Khan
Banaras	Liaquat Ali
Kanpur	Nana Sahab, Tantia Tope, Azimullah Khan
Lucknow	Hazrat Mahal (Begum of Awadh)
Jhansi	Rani Laxmi Bai
Bareilly	Khan Bahadur Khan
Awadh (Bihar)	Veer Kunwar Singh

The causes of failure of revolt include lack of efficient leadership, support of some Indian rulers to the Britishers, lack of common motive for participating in the revolt, inferior military equipments of rebels etc.

Socio-Religious Reform Movements

Movement	Founder	Idea
Brahmo Samaj	Raja Rammohun Roy	Propagated monotheism, opposed sacrifices idiolatry, superstition and sati.
Prathna Samaj	Atmaram Pandurang	Monotheism, upliftment of women, abolition of caste discrimination.
Arya Samaj	Dayanand Saraswati	Gave the slogan 'go back to the Vedas' denounced rites, idiolatry Brahmins supremacy etc.
Deccan Education Society	MG Ranade, GG Agarkar, VG Chiplinkar	To contribute to education and culture in western India, established Fergusson College at Pune (1885)
Ramakrishna Mission	Vivekananda	Revive Hinduism, against caste restrictions, superstition in Hinduism and overhaul of education system.
The Theosophical Society	Madam HP Blavatsky and Col. HS Olcott	Drew inspiration from Upanishads, philosophy of the Vedanta and transmigration of the souls.
Servants of Indian Society	Gopal Krishna Gokhale	Famine relief and improving tribal conditions in particular.

CHIEF NATIONAL ACTIVITIES

Formation of Indian National Congress (INC)

- The INC was formed when 72 delegates from all the presidencies and provinces of India met in Bombay, in December 1885. Allan Octavian Hume, a retired British official in India, called as 'Founder Father of the Congress' played a leading role in the formation of the INC.
- AO Hume established contact with some of the most important Indian leaders all over the country and received their cooperation in forming the Congress. The First Session of Indian National Congress was held on 8th December,1885 at Tejpal Sanskrit Pathshala, Bombay under the Presidentship of WC Banerjee.

Partition of Bengal

The partition was announced by **Lord Curzon** on 16th October, 1905 through a royal proclamation, reducing the old province of Bengal in size by creating East Bengal and Assam out of the rest of Bengal.

Swadeshi Movement

This movement had its origin in the anti-partition movement of Bengal. Lal, Bal, Pal and Aurobindo Ghosh played an important role. INC took the Swadeshi call first at the Banaras Session, 1905 presided over by GK Gokhale.

Muslim League (1906)

- It was set-up in 1906 by Aga Khan, Nawab Salimullah of Dhaka and Nawab Mohsin-ul-Mulk.
- The league supported the **Partition of Bengal** and opposed the **Swadeshi Movement,** demanded special safeguards to its community and a separate electorate for Muslims.
- This led to communal differences between the Hindus and the Muslims.

Demand for Swaraj

In the following sessions, demand for Swaraj arised

- **Calcutta Session** The INC, under the leadership of Dadabhai Naoroji, adopted *'Swaraj'* (Self-government) as the goal of Indian people.
- **Surat Session** The INC split into two groups: the Extremists and the Moderates, due to the debate on nature of Swadeshi Movement. Extremists were led by Lal, Bal, Pal while the Moderates by GK Gokhale.
- A trust was founded by Mohan Das Karam Chand Gandhi named as Navjiwan Trust with the idea of attaining third Swaraj.

Morley-Minto Reforms

- The reforms envisaged a separate electorate for Muslims, besides other constitutional measures.
- Lord Minto came to be known as the Father of Communal Electorate.

Ghadar Party

- It was formed by Lala Hardayal, Taraknath Das and Sohan Singh Bhakna. Its headquarters was at San Francisco.
- Its name was taken from a weekly paper, **Ghadar**, which had been started on 1st November, 1913 to commemorate the 1857 Revolt.

Home Rule Movement

- It was started by BG Tilak (April, 1916) at Poona and Annie Besant and S Subramania Iyer at Adyar, near Madras (September, 1916).
- Its objective was to establish self-government for India in the British Empire.
- Tilak supported the movement and joined Annie Besant. He raised the slogan **Swaraj is my Birth Right and I shall have it.**

Lucknow Pact

This pact between INC and Muslim League was signed following a war between Britain and Turkey which lead to anti-British feelings among Muslims. Both organisations jointly demand dominion status for the country.

August Declaration

- After the Lucknow Pact, the British policy was announced which aimed at "increasing association of Indians in every branch of the administration for progressive realisation of responsible government in India as an integral part of the British empire". This came to be called the August Declaration.
- The **Montague–Chelmsford reforms or the Act of 1919** was based on this declaration.

Rowlatt Act

- This act gave unbridled powers to the government to arrest and imprison suspects without trail. This law enabled the government to suspend the right of **Habeas Corpus**, which had been the foundation of civil liberties in Britain.

- **Rowlatt Satyagraha** was started against the act. This was the first countrywide agitation by Gandhiji.

Jallianwala Bagh Massacre

- People were agitated over the arrest of **Dr Kitchlu** and **Dr Satyapal** on 10th April, 1919.
- **General O' Dyer** fired at people who assembled in the Jallianwala Bagh, Amritsar. The Hunter Commission was appointed to enquire into it.
- Rabindranath Tagore returned his knighthood in protest.
- Sardar **Udham Singh** killed General Dyer in Caxton Hall, London.

Khilafat Movement

- Muslims were agitated by the treatment done with Turkey by the British in the treaty that followed the **First World War**.
- Ali brothers, **Mohd Ali** and **Shaukat Ali** started this movement. It was jointly led by the Khilafat leaders and the Congress.

Non-Cooperation Movement

- Congress passed the resolution in its Calcutta Session in September, 1920.
- It was the first mass-based political movement under Gandhiji. It included resignation from nominated offices and posts in the local bodies.
- Many refused to attend government *durbars* and boycott of British courts by the lawyers.
- It also included refusal of general public to offer themselves for military and other government jobs and boycott of foreign goods.

Chauri-Chaura Incident

- The Congress Session at Allahabad in December 1921, decided to launch a **Civil Disobedience Movement**. Gandhiji was appointed its leader.
- But before it could be launched, a mob of people at Chauri-Chaura (near Gorakhpur) clashed with the police and burnt 22 policemen on 5th February, 1922. This compelled Gandhiji to withdraw the Non-Cooperation Movement on 12th February, 1922.

Swaraj Party

Motilal Nehru, CR Das and NC Kelkar (called Pro-changers) demanded that the nationalist should end the boycott of the Legislative Councils, enter them and expose them.

Simon Commission

- It was constituted by John Simon, to review the political situation in India and to introduce further reforms and extension of parliamentary democracy.
- Indian leaders opposed the commission, as there were no Indians in it, they cried **Simon Go Back**.
- The government used brutal repression and at Lahore, **Lala Lajpat Rai** was severely beaten in lathi- charge and later succumbed to death.

The Nehru Report

After boycotting the Simon Commission, all political parties constituted a committee under the chairmanship of **Motilal Nehru** and **Tej Bahadur Sapru** to evolve and determine the principles for the Constitution of India. The report failed.

Lahore Session (1929)

- On 19th December, 1929, under the presidentship of **JL Nehru**, the INC, at its Lahore Session, declared **Poorna Swaraj** (complete independence) as its ultimate goal

- The tri-coloured flag adopted on 31st December, 1929, was unfurled and 26th January, 1930 was fixed as the **First Independence Day**, to be celebrated every year. Later, this day was chosen as the **Republic Day of India**.

Dandi March

It is also called the **Salt Satyagraha**. Gandhiji started his march from Sabarmati Ashram on 12th March, 1930 for the small village Dandi to break the Salt Law. He picked a handful of salt and inaugurated the **Civil Disobedience Movement**.

Civil Disobedience Movement

In the movement, countrywide mass participation by women was taken. The Garhwal soldiers refused to fire on the people at Peshawar.

First Round Table Conference

- It was the first conference arranged between the British and Indians as equals. It was held on 12th November, 1930 in London to discuss Simon Commission.
- Hindu Mahasabha and Muslim League participated in it. The conference failed due to absence of the Indian National Congress.

Gandhi Irwin Pact

- The government represented by Lord Irwin, and INC led by Gandhiji signed a pact on 5th March, 1931.
- In this, the INC called off the Civil Disobedience Movement and agreed to join the Second Round Table Conference.
- The government allowed the villagers on the coast to make salt for consumption and released the political prisoners. The **Karachi Session of 1931** endorsed the Gandhi Irwin Pact.

Second Round Table Conference

- Gandhiji represented the INC and went to London to meet British Prime Minister Ramsay McDonald.
- The conference however failed as Gandhiji could not agree with British Prime Minister on his policy of Communal Representation and refusal of the British Government on the basic Indian demand for freedom.

> **Poona Pact/Gandhi-Ambedkar Pact**
> The idea of separate electorate for the depressed classes was abandoned, but seats reserved for them in the Provincial Legislature were increased.
> Thus, Poona Pact agreed upon a joint electorate for upper and lower castes.

Demand for Pakistan

- In 1930, Iqbal suggested that the North-West provinces and Kashmir should be made Muslim states within the federation.
- In December 1943, the Karachi Session of the Muslim League adopted the slogan Divide and Quit. Chaudhary Rehmat Ali gave the term Pakistan in 1933.

August Offer

- It offered (i) Dominion status in the unspecified future (ii) A post-war body to enact the Constitution (iii) To expand the Governor-General's Executive Council to give full weightage to minority opinion.
- This was rejected by the INC, but was accepted by the Muslim League.

The Cripps Mission

- The British Government with a view to get cooperation from Indians in the Second World War, sent **Sir Stafford Cripps** to settle terms with Indian leaders.
- He offered dominion status to be granted after war.
- Congress rejected it. Gandhiji termed it as *'a post - dated cheque on a crashing bank'*.

The Revolt of 1942 and the Quit India Movement

- This revolt is also called the **Wardha Proposal,** a Leaderless Revolt.
- A resolution was passed on 8th August, 1942, at Bombay. Gandhiji gave the slogan **Do or Die**.
- On 1st August, the Congress was banned and its important leaders were arrested. Gandhiji was kept at the **Aga Khan Palace**, Pune. The people became violent.

The movement was, however, crushed by the government.

> **Indian National Army** (INA)
> **Subhash Chandra Bose** escaped to Berlin in 1941 and set-up the Indian League there. In July 1943, he joined the INA at Singapore. Ras Bihari Bose handed over the leadership to him.
> INA had three fighting brigades, named after Gandhi, Azad and Nehru. **Rani of Jhansi Brigade** was an exclusive women force. INA had its headquarters at Rangoon and Singapore.

Practice Exercise

1. Who founded the Hindu Shahi dynasty of Punjab?
(a) Vasumitra (b) Kallar
(c) Jayapala (d) Mahipala

2. 'Mitakshara', an authoritative treatise on Hindu law, was written by
(a) Jimutavahana (b) Hemadri
(c) Manu (d) Vagneswara

3. The famous Vedic saying 'War begins in the minds of men' is stated in
(a) Rig Veda (b) Atharva Veda
(c) Sama Veda (d) Mundaka Upanishad

4. Which one of the following four vedas contains an account of magical charms and spells?
(a) Rig Veda (b) Sama Veda
(c) Yajur Veda (d) Atharva Veda

5. Upanished are books on
(a) Religion (b) Yoga
(c) Law (d) Philosophy

6. The Khajuraho shrines built by Chandella rulers are dedicated to
(a) Vishnu and Shiva (b) Indra and Varun
(c) Shiva and Parvati (d) Vishnu and Brahma

7. Who founded the philosophy of Pustimarga?
(a) Chaitanya (b) Nanak
(c) Surdas (d) Ballabhacharya

8. Both Mahavira and Buddha preached during the regin of
(a) Ajatashatru (b) Bimbisara
(c) Nandivardhan (d) Uday

9. What is the name of Garhwal in Skand Purana?
(a) Kedarkhand (b) Kurmachal
(c) Jallandhar (d) Garhdesh

10. Buddhism split up into the Hinayana and Mahayana sects at the Buddhist Council held during the reign of
(a) Harsha
(b) Kanishka
(c) Ashoka
(d) Chandragupta Maurya

11. Buddhism made an important impact by allowing two sections of society into its fold. There were
(a) merchants and priests
(b) money lenders and slaves
(c) warriors and traders
(d) women and sudras

12. Which among the following is the sacred book of the Buddhists?
(a) Upanishad (b) Vedas
(c) Tripitaka (d) Aranyak

13. Who among the following is credited with the invention of Algebra?
(a) Aryabhatta (b) Bhaskara
(c) Apastamba (d) Medhatithi

14. Kalhana's well known work 'Rajatarangini' is an important source material for the study of which one of the following?
(a) Ancient Kamarupa
(b) Post-Mauryan Magadha
(c) Medieval Rajasthan
(d) Early Medieval Kashmir

15. The images in the temple of Angkorvat are those
(a) Buddha (b) Hindu Deities
(c) Tirthankaras (d) Cambodian Kings

16. Which one of the following is related to the origin of the caste system?
(a) Dasaranjana (b) The Purusha-Sukta
(c) Kalpasutra (d) The Brahmanas

17. In Jainism 'perfect knowledge' is referred to as
(a) Jina (b) Ratna
(c) Kaivalya (d) Nirvanas

18. Who among the following is not associated with medicine in Ancient India?
(a) Dhanvantri (b) Bhaskaracharya
(c) Charaka (d) Susruta

19. Which of the following pair is correct?
(a) Ashvaghosa - Vikramaditya
(b) Banabhatta - Harshavardhan
(c) Harisena - Kanishka
(d) Kalidasa - Samudragupta

20. The first discourse of Buddha in Sarnath is called
(a) Mahabhiniskraman
(b) Mahaparinivana
(c) Mahamastakabhisheka
(d) Dharmachakra Pravartan

21. Among the following who was the earliest visitor to India?
(a) Alberuni (b) Fa - Hien
(c) Hieun - Tsang (d) Megasthanes

22. Which of the following was not a kingdom in Ancient India?
(a) Avanti (b) Vatsa
(c) Hampi (d) Kosala

23. Which of the following temples was built by the Rashtrakutas?
(a) Ajanta (b) Ellora
(c) Mahabalipuram Cave (d) Khajuraho

24. Which one of the following chronological orders of the given dynasties of India is correct?
(a) Maurya - Nanda - Kanva - Sunga
(b) Nanda - Maurya - Sunga - Kanva
(c) Nanda - Maurya - Kanva - Sunga
(d) Maurya - Nanda - Sunga - Kanva

25. The main contribution of the Chola dynasty in the field of administration lies in
(a) systematic provincial administration
(b) a well planned revenue system
(c) a well organised Central Government
(d) an organised local self government

26. Which one of the following Kings controlled the famous silk route of Central Asia?
(a) Harsha (b) Chandragupta - II
(c) Ashoka (d) Kanishka

27. Who were the first to issue gold coins?
(a) Indo Greeks (b) Shakas
(c) Parthians (d) Kushans

28. The Kailash temple at Ellora was built by the
(a) Rashtrakuta (b) Cholas
(c) Pallavas (d) Chalukyas

29. The Vijay Stamble (Tower of Vitory) at Chittor was built by
(a) Rana Pratap (b) Rana Kumbha
(c) Rana Sanga (d) Bappa Raval

30. The Chalisa or the Group of forty was the nick name of
(a) forty leading slave officers of Iltutmish
(b) forty great scholars at the court of Iltutmish
(c) Turkish commanders of Iltutmish
(d) Turkish nobility created by Iltutmish

31. 'Tahqiq - i - Hind', a famous literary work, was written by
(a) Badauni
(b) Nizam - ud - din Ahmad
(c) Alberuni
(d) Minhaj - us - Siraj

32. In which region of India was the Suharawadi order of Sufism popular?
(a) Delhi and Bihar (b) Delhi and Doab region
(c) Punjab and Sind (d) Around Ajmer

33. The Delhi Sultanate virtually ended due to the invasion of
(a) Changez Khan (b) Babur
(c) Nadir Shah (d) Timor

34. India's famous Peacock Throne and the diamond Koh-e Noor were taken away by
(a) Ahmad Shah Abdali (b) Muhammad Ghori
(c) Nadir Shah (d) Robert Cive

35. Who laid the foundation of first independent Turkish Kingdom in India?
(a) Mohammad Qasim
(b) Qutubuddin Aibak
(c) Ghisuddin Balban
(d) Muhammad- bin-Tughlaq

36. Who among the following, destroyed the group of Forty Nobles?
(a) Bahram Shah (b) Iltutmish
(c) Razia (d) Balban

37. Who among the following Sultans built the fifth storeys of Qutub Minar?
(a) Qutubuddin Aibak (b) Iltutmish
(c) Firoz Shah Tughlaq (d) Sikandar Lodi

38. Who among the following Sultans of Delhi was the first to have paid to his soldiers in cash?
(a) Iltutmish
(b) Alauddin Khilji
(c) Muhammad- bin-Tughlaq
(d) Firoz Tughlaq

39. Moorish traveller, Ibn Battuta, came to India during the reign of
(a) Alauddin Khiliji
(b) Firoz Shah Tughlaq
(c) Balban
(d) Muhammad - bin - Tughlaq

40. Who among the following Mughal Emperors had the longest reign?
(a) Bahadur Shah (b) Jahandar Shah
(c) Farrukhsiyar (d) Muhammad Shah

41. The part of Delhi were Aibak laid the foundation of the first so called 'Seven cities' of medieval Delhi was
(a) Mehrauli (b) Shahjahanabad
(c) Din Panah (d) Hauz Khas

42. Which of the following is the most important statement which shows the real greatness of Akbar as a ruler?
(a) He tried to encourage inter - religious marriages
(b) He set up a revenue system based on average crop estimates
(c) He established Din-e-Ilahi incorporating the principles of many religions
(d) He tried to unite India into a single nation

43. 4th July, 1776 is important in world history because of
(a) Battle of Plassey
(b) Sea route of India was discovered
(c) English King Charles II was executed
(d) American Congress adopted the Declaration of Independence

44. Which of the following was the founder of 'Prarthana Samaj'?
(a) Devendranath Tagore
(b) Mahadeo Govind Ranade
(c) Keshab Chandra Sen
(d) Dr Atmaram Pandurang

45. Disciples of which one of the leaders in Bengal during the Indian freedom struggle were called Young Bengal?
(a) Keshab Chandra Sen
(b) Henry Derozio
(c) Surendra Nath Banerjee
(d) Madhusudan Datta

46. The first monarch of Magadh Kingdom in the 6th century BC was
(a) Bimbisara (b) Prasenajit
(c) Ajatashatru (d) Jarasandha

47. Who was the founder of Qutb Shahi dynasty?
(a) Adil Shah (b) Ibrahim Adil Shah II
(c) Ibrahim Qutb Shah (d) Quli Qutb Shah

48. Nadir Shah invaded India during the reign of
(a) Shah Alam (b) Bahadur Shah
(c) Muhammad Shah (d) Farrukhsiyar

49. Who united all the Sikhs and founded a kingdom in the Punjab?
(a) Guru Nanak
(b) Guru Gobind Singh
(c) Maharaja Ranjit Singh
(d) Guru Tegh Bahadur

50. The founder of the city of Agra was
(a) Alam Khan (b) Daulat Khan
(c) Bairam Khan (d) Sikandar Lodi

51. Who among the following introduced the famous Persian festival of Nauroj in India?
(a) Balban (b) Firoz Tughlaq
(c) Iltutmish (d) Alauddin Khilji

52. What is the correct chronological order in which of the following invaded India?
1. Huns 2. Kushans
3. Aryans 4. Greeks

Codes
(a) 4, 3, 2, 1 (b) 3, 4, 2, 1
(c) 4, 2, 3, 1 (d) 3, 4, 1, 2

53. Who wrote Mitakshara, a book on Hindu law?
(a) Nayachandra (b) Amoghavarsa
(c) Vijnaneswara (d) Kamban

54. The First Battle of Panipat was fought between
(a) Humayun and Shershah
(b) Rana Sanga and Babur
(c) Akbar and Hemu
(d) Ibrahim Lodhi and Babur

55. Which of the following battles was fought in AD 1192?
(a) First Battle in Tarain
(b) Second Battle of Tarain
(c) Battle of Talikota
(d) Battle of Khanwa

56. Who was the Indian ruler to face the Mahmud Ghaznavi?
(a) Prithviraj Chauhan (b) King Jaipal
(c) Jayachandra (d) Firdausi

57. The Second Battle of Tarain was fought between Muhammad Ghori and Prithviraj Chauhan in
(a) 1191 (b) 1192
(c) 1193 (d) 1194

58. The two great Mughal rulers who wrote their own memories are
(a) Babur and Humayun
(b) Humayun and Akbar
(c) Babur and Jahangir
(d) Jahangir and Shahjahan

59. The Mughal Emperor in India who gave Surat to the British East India Company was
(a) Babur (b) Akbar
(c) Jahangir (d) Aurangzeb

60. The first Indian ruler to organise Haj Pilgrimage at the expense of the state was
(a) Alauddin Khilji (b) Firoz Tughlaq
(c) Akbar (d) Aurangzeb

61. Match the following

	List I		List II
A.	Second Battle of Panipat	1.	Decline of Vijaynagar Empire
B.	Second Battle of Terrain	2.	British rule in India
C.	Battle of Talikota	3.	Turkish rule in India
D.	Battle of Plassey	4.	Mughal rule in India
		5.	Slave dynasty in India

Codes

	A	B	C	D		A	B	C	D
(a)	2	3	4	1	(b)	3	1	2	4
(c)	5	3	2	1	(d)	4	3	1	2

62. Who was the Governor General of India during the Revolt of 1857?
(a) Lord Canning (b) Lord Dalhousie
(c) Lord Dufferin (d) Lord Hardinge

63. Who was the founder-editor of the famous newspaper Kesari during the National struggle?
(a) Mahatma Gandhi (b) Jawaharlal Nehru
(c) Lokmanya Tilak (d) Muhammad Iqbal

64. The Ghadar Movement was founded by
(a) Ajit Singh (b) Lala Hansraj
(c) Lala Hardayal (d) None of these

65. The book 'Unto this Last' which influenced Gandhi was authored by
(a) Boris Yeltsin (b) John Ruskin
(c) Pushkin (d) Ruskin Bond

66. Which of the following published by Annie Besant?
(a) Al- Hilal (b) Commanweal
(c) Miral - ul- Akbhar (d) Native opinion

67. The name of the periodical among the following published by Mahatma Gandhi during his stay in South Africa.
(a) Navjiwan (b) India Gazette
(c) Afrikaner (d) Indian Opinion

68. Who said that "the real seat of taste is not the tongue, but the mind"?
(a) Aurobindo Ghosh
(b) Mahatma Gandhi
(c) Bal Gangadhar Tilak
(d) Swami Vivekananda

69. Shuddhi Movement (conversion of non-Hindus to Hinduism) was started by
(a) Swami Vivekananda
(b) Swami Shradhanand
(c) Mahatma Gandhi
(d) Raja Ram Mohan Roy

70. Which of the following features are common to Jainism and Buddhism?
I. Denial of the authority of Vedas
II. Condemnation of animal sacrifice
III. Pursuing severe ascetism
IV. Existence of soul
V. Rejection of existence of God

Select the correct answer using the codes given below.
(a) I, IV and V (b) I and II
(c) I, II, III and V (d) All of these

71. The pioneer of Indian Renaissance was
(a) Swami Vivekananda
(b) Swami Dayanand Saraswati
(c) Dadabhai Naoroji
(d) Raja Rammohan Roy

72. Who put forward 'Drain of Wealth Theory'?
(a) Dadabhai Naoroji
(b) Swami Vivekanand
(c) Mahatma Gandhi
(d) Gopal Krishna Gokhale

73. Who among the following were popularly known as Red Shirts?
(a) Congress Socialists
(b) Members of Azad Hind Fauj
(c) Khudai Khidmatgars
(d) People led by Rani Gaidinliu

74. Which religious reformer of Western India was known as 'Lokhitwadi'?
(a) Gopal Hari Deshmukh
(b) RG Bhandarkar
(c) Mahadev Govind Ranade
(d) BG Tilak

75. 'India Wins Freedom' is the autobiography of
(a) Abul Kalam Azad (b) Muhammad Ali
(c) Zakir Hussain (d) Syed Ahmed Khan

76. The Asiatic Society was established in Calcutta by
(a) Warren Hastings (b) Sir William Jones
(c) Raja Ram Mohan Roy (d) TB Macaulay

77. Who was the first European to translate the Bhagwad Gita into English?
(a) William Jones
(b) Charles Wilkins
(c) James Prinsep
(d) Sir Alexander Cunningham

78. The first English newspaper in India was started by
(a) Dadabhai Naoroji
(b) JA Hickey
(c) Lord William Bentinck
(d) Rabindra Nath Tagore

79. Which one among the following is regarded as the Magna Carta of Indian Education?
(a) Wood's Despatch (b) Hunter Commission
(c) Sadler Commission (d) Wardha Scheme

80. During the Mughal period which one of the following trade first come to India?
(a) Portuguese (b) English
(c) Dutch (d) Danish

81. Who was the first Portuguese Viceroy in India?
(a) Diaz
(b) Vasco da Gama
(c) Francisco de Almeida
(d) Albuquerque

82. Match the following

List I (Place of 1857 Revolt)	List II (Leader of Revolt)
A. Lucknow	1. Maulavei Ahmadullah
B. Kanpur	2. Kunwar Singh
C. Bihar	3. Nana Sahib
D. Rohilkhand	4. Beghum Hazrat Mahal

Codes

	A	B	C	D		A	B	C	D
(a)	2	3	4	1	(b)	4	1	2	3
(c)	2	1	4	3	(d)	4	3	2	1

83. The name of Lord Cornwallis is associated with the
(a) Dual government
(b) Maratha wars
(c) System of subsidiary alliances
(d) Permanent settlement

84. Sir Charles Wood's Despatch of 1854 dealt with
(a) administrative reforms
(b) social reforms
(c) economic reforms
(d) educational reforms

85. Through which educational report Calcutta University came into existence?
(a) Macaulay's Minute (b) Hunter Commission
(c) Charter Act (d) Wood's Despatch

86. Which of the following sought to change the character of Indian Government from unitary to federal?
(a) Government of India Act, 1919
(b) Government of India Act, 1935
(c) Indian Council Act, 1909
(d) Indian Independence Act, 1947

87. Which incident led Gandhiji to withdraw Non-Cooperation Movement?
(a) Kakori episode
(b) Chauri- Chaura episode
(c) Jallianwala Bagh episode
(d) Muzaffarpur episode

88. English education in India was introduced by
(a) Warren Hastings (b) Lord Rippon
(c) Lord Cornwallis (d) Lord William Bentinck

89. Which of the following laid the foundation of the British Civil Service in India?
(a) Warren Hastings (b) Lord Cornwallis
(c) Lord Wellesley (d) Lord Canning

90. The introduction of local self-government in the modern period of India is associated with the administration of
(a) Lord Ripon (b) Lord Irwin
(c) Lord Dufferin (d) Lord Canning

91. During which viceroy, Queen Victoria was crowned with Kaiser- i- Hind in Delhi Durbar?
(a) Hastings (b) Lytton
(c) Elgin (d) Lord Minto

92. Which one of the following pairs is correctly matched?
(a) Lord Cornwallis: Subsidiary Alliance
(b) Lord Dalhousie: Permanent Settlement of Bengal
(c) Lord Lytton : Doctrine of Lapse
(d) Lord Curzon : Partition of Bengal

93. Gandhiji give the call 'Do or Die' during
(a) Non - Cooperation Movement
(b) Civil Disobedience Movement
(c) Quit India Movement
(d) Industrial Satyagraha

94. The date 6th April, 1930 is known in Indian History for
(a) Dandi March by Mahatma Gandhi
(b) First Round table Conference
(c) Gandhi - Irwin Pact
(d) Jallianwala Bagh Massacre

95. Poona Pact was signed between
(a) Gandhiji and Lord Irwin
(b) Gandhiji and Jinnah
(c) Gandhiji and SC Bose
(d) Gandhiji and Ambedkar

Previous Year's Questions

96. Who is the author of the book 'Great Soul: Mahatma Gandhi and his Struggle with India', criticised for its content? **[CLAT 2011]**
(a) Nirad C Chaudhary (b) Joseph Lelyveld
(c) Khushwant Singh (d) Hermann Kallenbach

97. The first Shaka king in India was **[CLAT 2013]**
(a) Rudradaman (b) Menandar
(c) Maues (d) Damanrudra

98. The grant of Diwani of Bengal, Bihar and Orissa is associated with **[CLAT 2013]**
(a) Nawab Shuja-ud-Daula
(b) Nawab Asif-ud-Daula
(c) Shah Alam I
(d) Shah Alam II

99. Navjiwan Trust was instituted with the objectives of propagating peaceful means of attaining third Swaraj, by **[CLAT 2013]**
(a) Mohan Das Karam Chand Gandhi
(b) Lala Lajpat Rai
(c) Bal Gangadhar Tilak
(d) Dr Ambedkar

100. Kapilvastu Relics (fragments of Lord Buddha's bone), for the second time in 114 yr, recently travelled from India to **[CLAT 2013]**

(a) China (b) Sri Lanka
(c) Myanmar (d) Japan

101. The last British Emperor of India was **[CLAT 2013]**

(a) King George I (b) King George III
(c) King George V (d) King George VI

102. Capital of India was transferred from Calcutta to Delhi in the year **[CLAT 2013]**

(a) 1901 (b) 1911 (c) 1921 (d) 1922

103. Lord Buddha's image is sometimes shown with the hand gesture, called 'Bhumisparsha Mudra'. It signifies **[CLAT 2014]**

(a) Buddha's calling of the Earth to watch over Mara and to prevent Mara from disturbing his meditation
(b) Buddha's calling of the Earth to witness his purity and chastity despite the temptations of Mara
(c) the gesture of debate or discussion/argument
(d) Both (a) and (b)

104. Find out the correct chronological sequence of the following persons visit to India at one time or another (1) Fa-Hien (2) I-Tsing (Yijing) (3) Megasthanese (4) Hiuen-Tsang **[CLAT 2014]**

(a) 1, 3, 2, 4 (b) 1, 3, 4, 2
(c) 3, 1, 4, 2 (d) 3, 1, 2, 4

105. During the time of which Mughal Emperor did the East India Company establish its first factory in India? **[CLAT 2014]**

(a) Akbar (b) Jahangir
(c) Shahjahan (d) Aurangzeb

106. Who among the following, first translated the Bhagwat Gita into English? **[CLAT 2014]**

(a) Charles Wilkins
(b) Alexander Cunningham
(c) William Jones
(d) James Prinsep

107. Which was the first newspaper to be published in India? **[CLAT 2014]**

(a) Bombay Samachar (b) The Hindu
(c) Bengal Chronicle (d) Bengal Gazette

108. Which one of the following scripts of ancient India was mostly written from right to left? **[CLAT 2014]**

(a) Nandnagari (b) Brahmi
(c) Kharoshti (d) Sharada

109. Match List I with List II and select the correct answer using the codes given below the lists. **[CLAT 2014]**

	List I (Events)		List II (Results)
A.	Dandi March	1.	Communal electorate
B.	Chauri Chaura	2.	Illegal manufacture of salt
C.	Simon Commission	3.	Country-wise agitation
D.	Morley Minto Reforms	4.	Withdrawal of a movement

Codes

	A	B	C	D		A	B	C	D
(a)	1	2	3	4	(b)	4	3	2	1
(c)	2	4	3	1	(d)	1	4	3	2

110. Under the leadership of Mahatma Gandhi, the Civil Disobedience Movement, launched in 1930, started from **[CLAT 2014]**

(a) Sabarmati (b) Dandi
(c) Sevagram (d) Champaran

111. Match List I with List II and choose the correct answer **[CLAT 2014]**

	List I		List II
A.	Visakhadatta	1.	Surgery
B.	Varahamihira	2.	Drama
C.	Sushruta	3.	Astronomy
D.	Brahmagupta	4.	Mathematics

Codes

	A	B	C	D		A	B	C	D
(a)	1	3	4	2	(b)	2	1	3	4
(c)	2	3	1	4	(d)	3	4	1	2

112. What is the correct sequence of the following movements in chronological order? **[CLAT 2015]**

1. Civil Disobedience Movement
2. Khilafat Movement
3. Home Rule Movement
4. Quit India Movement

Codes

(a) 1, 2, 3, 4 (b) 4, 3, 2, 1
(c) 3, 2, 1, 4 (d) 2, 4, 1, 3

113. Who among the following was the author of Rajtarangini, commonly regarded as the first genuine history of India, written by an Indian? **[CLAT 2015]**

(a) Banbhatta
(b) Ravikirti
(c) Pushpananda
(d) Kalhana

114. Which of the following acts formally introduced the principle of elections for the first time? **[CLAT 2015]**

(a) Indian Councils Act, 1909
(b) Government of India Act, 1919
(c) Government of India Act, 1935
(d) India's Independence Act, 1947

115. Which among the following 18th century Indian rulers has been called 'Plato of his tribe'? **[CLAT 2015]**

(a) Sawai Jai Singh
(b) Badam Singh
(c) Suraj Mal
(d) Guru Gobind Singh

Answers

1	*b*	2	*d*	3	*b*	4	*d*	5	*d*	6	*a*	7	*d*	8	*a*	9	*a*	10	*b*
11	*d*	12	*c*	13	*a*	14	*d*	15	*b*	16	*b*	17	*c*	18	*b*	19	*b*	20	*d*
21	*c*	22	*c*	23	*b*	24	*b*	25	*d*	26	*d*	27	*a*	28	*a*	29	*b*	30	*a*
31	*c*	32	*c*	33	*c*	34	*c*	35	*b*	36	*d*	37	*b*	38	*d*	39	*d*	40	*d*
41	*a*	42	*c*	43	*d*	44	*d*	45	*b*	46	*a*	47	*d*	48	*c*	49	*c*	50	*d*
51	*a*	52	*b*	53	*c*	54	*d*	55	*b*	56	*b*	57	*b*	58	*c*	59	*c*	60	*c*
61	*d*	62	*a*	63	*c*	64	*c*	65	*b*	66	*b*	67	*d*	68	*b*	69	*b*	70	*b*
71	*d*	72	*a*	73	*c*	74	*a*	75	*a*	76	*b*	77	*b*	78	*b*	79	*a*	80	*a*
81	*c*	82	*d*	83	*d*	84	*d*	85	*d*	86	*b*	87	*b*	88	*d*	89	*a*	90	*a*
91	*b*	92	*d*	93	*c*	94	*a*	95	*d*	96	*b*	97	*c*	98	*d*	99	*a*	100	*b*
101	*d*	102	*b*	103	*d*	104	*c*	105	*b*	106	*a*	107	*d*	108	*c*	109	*d*	110	*a*
111	*c*	112	*c*	113	*d*	114	*a*	115	*c*										

CHAPTER 02

GEOGRAPHY

Geography is a scientific field that is devoted to the study of the Earth's landforms, Oceans environment and ecosystems and the interactions between the human society and their environment.

PHYSICAL AND WORLD GEOGRAPHY

Physical geography is imperative for understanding the countries and regions of the world in different ways. It is that bunch of science which deals with the natural environment.

The Universe

- The universe is commonly defined as the totality of everything that exists including all physical matter and energy, the planets, stars, galaxies and the contents of intergalactic space. The study of universe is called cosmology.
- A galaxy is a vast system of billion of stars, dust and light gases bound by their own gravity.
- Our galaxy is Milky Way Galaxy (Akash Ganga) formed after the Big Bang. Andromeda is the nearest galaxy to Milky Way.
- Big Bang was an explosion of concentrated matter in the universe that occurred 15 billion years ago. It led to the formation of galaxies of stars and other heavenly bodies.
- Stars are the astronomical objects made-up of hot burning gases and they shine by emitting their own light.
- Comets are made up of frozen gases. Hailey's Comet reappears within the gap of 76 years, last seen in 1986.
- Constellations are the units to enable the astronomers to identify the position of the stars. There are 88 known constellations.

- Satellites are the heavenly bodies that revolve around the planets. Moon is the natural satellite of the Earth.

Solar System

- The solar system comprises the sun, eight planets and their satellites (or moons) and thousands of other smaller heavenly bodies such as asteroids, comets and meteors.
- The sun is at the centre of the solar system and all the planets revolve around it in elliptical orbit. It is the nearest star to the Earth.
- Hydrogen and Helium are the main gases present in the sun. It has a surface temperature of about 6000°C.
- Planets are opaque (thick/cloudy) bodies revolving around and lighted by the sun. There are eight planets in the solar system.
- The sequence of planets according to their distance from the sun is Mercury, Venus, Earth, Mars, Jupiter, Saturn, Uranus and Neptune.
- The planets can be classified into two i.e. Inner planets which are nearer to the sun (Mercury, Venus, Earth and Mars) and outer planets which are far away from the sun (Jupiter, Saturn, Uranus and Neptune).
- Small planetary bodies that revolve around the sun and found in between the orbits of Mars and Jupiter are called asteroids.
- Meteors (shooting star) are fragments of rock coming towards the Earth. They are formed due to collision among the asteroids.
- Moon is also known as the fossil planet. It is the only natural satellite of the Earth.

Facts about Planets

Biggest Planet	Jupiter
Biggest Satellite	Gannymede
Blue Planet	Earth
Green Planet	Uranus
Brightest Planet	Venus
Brightest Planet outside solar system	Sirius (Dog Star)
Closest Star of solar system	Proxima Centauri
Coldest Planet	Neptune
Evening Star	Venus
Farthest Planet from Sun	Neptune
Planet with maximum number of satellites	Jupiter
Fastest revolution in solar system	Mercury
Hottest Planet	Venus
Densest Planet	Earth
Fastest rotation in solar system	Jupiter
Morning Star	Venus
Nearest Planet to Earth	Venus
Nearest Planet to Sun	Mercury
Red Planet	Mars
Slowest revolution in solar system	Neptune
Slowest rotation in solar system	Venus
Smallest Planet	Mercury
Smallest Satellite	Deimos
Earth's Twin	Venus
Only Satellite with an atmosphere like Earth	Titan

The Earth

- The Earth is the third planet from the sun. It is the only planet known to have an atmosphere contains free oxygen, water and life. It is known as *Blue Planet*.
- Earth spins on an imaginary line called an axis that runs from the North pole to the South pole, while also orbiting the sun. The rotation of Earth causes day and night and formation of high and low tides.
- Earth's motion is elliptical orbit around the sun in one year. It causes change of seasons and variation of the length of the days and nights at different times of the year.
- Equinoxes on Earth are the days when days and nights are equal. It happens twice a year i.e. 21st March and 23rd September.

- Seasons are the periods into which the year can be divided as a result of the climatic conditions. There are four seasons such as spring, summer, autumn and winter.
- In order to understand various locations on the Earth, it has been divided into three parts i.e. Equator, Longitude and Latitude. These are the imaginary lines drawn on the Earth'surface.
- Latitude lines circle the globe in an East-West direction. It measures how far North or South a point lies from the equator.
- The equator is at 0° latitude and separate Earth's Northern and Southern Hemisphere.
- Longitude lines run from the North pole to the South pole. It measures how far East or West a point on Earth lies from the Prime Meridian.
- The Prime Meridian, the line of longitude that passes through Greenwich, England, is the 0° longitude line.
- International Date line is the longitude where the date changes exactly by one day when it is crossed. 180° East and 180° West meridians is the same line which is called the International Date line.
- Eclipse is another phenomenon which take place at regular interval. When the light of the sun or the moon is blocked by another body, the sun or the moon is said to be in eclipse.
- Solar eclipse is caused when the moon comes in between the Earth and the Sun.
- Lunar eclipse is caused when the Earth comes between the moon and the Sun.

Interior of the Earth

- Earth's interior is divided into crust, mantle and core. It forms the different layers of the Earth.
- The crust is the outermost and the thinner layer of the Earth. This layer is also called SiAl (silica and aluminium).
- Mantle is the intermediate layer of the Earth in terms of both its location and density. The upper part of mantle is called Asthenosphere.
- The innermost layer of the Earth is called Core. The innermost part of the core may be called solid or crystalline.
- This layer is known as NiFe (due to large concentration of nickel and iron). The outer part of the core is believed to have the properties of a liquid.
- Other important features of Earth are earthquakes and volcanoes.
- Any sudden disturbance below the Earth's surface may produce vibrations or shaking in Earth's crust and some of these vibrations, when reach the surface are known as Earthquakes.
- The intensity of earthquake waves is recorded by *Seismograph*. Intensity of shaking is measured on the modified *Mercalli scale*.
- *Focus* is the point beneath the Earth where earthquake originates and epicentre is the point just above the focus on the Earth's surface.
- Volcanoes are the sudden eruption of hot magma (molten rock), gases, ash and other material from inside the Earth to its surface.
- The different types of volcanoes include Active volcano, Dormant volcano and Extinct volcano.
- Active volcanoes are those which erupt frequently e.g. Mauna Loa (Hawaii), Stromboli (Mediterranean Sea).
- Dormant volcanoes are those that have not erupted for past few year e.g. Fujiyama (Japan), Barren Island (Andamans).
- Extinct volcanoes are those which have not erupted for several centuries.
- The land near the edges of the Pacific ocean is known as *Ring of Fire* as hundreds of active volcanoes are found there.

Rocks and Landforms

- Earth's crust is made up of various types of rocks. On the basis of the mode of origin, rocks are of three types namely Igneous rocks, Sedimentary rocks and Metamorphic rocks.
- Igneous rocks are formed by the solidification of the molten magma e.g. Mica, Granite etc.
- Sedimentary rocks are formed due to accumulation of rock particles and organic matter in layers under tremendous pressure. e.g. Gravel, Peat, Gypsum etc.
- Metamorphic rocks were originally igneous or sedimentary, but have been changed by pressure, heat or action of water. e.g. Gneiss, Marble, Quartzite etc.
- There are four major landforms on Earth such as mountains, hills, plateau and plains.
- An uplifted portion of the Earth's surface is called a hill or a mountain. Mountains are classified into four types i.e. Fold mountains, Block mountains, Volcanic mountains and Residual or Dissected mountains.
- Fold mountains are formed by folding of crustal rocks by compressive forces. e.g. Himalayas (Asia), Alps (Europe) etc.
- When blocks of the Earth's crust are raised or lowered during the last stage of mountain building, block mountains are formed e.g. Vosges (France) etc.
- Volcanic mountains are formed by the matter thrown out from the volcanoes, e.g. Mt. Mauna Loa (Hawaii), Mt. Popa (Myanmar).
- Residual mountains are also known as relic mountains. These are formed as a result of weathering of previously existed mountains due to various agents causing erosion. e.g. Nilgiri hills, Girnar hills, Rajmahal hills etc.

Major Mountain Ranges

Range	Location	Length (km)
Andes	South America	7200
Himalayan, Karakoram and Hindu Kush	South Central Asia	5000
Rockies	North America	4800
Great Dividing Range	East Australia	3600
Atlas	North-West Africa	1930
Western Ghats	Western India	1610
Caucasus	Europe	1200
Alaska	USA	1130
Alps	Europe	1050

Major Mountain Peaks

Mountain Peak	Range	Location	Height (in metres)
Mt Everest (highest in the world)	Himalayas	Nepal-Tibet	8848
K2 (Godwin Austin)	Karakoram	India (PoK)	8611
Kanchenjunga	Kanchenjunga Himalaya	India	8586
Dhaulagiri	Himalayas	Nepal	8167
Annapurna	Himalayas	Nepal	8091
Gurla Mandhata	Himalayas	Tibet	7694
Tirich Mir	Hindu Kush	Pakistan	7708
Aconcagua	Andes	Argentina	6962

- A plateau is a portion of land that is more or less flat and level, elevated above the surrounding area. It may have steep slopes or vertical cliffs on one or more sides.
- Plains occur as lowlands and at the bottom of valleys but also on plateaus or uplands at high elevations.
- There are three types of plains, i.e. structural plain, erosional plain and depositional plain.

ATMOSPHERE

- The vast expanse of air which envelops the Earth all around is called the atmosphere. It extends to thousands of kilometres.
- The major constituents of air in the atmosphere are Nitrogen (78%), Oxygen (21%), Argon (0.93%) and Carbon dioxide (0.03%).
- Beside these, water vapour, dust particles, smoke, salts and other impurities are present in air in varying quantities.

Structure of Atmosphere

Layer	Height (km)	Feature
Troposphere	0-18 km	Contains 75% of the gases in the atmosphere. As height increases, temperature decreases – (temperature inversion) (about 6.5°C per 1 km ascent).
Stratosphere	18-50 km	This layer contains the ozone layer. The temperature remains fairly constant (– 60°C).
Mesosphere	50-80 km	This is the coldest region of the atmosphere. The temperature drops to about – 100°C.
Ionosphere	80-400 km	Radio waves are bounced off the ions and reflect waves back to the Earth. This generally helps radio communication.
Exosphere	Above 400 km	Upper part of exosphere is called Magnetosphere. The temperature keeps on rising constantly at high rate.

- A greenhouse gas is a gas in the atmosphere that absorbs and emits radiation within the thermal infrared range.
- The primary greenhouse gases in the Earth's atmosphere are water vapour, carbon dioxide, methane, nitrous oxide and ozone.

Wind System

- The pressure difference is the major cause of the genesis of the wind system. The air moves from high pressure to low pressure.
- The slope of pressure from high to low is called as pressure gradient which is also called as barometric slope.
- The direction of wind deviates from the expected one due to coriolis force caused by the rotation of the Earth.
- The different types of winds are Planetary wind, Periodic wind and Local wind.
- Planetary winds blow throughout the year from one latitude to another in response to latitudinal differences in air pressure. e.g. Trade winds, Westerlies and Polar winds.
- Periodic winds change their direction periodically with the change in pressure and temperature. e.g. monsoon, land and sea breeze etc.
- Local winds develop as a result of local differences in temperature. e.g. *Loo* which blows in summer.

Local Winds

Name	Nature of Wind
Chinook	Hot, dry wind in Rockies, also called '*Snow Eater*'.
Foehn	Hot, dry wind in the Alps.
Khamsin	Hot, dry wind in Egypt.
Sirocco	Hot, moist wind from Sahara to Mediterranean Sea.
Solano	Hot, moist wind from Sahara towards Iberian Peninsula.
Harmattan	Hot, dry wind blowing outwards from the interior of West Africa, also called *Guinea Doctor*.
Bora	Cold, dry wind blowing outwards from Hungary to the North of Italy (near Adriatic Sea).

Name	Nature of Wind
Mistral	Very cold wind, which blows from the Alps over France.
Punas	Cold, dry wind blowing down towards the Western side of Andes.
Blizzard	Very cold winds in Tundra region.
Purga	Cold wind in Russian Tundra.
Levanter	Cold wind in Spain.
Norwester	Hot wind in New Zealand.
Santa Ana	Hot wind in South California (USA).

- Cyclone is rapid inward circulation of air masses with a low pressure at centre. It is anti-clockwise in the Northern hemisphere and clockwise in the Southern hemisphere.
- Anti-cyclone is a rapid outward movement of air masses with a high pressure at centre. It is clockwise in the Northern hemisphere and anti-clockwise in the Southern hemisphere.
- Hurricane or tropical cyclone is a disturbance of about 650 km across, spinning around a central area of very low pressure.
- Large ocean wave that is caused by sudden motion on the ocean floor are called Tsunami. The motion could be an earthquake, volcanic eruption or underwater landslide.

SOURCES OF WATER IN THE WORLD

Oceans are the major source of water. They cover almost 71% of the Earth's surface. The oceans contain roughly 97% of the Earth's water supply.

Major Oceans of the World

Ocean	Important Information
Pacific	It is the largest and deepest ocean. Mariana Trench, the world's deepest trench is in Pacific ocean.
Atlantic	It has the longest coastline. It is the busiest ocean for trade and commerce since its sea routes connect the two most industrialised regions, namely Western Europe and North-Eastern United States of America. Atlantic ocean is still widening. Puerto Rico Trench is the deepest point of this ocean.
Indian	Only ocean named after a country. It is deeper than the Atlantic ocean. Java Trench is the deepest point of this ocean.
Arctic	It is the smallest ocean and lies within the Arctic circle. Most of the part of the ocean is frozen and hence it is least saline and the shallowest among all the oceans. Litke Deep is the deepest point of this ocean.

Rivers are another source of water on Earth. A river is a natural flowing water towards ocean, sea or another river. The bottom of the river channels is called the bed and the sides of the channel are called the banks.

Major Rivers of the World

River	Source	Important Facts
Nile	Tributaries of Lake Victoria, Africa	Longest river (6650 km)
Amazon	Glacier-fed lakes, Peru	Largest river and second longest river (6400 km)
Mississippi-Missouri	Source of Red Rock, Montana	Longest river in the USA (3770km)
Chang Jiang (Yangtze)	Tibetan plateau, China	Longest river in Asia (6300 km)
Ob	Altai Mountain, Russia	Seventh longest river (3650 km) form World's longest estuary 'Gulf of Ob'.
Huang He (Yellow)	Eastern part of Kunlan Mountain, West China	Second longest river in Asia (5464) and sixth longest in the world.

River	Source	Important Facts
Yenisei	Tannu-Ola Mountain, Western Tuva, Russia	Largest river system flowing to the Arctic ocean (5540)
Zaire (Congo)	Confluence of Lualab and Luapula rivers, Congo	World's deepest river with measured depths in excess of 220 m.
Niger	Guinea	Third longest river in Africa (4180 km)
Mekong	Tibetan highlands	World's 12th longest and Asia's 7th longest river (4350 km)
Danube	Black Forest, Germany	Second-longest river of Europe and longest river of European Union (2860 km)
Volga	Valdai plateau, Russia	Longest river of Europe (3530 km).

A **waterfall** is a place where water flows over a vertical drop or a series of steep drops in the course of a stream or river.

Important Waterfalls

Waterfall	Location	Facts
Angel Falls	Venezuela	World's highest uninterrupted waterfall
Tugela Falls	South Africa	Second tallest waterfall in the world
Jog Falls	Karnataka, India	Second highest plunge waterfall in India
Niagara Falls	Border of Ontario, Canada and New York	Made up of three waterfalls i.e. the American falls, the Bridal Veil falls and the Horseshoe falls.
Victoria Falls	South Africa	Described by CNN as one of the seven natural wonders of the world

A **lake** is an area of variable size filled with water surrounded by land.

Important Lakes of the World

Lake	Location	Facts
Superior	Canada and USA	Largest of the Great lakes of North America
Victoria	Tanzania (Africa)	One of the African Great lakes and the source of Nile river
Baikal (Nature's lake)	Russia	The oldest and deepest freshwater lake in the world
Malawi	Tanzania (Africa)	Second deepest lake on the African continent
Great Bear	Canada	Fourth largest in North America

A **canal** is a man-made waterway. Canals are built for a variety of uses including irrigation, land, drainage, urban water supply or for the purpose of transportation.

Important Canals of the World

Canal	Connects
Panama	Pacific ocean with Caribbean sea
Suez	Mediterranean sea to Red sea
Erie	Atlantic ocean to Great lakes
Kiel	North sea to Baltic sea

An **island** is any piece of sub-continental land that is surround by water.

Major Islands of the World

Island's Name	Country	Important Facts
Greenland	Denmark	The world's largest island
New Guinea	Indonesia	The world's second-largest island
Borneo	Brunei/Malasia /Indonesia	Third largest island in the world and the largest island in Asia
Madagascar	Madagascar	Fourth largest island in the world
Baffin Island	Canada	The largest in Canada Island
Sumatra	Indonesia	The largest island in Indonesia

NATURAL VEGETATION

- Natural vegetation refers to plants which have grown naturally and not planted by human beings. There are three major types of natural vegetation i.e. forest, deserts and grasslands.
- Forests can be classified as tropical rainforests, temperature deciduous forests and temperate coniferous forests.
- Deserts are arid or dry regions and receive less than 100 inches of rain per year. The world's deserts occupy almost one-quarter of the Earth's land surface.

Famous Deserts of the World

Name	Country/Regio	Important Facts
Sahara (Libyan, Nubian)	North Africa	Largest hot desert
Victorian (Great Sandy)	Australia	Largest desert in Australia
Arabian (Rub' al Khali, An-Nafud)	Arabia	Second largest desert
Dasht-e-Lut (Barren Desert)	Iran	Largest salt desert
Dast-e-Kavir (Salt Desert)	Iran	
Atacama	Northern Chile	Driest non-polar desert
Patagonian	Argentina	Largest desert in Argentina
Kalahari	Botswana	
Namib	Namibia	Oldest desert in the world (55-80 million years)

- Grasslands are areas dominated by grasses and have few or no trees. Grazing and roaming animals occur in abundance. They occupy one-quarter of the Earth's land area.

Famous Grasslands of the World

Grasslands	Countries
Steppe	Eurasia
Prairie	USA
Pampas	Argentina and Uruguay (South America)
Veld	South Africa
Downs	Australia
Canterbury	New Zealand

Mineral Resources

A naturally occurring substance that has a definite chemical composition is a mineral. Minerals are not evenly distributed over Earth's surface rather concentrated in a particular area or rock formations.

Minerals of the World

Mineral	Leading Producer
Gold	South Africa
Bauxite	Australia
Copper	Chile
Platinum	South Africa
Chromium	South Africa
Vanadium	China
Antimony	China
Tungsten	China
Phosphate	Morocco
Manganese	South Africa
Diamond	Russia
Iron ore	China
Petroleum	The USA/Saudi Arab

Mines of the World

Mine	Mineral
Kimberley (South Africa)	Diamond
Lumbabashi (Zaire)	Copper
Wankee (Zimbabwe)	Coal
Witwatersrand (South Africa)	Gold
Katanga (Zaire-Zambia)	Copper and Cobalt
Kasai Province (Zaire)	Bort Diamond

INDIAN GEOGRAPHY

- India is the 7th largest country in the world with an area of 3287263 sq km, which is 2.42% of world's area. India is the second most populous country in the world with a population of 1.21 billion (2011), which is 17.44% of the world population.
- Indian sub-continent is located in the Northern and Eastern hemisphere.
- India is surrounded by China, Nepal and Bhutan in the North; Myanmar, Bangladesh in East, Sri Lanka in the South and Pakistan in the West. In the South, the Gulf of Mannar and the Palk Strait separate India from Sri Lanka.
- Three oceans protect India's half of the boundary. In East Bay of Bengal, in the South Indian ocean and in West Arabian sea.
- The 82°30′ E longitude is taken as Standard Time Meridian of India i.e. Indian Standard Time (IST), as it passes through the middle of India.
- The Tropic of Cancer (23.5°N latitude) passes through 8 states (Gujarat, Rajasthan, Madhya Pradesh, Chhattisgarh, Jharkhand, West Bengal, Tripura and Mizoram).
- In the Indian sub-continent, India is the only country to share its land frontiers with every member country of the sub-continent.

India : Basic Information

Latitudinal extent	8°4′ North to 37° 6′ North
Longitudinal extent	68°7′ East to 97° 25′ East
North-South extent	3214 km
East-West extent	2933 km
Land frontiers	15200 km
Total coastline	7516.6 km
Number of states	28
Number of Union Territories	8
Land neighbours (7)	Pakistan, Afghanistan, China, Nepal, Bhutan, Bangladesh and Myanmar
States with longest coastline	Gujarat
Active volcano	Barren Island in Andaman and Nicobar Islands
Southernmost point	Indira Point or Pygmalion point in Great Nicobar
Southernmost tip of mainland	Kanyakumari
Northernmost point	Indira Col (Siachen)
Westernmost point	Ghaur Moti in Gujarat
Easternmost point	Kibithu in Arunachal Pradesh

Indian States Situated on the Border

Country	Indian States Situated on the Border
Pakistan	Gujarat, Rajasthan, Punjab, Jammu and Kashmir
Afghanistan	Jammu and Kashmir
China	Jammu and Kashmir, Uttarakhand, Himachal Pradesh, Sikkim and Arunachal Pradesh
Nepal	Uttar Pradesh, Uttarakhand, Bihar, West Bengal, Sikkim
Bhutan	Sikkim, West Bengal, Assam and Arunachal Pradesh
Bangladesh	West Bengal, Assam, Meghalaya, Tripura and Mizoram

Physical Features of India

- India is divided into five parts on the basis of physical division i.e. the Himalayan Range of mountains, the Peninsular plateau, the Great Indian plains, the Coastal plains and the Islands of India.

- Himalayas means 'Abode of Snow' and they are young fold mountains in the world.
- They stretch from the Indus river in the West to the Brahmaputra river in the East.
- They consist of three parallel ranges such as Himadri (Greater Himalayas), Himachal (Lesser Himalayas) and Shiwaliks (Outer Himalayas).

Mountain Peaks in India

Highest Peak	Height (m)	State
Mt K2	8611	PoK (India)
Kanchenjunga	8586	Sikkim
Nanda Devi	7817	Uttarakhand
Saltoro	7742	Jammu and Kashmir
Kangto	7090	Arunachal Pradesh
Reo Purgil	6816	Himachal Pradesh
Saramati	3841	Nagaland
Sandakphu	3636	West Bengal
Khayang	3114	Manipur
Anaimudi	2695	Kerala
Doda Beta	2636	Tamil Nadu

- There are some important passes in the Himalayan ranges of mountains in India. A mountain pass is a route through a mountain range or over a ridge.

Important Passes in India

Pass	Location	Connectivity
Karakoram Pass	Jammu and Kashmir	India to China
Burzil Pass	Jammu and Kashmir	Kashmir valley to Central Asia
Zojila Pass	Jammu and Kashmir	Srinagar to Leh
Shipki La Pass	Himachal Pradesh	Shimla to Gartok (Tibet)
Jelep La Pass	Sikkim	Kalimpong (West Bengal) to Lhasa (Tibet)
Pirpanjal Pass	Jammu and Kashmir	Jammu-Srinagar road passes
Banihal Pass	Jammu and Kashmir	Jammu-Srinagar NH-IA passes from this pass
Rohtang Pass	Himachal Pradesh	Kullu-Keylang road passes from this pass

- To the South of the Himalayas and to the North of the Peninsula lies the great plains of the North India.
- The plains are formed by depositional works of three major river systems i.e. Indus, Ganga and Brahmaputra.
- The vast plains of North India are alluvial in nature and the Western most portion is occupied by the desert.
- The plains are made of Bhangar (old alluvium), Khadar (new alluvium) in the river bed, Bhabar (porous gravel ridden plains at the foothills of Shiwalik and streams disappear here) and Terai (damp, thick forest area, where Bhabar streams reappear).
- The Indian plains are divided into four major plains i.e. the Punjab-Haryana plain, the Rajasthan plain, the Ganga plain and the Brahmaputra plain.
- The deserts found in the Western part of India are hot deserts. It is also known as Thar Desert. The cold deserts are found in the North-Eastern part of Jammu and Kashmir.
- Rising from the height of 150 m above the river plains up to an elevation of 600 – 1000 m in the irregular triangle known as the Peninsular Plateau.
- Some of the Indian plateaus are the central highland, the Deccan Plateau, Meghalaya plateau, the Bundelkhand upland, the Marwar upland and the Chhotanagpur plateau.
- Another important features of India are the coastal plains which are divided into Eastern Coastal Plain and Western Coastal Plain.
- The Eastern Coastal Plain extends from the detaic plains of the Ganga in the North to Kanyakumari in the South. It includes Utkal

Plain, Andhra Coastal Plain and Coromandal coast.

- The Western Coastal plain is about 1500 km long from Surat to Cape Comorin. The plain is sub-divided into Kachchh Plains, Kathiawar Plains, Gujarat Plains, Konkan Coast, Karnataka or Kanara Coast and Malabar Coast or Kerala Coast.
- The Islands are another important physical features of India. India has large number of islands, most of which are located in two groups i.e. Andaman and Nicobar group and Lakshadweep group.
- Group of Islands is called Archipelago.
- Andaman and Nicobar Islands is located in Bay of Bengal. There are nearly 203 Islands in Andaman group whereas there are 7 big and 12 small Islands in Nicobar group.
- Ten degree channel separates Andaman group from Nicobar group. Duncan passage lies between South Andaman and Little Andaman group.
- Lakshadweep Island is located in Arabian sea. Minicoy is the second largest and Southern most island of this group.
- Minicoy is separated from rest of the Lakshadweep by Nine degree channel. Eight degree channel separates Lakshadweep group from Maldives.

Drainage System of India

- Indian rivers can be divided into two main groups i.e. Himalayan rivers and Peninsular rivers.
- The Himalayan rivers are perennial rivers and have large basin. They are divided into three river systems i.e. the Indus system, the Ganga system and the Brahmaputra system.
- The Indus is the Western most of Himalayan rivers in India. It originates from a glacier in the Tibetan region near Mansarovar Lake.

Important Rivers of Indus River System

River	Source	Length (km)	Falls into
Indus	Near Mansarovar Lake	2880	Arabian sea
Jhelum	Verinag	724	Chenab
Chenab	Bara Lacha Pass	1180	Indus
Ravi	Near Rohtang Pass	725	Chenab
Beas	Near Rohtang Pass	460	Sutlej
Sutlej	Mansarovar-Rakas Lake	1450	Chenab

The Ganga system is the second major drainage system of India. It rises in the Gangotri glacier near Gaumukh in the Uttarakhand. Here it is known as the Bhagirathi.

- The Bhagirathi meets the Alaknanda at Dev Prayag, hereafter, it is known as the Ganga.

Important Rivers of Ganga River System

River	Source	Length (km)
Ganga	Gangotri glacier	2525
Yamuna	Yamunotri glacier	1376
Chambal	Near Mhow	960
Ghagra	Near Gurla Mandhata peak, South of Mansarovar	1080
Son	Amarkantak plateau	780
Damodar	Chhotanagpur plateau	541
Gandak	Tibet-Nepal border	425 (in India)
Kosi	Sikkim-Nepal-Tibet Himalaya	730 (in India)

- The Brahmaputra is one of the largest river of the world. It is known as Tsangpo in Tibet, Dihang or Siang in Arunachal Pradesh, Brahmaputra in Assam and Jamuna in Bangladesh.
- Brahmputra forms largest number of riverine islands. Majuli is the largest riverine island in the world.

- The Peninsular river system can be divided into East flowing rivers and West flowing rivers.
- The East flowing rivers form delta whereas the West flowing rivers do not form delta.

East Flowing Rivers

River	Source	Length (km)	Tributaries
Mahanadi	North foothills of Dandakaranya	857	Seonath, Hasdeo, Ib, Mand, Tel, Ong
Godavari	Triambak plateau of North Sahyadri near Nasik	1465 (Longest river of Peninsular India)	Penganga, Wardha, Wainganga, Indravati, Sabari, Manjira
Krishna	North of Mahabaleshwar in the Western Ghat	1400	Bhima, Tungabhadra, Ghatprabha, Malaprabha, Koyna.
Kaveri	Brahmgiri range in Western Ghat	800	Hemavati, Arkavati, Kabani, Bhavani, Amravati

West Flowing Rivers

River	Source	Length (km)	Tributaries
Sabarmati	Mewar in Aravali range	371	Hathmati, Sedhi, Wakul
Mahi	Rises from Vindhayan range	583	Som, Anas, Panam
Narmada (largest West flowing river in Peninsular India)	Amarakantak Plateau	1312	Hiran, Tawa, Banjar, Shar, Shakkar, Burhner
Tapi	Rises near Multai on the Satpura range	724	Purna, Betul, Arunavati
Luni (Salt river)	Rises from Aravalis	495	Jowai, Sukri, Jojari

Climate and Seasons of India

- India has tropical monsoon type of climate. It is greatly influenced by the presence of Himalayas in the North as they block the cold masses from Central Asia.
- The Tropic of Cancer divide India into two almost equal climatic zones i.e. the Northern zone (sub-tropic) and the Southern zone (tropic).
- Indian climate is characterised by distinct seasonality. Indian Meteorological Department (IMD) has recognised four distinct seasons.

Seasons and their Features

Season	Period	Precipitation	Features
Winter	November to March	Cause rainfall in Sub-Himalayan belt by Western disturbances	Clear sky, low temperature and high humidity range of temperature
Summer (Pre-Monsoon)	March to June	Only 1% rainfall of total Indian rainfall mostly by storms by convective current	Dry season, high temperature and low humidity
Rainy	June to September	Rainfall through South-West monsoon	High heat, high humidity, extensive cloud and several spells of moderate to heavy rainfall
Cool	Mid September to November	Retreacting monsoon causes rainfall in Tamil Nadu and adjoining areas of Andhra Pradesh and Kerala	No cloud, severe and devastating tropical cyclone, clear sky

Forests in India

- According to state records, the forest area covers 23.28% of the total land area of the country.
- Madhya Pradesh has the largest areas under forest followed by Arunachal Pradesh.
- The lowest forest percentage is in Haryana and Punjab because of the extensive agriculture.

Types of Forests in India

Forest Type	Distribution	Climatic Conditions	Characteristics
Tropical Evergreen Forests	Rainy slopes of Western Ghats. North-East India except Arunachal Pradesh. Andaman and Nicobar Islands.	Rainfall > 200 cm Relative Humidity > 70% Average temperature is about 24° C. Hot and humid climate.	Height of trees is 40 to 60 m. Leaves are dark, green and broad.
Tropical Moist Deciduous Forests	Eastern parts of Sahyadris (Western Ghats). North-Eastern part of Peninsula. Middle and lower Ganga valley. Foothills of Himalayas in Bhabar and Tarai region.	100 to 200 cm rainfall per annum. Moderate temperature	30 to 40 m high trees. Due to deficiency of water, they shed their leaves in spring (onset of summer).
Tropical Dry Deciduous Forests	Large parts of Maharashtra and Andhra Pradesh. Parts of Punjab, Haryana and Eastern parts of Rajasthan. Northern and Western parts of Madhya Pradesh.	50 to 100 cm rainfall. Moderate humidity	6 to 15 m high. Roots are thick and long.
Dry Forests or Arid Forests	Rajasthan and adjoining areas of Haryana, Gujarat and Punjab. Rainshadow area of Peninsular India.	Low rainfall (less than 50 cm per annum). Relative humidity is less.	Thorny vegetation. Roots are very long. Leaves are small.

Soils in India

- Soils is a valuable resource of India. Much of the Indian agriculture depends upon the extent and qualities of soil.
- Weathering prepares loose materials on the surface of the Earth and mixed with decayed organic matters, it forms soil.
- The nature of soil in a place is largely influenced by such factors as climate, natural vegetation and rocks.

Major Types of Soil in India

Types of Soils	States where Found/Occurrence	Compositions	Crops Grow
Alluvial	Punjab, Haryana, Uttar Pradesh, Bihar, Jharkhand	Rich in potash and lime, but deficient in nitrogen and phosphoric acid	Large variety of Rabi and Kharif crops such as wheat, rice, sugarcane, cotton and jute etc
Black (or Regur soil)	Deccan plateau, Valleys of Krishna and Godavari	Rich in iron, lime, aluminium, magnesium, calcium but lacks in nitrogen, phosphorus and humus	Cotton, sugarcane, jowar, tobacco, wheat, rice etc

Red	Eastern parts of Deccan plateau, Tamil Nadu	Rich in iron and potash but deficient in lime, nitrogen phosphorus and humus	Wheat, rice, cotton, sugarcane and pulses etc
Laterite	Summits of Eastern and Western Ghats, Assam hills	Rich in iron but poor in silica, lime, phosphorus, potash and humus	Tea, coffee, rubber, cashew and millets etc
Desert	West and North-West India, Rajasthan, North Gujarat and Southern Punjab	Rich in soluble salts but deficient in organic matter	Generally unsuitable for cultivation, but with irrigation useful for cultivation of drought-resistant lime, millets, barley, cotton, maize and pulses etc
Mountain	Hills of Jammu and Kashmir, Himachal Pradesh, Uttarakhand and Assam hills	Rich in iron and humus but deficient in lime	With fertilizers, tea, fruits and medicinal plants can be grown
Saline and Alkaline	Drier parts of Bihar, Jharkhand, Uttar Pradesh, Haryana, Punjab, Rajasthan and Maharashtra	Many salts, such as sodium, magnesium and calcium	Unfit for agriculture
Peaty and Marshy	Kerala, coastal regions of Odisha, Tamil Nadu and Sundarbans of West Bengal	Contain large amount of soluble salts and organic matter but lack in potash and phosphates	Useful for rice and jute cultivation

Biodiversity of India

India is a mega-diverse nation housing for around 10% of the world's species. It hosts three biodiversity hotspots i.e. the Western Ghats, the Himalayas and the Indo-Burma region.

Sanctuaries/National Parks Specific to Animals

Sanctuary/Reserve	State	Specific to
Rann of Kutch Wild Ass Sanctuary	Gujarat	Wild Ass
Kaziranga National Park	Assam	One-horned Rhinoceros
Periyar National Park	Kerala	Elephants
Gir National Park	Gujarat	Lions
Ghatigaon Sanctuary	Madhya Pradesh	The Great Indian Bustard
Sundarbans National Park	West Bengal	The Royal Bengal Tiger
Gahirmatha Turtle Sanctuary	Odisha	Olive Ridley Turtle
Vikramshila Gangetic Dolphin Sanctuary	Bhagalpur, Bihar	Dolphins
Ramdevara betta Vulture Sanctuary	Karnataka	Vulture
Daroji Bear Sanctuary	Hampi, Karnataka	Bear
Keibul Lamjao National Park	Loktak Lake (Bishnupur), Manipur	Sangai
Sri Lankemalleswara Wildlife Sanctuary	Andhra Pradesh	Jerdon's Courser
National Chambal Sanctuary	Uttar Pradesh Rajasthan and Madhya Pradesh	Gharial

List of Biosphere Reserves in India

Name	State	Key Fauna	Area (km^2)	Remark
Great Rann of Kutch	Gujarat	Indian Wild Ass	12454	Largest of India
Gulf of Mannar	Tamil Nadu	Dugong or Sea Cow	10500	UNESCO Site
Sundarbans	West Bengal	Royal Bengal Tiger	9630	UNESCO Site
Cold Desert	Himachal Pradesh	Snow Leopard	7770	—
Nandadevi	Uttarakhand		5860	UNESCO Site
Nilgiri	Tamil Nadu, Kerala and Karnataka	Lion-tailed macaque	5520	UNESCO Site
Dihang-Dibang	Arunchal Pradesh		5112	—
Pachmarhi	Madhya Pradesh	Squirrel, Flying Squirrel	4981	UNESCO Site
Seshachalam Hills	Andhra Pradesh		4755	—
Simlipal	Odisha	Gaur, Royal Bengal Tiger	4374	UNESCO Site
Achanakamar-Amarkantak	Madhya Pradesh, Chhattisgarh		3835	UNESCO Site
Manas	Assam	Golden Langur, Red Panda	2837	UNESCO Site
Khangchendzonga	Sikkim	Snow Leopard, Red Panda	2620	UNESCO Site
Agasthyamalai	Kerala, Tamil Nadu	Nilgiri Tahr, Elephants	1828	—
Great Nicobar	Andaman and Nicobar Islands	Saltwater Crocodile	885	UNESCO Site
Nokrek	Meghalaya	Red Panda	820	UNESCO Site
Dibru-Saikhowa	Assam	Golden Langur	765	—
Panna	Madhya Pradesh	Tiger, Chital, Bear	543	UNESCO Site

Agriculture in India

- India is essentially an agricultural land. Two-thirds of its population still lives on agriculture.
- Agriculture is a primary activity which includes farming, animal rearing and fishing.

There are three crop seasons in India

(i) Kharif—Autumn—Rice, Jowar, Bajra, Ragi
(ii) Rabi—Spring—Wheat, Barley, Peas, Rape seed
(iii) Zaid—Summer—Melon, Watermelon, Cucumber

- The different types of farming include Shifting agriculture, Intensive agriculture and Extensive agriculture.
- Green Revolution (1968) in India led to an increase and continuation in the production of foodgrains in India. The components of Green Revolution include use of high yield variety seeds, fertilizers, insecticides and pesticides.

Major Crops and Producing States

Crop Type	Crop Name	Major Producers
Cereals	• Wheat	• Uttar Pradesh, Punjab and Madhya Pradesh
	• Rice	• West Bengal and Uttar Pradesh
	• Gram	• Madhya Pradesh and Tamil Nadu
	• Barley	• Maharashtra, Uttar Pradesh and Rajasthan
	• Bajra	• Maharashtra, Gujarat and Rajasthan
Cash Crops	• Sugarcane	• Uttar Pradesh and Maharashtra
	• Poppy	• Uttar Pradesh and Himachal Pradesh
Oil Seeds	• Coconut	• Kerala and Tamil Nadu
	• Linseed	• Rajasthan, Madhya Pradesh and Haryana
	• Groundnut	• Gujarat, Andhra Pradesh and Tamil Nadu
	• Rape seed and Mustard	• Rajasthan, Madhya Pradesh and Haryana
	• Sesame	• Uttar Pradesh and Rajasthan
	• Sunflower	• Andhra Pradesh, Maharashtra and Karnataka
Fiber Crops	• Cotton	• Maharashtra and Gujarat
	• Jute	• West Bengal and Bihar
	• Silk	• Karnataka and Kerala
	• Hemp	• Madhya Pradesh and Uttar Pradesh
Plantations	• Coffee	• Karnataka and Kerala
	• Rubber	• Kerala and Karnataka
	• Tea	• Assam, West Bengal and Tamil Nadu
	• Tobacco	• Gujarat, Maharashtra and Madhya Pradesh
Spices	• Pepper	• Kerala, Karnataka and Tamil Nadu
	• Cashewnuts	• Kerala, Tamil Nadu and Andhra Pradesh
	• Ginger	• Kerala and Uttar Pradesh
	• Turmeric	• Andhra Pradesh and Odisha

Growing Conditions of Some Important Crops

Crop	Rainfall	Soil
Rice	1500-300 cm	Clay or Loamy, Alluvial
Wheat	80 cm	Well-drained loams and Clay loam
Cotton	50-75 cm	Block soil (Regur), Alluvial or Laterite soils
Sugarcane	100-150 cm	Any type of soil that can retain moisture
Sorghum (Jowar)	∠100 cm	Variety of soils including Clay and Sandy
Jute	Rainfall of 150 cm, with 90% humidity	Light sandy or Clay loams
Tea	125-375 cm, grown on hill slopes	Well drained, deep triable loams or forest soils rich in organic matter

Crop	Rainfall	Soil
Coffee	150-200 cm	Rich well-drained friable loams containing good amount of vegetable mould
Pearl Millet (Bajra)	40-50 cm	Sandy loams, Red and black soils
Finges Millet (Ragi)	50-100 cm	Red, sandy loams and light black
Pulses	50-75 cm	Dry, light soil
Rubber	150-200 cm	Rich well-drained soils
Tobacco	50-100 cm	Well-drained loamy soil, Alluvial or Black soils

Mineral Resources in India

Three types of minerals are as follows

1. **Metallic** Iron ore, copper, aluminium, tin, lead, gold and silver.
2. **Non-Metallic** Coal, mica, manganese, petroleum and sulphur.
3. **Radioactive** Uranium and thorium.

Mineral Resources of India

Mineral	States
Coal	West Bengal, Jharkhand, Odisha, Madhya Pradesh and Chhattisgarh
Copper	Madhya Pradesh, Rajasthan, Jharkhand, Karnataka
Gold	Karnataka, Andhra Pradesh
Iron	Madhya Pradesh, Goa, Karnataka, Andhra Pradesh and Odisha
Bauxite	Odisha, Jharkhand, Madhya Pradesh, Maharashtra, Andhra Pradesh, Gujarat and Tamil Nadu
Mica	Jharkhand, Bihar, Andhra Pradesh and Rajasthan
Petroleum	Assam, Gujarat, Mumbai High, Bassein (South of Mumbai High)
Uranium	Jharkhand, Rajasthan, Andhra Pradesh and Karnataka
Thorium	Kerala Coast, Rocks of Aravali in Rajasthan
Silver, Zinc and Lead	Rajasthan, Andhra Pradesh, Karnataka (Kolar mines)
Diamond	Panna (Madhya Pradesh), Banda (Uttar Pradesh)

Industries in India

- Growth in the Industrial sector is one of the vital figures that affect the Gross Domestic Product (GDP) in India.
- The economy of India is the 7th largest economy in the world.
- India is classified as a newly industrialised country with an average growth rate of 7% (approx.) over the last two decade.
- The Industry sector has held a constant share of its economic contribution (26% of GDP).

Industries in India

Industry	Distribution
Cotton Textile Industry	Maharashtra (Mumbai, Sholapur, Pune, Kolhapur, Satara, Wardha, Aurangabad and Amravati), Gujarat (Ahmedabad, Vadodra, Rajkot, Surat, Bhavnagar, Porbandar, Maurvi and Viramgam), Tamil Nadu (Chennai, Tirunevelli, Madurai, Tuticorin, Salem, Virudhnagar and Pollachi)
Petroleum Industry	Assam, Gujarat, Maharashtra, Bihar
Copper Industry	Gujarat, Andhra Pradesh, Maharashtra, Odisha, Uttarakhand
Jute Textile Industry	West Bengal, Bihar, Uttar Pradesh, Andhra Pradesh, Assam, Odisha, Tripura and Chhattisgarh
Silk Textile Industry	Karnataka is the leading producer followed by West Bengal, Bihar etc
Cement Industry	Madhya Pradesh, Andhra Pradesh, Gujarat, Tamil Nadu
Tea Industry	Nearly 98% of the production comes from Assam, West Bengal, Tamil Nadu and Kerala, while the rest comes from Karnataka, Terai region of Uttar Pradesh, Himachal Pradesh, Arunachal Pradesh Manipur and Tripura
Sugar Industry	Uttar Pradesh is the leading producer of sugar. Uttar Pradesh (Gorakhpur, Deoria, Basti, Gonda, Meerut, Saharanpur, Muzaffarnagar, Bijnor and Moradabad), Bihar (Darbhanga, Saran, Champaran and Muzaffarpur), Punjab
Iron and Steel Industry	Bhadrawati (Karnataka), Jamshedpur (Jharkhand), Durgapur, Burnpur (West Bengal), Bokaro (Jharkhand), Rourkela (Odisha), Bhilai (Chhattisgarh), Salem (Tamil Nadu) and Vishakhapatnam (Andhra Pradesh)
Ship Industry	Cochin Shipyard, Mumbai (Mazagon Dock), Hindustan Shipyard at Vishakhapatnam and Kolkata (Garden Reach workship), Mazagon Dock Limited at Mumbai builts vessels for Indian Navy
Aircraft Industry	Hindustan Aeronautics India Limited was formed by merging two aircraft factories at Bengaluru and Kanpur. Four other factories are at Nasik, Lucknow, Koraput (Odisha) and Hyderabad
Fertiliser Industry	The Fertiliser Corporation of India (FCI) was set-up in 1961. National Fertilizer Limited (NFL) was set up in 1974. Sindri (Bihar), Nangal, Trombay, Gorakhpur (Uttar Pradesh), Durgapur, Namrup, Cochin, Rourkela, Neyveli, Varanasi, Vadodra, Kanpur, Vishakhapatnam and Kota
Heavy Machinery Industry	Durgapur, Mumbai, Ranchi, Vishakhapatnam, Tiruchirapalli and Naini
Machine Tool Industry	It forms the basis for the manufacturing of industrial, defence equipments, automobiles, railway engines and electrical machinery
Heavy Electrical Equipments Industry	Bengaluru, Bhopal, Jammu, Tiruchirapalli, Ramchandrapuram (Hyderabad) and Jagdishpur (Uttar Pradesh)
Coal Industry	Odisha, Jharkhand, West Bengal, Bihar, Chhattisgarh, Telangana and Madhya Pradesh

Energy Resources in India

India is exploiting almost all the sources of energy such as hydroelectricity, thermal energy, nuclear energy, solar energy and wind energy.

Renewable Energy Plants

Types	Plants	States
Wind Energy	• Muppandal • Perungudi • Kayattar • Satara • Jogimati • Lamba, Mandvi	• Tamil Nadu • Tamil Nadu • Tamil Nadu • Maharashtra • Karnataka • Gujarat
Geothermal Energy	Manikaran Puga Valley Tattapani	Himachal Pradesh Jammu and Kashmir Chhattisgarh
Tidal Energy	Gulf of Khambat Gulf of Kachchh Sundarban	Gujarat Gujarat West Bengal
Wave Energy	Vizhinjam	Kerala
Solar Energy	Tirupati	Andhra Pradesh

The Major Atomic Power Stations

Power Station	Location
Tarapur	Maharashtra
Rawatbhata	Rajasthan
Kalpakkam	Tamil Nadu
Narora	Uttar Pradesh
Kakrapara	Gujarat
Kaiga	Karnataka
Kudankulam	Tamil Nadu

Major Thermal Plants

States	Names of the Plant
Haryana	Faridabad, Panipat
Punjab	Bhatinda, Ropar
Delhi	Badarpur Indraprastha
Rajasthan	Kota
Uttar Pradesh	Obra, Panki, Singrauli
Gujarat	Ukai, Sikka, Ahmedabad, Sabarmati
Madhya Pradesh	Satpura, Amarkantak, Pench
Chhattisgarh	Korba, Bhilai
Maharashtra	Nashik, Uran, Chandrapur, Trombay, Dabhol
Andhra Pradesh Telangana	Nellore, Vijayawada, Ramagundam Kothagudam
Tamil Nadu	Ennore, Tuticonn, Neyveli
Bihar	Barauni
Jharkhand	Bokaro
Odisha	Talcher, Rourkela
West Bengal	Kolkata, Titagarh, Durgapur
Assam	Kamrup, Bongagaon
Jammu and Kashmir	Pampore
Tripura	Rokhia

Transportation in India

- Public transport remains the primary mode of transport for most of the Indians.
- India has the second largest railway network in Asia and the fourth largest in the world after the USA, Russia and China.

The Indian railway operate in three different Gauges

(i) Broad Gauges (1.676 m)
(ii) Meter Gauges (1.000 m)
(iii) Narrow Gauges (0.761 and 0.610 m)

- The first Indian railway line was operated in 1853 between Bombay and Thane.
- The second train ran between Hawrah and Hoogly in 1854.
- The first electric train in India was 'Deccan Queen'. It was introduced in 1929 between Bombay and Poona.
- The headquarters of Indian Railway is in New Delhi.
- The fastest train in India is the Vande-Bharat Express (New Delhi-Varanshi) with maximum speed of 180 km/hour.

- The longest train route is 'Vivek Express' from Dibrugarh (Assam) to Kanyakumari (Tamil Nadu). It covers a distance of 4278 km (2658 miles).
- The first metro rail was introduced in Kolkata on 24th October, 1984 connecting two stations of Dumbum and Belgachia.
- The Mumbai Mono rail started in 2014 is the first operational Mono rail in India.

Railway Zones

Zone	Headquarters
Central Railway	Mumbai
Eastern Railway	Kolkata
Northern Railway	New Delhi
North-Eastern Railway	Gorakhpur
North Frontier Railway	Maligaon
Southern Railway	Chennai
South Central Railway	Secundrabad
South-Eastern Railway	Garden Reach, Kolkata
Western Railway	Mumbai (CST)
East Central Railway	Hajipur
East Coast Railway	Bhubaneshwar
North Central Railway	Allahabad
North-Western Railway	Jaipur
South-East Central Railway	Bilaspur
South Western Railway	Hubli
West Central Railway	Jabalpur
Metro Railway	Kolkata
Southern Coast	Visakhapatnam

- The next important transport in India is Roadways. India has one of the largest road networks in the world.
- It consists of National Highways, State Highways, District roads and village roads.
- The Golden Quadrilateral project connecting Delhi, Mumbai, Kolkata and Chennai is currently being processed.
- NH44 is the longest National Highway in India. It covers the North-South corridor and is officialy listed as running over 3745 km from Srinagar to Kanyakumari
- NH5 and NH17 run along the Eastern and the Western coast respectively.
- NH548 & 118 is the shortest highway in India (Both length 5-5 km).
- NH15 represents the border road in Rajasthan desert.

National Highways

NH1	New Delhi-Ambala-Jalandhar-Amritsar-Indo-Pak Border
NH2	Delhi-Mathura-Agra-Kanpur Allahabad-Varanasi-Kolkata
NH3	Agra-Gwalior-Nashik-Mumbai
NH4	Thane-Chennai (via Pune-Beigam)
NH5	Kolkata-Chennai
NH6	Kolkata-Dhule
NH7	Varanasi-Kanyakumari
NH8	Delhi-Mumbai (via Jaipur-Baroda-Ahmedabad)
NH9	Pune-Machilipatnam
NH10	Delhi-Fazilka
NH11	Jaipur-Bikaner
NH12	Jabalpur-Jaipur
NH24	Delhi-Lucknow
NH27	Allahabad-Mangawan
NH28	Barauni-Lucknow
NH29	Varanasi-Pharenda and terminating of Sonali
NH47A	Kundanoor-Willington Island in Kochi

- Airways is another important transport in India. On 18th February, 1911, first commercial plane flew in India between Allahabad and Nainital.
- JRD Tata was the first person to take a solo flight from Mumbai to Karachi in 1931.
- In 1953, all the private airline companies were nationalised. Indian Airlines and Air India came into existence.
- Some new airlines running are Spice Jet, Jet Airways, Kingfisher, Indigo etc.

Some Major International Airports in India

International Airports	City
Begumpet Airport	Hyderabad
Calicut International Airport	Calicut
Chhatrapati Shivaji International Airport	Mumbai
HAL Airport	Bengaluru
Goa Airport (Dabolim Airport)	Dabolim
Netaji Subhash Chandra Bose International Airport	Kolkata
Trivandrum International Airport	Thiruvananathapuram
Lokpriya Gopinath Bordoloi International Airport	Guwahati
Sardar Vallabhbhai Patel International Airport	Ahmedabad
Indira Gandhi International Airport (Delhi International Airport Ltd)	Delhi
Chennai International Airport	Chennai
Raja Sansi International Airport	Amritsar
Devi Ahilya Bai Holker International Airport	Indore

Apart from these, Waterways also play an important role. The government has recognised the following National Waterways of India.

Major Waterways of India

Numbers	Stretches of the Water Way	Specifications
NW1	Allahabad-Haldia (1620 km)	Along Ganga River
NW2	Sadiya-Dhubri (891 km)	Along Brahmaputra River
NW3	Kottapuram-Kollam (205 km)	Along Champakara and Udyogamandal Canal
NW4	Bhadrachalam to Rajahmundry and Wazirabad to Vijaywada (1095 km)	Along Godavari and Krishna River
NW5	Mangalgarhi to Paradeep and Talcher to Dhamara (623 km)	Along Mahanadi and Brahmini River System
NW6	Lakhimpur to Bhanga (121 km)	Along Barak River

The Waterways Authority in India divides Indian ports into three categories i.e. Major, Minor and Intermediate ports.

Eastern Coast Ports

Ports of Eastern Coast	Important Fact
Kolkata	Oldest port, India's riverine port having two dock system (Kolkata Docks & Haldia Docks)
Paradeep	It handles iron-ore and some amounts of coal and dry cargo.
Chennai	All weather port having deep drafted birth, oil jetties, iron-ore terminals etc.
Vishakhapatnam	Seaport and well known for its outstanding performance. It serves the Bhilai and Rourkela Steel Plant.
Tuticorin	Artificial deep sea harbour, all weather port offer direct weekly container service to USA.
Ennore	First corporatised major port in India.
Port Blair	It is one of the major seaport in India.

Western Coast Ports

Ports of Western Coast	Important Fact
Mumbai	It handles maximum traffic, natural harbour, it handles mostly petroleum and dry cargo.
Kandla	Tidal port and important traffic handled are crude oil, petroleum, edible oil, foodgrains.
Marmagao	It handles iron ore. It has a naval base.
New Mangalore	It is an all weather port.
Cochin	Major natural port in Willington Island.
Jawaharlal Nehru	It is called as Nhava Sheva.

- Largest container port of India is Jawaharlal Nehru (Nhava Sheva) port in Mumbai. The largest natural port is in Vishakhapatnam.
- Kandla in Gujarat is a tidal port. It has been made into a free trade zone.
- New Mangalore port is also called the *Gateway of Karnataka*.
- Mumbai port is the busiest port of India.

Demographic Profile of India

- India is the 2nd most populous country in the world with 1.3 billion people which is nearly 1/5th of the world's population.
- India has more than 50% of its population below the age of 25 years and more than 40% below the age of 35 years.
- The sex ratio is 944 females for 1000 males. It comprises 72.56 million males and 58.44 million females.
- Density of population per sq km has been 382 with Delhi being highest with 11,320.
- Literacy rate of India has gone up to 73% from previous figure of 64.83%.
- Population growth during the decade remained 17.7%.

Practice Exercise

1. The position of a planet when it is nearest to the Sun is called
   (a) perihelion (b) apihelion
   (c) apigee (d) perigee
2. Solar eclipes occurs when
   (a) Moon comes between the Sun and the Earth
   (b) the Sun comes between the Earth and Moon
   (c) the Earth comes between the Sun and Moon
   (d) None of the above
3. The lenght of its day and the tilt of its axis are almost identical to those of the earth. This is true of
   (a) Uranus (b) Neptune
   (c) Saturn (d) Mars
4. Who was the first person to land on the Moon?
   (a) Neil Armstrong and Edwin Aldrin
   (b) Neelam Sanjeeva Reddy and Einstein
   (c) Stephen Hawkins and Kingsley
   (d) None of the above
5. During a journey from Earth to Moon and back, the greatest energy required from the spaceships rocket is to overcome
   (a) the Moon's gravity at lunar landing
   (b) the Earth's gravity at take off
   (c) the Moon's gravity at take off
   (d) the Earth's gravity at re-entry into the atmosphere
6. What are comets?
   (a) Celestial bodies with long tail that revolve around the sun
   (b) Small stonelike objects
   (c) Planets between Mars and Jupiter
   (d) None of the above
7. One of the states through which the Tropic of Cancer passes is
   (a) Jammu and Kashmir (b) Himachal Pradesh
   (c) Bihar (d) Jharkhand
8. Rotation of the earth causes deflection of wind by
   (a) Coriolis force (b) Dynamic force
   (c) Gradient force (d) Gravity force
9. Seasonal contrasts are maximum in
   (a) low latitudes (b) high latitudes
   (c) mid latitudes (d) subtropic
10. Planetary winds are those that
    (a) change their direction with change of season
    (b) change their direction with day and night
    (c) never change their direction
    (d) blow up mountain slopes
11. Global warming will melt polar ice caps. The reason why this is a major environmental concern is because it will result in
    (a) increased rise of icebergs
    (b) increased opportunity for oil exploration
    (c) reduced hunting ranges for polar bears
    (d) coastal and land flooding
12. The world's most active volcano
    (a) Fujiyama (b) Cotopaxi
    (c) Kilauea (d) Vesuvius
13. The Tropic of Cancer passes through
    (a) Madhya Pradesh (b) Maharashtra
    (c) Manipur (d) Mizoram
14. Soils are usually formed by the process of
    (a) erosion (b) deposition
    (c) denudation (d) weathering
15. Match the following

List I		List II	
A.	Alluvial Soil	1.	Cotton
B.	Black Soil	2.	Rice
C.	Brown Soil	3.	Tea
D.	Red Soil	4.	Wheat

Codes

	A	B	C	D
(a)	2	3	1	4
(b)	2	1	3	4
(c)	3	1	2	4
(d)	4	1	3	2

16. Which one of the following is a 'cold water's current?
    (a) Gulf stream (b) Venezuala
    (c) Labradore (d) None of these

17. Srinagar is situated on the bank of the river
(a) Ravi (b) Sutlej
(c) Jhelum (d) Chenab

18. Which of the following peninsular rivers is westward flowing?
(a) Mahanadi (b) Godavari
(c) Tapti (d) Cauvery

19. Which of the following pairs is correct?
(a) Berlin - Danube (b) Baghdad - Tigris
(c) Rome - Seine (d) Paris - Tiber

20. The Tibetan river 'Tsangpo' enters India through the State of
(a) Arunachal Pradesh (b) Asom
(c) Manipur (d) Nagaland

21. Which one of the following pairs is not correctly matched?
(a) Indus - Shyok
(b) Ganga - Gandak
(c) Godavari - Musi
(d) Krishna - Tungabhadra

22. The Tigris river flows mainly through
(a) Turkey (b) Syria
(c) Iraq (d) Iran

23. Which of the following rivers falls into the Arabian sea?
(a) Godavari (b) Mahanadi
(c) Mahi (d) Krishna

24. Which of the following river makes Estuary?
(a) Narmada (b) Ganga
(c) Yamuna (d) Luni

25. Which one of the following lakes in India has the highest water salinity?
(a) Dal (b) Chilka
(c) Wular (d) Sambhar

26. The Sivasamudram Falls is on
(a) River Cauvery (b) River Subernarekha
(c) River Indravati (d) None of these

27. Which are the West-flowing rivers of southern India which flow into Arabian Sea?
(a) Chambal and Betwa
(b) Damodar and Mahanadi
(c) Narmada and Tapti
(d) Krishna and Cauveri

28. The largest river island in the world, Majuli is located in which of the following districts of Asom?
(a) Majuli
(b) Dibrugarth
(c) Dhemaji
(d) Tinsukia

29. Which of the following dams is not on the river Narmada?
(a) Koyana (b) Indira Sagar
(c) Sardar Sarovar (d) Gandhi Sargar

30. Which of the following are located in Meghalaya?
(a) Girnar Hills (b) Jaintia Hills
(c) Garo Hills (d) Javadi Hills

31. Wildlife Society of Orissa a voluntary organisation, has brought to the notice of the State Government that the wildlife species of the state is under potential threat of extinction because of
(a) increasing water pollution
(b) increasing urbanisation
(c) indiscriminate mining
(d) rampant poaching

32. Match the following

	List I		List II
A.	Manas	1.	Hangul
B.	Dachigam	2.	Elephant
C.	Mudumalai	3.	Tiger
D.	Kaziranga	4	Rhinoceros

Codes

	A	B	C	D		A	B	C	D
(a)	1	2	3	4	(b)	3	1	2	4
(c)	2	4	3	1	(d)	1	3	2	4

33. Nanda Devi peak forms a part of
(a) Asom Himalayas
(b) Kumaon Himalayas
(c) Nepal Himalayas
(d) Punjab Himalayas

34. Where is the Forest Reserve Institute of India located?
(a) Dehradun (b) Bhopal
(c) Lucknow (d) Delhi

35. Where is the Nanda Devi peak located?
(a) Himachal Pradesh (b) Uttarakhand
(c) Sikkim (d) Nepal

36. Which one of the following is located in the Bastar region?
(a) Bandhavgarh National Park
(b) Dandeli Sanctuary
(c) Rajaji National Park
(d) Indravati National Park

37. Taptapani, a hot spring of Odisha, is situated in the district
(a) Angul (b) Kalahandi
(c) Ganjam (d) Koraput

38. Nandi Hills are situated in the vicinity of
(a) Bangalore (b) Mysore
(c) Hubli (d) Chennai

39. On which river is Jayakwadi project located?
(a) Krishna (b) Godavari
(c) Narmada (d) Cauvery

40. Akal Wood Fossil Park is situated at
(a) Churu (b) Barmer
(c) Jaipur (d) Jaisalmer

41. The 'Nalsarover Bird Sanctuary' is located in
(a) Rajasthan (b) Gujarat
(c) Haryana (d) Kerala

42. Raja Rani, Roarer and Rocket are associated with
(a) Kauveri (b) Krishna
(c) Jog Falls (d) Sringeri

43. Where is Namdapha Wildlife Sanctuary located which is full of flora, fauna and avian with surprising dangers?
(a) Meghalaya (b) Mizoram
(c) Nagaland (d) Arunachal Pradesh

44. Land of the Blue Mountains, lies in the southern most outpost of the North Eastern states is
(a) Meghalaya (b) Mizoram
(c) Arunachal Pradesh (d) Tripura

45. The Vindhyas belong to which class of mountains?
(a) Block mountains (b) Fold mountains
(c) Volcanic mountains (d) Residual mountains

46. Iron ore mines are located in which of the following regions?
(a) Gulbarga (b) Bellary - Hospet
(c) Mysore - Pandya (d) Hubli - Dharwad

47. The State in India having dry season for only 3 to 4 months every year is
(a) West Bengal (b) Kerala
(c) Mizoram (d) Himachal Pradesh

48. Which of the following is correctly matched?
(a) Gulbarga - Karnataka
(b) Midnapur - Gujarat
(c) Wardha - Madhya Pradesh
(d) Cochin - Tamil Nadu

49. The three temples, the Shivadol, the Vishnudol and the Devidol are situated at which place of Asom?
(a) Silghat (b) Sibsagar
(c) Sadiya (d) Sarthebari

50. Which sea lea lies between Jordan and Israel?
(a) Red Sea (b) Caspian Sea
(c) Dead Sea (d) Black Sea

51. Ten Degree Channel is between
(a) Dover and Calais
(b) Alaska and Russia
(c) Little Andaman and Car Nicobar
(d) North Korea and South Korea

52. Niagra waterfall is situated nearest to
(a) Switzerland and Germany
(b) USA and Canada
(c) France and Italy
(d) Denmark and Swedem

53. Which of the following is the deepest landlocked protected port?
(a) Kandla (b) Vishakapatnam
(c) Haldia (d) Tuticorin

54. The canal joining Baltic Sea to North Sea is
(a) Kiel Canal (b) Suez Canal
(c) Panama Canal (d) None of these

55. The busiest and the most important route of the world is
(a) North Pacific Sea Route
(b) North Atlantic Sea Route
(c) South Atlantic Sea Route
(d) Indian Ocean Route

56. The Shompens are the tribal people of
(a) Andaman (b) Nicobar
(c) Lakshadweep (d) None of these

57. Grasses are almost absent in
(a) tropical moist deciduous forest
(b) tropical dry evergreen forest
(c) tropical semi evergreen forest
(d) tropical wet evergreen forest

58. Which of the following two places are connected by the road in India, which is constructed on the highest altitude in the world?
(a) Leh and Manali
(b) Jammu and Srinagar
(c) Sikkim and Darjeeling
(d) Srinagar and Leh

59. 'Brindavan Express' is run between
(a) Chennai and Tiruchi
(b) Chennai and Bangalore
(c) Chennai and Mysore
(d) Bangalore and Mysore

60. Which one of the following countries has the longest international boundary with India?
(a) Bangladesh (b) Bhutan
(c) China (d) Pakistan

Previous Years' Questions

61. Which one of the following tribes lives in the Niyamgiri Hills, which is at the heart of the controversy surrounding Vedanta Resources' mining operations? **[CLAT 2011]**
(a) Manna Dhora (b) Dongria Kondh
(c) Pardhan (d) Mal Pahariya

62. The longest highway in India runs from **[CLAT 2011]**
(a) Kolkata to Jammu
(b) Shillong to Amritsar
(c) Ambala to Nagercoil
(d) Varanasi to Kanyakumari

63. Which of the following oceans has the shape of the English letter 'S'? **[CLAT 2012]**
(a) Atlantic (b) Pacific
(c) Indian (d) Arctic

64. Which strait separates Europe from Africa? **[CLAT 2012]**
(a) Mallaica (b) Gibralter
(c) Berring (d) Palk

65. The longest irrigation canal in India is called
(a) Upper Bari Doab Canal **[CLAT 2012]**
(b) Indira Gandhi Canal
(c) Sirhind Cana
(d) Yamuna Canal

66. Which is the longest shipping canal in the world? **[CLAT 2012]**
(a) Panama Canal
(b) Suez Canal
(c) White Sea-Baltic Canal
(d) Kiel Canal

67. Which pair of states does not touch each other? **[CLAT 2013]**
(a) Meghalaya, Manipur
(b) Chhattisgarh, Uttar Pradesh
(c) Rajasthan, Punjab
(d) Jammu and Kashmir, Himachal Pradesh

68. Baglihar dam, is constructed on river **[CLAT 2013]**
(a) Ravi (b) Chenab (c) Indus (d) Sutlej

69. Which of the following planets has the maximum number of natural satellites? **[CLAT 2014]**
(a) Earth (b) Mars
(c) Jupiter (d) Saturn

70. Which one of the following does not remain to be a planet now? **[CLAT 2014]**
(a) Neptune (b) Uranus
(c) Pluto (d) Venus

71. The change in the colour of stars is linked to **[CLAT 2015]**
(a) variation in their surface temperature
(b) variation in their distance from the earth
(c) fluctuations in their composition and size
(d) irregular absorption or scattering in earth's atmosphere

72. Which of the following is incorrect option? **[CLAT 2015]**
(a) Within the Arctic and Antarctic circles, there is atleast one day in the year during which the Sun does not set and atleast one day on which it never rises
(b) At the North pole, there is darkness for half the year
(c) At summer solstice, the Sun shines vertically over the Tropic of Capricorn
(d) The Sun shines vertically over the equator twice in the year

73. Which one of the following railway zones and the corresponding headquarter pairs is not correctly matched? **[CLAT 2015]**
(a) North-Eastern Railways : Gorakhpur
(b) South-Eastern Railways : Chandigarh
(c) Eastern Railways : Kolkata
(d) South-East Central Railways : Bilaspur

74. .... is the fastest planet to revolve around the Sun. **[CLAT 2016]**
(a) Mercury (b) Jupiter
(c) Venus (d) Mars

75. Mars is also known as the **[CLAT 2016]**
(a) Blue Planet
(b) Red Planet
(c) Green Planet
(d) Brown Planet

76. World's longest rail tunnel is about **[CLAT 2017]**
(a) 1.47 kms
(b) 2.23 kms
(c) 57.09 kms
(d) 4.32 kms

Answers

1	*a*	2	*a*	3	*d*	4	*a*	5	*b*	6	*a*	7	*d*	8	*a*	9	*d*	10	*a*
11	*d*	12	*c*	13	*d*	14	*d*	15	*d*	16	*c*	17	*c*	18	*c*	19	*b*	20	*a*
21	*c*	22	*c*	23	*c*	24	*a*	25	*d*	26	*a*	27	*c*	28	*a*	29	*a*	30	*b*
31	*d*	32	*b*	33	*b*	34	*a*	35	*b*	36	*d*	37	*c*	38	*a*	39	*b*	40	*d*
41	*b*	42	*c*	43	*d*	44	*b*	45	*d*	46	*b*	47	*d*	48	*a*	49	*b*	50	*c*
51	*c*	52	*b*	53	*b*	54	*a*	55	*b*	56	*b*	57	*a*	58	*a*	59	*b*	60	*a*
61	*b*	62	*d*	63	*a*	64	*b*	65	*b*	66	*b*	67	*a*	68	*b*	69	*c*	70	*c*
71	*d*	72	*c*	73	*b*	74	*a*	75	*b*	76	*c*								

CHAPTER 03

INDIAN ECONOMY

India has emerged as the fastest growing major economy in the world as per the Central Statistics Organisation (CSO) and International Monetary Fund (IMF. the Government of India has forecasted that the Indian economy will grow at 7.1% in the financial year 2016-17.

There are three sectors of Indian economy namely primary sector, secondary sector and tertiary sector.

- The **primary sector** of the economy is involved in the extraction or harvesting of products from the Earth. Some of the activities include agriculture, mining, forestry etc.
- The **secondary sector** of the economy is involved in the production of finished goods. Activities include metal working, automobile manufacturing, textile etc.
- The **tertiary sector** of the economy is also called as the service sector. Some of the activities which are part of this sector are retail, transportation, banking etc.

NATIONAL INCOME OF INDIA

- National Income is the net value of all the final goods and services produced by its nationals during a financial year (1st April to 31st March).
- There are three methods for calculating National Income i.e. Product method, Income method and Consumption method.
- The first scientific attempt to measure National Income in India was made by Professor VKRV Rao in 1931-32.

- In 1949, National Income Committee was organised under the chairmanship of Professor PC Mahalanobis.
- **Gross Domestic Product** (GDP) is an important aspect of National Income. It refers to the total value of all the goods and services produced during a given period of time.
- The National Income is calculated by Central Statistical Organisation and National Sample Survey Organisation (NSSO) in India.

Planning in India

- In 1938, **National Planning Committee** was formed under the chairmanship of Jawaharlal Nehru.
- In 1944, Bombay plan was formulated by few Congress men and industrialists to make out a growth map of India.
- After independence, **Planning Commission** was established by Jawaharlal Nehru in 1950 for planned economic development of India.
- Planning Commission was an extra constitutional body, charged with the responsibility of making assessment of all resources of the country and augmenting deficient resources.
- **National Development Council** (NDC) was established by Nehru on 6th August, 1952 to discuss planning issues with States and Union Territories of India.
- In January 2015, NITI (National Institution for Transforming India) Ayog, a policymaking think-tank of government, was established. It replaces Planning Commission and aims to involve states in economic policymaking.
- The Chairman of NITI Ayog is Prime Minister and it also comprises Chief Ministers of states and heads of all Union Territories.

Five Year Plans

- The **First Plan** (1951-56) based on Harrod Domar model gave priority to agriculture. Economist KN Raj was the architect of this plan.
- The **Second Plan** (1956-61), also known as Nehru Mahalanobis plan emphasised on the development of basic and heavy industry.
- The **Third Plan** (1961-66), known as Gadgil Yojana aimed to be self-reliant and self-generating economy. The plan failed to achieve its target due to Indo-China war (1962) and Indo-Pak war (1965).
- From 1966 to 1969 it was a Plan Holiday. Due to the unfortunate failure of the Third plan, the Fourth plan was postponed and three annual plan were implemented.
- The **Fourth plan** (1969-74) laid special emphasis on improving the condition of underprivileged and weaker sections.
- The **Fifth Plan** (1974-79) aimed at removal of poverty and attainment of self-reliance.
- In 1978, Annual Plan was brought out by Janata Party Government under Morarji Desai. The focus of the plan was enlargement of the employment potential in agriculture and allied activities.
- The **Sixth Plan** (1980-85) aimed at removing poverty through strengthening of infrastructure for both agriculture and industry.
- The **Seventh Plan** (1985-90) focused to accelerate foodgrains production and to increase employment opportunities.
- From 1990-1992, Annual Plans were formulated. The Eighth Plan could not take off due to fast changing political situations at the centre.
- The **Eighth Plan** (1992-97) was also called as Rao-Manmohan Singh model. It is the first indicative plan. The aim was to bring improvement in Human Resource Development (education, health, employment).
- The **Ninth Plan** (1997-02) was known as input-output model. The aim was to attain social justice, rural development, job creation and growth with equitable distribution.

- The **Tenth Plan** (2002-07) was called as comprehensive input-output model. It aimed in the development of social infrastructure, employment and energy.
- The **Eleventh Plan** (2007-2012) was also known as Planning Commission Proforma. It aimed at job creation and availability of basic physical and educational services.
- The **Twelfth Plan** (2012-17) aimed at to achieve faster, sustainable and more inclusive growth.

The NITI Ayog established introduced the 15 Years Vision Plan which terminates the concept of 'Five Year Plan'.

DEMOGRAPHY OF INDIA

- Demography is the study of the size, territorial distribution and composition of population, change there in and the components of such changes.

There are four stages of demographic transition.

(i) At the first stage birth and death rates are both high.

(ii) At second stage, birth rate remains high, death rate falls.

(iii) At third stage, birth rate starts to fall and death rate continues to fall.

(iv) At the fourth stage, both birth and death rates are low.

- The year 1921 was a year of the great divide in the demographic history of India when mortality started to decline leading to acceleration in the rate of population growth.
- First census was held in 1872. The first synchronised census was held in 1881, since then at every ten years census is organised.
- The census 2011 is the 15th National Census Survey conducted by the census organisation of India.

Important Data related to Census 2011

Total Population	1210854977
Males	623.7 million
Females	586.46 million
Population (0-6 group)	15,87,89,287
Population Density	382
Literacy	74%
Sex Ratio	940/1000
Child Sex Ratio	914/1000

Human Development Index (HDI)

- HDI measures the average achievements in a country in three basic dimensions of the human development i.e. a long and healthy life, access to knowledge and a decent standard of living.
- The United Nations Development Programme (UNDP) introduced the HDI in its first Human Development Report (HDR) prepared under the stewardship of Mahbub-Ul-Haq in 1990. In the HDR 2016, India has been ranked 131 out of 188 countries in term of HDI.

Three dimensions of HDI are

(i) Life expectancy at birth rate

(ii) Education Index comprising means, year of schooling and expected year of schooling.

(iii) Gross National Income (GNI) per capita (PPP US $) Index.

Agriculture

- Agriculture sector is important in the Indian economy as it contributes 17% to the GDP and 10.2% to the exports. It provides livelihood to more than half of the population.
- **Green Revolution** was launched in the year 1966 as a part of new agricultural strategy. Initially, it included the Intensive Agriculture District Programme (IADP) and later the High Yielding Varieties Programme (HYVP).
- Green Revolution was the brain child of **Norman Borlaug**. In India, it was made successful by Dr **MS Swaminathan**. He is called the Father of Green Revolution in India.

- The achievements of Green Revolution were rise in the production of wheat and rice and increase in employment opportunities.

Major Agricultural Revolution

Revolution	Related to
Yellow Revolution	Oilseeds
White Revolution	Milk
Black Revolution	Petroleum Production
Red Revolution	Meat and Tomato Production
Round Revolution	Potato
Silver Fiber Revolution	Cotton
Blue Revolution	Fish
Pink Revolution	Shrimp
Grey Revolution	Wool
Evergreen Revolution	Overall development of agriculture
Green Revolution	Foodgrains
Golden Revolution	Horticulture
Silver Revolution	Egg and Poultry
Brown Revolution	Cocoa
Rainbow Revolution	Amalgamation of all above revolutions
Second Green Revolution	Change in agricultural production to feed and sustain the growing population

Industry

- Industry refers to an economic activity concerned with the processing of raw materials and manufacture of goods in factories.
- Industry sector has a share of 28% in the overall GDP in India.
- Industrial policies were launched in India in 1948, 1956, 1977, 1980 and 1991.
- The **Industrial Policy, 1956** is called the Economic Constitution of India. It gave the public sector a strategic role in the economy.
- The **Industrial Policy, 1991** aimed at ending license permit raj, integrating Indian economy with the outer world, removing restrictions on FDI, reforming public sectors and restricting the number of sector in which only government can participate.
- Public sector was promoted to capture commanding heights of the economy, i.e. to take up strategic role in the industrialisation of the country.
- In order to promote public sector, the different companies were categorised into Maharatnas, Navratnas and Miniratnas.
- In 2013, New Company bill was introduced. This replaced the six decades Old Company Act, 1956.
- The concept of Navratnas were started in 1997. At present, there are 8 Maharatnas, 16 Navratnas and 74 Miniratnas.

The Indian Currency System

- The present monetary system of India is based on inconvertible paper currency and is managed by the Reserve Bank of India (RBI).
- The present currency system is based on minimum reserve system of note issue. It was adopted in 1957.

Printing of Securities and Minting in India

Security Press	Station	Related to
India Security Press (1922)	Nashik	Postal material, Postal stamps etc
Security Printing Press(Estd. 1982)	Hyderabad	Union excise duty stamps
Currency Notes Press (1928)	Nashik	Bank notes from ₹ 1 to ₹ 100
Bank Notes Press (1974)	Dewas	Bank note of ₹ 20, ₹ 50, ₹ 100, ₹ 500
Modernised Currency Notes Press (1995)	Mysore (Kar) Salbani (West Bengal)	—
Security Paper (Estd. 1967-68)	Hoshangabad	Banks and currency notes paper

Demonetisation

Currency demonetisation is a radical financial step in which a particular currency's status as a legal tender is declared invalid. On 9th December, 2016, Reserve Bank of India withdrew the old ₹ 500 and ₹ 1000 notes as official mode of payment. The reason for this move given was that it will help to tackle black money, help to eliminate fake currency and to lower cash circulation in the country.

BANKING IN INDIA

- The first bank of limited liability managed by an Indian was Oudh Commercial Bank established in 1881. Subsequently Punjab National Bank (PNB) was established in 1894.
- The largest bank Imperial Bank of India was nationalised in 1955 and renamed as State Bank of India followed by formation of its seven associates in 1959.
- The Union Cabinet, on 15th June, 2016, approved the merger of five associate banks as well as Bharatiya Mahila Bank (BMB) with State Bank of India. It is the first move to consolidate the country's struggling public sector banks.
- India's first all women bank, Bharatiya Mahila Bank (BMB) was inaugurated in Mumbai on 19th November, 2013.
- The step toward 'Social Banking' was taken with the nationalisation of 14 Commercial Banks on 19th July, 1969. Six more Commercial Banks were nationalised on 15th August, 1980.
- All Commercial Banks (Indian and foreign), Regional Rural Banks and State Cooperative Banks are Scheduled Banks. Non-Scheduled Banks are those, which are not included in the Second Scheduled of the RBI Act, 1934.
- State Bank of India has the largest network of foreign offices followed by Bank of Baroda. Among private sector banks, ICICI Bank has the largest foreign presence.

Reserve Bank of India (RBI)

- RBI is the Central Bank of the country. It was set-up on the basis of Hilton Young Commission recommendation in April 1935 with the enactment of RBI Act, 1934. Its first Governor was Sir Osborne Smith.
- The main purpose of creating RBI was to separate currency and credit from Government of India.
- RBI was nationalised in 1949 and its first Indian Governor was CD Deshmukh.

Administration of RBI

- The headquarters of the RBI is in Mumbai.
- There are 14 Directors in Central Board of Directors besides the Governor, four Deputy Governors and one Government Official.

Role of RBI

- RBI controls the money market. It acts as guardian of banks and maintaining financial stability. Since 1952, Monetary Policy of the RBI emphasise on twin goals, i.e. economic growth and inflation control.
- RBI controls the money market through various tools like Bank Rate, Repo Rate, Reverse Repo Rate, Statutory Liquidity Ratio and Cash Reserve Ratio.
- **Bank rate** is the rate at which the RBI gives finance to commercial banks.
- **Repo rate** is the rate at which RBI lends short-term money to the banks against securities.

Payment Bank

Payment Banks differ from conventional banks as they are not allowed to lend to customers or issue credit cards.

These banks can accept deposits of up to ₹ 1 lakh and can offer current and saving account deposits. They can also issue debit cards and offer internet banking.

- **Reverse Repo rate** is the rate at which banks park short-term excess liquidity with the RBI.
- **Statutory Liquidity Ratio** (SLR) is the ratio of liquid asset which all commercial banks have to keep in the form of cash, gold and unrestricted approved securities.
- **Cash Reserve Ratio** (CRR) is the cash reserve which every bank needs to keep with the RBI.

MUDRA Bank

- Micro Units Development and Refinance Agency Bank (or MUDRA Bank) was launched on 8th April, 2015 with a corpus of ₹ 20000 crore and a credit guarantee corpus of ₹ 3000 crore.
- It is a public sector financial institution in India. It provides loans at low rates to small entrepreneurs. MUDRA Bank will be set-up through a statutory enactment. It is a 100% subsidiary of SIDBI.

  MUDRA Bank has launched three loan instruments
  - Shishu-covers loans upto ₹ 50000
  - Kishor-covers loans above ₹ 50000 and upto ₹ 5 lakh
  - Tarun-covers loans above ₹ 5 lakh and upto ₹ 10 lakh

All India Financial Institutions At a Glance

Financial Institutions and their Headquarters	Purpose
Industrial Finance Corporation of India (IFCI) 1948, New Delhi	To grant loans advances to industrial concerns and subscribe to debentures floated by them.
State Finance Corporations (SFCs), 1951	To finance the needs of the small-scale and medium sized industries in respective states.
Industrial Credit and Investment Corporation of India (ICICI) 1955, Mumbai	To stimulate the promotion of new industries and assist in modernisation of existing industries.
Industrial Development Bank of India (IDBI) 1964, Mumbai	To meet the financial needs of industrialisation and co-ordinate with all other agencies concerned with industrial development finance.
Industrial Investment Bank of India (IIBI), 1985	To assist the industrial units in Eastern region.
Small Industries Development Bank of India (SIDBI), Lucknow	To promote, finance and development Industry in small scale sector.
Unit Trust of India (1964) (UTI)	To stimulate and pool the savings of the middle and low income groups.
National Housing Bank (NHB) 1988, New Delhi	To track prices of residential properties in India.
EXIM Bank (1982), Mumbai	To finance, facilitate and promote foreign trade in India.
Tourism Finance Corporation of India Limited (TFCI)—1989, New Delhi	To provide assistance to tourism related activities/projects.
Mutual Funds	To mobilise the savings of the general public and invest them in stock market securities.
Venture Capital Funds	To give commercial support to new ideas and for the introduction and adaptation of new technologies.

Insurance Sector

- Insurance industry includes two sectors: **Life Insurance** and **General Insurance**.
- Life insurance in India was introduced by Britishers. A British firm in 1818 established the **Oriental Life Insurance Company** at Calcutta now Kolkata.
- Since the opening up, the number of participants in the Insurance Industry have gone up from 7 insurers (including Life Insurance Corporation (LIC) four public sector general insurers, one specialised insurer and the General Insurance Corporation (GIC) as the national re-insurer) in 2000 to 49 insurers as on 30th September, 2011.

Indian Financial System

- Financial system refers to the borrowing and lending of funds for the demand and supply of funds of all individuals institutions, companies and of the government.
- The Indian Financial System consists of two parts, *viz*, Indian money market and the Indian capital market.
- **Money Market** This is a market for 'near money' or it is the market for borrowing and lending of short-term funds.
- **Capital Market** Capital market is concerned with provision of raising long-term funds of maturity 1 year or more.

Stock Exchange in India

- Stock exchange or share market deals in shares, debentures and financial securities.
- There are 23 stock exchanges in India. Among them two are national level stock exchanges namely Bombay Stock Exchange (BSE) and National Stock Exchange (NSE). The rest 21 are Regional Stock Exchanges (RSE).

Bombay Stock Exchange (BSE)

- It is a stock exchange located on Dalal Street, Mumbai, Maharashtra. It is the 11th largest stock exchange in the world by market capitalisation as on 31st December, 2012.
- It was established in 1875. It was (formerly known as **Bombay** Stock Exchange Ltd.). It is the India's oldest stock exchange, one of Asia's oldest stock exchange and one of India's leading exchange groups.

National Stock Exchange (NSE)

- It is the country's leading stock exchange located in the financial capital of Mumbai, India.
- National Stock Exchange (NSE) was established in the mid 1990s as a demutualised electronic exchange.

Fiscal Policy

It is the means by which a government adjusts its spending levels and tax rates to monitor and influence a nation's economy.

Sources of Revenue

Main sources of revenue are customs duties, excise duties, service tax, taxes on property, corporate tax, income taxes.

Structure of Taxes

Direct Tax	Indirect Tax
Personal Income Tax	Excise Duty
Corporation Tax	Custom Duty
Wealth Tax	Sales Tax
Gift Tax	Service Tax
Land Revenue	Value Added Tax
Profession Tax	Passenger Tax
Stamp Duty and Registration Charges	Entertainment Tax
Securities Transaction Tax	Electricity Duty
Banking Cash Transaction Tax	Motor Vehicles Tax

Sources of Expenditure

- **Plan Expenditure** It consists expenditure on agriculture, rural development, irrigation and flood control, energy, industry, minerals, transport and communications etc.
- **Non-Plan Expenditure** It consists expenditure on payments, defence, subsidies and general services.

Public Debt

- **Internal Debt** It consists loans raised from the open market treasury bills issued to the RBI, Commercial Banks etc.
- **External Debt** It consists of loans taken from World Bank, International Monetary Fund (IMF), Asian Development Bank (ADB) and individual countries.

GST (Goods and Services Tax)

GST in India implemented from 1st July, 2017. Two components one levied by the centre (referred to as Central GST) and the other levied by the states (referred to as State GST), rates for which would be prescribed appropriately.

- **Central Taxes replaced by GST Bill** Central Excise Duty, Additional Duties of Excise and Customs, Special Additional Duty of Customs (SAD), Service Tax and Cesses and Surcharges on supply of goods and services.
- **State Taxes Subsumed in the GST Bill** Vat, Central Sales Tax, Purchase Tax, Luxury Tax, Entry Tax, Entertainment Tax, Taxes on advertisements, lottery, betting, gambling and State Cesses and Surcharges.
- Under GST, goods and services are taxed at the rates of 0%, 5%, 12%, 18% and 28%. There are special rate of 0.25% and 3% on rough precious and semi precious stones and 3% of gold.

Finance Commission

- Finance Commission is constituted to define financial relations between the centre and the state.
- The 14th Finance Commission appointed under the chairmanship of Dr YV Reddy gave its recommendation on principles which would govern the quantum and distribution of grant-in-aid along with other primary areas it deals with
- The 15th Finance Commission oppointed under the chairman of N.K. Singh. This Commission recommended path for fiscal deficit for the central and states will result in a reduction of total liabilities of (i) the centre from 62.9% of GPD in 2020-21 to 56.6% in 2025-26 (ii) the states on aggregate from 33.1% of GPD in 2020-21 to 32.5% by 2025-26.

Balance of Payment (BOP)

- The Balance of Payment (BoP) records the transactions in goods, services and assets between residents of a country with the rest of the world for a specified time period typically a year.
- There are two main accounts in the BoP, the Current Account and the Capital Account. In addition to that BoP comprises-errors and omissions and change in foreign exchange reserves.

Current Account

Current Account transactions are classified into merchandise (exports and imports) and invisibles.

Invisibles *These are transactions classified into three categories namely*

(i) Services travel (ii) Income (iii) Transfers

Capital Account

- Under Capital Account, capital inflows can be classified by instrument (debt/equity) and maturity (short/long-term).
- The main component of capital account include foreign investment, loans and banking capital.

Foreign Direct Investment (FDI)

FDI is a type of investment that involves the injection of foreign funds into an enterprises that operates in a different country of origin from the invester. FDI plays an extraordinary and growing role in global business.

The three main institutions that handle FDI related issues in India are

- The Foreign Investment Promotion Board (FIPB).
- The Foreign Investment Implementation Authority (FIIA)
- The Secretariat for Industrial Assistance (SIA).

Union Budget

- The budget is an extensive account of the government's finances, in which revenues from all sources and expenses of all activities undertaken are aggregated.
- The Finance Minister presents the Union Budget every year in the Parliament that contains the Government of India's revenue and expenditure for one fiscal year, which runs from 1st April to 31st March.

- **John Mathai** proposed the first budget of Republic of India in 1950 and also the creation of Planning Commission.

> Finance Minister **Morarji Desai** has given budget for the maximum number of times (10) followed by **P Chidambaram**, who has presented given 8 times union-budgets.

Major Types of Budgeting

There are three types of budgeting, which are given as under

1. **Outcome Budgeting** This type of budgeting tries to ensure that budget outlays translate into concrete outcomes.
2. **Zero-Based Budgeting** It is a method of budgeting, in which all budgetary allocations are set to nil at the beginning of a financial year.
3. **Gender Budgeting** It came into effect in 2004-05. To contribute towards the women empowerment and removal of inequality based on gender, role of budgeting has been accepted through this step.

Inflation, Deflation and Stagflation

- **Inflation** means a persistent rise in the general price level of goods and services leading to a fall in the currency's purchasing power.
- **Deflation** A general decline in prices, often caused by a reduction in the supply of money or credit. Deflation can be also caused by a decrease in government, personal or investment spending. The unemployment since there is a lower level of demand in the economy, which can lead to an economic depression.
- **Stagflation** When you have a slow economy with high inflation rates and unemployment stagflation is usually resultant. When the economy does not grow and prices continue to rise have a stagflation cycle in the economy.

International Financial Institutions

There are some International Financial Institutions, which are given as under

International Monetary Fund (IMF)

- IMF was conceived on 22nd July, 1944 and came into existence on 27th December, 1945, when 29 countries signed the agreement. It originally had 45 members. India is the founding member.
- IMF at present has 189 members and headquartered at Washington DC. The capital resources of the IMF comprise Special Drawing Rights (SDRs) and currencies that member pay under quotas calculated for them when they join the IMF.

World Bank (WB)

- World Bank is the institution created at the **Bretton Woods Conference** in 1944. Along with the IMF, it constitutes **'twin-sister'** of Bretton Woods.
- World Bank has 189 members and is headquartered in Washington DC.
- The World Bank provides loans to developing countries for capital programme and its official goal is reduction of poverty.
- International Finance Corporation (IFC) was established in 1956, to provide loans to private industries of developing nations.
- International Development Association (IDA), known as the **soft loan window** of the World Bank was established on 24th September, 1960.
- International Centre for Settlement of Investment Disputes (ICSID) was established in 1966, to provide facilities for the conciliation and arbitration of investment disputes between member countries. It has 157 members.

- Multilateral Investment Guarantee Agency (MIGA) was founded in 1988 to promote foreign direct investment into developing countries. It has 175 members.

World Trade Organisation (WTO)

- It was constituted on 1st January, 1995, under the **Marrakesh Agreement** and took the place of GATT (General Agreement on Trade and Tariff) as an effective formal organisation. GATT was an informal organisation, which regulated world trade since, 1948.
- It is headquartered at Geneva. At present, it has 164 members. (Afghanistan has become the 164th WTO member).

Asian Development Bank (ADB)

It was established in December, 1966 with the aim to accelerate economic and social development in Asia and Pacific region. It is headquartered at **Manila**, Philippines.

Asian Infrastructure Investment Bank (AIIB)

It is a Multilateral Development Bank (MDB) conceived for the 21st century. Chinese President Xi Jinping and Premier Li Keqiang announced the AIIB initiative during their respective visits to South-East Asian countries in October 2013.

Schemes Related to Various Sectors of Economy

Government of India in the process of poverty eradication, employment and reducing gender discrimination have been implementing various schemes and programmes towards development and empowered people through generating more employment and skill development as well.

Employment and Skill Development Schemes

Startup Standup India (15th Aug, 2015)	• 'Startup India' is a revolutionary scheme that has been started to help the people who wish to start their own business. • 'Standup India' Scheme facilitates bank loans between ` 10 lakh and ` 1 crore to at least one Scheduled Caste (SC) or Scheduled Tribe (ST) borrower and at least one woman borrower per bank branch for setting up a greenfield enterprise.
Pradhan Mantri Kaushal Vikas Yojana (April 2015)	• It provides encouragement to youth for development of employable skills by providing monetary rewards.
Pradhan Mantri Mudra Yojana (8th April, 2015)	• Under the Micro Units Development and Refinance Agency (MUDRA) Bank is a new institution being setup by Government of India for development and refinancing activities relating to micro units. • Under the scheme, three categories are– Shishu, Kishore and Tarun.
Prime Minister's Employment Generation Programme (PMEGP) (2008)	• This scheme aims to generate employment opportunities in rural as well as in urban areas through setting up of self-employment ventures/projects/micro enterprises.
Mahatma Gandhi National Rural Employment Guarantee Scheme (MGNREGS) (2nd Feb, 2006)	• The scheme was notified throughout the country with effect from 1st April, 2008. Renamed as MGNREGS from 2nd Oct, 2009. Swarna Jyanti Gram Rozgar Yojana and Food for Work Programme merged into it. • It aims at enhancing livelihood security to households in rural areas of the country by providing at least 100 days (150 days for rain hit areas) guaranteed wage employment in a financial year to every household, whose adult members volunteer to do unskilled manual work. It also mandates 33% participation for women. The primary objective of the scheme is to augment wage employment.

Financial Inclusion Related Schemes

Pradhan Mantri Jan Dhan Yojana (28th Aug, 2014)	• The aim of this scheme to tie every Indian in the rural or urban sector to the mainstream banking system. • Its offers a life cover of ₹ 30000 and Accidental insurance of ₹ 200000. • 100% financial inclusion.
Direct Benefit Transfer (DBT) (1st Jan, 2013)	• It is an attempt to change the mechanism of transferring subsidies launched by Government of India. • The programme aims to transfer subsidies directly to the people through their bank accounts.

Social Security Schemes

Atal Pension Yojana (9th May, 2015)	• This pension yojana is targeted at the unorganised sector in India. • It is available to people between 18 and 40 yrs of age with bank accounts. • The subscribers are required to opt for a monthly pension from ₹ 1000 to ₹ 5000.
Pradhan Mantri Jeevan Jyoti Bima Yojana (9th May, 2015)	• This scheme provide life insurance of ₹ 2 lakh with a premium of ₹ 330 per year. • This yojana is available to people between 18 and 50 yrs of age with bank account.
Pradhan Mantri Suraksha Bima Yojana (9th May, 2015)	• It is available to people between 18 and 70 yrs of age with bank accounts. • It has an annual premium of ₹ 12 for ₹2 lakh accidental and ₹ 1 lakh full disability.
Pradhan Mantri Ujjwala Yojana (1st May, 2016)	• It was launched to provide free LPG connections to women from Below Poverty Line (BPL) families.
Deen Dayal Upadhyaya Antyodaya Yojana (25th Sep, 2014)	• This scheme is for uplift of urban and rural poor through enhancement of livelihood opportunities through skill development and other means.

Women and Child Development Schemes

Beti Bachao, Beti Padhao (22nd Jan, 2015)	It aims to generate awareness and improve the efficiency of welfare services meant for women.
National Mission for Empowerment of Women (NMEW) (2010)	This scheme aims to achieve empowerment of women socially, economically and educationally by securing convergence of schemes.
Rajiv Gandhi Scheme for Empowerment of Adolescent Girls (RGSEAG) 'Sabla' (19th Nov, 2010)	It aims at empowering adolescent girls of 11 to 18 yrs by improving their nutritional and health status, upgradation of home skills, life skills and vocational skills.
Indira Gandhi Matritva Sahyog Yojana (IGMSY) (2010)	It aims to improve the health and nutrition status of pregnant, lactating women and infants.
Mid-Day Meal Scheme (largest feeding school programme in the world)	This scheme was launched for improving the nutritional status of children in Classes I-VIII in government, local body and government-aided schools. Its other objective was to enable the disadvantaged and the poor children to attend school regularly.

Infrastructure and Manufacture Development Schemes

PM Gati Shakti Scheme (25 Oct, 2021)	It is an multi-model connectivity plan with the aim of coordinated planning and execution of infrastructure projects to bring down logistics costs.
Shyama Prasad Mukherjee Rurban Mission (21st Feb, 2016)	This mission aims at development of rural growth clusters which have latent potential for growth, in all States and UTs, which would trigger overall development in the region.
Deen Dayal Upadhyaya Gram Jyoti Yojana (25th July, 2015)	The scheme has replaced the existing Rajiv Gandhi Grameen Vidyutikaran Yojana. It aims to provide electrification to all village.
Atal Mission for Rejuvenation and Urban Transformation (AMRUT) (25th June, 2015)	It aims to enable better living and drive economic growth stressing on the need for people centric urban planning development.
Namami Gange Scheme (13th May, 2015)	It aims to clean and protect the Ganga river in a comprehensive manner.
Housing for ALL by 2022 (21st June, 2015)	Under this scheme, more than 2.9 crore homes would be built across all the urban locations in the next 7 yrs.
Swachch Bharat Abhiyan (2nd Oct, 2014)	It is a national campaign by the Government of India, covering 4041 statutory cities and towns, to clean the streets, roads and infrastructure of the country.
HRIDAY - Heritage City Development and Augmentation Yojana (21st Jan, 2015)	This is scheme seeks to preserve and rejuvenate the rich cultural heritage of the country.
Sansad Adarsh Gram Yojana (11th Oct, 2014)	It is a rural development programme broadly focusing upon the development in the villages which includes social development, cultural development and spread motivation among the people on social mobilisation of the village community.
Make in India (25th Sep, 2014)	It is an initiative launched by the Government of India to encourage multinational, as well as national companies to manufacture their products in India.
Digital India (August) (2014)	It is a major flagship programme of the Government of India, aimed at transforming the country into a digitally empowered social and knowledge economy, as well as to revive the state of governance in the country. It is an 'Umbrella Programme' weaving together many existing schemes under multiple ministries and departments to ensure that its services are available to citizens electronically.
Pradhan Mantri Gramodya Yojana (PMGY) (2000)	It focuses on village level development in five critical areas, i.e. primary health, primary education, housing, rural roads and drinking water and nutrition with the overall objective of improving the quality of life of people in rural areas.

Agriculture Development Schemes

PM Kisan Samman Nidhi Yojna (Dec. 2018)	It is a central government scheme. This scheme provide ₹ 6000 per year financial assitance to those farmers have cultivable area upto 2 hectares. ₹ 6000 per year will be paid in three installments.
Pradhan Mantri Fasal Bima Yojana (18th Feb, 2016)	It is the new crop damage insurance scheme. It will replace the existing two crop insurance schemes National Agricultural Insurance Scheme (NAIS) and Modified NAIS.
Pradhan Mantri Krishi Sinchai Yojana (2nd July, 2015)	The primary objectives of this scheme are to attract investments in irrigation system at field level, develop and expand cultivable land in the country. It also aims is to enhance ranch water use in order to minimise wastage of water, enhance crop per drop by implementing water saving technologies and precision irrigation.

Practice Exercise

1. Which of the following body estimation National Income in India?
(a) RBI
(b) Planning Commission
(c) Finance Commission
(d) Central Statistical Organisation

2. National income is the same as
(a) Net Domestic Product at market price
(b) Net Domestic Product at cost factor
(c) Net National Product at market price
(d) Net National Product at factor cost

3. Net National Product (NNP) of a country is
(a) GDP minus depreciation allowances
(b) GDP plus net income from abroad
(c) GNP minus net income from abroad
(d) GNP minus depreciation allowances

4. GDP at factor cost is
(a) GDP minus indirect taxes plus subsides
(b) GNP minus depreciation allowances
(c) NNP plus depreciation allowances
(d) GDP minus subsidies plus indirect taxes

5. Which one of the following is not a method of measurement of National Income?
(a) Value Added Method
(b) Income Method
(c) Expenditure Method
(d) Investment Method

6. Planning Commission has been scrapped and replaced by a new think tank called
(a) National Institution for Transforming India Ayog
(b) National Rural Development Commission
(c) National Commission for Progress and Development
(d) National Research and Development Commission

7. ______ has developed the concept of Human Development Index in ____
(a) Mehboob-ul-Haq, 1990
(b) Avinash Dixit, 1999
(c) Jagdish Bhagwati, 1980
(d) Amartya Sen, 1970

8. Which of the following measures the value of a currency against a basket of other currencies?
(a) Real Exchange Rate
(b) Effective Exchange Rate
(c) Real Effect Exchange Rate
(d) Nominal Exchange Rate

9. Which of the following banks overtook Wells Fargo as the most valuable bank in USA?
(a) JS Morgan Chase (b) HSBC
(c) Citigroup (d) Bank of America

10. In India, three women had held the post of Deputy Governor of RBI. Which of the following is not amongst them?
(a) KJ Udeshi (b) Usha Thorat
(c) Dr Isher J Ahluwalia (d) Shyamala Gopinath

11. Bank rate is the rate at which
(a) a bank lends to the public
(b) the Reserve Bank of India lends to the public
(c) the Government of India lends to other countries
(d) the Reserve Bank of India gives credit commercial banks

12. ______ has become the first bank in India to introduce software robotics in power banking.
(a) HDFC (b) ICICI
(c) SBI (d) Yes Bank

13. Financial is a banking solutions software which was awarded, 'Core Banking Technology Provider of the Year' award in July 2012. Financial is from which software company?
(a) Wipro (b) TCS
(c) Infosys (d) Cognizant

14. Which of the following non-banking finance companies is not allowed to convert itself into a Bank?
(a) Birla Mutual Fund
(b) Tata Finance
(c) Peerless Finance
(d) Kotak Mahindra Finance Ltd.

15. ______ is not a component of the Li Keqiang Index.
(a) Bank loans
(b) Export
(c) Electricity consumption
(d) Railway freight

16. Train travel insurance in India is available at a premium of _____ with effect from 7th October, 2016.
(a) 1 rupee (b) 2 rupees
(c) 92 paisa (d) 1 paisa

17. What do you understand by Bear Raid?
(a) An attempt to bring down the price of strong short selling
(b) Simultaneous buying shares and debentures in view of getting more values in near future
(c) Higher rate of price paid for particular government share or debentures
(d) Any of the above

18. The foreign exchange reserves of India include
(a) gold (b) SDRs
(c) foreign currencies (d) All of these

19. Who propounded the 'market law'?
(a) Adam Smith (b) JB Say
(c) TR Malthus (d) David Ricardo

20. The term 'Paper Gold' means
(a) Special Drawing Rights (SDR) of the IMF
(b) Special accommodation facility of the World Bank
(c) Currencies Still on Gold Standard
(d) Deficit Financing

21. What is the NASDAQ?
1. World's first electronic stock market
2. World's largest shipping fleet
3. World's highest postal office
4. Another name for New York Stock Exchange

Select the correct answer using the codes given bleow
(a) 1 and 4 are correct (b) Only 1 is correct
(c) Only 4 is correct (d) All are incorrect

22. 'WPI' is used as an acronym for
(a) World Price Index
(b) Wholesale Price Indicators
(c) Wholesale Price Index
(d) World Price Indicators

23. The principal source of revenue to the State Government in India is
(a) Income Tax
(b) Sales Tax
(c) State Excise Duties
(d) Land Revenue

24. Depreciation is equal to
(a) Gross National Product- Net National Product
(b) Net National Product-Gross National Product
(c) Gross National Product-Personal Income
(d) Personal Income-Personal Taxes

25. 'Devaluation' means
(a) converting rupee into gold
(b) lowering of the value of one currency in comparison of some foreign currency
(c) making rupee dearer in comparison to some foreign currency
(d) None of the above

26. Which of the following is at the apex of Industrial Finance in India?
(a) Industrial Finance Corporation
(b) Reserve Bank of India
(c) Industrial Development Bank of India
(d) Industrial Credit and Investment Corporation of India

27. The term fiscal deficit means
(a) total receipts minus expenditure
(b) total receipts minus interest payments on external debt
(c) revenue receipts minus expenditure
(d) revenue receipts minus defence expenditure

28. Among the remedies of inflation, we cannot include
(a) better capacity utilisation
(b) lowering bank rate
(c) reducing budgetary deficit
(d) an efficient public distribution system

29. Structural unemployment arises due to
(a) deflationary conditions
(b) heavy industry bias
(c) shortage of raw material
(d) inadequate productive capacity

30. The largest revenue source in India is
(a) Sales Tax (b) Income Tax
(c) Excise Duty (d) Export Duty

31. What is the primary objective of the Governments in opting for deliberate devaluation of currency?
(a) Boosts import
(b) Boosts internal trade
(c) Boosts exports
(d) Increase gold reserves

32. ______ for States and ______ for Union Territories is the new limit of flexible fund decided by the government in the Centrally Sponsored Schemes in order to give more freedom of operation in these schemes.
(a) 25%, 30% (b) 20%, 30%
(c) 10%, 35% (d) 50%, 20%

33. One rupee note in India was issued by
(a) Reserve Bank of India
(b) Union Government of India
(c) Governor of Reserve Bank of India
(d) Central Bank of India

34. What is the name of the innovative Council proposed in the Railway Budget-2015 to promote innovation?
(a) Navachar (b) Rail Tech
(c) Kayakalp (d) Sankalp

35. Temporary tax levied to obtain revenue is called
(a) Cess (b) Sales tax
(c) Revenue tax (d) Surcharge

36. What does 'IPO' means in the securities market?
(a) Investment Plan Offer
(b) Investment Promotion Order
(c) Initial Public Offer
(d) Industrial Plan Order

37. The Union Government has decided to withdraw the benefit of subsidised LPG to the customers having income above
(a) ₹ 7.5 Lakh (b) ₹ 10 Lakh
(c) ₹ 12.5 Lakh (d) ₹ 15 Lakh

38. Nobel Prize in Economics for 2016 has been given to Oliver Hart and Bengt Holmstrom for their contribution to
(a) Contract theory
(b) Imperfect competition
(c) Game theory
(d) Limitations on state intervention in market economy

39. Which of the following Indian company got the top rank among Indian companies in Top 500 companies list of fortune India?
(a) Indian Oil Corporation
(b) ONGC
(c) RIL
(d) SAIL

40. Which country was chosen to chair Partnership in Population and Development (PPD) for the year 2015?
(a) India (b) China
(c) Sri Lanka (d) Ghana

41. The World Bank and IMF gives respectively
(a) long term and short term credits
(b) short term and long term credits
(c) both long term credits
(d) both short term credits

42. In the United Nations, who decides the quantum of contribution of each member to the income resources of the UN?
(a) Trusteeship Council
(b) Economic and Social Council
(c) Security Council
(d) General Assembly

43. Special Economic Zones in India means
(a) the places where industries get certain incentives and / or tax advantages
(b) the places where industries can operate without any control
(c) the places wherein any person can start any industry
(d) the places wherein the national labour laws do not apply

44. When the employer is held liable for the wrongful act of his employee, the liability is called
(a) absolute liability
(b) tortuous liability
(c) vicarious liability
(d) atrict liability

45. Which one of the following is the central theme of 'The Communist Manifesto' written by Marx and Engels?
(a) Tools of Production (b) Theory of State
(c) Abolition of State (d) Class Struggle

46. Trade Mark can be defined as
(a) the name of the company manufacturing different models of the same article
(b) a mark on one commodity irrespective of the fact as to its manufacturer
(c) a private limited firm and its goods
(d) a mark on the articles by the manufacturer to distinguish his make from those of others

47. ISO-9000 certificate is a stringent quality control standard for electronic goods that are essential for any Indian exporter to compete in international markets. It is issued by the
(a) Bureau of Indian Standards
(b) British Standards Institution
(c) UN Exports Agency
(d) International Organisation for Standardisation

48. The Ex-officio Secretary of NDC is
(a) Secretary of Finance Ministry
(b) General Secretary of Lok Sabha
(c) Secretary of Planning Commission
(d) Vice-Chairman of Planning Commission

49. Which of the following is not 'Free Trade Zone'?
(a) Kandla (b) Mumbai
(c) Visakhapatnam (d) Trivandrum

50. As per agreement on 10th July, 2012, the World Bank will extend additional credit of $ 10 million to which Indian State, towards implementation of 'Rural Livelihood' Project name "Jeevika"?
(a) Andhra Pradesh (b) Bihar
(c) Rajasthan (d) Maharashtra

Previous Year's Questions

51. Mahatma Gandhi National Rural Employment Guarantee Act (MGNREGA) completed how many years of operation in 2011? **[CLAT 2012]**
(a) 3 yrs (b) 4 yrs
(c) 5 yrs (d) 6 yrs

52. Excess of money supply as compared to supply of goods results in **[CLAT 2012]**
(a) depression
(b) deflation
(c) trade deficit
(d) inflation

53. The 'Eleventh Five Year Plan' envisaged the highest growth in the sector of **[CLAT 2012]**
(a) industry (b) agriculture
(c) services (d) manufacturing

54. To which country does India export the largest quantity of iron ore? **[CLAT 2012]**
(a) USA (b) Japan
(c) Egypt (d) Germany

55. As per the Indian Union Budget of 2012-13, the income tax exemption limit for persons below 65 yrs of age is **[CLAT 2012]**
(a) ₹ 175000 (b) ₹ 200000
(c) ₹ 250000 (d) ₹ 190000

56. Dr Norman Borlaug is famous as Father of the Green Revolution in 1960s. His initial goal was to create varieties of wheat adapted to the climate of **[CLAT 2013]**
(a) Mexico (b) India
(c) USA (d) China

57. In 2012-13, India's target is to restrict the fiscal deficit to x % of the GDP, where x is **[CLAT 2013]**
(a) 10 (b) 8.3 (c) 15 (d) 5.1

58. Duration of which Five Year Plan was 2007-2012? **[CLAT 2013]**
(a) X (b) XII (c) IX (d) XI

59. The First Five Year Plan of India was based on **[CLAT 2014]**
(a) John W Miller Model
(b) PC Mahalanobis Model
(c) Gadgil Yojana
(d) Herrod-Domar Model

60. Economic growth rate projected by the IMF for India in the fiscal year 2014-15 is **[CLAT 2014]**
(a) 5.4% (b) 5.5% (c) 5.6% (d) 5.7%

61. Which one of the following measures is not likely to aid in improving India's balance of payment position? **[CLAT 2014]**
(a) Promotion of import substitution policy
(b) Devaluation of rupee
(c) Imposition of higher tariff on imports
(d) Levying the higher duty on exports

62. Who is the Chairman of the 14th Finance Commission? **[CLAT 2014]**
(a) Dr M Govinda Rao (b) Dr Vijay Kelkar
(c) Dr YV Reddy (d) Dr Raghuram Rajan

63. Who was appointed as the 23rd Governor of the Reserve Bank of India? **[CLAT 2014]**
(a) KC Chakrabarty (b) Urijit Patel
(c) Raghuram Rajan (d) D Subbarao

64. In India, the interest rate on savings accounts in all the nationalised commercial banks is fixed by **[CLAT 2014]**
(a) Union Ministry of Finance
(b) Union Finance Commission
(c) Indian Banks' Association
(d) None of the above

65. The Chairperson of the Seventh Pay Commission is **[CLAT 2014]**
(a) Justice BN Srikrishna
(b) Justice DK Jain
(c) Justice AP Shah
(d) Justice AK Mathur

66. The Reserve Bank of India was established in the year **[CLAT 2014]**
(a) 1858 (b) 1935 (c) 1947 (d) 1950

67. Which of the following is a Direct tax? **[CLAT 2015]**
(a) Excise duty (b) Sales tax
(c) Income tax (d) None of these

68. Which of the following is the oldest share market in India? **[CLAT 2015]**
(a) Bombay (b) Madras
(c) Calcutta (d) Delhi

69. Which committee was constituted by the RBI to review Governance of Boards of Banks in India? **[CLAT 2015]**
(a) PJ Nayak Committee
(b) HR Khan Committee
(c) Harsh Vardhan Committee
(d) K Subramanian Committee

70. Which is the single policy rate to unambiguously signal the stance of monetary policy as recently recommended by the RBI? **[CLAT 2015]**
(a) PLR (b) Repo rate
(c) Bank rate (d) CLR

71. The recently announced 'Paramparagat Krishi Vikas Yojana' aims to boost **[CLAT 2015]**
(a) organic farming
(b) drip irrigation
(c) horticulture crops
(d) vegetable production

72. What is the name given to the dedicated TV channel for farmers that was announced in the Union Budget 2014-15 and ₹ 100 crore was set aside for its establishment? **[CLAT 2015]**
(a) Kisan (b) Farmers Show
(c) Krishi Channel (d) None of these

73. How much Foreign Direct Investment (FDI) in country's defence sector was proposed in the Union Budget 2014-15 presented on 10th July, 2014? **[CLAT 2015]**
(a) 51% (b) 49%
(c) 60% (d) 35%

74. Which of the following is the world's largest e-commerce company? **[CLAT 2015]**
(a) Amazon (b) Bay
(c) Alibaba (d) Flipkart

75. IRCTC has recently launched a new service called 'RuPay Prepaid cards', which will enable passengers to book their tickets, do shopping and pay service bills online. This service was launched in collaboration with which bank? **[CLAT 2015]**
(a) Union Bank of India
(b) State Bank of India
(c) ICICI Bank
(d) Bharatiya Mahila Bank

76. The 'Ease of Doing Business Index' is prepared and published by **[CLAT 2015]**
(a) World Trade Organisation
(b) World Bank Group
(c) United Nations
(d) European Union

77. In an attempt to curb black money, the government has made PAN mandatory for all financial transactions exceeding **[CLAT 2016]**
(a) ₹ 2 lakh (b) ₹ 1 lakh
(c) ₹ 4 lakh (d) ₹ 3 lakh

78. The currency of Thailand is **[CLAT 2016]**
(a) Ringgit (b) Rupee
(c) Peseta (d) Baht

79. Who is the Union Finance Minister of India? **[CLAT 2016]**
(a) Arun Jaitley
(b) Rajnath Singh
(c) DV Sadananda Gowda
(d) Sushma Swaraj

80. Which country is the first developed nation to default on debt of IMF? **[CLAT 2016]**

(a) Japan (b) The UK
(c) Greece (d) The USA

81. Who is the Chairperson of NITI Aayog? **[CLAT 2016]**

(a) Sushmita Mahajan
(b) Arun Jaitley
(c) Sushma Swaraj
(d) Narendra Modi

82. India's third largest trading partner during 2016 is **[CLAT 2017]**

(a) Kuwait (b) Dubai
(c) Saudi Arabia (d) UAE

83. Japan is threatening to drag India to WTO on issues relating to the export of its **[CLAT 2017]**

(a) Tea (b) Small ships
(c) Steel (d) Electronic goods

Answers

1	*d*	2	*a*	3	*d*	4	*a*	5	*d*	6	*b*	7	*a*	8	*c*	9	*a*	10	*c*
11	*d*	12	*b*	13	*b*	14	*d*	15	*d*	16	*c*	17	*a*	18	*d*	19	*b*	20	*a*
21	*b*	22	*a*	23	*c*	24	*a*	25	*b*	26	*c*	27	*b*	28	*d*	29	*b*	30	*c*
31	*c*	32	*a*	33	*a*	34	*c*	35	*a*	36	*c*	37	*b*	38	*a*	39	*c*	40	*b*
41	*a*	42	*d*	43	*a*	44	*c*	45	*d*	46	*d*	47	*a*	48	*c*	49	*d*	50	*c*
51	*d*	52	*d*	53	*a*	54	*b*	55	*b*	56	*a*	57	*d*	58	*b*	49	*a*	60	*a*
61	*a*	62	*c*	63	*c*	64	*d*	65	*d*	66	*b*	67	*c*	68	*a*	69	*a*	70	*b*
71	*a*	72	*a*	73	*b*	74	*c*	75	*a*	76	*b*	77	*a*	78	*d*	79	*a*	80	*c*
81	*d*	82	*d*	83	*c*														

Gravitational potential energy, $U = mgh$
Where, m is mass, g is acceleration to gravity and h is height of the body from the surface of the earth.

> Energy of a stretched or compressed spring, energy of water collected at a height and energy of spring in a watch are examples of potential energy.

Tranformation of Energy

Energy can be transformed from one form to another, by using some equipments which are discussed as follows.

Some Equipments used to Transform Energy

Equipment	Energy Transformed
Dynamo	Mechanical energy into electrical energy
Electric motor	Electrical energy into mechanical energy
Microphone	Sound energy into electrical energy
Loud speaker	Electrical energy into sound energy
Electric bulb	Electrical energy into light and heat energy
Solar cell	Solar energy into electrical energy
Çandle	Chemical energy into light and heat energy
Sitar	Mechanical energy into sound energy

Power

Rate of doing work is called power.

Its SI unit is watt.

$$\text{Power} = \frac{\text{Work}}{\text{Time}}$$

> 1 watt hour = 3600 joule
> 1 kilowatt hour = 3.6×10^6 joule
> 1 HP = 746 watt

GRAVITATIONAL FORCE (GRAVITATION)

- Every body in the universe attracts other body by a force called force of gravitation. The gravitational force of earth is called **gravity**.
- The acceleration produced in a body due to gravity is called acceleration due to gravity (g) and its value on the surface of the earth. is 9.8 m/s^2.
- Acceleration due to gravity is independent of shape, size and mass of the body.
- Value of g decreases with height and depth from earth's surface.
  - decreases due to rotation of earth.
  - is maximum at poles.
  - is minimum at equator.
  - decreases if angular speed of earth increases and increases if angular speed of earth decreases.
- The acceleration due to gravity at the **moon** is one-sixth that of at the earth. So, the weight of a person on the surface of the moon will be one-sixth of his actual weight on the earth.

Satellites

- Satellites are natural or artificial bodies revolving around a planet under its gravitational attraction.
- Moon is a **natural satellite** while INSAT-B is an **artificial satellite** of earth. The period of revolution of a satellite revolving near the surface of earth is 1 hour 24 minutes (84 minutes).
- Jupiter has the maximum number of natural satellites. The planet Jupiter has 67 conformed moons.
- **Geo-stationary satellite** revolves around the earth at a height of 36000 km. The orbit of geo-stationary satellite is called **parking orbit**.

- Geo-stationary satellite revolves in equatorial plane from **West to East**. Time period of rotation of geo-stationary satellite is 24 h.
- The **earth** rotates on its axis from **West to East.** This rotation makes the sun and the stars appear to be moving across the sky from **East to West**.
- Geo-stationary satellite is used to reflect TV signals and telecast TV programmes from one part of the world to another, in weather forecasting i.e. in predictions of floods and droughts.
- **Polar Satellite** revolves around the earth in polar orbit at a height of 800 km (app.) Time period of these satellites is 84 min. These are used for weather forecasting.

Escape Velocity

Escape velocity is that minimum velocity with which a body should be projected from the surface of earth, so as it goes out of gravitational field of earth and never return to earth.

- Escape velocity is $\sqrt{2}$ times the orbital velocity.
- Escape velocity at the earth's surface is 11.2 km/s
- Escape velocity at the moon's surface is 2.4 km/s. Due to low escape velocity, there is no atmosphere on the moon.

General Properties of Matter

Matter exist in three states, solid, liquid and gas.Some properties of these matter are discussed below

Elasticity

It is the property of a body by virtue of which the body acquires its original shape and size after the removal of deforming force.

e.g., Steel is more elastic than rubber.

Pressure

Pressure is defined as the force, acting normally a unit area of a surface.

$$\text{Pressure} = \frac{\text{Force}}{\text{Area}}$$

Its unit is N/m^2. It is a scalar quantity.

Some facts related with pressure

- Fluid pressure is the pressure exerted by liquid column at a surface given as, $p = hdg$, where d is the density of liquid and h is height of liquid column above the surface.
- In a static liquid at same horizontal level, pressure is same at all points.
- Pressure at a point in a liquid is proportional to the density of the liquid.
- Atmospheric pressure is measured by barometer.
- Sudden fall in barometric reading is the indication of storm.
- Slow fall in barometric reading is the indication of rain.
- Slow rise in the barometric reading is the indication of clear weather.

Archimedes' Principle

It states that when a body is partially or completely immersed in a liquid, there is an apparent loss in the weight of the body which is equal to the weight of liquid displaced by the body.

- The weight of water displaced by an iron ball is less than its own weight. Whereas water displaces by the immersed portion of a ship is equal to its weight. So, small ball of iron sinks in water but large ship floats.
- A fat person will quickly learn the swimming as compared to a slim person because he will displace more water so will be more balanced.
- Hydrogen filled ballon float in air because hydrogen is lighter than air. A person can lift more weight in water.

Laws of Floatation

A body floats in a liquid if,

- the density of the material of the body is less than that of the density of the liquid in which the object has to float.
- the upthrust force of the fluid on the body must be equal to the total weight of the body.
- the volume of the body submerged must be large so as to displace large amount of fluid.

Density

- Density is defined as mass per unit volume.
- Relative density is measured by hydrometer.
- The density of sea water is more than that of normal water.
- The density of iron is more than that of water but less than that of mercury. So, a solid chunk of iron sink in water but float in mercury.
- If ice floating in water in a vessel melts, the level of water in the vessel does not change.

Surface Tension

- The property of a liquid by the virtue of which it tries to minimise its free surface area is called surface tension.
- Surface tension decreases with rise in temperature and become zero at the critical temperature.
- The surface tension of clean water is higher than that of a soap solution.
- Formation of lead shots, spraying result in coldness, floatation of needle on water, dancing of camphor on water, are based on surface tension.
- Liquid drop form spherical shape due to surface tension.
- When kerosene oil is sprinkled on water, its surface tension decreases, due to which the excess of mosquitoes floating on the surface of water die due to sinking.
- When a ship enters in a sea from a river, it raise a bit because the density of saline water is higher.

Cohesive and Adhesive Force

Force of attraction applied between molecules of same substance is called cohesive force while attractive force between molecules of different substances is called adhesive force. A solid melts into liquid due to adhesive force.

Capillarity

The phenomenon of rise or depression of liquids in a capillary tube is called capillarity.

Bernoulli's Theorem

When an incompressible and non-viscous liquid (or gas) flows in streamlined motion from one place to another, then at every point of its path the total energy per unit volume (pressure energy + kinetic energy + potential energy) is constant.

Venturimeter, Bunsen's burner, atomizer, filter pump, motion of aeroplane and Maynus effect are based upon the Bernoulli's theorem.

HEAT

- Heat is a form of energy which produces us the sensation of warmth.
- Its units are calorie, kilocalorie or joule.

1 calorie = 4.18 joule

Temperature

- Temperature is the measurement of hotness or coldness of a body.
- When two bodies are placed in contact, heat always flows from a body at higher temperature to the body at lower temperature.
- An instrument used to measure the temperature of a body is called a **thermometer**.

- The **normal temperature** of a **human body** is 37°C or 98.4°F.
- – 40° is the temperature at which **Celsius** and **Fahrenheit** thermometers read same.
- The **clinical thermometer** reads from 96°F to 110°F.
- White roof keeps the house cooler in summer than black roof because white roof reflects more and absorbs less heat rays whereas black roof absorbs more and reflects less heat rays.

Thermal Expansion

- Thermal expansion is the increase in size of a body on heating.
- It can occur in solids, liquids and gases.

> - Telephone wires are kept loose to allow the wires for contraction in winter.
> - A gap is provided between two iron tracks of the railway track so that rails can easily expand during summer and do not bend.

Latent Heat

Latent heat of fusion of ice is 80 cal/g.

Hot water burns are less severe than that steam burns because steam has high latent heat.

Evaporation

- It is the slow process of conversion a liquid into vapours even below its boiling temperature.
- The amount of water vapour in air is called **humidity**.
- Relative humidity is measured by hygrometer.
- Relative humidity increases with the increase of temperature.

Transmission of Heat

- Transfer of heat from one place to other place is called transmission of heat.
- In solids, transmission of heat takes place by **conduction process**.
- In liquids and gases, transmission of heat takes place by **convection process**. In room, ventilaters are provided to escape the hot air by convection.
- Heat from the sun reaches the earth by **radiation**.

SIMPLE PENDULUM

- Simple pendulum is a heavy point mass suspended from a rigid support by means of an elastic inextensible string.
- The maximum time period of a simple pendulum is 84.6 min.
- A pendulum clock slow down in summers and becomes fast in winters.
- If a simple pendulum is suspended in a lift descending down with an acceleration, then time period of pendulum will increase. If the lift is ascending, then time period of pendulum will decrease. If a lift falling freely under gravity, then the time period of the pendulum is infinite.

Waves

A wave is a vibratory disturbance which propagates energy from one point to the another without any actual movement of matter.

Waves are broadly of two types

1. **Longitudinal Waves** In this wave, particles of the medium vibrate in the direction of propagation of wave. Waves on springs or sound waves in air are examples of longitudinal waves.
2. **Transverse Waves** In this wave, particles of the medium vibrate perpendicular to the direction of propagation of wave. Waves on strings under tension, waves on the surface of water are the examples of transverse waves.

Electromagnetic Waves

- The waves which do not require medium for their propagation i.e. which can propagate even through the vacuum are called electromagnetic waves.

- Light and heat are the examples of electromagnetic waves. This wave propagates with the velocity of light.
- Cathode rays, Canal rays, α-rays, β-rays, sound waves and ultrasonic waves are not electromagnetic waves.

Sound Waves

Sound waves are longitudinal waves. Based on their frequency range, sound waves are divided into following categories

- The sound waves which lie in the frequency range 20 Hz to 20000 Hz are called audible waves.
- The sound waves having frequencies less than 20 Hz are called infrasonic waves.
- The sound waves having frequencies greater than 20000 Hz are called ultrasonic waves.

LIGHT

- Light is a form of energy which is propagated as electromagnetic waves. Light is a transverse wave.
- Speed of light is maximum in vacuum and air i.e., 3×10^8 m/s.
- Light takes 8 min 19 sec to reach from sun to earth.

Reflection of Light

When a ray of light being incident on a boundary separating two media comes back into the same media, then this phenomenon is called reflection of light.

Laws of Reflection

- The incident ray, reflected ray and normal ray to the reflecting surface at the incident point all lie in the same plane.
- The angle of reflection is equal to the angle of incidence.

Reflection from Plane Mirror

- The image is virtual and laterally inverted.
- The size of image is equal to that of object.
- If an object moves towards a plane mirror with speed v, relative to the object the image moves towards with a speed $2v$.
- To see his full image in a plane mirror, a person requires a mirror of at least half of his height.

Spherical Mirrors

Spherical mirrors are of two types

(i) Concave mirror

(ii) Convex mirror

- Image formed by a convex mirror is always virtual, erect and diminished.

Uses of Concave Mirror

(i) As a shaving glass, (ii) As a reflector for the head lights of a vehicle and search light, (iii) In ophthalmoscope to examine eye, ear and nose by doctors and (iv) In solar cookers.

Uses of Convex Mirror

(i) As a rear view mirror in vehicle because it provides the maximum rear field of view and image formed is always erect and

(ii) In sodium reflector lamp.

Refraction of Light

- The bending of the ray of light passing from one medium to other medium is called refraction. When a ray of light enters from one medium to other medium, its frequency and phase do not change but wavelength and velocity changes.
- Refractive Index (μ)

$$= \frac{\text{Speed of light in vacuum}}{\text{Speed of light in the medium}}$$

Total Internal Reflection (TIR)

- If light is travelling from a denser medium to a rarer medium and the angle of incidence is more than the critical angle, then the light is reflected back into the denser medium. This phenomenon is called total internal reflection.

- Sparkling of diamond, mirage and looming, shinning of air bubble in water and optical fibre are examples of total internal reflection.

Lenses

Lens are generally of two types

(i) Convex lens
(ii) Concave lens

- When lens is dipped in a liquid of higher refractive index the focal length increases and convex lens behaves as concave lens and *vice-versa.*
- An air bubble trapped in water or glass appears as convex lens but behaves as concave lens.

Dispersion of Light

- When a ray of white light is passed through a prism, it gets splitted into its constituent colours. This phenomenon is called **dispersion of light**.
- The different colours in the spectrum area appeared in the following order, Violet, Indigo, Blue, Green, Yellow, Orange and Red (VIBGYOR).
- Wavelength of red colour is maximum and minimum for violet colour.
- Red, green and blue are primary colours.
- Green and magenta, blue and yellow, red and cyan are complementary colours.

Colour Combinations

Green + Red + Blue = White
Blue + Yellow = White
Red + Cyan = White
Green + Magenta = White
Green + Red = Yellow
Red + Blue = Magenta
Blue + Green = Cyan

Scattering of Light

The deviation of light from a comparably smaller sized particle in all directions is called scattering of light.

- Scattering of light is maximum in case of violet colour and minimum in case of red colour of light.

Human Eye

The human eye uses light and enables us to see objects around us. It works on the principle of refraction of light though a natural convex lens made of transparent living material and enables us to see things around us.

Least distance of distinct vision is 25 cm.

Defects of Eye

Myopia (Short sightedness)	A short sighted eye can see only nearer objects. Distant objects are not seen clearly. This defect can be removed by using concave lens of suitable focal length.
Hypermetropia (Long sightedness)	A long sighted eye can see distant objects clearly but nearer objects are not clearly visible. This defect can be removed by using a convex lens.
Presbyopia	In this defect, both near and far objects are not clearly visible. It can be removed by using bifocal lens.
Astigmatism	In this defect, eye cannot see horizontal and vertical lines clearly. This defect can be removed by using cylindrical lenses.

ELECTRICITY AND MAGNETISM

Electricity is associated with charge and electric current

Charge

- Charge is the basic property associated with matter due to which it produces and experiences electrical and magnetic effects.

- Similar charges repel each other and opposite charges attract each other.

Conductor	Conductors are those materials which allow electricity to pass through themselves. Metals like silver, iron, copper and earth acts like a conductor. Silver is the best conductor.
Insulator	Insulators are those materials which do not allow electricity to flow through themselves, wood, paper, mica, glass, ebonite are insulators.

Electric Current

Electric current is defined as the rate of flow of charge or charge flowing per unit time interval. Its unit is **Ampere**. It is a scalar quantity.

Ohm's Law

According to Ohm's law, the current (I) flowing through a conductor is directly proportional to the potential difference (V) across it.

$$I = \frac{V}{R}, \text{ where } R \text{ is the resistance.}$$

- If a wire is stretched or doubled on itself its resistance will change, but its specific resistance will remain unaffected.
- On increasing the temperature of the metal, its resistance increases.
- On increasing the temperature of semiconductor its resistance decreases.
- On increasing the temperature of electrolytes, their resistance decreases.
- The reciprocal of resistivity of a conductor is called its **conductivity**. Its unit is mho m^{-1}.

Magnets

- Magnet is a piece of iron or other materials that can attract iron containing object and that points North and South when suspended.
- When a magnet is freely suspended, its one pole always directs towards the North. This pole is called North pole. The other pole is called South pole.
- Similar poles repel each other and dissimilar poles attract each other.

ATOMIC AND NUCLEAR PHYSICS

Nuclear physics is the field of physics that studies the constituents (protons and neutrons) and interactions of atomic nuclei.

Cathode Rays

These rays were discovered by **Sir William Crooke**.

- These travel in straight lines.
- These produce fluorescence.
- These can penetrate through thin foils of metal.
- These are deflected by both electric and magnetic fields. These have velocity ranging 1-30th to 1-10th of the velocity of light.

Positive or Canal Rays

- These rays were discovered by **Goldstein**.
- The positive rays consist of positively charged particles.
- These rays travel in straight line.
- These rays are deflected by electric and magnetic fields.
- These rays are capable of producing physical and chemical changes.
- These rays can produce ionisation in gases.

X-Rays

- X-rays were discovered by **Roentgen**.
- X-rays are electromagnetic waves with wavelength range 0.1 Å–100 Å.
- X-rays travel in straight line. These show reflection, refraction, interference, diffraction and polarisation and are not deflected by electric and magnetic fields.

- Long exposure of X-rays is injurious to human body.
- X-rays shows photoelectric effect.

Uses of X-rays

- **In Medical Sciences** X-rays are used in surgery for the detection of fractures, diseased organs, foreign matter like bullet, stones etc. They are used in treatment of cancer and in skin diseases.
- **Engineering** X-rays are used in detecting faults, cracks, flaws and gas pockets in the finished metal products and in heavy metal sheets.
- **Scientific Work** X-rays are used in studying crystal structure and complex molecules.
- **In Custom Department** X-rays are used in custom department for detection of banned materials kept hidden.

Radioactivity

- It was discovered by **Henry Becquerel, Madame Curie** and **Pierre Curie** for which they jointly won Nobel Prize.
- The nucleus having protons 83 or more are unstable. They emit α, β and γ particles and became stable. The elements of such nucleus are called radioactive elements and the phenomenon of emission of α, β and γ particles is called **radioactivity**.
- **Robert Pierre** and his wife **Madame Curie** discovered a new radioactive element radium.
- The end product of all natural radioactive elements after emission of radioactive rays is lead.
- With the emission of an α-particle, atomic number is decreased by 2 and mass number is decreased by 4.
- With the emission of a β-particle atomic number is increased by 1 and mass number does not change.

Properties of Fundamental Particles

Particle	Mass (kg)	Charge (C)	Discoverer
Proton	1.672×10^{-27}	$+1.6 \times 10^{-19}$	Rutherford
Neutron	1.675×10^{-27}	0	Chadwick
Electron	9.108×10^{-31}	-1.6×10^{-19}	J J Thomson

Nuclear Fission

- The nuclear reaction in which a heavy nucleus splits into two nuclei of nearly equal mass is called nuclear fission.
  $_{92}U^{235} + {_0}n^1 \rightarrow {_{56}}Ba^{141} + {_{36}}Kr^{92} + 3\,{_0}n^1$ + energy
- Nuclear fission was first demonstrated by **Strassman** and **O Hahn**.
- **Atom Bomb** is based on nuclear fission. U^{235} and Pu^{239} are used as fissionable material.

Nuclear Fusion

- When two or more light nuclei combined together to form a heavier nucleus, then it is known as nuclear fusion.
- For the nuclear fusion, a temperature of the order of 10^8 K is required.
- **Hydrogen Bomb** was made by the American Scientist in 1952. This is based on nuclear fusion. It is 1000 times more powerful than atom bomb.

Nuclear Reactor or Atomic Pile

- Nuclear reactor is an arrangement in which controlled nuclear fission reaction takes place.
- First nuclear reactor was established in Chicago University under the supervision of Prof. Fermi.

Uses of Nuclear Reactor

(i) To produce electrical energy from the energy released during fission.

(ii) To produce different isotopes which can be used in medical, physical and agriculture science.

CHEMISTRY

Physical and Chemical Changes

- Physical changes are the change which only affect the physical properties like colour, hardness, density, melting point, etc. of matter but do not affect the composition and chemical properties of matter.
- Crystallisation, sublimation, boiling, melting, vaporisation, cutting of trees, dissolving sugar or salt in water etc. are physical changes.
- Chemical changes affect the composition as well as chemical properties of matter and result in the formation of a new substance.
- Burning of fuel, burning of candle and paper, electrolysis of water, photosynthesis, ripening of fruits etc. are examples of chemical changes.
- Burning of candle involves both physical and chemical changes.

Effect of change of Temperature and Pressure

- **The boiling point increases in the presence of impurities.** That's why boiling point of sea water is more than the boiling point of pure water (as the former contains impurity).
- **At high altitudes, the atmospheric pressure is less than sea level** and hence, water boils at a lower temperature (less than 100°C) and food takes more time to cook.
- **Inside the pressure cooker, pressure is higher** and hence, water boils at a higher temperature (i.e., boiling point of water increases) and food is cooked quickly.
- The air escaping from a punctured tyre is cold because the air escapes from a region of high pressure to low pressure.

Atom, Molecule and Element

- An atom is the smallest particle of the element that cannot usually exist independently and retain all its chemical properties.
- Atom is made up of electron, proton and neutron. Protons and neutrons reside in the nucleus (at the centre of atom) whereas electrons revolve around the nucleus.
  A molecule is the smallest particle of an element or a compound capable of independent existence under ordinary conditions.
- An element contains only one type of atom e.g. carbon (C), sulphur (S), diamond, graphite etc.

Isotopes and Isobars

- Isotopes have the same atomic number but, different mass number. e.g. there are three isotopes of hydrogen i.e. ${}_1H^1$, ${}_1H^2$, ${}_1H^3$.
- Isobars have the same mass number but different atomic number. e.g. ${}_{18}Ar^{40}$, ${}_{19}K^{40}$, and ${}_{20}Ca^{40}$.

Dating Techniques

- Radiocarbon dating is used to determine the age of carbon bearing materials like wood, animal fossil, etc.
- Uranium dating is used to determine the age of earth, minerals and rocks.

Acids and Bases

- Acids turn blue litmus red and give proton (H^+) in water. Bases turn red litmus blue and accept proton (H^+) from other substances or give ($\overline{O}H$). pH is the measure of acidity/basicity.
- pH value ranges from 1 to 14 on pH scale:

  pH > 7 for basic solutions

  pH = 7 for neutral solutions

  pH < 7 for acidic solutions

pH *of some important substances are as follows*

Gastric juice	1.0 to 3.0
Urine (Human)	4.8 to 8.4
Saliva (Human)	6.5 to 7.5
Tears	7.4
Milk (Cow)	6.3 to 6.6
Sea water	8.5

Metals and Non-metals

- Elements having a tendency to lose electron and form cation are called **metals**.
- Lithium is the lightest metallic element which is a very strong reducing agent.
- Aluminium is the most abundant metal of earth crust and iron comes second.
- The filament of an electric bulb is made of **tungsten**.
- Elements having a tendency to accept electron and form an anion are called non-metals.
- Non-metals are either solids or gases except bromine which is liquid.
- An alloy is a homogeneous mixture of two or more metals or a metal and a non-metal.
- Nichrome is an alloy of nickle, chromium and iron.
- The coil of the electric heater is made of nichrome.

Corrosion

- The oxidative deterioration of a metal surface by the action of environment is called corrosion. It is an electrochemical process.
- When exposed to air, iron surface turns brown due to the formation of hydrated ferric oxide ($Fe_2O_3 \cdot xH_2O$) which is also called **rust**, silver surface turns black due to the formation of silver sulphide (Ag_2S) and copper and bronze surfaces turn green due to the formation of basic copper carbonate, $Cu(OH)_2 \cdot CuCO_3$.
- **Corrosion of iron is called rusting** and accelerated by the presence of impurities, H^+, electrolyte such as NaCl and gases like CO_2, SO_2, NO_2 etc.
- Corrosion is prevented by electroplating, by applying oil, grease, paint, varnish etc. or by galvanisation (i.e. deposition of zinc layer over iron articles).
- A sliced apple, when exposed to air, turns brown after sometime. This is because apple contains iron which gets oxidised and gives a brownish colour to apple.

Renewable and Non-renewable Natural Resources

- **Renewable Resources** are available in excess, i.e., never ends, e.g. air, sunlight, etc.
- **Non-renewable Resources** are available in limited quantity and if used excessively these will end after a limited period of time. e.g. mineral, coal, petroleum, natural gas, etc.

Fuels

- The substances which produce heat and light on combustion are called fuels. A strong foul smelling substance, called ethyl mercaptan, C_2H_5SH, is added to LPG to detect its leakage as LPG is an odourless gas.
- The amount of heat obtained by complete combustion of per gram of a fuel is called **calorific value**.
- Vehicle carrying inflammable substances have metallic ropes touching the ground during motion in order to provide earthing for lightning. Fuels used in rocket are called **Rocket Propellants**. A mixture of liquid hydrogen and liquid oxygen is most common rocket propellant.

Coal

Coal is obtained by carbonisation of vegetable matter and is available in different varities : Peat (60% C), lignite or brown coal (70% C), bituminous coal (80% C), anthracite coal (90%C). Out of these, bituminous is the most common form.

Flame

Flame contains three parts based on colour and temperature:

1. **Innermost Part** is black due to the presence of unburned carbon particles. It has lowest temperature.
2. **Middle Part** is yellow due to incomplete combustion of fuel.
3. **Outermost Part** which is blue due to complete combustion of fuel, is the hottest and used by goldsmith (for melting) gold and silver.

Fire Extinguishers

- Water is the most common fire extinguisher, i.e. used to extinguish fire.
- Water extinguishes fire because as it evaporates, the vapours surround the burning substance, cutting off the oxygen supply, thus inhibiting burning process.
- Hot water will extinguish fire more quickly than cold water as hot water will evaporate faster. In case of electrical or oil (petrol) fires, water cannot be used as extinguisher. This is because water is a conductor of electricity and heavier than oil. Thus, oil floats over it and continues to burn.
- Carbon dioxide, which is generated by the reaction of baking soda with acid, is used to extinguish electrical or oil fires.
- Quality of petrol is measured in terms of octane number and that of diesel in terms of cetane number. TEL (Tetra Ethyl Lead) is an antiknock compound.

Safety Match

In safety match, the stick consists of a mixture of antimony trisulphide and potassium chlorate at its one end. The box side contains a mixture of powdered glass and red phosphorus.

Carbon and its Compounds

Carbon

- It is a member of group 14 on the Periodic Table, with symbol C and atomic number 6.
- It has three crystalline allotropes e.g. diamond, graphite and fullerenes.

Differences between Diamond and Graphite

Diamond	Graphite
Diamond is the ultimate abrasive.	Graphite is a very good lubricant, displaying super lubricity.
It is hard.	It is soft.
Diamond is an excellent electrical insulator.	Graphite is a good conductor of electricity.
Diamond is the best known naturally occurring thermal conductor.	Some forms of graphite are used for thermal insulation (i.e. firebreaks and heat shields)
Diamond is highly transparent.	Graphite is opaque.

Fullerenes

It is one of the allotropes of carbon.

It (C_{60}) looks like a soccer ball (or bucky ball).

It contains 20 six membered and 12 five membered rings of carbon atoms.

It acts as wonderful lubricant and the alkali metal compounds of C_{60} are used sas superconducting substance at the temperature range of 10-40 K.

Carbon Dioxide (CO_2)

It is an acidic oxide of carbon and is used by green plants for photosynthesis. It does not help in burning.

- Air and our breath contains carbon dioxide. Thus, when lime water is kept in air or we pass our breath into it, the lime water turns milky.
- When 'ENO' is dissolved in water, the appearance of effervescence is due to liberation of carbon dioxide gas.

Carbon Monoxide (CO)

- It is formed by incomplete combustion. It is a colourless, odourless gas.
- It contains a triple bond and are fairly polar, resulting in a tendency to bind permanently to haemoglobin molecules, displacing oxygen, which has a lower binding affinity.

Organic Compounds

- These are the compounds of mainly carbon and hydrogen or compounds of carbon and hydrogen with other elements like phosphorus, oxygen, nitrogen, sulphur, halogens etc.
- Urea is the first synthesised organic compound (by Wholer).
- Acetic acid was the first organic compound synthesised in the laboratory from its elements.

Hydrocarbons

These are the compounds of only carbon and hydrogen. *These are of following three types*

1. **Saturated Hydrocarbons** These compounds contain only single bonds. These are also called **alkanes** or **paraffins** and have general formula, C_nH_{2n+2}. where, $n = 1, 2, 3 \ldots$

   Methane is the first member of this group.
2. **Unsaturated Hydrocarbons** These have general formula, C_nH_{2n} for alkene and C_nH_{2n-2} for alkynes. These have atleast one double (=) or triple (≡) bond, and are called alkene and alkynes, respectively.

   > Ethylene (C_2H_4) is the first member of alkene and acetylene (C_2H_2) is the first member of alkyne.

3. **Aromatic Hydrocarbons** These have ring structure with alternate double bonds and follows $(4n+2)\,\pi e^-$ (Huckle's rule).

Functional Group

- It is an atom or group of atoms in a molecule, which is responsible for the chemical properties of the molecules.
- —OH is alcoholic group, —CHO is aldehyde group, >C=O is keto group, —COOH is carboxylic acid group, —O— ether group.

Homologous Series

It is a series of compounds in which adjacent members differ by a —CH_2 unit (14 unit mass). All members of a homologous series have same functional group and same chemical properties.

Isomerism

Compounds having the same molecular formula but different structure are called isomers and the phenomenon is called isomerism. e.g. C_2H_6O can have the following structure, CH_3OCH_3 and C_2H_5OH.

BIOLOGY

Biology (coined by **Lamarck** and **Treviranus** 1802), is branch of science which deals with study of living organisms. It mainly includes **Botany** (Study of plants), **Zoology** (Study of animals) and **Microbiology** (Study of micro-organisms).

Popular Scientists and Their Contribution

- **Charles Darwin** wrote *'Origin of Species'* and proposed 'Theory of Natural Selection'.
- **Mendel** (1866) proposed 'law of inheritance' and was called 'father of genetics'.
- **Anand Mohan Chakraborty** developed superbug (*Pseudomonas putida*) by genetic engineering.
- **Kohler** and **Milstein** discovered hybridoma technology.
- **Alec Zaffrey** discovered DNA fingerprinting.
- **Robert Hooke** (1665) discovered cell and wrote book *'Micrographia'*.
- **Watson** and **Crick** proposed double helical model of DNA.
- **Hargovind Khorana** artificially synthesised gene.
- **Kary Mullis** (1985) invented 'polymerase chain reaction'.

LIVING WORLD

In 18th century **Carolus Linnaeus** developed **binomial nomenclature** for living organisms i.e. scientific name consists of **genus** and **species**.

- **RH Whittaker** (1969) classified living organisms into five kingdoms—Monera, Protista, Fungi, Plantae and Animalia.
- Monera includes bacteria and *Mycoplasma* while Protista includes Protozoa and some eukaryotes.
- Viruses are sub-microscopic, obligate parasite, intracellular consisting of nucleoprotein.
- **WM Stanley** crystallised TMV.
- **Viroids** are smallest infectious single-stranded RNA molecules discovered by **TO Diener**.
- The largest bird is *Ostrich*, but it is flightless.
- The palaealithic period or prehistoric period or stone age was period when stone tools were made by humans.

THE CELL

- According to cell theory (proposed by **Schleiden** and **Schwann** (1838)) cell is the structural and functional unit of living organisms.
- An organism may be composed of single cell (**called unicellular**) or many cells (**called multicellular**).
- Cells are of two types i.e. **prokaryotic** (which lacks nucleus and membrane bound organelles) and **eukaryotic** (which have nucleus and membrane bound organelles).
- Prokaryotic cell is found in bacteria, mycoplasma and blue-green algae while eukaryotic cell is found in plants, animals and fungi.

Human Systems

The cells of human and other multicellular animals are organised into tissues. Two or more tissues group together to form organs. An organ system is a group of organs that function together to carry out the principal activities of the body.

1. Digestive System

Digestion is the process by which complex food is hydrolysed into simple components with the help of digestive enzymes.

Major Enzymes of Digestion

Enzyme	Source	Where Active	Substrate	Main Break-down Product
Carbohydrate Digestion				
Salivary amylase	Salivary glands	Mouth	Polysaccharides	Disaccharides
Pancreatic amylase	Pancreas	Small intestine	Polysaccharides	Disaccharides
Sucrase/Lactase	Small intestine	Small intestine	Disaccharides	Monosaccharides (e.g. glucose)

Protein Digestion				
Pepsin	Stomach mucosa	Stomach	Proteins	Peptide fragments
Trypsin and chymotrypsin	Pancreas	Small intestine	Proteins and polypeptide	Peptide fragments
Carboxypeptidase	Pancreas	Small intestine	Peptide fragments	Amino acids
Amino peptidase	Intestinal mucosa	Small intestine	Peptide fragments	Amino acids
Fat Digestion				
Lipase	Pancreas	Small intestine	Triglycerides	Free fatty acids, monoglycerides
Nucleic Acid Digestion				
Pancreatic nucleases	Pancreas	Small intestine	DNA, RNA	Nucleotides
Intestinal nucleases	Intestinal mucosa	Small intestine	Nucleotides	Nucleotides bases

Fat Soluble Vitamins

Vitamin	Name	Rich Food Source	Function	Deficiency Disease
A	Retinol	Fish liver oils, dairy products, liver. Most leafy vegetables and carrots contain carotene that can be converted into retinol.	Needed for healthy epithelial cells. Needed for regeneration of rhodopsin in red cells of the eye.	Dry skin, night blindness.
D	Calciferol	Fish oils, egg yolk, butter. It can be made by the action of sunlight on skin.	Promotes absorption of calcium from intestines. Necessary for formation of normal bone and reabsorption of phosphate from urine.	Rickets in children ('soft' bones that bend easily) osteomalacia painful bones in adults.
E	Tocopherol	Vegetable oils, cereal products and many other foods.	In rats, formation of red blood cells, affects muscles and reproductive system. Unclear in humans.	Mild anaemia and sterility in rats. Deficiency is rare in humans.
K	Phyllo-quinone	Fresh dark green vegetables. Also made by gut bacteria.	Formation of prothrombin (involved in blood clotting).	Delayed clotting time. May occur in new-born babies before their gut become established.

Water Soluble Vitamins

Vitamin	Name	Rich Food Source	Function	Deficiency Disease
B_1	Thiamine	Yeast, cereals, nuts, seeds, pork	Coenzyme in cell respiration, necessary for complete release of energy from carbohydrates	Beri-beri (severe muscle wastage, stunted growth, nerve degeneration)
B_2	Riboflavin	Liver, milk, eggs, green vegetables	Coenzyme in cell respiration. Precursor of FAD	Cracked skin, blurred vision
B_3	Niacin	Liver, yeast, whole cereals, beans	Coenzyme in cell respiration. Precursor of NAD/NADP	Pellagra (severe skin problems, diarrhoea, dementia)

Vitamin	Name	Rich Food Source	Function	Deficiency Disease
B_6	Pyridoxine	Meat, fish, eggs, cereals bran, some vegetables.	Interconversion of amino acids.	Skin problems, nerve disorder
B_5	Pentothenic acid	Animal tissue, whole grain cereals, legumes.	Need to manufacture adrenal hormone.	Unclear
B_{12}	Cyanocobalamin	Liver, milk, fish, yeast. None in plant foods.	Maturation of red blood cells in bone marrow. Maintenance of myelin sheath of nerves.	Pernicious anaemia, nerve disorders.
B_9	Folic acid	Liver, raw green vegetables, yeast, gut bacteria.	Formation of nucleic acids. Formation of red blood cells.	Anaemia, especially during pregnancy.
C	Ascorbic acid	Blackcurrant peppers, sprouts, citrus fruits.	Formation of collagen and intercellular cement.	Scurvy, poor wound healing.

2. Respiratory System

Respiration in an oxidative process involving oxidation of food substances such as carbohydrate, fat and proteins to form CO_2, water and release energy. Respiration may be anaerobic (i.e. without O_2) or aerobic (i.e. with O_2).

Respiratory Organs of Animals

Organs	Animals
Lungs	Reptiles, mammals
Gills	Fishes, tadpoles, prawns
Tracheae	Insects, centipedes, millipedes
Body surface	Protozoans, poriferans, coelenterates
Book lungs	Spider, scorpion, ticks, mites
Ctenidia	Mollusca (*Unio*)
Air bladder	Lung fish, bony fishes (*e.g. Labeo*)
Air sacs/lungs	Birds

3. Circulatory System

3.1 Blood

- Blood is a fluid connective tissue composed of plasma and cells.
- An adult person has 5-6 litre blood.
- It is slightly alkaline having pH 7.3-7.4.
- Plasma is pale yellow, transparent fluid which constitute about 60% volume of blood.
- Plasma is composed of 90-92% water, 7% organic substances (albumin, globulin and fibrinogen protein) and 1% inorganic substances.
- Red blood corpuscles (most abundant) are non-nucleated and contain haemoglobin, the respiratory pigment.
- White blood corpuscles are colourless, nucleated, granular and agranular.

- **Eosinophils** also called acidophils (2-8%) are phagocytic granulocytes and play important role in hypersensitivity.
- **Basophils** (2%) are non-phagocytic and increase during chickenpox.
- **Neutrophils** (65%) are phagocytic and increase during bacterial infection.
- **Monocytes** (05%) are agranulocytes called policeman of blood and increase during tuberculosis.
- **Lymphocytes** (26%) are agranulocytes producing antibodies and increase during viral infection.
- **Platelets** (thrombocytes) are non-nucleated.
- **Rh-factor** discovered by **Landsteiner** and **Veiner** in ***Rhesus*** monkey is responsible for erythroblastosis foetalis disease.
- Leukemia is a blood related disorder where the white blood cells get reduced in number.
- Important components of blood clotting are fibrinogen, prothrombin, thromboplastin, calcium ions and vitamin-K.

3.2 Heart

- Human heart is **myogenic** i.e. contraction is initiated by a **Sino-Atrial node** (SA node) located in right atrium. It is also called **pacemaker**.
- First heart sound is **lubb** and second heart sound is **dup.**
- Contraction of heart is called systole. (120 mm Hg) while relaxation of heart is called **diastole** (80 mm Hg).

3. Excretory System

- **Excretion** is the elimination of harmful waste products from the animal body to regulate the composition of the body fluids and tissues.
- Human excretory system is composed of a pair of kidneys, ureters, a urinary bladder and urethera.
- **Nephron** is the structural and functional unit of kidney.
- Colour of urine is pale yellow. It is due to presence of a pigment urochrome.
- Human urine contains 95% water, 2% salts, 2.6% urea and 0.3% uric acid.
- pH of urine is 6.0 (mildly acidic).

Main Excretory Organs

Excretory Organs	Animals
Contractile vacuole	*Amoeba*
Flame cells/solenocytes	Tapeworm
Renette cell	*Ascaris*
Nephridia	Earthworm
Malpighian tubules	Cockroach
Cocxal glands	Scorpion
Green glands	Prawn

4. Central Nervous System

The brain is the organising and processing centre. It is the site of consciousness, sensation, memory and intelligence. The brain receives impulses from the spinal cord and from 12 pairs of cranial nerves extending to the senses and to other organs. In addition, the brain initiates activities without environmental stimuli. Three major portions of the brain are recognised i.e. The hindbrain, midbrain and forebrain.

5. Endocrine System

Pituitary is the master gland, hypothalamus controls all glands and their functions liver is the largest gland in our body.

Human Diseases

It can be defined as any condition which impairs or disturbs the normal functioning of the body due to some reasons. Most of the diseases in human are caused due to bacteria and virus.

Some Human Diseases Caused by Virus

Disease	Pathogen	Incubation	Symptoms	Prevention and Control
Chickenpox (*Varicella*)	*Herpes zoster* virus	12-20 days	Dark red coloured rash or pox changing into vesicles, crusts and falling.	Varicella vaccine.
Smallpox	*Variola* virus	12 days	Appearance of rash changing into pustules, scaps.	Smallpox vaccine.
Poliomyelitis	Polio virus	7-14 days	Damages motor neurons causing stiffness of neck, convulsion, generally paralysis of legs.	Salk vaccine and Oral Polio Vaccine (OPV).
Measles (Rubella disease)	*Rubella* virus	10 days	Rubella (skin eruptions), coughing, sneezing, etc.	MMR (Measles Mumps Rubella) B-vaccine.
Mumps	Mumps virus	12-26 days	Painful enlargement of parotid and salivary glands.	Mumps-vaccine.
Rabies (Hydrophobia)	Rabies virus	10 days to 1-3 months	Spasm of throat and chest muscles, fears of water, paralysis and death.	Immunisation of infected person and pets-like dogs.

Some Human Diseases Caused by Bacteria

Disease	Pathogen	Incubation Period	Symptoms	Prevention and Control
Tuberculosis	*Mycobacterium tuberculosis*	2-10 weeks	Coughing, chest pain and bloody sputum with tuberculin.	BCG vaccine.
Diphtheria	*Corynebacterium diphtheriae*	2-6 days	Inflammation of mucosa of nasal chamber, throat, etc. respiratory track blocked.	DPT vaccine.
Cholera	*Vibrio cholerae*	6 h to 2-3 days	Acute diarrhoea and dehydration.	Sanitation, boiling of water and cholera vaccine.
Leprosy	*Mycobacterium leprae*	2-5 years	Skin hypopigmentation, nodulated skin, deformity of fingers and toes lepromin in skin tests.	Isolation.
Tetanus (Lock jaw)	*Clostridium tetani*	3-21 days	Degeneration of motor neurons, rigid jaw muscles, spasm and paralysis.	ATS and DPT vaccines.
Typhoid	*Salmonella typhi*	1-3 weeks	Classic typhoid fever.	TAB vaccine and screening of food and water.
Plague	*Pasteurella pestis*	2-6 days	Bubonic plague affects, lymph nodes, pneumonic plague affects lungs and septicemic plague causes anaemia.	Killing of rats and ratfleas, plague vaccine.
Gonorrhoea	*Neisseria gonorrhoeae*	2-10 days	Inflammation of urinogenital tract.	Practice safe sex.
Pneumonia	*Diplococcus pneumoniae*	1-3 days	Decrease in respiratory efficiency.	Isolation of infected person.
Salmonellosis	*Salmonella enteridis*	48 hours	Diarrhoea.	Isolation of infected person.

Practice Exercise

PHYSICS

1. A car is moving with high velocity when it takes a turn, a force acts on it outwardly because of
(a) centrifugal force (b) centripetal force
(c) gravitational force (d) All of these

2. A Geostationary satellite
(a) revolves about the polar axis
(b) has a time period less than that of the near earth satellite
(c) moves faster than a near earth satellite
(d) appears to be stationary

3. A bomb is dropped at a point from a moving aeroplane. The pilot observes that
(a) the bomb traverses a curved path and falls some distance behind that point
(b) the bomb traverses a curved path and falls some distance ahead
(c) the bomb drops vertically downward
(d) the bomb remains stationary in the air for some time

4. What happens to the level of mercury in the barometer tube when it is taken down a coal mine? It
(a) falls (b) remains unaltered
(c) rises (d) rises and then falls

5. A glass vessel is filled with water and a lid is fixed to it tightly. Then it is inside a freezer for hours. What is expected to happen?
(a) The water freezes to ice and the level of ice comes down
(b) The water in the glass vessel sim freezes to ice
(c) The glass vessel breaks due expansion as water freezes to ice
(d) The water does not freeze at all

6. In a barometer, mercury is preferred over water because
(a) mercury is a good conductor of heat
(b) mercury shines and therefore its level can be read easily
(c) mercury has high density and low vapour pressure
(d) mercury is available in pure form

7. Two cars, passing each other at high speed, are in danger of side swiping because
(a) of the increase in air pressure in the space between them
(b) of decrease in the velocity of air molecules between them
(c) of decrease in air pressure in the space between them
(d) increase in the velocity of air molecules between them

8. Old-written material, which cannot be read easily, can be read by
(a) cosmic rays
(b) ultraviolet rays
(c) infrared rays
(d) None of the above

9. The best conductor of electricity is
(a) filtered hot water
(b) distilled water
(c) filtered water at room temperature
(d) salt water

10. Nuclear fission is caused by the impact of
(a) proton (b) electron
(c) neutron (d) None of these

11. Which of the following is used as a coolant in nuclear reactors ?
(a) Heavy water (b) Cadmium
(c) Liquid sodium (d) Graphite

12. Which of the following has the least penetrating power?
(a) Alpha particles
(b) Beta particles
(c) Gamma rays
(d) All have the same penetrating power

13. Which of the following is responsible for the energy release by stars?
(a) Fission
(b) Fusion
(c) Chemical section
(d) Gravitational collapse

14. Which of the following are most penetrating?
(a) α-rays (b) β-rays
(c) γ-rays (d) X-rays

15. The nuclides having the same number of neutrons but different number of protons or mass number are known as
(a) isobars (b) isoelectronic
(c) isotopes (d) isotones

16. Cryogenic engines find applications in
(a) rocket technology
(b) frost-free refrigerators
(c) sub-marine propulsion
(d) researches in superconductivity

17. What will happen if the star having mass greater than five times of the sun, is dead?
(a) White dwarf will form (b) Neutron star will form
(c) Black hole will form (d) Nebula will form

18. In which of the following cases lies the broadcast band of FM?
(a) UHF (b) VHF (c) SHF (d) HF

19. When light passes from air into glass it experiences change in
(a) frequency and wavelength
(b) frequency and speed
(c) wavelength and speed
(d) frequency, wavelength and speed

20. Which of the following are the discoveries of Einstein?
(a) Radioactivity and photoelectric effect
(b) Radioactivity and theory of relativity
(c) Theory of relativity and photoelectric effect
(d) X-rays and photoelectric effect

21. A convex mirror makes a good rear-view mirror for a car because
(a) it does not form diminished images
(b) it has no focal point
(c) its images can be thrown on a screen
(d) it forms erect, reduced images

22. According to the law of conservation of energy,
1. energy can be created but not destroyed
2. energy can neither be created nor destroyed
3. energy can be transformed from one form to the other

(a) Only 1 (b) Only 2
(c) Both 2 and 3 (d) Only 3

23. Why is there a spluttering sound when water is sprinkled on hot oil?
(a) Boiling point of the water is higher than that of oil
(b) Boiling point of the oil is higher than that of water
(c) Oil and water do not mix
(d) Oil and water combine to form a compound

24. Which falls down faster in a vacuum-a feather, a wooden ball or a steel ball?
(a) A wooden ball
(b) A feather
(c) A steel ball
(d) All will fall down at the same speed in a vacuum because there will be no air resistance

25. Materials used for making cooking utensils should have
(a) low specific heat and high thermal conductivity
(b) high specific heat and high thermal conductivity
(c) low specific heat and low thermal conductivity
(d) high specific heat and low thermal conductivity

26. Machine parts get jammed in winter, because
(a) the viscosity of the lubricant used in machine parts increases with the decrease in temperature
(b) the viscosity of lubricant used in machine parts decreases with the decrease in temperature
(c) the inertia of machine parts decreases with the decrease in temperature
(d) the inertia of machine parts increases with the decrease in temperature

27. Usually light travels faster than sound. However, when we switch a television set on the picture comes later than the sound. The reason is that
(a) in TV transmission sound is transmitted first and picture is transmitted later
(b) there is always a delay in the picture tube getting switched on
(c) Emission of electrons from the picture tube takes time
(d) The wiring for picture tube is much longer compared to that for the speaker

28. Which of the following is good nuclear fuel?
(a) Uranium-238 (b) Neptunium-239
(c) Thorium-236 (d) Plutonium-239

29. 'mho' is the unit of
(a) resistance (b) specific resistance
(c) conductivity (d) None of these

30. When an electric bulb breaks, there is a mild bang due to
(a) the chemical reaction between the enclosed gases
(b) the compressed gases rushing out suddenly
(c) the air rushing in to fill the evacuated space
(d) None of the above

31. Transfer of heat energy from the sun to the moon takes place by
(a) radiation only
(b) radiation and conduction
(c) radiation and convection
(d) radiation, conduction and convection

32. The blue colour of the water in the sea is due to
(a) absorption of other colours by water molecules
(b) reflection of the blue light by the impurities in sea water
(c) reflection of blue sky by sea water and scattering of blue light by water molecules
(d) None of the above

33. Which of the following is used as a moderator in nuclear reactor?
(a) Ordinary water (b) Radium
(c) Thorium (d) Graphite

34. A weather balloon is not fully inflated on the ground because
(a) it cannot rise up in the air when fully inflated
(b) it cannot withstand the outside pressure if fully inflated
(c) if the balloon is fully inflated, it may not remain stable in a storm
(d) the air inside the balloon expands as it rises and may burst

35. One should not connect a number of electric appliances to the same power socket because
(a) the appliances will not get full voltage
(b) the appliances will not get proper current
(c) this can damage the appliances
(d) this can damage the domestic wiring due to overheating

36. Small drops of a liquid are spherical in shape because
(a) the earth attracts all the particles of the drop equally
(b) for a given volume, the surface area of a sphere is maximum
(c) the surface energy is maximum for the spherical shape
(d) the surface energy is minimum for the spherical shape

37. A ship rises as it enters the sea from a river because the
(a) water in sea is hard water
(b) larger quantity of water in the sea pushes the ship upwards
(c) density of sea water is lower than that of the river water
(d) density of sea water is higher than that of the river water

38. Consider the following statements
The fog during winter season is more on the day when
1. sky is clear
2. sky is cloudy
3. wind is blowing
Which of the statements given above is/are correct?
(a) Only 1 (b) 1 and 3
(c) Both 2 and 3 (d) Only 2

CHEMISTRY

1. Water is a compound because
(a) it exists as a solid, a liquid or a gas
(b) it contains hydrogen and oxygen
(c) it contains two different elements joined by chemical bonds
(d) it cannot be split up into simpler substances by chemical means

2. The element present in the largest amount in rocks and minerals is
(a) carbon (b) silicon
(c) hydrogen (d) aluminium

3. Which of the following is the lightest metal?
(a) Mercury (b) Silver
(c) Lithium (d) Lead

4. The most malleable metal is
(a) Silver (b) Gold
(c) Aluminium (d) Sodium

5. An atom of an element with mass number 23 and atomic number 11 will have
(a) 11 neutrons, 12 protons and 11 electrons
(b) 11 protons, 12 neutrons and 11 electrons
(c) 11 neutrons, 11 protons and 12 electrons
(d) 23 protons and 11 electrons

6. The filament of an electric bulb is made of
(a) iron (b) nichrome
(c) tungsten (d) graphite

7. The most abundant metal in the earth's crust is
(a) zinc (b) copper
(c) aluminium (d) iron

8. An alloy used in making heating elements for electric heating devices is
(a) solder (b) alloy steel
(c) nichrome (d) German silver

9. Galvanised iron sheets have a coating of
(a) tin (b) lead
(c) zinc (d) chromium

10. What is the purpose of adding baking soda to dough?
(a) To generate moisture
(b) To give a good flavour
(c) To give a good colour
(d) To generate carbon dioxide

11. An element that does not occur in nature but can be produced artificially is
(a) thorium (b) radium
(c) plutonium (d) uranium

12. Which of the following is the important ore of magnesium?
(a) Cessiterite (b) Malachite
(c) Carnallite (d) Galena

13. Which of the following pairs is not correctly matched?

	Mineral		**Industrial use**
(a)	Zirconium	—	Nuclear reactor
(b)	Manganese	—	Dry battery
(c)	Mica	—	Bleaching powder
(d)	Bauxite	—	Tanning

14. The element found on the surface of the moon is
(a) tin (b) tungsten
(c) tantalum (d) titanium

15. The average salinity of sea water is
(a) 2.0% (b) 2.5% (c) 3.0% (d) 3.5%

16. The metallic constituents of hard water are
(a) magnesium, calcium and tin
(b) iron, tin and calcium
(c) calcium, magnesium and iron
(d) magnesium, tin and iron

17. The high temperature superconductors are
(a) metal alloys
(b) ceramic oxides
(c) inorganic polymers
(d) pure rare earth metals

18. What are soaps?
(a) Salts of silicates
(b) Esters of heavy fatty acids
(c) Sodium or potassium salts of heavier fatty acids
(d) Mixture of glycerol and alcohols

19. In vulcanisation, natural rubber is heated with
(a) Carbon (b) Sulphur
(c) Silicon (d) Phosphorus

20. Which of the following is used as a filler in rubber tyres?
(a) Graphite (b) Coal
(c) Coke (d) Carbon black

21. Which one of the following fertilisers has more nitrogen content?
(a) Urea
(b) Ammonium nitrate
(c) Potassium nitrate
(d) Ammonium phosphate

22. Dialysis is used for people with defective kidneys. It involves the process of
(a) adsorption (b) osmosis
(c) electrophoresis (d) diffusion

23. Which of the following compounds are responsible for 'acid rain'?
1. Nitrogen dioxide
2. Silicon dioxide
3. Sulphur dioxide

4. Carbon monoxide

Select the correct answer from the codes given below

(a) 1 and 2 (b) 1 and 3
(c) 2 and 4 (d) 3 and 4

24. The substance coated on plastic tape-recorder tapes is
(a) zinc oxide (b) manganese oxide
(c) iron sulphate (d) None of these

25. Of the following metals which one used to pollute the air of a big city?
(a) Copper (b) Chromium
(c) Lead (d) Cadmium

26. Balloons are filled with
(a) helium (b) oxygen (c) nitrogen (d) argon

27. Which of the following is used in beauty parlours for hair setting?
(a) Chlorine (b) Sulphur
(c) Phosphorus (d) Silicon

28. Which of the following is the lightest gas?
(a) Nitrogen (b) Hydrogen
(c) Ammonia (d) Carbon dioxide

29. Carbon, diamond and graphite are together called
(a) isomers (b) allotropes
(c) isomorphs (d) isotopes

30. The variety of coal in which the deposit contains recognisable traces of the original plant material is
(a) anthracite (b) lignite
(c) peat (d) bitumen

BIOLOGY

1. Which one of the following is not a mammal?
(a) Bat
(b) Duck-billed platypus
(c) Shark
(d) Whale

2. The largest flower in the world is that of
(a) Lotus
(b) *Rafflesia*
(c) *Giant cactus*
(d) None of these

3. The acidic character of DNA and RNA are due to presence of
(a) purine bases (b) pyrimidine bases
(c) sugar fragments (d) phosphoric group

4. The number of DNA molecules per chromatid is/are
(a) one (b) two (c) three (d) four

5. Bacteriophage is a
(a) bacterium (b) fungus
(c) virus (d) mycoplasma

6. Sugar syrup is used for the preservation of fruits because it
(a) kills the microorganisms present in them
(b) helps to improve their taste and flavour
(c) drains moisture to inhibit growth of microorganisms
(d) mixes well with the fruits

7. Salt is used in our food because
(a) it makes the food tasty
(b) we sweat and lose salt
(c) it helps in production of hydrochloric acid required to digest the food
(d) it makes water absorb food particles better

8. What is the process by which a of lipid mass is converted into a number of small droplets?
(a) Saponification (b) Emulsification
(c) Oxidation (d) Dehydrogenation

9. Which one of the following vitamins is synthesised in the body by intestinal bacteria?
(a) Vitamin–B_1 (b) Vitamin–B_4
(c) Vitamin–D (d) Vitamin–K

10. Which of the following vitamins can be synthesised by our body ?

1. Vitamin–B_6 2. Vitamin–D
3. Vitamin–E 4. Vitamin–K

(a) 1 and 2 (b) 2 and 3
(c) 2 and 4 (d) 1 and 4

11. The vitamin which is generally excreted by humans in urine is
(a) vitamin–A
(b) vitamin–D
(c) vitamin–C
(d) None of these

12. A person who lives exclusively on milk, egg and bread is likely to become a victim of
(a) rickets (b) scurvy
(c) xerophathalmia (d) None of these

13. In the rabbit and horse, the appendix
(a) is very small
(b) helps in digestion of cellulose
(c) has no use
(d) stores food

14. What is the importance of roughage in our diet?
1. It helps in retaining water in the body.
2. It is necessary for normal functioning of the liver.
3. It adds bulk to the food and prevents constipation.

(a) 1 and 2 (b) 2 and 3 (c) 1 and 3 (d) Only 3

15. Which one of the following diseases is caused by the bite of a mad dog?
(a) Hydrocele (b) Hydrophobia
(c) Hydrocephalus (d) Hydroperitoneum

16. Which one of the following tests helps in diagnosis of cancer?
(a) X-ray (b) Urine test
(c) Blood test (d) Biopsy test

17. The most important requirement for the people of a flood hit area is
(a) smallpox vaccination
(b) BCG injection
(c) inoculation against cholera
(d) None of the above

18. During sleep a man's blood pressure
(a) increases (b) decreases
(c) remains constant (d) fluctuates

19. Match the following columns.

	Vaccine		Protects
A.	BCG	1.	Malaria
B.	BPL	2.	Sore throat
C.	Chloroquinin	3.	Tuberculosis
D.	Penicillin	4.	Rabies

Codes

	A	B	C	D		A	B	C	D
(a)	3	4	1	2	(b)	3	4	2	1
(c)	2	4	3	1	(d)	4	3	2	1

20. Which of the following are correctly matched?
1. Tse-tse fly-Sleeping sickness
2. Female *Anopheles* mosquito-Malaria
3. Sand fly- Kala-azar

(a) 1 and 2 (b) 2 and 3
(c) 1 and 3 (d) All of these

Previous Year's Questions

1. Light year is a unit of **[CLAT 2012]**
(a) distance (b) time
(c) sound (d) light intensity

2. Leukemia is a disease related to **[CLAT 2012]**
(a) kidney (b) throat (c) blood (d) eyes

3. Which is the largest gland in human body? **[CLAT 2012]**
(a) Pancreas (b) Liver (c) Thyroid (d) Pituitary

4. The largest living flightless bird is **[CLAT 2012]**
(a) Emu (b) Kiwi (c) *Ostrich* (d) Penguin

5. Light year is the unit of **[CLAT 2013]**
(a) time (b) distance
(c) light (d) None of these

6. Potential energy is described by the expression **[CLAT 2013]**
(a) PE = mgh (b) PE = ngh
(c) PE = oph (d) PE = pph

7. Palaeolithic period is also known as **[CLAT 2013]**
(a) Mesolithic age (b) Late stone age
(c) Old stone age (d) Neolithic age

8. The Environment Protection Act was passed by the Parliament of India in the year **[CLAT 2013]**
(a) 1976 (b) 1986 (c) 1996 (d) 2006

9. Dr Norman Borlaug is famous as father of the Green Revolution in 1960s. His initial goal was to create varieties of wheat adapted to the climate of **[CLAT 2013]**
(a) Mexico (b) India (c) USA (d) China

10. Which of the following planets has the maximum number of natural satellites? **[CLAT2014]**
(a) Earth (b) Mars (c) Jupiter (d) Saturn

11. The change in the colour of stars is linked to
(a) variation in their surface temperature **[CLAT 2014]**
(b) variation in their distance from the earth
(c) fluctuations in their composition and size
(d) irregular absorption or scattering in earth's atmosphere

12. Which one of the following does not remain to be a planet now? **[CLAT 2014]**
(a) Neptune (b) Uranus
(c) Pluto (d) Venus

13. Viruses are parasitic, having DNA/RNA but they can be crystallised and lack respiration. Therefore, they are treated as **[CLAT 2014]**
(a) living beings
(b) non-living beings
(c) Both (a) and (b)
(d) None of the above

14. Name the renowned Indian ecologist, who has been chosen for the prestigious 2015 Tyler Prize for Environmental Achievement on 23rd March, 2015? **[CLAT 2015]**
(a) MS Swaminathan (b) Kasthuri Rangan
(c) Jayaram Ramesh (d) Madhav Gadgil

15. Lysosomes, which are known as suicidal bags, are produced by which organelle? **[CLAT 2015]**
(a) Mitochondria
(b) Golgi body
(c) Peroxisome
(d) Ribosome

16. .... is the fastest planet to revolve around the Sun. **[CLAT 2016]**
(a) Mercury (b) Jupiter
(c) Venus (d) Mars

17. Mars is also known as the **[CLAT 2016]**
(a) blue planet (b) red planet
(c) green planet (d) brown planet

18. The country which cloned a buffalo calf first, is **[CLAT 2016]**
(a) Denmark (b) Sweden
(c) USA (d) India

19. India signed the 'Paris Agreement on Climate Change' in April, 2016 at **[CLAT 2016]**
(a) Paris (b) New Delhi
(c) Geneva (d) New York

20. Among the followig professors of Indian origin who has received Knighthood for the work as a coinventor of next generation DNA sequencing called solexa sequencing is **[CLAT2017]**
(a) Shankar Balasubramaniam
(b) P.C. Mahalanobis
(c) Mehnad Saha
(d) Satyendra Nath Bose

Answers

Physics

1	*d*	2	*c*	3	*c*	4	*c*	5	*a*	6	*b*	7	*c*	8	*c*	9	*a*	10	*c*
11	*b*	12	*c*	13	*c*	14	*c*	15	*b*	16	*d*	17	*b*	18	*c*	19	*c*	20	*d*
21	*d*	22	*c*	23	*b*	24	*d*	25	*d*	26	*b*	27	*c*	28	*d*	29	*b*	30	*c*
31	*a*	32	*c*	33	*a*	34	*d*	35	*d*	36	*d*	37	*d*	38	*a*				

Chemisty

1	*d*	2	*c*	3	*c*	4	*c*	5	*a*	6	*b*	7	*c*	8	*c*	9	*a*	10	*c*
11	*b*	12	*c*	13	*c*	14	*c*	15	*b*	16	*d*	17	*b*	18	*c*	19	*c*	20	*d*
21	*d*	22	*c*	23	*b*	24	*d*	25	*d*	26	*b*	27	*c*	28	*d*	29	*b*	30	*c*

Biology

1	*d*	2	*c*	3	*c*	4	*c*	5	*a*	6	*b*	7	*c*	8	*c*	9	*a*	10	*c*
11	*b*	12	*b*	13	*b*	14	*c*	15	*b*	16	*d*	17	*c*	18	*b*	19	*a*	20	*d*

Previous Year's Answers

1	*d*	2	*c*	3	*b*	4	*d*	5	*d*	6	*b*	7	*c*	8	*b*	9	*a*	10	*c*
11	*a*	12	*c*	13	*c*	14	*b*	15	*b*	16	*d*	17	*d*	18	*d*	19	*d*	20	*a*

CHAPTER 05

GENERAL KNOWLEDGE

General knowledge section is important section in the CLAT Entrance Exam. It covers facts of both India and the World. *Some of the significant event took place in India are listed below they are as follow*

INDIA

First in India

Census	1872
Regular Decadal Census	1881 onwards
Newspaper	Bengal Gazette (James Hickey) (Calcutta, 1780)
Persian Journal	Mirat-ul-Akhbar (Raja Ram Mohan Roy, 1822)
Vernacular Newspaper	Samachar Darpan (Bengali, 1818)
Hindi Newspaper	Udant Martand (1826)
First General Post Office	Kolkata GPO (1774)
Telephone line introduced in India	1851
First Passenger Train	Bombay to Thane (1853)
First Metro Train	Kolkata Metro (1984)
Expressway	Mumbai-Pune
First Silent Movie	Raja Harish Chandra (Dadasaheb Phalke,1913)
Talkie Movie	Alam Ara (Ardeshir Irani 1931)
English Movie	Noor Jahan (1934)

Satellite	Aryabhatta (19th April, 1975)
Indigenously made Satellite	INSAT-2A (1992)
Satellite dedicated exclusively for Education Purposes	EDUSAT
Successful Indigenous Launch Vehicle	SLV-3
Military Satellite	Rukmini (GSAT-7)
Lunar Mission	Chandrayaan-I (October, 2008)
Mars Orbital Mission	Mangalyaan
Aircraft Carriage Warship	INS Vikrant
Fighter Jet	Tejas (2001)
Battle Tank	Arjun
Indigenous Missile	Prithvi (1988)
Atomic Research Centre	Bhabha Atomic Research Centre, Tarapur
Nuclear Reactor	Apsara (1956), Trombay
First Ultra Mega Power Project	Mundra (Gujarat)
First Solar Sarovar	Bhuj (Kutchh Region)
First National Park	Hailey National Park (Jim Corbett, 1936)
First Marine National Park	Kutchh Region (Gujarat)
First Biosphere Reserve	Nilgiri (1986)
First Project Tiger	Jim Corbett (Uttarakhand, 1973)
Open University	Andhra Pradesh Open University (1982) (DR BR Ambedkar Open University)
State to establish Central Agricultural University	Manipur (1993)
Defence University	Indian National Defence University (Binola in Gurgaon, 2013)
Football Club	Mohun Bagan, Kolkata (1889)
Asian Games	Delhi (1951)
Cricket Tournament	The Bombay Triangular
Formula One Team	Force India

First in India (Female) Politics

First Woman President of India	Pratibha Devi Singh Patil
First Woman Prime Minister of India	Indira Gandhi
First Woman Speaker of Lok Sabha	Meira Kumar (2009)
First Woman Deputy Chairman of Rajya Sabha	Violet Alva (1962)
First Woman Cabinet Minister	Rajkumari Amrit Kaur (1947)
First Woman Chief Minister of an Indian State	Sucheta Kriplani (Uttar Pradesh,1963-67)
First Woman Mayor	Tara Charion (Madras)
First Woman Contestant for President Post	Manohara Holkar (1967)
First Woman Foreign Minister	Sushma Swaraj
First Female Governor	Sarojini Naidu (Uttar Pradesh)
First Woman Member of Parliament	Radhabai Subbarayan
First Actress to be nominated to Rajya Sabha	Nargis Dutt

Important Positions

First Indian Female Chairperson of INC	Sarojini Naidu (1925)
First Female President of INC	Annie Besant (1917)
First Woman IAS Officer	Anna Rajam George (1950)
First Female Chief Justice of HC	Leela Seth (1991)
First Female Judge	Anna Chandy (1948)
Chief Election Commissioner of India	V S Ramadevi (1990)
First Female DGP in India	Kanchan C Bhattacharya
First Female IPS	Kiran Bedi (1972)
First RBI Deputy Governor	K J Udesi
First Woman Chairperson of UPSC	Rose Millian Bathew
First Female Justice of Supreme Court	M Fathima Beevi (1989-92)
First Woman Artist who Performed in UNO	MS Subbulakshmi (1966)
First Woman Barrister of India	Cornelia Sorabji
First Woman Chairman of the UN General Assembly	Vijaya Laxmi Pandit

Expedition

First Woman to climb the Everest	Bachendri Pal (1984)
First Woman to climb Mount Everest Twice	Santosh Yadav (1992, 1993)
First Indian Woman to swim across the English Channel	Arti Saha (1959)
First Woman to swim across the Strait of Gibralter	Arti Pradhan (1988)
First Woman to Reach Antarctica	Maher Musa (1976)
First Woman to reach North Pole	Preety Sengupta
First Female Pilot in Indian Navy	Shivangi Singh

Sports

First Woman to Participate in Olympics	Nora Polley (1924, Tennis)
First Woman to win Grand Master in Chess	Bhagyashree Thipsay (1986)
First Woman to complete Century in World Cup Cricket	Thirush Kamini
To win Gold Medal in Pistol Shooting World Cup	Rahi Sarnobot
To win International Swimming Marathon	Archna Bharat Kumar Patel
First Woman to win Woman Tennis Association Title	Sania Mirza
First Woman to win Wimbledon India (Woman's Double)	Sania Mirza
First Woman to win Olympic Medal	Karnam Malleswari
First Woman to win a Gold in Asiad or Asian Games	Kamaljeet Sandhu

Space

First Woman to go into Space	Kalpana Chawla
First Woman to stay in the Space for the longest time	Sunita Williams
First Indian Airlines Pilot	Captain Durga Banerjee (1996)

Miscellaneous

First Test Tube Baby	Harsha *(Indira)*
First Miss Universe from India	Sushmita Sen (1994)
First Miss World from India	Reita Faria Powell (1966)
First woman to recieve Bharat Ratna	Indra Ganghi (1971)
First woman to recieve Gyanpith Award	Ashapurna Devi (1976)
First Female Excavation Engineer	Shivani Meena

First in India (Male)

Administration before Independence

First Governor-General of India	Lord William Bentinck (1833-35)
First British Governor-General of Bengal Presidency	Lord Warren Hastings (1774-85)
First Viceroy of India	Lord Canning (1858-62)
First Person to stay in Rashtrapati Bhawan (New Delhi)	Lord Irwin (1926-31)

Administration after Independence

First and Last Indian Governor-General of Free India	C Rajagopalachari (1948-1956)
First President of India	Dr Rajendra Prasad
First Vice-President of India	Dr S Radhakrishnan
First Prime Minister of India	Pandit Jawaharlal Nehru
First Minister of Education in Indian Government	Dr Abul Kalam Azad
First Non-Congress Prime Minister of India	Morarji Desai
First Scientist Nominated to the Lok Sabha	Meghnad Saha (1952)
First Muslim President of Indian Republic	Dr Zakir Hussain
First Home Minister of Independent India	Sardar Vallabhbhai Patel
First Sikh President	Giani Zail Singh
First Speaker of Lok Sabha	GV Mavalankar (1952-57)
First Deputy Chairman of Rajya Sabha	SV Krishna Moorthy Rao
The Prime Minister of India, who did not face the Parliament	Chaudhary Charan Singh
First Chairman of National Human Rights Commission	Rangnath Mishra
First Chief Election Commissioner of India	Sukumar Sen

Defence

First Commander-in-Chief of Free India	General KM Kariappa
First Marshal of the Indian Air Force	Arjan Singh (1964)
First Chief of Indian Navy	Vice-Admiral Ram Dass Katari
First Field Marshal of India	General SHFJ Manekshaw (1973)

Important Positions-Abroad

First Indian Judge in the International Court of Justice	Dr Nagendra Singh
First Indian Member of British House of Commons	Dadabhai Naoroji
First Indian American Elected as Voting Member of United States Congress	Dalip Singh Saund
First Indian American Governor in USA	Bobby Jindal
First Indian to become the Managing Director of World Bank	Gautam Kaji
First Indian Deputy Manager of the IMF	Prabhakar R R Narvekar

Sports

First Indian to play in Test Cricket	Ranjeet Singh (for English Cricket Team)
First Indian to complete Triple Centuries in Test Cricket	Virender Sehwag
First Indian to complete Double Century in One-day Cricket	Sachin Tendulkar
First Cricketer to get Padma Bhushan	C K Naidu
First Indian Cricketer to take a Wicket in his First Ball in ODI Cricket	Sadagoppan Ramesh
First Indian Cricketer to score a Test Century for the Indian Cricket Team	Lala Amarnath (1933)

Expedition

First Indian to climb Mount Everest 10 Times	Ang Rita Sherpa known as The Snow Leopard
First Indian to Climb Mount Everest without Oxygen	Ang Dorji Sherpa
First Indian to Reach the South Pole	Lieutenant Ram Charan (1960)
First Indian to Swim across English Channel	Mihir Sen (1958)

Miscellaneous

First Indian Doctor to do Successful Heart Transplant	Dr P Venugopal (1994)

Superlatives in India

Largest

The Largest Hindu Temple	Akshardham (Delhi)
The Largest Animal Fair	Sonepur (Bihar)
The Largest Prison	Tihar Jail, (Delhi)
The Largest District (in Population)	Medinipur (West Bengal)
The Largest Tribe	Gond
The Largest Saline Water Lake	Chilika Lake (Odisha)
The Largest Inland Salt Lake	Sambhar Lake (Rajasthan)
The Largest Fresh Water Lake	Wular Lake (Jammu and Kashmir)
The Largest Artificial Lake	Govind vallabh sant Sagar (Rihand Dam, Uttar Pradesh)
The Largest Desert	Thar (Rajasthan)
The Largest Delta	Sundarban (West Bengal)
The Largest Zoo	Arignar Anna Zoological Garden (Kolkata)
The Largest Gurudwara	Golden Temple (Amritsar)
The Biggest Church	Saint Cathedral at Old Goa (Goa)
The Largest Cave Temple	Kailash Temple (Maharashtra)
The Largest Mosque	Jama Masjid (Delhi)
The Largest Natural Port	Mumbai (Maharashtra)

The Largest Auditorium	Sri Shanmukhananda Hall (Mumbai)
The Largest Cave	Amarnath (Jammu and Kashmir)
The Largest Public Sector Bank	State Bank of India
The Largest Dome	Gol Gumbad, Bijapur (Karnataka)
The Largest Planetarium	Birla Planetarium (Kolkata)
The Biggest River Islands	Majuli, Brahmaputra River (Assam)
The Biggest Stadium	Narendra Modi Cricket Stadium (Ahmedabad)

Highest, Tallest

The Highest Award	Bharat Ratna
The Highest Gallantry Award	Param Vir Chakra
The Highest Hydel Power Station	Rongtong Hydel Project in Himachal Pradesh
The Highest Minar	Qutub minar (New Delhi)
The Highest Lake	Cholamu Lake (Sikkim)
The Highest Dam	Tehri Dam (Uttarakhand)
The Highest Waterfall	Kunchikal (Karnataka)
The Highest Road	Road at Urming La (in East Ladakh)
The Highest Airport	Leh Airport (Ladakh)
The Highest Peak	K_2 (8611m)
The Highest Gateway	Buland Darwaza (Fatehpur Sikri)
The Tallest Statue	Statue of Unity (Gujrat)

Longest

The Longest River Bridge	Dhola-Sadiya Bridge (Lohit river, Assam)
The State with Longest Coastline	Gujarat
The Longest River without Delta	Narmada (1312 unit)
The Longest Sea Bridge	Bandra-Worli Sea Link (officially called Rajiv Gandhi sea link)
The Longest Railway Platform	Gorakhpur (Uttar Pradesh)
The Longest National Highway	NH-44 (Srinagar to Kanyakumari, 3745 km)
The Longest River	The Ganga (2525 km)
The Longest Canal	Indira Gandhi Canal (650 km)
The Longest Dam	Hirakud Dam (Odisha)
The Longest Sea Beach	Marina Beach (Chennai)
The Longest River of Southern India	Godavari (1465 km)
The Longest Glacier	Siachen

Miscellaneous

The Smallest Inhabited Riverine Island in the World	Umananda, Brahmaputra (Assam)
The Deepest River Valley	Bhagirathi and Alaknanda
The Fastest Train	Vande Bharat Express between New Delhi and Varanasi
The Largest Concentration of Scheduled Tribes	Madhya Pradesh
The Oldest Refinery	Digboi (Assam)
The Largest Concentration of Scheduled Caste	Uttar Pradesh
The Shortest National Highway	NH-548 & 118 (Both length 5-5 km)
The Oldest Church	St. Thomas Church at Palayur, Trichur (Kerala) (built in 52 AD)

National Awards and Honours

Bharat Ratna

- Bharat Ratna is India's highest Civilian Award. It was first awarded in 1954. The actual award is designed in the shape of a Peepal leaf with Bharat Ratna inscribed in Devanagri script in the Sun Figure.
- The reverse side of the decoration Satyamev Jayate has been written in Hindi with an inscription of State emblem. The emblem, the Sun and the rim are of platinum. The inscriptions are in burnished bronze.

Winners of Bharat Ratna

1954	Dr Chandra Sekhar Venkat Raman, Dr Sarvepalli Radhakrishnan, Shri Chakravarti Rajagopalachari
1955	Pandit Jawaharlal Nehru, Dr Mokshagundam Visvesvaraya, Dr Bhagwan Das
1957	Pandit Govind Ballabh Pant
1958	Dr Dhondo Keshav Karve
1961	Dr Bidhan Chandra Roy, Shri Purushottam Das Tandon
1962	Dr Rajendra Prasad
1963	Dr Zakir Hussain, Dr Pandurang Vaman Kane
1966	Shri Lal Bahadur Shastri (Posthumously)
1971	Smt Indira Gandhi
1975	Shri Varahagiri Venkata Giri
1976	Shri Kumaraswamy Kamraj (Posthumously)
1980	Mother Teresa
1983	Shri Acharya Vinoba Bhave (Posthumously)
1987	Khan Abdul Ghaffar Khan (First Foreign Recipient)
1988	Shri Marudur Gopalan Ramachandran (Posthumously)
1990	Dr Nelson Rolihlahla Mandela, Dr Bhimrao Ramji Ambedkar (Posthumously)
1991	Shri Rajiv Gandhi (Posthumously), Sardar Vallabhbhai Patel (Posthumously), Shri Morarji Ranchhodji Desai
1992	Shri Maulana Abul Kalam Azad (Posthumously), Shri Satyajit Ray, Shri Jehangir Ratanji Dadabhai Tata
1997	Dr APJ Abdul Kalam, Smt Aruna Asaf Ali (Posthumously), Shri Gulzari Lal Nanda
1998	Smt MS Subbulakshmi, Shri Chidambaram Subramaniam
1999	Lokpriya Gopinath Bordoloi (Posthumously), Professor Amartya Sen, Loknayak Jayaprakash Narayan (Posthumously), Pandit Ravi Shankar
2001	Ustad Bismillah Khan, Lata Dinanath Mangeshkar
2009	Pandit Bhimsen Gururaj Joshi
2014	Sachin Ramesh Tendulkar (First Sportsman is get award), CNR Rao
2015	Atal Bihari Vajpayee, Madan Mohan Malaviya
2019	Bhupen Hazarika (Posthumously), Nanaji Deshmukh (Posthumously), Pranab Mukherjee

Padma Awards

The Padma awards are one of the highest civilian awards awarded on the eve of Republic Day. *They are as follow*

1. **Padma Vibhushan** It is the second highest civilian award after Bharat Ratna and is awarded by President of India.
2. **Padma Bhushan** Established on 2nd January, 1954, it is third highest civilian award. It is announced on the occasion of Republic Day every year.
3. **Padma Shri** It is the fourth highest civilian award. It is awarded irrespective of citizenship to recognise their distinguished contribution in various spheres of activities including the arts, education, industry, literature, sports, science etc.

Valour Awards

1. **Param Vir Chakra** (PVC) It is India's highest military decoration, awarded for the highest degree of valour or self-sacrifice in the presence of the enemy.
2. **Maha Vir Chakra** (MVC) It is the second highest military decoration in India and is awarded for acts of distinct gallantry in the presence of the enemy, whether on land, at sea or in the air. It may be awarded posthumously.
3. **Vir Chakra** It is an Indian gallantry award presented for acts of bravery in the battlefield. It is third in precedance in the war time gallantry awards and comes after the Param Vir Chakra and Maha Vir Chakra.
4. **Ashoka Chakra** It established on 4th January, 1952, is equivalent to the Param Vir Chakra and is awarded for the most recognizable bravery, or some daring or pre-eminent valour or self-sacrifice other than in the face of the enemy.

5. **Kirti Chakra** It may be awarded to civilians as well as military personnel, including posthumous awards. It is the peacetime award equivalent to the Maha Vir Chakra.
6. **Shaurya Chakra** It may be awarded to civilians as well as military personnel, sometimes posthumously. It is the peacetime award equivalent to the Vir Chakra.

Literary Award: Bharatiya Jnanpith Award

- The Jnanpith Award is a literary award in India alongwith Sahitya Akademy fellowship. It is one of the two most prestigious literary honours in the country.
- Any Indian citizen, who writes in any of the official languages of India is eligible for the award.

Film Awards

1. National Film Awards

- The National Film Awards are the most prominent film award ceremony in India, established in 1954 and it is administrated along with the International Film Festival of India and the Indian Panorama, by the Indian Government's Directorate of Film Festivals since 1973.
- Due to the national scale of the National Film Awards, it is considered to be the equivalent of the American Academy Awards known as oscars.

2. Filmfare Award

The Filmfare Award is presented annually by Filmfare Magazine of The Times Group. It honours professionals of artistic and technical excellence in the Hindi film industry of India.

3. Dada Saheb Phalke Award

- The Dada Saheb Phalke Award is India's highest award in cinema given annually at the National Film Awards ceremony by the Government of India for life- time contribution to Indian cinema.
- It was instituted in 1969, the birth centenary year of Dada Saheb Phalke, considered as the Father of Indian Cinema. Phalke Award carries a Swarna Kamal, a shawl and a cash prize of ₹ 10,00,000.
- First Award–Devika Rani

Sports Awards

1. Rajiv Gandhi Khel Ratna (Major Dhyan Chand Khel Ratna Award)

- The Rajiv Gandhi Khel Ratna (RGKR) is India's highest honour given for achievement in sports. The words 'Khel Ratna' literally means 'Sports Gem' in English.
- The award is named after the late Rajiv Gandhi, former Prime Minister of India. The award was instituted in the year 1991-1992 and was awarded by Government of India.
- Upto 2004-05, the cash component was ₹ 5,00,000. The money has been increased from ₹ 7,50,000 to ₹ 25,00,000.
- First Awardee—Viswanathan Anand (1991)

2. Dhyan Chand Award

- Dhyan Chand Award is India's highest award for lifetime achievement in sports and games, given by the Government of India.
- The award is named after the legendary Indian hockey player Dhyan Chand.
- The award was instituted in 2002. The award carries a cash prize of ₹ 5,00,000.
- First Award–Shohuraj Birajdar, Ashok Diwan, Apaena Ghosh

International Awards and Honours

Nobel Prize

- The Nobel Prizes are given in the memory of Alfred Bernhard Nobel, who died in 1896. He was a noted Swedish Chemist and Engineer, who discovered nitroglycerin and its use in the manufacturing of Dynamite.

- The award is given for works in 6 disciplines, *viz.*, Peace, Physics, Chemistry, Medicine, Literature and Economics.
- The awards are presented in Stockholm in an annual ceremony on 10th December, except the Peace Prize, which is awarded in Oslo, Norway.
- The nature of the award is a Gold Medal, Diploma, extension in Swiss Visa and Passport and 8 million SEK (Swedish Krona).

Indian Nobel Prize Laureates

Laureate	Year	Subject
Rabindranath Tagore	1913	Literature
CV Raman	1930	Physics
Mother Teresa	1979	Peace
Amartya Sen	1998	Economic Studies
Kailash Satyarthi	2014	Peace
Abhijeet Banerjee	2019	Economics

Ramon Magsaysay Award

- The Ramon Magsaysay Award is an annual award established to perpetuate former Philippine President Ramon Magsaysay.
- The prize was established in April 1957 by the trustees of the Rockefeller Brothers Fund based in New York city with the concurrence of the Philippine Government.
- The Ramon Magsaysay Award Foundation gives the prize to Asian individuals achieving excellence in their respective fields.

The Right Livelihood Award

- This award focuses on individuals and organisations for their outstanding work on behalf of the planet and its people. It is also known as *Alternative Nobel Prize*.
- It was established by Jakob Von Uexkull in 1980. It is to be given in the field of Environment, Human Rights, Sustainable Development, Health, Education and Peace.

Oscar Award

- The Academy Awards, informally known as the Oscar, are a set of awards given annually for excellence in cinematic achievement.
- It is organised and overseen by the *Academy of Motion Picture Arts and Sciences* (AMPAS) of United States. The awards were first given in 1929 at a ceremony created for the awards, at the Hollywood Roosevelt Hotel.
- The award ceremony was first broadcast to radio in 1930 and television in 1953.

Grammy Awards

- A Grammy Award is an honour awarded by the Recording Academy to recognise outstanding achievement mainly in the English-language music industry.
- It shares recognition of the music industry as that of the other performance award, such as the Emmy Awards (television), the Tony Awards (stage performance) and the Academy Awards (motion pictures).

Golden Globe Award

- The Golden Globe Award is an American award bestowed by the 93 members of the Hollywood Foreign Press Association (HFPA) recognising excellence in film and television, both domestic and foreign.
- The annual formal ceremony and dinner at which the awards are presented are a major part of the film industry's awards season, which culminates each year with the Academy Awards.

Man Booker Prize

- The name of Booker Prize has been renamed as Man Booker Prize in 2002.
- The award is given for fiction is a literary prize given each year for the best original hovel, written is the English language and published in the UK.

International Beauty Contests

Miss Universe

Formation	1952, Founded by-California Clothing Company, Pacific Mills
Type	Beauty Pageant
Headquarters	New York City, United States
Official Language	English
First Televised	In 1955, CBS began Nationally broadcasting the combined Miss USA and Miss Universe Pageant from 1960 and separately from 1955; in 2003, NBC took over the television rights.
Slogan	Redefined for Today
Logo	'The women with stars' was born in 1998 representing the beauty and responsibility of women around the Universe
First Winner (1952)	Armi Kuusela (Finland)
Indian Winners	(a) Susmita Sen (1994) (b) Lara Dutta (2000), Harnaaz Kaur Sandhu (2021)

Miss World

Formation	In 1951, by Morley, UK (It is the oldest surviving major International beauty pageant)
Type	Beauty Pageant
Headquarters	London, England
Location	United Kingdom
Official Language	English
Slogan	Beauty for a Purpose
First Winner (1951)	Kiki Hakansson (Sweden)
Indian Winners	(a) Reita Faria (1966) (First Asian Winner) (b) Aishwarya Rai (1994) (c) Diana Hayden (1997) (d) Yukta Mookhey (1999) (e) Priyanka Chopra (2000) (f) Manushi Chillar (2017)

Miss India

Miss India or Femina Miss India is a National Beauty Pageant in India. It is organised by Femina, a women's magazine published by Bennett, Coleman and Company Limited. Its headquarters is at Mumbai and it was formed in 1963.

Formation	1963, Organised by Femina, a women's magazine published by Benett, Coleman and Company Limited
Type	Beauty Pageant
Location	India
Headquarters	Mumbai, India
Membership	Miss World, Miss Earth, Miss International
Official Languages	Hindi/English
National Director	Nikhil Anand
Stripped of Title	In 1989, the winner Kalpana Pandit was stripped of her title for misrepresenting her nationality.

Indian Defence Military/Parliamentary Organisations

Formation Days

Organisation	Formation Day	Motto
Military Nursing Services	1st October, 1926	Service with a Smile
Indian Air Force	8th October, 1932	Touching the Sky with Glory
Central Reserve Police Force	27th July, 1939 (Raising Day)	Peace Keeper to the Nation
National Cadet Corps	15th July, 1948	Unity and Discipline
Territorial Army	9th October, 1949	—
Indo-Tibetan Border Police	24th October, 1962	Valour, Determination and Devotion to Duty
Border Security Force	1st December, 1965	Duty unto Death
Central Industrial Security Force	10th March, 1969	Protection and Security
Coast Guard	1st February, 1977	We Protect
National Security Guards	30th March, 1984	Sarvatra Sarvottam Suraksha

Indian Army Commands

Command	Headquarters
Western Command	Chandimandir (Haryana)
Eastern Command	Kolkata
Northern Command	Udhampur (J&K)
Southern Command	Pune
Central Command	Lucknow
Army Training Command	Shimla
South-Western Command	Jaipur

Indian Air Force Commands

Command	Headquarters
Western Command	New Delhi
Central Command	Allahabad
Eastern Command	Shillong
South-Western Command	Jodhpur
Training Command	Bengaluru
Maintenance Command	Nagpur
Southern Command	Thiruvananthapuram

Indian Navy Commands

Command	Headquarters
Eastern Command	Vishakhapatnam
Southern Command	Kochi
Western Command	Mumbai

Defence Research in India

- Defence Research and Development Organisation (DRDO) was established in 1958 to provide a solid base to the national security system.
- DRDO formulates and executes programmes of scientific research, design and develops new weapons required by the Armed Forces.
- Integrated Guided Missile Development Programme (IGMDP) was launched in 1983 with the aim of achieving self-sufficiency in missile development and production.
- Today it comprises five core missile programmes—the strategic Agni Ballistic Missile, the tactical Prithvi Ballistic Missile, the Akash and Trishul Surface-to-Air Missiles and the Nag Anti-Tank Guided Missile.

Indian Missiles

Prithvi-I (SS-150)	Road-mobile, short-range ballistic missile (Range : 150 km, Payload : 1000 kg, User : Army)
Prithvi-II (SS-250)	(Range : 250-350 km, Payload : 500 kg-1000 kg, User : Air Force, Army)
Prithvi-III (SS-350)	(Range: 350-600 km, Payload : 250 kg-500 kg, User: Army, Air Force, Navy)
Agni-I	(Range: 700-1,200 km, Type : MRBM, User : Army, Air Force)
Agni-II	(Range: 2,000-2,500 km, Type: IRBM, User : Army, Air Force)
Agni-III	(Range : 3,000-5,000 km, Type: IRBM, User : Army, Air Force)
Agni-IV	(Range: 2,500-3,700 km, Type : IRBM, User : Army, Air Force)
Agni-V	(Range : 5,000-8,000 km, Type : ICBM, User : Army, Air Force)
Agni-VI	(Range : 8,000-10,000 km, Type : ICBM, User : Army, Air Force)
Dhanush	Naval variant of the Prithvi short-range ballistic missile intended for launch from surface ships (Range : 350 km, User : Navy)
K-15	(Range : 750 km, Weight : 10 tonne, Warhead : 1 tonne, Length : 10 m)
K-4	(Range : 3,500-5,000 km, Speed : 7.5, Weight : 17 tonnes, Warhead : 1 tonne)
K-5	(Range : 6,000 km, Weight : Unspecified, Warhead : 1 tonne)
BrahMos	(Type : Supersonic, Range : 290 km, Status : Inducted)
Shaurya	(Type : Hypersonic, Range : 1000-1800 km, Status : Inducted, User : Army)
SRSAM	(Type : Hypersonic, Range : 15 km, Status : Inducted)
Pinaka	(Range : 40 km, Status : Inducted)
Nag	All-weather, top-attack, fire-and-forget anti-tank guided missile (Range: 4 km, Status : Inducted)
Akash	Medium range surface-to-air missile (Range: 30 km, Status : Inducted)
Phase-I	(Status : Development completed)
MRSAM	(Range : 70 km, User : Air Force)
Nirbhaya	(Range : 1000-1500 km)
Barak 8	(Range : 0.5-90 km)

Paramilitary and Reserved Forces

Indo-Tibetan Border Police (ITBP)	It was established in 1962, after the Chinese attack. It is basically employed in the Northern borders for monitoring the borders and also to stop smuggling and illegal immigration.
National Security Guard (NSG)	It was established in 1984. It has been established to counter the surface of militancy in the country. It is highly trained force which deals with militants effectively.
Central Industrial Security Force (CISF)	It was set-up in 1969 after the recommendations of Justice B. Mukherjee. Its objective is to monitor and provide security to the industrial complexes of Central Government.
Assam Rifles	It was established in 1835 and is the oldest paramilitary force in the country. Its main objective is to keep vigilance of international boarders in North-East and countering insurgency operations in Arunachal Pradesh, Manipur, Mizoram and Nagaland.
Border Security Force (BSF)	It was established in 1965. It keeps a vigil over the international borders against the intrusion in the country.
Central Reserve Police Force (CRPF)	It was set-up in 1939. Its main objective is to assist the State/Union Territory Police in maintenance of law and order. The 88th Battalion of CRPF, known as 'Mahila Battalion' (commissioned on 30th March, 1986) is the world's first paramilitary force comprising entirely women.
National Cadet Corps (NCC)	It was established in 1948. Its main objective is to stimulate interest among the youth in the defence of the country in order to build up a reserve manpower to expand armed forces.
Territorial Army (TA)	It was established in 1948. It is a voluntary, part time force (between 18 and 35 years), not professional soldiers, but civilians, who wish to assist in defence of the country.
Home Guards	It was established in 1962, to assist the police in maintaining security, to help defence forces and to help local authorities in case of any eventuality.

Indian Space Research

- The Indian space programme began in 1962 by the setting up of Indian National Committee for Space Research (INCOSPAR).
- Indian Space Research Organisation (ISRO) was set up in 1969 with its headquarters at Bengaluru.
- The Government of India established the Department of Space in 1972 to promote development and application of space science and technology for socio-economic benefits.
- Thumba Equatorial Rocket launching station near Thiruvananthapuram in Kerala was set up in 1963 for launching facilities.
- Sriharikota Range (SHAR) is a satellite launching station set up in Sriharikota in Andhra Pradesh. SHAR has been renamed as Satish Dhawan Space Centre in 2002.
- India launched its second satellite named Bhaskara I on 7th June, 1979 from Baikanur (Russia).
- The first Indian Remote Sensing Satellite was launched on 17th March, 1988.
- The first Indian Communication Satellite, *Apple* was launched on 19th June, 1981 from Kouru in French Guyana (South America). It was the first Indian satellite that was placed in geostationary orbit.
- India undertook demonstration of space applications for communication, broadcasting and remote sensing, designed and built experimental satellites— Aryabhatta, Bhaskara, **APPLE** and Rohini and experimental Satellite launch Vehicles-SLV-3 and ASLV.
- India successfully sent its Chandrayaan-1 spacecgraft to Moon in November 2008 and became the fourth individual country to sent a probe to the lunar surface.
- ISRO's PSLV-C 37 Successfully launched 104 fatelliters in filight, a world record.

India's Important Satellites

Satellite	Launch Date	Launch Vehicle	Type of Satellite
Mangalyan	24.09.2014	PSLV-C25	Exploring Planet Mars
IRNSS-1B	04.04.2014	PSLV-C24	Navigation Satellite
GSAT-14	05.01.2014	GSLVD5	Geo-Stationary Satellite
Mars Orbiter Mission Spacecraft	05.11.2013	PSLV-C25	Space Mission
GSAT-7	30.08.2013	Ariane-5 VA-215	Geo-Stationary Satellite
INSAT-3D	26.07.2013	Ariane-5 VA-214	Geo-Stationary/ Meteorological Satellite
IRNSS-1A	01.07.2013	PSLV-C22	Navigation Satellite
SARAL	25.02.2012	PSLV-C20	Earth Observation Satellite
GSAT-10	29.09.2012	Ariane-5VA-209	Geo-Stationary Satellite
RISAT 1	26.04.2012	PSLV-C19	Earth Observation Satellite
IRNSS-1D	28.03.2015	PSLV-C27	First Indian Regional Navigation Satellite System
GSAT-6	27.08.2015	GSLV-D6	Communication Satellite
Astrosat	28.09.2015	PSLV-C30	Multi-Wavelength Space Observatory
GSAT-15	11.11.2015	Ariane 5VA-227	Communication Satellite
IRNSS-1E	20.01.2016	PSLV-C31	5th Indian Regional Navigation Satellite System
IRNSS-1F	10.03.2016	PSLV-C32	6th Indian Regional Navigation Satellite System
IRNSS-1G	28.04.2016	PSLV-C33	7th Indian Regional Navigation Satellite System
Cartosat-2C	22.06.2016	PSLV-C34	Earth Observation/Remote Sensing Satellite
INSAT-3DR	08.09.2016	GSLV-F05	Meteorological Satellite
SCATSAT	26.09.2016	PSLV-C35	Miniature Satellite
GSAT-18	05.11.2016	Ariane 5 ECAVA-231	Communication Satellite
RESOURCESAT-2A	07.12.2016	PSLV-C36	Remote Sensing Satellite
INSAT-3DR	08.12.2016	GSLV-F05	Weather Satellite
Cartosat-2	15.02.2017	PSLV-C37	Remote Sensing Satellite
GSAT-7A	19.12.2018	GSLV-F11	Communication Satellite
Kalamset V2	25.01.2019	PSLV-C44	Communication Satellite
Chandrayan-2	22.07.2019	GSLV MK-III	Lunar Mission
GSAT-30	17.01.2020	Ariane 5VA-251	Communication Satellite

SPORTS (INDIA/WORLD)

Olympics

- The Olympic Games were held for the first time by the Greeks in 776 BC on Mount Olympus, in honour of the Greek God, Zeus.
- They were stopped by a royal order of the Roman Emperor Theodosius in AD 394.
- These games were revived in 1894 by the efforts of a French educator and historian Pierre de Coubertin, thats why he is considered the father of the modren olympic games and the first modern Olympic Games were started in Athens, the capital of Greece on 6th April, 1896.
- Separate Winter Olympic Games began in 1924.
- Women have been participating in the Olympic since 1912.
- The Olympic Games are organised after every four years.
- 2016 Summer Olympics were held in Rio de Janeiro.
- 2020 Summer Olympics were held in Tokoyo (Japan).

India's Performance in Olympics

Discipline	Year	Performance
Wrestling	1952	KD Jadhav won Bronze Medal in men's 52-57 kg Freestyle
	2008	Sushil Kumar won Bronze Medal in men's 66 kg Freestyle
	2012	Sushil Kumar won Silver Medal in men's 66 kg Freestyle
	2012	Yogeshwar Dutt won Bronze Medal in men's 60 Kg Freestyle
	2016	Sakshi Malik won Bronze Medal in women's 58 Kg Freestyle
	2020	Ravi Dhaiya won silver metal in men's 57 kg Freestyle.
	2020	Bajrang Punia won Bronze medal in men's 65 kg freestyle.
Hockey	1928	Won Gold Medal
	1932	Won Gold Medal
	1936	Won Gold Medal
	1948	Won Gold Medal
	1952	Won Gold Medal
	1956	Won Gold Medal
	1960	Won Silver Medal
	1964	Won Gold Medal
	1968	Won Bronze Medal
	1972	Won Bronze Medal
	1980	Won Gold Medal
	2020	Won Bronze Medal
Shooting	2004	Rajyavardhan Singh Rathore won Silver Medal in double trap
	2008	Abhinav Bindra won Gold Medal in Men's 10 m air rifle
	2012	Vijay Kumar won Silver Medal in 25 Rapid Fire Pistol
	2012	Gagan Narang won Bronze Medal in 10m Air Rifle
Athletics	1960	Milkha Singh-fourth in 400 m final Zora Singh- eighth in 50 km walk
	1964	Gurbachan Singh Randhawa -fifth in 100 m hurdles (final)
	1976	Sriram Singh-seventh in 800 m final Shivnath Singh-eleventh in the marathon
	1980	Sriram Singh-Semifinalist in 800 m
	1984	PT Usha-fourth in 400 m hurdles
	2020	Neeraj Chopra won Gold Medal in Javelin Throw.
Football (Soccer)	1956	Semi-finals
Tennis	1996	Leander Paes won Bronze Medal in men's singles event
Weightlifting	2000	Karnam Malleshwari won Bronze Medal in women's 69 kg category
	2020	Meerabai Chanu won Silver Medal in Women's 49 kg category.
Boxing	2008	Vijender Singh won a Bronze Medal (75 kg)
	2012	Mary Kom won a Bronze Medal in Women's flyweight
	2020	Luvlina Borgona won Bronze Medal in 64-69 kg Women Boxing
Badminton	2012	Saina Nehwal won a Bronze Medal in Women's singles
	2016	PV Sindhu won a Silver in women's singles
	2020	PV Sindhu won a Bronze in women's singles
Gymnastics	2016	Dipa Karmakar 4th place in the vault Final.

The Asian Games

- The Asian Games, also called the Asiad, are a multi-sport event held every four years among athletes from all over Asia.
- The games are regulated by the Olympic Council of Asia (OCA), under the supervision of the International Olympic Committee (IOC).
- The first Asian Games were held in 1951 in New Delhi.

The Commonwealth Games

- The event was first held in 1930 and with the exception of 1942 and 1946.
- Apart from many Olympic sports, the games also include some sports that are played predominantly in commonwealth countries, such as lawn bowls and netball.
- The four home nations of the United Kingdom-England, Scotland, Wales and Northern Ireland Send separate terms.
- Only six countries have attended every Commonwealth Games : Australia, Canada, England, New Zealand, Scotland and Wales.

- Australia has been the highest achieving team for twelve games, England for seven and Canada for one.

National Games of Different Countries

Country	Sport
USA	Baseball
Spain	Bull Fighting
Canada	Ice Hockey
New Zealand	Rugby Union
India	Field Hockey
Pakistan	Field Hockey
Bangladesh	Kabaddi
Sri Lanka	Volleyball
Russia	Chess
China	Table Tennis
Brazil	Football
France	Football
England	Cricket
Japan	Judo/Ju-Jitsu
Australia	Cricket
Malaysia	Badminton
Turkey	Oil Wrestling
Greece	Football
Scotland	Rugby Football
Indonesia	Badminton
Bhutan	Archery
Switzerland	Schwingen (Swiss Wrestling)

Important Cups and Trophies

Sport	Cup and Trophy
Cricket	Irani Trophy, Duleep Trophy, Ranji Trophy, Asia Cup, Deodhar Trophy, CK Naidu Trophy, Cooch-Behar Trophy
Football	Durand Cup, Nizam Gold Cup, Rovers Cup, Sanjay Gold Cup, Santosh Trophy, Subroto Mukherjee Cup, Vittal Trophy, Nehru Gold Cup
Hockey	Agha Khan Cup, Azlan Shah Cup, Nehru Trophy, Dhyan Chand Trophy, Beighton Cup, Scindia Gold Cup, Modi Gold Cup, Indira Gandhi Gold Cup, Rangaswami Cup, Khan Abdul Gaffar Cup
Golf	Canada Cup, Muthian Gold Cup, Ryder Cup, Walker Cup
Table Tennis	Corbillion Cup (women), Jayalaxmi Cup (women), Swaythling Cup (men)
Lawn Tennis	Davis Cup, Hamlet Cup, Australian Open, French Open, Wimbledon, US open
Badminton	Thomas Cup (men), Uber Cup (women), Narang Cup
Boxing	Aspy Adjania Trophy
Rowing	Wollington Trophy
Bridge	Ruia Trophy
Polo	Ezra Cup, Winchester Cup, Radha Mohan Cup

Terminologies in Sports

Sport	Terminology
Athletics	Baton, Bell lap, Decathlon, Discus, False start, Field, Foul, Hammer, heptathlon, High jump, Hurdles, Javelin, Lane, Lap, Long jump, Marathon, Cross country, etc.
Badminton	Alley, Back Alley, Backcourt, Balk, Baseline, Centre line, Clear, Court, Drive, Serve, Service court, Short service line, Shuttlecock, Smash, Wood Shot, etc.
Baseball	Pinching, Home run, Base runner, Throw, Perfect game, Strike, Put out, etc
Billiards	Cue, Cannon, Baulk, Pot scratch, Long jenny, Short jenny, Frame, Spider, Short and long rest, In-off, etc.
Boxing	Accidental Butt, Bleeder, Bolo punch, Bout, Brawler, Break, Buckle, Canvas, Card, Caught Cold, Clinch, Kidney punch, Liver shot, Low blow, Mauler, Knock out, Round, Ring stoppage, Punch, Upper-cut, Timing, Foot work, etc.
Bridge	Contract bridge, Duplicate bridge, Tricks, Suite, Rubber, Trump, Grand slam, Little slam, etc.
Billiards and Snooker	Pull, Cue, Hit, Object ball, Break shot, Scoring, Cushion billiards, etc.
Chess	Gambit, Stalemate, Move, Resign, Checkmate, etc.
Cricket	Hat-trick, Maiden, Follow-on, Declare, Bowled, Caught, Run-out, Leg before wicket (LBW), Stumped, Mid-off, Bouncer, Googly, Full toss, Drive, Cut, Pull, Hook, Flick, etc.

Sport	Terminology
Cycling	Sprint, Time trial, Point race, Trackrace, etc.
Football	Attacker, Back heel, Back Pass, Ball carrier, Bending the ball, Bicycle kick, Center spot, Corner flag, Corner kick, etc.
Golf	Ace, Albatross, Double eagle, all square, Approach putt, Apron, Ball mark, Ballooning, Beach, Birdie, Blind shot, etc.
Gymnastics	Aerial, Back handspring, Back somersault, Double back, Double twist, Flyaway, Front hip pullover, etc.
Hockey	Centre, Defender, Forward, Half, Penalty-stroke, Penalty corner, Push-in, Free-hit, Striking, etc.
Horse Racing	Race course, Steeplechase, Bets, Bookies, Jockey, Punter, etc.
Judo	Cocoa, Blue, White, Green belt, etc.
Polo	Mallet, Bunker, Chukker, Handicap, Goal, Sixty Yarder, etc.
Shooting	Bag, Bull's eye, Marksmanship, Plug, Skeet, etc.
Swimming	Add up, Anchor, Approved meet, Backstroke, Banner, Beep, Bonus Heat, Bottom, Breaststroke, etc.
Table Tennis	Backhand, Backspin, Block, Chop, Closed, Dead ball, Doubles, Drive, Drop shot, Expedite rule, Forehand, etc.
Tennis	Smash, Cross-court, Passing shot, Backhand, Forehand, Slice, Top-spin, Serve, Dropshot, Lob, Down-the-line, Deuce, Tie-breaker, Set, Game, Grand slam, Ace, volley, etc.
Volleyball	Assist, Attack, Attack line, Back row attack, Block, Center line violation, Chester, Coach kill, Whale, Yellow card, etc.
Weightlifting	Bulking, Shredded, Six pack, Feeling the burn, Power rack, Smith machine, Muscle memory, etc.
Wrestling	Free style, Hal nelson, Point , Heave, etc.

Number of Players in Different Sports

Sport	Number of Players (on one side)
Kabaddi	7
Cricket	11
Squash	1 or 2
Baseball	9
Tennis	1 or 2
Ice Hockey	6
Kho-Kho	9
Hockey	11
Football	11
Basketball	5
Badminton	1 or 2
Rugby Football	15
Polo	4
Water Polo	7
Volleyball	6
Table Tennis	1 or 2

Names of Playing Fields

Game	Playing Field	Game	Playing Field
Badminton	Court	Handball	Court
Athletics	Track	Tennis	Court
Baseball	Diamond	Golf	Course
Boxing	Ring	Hockey	Field
Football	Field	Ice Hockey/ Sketing	Ring
Cricket	Pitch	Wrestling	Ring/Arena
Archery, Shooting	Range	Judo, Karate	Mat
Swimming	Pool	Table Tennis	Board
Cycling	Vellodrome	Formula-1	Track

FAMOUS MONUMENTS

National Monuments of Major Countries

Monument	Country
Statue of Liberty (New York)	USA
Kremlin (Moscow)	Russia
The Great Wall of China	China
Eiffel Tower (Paris)	France
Leaning Tower of Pisa	Italy
Opera House (Sydney)	Australia
Christ the Redeemer	Brazil
Machu Picchu	Peru
Taj Mahal (Agra)	India
Tugu Negara (Kuala Lumpur)	Malaysia
The Great Sphinx (Giza)	Egypt

Famous Monuments of India

Site	Location	Founder/Builder
Anand Bhawan	Allahabad (Uttar Pradesh)	Motilal Nehru
Adhai Din Ka Johpda	Ajmer (Rajasthan)	Qutub-ud-din Aibak
Ajanta Caves	Aurangabad	Gupta Rulers
Akbar's Tomb	Sikandera (Uttar Pradesh)	Jahangir
Bharatpur Fort	Bharatpur (Rajasthan)	Raja Surajmal Singh
Bada Imambada	Lucknow (Uttar Pradesh)	Nawab Asaf-ud-daulah
Badrinath Temple	Chamoli (Uttarakhand)	Adi Shankaracharya
Brihadesswari Temple	Thanjavur (Tamil Nadu)	Raja Raja Chola I
Cochin Fort	Kerala	Portuguese
Dilwara Jain Temple	Mount Abu (Rajasthan)	Vimal Shah
Etamad-ud-daula's Tomb	Agra (Uttar Pradesh)	Noor Jahan
Ellora Caves	Aurangabad	Rashtrakuta Dynasty
Elephanta Caves	Mumbai	Rashtrakutas
Fatehpur Sikri	Agra (Uttar Pradesh)	Akbar
Fort William	Kolkata	Lord Clive
Gateway of India	Mumbai	British Government
Golconda Fort	Hyderabad (Andhra Pradesh)	Qutubshahi Dynasty
Golghar	Patna (Bihar)	British Government
Golden Temple	Amritsar (Punjab)	Guru Ram Das
Humayun's Tomb	Delhi	Hameeda Bano Beghum
Hauz Khas	Delhi	Ala-ud-din Khilji
Harmandir Sahib	Patna (Bihar)	Maharaja Ranjit Singh
Jama Masjid	Delhi	Shah Jahan
Jantar-Mantar	Delhi and Jaipur	Sawai Jai Singh
Jagannath Temple	Puri (Odisha)	Anantavarman Chodaganga Deva
Kankaria Lake	Ahmedabad	Sultan Qutub-ud-din
Kandaria Mahadev	Khajuraho (Madhya Pradesh)	Chandela Kings
Konark Sun Temple	Puri (Odisha)	King Nara Simhadeva (Eastern Ganga Dynasty)

Site	Location	Founder/Builder
Kashi Vishwanath Temple	Varanasi (Uttar Pradesh)	Ahilya Bai Holker
Laxmi Narayan Temple	Delhi	Birla Family
Laxman Jhula	Rishikesh (Uttarakhand)	Mehak Chauhan
Meenakshi Temple	Madurai (Tamil Nadu)	Kumari Kandam
Moti Masjid	Agra Fort (Uttar Pradesh)	Shah Jahan
Nahargarh Fort	Jaipur (Rajasthan)	Raja Jai Singh
Nishaat Bagh	Jammu and Kashmir	Asaf Ali
Old Fort (Purana Quila)	Delhi	Sher Shah Suri
President House	Delhi	British Government
Pichhola Lake	Udaipur (Rajasthan)	Nomadic gypsies
Prince of Wales Museum	Mumbai	George V
Red Fort	Delhi	Shah Jahan
Safdarjung ka Maqbara	Delhi	Shuja-ud-daulah
Sabarmati Ashram	Ahmedabad	Mahatma Gandhi
Somnath Temple	Saurashtra (Gujarat)	Bhimdev solanki
Siddivinayak Temple	Mumbai (Maharashtra)	Laxman Vithu and Deubai Patil
Shikharj	Parasnath (Jharkhand)	—
Shalimar Bagh (Garden)	Srinagar (Kashmir)	Jahangir
Taj Mahal	Agra (Uttar Pradesh)	Shah Jahan
Umaid Palace	Jodhpur (Rajasthan)	Maharaj Ummed Singh
Vijay Stambh	Chittorgarh (Rajasthan)	Rana Kumbha
Victoria Memorial	Kolkata	King George V

INDIAN ART AND CULTURE

Classical Dances of India

Dance	State	Dancer
Bharatnatyam	Tamil Nadu	Bala Saraswati, Leela Samson, Mrinalini Sarabhai, Sonal Mansingh
Kathak	Northern India (UP)	Bharti Gupta, Birju Maharaj, Durga Das, Gopi Krishna
Kuchipudi	Andhra Pradesh	Josyula Seetharamaiah, Vempati Chinna Satyam
Manipurai	Manipur	Guru Bipin Sinha, Jhaversi Sisters, Nirmala Mehta, Savita Mehta
Odissi	Odisha	Debaprasad Das, Dhirendra Nath Patnaik, Indrani Rahman
Kathakali	Kerala	Mrinalini Sarabhai, Guru Shankaram, Shankar Kurup
Mohiniyattam	Kerala	Pratima Devi, Sanyukta Panigrahi, Sonal Mansingh, Pankaj Charan Das

State and Folk Dance

State	Folk Dance
Andhra Pradesh	Kuchipudi, Ghantarmardala, Kottam Thedal
Assam	Bihu, Bichhua, Natpuja, Maharas
Bihar	Jat-Jatin, Panwariya, Bidesia
Gujarat	Garba, Dandiya Ras
Haryana	Jhumar, Phag, Dhamal
Himachal Pradesh	Jhora, Kinnauri Nati
Jammu and Kashmir	Rauf, Hikat, Damali
Karnataka	Yakshagan, Huttari, Kunitha
Kerala	Kathkali, Mohiniattam, Ottamullal
Maharashtra	Lavani, Koli, Gafa

State	Folk Dance
Odisha	Rak Mar Nacha, Ghumura, Goti Pua, Keisabadi
Bengal	Kathi, Gambhira, Dnali, Jatra
Punjab	Bhangra, Giddha, Jindua
Rajasthan	Ghumar, Kalbelia, Jhulan Leela
Tamil Nadu	Kumi, Kavadi
Uttar Pradesh	Nautanki, Rashila, Jaita
Uttarakhand	Garhwali, Jhora, Chappeli

Instrument and Vocalist

Carnatic	MS Subbalakshmi, Balamuralikrishna, Bombay Jaishree, HK Raghavendra, Aryakudi Ramanujan Iyenegar Venkataram, Sitarajam, Mani Krishnaswamy, Akhil Krishnan, ML Vasanthakumari, MD Ramanathan, GN Balasubramaniam
Dhrupad	Ustad Rahim Fahim-ud-din Dagar, Zahir-ud-din Dagar, Wasif-ud-din Dagar, Bundecha Bandhu, Pt Abhay Narayan Mallick, Pt Ritwik Sanyal, Uday Bhawalkar
Hindustani	Shubha Mudgal, Madhup Mudgal, Mukul Shivputra, Pandit Jasraj, Parveen Sultana, Naina Devi, Girija Devi, Ustad Ghulam Mustafa Khan, Gangubai Hangal, Krishna Hangal, V Rajput, Kumar Gandharva, Faiyyaz Khan, Mallikarjun Mansur.
Thumri	Ustad Bade Ghulam Ali Khan, Ustad Mazhar Ali Khan, Ustad Zawad Ali Khan, Poornima Chaudhary, Shanti Heerananda, Naina Devi, Rita Ganguly

Musical Instruments and Instrumentalists

Instrument	Instrumentalist
Stringed Instrument	
Been	Asad Ali Khan, Zia Moin-ud-din Khan
Santoor	Shiv Kumar Sharma
Sarod	Buddhadev Dasgupta, Ali Akbar Khan, Amjad Ali khan, Bahadur Khan, Sharan Rani, Zarin S Sharma
Sarangi	Ustad Binda Khan
Sitar	Ravi Shankar, Hara Shankar Bhattacharya, Nikhil Banerjee, Vilayat Khan, Mustaq Ali Khan
Surb Ahar	Sajjad Hussain, Annapurna
Veena	Doraiswamy Iyengar, Chittibabu, Emani Sankara Shastri, Dhanammal, S Bala Chandran, KR Kumaraswamy
Violin	Gajanan Rao Joshi, MS Gopal Krishnan, TN Krishnan, Baluswamy, Dikshitar, Dwaran Venkataswamy Naidu Lalyuli G Jayaraman, Mysore T Chowdiah, VG Jog
Wind Instrument	
Flute	TR Mahalingam, N Ramani, Hari Prasad Chaurasia, Pannalal Ghosh
Nadaswaran	Sheikh Chinna Moula, Neeruswamy Pillai, Rajaratanam Pillai
Shehnai	Bismillah Khan
Percussion (Striking Thumping) **Instrument**	
Mridangam	Palghat Mani Iyer, Karaikudi R Mani, Palghat Raghu
Pakhawag	Pt Ayodhya Prasad, Gopal Das, Babu Ram Shanker Pagaldas
Tabla	Zakir Hussain, Nikhil Ghosh, Kishan Maharaj, Alla Rakha Khan, Pandit Samta Prasad, Kumar Bose, Latif Khan
Kanjira	Pudukkotai Dakshinamurthi Pillai

Cultural Institution

Institution	Headquarters
Anthropological Survey of India, 1945	Kolkata
Archaeological Survey of India, 1861	New Delhi
Asiatic Society, 1784 (Sir William Jones)	Kolkata
Indira Gandhi National Centre for Arts, 1985	New Delhi
Lalit Kala Akademi (National Academy of Fine Arts), 1954	New Delhi
National Archives of India, 1981	New Delhi
National School of Drama, 1959	New Delhi
Sahitya Academi, 1954	New Delhi
Sangeet Natak Academi, 1953	New Delhi
Library of Tibetan Works and Archives	Dharmashala
Science City	Kolkata
Victorial Memorial Hall	Kolkata
Birla Industrial and Technological Museum	Kolkata
Central Institute of Buddhist Studies	Leh
Nava Nalanda Mahavihara	Nalanda (Bihar)
National Gallery of Modern Art	New Delhi

Practice Exercise

1. Which is the agency the Government has engaged to grade and standardise various agricultural products?
(a) Food corporation of India
(b) Directorate of Marketing and Inspection
(c) Bureau of Indian Standards
(d) Central Statistical Organisation

2. India Army School of Artillery is located at
(a) Bengal (b) Chennai
(c) Pune (d) Deolali

3. In which of the following states in Rangauathittu Bird Sanctuary located?
(a) Tamil Nadu (b) Kerala
(c) Karnataka (d) Andhra Pradesh

4. Kiel Canal connects
(a) Baltic Sea and North Sea
(b) Red sea and Mediterranean Sea
(c) Caribbean Sea and Pacific Sea
(d) Atlantic Ocean and Pacific Ocean

5. Among the following continents which one has the lowest growth rate of population?
(a) North America (b) South America
(c) Australia (d) Europe

6. Which of the these international tennis events is played on a grass court?
(a) US Open
(b) French Open
(c) Wimbeldon
(d) Australian Open

7. Match the following

List I	List II
A. Aurangabad	1. Auroville
B. Guwahati	2. Sarnath
C. Puducherry	3. Ellora Temples
D. Varanasi	4. Nilachal Hills

Codes

	A	B	C	D
(a)	3	4	1	2
(b)	2	1	4	3
(c)	3	1	4	2
(d)	2	4	1	3

8. Ogaden region has been a source of conflict between which countries?
(a) Morocco and Algeria
(b) Nigeria and Comeroon
(c) Angola and Zaubia
(d) Ethiopia and Somalia

9. Which of the following pairs is wrongly matched?

	Country		National Emblem
(a)	Pakistan	:	Crescent
(b)	Canada	:	White Lily
(c)	Australia	:	Kangaroo
(d)	USA	:	Lotus

10. Which one of the following is not related to United Nations?
(a) Multilateral Investment Guarantee Agency (MIGA)
(b) International Finance Corporation
(c) International Centre for Settlement of Investment Disputes
(d) Bank For International Settlements

11. Which organ of UNO is considered as World Parliament?
(a) General Assembly
(b) Security Council
(c) International Court of Justice
(d) Trusteeship Council

12. Which of the following is not associated with UNO?
(a) ILO (b) WHO
(c) Security Council (d) ASIAN

13. The headquarters of UNHCR is located at
(a) New York (b) Rome
(c) London (d) Geneva

14. First Municipal corporation was set up in 1687 in
(a) Bombay (b) Allahabad
(c) Madras (d) Calcutta

15. The first person to travel twice to space is
(a) Suman Sharma (b) Charles Simonyi
(c) David Kellermann (d) None of these

16. Ustad Vilayat khan is associated with
(a) Painting (b) Classical music
(c) Light Music (d) Instrumental Music

17. Match the following

	List I		List II
A.	Jainendra Kumar	1.	Writer
B.	Kubala Khan	2.	Euperor
C.	Marco Polo	3.	Traveller
D.	Jagdish Chandra Bose	4.	Scientist

Codes

	A	B	C	D
(a)	1	2	3	4
(b)	1	4	2	3
(c)	2	3	4	1
(d)	3	1	2	4

18. Who among the following was the first woman chief justice of a High Court?
(a) Geeta Mukherjee (b) Leila Seth
(c) Sujata Manohar (d) Rani Seth Malani

19. Who is the author of the book "Glimpses of world History"?
(a) Abul Kalam Azad (b) Jawaharlal Nehru
(c) S Gopalan (d) S Radhakrishnan

20. Match the following

	List I (Cup/Trophy)		List II (Sport)
A.	Deodhar Trophy	1.	Volley ball
B.	Durand Cup	2.	Football
C.	Davis Cup	3.	Cricket
		4.	Tennis

Codes

	A	B	C		A	B	C
(a)	3	2	4	(b)	3	1	4
(c)	2	3	1	(d)	1	2	4

21. Which one of the following days are observed as the World Environment Day?
(a) 28th February
(b) 4th March
(c) 5th June
(d) 16th September

22. Who invented the computer mouse?
(a) Charles Babbage (b) Bill Gates
(c) Douglas Engelbart (d) Narsimha Murthy

23. Swami Vivekananda's Birthday is observed in India as
(a) All Saints Day
(b) Hindu Renaissance Day
(c) National Youth Day
(d) World Religious Day

24. Which of the following in a Military Alliance?
(a) ASEAN (b) NAFTA
(c) NATO (d) EEC

25. Which one of the following countries is not a member of the Nordic council?
(a) Norway (b) Denmark
(c) Iceland (d) United Kingdom

26. Who among the following got the "Bharat Ratna" before becoming the President of India?
(a) R Venkataraman (b) Dr Rajendra Prasad
(c) Dr Zakir Hussain (d) V V Giri

27. Who is the first Non-Indian to receive the Bharat Ratna?
(a) Martin Luther King
(b) Mother Teresa
(c) Khan Abdul Ghaffar Khan
(d) Aubin Mehta

28. The first satellite to be sent into space was
(a) Pimeer (b) Luna I
(c) Sputnik (d) Apollo II

29. Selene - 1, the lunar orbiter mission belongs to which one of the following?
(a) China (b) European Union
(c) Japan (d) USA

30. Which of the following is author name of RDX?
(a) Cyanohydrian (b) Dextran
(c) Cyclonhexane (d) Cyclonite

31. Which of the following beaches is visited by Olive Ridley turtles annually for mass nesting?
(a) Chandipur
(b) Gahirmatha
(c) Gopalpur
(d) Paradwip

32. Among the Indian language, which one is spoken maximum in the world after Hindi?
(a) Telugu (b) Tamil
(c) Bengali (d) Malayalam

33. Which one of the following is the first National Park established in India?
(a) Bandipur (b) Corbett
(c) Velavadar (d) Periyar

34. In which of the following places was Asia's first Export Processing Zone (EPZ) set up?
(a) Santa Cruz (b) Kandala
(c) Cochin (d) Surat

35. The largest man-made canal in the world is
(a) Rhine Canal (b) Panama Canal
(c) Suez Canal (d) None of these

36. The headquarters of International Atomic Energy Agency is located in
(a) Geneva (b) Washington DC
(c) Vienna (d) London

37. The first newspaper in India was started by
(a) Dadabhai Naoroji
(b) J A Hickey
(c) Lord William Bentinck
(d) Rabindranath Tagore

38. The headquarters of ASEAN (Association of South East Asian Nations) is situated at
(a) Beijing (b) Mexico
(c) Kuala Lumpur (d) Jakarta

39. The first newspaper published in English language was
(a) The Bengal Gazette (b) The Hindu
(c) Young India (d) Native Opinion

40. The territory of Puducherry lies divided in the state of.
(a) Tamil Nadu, Andhra Pradesh and Maharashtra
(b) Tamil Nadu, Karanataka and Kerala
(c) Tamil Nadu, kerala and Andhra Pradesh
(d) Tamil Nadu, Karanataka and Goa

41. The Book 'Mother India' was written by
(a) Catherine Mayo (b) Lala Lajpat Rai
(c) Bal Gangadhar Tilak (d) Bipin Chandra Pal

42. Falklands Islands has been a disputed territory between
(a) Britain and Chile (b) Britain and Argentina
(c) Argentina and Chile (d) Mexico and USA

43. Vautawang Falls is located in
(a) Mizoram (b) Manipur
(c) Arunachal Pradesh (d) Tripura

44. The first woman to scale the world's 14 highest mountains is
(a) Dorothy Height (b) Oh Eun - Sun
(c) Aditi Malik (d) None of these

45. The first Lokpal Bill was introduced in the parliament in
(a) May 1968 (b) May 1980
(c) July 1982 (d) June 1985

46. D Oliverira Trophy is associated with
(a) Cricket (b) Hockey
(c) Chess (d) Football

47. Matatilla Multi-purpose project is located on
(a) River Betwa (b) River Rinand
(c) River Tapi (d) River Mahi

48. 'Romancing with Life' is a book written by
(a) Dilip Kumar (b) Debasheesh Dutta
(c) Dev Anand (d) Hema Malini

49. Which of the following cities is situated on the river Hudson?
(a) Paris (b) New York
(c) London (d) Montreal

50. Four Nobel Truths are associated with
(a) Jainism (b) Hinduism
(c) Buddhism (d) None of these

51. Who was the chairman of special committee to examine the Draft Constitution of India?
(a) Dr B R Ambedkar
(b) Sir Alladi Krishnaswary Iyer
(c) Sardar Patel
(d) Jawahar Lal Nehru

52. The headquarters of Central Water Tribunal is located on
(a) Kolkata (b) Delhi
(c) Mumbai (d) Chennai

53. When was SAARC established?
(a) 8th December, 1984 (b) 1st January, 1984
(c) 8th December, 1985 (d) 1st January, 1985

54. Which of the following volcanoes is situated in Mexico?
(a) Colema (b) Purance
(c) Sameru (d) Etna

55. Ebrahim Alkazi is a well known personality from the field of
(a) Folk Dance (b) Theatre
(c) Business (d) None of these

56. Who amongst the following has developed the concept of Human Development Index?
(a) Amartya Sen (b) A S Kadir
(c) Alva Myrdal (d) Mehboob-ul-Haq

57. The headquarter of United Nations Environment Programme (UNEP) is located in
(a) Kenya (b) Washington
(c) Moscow (d) Tokyo

58. Which of the following is the main purpose of "know your customer Guidelines" by RBI?
(a) To keep a check on money laundering
(b) To keep a check on money flow in market
(c) To bring more and more people in income tax net
(d) To know their customer well

59. Shipkila is the famous mountain pass of
(a) Himachal Pradesh (b) Jammu and Kashmir
(c) Sikkim (d) Uttarakhand

60. The Strait which Separated North and South Island's of New Zealand in
(a) Foveaus strait (b) Bass strait
(c) Cook strait (d) Torres strait

Previous Year's Questions

61. Julian Assange, the founder of WikiLeaks, was arrested in which of the following nations? **[CLAT 2011]**
(a) UK (b) Sweden
(c) USA (d) Denmark

62. Which of the following are the five countries that have decided to bid for 2017 World Athletics Championships? **[CLAT 2011]**
(a) Qatar, USA, China, Sri Lanka and Brazil
(b) Germany, Britain, Hungary, Qatar and Spain
(c) Germany, Qatar, India, Spain and China
(d) Germany, Britain, China, Qatar and Spain

63. Nagoya Protocol, signed by India on 30th October, 2010 is **[CLAT 2011]**
(a) an international treaty of bilateral investment between India and Japan
(b) an international treaty to ensure that local produce are exploited only under license and for the common good of the mankind
(c) an international treaty to ensure that the benefits of natural resources and their commercial derivatives are shared with local communities
(d) None of the above

64. Which one of the following films was officially selected to compete in the *Un-Certain Regard* (A Certain Glance) category at the 2010 Cannes Film Festival? **[CLAT 2011]**
(a) Udaan (b) My Name is Khan
(c) Wednesday (d) Dhobi Ghat

65. Why was Arundhati Roy investigated for sedition? **[CLAT 2011]**
(a) For committing contempt of court
(b) For saying that Kashmir is not an integral part of India
(c) For sympathising with the Maoists
(d) For condemning nuclear tests conducted by India

66. Damon Galgut's 'In a Strange Room' was recently in news for **[CLAT 2011]**
(a) Man Booker Prize shortlist
(b) Winning the Pulitzer Prize
(c) Winning the Orange Prize for fiction
(d) None of the above

67. Which of the following pair is incorrect? **[CLAT 2011]**
(a) Muammar Gaddafi : Syria
(b) Fidel Castro : Cuba
(c) Pol Pot : Cambodia
(d) Hosni Mubarak : Egypt

68. Who was recently in the news when the Supreme Court of India rejected her plea for Euthanasia, but paved the way for legalisation of passive euthanasia? **[CLAT 2011]**
(a) Aruna Shanbaug (b) Aruna Roy
(c) Mary Roy (d) Medha Patkar

69. Who replaced Lalit Modi as the IPL Chairman and Commissioner from this year's edition of the IPL? **[CLAT 2011]**
(a) Chirayu Amin (b) Rajiv Shukla
(c) Ratnakar Shetty (d) Shashank Manohar

70. 'The Naive and the Sentimental Novelist' is a 2010 publication of Harvard University Press of which of the following authors? **[CLAT 2011]**
(a) Orhan Pamuk (b) JM Coetzie
(c) Partha Chatterjee (d) Ben Okri

71. The recent Tunisian Revolution is known as **[CLAT 2011]**
(a) Orange Revolution (b) Jasmine Revolution
(c) Purple Revolution (d) Crescent Revolution

72. Rani Kumudini Devi, whose birth centenary is being celebrated in 2011, was the **[CLAT 2011]**
(a) first woman Barrister of India
(b) first woman Mayor of Hyderabad
(c) first woman Photographer in India
(d) first woman Doctor of India

73. Srikrishna Committee, which recently submitted its report, was constituted for which of the following issues? **[CLAT 2011]**
(a) Mumbai bomb blast case
(b) Malegaon blast case
(c) Telangana issue
(d) 2G Spectrum corruption issue

74. Which of the following teams has won the Santosh Trophy Football Championship in 2011? **[CLAT 2012]**
(a) Punjab (b) West Bengal
(c) Goa (d) Railways

75. World Computer Literacy Day is celebrated on **[CLAT 2012]**
(a) 14th November (b) 3rd November
(c) 2nd December (d) 5th July

76. Christian Lagarde heads the **[CLAT 2012]**
(a) World Bank
(b) UNICEF
(c) International Monetary Fund
(d) WHO

77. Le Corbusier, the architect of Chandigarh was a national of **[CLAT 2012]**
(a) Britain (b) Portugal
(c) France (d) Netherland

78. The seat of International Criminal Court is at **[CLAT 2012]**
(a) Hague (b) Geneva
(c) Washington (d) Tokyo

79. The largest living flightless bird is **[CLAT 2012]**
(a) Emu (b) Kiwi (c) Ostrich (d) Penguin

80. India became a member of UNO in **[CLAT 2012]**
(a) 1945 (b) 1947 (c) 1950 (d) 1952

81. The II Africa-India Summit was held in May 2011 in **[CLAT 2012]**
(a) New Delhi (b) Lagos
(c) Nairobi (d) Addis Ababa

82. Who said that, 'Man is a social animal'? **[CLAT 2012]**
(a) Socrates (b) Aristotle
(c) Kahn (d) Plato

83. Name the annual fair of Rajasthan that is famous for its camel trading even **[CLAT 2012]**
(a) Maru Mela (b) Pushkar Mela
(c) Suraj Kund Mela (d) Sonepur Mela

84. Who was awarded the UNESCO King Sejong Literacy Prize in 2011? **[CLAT 2012]**
(a) Nelson Mandela
(b) National Literacy Service, Burundi
(c) Medha Patkar
(d) National Literacy Mission, India

85. The 38th G-8 Summit held in 2012 in **[CLAT 2012]**
(a) USA (b) UK
(c) Germany (d) Canada

86. The UN Climate Change Conference 2011 was held in **[CLAT 2012]**
(a) New Delhi (b) Doha
(c) Durban (d) Geneva

87. First Indian to Ski to North pole is **[CLAT 2012]**
(a) Arun Nayyar
(b) Ajeet Bajaj
(c) Sq Ldr Sanjay Thapar
(d) Neal Paramjeet

88. 10th December is observed as **[CLAT 2012]**
(a) World Health Day (b) UN Day
(c) Red Cross Day (d) Human Rights Day

89. The book titled 'The Google Story' has been authored by **[CLAT 2012]**
(a) David A Vice (b) Shobha Dey
(c) Fredrick Forsyth (d) Vikram Seth

90. The famous Akshardham temple is situated in the city of **[CLAT 2012]**
(a) Jamnagar (b) Gandhinagar
(c) Jammu (d) Madurai

91. Which countries co-hosted the One-day Cricket World Cup in 2011? **[CLAT 2012]**
(a) India, Bangladesh and Sri Lanka
(b) India, Bangladesh and Pakistan
(c) India, Sri Lanka and Pakistan
(d) India, Sri Lanka, Bangladesh and Pakistan

92. Who was awarded the Nobel Prize for literature in 2011? **[CLAT 2012]**
(a) Paul Lauterbur (b) Bill Clinton
(c) Tomas Transtromer (d) Shirin Ebadi

93. Who was leading in the Republican primaries to contest the American Presidential Election Scheduled in November, 2012? **[CLAT 2012]**
(a) Sara Palin (b) Newt Gingrich
(c) Rick Santorum (d) Mitt Romney

94. Government of India has launched a publicity campaign for Census 2011, in association with which of the following UN Organisation? **[CLAT 2012]**
(a) United Nations Development Programme (UNDP)
(b) World Health Organisation (WHO)
(c) United Nations Children's Fund (UNICEF)
(d) United Nations Population Fund (UNPF)

95. First Woman Director -General of Police in India was **[CLAT 2012]**
(a) Kanchan Choudhary (b) Kavita Choudhary
(c) Kiran Bedi (d) Aswathy Tonge

96. Identify the Indian Tennis player who has turned Hollywood filmmaker? **[CLAT 2012]**
(a) Vijay Amritraj (b) Mahesh Bhupathi
(c) Leander Paes (d) Ashok Amritraj

97. Where did the Olympic Games held in 2012? **[CLAT 2012]**
(a) Tokyo (b) Berlin
(c) London (d) Toronto

98. Taiwan was earlier known as **[CLAT 2012]**
(a) Fuchow (b) Marshal Island
(c) Formosa (d) Macau

99. The IV Summit of BRICS was held in New Delhi on **[CLAT 2012]**
(a) 11th January, 2012 (b) 1st April, 2012
(c) 29th March, 2012 (d) 28th February, 2012

100. Who out of the following was the recipient of Dhyan Chand Award in 2011? **[CLAT 2012]**
(a) Satish Pillai (b) Hukam Singh
(c) Shabbir Ali (d) Mukh Bain Singh

101. Name the actor who has been honoured with the Dadasaheb Phalke Award in 2012? **[CLAT 2012]**
(a) Naseeruddin Shah (b) Kamal Hasan
(c) Soumitra Chatterjee (d) Amol Paleker

102. In which city was 'Osama Bin Laden' killed in May 2011? **[CLAT 2012]**
(a) Islamabad (b) Abbottabad
(c) Faisalabad (d) Peshawar

103. Priyanka Chopra has been named National Ambassador of **[CLAT 2012]**
(a) WHO
(b) UNICEF
(c) UNESCO
(d) International Red Cross Society

104. The first ever formula one race in India was held in **[CLAT 2012]**
(a) Greater Noida (b) New Delhi
(c) Faridabad (d) Pune

105. Whose teaching inspired the French Revolution? **[CLAT 2012]**
(a) Rousseau (b) Locke
(c) Hegel (d) Wagner

106. An indigenous nuclear submarine still under construction has been named as **[CLAT 2012]**
(a) Chakra (b) Sudarshan
(c) Arihant (d) Ghaatak

107. In which city was the Arab Summit held in the last week of March 2012? **[CLAT 2012]**
(a) Bagdad (b) Cairo (c) Beirut (d) Riyadh

108. The Chairman of Fundamental Rights sub-committee of the Constituent Assembly was **[CLAT 2013]**
(a) Dr Rajendra Prasad (b) Dr BR Ambedkar
(c) Pt Jawaharlal Nehru (d) JB Kripalani

109. In the name P Chidambaram, the Ex. Union Finance Minister, what does 'P' stands for? **[CLAT 2013]**
(a) Palghat (b) Pallakudi
(c) Palaniappan (d) Perumal

110. A feature 'Bluetooth' now common in mobile phones, gets its name from a **[CLAT 2013]**
(a) Chinese 10th Century King
(b) UK Software Company
(c) Greek Goddess
(d) Danish 10th Century King

111. How many medals did India win in London Olympics 2012? **[CLAT 2013]**
(a) 3 (b) 4
(c) 5 (d) 6

112. The present Pope chosen in March 2013, Hails from which country ? **[CLAT 2013]**
(a) Brazil (b) Mexico
(c) Argentina (d) Panama

113. Which is the richest temple in India? **[CLAT 2013]**
(a) Balaji temple of Tirupathi
(b) Padmanabha Swamy temple of Thiruvananthapuram
(c) Shirdi Sai Baba temple
(d) Jagannatha temple of Puri

114. Hugo Chavez, who died on 5th March, 2013 after losing his battle with cancer, was the President, of which country? **[CLAT 2013]**
(a) Argentina (b) Cuba
(c) Brazil (d) Venezuela

115. Sushil Kumar, who won a Silver Medal in London Olympics in 2012 is associated with **[CLAT 2013]**
(a) shooting (b) boxing
(c) wrestling (d) weightlifting

116. Vijay Kumar, who clinched a Silver Medal in London Olympics in 2012 is associated with **[CLAT 2013]**
(a) boxing (b) shooting
(c) weightlifting (d) wrestling

117. In the month of March, 2013 the Supreme Court of India issued a notice that the Sailors/Marines of the following country shall not leave India without the permission of the Supreme Court. **[CLAT 2013]**
(a) Germany (b) Maldives
(c) Italy (d) Nepal

118. The leaning tower of Pisa does not fall because **[CLAT 2013]**
(a) it is tapered at the top
(b) it covers a large base area
(c) its CG is inside the tower
(d) the vertical line passing through the CG of the tower falls within its base

119. The earlier name of which city was New Amsterdam ? **[CLAT 2013]**
(a) Chicago (b) California
(c) Washington DC (d) New York

120. Who founded the Red Cross? **[CLAT 2013]**
(a) Henry Dunant (b) Alexander
(c) James Cook (d) Bismark

121. South African Paralympics icon Oscar Pistorius has been accused of killing **[CLAT 2013]**
(a) Julia Kamp (b) Reeva Steenkamp
(c) Pistorius Kamp (d) Shakeera Kamp

122. The headquarter of European Union is situated in **[CLAT 2013]**
(a) England (b) Germany
(c) France (d) Belgium

123. On which date 'International Women's Day' is celebrated? **[CLAT 2013]**
(a) 18th March
(b) 8th March
(c) 28th March
(d) 18th February

124. On which date Maha Kumbh Mela started in Prayag on 2013 ? **[CLAT 2013]**
(a) 14th January, 2013
(b) 1st January, 2013
(c) 26th January, 2013
(d) 4th January, 2013

125. In which place, on 21 February, 2013, two powerful explosive devices planted on bicycles had exploded in Hyderabad? **[CLAT 2013]**
(a) Dilrubnagar (b) Dilsukhnagar
(c) Dilkushnagar (d) Dilshaknagar

126. Carlos Slim, who tops the list of world's wealthiest people, for the fourth year in a row, belongs to which country? **[CLAT 2013]**
(a) USA (b) England
(c) Mexico (d) Germany

127. India in 2008 successfully put Chandrayaan-1 into its initial orbit by **[CLAT 2013]**
(a) PSLV-C12 (b) PSLV-C11
(c) PSLV-14 (d) GSLV-D3

128. Vishwaroopam has a 2013 Tamil spy thriller film written, directed and coproduced by ________, who also enacts the lead role. **[CLAT 2013]**
(a) Prakash Raj
(b) Rajni Kant
(c) Kamal Hassan
(d) Chiranjeevi

129. 'Paradise Regained' was written by **[CLAT 2013]**
(a) John Milton (b) Michel Angelo
(c) John Keats (d) Lord Byron

130. Where was 16th NAM Summit held? **[CLAT 2013]**
(a) Tehran (b) Mehran
(c) Turban (d) Bagdad

131. POSCO steel project to come up, but being strongly protested by the people is located in **[CLAT 2013]**

(a) Chhattisgarh
(b) Jharkhand
(c) Odisha
(d) Andhra Pradesh

132. Match List I with List II and select the correct answer using the codes given below the lists. **[CLAT 2014]**

List I (Person)	List II (Position)
A. Nagendra Singh	1. Chief Election Commissioner of India
B. SH Kapadia	2. President of the International Court of Justice
C. NR Madhava Menon	3. Former Chief Justice of India
D. VS Sampath	4. Legal educator and Founder-Director of National Law School of India University

Codes

	A	B	C	D		A	B	C	D
(a)	2	3	1	4	(b)	4	3	2	1
(c)	1	2	4	3	(d)	2	3	4	1

133. Law Day is observed on **[CLAT 2014]**

(a) 26th January (b) 26th May
(c) 15th August (d) 26th November

134. Which year was designated by the United Nations as International Women's Year? **[CLAT 2014]**

(a) 1974 (b) 1975
(c) 1976 (d) 1977

135. Match List I with List II and select the correct answer using the codes given below the lists. **[CLAT 2014]**

List I (Author)	List II (Work)
A. Devaki Nandan Khatri	1. Chandrakanta
B. Premchand	2. Durgeshnandini
C. Bankim Chandra Chattopadhyay	3. Nil Darpan
	4. Seva Sadan

Codes

	A	B	C		A	B	C
(a)	4	3	1	(b)	1	4	3
(c)	2	1	3	(d)	1	4	2

136. Which one of the following is not correctly matched? **[CLAT 2014]**

	Headquarters		**United Nations Specialised Agency**
(a)	International Civil Aviation Organisation	:	Montreal
(b)	World Trade Organisation	:	Geneva
(c)	United Nations Industrial Development Organisation	:	Brussels
(d)	International Fund for Agricultural Development	:	Rome

137. Mention the correct abbreviation for ATM. **[CLAT 2014]**

(a) Automated Teller Machine
(b) Any Time Money
(c) All Time Money
(d) Auto-limited Teller Machine

138. Which country Malala Yousafzai belongs to? **[CLAT 2014]**

(a) Pakistan (b) Afghanistan
(c) The USA (d) England

139. Which one of following is the highest peacetime gallantry award of India? **[CLAT 2014]**

(a) Param Vir Chakra
(b) Ashok Chakra
(c) Maha Vir Chakra
(d) Kirti Chakra

140. Who recently became the first woman chief of the State Bank of India? **[CLAT 2014]**

(a) Arundhati Bhattacharya
(b) Shubhalakshmi Panse
(c) Vijaylakshmi Iyer
(d) Chanda Kochhar

141. Who was the first winner of the prestigious Jnanpith Award? **[CLAT 2014]**

(a) Tarasankar Bandyopadhyay
(b) Kuppali Venkatappagowda Puttappa
(c) G Sankara Kurup
(d) Umashankar Joshi

142. The 9th Ministerial Conference of the WTO, held during 3rd to 6th December, 2013, was concluded at **[CLAT 2014]**

(a) Geneva, Switzerland
(b) Kaula Lumpur, Malaysia
(c) Warsaw, Poland
(d) Bali, Indonesia

143. Who was sworn in as the Prime Minister of Italy on 22nd February, 2014? **[CLAT 2014]**
(a) Oleksandr Turchynov
(b) Matteo Renzi
(c) Enrico Letta
(d) Giorgio Napolitano

144. Who was among the following honoured with Arjun Award in Chess for the year 2013? **[CLAT 2014]**
(a) Kavita Chahal
(b) Parimarjan Negi
(c) Ronjan Sodhi
(d) Abhijeet Gupta

145. Which one of the following satellites was successfully launched by the ISRO's Polar Satellite Launch Vehicle (PSLV-C24) on 4th April, 2014? **[CLAT 2014]**
(a) IRNSS-1B (b) GSAT-14
(c) INSAT-3D (d) SARAL

146. In which year, Defence Research and Development Organisation (DRDO) was formed by the amalgamation of the Technical Development Establishment (TDE) of the Indian Army and the Directorate of Technical Development and Production (DTDP) with the Defence Science Organisation (DSO) **[CLAT 2014]**
(a) 1955 (b) 1958 (c) 1959 (d) 1963

147. Nobel Prize in Literature for the year 2013 was awarded to **[CLAT 2014]**
(a) Mo Yan (b) James E Rothman
(c) Lars Peter Hansen (d) Alice Munro

148. Till date (2014), how many people have been awarded the Bharat Ratna Award? **[CLAT 2014]**
(a) 40 (b) 41 (c) 42 (d) 43

149. Who among the following has been recently appointed as brand ambassador for Central Reserve Police Force (CRPF)? **[CLAT 2014]**
(a) Aamir Khan
(b) Mahendra Singh Dhoni
(c) MC Mary Kom
(d) Sania Mirza

150. Who is winner of the coveted Dadasaheb Phalke Award for the year 2013?
(a) Javed Akhtar (b) Gulzar
(c) AR Rahman (d) Indeevar

151. Recently, in which country did Indian Prime Minister Narendra Modi inaugurate the first of the eight Coastal Surveillance Radar Systems (CSRS) being set-up by India? **[CLAT 2015]**
(a) Mauritius (b) Maldives
(c) Sri Lanka (d) Seychelles

152. Young Indian shuttler K Srikanth on 15th March, 2015 won which of the following major badminton championship? **[CLAT 2015]**
(a) China Grand Prix Gold
(b) Australian Grand Prix Gold
(c) Swiss Grand Prix Gold
(d) Indonesian Grand Prix Gold

153. In February, 2015, which Indian cricket legend had been inducted into the ICC Hall of Fame? **[CLAT 2015]**
(a) Rahul Dravid (b) Anil Kumble
(c) Saurav Ganguly (d) Mhd. Azharuddin

154. The 'Friends for Life'—an elephant conservation project, has been launched by World Wide Fund for Nature-India and .... **[CLAT 2015]**
(a) Aditya Birla Group (b) Muthoot Group
(c) Manapuram Group (d) Reliance Limited

155. The Ufa city, where annual BRICS Summit-2015 was held, is in which country? **[CLAT 2015]**
(a) China (b) Russia
(c) South Africa (d) Brazil

156. Indian Space Research Organisation (ISRO) will recently conferred 'Space Pioneer Award' by the National Space Society (NSS) to which country over the historic feat on successfully sending an orbit to Martian atmosphere in its very first attempt? **[CLAT 2015]**
(a) France (b) European Union
(c) China (d) The USA

157. Name India's Beyond Visual Range (BVR) air-to-air missile which was successfully test fired on 19th March, 2015 from a Sukhoi-30 fighter aircraft? **[CLAT 2015]**
(a) Astra (b) K-100
(c) Mitra (d) Tejas

158. Which one of the following is essentially a solo dance now-a-days performed in group as well? **[CLAT 2015]**
(a) Kuchipudi (b) Kathak
(c) Manipuri (d) Mohiniattam

159. An Indian industrialist on whose 175th birth anniversary, Union Government launched the commemorative native stamp on 6th January, 2015? **[CLAT 2015]**

(a) GD Birla
(b) TV Sundaram Iyengar
(c) Kasturbhai Lalbhai
(d) Jamsetji Nusserwanji Tata

160. Which one of the following is the online grievances monitoring portals launched by Union Government for Indians living abroad? **[CLAT 2015]**

(a) Madad (b) Sankalp
(c) Maithri (d) Raksham

161. National Industrial Corridor (NIC) that was proposed to be established in the Union Budget 2014-15, have its headquarters at which city? **[CLAT 2015]**

(a) Pune (b) Bhubaneswar
(c) Bengaluru (d) Hyderabad

162. Who among the following is India's first Chief of Cyber Security? **[CLAT 2015]**

(a) BJ Srinath (b) Gulshan Rai
(c) AS Kamble (d) Amardeep S. Chawla

163. 'Beyond the Lines'—an autobiography is authored by **[CLAT 2016]**

(a) Justice Krishna Iyer (b) Arun Shourie
(c) Soli Sorabjee (d) Kuldip Nayar

164. The 'Paris Agreement' was adopted in the twenty-First Session of Conference of Parties in the month of **[CLAT 2016]**

(a) November, 2015
(b) February, 2016
(c) December, 2015
(d) January, 2016

165. Who was conferred the Rajiv Gandhi Khel Ratna Award during August, 2015? **[CLAT 2016]**

(a) Saina Nehwal (b) Virat Kohli
(c) Dhoni (d) Sania Mirza

166. In April, 2016, the Duke and Duchess of Cambridge visited India. Their names are **[CLAT 2016]**

(a) Prince William and Kate Middleton
(b) Prince Robert and Kateler
(c) Prince Charles and Cathy
(d) Prince Hillery and Victoria

167. In 2015, Prime Minister Narendra Modi launched a new campaign, 'Startup India, Standup India'. The campaign is aimed at **[CLAT 2016]**

(a) promoting free education to all children below the age of 14 years and assuring them jobs after obtaining higher education
(b) promoting bank financing for Startups and offer incentives to boost entrepreneurship and job creation
(c) making India digital
(d) promoting Swachch Bharat

168. Which organisation has the motto 'Be Prepared'? **[CLAT 2016]**

(a) National Disaster Management Authority
(b) Boys' Scout
(c) National Cadet Corps
(d) National Service Scheme

169. Which state has the largest number of foreign students in India? **[CLAT 2016]**

(a) Karnataka (b) Maharashtra
(c) Haryana (d) Uttar Pradesh

170. Which state has become the first state to introduce compulsory gender education at the graduate level? **[CLAT 2016]**

(a) Kerala (b) Telangana
(c) Punjab (d) Andhra Pradesh

171. Which day is celebrated as 'World Consumer Rights Day'? **[CLAT 2016]**

(a) 5th June (b) 15th July
(c) 5th September (d) 15th March

172. Prime Minister, Narendra Modi, in March, 2016, launched an ambitious programme 'Setu Bharatam'. The programme is aimed at **[CLAT 2016]**

(a) making all National Highways railway level crossing free by 2019
(b) providing travel concession to senior citizens throughout India
(c) linking all major cities and towns by rail, air and road by 2019
(d) providing travel concession to women and children throughout India

173. Who lit the torch from the Sun's rays reflected in a parabolic mirror during the Olympic flame lighting ceremony for the Rio 2016 Olympic Games at the site of ancient Olympia in Greece on 22nd April, 2016? **[CLAT 2016]**

(a) Ronaldo
(b) Katerina Lehou
(c) Joanie Laureh aka Chyna
(d) Katerina Kaif

174. A Japanese Maglev, which is the fastest passenger train in the world, has broken its own record in 2015. The train reached .... km/h in the test run. **[CLAT 2016]**
(a) 503 (b) 453 (c) 603 (d) 403

175. The country which cloned a buffalo calf first, is **[CLAT 2016]**
(a) Denmark (b) Sweden
(c) the USA (d) India

176. Country's first 'visually challenged friendly' railway station is **[CLAT 2016]**
(a) Tirupathi (b) New Delhi
(c) Varanasi (d) Mysuru

177. Who was crowned as the winner of Femina Miss India 2016 and who will represent India at the Miss World pageant? **[CLAT 2016]**
(a) Sushobita Kapoor
(b) Priyadarshini Chatterjee
(c) Pankhuri Gidwani
(d) Sushruthi Krishna

178. Who is the Chairperson of National Human Rights Commission? **[CLAT 2016]**
(a) Justice DK Jain (b) Justice BS Chauhan
(c) Justice HL Dattu (d) Justice Balakrishna

179. At the Asian Indoor Athletics Championships held at Doha in February, 2016, who among women won the gold medal in long jump? **[CLAT 2016]**
(a) Irina Ektova of Kazakhstan
(b) Olga Rypakova of Kazakhstan
(c) Mayooka Johny of India
(d) Prajusha of India

180. Who is the President of Sri Lanka? **[CLAT 2016]**
(a) Ranil Wickremasinghe
(b) Jayawardane
(c) K Sripavan
(d) Maithripala Sirisena

181. Who is the author of 'Crime & Punishment'? **[CLAT 2016]**
(a) Harold Joseph Laski (b) Karl Marx
(c) Fyodor Dostoevsky (d) Geoffrey Chaucer

182. How many Indian universities/ institutes figure among the top-200 in BRICS rankings? **[CLAT 2016]**
(a) 20 (b) 16 (c) 6 (d) 26

183. India signed the 'Paris Agreement on Climate Change' in April, 2016 at **[CLAT 2016]**
(a) Paris (b) New Delhi
(c) Geneva (d) New York

184. Which state of India was declared in January, 2016 as the 'First Organic Farming State of India'? **[CLAT 2016]**
(a) Haryana (b) Punjab
(c) Kerala (d) Sikkim

185. The largest diaspora in the world is from **[CLAT 2016]**
(a) China (b) India
(c) Mexico (d) South Africa

186. Who has written the book 'Indomitable Spirit'? **[CLAT 2016]**
(a) Arundhati Roy (b) Narendra Modi
(c) Justice Krishna Iyer (d) APJ Abdul Kalam

187. Punjabi has become the .... most common language in the Parliament of Canada. **[CLAT 2016]**
(a) fourth (b) second (c) fifth (d) third

188. The maximum number of 'Smokeless Villages' are found in the State of **[CLAT 2016]**
(a) Rajasthan (b) Telangana
(c) Karnataka (d) Punjab

189. Name the Indian gymnast who has become the first female Indian gymnast to qualify for the Olympics. **[CLAT 2016]**
(a) Anjubala (b) Dipa Karmakar
(c) Bisweshwari Nandi (d) Rupinder Kaur

190. The first statue of a woman in Parliament Square in England is that of **[CLAT 2017]**
(a) Queen Elizabeth-II (b) Mother Teresa
(c) Margaret Thatcher (d) Millicent Fawcett

191. Immediately before Antonio Guterres was appointed the U N Secretary General in October 2016, he was **[CLAT 2017]**
(a) Commissioner General of UNRWA
(b) United Nations High Commissioner for Human Rights
(c) The Prime Minister of Portuguese
(d) United Nations High Commissioner for Refugees

192. Which country 3D-Printed a home of 37 sq. mts? **[CLAT 2017]**
(a) Taiwan (b) South Korea
(c) Spain (d) Russia

193. The bowler who has claimed the fastest 250 wickets in Cricket test matches is **[CLAT 2017]**
(a) Rangana Herath (b) Ravichandran Ashwin
(c) Dennis Lillee (d) Anil Kumble

194. Prithvi Defence Vehicle is **[CLAT 2017]**
(a) the name of a single seated aircraft developed by HAL
(b) the name of an amphibious Naval Vessel
(c) the name of India's Nuclear Intercepter Missile
(d) the name of a newly developed tank

195. Who called the immigration the 'Trojan horse of Terrorism'? **[CLAT 2017]**
(a) Donald Trump, President of the U.S
(b) Angela Merkel, Chancellor of Germany
(c) Theresa May, Prime Minister of U K
(d) Viktor Orban, Prime Minister of Hungary

196. The top destination for domestic tourists in India for the past three consecutive years has been **[CLAT 2017]**
(a) Kerala (b) Odisha
(c) Tamil Nadu (d) Rajasthan

197. The first Commercial Court and Commercial Disputes Resolution Centre was inaugurated at **[CLAT 2017]**
(a) Visakhapatnam, Andhra Pradesh
(b) Mumbai, Maharashtra
(c) Ahmedabad, Gujarat
(d) Raipur, Chhattisgarh

198. Name the President elect of France who is likely to take the oath on 14th May 2017? **[CLAT 2017]**
(a) Emmanuel Macron (b) Francois Fillon
(c) Marine Le Pen (d) Francois Holland

199. Volvo has launched the world's largest bus that can carry upto **[CLAT 2017]**
(a) 260 passengers (b) 300 passengers
(c) 150 passengers (d) 320 passengers

200. Which of the following country enacted a law during August 2016 providing for the right to register the marriages of Hindus? **[CLAT 2017]**
(a) Pakistan (b) Afghanistan
(c) Iran (d) Saudi Arabia

Answers

1	*c*	2	*d*	3	*c*	4	*a*	5	*d*	6	*c*	7	*a*	8	*d*	9	*d*	10	*d*
11	*a*	12	*d*	13	*d*	14	*c*	15	*b*	16	*d*	17	*a*	18	*b*	19	*d*	20	*a*
21	*c*	22	*c*	23	*c*	24	*c*	25	*d*	26	*c*	27	*c*	28	*c*	29	*c*	30	*d*
31	*b*	32	*c*	33	*b*	34	*b*	35	*c*	36	*c*	37	*b*	38	*d*	39	*a*	40	*c*
41	*a*	42	*b*	43	*a*	44	*a*	45	*a*	46	*a*	47	*a*	48	*c*	49	*b*	50	*c*
51	*b*	52	*c*	53	*c*	54	*a*	55	*b*	56	*d*	57	*a*	58	*d*	59	*a*	60	*c*
61	*a*	62	*b*	63	*d*	64	*a*	65	*b*	66	*a*	67	*c*	68	*a*	69	*a*	70	*a*
71	*b*	72	*b*	73	*c*	74	*b*	75	*c*	76	*c*	77	*c*	78	*a*	79	*c*	80	*a*
81	*d*	82	*a*	83	*b*	84	*b*	85	*a*	86	*c*	87	*b*	88	*d*	89	*a*	90	*b*
91	*a*	92	*c*	93	*d*	94	*c*	95	*a*	96	*a*	97	*c*	98	*c*	99	*c*	100	*c*
101	*c*	102	*b*	103	*b*	104	*a*	105	*a*	106	*a*	107	*a*	108	*d*	109	*c*	110	*d*
111	*d*	112	*c*	113	*b*	114	*d*	115	*c*	116	*b*	117	*c*	118	*d*	119	*d*	120	*a*
121	*b*	122	*d*	123	*b*	124	*a*	125	*b*	126	*c*	127	*b*	128	*c*	129	*a*	130	*a*
131	*b*	132	*d*	133	*d*	134	*b*	135	*d*	136	*c*	137	*a*	138	*a*	139	*b*	140	*a*
141	*c*	142	*d*	143	*b*	144	*d*	145	*a*	146	*b*	147	*d*	148	*d*	149	*c*	150	*b*
151	*b*	152	*c*	153	*b*	154	*b*	155	*b*	156	*d*	157	*a*	158	*c*	159	*d*	160	*a*
161	*a*	162	*b*	163	*d*	164	*c*	165	*d*	166	*a*	167	*b*	168	*b*	169	*a*	170	*b*
171	*d*	172	*a*	173	*b*	174	*c*	175	*d*	176	*d*	177	*b*	178	*c*	179	*c*	180	*d*
181	*c*	182	*b*	183	*d*	184	*d*	185	*b*	186	*d*	187	*d*	188	*c*	189	*b*	190	*d*
191	*d*	192	*d*	193	*b*	194	*c*	195	*d*	196	*c*	197	*d*	198	*a*	199	*b*	200	*a*

PRACTICE SETS
(1-3)

CLAT ENTRANCE

PRACTICE SET 1

Instructions

- *There are total 200 questions in this practice set.*
- *For every correct attempt the students will be awarded 1 mark.*
- *All the questions are in MCQs form.*

English Language

Directions (Q. Nos. 1-5) *Sentences are given with blanks to be filled in with the appropriate word(s). Four alternatives are suggested for each question.*

1. The farmer had .... land and many servants.

(a) very little (b) some
(c) a lot of (d) many

2. The criminal together with his associates .... arrested.

(a) are (b) was
(c) were (d) have

3. By the time I reach America, it .... morning.

(a) is
(b) would be
(c) must be
(d) was

4. When he got married he .... a life insurance policy.

(a) took up
(b) took out
(c) took in
(d) took over

5. In the last few days, ... to help him?

(a) anything has been done
(b) is anything done
(c) something is done
(d) has anything been done

Directions (Q. Nos. 6-10) *In the following questions, you have a brief passage with five questions following the passage. Read the passage carefully and choose the best answer to each question out of the four alternatives and indicate your correct alternative.*

Read not to contradict and confuse, nor to believe and take for granted, nor to find talk and discourse, but to weigh and consider. Some books are to be tasted, others to be swallowed, and some few to be chewed and digested. That is some books are to be read only in parts; others to be read, but not curiously; and some few to be read wholly, and with diligence and attention. Some books may also be read by deputy, and extracts made of them by others but that would be only in the less important arguments and the meaner sort of books; else distilled books are like common distilled waters, flashy things. Reading maketh a full man, conference a ready man and writing an exact man.

6. What should be the purpose of reading a book?

(a) To contradict
(b) To weigh and consider
(c) To take it for granted
(d) To understand the contents

7. Why are some books to be tasted?

(a) To be read with great care
(b) To be read with great attention
(c) To be read only in parts
(d) To be read for fun

8. How is man's character influenced by the art of writing?
(a) It makes him a great writer
(b) It makes him a ready man
(c) It makes him a full man
(d) It makes him an exact man

9. What kind of books is to be read by the deputy?
(a) Extraordinary books
(b) Ordinary books
(c) Interesting books
(d) Meaner sort of books

10. What is meant by 'chewed and digested'?
(a) Thoroughly read and understood
(b) Partly read and understood
(c) Understood without any effort
(d) None of the above

Directions (Q. Nos. 11-12) *In the following questions, out of the four alternatives, choose the one which best expresses the meaning of the given **bold** word in **CAPITAL LETTERS** and indicate your correct alternative.*

11. IMPAIR
(a) Weaken (b) Couple
(c) Double (d) Repair

12. MOROSE
(a) Genial (b) Gentle
(c) Gloomy (d) Idle

Directions (Q. Nos. 13-15) *In the following questions, out of the four alternatives, choose the one opposite in meaning to the given **bold** word in **CAPITAL LETTERS** and indicate your correct alternative.*

13. AMELIORATE
(a) Decay (b) Decline
(c) Worsen (d) Destroy

14. VINDICTIVE
(a) Careless
(b) Forgiving
(c) Heedless
(d) Refined

15. CAMARADERIE
(a) Curiosity
(b) Ferocity
(c) Impetuosity
(d) Animosity

Directions (Q. Nos. 16-20) *Which of the phrases (a), (b), (c) and (d) given below each sentence should replace the word/phrase in **bold** in the sentence to make it grammatically correct.*

16. The industrialisation process underwent a **sea change** during the 19th century.
(a) A sea of change
(b) A sea changes
(c) A sea changed
(d) No correction required

17. The solution to my problem is a long-term one which can **only be tackle** by official agencies.
(a) Only is tackle (b) Only be tackled
(c) Only tackle (d) Tackle

18. The employer wanted to **strike balance** between withholding his position and getting into a rapid exchange of opinions.
(a) Strike a balance
(b) Striking balance
(c) Have stroked a balance
(d) Have strike a balance

19. The students of the football team engaged in **playing fairly**.
(a) Playing fair (b) Fair play
(c) Fairness play (d) Fairness

20. As **good luck will have it**, it did not rain on the day of the wedding.
(a) Good luck has it
(b) Good luck having
(c) Good luck have it
(d) Good luck would have it

Directions (Q. Nos. 21-25) *Read each sentence to find out whether there is any grammatical error or idiomatic error in it. The error will be in one part of the sentence. The letter of that part is the answer.*

21. The friends met again after (a) / many years, and could not stop laughing (b) / at the tricks that they had played (c) / to their teachers. (d)

22. A lion lives in a forest (a) / was loyally served by (b) / a jackal that used to accompany the lion (c) / wherever it went. (d)

23. Unable to control his natural instinct, (a) / the jackal howled at the top (b) / by his voice in the middle (c) / of the night. (d)

24. On one occasion (a) / the farmer was rewarded to (b) / a cow by a rich man (c) / for his service.(d)

25. Rakesh anger asked (a) / his son to tell him (b)/ what had happened to (c)/ the food and drinks kept in the fridge. (d)

Directions (Q. Nos. 26-35) *In these questions, in the following passage, some of the words have been left out and the blanks have been numbered from 26 to 35. First read the passage over and try to understand what it is about. Then fill in the blanks with the help of the alternatives given. Indicate your correct alternative.*

The inevitable effect of mechanical production is uniformity, and although uniformity may lead to monotony, it need not lack beauty. In fact, modern improvement in popular ...**(26)**... is mainly the result of better design ...**(27)**... standardised, goods; and the average ...**(28)**... is buying better design goods, because those goods are ...**(29)**..., because the problem of taste has been ...**(30)**... for him. Good taste is not always ...**(31)**... and most people manage to get ...**(32)**... without it. It is fortunate therefore, that so many of the ... **(33)**... of life are now chosen for us by ... **(34)**.... Even among luxuries, the margin for ... **(35)**... taste is constantly being reduced.

26. (a) craft (b) technology (c) ideas (d) taste

27. (a) on (b) of (c) in (d) for

28. (a) shopper (b) client (c) man (d) businessman

29. (a) gaudy (b) accessible (c) reliable (d) durable

30. (a) tackled (b) simplified (c) resolved (d) solved

31. (a) genuine (b) laboured (c) impulsive (d) inborn

32. (a) ahead (b) along (c) through (d) around

33. (a) amenities (b) comforts (c) luxuries (d) necessities

34. (a) connoisseurs (b) artists (c) experts (d) scientists

35. (a) local (b) particular (c) impersonal (d) personal

Directions (Q. Nos. 36-40) *In the following items, each passage consists of six sentences. The first sentence (S_1) and the final sentence (S_6) are given in the beginning. The middle four sentences in each have been removed and jumbled up. These are labelled P, Q, R and S. You are required to find out the proper sequence of the four sentences and indicate your correct answer accordingly.*

36. S_1: When you have to study for examination, you have many things to do.

S_6: The final aim, of course, is to pass the examination that is two months away.

P: Suppose you have only two months to do it.

Q: The time-table tells you what you have to do everyday and for how many hours.

R: You have to read a number of books, learn tables and formulas.

S: Then the best way is to make a time-table for yourself.

Which one of the following is the correct sequence?

(a) R P S Q (b) S R Q P (c) Q R S P (d) P S Q R

37. S_1: The umpire has to do a lot of hard work before qualifying to surpervise a match.

S_6: So an umpire must keep abreast of time and apply the rules as occasion demands.

P: However, umpires are human and are sometimes prone to make mistakes.

Q: The rules of the game are being constantly changed.

R: The pljayers should gracefully and sportingly accept these mistakes.

S: He is aware of the responsibilities that go with the ob.

Which one of the following is the correct sequence?

(a) Q R R S (b) S P R Q (c) S R P Q (d) Q R P S

38. S_1 : Mohan came to the city to meet a friend.

S_6 : He should not have behaved so rudely

P : Mohan asked her to join them for tea.

Q : Mohan's friend who had some grudge against Shiela quickly got up and left the restaurant without saying a word.

R : While they were having tea at a restaurant Sheila, a former fellow student of theirs, came in.

S : Though Sheila knew Mohan's friend was a bad fellow, she accepted the invitation.

Which one of the following is the correct sequence?

(a) P R S Q (b) R P S Q
(c) P R Q S (d) R P Q S

39. S_1 : When the Romans invaded Britain about 2000 years ago, their calendar was calculated on the phases of the moon.

S_6 : The astronomer's name was Sosigenes and his calendar had a year of 365 days.

P : This calender had gradually become so out of line with the seasons that it was two or three months behind.

Q : The Emperor Julius Caesar was determined to correct it.

R : Caesar had been to Egypt and seen the advantages of a calender which used only the sun.

S : So he sought help from a Greek astronomer who lived in the Egyptian city of Alexandria.

Which one of the following is the correct sequence?

(a) R Q P S (b) P Q R S
(c) P S R Q (d) R S P Q

40. S_1 : Education is in great demand today in India.

S_6 : Things have changed considerably now.

P : These people were accustomed to applying their intelligence to the profession of their fathers.

Q : Sinrce independence it has spread to backward classes.

R : They had no idea that they could train themselves to do something else.

S : Besides this training they had little book leaning.

Which one of the following is the correct sequence?

(a) P Q R S
(b) Q P R S
(c) P Q S R
(d) Q P S R

General Knowledge

41. When was the National Anthem of India first sung?

(a) 1947 (b) 1950
(c) 1896 (d) 1911

42. The National Anthem was adopted by the Constitutent Assembly on

(a) 27th December, 1950
(b) 15th August, 1947
(c) 24th January, 1950
(d) 26th January, 1947

43. What is the size of three horizontal stripes of the National Tricolour Flag of India?

(a) White stripe is larger than the other two
(b) There is no fixed ratio of size of the three stripes
(c) All the three stripes are equal in size
(d) Green stripe is slightly larger than saffron and saffron is slightly smaller than white

44. National Flag of India was presented to the Nation on behalf of

(a) Indian National Congress
(b) people of India
(c) women of India
(d) freedom fighters

45. Which one of the following is said to be the 'cartoon capital' of India?

(a) Mumbai (b) Hyderabad
(c) Bengaluru (d) Noida

46. What is 'wi-fi' in information technology?

(a) Wire-fidelity (b) With fidelity
(c) Wireless fidelity (d) None of these

47. What is not applicable in the context of computers?

(a) Folder (b) File
(c) Briefcase (d) Attaché

48. What is ISP?

(a) International Service Programme
(b) Internet Service Provider
(c) Integrated Service Package
(d) None of the above

49. Alam Ara, the first talkie of India was produced in the year

(a) 1931 (b) 1913
(c) 1923 (d) 1919

50. Which year was observed as the year of women's empowerment?
(a) 2000 (b) 2001 (c) 2002 (d) 2003

51. The parameter of assessing the popularity of TV programmes is
(a) TVR (b) TPR (c) TCR (d) TRP

52. Who is Ram Mohan?
(a) Well known cartoonist
(b) Well known Animation artist
(c) Well known musician
(d) None of the above

53. Writer of 'Malgudi Days', the novel based on a South Indian imaginary locale is
(a) R.K. Lakshman (b) Ruskin Bond
(c) R.K. Narayanan (d) None of the above

54. Which of the following pairs are correctly matched?

Rivers	Ocean/Sea
1. Yangtze Kiang	East China Sea
2. Euphrates	Aral Sea
3. Lena	Arctic Ocean
4. Mekong	Japan Sea

Select the correct answer using the codes given below
(a) 1 and 2 (b) 2 and 3
(c) 1 and 3 (d) 3 and 4

55. Which one of the following topographic units receives the first monsoon in summer?
(a) Western Ghats (b) Himalayas
(c) Meghalaya Plateau (d) Eastern Ghats

56. Which one of the following nations has recently pushed back its time and synchronised with the tandard time?
(a) Sri Lanka (b) Bangladesh
(c) Bhutan (d) Nepal

57. Which of the following countries is not in the African continent?
(a) Togo (b) Sierra Leone
(c) Costa Rica (d) Mauritania

58. Which one of the following pairs is not correctly matched?

	Lake	**Location**
(a)	Superior	US-Canada
(b)	Baikal	Russia
(c)	Great Bear	Canada
(d)	Great Slave	Russia

59. Match List I with List II and select the correct answer using the codes given below the lists.

List I (Lake)	**List II** (State)
A. Chilka Lake	1. Andhra Pradesh
B. Kolleru Lake	2. Kerala
C. Sambhar Lake	3. Odisha
D. Vembanad Lake	4. Rajasthan

Codes

	A	B	C	D		A	B	C	D
(a)	2	1	4	3	(b)	2	4	1	3
(c)	3	4	1	2	(d)	3	1	4	2

60. Indian Standard Time is governed by which of the following longitude?
(a) 72½° East longitude
(b) 77½° East longitude
(c) 80° East longitude
(d) 82½° East longitude

61. Which one of the following Indian States leads in the production of rubber?
(a) Tamil Nadu (b) Karnataka
(c) Kerala (d) Andhra Pradesh

62. Which one of the following pairs is not correctly matched?

	Name of the Mountain Range	**Location in the Himalayas**
(a)	Zanskar Range	Kashmir
(b)	Dhauladhar Range	Himachal Pradesh
(c)	Singalila Range	Arunachal Pradesh
(d)	Kumaon Range	Uttarakhand

63. Between which ranges does the Kashmir valley in the Himalayas lie?
(a) Siwalik and Pir Panjal
(b) Pir Panjal and Dhauladhar
(c) Zaskar and Pir Panjal
(d) Dhauladhar and Zaskar

64. Air is a/an
(a) compound (b) element
(c) mixture (d) electrolyte

65. Which of the following is the best conductor of electricity?
(a) Ordinary water (b) Sea water
(c) Boiled water (d) Distilled water

66. Balloons are filled with
(a) helium (b) oxygen
(c) nitrogen (d) argon

67. The charcoal used to decolourise raw sugar is
(a) animal charcoal
(b) sugar charcoal
(c) coconut charcoal
(d) wood charcoal

68. The most abundant metal in the Earth's crust is
(a) zinc (b) copper
(c) aluminium (d) iron

69. Which of the following is a popular festival of Asom?
(a) Durga Puja (b) Bihu
(c) Onam (d) Baisakhi

70. Who among the following was the exponent of Visistadvaita philosophy?
(a) Vallabhacharya (b) Sankaracharya
(c) Ramanujacharya (d) Madhvacharya

71. Which of the following powers did not fight for the Tungabhadra Doab?
(a) Pallavas and Chalukyas
(b) Cholas and later Chalukyas of Kalyana
(c) Golconda and Ahmadnagar Sultanates
(d) Vijaynagar and Bahmani Kingdoms

72. Where was the first university in modern India founded?
(a) Mumbai (b) Kolkata
(c) Lahore (d) Chennai

73. Which one of the following is the correct chronological order of the invasions of North-West India after the fall of the Mauryas?
(a) Bactrian Greeks–Parthians–Kushans–Hunas
(b) Bactrian Greeks–Kushans–Parthians–Hunas
(c) Parthians–Bactrian Greeks–Hunas–Kushans
(d) Parthians–Hunas–Bactrian Greeks–Kushans

74. Who among the following was the wife of emperor Ashoka who influenced him?
(a) Chandalika (b) Charulata
(c) Gautami (d) Karuwaki

75. Chand Bibi, the famous Muslim ruler, belonged to which of the following kingdoms?
(a) Bijapur (b) Golconda
(c) Ahmednagar (d) Berar

76. The famous Kailasa temple cut out of the solid rock at Ellora was built under the patronage of the
(a) Cholas (b) Kadambas
(c) Pallavas (d) Rashtrakutas

77. The temple which is called the 'Khajuraho of Asom' is
(a) Kamakhya
(b) Tirupati Balaji
(c) Madankamdeva
(d) Umananda

78. The first Battle of Panipat was fought between
(a) Humayun and Shershah
(b) Rana Sanga and Babur
(c) Akbar and Hemu
(d) Ibrahim Lodhi and Babur

79. Who among the following is the Chairman of the Steering Committee to oversee the functions of the National Authority Chemical Weapons Convention (CWC)?
(a) The President
(b) The Prime Minister
(c) The National Security Adviser
(d) The Cabinet Secretary

80. Who presides over the joint sitting of the Lok Sabha and the Rajya Sabha?
(a) The Speaker of the Lok Sabha
(b) The Vice-President
(c) The President
(d) The Union Minister of Parlia-mentary Affairs

81. The electoral college that elects the Vice-president of India consists of
(a) members of Rajya Sabha only
(b) elected members of both the Houses of Parliament
(c) members of both the Houses of Parliament
(d) members of the Rajya Sabha and the Legislative Assemblies of States

82. Which one of the following political theories advocates the withering away of the State and ushering in a new society in which there will be no State and no ceasses?
(a) Liberalism
(b) Democratic Socialism
(c) Marxism
(d) Fabian Socialism

83. At which of the following places, the Buddhist council was not held?
(a) Vaishali (b) Pataliputra
(c) Rajagriha (d) Kannauj

84. Who among the following has composed the song *'Ay Mere Watan Ke Logon'*?
(a) Jai Dev (b) Anil Biswas
(c) C Ramchandra (d) Madan Mohan

85. The SAARC movement was launched for
(a) political alliances
(b) regional cooperation
(c) cultural exchanges
(d) military strategy

86. The headquarters of International Labour Organisation is at
(a) Paris (b) New York
(c) Hague (d) Geneva

87. The highest civilian award of India 'Bharat Ratna' has been awarded to only two foreigners so far. One of them is Nelson Mandela. The other is
(a) Abdul Ghaffar khan
(b) Mikhail Gorbachev
(c) Marshal Tito
(d) Abdul Wali Khan

88. The Shanti Swarup Bhatnagar Award is given by which of the following organisations?
(a) Council for Scientific and Industrial Research
(b) Indian Council for Agricultural Research
(c) Indian National Science Academy
(d) ISRO

89. Fiscal deficit in the Union Budget means
(a) the sum of budgetary deficit and the net increase in internal and external borrowings
(b) the difference between current expenditure and current revenue
(c) the sum of monetized deficit and budgetary deficit
(d) net increase in Union Government's borrowings from the Reserve Bank of India

90. Revenue of the State Governments are raised from the following sources, except
(a) entertainment tax
(b) expenditure tax
(c) agricultural income tax
(d) land revenue

Mathematics

91. In how many different ways can the letters of the word 'ARISE' be arranged?
(a) 90 (b) 60 (c) 180 (d) 120

92. A car runs at the speed of 50 km/h when not serviced and runs at 60 km/h when serviced. After servicing, the car covers a certain distance in 6 h. How much time will the car take to cover the same distance when not serviced?
(a) 8.2 h (b) 6.5 h (c) 8 h (d) 7.2 h

93. The ratio of the incomes of A and B is 5 : 4 and the ratio of their expenditure is 3 : 2. If at the end of each year, each saves ₹ 1600, then the income of A is
(a) ₹ 3400 (b) ₹ 3600
(c) ₹ 4000 (d) ₹ 4400

94. The difference between simple and compound interest @ 10% per annum on a sum of ₹ 1000 after 4 yr is
(a) ₹ 31 (b) ₹ 32.10
(c) ₹ 40.40 (d) ₹ 64.10

95. The edges of a cuboid are in the ratio 1 : 2 : 3 and its surface area is 88 cm^2. The volume of the cuboid is
(a) 24 cm^3 (b) 48 cm^3
(c) 64 cm^3 (d) 120 cm^3

96. A dog takes 4 leaps for every 5 leaps of a hare but 3 leaps of a dog are equal to 4 leaps of the hare. Compare their speeds in terms of ratio of their speed
(a) Dog's speed : Hare's speed = 15 : 16
(b) Dog's speed : Hare's speed = 16 : 15
(c) Dog's speed : Hare's speed = 3 : 5
(d) Dog's speed : Hare's speed = 5 : 3

97. The present ages of three persons are in proportions 4 : 7 : 9 : 8 yr ago, the sum of their ages was 56. Find their present ages (in yr)
(a) 20, 35, 45 (b) 8, 20, 28
(c) 16, 28, 36 (d) 20, 36, 46

98. A car covers a distance of 715 km at a constant speed. If the speed of the car would have been 10 km/h more, then it would have taken 2 h less to cover the same distance. What is the original speed of the car?
(a) 45 km/h (b) 50 km/h
(c) 55 km/h (d) 65 km/h

99. A is 50% as efficient as B. C does half of the work done by A and B together. If C alone does the work in 40 days, then A, B and C together can do the work in
(a) $13\frac{1}{3}$ days (b) 15 days
(c) 20 days (d) 30 days

100. A person covered some distance in 12 h. He covered half the distance by rail @ 75 km/h and the rest by car @ 45 km/h. The total distance covered by him was
(a) 450 km (b) 675 km
(c) 337.5 km (d) 1350 km

101. The ratio between the curved surface area and the total surface area of a right circular cylinder is 1 : 2. If the total surface is 616 sq. cm, the volume of the cylinder is
(a) 1848 cm^3 (b) 1232 cm^3
(c) 1078 cm^3 (d) 980 cm^3

102. A sphere and a cube have equal surface areas. The ratio of the volume of the sphere to that of the cube is
(a) $\sqrt{\pi} : \sqrt{6}$ (b) $\sqrt{\pi} : \sqrt{6}$
(c) $\sqrt{\pi} : \sqrt{3}$ (d) $\sqrt{6} : \sqrt{\pi}$

103. A sum of ₹ 12000 doubles in 5 yr at CI. What will be the amount after 20 yr?
(a) ₹ 120000 (b) ₹ 192000
(c) ₹ 124000 (d) ₹ 96000

104. A sum of ₹ 800 amounts to ₹ 920 in 3 yr at SI. If the rate of interest is increased by 5%, then the amount will increase to
(a) ₹ 950 (b) ₹ 980 (c) ₹ 1010 (d) ₹ 1040

105. $\left[1+\cfrac{1}{1+\cfrac{1}{1+\cfrac{1}{3}}}\right]+1\frac{4}{7}$
(a) $1\frac{1}{3}$ (b) $1\frac{1}{4}$ (c) $1\frac{1}{7}$ (d) 1

106. If 272/3 × 81 – 1/2 = 3x, the value of x is
(a) 1 (b) 0 (c) 1 (d) 2

Directions (Q. Nos. 107-110) *What approximate value should come in place of the question mark (?) in the following questions? (You are not expected to calculate the exact value.)*

107. 3735 + 13064 × 346 = ?
(a) 89 (b) 83 (c) 76 (d) 79

108. 54 × 746 ÷ 32 = ?
(a) 1259 (b) 1268
(c) 1196 (d) 1248

109. 7414 + 3698 + 1257 + 1869 = ?
(a) 14328 (b) 14438
(c) 13428 (d) None of these

110. (98360 + 25845 – 36540) ÷ 2500 = ?
(a) 36 (b) 30 (c) 32 (d) 35

Legal Aptitude & Indian Constitution

111. A candidate for the Lok Sabha and Assembly elections, as per the rulings of Supreme Court of India shall have to disclose
(a) assets and antecedents
(b) educational qualifications
(c) previous nomination
(d) Both (a) and (b)

112. The State shall endeavour to provide early childhood care and education for all children until they complete the age of Fourteen years. This provision is made in the Constitution 86th Amendment in
(a) Article 45 of the Constitution
(b) Article 245 of the Constitution
(c) Article 345 of the Constitution
(d) Article 145 of the Constitution

113. The concept of 'Hindutva' is well interpreted by the Supreme Court in
(a) the Minerva Mills case
(b) the Babri Masjid case
(c) the Golak Nath case
(d) the Manohar Joshi case

114. The High Courts at Bombay, Calcutta and Madras were established under the
(a) Indian High Courts Act, 1861
(b) Indian High Courts Act, 1865
(c) Indian High Courts Act, 1911
(d) Government of India Act, 1919

115. 'A' enters 'Z' house through a window. Here 'A' commits
(a) trespass (b) house trespass
(c) house breaking (d) All of these

116. Which Section of the Indian Evidence Act is not on 'shifting of burden of proof'?
(a) Section 101 (b) Section 102
(c) Section 105 (d) Section 108

117. The illustration that, 'A' and 'B' are jointly tried for the murder of 'C'. It is proved that A said, 'B' and I murdered 'C'," relates
(a) Section 30 of the Indian Evidence Act
(b) Section 24 of the Indian Evidence Act
(c) Section 25 of the Indian Evidence Act
(d) Section 27 of the Indian Evidence Act

118. A Hindu married woman of 32 years of age adopts a male child of 8 years with the consent of her husband. The adoption is
(a) valid
(b) not valid
(c) voidable at the option of husband
(d) None of the above

119. Which is the secondary source of Muslim Law under the following?
(a) Custom (b) Ijmaa
(c) Qiyas (d) None of these

120. What are the wife's rights when husband does not pay the dower?
(a) Refuse consummation
(b) File suit for recovery of dower
(c) Keep possession over dead husband's property
(d) All of the above

121. In Sunni-te Law, the guardian of the minor's property is
(a) mother (b) father
(c) mother's mother (d) father's father

122. A person employed to do any act for another or to represent another in dealings with the third person is
(a) aprincipal (b) apawnor
(c) an agent (d) abailor

123. The following is not the exception to the rule of hearsay
(a) dying declaration
(b) res gesture
(c) medical Expert's opinion
(d) confession

124. Which one of the following is not a document under the Indian Evidence Act?
(a) An inscription on a stone of a building
(b) A photograph
(c) A printout of a message sent through mobile or computer
(d) A knife recovered by police from the possession of an accused and produced in the court

125. In which of the following cases hearsay evidence is not admissible?
(a) Statement of experts expressed in treaties, if the author is dead or cannot be found
(b) Where eye-witness told the facts to another person, statement of that person
(c) If the statement is of a deceased person, when it related to cause of his death
(d) If the statement is part of the transaction-in-issue

126. Which one of the following Sections of the Indian Evidence Act says 'facts admitted need not be proved'?
(a) Section 18 (b) Section 21(v)
(c) Section 55 (d) Section 58

127. How many kinds of hurts are included under grievous hurt under Section 320 of the Indian Penal Code?
(a) 5 (b) 6 (c) 7 (d) 8

128. Which one of the following cases is not correctly matched?
(a) McNaughten's Case–Section 84 of IPC
(b) DPP versus Beard–Section 84 of IPC
(c) Basudeo versus State–Section 86 of IPC
(d) Bhawoo uiwaji *ver* Mooljee Dayal–Section 79 of IPC

129. 'A' attempts to pick the pocket of 'Z' by thrusting his hand into 'Z's pocket. 'A' fails in his attempt as 'Z' had nothing in his pocket. What offence 'A' has committed?
(a) Theft
(b) Attempt to commit theft
(c) Mischief
(d) No offence

130. Which one of the following Sections of the Code of Criminal Procedure provides for anticipatory bail?
(a) Section 436 (b) Section 438
(c) Section 439 (d) Section 437

131. Which of the following are liable under Section 125(1)(d) of the Code of Criminal Procedure for payment of maintenance to their parents, who are unable to maintain themselves?
(a) Sons only
(b) Daughters only
(c) Sons and daughters both
(d) None of the above

132. Under Section 15 of the Code of Civil Procedure, every suit shall be instituted in
(a) district court
(b) the court of lower grade
(c) the court of higher grade
(d) All of the above

133. In which of the following cases the principles relating to the defence of intoxication were laid down?
(a) McNaughten Case
(b) Director of Public Prosecution versus Beard
(c) R versus Dudley and Stephen
(d) R versus Prince

134. A Sunni Muslim performs marriage during the period of '*Iddat*', the marriage is
(a) void (b) valid
(c) irregular (d) voidable

135. Rule against perpetuity will not be applicable in
(a) perpetual transfer for gift
(b) personal contracts
(c) vested interest
(d) All of the above

136. Which one of the following provisions of the Transfer of Property Act relates to 'usufructuary mortgage'?
(a) Section 58 (a)
(b) Section 58 (b)
(c) Section 58 (d)
(d) Section 58 (e)

137. Which Provisions of the Transfer of Property Act defines 'lease'?
(a) Section 105 (b) Section 106
(c) Section 107 (d) Section 108

Directions (Q. Nos. 138-140) *Answer the Questions by application of the following legal principle.*

Principle When two or more persons agree to do, or cause to be done, an illegal act, or an act which is not illegal by illegal means, such an agreement is designated a criminal conspiracy provided that no agreement except an agreement to commit an offence shall amount to a criminal conspiracy unless some act besides the agreement is done by one or more parties to such agreement in pursuance thereof.

It is immaterial whether the illegal act is ultimate object of such agreement, or is merely incidental to that object.

138. John, Thomson, Robert, Smith and Chriss entered into an agreement to destroy an office building of the Government of India. John purchased AK-47 rifles and guns and explosive. Thomson supplied vehicles. Robert contributed money. Smith and Chriss made arrangements, conducted meetings and made plans for the commission of the act. John, Thomson and Robert before reaching the office building were apprehended by police and were shot dead. Decide about the offence of Smith and Chriss
(a) Smith and Chris are not guilty of conspiracy as they had not gone in the vehicle for committing crime
(b) liability of Smith and Chriss comes to end with the death of main accused persons viz John, Thomson and Robert
(c) as no offence is committed no one is responsible
(d) Smith and Chris are to be punished as it is immaterial in the criminal law, whether illegal act is ultimate object of the agreement or merely incidental to that object

139. In case of conspiracy, there must be
(a) two or more persons
(b) more than one person
(c) Both (a) and (b)
(d) Only (b) is correct and (a) is incorrect

140. The gist of the offence of criminal conspiracy is
(a) agreement is necessary between two or more persons to do or cause to be done an illegal act
(b) a legal act by illegal means followed by an overt act to be done or cause to be done according to agreement
(c) Both (a) and (b)
(d) None of the above

Directions (Q. Nos. 141-145) *Given below is a statement of legal principle, followed by a factual situation. Apply the principle to the facts and select the most appropriate answer among the alternatives given.*

141. Principle There is no liability is tort in cases of inevitable accidents.

Facts The defendant who was one of a showing party, fixed on a peasant. One of the bullets from his gun glanced off the bough of a tree and accidentally wounded the plaintiff who was engaged in carrying cartridges and game for the party.

(a) Defendant is liable
(b) Defendant is not liable because it is an inevitable accident and could not possible to prevent
(c) Defendant is liable because he had not act in this way
(d) None of the above

142. Principle Culpable homicide is murder, if the act by which the death is caused is done with the intention of causing death.

Facts X is in cultivating possession of agricultural land belonging to 'Z'. A suit is pending before the court for recovery of the said land. 'X' along with 'Y' intending to kill 'Z' to keep the disputed land in possession, plan and set fire to his house by locking 'Z' from outside just before midnight and by preventing other from coming to his rescue. 'Z' is roasted alive. Decide.
(a) 'X' and 'Y' guilty of murder
(b) 'X' and 'Y' are not guilty of murder
(c) 'X' and 'Y' are guilty of culpable homicide not, amounting to murder
(d) None of the above

143. Principle A contract is an agreement which the law will enforce. All agreements are contract if they are made with free consent by parties competent to contract for a lawful consideration and with a lawful object.

Facts 'A', a young man and 30 yr old businessman of sound mind without any consideration agrees to give 'B' ₹ 10000. 'A' fails to fulfil his promise, 'B' sues 'A' for the amount
(a) 'B' will succeed as 'A' has the capacity to make the contract
(b) 'B' will succeed as 'A' made the promise of his own free will
(c) 'B' will succeed as the money is not being paid for any illegal object
(d) 'B' will fail as the agreement is without consideration

144. Principle A contract without consideration is void. When at the desire of one party, the other party does something the consideration is said to flow from the later to the former.

Facts A house was on fire and a child was trapped inside the house, everyone was shouting for help. A brave on looker, hearing the shouting of child, went inside the house and brought it out. The grateful father of the child promised to pay the rescuer ₹ 10000 subsequently be rendered the promise. The rescuer sued the promisee for the breach.
(a) Commercial consideration cannot be applied to humanitarian help
(b) The father of the child must pay for the service rendered by the rescuer
(c) The recover is not entitled to the payment, since he acted on his own
(d) None of the above

145. Principle No person can be judge in his own cause.

Facts An admission test is to be held to select the best students for admission on merit. The father of a candidate without disclosing that his son is appearing in the test is involved in conducting test. Objections are taken on the ground that the sanctity of the test is vitiated as a person undirected in the test has taken part in conducting it. Decide
(a) test is valid because father of candidate is not a judge in this case
(b) admission test is vitiated because father is a party of conducting the test and hence in a position to affect the result
(c) objection not on sound ground
(d) None of the above

146. Two terms tentrue of US President was fixed in
(a) 1748 (b) 1848
(c) 1948 (d) None of these

147. The US Senate comprises
(a) 98 members (b) 100 members
(c) 102 members (d) None of these

148. The term of US House of Representative is
(a) 2 years (b) 3 years
(c) 4 years (d) None of these

149. Gerald Ford was US President by
(a) Appointment (b) Election
(c) Succession (d) None of these

150. The quorum of the House of Commons is
(a) 40 members (b) 50 members
(c) 60 members (d) None of these

151. The Labour Party was founded in Britain in
(a) 1900 (b) 1901
(c) 1902 (d) None of these

152. The Speaker of the House of Commons owes allegiance to
(a) Majority Party (b) Opposition Party
(c) No Party (d) None of these

153. The judges of the Indian Supreme Court are appointed by
(a) The Prime Minsiter (b) The President
(c) Parliament (d) None of these

154. Indian Parliament is
(a) Unicameral (b) Bicameral
(c) Tricameral (d) None of these

155. Relevancy and admissibility under the Indian Evidence Act are
(a) synonymous
(b) co-extensive
(c) Neither (a) nor (b)
(d) Both (a) and (b)

156. What is correct as regards the admissibility of self-regarding statements?
(a) Self-harming statement is admissible, but a self-serving statement is not generally admissible
(b) Self-serving statement is admissible, but a self-harming statement is not generally admissible
(c) Self-serving and self-harming statements both are generally admissible
(d) Self-serving and self-harming statements both are generally inadmissible

157. Motives of preparation and conduct are underwhich Section of Evidence Act?
(a) Under Section 6 of Evidence Act
(b) Under Section 7 of Evidence Act
(c) Under Section 8 of Evidence Act
(d) Under Section 9 of Evidence Act

158. Contractual rights and duties are created by
(a) state (b) statute
(c) parties (d) custom or usage

159. Voidable contract is one
(a) which is lawful
(b) which is invalid
(c) which is valid as long as it is not avoided by the party entitled to do so
(d) which is unlawful

160. A contract creates
(a) rights in personam
(b) rights in rem
(c) no obligations
(d) only obligations and no rights

Logical Reasoning

161. How many meaningful English words can be made with the letters 'OEHM' using each letter only once in each word?
(a) None (b) One (c) Two (d) Three

162. Sneha correctly remembers that her father's birthday is before 16th June but after 11th June whereas her younger brother correctly remembers that their father's birthday is after 13th June but before 18th June and her elder brother correctly remembers that their father's birthday is on an even date. On what date in June is definitely their father's birthday?
(a) Sixteenth
(b) Twelfth
(c) Fourteenth or Sixteenth
(d) None of the above

Directions (Q. Nos. 163-166) *Study the following arrangement carefully and answer the questions given below.*

Q 9 K # P @ 3 E N S A C ★ G © U M 7 F I V % 4 Z 8 Y

163. If all the numbers are dropped from the above arrangement, which of the following will be the seventeenth from the right end?
(a) E (b) P (c) I (d) @

164. Which of the following is the sixth to the left of the fifth to the left of 'V'?
(a) 3 (b) A (c) N (d) S

165. Which of the following is the eighth to the right of the fourteenth from the left end of the above arrangement?
(a) V (b) 4 (c) % (d) E

166. Four of the following five are alike in a certain way based on their positions in the above arrangement and so form a group. Which is the one that does not belong to that group?
(a) IM% (b) CNG (c) 3#N (d) UGC

167. How many such symbols are there in above arrangement, each of which is immediately preceded by an alphabet and immediately followed by a number?
(a) None (b) One
(c) Two (d) Three

168. Four pairs of words are given below out of which the words in all pairs except one, bear a certain common relationship. Choose the pair in which the words are differently related.

(a) Watt Power (b) Ampere Current
(c) Pascal Pressure (d) Radian Degree

169. The letters skipped in between the adjacent letters in the series are followed by equal space. Which of the following series observes this rule?

(a) SUXADF (b) RVZDFG
(c) HKNGSW (d) RVZDHL

170. Which of the following will be the third digit of the fourth number after the following numbers are arranged in descending order after reversing the positions of the digits within each number?

645, 869, 458, 347, 981, 792

(a) 4 (b) 6 (c) 8 (d) 9

171. P is 60 m South-East of Q. R is 60 m North-East of Q. Then, R is in which direction of P?

(a) North (b) North-East
(c) South (d) South-East

172. Choose the one which is different from the rest.

(a) 248 (b) 326
(c) 392 (d) 414

173. Three of the four groups of letters given below are alike in a certain way while one is different. Choose the odd one

(a) GWOURV (b) LZKMSU
(c) JOEHNP (d) SFXPMG

174. The letters skipped in between the adjacent letters in the series are followed by equal space. Which of the following series observes this rule?

(a) HKNGSW (b) EIMQVZ
(c) SUXADF (d) RVZDHL

175. A boy started walking positioning his back towards the sun. After some time, he turned left, then turned right and then towards the left again. In which direction is he going now?

(a) East or West
(b) North or West
(c) South or West
(d) North or South

Directions (Q. Nos. 176-180) *Read the following passage carefully and answer the questions given below it.*

A, B, C, D, E, F, G and H are sitting around a circular table, facing the centre. A sits third to the left of C and second to the right of E. B sits second to the right of D who is not an immediate neighbour of E. H sits second to the left of F. G is not an immediate neighbour of D.

176. Which of the following pairs has only one person sitting-between them, if the counting is done in clockwise direction?

(a) F, G (b) H, G (c) H, C (d) H, B

177. Who sits third to the right of E?

(a) D (b) G (c) F (d) B

178. What is the position of G with respect to A's position?

(a) Immediately to the right
(b) Second to the left
(c) Third to the right
(d) Third to the left

179. Who sits between E and A?

(a) F (b) D
(c) G (d) None of these

180. Starting from A's position, if all the eight are arranged in alphabetical order in clockwise direction, the seating position of how many members (excluding A) would remain unchanged?

(a) None (b) One
(c) Two (d) Three

Directions (Q. Nos. 181-185) *Below in each question are given two statements I and II. These statements may be either independent causes or may be effects of independent causes or a common cause. One of these statements may be the effect of the other statement. Read both the statements and then decide which of the following answer choice correctly depicts the relationship between these two statements. Mark answer*

(a) if Statement I is the cause and Statement II is its effect
(b) if Statement II is the cause and Statement I is its effect
(c) if both Statements I and II are effects of independent causes
(d) if both Statements I and II are effects of some common cause

181. I. The Government has amended tax laws to boost export.

II. The export sector has been passing through difficult times due to heavy tax burdens.

182. I. Budgetary allocation for building a better railway network eg, constructing new railway lines has increased.

II. There has been a substantial drop in the number of passenger opting for air travel.

183. I. The production of pulses has dropped for the third consecutive year.

II. India has decided to import pulses this year.

184. I. The Bank has provided a link on its website to obtain feed-back from customers.

II. Customers have been complaining about poor services in the Bank's branches.

185. I. Indian citizens are willing to incur the cost of using environment friendly technology.

II. Many countries are taking steps to cut their carbon emissions.

186. It was 9.35 am in Rakhi's watch, which kept correct time, when Reena informed her that the last bus left the bus stop at 9.25 am Reena's watch is 5 min fast. The frequency of the bus is every 20 min. For how long Rakhi must wait to catch the next bus?

(a) 5 min (b) 10 min
(c) 15 min (d) 25 min

187. Which of the following should come next in the given sequence of numbers?

2 4 3 2 4 3 1 2 4 3 1 2 2 4 3 1 2 3 2 4 3 1 2 3

(a) 2 (b) 3
(c) 4 (d) 5

188. In a certain code DESPAIR is written as TFEQSJ(B) How is NUMERAL written in that code?

(a) OVNFMBS (b) NVOFSBN
(c) NVOMFBS (d) NVOFMBS

189. If it is possible to make only one meaningful word with the first, second, sixth and tenth letters of the word DISCLAIMER, which of the following will be the third letter from the left? If no such word can be made, give 'X' as your answer and if more than one such words can be made, give 'Y' as the answer.

(a) I (b) R (c) D (d) X

190. How many such digits are there in the number 27561493 each of which is as far away from the beginning of the number as when the digits are arranged in descending order within the number?

(a) None (b) One
(c) Two (d) Three

Directions (Q. Nos. 191-195) *In each question below, is given a statement followed by two assumptions numbered I and II. An assumption is something supposed or taken for granted. You have to consider the statement and the following assumptions and decide which of the assumptions is implicit in the statement.*

191. Statement The General Administration Department has issued a circular to all the employees informing them that henceforth the employees can avail their lunch break at any of the half-hour slots between 1.00 pm. and 2.30 pm.

Assumptions

I. The employees may welcome the decision and avail lunch break at different time's slots.

II. There may not be any break in the work of the organization as the employees will have their lunch break at different time slots.

(a) Only assumption I is implicit
(b) Only assumption II is implicit
(c) Either I or II is implicit
(d) Neither I nor II is implicit

192. Statement Do not copy our software without our permission–A notice.

Assumptions

I. It is possible to copy the software.

II. Such warning will have some effect.

(a) Only assumption I is implicit
(b) Only assumption II is implicit
(c) Either I or II is implicit
(d) Both I and II are implicit

193. Statement Municipal Corporation has decided to ban the entry of vehicles from sub-urban areas to the main city through main routes during peak hours to avoid traffic congestion.

Assumptions

I. The people of sub-urban areas should not bring their vehicles during peak hours.

II. There is no traffic congestion by the vehicles of people residing in the main city.

(a) Only assumption I is implicit
(b) Only assumption II is implicit
(c) Either I or II is implicit
(d) Neither I nor II is implicit

194. **Statement** Science is a sort of news agency comparable in principle to other new agencies. But this news agency gives us information which is reliable to an extraordinary high degree due to elaborate techniques of verification and its capacity to survive centuries. So, science should be read with as much interest as we read news.

Assumptions

I. Science encourages investigative spirit.

II. People read news out of interest.

(a) Only assumption I is implicit
(b) Only assumption II is implicit
(c) Either I or II is implicit
(d) Both I and II are implicit

195. **Statement** All the employees are notified that the organisation will provide transport facilities at half cost from the nearby railway station to the office except those who have been provided with travelling allowance.

Assumptions

I. Most of the employees will travel by the office transport.

II. Those who are provided with travelling allowance will not read such notice.

(a) Only assumption I is implicit
(b) Only assumption II is implicit
(c) Either I or II is implicit
(d) Neither I nor II is implicit

196. In a certain code 'PLANT' is written as '$@2*©' and 'YIELD' is written as 'b64@%'. How is 'DELAY' written in that code?

(a) b4*2% (b) b4@2%
(c) %42@b (d) %4@2b

197. How many meaningful English words can be formed with the letters ARILT using each letter only once in that word?

(a) None (b) One
(c) Two (d) Three

198. D said, "A's father is the only brother of my sister's son." How is A's father related to D?

(a) Cousin
(b) Nephew
(c) Aunt
(d) Data inadequate

Directions (Q. Nos. 199-200) *The following questions are based on the five three letter words given below—PUN SAD CRY FOE STY If each of the words is rearranged in alphabetical order then.*

199. If it is possible to make only one meaningful English word using each letter only once, from the first letters of each of the five words after the letters of each word are rearranged in alphabetical order, the last letter of that word is your answer. If more than one word can be formed, 'X' is the answer and if no such word can be formed then 'W' is the answer.

(a) E (b) N
(c) X (d) W

200. How many words will remain unchanged even after their rearrangement in alphabetical order?

(a) None (b) One
(c) Two (d) Three

ANSWERS

1	(c)	**2**	(b)	**3**	(b)	**4**	(c)	**5**	(d)	**6**	(b)	**7**	(c)	**8**	(d)	**9**	(d)	**10**	(a)
11	(a)	**12**	(c)	**13**	(c)	**14**	(b)	**15**	(d)	**16**	(d)	**17**	(b)	**18**	(a)	**19**	(b)	**20**	(d)
21	(d)	**22**	(a)	**23**	(c)	**24**	(b)	**25**	(a)	**26**	(d)	**27**	(b)	**28**	(a)	**29**	(a)	**30**	(c)
31	(d)	**32**	(c)	**33**	(a)	**34**	(a)	**35**	(d)	**36**	(a)	**37**	(a)	**38**	(b)	**39**	(b)	**40**	(b)
41	(d)	**42**	(c)	**43**	(c)	**44**	(c)	**45**	(c)	**46**	(c)	**47**	(d)	**48**	(b)	**49**	(a)	**50**	(b)
51	(d)	**52**	(b)	**53**	(c)	**54**	(c)	**55**	(a)	**56**	(a)	**57**	(c)	**58**	(d)	**59**	(d)	**60**	(d)
61	(c)	**62**	(c)	**63**	(c)	**64**	(c)	**65**	(b)	**66**	(a)	**67**	(d)	**68**	(c)	**69**	(b)	**70**	(c)
71	(c)	**72**	(b)	**73**	(a)	**74**	(d)	**75**	(c)	**76**	(d)	**77**	(c)	**78**	(d)	**79**	(d)	**80**	(a)
81	(c)	**82**	(c)	**83**	(d)	**84**	(c)	**85**	(b)	**86**	(d)	**87**	(a)	**88**	(a)	**89**	(a)	**90**	(c)
91	(c)	**92**	(d)	**93**	(c)	**94**	(d)	**95**	(b)	**96**	(b)	**97**	(c)	**98**	(c)	**99**	(b)	**100**	(b)
101	(c)	**102**	(d)	**103**	(b)	**104**	(d)	**105**	(d)	**106**	(b)	**107**	(b)	**108**	(a)	**109**	(d)	**110**	(d)
111	(a)	**112**	(a)	**113**	(d)	**114**	(a)	**115**	(c)	**116**	(a)	**117**	(a)	**118**	(b)	**119**	(a)	**120**	(d)
121	(b)	**122**	(c)	**123**	(c)	**124**	(d)	**125**	(b)	**126**	(d)	**127**	(d)	**128**	(b)	**129**	(b)	**130**	(b)
131	(c)	**132**	(b)	**133**	(b)	**134**	(c)	**135**	(b)	**136**	(c)	**137**	(a)	**138**	(b)	**139**	(b)	**140**	(b)
141	(b)	**142**	(a)	**143**	(d)	**144**	(c)	**145**	(b)	**146**	(d)	**147**	(b)	**148**	(a)	**149**	(c)	**150**	(a)
151	(a)	**152**	(c)	**153**	(b)	**154**	(b)	**155**	(c)	**156**	(a)	**157**	(c)	**158**	(c)	**159**	(c)	**160**	(d)
161	(b)	**162**	(d)	**163**	(d)	**164**	(d)	**165**	(c)	**166**	(d)	**167**	(c)	**168**	(d)	**169**	(d)	**170**	(a)
171	(a)	**172**	(c)	**173**	(d)	**174**	(d)	**175**	(d)	**176**	(b)	**177**	(c)	**178**	(d)	**179**	(d)	**180**	(a)
181	(b)	**182**	(c)	**183**	(a)	**184**	(b)	**185**	(d)	**186**	(a)	**187**	(c)	**188**	(d)	**189**	(a)	**190**	(b)
191	(b)	**192**	(b)	**193**	(d)	**194**	(d)	**195**	(a)	**196**	(d)	**197**	(c)	**198**	(b)	**199**	(c)	**200**	(c)

PRACTICE SET 2

Instructions

- *There are total 200 questions in this practice set.*
- *For every correct attempt the students will be awarded 1 mark.*
- *All the questions are in MCQs form.*

English Language

Directions (Q. Nos. 1-5) *Four alternatives are given for the Idiom/Phrase* **bold** *in the sentence. Choose the alternative which best expresses the meaning of the Idiom/Phrase and mark it in the Answer-Sheet.*

1. Don't worry about the silly row. It was just **a storm in a tea cup.**
(a) important matter dealt with ease
(b) hot tea being served
(c) commotion over a trivial matter
(d) confusion and chaos

2. Syria is now **currying favour with** America.
(a) pleasing
(b) favouring
(c) obliging
(d) ingratiating itself with

3. We tend to **take for granted** the conveniences of modern life.
(a) to consider
(b) to admit
(c) to accept readily
(d) to care for

4. The prodigal son was left **high and dry** by his friends, when he lost all his money.
(a) wounded
(b) alone
(c) depressed
(d) neglected

5. The success of his first novel completely **turned his head.**
(a) made him vain
(b) made him look back
(c) changed him completely
(d) made him think

Directions (Q. Nos. 6-10) *In the following questions, you have a brief passage with five questions following the passage. Read the passage carefully and choose the best answer to each question out of the four alternatives and indicate your correct alternative.*

Florence Nightingle was born in the year 1820 in a small town in Italy. Her parents were famous and rich. They looked after little Florence very carefully. But, Florence was thin and sickly.

One day little Florence said to her father, "father, I would like to be a nurse". The little girl's father said, "My dear, I do not think you can be a nurse. Nursing is hard work." "I will try", said Florence. Soon she began to learn nursing at home.

One day, Florence was returning home early from school. On the way, she saw a dog lying on the road. It was crying bitterly. An unkind boy hit the poor creature with a big stone. It hurt right leg and it was bleeding badly. Florence became very sad. She gently carried the dog home and nursed the wound. She tied a bandage tightly round the leg. In a week the dog was quite well. Soon the dog became friendly with Florence. It wagged its tail and jumped around her playfully and licked Florence all over, as if, it wanted to say, "Thank you, little nurse, thank you".

6. Florence wanted to become
(a) an animal lover (b) a teacher
(c) a nurse (d) an MLA

7. When Florence expressed her desire to become a nurse her father
(a) agreed readily
(b) was very doubtful
(c) kept silent
(d) None of the above

8. On the way, she saw
(a) an unkind boy hitting a dog
(b) a wounded dog lying on the road
(c) a dog limping across the road
(d) None of the above

9. Florence nursed the wounded dog because
(a) she wanted to be a nurse
(b) her father told her to do so
(c) she felt pity for the dog
(d) None of the above

10. The dog licked Florence all over to
(a) clean her body
(b) express thanks
(c) show its anger
(d) None of the above

Directions (Q. Nos. 11-13) *In this section, each of the following items consists of a word in CAPITAL LETTERS, followed by four words. Select the word that is most similar in meaning.*

11. DISDAIN
(a) Disown (b) Condemn
(c) Hate (d) Criticise

12. BEWITCING
(a) Enchanting (b) Magical
(c) Affected (d) Ensnaring

13. RAPACITY
(a) Anger (b) Cruelty
(c) Pride (d) Greed

Directions (Q. Nos. 14-15) *In this section, each of the following items consists of a word in CAPITAL LETTERS, followed by four words. Select the word that is farthest in meaning to the bold word in capital letters.*

14. EPHEMERAL
(a) Temporal (b) Stable
(c) Permanent (d) Earthly

15. OBLIGATORY
(a) Doubtful (b) Voluntary
(c) Sincerely (d) Faithfully

Directions (Q. Nos. 16-20) *Which of the phrases (a), (b), (c), (d) given below each sentence should replace the phrase printed in **bold** type to make the sentence grammatically correct?*

16. Newspapers have great power **because** their enormous circulation.
(a) on account (b) because of
(c) as a result (d) owing

17. The crowd **which has gather** to protest against the decision slowly returned to their homes.
(a) which had gathered
(b) which have gather
(c) gathering up
(d) which gathers around

18. He will be handling the next project since he has **vastly experience** in this business.
(a) vast experience (b) vastly experienced
(c) a vast experiencing (d) the vast experience

19. Children now a days are watching **too much** television.
(a) to much of
(b) more of
(c) very much of
(d) No correction required

20. The bridge in **connection with** the two cities will remain closed for security reasons.
(a) connects between
(b) in connection to
(c) being connected from
(d) connecting

Directions (Q. Nos. 21-25) *Read each sentence to find out whether there is any grammatical error or idiomatic error in it. The error will be in one part of the sentence. The letter of that part is the answer.*

21. The foreign company has so far declined to (a)/directly comment on the Indian company's move, (b) / which analysts is say is a sign the company wanting to (c) / fight for its presence in the market. (d)

22. A property dealer was (a)/shoot dead by four unidentified jacket-clad men (b) / while taking a morning walk (c) / in a park. (d)

23. To curbing the spread of violence, (a)/authorities brought under curfew (b)/ more areas in the State, where (c) / three youths were killed. (d)

24. Not only was the actress over the moon (a) / as winning an award, but was (b)/also deeply touched by the support (c) / she got from the industry. (d)

25. Hectic schedules can (a)/take a toll on anybody and (b)/the solutions to this is (c)/a quick holiday to some exotic location. (d)

Directions (Q. Nos. 26-30) *Each sentence below has a blank/s, each blank indicating that something has been omitted. Choose the word/s that best fit/s the meaning of the sentence as a whole.*

26. We .... decided .... buy a new car.
(a) have, to (b) has, is
(c) are, in (d) is, to

27. Rohan .... asleep while watching the film.
(a) is (b) found (c) fall (d) fell

28. Priti passed her exams with colours.
(a) falling (b) seeing
(c) different (d) flying

29. She translated an English passage to Hindi without using a ....
(a) meaning
(b) dictionary
(c) symbols
(d) language

30. Tina finds it difficult to talk to people as she .... introvert.
(a) was a (b) can the
(c) is an (d) being a

Directions (Q. Nos. 31–35) *Out of the four alternatives, choose the one which can be substituted for the given words/sentence.*

31. Belief that God is in everything and that everything is God.
(a) Atheism (b) Pantheism
(c) Scepticism (d) Animism

32. A picture of a person or a thing drawn in such a highly exaggerated manner as to cause laughter.
(a) Cartoon (b) Cacography
(c) Cartography (d) Caricature

33. The state of being miserable bereft of all possessions.
(a) Dependant (b) Complacent
(c) Destitute (d) Omnipresent

34. That which cannot be called back.
(a) Irresponsible (b) Irrevocable
(c) Irredeemable (d) Incalculable

35. One who journeys from place to place.
(a) Quack (b) Cannibal
(c) Itinerant (d) Courier

Directions (Q. Nos. 36-40) *A few foreign language phrases, which are commonly used, are given below. Select the correct meaning of each phrase.*

36. Raison d'etre
(a) Logical conclusion (b) Reason for existence
(c) Free choice (d) Dubious argument

37. Quantum ramifactus
(a) The amount of damage suffered
(b) The amount of damage caused
(c) The amount of damage paid
(d) The amount of damage received

38. Vis-a-vis
(a) Direct (b) Opposite
(c) Face-to-face (d) Agree

39. Ex aquo et bono
(a) In equity and good conscience
(b) For the public good
(c) The thing speaks for itself
(d) In good faith

40. Lex est norma recti
(a) Law is rule of right
(b) Law rules the right
(c) Law is a rule of State
(d) Law follow equity

General Knowledge

41. Who composed the National Song of India?
(a) Rabindranath Tagore
(b) Bankim Chandra Chatterjee
(c) Shri Aurobindo
(d) Mahatma Gandhi

42. The first date of our National Calendar corresponds to which date of the Gregorian Calendar?
(a) 1st April, 1950
(b) 22nd March, 1950
(c) 22nd March, 1957
(d) 31st March, 1957

43. The TV ad of Fair & Lovely presented which well-known cricket personality doing commentary?
(a) Sunil Gavaskar (b) Sachin Tendulkar
(c) Ravi Shastri (d) K Srikant

44. 'You said it', the pocket cartoon in 'Times of India' is the composition of
(a) Sudhir Dar (b) Sudhir Tailang
(c) RK Lakshman (d) RK Narayanan

45. 'Reuter' is
(a) a news agency (b) a newspaper
(c) a TV channel (d) a monthly magazine

46. Employment News is published by
(a) Publications Division
(b) Press Information Bureau
(c) Ministry of Employment
(d) DAVP

47. Gyandarshan and Gyanvani are
(a) house magazines of Doordarshan and Aakashvani
(b) divisions of Prasar Bharti
(c) interactive educative broadcast of IGNOU
(d) broadcast for teachers

48. Which one is not a journalist?
(a) MJ Akbar (b) Pranoy Roy
(c) Shahid Kapoor (d) Sayeed Naqvi

49. 'Times of India' is a member of the following publication group.
(a) Bennet and Coleman
(b) Express
(c) Living Media
(d) Malayala Manorama

50. Author of 'Dwikhandita' is
(a) Sharat Chandra (b) Taslima Nasreen
(c) Jhumpa Lahiri (d) None of these

51. A branch of Indian Institute of Mass Communication has recently been established at
(a) Sambalpur (b) Dhenkanal
(c) Bhubaneshwar (d) Mayurbhanj

52. Which one of the following pairs is not correctly matched?

Line	Country
(a) Durand Line	Pakistan and Afghanistan
(b) Maginot Line	France and Germany
(c) 38th Parallel	Russia and Finland
(d) Radcliffe	India and Pakistan

53. The atmospheric layer reflecting radio waves is called
(a) Ozonosphere (b) Ionosphere
(c) Statosphere (d) Mesosphere

54. The deepest surface depression of the Earth is
(a) Kurile trench
(b) Mariana trench
(c) Tonga-Kermadec trench
(d) Benfley Subglacial trench

55. Shale is metamorphosed into which of the following rock?
(a) Graphite (b) Gneiss
(c) Marble (d) Slate

56. A metal is exposed to the atmosphere for sometime. It becomes coated with green carbonate the metal must be
(a) silver (b) copper
(c) aluminium (d) zinc

57. Indravati is a tributary of which river?
(a) Ganga (b) Godavari
(c) Krishna (d) Mahanadi

58. Match List I with List II and select the correct answer using the codes given below the lists

List I (Town)	List II (Industry)
A. Bhadravathy	1. Gem cutting
B. Coimbatore	2. Electrical motors
C. Kapurthala	3. Steel
D. Surat	4. Railway coach

Codes

	A	B	C	D		A	B	C	D
(a)	1	2	4	3	(b)	3	2	4	1
(c)	1	4	2	3	(d)	3	4	2	1

59. Where is Thattekad Bird Sanctuary located?
(a) Kerala (b) Tamil Nadu
(c) Karnataka (d) Andhra Pradesh

60. In which one of the following States of India is the Pamayangtse Monastery situated?
(a) Nagaland (b) Himachal Pradesh
(c) Sikkim (d) Arunachal Pradesh

61. The gas used to extinguish fire is
(a) neon (b) nitrogen
(c) carbon dioxide (d) carbon monoxide

62. In which of the following activities Silicon Carbide is used?
(a) Making cement and glass
(b) Disinfecting water and ponds
(c) Making castes for statues
(d) Cutting very hard substances

63. The element common to all acids is
(a) oxygen (b) hydrogen
(c) nitrogen (d) sulphur

64. Gobar gas contains mainly
(a) methane (b) carbon dioxide
(c) butane (d) carbon monoxide

65. The most malleable metal is
(a) silver (b) gold
(c) aluminium (d) sodium

66. Which of the following events made the English East India Company the legitimate masters of the Bengal Subah?
(a) Battle of Buxar, 1764
(b) Battle of Plassey, 1757
(c) Farrukh Siyar's Farman, 1717
(d) Ibrahim Khan's Farman, 1690

67. Which one of the following pairs is not correctly matched?
(a) Janjira Fort : Maharashtra
(b) Asirgarh Fort : Madhya Pradesh
(c) Daulatabad Fort : Rajasthan
(d) Gingee Fort : Tamil Nadu

68. Our National song has been taken from
(a) the essay 'Bharat Vidhata' written by Bankim Chandra Chattopadhyaya
(b) the magazine 'Tatva Bodhini' edited by Nobel laureate Rabindranath Tagore
(c) the novel 'Durgesh Nandini' written by Bankim Chandra Chattopadhyay
(d) the novel 'Anand Math' written by Bankim Chandra Chattopadhyay

69. Who designed the National Flag of independent India?
(a) Bankim Chandra Chatterjee
(b) Rabindranath Tagore
(c) Mahatma Gandhi
(d) Pingley Venkayya

70. Who is believed to have composed the treatise 'Nratya Shastra'?
(a) Brihannala (b) Menaka
(c) Bharata (d) Rambha

71. The Economic and Social Commission for Asia and Pacific (ESCAP) is located at
(a) Manila (b) Singapore
(c) Kuala Lumpur (d) Bangkok

72. The pioneer of Indian Renaissance was
(a) Swami Vivekananda
(b) Swami Dayananda Saraswati
(c) Dadabhai Naoroji
(d) Raja Rammohan Roy

73. The famous 'Satriya dance' of Asom got national recognition in the year
(a) 1999
(b) 2000
(c) 2001
(d) 1998

74. Which of the following is the most important statement which shows the real greatness of Akbar as a ruler?
(a) He tried to encourage inter-religious marriages
(b) He set-up a revenue system based on average crop estimates
(c) He established Din-i-Ilahi incorporating the principles of many religions
(d) He tried to unite India into a single nation

75. Which of the following has been the field of activity of Pt Bhimsen Joshi?
(a) Literature
(b) Classical music (Vocal)
(c) Education
(d) Journalism

76. When did the United Nations Organisation come into existence?
(a) 24th October, 1945
(b) 24th October, 1943
(c) 26th November, 1945
(d) 26th November, 1943

77. According to the Preamble of the Constitution, India is a
(a) Sovereign Democratic Socialist Republic
(b) Sovereign Socialist Secular Republic
(c) Sovereign Democratic Republic
(d) Sovereign Socialist Secular Democratic Republic

78. Match List I with List II and select the correct answer using the codes given below the lists

List I (State)		**List II** (Full statehood granted in)
A. Goa	1.	1966
B. Haryana	2.	1972
C. Meghalaya	3.	1975
D. Sikkim	4.	1988

Codes

	A	B	C	D
(a)	3	1	2	4
(b)	4	2	1	3
(c)	3	2	1	4
(d)	4	1	2	3

79. Consider the following statements
1. In the Lok Sabha, 12 members are nominated by the President of India.
2. In the Rajya Sabha, a maximum of 2 members of the Anglo-Indian community can be nominated by the President of India.

Which of the statement(s) given above is/are correct?
(a) Only 1
(b) Only 2
(c) Both 1 and 2
(d) Neither 1 nor 2

80. Who among the following has not been a Chief Justice of India?
(a) RC Lahoti (b) GB Pattanaik
(c) SS Gill (d) VN Khare

81. The International Court of Justice is located at
(a) Geneva (b) Hague
(c) Amsterdam (d) Vienna

82. Who is the first Asian Winner of Nobel Prize?
(a) CV Raman
(b) Rajiv Gandhi
(c) Rabindranath Tagore
(d) Mother Terresa

83. The Nobel Peace Prize is awarded in which city?
(a) Oslo (b) Stockholm
(c) Brussels (d) Geneva

84. 'Ashoka Chakra' is awarded for
(a) acts of gallantry in the presence of enemy
(b) gallantry by children
(c) outstanding contribution to literature
(d) the most conspicuous bravery or self sacrifice on land, air or sea but not in the presence of the enemy

85. Which are the two states (other than UP) having the highest representation in Lok Sabha?
(a) Bihar and Madhya Pradesh
(b) Bihar and Maharashtra
(c) Karnataka and Andhra Pradesh
(d) Tamil Nadu and Rajasthan

86. The International Human Rights Convention adopted by the United Nations in 1990 relates to
(a) disabled (b) stateless persons
(c) migrant workers (d) children

87. The five permanent members of UN Security Council are
(a) Japan, West Germany, USSR, UK and USA
(b) Canada, China, France, USSR and USA
(c) Germany, China, USSR, UK and USA
(d) China, France, USSR, UK and USA

88. Where is the Judicature of Odisha?
(a) Bhubaneswar (b) Cuttack
(c) Both 'a' and 'b' (d) None of these

89. Which of the following is associated with Sufi Saints?
(a) Tripitaka (b) Dakhma
(c) Khanqah (d) Synagogue

90. Which of the following treaties brought an end to the independent existence of Peshwa Baji Rao II?
(a) The Treaty of Purandhar
(b) Convention of Wadgaon
(c) Treaty of Bassein
(d) Treaty of Salbai

Mathematics

91. The ratio of ducks and frogs in a pond is 37 : 39 respectively. The average number of ducks and frogs in the pond is 152. What is the number of frogs in the pond?
(a) 148 (b) 152 (c) 156 (d) 144

92. What approximate amount of compound interest can be obtaied on an amount of ₹ 9650 at the rate of 6.c.p.a. at the end of 3 yr?
(a) ₹ 1737 (b) ₹ 1920 (c) ₹ 1720 (d) ₹ 1843

93. The diagonal of a square is cm. The diagonal of another square whose area is double that of the first square is
(a) 8 cm (b) 12 cm (c) 6 cm (d) 16 cm

94. Half of 1 per cent is equal to
(a) 0.005 (b) 0.05 (c) 0.02 (d) 0.2

95. The maximum length of a pencil that can by kept in a rectangular box of dimensions 8 cm × 6 cm × 2 cm, is
(a) $2\sqrt{13}$ cm (b) $2\sqrt{14}$ cm
(c) $2\sqrt{26}$ cm (d) $10\sqrt{2}$ cm

96. In a school 10% of the boys are same in number as th of the girls. What is the ratio of boys to girls in the school?
(a) 3 : 2 (b) 5 : 2 (c) 2 : 1 (d) 4 : 3

97. The ratio of the speeds of two trains is 7 : 8. If the second train runs 400 km in 4 h, then the speed of the first train is
(a) 70 km/h (b) 75 km/h
(c) 84 km/h (d) 87.5 km/h

98. The number of prime factors of
6) 10 × (7) 17 × (55) 27
(a) 54 (b) 64
(c) 81 (d) 91

99. A and B entered into a partnership investing ₹ 12000 and ₹ 9000 respectively. After 3 months C also joined them with a capital of ₹ 15000. The share of C in the half yearly profit of ₹ 9500 is
(a) ₹ 3500 (b) ₹ 3000
(c) ₹ 2500 (d) ₹ 4000

100. A circular wire of radius 42 cm is cut and bent in the form of a rectangle whose sides are in the ratio of 6 : 5. The smaller side of the rectangle is
(a) 30 cm (b) 60 cm
(c) 72 cm (d) 108 cm

101. The marked price of a table is ₹ 3000 and is available at successive discounts of 20% and 10% respectively. If there is an additional discount of 5% on cash payment, then what is the cash price of the table?
(a) ₹ 2400 (b) ₹ 2160
(c) ₹ 2100 (d) ₹ 2052

102. A person sold 320 mangoes for the CP of 400 mangoes. His gain percent is
(a) 10% (b) 15% (c) 12½% (d) 25%

103. Of the three numbers, second is twice the first and is also thrice the third. If the average of the three numbers is 44, the largest number is
(a) 24 (b) 36
(c) 17 (d) 72

104. is equal to
(a) 2.5 (b) 0.025
(c) 0.0025 (d) 0.0000025

Directions (Q. Nos. 105–110) *What should come in place of the question mark (?) in the following questions?*

105. 196 × 948 ÷ 158 = ?
(a) 1156 (b) 1200
(c) 1188 (d) 1176

106. (786 × 64) ÷ 48 = ?
(a) 1050 (b) 1024
(c) 1048 (d) 1036

107. 3.5 + 11.25 × 4.5 – 32.5 = ?
(a) 18.275 (b) 21.625
(c) 32.375 (d) 25.45

108. (2640 ÷ 48) × (2240 ÷ 35) = ?
(a) 3520 (b) 3515
(c) 3495 (d) 3490

109. If one side one diagonal of a rhombus are 5 cm and 8 cm respectively then its area is
(a) 20 cm^2
(b) 24 cm^2
(c) 40 cm^2
(d) 26 cm^2

110. The ratio between the area of a square of side 'a' and an equilateral triangle of side 'a' is
(a) 2 : 1 (b) 4 : 3
(c) $2:\sqrt{3}$ (d) $4:\sqrt{3}$

Legal Aptitude & Indian Constitution

111. The power to decide an election petition is vested in the
(a) Parliament
(b) Supreme Court
(c) High Courts
(d) Election Commission

112. The number of writs that can be prayed for and issued by the Supreme Court and/or a High Court is
(a) 3 (b) 4
(c) 5 (d) 6

113. The pension of a high court judge is charged to the
(a) Consolidated Fund of India
(b) Consolidated Fund of the State where he last served
(c) Consolidated Funds of the different States where he has served
(d) Contingency Fund of India

114. Ignorance of law is
(a) not an excuse in Indian Law
(b) is an excuse in Indian Law
(c) no such legal principle is followed in Indian Law
(d) partly an excuse in Indian Law

115. The special status of Jammu and Kashmir implies that the State has
(a) a separate Judiciary
(b) a separate Constitution
(c) a separate administrative-structure
(d) Both 'a' and 'b'

116. Presumption that the younger survived the elder under Section 21 of the Hindu Succession Act, 1956 is a
(a) presumption of fact
(b) mixed presumption of fact and law
(c) rebuttable presumption of law
(d) irrebuttable presumption of law

117. Which Section of the Indian Penal Code deals with those conditions, when consent is said to be, not free consent?
(a) Section 87
(b) Section 90
(c) Section 92
(d) Section 89

118. Section 113-B, 'presumption as to dowry death' was added to the Indian Evidence Act in
(a) 1986
(b) 1983
(c) 1961
(d) 1962

119. A Hindu couple having the decree of judicial separation wants to live together
(a) they can live together
(b) they cannot live together
(c) they can live together after remarriage
(d) they can live together only after the permission of the court

120. A Hindu male of 28 years of age adopts a female child of 13 years of age. The adoption is
(a) valid
(b) voidable
(c) illegal
(d) void

121. A Hindu dies intestate leaving behind two sons, one daughter and widow. His property shall devolve to
(a) sons only
(b) sons and daughter only
(c) widow only
(d) sons, daughter and widow all

122. Which of the following modifies the application of Muslim Law?
(a) Shariat Act, 1937
(b) Muslim Marriage Dissolution Act, 1939
(c) Muslim Woman (Protection of Rights on Divorce) Act, 1986
(d) All of the above

123. Under Muslim Law, marriage is
(a) an institution legalizing male and female conjugal relations
(b) a civil contract
(c) Sunnet
(d) All of the above

124. In the absence of mother, which of the following females has the first priority to have the custody of a Muslim child?
(a) Father's mother
(b) Mother's mother
(c) Sisters
(d) Maternal aunt

125. After divorce a Muslim woman
(a) cannot remarry
(b) can remarry immediately
(c) can marry only after completion of *'Iddat'* period
(d) None of the above

126. The phrase 'procedure established by the law' means
(a) the judges in India cannot question the fairness or validity of a law, provided it is within the limits of the Constitution
(b) judges in India can question the fairness or validity of an undue law even if it is within the limits of the Constitution
(c) judges in India can declare a law invalid simply because in their opinion the law is not due or is unjust
(d) None of the above

127. Insurance is a
(a) contingent contract
(b) wagering contract
(c) contract of indemnity
(d) contract of guarantee

128. 'A' is charged with travelling on a railway without a ticket, the proving that he had a ticket is on
(a) prosecution
(b) accused
(c) complainant
(d) prosecution witness

129. Who amongst the following is an expert under the Indian Evidence Act
(a) hand writing expert
(b) finger print expert
(c) ballistics expert
(d) All of the above

130. Case of Pakala Narayan Swami *versus* King Emperor is related with
(a) Section 6 of the Indian Evidence Act
(b) Section 21(1) of the Indian Evidence Act
(c) Section 32(1) of the Indian Evidence Act
(d) Section 41 of the Indian Evidence Act

131. Adultery is an offence committed
(a) with the consent of a married woman
(b) with the consent of a woman
(c) without the consent of a woman but with the consent of her husband
(d) with the consent of a minor girl

132. The maxim '*Ignorantia facit excusat*' relates to
(a) Section 75 of the Indian Penal Code
(b) Section 76 of the Indian Penal Code
(c) Section 77 of the Indian Penal Code
(d) None of the above

133. A Chief Judicial Magistrate may pass a sentence of imprisonment
(a) not exceeding seven years
(b) exceeding seven years
(c) for life
(d) None of the above

134. Section 2(h) of the Code of Criminal Procedure defines the term
(a) Investigation (b) Charge
(c) Inquiry (d) Offence

135. Which Section of the Code of Criminal Procedure provides a protection to the members of Armed Forces from arrest?
(a) Section 41 (b) Section 45
(c) Section 46 (d) Section 50

136. If parties to a Hindu marriage are sapinda to each other, the marriage is
(a) void (b) voidable
(c) valid (d) None of these

137. Under Mitakshara School Coparcenary interest devolves by
(a) representation (b) survivorship
(c) obstructed heritage (d) unobstructed heritage

138. Which one of the following Sections of the Transfer of Property Act defines "Transfer of Property"?
(a) Section 3 (b) Section 4
(c) Section 5 (d) Section 6

139. The gift of future property is
(a) void (b) voidable
(c) valid (d) conditionally void

140. In which of the following conditions the lease can be terminated
(a) efflux of time
(b) on termination of lessor's interest or power
(c) on merger
(d) All of the above

141. In case of gift, the done dies before acceptance, then
(a) gift is voidable
(b) gift is valid
(c) gift is void
(d) None of the above

142. Amongst the following who is not a Revenue Officer as defined under the Madhya Pradesh Land Revenue Code?
(a) Commissioner
(b) Collector
(c) Settlement Officer
(d) Chairman, Board of Revenue

143. The member of a State Public Service Commission can be removed on the ground of misbehaviour only after an enjuiry has been conducted by the
(a) Supreme Court of India
(b) High Court of the State
(c) Committee Appointed by the President
(d) None of the above

144. A Bhumiswami can seek partition of his agricultural land amongst his legal heirs during his life time by applying to the
(a) Patwari
(b) Village Kotwar
(c) Tahsildar
(d) Superintendent of Land Record

145. Which amongst the following is not the duty of a Patel appointed under the Madhya Pradesh Land Revenue Code?
(a) To collect and pay Land Revenue into the Gram Kosh
(b) To furnish reports regarding State of his village
(c) To prevent encroachment on waste land, public path and roadways
(d) To maintain land records

146. A mortgage by deposit of title deed is called
(a) Anomalous mortgage
(b) English mortgage
(c) Equitable mortgage
(d) Usufructuary mortgage

147. Which of the following is not an actionable claim?
(a) Right to a Provident Fund Account
(b) Promise to pay ₹ 500 if the promisee succeed in LLB examination
(c) A greement to pay ₹ 500 if the promisee marries a particular woman
(d) Right to claim benefit of a contract coupled with a liability

148. .... is defined as a security for repayment of a loan.
(a) Pledge (b) Mortgage
(c) Lease (d) None of these

149. The normal term of office of a member nominated to a Gram Nyayalaya constituted under the Madhya Pradesh Gram Nyayalaya Adhiniyam 1996 is
(a) two years
(b) three years
(c) five years
(d) six years

150. The Preamble says that the State in India will assure the dignity of the individual. The Constitution seeks to achieve this object by guaranting
(a) equal Fundamental Rights to each citizen
(b) the right to adequate means of livelihood to each individual
(c) just and humane conditions of work to each individual
(d) equal wages for equal work to each individual irrespective of sex

Directions (Q. Nos. 151–160) *Given below is a statement of legal principle, followed by a factual situation. Apply the principle to the facts and select the most appropriate answer among the alternatives given.*

151. Principle No legal remedy exists for an injury caused by an act, for which one has consented.
Facts The driver of a van with restive horses cried for help. The plaintiff went and attempted to hold the horse but it throw him on the ground causing him injuries, in respect of which he sued the defendant.
(a) The suit is dismissed because the plaintiff must have known that his attempt to hold the horse with the risk
(b) The suit is not dismissed and plaintiff must be compensated because driver cry for help and he is in problem
(c) Plaintiff should be able to recover as the driver failed to take precautions of horse
(d) Plaintiff should not be able to recover as he consented to the risk

152. Principle A master is liable for the wrongs committed by the servant in the course of his employment
Facts During the poonam celebrations which was attended by lakhs of people, the plaintiff was seriously injured by the explosion caused by igniting explosive powder filled coconut shells. During the festival all sorts of explosion are fired and fire-works mark the poonam celebrations. Many contractors are engaged to make the explosive devices. During the celebrations, one shell, instead of going vertically into the sky fell tangentially on the crowd and injured the plaintiff.
(a) Master is liable because it is fault of employees who had made the coconut shells known as Minnal gundus
(b) Master is not liable because plaintiff is a volunteer and that he has come to watch the celebrations
(c) Master is not liable because it is fault of employees
(d) Master is not liable because employees had been taken care in handling the explosive

153. Principle When any person dis-honestly takes any moveable property out of the possession of any other person without his consent, he is guilty of theft.
Facts A entered the drawing room of Y. A picked up the H.M.T. Quartz wristwatch lying on the table and hide it in a corner and left immediately whether A was committed theft.
(a) A commits theft because he has moved the watch from Y's table without his consent
(b) A does not commit theft because he has not left Y's house with watch
(c) A does not commit theft because Y is careless with his valuables
(d) A commits theft at the moment he picks up the watch dishonestly and intended to keep it

154. Principle An agreement is contract if it is made by the free consent of the parties competent to contract, for a lawful considera- tion and with a lawful object, and they are not hereby expressly declared to be void.

Facts Ram agrees to sell Shyam a house worth ₹ 15 lakhs for ₹ 5000. Is the agreement between Ram and Shyam a contract? Decide.

(a) No, because Shyam has played foul on Ram
(b) Yes, because inadequacy of consideration does not make an agreement void
(c) No, because there is no free and express consent
(d) No, because consideration is inadequate

155. Principle

1. No consideration—no contract
2. Consideration is something done or abstinence of a party at the desire of another party
3. Consideration must have value in the eye of law.

Facts Innovative Educational Trust manages a school named Bharat Vidyaniketan. Ram, the parent of a student in the school suggested to the trust that it could build a new library building for which he would bear a part of the cost. The school authority accepted the suggestion and started construction of the building. Ram has suffered a loss in business, now he refuses to pay the part he had offered earlier.

(a) Ram is liable to pay because based upon his promise, the school authority started construction of the building
(b) Ram is not liable to pay because, as the building was for the benefit of the school and he has nothing to do with it by way of enjoying and benefit
(c) Ram is liable to pay because Ram's child is a student in the same school
(d) None of the above

156. Principle Damages cannot be claimed against a risk to which consent has been given. The principle does not apply to rescue cases.

Facts A and B brought tickets to have a view of a football match. During the course of the game a hand kick from one of the players caused the ball to hit *A* on his face, causing bleeding and nausea from nose. After half time the organizers allowed entry of more spectators, then the seating capacity of the stadium. In the resulting stampede C and D who were watching the match since the beginning got injured.

(a) A shall not be able to recover as by purchasing a seat in a football game he consented to all the risks of such watching
(b) A shall not be able to recover as he consented to the risk of the ball
(c) A shall be able to recover as he consented to watch the game not to be injured in it
(d) A shall be able to recover as the organisers failed to take precautions against the ball

157. Principle

1. Any person may use reasonable force in order to protect his property or person.
2. However, the force employed must be proportionate to the apprehended danger.

Facts A person walking at a night on a lonely road. A robber came with a knife and said to the person, "your life or your purse". Person pulled out his revolver. On seeing it, robber ran. Person shot robber in his leg.

(a) Person will not be punished as the force he used was proportionate to the apprehended injury
(b) As robber ran to escape there was no longer a threat to person's property so person will be punished
(c) Person will not be punished as there was danger to his property
(d) Person will be punished as the force employed was disproportionate to the apprehended injury

158. Principle When any person dishonestly takes away moveable property out of the possession of any other person without his consent, he is guilty of theft.

Facts A finds a mobile on the road and he keeps it.

(a) A commit theft because he does not report to owner of the mobile
(b) A does not commit theft because the mobile was not taken away from the possession of any body
(c) A commit theft because he does not report to police
(d) None of the above

159. Principle An agreement is enforceable at law if parties competent to contract enter into it with free consent, for consideration. And the contract is not contrary to law and against public policy.

Facts A Minor enter into an agreement to sell his flat at Delhi for a sum of ₹ 10 lakhs. Minor's father is very annoyed with Minor at the transaction and does not allow to delivers. The buyer files a suit for a specific performance.

(a) The buyer will not succeed because *A*'s father does not approve of the contract
(b) The buyer will succeed because *A* freely entered into the contract
(c) The buyer will not succeed because *A* is Minor
(d) The buyer will succeed because the agreement is with consideration

160. Principle An unfair trade practice includes a trade practice which for the purpose of sale, falsely represents that the goods are of a particular standard, quality or grade.

Facts P & Co issues an advertisement that their tooth paste is 102% better than the tooth paste of C & Co. Is this can an unfair trade practice?

(a) No, this is not unfair trade practice as this is a normal practice in trade
(b) No, because the facts in this advertisement are correct
(c) Yes, because the fact, relating to the product are not correct
(d) None of the above

Logical Reasoning

161. How many such pairs of digits are there in number '36725918' each of which has as many digits between them in the number as when the digits are arranged in descending order within the numbers?

(a) None
(b) One
(c) Two
(d) Three

162. What should come next in the following number series?

6 8 8 1 2 6 8 6 1 2 3 6 8 8 1 2 3 4 6 8 6 1 2 3 4 5 6 8?

(a) 6 (b) 1
(c) 4 (d) 8

163. How many such digits are there in the number '37152869' each of which is as far away from the beginning of the number as when the digits are arranged in ascending order within the number?

(a) None (b) One (c) Two (d) Three

Directions (Q. Nos. 164–172) *In each of the questions below are given four statements followed by three conclusions numbered I, II and III. You have to take the given statements to be true even if they seem to be at variance from commonly known facts. Read all the conclusions and then decide which of the given conclusions logically follows from the given statements disregarding commonly known facts.*

164. Statements

All coins are glasses.
Some glasses are cups.
Some cups are boxes.
All boxes are pins.

Conclusions

I. Some coins are cups.
II. Some pins are glasses.
III. Some cups are pins.

(a) None follows
(b) Only I follows
(c) Only III follows
(d) II and III follow

165. Statements

Some pens are pencils.
All pencils are caps.
All caps are buses.
Some buses are trains.

Conclusions

I. Some trains are caps.
II. Some pens are buses.
III. Some pencils are trains.

(a) Only I follows
(b) Only II follows
(c) I and III follow
(d) None follows

166. Statements

All shirts are skirts.
All skirts are banks.
All banks are roads.
All roads are brushes.

Conclusions

I. All banks are skirts.

II. All roads are banks.

III. Some brushes are shirts.

(a) Only I follows
(b) Only III follows
(c) I and III follow
(d) I, II and III follow

167. Statements

Some fishes are plates.
Some plates are spoons.
Some spoons are plants.
All plants are crows.

Conclusions

I. Some plates are crows.

II. Some crows are spoons.

III. Some plants are spoons.

(a) Only I follows
(b) I and II follow
(c) None follows
(d) II and III follow

168. Statements

Some eggs are hens.
Some hens are ducks.
All ducks are pigeons.
All pigeons are sparrows.

Conclusions

I. All ducks are sparrows.

II. No egg is duck.

III. Some sparrows are hens.

(a) Only I follows (b) I and II follow
(c) Only III follows (d) I and III follow

169. Statements

No man is tiger.
No tiger is cat.
Some cats are lions.
Some lions are tigers.

Conclusions

I. Some tigers are cats.

II. Some cats are men.

III. Some lions are men.

(a) None follows
(b) Only III follows
(c) I and II follow
(d) Only I follows

170. Three of the following four are alike in a certain way and so form a group. Which is the one that does not belong to that group?

(a) Papaya (b) Mango
(c) Jackfruit (d) Watermelon

171. Number of letters skipped in between adjacent letters of the series starting from behind are increased by one. Which of the following series observes this rule?

(a) ONLKI (b) OMKIG
(c) OMJFA (d) OIGDC

172. If the first and second digits in the squence 7 9 8 4 5 3 6 7 8 3 4 5 are interchanged, also the third and fourth digits, the fifth and sixth digits and so on. Which digit would be the sixth counting from your right?

(a) 5 (b) 6
(c) 7 (d) 8

Directions (Q. Nos. 173–177) *In each question below, is given a statement followed by two assumptions numbered I and II. An assumption is something supposed or taken for granted. You have to consider the statement and the following assumptions and decide which of the assumptions is implicit in the statement. Give answer*

(a) if only assumption I is implicit
(b) if only assumption II is implicit
(c) if neither I nor II is implicit
(d) if both I and II are implicit

173. Statement To achieve economic development, people should work hard.

Assumptions

I. Achieving economic development is desirable.

II. Working hard is not impossible.

174. Statement He is too industrious to be poor.

Assumptions

I. Very industrious people also can be poor.

II. Very lazy people also can be rich.

175. Statement Visitors may use lift at their own risk.

Assumptions

I. Using lift is not always safe.

II. Visitors do not want to use lift.

176. Statement This book is so designed that even a layman can easily learn science in the absence of a teacher.

Assumptions

I. Learning science by everybody is desirable.

II. A layman generally finds it difficult to learn science on his own.

177. Statement Although the rates of this hotel are comparable with other hotels, the amenities provided here are far superior.

Assumptions

I. Rates are independent of amenities provided.

II. Rates are dependent on amenities provided.

Directions (Q. Nos. 178-184) *Find out the correct answer out of the four alternatives given below each question and then mark it in your answersheet.*

178. Ice : Coolness :: Earth : ?

(a) Forest (b) Weight
(c) Gravitation (d) Ocean

179. Coconut : Shell :: Letter : ?

(a) Mail (b) Letter-box
(c) Stamp (d) Envelope

180. Income is related to profit in the same way as expenditure is related to

(a) loss
(b) surplus
(c) balance
(d) sale

181. Much is related to many in the same way as measure is related to

(a) calculate (b) count
(c) weigh (d) measurement

182. Clue is related to mystery in the same way as warning is related to

(a) precaution (b) disaster
(c) risk (d) danger

183. Select the series in which the letters skipped in between adjacent letters do not decrease in order

(a) MGVFK (b) PJXHM
(c) EQZFI (d) GWIQU

184. If 'M' denotes '+', 'N' denotes '÷', 'R' denotes '–' and 'Q' denotes 'x' then

15 M 12 Q 5 R 40 N 8 = ?

(a) 70 (b) 130
(c) 45 (d) 60

Directions (Q. Nos. 185-190) *Below in each question are given two statements (I) and (II). These statements may be either independent causes or may be effects of independent causes or a common cause. One of these statements may be the effect of the other statement. Read both the statements and then decide which of the following answer choice correctly depicts the relationship between these two statements. Mark answer*

(a) if Statement I is the cause and statement II is its effect
(b) if Statement II is the cause and statement I is its effect
(c) if both Statements I and II are effects of independent causes
(d) if both Statements I and II are effects of some common causes

185. I. There has been mass recruitment of IT professionals by Indian IT companies.

II. Many developed countries are increasingly outsourcing IT related functions to India and China.

186. I. Many farmers have given up jute cultivation as it is no longer economically viable.

II. The textile ministry has proposed a hike in the Minimum Support Price of jute.

187. I. The government is considering changes in the Land Acquisition Act.

II. Several large infrastructure development projects have been stalled due to unavailability of land.

188. I. The Government is considering the possibility of involving private sector companies in highway construction projects.

II. The implementation of many highway projects undertaken by government agencies is behind schedule in various states.

189. I. The price of aircraft fuel has risen during the past few months.

II. Many passenger airlines in India have been forced to cut their air fares by about 10 percent.

190. If 'yellow' is called 'red', 'red' is called 'blue', 'blue' is called 'white', 'white' is called 'black', 'black' is called 'green', and 'green' is called 'violet', what is the colour of clear sky?

(a) Green (b) Violet
(c) Yellow (d) None of these

Directions (Q. Nos. 191–195) *Study the following information carefully and answer the given questions*

A, B, C, D, E, F, G and H are eight friends sitting around a circular table facing the centre. A sits second to the left of D who is third to the left of E. C sits third to the right of G who is not an immediate neighbour of E. H sits third to the right of B who sits second of the right of G.

191. Who sits between D and C?

(a) Only B
(b) Only C and A
(c) Only G
(d) Only E

192. Who sits second to the right of E?

(a) E (b) F
(c) G (d) 0C

193. What is the position of A with respect to H?

(a) Third to the left
(b) Third to the right
(c) Second to the left
(d) Second to the right

194. Four of the following five are alike based upon their seating arrangements and so form a group. Which is the one that does not belong to that group?

(a) CH (b) FG
(c) DA (d) BE

195. Which of the following pairs has the second person sitting to the immediate left of the first person?

(a) DB (b) EH
(c) FA (d) None of these

Directions (Q. Nos. 196–200) *Read the following information carefully and answer the questions, which follow*

'P ÷ Q' means 'P is son of Q'.
'P × Q' means 'P is sister of Q'.
'P + Q' means 'P is brother of Q'.
'P – Q' means 'P is mother of Q'.

196. How is T related to S in the expression 'T × R + V ÷ S'?

(a) Sister
(b) Mother
(c) Aunt
(d) None of the above

197. How is T related to S in the expression 'T × R ÷ V – S'?

(a) Father (b) Sister
(c) Daughter (d) Aunt

198. How is S related to T in the expression 'T + R – V + S'?

(a) Uncle
(b) Nephew
(c) Son
(d) Cannot be determined

199. Which of the following means that 'S is the husband of T'?

(a) T × R – V + S
(b) T – R ÷ V × S
(c) T – R + V ÷ S
(d) T ÷ R × V + S

200. How is V related to T in the expression 'T ÷ R + V × S'?

(a) Aunt (b) Nephew
(c) Niece (d) Uncle

ANSWERS

1	(c)	**2**	(d)	**3**	(c)	**4**	(d)	**5**	(a)	**6**	(c)	**7**	(b)	**8**	(b)	**9**	(c)	**10**	(b)
11	(c)	**12**	(a)	**13**	(d)	**14**	(c)	**15**	(b)	**16**	(b)	**17**	(a)	**18**	(c)	**19**	(d)	**20**	(c)
21	(c)	**22**	(b)	**23**	(a)	**24**	(b)	**25**	(c)	**26**	(a)	**27**	(d)	**28**	(d)	**29**	(b)	**30**	(c)
31	(b)	**32**	(a)	**33**	(c)	**34**	(c)	**35**	(c)	**36**	(b)	**37**	(a)	**38**	(c)	**39**	(a)	**40**	(a)
41	(b)	**42**	(b)	**43**	(d)	**44**	(c)	**45**	(a)	**46**	(c)	**47**	(d)	**48**	(c)	**49**	(d)	**50**	(b)
51	(c)	**52**	(c)	**53**	(b)	**54**	(b)	**55**	(d)	**56**	(b)	**57**	(b)	**58**	(b)	**59**	(a)	**60**	(c)
61	(c)	**62**	(d)	**63**	(b)	**64**	(a)	**65**	(b)	**66**	(c)	**67**	(c)	**68**	(d)	**69**	(d)	**70**	(c)
71	(d)	**72**	(d)	**73**	(c)	**74**	(d)	**75**	(b)	**76**	(a)	**77**	(d)	**78**	(d)	**79**	(d)	**80**	(c)
81	(b)	**82**	(c)	**83**	(a)	**84**	(d)	**85**	(b)	**86**	(d)	**87**	(d)	**88**	(b)	**89**	(c)	**90**	(c)
91	(c)	**92**	(d)	**93**	(a)	**94**	(a)	**95**	(c)	**96**	(b)	**97**	(d)	**98**	(d)	**99**	(c)	**100**	(b)
101	(d)	**102**	(d)	**103**	(d)	**104**	(d)	**105**	(d)	**106**	(c)	**107**	(b)	**108**	(a)	**109**	(b)	**110**	(d)
111	(c)	**112**	(c)	**113**	(a)	**114**	(b)	**115**	(b)	**116**	(c)	**117**	(b)	**118**	(a)	**119**	(a)	**120**	(d)
121	(d)	**122**	(d)	**123**	(d)	**124**	(b)	**125**	(c)	**126**	(a)	**127**	(a)	**128**	(b)	**129**	(d)	**130**	(c)
131	(a)	**132**	(b)	**133**	(a)	**134**	(a)	**135**	(b)	**136**	(a)	**137**	(b)	**138**	(c)	**139**	(a)	**140**	(d)
141	(c)	**142**	(d)	**143**	(b)	**144**	(c)	**145**	(d)	**146**	(c)	**147**	(d)	**148**	(b)	**149**	(c)	**150**	(a)
151	(a)	**152**	(a)	**153**	(d)	**154**	(b)	**155**	(a)	**156**	(a)	**157**	(b)	**158**	(b)	**159**	(c)	**160**	(c)
161	(c)	**162**	(d)	**163**	(c)	**164**	(c)	**165**	(b)	**166**	(b)	**167**	(d)	**168**	(d)	**169**	(a)	**170**	(c)
171	(c)	**172**	(c)	**173**	(d)	**174**	(c)	**175**	(a)	**176**	(b)	**177**	(c)	**178**	(c)	**179**	(d)	**180**	(a)
188	(b)	**182**	(d)	**183**	(b)	**184**	(a)	**185**	(b)	**186**	(a)	**187**	(d)	**188**	(b)	**189**	(c)	**190**	(d)
191	(a)	**192**	(b)	**193**	(d)	**194**	(c)	**195**	(d)	**196**	(d)	**197**	(b)	**198**	(d)	**199**	(c)	**200**	(a)

PRACTICE SET 3

Instructions

- *There are total 200 questions in this practice set.*
- *For every correct attempt the students will be awarded 1 mark.*
- *All the questions are in MCQs form.*

English Language

Directions (Q. Nos. 1-5) *Out of the four alternatives, choose the one which can be substituted for the given words/sentence and indicate it by choosing the appropriate alternative.*

1. The dead skin cast off by a snake.
(a) Bough (b) Slough
(c) Peeling (d) Borough

2. Science dealing with bird life.
(a) Zymology (b) Ornithology
(c) Etymology (d) Philology

3. One who is from 60 to 69 years old.
(a) Sexton (b) Sexologist
(c) Sexagenarian (d) Sextuplet

4. Someone who keeps bees.
(a) Apiarist (b) Horticulturist
(c) Ornithologist (d) Pathologist

5. Speaking one's thoughts aloud to oneself.
(a) Apostrophise (b) Memorise
(c) Soliloquize (d) Solemnise

Directions (Q. Nos. 6-15) *In the following questions, you have a brief passage with ten questions following the passage. Read the passage carefully and choose the best answer to each question out of the four alternatives and indicate your correct alternative.*

In a small hill town, there lived a thief. He was very smart and before breaking into houses for theft he used to enquire about the lifestyles of the people staying in that house. Then at the dead of night he used to commit theft.

Dhanpatrai was a moneylender living in the same town. He was thrifty and never wasted money. He had a daughter named Laxmi. The thief knew that Dhanpatrai was rich and he had a lot of jewellery with him. Smartly the thief found out the location of the house and designed the theft. One night, getting up to the roof of the house he started removing the roof-covering made of earthen tiles.

The moneylender heard the sound and was sure that a thief was on the roof of the house. Now, he had to create some ploy. He hit upon a plan. "Laxmi, Laxmi" he called out to his daughter who was sleeping. "Laxmi, I hope our money-box and jewellery are kept in the ceiling," he asked cleverly.

Generally, in hill area, to keep house warm in winter, houses have a thatched roofing and below that, a wooden ceiling. Certain things used to be kept in the space between the roofing and wooden ceiling. So, when the thief heard the question put by Dhanpatrai, he thought that there was a ceiling below the thatched roof. So, he jumped down.

But actually in the house there was no wooden ceiling. So, the thief fell to the floor of the house which was about fifteen feet below and broke his leg.

Immediately, the moneylender called all the neighbours and they handed over the thief to the police. He saved his house from being burgled, with his ingenuity.

6. What was the role of Laxmi in this episode?
(a) She called people and scared the thief
(b) Laxmi sent the people for police
(c) She asked Dhanpatrai to call the people
(d) Her name was used to misguide the thief

7. How did the thief enter the house of Dhanpatrai?
1. By removing the tiled top of the house.
2. By removing the wooden ceiling.
3. By opening the door with duplicate key.

(a) Only 1 (b) Only 2
(c) Only 3 (d) Both 1 and 2

8. Where was the jewellery actually kept?
(a) Inside the bed on which Laxmi was sleeping
(b) On the thatched roof top
(c) Below the pillow of Dhanpatrai
(d) There is no mention of jewellery's location

9. What was the quality of the thief?
(a) He was expert in removing roof tops
(b) Before theft he used to study the lifestyles of residents
(c) He was accurate in identifying his victim
(d) He was liked by the people and the police

10. Who was Dhanpatrai?
(a) The father of the thief
(b) The moneylender who used to keep valuables on the roof
(c) A cunning and crafty man
(d) The father of Laxmi

11. Who called the police?
(a) The son of Dhanpatrai
(b) The daughter of Dhanpatrai
(c) Dhanpatrai himself
(d) None of the above

12. Which quality of Dhanpatrai protected his house?
(a) His thrifty behaviour
(b) His deep affection for the daughter
(c) The cleverness with which he handled the situation
(d) His past decision of not thatching the roof top

13. Why did the thief choose Dhanpatrai's house for the act?
(a) There was hardly any house left in the town for theft
(b) Dhanpatrai was living with his daughter
(c) The house did not have wooden ceiling
(d) He had the information that Dhanpatrai was rich

14. Which of the following statements is true in the context of the passage?
(a) The daughter of Dhanpatrai was too weak to handle the thief
(b) The people of the town did not like Dhanpatrai
(c) Dhanpatrai played a trick with the thief
(d) Dhanpatrai did not have money for wastage

15. The thief would have escaped unhurt had there been ……….
(a) a dog in the house
(b) a wooden ceiling below the thatched roof
(c) very few policemen to catch him
(d) no alertness on the part of Dhanpatrai's son

Directions (Q. Nos. 16-20) *In each of the following sentences, a word or phrase is written in italicised letter. For each italicised part, four words/phrases are listed below each sentence. Choose the word nearest in meaning to the italicised part.*

16. A million cinemas a year bring the same *stale bladerdash.*
(a) adventure (b) nonsense
(c) thriller (d) romance

17. There must be lively discussion of Indian authors if we are to *foster* our knowledge.
(a) promote (b) cherish
(c) nourish (d) nurture

18. Buoyed by these visions of the future of his son, the artist *soldiered on*.
(a) continued bravely
(b) stopped further
(c) struggled hard
(d) fought on

19. Last fortnight, the rains came to the parched soils of India after the merciless drought had already *sapped* the vitality and livelihood of millions of peasants.
(a) decreased (b) demolished
(c) destroyed (d) drained away

20. The boy gave a *vivid description* of all that happened.
(a) brilliant (b) fresh
(c) explanatory (d) picturesque

Directions (Q.Nos. 21-25) *Which of the phrases (a), (b), (c) and (d) given below each sentence should replace the word/phrase printed in bold in the sentence to make it grammatically correct?*

21. Since, Riya did not want to be disturbed while studying, she left the phone **off hooks**.
(a) off the hook (b) off hooking
(c) for the hook (d) of hook

22. Since, Shilpa was overburdened with work, Deepa decided to **gave her hand**.
(a) giving hands (b) give her a hand
(c) giving her handful (d) gave her hands

23. Despite having passed out from school over ten years back, most schoolmates **has keep touch** with each other.
(a) are kept touched
(b) is keeping touch
(c) keep touched
(d) had kept in touch

24. Sheela **has well awareness of** the fact that her actions would have terrible repercussions.
(a) was well aware of
(b) has aware for
(c) is aware to
(d) is in awareness with

25. Shashi tried **as hard he would** to win the race but failed to do so.
(a) as hardly so he could (b) as hard as he could
(c) hardly so as (d) so hard that could

Directions (Q. Nos. 26-30) *Read each sentence to find out whether there is any grammatical error or idiomatic error in it. The error will be in one part of the sentence. The letter of that part is the answer.*

26. Since, the online education system (a)/ has been poorly designed there (b)/ are not many institute (c)/ that offer this facility. (d)

27. Unless the new resolution is (a)/completely reviewed it (b)/ will cause a great deal of (c)/ trouble for new employees. (d)

28. After careful scrutiny of the report (a)/ variety mistakes that had been (b)/ made by the research (c)/ department were found. (d)

29. His industrious nature (a)/ and calm temperament (b)/ have endeared him (c)/ to his colleagues and one's superiors. (d)

30. The celebrities that organised (a)/ the marathon were aiming (b)/ to create an awareness (c)/ about the treatment of diabetes. (d)

Directions (Q. Nos. 31-35) *Pick out the most effective word/group of words from those given to fill in the blanks to make the sentence meaningfully complete.*

31. Although he appears to be very .... in his speech, he is very good at heart.
(a) strong (b) fine
(c) rude (d) innocent

32. He was wrongly punished although he was not ....
(a) fault
(b) mistaken
(c) erroneous
(d) guilty

33. .... you complete the assignment in time, you will not be allowed to proceed on leave.
(a) If (b) Unless
(c) Before (d) When

34. In the .... two months, we will not be able to meet him.
(a) past (b) last
(c) farther (d) next

35. The festival of Deepawali was .... by all of us.
(a) performed (b) enjoyed
(c) spent (d) engaged

Directions (Q.Nos. 36-40) *The first and the last parts of the sentence/passage are numbered (1) and (6). The rest of the sentence/passage is split into four parts and named (P), (Q), (R) and (S). These four parts are not given in their proper order. Read the sentence/passage and find out which of the four combinations is correct.*

36. 1. For thousands of millions of years the Moon has been going round the Earth.
P. However, some of them will still be going round the Earth thousands of years from now.
Q. These artificial satellites are very much smaller than the Moon.
R. Today, however, the Earth has many other satellites, all made by man.
S. During this time, the Moon has been the only satellite of the Earth.
6. Artificial satellites do not fall because they are going too fast to do so.
(a) P R S Q (b) Q S R P
(c) S R P Q (d) S R Q P

37. 1. Sir Edmund Hillary and Tenzing Norgay were the first to reach the peak of Mount Everest in 1953.

P. While a Nepalese and a Japanese climber have done it three times, the Italian climber Reinhold Messner has done it twice.

Q. Some 164 men and women mountaineers from 21 nations have made the ascent.

R. The mountain still continues to enthral.

S. Since, then, there has been a succession of climbs.

6. Those wanting to climb Everest must file an application, with the Nepal Tourism Ministry.

(a) P Q R S (b) S R Q P
(c) S Q P R (d) S P R Q

38. 1. There is a lot of luck in drilling for oil.

P. The samples of soil are examined for traces of oil.

Q. The drill may just miss the oil although it is near.

R. Sometimes, it may strike oil at a fairly high level.

S. When the drill goes down it brings up soil.

6. If they are disappointed at one place, the drillers go to another.

(a) Q P R S (b) Q R S P (c) P S R Q (d) S R Q P

39. 1. India is a very old country with a great past.

P. Since, August 1947, she had been in a position to pursue her own foreign policy.

Q. But it is a new country also, with new urges and new desires.

R. But even so, she could not forget the lesson of her great leader.

S. She was limited by the realities of the situation which she could not ignore or overcome.

6. She tried to adapt theory to reality.

(a) P Q R S (b) Q P S R
(c) S R P Q (d) R S P Q

40. 1. Of all the living creatures on the earth, insects are the most plentiful.

P. In some countries, they are farmers' greatest enemy.

Q. Locusts are perhaps the most dangerous of all, for they will eat almost any green plant and leave cultivated lands bare.

R. Some varieties are very useful to man, like bees from which we get honey and wax, and silkworms which supply us with silk.

S. Other varieties, however, are extremely harmful and do a great amount of damage, especially to crops.

6. Common flies, cockroaches, termites, mosquitoes and lice are some other insects harmful to man.

(a) P S R Q (b) S R P Q
(c) R S Q P (d) Q S R P

General Knowledge

41. Who was the first woman President of Indian National Congress?
(a) Mrs Vijayalakshmi Pandit
(b) Mrs Sarojini Naidu
(c) Dr Annie Besant
(d) None of the above

42. Who was the first woman Chief Justice of a High Court in India?
(a) Miss M Fathima Beevi
(b) Miss Anna Chandi
(c) Anna George Malhotra
(d) Miss Leila Seth

43. Which of the following statements concerning Indian National Flag is correct?
(a) No other Flag is to be placed above it
(b) No other Emblem is to be placed above it
(c) The flag is not to be carried flat
(d) All the above statements are correct

44. Our National Song is
(a) Sare Jahan se Achcha (b) Jana Gana Mana
(c) Vande Mataram (d) All of these

45. Which is not a film certificate given by Central Film Certification Board?
(a) U (b) A
(c) U/A (d) A/U

46. What is 'middle cinema'?
(a) Films made for middle-aged people
(b) Films made for the middle class
(c) A combination of art and commercial films
(d) Films made in the decade of 50s

47. Which one is not an element of the process of mass communication?
(a) Message (b) Channel
(c) Receiver (d) Telephone

48. English magazine 'The Week' is a member of the group
(a) Bennet and Coleman
(b) Express
(c) Delhi Press
(d) Malayala Manorama

49. Which one is the oldest news agency of India?
(a) UNI (b) PTI
(c) ANI (b) UPI

50. The journalist accused by Sonu Nigam with the allegation of male casting couch?
(a) Subhash K Jha (b) Prakash K Jha
(c) Prashant Thakkar (d) None of these

51. "Because you deserve to know" is the punchline of which newspaper?
(a) The Hindu
(b) The Times of India
(c) The Indian Express
(d) The Hindustan Times

52. Where are the hot deserts generally found?
(a) On the Eastern margins of the tropics
(b) On the Western margins of the tropics
(c) Nearer the Equator
(d) In the middle of the continents

53. Why are winters more severe in Southern Hemisphere that in Northern Hemisphere?
(a) Earth is titled towards the Sun in the Northern Hemisphere
(b) Northern Hemisphere receives more sunlight
(c) Because of more iceberg activity in Southern Hemisphere
(d) Southern Hemisphere is less in habited

54. On which of the following dates is your shadow at noon the smallest?
(a) 25th December (b) 21st March
(c) 22nd June (d) 14th February

55. Ozone layer in atmosphere
(a) produces rain
(b) produces pollution
(c) provides safty to life on Earth from ultraviolet radiation
(d) produces oxygen in the atmosphere

56. Tetraethyl lead is used as
(a) mosquito repellent
(b) pain killer
(c) fire extinguisher
(d) petrol additive

57. Which of the following is used in beauty parlours for hair setting?
(a) Phosphorus (b) Sulphur
(c) Chlorine (d) Silicon

58. Which of the following is a non-metal that remains liquid in room temperature?
(a) Bromine (b) Chlorine
(c) Helium (d) Phosphorus

59. From which mineral is radium obtained?
(a) Limestone (b) Haematitie
(c) Pitchblende (d) Rutile

60. What is laughing gas?
(a) Carbon Dioxide
(b) Sulphur Dioxide
(c) Nitrogen Dioxide
(d) Nitrous Oxide

61. Who is considered as the greatest of all the Vijayanagar rulers?
(a) Krishnadeva Raya (b) Vira Narasimha
(c) Sadasiva Raya (d) Rama Raya

62. Which was the only Indus site with an artificial brick dockyard?
(a) Lothal (b) Kalibangan
(c) Harappa (d) Mohenjodaro

63. Nalanda University was a great centre of learning, especially in
(a) Buddhism (b) Jainism
(c) Vaishnavism (d) Tantra

64. 'Lakh Baksh' was a title given to the ruler
(a) Iltutmish
(b) Balban
(c) Raziya
(d) Qutub-ud-Din Aibak

65. The Rathas of Mahabalipuram was built during the reign of the
(a) Palas (b) Cholas
(c) Rashtrakutas (d) Pallavas

66. Which among the following is a martial dance?
(a) Kathakali
(b) Bamboo dance of Meghalaya
(c) Chhau of Mayurbhanj
(d) Bhangra of Punjab

67. Where did the dance form 'Mohini Attam' develop?
(a) Manipur (b) Kerala
(c) Karnataka (d) Tamil Nadu

68. Kabir was a pupil of which personality?
(a) Vallabhacharya (b) Ramanand
(c) Chaitanya (d) Madhvacharya

69. India and Pakistan were partitioned under which of the following plans of the British colonial government?
(a) Mountbatten Plan (b) Cripps Plan
(c) Chelmsford Plan (d) Wavell Plan

70. With which of the following religions are monastries, temples and stupas associated?
(a) Buddhism (b) Jainism
(c) Hinduism (d) Christianity

71. Who among the following had the longest tenure as the Prime Minister of India?
(a) Morarji Desai (b) Charan Singh
(c) VP Singh (d) Lal Bahadur Shastri

72. Who presides over the meetings of the Lok Sabha?
(a) Speaker (b) Vice-President
(c) Prime Minister (d) President

73. Where is the headquarters of the UNO?
(a) Geneva (b) The Hague
(c) New York (d) Paris

74. What is the maximum time interval permissible between two successive sessions of the Parliament?
(a) Four months (b) Six months
(c) Eight months (d) Nine months

75. What is the minimum age laid down for a candidate to seek election to the Lok Sabha?
(a) 18 yr (b) 21 yr
(c) 25 yr (d) 30 yr

76. The Indian Universities were first founded during the time of
(a) Macaulay
(b) Warren Hastings
(c) Lord Canning
(d) Lord William Bentinck

77. The most important sufi shrine in India is located at
(a) Pandua (b) Bidar
(c) Ajmer (d) Shahjahanabad

78. The Parliament can make law for the whole or any part of India for implementing international treaties
(a) with the consent of all the states
(b) with the consent of majority of states
(c) with the consent of states concerned
(d) without the consent of any state

79. Rajya Sabha can delay the Finance Bill sent for its consideration by the Lok Sabha for a maximum period of
(a) one month (b) one year
(c) seven days (d) fourteen days

80. Ras Leela, Yaosang, Lai Haraoba are the festivals of
(a) Assamese people (b) Karbi people
(c) Manipuri people (d) Bodo people

81. Who was the founder of sultanate of Gujarat?
(a) Ahmad Shah
(b) Muhammad Shah
(c) Dilawar Khan
(d) Zafar Khan

82. The 'Ajivikas' were a
(a) sect contemporary to the Mahavira
(b) breakaway branch of the Buddhists
(c) sect founded by Charvaka
(d) sect founded by Shankaracharya

83. What does the Constitution (Ninety Second Amendment) Act, 2003 deal with?
(a) Creation of a separate National Commission for Scheduled Tribes
(b) Cyber Crime
(c) Inclusion of Bodo, Dogri, Maithili and Santhali languages in the Eighth Schedule
(d) Making right to free and compulsory education a fundamental right

84. Which type of ancient script did the Harappans use?
(a) Pictographic (b) Linear
(c) Hieroglyphic (d) Symbolic

85. What is the name of the major base of Indian Navy at Karwar?
(a) INS Kadamba
(b) INS Vikramaditya
(c) INS Harshvardhan
(d) INS Kushan

86. Saraswathi Samman is given annually for outstanding contribution to
(a) classical music (b) education
(c) literature (d) fine arts

87. Which is the oldest paramilitary force in the country?
(a) Border Security Force (BSF)
(b) Assam Rifles
(c) Indo-Tibetan Border Police (ITBP)
(d) Coast Guard

88. The 'Cannes Award' is given for excellence in which field?
(a) Films (b) Journalism
(c) Literature (d) Economics

89. Which of the following countries is not a member of Group 15 developing countries?
(a) Mexico (b) Malaysia
(c) Brazil (d) Bolivia

90. The United Nations Conference on Trade and Development (UNCTAD) is located at which of the following places?
(a) Geneva (b) Rome
(c) Paris (d) Vienna

Mathematics

91. The number of employees in Companies A, B and C are in a ratio of 4 : 5 : 6 respectively. If the number of employees in the three Companies is increased by 25%, 30% and 50% respectively, what will be the new ratio of employees working in Companies A, B and C respectively?
(a) 13 : 10 : 18 (b) 10 : 13 : 17
(c) 13 : 15 : 18 (d) None of these

92. A milkman sells 120 litres of milk for ₹ 3360 and he sells 240 litres of milk for ₹ 6120. How much concession does the trader give per litre of milk, when he sells 240 litres of milk?
(a) ₹ 2 (b) ₹ 3.5 (c) ₹ 2.5 (d) ₹ 1.5

93. A train starts with the speed of 70 km/h with its speed increasing every two hours by 10 km/h. In how many hours will it cover 345 km?
(a) 2¼ h (b) 4 h 5 m
(c) 4½ h (d) None of these

94. If 3/5th of a cistern is filled in 1 minute, how much more time will be required to fill the rest of it?
(a) 40 s (b) 30 s (c) 36 s (d) 24 s

95. What is the smallest number by which 3600 be divided to make it a perfect cube?
(a) 9 (b) 450 (c) 50 (d) 300

96. X got 30% concession on the labelled price of an article and sold it for ₹ 8750 with 25% profit on the price she bought. What was the labelled price?
(a) ₹ 16000 (b) ₹ 12000
(c) ₹ 10000 (d) None of these

97. In 10 yr, A will be twice as old as B was 10 yr ago. If A is now 9 yr older than B, the present age of B is
(a) 29 yr (b) 19 yr (c) 49 yr (d) 39 yr

98. A train crosses a pole in 15 s, while it crosses 100 m long platform in 25 s. The length of the train is
(a) 125 m (b) 135 m (c) 159 m (d) 175 m

99. A can do a piece of work in 12 days and B can do it in 18 days. They started the work together but A left 3 days before the completion of the work. The total number of days to complete the work is
(a) $6\frac{3}{5}$ days (b) 9 days
(c) $9\frac{1}{5}$ days (d) $10\frac{1}{5}$ days

100. A man walking at the rate of 6 km/h crosses a square field diagonally in 9 s. The area of the field is
(a) 125 sq cm (b) 112.5 sq cm
(c) 110 sq cm (d) $100\sqrt{2}$ sq. m

101. A trader marks his goods 25% above the CP but discounts 15% on the marked price. His gain per cent in the deal is
(a) 5% (b) $6\frac{1}{4}\%$ (c) $7\frac{1}{2}\%$ (d) 10%

102. On selling each of the two radios for ₹ 5000, a person neither gained nor lost. If he had sold one radio at 25% gain, then at what per cent loss did he sell the other radio?
(a) $16\frac{2}{3}\%$ (b) $18\frac{2}{9}\%$ (c) 25% (d) $26\frac{2}{3}\%$

103. A house owner wants to get his house painted. He is told that this would require 25 kg of paint. Allowing for 15% wastage and assuming that the paint is available in 2 kg tins, the number of tins required for painting the house is
(a) 15 (b) 12 (c) 10 (d) 20

104. Price of foodgrains have risen by 10% and of other items of consumption by 15%. If the ratio of an employee's expenditure on food-grains and other items is 2 : 5, by how much should his salary be increased so that he may maintain the same level of consumption as before, assuming that his present salary is ₹ 3500?
(a) ₹ 300 (b) ₹ 350 (c) ₹ 375 (d) ₹ 475

105. The value of in standard form, is

(a) 1.1×10 (b) 1.1×10^2
(c) 1.1×10^3 (d) 1.1×10^4

Directions (Q. Nos. 106-110) *What should come in place of the question mark (?) in the following number series?*

106. 1, 9, 25, 49, ?, 169

(a) 100 (b) 64 (c) 81 (d) 121

107. 3, 23, 43, ?, 83, 103

(a) 33 (b) 53
(c) 63 (d) 73

108. 748, 737, 715, 682, 638, ?

(a) 594 (b) 572
(c) 581 (d) None of these

109. 121, 117, 108, 92, 67, ?

(a) 31 (b) 29 (c) 41 (d) 37

110. 50, 26, 14, ?, 5, 3.5

(a) 6 (b) 8
(c) 10 (d) 12

Legal Aptitude & Indian Constitution

111. What does the abbreviation POTA means

(a) Prevention of Terrorism Act
(b) Prevention of Terrorists Act
(c) Punishment of Terrorists Act
(d) None of the above

112. An accused below the age of 18 years for committing an offence can be tried under

(a) Indian Penal Code (45 of 1860)
(b) Juvenile Justice (Care and Protection of Children) Act, 2000
(c) Both (a) and (b)
(d) being a minor, he is not to be punished

113. Economic Justice, an important objective of the Constitution of India, is embeded in the

(a) Preamble
(b) Preamble and Directive Principles
(c) Directive Principles
(d) Fundamental Rights

114. "No action lies against the Government for injury done to an individual in the course of exercise of its sovereign functions". All of the following actions are covered by the above provision, except

(a) improper arrest, negligence or trespass by police officers
(b) loss of movables from government custody owing to negligence of its officers
(c) injury due to the negligence of servants of the government employed in a railway or a dockyard
(d) administration of justice

115. Rule 2 under Section 10 of the Hindu Succession Act, 1956 is

(a) per capita rule
(b) per stirpes
(c) per stirpes per capita rule
(d) rule of exclusion

116. Which one of the following mortgages does not require writing and registration?

(a) Usufructuary mortgage
(b) Simple mortgage
(c) English mortgage
(d) Mortgage by deposit of title deeds

117. Which one of the following is not correctly matched?

(a) Child witness	:	Section 118
(b) Dumb witness	:	Section 120
(c) Hostile witness	:	Section 154
(d) Expert witness	:	Section 45

118. Hindu law does not apply to a person who is a Hindu by

(a) birth (b) conversion
(c) re-conversion (d) None of these

119. Provision of Section 24 of the Hindu Marriage Act, 1955 corresponds to

(a) Section 36 of the Special Marriage Act, 1954
(b) Section 36 of the Indian Divorce Act, 1869
(c) Both (a) and (b)
(d) None of the above

120. Under Hindu Succession Act, 1956, who amongst the following is not in Class I heir?

(a) Father
(b) Mother
(c) Son
(d) Daughter

121. Who can be a guardian in minor's marriage in Sunni Law?

(a) Mother in the presence of father
(b) Grandmother in the presence of mother
(c) Maternal uncle in the presence of real uncle
(d) Father

122. A person who goes underground or evades the jurisdiction of the court is known as
(a) Offender (b) Underground
(c) Absentee (d) Absconder

123. A person whose fundamental rights are violated can move the High Court under
(a) Article 20 (b) Article 226
(c) Article 32 (d) Article 22

124. 'A' and 'B' contract to marry each other, before the time fixed for the marriage, 'A' goes mad, the contract becomes
(a) Voidable Contract
(b) Conditional Contract
(c) Contingent Contract
(d) Void Contract

125. Under Section 17 of the Indian Evidence Act, the 'admission' is
(a) written only (b) oral only
(c) Both written and oral (d) None of these

126. Which one of the following cases does not relate to 'dying declaration'?
(a) Queen Emperess *Vs* Abdullah
(b) Pakala Narayan Swamy *Vs* King Emperor
(c) Zatar *Vs* State of UI
(d) Ratangond *Vs* State of Bihar

127. Which of the following sections was amended by the Indian Technology Act, 2000?
(a) Section 6 of the Indian Evidence Act
(b) Section 17 of the Indian Evidence act
(c) Section 32 of the Indian Evidence Act
(d) Section 41 of the Indian Evidence Act

128. Which one of the following cases is not related to *Mens rea?*
(a) R *Vs* Prince
(b) Queen *Vs* Tolson
(c) Sherras *Vs* De Rutzen
(d) Barendra Kumar Ghosh *Vs*

129. How many exceptions have been provided for the offence of defamation under Section 499 of the Indian Penal Code?
(a) 4 (b) 10 (c) 6 (d) 9

130. In which of the following offences under the Indian Penal Code, preparation of the offence is punishable?
(a) Murder
(b) Dowry death
(c) Waging war against Government of India
(d) Theft

131. Which one of the following cases is a case relating to Section 34 of the Indian Penal Code?
(a) KM Nanavati *Vs* State of Maharashtra
(b) Niharendu Dutta *Vs* King Emperor
(c) Barendra Kumar Ghosh *Vs* King Emperor
(d) Kedar Nath *Vs* State of West Bengal

132. Which one of the following Sections of the Indian Penal Code defines 'affray'?
(a) Section 159 (b) Section 160
(c) Section 161 (d) Section 148

133. Which Section of the Code of Criminal Procedure provides that "no statement made by any person to a police officer if reduced to writing, be signed by the person making it"?
(a) Section 161
(b) Section 162
(c) Section 163
(d) Section 164

134. On being submitted the sentence of death by Court of Sessions, the High Court may
(a) confirm the sentence
(b) annual the conviction
(c) may pass any other sentence warranted by law
(d) All of the above

135. Which one of the following sections of the Code of Civil Procedure deals with 'Revision'?
(a) Section 110
(b) Order VI, Rule 13
(c) Section 115
(d) Section 120

136. Which one of the following authorities is not entitled to try a case summarily under the Code of Criminal Procedure?
(a) Chief Judicial Magistrate
(b) Metropolitan Magistrate
(c) Judicial Magistrate of the First Class
(d) 2nd Class Judicial Magistrate

137. Order 42 of the Code of Civil Procedure deals with
(a) appeal to Supreme Court
(b) appeal by indigent person
(c) appeal against orders
(d) appeal from appellate, decrees

138. Which of the following sections of the Code of Civil Procedure defines the 'Mesne Profit'?
(a) Section 2(4) (b) Section 2(14)
(c) Section 2(6) (d) Section 2(12)

139. In regard to a Hindu marriage, 'Sapinda relationship' of any person is counted upto
(a) fifth generation in the line of ascent through father only
(b) third generation in the line of ascent through mother only
(c) Both (a) and (b)
(d) None of the above

140. Who applied Qiyas for the first time as source of Muslim Law?
(a) Imam Abu Hanifa
(b) Imam Yusuf
(c) Imam Later
(d) Imam Ahmad

141. In Shia School of Muslim Law the amount of Mehar is
(a) not legally fixed
(b) 10 dirhams
(c) 100 dirhams
(d) 500 dirhams

142. Doctrine of 'cypres' is related with
(a) marriage (b) dower
(c) gift (d) wakfs

143. Dissolution of Muslim marriage by agreement is known as
(a) Talaq in Ahsan (b) Illa
(c) Zihar (d) Khula

144. Which one of the following sections of the Transfer of Property Act, defines 'Notice'?
(a) Section 2
(b) Section 3
(c) Section 5
(d) Explanation H of Section 3

145. The provision of fraudulent transfer is given in
(a) Section 49 of the Transfer of Property Act, 1882
(b) Section 50 of the Transfer of Property Act, 1882
(c) Section 51 of the Transfer of Property Act, 1882
(d) Section 53 of the Transfer of Property Act, 1882

146. Which of the following properties cannot be transferred?
(a) Share in copyright
(b) Interest in mortgaged property
(c) Right to future maintenance
(d) Immovable property

147. Which of the following sections of the Transfer of Property Act deals with 'effect of holding over a lease'?
(a) Section 114 A (b) Section 115
(c) Section 115 A (d) Section 116

148. The doctrine of 'lis pendens' is explained in famous case of
(a) Bellamy *Vs* Sabine
(b) Musahur Sahu *Vs* Hakim Lal
(c) Muhammad Shafi *Vs* Muhammad Sayed
(d) Tulk *Vs* Moxhay

149. The mortgagors right to redeem the mortgaged property accrues
(a) at any time after the mortgage
(b) at any time after the mortgage money has become due
(c) at any time when the mortgagor wants
(d) at any time mortgagee demands the money

150. Who is competent to transfer a revenue case from one District to another under Section 29 of the MP Land Revenue Code?
(a) State Government (b) Board of Revenue
(c) Chief Secretary (d) Revenue Minister

Directions (Q. Nos. 151-160) *Given below is a statement of legal principle, followed by a factual situation. Apply the principle to the facts and select the most appropriate answer among the alternatives given.*

151. Principle No legal remedy exists for an injury caused by an act, for which one has consented.

Facts In the One Day International Cricket Match between India and Pakistan, Sehwag hit a full toss delivery of Shoaib Akhtar over the boundary for a six. The ball fell on the body of one of the spectator and injured him. Spectator sues organiser of the match for reimbursement of the medical bill he paid for treatment.
(a) Spectator can recover the costs of his medical expense from Sehwag
(b) Spectator should be compensated as he purchased the ticket to get entertainment and not to get injured
(c) No body would be liable to pay anything to spectator because he voluntarily exposed himself to risk
(d) Organiser is liable as it did not ensure that the spectators were protected from the risks of such injuries

152. Principle A master is liable for the wrongful acts of his servants committed in the course of employment.

Facts The plaintiff had dispatched hundreds of cannisters full of mustard oil which was manufactured by them and sold under their brand. At the railway station, a few hundred cannisters were seized by the Sanitary Inspector and were loaded in a truck which was used for carrying rubbish and night soil. By this act plaintiff suffered a huge loss because their customers refused to take delivery of the tins on the ground that they had been carried in municipal vehicle which was used to carry rubbish and night soil and unfit for human consumption.

(a) Sanitary Inspector is liable for his act
(b) Plaintiff cannot succeed because it is duty of Sanitary Inspector to check the quality of oil
(c) Municipality held to be liable because his employees handled the cannisters negligently
(d) No any one liable

153. Principle When any person dishonestly takes any moveable property, out of the, possession of any other person without his consent, he is guilty of theft.

Facts A entered the study room of Y and takes away a book with the intention to return it.

(a) A commit theft because the book has been taken without Y's consent
(b) A does not commit theft because he intends to return the book
(c) A commit theft because he has moved the book from Y's house
(d) A commit theft because he has taken a book which is moveable property

154. Principle

1. A person who is usually of sound mind, but occasionally of unsound mind may not make a contract when he is of unsound mind.
2. A person who is usually of unsound mind but occasionally of sound mind may make a contract when he is of sound mind.

Facts A property worth about ₹ 25000 was agreed to be sold by a person for ₹ 7000 only. His mother proved that he was a born idiot incapable of understanding the transaction. Decide

(a) sale is void
(b) sale is not void because he was idiot but know about the money
(c) sale is not void because money was already accepted
(d) None of the above

155. Principle Liability of a person depends upon his act.

Facts One evening a delivery boy from M/s KT Dass and Co. delivered a carton of sweets at Mr Chatterjee's residence. The delivery boy told Mrs Chatterjee that the sweets were ordered by her husband. When Mr Chatterjee came home in the evening, he told his wife that he did not order any sweets. Nevertheless, the entire family finished all the sweets. Next day morning the delivery boy came again to Mr Chatterjee's residence and explained that by mistake he delivered to the carton to them, in fact it was to be delivered to their next door neighbour, Mr Banerjee. When Mr Chatterjee told him that they had already consumed the sweets, the boy on behalf of his employer asked Mr Chatterjee to pay the price of sweets.

(a) M/s KT Dass and Co. have no right to claim the price because there was a serious mistake on the part of their employee
(b) M/s KT Dass and Co. cannot claim the price because the sweets were not ordered by Mr and Mrs Chatterjee at all
(c) M/s KT Dass and Co. cannot claim the price because there was no contract or agreement between them
(d) M/s KT Dass and Co. are entitled to claim the price from Mr and Mrs Chatterjee because they consumed the sweets without ascertaining why they were delivered to them and because they enjoyed the sweets though they did not order them

156. Principle Mere silence as to the facts likely to affect the willingness of a person to enter into a contract is not a fraud, unless the circumstances of the case are such that, on close examination it is found to be the duty of the person keeping silent to speak, or unless his silence is, in itself, equivalent to speech.

Facts X sells by auction to Y, a horse which X knows to be of unsound state of mind. X says nothing to Y about the horse's unsound state of mind. Give the correct answer.

(a) X can be held liable for fraud
(b) X can be held liable for misrepresentation
(c) X cannot be held liable, because he did not say anything positive about the mental state of the horse
(d) X cannot be held liable because it is the buyer who must be aware of the things

157. Principle A person is said to be of sound mind for the purpose of making a contract if, at the time when he makes it, he is capable of understanding it and of forming a rational judgement as to its effect upon his interests.

Facts Mr X who is usually of sound state of mind, but occasionally of unsound state of mind, enters into a contract with Mr Y when he was of unsound state of mind. Mr Y having come to know about this fact afterwards, wants to file a suit against Mr X. **(2011)**

(a) Mr X cannot enter into contract, because he is of unsound state of mind when he entered into contract
(b) Mr X can enter into contract but the burden is on the other party to prove that he was of unsound state of mind at the time of contract
(c) Mr X can enter into contract but the burden is on Mr X to prove that he was of sound state of mind at the time of contract
(d) None of the above

158. Principle Every person, who is of the age of majority, is competent to contract according to the law to which he is subject.

Facts A minor mortgaged his house in favour of Thakur Das, a money lender, to secure a loan of ₹ 20000. A part of this, i.e. ₹ 10500 was actually advanced to him. While considering the proposed advance the attorney who was acting for the money lender, received information that plaintiff was still a minor. Subsequently, the minor commenced an action stating that he was underage when he executed the mortgage and the same should therefore, be cancelled. He prayed for setting aside the mortgage. The mortgage money lender prayed for the refund of ₹ 10500 from the minor.

(a) As a minor's contract is void and money advanced to a minor can be recovered
(b) A minor's contract is void a initio any money advanced to a minor cannot be recovered
(c) A minor's contract is voidable; any money advanced to a minor can be recovered
(d) Advanced money can be recovered because minor has given wrong information about his age

159. Ramu applied for the post of director in an organisation. The governing body of the organisation passed a resolution appointing him to the post. After the meeting, one of the members of the governing body informed him privately of the resolution. Subsequently, the resolution was rescinded. Ramu claims damages, which one of the following is the correct legal proposition in the case?

(a) Ramu cannot claim damages as he had not resigned, from his existing post in anticipation of getting the appointment letter
(b) Ramu cannot claim damages as there was no formal communication
(c) Ramu can claim damages as governing body cannot rescind the resolution once passed
(d) Ramu can claim damages as there was private communication

160. Principle Every agreement in restraint of the marriage of any person, other than a minor, is void.

Facts Qadir Khan died in a road accident. Two co-widows, Sultana and Marjina enter into an agreement that if any of them will remarry, would forfeit her right to her share in the deceased husband's property.

(a) The agreement is void because it was restraint of marriage
(b) The agreement is not void because no restraint was imposed upon either of two widows for remarriage
(c) The restraint was partial so agreement is valid
(d) None of the above

Logical Reasoning

161. In a certain code PAGE is written as '3%7@', SORE is written as 8©9@. How is 'PEAS' written in that code?

(a) 3@©8 (b) 3@%9
(c) 3@%8 (d) 3%@8

162. Among A, B, C, D and E each scoring different marks in a test, C scored more than D but not as much as E. E scored more than A who scored less than B. Who score third highest marks?

(a) B (b) A
(c) C (d) Data inadequate

163. How many such pairs of letters are there in the word 'CONFIRM' each of which has as many letters between them in the word as in the English alphabet?
(a) None (b) One (c) Two (d) Three

Directions (Q. Nos. 164-173) *Study the following information carefully and answer the questions given below.*

A, B, C, D, E, F, G and H are sitting around a circle facing the centre. C is fourth to the left of F who is fifth to right of E. D is third to the right of A who is not immediate neighbour of E of F. B is third to left of H who is not immediate neighbour of E.

164. Four of the following five are alike in a certain way based on their positions in the above sitting arrangement and so form a group. Which is the one that does not belong to that group?
(a) HFE (b) DCG (c) BHF (d) AEF

165. Who is between D and E?
(a) C (b) B
(c) A (d) Data inadequate

166. Which of the following pairs are sitting between A and D?
(a) FB (b) GB (c) FG (d) FE

167. Who is third to the right of E?
(a) B (b) F
(c) D (d) None of these

168. Who is to the immediate right of A?
(a) G (b) B
(c) F (d) Data inadequate

169. What is D's position with respect to B?
(a) Immediate right (b) Fourth to the right
(c) Third to the left (d) Immediate left
(a) Only (a) (b) Only (b)
(c) Both (b) and (c) (d) Only (d)

170. In which of the following pairs is the first person sitting to the immediate left of the second person?
(a) CH (b) GA
(c) BD (d) FG

171. Three of the following four are similar in relation to their positions in the English alphabet and hence form a group. Which one does not belong to that group?
(a) SPEAK: PZVKH (b) HUSKY: BPGFS
(c) BRAIN: MRZIY (d) BREAK: PZVIY

172. If the letters of the word 'PROTECTION' which are at odd numbered position in the English alphabet are picked up and are arranged in alphabetical order from left and if they are now substituted by Z, Y, X and so on, beginning from left which letter will get substituted by X?
(a) E (b) O
(c) T (d) I

173. The letter I, J, K, L, M, N, O, P, Q, R, S, T in their order are substituted by twelve numbers but not in that oder. 3 is assigned to R. The difference between R and M is 7. The difference between K and M is 2. What number is assigned to K?
(a) 8 (b) 12 (c) 7 (d) 11

Directions (Q. Nos. 174-183) *In questions given below, statements 1 and 2 are followed by conclusions I and II. Taking the statements to be right although they may seem at variance with commonly accepted facts, mark your answers as under*

(a) If only conclusion I follows
(b) If only conclusion II follows
(c) If both I and II follow
(d) Neither I nor II follows

174. Statements
1. All hands are machines.
2. All machines are wheels.

Conclusions
I. All wheels are hands.
II. All hands are wheels.

175. Statements
1. Some buds are leaves.
2. Some leaves are red.

Conclusions
I. Some buds are red.
II. Some leaves are not buds.

176. Statements
1. Some stones are shells.
2. All shells are pearls.

Conclusions
I. Some stones are pearls.
II. All pearls are shells.

177. Statements
1. Brown is red and blue is green.
2. Green is pink and yellow is red.

Conclusions
I. Yellow is brown.
II. Pink is blue.

178. Statements
1. Merchants who do not own cars do not have bicycles either.
2. Those who do not have bicycles have tricycles.

Conclusions
I. Some merchants have only tricycles.
II. No one has both, the car and the tricycles.

179. A man was walking in the evening just before the Sun set. His wife said that, his shadow fell on his right. If the wife was walking in the opposite direction of the man, then which direction the wife was facing?
(a) North (b) West (c) South (d) East

180. Choose that set of numbers from the four alternative sets, that is similar to the given set.
Given set (246, 257, 358)
(a) (145, 235, 325) (b) (143, 253, 246)
(c) (273, 365, 367) (d) (233, 343, 345)

181. Three of the following four are alike in a certain way and hence form a group. Which one of the following does not belong to that group?
(a) 7 (b) 9 (c) 17 (d) 33

182. 136 vehicles are parked in a parking lot in a single row. After the first car there is one scooter. After the second car, there are two scooters. After the third car, there are three scooters and so on. Work out the number of scooters in the second half of the row.
(a) 61 (b) 62 (c) 63 (d) 64

183. Find the oddman out.
(a) MOndAy (b) tUESdAy
(c) WEdNESdAy (d) thUrSdAy

Directions (Q. Nos. 184-190) *Find out the missing term in the following letter-number series.*

184. H 4 W, I 18 V, K 48 T, N 100 Q,?, W 294 H
(a) P 1485 S (b) R 180 M
(c) S 198 I (d) T 206 K

185. 1 ED, 2 FD, 3 KH,?, 15 KG, 48 KF
(a) 12 PX (b) 6 RI
(c) 9 LV (d) 8 TQ

186. M 4, T 7, P 7, Q 10, S 10, N 13,?, K 16
(a) V 4 (b) K 7 (c) T 13 (d) G 15

187. R 5 P, T 6 M, V 9 J, X 15 G,?
(a) A 12 L (b) I 18 X
(c) Z 25 D (d) U 20 Q

188. DGK 0, GKP 3,?, PVC 15
(a) GKV 5 (b) KPV 8
(c) PVZ 9 (d) KPU 11

189. Seema correctly remembers that she took leave after 21st October and before 27th October. Her colleague Rita took leave on 23rd October but Seema was present on that day. If 24th October was a public holiday and 26th October was Sunday, on which day in October did Seema take leave?
(a) 22nd October (b) 25th October
(c) 22nd or 25th October (d) Data inadequate

190. If 'A × D' means 'A is the sister of D', 'A + D' means 'D is the daughter of A' and 'A ÷ D' means 'A is the mother of D', then how will N is the aunt of M be denoted?
(a) M + L × N (b) M ÷ L + N
(c) L × N ÷ M (d) N × L ÷ M

Directions (Q. Nos. 191-195) *In each question below is given a statement followed by two courses of action numbered I and II. A course of action is a step or administrative decision to be taken for improvement, follow-up or further action in regard to the problem, policy etc. On the basis of the information given in the statement, you have to assume everything in the statement to be true and then decide which of the suggested courses of action logically follows for pursuing.*

Give answer
(a) if only course of action I follows
(b) if only course of action II follows
(c) if either course of action I or course of action II follows
(d) if both courses of action I and II follow

191. Statement An increasing number of graduates produced by Indian universities are unemployable.

Courses of action
I. Colleges and Institutes of higher learning should be given greater autonomy to decide course content.
II. World class foreign universities should be encouraged to set up campuses in India.

192. Statement Heavy rains hit the state during October, just before the State Assembly elections and caused heavy damage to standing crops in most parts of the state.

Courses of action

I. Elections should be postponed to give candidates the opportunity to campaign.

II. The Government should announce a relief package for those who are affected.

193. Statement Cell phone users have found that tariff plans are not as attractive as promoted by telecome companies and complained to regulatory authority about the same.

Courses of action

I. The regulatory authority should direct telecome companies to be transparent on the tariff structure of all plans.

II. The government should restrict the number of telecome companies operating in the country.

194. Statement A number of school children in the local schools have fallen ill after the consumption of their subsidised tiffin provided by the school authority.

Courses of action

I. The tiffin facility of all schools should be discontinued with immediate effect.

II. The government should implement a system to certify the quality of tiffin provided by the school.

195. Statement The dolphin population in India has been decreasing sharply over the past few years.

Courses of action

I. Dolphins should be declared an endangered species and be bred in aquariums or protected areas.

II. Locals should be enlisted to protect dolphins.

Directions (Q. Nos. 196-200) *In each question below, is given a statement followed by two assumptions numbered I and II. An assumption is something supposed or taken for granted. You have to consider the statement and the following assumptions and decide which of the assumptions is implicit in the statement.*

196. Statement The economic condition of the country has gone from bad to worse.

Assumptions

I. The government has failed to tackle economic problems.

II. People are not cooperating with the government.

(a) Only assumption I is implicit
(b) Only assumption II is implicit
(c) Either I or II is implicit
(d) Both I and II are implicit

197. Statement The next meeting of the Governing Board of the Institute will be held after one year.

Assumptions

I. The Institute will remain in function after one year.

II. The Governing Board will be dissolved after one year.

(a) Only assumption I is implicit
(b) Only assumption II is implicit
(c) Either I or II is implicit
(d) Neither I nor II is implicit

198. Statement Market trends are changing continuously and with increasing competitiveness, the consumer's demands with respect to the prices and quality are gradually increasing.

Assumptions

I. The consumers did not care for the prices and quality earlier.

II. Market competitiveness is not favourable for the consumers.

(a) Only assumption I is implicit
(b) Only assumption II is implicit
(c) Either I or II is implicit
(d) Neither I nor II is implicit

199. Statement "A visit of school children to forest to widen their knowledge of natural resources has been arranged." A notice in the school.

Assumptions

I. Forests are full of natural resources.

II. Children are likely to learn from their interaction with the new environment.

(a) Only assumption I is implicit
(b) Only assumption II is implicit
(c) Either I or II is implicit
(d) Both I and II are implicit

200. Statement In view of the violent situation due to students' agitation the state government has decided to close down all the educational institutions in the state for two weeks with immediate effect.

Assumptions

I. The students' agitation may subside after two weeks.

II. The students may not find a place to come further and continue agitation after the closure of the educational institutions.

(a) Only assumption I is implicit
(b) Only assumption II is implicit
(c) Either I or II is implicit
(d) Both I and II are implicit

ANSWERS

1	(b)	**2**	(b)	**3**	(c)	**4**	(a)	**5**	(c)	**6**	(d)	**7**	(a)	**8**	(d)	**9**	(c)	**10**	(d)
11	(c)	**12**	(d)	**13**	(d)	**14**	(c)	**15**	(b)	**16**	(b)	**17**	(d)	**18**	(a)	**19**	(d)	**20**	(d)
21	(a)	**22**	(b)	**23**	(c)	**24**	(a)	**25**	(b)	**26**	(c)	**27**	(d)	**28**	(b)	**29**	(d)	**30**	(c)
31	(c)	**32**	(d)	**33**	(b)	**34**	(a)	**35**	(b)	**36**	(d)	**37**	(c)	**38**	(c)	**39**	(b)	**40**	(c)
41	(c)	**42**	(d)	**43**	(d)	**44**	(c)	**45**	(d)	**46**	(c)	**47**	(d)	**48**	(d)	**49**	(b)	**50**	(a)
51	(d)	**52**	(b)	**53**	(b)	**54**	(c)	**55**	(c)	**56**	(d)	**57**	(b)	**58**	(a)	**59**	(c)	**60**	(d)
61	(a)	**62**	(a)	**63**	(a)	**64**	(d)	**65**	(d)	**66**	(c)	**67**	(b)	**68**	(b)	**69**	(a)	**70**	(a)
71	(a)	**72**	(a)	**73**	(c)	**74**	(b)	**75**	(c)	**76**	(c)	**77**	(c)	**78**	(d)	**79**	(d)	**80**	(c)
81	(d)	**82**	(a)	**83**	(c)	**84**	(a)	**85**	(a)	**86**	(c)	**87**	(b)	**88**	(a)	**89**	(d)	**90**	(a)
91	(d)	**92**	(c)	**93**	(c)	**94**	(a)	**95**	(b)	**96**	(c)	**97**	(d)	**98**	(c)	**99**	(b)	**100**	(b)
101	(b)	**102**	(a)	**103**	(a)	**104**	(d)	**105**	(c)	**106**	(d)	**107**	(c)	**108**	(d)	**109**	(a)	**110**	(b)
111	(a)	**112**	(b)	**113**	(b)	**114**	(c)	**115**	(a)	**116**	(d)	**117**	(b)	**118**	(d)	**119**	(c)	**120**	(a)
121	(d)	**122**	(d)	**123**	(b)	**124**	(d)	**125**	(c)	**126**	(c)	**127**	(b)	**128**	(d)	**129**	(b)	**130**	(c)
131	(c)	**132**	(a)	**133**	(b)	**134**	(c)	**135**	(c)	**136**	(d)	**137**	(d)	**138**	(d)	**139**	(c)	**140**	(a)
141	(a)	**142**	(d)	**143**	(d)	**144**	(b)	**145**	(d)	**146**	(c)	**147**	(d)	**148**	(a)	**149**	(b)	**150**	(b)
151	(c)	**152**	(c)	**153**	(b)	**154**	(a)	**155**	(d)	**156**	(a)	**157**	(a)	**158**	(d)	**159**	(b)	**160**	(a)
161	(c)	**162**	(d)	**163**	(c)	**164**	(d)	**165**	(b)	**166**	(c)	**167**	(d)	**168**	(a)	**169**	(d)	**170**	(a)
171	(b)	**172**	(d)	**173**	(b)	**174**	(b)	**175**	(b)	**176**	(a)	**177**	(c)	**178**	(d)	**179**	(c)	**180**	(a)
181	(b)	**182**	(c)	**183**	(b)	**184**	(b)	**185**	(b)	**186**	(c)	**187**	(c)	**188**	(b)	**189**	(c)	**190**	(d)
191	(a)	**192**	(b)	**193**	(a)	**194**	(b)	**195**	(d)	**196**	(a)	**197**	(a)	**198**	(d)	**199**	(d)	**200**	(d)